ICCA
CONGRESS SERIES NO. 13

INTERNATIONAL ARBITRATION CONGRESS
MONTRÉAL, 31 MAY - 3 JUNE 2006

KLUWER LAW
INTERNATIONAL

INTERNATIONAL COUNCIL FOR COMMERCIAL ARBITRATION

INTERNATIONAL ARBITRATION 2006:

BACK TO BASICS?

GENERAL EDITOR: ALBERT JAN VAN DEN BERG

with the assistance of the
International Bureau of the
Permanent Court of Arbitration
The Hague

ISBN 9789041126917

Published by:
Kluwer Law International
P.O. Box 316
2400 AH Alphen aan den Rijn
The Netherlands

Sold and distributed in North, Central and South America by:
Aspen Publishers, Inc.
7201 McKinney Circle
Frederick, MD 21704
United States of America

Sold and distributed in all other countries by:
Turpin Distribution Services Ltd
Stratton Business Park
Pegasus Drive
Biggleswade
Bedfordshire SG18 8TQ
United Kingdom

Printed in the Netherlands on acid-free paper

Preface

ICCA Congress Series no. 13 comprises the proceedings of the 18th ICCA Congress, hosted by the ICCA Montréal 2006 Organizing Committee on 31 May to 3 June 2006 in Montréal, Quebec, Canada. We are very grateful to the Organizing Committee and their sponsors for their efforts on behalf of ICCA. The touristic attractions of Montréal combined with the outstanding program devised by the ICCA Program Committee resulted in a fully-subscribed Congress; for the first time in the history of ICCA Congresses and Conferences, registration had to be closed, but fortunately, in the end, everyone who wished to attend was able to do so. We are greatly appreciative of the hospitality and flexibility of our hosts in making everyone welcome.

Under the general title of "International Arbitration 2006: Back to Basics?", the sessions were divided into two simultaneous Working Groups: Working Group A "Re-examining the Arbitration Agreement" and Working Group B "Contemporary Practice in the Conduct of Proceedings". The sessions in Working Group A were in the format of a Reporter who presented a Report on the topic of the session, together with several Commentators who gave their specific views on the topic based on their backgrounds and experiences. Working Group B combined sessions in the form of Roundtables, presided by a Moderator who led the participants in the Roundtable in a discussion of the topic with sessions in the Reporter-Commentator format. The final session was a plenary Working Group C on the subject of "International Arbitration and the Generation of Legal Norms" with Reports on Commercial Arbitration and Transnational Public Policy, and Treaty Arbitration and International Law. Each session allowed ample time for discussion with the participants who in many cases had been able to study the papers ahead of time as many of them had been made available on the Congress website.

The Closing Ceremony honored Prof. Pieter Sanders with the presentation of the first ICCA Lifetime Merit Award by the President of ICCA, Gerold Herrmann.

Many thanks go to the Moderators of the Sessions who had the task of collecting and coordinating the contributions for their session, urging the members of the panel to submit their contributions on time and guiding the discussion! The Moderators of the sessions were as follows:

Working Group A: *Re-Examining the Arbitration Agreement*
- The Arbitration Agreement: Still Autonomous?, moderated by Werner Melis
- Jurisdiction to Determine Jurisdiction, moderated by Loukas Mistelis
- Control of Jurisdiction by Injunctions Issued by National Courts, moderated by Carlos Nehring Netto
- Protection of Jurisdiction by Injunctions Issued by Arbitral Tribunals, moderated by Margrete Stevens
- Applicable Law: Consensus or Confusion?, moderated by Ivan Szasz
- Jurisdiction Over Non-signatories: National Contract Law or International Arbitral Practice?, moderated by Ulf Franke
- Treaties as Agreements to Arbitrate, moderated by Gabrielle Kaufmann-Kohler

Working Group B: *Contemporary Practice in the Conduct of Proceedings*
- Document Production, moderated by Arthur Marriott;

- Fact Testimony, moderated by Marc Lalonde
- Evidentiary Privileges, moderated by William K. Slate
- Arbitral Provisional Measures: The Actual Practice, moderated by Fali S. Nariman
- Legal Experts, moderated by Karl-Heinz Böckstiegel
- Damages and Technical Experts, moderated by John Beechey
- Techniques for Eliciting Expert Testimony, moderated by Yves Derains
- Oral Argument, moderated by V.V. Veeder

Working Group C: *International Arbitration and the Generation of Legal Norms*
- Plenary Session, moderated by Donald Francis Donovan.

The next ICCA Conference will be held in Dublin on 8 to 10 June 2008 and an important part of the program will be the celebration of the fiftieth anniversary of the New York Convention on the Recognition and Enforcement of Foreign Arbitral Awards, concluded on 10 June 1958. Information on the Congress, as it becomes available, will be posted on the ICCA website at <www.arbitration-icca.org> and on the Dublin 2008 Organizing Committee website at <www.iccadublin2008.org>.

The publication of this volume marks another anniversary, ten years of cooperation between the International Bureau of the Permanent Court of Arbitration and ICCA regarding the ICCA publications. I would like to express my thanks on behalf of ICCA to the Secretary-General, Tjaco T. van den Hout, and to his predecessor, Hans Jonkman, for their decade of support in providing a seat for ICCA's publication activities and supporting us with the PCA's facilities.

My further thanks go to the more than fifty contributors to this volume for their outstanding papers. Their work enriches the ICCA programs and its publications which could not exist without them.

My final thank you goes to the ICCA Publications staff, and in particular to Ms. Alice Siegel and Ms. Judy Freedberg, for their herculean efforts in compiling and editing this hefty volume.

Albert Jan van den Berg
July 2007

TABLE OF CONTENTS

WORKING GROUP B: CONTEMPORARY PRACTICE IN THE CONDUCT OF PROCEEDINGS

CLOSING CEREMONY

Working Group A

1. The Arbitration Agreement: Still Autonomous?

The Arbitration Agreement:
Still Autonomous?

*Philippe Leboulanger**

I.   INTRODUCTION

I wonder whether there was not some irony – or provocation – on the part of the ICCA Program Committee in the choice of a French lawyer to address this topic and to answer such a question! In French law the arbitration agreement is conceived as a sort of "watertight compartment" placed in a spaceship flying in the stratosphere, where it escapes almost all influence from the earth. Actually, there is no other country on our planet where the arbitration agreement is more autonomous than in France, and, I should say, more autonomous than ever!

The explanation of this very liberal conception may be found in the rule contained in the Civil Code which, during almost two centuries, declared the arbitration agreement void unless otherwise provided for by the law. French law was thus built against this prohibition which was abandoned only five years ago in domestic arbitration!

The evolution towards an extremely liberal regime had already been predicted by Philippe Fouchard in 1965 in his doctoral thesis where he wrote:

> "In international trade the arbitration agreement will be the first instrument of the autonomy that the (arbitration) community seeks to obtain vis-à-vis the state frames."[1]

Originally, the concept of arbitration was seen as "a primitive form" of justice,[2] "mainly conceived as an institution of peace, the purpose of which was not primarily to ensure the rule of law but rather to maintain harmony between persons who were

---

* *Avocat au Barreau de Paris*, Leboulanger & Associés; lecturer on International Arbitration and International Trade Law, University of Paris II (Panthéon-Assas). The author acknowledges the assistance of Irina Pongracz, J.D. Missouri University, *Avocat au Barreau de Paris*, in the preparation of this article.

1. Philippe FOUCHARD, *L'Arbitrage Commercial International* (Dalloz 1965) p. 54.
2. HOLDSWORTH, *History of English Law*, Vol. XIV (1964) p. 187.

3

destined to live together".[3] Well designed, the process could indeed provide the benefits that its proponents claim for it: proceedings that are simpler, quicker and less costly than litigation and that produce final and enforceable decisions.

Today, international commercial arbitration has become the usual method of adjudicating international commercial disputes and Philippe Fouchard's prediction proved to be right:

> "the principle of autonomy or (separability) of the arbitration agreement is the cornerstone of the whole system, which would certainly not exist without such principle". [4]

This principle ensures the parties' intent to arbitrate any disputes which arise out of their contractual relationship without undue court interference, notwithstanding a party's challenge to the validity of the contract or the arbitration agreement it contains.[5] It is considered that once parties have validly given their consent to arbitration, the obligation to arbitrate survives because it is separable from the rest of the contract.[6]

The doctrine of autonomy of the international arbitration agreement is "traditionally" understood as implying its continuous validity notwithstanding the flaws which may affect the underlying contract, meaning its independence from both the main contract and from the lex contractus (II).

Despite its role as one of the conceptual pillars of international arbitration law, the notion of "autonomy" of the arbitration agreement is still subject to considerable controversy, one important criticism of it being that "procedural" dispute resolution provisions, such as arbitration agreements, cannot, in reality, be separate and distinct from the "substantive" provisions of the same contract. Many arguments are raised as to the actual limits of the doctrine so that it is still submitted today that its universal recognition might mask in reality important differences in scope and application.

In this sense, extensive application of the notion of autonomy, affirmed in many civil legal systems, allowed numerous scholars to envisage the complete autonomy of the arbitration agreement in international commercial arbitration law (III.1).[7] In the

---

3. René DAVID, *Arbitration in International Trade* (Kluwer 1985) p. 29.
4. Philippe FOUCHARD, *"Où va l'Arbitrage International?"*, 34 McGill Law Journal (1989, no. 3) p. 435.
5. Emmanuel GAILLARD and John SAVAGE, eds., *Fouchard, Gaillard, Goldman, On International Commercial Arbitration* (Kluwer International Law 1999) p. 197; Julian D.M. LEW, Loukas A. MISTELIS, Stephan M. KRÖLL, *Comparative International Commercial Arbitration* (Kluwer International Law 2003) p. 99; Alan REDFERN and Martin HUNTER, *Law and Practice of International Commercial Arbitration*, 4th edn. (Sweet & Maxwell 2004) p. 9; W. Laurence CRAIG, William W. PARK, Jan PAULSSON, *International Chamber of Commerce Arbitration*, 3d edn. (Oceania Publications 2004) p. 48; Jean-François POUDRET and Sébastien BESSON, *Droit comparé de l'arbitrage international* (Bruylant 2002) pp. 133-150.
6. *Ibid.*
7. Jean-Pierre ANCEL, *"L'actualité de l'autonomie de la clause compromissoire"*, *Travaux du comité français de droit international privé 1991-1992* (Pédone 1994) pp. 75-107; see also Emmanuel GAILLARD

common law tradition, in the United States for the most part, the doctrine was undergoing a wave of academic reappraisal and US courts have been struggling with its limits (III.2).[8] Some more criticism has been generated in relation to the so-called "automatic transmission" of the arbitration agreement with the rights under the main contract. In various legal systems, it is generally admitted that the arbitration agreement follows the main contract when the contract is assigned. Often it is argued that such an automatic transmission challenges the scope of the principle of autonomy in the sense that it represents a limit to the autonomy of the arbitration agreement (III.3).

This Report is devoted to an analysis of the evolution of the doctrine, its universal recognition and whether differences in application among national legal systems might justify questioning the autonomy of the arbitration agreement.

II. THE DOCTRINE OF AUTONOMY

In the course of three centuries of history, the autonomy of the arbitration agreement has acquired worldwide recognition (1), and courts and commentators alike developed the doctrine and justified its consequences (2).

1. Origins and Evolution

In the international context, the arbitration agreement is deemed to be autonomous or presumptively "separable" or "severable" from the underlying contract in which it is found or to which it relates. As pointed out by Justice Schwebel:

> "when the parties to an agreement containing an arbitration clause enter into that agreement, they conclude not one but two agreements, the arbitral twin of which survives any birth defect or acquired disability of the principal agreement" [9]

According to this definition of the autonomy, firstly, the arbitration agreement should remain unaffected by the fate of the main contract, that is its possible nullity, termination, or non-existence and secondly, the arbitrator should have jurisdiction to

---

and John SAVAGE, eds., *op. cit.*, fn. 5, p. 218.

8. Some American commentators seem to treat the doctrine of separability as some sort of inexplicable aberration, a doctrinal mystification, or fiction. It has been maintained that "[s]eparability perverts contract law because it assumes away the fundamental principle of contract consent", or "if a contract is induced by fraud it would appear that none of the provisions of the contract would be valid, including the arbitration provision", in Richard C. REUBEN, "First Options, Consent to Arbitration and the Demise of Separability: Restoring Access to Justice for Contracts with Arbitration Provisions", 56 Southern Methodist University Law Review (2003), p. 819 at p. 827 and pp. 841-842; see also, Alan Scott RAU, "Everything You Really Need to Know About 'Separability' in Seventeen Simple Questions", 14 American Review of International Arbitration (2003, no. 1) pp. 1-120, at p. 3 and p. 81.

9. Stephen M. SCHWEBEL, "The Severability of the Arbitration Agreement", *International Arbitration: Three Salient Problems* (Grotius Publications, Cambridge 1987) pp. 1-60, at p. 5.

rule on any complaint relating to the existence or the validity of the main contract as long as there are no grounds for declaring the arbitration agreement invalid.[10]

a.   Origins of the doctrine

The separability of the arbitration agreement was established already in English arbitration legislation: the 1698 Arbitration Act. The Act granted arbitration clauses the same power as a rule of court if the parties had agreed to this.[11] Subsequent English case law, however, rendered the arbitration agreement incapable of judicial enforcement and delayed the evolution of Anglo-American arbitration law.[12] Similarly, the 1804 Napoleonic Code outlawed the enforcement of arbitral clauses, which influenced French domestic arbitration law for two centuries.[13] Early in the twentieth century, the principle of autonomy re-emerged in the international arena. Switzerland seems to be the first nation to have acquired a fixed separability doctrine when, in 1931, the *Tribunal Fédéral* declared that the invalidity of the main contract could not affect the arbitration clause. This view has been consistently applied ever since[14] and is enshrined in the Swiss Private International Law Act 1987 (PILA).[15]

In England, following a long line of contradictory judicial decisions,[16] the House of Lords confirmed the separability of the arbitration clause in 1942 when the Lords ruled that such a clause may be wide enough to cover a dispute as to whether the underlying contract has been repudiated or frustrated.[17] Half a century later, in the well-publicized 1992 decision *Harbour Assurance Co. (UK) Ltd. v. Kansa General International Insurance Co. Ltd. and Others*,[18] English judges expressly recognized the separability principle as part of English law:

---

10. Antonias DIMOLITSA, "Separability and Kompetenz-Kompetenz" in *International Commercial Arbitration: Improving the Efficiency of Arbitration Agreements and Awards: 40 Years of Application of the New York Convention*, ICCA Congress Series no. 9 (1999) (hereinafter *ICCA Congress Series no. 9*) p. 217.

11. Adam SAMUEL, "Separability of Arbitration Clauses – Some Awkward Questions about the Law of Contracts, Conflict of Laws and the Administration of Justice", Arbitration and Dispute Resolution Law Journal (2000) p. 36.

12. *Kill v. Hollister*, 1 Wils. 129 (1746).

13. Until the law of 15 May 2001, Art. 2061 of the French Civil Code (CC) provided that in domestic arbitration "the arbitration agreement was considered null if not otherwise provided by the law".

14. For a complete guide to Swiss case law on the principle of autonomy, see Christoph MÜLLER, *International Arbitration – A Guide to the Complete Swiss Case Law (Unreported and Reported)* (Bruylant 2004) pp. 45-47.

15. Jean-François POUDRET and Sébastien BESSON, *op. cit.*, fn. 5, p. 133.

16. See, e.g., *Smith Coney and Barett v. Becker Gray and Co.* [1916] 2 Ch. 86; *Hirji Mulji v. Cheong Yue Steamship Company Ltd.* [1926] All E.R. 51; *Joe Lee Ltd v. Lord Dalmeny* [1927] Ch. 300.

17. See, e.g., *Hayman v. Darwin Ltd.* [1942] A.C. 356; *David Taylor and Son Ltd v. Barrett Trading Company* [1953] 1 W.L.R. 562; *Ashville Investments Ltd v. Elmer Contractors Ltd.* [1988] 3 W.L.R. 867. See also Hong-Lin YU, "Five Years On: A Review of the English Arbitration Act 1996", 19 Journal of International Arbitration (2002, no. 3) p. 209.

18. *Harbour Assurance Co. (UK) Ltd. v. Kansa General International Insurance Co. Ltd.* [1992] 1 Lloyd's Rep. 81 (Q.B.(Com. Ct.) 1991); *Harbour Assurance Co. (UK) Ltd. v. Kansa General International Insurance Co. Ltd.* [1993] Q.B. 701; [1993] 3 W.L.R. 42; [1993] 3 All E.R. 897.

a) "In English law the principle of separability of an arbitration clause in a contract could give an arbitrator jurisdiction to determine the validity or invalidity of the relevant contract provided that 'the arbitration clause itself was not directly impeached'; and
b) in every case the logical question was not whether the issue of illegality went to the validity of the contract but whether it went to the validity of the arbitration clause. In this case illegality did not affect the validity of the arbitration clause, which on its proper construction was wide enough to cover a dispute as to the initial illegality of the contract."

In the United States, in order to overcome judicial resistance to arbitration, Congress enacted in 1925 the Federal Arbitration Act (FAA) which regretfully remained silent on the issue of separability.[19] A pro-arbitration opening could be signaled in subsequent case law when US justices affirmed that "[T]he FAA created a body of federal substantive law which was applicable in state and federal court"[20] and "[it] embodies the national policy favoring arbitration and places arbitration agreements on equal footing with all other contracts."[21]

In France, the doctrine was consecrated in the 1963 landmark *Gosset* decision where the *Cour de cassation* held that in international disputes the arbitration agreement is separable from the main contract and juridically autonomous:

"[T]he arbitration agreement, whether concluded separately or included in the contract to which it relates, shall ... have full legal autonomy and shall not be affected by the fact that the aforementioned contract may be invalid."[22]

This principle has been reiterated in identical terms in many subsequent decisions and regularly reaffirmed by the *Cour de cassation* so that it became a substantive rule of French international arbitration law.[23] It is safe to say that today French courts consider an

---

19. Federal Arbitration Act (FAA), 9 U.S.C. Sects. 1-16, Sect. 2 provides:

"A written provision in ... contract ... to settle by arbitration a controversy thereafter arising out of such contract ... or an agreement in writing to submit to arbitration an existing controversy arising out of such a contract ... shall be valid, irrevocable, and enforceable, save upon such grounds as exist at law or in equity for the revocation of any contract."

20. *Southland Corp. v. Keating*, 465 U.S. 1, 104.
21. As referred to by Justice SCALIA in *Buckeye Check Cashing, Inc. v. John Cardegna, et al.*, 2006 WL 386362 (U.S. 21 Feb. 2006), hereinafter *Cardegna*.
22. *Cour de cassation*, 7 May 1963 (*Ets. Raymond Gosset v. Carapelli*), Juris Classeur Périodique, Ed. G., Pt. II, No. 13405 (1963).
23. *Cour de cassation*, 4 July 1972 (*Hecht v. Buisman's*), Juris Classeur Périodique, Ed. G., Pt. II, No. 16927 (1971) with note B. GOLDMAN; Court of Appeal, Paris, 13 December 1975 (*Menicucci v. Mahieux*), Journal du Droit International (1977) p. 106 with note E. LOQUIN; For a detailed list of related French case law see also Emmanuel GAILLARD and John SAVAGE, eds., *op. cit.*, fn. 5, p. 198; Jean-Pierre ANCEL, *op. cit.*, fn. 7, p. 77.

international arbitration agreement to be independent of the main contract regardless of both the position of any foreign law applicable to the contract and that of the rules governing the arbitration agreement itself.[24]

The doctrine of autonomy had a similar spectacular evolution in the international arena, where leading institutional arbitration rules and national arbitration laws specifically provide for it.

b. Worldwide recognition

The autonomy of the arbitration agreement has been accepted by all norms of private origin. The International Chamber of Commerce (ICC) was the first leading institution to recognize in 1955 the principle of autonomy,[25] followed, in 1976, by the United Nations Commission on International Trade Law (UNCITRAL) Arbitration Rules.[26] Arbitration rules such as the LCIA[27] Rules, the AAA[28] International Arbitration Rules

---

24. See Sect. III(*1*).

25. Art. 6(4) of the ICC 1998 Rules provides:

"Unless otherwise agreed, the Arbitral Tribunal shall not cease to have jurisdiction by reason of any claim that the contract is null and void or allegation that it is non-existent provided that the Arbitral Tribunal upholds the validity of the arbitration agreement. The Arbitral Tribunal shall continue to have jurisdiction to determine the respective rights of the parties and to adjudicate their claims and pleas even though the contract itself may be non-existent or null and void."

On the history of this provision see Yves DERAINS and Eric A. SCHWARTZ, *A Guide to the New ICC Rules of Arbitration* (Kluwer Law International 1998) p. 104.

26. Art. 21(2) of the UNCITRAL Arbitration Rules provides:

"[f]or the purposes of article 21 [i.e., the determination by the arbitral tribunal on its jurisdiction], an arbitration clause which forms part of a contract and which provides for arbitration under these Rules shall be treated as an agreement independent of the other terms of the contract. A decision by the arbitral tribunal that the contract is null and void shall not entail ipso jure the invalidity of the arbitration clause."

27. The London Court of International Arbitration (LCIA). Art. 23(1) of the LCIA Arbitration Rules, adopted to take effect as of 1 January 1998, provides:

"The Arbitral Tribunal shall have the power to rule on its own jurisdiction, including any objection to the initial or continuing existence, validity or effectiveness of the Arbitration Agreement. For that purpose, an arbitration clause which forms or was intended to form part of another agreement shall be treated as an arbitration agreement independent of that other agreement. A decision by the Arbitral Tribunal that such other agreement is non-existent, invalid or ineffective shall not entail ipso jure the non-existence, invalidity or ineffectiveness of the arbitration clause."

28. The American Arbitration Association (AAA) is a public service organization headquartered in New York. Art. 15 of the AAA's International Arbitration Rules provides:

"The tribunal shall have the power to determine the existence or validity of a contract of which an arbitration clause forms a part. Such an arbitration clause shall be treated as an agreement independent of the other terms of the contract. A decision by the tribunal that the contract is null

or the WIPO[29] Arbitration Rules provide for practically identical provisions as those of Art. 21(2) of the UNCITRAL Arbitration Rules.

The most important evolution in the field of separability was nevertheless noticed once nations started to enact "modern" arbitration statutes that acknowledged the doctrine of autonomy. This trend corresponded in some way to the adoption of the UNCITRAL Model Law in 1985. On 21 June 1985 the UNCITRAL adopted the "Model Law on International Commercial Arbitration" (hereinafter the UNCITRAL Model Law).[30] A few months later, on 11 December 1985, the United Nations General Assembly approved the UNCITRAL Model Law and recommended that "all States give due consideration" to this model. Whether the extensive adoption of the UNCITRAL Model Law intervened as a result of the above recommendation could be argued. Nonetheless, in the past two decades many countries have enacted modern arbitration statutes which expressly recognized the separability doctrine[31] or adopted the UNCITRAL Model Law including Art. 16 which precisely refers to the doctrine of autonomy.[32]

---

and void shall not for that reason render invalid the arbitration clause."

29. The World Intellectual Property Organization (WIPO). See Art. 36 of the WIPO Arbitration Rules.
30. Art. 16(1) of the UNCITRAL Model Law provides that: "... an arbitration clause which forms part of a contract shall be treated as an agreement independent of the other terms of the contract". See Matthew B. COBB, "Article 16(1) of the UNCITRAL Model Law: The Related Doctrines of Kompetenz-Kompetenz and Separability", 16 Mealey's International Arbitration Report (2001, no. 6) p. 32.
31. See Art. 178(3) of the 1987 Swiss Private International Law Act (PILA) which provides that "the validity of an arbitration agreement cannot be contested on the ground that the main contract may not be valid"; Art. 1053 of the Netherlands Code of Civil Procedure which states that "an arbitration agreement shall be considered and decided upon as a separate agreement"; Art. 1607 (1) and (2) of the Belgian Judicial Code (Law of 4 July 1972); Art. 8 of the 1988 Spanish Arbitration Act which specifically provides: "The nullity of a contract will not necessarily result in the nullity of the arbitration agreement accessory to it"; Art. 808, para. 3 of the Italian Code of Civil Procedure which provides that "the validity of the arbitration agreement is assessed independently of that of the main contract". Arbitration statutes have also been enacted in France (1981), England (1996) and Sweden (1999). We should not omit to mention that many Arab and Latin American countries have followed the same course: Algeria (1993), Tunisia (1993), Egypt (1994), Brazil (1996).
32. Legislation based on the UNCITRAL Model Law has been enacted in: Australia, Austria (with the exception of Art. 16.1 related to the autonomy of the arbitration agreement, see in this sense Andreas REINER, "La Réforme du Droit autrichien de l'arbitrage par la loi du 13 janvier 2006", Rev. arb. (2006) p. 401 at p. 410), Azerbaijan, Bahrain, Bangladesh, Belarus, Bulgaria, Cambodia, Canada, Chile, in China: Hong Kong Special Administrative Region, Macau Special Administrative Region; Croatia, Cyprus, Denmark, Egypt, Germany, Greece, Guatemala, Hungary, India, Iran (Islamic Republic of), Ireland, Japan, Jordan, Kenya, Lithuania, Madagascar, Malta, Mexico, New Zealand, Nicaragua, Nigeria, Norway, Oman, Paraguay, Peru, the Philippines, Poland, Republic of Korea, Russian Federation, Singapore, Spain, Sri Lanka, Thailand, Tunisia, Turkey, Ukraine, within the United Kingdom of Great Britain and Northern Ireland: Scotland; in Bermuda, overseas territory of the United Kingdom of Great Britain and Northern Ireland; within the United States of America: California, Connecticut, Illinois, Louisiana, Oregon and Texas; Zambia and

Canada[33] and most of the countries that are members of the British Commonwealth such as Australia and Hong Kong are among the proponents of the doctrine.[34] England recognized the principle of autonomy in case law and then in specific statutory law. Overcoming the English legislators' reticence vis-à-vis the adoption of the UNCITRAL Model Law,[35] Art. 7 of the English Arbitration Act of 1996 (AA 1996) finally confirmed the principle of autonomy in very clear terms:

> "Unless otherwise agreed by the parties, an arbitration agreement which forms or was intended to form part of another agreement shall not be regarded as invalid, non-existent or ineffective because that other agreement is invalid, or did not come into existence or has become ineffective, and it shall for that purpose be treated as a distinct agreement."[36]

In the United States, while the UNCITRAL Model Law was not implemented at the

---

Zimbabwe.

33. The concept of an independent agreement is provided for in most of the domestic Acts which were inspired by the UNCITRAL Model Law. See, in this sense, Art. 2642 of the Civil Code of Quebec which provides:

"An arbitration agreement contained in a contract is considered to be an agreement separate from the other clauses of the contract and the ascertainment by the arbitrators that the contract is null does not entail the nullity of the arbitration agreement."

The Ontario domestic Act provides:

"If the arbitration agreement forms part of another agreement, it shall, for the purpose of a ruling on jurisdiction, be treated as an independent agreement that may survive even if the main agreement is found to be invalid."

See generally J. Brian CASEY and Janet MILLS, *Arbitration Law of Canada: Practice and Procedure*, (2005) p. 49.

34. Andrew ROGERS, "Separability – The Indestructible Arbitration Clause", 10 Arbitration International (1994) p. 77 at p. 80.

35. The drafters of the English Arbitration Act 1996 (AA 1996) considered wholesale adoption of the Model Law to be a step too far and unnecessary mainly because England had an up-to-date arbitration regime supported by an extensive body of jurisprudence. See in this sense Charles CHATTERJEE, "Legal Aspects of Severability of Arbitration Clauses: an English Perspective", The Arbitration and Dispute Resolution Law Journal (1996) p. 297 at p. 310.

36. As an important study on the English Arbitration Act concluded: "Whatever degree of legal fiction underlying the doctrine, it is not generally considered possible for international arbitration to operate effectively in jurisdictions where the doctrine is precluded [...] international consensus on autonomy has now grown very broad", in UK Department of Trade and Industry Consultation document on Proposed Clauses and Schedules for an Arbitration Bill, reprinted in 10 Arbitration International (1994) p. 189, at p. 227. After citing leading cases from Switzerland, France, the United States, Germany and Russia, the study considered that English law "fits firmly into the mainstream of this international consensus", and recommended the statutory recognition of the doctrine, which finally led to its incorporation at Sect. 7 of the Arbitration Act 1996. See also CRAIG, PARK, PAULSSON, *op. cit.*, fn. 5, p. 50.

federal level,[37] some states have nonetheless adopted it with a view to promoting international arbitration within their boundaries.[38] Even if the judicial position of the doctrine of separability varies from state to state and despite the absence of an updated uniform legislation on international commercial arbitration,[39] US courts have manifested a spectacular *favor arbitrandum* starting with the Supreme Court's majority opinion in the 1967 *Prima Paint v. Flood & Conklin Manufacturing Co.*[40]

This landmark decision is generally credited with making the separability doctrine US law.[41] The doctrine also received a broad application at state level where state lower courts have held that the separability of the arbitration agreement was a principle of

---

37. Sébastien BESSON, "The Utility of State Laws Regulating International Commercial Arbitration and their Compatibility with the FAA", 11 American Review of International Arbitration (2000) p. 211.

38. Besides the States that adopted the UNCITRAL Model Law, *op. cit.*, fn. 32, other states, e.g., Georgia, passed specific legislation related to international arbitration and expressly acknowledged the separability principle. In this sense, Art. 9-9-34 Georgia Code Ann., Title 9, Chapter 9 provides:

   "The arbitrators may rule on their own jurisdiction, including any objections with respect to the existence or validity of the arbitration agreement. For that purpose, an arbitration clause which forms part of a contract shall be treated as an agreement independent of the other terms of the contract. A decision by the arbitrators that the contract is null and void shall not thereby invalidate the arbitration clause."

39. For a broad analysis of the US statutory law on arbitration, see Kimbell Sherman ELLIS, "Mandatory Arbitration, July 2005", <www.afsaonline.org/CMS/fileREPOSITORY/Mandatory%20Arbitration%20ReportJuly%202005.pdf>; Jon O. SHIMABUKURO, "The Federal Arbitration Act: Background and Recent Developments", Report for Congress, updated 17 June 2002, <www.thememoryhole.org/crs/RL30934.pdf>; Timothy J. HEINSZ, "The Revised Uniform Arbitration Act: An Overview", 56 Dispute Resolution Journal (2001, no. 2) p. 28.

40. 388 U.S. 395 (1967).

41. It is worth mentioning that the majority opinion in *Prima Paint* never expressly adopted the separability doctrine. The Supreme Court held only that under a broad arbitration clause to which the FAA applies, a claim of fraud in the inducement of a contract generally – as opposed to a claim of fraud in the inducement of the arbitration clause itself – must be referred to the arbitrators rather than decided by the courts. The Court based its holding on the language of Sect. 4 of the FAA that requires a court, on a petition to compel arbitration, to refer the case to arbitration "upon being satisfied that the making of the agreement for arbitration or the failure to comply therewith is not in issue". As the dissent notes, the language of Sect. 4 of the FAA nowhere

   "provides an 'explicit answer' to the question of whether the arbitration clause is 'separable' from the rest of the contract in which it is contained. Sect. 4 merely provides that the court must order arbitration if it is 'satisfied that the making of the agreement for arbitration ... is not in issue'. That language, considered alone, far from providing an 'explicit answer', merely poses the further question of what kind of allegations put the making of the arbitration agreement in issue."

388 U.S. at 410.

federal law applicable in state courts[42] and was recently reaffirmed by the US Supreme Court in *Buckeye Check Cashing, Inc. v. John Cardegna et al.*[43]

This universal recognition, also affirmed in arbitral case law,[44] led some eminent scholars to consider the autonomy of the arbitration agreement as a "true transnational rule of international commercial arbitration".[45] The assertion is far from being false. In fact, international commercial arbitration is practiced as a body of transnational law because a large number of countries currently apply the same major principles and concepts. According to some scholars, this uniformity has principally two sources: the widespread acceptance of international arbitration treaties,[46] on the one hand, and the influence of the UNCITRAL Model Law which has served as the paradigm for most recently enacted "modern" national arbitration statutes,[47] on the other hand.

The issue is nevertheless open to debate. One might correctly advance that these conventions are implicitly in favor of the autonomy of the arbitration agreement and did not hinder its widespread recognition,[48] whereas someone else could, on the contrary, contend that these conventions were "indifferent" to the principle of autonomy, mainly due to the fact that none of them expressly referred to it.[49] Or maybe it would be safer

---

42. See generally Sébastien BESSON, *op. cit.*, fn. 37, p. 217.

43. *Buckeye Check Cashing, Inc. v. John Cardegna et al.*, *op. cit.*, fn. 21. See also infra Sect. III.2.

44. In *Elf Aquitaine Iran v. National Iranian Oil Co. (NIOC)*, ICCA *Yearbook Commercial Arbitration* XI (1986) (hereinafter *Yearbook*) p. 97, the arbitral tribunal reasoned in the following terms:

> "The autonomy of an arbitration clause is a principle of international law that has been consistently applied in decisions rendered in international arbitrations, in the writings of most qualified publicists on international arbitration, in arbitration regulations adopted by international organizations and treaties. Also, in many countries, the principle forms part of national arbitration law.
> (....)
> [T]he arbitration clause binds the parties and is operative and unimpaired by the allegation by NIOC that the Agreement, as a whole, is null and void 'ab initio'."

45. Emmanuel GAILLARD and John SAVAGE, eds., *op. cit.*, fn. 5, p. 228.

46. UN Convention on the Recognition and Enforcement of Foreign Arbitral Awards, 10 June 1958, 21 U.S.T. 2517, 330 U.N.T.S. 3 (hereinafter New York Convention) is presently signed by 142 States. For an up-to-date list of contracting States see <http://www.uncitral.org/uncitral/en/uncitral_texts/arbitration/NYConvention_status.html>. Similarly, the 1965 Washington Convention establishing ICSID was signed by 155 States, *Yearbook* XXXI (2006) p. 1513.

47. See <http://www.uncitral.org/uncitral/en/uncitral_texts/arbitration/1985Model_arbitration_status.html>.

48. Peter SCHLOSSER, *Das Recht der Internationalen Privaten Schiedsgerichtsbarkeit* (1975) Sect.316 ; See also Stephen M. SCHWEBEL who maintains that the New York Convention adopts separability by "implication", *op. cit.*, fn. 9 at p. 22, and Antonias DIMOLITSA, *op .cit.*, fn. 10 at p. 217.

49. See Albert Jan VAN DEN BERG, *The New York Arbitration Convention of 1958* (1981) p. 146. Considering Art. II(3) of the New York Convention which only provides that:

> "The court of a Contracting State, when seized of an action in a matter in respect of which the parties have made an [arbitration] agreement within the meaning of this article, shall, at the request of one of the parties, refer the parties to arbitration, unless it finds that the said

to consider that the drafters of the above conventions left the issue of separability to be decided by relevant national legal systems?

Judges, legislators and arbitrators, all affirmed the principle and applied it in international commercial arbitration. A stream of ink flowed during the past decades and multiple arguments were developed by the arbitration milieu in order to justify "the legal fiction" of the autonomy.

2. Justification and Consequences of the Autonomy

The importance of a valid arbitration agreement in a world where international commercial arbitration transcends national boundaries has led commentators throughout the world to search for the rationale behind the doctrine of autonomy in order to justify its existence and its role.

a. The rationale behind autonomy

The doctrine can be explained by practical and theoretical reasons. From a practical point of view, the requirements of international trade where arbitration became an effective method of dispute resolution and the parties' need for security, away from the uncertainties of the national procedure laws, justify by themselves the need that the arbitration agreement be legally protected in order to assure its efficiency.

When the arbitration agreement incorporates institutional rules – like the ICC, the UNCITRAL or the LCIA Arbitration Rules – which expressly provide that an arbitration clause is separable from the parties' underlying contract, then the autonomy could equally be justified on the basis of the so-called parties' "express" agreement.[50] In the absence of similar express provisions, courts or arbitrators might look for the party's implied intent to refer to arbitration any dispute related to the main contract,[51] so that parties would be less capable of vitiating their arbitration obligation by the simple expedient of declaring the agreement void.

It could also be argued that the security of efficient international business practices implies that parties from different legal traditions would have their expectations fulfilled in that any disputes would be solved in a neutral, non-national arbitral forum, regardless any challenges to the validity of their underlying contract.[52]

[arbitration] agreement is null and void, inoperative or incapable of being performed",

the author of the influential study of the New York Convention affirmed that the New York Convention is "indifferent" as to separability.

50. See Art. 6 of the ICC Rules, Art. 21 of the UNCITRAL Rules, and Art. 23 of the LCIA Rules.
51. For more developments on this issue see Alan Scott RAU, op. cit., fn. 8.
52. The High Court in Harbour Assurance Co. (UK) v. Kansa Gen. Int'l Ins. Co., 1 Lloyd's Rep. 81 (Q.B. 1992) explained the doctrine of separability as follows:

"First, there is the imperative of giving effect to the wishes of the parties unless there are compelling reasons of principle why it is not possible to do so.... Secondly, if the arbitration clause is not held to survive the invalidity of the contract, a party is afforded the opportunity to evade his obligation to arbitrate by the simple expedient of alleging that the contract is void. In such cases

From a theoretical point of view, it has been pointed out that "[T]he very concept and phrase 'arbitration agreement' itself imports the existence of a separate or at any rate separable agreement, which is or can be divorced from the body of the principal agreement if needs be."[53]

Separate treatment of the contract and its arbitration agreement is often explained on the ground that there are "different kinds of agreements": the arbitration agreement concerns issues of procedural dispute resolution, while the contract concerns the substantive rights and obligations of the parties in their contractual relationship. Many academics[54] and arbitrators[55] rely therefore on the "procedural" or "jurisdictional" nature of the arbitration agreement to justify its "separable" or "independent" character.

This approach did not receive a unanimous welcome. It was argued, for example, that the arbitration agreement cannot be conceived as an independent contract since it is one among the other clauses that create a unique agreement and it does not exist without the main contract.[56] However, French scholars are of the opinion that the arbitration agreement is nonetheless separable from the main contract since it helps to define the process that will determine the future of the agreement and it is therefore "ancillary" to the substantive provisions of that agreement.[57]

It has also been suggested that the arbitration agreement is an "accessory" to the right of action which goes together with the substantive provisions of the contract: in such a

---

courts of law then inevitably become involved in deciding the substance of a dispute. Moreover, in international transactions where the neutrality of the arbitral process is highly prized, the collapse of this consensual method of dispute resolution compels a party to resort to national courts where in the real world the badge of neutrality is sometimes perceived to be absent. For parties the perceived effectiveness of the neutral arbitral process is often a vital condition in the process of negotiation of the contract. If that perception is absent, it will often present a formidable hurdle to the conclusion of the transaction. A full recognition of the separability principle tends to facilitate international trade."

53. Stephen M. SCHWEBEL, op. cit., fn. 9, at p.3.
54. Christophe SERAGLINI in Jacques BEGUIN and Michel MENJUCQ, eds., Droit du commerce international (Lexis Nexis Litec 2005) p. 883 ; Jean-Baptiste RACINE, "Réflexions sur l'autonomie de l'arbitrage commercial international", Rev. arb. (2005) p. 305 at p. 313; Jean-Pierre ANCEL, op. cit., fn. 7, p. 82.
55. In Sojuznefteexport v. Joc Oil. Ltd., Yearbook XVIII (1993) p. 92, for example, the arbitral tribunal considered the procedural character of the arbitration agreement in order to justify its autonomy from the underlying contract in the following terms:

"Taking into account the cited facts and observations as to the nature of the arbitration agreement (clause), the Commission has come to the conclusion that, by virtue of its procedural content and independently of the form of its conclusion, it is autonomous in relation to the material-legal contract. An arbitration clause, included in a contract, means that there are regulated in it relationships different in legal nature, and that therefore the effect of the arbitration clause is separate from the effect of the remaining provisions of the foreign trade contract."

56. Jean-François POUDRET and Sébastien BESSON, op. cit., fn. 5, p. 134.
57. Pierre MAYER, "The Limits of Severability of the Arbitration Clause" in ICCA Congress Series no.9, p. 261. For the French version, see Rev. arb. (1998) pp. 359-368.

view, the arbitration agreement exists as long as the right of action exists, even if the main contract no longer exists.[58] One can recall that English courts, for example, prior the 1996 statutory enactment of the doctrine of autonomy, took a similar approach in considering the "collateral" nature of the arbitration agreement in order to justify its separability from the main contract.[59]

This is also the Swiss view according to which an arbitration agreement is an "agreement on jurisdiction", a procedural contract which is autonomous and independent from the main contract in which it is contained.[60] Even if the arbitration agreement is formally linked to the substantive main contract in the same document, Swiss courts interpreted it as a procedural agreement, independent to the extent that in case of doubt it has to be assumed that the parties did not want to submit to arbitration only disputes concerning the execution of their mutual obligations under the contract, but also disputes concerning whether a contract has been validly concluded.

Whatever rationale one might consider in order to explain the autonomy of the arbitration agreement, it is undeniable that the doctrine is now embedded in most modern arbitration laws and practice upon which international arbitrators rely, irrespective of their seat and of the law governing the proceedings.[61]

It is worth then mentioning the consequences of the autonomy for at least two reasons. First, they express the doctrine of autonomy and its application in the international arena, and secondly, some of them were more welcomed than others, providing scholars with arguments against the autonomy itself.

b.   *The consequences of the principle of autonomy*
The two direct, most important consequences of the doctrine are, first, that the status of the main contract does not affect the arbitration agreement, and second, that the substantive law governing the formation or the validity of the arbitration agreement may be different from that governing the underlying contract. The doctrine's main corollary is the principle of competence-competence.

i.   Independence of the arbitration agreement from the main contract
The arbitral tribunal can consider the challenge to the validity of the main contract without questioning its own legitimacy and jurisdiction. This rule has been controversial

---

58. Eric LOQUIN, *"L'arbitrage du commerce international"* in *Dictionnaire Joly – Pratique des contrats internationaux* (2001) Livre X, n° 102, p. 50 ; Sylvain BOLLÉE, *"La clause compromissoire et le droit commun des conventions"*, Rev. arb. (2005) p. 917 at p. 925.

59. In this sense, Lord Diplock in *Paal Wilson and Company A/S v. Partenreederei* [1986] 3 W.L.R. 1149 at p. 1168 said that:

"an arbitration clause is collateral to the main contract in which it is incorporated and gives rise to collateral primary and secondary obligations of its own. Those collateral obligations survive the termination of all primary obligations assumed by the parties under the other clauses in the main contract."

60. Christoph MÜLLER, *op. cit.*, fn. 14, p. 45.
61. Emmanuel GAILLARD and John SAVAGE, eds., *op. cit.*, fn. 5, p. 198.

to the extent that it has been sustained that even if an arbitration agreement might not be affected by the nullity of the underlying contract, it will not survive its non-existence. In order to justify this difference in the application of the rule, case law developed the distinction between voidable and void ab initio contracts. Such distinction, even though rejected in many modern statutes and conventions, still existed in case law not long ago.

Most of the jurisdictions in favor of such a limited application of the separability doctrine have lately revised their position so that today, it is safe to affirm that, if an arbitral tribunal or court concludes that the entire underlying contract was void, that conclusion would not necessarily deprive the arbitration agreement of validity.[62]

ii.   Independence of the arbitration agreement from the lex contractus

The autonomy of the arbitration agreement also means that such agreements *may* be, but not necessarily should be governed by a law different from that governing the main contract. Therefore, when the parties did not expressly make a choice, the substantive law governing the formation or the validity of the arbitration agreement may be different from both the law applicable to the substance of the contract and to the arbitral proceedings.[63] Such determination rests either on the application of the traditional choice-of-law rules or, as French case law lately acknowledged it, on the application of the substantive rules method. Nevertheless, in comparative law, the traditional choice-of-law method is still the most commonly encountered method,[64] and the major conventions on arbitration refer to it.[65]

Four possible alternatives for the law governing an arbitration agreement should therefore be relevant when using such a method:

(a) the law expressly or impliedly chosen by the parties to govern the arbitration agreement itself;
(b) the law of the arbitral *situs*;[66]

---

62. See infra Sect. III.2.
63. Emmanuel GAILLARD and John SAVAGE, eds., *op. cit.*, fn. 5, p. 212.
64. See, e.g., Art. 1074 of the Netherlands Code of Civil Procedure, which addresses the validity of an arbitration agreement under "the law applicable thereto"; Art. 61 of the Spanish Law 36/1988 on Arbitration of 5 December 1988 which requires that the law designated by the parties to govern the arbitration agreement "has some connection with the ... dispute"; Art. 48 of the 1999 Swedish Arbitration Act according to which the arbitration agreement is governed by the law chosen by the parties or, absent such choice, by the law of the place of arbitration.
65. Art. V(1)(a) of the 1958 New York Convention which provides that recognition and enforcement of an award may be refused if the arbitration agreement is not "valid under the law which the parties have subjected it or, failing any indication thereon, under the law of the country where the award was made"; and Art. IX(1) of the 1961 European Convention which employs similar language.
66. In practice, in the absence of any expressed or implied choice by the parties, the choice of law applicable to international arbitration agreements is influenced by both the New York Convention and national law. In this sense, the Convention implicitly submits the determination of the arbitration agreement's existence or validity to the law chosen by the parties or, failing any indication thereon, to the law of the arbitral *situs*. There is a similar provision in the Model Law at Art. 34(2)(a) and at Art. 178 Swiss PILA. There are several jurisdictions in which a court or

(c) the law governing the parties' main contract;[67] and
(d) the law of the forum where judicial enforcement is sought.[68]

In France, the doctrine of autonomy has been used to detach the arbitration agreement from all national laws, meaning that in international cases, no law applies to arbitral clauses except basic rules relating to the existence and scope of the agreement and international public policy.

iii.   Arbitrators' jurisdiction to rule on their own jurisdiction
Viewed as an indirect consequence of the separability doctrine, the principle of competence-competence gives arbitrators the power to consider their own jurisdiction. Most international arbitration statutes and institutional arbitration rules address the separability doctrine and the principle of competence-competence together. Consequently, the autonomy of the arbitration clause is often confused with the notion of competence-competence.

In reality, the two principles are distinct and many commentators warn against

---

arbitral tribunal has taken the law of the seat of the arbitration as the appropriate law to govern the parties' arbitration agreement. In this sense, see *Bulgarian Foreign Trade Bank Ltd v. Al Trade Finance Inc.*, Swedish Supreme Court, 27 October 2000, Case No. T 1881-99, *Yearbook* XXVI (2001) p. 291; *XL Insurance Ltd. v. Owens Corning* [2002] 2 Lloyd's Rep. 500; *Matermaco SA v. PPM Cranes Inc. and Legris Industries SA.*, 20 September 1999, *Tribunal de Commerce*, Brussels, *Yearbook* XXV (2000) pp. 673-677, also cited in Alan REDFERN and Martin HUNTER, *op. cit.*, fn. 5, p. 127. It is also worth mentioning that English courts increasingly place more weight on the parties' selection of a particular arbitral *situs*, regarding this as an implied choice-of-law governing the arbitration agreement. See to this effect *XL Insurance Ltd v. Owens Corning*, 2 Lloyd's Law Rep. 500 (2000) where the Court said: "by stipulating for arbitration in London under the provisions for the [English Arbitration] Act ... the parties chose English law to govern the matters which fall within those provisions, including the formal validity of the arbitration clause and the jurisdiction of the arbitral tribunal; and by implication chose English law as the proper law of the arbitration clause".

67. According to Professor Lew, "there is a very strong presumption in favour of the law governing the substantive agreement which contains the arbitration clause also governing the arbitration agreement. This principle has been followed in many cases. This could even be implied as an agreement of the parties as to the law applicable to the arbitration clause", in Julian D.M. LEW, "The Law Applicable to the Form and Substance of the Arbitration Clause" in *ICCA Congress Series no. 9*, p. 114. This presumption was recently reaffirmed in English case law in *Sonatrach Petroleum Corporation (BVI) v. Ferrell International Ltd.* [2002] 1 All E.R. (Comm.) 627, also cited in Alan REDFERN and Martin HUNTER, *op. cit.*, fn. 5, p. 125. See also, Art. 178(2) of the Swiss PILA and the provisions of many institutional rules dealing with applicable law which are expressly directed at the law governing the merits of the parties' dispute, such as: UNCITRAL Rules Art. 33; 1998 ICC Rules Art. 17; AAA International Rules Art. 29.

68. That was the position of US courts prior enactment of the FAA. This approach considered the validity and enforceability of an arbitration agreement as a "procedural" or "remedial" matter governed by the law of the judicial forum in which the [arbitration] agreement was invoked. Presently Sects. 187 and 188 of the *Restatement (Second) Conflict of Laws* generally give effect to the parties' contractual choice of law or, failing such agreement, provide for application of the law of the state with the most significant relationship to the parties' [arbitration] agreement. For a detailed discussion on this topic, see G.A. BORN, *International Commercial Arbitration*, 2nd edn. (2001) p. 108.

confusing their analysis.[69] The autonomy of the arbitration agreement operates with respect to flaws in the main contract which might affect the arbitrator's jurisdiction whereas the principle of competence-competence gives arbitrators jurisdiction to decide on challenges to the arbitration clause itself,[70] representing therefore only a procedural tool of the separability doctrine.[71] It is correct then to affirm that the only common function that separability and competence-competence can provide is that both principles create mechanisms to prevent a bad-faith party from stopping the arbitral proceedings before they have begun.[72]

Considering this brief overview of the origins and evolution of the doctrine of autonomy, we should analyze now its current status: its achievements or its presumptive limits as voiced up by international scholars.

III. IS THE ARBITRATION AGREEMENT STILL AUTONOMOUS?

As already mentioned, the doctrine of autonomy has gained worldwide recognition and application in the field of international commercial arbitration. We are, nevertheless, asked whether the arbitration agreement is still autonomous. This question seemed legitimate in view of the inconsistent application of the doctrine of autonomy in some legal systems which has allowed ongoing doctrinal criticism as to its true meaning.

In order to respond correctly to this doctrinal inquiry, recent case law development should be scrutinized. It might be preferable therefore to start with France where courts and scholars alike draw increasingly widespread conclusions from the doctrine of autonomy to consider the arbitration agreement independent from all national laws (1).

Then, in order to acquire an objective point of view, one should consider the latest developments in US case law. The Supreme Court recently revised its position and affirmed the force of the doctrine in US international arbitration law. One might be led to conclude that the "immunity" of the arbitration agreement, as perceived in the civil law tradition, has at last crossed the ocean (2).

---

69. As William PARK underlined it, the differences between the two principles are as follows:

"Separability says nothing about the validity of the arbitration clause itself. The fact that an arbitration clause might be valid notwithstanding infirmities in other contract terms does not mean that the clause will be valid, or that an arbitrator's erroneous decision on the clause's validity will escape judicial scrutiny. Separability and competence-competence intersect only in the sense that arbitrators who rule on their own jurisdiction will look to the arbitration clause alone, not to the entirety of the contract."

in William W. PARK, "Determining Arbitral Jurisdiction: Allocation of Tasks between Courts and Arbitrators", 8 American Review of International Arbitration (1997) p.133.

70. C. SVERNLOV, "The Current Status of the Doctrine of Separability", 8 Journal of International Arbitration (1991, no. 4) pp. 37-49.

71. Jean-François POUDRET and Sébastien BESSON, op. cit., fn. 5, p. 133.

72. William W. PARK, "The Arbitrability Dicta in First Options v. Kaplan: What Sort of Kompetenz-Kompetenz Has Crossed the Atlantic?", 12 Arbitration International (1996, no. 2) pp. 137-159.

Finally, the circulation of the arbitration agreement with the main contract, notwithstanding its autonomy, might be considered as another important achievement of the principle of autonomy when it is justified on the basis of the validity of the arbitration agreement independently of that of the main contract (3).

1. The Extensive Meaning of Autonomy

Expanding the initial meaning of the principle of autonomy, namely to protect the arbitration agreement from any challenges raised to the validity of the main contract, French case law evolved toward the concept of "full autonomy", a revolutionary position, considering that the existence, the validity and the scope of the arbitration agreement, in international commercial arbitration, should be determined by reference to substantive rules, independently of any applicable national law,[73] and thus detached from the traditional conflict-of-law rules (a). Today, the principle of validity is also applied to characterize arbitration agreements concluded by a State or a State entity (b).

a. The French approach: the substantive rules method

i. The substantive rules method
As early as 1972, the Paris Court of Appeal held for the first time ever that, even if one considers that the existence and validity of an arbitration agreement should be determined by reference to a particular national law, as a result of the principle of separability such law will not necessarily be that governing the main contract.[74] Considering that the arbitration agreement is valid purely on the basis of the principle of autonomy, without any reference to the law governing it, French courts established a so-called "principle of validity" and concluded that the international arbitration agreement has validity and effectiveness of its own and is not subject to the traditional choice-of-law method.[75] The concept of linking the agreement to a particular law disappeared entirely and the principle of autonomy evolved into a substantive rule imposing the validity of the international arbitration agreement subject to only two exceptions concerning French mandatory rules and international public policy.[76]

---

73. Court of Appeal, Paris, 13 December 1975 (*Menicucci v. Mahieux*), Journal du Droit International (1977) p. 104 with note E. LOQUIN.

74. Court of Appeal, Paris, 25 January 1972 (*Quijano Aguero v. Marcel Laporte*), Rev. arb. (1973) p.158.

75. *Cour de cassation*, 4 July 1972 (*Hecht v. Buisman's*), Journal du Droit International (1972) p. 843, 845 with note B. OPPETIT.

76. Court of Appeal, Paris, 17 December 1991 (*Gatoil v. National Iranian Oil Co.*), Rev. arb. (1993) p. 281, where the French court reaffirmed the notion of "international substantive rules" as follows:

"in the field of commercial arbitration, the principle of autonomy of the arbitration agreement is of general application, as an international substantive rule upholding the legality of the arbitration agreement, quite apart from any reference to a system of choice of law, because the validity of the agreement must be judged solely in the light of the requirements of international public policy".

This approach, which marks the abandonment of the conflict-of-law rules method in the appreciation of the validity of an international arbitration agreement, was affirmed by the French *Cour de cassation* in the 1993 landmark *Dalico* decision in the following terms:

> "pursuant to a substantive rule of international arbitration law, the arbitration agreement is legally independent of the main contract which incorporates it either directly or by reference, and ... its existence and validity are to be appreciated, subject to the mandatory rules of French law and international public policy, based on the mutual intent of the parties, without a need for a reference to any national law".[77]

Reviewing the past thirty years, one might observe that the French *Cour de cassation*, in search of the right definition, subsequently qualified the arbitration agreement first as autonomous, then independent from the main contract, and finally as having a validity and efficiency of its own.[78] This last conception of the autonomy has been recently reaffirmed by the Court and today it represents the solution in the French law of international arbitration.[79]

ii.   Critics of the substantive rules method

Even though accepted by a majority of the doctrine, some authors pointed out that an arbitration agreement is a fortiori a contract and that it cannot be considered valid unless it satisfies relevant conditions as to its form and substance under a law which governs that contract.[80] In other words, an arbitration agreement cannot be an agreement without a law, a so-called *contrat sans loi*.

Actually, under French law the arbitration agreement is not a contract without a governing law but a contract without a choice of law and the validity of the arbitration agreement is derived from those principles that the *Cour de cassation* called "mandatory rules of French law" and "international public policy", the so called *Dalico* rules.[81] These rules were interpreted as the expression of a certain "French imperialism" in that the *Cour de cassation* intended to include French rules on arbitrability in the body of rules

---

77. *Cour de cassation*, 20 December 1993 (*Comité populaire de la municipalité de Khoms El Mergheb v. Dalico Contractors*), 121 Journal du Droit International (1994) p. 432, with note E. GAILLARD and note E. LOQUIN at p. 690; 1994 Rev. arb. (1994) p. 116, with note H. GAUDEMET-TALLON; Revue critique de droit international privé (1994) p. 663, with note P. MAYER.

78. *Cour de cassation*, 5 January 1999 (*M. Zanzi v. J. de Cornick et autres*), Rev. arb. (1999) p. 260 with note P. FOUCHARD.

79. *Cour de cassation*, 7 June 2006 (*Copropriété maritime Jules Verne, et al. v. Sté ABS American Bureau of Shipping, et al.*) no. 03-12.034, Juris-Data no. 2006-033853; *Cour de cassation*, 25 October 2005 (*Société Omenex v. M. Hugon*), Rev. arb. (2006) p. 103 with note Jean-Baptiste RACINE ; Journal du Droit International (2006) p. 996 with note F.X. TRAIN.

80. See Hélène GAUDEMET-TALLON, note following Court of Appeal, Paris, 26 March 1991 (*Comité populaire de la municipalité de Khoms El Mergheb v. Dalico Contractors*), Rev. arb. (1991) p. 469.

81. Emmanuel GAILLARD and John SAVAGE, eds., *op. cit.*, fn. 5 and *Dalico*, see fn. 77.

based upon which the validity of the international arbitration agreement will be checked.[82]

However, the true significance of this method, as sustained by a majority of commentators, consists in determining the validity of an international arbitration agreement solely by reference to the French conception of international public policy. Such a conception does not lead to the exclusion of the law normally applicable, but consists of "the French legal system view of the fundamental requirements of justice in an international context"[83] where the notion of "mandatory rules of French law" and "international public policy" such as used in the 1993 *Dalico* decision are synonymous and stand for a limited body of rules which must be observed for an arbitration agreement be effective.

By using the substantive rules method, French courts clearly want to guarantee the validity of the arbitration agreement and its absolute efficiency and in doing so they consider that they give force to the real intent of the parties.[84]

Justified then on the basis of a validity and efficiency of its own, depending only on the parties' intent, French scholars asked themselves whether in international commercial arbitration, the existence of a principle of the validity of the international arbitration agreement should not be affirmed,[85] so that its objective "to establish a particular legal protection for this particular agreement" will be respected.[86]

b. *The international validity of the arbitration agreement concluded by a State or a State Entity*

One important application of the substantive rules method that French courts subsequently developed in the field of subjective arbitrability consists in that States or State entities cannot hide behind their own domestic law to request the nullity of the arbitration agreement.[87] This development, sometimes described as "a-national"

---

82. See Eric LOQUIN, note following *Cour de cassation*, 20 December 1993 (*Comité populaire de la municipalité de Khoms El Mergheb v. Dalico Contractors*), *op. cit.*, fn. 77, pp. 698-699.

83. See H. SYNVET, note following Court of Appeal, Paris, 17 December 1991 (*Gatoil v. National Iranian Oil Co.*), *op. cit.*, fn. 76, p. 294; See also Emmanuel GAILLARD and John SAVAGE, eds., *op. cit.*, fn. 5, p. 233.

84. *Cour de cassation*, 5 January 1999 (*Banque Worms v. R. Bellot and SNTM-Hyproc*), Rev. arb. (2000) p. 84 with note Daniel COHEN.

85. Jean-Baptiste RACINE, "*Réflexions sur l'Autonomie de l'Arbitrage Commercial International*", Rev. arb. (2005) p.305.

86. Jean-Pierre ANCEL, *op. cit.*, fn. 7.

87. This principle was expressed for the first time in French case law in *Cour de cassation*, 2 May 1962 (*Trésor Public v. Galakis*), Juris Classeur Périodique Ed. G., Pt. II, No. 14,798 (1966) and reaffirmed namely in Court of Appeal, Paris, 17 December 1991 (*Gatoil v. National Iranion Oil Co.*), Rev. arb. (1993) p. 281 (for an English translation see 7 International Arbitration Report (1992), where the court considered that:

"international public policy ... [prohibited] NIOC from availing itself of restrictive dispositions in its national law to withdraw a posteriori from the arbitration to which the parties agreed ... similarly, neither can Gatoil base its objections to the capacity and powers of NIOC upon the

arbitration, provides that international arbitrations are completely outside the regulatory reach of national laws and national juridical authority. The limits imposed on arbitration in domestic law do not impinge upon international arbitral agreements, proceedings, or awards.[88] Viewed as an indirect consequence of the doctrine of autonomy, the international validity of an arbitration agreement concluded by a State or a State entity has been adopted in international conventions[89] and in comparative law.[90] Also accepted in the international arbitral practice,[91] this principle has thus affirmed the absolute

---

dispositions of Iranian law since international public policy is not concerned by conditions set in this domain in the international legal order".

See also Jean-Pierre ANCEL, *op. cit.*, fn. 7, p. 75.

88. Thomas E. CARBONNEAU, *Cases and Materials on the Law and Practice of Arbitration*, 3d edn. (Juris Publishing 2002) p. 31.

89. See Art. II(1) of the 1961 European Convention, *Yearbook* XX (1995) p. 1006, which provides:

"[i]n cases referred to in Article I, paragraph 1, of this Convention [i.e., arbitration agreements and awards within the scope of the Convention], legal persons considered by the law which is applicable to them as 'legal persons of public law' have the right to conclude valid arbitration agreements".

90. Art. 177(2) of the Swiss PILA provides:

"If a party to the arbitration agreement is a state or an enterprise or organization controlled by it, it cannot rely on its own law in order to contest its capacity to be a party to arbitration or the arbitrability of a dispute covered by the arbitration agreement."

Similarly, Greek, English and Italian Courts have held that in principle state-owned entities cannot rely on particular domestic law provisions to avoid the application of arbitration agreements to which they are parties.

91. This principle was first formulated, in arbitral case law, in the 1971 ICC Award no. 1939:

"International public policy would be strongly opposed to the idea that a public entity, when dealing with foreign parties, could openly, knowingly, and willingly, enter into an arbitration agreement, on which its co-contractor would rely, only to claim subsequently, whether during the arbitral proceedings or on enforcement of the award, that its own undertaking was void."

Subsequently, in *Framatome v. Atomic Energy Organization of Iran* (AEOI)(1982), the respondent argued that the Iranian Constitution, which makes the submission to arbitration of disputes concerning state property conditional upon the approval of the Council of Ministers and notification to the Parliament, made the relevant arbitration agreement void. The arbitral tribunal disagreed in the following terms:

"It is superfluous to add that there is a general principle, which today is universally recognized in relations between states as well as in international relations between private entities ... whereby the Iranian state would in any event ... be prohibited from reneging on an arbitration agreement entered into by itself or, previously, by a public entity such as AEOI.
   The position of the current positive law of international relations is ... that a government bound by an arbitration clause – and this observation applies equally to obligations assumed directly and those assumed through an intermediary of a public organ ... cannot validly free itself from that

autonomy of the arbitration agreement, namely its power to "evacuate" the parties' national law unfavourable to the validity of the arbitration agreement,[92] and confirmed the fact that international commercial arbitration is de facto an autonomous and self-regulating international system of adjudication, subject only to the normative restraints contained in international conventions or that exist as a matter of customary international arbitral practice.

Could we therefore already conclude that the arbitration agreement is still autonomous? In my opinion, we should. I believe that nowhere in the world can the arbitration agreement find such a supportive protection from state courts as in France. But the "immunity" of the arbitration agreement from any flaws in the main contract to which it is related might also justify its absolute autonomy such as interpreted by many legal systems.

2.   The "Immunity" of the Arbitration Agreement

In the terminology of the New York Convention and of the UNCITRAL Model Law, the arbitration agreement is not enforceable if it is "null and void", "inoperative" or "incapable of being performed", the basic objections to its validity being those which are available under generally applicable contract law to contest the validity of any contract. In particular, these grounds include fraudulent inducement, fraud, illegality, unconscionability or duress, and waiver.

The validity of the arbitration agreement is also challenged on the basis of flaws in the main contract. In such situations, it is widely accepted, both in comparative law and in international arbitral case law that the purpose of the principle of autonomy is to ensure the "immunity" of the arbitration agreement, so that it remains unaffected by defects in the main contract. When they enter into an arbitration agreement, the parties intend – unless otherwise provided – to arbitrate *all* their disputes including those that the main contract is "non-existent", "null" or "void". It is thus generally accepted, by most national laws[93] and arbitration rules[94] that such claims shall not render the arbitration agreement invalid, or deprive the arbitral tribunal of jurisdiction.

---

obligation by an act of its own will, for example by a change in its internal law or by unilateral repudiation of the contract."

92. Jean-Pierre ANCEL, *op. cit.*, fn. 7, p. 86.

93. See Swiss PILA (1987) Art. 178(7); English AA 1996 Sect. 7; UNCITRAL Model Law (1985) Art. 16(1).

94. See ICC Arbitration Rules Art. 6(4); AAA International Arbitration Rules Art. 15(2); LCIA Rules Art. 23(1); UNCITRAL Arbitration Rules Art. 21(2); WIPO Arbitration Rules Art. 36.

However, some jurisdictions, principally the US courts,[95] have constantly operated on the basis of the distinction between contracts void ab initio[96] and voidable contracts[97] in order to decide on the fate of the arbitration agreement (a). At a certain time, French courts had a similar changing approach, considering that the validity of the arbitration agreement depends on the existence of the underlying agreement to which it relates (b).

This distinction has been interpreted as a limitation to the doctrine of autonomy, even though today it is considered, at least in the continental tradition, that the arbitration agreement has become "immune" to all causes that might render the main contract invalid, and that any challenges to the arbitration agreement itself should be reserved solely for the arbitrators' determination.[98]

It is important therefore to determine whether the distinction between void ab initio and voidable contracts as operated in some legal systems, still represents a real limitation to the doctrine of autonomy and allows one to question the autonomy of the arbitration agreement.

a.   The "void/voidable" distinction in US law

While the doctrine of separability is part of the US law since the 1967 landmark *Prima Paint* decision,[99] subsequent case law interpreted this decision restrictively on the basis of the *void/voidable* distinction.[100] On one hand, American courts had no trouble

---

95. A similar distinction had also prevailed in English law prior to *Harbour Assurance Company (UK) Ltd. v. Kansa General International Insurance Co. Ltd.* decision which overturned it considering that the doctrine of validity extends to claims of initial invalidity of the contract.

96. A contract that is void ab initio is one that produces no legal effect. "If an agreement is void, it cannot be a contract" in Samuel WILSTON & Richard A. LORD, *A Treatise on the Law of Contract*, 4th edn. (1990) p. 50; See generally the US *Restatement (Second) of Contracts* (1979) Sect.7 according to which a void contract is one that contains "a promise for breach of which the law neither gives a remedy nor otherwise recognizes a duty of performance by the promisor".

97. A voidable contract is an agreement that "unless rescinded ... imposes on the parties the same obligations as it if were not voidable" in *Black's Law Dictionary* (West Group 2000); According to the *Restatement (Second) of Contracts* (1979) Sect. 7, "a voidable contract is one where a party has the power to avoid the legal relations created by the contract. Typical instances for voidable contracts are those where one party is an infant, or where the contract is induced by fraud, duress or undue influence or mistake."

98. See Jean-Pierre ANCEL, *op. cit.*, fn. 7.

99. The US Supreme Court in *Prima Paint*, see fn. 40, held that:

"if the claim is fraud in the inducement of the arbitration clause itself – an issue which goes to the making of the agreement to arbitrate – the federal court may proceed to adjudicate. But the statutory language [of the Federal Arbitration Act] does not permit the federal court to consider claims of fraud in the inducement of the contract generally."

100. In *Three Valleys Municipal Water District v. E.F. Hutton*, 925 F.2d 1136 (9th 1991), the Court held that:

"If the dispute is within the scope of an arbitration agreement, an arbitrator may properly decide whether a contract is 'voidable' because the parties have agreed to arbitrate the dispute. But, because an 'arbitrator's jurisdiction is rooted in the agreement of the parties', a party who

applying separability to claims that a contract containing an arbitration clause is voidable in order to combat delaying tactics of one party alleging invalidity of the arbitration agreement. On the other hand, they regularly refused to apply the doctrine of separability to contracts claimed to be void ab initio, considering that the arbitration agreement was affected by the invalidity as well.[101]

Courts and commentators alike suggested that a valid arbitration agreement cannot be severed from a "contract" that never came into legal existence. According to general principles of contract law, if the agreement has never been entered into, the arbitration clause never came into force, or if the agreement was not validly entered into, prima facie, it was invalid as a whole, i.e., on all of its parts, including the arbitration clause.

For nearly forty years, the US Supreme Court did not have the opportunity to retake a position on the application of the doctrine of separability as initially defined in *Prima Paint*. Then we witnessed the *Cardegna* "saga". Following the decision of the Florida Supreme Court in re *Cardegna v. Buckeye Check Cashing Inc.*,[102] where it was ruled that the doctrine of separability did not apply to allegations that the contract was void (as illegal) as opposed to being merely voidable (due to fraud), the US Supreme Court redefined the limits of the doctrine of autonomy and laid out three principles for arbitration. Firstly, as a matter of substantive federal arbitration law, an arbitration provision is severable from the remainder of the contract. Secondly, unless the challenge is to the arbitration clause itself, the issue of the contract's validity is considered by the arbitrator in the first instance. Thirdly, this rule applies both in state as well as in federal courts.[103]

Reaffirming the principle of separability, the US Supreme Court redefined its limits in a very extensive way, in the sense that today the *void/voidable* distinction no longer

---

contests the making of the contract containing the arbitration provision cannot be compelled to arbitrate the threshold issue of the existence of an agreement to arbitrate."

101. The courts' basic rationale for refusing to apply the doctrine of autonomy to claims that the contract containing the arbitration agreement never came into existence or was otherwise void was expressed as follows: "something can be severed only from something else that exists" in *Pollux Marine Agencies v. Louis Dreyfus Corp.*, 455 F. Supp. 211, 219 (S.D.N.Y. 1978). "The destruction of [the underlying] transaction carried over to the arbitration agreement, the arbitrators are deprived of their jurisdiction, and an award already rendered would lose all legal effect" in *Teledyne, Inc. v. Kone Corp.*, 892 F.2d 1404, 1410 (9th Cir. 1990).

102. *Cardegna v. Buckeye Check Cashing Inc.*, 894 So. 2d 860 (Fla 2005). Briefly, Cardegna brought a putative class action against Buckeye Check Cashing, alleging that Buckeye's loan agreements contained usurious interest rates and violated Florida lending and consumer protection laws. Cardegna argued that the entire contract was void for illegality, and that the arbitration clause was therefore also void. Buckeye moved to compel arbitration. The trial court denied the motion, holding that a court rather than an arbitrator should resolve a claim that a contract is void ab initio. The District Court of Appeal of Florida for the Fourth District reversed, holding that because respondents did not challenge the arbitration provision itself, but instead claimed that the entire contract was void, the agreement to arbitrate was enforceable, and the question of the contract's legality should be decided by the arbitrator. Respondents appealed and the Florida Supreme Court reversed, reasoning that such an issue should be determined by courts and not arbitrators.

103. *Cardegna v. Buckeye Check Cashing Inc.*, 2006 WL 386362 (U.S. 21 Feb. 2006), *op. cit.*, fn. 21.

plays a role in US arbitration law. It may now be properly stated that if at one time US commentators more or less justifiably questioned the autonomy of the arbitration agreement, such inquiry has now become less than effective.

French case law, always in favor of the autonomy of the arbitration agreement, had, at a certain time, accidentally upheld the *void/voidable* distinction, limiting therefore the application of the doctrine of autonomy. While it is worth mentioning it, such isolated case law does not represent the present rule of law in French international arbitration law.

b. The "void/voidable" distinction in French case law

As already mentioned, French case law acknowledged the principle of autonomy since the 1963 landmark *Gosset* decision and regularly affirmed it until the 1990 isolated *Cassia* decision where the *Cour de cassation* did not apply the principle because the main contract to which the arbitration agreement related was non-existent.[104] Subsequent case law upheld the *Cassia* rule considering the validity and efficiency of the arbitration agreement limited only by the existence in the form of the underlying agreement.[105] Such an unfortunate decision compromised the effectiveness of the autonomy of the arbitration agreement and went against the principle's main purpose being to ensure that the arbitration agreement remains unaffected by flaws in the underlying contract. Some of the most important achievements of the autonomy were suddenly questioned by the *Cour de cassation*: the principle of the absolute validity of the arbitration agreement and its independence from the traditional choice of laws rules.

Where the arbitration agreement could be held void or non-existent if directly affected by such cause, French courts have traditionally considered that the existence and validity of the arbitration agreement should never be considered in connection with the existence and validity of the main contract.[106] It is correct to affirm that the *Cassia* decision imposed a limited application of the doctrine to the point that commentators

---

104. *Cour de cassation*, 10 July 1990 (*Pia investments Ltd. v. Cassia*), Rev. arb. (1990) p. 851, holding that:

> "in international arbitration, the autonomy of the arbitration clause presupposes the formal existence of the main contract containing it…".

105. Court of Appeal, Paris, 19 January 1999 (*Société CIC International Ltd. v. Ministre de la Défense de la République d'Allemagne*), Rev. arb. (1999) p. 601 where it was held that:

> "*en matière internationale et parce qu'elle se rapporte au droit d'ester en justice et non au droit substantiel, la clause d'arbitrage, ainsi séparable du reste du contrat où elle figure, a une validité et une efficacité propres don't les seules limites sont l'existence en la forme de la convention qui la contient*".

in international law and because it refers to the right of action and not to a substantive right, the arbitration agreement, although separable from the underlying contract, has a validity and efficiency of its own limited only by the existence in the form of the underlying agreement; consequently, it is not vitiated by the possible defects affecting the act in which it is contained, as long as its continuous existence is proved. (author's translation)

106. Emmanuel GAILLARD and John SAVAGE, eds., *op. cit.*, fn. 5, p. 363.

could have questioned the status of the autonomy of the arbitration agreement. Fortunately, recent case law reaffirmed the French "traditional" solution in that the international arbitration agreement enjoys a complete autonomy, meaning its own validity and efficiency independent of that of the main contract.[107]

c. *The "void/voidable" distinction: an artificial limitation to the doctrine of autonomy*
There are more than a few who consider today, at least in the continental tradition, that the arbitration agreement became "immune" from all causes related to the main contract that might limit its validity, such that any challenges to the arbitration agreement itself are reserved for the arbitrators' determination solely.[108] In the common law tradition, this distinction has encountered severe criticism and is not accepted anymore.

The legal "fiction" of the autonomy is becoming increasingly "real" and numerous arguments have been raised in favor of the "complete" autonomy and against its "artificial limitation" imposed by some state courts on the basis of the *void/voidable* distinction. Firstly, limiting the autonomy on the basis of this distinction was inconsistent with the main foundation of the doctrine of separability which considers the arbitration agreement and the main contract as two separate agreements. The first one can come into existence without the second one, and different national laws may apply to the formation of each of them. Accordingly, in order to apply, the doctrine of autonomy does not require the existence of a valid underlying contract.

The artificial character of the distinction is even more obvious when one considers that the only difference between void and voidable contracts is that the former never officially exists at law, while the latter requires an action by one party to extinguish its existence. In either case, the agreement of the parties is not legally binding. If one accepts that the doctrine of separability allows the arbitration agreement to stand as a clear manifestation of the parties' intent to arbitrate cases where the main contract is voidable, then a similar logic should apply to contracts alleged to be void ab initio because the intention of the parties to submit the dispute to arbitration is not automatically called into question when the main contract did not come into existence. Otherwise, the application of the *void/voidable* distinction would go against the parties' intent that any dispute about their legal relationship be arbitrated and would frustrate therefore their expectations.

In a similar way, the circulation of the arbitration agreement has also given rise to a reappraisal of the doctrine of autonomy, being frequently interpreted as a limitation to it.

---

107. See *Cour de cassation*, 25 October 2005 (*Société Omenex v. M. Hugon*), *op. cit.*, fn. 79 where the Court stated that:

"in application of the principle of validity of the arbitration agreement and of its autonomy in international law, neither the nullity nor the non-existence of the underlying contract affects it".

108. *Tribunal Fédéral*, 1994, (*National Power Corp. v. Westinghouse*) ATF 119 II 380, ASA Bulletin (1994) p. 246. See also Jean-Pierre ANCEL, *op. cit.*, fn. 7.

3. The Circulation of the Arbitration Agreement

In various legal systems the assignment of rights under the main contract entails the circulation of the arbitration agreement. Is it therefore possible to logically uphold that the arbitration agreement is independent of the main contract and, at the same time, that it is transmitted, when the underlying contract is assigned? Or should we agree that such an automatic transmission challenges the scope of the doctrine, in the sense that it represents a limit to the autonomy of the arbitration agreement itself?

Civil law and common law systems have no specific statutory rules dealing with this issue (a). In the absence of such distinctive rules, courts and academics have expressed conflicting views which question the effective meaning of the autonomy (b).

a. The circulation of the arbitration agreement: a jurisdictional overview

In civil law countries (except in Italy), courts generally consider their national statutory rules concerning the scope and the effects of the assignment of contractual rights in order to interpret the assignment of the arbitration agreement. Under most of these rules, an arbitration agreement is automatically transmitted when the main contract is assigned, as incident to the assigned claim, thus binding the assignee to the arbitration agreement.

Swiss courts, for instance, have consistently accepted the assignment of the arbitration agreement with the rights under the main contract reasoning that in the case of a transfer of a contractual relationship, the arbitration agreement, due to its accessory nature, is also transferred.[109] As far as the assignment of claim is concerned, such an effect is derived from Art. 170(1) of the Swiss Code of Obligations, whether the arbitration agreement is considered as a preferential right or as an ancillary right.[110] Accordingly, they hold as a rule that an arbitration agreement may be presumed to have been transferred together with the assigned claim unless such transfer is restricted by law, contract or the nature of the contract.[111]

German courts have similarly insisted on the automatic assignment of the arbitration agreement and, drawing an analogy with the rules of the German Civil Code which governs the scope of the contractual assignment,[112] considered the arbitration agreement

---

109. *Tribunal Fédéral*, 7 August 2001, 4P.124/2001, 20 ASA Bulletin (2002, no. 1) p. 88.
110. Art. 170 Swiss Code of Obligations provides that:

> "1. The assignment of a claim includes the transfer of the preferential rights and other ancillary rights, except those which are inseparable from the assignor.
> (....)
> 3. The related rights to the assigned contract are supposed to be assigned with the original debt."
> (author's translation)

111. See *Tribunal Fédéral*, 9 May 2001 (*Nextrom Holding S.A. and Nextrom S.A v. Watkins International S.A.*), 20 ASA Bulletin (2002, no. 1) p. 80; *Müller v. Bossard*, published in the Official Court Reporter (ATF) 103 II 75; *Tribunal Fédéral*, 13 October 1992 (*Transkei v. F.J. Berger and Steyr-Daimpler-Puch AG*), ASA Bulletin (1993) p. 68.
112. See Art. 401 of the German Civil Code (BGB) that provides:

to be a characteristic of the assigned claim, an intrinsic attribute of the right which has passed on to the assignee.[113]

French courts hold today that the international arbitration agreement is enforceable against all parties that succeed in rights to the initial parties.[114] It is worth mentioning nevertheless that until not long ago, their position as to the automatic transmission of the arbitration agreement varied depending on whether it was related to a chain of contracts or to one individual contract.[115] In the first case, the *Cour de cassation* refused the automatic transmission of the arbitration agreement, holding that the arbitration agreement remains subject to the principle of privity of contracts and could not therefore circulate unless the parties have expressly[116] or at least implicitly[117] provided otherwise. In the case of the assignment of individual contractual rights or the assignment of the entire contract, French courts characterized the arbitration agreement as an accessory right attached to the claim and held therefore its automatic transmission whether it was referring to the assignment of a right under the contract or of the entire contract.[118]

The automatic circulation of the arbitration agreement has been recently limited by the Italian Supreme Court which, in a decision of 19 September 2003, considered that the arbitration agreement cannot be transferred automatically without the assignee's express agreement.[119]

In the common law tradition, the issue of the circulation of the arbitration agreement is less settled. US courts recognized, at a certain time, the automatic transmission of the

---

"(1) When a claim is assigned, mortgages on real estate or on ships, pledges or liens put up for such claim, and all rights resulting from suretyships pass over to the new creditor.
(2) A privilege attached to the claim and enforceable vis-à-vis other creditors in attachment or insolvency proceedings can also be asserted by the new creditor."

113. Otto SANDROCK, "'Intra' and 'Extra-Entity' Agreements to Arbitrate and their Extension to Non-Signatories Under German Law", 19 Journal of International Arbitration (2002, no. 5) pp. 423-442.

114. *Cour de cassation*, 8 February 2000 (*Société Taurus Films v. Les Films du Jeudi*), Rev. arb. (2000) p. 280.

115. Pierre MAYER, "*La circulation des conventions d'arbitrage*", Journal du Droit International (2005) p. 251 at p. 253.

116. *Cour de cassation*, 6 November 1990 (*Fraser v. Compagnie européenne des Pétroles*), Rev. arb. (1991) p. 73; Court of Appeal, Paris, 22 March 1995 (*SMABTP v. Statinor*), Rev. arb. (1997) p. 550 at p. 552 where the Court held that "the assumption of obligations requires knowledge of such obligations on the part of the assignee"; See also Philippe DELEBEQUE, "*La transmission de la clause compromissoire: à propos de l'arrêt de la Cour de cassation du 6 novembre 1990*", Rev. arb. (1991) p. 19.

117. See generally Emmanuel GAILLARD and John SAVAGE, eds., *op. cit.*, fn. 5, p. 427.

118. Art. 1692 French CC stipulates that: "the sale or assignment of a claim includes all accessories attached thereto, such as a right against the surety and any right of property or mortgage securing the same". (author's translation)
    See also *Cour de cassation*, 8 February 2000 (*Société Taurus Films v. Les Films du Jeudi*), *op. cit.*, fn. 114 at p. 280.

119. Unpublished decision cited in Pierre MAYER, *op. cit.*, fn. 115.

arbitration agreement with the main contract. However, as of today, more judgments consider such assignment contingent upon the express consent of the parties.[120]

Neither arbitration rules nor international conventions address this issue on which there is no general consensus in comparative law. The circulation of the arbitration agreement might be thus a good test to evaluate the level of its autonomy.

b.   The circulation of the arbitration agreement: autonomy or dependence?

According to its traditional meaning, the arbitration agreement is autonomous from the main contract. A higher degree of autonomy would therefore suggest that the arbitration agreement cannot be qualified as an accessory right presumed to be automatically transferred to the assignee but rather requires the two parties to expressly consent to its transfer. A lesser degree of autonomy could support the presumption as to its accessory nature vis-à-vis the main contract and therefore justify its automatic assignment. Nevertheless, most jurisdictions still treat the arbitration agreement as an integral part of the contract when dealing with this issue. How could it be possible then to explain the automatic transmission of the arbitration agreement and combine it with the doctrine of autonomy?

In this sense, it should be admitted that a difficult task rests with French courts and scholars, which have recognized the "full" autonomy of the arbitration agreement and still upheld its automatic transmission.[121]

Arguments such as the arbitration agreement's ancillary nature,[122] or its "validity" and "own effectiveness"[123] were raised before the *Cour de cassation* resolved the difficulty by advancing the concept of "autonomous circulation" of the arbitration agreement according to which:

"an international arbitration agreement, legally independent of the main contract,

---

120. See in this sense, *Marubeni Corporation, et al. v. Mobile Bay Wood Chip Center, et al.*, 16 June 2003, 2003 WL 22466216 (S.D. Ala.), Yearbook XXIX (2004), p. 937; *Chemrite (Pty) Ltd., et al. v. Bel-Ray Co., Inc.*, 181 F.3d 435 (1999), Yearbook XXV (2000), p. 991.

121. See *Cour de cassation*, 12 July 1950 (*Montané v. Compagnie des chemins de fer portugais*), 77 Journal du Droit International (1950) p. 1206 with note B. GOLDMAN; Court of Appeal, Aix, 9 January 1997 (*SNTM Hyproc v. Banque Générale du Commerce*), Rev. arb. (1997) p. 76 with note D. COHEN, where the court held that the assignee of a contract who enjoys the benefit of the rights assigned cannot avoid the application of the arbitration agreement contained in that contract; Court of Appeal, Paris, 20 April 1988 (*Clark International Finance v. Sud Matériel Service*), Rev. arb. (1988) p. 570, where the court held that no express provision is required from the assignee to accept the arbitration agreement, rather an express provision is required to exclude it from the assignment of the main contract. See also, Eric LOQUIN, "*Contradictions de l'arbitrage international français*", Gazette du Palais (2002, N° 1) p. 7 at p. 11.

122. Pierre MAYER, *op. cit.*, fn. 57, p. 262.

123. *Cour de cassation*, 19 October 1999 (*Banque Worms v. R. Bellot et SNTM-Hyproc*), Rev. arb. (2000) p. 85.

circulates with it regardless the validity of the assignment of rights under the main contract." [124]

It is thus obvious that the "autonomous circulation" of the arbitration agreement no longer negatively affects the doctrine of autonomy. The arbitration agreement is fully autonomous since its own circulation is also autonomous.

IV.   CONCLUSION

The doctrine of autonomy is an interesting academic challenge. It tells us a lot about our conception of contracts as a whole, dispute resolution in general and our techniques for making law to suit practical needs of the business community. Every modern regime of arbitration takes separability as the cornerstone of the entire structure: entrusting the validity of the underlying contract to arbitrators seems universally recognized as being necessary both to guard the integrity of arbitral decision-making on the merits, and to allow the process to get smoothly underway. Differences in application exist. But, there is a strong tendency towards uniformity, leading the international community to the recognition of the autonomy of the arbitration agreement.

Accordingly, I really consider that, today, the few slight differences in application should not entitle one anymore to question the autonomy of the arbitration agreement.

---

124. *Cour de cassation*, 28 May 2002 (*Société Burkinabé des ciments et matériaux (Cimat) v. Société des ciments d'Abidjan (SCA)*), Rev. arb. (2003) p. 397.

The Autonomy of the Arbitration Agreement: Some Thoughts on the US Experience

*Joseph E. Neuhaus**

I.   INTRODUCTION

1.   Separability Doctrine

Where a contract contains an arbitration clause, the separability doctrine provides that the validity of the arbitration clause has to be determined separately from that of the contract as a whole, even though the arbitration clause is merely a part of the contract. The consequence of the doctrine is that the arbitration agreement may survive the invalidity of the underlying contract. The need for "separability" is obvious: without it, a finding that the contract is invalid would deprive the arbitrators of their jurisdiction, because under ordinary contractual principles a clause shares the fate of the contract in which it is contained. Philippe Leboulanger ably explores this in greater depth in his Report.[1]

Neither the Federal Arbitration Act (FAA) nor the New York Convention mentions the autonomy or separability of the arbitration agreement. The case that is commonly seen as establishing the doctrine in the US is *Prima Paint Corp. v. Flood & Conklin Mfg. Co.*, 388 U.S. 395 (1967). In that case, the parties had entered into a consulting agreement containing an arbitration clause. When the plaintiff filed suit seeking rescission of the entire agreement on the basis of fraudulent inducement, the plaintiff also moved to stay arbitration. The Supreme Court held that the challenge to the entire contract had to be decided by the arbitrators, noting that "if the claim is fraud in the inducement of the arbitration clause itself – an issue which goes to the 'making' of the agreement to arbitrate – the federal court may proceed to adjudicate it. But the statutory language [of FAA Sect. 4] does not permit the federal court to consider claims of fraud in the inducement of the contract generally." *Prima Paint*, 388 U.S. at 403-404.

---

*   Partner and co-coordinator of the international arbitration practice, Sullivan & Cromwell LLP. I gratefully acknowledge the extremely able assistance of Andreas Stier, an associate at Sullivan & Cromwell LLP, in the preparation of this Commentary.
1. See this volume, pp. 3-31.

The holding of the Supreme Court implies that the arbitration agreement is separable from the underlying contract: once the court is satisfied that the making of the arbitration agreement, as opposed to the underlying contract, is not in issue, it sends the case to arbitration. That means, for purposes of determining its validity, the arbitration agreement must be separable from the underlying contract.

2. *First Options*

Since another leading US Supreme Court case, *First Options of Chicago, Inc. v. Kaplan*, 514 U.S. 938 (1995), is frequently mentioned in discussions of the autonomy of the arbitration agreement, it is worth briefly reviewing its relationship to the doctrine.

In *First Options*, the Supreme Court ruled on the scope of judicial review of the arbitrators' finding regarding their competence. The Supreme Court held that the arbitrators' decision on whether or not they have jurisdiction to decide the merits of a particular dispute is subject to independent review by the courts. The Supreme Court noted, however, that where there is "clear and unmistakable" evidence that the parties agreed that the arbitrator should decide questions of arbitrability, "the court should give considerable leeway to the arbitrator, setting aside his or her decision only in certain narrow circumstances". 514 U.S. at 943.

Thus, *First Options* concerns review of the arbitrators' decision on arbitrability after the fact. It has, however, been applied by courts in deciding whether the court should address the scope of an arbitration clause in deciding whether to refer the parties to arbitration. In either case, *First Options* is a principle of interpretation of the scope of the arbitration clause. The separability principle goes to whether the clause, whatever it means, is valid in the face of a challenge to its validity.

II. VOID/VOIDABLE DISTINCTION

1. *Buckeye*

The Supreme Court in *Buckeye Check Cashing v. Cardegna*, 126 S. Ct. 1204 (2006) has eliminated the *void* (absolute nullity)/*voidable* (valid until annulled) distinction. It reversed the judgment of the Florida Supreme Court that, relying on the distinction between *void* and *voidable* contracts, had declined to apply *Prima Paint*'s rule of severability. The Florida Supreme Court had held that if the underlying contract indeed violated Florida's usury laws, the contract would be *void* and all of its provisions, including the arbitration clause, would be nullified as well.

The Supreme Court pointed out that *Prima Paint* rejected the application of state severability rules to the arbitration agreement without discussing whether the challenge would have rendered the contract *void* or merely *voidable*.

To most arbitration practitioners, the analysis in *Buckeye* is a fairly straightforward application of the principle of the autonomy of the arbitration agreement. In many cases a claim that a contract is *void* is based on grounds that do not call into question the agreement to arbitrate, and conversely, a claim that the contract is *voidable* can nullify the arbitration agreement.

2. *Why Did Courts Start to Distinguish Between Void and Voidable Contracts, if Prima Paint Did Not Make This Distinction?*

Some courts read *Prima Paint* as standing for the proposition that attacks on the underlying contract *always* go to the arbitrators. "The *Prima Paint* doctrine [...] extends to all challenges to the making of a contract." *Rhoades v. Powell*, 644 F. Supp. 645, 653 (E.D. Cal. 1986) (plaintiff sought rescission – without indicating the basis – of customer agreements, not arbitration clauses alone). "The basis of the underlying challenge to the contract does not alter the [*Prima Paint*] principle." *Unionmutual Stock Life Insurance v. Beneficial Life*, 774 F.2d 524, 529 (1st Cir. 1985) (frustration of purpose as ground for rescission).

Courts were confronted, however, with situations in which the underlying contract was attacked on grounds that also vitiated the arbitration agreement, such as, for example, mental incapacity. Here, it would be inappropriate to send the dispute to arbitration because the parties did not validly waive their right to a trial. Therefore, it was suggested that *Prima Paint* only applied to *voidable*, but not to *void* contracts. This allowed the courts to consider attacks on the underlying contract on grounds that the contract was *void*. While the reading of *Prima Paint* was flawed, these courts came to the correct results. *Three Valleys Mun. Water Dist. v. E.F. Hutton & Co., Inc.*, 925 F.2d 1136, 1140 (9th Cir. 1991) (challenge that signatory had no authority to enter into contract containing arbitration clause – held: district court's order directing arbitration reversed and remanded; on remand district court must first determine whether the signatory had authority); *Sandvik AB v. Advent Int'l Corp.*, 220 F.3d 99 (3rd Cir. 2000) (defendant denied existence of the contract that contained an arbitration clause on the ground that the signatory lacked authority, but argued that the arbitration agreement was separable and valid, defendant moved to compel arbitration – held: order of the district court denying motion to compel arbitration affirmed).

III.   STRANGERS TO THE CONTRACT

Although *Buckeye* jettisons the *void/voidable* distinction that resulted from the "stranger-to-the-contract" problem, the "problem" still exists: if a party claims never to have agreed to arbitration, it is unjust to make him or her arbitrate.

In *Buckeye*, Justice Scalia distinguished between the issue of the contract's validity and the issue of whether any agreement between the alleged obligor and obligee was ever concluded. He noted that the Court's opinion only addressed the first issue. 126 S.Ct. at 1208.

There are grounds that prevent *any* contract from coming into existence – including the arbitration agreement. This is not a limitation of the separability doctrine. The doctrine only provides that the invalidity of the underlying contract does not *necessarily* invalidate the arbitration agreement.

1.   How Do Courts Limit Frivolous "Stranger-to-the-Contract" Claims?

A party seeking to avoid arbitration can easily allege that he or she is a stranger to the contract containing the arbitration clause on the supposed ground, for example, that he or she never intended to enter into the contract, the signatory was acting *ultra vires*, there was no "meeting of the minds", or the signature was forged.

Unlike the standard rule, whereby a mere assertion of a fact generally entitles a party to stay in court, at least for a while, in the arbitration context US courts have frequently placed pleading and evidentiary hurdles to attempt to ensure that cases are not side-tracked into lengthy court proceedings by ill-founded challenges to the existence of an arbitration agreement. Courts have required, for example, an unequivocal denial that the agreement had been made, accompanied by *supporting affidavits*. *Par-Knit Mills, Inc. v. Stockbridge Fabrics Co., Ltd.*, 636 F.2d 51, 55 (3rd Cir. 1980); *Interocean Shipping Co. v. National Shipping & Trading Corp.*, 462 F.2d 673 (2nd Cir. 1972). Some courts have articulated the test as one requiring that a claim by a party that a contract never existed at all must be supported by *substantial evidence*. *Chastain v. Robinson-Humphrey Co.*, 957 F.2d 851 (11th Cir. 1992).

2.   Confusion in This Area and Some Courts Have Gotten It Wrong

a.   Mental incapacity
In *Primerica Life Insurance Co. v. Brown*, 304 F.3d 469 (5th Cir. 2002), a borrower brought an action against the lender for breach of contract. The lender moved to compel arbitration. The parties agreed with the district court's finding that the borrower had been "profoundly retarded since birth". Having determined that the borrower "lacked the capacity to contract under Mississippi law", the district court refused to compel arbitration. The Fifth Circuit, however, reversed, holding that the borrower's capacity defense is a defense to his entire agreement and not a specific challenge to the arbitration clause that, under *Prima Paint*, must be submitted to the arbitrator.

b.   Inability to read English
In *Villa Carcia v. Merrill Lynch*, 833 F.2d 545 (5th Cir. 1987), an investor brought suit against a brokerage firm and employees for violations of the Securities Exchange Act of 1934 and state law. The defendants moved to compel arbitration. The district court denied the motion and the defendants appealed. The Fifth Circuit vacated the district court's judgment, holding that even if the plaintiff signed the agreement believing it to be only a signature exemplar, and even if the plaintiff's inability to read English prevented him from reading the agreement, these are issues that should be decided by an arbitrator, not the district court, since they go to the formation of the entire agreement rather than to the formation of the arbitration provision

3.   Cases That Have Been Correctly Decided

a.   Forged signature
In *Chastain v. Robinson-Humphrey Co.*, 957 F.2d 851 (11th Cir. 1992), a securities firm moved to compel arbitration of a customer's securities claims. The plaintiff customer

argued that she never agreed to either the customer agreements or the arbitration clauses and that her signature on the agreement was a forgery. The defendant admitted that the signature was not the plaintiff's but argued that the plaintiff must arbitrate because of a purported contract. The defendant's theories were: (1) that the plaintiff's father had authority to bind his daughter; and (2) that the plaintiff ratified the customer agreements through her conduct. The Eleventh Circuit held that the district court should proceed to a trial on the issue of whether or not the plaintiff is bound by the arbitration language in the customer agreements. The Eleventh Circuit noted that in a case where the party seeking to avoid arbitration has not signed any contract requiring arbitration, that party is challenging the very existence of *any* agreement, *including the existence of an agreement to arbitrate*. The court also said that "*Prima Paint* has never been extended to require arbitrators to adjudicate a party's contention, *supported by substantial evidence*, that a contract never existed at all."

b.   Signatory lacked mental capacity to assent

In *Spahr v. Secco* , 330 F.3d 1266 (10th Cir. 2003), the plaintiff who suffered from dementia and Alzheimer's disease brought suit in state court against a stockbroker and her firm, alleging inter alia breach of fiduciary duty. The defendants removed the case to federal court and filed a motion to stay the proceedings and order arbitration, pursuant to an agreement signed by the plaintiff. The district court denied the motion on the basis that the entire agreement which contained the arbitration clause was unenforceable due to the plaintiff's mental incapacity. The Tenth Circuit affirmed, noting that courts may easily apply the *Prima Paint* rule when the challenge is fraud because fraud can be directed at the underlying contract or at the arbitration clause itself. But *Prima Paint* "cannot be applied with precision when a party contends that an entire contract containing an arbitration provision is unenforceable because he lacked the mental capacity to enter into the contract". Since a mental capacity challenge can logically only be directed at the entire contract, the "making" of an agreement to arbitrate was at issue under Sect. 4 FAA.

4.   Stranger Seeking to Compel a Signatory to Arbitrate: Who Decides?

So far, we have dealt with situations where a purported stranger to the contract seeks to *avoid* arbitration. The considerations here are straightforward: if a person has not agreed to waive his or her right to a trial, he or she should not be forced to go to arbitration. But different considerations arguably may apply where a purported stranger seeks to *enforce* an arbitration agreement against a signatory. For example, *Minera Alumbrera Ltd. v. Fluor Daniel, Inc.*, 1999 WL 269915 (S.D.N.Y. 1999) (non-signatory guarantor sought to take advantage of an arbitration clause contained in the underlying contract on theories of *alter ego*, incorporation by reference and estoppel). Here it may be argued that the autonomy principle is not involved at all. The challenge is not to the *validity* of the arbitration agreement with respect to the party opposing arbitration. As to that party, the challenge is merely to the *scope* of the clause: the question is whether the agreement extends to the purported stranger. Further, unlike when a claimed stranger to the contract is being dragged to arbitration, is it unjust to send someone to arbitration who has agreed to arbitrate, especially given that the arbitrators will first rule on their competence?

This example suggests, or highlights, a limitation on the principle that a challenge to the validity of the arbitration agreement is considered by the courts under the separability doctrine. For this principle to operate, the challenge arguably should be to the "validity" of the clause as applied to the particular party opposing arbitration, and not merely to its scope. It is doubtful that current law in the United States includes this limitation, however. *Minera Alumbrera*.

IV. ASSIGNMENT AND THE SEPARABILITY DOCTRINE

Philippe Leboulanger suggests that the "automatic assignment of the arbitration agreement" challenges the scope of the autonomy principle, and invites comment. In my view, the concept of autonomy has no application in the assignment context.

One cannot sensibly separate the substantive rights under a contract from the right to arbitrate claims with respect to those rights. If the assignor assigned his or her rights under the contract, the assignor has nothing left to arbitrate. Also, one cannot by assignment alter or eliminate the obligor's right to arbitrate. Thus, the assignee could not force the obligor to court on a theory that the right and obligation to arbitrate was not assigned. The right to arbitrate has to go with the substantive right.

There is also no purpose for the doctrine in the assignment context. Under the doctrine (1) an arbitration agreement can be valid even though the underlying contract is invalid, which overcomes the jurisdictional problem where arbitrators conclude that the contract is invalid; (2) the law governing the arbitration clause may be different from that governing the underlying contract; and (3) the arbitration clause can survive the termination/expiry of the underlying contract. Each of these effects of separability facilitates the arbitration process and aligns with the parties' likely intent in the typical contract. No such purpose is served by separating the arbitration clause from the fate of the underlying contract rights and obligations in the assignment context. Most important, because arbitration makes no sense divorced from the substantive rights, this treatment accords with likely intent.

V. A-NATIONAL ARBITRATION

Under the separability doctrine the law governing the underlying contract can be different from the law that governs the arbitration clause. *Restatement (Second) Conflict of Laws* summarizes the prevailing approach. *Restatement* Sect. 218 provides that the "validity of an arbitration agreement, and the rights created thereby, are determined by the law selected by application of the rules of Sects. 187-188". According to Sects. 187-188, a contractual choice-of-law clause will generally be given effect. In the absence of an explicit choice-of-law clause, the law of the *state* with the most significant relationship will be applied to the arbitration agreement. Thus, Sect. 188 provides, in part,

"(1) The rights and duties of the parties with respect to an issue in contract are determined by *the local law of the state* which, with respect to that issue, has the most significant relationship to the transaction and the parties...." (Emphasis added.)

If the parties agreed upon a place of arbitration, the law of that *state* will most likely be applied to determine whether or not the arbitration agreement is valid. The author is not aware of any US case that has chosen an a-national solution *à la Dalico*.

VI.   HOW AUTONOMOUS IS THE ARBITRATION AGREEMENT?

There is another form of "autonomy" of the arbitration agreement that has arisen in recent US cases, and that is whether the arbitration agreement is separable from procedural terms and conditions such as a class action waiver. An argument can be made that under this form of the separability doctrine the validity of the agreement to arbitrate should be determined separately from other provisions, especially if those provisions govern procedural aspects of the arbitration.

This was the conclusion reached by the arbitrator in *Gipson v. Cross Country Bank*, 354 F. Supp. 2d 1278 (D. Ala. 2005). Disregarding a court's prior ruling on the issue, the arbitrator issued an order that it was for him to decide whether the class action prohibition clause was valid because that question did not go to the issue of the validity of the arbitration clause. In other words, the arbitrator considered the arbitration clause to be separable from the class action waiver.

The district court ruled, however that, while under *Green Tree* the arbitrator decides whether the contract forbids class arbitration when the arbitration clause was *silent* on the issue, it was for the courts to decide when the arbitration clause expressly prohibited class actions. The rationale for this decision, though not expressed, seems to be that the arbitration agreement is not separable from the class action waiver and the invalidity of the latter dooms the former.

Re-examining the Arbitration Agreement: Is It Still Autonomous? The Common Law Canadian Experience

J. Brian Casey[*]

I. INTRODUCTION

Historically in England agreements to arbitrate were not enforced in the courts of equity, and while a party could sue for damages in the common law courts, any damage award would be minimal. This changed with the adoption of Sect. 11 of the Common Law Procedure Act, 1854,[1] which provided for indirect enforcement by staying any court action found to have been brought in violation of an arbitration agreement. In common law jurisdictions the extent to which a State permits arbitration agreements to oust the jurisdiction of its courts is essentially a matter of policy as reflected in the State's legislation both as regards enforcement, interpretation and scope.

Canada, like most common law jurisdictions, has evolved the doctrine of autonomy with respect to arbitration clauses. In so doing, however, it has not followed the French lead in embracing the concept of full autonomy and, it is doubtful it would do so.

II. RECOGNITION OF THE PRINCIPLE OF AUTONOMY IN CANADA

Each Province and the Federal government have adopted the Model Law for international arbitration. Under the Model Law, Art. 16(1), the arbitral tribunal may rule on its own jurisdiction, including any objections with respect to the existence or validity of the arbitration agreement. For that purpose, an arbitration clause which forms part of a contract shall be treated as an agreement independent of the other terms of the contract. A decision by the arbitral tribunal that the contract is null and void shall not entail *ipso jure* the invalidity of the arbitration clause. The concept of an independent

---

[*] Partner, Baker & McKenzie LLP.
1. *Chitty on Contracts*, 23rd edn. (Sweet & Maxwell, London 1968) p. 350.

agreement is also provided for in most of the domestic Arbitration Acts in Canada. The Ontario Domestic Act[2] provides:

> "If the arbitration agreement forms part of another agreement, it shall, *for the purposes of a ruling on jurisdiction*, be treated as an independent agreement that may survive even if the main agreement is found to be invalid."

Art. 2642 of the Civil Code of Quebec states:

> "An arbitration agreement contained in a contract is considered to be an agreement separate from the other clauses of the contract and the ascertainment by the arbitrators that the contract is null does not entail the nullity of the arbitration agreement."

It is important to note that the legislation in the common law provinces speaks of an independent or separate agreement for the purposes of its survival and scope, notwithstanding the fate of the main contract. Nowhere does the legislation talk in terms of a fully autonomous agreement. Arguably the Quebec Civil Code provision is broader. It is clear from the common law legislation, the so-called "autonomy" of the arbitration agreement is not to be considered "full autonomy". For certain purposes it may be treated as a separate contract, but not for all purposes, unless it can be demonstrated that was the intention of the parties.

Under the common law, the arbitration clause has been treated as a secondary or ancillary contract. Such contracts have their own existence, but are incidental to and remain connected to the primary contract. The reason for the existence of the secondary contract is to be found in the existence of the primary contract. As such, the secondary contract will be interpreted from this autonomous but ancillary position.

III.   THE CONSEQUENCES OF AUTONOMY

1.   *Contract Formation*

a.   *Consensus ad idem*
Ordinary contract law applies to determine whether or not there is an arbitration agreement. There must be an offer and an acceptance in circumstances in which the parties are *ad idem*. The consideration is the mutual covenant to submit disputes to arbitration. For example, in the case of *Tywood Industries Ltd. v. St. Anne-Nackawic Pulp & Paper Co.*,[3] in response to an invitation to tender that contained no provisions respecting arbitration, the plaintiff submitted a quotation on its standard form which also did not refer to arbitration. The plaintiff's quotation was accepted by a purchase

---

2. Ontario Arbitration Act, 1991 S.O. 1991, Chapter 17. Reference hereafter to the Ontario Domestic Act is a reference to this statute.
3. (1979), 25 O.R. (2d) 89 (H.C.).

order issued by the defendant. The defendant's standard form purchase order provided that all disputes arising from the agreement would be settled by arbitration. When the plaintiff brought an action in court for the price of goods sold and delivered, the defendant brought a motion to stay the proceedings on the grounds that an arbitration ought to be held. The court dismissed the application. Mr. Justice Grange of the Ontario court found the conduct of both parties indicated that neither had considered any terms other than those found on the face of the documents, namely the specifications and the price, and that, while each had attempted to impose upon the other their standard form provisions, there was doubt that the arbitration clause had ever been accepted by the plaintiff. The *Tywood* decision has been followed in the Ontario case of *Magnotta Winery Corp. v. Ziraldo*[4] which re-iterated that issues respecting offer, acceptance, consensus *ad idem* and the interpretation of an arbitration clause are to be determined in accordance with ordinary contract principles except where modified by the Model Law or a domestic Act.

Contrasting the *Tywood* decision is the case of *Fung Sang Trading Ltd. v Kai Sun Sea Produas & Food Ca Ltd.*, a case of the High Court of Hong Kong.[5] In that case the defendant argued there was doubt as to whether the contract for the delivery of goods had ever been completely entered into. There had been correspondence back and forth, and conflicting affidavits were filed. The court, following the Model Law (which has been adopted in Hong Kong), held it was up to the arbitrators to decide whether or not the contract was entered into. In so doing, the court had no difficulty separating the issue of whether the contract was entered into from the issue as to whether an arbitration agreement had been sufficiently proven and ought to be enforced.[6] Once the arbitration agreement was sufficiently proven, the court found the arbitral tribunal had the jurisdiction to rule on the existence of the contract.

b.   Offer and acceptance

In the Ontario case of *Kanitz v. Rogers Cable Inc*,[7] Mr. Justice Nordheimer of the Superior Court of Justice dealt with the question of whether the posting on a web site of an amended customer user agreement, which included an arbitration clause, was sufficient to compel the customers to arbitrate. The customers were users of a high-speed internet service and had agreed that the user agreement which they had signed could be modified from time to time by the company, so long as they received notice. The continued use by the customer of the service, after notice, was to be taken as acceptance of the change. An amended user agreement was introduced which included an arbitration clause. Notice of the amended agreement was put on the company's home page and on the

---

4. [1999] O.J. No. 3968 (Ont. S.C.J.).

5. ICCA *Yearbook Commercial Arbitration* XVII (1992) p. 289. For a case in which the court found that letters back and forth between the parties never did result in the parties being *ad idem*, see *Frota Oceania Brasiliera S.A. v. Steamship Mutual Underwriting Association*, [1996] 2 Lloyd's Rep. 461 (C.A.).

6. Also see *Zambia Steel & Building Supplies Ltd. v. James Clerk & Eaton Ltd.*, [1986] 2 Lloyd's Rep. 225 (C.A.), in which an agreement to arbitrate was taken from an exchange of a quotation and purchase order.

7. (2002), 58 O.R. (3rd) 299.

Customer Support site. The judge found that given the nature of the service being provided, the postings on the web sites were sufficient notice and the arbitration clause was enforceable. The court also agreed with and followed the decision in *Rudder v. Microsoft Corp.*[8] to the effect that having to scroll down through an agreement on a computer screen to find the arbitration clause did not make it obscure or in the "fine print".

c.   Incorporation by reference

It is possible to incorporate an arbitration agreement by reference. For example, standard conditions may be set out in a document separate from the contract, but referenced therein. If the standard conditions include an arbitration clause, this may be a sufficient reference to bind the parties to arbitrate.[9] Reference to another document, which by its nature may not make it clear that an arbitration clause is being incorporated may not be sufficient. The reference must be clear.[10]

Bills of lading have posed a special problem. Both English and Canadian courts have been consistent in finding that general words such as "all terms, conditions and exceptions of governing charter party are hereby incorporated herein" as appears in a bill of lading are not sufficient to incorporate an arbitration clause included in the charter party. The rationale appears to be, in part, founded on commercial necessity. The bill of lading is a negotiable instrument and therefore before one could hold a third party to terms that might not ordinarily come to mind, clear and explicit language would be required.[11] By accepting a bill of lading that is subject to the terms of the charter-party agreement, a purchaser might not necessarily believe or even be put on notice that he was adopting an arbitration agreement.[12]

The English Act in Sect. 6(2) provides that reference in an agreement to a written form of arbitration clause or to a document containing an arbitration clause does constitute an arbitration agreement if the reference is such "as to make that clause part of the Agreement". It may be that under this Act, a more general reference to a document containing an arbitration clause will be sufficient to effect incorporation but, presumably, much will turn on the individual facts of each case.

---

8. (1999), 2 C.P.R. (4th) 474.

9. *Secretary of State for Foreign and Commonwealth Affairs v. The Percy Thomas Partnership* [1998] C.I.L.L. 1342.

10. *The Rena K,* [1979] 1 All E.R. 397 (H.L.); *Nanisivik Mines Ltd. v. Canarctic Shipping Co.* (1994), 113 D.L.R. (4th) 536 (Fed. C.A.).

11. *Mendes v. Ice Pearl (The),* [1996] 6 W.W.R. 411, 18 B.C.L.R. (3d) 182.

12. Where new bills of lading were issued incorporating an arbitration clause from the existing charter party, the BCSC held that at the time of their issuance, none of the parties intended the bills of lading to create a new contractual obligation requiring arbitration of a claim between the ship owner and the shipper. The application for a stay of proceedings was therefore dismissed. See *Conagra (International) S.A. v. Seamotion Navigation Ltd.* (24 February 1995), Doc. Vancouver A934848 (B.C.S.C.); see also *Welex AG v. Rosa Maritime Ltd.,* [2003] EWCA Civ. 938.

2.   *Other Consequences of Autonomy*

In Canada, the courts are prepared to give effect to secondary contracts even in situations in which there are allegations that the main contract is void *ab initio*. In the case of *Ash v. Lloyds*,[13] the court dealt with an exclusive jurisdiction clause which, like an arbitration clause is considered a secondary contract. Mr. Justice Carthy speaking for the court at page 758 said:

> "The plaintiffs argue that the exclusive jurisdiction clauses should be ignored because if there has been fraud in the circumstances surrounding the procurement of the contracts then the contracts are *void ab initio* and the clauses relating to forum are of no effect. I agreement with McKeown, J. and with the authorities he cites to the effect that an allegation that a contract is *void ab initio* does not make it so until a final judgment of the court. If the plaintiffs can commence an action with an allegation of fraud which would void the contract and thus vitiate a choice of jurisdiction clause from the outset, then they may succeed on the merits while enjoying their own choice of jurisdiction or fail on the merits while depriving the defendant of the contracted choice. These clauses are too important in international commerce to permit that anomalous result to flow."

In the United Kingdom, the same result has been obtained in *Harbour Assurance Co. (UK) Ltd. v. Kansa General International Assurance Co. Ltd.*[14] where the plaintiff had brought an action for a declaration that certain insurance policies were void for non-disclosure of material facts. In addition, it was claimed the contracts were void for illegality as the defendants were not registered under the Insurance Companies Act. The Court of Appeal confirmed the principle of the separability of the arbitration clause. The arbitrator could determine the initial validity or invalidity of the contract provided that the arbitration clause itself was not directly impeached. In other words, the allegation of illegality or wrongdoing must have been directed to the arbitration agreement not simply the contract for insurance.

a.   Repudiation
Arbitration agreements, as with any commercial contract, may be repudiated. In the case of *John Downing v. Al Tameer Establishment*,[15] the English Court of Appeal held that where a plaintiff was advised by a defendant that they considered there was no contract between the parties and this repudiation was accepted by the plaintiff who then issued a writ of summons, the court held that the issuing of the writ indicated that not only the primary contract was repudiated but the arbitration clause itself had been repudiated.

---

13. (1992) 9 O.R. (3d) 755 (C.A.), leave to appeal to the Supreme Court of Canada refused (1993), 10 O.R. (3d) xv.
14. [1993] 3 All. E.R. 897 (C.A.).
15. [2002] EWCA Civ 721 (22 May, 2002).

b. Privity of contract

As the arbitration agreement is a contract governed by the ordinary principles of contract law, associated or connected parties may have all of the rights and obligations under the arbitration agreement by operation of law in a number of situations; for example, the named party is the personal representative of another, or is trustee of a beneficiary, or is the agent for a named or unnamed principal. Similarly a trustee in bankruptcy who has adopted the contract may enforce it and conversely will be bound to arbitrate under it. Absent such circumstances privity of contract applies to the arbitration agreement.

The Privy Counsel case, *The Bay Hotel and Resort Ltd. v. Cavalier Construction Co. Ltd.*[16] dealt with the situation in which the party to the contract, Cavalier Construction, formed a subsidiary to actually carry out the construction under the contract. In an action for damages, the Privy Counsel held that the arbitrator had erred in joining the subsidiary as claimant. In the words of Lord Cooke of Thorndon on behalf of the court: "... there appears to be no clear instance of a party who has not consented and is not estopped being held bound to arbitrate with a claimant who is not a party to the arbitration agreement".

c. Choice of law

In theory, since the arbitration clause is a separate contract, the parties may also choose a law different from the governing law of the primary contract under which the arbitration agreement is to be governed and interpreted. However, in recognizing that the arbitration agreement is a secondary contract, it must be read in light of the primary contract. It does not exist in a vacuum. For example, where one clause of a contract provided that the parties agreed to submit all disputes to arbitration, but another clause in the contract provided that for breach of the agreement a party may maintain an action for damages, the second clause was interpreted as qualifying the arbitration clause and the party could litigate at its option.[17] In another example, in the case of *Huras v. Primarerica Financial Services Ltd.*,[18] there was an arbitration agreement that provided for arbitration of any disputes arising out of the contract of employment with the plaintiff. The employee brought a class action in the Ontario Court alleging she, as representative plaintiff and all members of the class, ought to have been paid the minimum wage under Ontario legislation during the three-month training period she was required to undergo. The training period was required before she could become an employee. The Ontario Court of Appeal held that while the arbitration agreement was certainly valid, it only applied to disputes related to the contract of employment. It had no application to the training period prior to the commencement of employment.

In trying to determine the intention of the parties with respect to what law they expected would govern the arbitration clause, the courts in Canada will look to the primary contract and, as a matter of course, apply the choice of law agreed to by the parties. It would require clear evidence to demonstrate that the parties were in

---

16. [2001] UKPC 34.
17. *Alberta Power Ltd. v. McIntyre Porcupine Mines Ltd.* (1975), 59 D.L.R. (3d) 303 (Alta. C.A.).
18. (2000) 137 O.A.C. 79 (Ontario C.A.).

agreement that some other law was to apply to the arbitration clause in order to displace the clear intention of the parties as set out in their choice of law clause in the primary contract.

If there is no law specified in the primary contract, in Canada one is left with the Model Law which provides the arbitral tribunal shall apply the law determined by the "conflict of law rules which it considers applicable".[19] In such a circumstance, the arbitral tribunal would not be permitted to choose such rules of law or other remedial interpretive power it considered "appropriate". In interpreting the scope of the arbitration clause, the tribunal must therefore first determine to what law the arbitration agreement is subject and then interpret the words of the clause in light of and in a manner consistent with that law. That law will in the ordinary course be the law of the primary contract.

This is consistent with the Model Law and the New York Convention with respect to judicial review and enforcement. Both provide for challenge on the ground that the arbitration agreement was not valid "under the law to which the parties have subjected it".[20]

Under the Ontario Domestic Act, a broader scope is given to the tribunal. Sect. 32(1) provides that if the parties have not designated any rules of law, the tribunal may apply the "rules of law it considers appropriate in the circumstances". It is thus conceivable that in an arbitration conducted under the Ontario Domestic Act there may be (at least in theory) the prospect that the arbitral tribunal could choose a law for the arbitration agreement separate and distinct from that found to govern the primary contract. No reported Canadian case has dealt with this prospect to date.

IV.   LIMITS TO THE PRINCIPLE OF AUTONOMY

The word "autonomy" may be an unfortunate choice of words to describe the independent nature of the arbitration agreement. Autonomy carries with it the concept of self-governance and complete independence. A secondary contract in common law is not completely independent. It has independence for some specific, necessary purposes but it would be an error to try and import full autonomy to the clause. It is not meant to be autonomous for all purposes. If one starts with the concept that the arbitration clause is a secondary contract, it leads you to the conclusion that it has partial but not "full" autonomy.

1.   *Choice of Law Revisited*

In the *Peterson Farms* decision[21] the English court refused to adopt the reasoning of an ICC tribunal that the scope of the arbitration clause should be determined by reference to some general interpretive power, rather than the law provided for in the contract. In

---

19. Model Law Art. 28(2).
20. E.g., Model Law Arts. 34(2)(a)(i) and 36(1)(a)(i).
21. *Peterson Farms Inc. v. C&M Farming Ltd.*, [2002] EWHC 121 (Comm), 4 February 2004.

this case the contract provided: "This Agreement shall be interpreted and construed in accordance with the laws of Arkansas, USA." The tribunal had held that due to the severability and autonomy of the arbitration clause they were not bound to follow the choice of law clause in interpreting the scope of the clause. In this way they were able to include other parties under a "group of companies" doctrine, which was unknown to Arkansas law. As a result of the choice of law clause, Langley J. held there was "... no basis for the tribunal to apply any other law...".[22] A Canadian court would come to the same conclusion that the law applicable to determine the scope and effect of the arbitration clause will be, in the absence of any other evidence, the same law as the parties had agreed would apply to the primary agreement. It is the intention of the parties that is important. This intention is to be determined from giving meaning to all of the words used by the parties in their contract and the application of the concept of primary and secondary contracts. The common law would not consider this to be a limit on the principle of autonomy of the arbitration agreement, but simply the consequence of applying the principles of contract construction. Nothing prevents the parties from specifying a different law for the arbitration agreement or, for that matter making it a completely independent agreement.

2.   Assignment

As a secondary contract, the arbitration agreement follows the primary contract where the primary contract is assigned. In the cases of *ABN AMRO Bank Canada v. Krupp Mak Maschenenbau GmbH*[23] and *PetroCanada v. 366081 Limited*[24] the courts have held that both benefits and burdens must follow when a contract is assigned and accordingly the arbitration clause must also be considered to have been assigned. This requires a careful analysis of the assignment however to determine what precisely has been assigned.

The assignment of the accounts receivable from a company may include the obligation to arbitrate. In those cases, the assignee takes an assignment of the right to directly pursue the payor for non-payment. Accordingly in so doing, it is taking the benefit of the contract and the payor may then assert against the assignee the obligation to arbitrate. Arguably the reverse may not be the case should the payor wish to bring arbitration directly against the assignee for matters relating to a breach of contract by the assignor. For example, in the case of *Simex Inc. v. Imax Corporation*,[25] a film production agreement between Midland Production Corp. and Ridefilm Corporation called for the arbitration of any dispute arising out of the contract. The contract stated that title to the film, was to be at all times in the name of Ridefilm. Ridefilm, in a transfer agreement, sold its assets to SimEx Inc. When certain royalties were not paid to Midland, it attempted to bring arbitration against SimEx without success. The court held that as the production agreement itself had not been assigned, but only the film assets of Ridefilm, Midland had no claim against SimEx which could be brought by way of arbitration.

---

22. *Ibid.*, at para. 47.
23. (1996) 135 D.L.R. (4th) 134.
24. (1995) 25 B.L.R. (2d) 19.
25. (2005) CanLII 46629 Ont. C.A.

3. The Service of Notice of Arbitration

Another interesting question of the interplay between the arbitration agreement and the primary contract can arise with respect to the service of documents. Many contracts provide for very explicit methods of service of notices or demands. These may be at odds with the notice provisions contained in some arbitral institution's rules referred to in the arbitration agreement. Can a party follow the institution's rules and ignore the contract notice provisions with impunity?

V. CONCLUSION

The principle of the autonomy of the arbitration agreement is alive and well in common law jurisdictions insofar as it relates to the survival and interpretation of the arbitration agreement, regardless of the ultimate validity of the primary contract. It is not however to be treated generally as completely independent of the primary contract in matters of its interpretation, or the law to which it is subject. As with all secondary or ancillary contracts the arbitration agreement will be subject to the intention of the parties as manifested in the primary contract unless there is an express intention to the contrary.

The Arbitration Agreement: Still Autonomous?
A Brazilian Perspective

*Gilberto Giusti**

I.   INTRODUCTION – ARBITRATION AS A NEW PRACTICE IN BRAZIL

When speaking about arbitration in Brazil, one must have in mind that, although this mechanism of solving disputes has long been present in Brazilian legislation, the actual practice of arbitration is quite recent in Brazil.

There were basically two reasons why arbitration was not customarily practiced in Brazil until recently. First, the arbitration clause lacked binding force, which hampered the practical use of arbitration in Brazil for many years. Even if an agreement contained an arbitration clause establishing that the parties had consented to resolve any controversy between them by arbitration, there was no way of compelling the other party to adhere in fact to arbitration. The arbitration clause was consequently not binding. It was merely an affirmative covenant, non-performance of which by the other party gave rise at most to the right to claim damages.

Further, the arbitration award had to be confirmed by the state court that would have had jurisdiction to judge the dispute originally if it had been submitted to the courts. Even if the state court limited itself to considering the formal aspects of the award, it involved red tape that discouraged the use of arbitration.

As to foreign awards, meaning those rendered anywhere outside Brazil, they also had to be enforced by the Judiciary of the place where they were made. The judgment of the foreign court enforcing the award was then submitted for confirmation by the Federal Supreme Court of Brazil, and only then would it be enforceable in Brazil.

So, despite the many virtues attributed to arbitration for the resolution of disputes – such as speed, confidentiality, expertise and respect for the parties' free will – until a few years ago little was heard of the actual use of arbitration to settle disputes in Brazil.

This situation could not continue, in view of the complaints of businessmen and jurists, who were calling for a more expeditious and specialized justice.

In 1995 a reform movement started in Brazil that brought about positive changes in the Code of Civil Procedure. And in 1996, the Brazilian Arbitration Law, Law No. 9,307, was enacted governing arbitration in Brazil and repealing the rules on the matter under the Civil Code and the Code of Civil Procedure.

---

*   Partner and co-coordinator of the arbitration team, Pinheiro Neto Advogados, São Paulo, Brazil.

This Law brought about the long hoped for binding effect and compulsory enforcement of the arbitration clause. The new Law makes a clear distinction between the arbitration clause (*cláusula compromissória*), on the one hand, and the arbitration agreement (*compromisso arbitral*), on the other, both being different species of the genus "arbitration arrangement". Thus, if the parties wish to submit their disputes to arbitration, they must enter into an arbitration arrangement, which initially will be an arbitration clause inserted in the contract, and then, if a dispute arises, an arbitration agreement.

The Brazilian Arbitration Law also dispenses with the confirmation of the award by the state court. Today, the award has the same validity and effectiveness as a judicial decision, and can be enforced directly against the losing party without the need for prior confirmation by the courts. This also applies to awards made abroad, which no longer need be enforced by the courts of the country where they are rendered. All that is now required is the confirmation by the Superior Court of Justice, which should analyze whether the foreign award is not contrary to national sovereignty and good morals.

It is also important to mention that the Brazilian Arbitration Law permits the parties to agree, in an arbitration clause and/or in an arbitration agreement, to adopt the rules of an institutional arbitration body or specialized entity, whether or not Brazilian. The law further permits the parties to establish the venue for arbitration, which may be in Brazil or abroad, as well as the language in which it will be carried out. Accordingly, it is now perfectly possible under Brazilian law for the parties, whether or not Brazilians, to settle their disputes by arbitration in accordance with the rules of any specialized arbitral body.

Shortly after the Brazilian Arbitration Law was published, there was a great deal of controversy as to the constitutionality of some of its provisions. The constitutionality of the arbitration mechanism itself was not questioned, but rather the judicial enforceability of the arbitration clause as provided for in Art. 7 of said law. This is because Art. 5, XXXV of the Brazilian Federal Constitution prohibits the exclusion from consideration by the courts of any violation or threat to a right. It was thus contended that the obligation to submit to a private arbitration tribunal would run counter to said constitutional precept.

This issue was taken to the Federal Supreme Court of Brazil in the context of a question of unconstitutionality raised in connection with an action to enforce a Spanish award. The Supreme Court took several years to render a decision in this respect. Judgment was finally rendered on 12 November 2001 and, by opinion of seven against four of the Federal Supreme Court Justices, the provisions of the Brazilian Arbitration Law on specific performance of the arbitration clause were held to be constitutional.

The Federal Supreme Court judgment signaled that arbitration could develop as a reliable dispute settlement mechanism in Brazil. Another major contribution to this was the ratification by Brazil of the Convention on the Recognition and Enforcement of Foreign Arbitral Awards, signed in New York on 10 June 1958. On 23 July 2002, the then President of the Republic, Fernando Henrique Cardoso, signed Decree No. 4,311, approving the wording of the New York Convention and validating its terms throughout Brazil. Ratification of the New York Convention by Brazil was warmly welcomed by the Brazilian legal and business communities.

As seen, arbitration has had an extraordinary evolution in Brazil in recent years. Vital aspects of this mechanism have been dealt with in legal writings and case law, as they tend increasingly to recognize the validity of arbitration clauses and the effectiveness of arbitration awards.

II.   THE PRINCIPLE OF SEPARABILITY OF THE ARBITRATION CLAUSE

In the first years after the Brazilian Arbitration Law came into force, Brazilian court rulings were still split, and judgments against the binding force of the arbitration clause were commonplace. But since the Federal Supreme Court found the Brazilian Arbitration Law constitutional in 2001, the judgments of the Brazilian courts have converged into a common stance that the arbitration clause is valid and binding on the parties, and that the arbitral award is as effective as a final and conclusive decision of the courts.

The Brazilian Arbitration Law embodies the most widely accepted principles found in arbitration laws worldwide, including the separability of the arbitration clause as per Art. 8 of said law:

> "*Article 8*
> The arbitration clause is separable from the contract where it is incorporated, so that the invalidity of the contract shall not necessarily render the arbitration clause null and void."

As can be seen, the Brazilian Arbitration Law expressly mandates that the arbitration clause is separable from the contract in which it is contained. The parties' commitment to refer their disputes to arbitration is separate from the other rights and obligations inherent to the subject matter of the agreement.

Furthermore, the Brazilian Arbitration Law states that the arbitrator himself has competence to decide on any dispute about the arbitration agreement, thus acknowledging the renowned principle of *Kompetenz-Kompetenz*. This principle is espoused by the same Art. 8, Sole Paragraph of the Brazilian Arbitration Law:

> "*Sole Paragraph:*
> The arbitrator shall decide – either ex-officio or at the parties' request – on the existence, validity and enforceability of the agreement to arbitrate and of the contract bearing the arbitration clause."

Brazilian court rulings have increasingly accepted the validity and binding nature of both the arbitration clause and the arbitral award, but the same does not hold true as regards the principles set out in Art. 8 and its Sole Paragraph of the Brazilian Arbitration Law.

Some Brazilian legal scholars still frown at the idea that a dispute resolution clause is separable from the other terms and conditions of the legal document where it is inserted (and, as such, even surviving the voidability of such document). Likewise, the deep-seated tradition in Brazil of unrestricted access to the courts has somewhat hampered the acceptance of an arbitrator's authority to deliberate on his own competence, and even to decide on the existence and validity of an arbitration clause.

Court rulings on this matter are still scarce, but in some cases, in an attempt to escape arbitration, litigants have resorted to the courts and obtained anti-suit injunctions on grounds of the supposed voidability of the contract where the arbitration clause was inserted, or of the supposed invalidity of the arbitration clause itself.

These moves have occurred in the recent past, notably with regard to contracts executed with Public Administration entities (independent agencies, government-owned companies, mixed-capital companies); in these cases, the arbitration clauses were challenged on the allegation that they would apply to rights that could not be disposed of by those acting on behalf of the Public Administration. Instead of delegating this issue to the already constituted or about to be constituted arbitral tribunal, the courts have declared themselves competent to void such arbitration clauses.

However, we strongly believe that, just as Brazilian courts have increasingly accepted the presence of arbitration in our legal reality, they will also acknowledge both the separability of an arbitration clause and the principle of *Kompetenz-Kompetenz*. For this reason, in the specific case of Brazil, instead of asking "The Arbitration Agreement: Still Autonomous?", we should perhaps ask "When will the autonomy of the arbitration agreement be fully recognized?". We are confident that such recognition will happen in the near future.

Working Group A

2. Jurisdiction to Determine Jurisdiction

The Arbitrator's Jurisdiction to Determine Jurisdiction

*William W. Park**

> *The boundaries of my language signify the borders of my world.*
> *Ludwig Wittgenstein*[1]

---

* Professor of Law, Boston University; Member of ICCA. Thanks are due to Alan Rau and Adam Samuel for helpful comments on an early draft. © 2007, William W. Park.

1. *Die Grenzen meiner Sprache bedeuten die Grenzen meiner Welt.* Ludwig WITTGENSTEIN, *Tractus Logico-Philosophicus* (1921), at Sect. 5.6. In the original, the juxtaposition of boundaries (*Grenzen*) and the verb to signify (*bedeuten*) is particularly striking, since linguistic meaning usually grounds itself in distinctions and demarcation. An Austrian philosopher who taught at Cambridge in the early 20th century, Wittgenstein continues to influence legal theory in certain quarters. See Eduardo SILVA ROMERO, *Wittgenstein et la philosophie du droit* (2002) Sect. 271 at pp. 353-355; B.F. McGUINNESS, T. NYBERG and G.H. von WRIGHT, eds., *Protractatus, An Early Version of Tractatus logico-philosophicus* (D.F. PEARS and B.F. McGUINNESS, trans., 1971); *Tractatus logico-philosophicus* (Pierre KLOSSOWSKI, trans., 1961), providing a slightly nuanced rendering of the cited phrase, *"Les limites de mon langage signifient les limites de mon propre monde."* Ibid. at p. 86.

I.   INTRODUCTION: THE LIMITS OF LANGUAGE

Legal phrases, maxims and rules often enhance efficient dispute resolution by providing intellectual hooks on which to hang analysis, as well as mental handles with which to arrange otherwise complex arguments. Like the questions we ask, the language of the law can shape the choices ultimately made by arbitrators and judges.

Words can beget misunderstanding as well as insight, however. Expressions which bear multiple meanings often find themselves employed with promiscuous disregard to context and function.

The disorienting effect of language finds illustration in the principle that arbitrators may rule on their own authority. Often expressed as *Kompetenz-Kompetenz*[2] (literally "jurisdiction on jurisdiction"), the precept has been applied to questions such as *who* must arbitrate, *what* disputes must be arbitrated, and *which* powers arbitrators may exercise.[3]

As we shall see, this much-vexed principle possesses a chameleon-like quality that changes color according to the national and institutional background of its application. The basic rule that arbitrators may decide on their own jurisdiction says nothing about who ultimately decides a particular case. Rather, the rule states only that the question of "who decides what" may itself be addressed by an arbitrator. At least until a competent court directs otherwise, arbitral proceedings need not stop just because one side challenges the arbitrator's authority.

To say that arbitrators may make jurisdictional decisions tells only part of the story.[4] Every jurisdictional ruling by an arbitrator begs two further questions, one relating to timing and the other to finality.

The timing question asks when judges should intervene in the arbitral process to monitor possible jurisdictional excess. If an unhappy respondent denies having agreed to arbitrate, a court might be requested to declare the arbitration clause invalid. Should a judge entertain a "mid-arbitration" request to stop the proceedings? Or should the respondent be required to wait until an award has been rendered, and only then seek vacatur for alleged jurisdictional excess?

---

2. Normally interchangeable, *compétence-compétence* and *Kompetenz-Kompetenz* often take their usage by the speaker's preference for a German or a French formulation. Given a slight scholarly preference for the German phrase, that formulation will be used in this paper. See generally Pierre MAYER, "*L'Autonomie de l'arbitre dans l'appréciation de sa propre compétence*", 217 Recueil des Cours (Académie de droit international de La Haye 1989) p. 320; Emmanuel GAILLARD, "*L'effet negative de la compétence-compétence*", in J. HALDY, J-M. RAPP and P. FERRARI, eds., *Études de procédures et d'arbitrage en l'honneur de Jean-François Poudret* (1999) p. 385; Adam SAMUEL, *Jurisdictional Problems in International Commercial Arbitration* (1989) Chaps. 4 and 5, pp. 177-274.

3. When the very existence of the arbitration agreement is challenged, the term "arbitrator" may turn out to be a misnomer. However, to avoid an unduly heavy style, discussions of arbitral jurisdiction often speak of "arbitrator" (rather than "alleged arbitrator") even when that status remains an open question. In that context, the term is used for convenience, with no intent to presume ultimate conclusions on the matter.

4. While thoughts may be simultaneous, words remain sequential, creating a chronically inadequate container for legal truth, reminiscent of the "treasure in earthen vessels" mentioned in Paul's Second Epistle to the Corinthians (II Cor. 4:7).

Each alternative carries its own risks and opportunities for mischief. Delay in judicial scrutiny can subject respondents to the expense of unauthorized proceedings before overreaching arbitrators.[5] However, early access to courts increases opportunities for dilatory tactics. In the business world, determining the scope of arbitration clauses may implicate time-consuming investigations into complex questions of fact and law related to matters such as agency relationships and the corporate veil.[6]

The second question relates to the effect that judges should give to arbitrators' jurisdictional rulings. In what circumstances (if any) should an arbitrator's decision on his or her authority be final?

Legal systems differ on whether and when an arbitrator's decision on his or her authority should foreclose judicial determination on the matter. Some countries (notably the United States) implement the litigants' agreement to have arbitral authority determined by the arbitrators themselves. Judges, of course, must still ask what (if anything) the parties actually expected the arbitrator to decide.[7] Assuming such an agreement exists, however, it will be respected.

Other countries (notably Germany) seem to preclude such agreements to arbitrate arbitrability. This approach sacrifices liberty of contract in order to provide an extra measure of protection against inadvertent loss of the proverbial day in court.

This dual line of inquiry, looking at timing of judicial intervention and effect of arbitral determinations, can remove much of the mystification afflicting jurisdictional discourse in arbitration law. From a policy perspective, the correct answers will not always be self-evident. However, asking the right questions, rather than simply reciting a catch-phrase, permits attention to costs and benefits of each alternative, enhancing the transactional security and economic cooperation that can be facilitated by arbitration.[8]

---

5. Under some circumstances (depending on the applicable institutional rules and arbitral situs) the arbitrators may award costs against the losing party, including attorneys' fees. Not always, however, as proven by recent American case law. See *CIT Project Finance v. Credit Suisse First Boston*, 799 NYS2d 159, 2004 WL 2941331 (2004), holding an award of attorneys' fees to be permissible only if explicitly provided in the parties' agreement.

6. See, e.g., *Intergen v. Grina*, 344 F. 3d 134 (1st Cir. 2003) (litigation between two parent entities, neither of which had signed arbitration clause, with one side seeking a "plaintiff friendly" court); *Bridas v. Turkmenistan*, 447 F. 3d 411 (5th Cir. 2006) (government manipulation of oil company made it the state's alter ego); *Sarhank v. Oracle Corp.*, 404 F. 3d 657 (2d Cir. 2005) (parent should not answer pursuant to arbitration clause signed by subsidiary); *Kazakhstan v. Istil Group*, [2006] EWHC 448 (Comm.) Queen's Bench (vacating award against Kazakhstan for lack of substantive jurisdiction.); *Fluor Daniel Intercontinental v. General Electric Co.*, 1999 WL 637236 (S.D.N.Y., 20 August 1999) (estoppel required signatories of arbitration clauses to arbitrate with nonsignatory).

7. In many instances the question will be more along the lines of what the parties' expectations would have been had they given the matter any thought.

8. While the rationale for arbitration varies according to context, its core value lies in the same principles that justify freedom of contract. Business managers can negotiate a "fix to fit the fuss" as people in the American South say. For international contracts, arbitration enhances neutrality (and thus predictability) and secures a significant treaty enforcement mechanism. In business-to-business transactions, arbitration can facilitate access to expertise, particularly in construction and reinsurance. By contrast, the motivator for American consumer arbitration often lies in avoiding jury trial. This does not mean that arbitration commends itself for all agreements. See Theodore

57

II. THE BASICS

1. An Anti-sabotage Mechanism

a. The principle in primitive form

In its most primitive form, the principle that arbitrators may rule on their jurisdiction serves as a measure to protect against having an arbitration derailed before it begins. The arbitral tribunal (and/or the relevant arbitral institution) need not halt the proceedings just because one side questions its authority. The principle reduces the prospect that proceedings will be derailed through a simple allegation that an arbitration clause is unenforceable, due to any number of contract law defenses. In most legal systems,[9] arbitrators can get on with their work until ordered to stop by a judge with authority to do so.[10]

The rule is not foolproof, of course, given the eternal ingenuity with which fools often acquit themselves. Recalcitrant parties can still mount troublesome court

---

EISENBERG and Geoff MILLER, *The Flight from Arbitration: An Empirical Study of Ex Ante Arbitration Clauses in Publicly-Held Companies' Contracts* (30 August 2006), Cornell Legal Studies Research Paper Series, which studies more than 2,000 contracts contained as exhibits in 2002 for Form 8-K SEC filings, required under American securities laws for material events. The study finds that only eleven percent of the contracts included arbitration clauses. The highest rates were to be found at thirty-seven percent and thirty-three percent for employment and licensing contracts respectively.

9. Exceptions do exist, however. In China, for example, the power to rule on the validity of an arbitration agreement is given to "the arbitration commission" (which is to say, the supervisory arbitral institution) rather than the arbitrators. The assumption seems to be that ad hoc arbitration does not take place in China. Art. 20 of the Arbitration Law of the People's Republic of China (effective 1 September 1995) provides, "If a party challenges the validity of the arbitration agreement, he may request the arbitration commission to make a decision or apply to the People's Court for a ruling. If one party requests the arbitration commission to make a decision and the other party applies to the People's Court for a ruling, the People's Court shall give a ruling." See translation in Cheng DEJUN, Michael J. MOSER and WANG Shengchang, *International Arbitration in the People's Republic of China*, 2nd edn. (2000) at p. 727. Art. 26 of the same statute provides that an arbitration agreement must designate an "arbitration commission". While this term clearly includes Chinese arbitration institutions, it is not entirely certain to what extent foreign associations fall within its purview. See discussion in Jingzhou TAO and Clarisse VON WUNSCHHEIM, "Articles 16 and 18 of the PRC Arbitration Law: The Great Wall of China for Foreign Arbitration Institutions", 23 Arb. Int'l (2007, no. 2) pp. 309-326.

10. Anti-arbitration injunctions issued by courts with questionable authority over the arbitration raise issues beyond the scope of this paper. See Emmanuel GAILLARD, "Reflections on the Use of Anti-Suit Injunctions in International Arbitration" in L. MISTELIS and J. LEW, eds., *Pervasive Problems in International Arbitration* (2006) p. 203. See also Hakeem SERIKI, "Anti-Suit Injunctions and Arbitration: A Final Nail in the Coffin?", 23 J. Int'l Arb. (2006, no. 1) p. 25. For the time being, let us assume that a Massachusetts court monitors an arbitration taking place in Boston, that a Paris judge is asked to recognize an award rendered against a French company, or that a Swiss judge is called to enforce an award by attaching assets in a Geneva bank. We can leave for another day the circumstances under which a court in Mumbai or Karachi might attempt to enjoin an arbitration in London.

challenges (even if not ultimately successful) designed to slow the train.[11] However, the principle does avoid conceptual barriers to arbitration that would exist if legal systems considered jurisdictional powers of judges and of arbitrators to be mutually exclusive.[12]

On occasion, analogies have been made between arbitral jurisdiction and the power of courts to construe constitutional provisions related to their authority. Such comparisons should be resisted. Few non-circular options exist for interpreting judicial authority, at least in western legal systems. By contrast, in commercial arbitration the enforcement of arbitral authority (initially a matter of the litigants' consent[13]) normally rests with national courts, which must undertake some investigation into the legitimacy of that authority as part of the enforcement process.

b.   Diversity: The Timing and Impact of Court Intervention
Although most countries accept that a jurisdictional objection does not automatically stop an arbitration, little consensus exists on the other aspects of an arbitrator's ruling on his or her authority. National practice diverges in both (i) the timing of court examination of arbitral authority and (ii) the impact that an arbitrator's jurisdictional ruling will have in a judicial proceeding.

Diversity results from the fact that an arbitrator's jurisdictional power, at least in commercial arbitration,[14] derives from national law and institutional rules,[15] not from the treaty framework imposed by the New York Convention.[16] Consequently, the

---

11. See generally Philippe FOUCHARD, Emmanuel GAILLARD and Berthold GOLDMAN, *Traité de l'arbitrage commercial international* (1996) Sects. 660-682; W. Laurence CRAIG, William W. PARK and Jan PAULSSON, *International Chamber of Commerce Arbitration*, 3rd edn. (2000), at pp. 48-49 and 512-515; W. Michael REISMAN, W. Laurence CRAIG, William W. PARK and Jan PAULSSON, *International Commercial Arbitration* (1997) at pp. 524-540 and 645-664; Antonias DIMOLITSA, "*Autonomie et Kompetenz-Kompetenz*", Rev. arb. (1998) p. 305.

12. While few modern legal systems follow such an approach, vestiges can still be found in some court decisions. See *MBNA America Bank v. Loretta Credit*, 281 Kansas 655 (2006), discussed infra.

13. Without such consent, there would be insufficient connections to the parties or transaction sufficient to justify any jurisdiction at all. The state does, of course, provide support for the parties' agreement, principally in the form of judicial enforcement of the award, conditioned on the respect for minimum standards of procedural fairness. The consent underlying arbitration remains qualitatively different from the implied submission to government courts that arguably results from living in society. Arbitration agreements empower a particular adjudicator to decide specific questions with respect to a limited number of persons, constrained by a contractually conferred mission.

14. A different regime obtains for investment arbitration under the ICSID Rules, under which awards are subject to review not by national courts, but by an internal annulment process. See Art. 52 of the Washington Convention. Treaty foundations also exist for other supra-national adjudicatory bodies, such as the European Court of Justice, the International Court of Justice and the European Court of Human Rights.

15. For institutional incarnations of the principle, see, e.g., ICC Rules Art. 6, UNCITRAL Rules Art. 21, AAA International Rules Art. 15, LCIA Rules Art. 23 and ICSID Rules Art. 41.

16. Convention on the Recognition and Enforcement of Foreign Arbitral Awards, 330 U.N.T.S. 38, 21 U.S.T. 2517, T.I.A.S. No. 6997 (1958). Twenty-four countries originally signed the Convention. The rest have joined by accession or succession. The most recent adherents include Afghanistan, Liberia, Pakistan and the United Arab Emirates, bringing to one hundred thirty-eight

expression *Kompetenz-Kompetenz* has thus taken on several lives, giving rise to a constellation of related but distinct notions often subject to undue mystification.[17] While commentators sometimes refer to "the internationally recognized doctrine" of *Kompetenz-Kompetenz*,[18] it would be more accurate to speak of doctrines in the plural.[19] Variations derive both from disparate implementations of the principle and from divergent views on what exactly is meant by a "jurisdictional question".[20]

To illustrate, if German courts are asked to hear a matter which one side asserts is subject to arbitration, they would decide immediately on the validity and scope of the arbitration agreement.[21] In neighboring France, challenge of arbitration clauses must normally wait until an award has been rendered.[22]

Across the Channel in England, litigants have a right to declaratory decisions on arbitral authority only if they take no part in the arbitration.[23] In Germany the

---

(138) the total number of countries bound by the treaty. Although the Convention requires courts to respect arbitration agreements and awards, grounds for invalidating an arbitration clause lie with national law. For example, Art. V(1)(*a*) speaks of the parties' incapacity "under the law applicable to them" or the agreement's invalidity under "the law to which the parties have subjected it". In this, the Convention is not unlike Sect. 2 of the U.S. Federal Arbitration Act, which leaves the validity of an arbitration agreement to state contract law.

17. Unfortunately, more than one symposium has given the principle an unfortunate oversimplification, with sweeping generalizations that derive either from the ignorance of a novice or (in some instances) the polemical mischief of someone who knows better but for ideological reasons suggests that "international jurisdictional standards" represents a synonym for the way things are done in France.

18. David JOSEPH, *Jurisdiction and Arbitration Agreements and Their Enforcement* (2005) Sect. 13.23, at p. 392. Compare Laurent LÉVY, "Anti-Suit Injunctions Issued by Arbitrators" in E. GAILLARD, ed., *Anti-Suit Injunctions in International Arbitration* (2005) p. 115 suggesting that "in upholding their jurisdiction, arbitrators implicitly declare that any other court ... is prevented from ruling on the same matter". *Ibid.* at p. 117. While consistent with French doctrine, this position would not represent expectations of most American arbitrators, familiar with possible judicial decisions on jurisdiction during arbitral proceedings. Other perspectives published in this collection include essays by Axel Baum, Frédéric Bachand, Matthieu de Boisséson, José Carlos Fernández Rozas, Philippe Fouchard, Christopher Greenwood, Konstantinos Kerameus, Julian Lew, Michael Schneider and Steven Schwebel.

19. In some literature, it has also been suggested that so-called "anti-suit injunctions" issued against arbitration violate the principle that arbitrators determine their own jurisdiction. See Emmanuel GAILLARD, "*Il est interdit d'interdire*", 2004 Rev. Arb. (2004) p. 47, discussed infra. The usefulness of such a perspective depends on what version of *Kompetenz-Kompetenz* principles are taken as a standard baseline.

20. As models for various wrinkles on the problem of *Kompetenz-Kompetenz*, the current paper focuses on the law of six legal systems: England, France, Germany, Switzerland, the United States and the UNCITRAL Model Law. This selection was made to further analytic clarity, and in no way implies a lack of interest or importance with respect to other legal systems.

21. German Code of Civil Procedure (*Zivilprozessordnung* – ZPO) Sect. 1032(1).

22. New French Code of Civil Procedure (*Nouveau code de procédure civile*– NCPC) Art. 1458. In some countries, notably Greece, distinctions seem to be made between decisions confirming jurisdiciton (review permitted) and denying jurisdiction (review not permitted). See Stelious KOUSSOULIS, *Jurisdictional Problems in International Arbitration* (2000) at pp. 59-62.

23. 1996 English Arbitration Act Sect. 72.

admissibility of such applications depends on whether the tribunal has already been constituted.[24] By contrast, it seems that courts may entertain applications for jurisdictional declarations at any time in Sweden[25] and Finland.[26]

In Switzerland, courts asked to appoint an arbitrator will normally apply a prima facie standard in deciding whether the arbitration clause is valid, but engage in full consideration of jurisdiction (at least as to law) in the context of award review.[27] American courts, however, may order full examination of the validity of an arbitration clause at *any* stage of the arbitral process to determine whether, as a matter of fact and law, the parties have indeed agreed to arbitrate.[28]

The United States generally permits parties to give arbitrators the final word on some aspects of arbitral power.[29] A similar result would seem to obtain in Finland.[30] In other countries, however, the effect of such agreements remains far from clear.[31]

In light of this multiplicity of applications, the temptation exists to suggest that the term *Kompetenz-Kompetenz* be exiled from the arbitration lexicon, and that scholars abandon any hope of rationalizing the principle. Such radical change would be ill-advised, however. Only the most compelling reasons justify banishment of time-

---

24. ZPO Sect.1032(2), permitting applications only before the tribunal's constitution.
25. 1999 Swedish Arbitration Act Sect. 2, discussed in Kaj HOBÉR, "Arbitration Reform in Sweden", 17 Arb. Int'l (2001) p. 351 at pp. 357-358; Christopher SEPPÄLÄ, "Comment on Sect. 2 of the Swedish Arbitration Act of 1999 Dealing with the Right of Arbitrators to Rule on Their Own Jurisdiction" in Lars HEUMAN and Sigvard JARVIN, eds., *The Swedish Arbitration Act of 1999 Five Years On: A Critical Review of Strengths and Weaknesses* (2006) p. 45; Symposium Proceedings, University of Stockholm, October 2004.
26. Petri TAIVALKOSKI, *"Le nouveau droit finlandais de l'arbitrage international"* in Laurent GIOUIFFES, Pascale GIRARD, Petri TAIVALKOSI and Gabriele MECARELLI, eds., *Recherche sur l'arbitrage en droit international et comparé* (1997) p. 126. Making reference to Sect. 50 of the 1992 Arbitration Act (23 October 1992/967), Dr. Taivalkoski writes, *"Quant à la demande principale concernant la validité de la convention d'arbitrage, le droit finlandais prévoit la possibilité d'intenter une action déclaratoire de nullité contre la convention d'arbitrage indépendamment de toute action au fond." Ibid.* at p. 158 .
27. Swiss Private International Law Act (*Loi fédéral sur le droit international privé* – LDIP) Arts. 7 and 179(3).
28. *Sandvik AB v. Advent Int'l Corp.* 220 F. 3d 99 (3d Cir. 2000).
29. See discussion of *First Options*, infra.
30. Gustaf MÖLLER, "The Arbitration Agreement", *Law and Practice of Arbitration in Finland* (Finnish Arbitration Association 2004) p. 7, noting as follows:

"[T]he parties may by a separate arbitration agreement confer on the arbitrators the power to finally determine the matter of jurisdiction in a final and binding award. A specific separate arbitration agreement as to the jurisdiction of the arbitral tribunal will give the tribunal the power to decide this question and has the effect that a party expressly waives his right to challenge the award on jurisdiction. Conversely, if the arbitral tribunal – subject to a specific agreement to make a final decision on jurisdiction – finds that it has no jurisdiction, such decision would be final."

Ibid. at 17.
31. See discussion of jurisdictional agreements in German law, infra.

honored notions.[32] The remedy for confusion will normally lie in a fuller appreciation of the contextual application of the term, a task to which we now turn.

The modest suggestions of this paper are threefold. First, discourse about arbitral jurisdiction suffers considerable damage through loose jargon divorced from national practice. What matters is *when* courts examine the parties' actual agreements about arbitral authority and the *effect* (if any) that judges give those agreements. Second, agreements to submit jurisdictional questions to arbitration should be honored but not presumed. Finally, although arguments about the timing of judicial intervention remain finely balanced, the weightier considerations argue for postponing most jurisdictional inquiry until after the award has been rendered.

2. Judicial Intervention: When and to What Extent?

a. The shadow of public power

On its face, *Kompetenz-Kompetenz* addresses the powers of arbitrators, in particular their right to make jurisdictional rulings. The flip side of the equation, however, reveals a rule about courts, and the limitations on judges' ability to hear certain matters imposed when litigants decide (or allegedly decide) to submit controverted questions to private dispute resolution. This reverse perspective highlights the heart of understanding how the principle works in practice.

Although private, arbitration proceeds in the shadow of public coercion. Arbitrators have no marshals or sheriffs, and thus parties often ask judges to stay litigation, compel arbitral proceedings, seize assets or grant res judicata effect to an award so as to preclude competing court actions. The contours of arbitral power thus concern not only arbitrator and litigants, but also national legal systems which must establish guidelines for when and to what extent courts may intervene to review or to pre-empt the arbitrator's jurisdictional ruling.

From the perspective of a national legal system, challenges to an arbitrator's authority raise two distinct questions. The first relates to the point in the arbitral process when courts ought to examine arbitral authority to prevent or correct an excess of jurisdiction.[33] The second addresses the matter of when (if ever) courts should defer to an arbitrator's jurisdictional determination as final.

---

32. One recalls the words of Jean PORTALIS, an illustrious author of the French Civil Code:

> "*Tout ce qui est ancien a été nouveau; l'essentiel est d'imprimer aux institutions nouvelles le caractère de permanence et de stabilité qui puisse leur garantir le droit de devenir anciennes.*" (All which is old was once new; the essential is to imprint on new institutions the character of permanence and stability capable of guaranteeing their right to become old.)

> *Discours préliminaire sur le projet de Code civil* (1804).

33. The somewhat awkward phraseology, "preventing or correcting" imposes itself by virtue of the fact that judges sometimes intervene at the beginning of the process (to compel arbitration or to consider competing court litigation) and sometimes at the end (to review awards).

b.   Timing

The first inquiry concerns the *timing* of judicial intervention. Paradigms range from the American approach (courts may intervene at any moment) to the French model (courts wait until after an award is rendered). The difference becomes significant when one side to the dispute makes application to a court with supervisory (curial) competence over the arbitration, asking that the proceedings be stopped or that a case be heard notwithstanding an alleged arbitration clause.[34]

Between these two extremes, many legal systems provide hybrid timing solutions that vary according to the specific posture in which arbitral jurisdiction has been challenged. One standard might apply when a legal action is brought in respect of matters purportedly referred to arbitration. Another standard might pertain to a motion for declaratory judicial determination of preliminary jurisdictional questions. Distinctions might be made depending on whether the applicant has or has not taken part in the arbitration.[35]

c.   Effect of an arbitrator's determination

The other question relates to the *effect* of an arbitration agreement on jurisdictional questions. A legal system might take the position that all arbitral decisions on jurisdiction may be reviewed de novo by the appropriate court.[36] However, such is not the only option, or even the most sensible one. An alternative would be for courts to ask what jurisdictional matters the parties agreed the arbitrator would decide, and to defer accordingly.

Each option presents its own risks, requiring lawmakers to navigate between policy dangers much as Odysseus had to sail between Scylla and Charybdis. If courts may defer to arbitrators on jurisdictional matters, intellectual sloppiness (or a desire to clear dockets) might lead judges to accept mere contract recitals rather than to engage in rigorous inquiry into what the parties really meant. The other risk lies in undue rigidity, precluding recognition even of the litigants' clearly expressed wishes for finality in arbitral determinations about jurisdiction issues.

In systems where courts may defer to an arbitrator's jurisdictional determination, judges must still examine arbitral authority. However, the analysis takes place at a different level, asking whether the parties intended an arbitrator to have the last word

---

34. On the costs and benefits of different timing options, see Christopher SEPPÄLÄ, *op. cit.*, fn. 25, p. 45.

35. In England, for example, one can see the interaction of 1996 English Arbitration Act Sects. 9 (stay of legal proceedings in respect of matters referred to arbitration), 30 (jurisdiction to determine jurisdiction), 32 (application for judicial determination of preliminary questions) and 72 (person who takes no part in arbitration may apply for court declaration). Compare the situation with respect to pre-award judicial intervention in Germany, Sweden and Switzerland, all discussed infra.

36. In most cases, courts *will* have the last word on jurisdiction, rendering misplaced the fretting about arbitrators' "unfettered discretion" such as evidenced in *Ottley v. Sheepshead Nursing Home*, 688 F. 2d 882 (2d Cir. 1982) at 898 (Lombard, J, dissenting).

on a particular jurisdictional issue. The pertinent question is what the contract provides.[37]

With the obvious exception of challenges based on public policy (non-arbitrable subjects), analysis would normally focus on the parties' pre-dispute intent. Courts must examine the facts of each case as they bear on the parties' pre-dispute expectations. If (and only if) the litigants intended arbitration of a particular jurisdictional question, the matter would be given to the arbitrator for ultimate disposition, not just an expression of preliminary views. However, in all events courts would first look seriously at the parties' expectations.

d.   A cautionary tale about an (allegedly) lazy professor
The point about the binding nature of an agreement to arbitrate jurisdiction might be illustrated by the following scenario. Imagine a publication dispute between a law journal and a learned professor. Having written an article for the journal, the professor asserts that the editor agreed to pay a $1,000 royalty. On failure to pay, she files an arbitration claim based on what she believes to constitute a valid arbitration clause in the license to publish.

"No way!" the editor replies. "On its face, the clause provides that an arbitrator has jurisdiction *only* over claims filed within thirty days after the dispute arises. This lazy professor missed that deadline, having waited to file her claim on the 4th of July, more than two months after our early May disagreement on the matter."

The professor sees things quite differently. She replies that no differences arose until the middle of June. She recalls no discussion in May, and challenges the editor's recollection.

To settle the matter, the author and the journal sign a written agreement to have an arbitrator determine when the disagreement arose: the first week of May or the middle of June. They agree that the same proceeding will address entitlement to the $1,000, and that both questions will be addressed by an eminent French scholar whom they jointly appoint as sole arbitrator.

After hearing the witnesses and reading the parties' submissions, the arbitrator finds no evidence of a disagreement before the 15th of June.[38] This means the author's claim was timely filed on the 4th of July. Further, the arbitrator finds that the editor did indeed agree to pay $1,000 for the article.

Does any sound policy give the editor a jurisdictional escape hatch? Having agreed to submit the time limits to arbitration, why should the editor be allowed to renege on the

---

37. The alternative of no judicial review does not necessarily conflict with the first and second timing alternatives. It might be that an American court, examining jurisdiction early in the game when a motion is made to compel arbitration, comes to the conclusion that the parties intended for the relevant issue to be given to the arbitrator for decision. As discussed below, the two timing extremes are represented by the French model (which defers judicial intervention until the award stage) and the situation in the United States (where courts may address arbitral jurisdiction at any moment).

38. The time limits in this scenario, we remember, are restrictions on arbitral authority, not statutes of limitations. The latter remain substantive. The hypothetical presumes that the challenge is launched against the right to arbitrate, not substantive recovery.

bargain and ask courts to decide de novo when the disagreement occurred? Although a judge might be skilled at weighing the evidence, the parties submitted the question to arbitrators.

Any such a second bite at the jurisdictional apple would seem inconsistent with the whole thrust of modern arbitration law, which aims to give res judicata effect to arbitral awards based on valid agreements. Any arbitral award should, of course, be subject to challenge for jurisdictional infirmity, such as physical coercion or forgery in the arbitration clause. However, an agreement accepted with informed consent, followed by fair proceedings, should bind both sides. Having lost the arbitration, the editor should not be permitted to refuse the author her $1,000 fee by re-opening the dispute. Indeed, if the award is made abroad, refusal to grant recognition might well violate the New York Convention.

In this cautionary scenario, a particular issue (the date of the editor/author disagreement) started out being characterized as "jurisdictional" but ended (by the parties' consent) as a matter of the "substantive merits" in their dispute. There is nothing unusual about such transformation. Without going as far as the proverbial Humpty Dumpty,[39] most thoughtful people accept that words have different meanings in different contexts, and that language would be misapplied if labels used against one background are transferred to another with no adjustment to take into account their function.[40]

e. A word on procedural context

The way courts evaluate arbitration clauses often depends on the procedural context in which the clauses present themselves. Some countries apply different standards to pre-award and post-award judicial scrutiny, distinguishing between prima facie and full review. On occasion, legal systems permit jurisdictional challenges brought in the course of court actions ("stop the lawsuit so we can arbitrate") but deny requests for declarations about ongoing arbitrations ("stop the arbitration because we should be in court").[41] In some instances a court will address jurisdiction differently depending on whether or not the arbitration has actually begun.[42] Different rules might also apply

---

39. In an episode from the sequel to *Alice in Wonderland*, Humpty Dumpty asserted, "When I use a word, it means just what I choose it to mean – neither more nor less." Lewis CARROLL, *Through the Looking Glass* (1872). The whimsical reference serves as a warning against careless vocabulary. However, language can also be misapplied if labels in one context are transferred automatically to another, with no adjustment to take into account their purpose.

40. Some things are said to go without saying. Nevertheless, they may go much better *with* the saying. For example, the word "run" can be used as a verb and noun, with quite different meanings, depending on its context. When we have a head cold, our noses run. As a financial institution fails, there may be a run on the bank.

41. In systems that permit injunctions, like the United States, motions for declarations related to arbitrations would likely be combined with motions to enjoin or to compel the arbitral proceedings.

42. See discussion of German ZPO Sect. 1032(2) and French NCPC Art. 1458. In many countries, of course, the various procedural postures are not always easily separated. In the United States, for example, applications to stay lawsuits and motions to compel arbitration are often made before

according to whether the arbitration is conducted locally or abroad.[43]

Several scenarios merit consideration. First, applications to review awards (partial or final) may be brought at the place of arbitration as motions to vacate or to confirm. Review might also be sought at the enforcement situs through motions to recognize or enforce the award. Second, a respondent in a court action might assert an arbitration clause as a bar to a lawsuit brought on the merits of claim, usually for breach of contract. Finally, a litigant considering that a dispute should be heard in court rather than in arbitration may petition for a judicial declaration (combined with an injunction in some countries) about the scope or validity of an arbitration clause. Such actions might be brought either before or during the arbitration.

f.   Review standards

Differences relate not only to when and whether courts may address arbitral jurisdiction, but on the standards of review applied when they do examine the validity of the arbitration clause. The most significant dividing line relates to whether the judge will make a full inquiry into the parties' intent, or simply a summary examination, applying what is sometimes called a prima facie standard.

For example, a seller might bring a judicial action to collect the price of an engine. In response, the buyer (who alleges the engine was defective) might move to stay litigation, asserting that the parties had agreed to arbitrate their dispute. The seller might reply with allegations that the arbitration clause was void.

In the alternative, the buyer might file an arbitration for product malfunction, alleging an engine explosion that caused personal injury and loss of profits. Here it would be the seller (preferring to be in court) who asks a judge to address the validity and scope of the arbitration agreement, perhaps arguing that the person who signed the clause lacked authority, or that the clause was not broad enough to cover the tort action for personal injury or the financial claim for lost profits.

German law illustrates how these procedural postures evoke different judicial responses. Courts in Germany would address challenges to the arbitration clause in the context of a lawsuit, with the buyer arguing that the claim should be heard by arbitrators. A judge could also hear the seller's application (if brought before arbitration began) for a declaration that the arbitration clause was invalid. However, if the arbitration was in progress (and no lawsuit had been brought), the arbitrators would simply rule on their own jurisdiction and proceed with the case. Judicial pronouncement on the allegedly defective arbitration clause would await challenge to an award, whether partial or final.[44]

---

the same court at the same time. See, e.g., *Intergen v. Grina*, 344 F. 3d 134 (1st Cir. 2003), 344 F. 3d 134, in which the defendants in a lawsuit moved both to compel arbitration and to stay legal proceedings. See discussion in George SMITH and Sarah HOLLOWAY, *"Intergen N. V. v. Grina:* Fundamental Contract Principles Trump Policy Favoring International Arbitration Where Nonsignatories Are Involved", 20 ADR and The Law (AAA 2006) p. 266.

43. Such seems to be the case in Switzerland, as discussed infra.

44. See German ZPO Art. 1032(1) and Art. 1032(2). Applications for declaratory relief seem permitted only before the tribunal has been constituted. Compare 1996 English Arbitration Act Sect. 9 and Sect. 72.

Matters get even more complicated in legal systems where different standards of review apply according to the procedural posture of the arbitration. French judges, for example, asked to hear a claim can address the validity of an arbitration clause *only* in the most superficial manner, and *only* in the event no arbitral tribunal has been constituted. At that point the court can ask whether the clause was clearly void (for example, the document might lack any signature), but must put off until later any more complex questions (such as disputes about whether the scope of the arbitration clause covers the dispute).[45] Once the arbitration has started, however, judges must sit on their hands until the award is made, when they provide a full examination of alleged defects in the arbitration clause.[46]

In some countries, courts distinguish between arbitration held at home or abroad. Swiss courts, for example, make a full and comprehensive review of the validity of the arbitration clause when the arbitration has its seat abroad. By contrast, when the arbitration is held in Switzerland, judges engage only in a summary examination of arbitral jurisdiction (*examen sommaire*). Full review must wait until the award stage.

In other nations (such as the United States) courts engage in full examination of arbitral power regardless of whether the arbitration has begun, and irrespective of whether they are being asked to hear the merits of the claims. The court might decide that the lawsuit should stop and the arbitration should proceed. Or vice versa. Or, the court might pass this jurisdictional question back to the arbitrators themselves for their determination.

g. The judge's role: Preventive or remedial?

As a general matter, pre-award requests for declarations and injunctions implicate a *preventive* role for courts. The jurisdictional foundation of an arbitral proceeding must be monitored before anyone knows what the arbitrator will decide. The arbitrator's jurisdiction becomes an issue because judges are asked to make a respondent participate, or to tell a claimant that the arbitration lacks jurisdictional foundation.[47]

By contrast, when arbitral jurisdiction becomes an issue in the endgame, after an award is rendered, judges exercise a *remedial* function, correcting mistakes that allegedly occurred earlier in the arbitral process. The validity of an award might be subject to judicial scrutiny at the arbitral seat, through motions to vacate or to confirm under local law.[48] Or the award might be subject to scrutiny when presented for recognition abroad,

---

45. See also French NCPC Art. 1458.

46. NCPC Art. 1458, permitting pre-arbitration review only to determine if the arbitration clause is *manifestment nulle*. Standards for judicial review are contained in other provisions, for example Art. 1502 for international arbitration.

47. 9 U.S.C. Sect. 4 provides that courts may compel arbitration "upon being satisfied that the making of the agreement for arbitration ... is not in issue".

48. 9 U.S.C. Sect. 10 permits vacatur of an award "where the arbitrators exceeded their powers". For a US Supreme Court pronouncement on determining arbitral jurisdiction at the award stage, see *First Options of Chicago v. Kaplan*, 514 U.S. 938 (1995). In international cases, the New York Convention Art. V provides that courts need not recognize an award if the arbitration agreement "is not valid" (Art. V(1)(a)) or if the award "deals with a difference not contemplated by or not falling within the terms of the submission to arbitration". (Art. V(1)(c)).

by a winning claimant seeking to attach assets or a prevailing respondent asserting the award's res judicata effect to block competing litigation. Normally (but not always) the New York Arbitration Convention would be invoked.[49] At this point, a different set of options present themselves. Courts then face the choice of either giving effect to the award (by confirmation, recognition or enforcement) or rejecting its validity (by vacatur or non-recognition).

3.   Three Meanings of Kompetenz-Kompetenz

When questions are raised about the validity or scope of a particular arbitration clause, one option would be for the arbitration to stop automatically, until matters have been clarified by a judge. It is against this extreme position, which denies arbitrators any right at all to rule on their own authority, that one must begin to explore the various meanings of *Kompetenz-Kompetenz*.[50]

If a legal system does allow the arbitration to proceed in the face of a jurisdictional challenge, the story could unfold in several ways. At least three different approaches might be envisaged.

First, the arbitrators might offer an opinion on the limits of their own authority, but without in any way restricting the court's consideration of the same question. Although the arbitration does not necessarily stop, neither do related judicial actions. Courts proceed pursuant to whatever motions might be available under local law.

Second, courts could refrain from entertaining any jurisdictional motions until *after* an award had been rendered. The arbitrators would then have the first word on jurisdiction.[51]

The third meaning given to *Kompetenz-Kompetenz* requires that courts defer completely to an arbitrator's decision about his or her own authority. The arbitrator gets the last word as well as the first. However, such a result requires that judges first determine that the parties did in fact agree to such finality.[52]

---

49. For a case where an award was found subject to *neither* the domestic provisions (Chapter 1) of the Federal Arbitration Act or the international provisions (Chapter 2), see *Bechtel Co v. Department of Civil Aviation of Dubai*, 360 F. Supp. 2d 136 (D.D.C. 2005). For a case implicating *both* national statute and the New York Convention, see *Yusuf Ahmed Alghanim & Sons v. Toys "R" Us*, 126 F. 3d 15 (2d Cir. 1997).

50. See, e.g., the Kansas Supreme Court decision in *MBNA America Bank v. Loretta K. Credit*, discussed infra.

51. As explained more fully below, some legal systems distinguish between judicial consideration of arbitral jurisdiction in connection with (i) request for a declaratory judgment and (ii) the context of a court action on the merits of the claim. Moreover, distinctions are often made between applications that can be filed before, as opposed to after, an arbitral tribunal has been constituted. Finally, varying evidentiary standards (full review as contrasted with summary examination) frequently apply depending on when (before or after the award is rendered) the court examines arbitral authority.

52. Depending on the legal system, judicial proceedings to address the finality of the arbitrator's ruling could take place either before or after the award had been rendered. This question of timing would be a separate issue from the matter of finality.

a.   No automatic stop to the arbitration

Under the first hypothesis, the arbitrator's right to make jurisdictional rulings operates in tandem with a rule allowing judges to examine an arbitrator's jurisdiction before an award has been rendered. In some countries, courts may step in from day one, at any time in almost any circumstance.[53] In others, courts might have full power to address arbitral jurisdiction in the context of lawsuits on the merits of the claim, but only limited margin to maneuver through declaratory judgments.[54]

The arbitrator's right to rule on jurisdiction holds significant practical value (at least for the party wishing to arbitrate) notwithstanding the possibility of court intervention. A recalcitrant respondent cannot bring the proceedings to a halt just by challenging jurisdiction.[55] Moreover, whether courts ultimately substitute their own views for those of the arbitrators depends on the facts of each case. In some instances a judge might order the proceedings suspended, either permanently or until the jurisdictional facts have been determined.[56] In others, the arbitration clause may be found to be robust enough to cover the controverted dispute.[57]

As mentioned, even in countries that permit courts to address arbitral jurisdiction before an award is rendered, distinctions are often made between judicial actions on the merits of a dispute (where a defendant asserts the action is preempted by an arbitration clause) and requests for declaratory judgments about potential or ongoing arbitrations (where a respondent asserts defects in the arbitration clause). With respect to court actions on the merits, judges usually possess full power to address jurisdictional questions, particularly in countries following the UNCITRAL Model Arbitration Law.

---

53. In the United States, for example, courts address arbitration questions in connection with motions to stay court proceedings or to compel arbitration, as well as to confirm or vacate awards. Limits do exist on appellate review of lower court orders on arbitration. See 9 U.S.C. Sect. 16. For US cases, see *Three Valleys Municipal Water District v. E.F. Hutton*, 925 F. 2d 1136 (9th Cir. 1991) (courts determine whether contracts void because of signatory's lack of power to bind principals); *Engalla v. Permanente Med. Group*, 938 P.2d 903 (Cal. 1997) (malpractice claim against health care provider referred to ad hoc arbitration that left administration to the parties rather than independent institution; habitual delays in the process found to constitute evidence of fraud by health care provider). See also *Brake Masters Systems Inc. v. Gabbay*, 206 Ariz. 360, 363 (2003), stating, "Our arbitration statutes and the weight of authority from other jurisdictions allow either a pre-arbitration or a post-arbitration determination of arbitrability."

54. See German ZPO Sect. 1032(2).

55. See US Supreme Court decisions in *Howsam*, *Bazzle* and *First Options*, discussed infra. For an English case expressing a similar view, see, e.g., *Christopher Brown Ltd v. Genossenschaft Oesterreichischer Waldbesitzer*, [1954] 1 Q.B. 8, stating that arbitrators whose authority is challenged are entitled to inquire into the merits of the jurisdictional issue, not for the purpose of binding the parties, but to satisfy themselves (as a preliminary matter) about whether they ought to proceed with the arbitration or not. The same basic principle has been enacted into the 1996 English Arbitration Act at Sect. 30, although the Act now provides timing limitations on judicial review. See discussion of Act Sect. 72, infra.

56. See discussion infra of *Sandvik v. Advent*.

57. See discussion infra of *Pacificare v. Book*.

For declaratory decisions, however, the law sometimes limits the circumstances in which such applications may be made.[58]

In this regard, it is important not to confuse the allocation of functions between arbitrators and the supervisory arbitral institution with the allocation of responsibility between arbitrators and national courts. For example, under the Arbitration Rules of the International Chamber of Commerce, if the ICC Court is *"prima facie* satisfied" that an arbitration agreement may exist, any jurisdictional challenge of a deeper nature goes to the arbitrators. This does not mean, however, that national courts will be deprived of power to make jurisdictional determinations when asked to stay litigation, enjoin arbitration or vacate an award.[59]

b. Giving arbitrators the first word
In other legal systems, recourse to courts must wait until the end of arbitration, *after* an award has been rendered. This version of *Kompetenz-Kompetenz* lays down rules about the stages in the arbitral process at which judges may intervene. The positive part of the principle addresses itself to arbitrators, permitting them to decide challenges to their own authority. The so-called "negative effect" of the principle speaks to courts,[60] telling the judge to wait until arbitration ends before inquiring about the validity or effect of an arbitration clause.[61]

Best exemplified by French law, this approach means that if an arbitrator has already begun to hear a matter, courts must decline to hear the case. The judge has a limited jurisdiction to hear a case only if the arbitration has not begun, and only if the alleged arbitration agreement is found to be clearly void (*manifestement nulle*). Given the importance of French doctrine in this field, the full text merits consideration:

"When a dispute which has been brought before an arbitral tribunal pursuant to

---

58. In England, only a person who takes no part in arbitration would normally be permitted to seek a court declaration on the arbitrator's jurisdiction. 1996 English Arbitration Act, Sect. 72. In Germany an application for a court declaration on the arbitration clause may be made only before the arbitral tribunal is constituted. The arbitration proceedings, however, may still be commenced while the court action is pending. See ZPO Sect. 1032(3). By contrast, in the United States courts may direct proceedings stayed during determination of issues on which arbitral jurisdiction depend. See *Sandvik AB v. Advent Int'l Corp.*, 220 F. 3d 99 (3d Cir. 2000).

59. But see *Apollo v. Berg*, 886 F. 2d 469 (1st Cir. 1989), discussed infra, where the court relied in part on the ICC Rules to limit the court's own review function. When the defendant questioned whether the arbitration clause remained valid after contract assignment, the federal court turned the matter over to the arbitrators themselves.

60. Emmanuel GAILLARD, *op. cit.*, fn. 2, p. 385 . The "negative effect" might be considered as part of the arsenal of doctrinal tools to combat dilatory tactics of a party wishing to sabotage the proceedings. See Emmanuel GAILLARD, *"Les manoeuvres dilatoires des parties et des arbitres dans l'arbitrage commercial international"*, Rev. arb. (1990) p. 759.

61. The negative effect of arbitration clauses sometimes extends beyond jurisdictional matters, to judicial orders for provisional measures, see Elliott GEISINGER, *"Les relations entre l'arbitrage commercial international et la justice étatiqe en matière de mesures provisionnelles"*, 127 Semaine Judiciaire (December 2005) p. 375 ; Jean-François POUDRET and Sébastien BESSON, *Droit comparé de l'arbitrage international* (2002), Sect. 6.3.2.2, at pp. 554-555.

an arbitration agreement is brought before a governmental court, the court must declare itself without jurisdiction. If the dispute has not yet been brought before the arbitral tribunal, the court must also declare itself without jurisdiction unless the arbitration agreement is clearly void."[62]

At issue here is the timing, rather than the extent, of judicial review. Going to court at the beginning of the proceedings can save expense for a defendant improperly joined to the arbitration. On the other hand, judicial resources may be conserved by delaying review until the end of the process, by which time the parties might have settled.

Even in countries that allow judicial intervention before an award is rendered, a core element of modern arbitration law resides in recognition of separate spheres of responsibility for courts and arbitrators. Pale hints of the negative aspect of *Kompetenz-Kompetenz* can be found, for example, in a recent US Supreme Court decision which adopted a "wait and see" approach with respect to public policy questions related to arbitration of treble damages claims.[63]

This is not to say, however, that the French timing mechanism itself has gained widespread acceptance. Such across-the-board deference to arbitrators (or alleged arbitrators) commands no wide international consensus. Outside the French hexagon, legal systems follow a more flexible and nuanced approach with respect to court intervention. Significant departures from French practice can be seen not only in the United States, but also in important arbitral venues such as England, Sweden and Switzerland, as well as nations such as Germany which follow the UNCITRAL Model Arbitration Law.[64]

The point is not trivial, since scholars sometimes cloak the Gallic perspective with wider acceptance than may actually be the case. Readers even encounter references to principles "generally recognized in comparative law"[65] which, on closer examination,

---

62. See NCPC Art. 1458:

> "*Lorsqu'un litige dont un tribunal arbitral est saisi en vertu d'une convention d'arbitrage est porté devant une juridiction de l'État, celle-ci doit se déclarer incompétente.*
> *Si le tribunal arbitral n'est pas encore saisi, la juridiction doit également se déclarer incompétente à moins que la convention d'arbitrage ne soit manifestement nulle.*"

Art. 1458 falls within Title I of Book IV of the NCPC and thus retains residual application to international arbitration. See NCPC Art. 1507 and Décret du 12 mai 1981, Arts. 55 and 56.

63. See discussion infra of *Pacificare v. Book*.

64. See discussion infra, Sect. II.4.

65. See Emmanuel GAILLARD, *op. cit.*, fn. 19, p. 47, suggesting that anti-suit injunctions (courts prohibit lawsuits or arbitrations through contempt-of-court sanctions) "fail to recognize this principle very generally accepted in comparative law". (Anti-suit injunctions "*méconnaissent ce principe [compétence-compétence] principe très généralement reconnu en droit comparé*".) *ibid.* para. 21, p. 61. While not explicitly addressing "positive" (arbitrator rights) and "negative" (judicial restraint) principles, the essay's context (court actions that trump arbitration) clearly infers reference to the latter. The essay's title derives from a leftist slogan ("It is forbidden to forbid") of the May 1968 Paris uprisings, when university walls sported gems such as *Ni Dieu ni maître!* (Neither God nor master!), *La lutte continue* (The struggle continues) and *Sexe, c'est bien, a dit Mao, mais pas trop*

describe nothing more than the parochial French approach (however commendable). Whatever the optimum policy might be on timing judicial intervention, the temptation to blur lines between the "is" and the "ought" of legal doctrine must be resisted.[66]

c. The arbitrator's decision is final

i. Jurisdiction as a question of substantive merits

Regardless of when judges entertain motions on arbitral jurisdiction, the parties might agree, expressly or impliedly, to subject the jurisdictional question to arbitration. In legal systems following this third approach, jurisdictional questions themselves are considered capable of settlement by arbitration, pursuant to agreement by the parties.[67] Under these circumstances, an arbitrator's determination on his or her own authority will be final. The parties' agreement transforms the jurisdictional difference into a disputed question of fact or law, whose substantive merits the litigants submit to final determination by an arbitrator.[68]

The application of this line of reasoning will in all events depend on the facts of each case. In some instances, the parties may indeed have agreed to submit a jurisdictional question to final and binding arbitration. In other instances, an assertion that they have done so will be preposterous, unable to withstand analysis except by ignoring reality in

---

souvent. (Sex is good, said Chairman Mao, but not too often). Professor GAILLARD presents a more subtle message in "*La reconnaissance, en droit Suisse, de la seconde moitié du principe d'effet négative de la compétence-compétence*" in *Global Reflections on International Law, Commerce and Dispute Resolution: Liber Amicorum in Honour of Robert Briner* (2005) p. 311 at p. 312: "*La même unanimité [compétence des arbitres pour connaître de leur compétence] ne se retrouve pas en droit compare lorsque la règle s'adresse non plus aux arbitres mais aux juridictions étatique.*" (The same unanimity [jurisdiction on jurisdiction] does not appear in comparative law when the rule addresses itself to courts.)

66. As a policy matter, Professor Gaillard suggest that "anti-suit injunctions negate the very basis of arbitration, that is, the parties' consent to submit their disputes to arbitration". See Emmanuel GAILLARD, *op. cit.*, fn. 10, at p. 213. While true in many cases, this approach might on occasion presume its own conclusion, in that some legal systems see the "basis of arbitration" as more limited than full party autonomy. The policy underpinning for the "negative" jurisdictional principle was also summarized by Professor Gaillard in his contribution to the Briner *Festschrift*, cited supra:

> "*Il convient également [en plus de permettre aux arbitres de poursuivre leur mission lorsque leur compétence est contestée] de s'assurer que le même contentieux ne puisse être aussitôt porté devant les juridictions étatiques qui, en l'absence de convention d'arbitrage, auraient été compétentes pour connaître le fond de l'affaire.*" (One must also [in addition to allowing arbitrators to pursue their mission when jurisdiction is contested] provide that the same dispute is not brought before state courts which, in the absence of an arbitration clause, would be competent to address the merits of the matter.)

Ibid. at p. 312.

67. On the notion of "merits" in an international arbitration, see Veijo HEISKANEN, "Dealing with Pandora: The Concept of 'Merits' in International Commercial Arbitration", 22 Arb. Int'l (2006, no. 4) pp. 597-611.

68. For an illustration, see the "cautionary tale" discussed infra in connection with the new German approach to *Kompetenz-Kompetenz*.

favor of fiction. The parties' agreement, determined on a case-by-case basis, will determine whether this brand of *Kompetenz-Kompetenz* makes sense. In each instance, the question for judges will be: What did the parties intend to submit to arbitration?

Legal systems disagree on whether judges should ever be permitted to accord finality to an arbitrator's decision on his or her authority, even on a finding of the parties' prior consent. In practice, giving arbitrators the last word on jurisdictional questions means that some litigants may well lose their access to court. The peril derives not so much from isolated mistakes, whether by arbitrators or by courts, but from the risk that an overburdened judiciary might fall into a systematic proclivity toward granting jurisdictional authority to arbitrators, even when contracts are ambiguous on the matter.

Long gone are the days when judges exhibited blanket hostility to arbitration. Today, courts often perceive arbitration as a way to clear crowded dockets. Even the best of judges may be tempted to exchange rigorous reasoning for the convenience of a finding that the parties really did want jurisdictional questions addressed by arbitrators. Such a tendency seems to have been a factor in recent changes in German law, which now reduces the prospect of never-bargained-for arbitrations by requiring that all questions of arbitral authority go to judges.[69]

This approach, however, may create even more problems than it resolves. A judicial monopoly on final resolution of jurisdictional questions imposes serious restrictions on party autonomy, particularly among sophisticated business managers. The result is a serious limit on the liberty of contract that has long bolstered healthy commercial transactions in free economies.

ii.   German doctrine: Then and now

Prior to Germany's adoption of the UNCITRAL Model Law in 1998, court decisions had recognized that an arbitral tribunal might be granted the power to rule on its own jurisdiction pursuant to a specific clause, accepted by both parties, that implicitly dispensed with subsequent judicial review. In a landmark decision, Germany's highest court, the *Bundesgerichtshof*, had decided that the parties to a commercial contract could submit the question of arbitral authority to final and binding arbitration.[70] What the court called a *Kompetenz-Kompetenz-Klausel*, or "jurisdiction on jurisdiction clause", was deemed sufficient to insulate the arbitrator's decision on the matter from judicial scrutiny.

Currently, the prevailing opinion in Germany (both scholarly and judicial) seems to hold that such *Kompetenz-Kompetenz* clauses are invalid. German case law has held that the parties may not restrict judges from examining arbitral jurisdiction in the context

---

69. See references to work by Peter SCHLOSSER and decisions of the BGH, discussed infra.
70. BGH, 5 May 1977, III ZR 177/74. Reported in 68 BGHZ 356, at 358. See discussion in Peter SCHLOSSER, *Das Recht der internationalen privaten Schiedsgerichtsbarkeit* (1989) at Sect. 556. See generally, Jan K. SCHÄFER, Richard H. KREINDLER and Reinmar WOLFF, *Schiedsgerichtsbarkeit Kompendium für die Praxis* (2006) at Sects. 191-193.

of challenges to either interim or final awards.[71] Whether such a position constitutes sound doctrine remains open to debate, as discussed later.

iii.   French and Swedish perspectives

French law seems to include a more nuanced position with respect to the finality of an arbitrator's jurisdictional determinations.[72] Unlike Germany, France has known no marked break with prior case law, which may account for the fact that the Gallic position seems to be elaborated through scholarly comment.[73]

As a starting point, it is clear that the legal framework for judicial review of awards bears a mandatory character. The grounds on which courts set awards aside (enumerated in the *Nouveau code de procedure civile*) may not be abrogated by contract.[74]

Less evident, however, is the proposition that a ban on waiver of statutory annulment standards necessarily means limitation of the questions which by contract may be submitted for final determination by arbitrators. What might be a jurisdictional question in some contexts could become a matter of the merits in an arbitration where both sides clearly submitted the issue to arbitration.

---

71. See BGH, 13 January 2005, III ZR 265/03. Reported NJW 16/2005 at 1125. The case states that a court may decide on arbitral jurisdiction without waiting for a preliminary award to be rendered under ZPO Sect. 1040 (the equivalent of Art. 16 of the UNCITRAL Model Law). See also BGH decision (February 2006) reported in SchiedsVZ (2006) p. 161, at p. 164, finding no violation of *ordre public* when jurisdiction was addressed only in a final (rather than preliminary) award, given that courts would have the opportunity to address the matter then. Review of a final award would normally be made under ZPO Sect. 1059, while review of a preliminary jurisdictional award would proceed under ZPO Sect. 1040. As discussed infra, other provisions of German law relevant to arbitral jurisdiction in other contexts include ZPO Art. 1032(1) (courts before which an action is brought shall consider the validity of an arbitration clause raised as a defense to the action) and ZPO 1032(2) (application for determining the admissibility of arbitration may be brought prior to constitution of the arbitral tribunal).

72. See, e.g., Laurence FRANC, "Contractual Modification of Judicial Review of Arbitral Awards: The French Position", 10 Am. Rev. Int'l Arb. (1999) p. 215, suggesting that French law prohibits party agreement on any modification of judicial review.

73. See Philippe FOUCHARD, Emmanuel GAILLARD and Berthold GOLDMAN, *op. cit.*, fn. 11, Sect. 659 (at p. 414), asserting that the arbitral power to make jurisdictional rulings has "all too often" been understood as giving arbitrators power to decide alone on their authority, which would be "neither logical nor acceptable". (*"Trop souvent encore, le principe de la compétence-compétence est compris comme donnant aux arbitres le pouvoir de décider seuls de leur investiture, ce qui ne serait ni logique, ni acceptable."*) The French original speaks of arbitral *"investiture"*, which might be interpreted as appointment, a narrower notion than jurisdiction. However, the English version clearly uses the term "jurisdiction". See E. GAILLARD and J. SAVAGE, eds. *Fouchard Gaillard Goldman* (1999) at Sect. 659 (p. 400).

74. For cases in which French courts have voided arbitration clauses attempting to change judicial review, see *Cour d'appel de Paris*, 27 Oct. 1994, *Diseno v. Société Mendes*, Rev. arb. (1995) p. 261. See generally cases cited in *Fouchard Gaillard Goldman, op. cit.*, fn. 11, Sect. 1597, speaking of the "mandatory nature" of the organization of challenge to awards (*le caractère impératif de l'organisation des voies de recours*). For a critique of the logic of the French position, see Alan Scott RAU, "The Culture of American Arbitration and the Lessons of ADR", 40 Tex. Int'l L.J. (2005) p. 449, at p. 454 n. 22.

For example, one party to a bill of lading might contend that it incorporated by reference the arbitration clause in a related charter party. Posed in those terms, the matter would normally be a jurisdictional question ultimately to be determined by courts. However, nothing in French law suggests that the two parties cannot, in a clear and distinct agreement, agree to be bound by an arbitrator's determination on that question.

Sweden seems to take a similar position, albeit in a more explicit fashion. After providing that arbitrators may rule on their own jurisdiction, Sect. 2 of the Swedish Arbitration Act adds that this principle "shall not prevent a court from determining such a question" and that the decision of arbitrators on their jurisdiction "is not binding" but rather subject to the full panoply of grounds for challenging awards.[75] Again, it is not certain that the mandatory nature of judicial review necessarily prohibits parties from submitting jurisdictional questions to arbitration if they so wish.

iv.   The American "arbitrability question"
In the United States, a clear line of judicial pronouncements holds that in some situations arbitrators may rule on their own powers without subsequent de novo review by courts. In the sense used by American courts, such grants of jurisdictional power are *not* legal fictions, but require evidence of the parties' real intent expressed in concrete language either in the main contract or in a separate agreement.

Jurists from outside the United States may find the terminology unfamiliar. Court decisions speak of the "arbitrability question" in the same way that the rest of the world refers to a jurisdictional issue. If an "arbitrability question" has been submitted to arbitration, then courts defer to the arbitrator on the matter.

Admittedly, the words "*Kompetenz-Kompetenz* clause" do not figure in American cases. However, after the "arbitrability question" decisions have been broken down and decorticated, one finds that judges in the United States have been using the same conceptual framework as the pre-1998 German cases. In this context, one might recall how the middle-aged cloth merchant in Molière's *Bourgeois Gentilhomme* learned, much to his delight, that he had actually been speaking prose all along, without ever being aware of this rhetorical skill.[76] The difference, however, is that courts in the United States seem happily oblivious to the link between American legal notions and the doctrines elaborated in the rest of the world to meet similar juridical problems.

In addressing jurisdiction, American courts sometimes say the issue is not only "who decides what", but also "who decides who decides". This formulation provides another

---

75. Arbitration Act 1999, 4 March 1999. See generally, Christopher SEPPÄLÄ, *op. cit.*, fn. 25.
76. Jean-Baptiste POQUELIN (MOLIÈRE), *Le Bourgeois Gentilhomme* (The Would-Be Gentleman) (1670), Act II, Scene 4. Monsieur Jourdain, a *nouveau riche* draper, has hired a philosophy teacher to increase his oratorical skill. On learning that language which is not poetry is prose, the newly enlightened merchant exclaims with amazement and pride, "*Par ma foi! il y a plus de quarante ans que je dis de la prose sans que j'en susse rien.*" ("My Lord! For more than forty years I have been saying prose without knowing anything at all of the matter.")

way of asking when arbitrators may determine the contours of their own decision-making authority.[77]

The American approach often involves the transformation of a jurisdictional matter (normally for courts) into the substantive merits in the arbitration itself (for the arbitrators). Jurisdictional challenges usually relate to the arbitrator's authority to decide an issue or to exercise a particular procedural power. Once it has been determined that the parties agreed to entrust to the arbitrator the adjudication of disputes on such questions, then almost by definition the question is no longer one of jurisdiction. Arbitrators receive their power from the parties' consent. If a court decides that the parties asked the arbitrator to decide a matter (for example, time eligibility requirements for arbitration), then in essence this constitutes the court's jurisdictional determination.

When the very existence of an agreement to arbitrate is disputed, however, courts will generally refuse to compel arbitration until they resolve whether the arbitration clause exists at all.[78] In some events, the existence and content of the parties' agreement may have to be determined by a jury.[79]

The recent decision in *Alliance Bernstein Investment v. Schaffran*[80] illustrates the various ramifications of the American approach. A former employee of a New York hedge fund alleged wrongful termination, claiming that he had been fired for cooperating with government investigations into wrongdoings by his employer.[81]

The employment relationship was subject to rules of the National Association of Securities Dealers (NASD), which provided for mandatory arbitration with one important exception: claims of employment discrimination.[82] Normally, the arbitration

---

77. See, e.g., Alan Scott RAU, "The Arbitrability Question Itself", 10 Am. Rev. Int'l Arb. (1999) p. 287. See also discussion infra of *First Options v. Kaplan*.

78. See *Sandvik AB v. Advent Int'l Corp*, 220 F. 3d 99 (3d Cir. 2000).

79. *China Minmetals Materials Ltd. v. Chi Mei*, 334 F. 3d 274 (3d. Cir. 2003), involving allegations of a forged contract in a dispute about what (if anything) a New Jersey company (Chi Mei) agreed to sell to a Chinese corporation (Minmetals). The court stated,

"If there is doubt as to whether such an agreement exists, the matter, upon a proper and timely demand, should be submitted to a jury. Only when there is no genuine issue of fact concerning the formation of the agreement should the court decide as a matter of law that the parties did or did not enter into such an agreement."

Ibid. at p. 281.

80. 445 F. 3d 121 (2d Cir. 2006). Contrary to the suggestion by some commentators, this case seems to be focused on jurisdiction from a contractual perspective, not subject matter arbitrability in the public policy sense. Compare note in 17 World Arb. & Med. Rep. (2006) p. 171 at p. 172.

81. In particular, the former employee asserted that his employer had violated the "whistle blower" provisions of the Sarbanes-Oxley Act, 18 U.S.C. Sect. 1514A.

82. NASD Rule 10201(b) provides that "a claim alleging employment discrimination ... in violation of a statute is not required to be arbitrated" unless the parties have explicitly agreed to arbitration of the discrimination action either before or after the dispute arose. In other words, the submission of a discrimination claim must be specific, rather than covered in a broad "blanket" arbitration clause covering disputes in general.

clause would have been invoked by the employer, on the assumption that juries tend to possess a more sympathetic predisposition toward employees.[83]

In this case roles were reversed. For reasons that are not entirely clear from the face of the decision, the employer (not the employee) moved for a declaratory judgment that the "whistle blower" action (alleging retaliation for cooperation with government investigator) constituted an "employment discrimination" claim by the employee, and thus was not subject to arbitration. The arbitrator's authority thus depended on whether the employee's claim could be characterized as an "allegation of discrimination" within the meaning of the NASD Rules.

The court did not see its role as deciding whether or not the arbitrator possessed jurisdiction to hear the claim.[84] Rather, the question was *who* (judge or an arbitrator) would decide whether the allegations of termination for "whistle blowing" were subject to arbitration, or instead amounted to the type of discrimination claim that was carved out of the scope of the arbitration clause.[85]

The starting point for analysis lay in the relevant NASD Rules, under which the arbitrators were expressly "empowered to interpret and determine the applicability of all provisions under the [NASD] Code" in a way that was "final and binding" on the parties.[86] The court's job, therefore, was to ascertain what the parties meant by that language.[87]

According to the Second Circuit, a presumption exists that the parties would normally intend an "arbitrability question" to be determined by a judge.[88] The

---

83. Not all wrongful dismissals will be the result of discrimination. For example, an employee might be wrongfully terminated because he is fired without reason in violation of his or her contract, or for a reason not otherwise permitted by law, such as reporting on the misbehavior of a boss. Discrimination has traditionally been conceptualized as dismissal for reasons of bias based on race, religion or gender. In this case, the question was whether the allegedly unfair termination (retaliation) was to be characterized as "discrimination" or simply a firing that was contrary to the law for other reasons.

84. The claim of non-arbitrability related to the scope of a contract provision (NASD Rule 10201), not any public policy limits on arbitration of "whistle-blower" claims. If public policy had been at issue, the result would likely have been different.

85. In its opening paragraph, the court stated that the issue before it was not "whether the claims *must* be arbitrated, but rather ... *who* will decide the arbitrability question". 445 F. 3d 121 (2d Cir. 2006). The distinction is sometimes ignored. A recent summary of *Alliance Bernstein* suggested that the case "held that an employee's claim [for violation of the statute] is for an arbitrator to decide. See 17 World Arb. & Med. Rep. (2006) p. 171. While the commentary later states the holding correctly, the introductory slip of the pen reveals a general tendency to conflate the two issues.

86. NASD Rule 10324 provides, "The arbitrators shall be empowered to interpret and determine the applicability of all provisions under this Code and to take appropriate action to obtain compliance with any ruling by the arbitrator(s). Such interpretations and actions to obtain compliance shall be final and binding upon the parties."

87. Since American contract law is generally a matter for states, the court normally looks to state law for guidance about the parties' intent. See *First Options v. Kaplan*, 514 U.S. 938, at 944 (1995); *John Hancock Life Ins. v. Wilson*, 254 F. 3d 48, at 53 (2d Cir. 2001).

88. *First Options*, supra, at 944-945.

presumption might, however, be overcome.[89] To do so would require "clear and unmistakable" evidence that the parties wished the question to be decided by arbitrators.[90] This intent could be found, for example, in a separate agreement providing for arbitration of "any and all controversies" including interpretation of the provisions of the relevant arbitration rules.[91]

In *Alliance Bernstein* the court was careful to keep close to the language of the arbitration provisions. The language of the relevant rule did not provide for "any and all" matters to be arbitrated, but only for power to "interpret and determine the applicability of" provisions under the NASD code, which would include the scope of the exclusion for discrimination claims.[92] Since there was no disagreement that both sides had accepted the NASD rules,[93] the parties' intent to arbitrate their differing interpretations of the rules could be ascertained from the four corners of the documentation before the court. The arbitrator's decision on this matter would not be subject to later judicial second guessing. Rather, the "whistle blower" claim would be subject to arbitration if, and only if, the arbitrator so determined.

The court found the question of whether "whistle blower" claims were arbitrable was for the arbitrators, and thus insulated that finding from review for "excess of powers" under the Federal Arbitration Act.[94] The award might well be attacked on other jurisdictional grounds, however. For example, the arbitrator would still lack power if an irregularity could be found in signature of the agreement containing the reference to arbitration. Perhaps the person who signed was not authorized to do so. Or, the

---

89. See also *PaineWebber v. Bybyk*, 81 F. 3d 1193 (1996), holding that whether an investor's claims against a brokerage firm were subject to arbitration was a question for the arbitrators. The matter in *Bybyk* involved NASD time limitations on eligibility for arbitrations. Although the court on occasion referred loosely to these arbitration eligibility requirements as a "statute of limitations" the case did not concern a proper statute of limitations arising under the applicable law, which would clearly have been for the arbitrator. See discussion of "admissibility" *infra*.

90. *Contec Corp. v. Remote Solution Co.*, 398 F. 3d 205, at 208 (2d Cir. 2005). The case at bar was covered by the American Arbitration Association Commercial Arbitration Rules (for domestic transactions), which provided in Rule R-7 that "the arbitrator shall have power to rule on his or her own jurisdiction, including any objections to the existence, scope or validity of the arbitration agreement". One might note that this language could be subject to misinterpretation if the "arbitrability question" presented was whether one side had indeed signed the arbitration agreement. Clearly, arbitrators cannot pull themselves up by their own jurisdictional bootstraps. Questions of "scope" of an arbitration clause (which might be subject to an arbitrator's binding jurisdictional determination) must be distinguished from questions about who is a party (on which an arbitrator will rarely have the last word, absent a clear separate agreement on the matter, concluded by the very party contesting jurisdiction).

91. In cases where only one party to the dispute is a member of the NASD, a separate agreement would be required to indicate such a clear intent to arbitrate jurisdictional questions. See *John Hancock*, 254 F. 3d at 54-55.

92. NASD Rule 10324.

93. The employer was a member of the NASD itself, and the employee had signed a so-called "Form U-4" agreeing "to arbitrate any dispute, claim or controversy that may arise between me and my firm ... under the rules, constitutions or by-laws" of the NASD.

94. 9 U.S.C. Sect. 10(4).

signature might have been compelled by a gun at the head. Or, maybe the signature was a forgery. But the decision on jurisdiction over the "whistle blower" claim could not be disregarded because a judge later disagreed with the arbitrator's interpretation of the rules.

Under this approach, once a precise question has clearly been delegated to an arbitrator, it ceases to be "jurisdictional" in the context of the case to which it is relevant. Since the arbitrator has been empowered to hear the matter, any further inquiry must be limited to "What did the arbitrator decide?" That decision might relate to a matter which, in the abstract, would be characterized as jurisdictional. However, the parties' intent prevails, and the arbitrator will determine the matter in a final way.

Such allocation of functions between judges and arbitrators explains itself principally by reference to contract principles.[95] Absent an express or implied waiver of the right to go to court, a litigant will not normally be denied recourse to otherwise competent tribunals. But once such a waiver has been given in the form of an arbitration clause, it is hard to see why a litigant should be permitted to renege on this bargain to arbitrate.

Reasonable people, of course, might argue about what the parties had in mind when they made their bargain. One judge might think that another judge got it wrong, or was misguided, in her reading of how the relevant arbitration rules or contract affected the questions that would be submitted to arbitration. But these debatable matters of fact do not call into question the jurisdictional principle that the parties to a dispute may empower arbitrators to decide controversies about the preconditions to arbitration.

American judges who review questions of jurisdiction must look beyond labels, and instead fix their scrutiny on the parties' real deal. If two litigants intended to submit a question to final and binding arbitration, then the arbitral determination holds, regardless of whether the question would initially have fallen within the arbitrator's mission. In this sense, the *Kompetenz-Kompetenz* clause remains alive and well in the United States.

In defining "arbitrable questions", courts are in the business of drawing lines between jurisdiction and merits, often in a manner that enlarges the arbitrator's authority. Although issues of substance (merits of the dispute) and jurisdiction (arbitrator's right to hear the case) should be treated differently by courts, the two categories are not fixed immutably in the real world. A particular question might be characterized as "substantive merits" in one dispute and "jurisdiction" in another. If indeed the parties to an arbitration agreement clearly intend for a matter to be decided by arbitration, then a "jurisdictional" label would be inappropriate if it were to lead courts to usurp the arbitral function. To ignore this possibility might, in some circumstances, put a country in breach of its New York Convention obligations. The wrinkles on this topic are sizable, and thus it has been addressed in greater detail below in the discussion of the new German arbitration law.

---

95. Regulatory impulses also come into play, although usually only at the margins. Even if the parties to a dispute authorize adjudication through arbitration, courts will hesitate to enforce private decision-making that runs afoul of public policy, either by virtue of touching subjects too sensitive to be removed from government tribunals (e.g., claims of discrimination) or because the decision-making process is tainted with bias or corruption.

4.   Paradigms and Hybrids: Another Look at Timing

a.   Policy concerns

Fixing the point in time for court intervention involves a relatively clear (albeit difficult) choice between costs and benefits related to the expenditure of either public or private resources. Under one model, a party unhappy with having to arbitrate may go to court at *any* moment for the purpose of contesting arbitral power. Another paradigm, however, provides for court challenge of arbitral authority only *after* an award is rendered.

Court challenge to jurisdiction at the beginning of the process can save time and expense for the litigants. If a judge finds the alleged arbitral clause to be void, or too narrow in scope to cover the dispute, then neither side need waste time or money in arbitration. The parties are free to pursue their litigation in the appropriate judicial forum.

By contrast, government funds can be preserved by delaying judicial review until after the award has been rendered. In many legal systems, similar or analogous concerns about economy of judicial resources impose restraints on appeal of interlocutory lower court decisions.[96]

If questions of authority are left to the end game, perhaps there will not even be a jurisdictional challenge in court. The case might settle, or the party resisting arbitration might prevail. And if the matter does go to court, the arbitrator may have done much of the intellectual heavy lifting, sorting facts and law to provide the reviewing judge a helpful analytic road map.

b.   Extremes: France and the United States

i.   United States

American arbitration law traditionally has given parties a right to raise a matter of arbitral authority at any time, whether before or after the award. Such determinations would usually be made pursuant to litigation under Sects. 3 and 4 of the Federal Arbitration Act, providing for stay of court litigation and orders to compel arbitration.[97]

---

96. See, e.g., Sect. 16 of the U.S. Federal Arbitration Act (9 U.S.C. Sect. 16). See also discussion of the "collateral order" doctrine in *Lauro Lines SRL v. Chasser*, 490 U.S. 495 (1989) and *Digital Equipment Corp. v. Desktop Direct, Ind.*, 511 U.S. 863 (1994). See also 28 U.S.C. Sect. 1292(b), involving appeal when an order involves "a controlling question of law as to which there is substantial ground for difference of opinion". See also, *International Ass'n of Machinists and Aerospace Workers Local Lodge*, 410 F. 3d 204 (5th Cir. 2005); *ATAC Corp. v. Arthur Treacher's, Inc.*, 280 F. 3d 1091 (6th Cir. 2002); *Salim Oleochemicals v. M/V Shropshire*, 278 F. 3d 90 (2d Cir. 2002). For conversations on this topic, thanks are due to Ward Farnsworth, Gary Lawson and Louise Ellen Teitz.

97. See generally discussion in *Three Valleys Municipal Water District v. E.F. Hutton*, 925 F. 2d 1136 (9th Cir. 1991). In *Allied-Bruce Terminix v. Dobson*, 513 U.S. 265 (1995) and *Vimar Seguros y Reaseguros v. Sky Reefer*, 515 U.S. 528 (1995) judges determined arbitral jurisdiction at the outset of the process, rather than waiting to see what the arbitrators would decide. See also the US Supreme Court decisions in *Pacificare*, *Howsam*, *Bazzle*, and *Buckeye*, infra.

This approach means that a party who never agreed to arbitrate will not need to waste time and money in a proceeding that lacks an authoritative foundation. Moreover, either side can request clarification about the scope of the arbitrator's power before substantial sums are spent needlessly. The prospect of award vacatur on jurisdictional grounds cannot be excluded, but it may be less likely to hang as a Sword of Damocles in cases of obvious jurisdictional defect.

ii.   France

By contrast, the French model delays court consideration of jurisdictional matters until the award review stage.[98] This approach reduces the prospect of dilatory tactics designed to derail an arbitration. A bad-faith respondent will be less able to add the cost of a court challenge at the same time that the arbitration is going forward.[99]

Another benefit from the French paradigm lies in its potential for higher quality jurisdictional review by judges, who will be able to benefit from the arbitrators' earlier consideration of the matter. And government resources may be conserved for the simple reason that a settlement might obviate the need for judicial review.

A cynic, of course, might note that the French rule can have practical advantages for arbitrators themselves, who will not be declared incompetent until after collecting their fees. But as Rudyard Kipling might have written, that is another story.

c.   Hybrids: England, Switzerland and the UNCITRAL Model

Countries that delay judicial intervention until the award stage aim to preserve government resources. By contrast, legal systems that permit court rulings on arbitral jurisdiction at any moment allow litigants to avoid the expense of an invalid proceeding.

Attempts to find a middle way in the timing of jurisdictional challenge have not always proved easy. Like the man who hoped to get his girlfriend drunk without emptying the wine bottle,[100] efforts at meeting both goals have often served disappointment.

Nevertheless, some legal systems do explore hybrid solutions. England, Switzerland and the UNCITRAL Model provide examples.

i.   England[101]

The position in England seems once to have been roughly analogous to that in the United

---

98. NCPC, Art. 1458.

99. For a case of the *Cour de cassation* interpreting the French version of *compétence-compétence* in the context of an ICC arbitration, see *SARl Métu System France*, Cass. 1re civ., C., 1 December 1999, holding that only the clear nullity of an arbitration agreement would bar application of the principle by which an arbitrator was permitted to rule on his own jurisdiction.

100. In Italian, the observation traditionally takes on a more matrimonial nuance: *Non puoi avere la botta piena e la moglie ubbriaca.*

101. Since the 1996 English Arbitration Act does not apply in Scotland, but governs arbitrations with their juridical seat in England, Wales or Northern Ireland, this paper will resist reference to "British" arbitration law. Since 1536 England and Wales have been part of the same legal system. However, to avoid the cumbersome expression "England and Wales or Northern Ireland", more convenient terms such as "English arbitration" or "arbitration in England" will be used.

States, in that arbitrators addressed jurisdiction subject to general control by the competent court.[102] Such remains the case with respect to final awards, where dissatisfied litigants may challenge arbitrators' mistakes on substantive and procedural jurisdiction.[103] Things have become a bit more complex since 1996.[104] Today, the English Arbitration Act gives an arbitral tribunal the right to rule on its own substantive jurisdiction.[105] The right to challenge arbitral jurisdiction by declaration or injunction is open only to a person "who takes no part in the proceedings".[106] This power can be particularly useful in connection with what are sometimes called "unilateral" arbitration clauses, which permit one side the option to litigate in court rather than to arbitrate. If the other side begins an arbitration before the option has been exercised, the power to request a declaration provides the machinery for vindicating the right to litigate.[107]

Most challenges to substantive competence must wait until an award has been rendered.[108] At that time courts will have an opportunity to review excess of authority as well as the arbitrators' improper arrogation of powers.[109] On occasion, a jurisdictional ruling may also give rise to allegations of procedural irregularity.[110]

---

102. See, e.g., opinion by Devlin, J., in *Christopher Brown Ltd v. Genossenschaft Oesterreichischer Waldbesitzer*, [1954] 1 Q.B. 8. See Michael J. MUSTILL and Stewart C. BOYD, *Commercial Arbitration* (1982 edn.) at pp. 514-515, discussing the possibility of declaratory relief on questions of jurisdiction under the law as it stood prior to 1996.

103. See 1996 English Arbitration Act Sect. 67 (substantive jurisdiction) and 68(2) ("serious irregularity" defined to include "the tribunal exceeding its powers").

104. The Chartered Institute of Arbitrators has attempted to provide comprehensive enlightenment through two valuable studies: "Guidelines for Arbitrators as to How to Deal with Challenges to Their Jurisdiction", 68 Arbitration (2002, no. 3) p. 276 and "Guideline on Jurisdictional Issues in International Arbitration", 70 Arbitration (2004, no. 4) p. 308, also reproduced in 17 World Trade & Arb'n Materials (April 2005) p. 113 . See also Peter AEBERLI, "Jurisdictional Disputes under the Arbitration Act 1996: A Procedural Route Map", 21 Arb. Int'l (2005) p. 253.

105. 1996 English Arbitration Act Sect. 30.

106. 1996 English Arbitration Act Sect. 72. Non-participants may challenge jurisdictional defects regardless of whether failure to participate was by choice or by inadvertence, and regardless of whether in hindsight non-participation seems justified. The 1996 English Arbitration Act in Sect. 30 provides for arbitrators to determine their own jurisdiction as a preliminary matter but in Sect. 67 also permits judicial challenge of any jurisdictional determination. In Sect. 9 the 1996 English Arbitration Act provides for stay of litigation only if the court is satisfied that the arbitration agreement is not "null and void, inoperative or incapable of being performed".

107. See *Law Debenture Trust Corp. v. Elektrim*, [2005] 1 All E.R. 476, 2005 WL 1630790. The case is discussed in Simon NESBITT and Henry QUINLAN, "The Status and Operation of Unilateral or Optional Arbitration Clauses", 22 Arb. Int'l (2006) p. 133.

108. 1996 English Arbitration Act Sect. 67.

109. See 1996 English Arbitration Act Sect. 68. See *Lesotho Highlands Development Authority v. Impreglio SpA* [2005] UKHL 43.

110. For a case in which an arbitrator's jurisdictional decision was challenged on grounds of procedural irregularity, see *Aoot Kalmneft v. Glencore International A.G.* ([2002] 1 Lloyd's Rep. 128 (Queen's Bench, 27 July 2001), 2001 WL 825106). An ad hoc London arbitration addressed a dispute between an oil trading company and an oil production entity in Kalmykia. The oil trader claimed that it had paid for oil never delivered, while the production company alleged it had been the victim of fraud by one of its officers, who allegedly had no authority to conclude the agreement.

The Act does permit application for judicial determination on a "preliminary point of jurisdiction". In this latter context, courts may consider the matter only on agreement of all parties, or if the arbitral tribunal grants permission and a court finds that addressing the question is likely to produce substantial savings in costs.[111]

Otherwise, a party seeking annulment of an arbitrator's decision for excess of jurisdiction may do so only after attempting to remedy the problem through the appropriate arbitral procedures. In the interest of arbitral efficiency, court challenges to awards can only be brought after any available institutional review.[112] And a "use it or lose it" principle requires that challenges for excess of authority must be made "forthwith" or within the time provided by the arbitration agreement.[113] To rebut the presumption that the right to object has been waived, the challenging party must show that it did not know, and could not with reasonable diligence have discovered, the grounds for objection.[114] In this respect, the Act leads to a result different from the one obtaining in Switzerland, where defendants may lose their right to challenge an award's jurisdictional underpinnings by boycotting the proceedings.[115]

Arbitral jurisdiction might also be tested in court if one party brings a court action for a claim which the other party says is covered by the arbitration agreement. Arbitral authority is put at issue in a motion to stay legal proceedings, and the point is decided then and there. Like analogous provisions in Art. 8 of the UNCITRAL Model Law,

---

In an interim decision, the sole arbitrator ruled that he had jurisdiction. The production entity challenged this award inter alia on the grounds that a finding of validity for the arbitration clause prejudged the case on the merits. By finding that the officer had authority to commit to arbitration, the arbitrator gave an implicit preview of his views with respect to the binding nature of the main agreement. Justice Coleman rejected the challenge, finding that an arbitrator may "rule on his own jurisdiction at the outset, even if that involves deciding whether there was a binding contract to arbitrate and even if his decision on that matter gives rise to a conclusion in respect of a major issue on the merits of the underlying claim in the arbitration". *Ibid.*, Paragraph 84. See discussion in Robert KNUTSON, "Procedural Fairness, Kompetenz-Kompetenz and English Arbitral Practice", 6 LCIA News (November 2001) p. 5.

111. 1996 English Arbitration Act Sect. 32. If the parties have not all agreed, an application requires permission of the arbitral tribunal. In this latter instance, the court must be satisfied not only of potential cost savings, but also that the application was made without delay and that there is "good reason" why the matter should be judicially decided.

112. 1996 English Arbitration Act Sect. 70(2) speaks of "any available arbitral process of appeal or review". However, courts are not necessarily bound by the arbitral institution's decision on the matter. Challenge to an award must also be delayed until exhaustion of any application to correct an award under the Act Sect. 57, in default of the parties' agreement otherwise.

113. 1996 English Arbitration Act Sect. 73(1). In some instances, the arbitral tribunal may set the appropriate time limits for challenge.

114. *Ibid.*, Sect. 73. The English Act is more severe than the analogous provisions in Art. 4 of the UNCITRAL Model Arbitration Law, which covers only a party who actually "knows" of a procedural defect.

115. See *Westland Helicopters v. Emirates Arabs Unis, Arabie Saoudite, Etat du Qatar, ABH et Arab Organization for Industrialization (AOI)*, Swiss *Tribunal fédéral*, 19 April 1994, 120 II 155 ATF (1994), also reported in 12 ASA Bull. (1994) p. 404.

English arbitration law contemplates that in some instances there might be simultaneous proceedings by courts and arbitrators regarding the competence of the arbitral tribunal.[116]

ii. Switzerland[117]

Although not free from scholarly debate,[118] Swiss case law seems to distinguish between arbitration held inside and outside of the country. Federal statute provides that arbitral tribunals shall rule on their authority, normally through interlocutory decisions,[119] and that objections to jurisdiction must be raised before the tribunal prior to any defense on the merits.[120] Moreover, state courts must decline jurisdiction unless they find that the arbitration clause is void, inoperative or incapable of being applied.[121]

If the seat of the arbitration is in Switzerland, courts engage in only summary examination of arbitral authority.[122] When the arbitral seat lies outside of Switzerland, however, the *Tribunal fédéral* has called for a fuller and more comprehensive examination

---

116. 1996 English Arbitration Act Sect. 9. This section requires a stay of proceedings only so far as they concern that matter to be referred to arbitration and only if the court is satisfied that the arbitration agreement is not "null and void, inoperative or incapable of being performed".

117. See generally, Bernhard BERGER & Franz KELLERHALS, *Internationale und interne Schiedsgerichtsbarkeit in der Schweiz* (2006) at Ch. 2, Sect. 7(II), paras. 607-617; Pierre LALIVE, Jean-François POUDRET and Claude REYMOND, *Le Droit de l'arbitrage* (1989), at pp. 379-386; Werner WENGER, "Commentary on Article LDIP 186" in *International Arbitration in Switzerland* (2000) pp. 459-477. See also Zina ABDULLA, "The Arbitration Agreement" in G. KAUFMANN-KOHLER & B. STUCKI, eds., *International Arbitration in Switzerland* (2004) p. 15 at pp. 29-32.

118. See work by J.-F POUDRET and G. COTTIER, discussed infra. See also Werner WENGER, *Kommentar zum schweizerischen Privatrecht, Internationales Privatrecht* (Basel) discussed in *Tribunal fédéral*, ATF 122 III 139, (*Fondation M v. Banque X*, 29 April 1996) and Andreas BUCHER, *Le nouvel arbitrage international en Suisse*, at p. 55, n. 130, discussed in *Tribunal fédéral*, ATF 121 III 38 (*Compagnie de Navigation et Transports SA v. MSC Mediterranean Shipping Company SA*, 16 January 1995).

119. Art. 186 of the *Loi fédérale sur le droit international privé* (LDIP) provides that such jurisdictional rulings should be made "*en general/in der Regel*".

120. *Ibid.*, Art. 186(2).

121. *Ibid.*, Art. 7, providing for courts to verify that the arbitration clause is not "*caduque, inopérante ou non susceptible d'être appliqué*".

122. *Tribunal fédéral*, ATF 122 III 139, *Fondation M v. Banque X* (29 April 1996), which holds at consideration 2(b):

"*Il est généralement admit que, si le juge étatique est saisi d'une exception d'arbitrage et que le tribunal arbitral a son siège en Suisse, le juge se limitera à un examen sommaire de l'existence prima facie d'une convention d'arbitrage, afin de ne pas préjuger de la décision du tribunal arbitral sur sa propre compétence.*" (It is generally accepted that if a state judge hears a defense based on arbitration, and the arbitral tribunal has its seat in Switzerland, the judge will limit himself to a summary examination of the prima facie existence of the arbitration agreement, in order not to prejudge the arbitral tribunal's decision on its own jurisdiction.)

of the validity of the arbitration agreement.[123] This inquiry would generally occur at the time the clause is invoked in a Swiss court action on the merits of the dispute, allegedly brought in disregard of the agreement to arbitrate. In applying Art. II of the New York Convention (requiring reference to arbitration unless the clause is void, inoperative or incapable of being performed), courts would *not* limit themselves to a summary (prima facie) examination of the validity of the agreement to arbitrate.

The logic of this distinction (which has not gone unquestioned[124]) seems to be that when arbitration occurs abroad, Swiss courts might not get a chance at a later time to correct an arbitrator's erroneous decision about jurisdiction under the questionable agreement. By contrast, most arbitration conducted inside Switzerland will be subject to judicial review on the grounds enumerated in the federal conflicts-of-law statute, which include excess of jurisdiction.[125]

Comparisons are sometimes made between jurisdictional review in France and in Switzerland. Notwithstanding some inferences to the contrary, one can see as many (or more) differences as similarities. For arbitrations inside the forum state, both countries delay full judicial review of arbitral authority until the award stage. There the similarity ends, however. Swiss law contains nothing equivalent to the extreme French position that requires courts, while the arbitration is ongoing, to refrain from addressing even the clearest indications of an arbitration clause's invalidity.[126] On the contrary, Swiss courts verify the validity of arbitration clauses in a summary fashion (prima facie) when asked either to appoint an arbitrator or to hear disputes allegedly subject to arbitration.[127] And as already noted, when the arbitral seat is outside Switzerland, Swiss

---

123. *Tribunal fédéral*, ATF 121 III 38, *Compagnie de Navigation et Transports SA v. MSC Mediterranean Shipping Company SA* (16 January 1995). The court stated at consideration 3(b),

> "*En revanche, si le tribunal arbitral a son siège à l'étranger, le juge étatique suisse, devant lequel une exception d'arbitrage est soulevée, doit statuer sur ce moyen de défense avec plein pouvoir d'examen quant aux griefs soulevés, et en particulier celui déduit de l'article II al. 3 de la Convention de New York, sans pouvoir se limiter à un examen prima facie.*"

> (By contrast [to arbitration conducted inside Switzerland] if the arbitral tribunal has its seat abroad, the state judge before whom the arbitration exception is raised must decide on this defense with full powers of examination concerning the grounds for challenge, and in particular that of Art. II (3) of the New York Convention, without limiting himself to a prima facie examination.)

124. See Jean-François POUDRET and Gabriel COTTIER, "*Remarques sur l'Application de Article II de la Convention de New York*", 13 ASA Bull. (1995) p. 383. The authors write, "*Si cette solution doit certes être approuvée, la motivation qui la soutient repose toutefois sur une distinction peu convaincante et même infondée....*" *Ibid.*, at p. 387. See also works by WENGER and BUCHER, cited supra, fn. 118.

125. *Loi fédérale sur le droit international privé*, Art. 190. In some instances the parties may waive challenge to the award. See discussion infra of LDIP Art. 192.

126. Art. 1458, *Noveau code procédure civile*.

127. See Arts. 7 and 179(3) of the *Loi fédérale sur le droit international privé*. See decision of Swiss *Tribunal fédéral*, ATF 122 III 139, *Fondation M v. Banque X*, discussed supra and in François PERRET, "Parallel Actions Pending Before an Arbitral Tribunal and a State Court", ASA Special

courts are free to engage in a full inquiry into the validity of the arbitration clause.

Moreover, Swiss case law has held that an arbitrator will be deprived of jurisdiction to hear a matter if a case has already begun before a foreign court. This application of *lis pendens* has been criticized, since it permits a bad-faith litigant to paralyze an arbitration by starting litigation abroad before a Swiss arbitral proceeding has begun.[128] Recent federal legislation gives arbitrators sitting in Switzerland the right to rule on their own jurisdiction even if a foreign court has already been seized of the matter.[129]

In some events an arbitrator's excess of jurisdiction may escape any judicial scrutiny, even if the arbitral seat lies in Switzerland. Although proper monitoring for excess of authority would normally be provided under the federal conflicts-of-law statute,[130] the parties may by agreement dispense with such review if both sides are non-Swiss.[131]

Series No. 15 (January 2001) at pp. 65-66. With respect to consideration of arbitration clauses prior to appointment of an arbitrator, the federal statute calls for an *examen sommaire* (summary examination).

128. See *Fomento de Construcciones y Contrats S.A. v. Colon Container Terminal S.A.*, Swiss *Tribunal fédéral*, 14 May 2001 (Ie Cour Civile), BGE 127 III 279/ATF 127 III 279; reported in 2001 Rev. arb., p. 835 (commentary by Jean-François POUDRET); Elliot GEISINGER and Laurent LÉVY, "Applying the Principle of Litispendence", Int'l A.L.R. (2000, no. 4). See also Adam SAMUEL, "Formento – A Tale of Litispendence, Arbitration and Private International Law in BREDIN, LALIVE, POUDRET AND TERRÉ, eds., *Liber Amicorum Claude Reymond: Autour de L'Arbitrage* (Litec, Paris 2004) p. 255. Under Art. 9 of the Swiss LDIP, an arbitral tribunal in Geneva was required to suspend its work in deference to a judicial action begun in Panama. Some observers consider the case might have been better decided on the rationale that participation in the Panama litigation constituted a waiver of the right to arbitrate. See also, Matthias SCHERER and Teresa GIOVANNINI, "Geneva Court Will Not Enforce Foreign Anti-Arbitration Injunction", IBA Arbitration Committee Newsletter 42 (September 2006) (commenting on decision of Geneva Tribunal of First Instance, 2 May 2005, rejecting an application to stay arbitration (ASA Bull. (2005) p. 728, with note by M. STACHER).For a more general perspective on parallel court proceedings, see Martine STÜCKELBERG, "*Lis Pendens and Forum Non Conveniens* at the Hague Conference", 26 Brooklyn J. Int'l L. (2001) p. 949. For another perspective on anti-suit injunctions, see John FELLAS, "Anti-Suit Injunctions in Aid of Arbitration", 20 Int'l Arb. Rep. (April 2005) p. 25.

129. See Art. 186, al 1bis, LDIP, which provides as follows:

"*Il [le tribunal arbitral] statue sur sa compétence sans égard à une action ayant le même objet déjà pendante entre les mêmes parties devant un autre tribunal étatique ou arbitral, sauf si des motifs sérieux commandent de suspendre la procédure.*" [The arbitral tribunal decides on its jurisdiction without regard to an action with the same object pending between the same parties before another national court or arbitral body, unless serious reasons demand suspension of the procedure.]

Modification du 6 octobre 2006. The provision is expected to enter into force early in 2007, either the day of its acceptance by the voters in the event a referendum, or (if no referendum is held) on the first day of the second month following the deadline for a referendum, which has been fixed at 25 January 2007. See also *Communiqué, Département fédéral de justice et police* (Alexander MARKUS, Office fédéral de la justice) 17 May 2006.

130. *Loi fédérale sur le droit international privé*, Art. 190(2)(b) and (c).

131. *Loi fédérale sur le droit international privé*, Art. 192. Non-Swiss parties are defined as having neither domicile, habitual residence or business establishment in Switzerland.

iii.   The UNCITRAL Model Law

Countries that follow the UNCITRAL Model Arbitration Law provide yet another twist on the timing of judicial review. The statute dates from 1985, when the United Nations sponsored a Model Law on International Commercial Arbitration[132] which has been enacted in more than fifty countries.[133]

The UNCITRAL Model gives the arbitral tribunal an explicit right to determine its own jurisdiction in the form of a "preliminary" award, subject to challenge on a request from a party within thirty days.[134] Arbitrators, of course, may choose to delay decisions on jurisdictional matters until the final award.

The Model Law does not prevent courts from finding an arbitration clause to be void in the context of a judicial action on the substantive merits of the case, assuming judicial jurisdiction exists over the relevant parties and/or dispute.[135] The Model Law envisions the possibility of simultaneous proceedings by courts and arbitrators regarding the competence of the arbitral tribunal.[136] Art. 8 provides that a court must refer parties to arbitration only if it finds the arbitration agreement not to be "null and void, inoperative or incapable of being performed".

Controversy does exist on the standard for pre-award review. Some authorities hold to "full review" while others adopt a "*prima facie* review" approach that refers parties to arbitration unless the arbitration clause appears void on its face.[137]

The "prima facie" approach leaves open the question of whether a court's decision is subject to being re-opened at a later stage. A judge might say, "I've given the clause a quick glance, and it looks fine to me." Presumably this would not preclude a later

---

132. Drafted by the U.N. Commission for International Trade Law (UNCITRAL), the Model Law on International Commercial Arbitration received General Assembly approval on 11 December 1985. See U.N. General Resolution 40/72, 40 GAOR Supp. No. 53, A/40/53, at 308. See generally Howard M. HOLTZMANN and Joseph E. NEUHAUS, *Guide to the UNCITRAL Model Law on International Commercial Arbitration* (1989); Henri C. ALVAREZ, Neil KAPLAN and David W. RIVKIN, *Model Law Decisions* (2003); Pieter SANDERS, *The Work of UNCITRAL on Arbitration and Conciliation* (2nd edn., 2004).

133. The geographically and culturally diverse countries that have adopted the UNCITRAL Model Law include Australia, Canada, Egypt, Germany, Hong Kong, India, Iran, Mexico, Nigeria, Russia, Scotland, Singapore, Spain, and New Zealand. Within the United States, California, Connecticut, Illinois, Oregon, and Texas have adopted the Model Law on a state level.

134. Art. 16, Model Arbitration Law of the United Nations Commission on International Trade Law.

135. See Howard HOLTZMANN and Joseph NEUHAUS, *op. cit.*, fn. 132, at p. 306:

"This provision provoked debate between those who considered that the court should have power to stay the arbitral proceedings in order to prevent potentially needless arbitration and those who would have ... had the court suspend its own proceedings in order to avoid delay and needless court intervention."

136. Holtzmann and Neuhaus note that "a court might still consider the jurisdiction of the tribunal in considering whether a substantive claim should be referred to jurisdiction...". See Howard HOLTZMANN and Joseph NEUHAUS, *op. cit.*, fn. 132, at p. 486.

137. See Frédéric BACHAND, "Does Article 8 of the Model Law Call for Full or Prima Facie Review of the Arbitral Tribunal's Jurisdiction?", 22 Arb. Int'l (2006) p. 463.

jurisdictional attack on the award, which under the UNCITRAL Model Law would be available for invalidity of the arbitration agreement or arbitral decisions falling outside the scope of the arbitration submission. By contrast, if the judge's quick glance determines the clause is void, the parties would seem to be stuck with that decision, since by definition there would be no award to review.

5. *The First Word and the Last*

a. *Base-line positions*

One way to summarize the different base-line positions on determinations of arbitral authority might be to ask when arbitrators have the first word on their jurisdiction, and when they have the last. Here is how the landscape might be described.

1. In most modern legal systems, an arbitrator will have the "first word" on his/her jurisdiction, unless a court of competent jurisdiction says otherwise. The arbitral tribunal need not stop the proceedings just because a party questions some aspect of arbitral authority.

2. The fact that arbitrators *can* have the first word does not mean that they always *do* have the "first word". A litigant might go to court to challenge arbitral jurisdiction without waiting for an award. Such is the situation in the United States and Germany.

3. By contrast, in other countries courts must generally wait to examine jurisdiction until an award is rendered. This is the rule in France, subject to certain narrow exceptions.

4. In all major legal systems, the "last word" on arbitral jurisdiction will normally be for courts at the time an award is subject to scrutiny in the context of a motion to vacate, confirm or grant recognition.

5. Countries differ dramatically, however, on whether and when the parties may entrust a jurisdictional matter to final and binding arbitration, thus in effect transferring the "last word" from the courts to the arbitrators. In the United States, deference to an arbitrator's jurisdictional decision requires a finding that "the arbitrability question" has clearly been given to the arbitrators. Courts might make this finding either at the beginning of the arbitral process (when one side tries to compel arbitration) or at the end (when an award is presented for review). Other legal systems (notably Germany) deny deference to agreements that purport to subject jurisdictional questions to final determination by arbitrators. Results may depend on whether the purported agreement on jurisdiction takes the form of a separate agreement or a clause in the main commercial contract.

b. *The devil in the detail*

Being human, judges like arbitrators sometimes get it wrong. Errors can creep into a judge's understanding of the parties' intent on jurisdictional questions. The results may be either denial of a party's day in court (in a so-called "pro-arbitration" decision) or disregard of the parties' bargain to arbitrate (in a so-called "anti-arbitration" decision).

Although trivial, the point is of utmost importance in connection with rules on arbitral jurisdiction. The establishment of any principle bears a danger of misapplication, a fact that might be taken into account by policy-makers in determining whether the rule is likely to provide an optimum balance of efficiency and fairness.

Some risks are greater than others. By allowing parties to grant arbitrators final authority on jurisdictional matter, a legal system increases the peril that faulty contract interpretation will result in some litigants being denied their day in court. Judges might take a mere contract recital for a manifestation of genuine party consent. The problem is particularly delicate in complex large-scale commercial fact patterns, where legal principles often end up being indicative rather than dispositive.[138]

The complexity of other policy concerns facing legislators can be seen in the various wrinkles engrafted on the major guidelines set down for establishment of arbitral jurisdiction. As has been mentioned elsewhere, these include (i) special rules on declaratory court decisions,[139] (ii) mechanisms to address preliminary points of arbitral jurisdiction,[140] (iii) varying appellate procedures for decisions that implicate arbitral jurisdiction,[141] (iv) different standards by which courts address arbitral jurisdiction before (as opposed to after) an arbitration has begun, or before (as opposed to after) an award has been rendered.[142] As to the wisdom of these nuances, only time will tell.

---

138. In contrast, the US federal court decisions set forth relatively firm rules for problems that repeat themselves with routine regularity in American arbitration: class actions in consumer lending, and time limits in securities complaints against brokers. See discussions of *Bazzle* and *Howsam*, infra.

139. Some countries such as England and Germany restrict the right of courts to provide declaratory decisions about arbitral authority, but not the power to address arbitral jurisdiction in the context of an action on the underlying dispute.

140. Compare UNCITRAL Art. 16 (immediate appeal of jurisdictional ruling) with Sect. 32 of the 1996 English Arbitration Act, which permits an application to the court for a determination on substantive jurisdiction if made by all parties or with the permission of the arbitral tribunal. English law also provides for interim awards on jurisdiction, subject to court review. See Sects. 31(4) and 67 of the 1996 English Arbitration Act. On the policies behind bifurcated hearings to address jurisdictional decisions separately, see John GOTANDA, "An Efficient Method for Determining Jurisdiction in International Arbitrations", 40 Columbia J. Trans. L. (2001) p. 11.

141. For the position in the United States, see 9 U.S.C. Sect. 16, providing different standards for appeal of lower court decisions on arbitral jurisdiction, depending on whether the court finds for or against the arbitrator's power.

142. French courts address arbitral jurisdiction only if the arbitral tribunal has not yet been "seized" of the matter, and must limit their inquiry to whether an arbitration clause is clearly void (*manifestement nulle*). NCPC Art. 1458. Compare the situation under UNCITRAL Art. 8. Similarly, in Switzerland courts generally review an arbitration clause on a prima facie basis (*examen sommaire*) before the award, but reserve plenary review following an arbitrator's decision. LDIP Arts. 7 and 179(3).

III.   CLARIFICATIONS

1.   Supra-national Adjudicatory Bodies

In most instances, *Kompetenz-Kompetenz* refers to how national courts exercise supervisory competence, as discussed earlier. However, the phrase *Kompetenz-Kompetenz* has also been applied in forms of international dispute resolution that proceed largely independent of close national court supervision, including the practice of the Permanent Court of Arbitration and arbitration under the rules of ICSID, the International Centre for the Settlement of Investment Disputes.[143] The import of this jurisdictional principle takes on a different cast when the arbitral tribunal is not subject to immediate and well-established forms of control by national courts.

An example of arbitration removed from the review of national courts can be found in the ICSID system, which pursuant to treaty provides a structure for arbitration of investment disputes between host states and foreigners.[144] ICSID tribunals render their awards outside the framework of national arbitration statutes. The Convention forecloses challenge to awards on normal statutory grounds[145] in favor of ICSID's special system of quality control under its own internal challenge procedure.[146]

Consequently, jurisdictional determinations are by necessity subject to the arbitrators' jurisdiction alone, absent evidence that the parties never consented in any way to ICSID arbitration.[147] While this may at first blush appear to be similar to the

---

143. See generally cases summarized in Pierre LALIVE, "Some Objections to Jurisdiction in Investor-State Arbitration", in *International Commercial Arbitration: Important Contemporary Questions*, ICCA Congress Series no. 11, p. 376 at pp. 378-380.

144. The Convention on the Settlement of Investment Disputes Between States and Nationals of Other States, Washington 18 March 1965 (ratified by 140 nations) established the International Centre for Investment Disputes (ICSID) to hear disputes between Convention states and investors from another party to the Convention. See generally Emmanuel GAILLARD, *La Jurisprudence du CIRDI* (2004); Rudolf DOLZER and Margrete STEVENS, *Bilateral Investment Treaties* (1995); Abby Cohen SMUTNY, "Arbitration Before the International Centre for Investment Disputes", 3 Bus. Law Int'l (September 2002) p. 367.

145. For ICSID arbitration in the United States, this rule has never been tested in a court action raising the conflict between the Federal Arbitration Act (allowing motions to vacate awards) and the Washington Convention (which excludes such vacatur). The US Constitution in Art. VI(2) lists both treaties and federal statutes as the "supreme Law of the Land", without establishing a hierarchy. On some matters statutes clearly override treaties. See, e.g., Pub. L. No. 96-499 Sect. 1125, providing that no treaty shall require "exemption from (or reduction of) any tax imposed" on gains from disposition of US realty. When Congress is silent courts look to canons of statutory interpretation such as "last in time prevails" or "specific restricts general". See Detlev VAGTS, "The United States and its Treaties: Observance and Breach", 95 Am. J. Int'l L. (2001) p. 313.

146. See Convention on the Settlement of Investment Disputes Between States and Nationals of Other States Art. 52, ICSID Basic Documents 25 (1985). See generally W. Michael REISMAN, *Systems of Control in International Adjudication and Arbitration* (Duke 1992) pp. 46-50.

147. Convention Art. 41 provides that "The Tribunal shall be the judge of its own competence." See also Rules of Procedure for Arbitration Proceedings, Rule 41. The Centre's jurisdiction is addressed in Art. 25 of the Washington Convention itself.

situation in other forms of arbitration,[148] there is no judiciary to exercise supervisory power, since Art. 26 of the Washington Convention provides that consent to ICSID jurisdiction shall (unless otherwise stated) be deemed to constitute consent to arbitration "to the exclusion of any other remedy".[149]

Similar non-national *Kompetenz-Kompetenz* principles might be appropriate for the emerging field of tax treaty arbitration. Recent proposals have been elaborated by the Organization for Economic Cooperation and Development[150] and in research sponsored by the International Fiscal Association (IFA).[151]

2. Applicable Law

If a question arises about whether an arbitral tribunal has jurisdiction to decide its jurisdiction, what procedural law should be applied to test the limits of the principle? The quick answer (not very helpful) would be that the matter will be determined under whatever arbitration principles might be deemed appropriate by the forum where the challenge arises. For example, if the arbitrators' jurisdictional determination has been questioned before French courts, the applicable procedural law would be the *Nouveau code de procédure civile*; if in the United States, the Federal Arbitration Act; in England, the 1996 Arbitration Act. And should a litigant, by some extraordinary boldness, challenge the principle of *Kompetenz-Kompetenz* in ICSID arbitration the judges seized of the matter would (one hopes) look to the 1965 Washington Convention.

The answer is much more complex in reality. National legal systems quite rightly look to other legal systems through a variety of mechanisms, including reference to a transnational procedural lex mercatoria[152] or in some cases the law applicable to the

---

148. See Christoph SCHREUER, The *ICSID Convention* (2001) at p. 521, comparing ICSID Art. 41 with ICC Rule 6 and Art. 21 of the UNCITRAL Arbitration Rules.

149. See *ibid.* at p. 347, noting that consent to ICSID arbitration means that "the parties have lost their right to seek relief in another forum, national or international".

150. See Proposals for Improving Mechanisms for Resolution of Tax Treaty Disputes, Public discussion draft, February 2006 (OECD Committee on Fiscal Affairs), proposing amplification of the "Mutual Agreement Procedure" in Model Income Tax Convention Art. 25.

151. William W. PARK and David R. TILLINGHAST, *Income Tax Treaty Arbitration* (2004). In this connection, the IFA-sponsored study makes the following proposal:

"In the event that an arbitral tribunal fails to decide a claim because it deems the matter to be outside the scope of the convention, and thus governed solely by national law, either Contracting State or the taxpayer may challenge this finding before a Jurisdictional Review Panel. This Panel shall be constituted according to the process provided in Art. 5. The Panel shall consider de novo whether the claim is governed by the Convention. The decision of the Panel shall be final. Following a decision that a claim is governed by this Convention, a new arbitral tribunal shall be constituted pursuant to Art. 5 and shall be bound by the Panel's jurisdictional determination."

Ibid., p. 97, including Proposed Art. 8(c) of Supplement to Double Tax Convention Art. 25.

152. *Rhône Méditerranée v. Achille Lauro*, 712 F. 2d 50 (3d Cir. 1983). See also *Isover St. Gobain v. Dow Chemical France et al.*, ICC Case 4131 (1982) in Sigvard JARVIN and Yves DERAINS, eds., *ICC Collection of Arbitral Awards, Volume I: 1974-1985* (1990), upheld by the Paris *Cour d'appel*, 21

merits.[153] In a federal system, the laws of different political subdivisions might compete. Depending on the issue, procedural questions in the United States might be subject to one of three different chapters of the Federal Arbitration Act,[154] as well as state contract principles regarding interpretation of the New York Convention.[155] Or state law might apply, either by virtue of the arbitral seat[156] or the parties' choice.[157]

3. The Autonomy of the Arbitration Clause

A frequent source of confusion about the arbitrator's right to rule on his or her jurisdiction lies in the interaction of *Kompetenz-Kompetenz* principles and the doctrine of "separability" or the "autonomy" of the arbitration clause.[158] Many eminent authorities have addressed the interaction of the two principles,[159] which when all is said and done are designed to create presumptions that help the arbitration process run smoothly.[160]

October 1983, Rev. Arb. (1984) p. 98; English language extracts in ICCA *Yearbook Commercial Arbitration* IX (1984) (hereinafter *Yearbook*) p. 132.

153. *Pepsico v. Officina Central de Asesoria*, 945 F. Supp. 69 (S.D.N.Y. 1996). See also DICEY, MORRIS and COLLINS, *The Conflict of Laws*, 14th edn., L. COLLINS, gen. ed. (2006), Rule 57(1), at p. 712, suggesting that "the material validity, scope and interpretation of an arbitration agreement" are governed by the parties' chosen law or (in the absence of choice) the law most closely connected with the arbitration agreement, normally that of the arbitral seat. This formulation is a considerable improvement over that in the prior edition, which included the "effect" of an arbitration agreement in the ambit of applicable law." While true as far as it goes, the rule fails to mention that the "effect" of arbitration agreements can also be determined by the arbitration law of the arbitral seat, the treaty context, and law of the recognition forum, regardless of the parties' choice.

154. FAA Ch. 2 implements the New York Convention, and Ch. 3 the Panama Convention.

155. Art. II of the New York Convention requires "an arbitral clause in a contract or an arbitration agreement, signed by the parties...". See *Kahn Lucas v. Lark Int'l* , 186 F. 3d 210 (2d Cir. 1999), holding that "signed by the parties" applies to arbitral clauses in contracts as well as separate arbitration agreements. For a contrary holding, see *Sphere Drake Ins. PLC v. Marine Towing, Inc.*, 16 F. 3d 666, 669 (5th Cir.1994). Little evidence indicates how many arbitrators reflect on the comma before taking jurisdiction.

156. *New England Energy v. Keystone Shipping Co.*, 855 F. 2d 1 (1st Cir. 1988).

157. *Mastrobuono v. Shearson Lehman Hutton*, 514 U.S. 52 (1995); *Volt Information Sciences v. Board of Trustees*, 489 U.S. 468 (1989).

158. See Alan Scott RAU, "Everything You Really Need to Know About 'Separability' in Seventeen Simple Propositions", 14 Am. Rev. Int'l Arb. (2003) p. 121; Adam SAMUEL, "Separability of Arbitration Clauses — Some Awkward Questions about the Law on Contracts, Conflict of Laws and the Administration of Justice", ADR Law J. (2000) p. 36; Christian HERRERA PETRUS, "Spanish Perspectives on the Doctrines of Kompetenz-Kompetenz and Separability: A Comparative Analysis of Spain's 1988 Arbitration Act", 11 Am. Rev. Int'l Arb. (2000) p. 397.

159. See, e.g., Pierre MAYER, *op. cit.*, fn. 2, at pp. 339-352.

160. Redfern and Hunter state,

"There are essentially two elements to this [jurisdictional] rule: first, that an arbitral tribunal can rule on its own jurisdiction; and secondly that, for this purpose, the arbitration clause is separate and independent from the terms of the contract containing the transactions between the parties."

Kompetenz-Kompetenz is distinct from, but intersects functionally with, the notion that an arbitration agreement can be operationally detached from the main contract in which it is found. Often conceptualized as a matter of "separability", the principle that an arbitration clause possesses contractual autonomy permits the arbitrators to do their job, notwithstanding what their award might say about the validity of the contract in dispute. The separability doctrine gives the arbitration clause the status of a contract autonomous from the principal agreement in which it is encapsulated.[161] Thus arbitrators may decide issues relating to the validity of the main contract (such as allegations of fraud in the inducement, or "per se" violations of antitrust law) without risk that their power will disappear retroactively. The autonomy of the arbitration clause recognizes the contracting parties' presumed intent that the arbitrator should be empowered to decide on the validity or survival of the principal commercial contract. Otherwise the arbitrators might be stripped of power at the very moment when evaluating important aspects of the parties' business relationship.[162]

Separability and *Kompetenz-Kompetenz* can serve much of the same function, in that both notions create mechanisms to prevent a bad-faith party from stopping the arbitral proceedings before they have begun. The autonomy of the arbitration clause operates with respect to defects in the main contract which might otherwise taint the arbitrator's jurisdiction. The doctrine of *Kompetenz-Kompetenz*, on the other hand, gives the arbitrator the right to pass upon even alleged infirmities in the arbitration clause itself.

To illustrate the difference between the separability of the arbitration clause and *Kompetenz-Kompetenz*, assume that an arbitration clause has been included in a marketing agreement by which a consultant agreed to help an American corporation obtain a public works contract in the Ruritania. It might be alleged both that (i) the person who signed

---

Alan REDFERN, Martin HUNTER, Nigel BLACKABY and Constantine PARTASIDES, *Law and Practice of International Commercial Arbitration*, 4th edn. (2004), Sect. 5-42, at p. 254. See also Julian D.M. LEW, Loukas A. MISTELIS and Stefan KRÖLL, *Comparative International Commercial Arbitration* (2003), Sect. 14-19 at p. 334. These authors write,

"While competence-competence empowers the arbitration tribunal to decide on its own jurisdiction, separability affects the outcome of this decision.... Without the doctrine of separability, a tribunal making use of its competence-competence would potentially be obligated to deny jurisdiction on the merits since the existence of the arbitration clause might be affected by the invalidity of the underlying contract."

161. See *Prima Paint Corp. v. Flood & Conklin Mfg. Co.*, 388 U.S. 395 (1967). Surprisingly, one recent decision has invoked *First Options v. Kaplan* to question the validity of the separability doctrine. See *Maye v. Smith Barney*, 897 F. Supp. 100 (S.D.N.Y. 1995)

162. Many countries permit the arbitration agreement to be subject to a different law than that of the main contract. On separability, see generally Peter GROSS, "Separability Comes of Age in England", 11 Arb. Int'l (1995) p. 85 , discussing *Harbour Assurance Co. (U.K.) v. Kansa General International Assurance Co.*, [1993] 3 All E.R. 897; Matthieu de BOISSESON, *Droit Français de l'Arbitrage*, 2nd edn., (1990) at pp. 482-484 and pp. 491-493 (Sects. 575 and 579); and cases discussed in Adam SAMUEL, *op. cit.*, fn. 2, at pp. 155-172. See generally Adam SAMUEL, "Separability and the US Supreme Court Decision in *Buckeye v. Cardegna*", 22 Arbitration International (2006) p. 477; Adam SAMUEL, *op. cit.*, fn. 158, p. 36.

the agreement for the American corporation was not authorized to do so and (ii) the consulting agreement was void because the payments thereunder were earmarked in part to bribe government officials.[163] Separability notions would permit the arbitrators to find the main contract void for illegality without destroying their power under the arbitration clause to do so.[164] Separability would not, however, prevent the court from determining whether the individual who signed the agreement was authorized to bind the corporation to arbitrate; nor would separability save from ultimate annulment or non-recognition an award based on an arbitrator's erroneous assumption about such corporate power.[165]

On the other hand, French principles permit the arbitrators to go to the end of the proceedings and decide the matter of the corporate signature, rather than having the question referred to the appropriate court at the outset of the arbitration.[166] However, without a separability principle, the arbitrators' right to rule on their own jurisdiction would not save the validity of an award that had declared the main contract void because of illegality.

The situation in American case law has been subject to several key decisions of the US Supreme Court. In the landmark American *Prima Paint* decision,[167] a claim was brought for fraud in the inducement of the purchaser of a paint business. The buyer sought rescission in court rather than before the bargained-for arbitral tribunal. The court in essence asked, "Who, court or arbitrator, shall decide whether there was fraudulent inducement of a contract?" Without the autonomy of the arbitration clause, the question would have been for the court, since an arbitrator could not have declared the main agreement to be rescinded without thereby invalidating the arbitration clause. Separability of the arbitration clause permitted the fraud charge, with respect to the main agreement, to be characterized as related to the merits of the case, rather than to the jurisdiction of the arbitrator.

---

163. Or the illegality might derive from a violation of antitrust law, or a lender not being authorized to engage in banking in the relevant jurisdiction. See *Worthen B. & T. Co. v. United Underwrit. Sales Corp.*, 251 Ark. 454 (1971); but see *Shepard v. Finance Associates of Auburn, Inc.*, 366 Mass. 182 (1974). Compare *Harbour v. Kansa Harbour Assurance*, [1993] Q.B. 701 and 10 Arb. Int'l (1994) p. 194; Peter GROSS, *op. cit*, fn. 162, p. 85.

164. Contracts to engage in bribery are generally void throughout the world, while contracts to arbitrate are not. A court probably could, however, refuse to enforce the award if the arbitrator had decided that the contract did *not* implicate bribery when in fact (in the court's view) it did. While the arbitrator's finding on the validity of the contract would normally be entitled to deference, many statutes and treaties contain explicit provisions for judicial refusal to enforce awards that violate public policy. See, e.g., French NCPC Art. 1502(5) and New York Convention Art. V(2)(b).

165. See, e.g., *South Pacific Properties v. Egypt*, French *Cour de Cassation* (6 January 1987), Rev. Arb. (1987) p. 469, note Ph. LEBOULANGER. Translation and note by Emmanuel GAILLARD, 26 I.L.M. (1987) p. 1004.

166. German law as it now stands might permit the parties to enter into a "*Kompetenz-Kompetenz* clause" that could insulate the arbitrator's findings on the signature from any judicial review, although it is not clear whether such findings would withstand a challenge to the validity of the *Kompetenz-Kompetenz* clause itself.

167. *Prima Paint Corp. v. Flood & Conklin Mfg. Co.*, 388 U.S. 395 (1967).

The principle was recently affirmed in *Buckeye Check Cashing, Inc. v. Cardegna* where the US Supreme Court affirmed the doctrine in the context of a consumer dispute heard in state court and involving an alleged violation of state statute.[168] This classic separability case involved a challenge to arbitral jurisdiction based on the alleged invalidity of a loan agreement. Had the view of the state court prevailed, the arbitrators would have had no power to consider their own jurisdiction. From the start, the charge of "void contract" would have taken away that opportunity, since the allegedly invalid loan agreement would have been inseparably linked to the arbitration clause.[169]

---

168. 126 S.Ct. 1204 (2006). A decision by Justice Scalia found that the Florida Supreme Court failed to adhere to the teachings of *Prima Paint* in a putative class action against a check cashing service accused of making usurious loans in violation of Florida law. Claimants argued that because the contract was allegedly void, the arbitration clause was unenforceable. The action was brought by the borrowers, with lenders seeking to compel arbitration. The Court held that the illegality did not invalidate the arbitration clause, which was separable (autonomous) from the main agreement. Although the Court reached the right result, a bit of careless phraseology has the potential to create mischief in subsequent cases. Justice Scalia asserted,

> "Applying them [general arbitration principles] to this case, we conclude that because respondents challenge the Agreement, but not specifically its arbitration provisions, those provisions are enforceable apart from the remainder of the contract. The challenge should therefore be considered by an arbitrator, not a court."

Ibid. at 1209 These sentences imply both too little and too much. First, an arbitration clause might well be invalid even if a challenge aims at the main agreement, as in event of forgery or lack of capacity. Second, arbitrators do not lose the right to "consider" jurisdiction simply due to challenge launched against the arbitration provisions. Instead, any consideration of the provisions is simply subject to judicial scrutiny, absent the parties' agreement otherwise. Justice Alito did not participate and Justice Thomas dissented on the basis that the FAA does not apply in state court proceedings to displace a state law prohibiting enforcement of an arbitration clause. See generally, Alan Scott RAU, "Separability in the United States Supreme Court", 2006 Stockholm Int'l Arb. Rev. (2006) p. 1; Adam SAMUEL, *op. cit.*, fn. 162, p. 477.

169. Whether the arbitration law of the United States should allow arbitration of such consumer disputes remains open to question. In Europe the pre-dispute arbitration clause in the usurious loan agreement would most likely be void. See Art. 6.1 of the 1993 European Union Directive on Unfair Contract Terms, which invalidates "unfair" contract terms in consumer contracts. Arts. 3 and 4.1 set out the basic notion of an unfair contract, which include terms not individually negotiated if they cause a significant imbalance in the parties' rights and obligations arising under the contract. An annex contains an indicative and non-exclusive list of "the terms which may be regarded as unfair" including paragraph "q" which presumes a term to be unfair if it has the effect of "excluding or hindering the consumer's right to take legal action or exercise any other legal remedy, particularly by requiring the consumer to take disputes exclusively to arbitration not covered by legal provisions...".

IV. TAXONOMY: WHAT IS A JURISDICTIONAL QUESTION?

1. Existence, Scope and Public Policy

In practice, an arbitrator's right to decide a question will often depend on how that question is characterized by the reviewing court. Labeling matters as "jurisdictional" puts them into the realm where judges would normally expect to exercise some scrutiny, depending on the circumstances of the case and the approach of the relevant legal system.

To reduce the risk of simply presuming one's own conclusions about what is or is not jurisdictional, it might be helpful to suggest three common categories of defects in arbitral authority.

(i) *Existence of an arbitration agreement.* In some instances there may be no binding agreement to arbitrate (for example, due to absence of signatory authority), or strangers to the agreement might have been joined through fraud, forgery or duress.[170]

(ii) *Scope of authority.* An arbitrator might be asked to decide substantive questions which the arbitration clause never submitted to his or her determination. Or the arbitrator might disregard party-agreed rules on how the arbitration was to be conducted, perhaps by exceeding limits on arbitral powers.[171]

(iii) *Public policy.* An arbitration might purport to address subjects that a relevant legal system says may not be arbitrated (subject matter arbitrability[172]), or which a court feels lie within its exclusive purview.[173] Or an award might give effect to illegal conduct.[174]

The first two flaws relate to the contours of the parties' contract. The third derives from public policy, regardless of what the parties might have agreed.

There is no magic in this tripartite classification, which commends itself only as a

---

170. See, e.g., *Chastain v. Robinson-Humphrey*, 957 F. 2d 851 (11th Cir. 1992) (forgery); *Gibson v. Neighborhood Health Clinics*, 121 F. 3d 1126 (7th Cir. 1997). See also decisions in *Sphere Drake v. All American Insurance*, *Three Valleys* and *Sandvik*, discussed infra. See generally, Bernard HANOTIAU, *Complex Arbitrations* (2005).

171. On occasion, arbitral institutions may also play a role in excess of authority. For example, if disputes are to be settled by arbitrators appointed by the International Chamber of Commerce International Court of Arbitration, a tribunal should not normally be constituted by the American Arbitration Association or the London Court of International Arbitration. See *Maritime International Nominees Establishment (MINE) v. Republic of Guinea*, 693 F. 2d 1094 (D.D.C. 1982).

172. Subject matters that have traditionally been sensitive (notwithstanding that many are not considered arbitrable) include competition law, securities regulation, bankruptcy and intellectual property. See, e.g., Alain PRUJINER, "*Propriété intellectuell et arbitrage: quelques réflexions après l'arrêt Caillou*" in *Cahiers de Propriété Intellectuelle, Mélanges Victor Nabhan* (2004).

173. See discussion infra of *United States v. Stein*, concerning the right to legal fees in a criminal tax investigation.

174. An arbitrator would not likely be permitted to render an award giving effect to a sale of illegal arms to terrorists or ordering payment for slaves or heroin. Nor would an arbitrator be permitted to reinstate a pilot dismissed from employment for showing up drunk at the cockpit. See discussion infra.

starting point for analysis. Jurisdiction remains a notoriously slippery term. Different statutes employ different terms, and divergent intellectual pigeon-holes to organize grounds for jurisdictional challenge.[175] In the real world, an alleged problem sometimes involves a combination of factors, or represents shades of gray on a jurisdictional continuum.

Violations of public policy, of course, will defeat the enforcement of arbitration agreements regardless of the parties' wishes, at least within the forum whose norms have been offended.[176] The problem with public policy, of course, lies in its malleability and potential for mischief when applied through a parochial lens. Although courts can hardly be expected to enforce an arbitration agreement related to an arms sale to terrorists, the "public policy" shibboleth frequently finds itself invoked with respect to concerns of much less magnitude.[177]

The other two categories of jurisdictional shortcoming (existence and scope of the clause) might be remedied by the parties' agreement.

If the challenge relates to the very validity of the arbitration clause, the issue could be submitted to final arbitral determination through a second agreement legitimately concluded by the party sought to be bound. Such a result has been accepted in some legal systems,[178] but not others.[179] Without such a subsequent agreement, however, arguments about proper parties will inevitably be subject to review by a court asked to enforce the award.[180]

Problems of scope might be addressed in the initial arbitration clause itself. At the time of concluding their transaction, foresighted parties could give arbitrators explicit authority to adjudicate challenges to the extent of their powers and the range of matters covered by the arbitration clause. Again, the extent to which a grant of jurisdictional power will be recognized in court depends on the relevant judicial system.

---

175. Compare: 1996 English Act Sect. 67 and Sect. 68, French NCPC Art. 1502, Swiss LDIP Art. 190, FAA Sect. 10, UNCITRAL Model Law Art. 34.

176. It might be that one country finds it intolerable for the arbitrator to have applied the parties' choice-of-law clause in a way that disregards its competition law, while another country might be offended if the arbitrator does ignores the choice-of-law clause.

177. See, e.g., *Nagrampa v. MailCoups Inc.*, 469 F. 3d 1257 (9th Cir. 2006), refusing to recognize an arbitration agreement because it would have required a California resident to travel to Boston for arbitration, notwithstanding that she was an admittedly savvy businesswoman who "knew her industry inside and out". *Ibid.* at 1310 (dissent by Kozinski). Finding an arbitration clause unconscionable (a matter held to be for judge rather than arbitrator), the Ninth Circuit reversed a lower court decision dismissing a California state action brought by the franchisee. The prize for parochialism may well go to *Laminoirs-Trefileries-Cableries de Lens, S.A. v. Southwire Co.*, 484 F. Supp. 1063, 1068-1069 (N.D. Ga. 1980), vacating award simply because it applied a French interest rate to an international contract involving a company from France.

178. See *Astro Valiente Compania Naviera v. Pakistan Ministry of Food & Agriculture (The Emmanuel Colocotronis No. 2)* [1982] 1 W.L.R. 1096, 1 All E. R. 578 (disagreement on whether charter party terms incorporated into a bill of lading). See also discussions of the law in the United States (infra) and Finland (supra).

179. See discussion infra of the German BGH decision of 13 January 2005.

180. The subsequent arbitration agreement would in essence transform a jurisdictional question (in the first dispute) into one of the substantive merits (in the second).

Even if a legal system does not give final effect to an arbitrator's jurisdictional ruling, it might well accord interim deference by delaying judicial review until after an award. The timing for challenge, however, remains a question separate from the effect of the jurisdictional decision and the parties' intention in that regard.

2. Common Trouble Spots

An arbitrator's jurisdiction to hear a matter will normally depend on several distinct lines of inquiry: (i) the existence of an agreement to arbitrate; (ii) the scope of the agreement with respect to parties, subject matter and procedural powers; (iii) public policy that might override the agreement, by making the subject non-arbitrable or the governing law inapplicable.

With respect to the first two contract-related categories, common questions arise with respect to implied agency; waiver of right to arbitrate (for example, by initiation of court litigation or undue delay), survival of an arbitration clause after assignment and authority of a corporate officer.

Even if a valid arbitration agreement exists, its substantive and procedural limits may be circumscribed in ways that require serious examination. Did the parties intend that tort claims arising out of the contract would be subject to the arbitrator's jurisdiction? Were statutory causes of action (for example, relating to antitrust violations) included within the arbitrator's mission? Did the arbitrators exceed their authority by disregarding the applicable law[181] or the basic terms of the contract?[182] While some countries create presumptions about certain aspects of jurisdiction,[183] care must be taken that they not be misapplied.

The process for constitution of the arbitral tribunal also affects arbitral power. Arbitrators possess jurisdiction only if appointed according to the parties' agreement. If the parties agreed to arbitration by a tribunal appointed by the International Chamber of Commerce, there is no basis to oblige the defendant to participate in an arbitration convened by the American Arbitration Association.[184] Interpreting the parties' intent as to the constitution of the arbitral tribunal becomes particularly problematic when courts are called to repair pathological clauses lacking particulars about the arbitral situs or

---

181. For example, arbitrators who apply provisions of US antitrust law, notwithstanding the merchants' agreement that the contract shall be subject to the laws of another country, might exceed their jurisdiction, unless the mandatory norms of the United States (as place of performance) preempt the contractually designated law. See *Mitsubishi Motors Corp. v. Soler Chrysler-Plymouth*, 473 U.S. 614 (1985).

182. See, e.g., *Mobile Oil v. Asamera*, 487 F. Supp. 63 (S.D.N.Y. 1980).

183. In England, for example, the House of Lords decision in *Lesotho Highlands* (discussed infra) might be seen as creating the presumption that arbitrators who exercise statutory powers do so within their mandate, notwithstanding that the powers have been exercised incorrectly.

184. For an analogous problem, see *Guinea v. MINE*, 693 F. 2d 1094 (D.C.C. 1982), and Geneva *Office des Poursuites*, 26 I.L.M. (1987) p. 382.

institutional rules.[185] In some cases, the arbitrators' qualifications will be established in part by the institutional rules to which the arbitration agreement refers.[186]

Procedural powers exercised by arbitrators can also become jurisdictional issues. Did the parties authorize the arbitrators to consolidate two proceedings? Did the parties authorize the arbitrators to punish a party for failing to produce documents? Did the parties authorize the arbitrators to award compound interest?

Sound analysis will depend on the contextual configuration in which jurisdictional questions are asked. The problem areas sketched below have in the past fertilized disagreements about arbitral authority.

a. Who is a party?

When arbitrators assume jurisdiction over a nonsignatory to the arbitration agreement (perhaps because two or more corporations are related through common ownership), the task of determining who agreed to arbitrate may be complicated by the form in which contract documents were signed.[187] Corporate restructuring provides another fertile source for confusion as to the proper party to an arbitration agreement.[188]

b. Meaning of contract terms

In commercial arbitrations, disputes frequently raise questions about what controverted events are covered by the clause, and what procedural powers have been given to an

---

185. See, e.g., *Jain v. De Méré*, 51 F. 3d 686 (7th Cir. 1995); *National Iranian Oil Company v. Ashland Oil, Inc.*, 817 F. 2d 326 (5th Cir. 1987); *Marks 3-Zet-Ernst Marks GmbH v. Presstek, Inc.*, 455 F. 3d 7 (1st Cir. 2006). In the last case, the contract between German and American entities provided only for "arbitration in the Hague under the International Arbitration rules".

186. For example, the rules of the International Chamber of Commerce require arbitrator "independence". Arbitration qualifications incorporated into a contract through reference to institutional rules often overlap public policy limits on biased arbitrators, just as arbitration rules on notice and the right to present one's case will frequently echo due process requirements of municipal arbitration law.

187. For example, in *South Pacific Properties v. Egypt*, an arbitral tribunal had to determine whether the government of Egypt was bound by an arbitration clause in an investment contract concluded by an Egyptian state-owned corporation but also initialled by a government minister with the ambiguous words "approved, agreed and ratified". *Egypt v. Southern Pacific Properties, Ltd.*, Judgment of 12 July 1984, Cour d'appel, Paris 1987 J.D.I. (Clunet) p. 129; Rev. arb. (1986) p. 75. See 23 I.L.M. p. 1048 (E. GAILLARD trans. 1984). Affirmed by *Cour de cassation* Judgment of 6 Jan. 1987, Cass. civ. Ire, 1987 J.D.I. (Clunet) p. 469 (with commentary by Ph. LEBOULANGER), reprinted in 26 I.L.M. p. 1004 (E. GAILLARD trans. 1987). The ICC award itself (Case No. 3493) is published in 22 I.L.M. p. 752 and Rev. arb. (1986) p. 105. Following a subsequent ICSID award against Egypt (ICSID Case No. ARB/84/3, 20 May 1992), the parties reached a final settlement in December 1992. See 8 Int. Arb. Rep. (January 1993) p. 328.

188. See also discussion supra of US Court of Appeals decisions in *Sarhank*, *Intergen*, and *Bridas v. Turkmenistan*; English Queen's Bench decision in *Kazakhstan v. Istil* and US district court decision in *Fluor Daniel v. General Electric*.

arbitrator. For example, a party might assert that a transaction occurred before the arbitration clause entered into effect, or that the arbitrator's power to award punitive damages had been expressly circumscribed.[189]

c.   Waiver, delay and other post-contract events

Arbitrators are often presented with questions arising out of events subsequent to contract formation. Invalidity might be asserted on the basis of assignment,[190] waiver of the right to arbitrate,[191] failure to observe statutory or contractual time limits, or undue delay in pursuing a claim.[192] For example, the arbitrator might be asked to determine whether one party's recourse to courts constitutes waiver of the right to compel arbitration, or whether delay in bringing a claim bars arbitration by virtue of a statute of limitations or an eligibility requirement contained in arbitration rules.[193]

d.   Ab initio invalidity of the arbitration agreement

The validity of an arbitration clause may be in doubt not only because of gross consensual defects related to physical duress and forgery, but also due to the lack of authorized signatures required by the corporate by-laws or inadequate incorporation of institutional arbitral rules.[194]

e.   Procedure

In addition to excess of jurisdiction with respect to substantive contract questions, an arbitral tribunal may act outside the limits to their authority set by the parties with respect to procedural matters. The arbitral tribunal may be improperly constituted (under a set of institutional rules other than the ones specified in the contract), or the arbitral tribunal may deny one side its right to be heard during the arbitral proceedings.

---

189. See also discussion infra of the Scalia opinion in *Pacificare*.

190. *Apollo v. Berg*, 886 F. 2d 469 (1st Cir. 1989).

191. *Cabintree v. Kraftmaid*, 50 F. 3d 388 (7th Cir. 1995).

192. *Smith Barney Harris Upham & Co. v. Luckie*, 85 N.Y.2d 193, 647 N.E.2d 1308 (1995).

193. See, e.g., *Paine Webber v. Landay*, 903 F. Supp. 193 (D. Mass. 1995) (six-year time limit for bringing claim under NASD Code of Arbitration Procedure held to be a question for arbitrator to decide); *Smith Barney v. Luckie*, New York Ct. App., 21 Feb. 1995, 63 U.S. Law Week 2531 (7 March 1995) (statute of limitations questions must be resolved by courts; New York law not pre-empted by Federal Arbitration Act). Compare New York cases cited in *Paine Webber v. Landay* at n. 5 of Judge Woodlock's opinion. See also *Zwitserse Maatschappij van Levensverzekering en Lijfrente v. ABN International Capital Markets*, 996 F. 2d 1478 (2d Cir. 1993) (initiation of judicial proceedings in The Netherlands resulted in waiver of right to arbitrate); *Khalid Bin Alwaleed Foundation v. E.F. Hutton*, U.S. Dist. Ct. N. D. Ill., E.D. (1990), reported in *Yearbook* XVI (1991) p. 645 (US no. 109) (participation in pre-trial discovery did not constitute waiver of right to arbitrate).

194. See *Three Valleys Municipal Water District v. E.F. Hutton & Co.*, 925 F.2d. 1136 (9th Cir. 1991), concerning securities law violations brought by government entities against investment company. The government entities resisted arbitration on the grounds that the individual who signed the agreements allegedly on their behalf did not have authority to do so. The Court of Appeals held that whether the signatory had authority to bind the plaintiffs was a question for the courts to decide, and remanded the case to the district court for a determination on the matter.

An increasingly important source of jurisdictional difficulty lies in the multiparty dimension of many business disputes. Problems arise from attempts to consolidate related arbitrations[195] and to appoint arbitrators for claims against more than one defendant.[196] For better or for worse, the Federal Arbitration Act does not authorize forced consolidation of different arbitration proceedings, even if they present similar questions of law and fact.[197]

Since specific examples often provide greater insight than general definitions,[198] a list of illustrative jurisdictional problems has been appended to this essay.[199] In no way do these scenarios exhaust the variety of situations in which the arbitrator's right to make a jurisdictional ruling could become an issue. Rather, they are presented as further examples of when and how challenges to arbitral power arise.

3.   Admissibility

Often we understand what something is by considering what it is not. The essence of arbitral jurisdiction might be put into starker relief through a comparison with what is sometimes called "admissibility".

A precondition to arbitration (limiting an arbitrator's right to hear the case) is not the same thing as a precondition to recovery (restricting one side's right to obtain damages). For example, arbitrators might well have authority to hear a dispute over mismanagement of a brokerage account, but deny the claim on the basis that the statute of limitations had passed.[200]

Notions of admissibility would normally be used to describe constraints on the right

---

195. Consolidation difficulties are illustrated by the now legendary story of the Macao sardine case as retold in Michael KERR, "Arbitration v. Litigation", 3 Arb. Int'l (1987) p. 79.

196. *Siemens and BKMI v. Dutco, Cour de cassation* (France), 7 January 1992, *Chambre Civile* No. 1, Cass., Rev. arb. (1992) p. 470. (two defendants and a three-person arbitral tribunal).

197. See *United Kingdom v. Boeing*, 998 F. 2d 68 (1993). The United Kingdom moved to consolidate arbitrations with Boeing and Textron, Inc., both of which had contracted with British Ministry of Defense to develop an electronic fuel system. The court ruled that consolidation of separate proceedings cannot be ordered absent the parties' consent. An earlier decision in *Neurus Shipping*, 527 F. 2d 966 (2d Cir. 1975), was distinguished on its facts. In the United States, forced consolidation will be possible only in a jurisdiction (like Massachusetts) that does provide for joinder of related parties. See *New England Energy, Inc. v. Keystone Shipping Co.*, 855 F. 2d 1 (1st Cir. 1988), discussed infa.

198. Sylvia Plath once observed that "the concrete can save when the abstract might kill". Sylvia PLATH, *The Journals of Sylvia Plath* (1982) p. 287.

199. See Appendix, pp. 147-153.

200. Other illustrations of preconditions to recover can be found in long-term supply contracts, which often provide for arbitration of disputes about price adjustments. Frequently, price modification will require the arbitrators (i) first to find a change in market conditions, and (ii) then to establish how far (and in what direction) the prices should be modified to reflect such changed conditions. Both questions remain matters of the substantive merits of the case, since the parties intended them to be addressed by the arbitrators rather than courts. The two-fold nature of the arbitrators' task simply represents the parties' assessment of the most efficient and logical way for analysis to proceed.

to file claims in cases clearly subject to arbitration. Since the matter is properly before the arbitrators, their decisions would usually *not* be reviewable in court.[201] Admissibility might relate to whether a claim is ripe enough (or too stale) for adjudication, or to arbitral preconditions (such as mediation) or time-bars (a prohibition on claims more than six years after the alleged wrong).[202]

In some instances, jurisdictional and admissibility questions may overlap. For example, a brokerage contract might be subject to rules that make an investor's claim ineligible for arbitration unless filed within six years after the allegedly inappropriate advice or trade. In addition, a statute of limitations might exist in the law applied to the merits of the dispute. The latter question (statute of limitations) would clearly fall to the arbitrators as part of their decision on the merits.[203] The former (eligibility for arbitration) might or might not be for arbitrators, depending on the parties' intent as evidenced in the applicable arbitration rules.

It may not always be apparent why distinctions should be made between (i) the time-bar in a statute of limitations and (ii) a time restriction on arbitration eligibility. However, the difference is crucial. The statute of limitations (a matter of admissibility) bars recovery itself, whether before courts or arbitrators. The limitation applies to the claimant's right to receive damages, regardless of the forum. By contrast, the jurisdictional limit, restricting eligibility for arbitration, says only that the case must be brought in court rather than before the arbitrator.

Preconditions to arbitration do not always lend themselves to facile analysis. In one intriguing case, *Vekoma v. Maran Coal*,[204] Switzerland's highest court annulled an award in which the arbitrators had declared themselves competent to hear a claim arguably

---

201. There might, however, be some situations in which valid jurisdictional challenges could be mounted to improper decisions on admissibility. If a contract says no actions may be filed before 2010, a putative award in 2005 would appear to most observers as an *excès de pouvoir* (subject to annulment) rather than simply an unreviewable mistake about calendars.

202. For a comparison of jurisdiction and admissibility in investment arbitration, see Ian A. LAID, "A Distinction without a Difference? An Examination of the Concepts of Admissibility and Jurisdiction in *Salini v. Jordan* and *Methanex v. USA*" in T. WEILER, ed., *International Investment Law and Arbitration: Leading Cases from the ICSID, NAFTA, Bilateral Treaties and Customary International Law* (2005) p. 201. See also contribution by Jan PAULSSON ("Jurisdiction and Admissibility")to the *Festschrift* in honor of Robert Briner, *op. cit.*, fn. 65, pp. 601-617.

203. Statutes of limitations relating to arbitration law (rather than the underlying claim) are for judges. For example, in a motion to compel arbitration opposed on the basis that it was made too late, an American court found that the Federal Arbitration Act failed to provide its own statute of limitations, and thus borrowed analogous limitations from state law principles at the place where the court was sitting. See *National Iranian Oil v. Mapco Int'l*, 983 F. 2d 485 (3d Cir. 1992).

204. See *Tribunal fédéral (Bundesgericht)* decision in *Transport en Handelsmaatschappij Vekoma B. V. v. Maran Coal Co.*, Civil Division I, 17 August 1995, reprinted 14 ASA Bull. (1996, no. 4) p. 673 with commentary by Philippe SCHWEIZER. See generally, Paul FRIEDLAND, "Swiss Supreme Court Sets Aside an ICC Award", 13 J. Int'l Arb. (1996, no. 1) p. 111; Pierre KARRER and Claudia KÄLIN-NAUER, "Is There a Favor Iurisdictionis Arbitri?", 13 J. Int'l Arb. (1996, no. 3) p. 31; François KNOEPFLER and Philippe SCHWEIZER, "*Jurisprudence suisse en matière d'arbitrage international*", Rev. suisse dr. int'l & dr. européen (1996) p. 573. Compare an arbitral tribunal's treatment of missed deadlines, deemed not to rise to the level of a jurisdictional defect. *Tribunal fédéral* Decision of 24 March 1997, 15 ASA Bull. (1997) p. 316.

brought after the contractually stipulated time limits. The contract required claims to be filed within thirty days after the parties agreed that their differences could not be resolved by negotiation. The arbitrators found that settlement negotiations had broken down in April 1992, and thus a May filing was timely. The respondent took the position that failure to settle occurred in January, when a letter from the claimant met with silence.

The court vacated the award, finding the arbitration clause lapsed by May when the claim was filed. Saying that negotiations might fail as a matter of either fact or law ("*tatsächlich oder normativ*"), the court found failure as a matter of law when the January offer went unanswered.[205] Whether the court was right to review the arbitrators' determination about time limits depends largely on the parties' intention in drafting their contract. Here as elsewhere, jurisdictional determinations often remain very fact sensitive.

One questionable aspect of this decision is that the Swiss court apparently deemed its review powers greater on questions of law than of fact, perhaps analogizing to review of cantonal court decisions. As a policy matter, this distinction is highly problematic. If arbitrators wrongly assume Company A acted as agent for Company B in signing an arbitration clause, they exceed their authority as to Company B whether from misunderstanding the law of agency or from a factual mistake about who signed the contract.

At this point, the distinction between "admissibility" and "jurisdiction" might provide a helpful segue into a deeper analysis of the nature of jurisdictional challenges. As we shall see, it is not always an easy task to distinguish between a decision that goes beyond the arbitrator's mandate and one that is simply wrong.

4. The Nature of Authority: Out of Bounds or Just Wrong?

a. Party consent

The party raising questions about the arbitrator's authority is not just saying that the arbitrators have made (or might make) an incorrect decision about whatever question has been put at issue. Rather, jurisdictional challenges argue that arbitrators have gone (or will go) out of bounds whatever their decision, whether right or wrong. At stake is *not* whether claimant breached the contract or owes $10 million, but rather the identity of the forum (arbitration or court proceeding) that will address and adjudicate the questions of contract breach and damages. Even if the respondent did breach, and does owe the money, an arbitrator lacking jurisdiction would not be authorized to hear the arguments.

A jurisdictional challenge asserts that the arbitrator has no right at all to hear a matter or exercise a procedural power. The challenge may be directed at the case in its entirety, a particular question (such as a competition counterclaim), or the exercise of

---

205. See 14 ASA Bull. (1996) pp. 676-678, at para. 3.

a procedural power (such as imposing sanctions for failure to produce documents or granting interest). The problem may also rest with the absence of a precondition to arbitration, such as the expiry of time limits.[206]

The labels applied to excess of authority may vary from country to country, with related terms ("jurisdiction", "authority", "powers" and "mission") often used almost interchangeably, or with slight contextual nuances to indicate *what* the arbitrator was authorized to decide rather than *how* the arbitrator was authorized to decide. In some legal systems, excess of authority may overlap with notions related to clear legal error. For example, courts in the United States have given themselves power to set aside awards for "manifest disregard of the law",[207] a malleable term most often applied when arbitrators have exceeded their authority,[208] also a statutory basis for vacatur.[209]

These jurisdictional questions remain neutral as to the merits of the case. It makes no difference whether claimant or respondent is right on the question of contract interpretation. The only issue is whether the arguments should be heard by arbitrators rather than courts.

Attempts to grapple with the nature of arbitral jurisdiction often fall prey to two divergent intellectual tendencies. The first conflates substantive errors on the merits (misinterpretation of the law) with errors of jurisdiction for the purpose of subjecting arbitral decisions to judicial review. After all, it might be argued, the parties never authorized the arbitrators to make a mistake. Thus from one perspective, each time the arbitrators go wrong in law they go beyond their mandate.[210] According to this view,

---

206. A precondition to recovery, of course, is not the same thing as a precondition to arbitration. For example, arbitrators might well have the right to hear a case, but deny the claim on the basis that the statute of limitations had passed. The distinction is sometimes referred to as between jurisdiction and "admissibility". See discussion infra.

207. See, e.g., Noah RUBINS, "'Manifest Disregard of the Law' and Vacatur of Arbitral Awards in the United States", 12 Am. Rev. Int'l Arb. (2002) p. 363; Hans SMIT, "Manifest Disregard of the Law in New York Court of Appeals", 15 Am. Rev. Int'l Arb. (2004) p. 315. See also Stephan WILSKE and Nigel MACKAY, "The Myth of the 'Manifest Disregard of the Law' Doctrine", 24 ASA Bull. (2006) p. 216.

208. See Alan Scott RAU, *op. cit.*, fn. 74, at pp. 530-533, analyzing the doctrine through the lens of two recent Court of Appeals cases, *Hoeft v. MVL Group*, 343 F. 3d 57 (2d Cir 2003) and *George Watt & Son v. Tiffany*, 348 F. 3d 577 (7th Cir. 2001).

209. For a recent rejection of a losing party's "manifest disregard" challenge, see *St. John's Mercy Medical Center v. Delfino*, 414 F. 3d 882 (8th Cir. 2005) ("The arbitrator did not cite relevant law and then ignore it...."). By contrast, the court did vacate for "manifest disregard" in *Patten v. Signator Insurance Agency*, 441 F. 3d 230 (4th Cir. 2006), where the arbitrator dismissed a claim against an insurance company by one of its sales agents, invoking a time limitation in an earlier contract with a different company. In theory the court distinguished non-reviewable error in contract interpretation from reviewable excess of authority. The court then lost its way, however, and went on to cite substantive Massachusetts law to find that the award was in "manifest disregard of the law".

210. Such was the position once taken in England by Lord Denning, who once suggested (albeit in an administrative context) that "Whenever a tribunal goes wrong in law it goes outside the jurisdiction conferred on it and its decision is void." See Lord DENNING, *The Discipline of the Law* (1979) p. 74. See also *Pearlman v. Keepers and Governors of Harrow School*, [1978] 3 W.L.R. 736, 743 (C.A.) ("The distinction between an error which entails absence of jurisdiction and an error

since mistakes are not authorized, by definition they constitute an excess of authority.

The reverse tendency conflates jurisdictional questions with the dispute's substantive merits, but for the opposite purpose: to deny courts the opportunity to second-guess arbitrators. Rather than saying that mistakes of law are questions of jurisdiction, some American courts find that jurisdictional questions have become questions of substance, submitted to the arbitrators by virtue of the parties' agreement. Such a characterization exercise has been performed on questions such as time-bars to arbitral authority, the right to consolidate cases, and the power to grant punitive damages.[211]

An intellectually rigorous test of what constitutes jurisdictional flaw has not been easy to find in commercial arbitration.[212] While a "we-know-it-when-we-see-it" test provides a starting point for analysis, the absence of intellectual rigor will not make the approach satisfying for very long. While accepting the difficulty of completely eliminating cultural blinders, few thoughtful people suggest that the law should adopt a purely subjective approach devoid of principled articulation. As with most legal problems, the difficulties usually lie at the fringes.[213] However, definitional difficulty does not mean that vital distinctions cease to exist between a decision that is simply wrong and one that exceeds the authority of the purported decision-maker.[214]

---

made within jurisdiction is [so] fine ... that it is rapidly being eroded."). See generally the House of Lords decision in *Anisminic Ltd. v. Foreign Compensation Commission* [1969] 2 AC 147, [1969] 1 All ER 208. Happily for the health of English law, the House of Lords in 2005 rejected this position in the *Lesotho Highlands* decision.

211. See discussion infra in Part V.

212. For an inquiry into similar questions in public international law, see W. Michael REISMAN, *Nullity and Revision* (1971). See also Alex LEES, "The Jurisdictional Label: Use and Misuse", 58 Stanford L. Rev. (2006) p. 1457, addressing more rigid applications of jurisdictional rules that operate "to shift authority from one law-speaking [sic] institution to another". *Ibid.* at p. 1460. The matter was addressed by the US Supreme Court in *Kontick v. Ryan*, 540 U.S. 443 (2004) (bankruptcy time prescription for creditor objections not jurisdictional in the sense of dispositive), which described jurisdiction as a word with "many, too many, meanings". *Ibid.* at p. 454.

213. In some instances, the very same facts might be relevant both to the merits of a dispute and to jurisdiction. See *Jackson v. Fie Corporation*, 302 F. 3d 515 (5th Cir. 2002), involving enforcement of a default judgment arising from the misfire of a pistol allegedly made by an Italian manufacturer. Testimony of the plaintiff's firearms expert (stating the gun was made by Fratelli Tanfoglio) proved relevant both to the merits of the products liability action and the court's personal jurisdiction over the foreign company.

214. The world of education illustrates the difference between simple mistake and excess of authority. In American law faculties, the professor who teaches a course normally bears responsibility for grading exams. If the lecturer decides that a paper merits a "B", then the student receives a "B", perhaps adjusted for classroom participation, again by the professor. Now assume that a colleague happens by chance to read the exam, and finds the grade excessively severe (the student deserved an "A") or unduly generous (the paper merits only a "C"). The second professor's views do not matter, whether correct or not. Each professor bears the authority and duty to grade his or her exams. That being said, not all authors would agree that a distinction can be made between the merits of a dispute and jurisdiction, at least in the context of court actions. See Evan Tsen LEE, "The Dubious Concept of Jurisdiction", 54 Hastings Law J. (2003) p. 1613, examining links between words such as "power" and "ability" in the context of jurisdiction. One wonders whether

In deciding challenges to arbitral authority, the parties' intent should serve as the touchstone and the lodestar. If the arbitrators have addressed (or are likely to address) questions that the parties submitted to arbitration, they do not exceed their power.

b. The arbitrator's job: competing principles

Judicial deference to an arbitrator's jurisdictional determination implicates several principles sometimes in tension one with another.[215] First, the arbitrators' decisions are normally final on the questions submitted to them, usually referred to as the merits of the dispute. Second, the arbitrators' decisions are *not* final on issues that the parties did not submit, which is to say, which fall outside the scope of the arbitral authority. Finally, courts will not defer to arbitrators' decisions that violate basic notions of public policy in the forum asked to endorse or give effect to the award.

Renunciation of the right to seek justice through government courts means that an arbitrator has the right to get it wrong, in the sense of evaluating a controverted event differently than would the otherwise competent judge.[216] Assuming the risk of a bad award on the merits of the dispute does not, however, mean giving arbitrators power to decide matters never submitted to them. The arbitrator's job is to decide the case. The court's job is to support the arbitral process, but only to the extent it does not exceed the mission conferred by the parties or the limits of public policy.

This distinction between a mistake on the merits and an excess of authority goes to the heart of what arbitration is all about. Arbitration is a consensual process unfolding within an enclosure created by contract. Litigants accept the risk of arbitrator mistake only for decisions falling within the borders of arbitral authority. A simple error is normally not subject to challenge, since the parties asked an arbitrator to decide the legal and factual merits of their dispute. But no court should recognize an award falling beyond the arbitral authority that gives legitimacy and integrity to the process.

Most modern arbitration statutes acknowledge this prohibits appeals related to the substantive merits of an award. Unlike judges, arbitrators do not normally find their decisions reversed for mistake of law. Arbitration statutes do, however, allow challenge

---

the thesis has not been overstated. Simply because the line between merits and jurisdiction sometimes runs thin does not mean the line never exists.

215. By deference, of course, one means something more than hypocritical adornment to soften the blow of an annulment, where a judge prefaces the vacatur with words such as, "With greatest respect for the distinguished arbitrator" while really thinking that this is an award that must be seen to be believed.

216. In mandated, court-annexed "arbitration" within the United States however, the parties normally retain a right to a de novo trial, making the so-called arbitrator a conciliator in reality. See 28 U.S.C. Sect. 655. See generally Lisa BERNSTEIN, "Understanding the Limits of Court-Connected ADR: A Critique of Federal Court-Annexed Arbitration Programs", 141 U. Penn. L. Rev. (1993) p. 2169. Some state statutes, however, seem to ignore the principle of consensuality. See, e.g., Minnesota's statute requiring arbitration of motor vehicle accident claims not in excess of ten thousand dollars ($10,000) (Minn. Statutes Sect. 65B.525), where the state has in essence given an adjudication franchise to the American Arbitration Association.

to awards that go beyond the arbitrators' mission,[217] whether described as an "excess of jurisdiction", "excess of authority" or "excess of powers".[218]

A party disappointed by an award will sometimes attempt a "back-door" appeal through arguments which depict the arbitrator's mistake as an excess of authority rather than a contract misinterpretation. Errors of law in contract interpretation seem to lend themselves to being portrayed as excess of jurisdiction. An award allowing lost profits, for example, might be portrayed as an arrogation of power not granted by the contract.[219]

Sound distinctions between simple mistake and excess of authority rest on two fundamental principles. First, an agreement to arbitrate normally means accepting that the arbitrator might make a mistake in evaluating the merits of the parties' claims and defenses. It would make little sense to say that an award will be final and binding if litigants automatically get a second bite at the apple, turning arbitration into foreplay to court proceedings.

c.   *Consent and presumptions*

Equally important, however, is the principle that litigants in arbitral proceedings do not expect to be bound by overreaching intermeddlers. Decisions on matters never submitted to arbitration deserve no more deference than the opinions of a random commuter passing through the Paris Métro or New York's Grand Central Station. This distinction remains central to the degree of deference that courts should grant an award that appears to tread on jurisdictional matters.

While such extreme examples may be rare (due to the *in terrorem* effect of judicial scrutiny), they do exist. Until enjoined by a federal court, a Florida "arbitration service" recently conducted one hundred and fourteen "arbitrations" against a bank. In each instance, a credit card holder received an "award" in the precise amount of the cardholder's outstanding debt, even though the bank had never signed an agreement that authorized the arbitration service to decide these disputes.[220]

---

217. Some arbitral regimes permit annulment for excess of authority only when a tribunal "manifestly" goes beyond its powers. See Art. 53(1)(b) of the 1965 Washington (ICSID) Convention, insightfully discussed in Philippe PINSOLLE, "Manifest Excess of Power and Jurisdictional Review of ICSID Awards", 2 Transnat'l Dispute Management (April 2005) p. 39.

218. For the purpose of this analysis, the terms jurisdiction, authority, and powers are used interchangeably. Slight nuances might exist in certain contexts. For example, "excess of jurisdiction" might apply to *what* the arbitrator is authorized to decide, and "excess of powers" to *how* the decision is made. However, each expression describes arbitrator behavior that goes beyond what is permitted by the relevant legal and contractual framework. See generally statement by Lord Phillips in *Lesotho Highlands* (discussed infra) acknowledging that "the concept of an excess of power that is not an excess of jurisdiction is not an easy one". *Lesotho Highlands Development Authority v. Impreglio SpA* [2005] UKHL 43 (30 June 2005), at paragraph 51.

219. See *Parsons & Whittemore Overseas v. Société Générale* (RAKTA), 508 F. 2d 969 (2d Cir. 1974).

220. *Chase Manhattan Bank v. National Arbitration Council*, 2005 WL 1270504 (M.D. Fla. 2005). One Mr. Charles Morgan acted as sole arbitrator under the auspices of the National Arbitration Council (NAC), of which he was sole proprietor. The arbitration clause in the credit agreement listed three arbitral institutions: American Arbitration Association, JAMS and National Arbitration Forum. The court granted an injunction against NAC and Mr. Morgan from

In the more normal line of cases, analysis is complicated by the different thresholds that exist for various types of consent. In some instances consent must be explicit or in writing. On other occasions, circumstances might permit consent to be inferred or presumed.

This should not be surprising, given the varying manifestations of consent in aspects of life other than arbitration. Only the most unromantic (or unrealistic) individual would argue that a woman's consent to be kissed by her boyfriend must be in writing. A glance or a phrase can supply the invitation. Her consent to be married, however, normally requires a higher degree of formality, evidenced by ceremony and explicit words of acceptance.

Similarly, in determining consent to arbitrate jurisdictional questions, the nature of the evidence required varies according to the character of the challenge. On one extreme, a company might say it never agreed to arbitrate anything at all. To meet this challenge, the other side would normally need to produce a written agreement of some sort. At the other end of the spectrum, the parties might differ over whether the arbitrator appointed to decide their dispute has power to award compound interest. Here, one might rely on inferences or presumptions drawn from generally accepted arbitral practice. In the middle might fall questions about the validity of an arbitration clause following an assignment, where the parties' intent can be ascertained by inferences in some situations but not others.[221]

In short, consent implicates a continuum of commitment. Once the major step (an agreement to arbitrate) has been taken, the details (arbitrator power on matters such as interest or assignment) might yield more easily to presumptions.[222]

d. Public policy

In order to reflect the interests of persons not party to the arbitration agreement, legal systems sometimes draw boundaries around an arbitrator's jurisdiction. Such "externalities" relate to sensitive public norms that affect all of society. The restrictions on arbitral power usually take the form of either limits on subjects that may be arbitrated (either in general or for a specific case) or refusal to give effect to awards whose content offends the recognition forum's most basic notions of morality or justice.

i. General subject matter limits

An arbitrator's decision may be "out of bounds" not only because it lacks any foundation in the parties' mutual consent, but also due to the arbitration's legal framework

---

conducting arbitrations or issuing awards involving the bank (Chase), and from accepting any monies from Chase cardholders for arbitration services.

221. See *AC Equipment Ltd. v. American Engineering Corp.*, 215 F. 3d 151 (2d Cir. 2003), where a subcontractor challenged the contractor's assignment of their agreement, arguing that the assignment invalidated the ad hoc arbitration clause. The court held that arbitration could be compelled, and an arbitrator appointed, without judicial hearings on the assignment's validity. The court distinguished the situation in which a subcontractor argues that it never agreed to arbitrate at all.

222. For an exploration of consent as a series of concentric circles, see Alan Scott RAU, *Federal Common Law and Arbitral Power*, forthcoming 2007.

applicable regardless of any agreements between the litigants. Notwithstanding the protagonists' desires, arbitration has on occasion been limited for "public policy" (*ordre public*) reasons with respect to sensitive subject matters such as competition law, securities regulation or civil rights violations.[223]

An attempt to empower an arbitrator to hear a particular dispute might be impermissible because the state has taken a monopoly on implementation of the law in areas where arbitrators (much like foxes guarding a chicken coop) present too great a risk of getting it wrong. Public policy may be invoked as a catch-all prohibition on the arbitration of certain categories of disputes, as well as to protect the integrity of the arbitral process in matters such as arbitrator bias or lack of due process.

Public policy limits on arbitrability *per se* are less important than they used to be, in the sense that courts now tend to allow arbitration to proceed with respect to public law claims related to antitrust, securities regulation, patents, bankruptcy and state franchise statutes.[224] Nevertheless, there still exist situations in which courts might feel it proper to deny arbitrators jurisdiction to hear questions relating to certain statutory claims, out of concern that the arbitrator might "get it wrong" in a way that injures vital public interests. To revive an old metaphor, allowing deference to arbitrators' determinations of acceptable public policy would be similar to leaving matters of war entirely to generals. In connection with vital public law claims, it would be hard to see how any submission of arbitrability to the arbitrator (regardless of whether it was in fact accepted by the parties) could be immune from independent judicial review.

Challenges to jurisdiction based on public policy do not yield to the same kind of analysis as jurisdictional limits based on the parties' agreement. The parties cannot expect the state to respect a grant of arbitral power on a subject matter that the state deems non-arbitrable. Similarly, arbitrators would not normally be permitted to determine their jurisdiction in any final and binding way in an award that furthers the parties' fraud.[225]

---

223. It is important to distinguish between invocation of public policy as a bar to arbitration, and the imposition of public policy to limit the way an arbitrator can or must decide the case. In the latter connection, See *Eco Swiss China Time Ltd. v. Benetton International NV*, European Court of Justice, Case 126/97 (ECR I-3055, 1999), concerning an application to annul an award contrary to European Community competition law. On public policy in arbitration, see generally, Homayoon ARFAZADEH, *Ordre public et arbitrage international à l'épreuve de la mondialisation* (2005) Ch. II, pp. 79-128.

224. For examples of the abandonment of earlier judicial hostility to arbitration of statutory claims that implicate vital societal interests, see generally, William W. PARK, *International Forum Selection* (1995) at pp. 97-100.

225. For example, a federal Court of Appeals in the United States upheld vacatur of an award in which the re-incorporation ("redomestication") of a captive insurance company from Massachusetts to Bermuda was deemed to be a fraud on the public regulatory authorities. See *Commercial Union v. Lines*, 378 F. 3d 204 (2d Cir. 2004). A captive insurance company called EMLICO reinsured with Commercial Union a portion of its liability under policies that EMLICO issued to General Electric, its only policy holder. General Electric sought to recover asbestos clean-up costs from EMLICO, which in turn sought to recover these from Commercial Union. EMLICO allegedly had transferred its corporate domicile to Bermuda by deceiving the Massachusetts Insurance Commissioner about its solvency. The district court was directed to determine whether the

ii.   Restrictions for specific cases

In some instances, public policy might limit arbitration of a particular dispute rather than an entire subject matter. The imposition of such jurisdictional restrictions can be illustrated by the decision in *United States v. Stein*.[226] Said to be the largest criminal tax case in American history, the case involves the indictment of former partners of the KPMG accounting firm, who were accused of conspiracy and tax evasion in connection with abusive tax shelters.[227] The partners asserted that by contract KPMG must advance the legal fees incurred for their defense. The firm argued that this "advancement claim" must be arbitrated pursuant to the terms of a partnership agreement

When the partners brought a court action to enforce their claim for the legal fees, the firm moved to dismiss the action on the basis of the arbitration clause. The court thus had to consider whether the dispute over the right to legal fees was itself subject to arbitration.

The case holds that arbitration of the legal fees issue would violate public policy even assuming the existence of a valid arbitration agreement.[228] The reasoning requires a bit of background. Federal prosecutors had been found to have violated the partners' Constitutional rights to counsel by pressuring KPMG (under threat of indictment and destruction of its business) to refuse advancement of the legal fees.

Acknowledging the principle that ambiguity in the scope of an arbitration clause would normally be decided in favor of arbitration, the court nevertheless took jurisdiction to decide on the question of legal fees. The policy in favor of arbitration was outweighed by a stronger federal policy in favor of prompt and fair criminal trials. The court considered arbitration of the legal fees issue would undermine this policy.

The court posited that arbitration involves "unpredictable timing and the likelihood of delay" and thus "would force the court to do violence to one important public interest or another". The interest that tipped the scale was the prompt determination of whether the defendants had proper counsel, or rather needed appointment of a lawyer at public expense.

One might disagree with the court's assumption about the delay occasioned by arbitration rather than litigation. However, it is not hard not to understand the concern that private arbitration should not derail a large criminal case, even if one does not accept the court's suggestion that arbitration is slow and unpredictable.

c.   *Content of the award*

Questions related to subject matter arbitrability intersect with, but are distinct from, problems derived from awards that violate public policy by reason of their content. For

---

Bermuda liquidation of EMLICO affected the results in the arbitration. The fraud at issue was not in the procurement of the re-insurance contract, nor in the procurement of the award (for example, by bribery), but rather fraud on a governmental body that potentially affected the outcome of the arbitration.

226. 2006 WL 2556076 (S.D.N.Y. 2006); stay pending appeal denied, 2006 WL 2724079.

227. Employees as well as partners were indicted. For ease of articulation, however, the term "partners" will be used for both categories of defendants.

228. The decision also addresses rights of several allegedly "non-party" defendants who asserted that they had never agreed to arbitrate.

example, an arbitrator might well have jurisdiction to decide an antitrust question. But he or she cannot ignore the relevant law and policies without risking having the award refused recognition on the grounds that it violates public policy[229] or gives effect to illegal conduct.[230]

Mandatory norms of the place of performance may limit an arbitrator's jurisdiction regardless of the applicable law. An arbitrator who ignores American antitrust laws, in connection with sales to New York consumers, can expect his or her award to be vacated (assuming an arbitral situs within the United States) even though the contract provides for Swiss law to be applicable.[231]

In this connection, arbitrators may find themselves in a double bind. In applying the mandatory norms of the place of performance, an arbitrator may exceed his or her jurisdiction under the law of a country called to enforce the award or monitor the integrity of the process. In the above example, the arbitrator who applied American antitrust rules even though the parties asked for a decision according to Swiss principles could expose the award to annulment for excess of authority in an arbitral situs that did not share the United States' perspective on the proper role of competition law.

---

229. See *Mitsubishi Motors v. Soler Chrysler Plymouth*, 473 U.S. 614, 638 (1985), where the Court asserted (rightly or wrongly) that "having permitted the arbitration to go forward, the national courts of the United States will have the opportunity at the award-enforcement stage to ensure that the legitimate interest in the enforcement of the antitrust laws has been addressed [because the New York Convention] reserves to each signatory country the right to refuse enforcement of an award where the "recognition or enforcement of the award would be contrary to the public policy of that country". While the efficacy of the arbitral process requires that substantive review at the award-enforcement stage remain minimal, it would not require intrusive inquiry to ascertain that the tribunal took cognizance of the antitrust claims and actually decided them.

230. Obvious examples include awards ordering payment for sales of slaves, heroin or illegal arms to terrorists. If an airline pilot is dismissed from employment for showing up drunk at the cockpit, courts can be expected to vacate an award reinstating the pilot. See *Delta Air Lines, Inc. v. Air Line Pilots Ass'n, Intern.*, 861 F. 2d 665 (11th Cir. 1988), involving pilot who was intoxicated while flying a commercial plane from Bangor, Maine, to Boston, Massachusetts. Focusing on the regulations promulgated by the Federal Aviation Administration, the court considered the case non-arbitrable, stating the airline "was under a duty to prevent the wrongdoing of which its Pilot-In-Command was guilty, and it could not agree to arbitrate that issue". *Ibid.* at p. 674. This non-arbitrability approach denies effect to an arbitral finding on the facts that the pilot had not been drunk. Such violation of public policy in the process of performing employment duties was distinguished from situations in which public policy was violated outside employment, giving rise to no workplace violation of a duty. In such instances, an arbitrator might be given greater leeway with respect to bad behavior. See *United Paper Workers v. Misco*, 484 U.S. 29 (1987) (marijuana found in car) and *Florida Power Corp. v. IBEW*, 847 F. 2d 680 (11th Cir. 1988) (drunk driving on employee's own time).

231. See fn. 16, *Mitsubishi Motors Corp. v. Soler Chrysler-Plymouth*, 473 U.S. 614 (1985). Pro-consumer usury prohibitions might also impose themselves on the arbitration of a loan transaction expressly made subject to the laws of a country without limits on interest rates.

V.   ITEMS FOR FURTHER CONSIDERATION

Inevitably, no matter how good a legal doctrine, questions arise about its application in specific situations. The devil always lurks in the details. The following discussion takes as its springboard several questions drawn from the French, German, English and American legal systems. Raising these queries in no way suggests that the legal systems mentioned have proven inadequate. Rather, the various lines of inquiry reflect a call for further dialogue.

1.   "Manifestly Void" Clauses in France

As mentioned earlier, in French law the arbitrators' power to decide on their own competence operates in tandem with an explicit provision that puts off jurisdictional challenges until after an award is rendered. The *Nouveau code de procédure civile* provides that if a claim has already been presented to the arbitrators (literally, if the tribunal has been "seized" of a matter) courts must declare themselves without jurisdiction to hear the case. If arbitration has *not* yet begun, courts must also declare themselves lacking jurisdiction unless the arbitration agreement is "clearly void" (*manifestement nulle*).[232]

The theory seems to be that a party wrongfully hindered in bringing its arbitration claim deserves more solicitude than does a party improperly joined to an arbitral proceeding. To deal with the former risk (dilatory tactics to disrupt arbitration), courts are given only limited power to examine the validity of the arbitration clause before the arbitration has begun, and none at all after proceedings have started.

Following an award, however, judicial review will take place on the grounds provided by the French arbitration statute, which for international arbitration covers a

---

232. NCPC Art. 1458. The full text reads as follows,

> "When a dispute for which an arbitral tribunal has been constituted [literally "seized" of the dispute] pursuant to an arbitration agreement is brought before a governmental court, the court must declare itself without jurisdiction. If the arbitral tribunal has not yet been constituted [literally "seized" of the dispute], the court must also declare itself without jurisdiction unless the arbitration agreement is clearly void." (Author's translation)

> *"Lorsqu'un litige dont un tribunal arbitral est saisi en vertu d'une convention d'arbitrage est porté devant une juridiction de l'État, celle-ci doit se déclarer incompétente. Si le tribunal arbitral n'est pas encore saisi, la juridiction doit également se déclarer incompétente à moins que la convention d'arbitrage ne soit manifestement nulle."* (In the original)

> Although certain provisions of domestic French arbitration law do not apply to international arbitration, such is not the case for Art. 1458, which falls within Title I of Book IV of the NCPC. See NCPC Art. 1507 and *Décret du 12 mai* 1981, Arts. 55 and 56, providing for non-application of certain provisions in Titles IV, V and VI.

number of jurisdictional defects: decision in the absence of an arbitration agreement, irregular composition of the arbitral tribunal, and failure to respect the mission given to the arbitral tribunal.[233]

This system conserves judicial resources by delaying review until the end of the process, when the parties may have settled or the arbitrator might have gotten it right. Some authors have called this sequence a "guarantee of good administration of justice".[234]

One source of puzzlement to many non-French lawyers lies in the fact that the exception for clauses that are *manifestement nulle* applies only when the arbitration has not begun. Why should this be so? Faced with a clause that is clearly void, why should a court find its hands tied in declaring the nullity of the proceedings simply because a purported arbitration has already begun? Perhaps the answer lies in the fact that the parties are already before a judge, and thus the risk of delay is less than if no judicial action had yet begun.

A "manifestly void" clause would seem inoperative regardless of how far along the sham procedures had run. To some observers, it seems strange to delay judicial intervention in an arbitration with no consensual underpinning simply because someone has set a process in motion.

Perhaps, at the beginning of an arbitration, courts might limit their task to determining whether they can be prima facie satisfied that the arbitration clause exists, deferring an in-depth analysis of jurisdiction to the moment when the award itself must be reviewed. But why should *all* examination of jurisdiction be forbidden?

Since arbitration remains consensual at its core, one might even ask how a purported tribunal can be "seized" of any matter on the basis of a void clause. There exists a risk of loading the analytic dice by using the term "arbitration" to refer to a process that was never accepted by the two sides. As a definitional matter, when a signature on an alleged arbitration agreement was clearly forged, or signed with a gun at her head, to label someone an arbitrator would not provide decision-making authority any more than calling a dog's tail a "leg" would give the animal five limbs instead of four.[235] Without a grant of authority from the litigants, a would-be arbitrator is no more than a shameless volunteer.

---

233. NCPC Art. 1502, for international cases. Review in domestic arbitration can be found in Art. 1483, which provides for annulment of an award containing analogous jurisdictional defects.

234. Pierre MAYER, *op. cit.*, fn. 2, at p. 350, suggesting, "*L'examen successif est une garantie de bonne administration de la justice; le juge pourra s'inspirer de la motivation adoptée par l'arbitre, ou y trouver au contraire une faille révélatrice.*" However, Mayer also argues that when a court action has been begun before arbitration, the judge should address the alleged jurisdictional defect without regard to whether "manifest" or not. *Ibid.* at p. 346. Moreover, good reason exists to suspect that Professor Mayer's views may have evolved during the past few years, to the point that he would favor an immediately available summary court proceeding to decide whether an arbitration clause was clearly void.

235. Abraham Lincoln once asked, "If I call a tail a leg, how many legs does a dog have? Five?" He then answered, "No. Four. Calling a tail a leg does not make it so."

2. The New Approach in Germany

a. The Kompetenz-Kompetenz clause[236]

Like the length of women's dresses, arbitration law often experiences its own fashion changes from one season to another. Perhaps the most radical of such style shifts can be found in the German approaches to arbitrators' jurisdictional determinations.

At one time, German courts recognized contract provisions that granted arbitrators a right to rule on their own authority in a final (rather than temporary) way.[237] In a landmark case arising from a charterparty of a refrigerated transport ship, Germany's highest court admitted the possibility of an agreement on jurisdiction (*eine Kompetenz-Kompetenz-Klausel*). The arbitral tribunal was given power to render a jurisdictional decision on whether the charterer's agent was bound to arbitrate, subject to no judicial second-guessing.[238] The job of deciding whether in fact such a clause existed in the relevant freight contract (so as to bind the party resisting arbitration) was remanded to the lower court. This principle followed the lines of an earlier *Bundesgerichtshof* decision redered almost a quarter century earlier,[239] and was confirmed in a case decided as late as 1991,[240] the same year the German Ministry of Justice established a reform commission whose work ultimately led to enactment of a new arbitration law.

b. The 1998 reforms

In 1998 Germany adopted the UNCITRAL Model Arbitration Law.[241] During the drafting stage, the official commentary on Art. 1040 *Zivilprozessordnung* (ZPO) (the equivalent of UNCITRAL Model Law Art. 16) stated that courts would always have the last word on arbitral jurisdiction.[242] In essence, questions of arbitrator jurisdiction were shifted to the category of non-arbitrable subject matters. This principle has been affirmed by authoritative commentary, asserting that *Kompetenz-Kompetenz* clauses are

---

236. For helpful comments on the German cases, thanks are due to Professor Peter Schlosser, Professor Klaus Peter Berger, and Dr. Ulrich Lohmann.

237. See generally Peter SCHLOSSER, "The Competence of Arbitrators and of Courts", 8 Arb. Int'l (1992) p. 189 at pp. 199-200. See also Klaus Peter BERGER, *International Economic Arbitration* (1993) at p. 359; Klaus Peter BERGER, *International Wirtschaftsschiedsgerichtsbarkeit* (1992) at p. 253.

238. BGH, Decision of 5 May 1977, III ZR 177/74. Reported in 68 BGHZ 356, at 358. See discussion in Peter SCHLOSSER, *op. cit.*, fn. 70, at Sect. 556.

239. BGH II ZR 323/55, decided in 1953.

240. BGH II ZR 68/90. See BGH Neue Juristische Wochenschrift (NJW) 1991, 2215.

241. On the 1998 German law, see Friedrich NIGGEMANN, "*Chronique de Jurisprudence Étrangère: Allemagne*", Rev. arb. (2006) p. 225; Otto SANDROCK, "Procedural Aspects of the New German Arbitration Act", 14 Arb. Int'l (1998) p. 33 ; Peter SCHLOSSER, *ADR II*, Institute of Comparative Law, Chuo University, Japan, Takeshi KOJIMA, ed. (2004) p. 335; Klaus Peter BERGER, "*Das neue Schiedsverfahrensrecht in der Praxis – Analyse und aktuelle Entwicklungen*", in *Recht der Internationalen Wirtschaft (RIW)*, vol. 1 (2001).

242. See *Entwurf eines Gesetze zur Neuordnung des Schiedsverfahrensrechts* July 1995, at p. 132 (Draft Commentary on German adoption of the UNCITRAL Model Arbitration Law).

against public policy[243] and that courts may intervene at any time to decide arbitral competence.[244] As discussed below, it remains to be seen whether the logic of these commentators and judicial decisions will be pushed to cover even separate contracts on arbitral authority, rather than simple jurisdictional clauses contained in a single commercial agreement.

Current case law has endorsed a prophylactic rule that seems to bar such clauses, regardless of what the evidence might show about the parties' intent. The prohibition on *Kompetenz-Kompetenz* clauses was confirmed clearly in 2005 by the *Bundesgrichtshof*[245]

---

243. Joachim MÜNCH, *Münchener Kommentar ZPO*, 2. Auflage, Band 3, Sect. 1040 (München 2001), at 1183 (Rdnr. 26). This commentary argues that the interplay of Sect. 1040 subsections 1 (tribunal may rule on its jurisdiction) and 3 (one month period for challenge of ruling) establish a mandatory character of judicial jurisdiction. Consequently, the commentary characterizes *Kompetenz Kompetenz* clauses as *unwirksam, weil gegen zwingendes Recht verstossend* (inoperative because they violate mandatory law). See also Klaus-Peter BERGER, *Private Dispute Resolution in International Business*, Volume I (2006), at Question 7; Klaus-Peter BERGER, "The Implementation of the UNCITRAL Model Law in Germany", 13 Int. Arb. Rep. 38 (January 1998).

244. Peter SCHLOSSER in STEIN/JONAS, *Kommentar zur Zivilprozessordnung*, 22. Auflage, Band 9 (Tübingen 2002) Sect. 1040, Rdnr. 2, at p. 489, with cross-reference to Schlosser's own comments at Sect. 1032, Rdnr. 11. Professor Schlosser writes, *"Aus der vorläufigen Kompetenz-Kompetenz des Schiedsgerichts folgt auch nicht, dass es das 'erste Wort' bezüglich der Wirksamkeit der Schiedsvereinbarung erhalten hätte."* (It does not follow from the arbitrator's preliminary *Kompetenz-Kompetenz* that he has the "first word" regarding the validity of the arbitration agreement.) In referring to the "first word" on jurisdiction, Professor Schlosser sought to draw attention to the way Germany's practice (permitting courts to rule on jurisdiction before an arbitral award) differs from the legal position in France, where court review of jurisdiction generally waits until after the award has been rendered. German law provides that courts will always have the "last word" on jurisdiction, and in some instances may also have the "first word" as well.

245. BGH, Decision of 13 January 2005, III ZR 265/03. Reported NJW 16/2005 at 1125. The case is also reported on the DIS database, with notes by HUBER/BACH and WAGNER/QUINKE. An alleged loss on a brokerage account (typical in arbitration cases) brought a court action for recovery notwithstanding the arbitration clause. In the course of confirming the duty to arbitrate, the Court re-emphasized that any jurisdictional decision would be subject to review. On its facts, the BGH pronouncement gives little difficulty. There was in fact no award review at all, let alone a challenge to a first award establishing jurisdictional principles for a second arbitration. In Anglo-American legal thought, the court's decision might be labeled *dictum*. See also BGH decision of 23 February 2006 (III ZB 50/05), reported 2006 SchiedsVZ (May/June 2006) p. 161, reversing the Karlsruhe OLG refusal to recognize an award rendered in Minsk under the rules of the Belarus (White Russia) Chamber of Commerce. Germany's highest court rejected the contention that international public policy (*ordre public inernational*) had been violated by an arbitral tribunal's jurisdictional ruling in a final award on the merits. According to the BGH, no policy violation occurs if the final jurisdictional ruling rested with the government courts, as was the case in Byelarus. SchiedsVZ (2006) p. 161, at p. 164.

in a decision which had followed a shift in approach announced three years earlier in a case expressing concern that a wrongful assertion of arbitral jurisdiction might result in deprivation of a party's "lawful judge" (*gesetzlich Richter*).[246]

The significance of the 2005 decision lies not only in its statements about *Kompetenz-Kompetenz* clauses, but also in its affirmation that judges may provide jurisdictional input *before* an arbitrator's decision on the matter. Thus courts not only have the "last word" on the arbitrator's jurisdiction, but in some instances the "first word" as well.

To a large extent, this new approach seems to derive from a fear of sloppy judicial decision-making. Rather than a rigorous analysis to determine the existence of a genuine agreement to arbitrate jurisdiction, judges were apparently inclined to leave jurisdictional issues to the arbitrators, almost automatically finding *Kompetenz-Kompetenz* clauses on scanty evidence. In the backlash, legislators and scholars expressed the opinion (rightly or wrongly) that the UNCITRAL Model Law was inconsistent with such a practice.[247]

In discussing the prior lack of analytic rigor, one of Germany's most eminent scholars suggests that prior to 1998 his country's judiciary had become inclined to find *Kompetenz-Kompetenz* clauses even where they did not exist, thus clearing the judicial dockets even as to a party that had no real intent to waive its right to a court hearing.[248] Professor Schlosser tells of a case in which a corporate liquidator had begun an action in Germany for a determination that certain goods were not the property of the respondent, a matter which arose by operation of law apart from the contract subject to arbitration. The parties to the relevant arbitration agreement had agreed as follows: "For all disputes arising out of this contract the contracting parties submit themselves to the Chamber of Commerce of Geneva." The *Bundesgerichtshof* instructed the lower court to verify the existence of an *oral* agreement to arbitrate by which the arbitral tribunal would have had jurisdiction to decide the scope of the written agreement to arbitrate.[249]

The German arbitration statute has an express provision permitting declaratory court judgments on the validity of arbitration clauses, provided application is made prior to constitution of the arbitral tribunal.[250] Moreover, German judges may examine fully the validity of the arbitration clause either in the context of a court action on the merits of

---

246. BGH, Decision of 6 Juni 2002, III ZB 44/01. This decision involved an arbitral tribunal's finding that it lacked jurisdiction. However, the court in *dictum* contrasted the facts of its case with the opposite scenario, where an arbitral tribunal wrongfully assumes jurisdiction thereby depriving a party of its "lawful judge" (*gesetzlich Richter*).

247. See BT-Drucksache 13/5274 at 26 and 44, cited by the *Bundesgerichtshof* in its decision of 13 January 2005, at 5 and 6. See also *Entwurf eines Gesetze zur Neuordnung des Schiedsverfahrensrechts* July 1995, at 132 (draft commentary on German adoption of the UNCITRAL Model Arbitration Law), discussed supra.

248. Peter SCHLOSSER, op. cit., fn. 241, p. 335, at p. 340.

249. SCHLOSSER, *ibid.,* at pp. 342-343, citing Juristenzeitung 1989, p. 201.

250. ZPO Sect. 1032(2) which provides, "*Bei Gericht kann bis zur Bildung des Schiedsgerichts Antrag auf Feststellung der Zulässigkeit oder Unzulässigkeit eines schiedsrichterlichen Verfahrens gestellt werden.*" (Prior to the constitution of the arbitral tribunal, an application may be made to the court to determine whether or not arbitration is admissible.)

a claim[251] or an annulment action of either an interim jurisdictional decision[252] or final award.[253]

It should be noted, however, that German scholars are not unanimous on all questions related to court review of arbitrators' jurisdiction. Some writers say that judicial review is mandatory, and thus the parties cannot by agreement create a de facto waiver of those provisions through an agreement giving a jurisdictional question to arbitrators.[254] Others, however, appear to accept that the parties may waive grounds for award vacatur that are designed to protect private interests,[255] as opposed to public order.[256] The result of this latter approach would be that courts might give respect to agreements subjecting jurisdictional questions to final arbitration, provided such questions are clearly identified.

c. The parties' expectations

At the risk of appearing presumptuous (always a hazard for a foreign lawyer), one might ask whether a blanket denial of *Kompetenz-Kompetenz* clauses constitutes an overreaction which might in some cases disregard the parties' legitimate expectations. The text of the law provides simply that arbitrators may rule on their own jurisdiction, that jurisdictional challenges must be raised in a timely fashion, and that the arbitrators' rulings on the matter would normally (*in der Regel*) take the form of an interim decision subject to judicial review on a request filed within thirty days of the ruling.[257]

These provisions say nothing about when or whether these arbitral decisions should be final. The statute here is silent about whether parties may create a special contractual regime submitting jurisdictional questions to final decision by an arbitrator. While such agreements may be rare in practice,[258] they might in some cases exist.

If the parties have two disputes (one related to the merits, and the other to

---

251. ZPO Sect. 1032(1). Compare the practice obtaining in France under NCPC Art. 1458, which allows pre-award court pronouncements on arbitration clauses only if the clause is *"manifestment nulle"* and only if the arbitration has not yet begun.

252. ZPO Sect. 1040(3), analogous to UNCITRAL Model Law Art. 16(3).

253. ZPO Sect. 1059.

254. Judicial review would normally occur under either under ZPO Sect. 1040(3) or ZPO Sect. 1059, depending on whether the award is interim or final.

255. See GEIMER in ZÖLLER, *ZPO*, 25. Aufl., 2005, Sect. 1059, Rdnr. 2 and 80; SCHWAB and WALTER, *Schiedsgerichtsbarkeit*, 7. Aufl., 2005, Kap. 6, Rdnr. 10; ALBERS in BAUMBACH, LAUTERBACH, ALBERS and HARTMANN, *ZPO*, 64. Aufl., München 2006, Sect. 1059, Rdnr. 2. See also GEIMER, *Internationales Zivilprozessrecht* (5. Aufl., Köln 2005) at pp. 130-131 (notes 309-311), addressing procedural party autonomy in relation to foreign judgments. Geimer posits that parties should be able to waive grounds for non-recognition designed to protect one of the parties, as opposed to government interests (*unmittelbare Staatsinteressen*), and to create by agreement a reliable environment for the resolution of their dispute.

256. Clearly the grounds for vacatur under ZPO 1059(2) (public policy and subject matter arbitrability) should not be waivable, since these matters directly implicate government (rather than private) interests.

257. ZPO Sect. 1040

258. In the adversarial context of preliminary jurisdictional rulings under ZPO Sect. 1040 (UNCITRAL Model Law Art. 16), parties rarely agree on very much, let alone a *Kompetenz-Kompetenz* clause.

jurisdiction), and wish to submit each to arbitration, it is hard to see why they should be prevented from doing so. Courts should, of course, have the opportunity to verify the reality of the alleged consent to arbitration. Judicial review would in all events involve examination of the validity of the initial agreement allegedly granting the arbitrators power on jurisdictional questions such as the scope of their procedural powers or the range of issues covered by the arbitration clause.

The grounds for judicial review envisaged in ZPO Sects. 1040 (for interim decisions) or 1059 (for final awards) certainly remain matters of public policy, and include lack of arbitral authority.[259] However, it would seem an elevation of form over substance to suggest that a question of arbitral authority which relates only to what the parties agreed (bearing no relation to any issue of substantive *ordre public*) must remain non-arbitrable (thus eluding a final decision by the arbitrator) notwithstanding an express contractual stipulation to the contrary.

The matter may well turn out to be a question of what is meant by a decision on the "merits". As suggested in the cautionary tale set forth earlier in this paper,[260] the parties may well wish, in some cases, to grant arbitrators power to decide a jurisdictional question in the same way they would decide some other questions of contract interpretation. If so, it would be unfortunate if the new German position on *Kompetenz-Kompetenz* clauses applied to separate agreements on arbitral authority,[261] and indeed inconsistent with the goal of the UNCITRAL Model Law, to give binding effect to legitimate arbitral decisions.

Whether made in Germany or abroad, an award should be subject to challenge for jurisdictional infirmity.[262] However, neither side should be permitted to renege on a freely accepted arbitration agreement followed by fair proceedings, even if the agreement covers matters relating to arbitral authority.

d.   Avoiding extremes

It is not difficult to sympathize with the concerns of German courts, legislators and scholars in connection with the confusion and potential abuse caused by earlier decisions. Loose talk about arbitrators determining their own jurisdiction can give rise to inappropriate overreaching. A contract's jurisdictional clause does not necessarily

---

259. ZPO Sect. 1059, analogous to UNCITRAL Model Law Art. 34, permits vacatur for invalid arbitration agreement, inability to present one's case, an award that deals with a matter not falling within the arbitration submission, or improper constitution of the arbitral tribunal.

260. See discussion supra in Part II.2.d. The time limits in that scenario, we remember, are restrictions on arbitral authority, not statutes of limitations. The latter remain substantive in German law. BGB Sects. 195 et seq. The hypothetical presumes that the restrictions limit the right to arbitrate, not substantive recovery.

261. ZPO Sect. 1059(1)(c) (analogous to UNCITRAL Model Law Art. 34) permits an award to be set aside if it deals with a dispute beyond the scope of the arbitration submission, and Sect. 1059(1)(d) permits setting aside of the arbitral award if the procedure is not in accordance with the parties' agreement.

262. See discussion in NIGGEMANN, *Chronique de Jurisprudence Étrangère*, supra, fn. 241, at p. 235: "*les tribunaux allemands constatent régulièrement que la décision du tribunal arbitral étranger sur sa compétence ne les lie pas*". Niggemann goes on to cite New York Convention Art. V(1)(*a*), related to absence of a valid arbitration agreement.

give the arbitrator competence, any more than pieces of paper can by themselves agree to anything.[263] Only individuals agree, whether in their own capacity or as agents for legally cognizable collectivities. Jurisdiction must be determined according to all the facts and circumstances, not simplistic recitals.

The prospect that a legal principle may be misused does not necessarily justify a rule that leads to a different type of error. With respect to arbitral jurisdiction, risks exist at two extremes. On the one hand, courts should not assume the finality of an arbitrator's jurisdictional determination merely on the basis of contract recitals taken out of context. On the other extreme, no good reason has been advanced to prohibit genuine consent to arbitration on questions related to the existence of an arbitrator's power.

As a matter of policy, sophisticated business managers have long been permitted to agree on final decisions about contract liability and damages. Such decisions normally benefit from a presumption of deference to the parties' pre-dispute wishes. Likewise, business managers may agree to arbitrate such matters. No good reason seems to prevent similar agreements about the jurisdictional prerequisites to such arbitration.[264]

If the "old style" German Kompetenz-Kompetenz was abused, the remedy might be better education of judges and lawyers about the dangers of overreaching arbitrators. With thoughtfulness and care, policy-makers should be able to avoid both extremes in the pursuit of reasonable counterpoise in the articulation and application of jurisdictional rules.

3. Arbitral Jurisdiction and Contract Interpretation

a. The litigants' role in creating arbitral authority

In a commercial agreement, broadly drafted arbitration clauses often give the arbitrator authority to construe contract language as well as to establish the facts. In an international context, this interpretative function will occasionally involve determining which governing law applies.

On occasion, the parties may wish to be more explicit about either the powers granted, or the restrictions imposed, with respect to the arbitrator's powers. Sometimes this may be done through explicit contract language or through incorporation of provisions in the relevant arbitration rules. For example, an arbitrator might be granted, or denied, the right to award attorneys' fees[265] or to permit third parties to intervene.[266]

---

263. See Judge Easterbrook's opinion in *Sphere Drake v. All American Insurance Co.*, 256 F. 3d 587 (7th Cir. 2001), at 590.

264. In a consumer context, sound public policy might call for a higher level of judicial paternalism. See David QUINKE, *Börsenschiedsvereinbarungen und prozessualer Anlegerschutz* (Carl Heymans Verlag 2005). This question was expressly left open by the BGH above-cited decision of 13 January 2005.

265. Art. 31 of the AAA International Rules permits arbitrators to follow the European practice by awarding "the reasonable costs for legal representation of a successful party". By contrast, New York CPLR Sect. 7513 endorses the so-called "American rule" by providing that attorneys' fees are permissible only if provided in the parties' agreement. At least one court has held that reference to the AAA Rules does not satisfy the requirements of New York law. See *CIT Project Finance v. Credit Suisse First Boston*, 799 NYS2d 159, 2004 WL 2941331 (2004). This slip opinion

What should happen when arbitrators misconstrue (in the eyes of the reviewing court) contract language relating to their authority? Challenges to an arbitrator's exercise of specific powers can set the stage for a battle between two equally important presumptions: (i) the last word on contract interpretation is normally for the arbitrator; but (ii) absent the parties' agreement otherwise, the final say on arbitral jurisdiction remains for the courts. As in so many other matters related to arbitral jurisdiction, the resolution of such conflicts will depend on the particular facts and circumstances of the case. Set forth below are two contexts in which courts have struggled with this tension.

b.   *Paradigm cases: Foreign currency and punitive damages*

i.   The House of Lords in *Lesotho Highlands*
One distinctive feature of English arbitration law is its detail. The 1996 Act seems to contain more specific rules about particular arbitral or judicial powers than any other major arbitration statute.

Most of these rules, however, contain an important escape hatch: they apply unless the parties have otherwise agreed, which is entirely as it should be in a legal system that values party autonomy and flexibility. For example, arbitrators are given authority to order security for costs (Sect. 38), to dismiss a claim for inordinate delay by the claimant (Sect. 41), to make an award in "any currency" (Sect. 48), or to award compound interest (Sect. 49). In all cases, however, the relevant arbitral powers are circumscribed by the qualifier "unless otherwise agreed" by the parties.[267] Granting a

---

may be distinguished on its facts, given that the relevant clause was drafted restrictively, giving the arbitrator power to decide only a narrow question whose resolution did not dispose of the claim. The approach applied more generally permits arbitrators to determine the parties' intent with respect to legal fees. See *PaineWebber v. Bybyk*, 81 F. 3d 1193 (2d Cir. 1996). See also *Shaw Group v. Triplefine International Corp.*, 322 F. 3d 115 (2nd Cir. 2003) and *Stone & Webster v. Triplefine International Corp.*, 118 Fed. Appx. 546 (2d Cir. 2004), involving attorneys' fees in an ICC arbitration. The two *Triplefine* decisions related to the same dispute, although the first decision also included Stone & Webster's parent the Shaw Group. In the *Shaw* decision the Second Circuit vacated a lower court decision that had enjoined a party from claiming as contract damages attorneys' fees incurred in opposing motions to stay arbitration. In the *Stone & Webster* decision the court affirmed an award of attorneys' fees (for the arbitration and the court action) notwithstanding the argument that they were precluded by N.Y. P.P.L.R. Sect. 7513, which imposes the so-called "American rule" of denying legal fees in breach of contract cases "unless otherwise provided in the agreement to arbitrate". The decision upheld the parties' right to waive the provisions of New York law by reference to institutional rules (such as those of the ICC) which provide for arbitrators to allocate legal expenses.

266. See, e.g., See Rules 22.1(h), LCIA Arbitration Rules, allowing a willing third person to be joined to a proceeding notwithstanding the objection of one of the parties.

267. Similarly, courts are given powers subject to the parties' agreement otherwise. The most notable example can be found in Sect. 69, which gives courts the right to correct an error of law. The Act provides for appeal on question of law (defined as questions of English law) but permits appeal to be waived either before or after the dispute arises. This opportunity for waiver of merits review meets the goal of arbitral finality expected by those members of the international business community who arbitrate in London for reasons of convenience and expertise, rather than to hear high-priced QC's engage in clever courtroom debate of matters already decided by the arbitrators. As under prior law, exclusion of merits review can be made by reference to

"power" to an arbitrator constitutes another way of saying that the arbitral tribunal has jurisdiction to do something, whether order security for costs, award interest or make a decision denominated in a particular currency.

In connection with these jurisdictional grants, the question that then arises is, "Who decides whether the parties have otherwise agreed?" Who determines whether a particular form of authority has been taken from arbitrators? A mistake in contract interpretation should not normally be reviewable. The arbitrators' job is to interpret the parties' agreement. But what happens if the part of the contract they interpret relates directly to their powers?

On the one hand, an award might well be recognized even though arbitrators imperfectly exercised powers granted by the statute. If the contract says that an arbitral tribunal is authorized to award compound interest, there would normally be no cause for annulment simply because the chosen rate was different than the one that a reviewing court might have considered appropriate.

On the other hand, the principle that arbitrators interpret contract language cannot stand for the proposition that they can create their own jurisdiction *ex nihilo*. If a contract says that arbitrators have no authority to award treble damages, it is hard to see how they could interpret the limitation as a grant.

What an arbitrator might find, however, is that the ban on treble damages was void under the applicable law. If so, the award could award exemplary damages if justified by the portions of the contract that were not tainted by invalidity. Similar findings might be made with respect to other contract restrictions, such as a limitation of liability clause that fixed a ceiling on recovery at a percentage of the price of goods sold, or excluded consequential damages. In all cases, however, the finding would need to be made as a matter of contract construction (the task given to the arbitrator), not interpretation of the arbitration law.

The matter has sometimes been subject to a certain ambiguity. The principal speech by Lord Steyn in the House of Lords decision in *Lesotho Highlands* suggested that the Arbitration Act gave "unconstrained" power to make an award in any currency.[268] His colleagues disagreed, however.[269] Lord Steyn then went on to posit that the power was not unconstrained, and that arbitrators had erred in interpreting either the contract or the Arbitration Act. In either event, he said, the arbitrators would have done no more than commit error of law.[270]

The possibility of a mistake in the interpretation of the Arbitration Act, however, might be more troublesome. Interpretation of arbitration statutes normally falls to

---

institutional arbitration rules providing for waiver of appeal.

268. *Lesotho Highlands Development Authority v. Impreglio SpA* [2005] UKHL 43 (30 June 2005), reversing the Court of Appeal decision found at [2004] All ER (Comm.) 97 (CA 2003). *Ibid.*, at paragraph 22. See generally William W. PARK, "The Nature of Arbitral Authority: A Comment on *Lesotho Highlands*", 21 Arb. Int'l (2005) p. 483 .

269. Lords Hoffmann, Scott and Rodgers agreed that error of law does not equal excess of power. However, they disagreed with Lord Steyn's construction of Sect. 48 concerning an arbitrator's power to order payment of money in any currency. Lord Phillips (at paragraphs 43-54) went further and stated that the arbitrators had purported to exercise a discretion that the statute did not give them.

270. Paragraph 23, HL decision of 30 June 2005.

courts. Arbitrators cannot, simply by their own bare assertion, create powers they do not have. If an arbitration statute requires awards to be denominated in Sterling, it is hard to see how an arbitrator's *ipse dixit* can generate authority to award Swiss Francs.

The difficulty arises because a decision on whether the parties have "agreed otherwise" amounts not only to an interpretation of the contract, but also to a de facto construction of how the Arbitration Act should be applied in a particular circumstance. By deciding that the parties have or have not "agreed otherwise" the arbitrators expand or contract their own authority accordingly.

In *Lesotho Highlands*, Lord Steyn made clear that the most that might have occurred in the case at bar was an erroneous exercise of powers that actually existed.[271] An award of Swiss Francs might be an imperfect exercise of arbitral power, but would not be a jurisdictional invention.

The contours of arbitrator power, however, may be more difficult to ascertain in other situations. For example, a contractual choice-of-law clause might designate a legal system that prohibits arbitrators from awarding punitive damages.[272] But such a clause could perhaps be read to designate substantive only state contract law, not including arbitral procedure.[273] Moreover, as the US Supreme Court has noted, it is not always obvious when damages are punitive rather than compensatory.[274] To what extent, then, do arbitrators have the power to confer on themselves, in a final and binding way, authority to grant punitive damages?

The decision in *Lesotho Highlands* cannot stand for the proposition that arbitrators may purposefully ignore their mandate. The arbitrators awarded currencies considered "appropriate in the circumstances" after having taken careful note of the contract stipulations[275] and looked only to currencies and exchange rates in the parties' agreement. Nothing suggests that their award was a fig leaf to cover intentional disregard of the contract.

The risk of pernicious arbitrator willfulness was noted by one observer, whose comment on *Lesotho Highlands* raised the specter of arbitrators "misapplying the Arbitration Act", "ignore[ing] the parties' agreement as to applicable law" and "riding rough-shod through choice-of-law provisions".[276] Beyond cavil, those who care for the health of arbitration must remain vigilant to such dangers, mindful of the difficulty in drawing the line between an arbitrator's innocent misconstruction of the parties' contract and a full-scale disregard of the arbitral mission.

---

271. Paragraph 24, HL decision of 30 June 2005.

272. See, e.g., New York law as expressed in *Garrity v. Lyle Stuart, Inc.*, 40 N.Y.2d 354 (1976).

273. *Mastrobuono v. Shearson Lehman Hutton*, 514 U.S. 52 (1995), upholding an award for punitive damages in a dispute covered by a New York choice-of-law clause.

274. See *Pacificare Health Systems v. Book*, 538 U.S. 401 (2002), where a unanimous Court upheld the right to compel arbitration of claims under the Racketeer Influenced and Corrupt Organizations (RICO) Act, which provides for treble damages, notwithstanding a contractual prohibition on punitive damages. The Court suggested that treble damage awards sometimes serve "remedial purposes" that are compensatory in nature.

275. See portions of award cited in Paragraph 10, HL decision of 30 June 2005.

276. See Adam SAMUEL, "*Lesotho Highlands*: Denaturing an Arbitration Statute and an Express Choice of Law Does Not Involve the Arbitrator Exceeding his Powers", 23 J. Int'l Arb. 259 (2006, no. 3), at pp. 261, 262 and 263, respectively.

That being said, the House of Lords decision in itself gives no mandate for such bad behavior. An arbitrator might well apply a power given to him or her by the Arbitration Act, but do so in an imperfect way. This might occur, for example, if the arbitrator applied interest or currency rates different from those that the reviewing judge would have considered appropriate. A wrong decision with respect to exercise of clearly granted powers does not always equal an excess of authority.

ii.   Punitive damages: The Supreme Court in *Pacificare*
In *Pacificare Health Systems v. Book*[277] a group of doctors had filed a nationwide class action against several health maintenance organizations, alleging that the organizations had conspired to refuse proper reimbursement for services provided under the health plans accepted by the physicians. The legal basis for the doctors' action included claims under the Racketeer Influenced and Corrupt Organizations Act, commonly known as RICO.[278] This line of attack was attractive for the plaintiff physicians because the RICO statute allows awards of treble damages, amounting to three times any actual damage proven. There was a catch, however. The physicians had agreed to resolve disputes with the health care providers through arbitration; And some of the arbitration agreements to which they had agreed were explicit in prohibiting arbitrators from awarding punitive damages.[279]

The Supreme Court allowed the arbitrators themselves to determine, as an initial matter, whether they could grant treble recovery under the RICO, notwithstanding the contract limitation on punitive damages. While the case is sometimes presented as an example of judges deferring to arbitrators on jurisdictional matters, the court in fact followed a different (and rather murky) line by denying that it was engaged in jurisdictional analysis at all. As discussed below, Justice Scalia asserted that it was not clear (at least to him) that the power to award punitive damages presented a gateway "arbitrability question", which is to say, a jurisdictional issue.

The lower courts had refused to require the physicians to arbitrate, reasoning that if arbitrators could not award punitive damages this would deny meaningful relief for

---

277. 538 U.S. 401 (2003), reversing *In re Humana Inc. Managed Care Litigation*, 285 F. 3d 971 (11th Cir. 2002).
278. 18 U.S.C. Sects. 1961-1968. While some readers might be puzzled that a health care provider was influenced by racketeers, those familiar with RICO know that it has long been commonplace to include racketeering counts in ordinary business litigation. Sect. 1962 makes it unlawful to invest income derived from a "pattern of racketeering" in any business engaged in interstate or international commerce. Sect. 1961 defines racketeering to include not only acts and threats of things such as murder, kidnapping, arson, robbery and bribery, but also acts indictable under several sections of federal criminal law. Frequently RICO civil claims are based on alleged conspiracy to commit mail and wire fraud, as defined in 18 U.S.C. Sects. 1341 and 1342. Sect. 1964 provides that persons injured by violations of RICO shall recover "threefold the damages he sustains" as well as attorney's fees.
279. The various agreements provided either that (i) "punitive damages shall not be awarded [in the arbitrations], (ii) "arbitrators ... shall have no authority to award any punitive or exemplary damages" or (iii) "arbitrators ... shall have no authority to award extra contractual damages of any kind, including punitive or exemplary damages".

violations of RICO. Presumptively, RICO claims were of such public importance as to be non-waivable in a pre-dispute arbitration agreement. The health care organizations appealed.

In a relatively brief opinion by Justice Scalia, a unanimous Supreme Court upheld the health care organizations' right to compel arbitration. The key to the Court's reasoning lies in its assumption about the ambiguity of the term "punitive damages" and the nature of treble damages in the RICO statute. The Court suggested that some judicial decisions had given treble damage a compensatory character, "serving remedial purposes in addition to punitive objectives".[280] Consequently, the Court expressed agnosticism about whether an arbitrator would or would not interpret the punitive damage prohibitions in a way that might cast doubt on the permissibility of treble damages. "We do not know how the arbitrator will construe the remedial limitations," wrote Justice Scalia, and thus it would be "mere speculation" (using the vocabulary of an earlier decision[281]) to presume that arbitrators might deny themselves the power to grant punitive damages. It was that very prospect (that treble damages might be found beyond the arbitrators' jurisdiction) which had troubled the lower court, anxious to protect the physicians' right to recovery. Consequently, the Court would not take upon itself the authority to decide "the antecedent question" of how the ambiguity concerning punitive damages is to be resolved.[282]

In essence, the Court decided not to decide, but to pursue a "wait and see" policy. On the theoretical level, therefore, the case cannot be said to give the arbitrators power to make final a determination on the matter of their authority.

Justice Scalia added to the suspense with an intriguing footnote. "If the conceptual ambiguity [about what the prohibition on punitive damages might mean] could itself be characterized as raising a 'gateway' question of arbitrability," he reasoned, then "it would be appropriate for a court to answer it [the arbitrability question] in the first instance."[283] The Court then concluded, "Given our presumption in favor of arbitration ... we think the preliminary question whether the remedial limitations at issue here prohibit an award of RICO treble damages is not a question of arbitrability."[284]

What the Court seems to be saying is that arbitrators would construe a particular expression in the contract ("punitive damages") in the same way they interpret any other contract phrase, taking into account the context of the parties' relationship and other

---

280. Referring to statutory remedies such as those at issue in RICO claims, Justice Scalia described treble damages as lying "on different points along the spectrum between purely compensatory and strictly punitive awards". 538 U.S. 405.

281. *Vimar Seguros y Reaseguros, S.A. v. M/V Sky Reefer*, 515 U.S. 528 (1995).

282. 538 U.S. 407.

283. 538 U.S. 407. But the footnote continues that the phrase "question of arbitrability" should be applicable only in the kind of narrow circumstance where contracting parties "would likely have expected a court to have decided the gateway matter, where they are not likely to have thought that they had agreed that an arbitrator would do so, and, consequently, where reference of the gateway dispute to the court avoids the risk of forcing parties to arbitrate a matter that they may well not have agreed to arbitrate". There are those who might observe, however, that the heart of arbitral jurisdiction turns on what the parties were "likely to have thought" about the decisions an arbitrator was supposed to make.

284. 538 U.S. 407, at n. 2.

terms in the agreement. While the meaning given to these terms might affect one side's recovery, it would not enlarge arbitral authority, given that it is already broadly defined under the common arbitration clause which gives arbitrators the job of interpreting the language in the parties' agreement and the applicable law, even (and especially) in close cases.[285]

From one perspective, Scalia might be saying no more than that the matter is not ripe for determination until the court knows whether the arbitrators will in fact exceed their jurisdiction or violate public policy.[286] The troubling aspect of this decision lies in its susceptibility to misinterpretation, as in essence giving arbitrators de facto power to determine their own jurisdiction to award treble damages, simply by the way they would interpret the notion of punitive damages. If the arbitrators held that treble damages under RICO were not "punitive" in the context of the physicians' claims, then by definition these damages would be within their jurisdiction.

Such a result may not be implausible under the circumstances. Arguments have been made that treble damages make "rough justice" compensation for the disruption that may result from contract breach but be difficult to quantify. The slope, however, does not continue indefinitely. At some point language ceases to be elastic, and the parties' words impose definite boundaries on what arbitrators can do.

4. The "Arbitrability Question" in the United States

a. Legal framework

i. Overview
In the United States, questions otherwise labeled "jurisdictional" often find themselves being classified as matters for the arbitrators to decide along with the merits of the dispute. As we shall see, this characterization exercise lies at the heart of judicial deference to the arbitral process.

---

285. Illustrations of this point arise in many interesting arbitrations. Here are a few.

(1) Professional specialty. A statute might make limitation of liability clauses valid only in contracts between persons "in the same profession" (French law refers to contracts "*entre professionels de la même specialité*"). Since two professional lives are rarely completely alike, the arbitrator must determine how narrow to draw the concept of professional "specialty".

(2) "Subject to ..." A contract might make one obligation "subject to" a particular event. Does the expression mean "On condition that" or "Unless"? Both usages exist. "Bob must take the exam, subject to [unless] being excused by the Dean. But, "Christine will have dinner at home, subject to [on condition that] her plane lands on time.

(3) A licensee might be entitled to sub-license to an entity that sells a "range" of the licensee's products. If the licensee sells three dozen products, how many constitutes a "range"? Presumably we need more than one, but not necessarily thirty-six.

286. Of course, when an arbitration award can be enforced against assets abroad, this may be of little consequence.

Unlike the arbitration laws of France,[287] and to a lesser extent England,[288] the Federal Arbitration Act creates no statutory presumption that courts should await the award before pronouncing themselves on an arbitrator's authority to hear a dispute.[289] Early in the arbitral process, courts can decide whether a particular matter has been (or can be) submitted to arbitration, usually in the context of a motion to compel arbitration or to stay litigation.[290] Courts remain free to entertain motions related to arbitral jurisdiction at any moment from the start of proceedings onward. Moreover, when the existence of an agreement to arbitrate is open to doubt, courts may order the question resolved by a jury.[291]

In other ways, however, American arbitration law has been extremely generous in giving arbitrators both the first and the last word in determining their own authority. The statutory scheme for international arbitration has been integrated with a practice of sending jurisdictional questions to arbitrators if there is evidence that such is the path intended by the parties.[292]

The conceptual underpinning of this approach relies on a finding that "the parties intended that the question of arbitrability [used in the sense of jurisdiction] shall be decided by the arbitrator".[293] With a different vocabulary, American courts have in essence adopted the old German concept of a *Kompetenz-Kompetenz* clause, by which the parties may agree to submit a jurisdictional matter to final and binding arbitration.[294] As discussed more fully below, jurisdictional differences have been manipulated into the

---

287. See NCPC Art. 1458, discussed supra.

288. See 1996 English Arbitration Act, Sect. 72, discussed supra, which provides for the right to challenge the arbitration agreement or jurisdiction through a motion for declaration or injunction only when the person alleged to be a party to the arbitration "takes no part in the proceedings". See also Sects. 70(2) (applications and appeals may be brought only after exhaustion of available arbitral process) and 73 (loss of right to object to lack of jurisdiction if a litigant takes part in an arbitration without raising the matter in the proceedings).

289. For the German position on the matter, see BGH decision of 13 January 2005, discussed *supra*.

290. FAA Sect. 3 provides that federal courts shall stay competing litigation "upon being satisfied that the issue involved in such [judicial] suit or proceeding is referable to arbitration...".

291. See *Sandvik AB v. Advent Int'l Corp* 220 F. 3d 99 (3d Cir. 2000); *China Minmetals Materials Ltd. v. Chi Mei*, 334 F. 3d 274 (3d. Cir. 2003).

292. For a survey of cases along these lines, see Robert B. DAVIDSON, "Recent U.S. Cases Affecting the Power of an International Arbitral Tribunal to Determine its own Jurisdiction" in Lars HEUMAN and Sigvard JARVIN, eds., *op. cit.*, fn. 25.

293. See *PaineWebber Inc. v. Bybyk*, 81 F. 3d 1192, at 1198-1199 (2d Cir. 1996). See also *Alliance Bernstein Investments*, discussed supra. The principle has also been extended to class actions in *JSC Surgutneftegaz v. Harvard College*, 167 Fed. Appx. 266 (2nd Cir. 2006), 2006 WL 354282, affirming 2005 WL 1863676 (S.D.N.Y. 2005). Here investors brought a class action arbitration over dividend policy of a Russian company, whose shares were evidenced by American Depository Receipts (ADR's) held in New York. The court found "the intent of the parties to commit the question of arbitrability to the arbitrator". Slip opinion at 3. The contest was not about the existence of the arbitration clause (accepted by both sides) but rather about whether its scope was broad enough to cover the parties' dispute.

294. American courts are often unwilling to use the same vocabulary as other nations, preferring to talk of "the arbitrability question" rather than jurisdiction. See *First Options of Chicago. v. Kaplan*, 514 U.S. 938, 943 (1995); *PaineWebber, Inc. v. Elahi*, 87 F. 3d 589, 596-598 (1st Cir. 1996).

realm of substantive questions whose resolution the parties are deemed to have given to the arbitrators.

ii. Void and voidable clauses

In the past, judicial decisions often distinguished between "void" and "voidable" clauses. Under this view, only courts may decide challenges based on allegations that the agreement is void ab initio, rather than simply voidable at one side's election.[295]

The instinct behind such decisions is understandable. *Ex nihilo nihil fit*: nothing comes from nothing. Consequently, a void clause cannot serve as the source of authority for any putative arbitrator.[296]

However well-intentioned, the void/voidable distinction seems unnecessary. The better approach would be for courts to ask simply, "What did the parties intend?" If the arbitration clause was for some reason invalid, then there would be no party intent to arbitrate anything. In some cases the invalidity might taint the entire contract, as in the event of forgery or unauthorized signature. In other instances, the invalidity might touch only the arbitration clause, and might be the result of fraudulent misrepresentations about the arbitral process which gave one side the right to rescind that aspect of the transactions.[297]

What should matter is simply that the arbitration clause was invalid, regardless of how that came to be.[298] Mercifully, the void/voidable distinction was finally laid to rest by the US Supreme Court in its recent *Buckeye* decision.[299] An action against a check cashing service, accused of making illegal usurious loans, was brought by borrowers in derogation of the arbitration clause. The Court found that the allegation of "void loan agreement" did not deprive the arbitrators of the right to decide that very issue, as long as the arbitration clause itself remained sound.

b. The dictum in First Options

To understand the "arbitrability question" approach, the most convenient starting point

---

295. See *Sandvik AB v. Advent Int'l Corp* 220 F. 3d 99 (3d Cir. 2000); *Three Valleys Municipal Water District v. E.F. Hutton & Co.*, 925 F. 2d 1136 (9th Cir. 1991); *Canada Life Ass. Co. v. Guardian Life Ins. Co.*, 242 F. Supp. 2d 344 (S.D.N.Y. 2003); *Sphere Drake Ins. v. All American Ins. Co.*, 256 F. 3d 587 (7th Cir. 2001).

296. *Pollux Marine Agencies v. Louis Dreyfus Corp.*, 455 F. Supp. 211 (S.D.N.Y. 1978). In this connection, analytic links are often between an arbitrator's jurisdictional power and the separability (autonomy) in the arbitration clause. If the voidness or illegality of the main agreement does not strike the arbitration clause, the arbitrator continues to have power to make a jurisdictional determination. By contrast, if the invalidity does infect the agreement to arbitrate (as might happen in a forged document) the arbitrator would clearly lack authority. See *Harbour Assurance Co. Ltd. v. Kansa General Int'l Ins. Co.*, [1993] Q.B. 701.

297. See *Engalla v. Permanente Med. Group*, 938 P.2d 903 (Cal. 1997), involving a malpractice claim against a health care provider in which habitual delays in arbitration were found to constitute fraud by the provider.

298. For a view along these lines (albeit pursuant to a slightly different line of reasoning), see Robert H. SMIT, "Separability and Competence-Competence in International Arbitration: Ex Nihilo Nihil Fit? Or Can Something Indeed Come From Nothing?", 13 Am. Rev. Int'l Arb. (2002) p. 19 at pp. 34-36.

299. *Buckeye Check Cashing, Inc. v. Cardegna*, 126 S.Ct. 1204 (2006), discussed supra.

might be *First Options of Chicago v. Kaplan*.[300] In *dictum*, this US Supreme Court decision supplied a verbal hook on which much subsequent case analysis has been hung. Almost invariably, these cases cite *First Options* for the dual proposition that (i) contracting parties may agree to arbitrate jurisdictional matters (questions about "arbitrability") but (ii) such agreement must be founded on clear evidence.

Prior to that decision, general American contract principles certainly existed to provide a doctrinal foundation for deference to arbitrators' decisions on their authority. *First Options*, however, supplied a high level of visibility and authoritative endorsement for such deference.[301]

In *First Options*, an arbitral award had been rendered against both an investment company and its owners with respect to debts owed to a securities clearinghouse. The owners (husband and wife) argued that they had never signed the arbitration agreement, and consequently were not bound by the award. The Supreme Court carefully distinguished between three questions: (i) did the Kaplans owe money? (ii) did the Kaplans agree to arbitrate? and (iii) who (court or arbitrator) should decide whether the Kaplans agreed to arbitrate?

On the facts of the case, the Supreme Court affirmed the lower court's finding that the owners had not agreed to arbitrate, without any judicial deference to the arbitrator's determination.[302] Whether Manuel and Carol Kaplan were bound to arbitrate by virtue of a clause signed by their investment company was a question for courts. It was for a judge, not arbitrator, to provide the ultimate determination on whether Mr. and Mrs. Kaplan were in fact bound to arbitrate by reason of the actions of their investment company, on theories such as agency, alter ego, or lifting the corporate veil.

Although unnecessary to the holding of the case, the Supreme Court went further and suggested that in some situations (although not under the facts of *Kaplan*) "the

---

300. 514 U.S. 938, 943. See generally, William W. PARK, "The Arbitrability Dicta in *First Options v. Kaplan*: What Sort of Kompetenz-Kompetenz Has Crossed the Atlantic?", 12 Arb. Int'l (1996) p. 137, reprinted 11 Int'l Arb. Rep. (Oct. 1996) p. 28; William W. PARK, "Determining Arbitral Jurisdiction: Allocation of Tasks Between Courts and Arbitrators", 8 Am. Rev. Int'l Arb. (1997) p. 133; reprinted in ADR Law J. (March 2000) p. 19. For an academic tourney on some of the issues raised in *First Options*, see Thomas CARBONNEAU, "Comment Upon Professor Park's Analysis of the Dicta in *First Options v. Kaplan*", 11 Int'l Arb. Rep. (November 1996) p. 18; Alan Scott RAU, "Arbitration As Contract: One More Word About *First Options v. Kaplan*", 12 Int'l Arb. Rep. (March 1997) p. 1; Thomas CARBONNEAU, "*Le Tournoi* of Academic Commentary on Kaplan: A Reply to Professor Rau", 12 Int'l Arb. Rep. (April 1997) p. 35. See also, Shirin PHILIPP, "Is the Supreme Court Bucking the Trend? *First Options v. Kaplan* in Light of European Reform Initiatives in Arbitration Law", 14 B.U. Int'l L. J. (1996) p. 119.

301. See *A T & T Technologies v. Communications Workers*, 475 U.S. 643 (1986), discussed infra. See also Alan Scott RAU, *op. cit.*, fn. 74, at p. 464, note 69, suggesting that the *dictum* of *First Options* can be "found fully developed in earlier Supreme Court decisions". Not all observers have noticed such full development.

302. The Supreme Court also dealt with the standard a court of appeals should apply when reviewing a district court decision relating to vacatur or confirmation of an arbitral award under Sect. 10 of the Federal Arbitration Act. The Court held that a district court's findings of fact should be accepted unless "clearly erroneous", but that questions of law should be decided de novo. The Third Circuit agreed with the owners that they were not bound by the arbitration agreement, and therefore had reversed the district court confirmation of the award against them.

arbitrability question itself" might be submitted to arbitration.[303] In such a situation, the courts must defer ("give considerable leeway") to arbitrators' decisions on the limits of their own jurisdiction. However, the burden of showing that a nonsignatory intended to arbitrate remained with the party seeking arbitration.[304]

The *dictum's* critical language (which in some situations may eclipse the holding of the case) reads as follows:

> "If [the parties agreed to submit arbitrability to arbitration] then the court's standard for reviewing the arbitrator's decision about the matter should not differ from the standard courts apply when they review any other matter that the parties have agreed to arbitrate.... That is to say, the court should give considerable leeway to the arbitrator, setting aside his or her decision only in certain narrow circumstances."[305]

Given the longevity of Supreme Court *dictum* in the field of arbitration,[306] its teaching on "the arbitrability question" can be expected to weigh heavily on the future allocation of functions between courts and arbitrators. At the least, the *dictum* now requires judges to ask not only whether arbitrators exceeded their powers, but also whether the arbitrators were given authority to decide a jurisdictional matter in a way deserving deference.[307]

---

303. 514 U.S. 938 (1995).

304. In the United States, given the absence of any federal common law, the bindingness of an arbitration clause would be a matter for state law principles.

305. For the proposition that arbitrability can be submitted to arbitrators, the Court cited to alleged authority in labor arbitration: *A T & T Technologies v. Communications Workers*, 475 U.S. 643, 649 (1986) and *Steelworkers v. Warrior & Gulf Navigation*, 363 U.S. 574, 583, n. 7 (1960). Invocation of these labor cases must be approached with caution. In the United States, the statutory basis for labor arbitration lies in Sect. 301 of the Labor-Management Relations Act of 1947 (commonly called the "Taft-Hartley Act") rather than the Federal Arbitration Act. See *Textile Workers v. Lincoln Mills*, 353 U.S. 448 (1957). Admittedly, the law under the FAA and the LMRA has seen a convergence, with courts routinely citing cases decided under one statute in connection with another. Neither of the two cited cases actually found an agreement to arbitrate the question of arbitrability. In *AT&T Technologies* the Court held that the lower court's decision to allow the arbitrator to decide arbitrability was error. *Warrior & Gulf* said that "it is clear ... in this case [that] the question of arbitrability is for the courts to decide". 363 U.S. 583, n. 7.

306. See, e.g., the Court's obscure pronouncement on arbitrator "manifest disregard" of the law in *Wilko v. Swan*, 346 U.S. 427 (1953), which has continued to be invoked long after the holding in the case was overruled.

307. See, e.g., *PaineWebber v. Elahi*, 87 F. 3d 589 (1st Cir. 1996). For an early expression of scholarly concern over the potential for confusion, see Thomas E. CARBONNEAU, "Beyond the Trilogies: A New Bill of Rights and Law Practice Through the Contract of Arbitration", 6 Am. Rev. Int'l. Arb. (1995) p. 1. See also Thomas E. CARBONNEAU, *Cases and Materials on the Law and Practice of Arbitration*, 3rd edn. (2002) at pp. 20-21

c. Possible applications of the dictum

i. Multiple contexts of "arbitrability"

The *dictum* may in some instances lend itself to mischief if applied by courts seeking to reduce their workload. Situations will certainly exist in which parties might agree to submit a particular question to binding arbitration, even though that question would normally be characterized as jurisdictional. However, awards may still be reviewed for excess of authority under Sect. 10 of the Federal Arbitration Act. At some point in any chain of agreements, a consensual basis must exist for arbitral authority over those questions.

One difficulty with the *dictum* is that the term "arbitrability" can cover so many different matters: whether a person ever agreed to arbitrate at all; the scope of an admittedly valid arbitration clause; and public policy limits on what arbitrators can and cannot decide. Only the second of those issues (scope of the parties' agreement) would normally be capable of delegation to arbitrators in a single agreement. The third category (public policy) would never be capable of delegation.

ii. Existence of arbitration clause

Perhaps the most serious challenge to the *dictum* arises in connection when a respondent in an arbitration asserts that it never agreed to arbitrate, or a respondent in a judicial action claims the benefit of an arbitration clause. Delegation of jurisdictional authority on that question would normally require a separate agreement. A contract clause purporting to give arbitrators power to determine their own authority does not, in itself, insulate from judicial review a decision to add a party that never agreed to arbitrate.[308] The mere narration or recital of the arbitrator's power on a printed form cannot be confused with a genuine grant of authority.

The suggestion that arbitrators can determine their own jurisdiction with respect to the identity of the parties, without a separate agreement submitting that question to arbitration, brings to mind the picture of Baron Münchhausen pulling himself up by his own pigtail. In many cases such a principle will assume the very proposition (arbitral jurisdiction) that remains to be proven. In the absence of an arbitration agreement accepted by the person alleged to be bound with respect to the dispute in question, the person rendering the award would seem better characterized as a vigilante, intermeddler or imposter.

This does not mean that a contract may never be interpreted as giving the arbitrator power to determine whether a particular person agreed to arbitrate at all. Rather, such agreements must be truly distinct from, and chronologically subsequent to, the alleged principal agreement. For example, a buyer might sign a purchase contract with a seller corporation. When a dispute arises, the seller might allege that an arbitration clause in the contract bound not only the seller corporation, but also its parent entity. Or, the

---

308. In some instances, of course, a person who did agree to arbitrate may be required, by the terms of the contract or agreed-upon arbitration rules, to accept joinder of a third party. See LCIA Rule 22.1(h), allowing a willing third party to be joined to a proceeding notwithstanding the objection of one of the existing litigants. In such a case, however, the objecting party has accepted the process for joinder by contracting for application of the LCIA Rules.

seller's parent might claim the benefit of the arbitration clause in attempting to avoid a court action brought against the parent by the seller. The theory might be advanced that the subsidiary had contracted as agent for the parent, or that the parent was the alter ego of the subsidiary.

After a dispute arises, nothing would prevent the parent from agreeing to ask an arbitrator to determine whether it was in fact bound by the arbitration clause. The arbitral tribunal to whose authority the parent has consented under the second agreement would be convened to determine whether the parent bound itself under the first agreement. In such a case, an arbitral tribunal so constituted would do no more than decide the merits of a question of fact and/or law about whether the initial agreement empowered the arbitrator to the extent asserted.[309]

iii. Scope

Questions related to the scope of an arbitration clause lend themselves more easily to application of the "arbitrability question" *dictum*. Depending on the facts and circumstances evidencing the parties' intent, an arbitration agreement might permit arbitrators to decide what controverted questions are covered by the clause, or to interpret the extent of their powers.

Not all contract terms, however, lend themselves to such final interpretation by arbitrators. For instance, courts presumably would not accept an arbitrator's erroneous finding that a contracting party named Alpha Corporation really referred to Omega Limited when the two entities were in fact completely unrelated to one another. An arbitrator's construction of contract terms cannot change the parties' identity.[310]

d. Broad and "open-ended" clauses

In practice, courts often address jurisdictional questions by reference to the nature of the arbitration clause itself. A "broad" arbitration clause will be seen as evidence of an intent to submit many (albeit not all) jurisdictional questions to the arbitrator. Such expansive, widely drafted clauses often talk about "all controversies, disputes and questions" that might be "related to or arising out of" the parties' agreement.[311]

While many contracts do contain such broadly drafted clauses, they are not universal.[312] On occasion, the parties may submit to arbitration only a single narrow

---

309. This is exactly what happened in *Astro Valiente Compania Naviera v. Pakistan Ministry of Food & Agriculture (The Emmanuel Colocotronis No. 2)*, [1982], 1 W.L.R. 1096, 1 All E. R. 578. Buyers of wheat at first refused to arbitrate a dispute with the shipper over demurrage, on the theory that the arbitration clause in the charter party had not been incorporated in the bill of lading which by the charter party's terms was to "supersede" the charter party. The parties submitted to ad hoc arbitration the question of whether the arbitration clause had been incorporated into the bill of lading.

310. See discussion of the Scalia opinion in *Pacificare*.

311. See, e.g., *Fraternity Fund Ltd. v. Beacon Hill Asset Mgt.*, 371 F. Supp. 2d 571 (S.D.N.Y. 2005); *Ryan Beck & Co. v. Fakih*, 268 F. Supp. 2d 210 (E.D.N.Y. 2003).

312. For an example of a narrow clause, see *Bristol-Myers Squibb v. SR International Business Insurance Co. Ltd.*, 354 F. Supp. 2d 499 (S.D.N.Y. 2005), which held that an arbitration clause making reference to "any dispute or difference arising under" the insurance policy did not cover fraud. The insurer sought to rescind policies and the policyholder sought a declaratory judgment that

question of fact, reserving the rest of the dispute to the competent courts.[313] Consequently, scholars, judges and policy-makers must be careful about presuming their own conclusion on what arbitration clauses do and do not cover.

In disputes where challenges to an arbitrator's jurisdiction do *not* implicate the existence of the arbitration clause, intriguing questions arise with respect to broadly drafted clauses that might give arbitrators absolute power to determine their own jurisdiction. Such "open-ended" clauses might cover "all disputes ever arising between the parties" and would not include the typical language requiring that arbitration arise from or be related to a particular contractual relationship. A related problem might derive from a master agreement subject to an arbitration provision, followed by several more limited contracts that do not themselves contain arbitration clauses.

While such open-ended language would reduce the prospect of judicial second-guessing of the arbitrator, the situation would not always be problem-free. Imagine that a university president asks a lawyer to represent his wayward child in litigation arising out of an auto accident. A retainer agreement signed by the president includes an arbitration clause stating that the arbitral tribunal will have power to decide questions relating to its own jurisdiction. After a dispute about the number of hours spent on the accident case is referred to a properly constituted arbitral tribunal, the lawyer (who is also an adjunct member of the university's law faculty) includes in her submission to the arbitrator a claim for a substantial salary increase for the course she teaches. Must a judge defer to an arbitral tribunal's decision to hear the salary claim as well as the retainer disagreement? Normally one would think not, at least if the president was contracting in a personal capacity (as parent) rather than as an academic administrator.

e. Judicial deference toward contract recitals

Even before the US Supreme Court decision in *First Options v. Kaplan*, some American judicial decisions gave evidence of deference to contract recitations which suggested (either explicitly or by reference to arbitration rules) that arbitrators were able to rule

---

the question of fraud was outside the scope of the arbitration. The court felt bound by the earlier precedent of *In Re Kinoshita*, 287 F. 2d 951 (2d Cir. 1961), which while out of step with modern law stilled controlled on narrow facts. For a case distinguishing *Kinoshita* (rightly or wrongly) see *S.A. Mineracao da Trindade-Samitri v. Utah Int'l, Inc.*, 745 F. 2d 190 (2d Cir. 1984) (words "whenever any question or dispute shall arise or occur under" the agreement held broad enough to include claims of fraudulent inducement to contract). Compare *Louis Dreyfus Negoce S.A. v. Blystad Shipping & Trading Inc.*, 252 F. 3d 218, 223 (2d Cir. 2001). *ACE Capital Re Overseas Ltd. v. Central United Life Insurance* Co., 307 F. 3d 24 (2d Cir. 2002).

313. See, e.g., *CIT Project Finance v. Credit Suisse First Boston*, 799 NYS2d 159, 2004 WL 2941331 (2004), holding that arbitrators may not grant attorneys' fees. The court reached this somewhat surprising conclusion notwithstanding Art. 31 of the AAA International Rules, which provides that arbitrators follow the European "loser pays" practice of awarding "reasonable costs for legal representation of a successful party". The court relied on N.Y. CPLR Sect. 7513, permitting an award of attorneys' fees only if provided in the parties' agreement. The arbitration clause at issue gave the arbitrators power only over a specific issue of fact, reserving most of the dispute to courts. By contrast, when the contract contains a broad clause, courts allow arbitrators to address the parties' intent on legal fees. See *PaineWebber v. Bybyk*, 81 F. 3d 1193 (2d Cir. 1996); *Shaw Group v. Triplefine International Corp.*, 322 F. 3d 115 (2nd Cir. 2003); *Stone & Webster v. Triplefine International Corp.*, 118 Fed. Appx. 546 (2d Cir. 2004).

in a final and binding way on their own jurisdiction.[314] One problematic example can be seen in the decision by the Court of Appeals in *Apollo Computer v. Berg*.[315]

A contract between a Massachusetts computer company and a Swedish distributor was terminated and the rights of the bankrupt Swedish distributor were assigned to a third party. The Massachusetts company claimed that the non-assignment clause in the contract covered the arbitration clause itself, which became void as a consequence of the assignment.

The court held that the arbitrators' jurisdiction over the claims was a question for arbitrators themselves to decide. The arbitral tribunal was appointed pursuant to the Arbitration Rules of the International Chamber of Commerce, which calls for the ICC to refer to the arbitrators any objections to the validity of an arbitration agreement, as long as the ICC is prima facie satisfied that an arbitration agreement may exist.[316] On this basis the American court reasoned that the parties had agreed to submit the arbitrability question to the arbitrators.

On closer examination the reasoning in *Apollo* might reveal itself as an exercise in presuming a conclusion. The problem is not that the parties lacked the power, as a matter of contract law, to submit the jurisdictional question to arbitration. Rather, it is simply not certain that they actually did so.

If a full examination of the facts reveals that the arbitration agreement was in fact automatically terminated by the assignment, then ICC Arbitration Rules become relevant. This would be relatively evident had the arbitration clause contained a proviso, typed in large bold letters, to the effect that "The Arbitration clause is void after assignment." In such circumstances, it is hard to imagine that any arbitrators could accord themselves jurisdiction in a final and binding way. A similar result would seem to obtain if the parties' had evidenced their intent through selection of an applicable law that yielded the same result.

A better approach might have been simply to make a finding about the effect of the assignment under Massachusetts law, which seemed to provide that a general non-assignment clause bars the delegation of duties, but not the assignment of rights, including the right to arbitrate. Indeed, such was the approach of the federal district court in this case.[317] For better or for worse, the Court of Appeals refused to address the issue, instead resting its decision on the principle that the effect of the assignment was a question for the arbitrators.

---

314. Instances in labor arbitration have already been mentioned. See *AT&T Technologies v. Communications Workers*, 475 U.S. 643 (1986), discussed infra.

315. 886 F. 2d 469 (1st Cir. 1989), at 473. See also sequel to *Apollo* in *Hewlett Packard, Inc. v. Berg*, 61 F. 3d 101 (1st Cir. 1995), vacating a confirmation order and remanding for further proceedings the award confirmed in 867 F. Supp. 1126 (D. Mass. 1994). Similar questions were discussed in *S.G.S. v. Raytheon*, 643 F. 2d. 863 (1st Cir. 1981).

316. ICC Rules, Art. 6(2) (1998 version). At the time, the applicable rule was found in Art. 8, and referred to the "*prima facie* existence" of the arbitration agreement, rather than the ICC Court being prima facie satisfied.

317. 886 F. 2d at 407. For a general discussion of the assignment of rights under UNIDROIT principles, see Wolfgang WIEGANT and Corinne ZELLWEGER-GUTKNECHT, "Assignment", in UNIDROIT Principles: New Developments and Applications (ICC Bulletin, Court of Arbitration, 2005 Special Supplement) p. 27.

For a private arbitral institution like the International Chamber of Commerce to leave the difficult issues to the arbitrator may be acceptable as an efficiency device if national courts later exercise a fuller control over the clause's validity.[318] However, the aggregate social and economic consequences of such a prima facie approach are likely to be less acceptable when a judge imposes state power to enforce an arbitral award without an independent examination of the authenticity and scope of the alleged arbitration agreement. The result may well be a loss of confidence by the business community in both the arbitral system and the judiciary that enforces arbitration agreements and awards.

f. *Amplifying First Options in subsequent case law*
Recent decisions of the US Supreme Court provide a perspective on how American jurisdictional methodology plays itself out in practice. The following two cases, *Howsam* and *Bazzle*, address which threshold preconditions for arbitration are to be determined by judges and which are for arbitrators.[319]

1. Time limits
Securities arbitration has been a particularly fruitful ground for jurisdictional conflict with respect to time limits. The investor generally tells of a "nest egg" lost due to a financial adviser's misconduct, with golden retirement years turned into a financially harsh old age due to unsuitable investments. The adviser, of course, replies that the customer was well aware of the risks and pushed hard for aggressive growth stocks.[320]

The reason time-bars are so frequently invoked in brokerage disputes is that the investor is a bit like a casino gambler: happy when winning, but likely to complain in the event of a loss.[321] If stock rises in value, there would be no loss and thus no grumbling that the investment advice was "unsuitable". Only when things later go sour will the

---

318. Even for arbitral institutions, however, this approach may not be free from problems. An arbitration agreement with a forged signature, or a real signature forced by a gun at the head, ought to be no less a complete nullity because it gives the appearance of being valid.

319. See generally William W. PARK, "The Contours of Arbitral Jurisdiction: Who Decides What?", 3 Int'l Arb. News (ABA, Summer 2003) p. 2, reprinted in 18 Int'l Arb. Rep. (August 2003) p. 21. A third Supreme Court opinion in *Pacificare Health Systems v. Book* is often discussed in connection with *Howsam* and *Bazzle*. In a puzzling footnote the Court stated that the question at issue was "*not* a question of arbitrability". 538 U.S. 407 at n. 2. (Emphasis added.) In light of its somewhat different rationale (courts wait to see how the arbitrators will decide) *Pacificare* has been discussed earlier, along with *Lesotho Highlands*, in relation to the impact of contract interpretation on arbitral jurisdiction.

320. The so-called "Seven Deadly Sins" of securities transactions are hardly as exciting as the classic offenses: lust, gluttony, sloth, anger, envy, pride and greed – although the last of these often plays a role in broker misbehavior. The catalogue of common transgressions includes (i) churning, (ii) unauthorized trading, (iii) unsuitable trading, (iv) intentional misrepresentation, (v) broker ignorance, (vi) misappropriation and (vii) outside business activities of the employee relating to investment marketing that is attributed to the employer. See David E. ROBBINS, "Seven Deadly Sins that Lead to Arbitration Disaster", 820 PLI/Corp, Practising Law Institute, Corporate Law and Practice Course Handbook Series (July-August 1993) p. 489.

321. While the investment in *Howsam* had occurred sometime between the account opening in 1986 and its closing in 1994, the arbitration was begun only in 1997.

broker be accused of misbehavior, even though the purchase of securities might be many years in the past.[322]

For decades, the question of what jurisdictional determinations could be made by an arbitrator was moot, since the basic distrust of arbitrators (the foxes who would guard the chicken coop) generally meant there was no arbitration of securities transactions. Except in international cases,[323] courts traditionally refused to enforce arbitration clauses that implicated either the 1933 Securities Act or the 1934 Securities Exchange Act.[324] Interpreting these two pieces of legislation was considered too important for the private sector. Therefore, since most investment portfolios contain stocks and bonds, accusations of misfeasance by financial advisers generally ended up in court.

In 1989 the situation changed due to liberalization of limits on subject matter arbitrability by the US Supreme Court.[325] In part the attitude shift may have been due to the SEC playing a more active role in supervising the self-regulatory organizations (such as the National Association of Securities Dealers (NASD)), under whose auspices securities arbitration proceeded. And in part the change in attitude might have been related to the perceived need to relieve congestion in judicial dockets.

In any event, the result was a wholesale adoption of arbitration by the securities industry to a point where many securities law questions are no longer addressed by courts at all. Much of the law has thus been frozen during the past dozen years, with few judicial precedents to fertilize legal development.

In *Howsam v. Dean Witter*[326] the drama played itself out through an investment in limited partnerships whose performance proved unsatisfactory, causing the investor to allege broker misrepresentation of the investment's quality. The brokerage firm then filed suit in federal court requesting an injunction against the arbitration on the ground that the original investment advice was more than six years old, and thus barred by the NASD "eligibility rule" requiring that any claim be brought within six years of the relevant occurrence.[327] The Supreme Court gave the arbitrators a green light to determine whether their power to hear the case was affected by time limits contained in the arbitration rules.

---

322. One recalls the vignette from the 1942 movie *Casablanca*, starring Humphrey Bogart and Ingrid Bergman. The French police captain, played by Claude Rains, closed down Rick's Café because he was "shocked" to find gambling going on – all the while being quite happy to take his winnings.

323. See *Scherk v. Alberto-Culver Co.*, 417 U.S. 506 (1974) (securities disputes arbitrable in a German-American contract at a time when prohibited in a domestic contract).

324. See *Wilko v. Swan*, 346 U.S. 427 (1953), overruled in *Shearson/American Express v. McMahon*, 482 U.S. 220 (1987) (fraud claims under Exchange Act Sect.10b). Ironically, *Wilko* has lived on in its *dictum* which posited "manifest disregard of the law" as an extra-statutory ground for judicial review.

325. See *Rodriguez de Quijas v. Shearson/American Express*, 490 U.S. 477 (1989), concerning Securities Act Sect.12(2) claims.

326. 537 U.S. 79 (2002). The unanimous decision was written by Justice Breyer. A concurrence by Justice Thomas rested solely on the basis that New York law (applicable to the contract in question) had held that time-bars under the NASD Rules are for arbitrators to decide.

327. NASD Code of Arbitration Sect. 10304 (formerly Rule 15), states that no dispute "shall be eligible for submission to arbitration ...where six (6) years have elapsed from the occurrence or event giving rise to the ... dispute".

Resolving a split among the circuits over who (judge or arbitrator) decides on "eligibility" requirements, the US Supreme Court in *Howsam* held that time limits were for the arbitrator. An opinion by Breyer paid lip service to the principle that judges would normally decide gateway jurisdictional matters unless the parties clearly provided otherwise. However, the Court presumed (rightly or wrongly) the parties' intent that the NASD Rules be construed by the arbitrators themselves, who were supposed to possess (according to the Court) special familiarity and expertise in interpreting these rules.[328]

ii.   Class actions

A plurality of the Court followed a similar line of reasoning in *Green Tree Financial Corp v. Bazzle*,[329] which involved an attempt at class action arbitration of disputes arising from consumer loans used to purchase mobile homes and finance residential improvements.[330] Once again, the Supreme Court punted the question to the arbitrator himself.[331]

In violation of South Carolina's Consumer Protection Code, the lender allegedly neglected to give borrowers notice about the right to name their own lawyers and insurance agents. Two groups of borrowers filed separate suits in the South Carolina state courts seeking class certification of their claims against the lender. The first court certified the class and compelled class arbitration pursuant to the loan agreement's arbitration clause. The second court initially denied the lender's motion to compel arbitration, but was reversed and the case proceeded to arbitration before the same arbitrator.

After the arbitrator awarded the two classes $10.9 million and $9.2 million (respectively) plus attorney's fees, the South Carolina Supreme Court consolidated the lender's appeals and ruled that the relevant loan contracts permitted class actions in

---

328. The court also noted that Sect. 10324 of the NASD Rules (formerly Rule 35) gave arbitrators power to "interpret and determine the applicability of all provisions under the [NASD] Code". For other cases on time limits, see *MCI Telecommunications Corp. v. Exalon Industries, Inc.*, 138 F. 3d 426 (1st Cir. 1998) (time limits for challenging award do not apply when existence of an arbitration agreement is challenged). But *contra* see *MBNA America Bank v. Hart*, 710 N.W.2d 125 (N.D. 2006); *MBNA America Bank v. Swartz*, 2006 WL 1071523 (Del. Ch) (time-bar for challenging clause).

329. 539 U.S. 444 (2003). The interesting plurality decision split 4-1-3-1. Four Justices concluded that it was for the arbitrator to decide whether the contracts allowed class action arbitration. One concurred in the judgment although he would have preferred to affirm the South Carolina decision that ordered arbitration to proceed as a class action. Three Justices dissented on the basis that any imposition of class-wide arbitration contravened the parties' contract, and one dissented on the ground that the FAA should not apply in state courts.

330. In federal court, class actions would be permitted under FRCP Rule 23. Several arbitral institutions (including the American Arbitration Association) have established rules for class action arbitration patterned on these provisions.

331. Commentary on this case includes Hans SMIT, "Class Actions and Their Waiver in Arbitration", 15 Am. Rev. Int'l Arb. (2004) p. 199; Bernard HANOTIAU, "A New Development in Complex Multiparty-Multicontract Proceedings: Classwide Arbitration", 20 Arb. Int'l (2004) p. 39.

arbitration.[332] The US Supreme Court granted certiorari to determine whether the state court holding was consistent with the Federal Arbitration Act. The plurality opinion by Justice Breyer announced that the permissibility of class action arbitration was a matter of contract interpretation for the arbitrator, not the courts. For Justice Breyer and his plurality, the question was "what kind of arbitration proceeding [had] the parties agreed to?" If the contract is silent, the question was for the arbitrator, they said.[333] The state court decision was vacated and remanded for further consideration.[334]

It is of course possible that litigants might agree to give an arbitrator broad power to determine whether an arbitration clause includes the possibility of class action, as suggested by the Breyer opinion in *Bazzle*. However, such a conclusion is by no means obvious from the language of the relevant contracts, each of which was accepted by an individual borrower and provided for an arbitrator to be selected for all disputes arising from "this contract" – a reference to the singular, not plural. In commercial arbitration, the normal presumption has always been that parties agree to arbitrate with particular claimants or respondents, not with the whole world. Prior to *Bazzle*, the FAA did not authorize forced joinder of different arbitrations arising out of related claims[335] except as agreed by the parties[336] or when conducted pursuant to a statute that explicitly so provides.[337]

---

332. The South Carolina Supreme Court had determined that the loan contracts were silent in respect of class action. By contrast, on the US Supreme Court the dissenting opinion by Justice Rehnquist found that the contracts forbid class arbitration, while the opinion by Justice Breyer delivered for the Court essentially ducked the issue and held that it was for the arbitrator to determine whether the contract allowed class arbitration.

333. With respect to the implications of silence, one is reminded of the playful comparisons of European legal systems. In Germany, all which is not permitted is forbidden. In France, all which is not forbidden is permitted. To which some add that in Italy all which is forbidden is also permitted.

334. A dissent by Chief Justice Rehnquist (joined by Justices O'Connor and Kennedy) argued that any imposition of class-wide arbitration contravened the parties' contract as a matter of law. Justice Thomas dissented on the ground that the Federal Arbitration Act should not apply in state courts. Justice Stevens concurred in the judgment but dissented from its reasoning. Believing that the state court was correct as a matter of law that class action arbitration was permitted, Stevens would have affirmed the South Carolina decision. However, to avoid the absence of any controlling majority (only three out of nine Justices agreed with Rehnquist) Stevens concurred with Breyer in the judgment.

335. See *Government of U.K. v. Boeing Co.*, 998 F. 2d 68 (2nd Cir. 1993) (denying consolidation of arbitrations with Boeing and Textron, Inc. relating to contract with the British Ministry of Defense to develop an electronic fuel system).

336. As between the same parties, Art. 4(6) of the ICC Rules permits the Court to join claims until the signing of the Terms of Reference. Thereafter, addition of any new claim must be authorized by the arbitral tribunal. Compare Art. 22(h) of the Arbitration Rules of the London Court of International Arbitration, permitting the arbitral tribunal to allow third persons to be joined in an arbitration provided the third person has consented in writing to joinder.

337. For example, Massachusetts Gen. Laws, c. 251, Sect. 2A, calls for consolidation as provided in the Massachusetts Rules of Civil Procedure, which in Rule 42 permits joinder of actions "involving a common question of law or fact". *New England Energy, Inc. v. Keystone Shipping Co.*, 855 F. 2d 1 (1st Cir. 1988) has held that a federal court sitting in Massachusetts may order consolidation of related arbitrations pursuant to state statute Compare California Code of Civil

In passing, one might ask to what extent the result in *Bazzle* was influenced by the somewhat unusual language in the arbitration clause. Arbitration was to resolve not only contract-related disputes, claims or controversies, but also controversies arising from or relating to "the relationships that result from this contract".

In one post-*Bazzle* case (on appeal as of this writing), a federal district court vacated an arbitral award that had interpreted a maritime transport contract to include a class action stipulation.[338] In finding "manifest disregard of the law" the court stressed both the maritime nature of the contracts (as to which expert testimony established a clear presumption against class actions) and the principle of New York law that when contracts are silent on an issue no agreement has been reached.[339]

As to the parties' intent, the court might well have reached the right result. Given the long tradition of non-consolidation for international maritime arbitration, something quite special would be needed to justify a determination that the litigants granted the arbitrators authority to create a class action process.[340]

Even if the court might have been correct on contract interpretation, it is by no means certain that the arbitrators' mistake (if it was one) could be characterized as "manifest disregard" of law. The job of interpreting the parties' intent falls to the arbitrators. This task, which implicates mixed questions of fact and law, as well as evaluation of industry custom and practice, has always been entrusted to the arbitrators.[341]

A new twist was added by a Court of Appeals decision arising from customer disputes with a cable television provider. *Kristian v. Comcast Corp.*[342] held that a ban on class actions would invalidate the arbitration agreement,[343] but for the possibility of severing the class action prohibition. In an action for antitrust violations under both state and federal law, the court applied a consumer protection rationale to conclude that the validity of the ban on arbitrability of the class action should be decided by courts rather than arbitrators. The court allowed the arbitration to proceed only after striking down and severing this prohibition.

Procedure, Sect. 1281.3.

338. *Stolt-Nielsen S.A. v. Animalfeeds Int'l Corp.*, 435 F. Supp. 2d 383 (S.D.N.Y. 2006).

339. *Ibid.* 387.

340. In some instances (not applicable in *Animalfeeds*) a state statute might provide otherwise. See *New England Energy v. Keystone Shipping Co.*, 855 F.2d 1 (1st Cir. 1988), applying Massachusetts law. On the law concerning consolidation before *Bazzle*, see *United Kingdom v. Boeing*, 998 F.2d 68 (1993), discussed supra.

341. Perhaps the court believed the arbitrators to have concluded that *Bazzle* dictated an interpretation of the contract which favored class arbitration. While this would indeed be a misreading of *Bazzle*, it seems more than unlikely that this particular panel (Gerald Aksen, Kenneth Feinberg and William Jentes) could have made that mistake. The court itself seems to have misstated *Bazzle*, suggesting that the interpretation of the agreement was for the arbitrator only "in the first instance" rather than as a final matter. *Ibid.*, at 384.

342. 2006 WL 1028758 (1st Cir. 2006). See also *Discover Bank v. Superior Court*, 113 P. 3d 1100 (2005), declaring a class action waiver to be unconscionable and *Strand v. U.S. Bank N.A.*, 693 N.W.2d 918 (N.D. 2005), upholding such waivers.

343. The arbitration clause itself provided (in bold face capitals!) that "there shall be no right or authority for any claims to be arbitrated on a class action or consolidated basis".

g.   Consumer transactions

i.   Legal framework: Justice Astbury's ghost

Unlike most of Europe, the United States provides no statutory scheme of general application to protect the interests of ill-informed consumers and employees who may be dispatched by an arbitration clause to seek uncertain remedies at inaccessible locations. For the past eighty years, a venerable but antiquated federal arbitration statute has stubbornly resisted distinctions between business and consumer arbitration, and has pre-empted state law that tried to protect the so-called little guy.

This does not mean, however, that courts cannot reach the same result (protecting consumer against abusive clauses) through ordinary contract principles. On a case-by-case basis, doctrines such as "unconscionability", "excessive cost" and "mutuality of remedy" have been pressed into service to safeguard the interests of weaker parties to adhesion contracts.[344] Indeed, in one Alabama case the court found a loan agreement's *Kompetenz-Kompetenz* clause in itself to indicate unconscionability.[345]

To a large extent, this American exceptionalism finds its roots in yet another national idiosyncrasy: the role of the civil jury in deciding contract claims, often beginning with a bias in favor of the consumer or employee (the proverbial "little guy") against the manufacturers and employers. Concerned about the lack of rationality in jury verdicts, the business community sees arbitration as a more reasonable alternative to court litigation. This legal oddity has given to arbitration law in the United States an evolutionary path distinct from that of most of its trading partners.

Resistance to reform has come largely from arbitration's institutional establishment, which (perhaps understandably) perceives itself as providing a bulwark of adjudicatory evenhandedness. The fear is often expressed that any move toward a more modern arbitration law might open a Pandora's Box of upheaval, led by an unholy alliance of consumer advocates and plaintiffs' lawyers who see arbitration as a scam to protect crooked finance companies and abusive bosses.[346]

The institutional establishment's opposition to change brings to mind remarks

---

344. See, e.g., *Kloss v. Jones* (discussed infra); *Circuit City Stores, Inc. v. Adams*, 279 F. 3d 889, 891-892 (9th Cir. 2002) (limitation of damages and unilateral nature of the clause found unconscionable). See also *Ting v. AT&T*, 182 F. Supp. 2d 902, 927-936 (N.D. Cal. 2002). For a view questioning mainline consumer protectionist thought, see Stephen J. WARE, "The Case for Enforcing Adhesive Arbitration Agreements – With Particular Consideration of Class Actions and Arbitration Fees", 5 J. Am. Arb. (2006) p. 251. For a contrasting view, see Jean R. STERNLIGHT, "The Rise and Spread of Mandatory Arbitration as a Substitute for the Jury Trial", 38 U. San Francisco L. Rev. (2003) p. 17. See generally, Edward BRUNET, Richard SPEIDEL, Jean STERNLIGHT and Stephen WARE, *Arbitration Law in America: A Critical Assessment* (2006) Ch. 5 (Consumer Arbitration).

345. *American General Finance v. Branch*, 793 So. 2d 738 (2001). The in question provided, "Borrower and Lender further agree that all issues and disputes as to the arbitrability of claims must b of Such authority of the arbitrator to determine its [sic] own authority may also be resolved by the arbitrator". *Ibid.*, p. 741. Other indicia of unconscionability included the breadth of the arbitration clause (applicable to every dispute or controversy) and the lender's exemption from arbitration in certain cases.

346. See, e.g., John M. TOWNSED, "The Federal Arbitration Act is Too Important to Amend", 4 Int'l Arb. News (ABA, Summer 2004) p. 19.

attributed to Sir John Astbury, the English judge who declared the 1926 British General Strike to be illegal. As mobs took to the streets and workers rioted throughout Britain, some political leaders talked of conciliation and change. To which Astbury reportedly replied, "Reform? Reform? Are things not bad enough already?"[347]

ii.   Jurisdiction in credit and securities operations

For better or for worse, the absence of any federal consumer protection regime for arbitration has engendered reactions at the state level. Two cases merit special attention, each one relating to a financial transaction in which the arbitration clause played a role in a scheme to take advantage of a relatively unsophisticated party.

One of the most creative efforts to protect weaker parties came out of Montana, which in *Kloss v. Jones*[348] attempted to impose public policy limits on the entirety of an arbitrator's jurisdiction. In refusing to compel arbitration against a financial adviser accused of negligence and breach of fiduciary duty, the Montana Supreme Court held the arbitration clause to be an impermissible attempt to waive basic rights guaranteed by the Montana constitution.

Kloss bears out the adage that "hard facts can make difficult law" – or at least problematic rules. After a ninety-five-year-old widow had been persuaded by her investment adviser to create a trust, the adviser proceeded to fund the trust by selling assets from her personal brokerage account. When the widow's nephew learned of the sell-off, he helped her begin litigation against the adviser for fraud, breach of fiduciary duty and deceptive business practices. The adviser invoked the arbitration clauses contained in the account-opening documents, likely fearing a less than sympathetic hearing before a jury.

The Montana Supreme Court found that the arbitration clause involved a waiver of rights guaranteed by the Montana Constitution: access to courts and trial by jury. The arbitration clause, contained in a contract of adhesion, had purported to waive these "sacred" and "inviolable" rights.[349] This waiver was not within the weaker party's "reasonable expectation" and thus was held to be unenforceable.

This avenue of attack is significant. The state court addressed waiver of constitutional rights in general, rather than saying that an arbitration clause was *per se* unconscionable, thus running less risk of conflict with the Federal Arbitration Act (FAA). While the FAA implements a policy favorable to arbitration, it contains a significant (albeit unintended) escape hatch by providing that arbitration clauses are enforceable except "on such grounds as exist at law or in equity for the revocation of any contract".[350] Since the

---

347. Attributed to Mr. Justice Astbury (1860-1939), who sat on the Chancery Bench from 1913 to 1929, and was elevated to the Privy Council in 1929.

348. 310 Mont. 123, 54 P.3d 1 (2002), on reh'g 57 P.3d 41, cert. denied, 538 U.S. 956 (2003). For a rather harsh critique of *Kloss*, see Carroll E. NEESEMANN, "Montana Court Continues its Hostility to Mandatory Arbitration", ABA Dispute Resolution J. (February/April 2003) p. 22, suggesting that the decision "makes the failure to read a provision (any provision, not just an arbitration clause) in an adhesion contract a complete defense to enforceability". Of course, in fact the Montana decision did not refer to "any provision" but concerned only waiver of constitutional rights not within the weaker party's "reasonable expectation".

349. *Ibid.*, Special Concurrence by Nelson, at paragraph 55.

350. 9 U.S.C. Sect. 2.

United States has no general federal law of contracts,[351] one must look to state law for the basic common law grounds for contract revocability.

Some states have attempted to push revocability beyond classic common law defenses such as fraud and duress, and occasionally impose special grounds for revocability of arbitration clauses, usually within the context of consumer or employee protection legislation. Such legislation has been held invalid, however, to the extent the state targets arbitration for special burdens that would defeat the policy of the FAA.[352] In other words, a state might say that all contracts must be in capital letters, but could not say that only arbitration clauses must be in capital letters.[353]

Here we return to our nonagenarian widow in Montana. When the court in *Kloss v. Jones* struck down the arbitration clause, it did not single out arbitration itself for attack. Rather the court applied principles of law "generally applicable to all contracts" in order to protect citizens against waiver of constitutional rights. Arguably, therefore, the refusal to enforce the arbitration clause did not run afoul of federal arbitration policy.

Kloss serves as a reminder that an arbitrator's power to address jurisdictional matters will be limited by public policy, which can always circumscribe the type of disputes that may be sent to arbitration.

A much less digestible decision recently came out of Kansas. Although the state Supreme Court had its heart in the right place (if courts have hearts anywhere), the reasoning remains highly problematic as a guide for the adjudication of future cases.

In *MBNA America Bank v. Credit*,[354] the court vacated an arbitration award used to collect on a credit card debt of one Ms. Loretta K. Credit. The bank had been unable to produce an arbitration agreement, and reason existed to suspect that the arbitration service provider might have been showing a systematic sympathy to financial institutions inconsistent with the impartiality one expects of arbitral institutions.

To reach its decision, the court need only have noted that the bank had provided no evidence of an agreement to arbitrate. Unfortunately, however, the court added dictum

---

351. Sixty-five years ago in *Erie R.R. v. Tompkins*, 304 U.S. 64 (1938), the US Supreme Court (attempting to prevent forum shopping between state and federal fora) stated, "Except in matters governed by the Federal Constitution or by acts of Congress, the law to be applied in any case is the law of the state." *Ibid.* at p. 78.

352. For example, at one point Montana passed a law stating that an arbitration clause was revocable unless in capital letters and underlined. See *Doctor's Associates v. Casarotto*, 517 U.S. 681 (1996). Massachusetts also attempted (unsuccessfullly) a similar restriction on securities arbitration. See *Securities Industry Assoc. v. Connolly*, 883 F. 2d 1114 (1st Cir. 1989). For other attempts to rationalize the role of state arbitration law, see *Mastrobuono v. Shearson Lehman Hutton*, 514 U.S. 52 (1995); *Allied-Bruce v. Dobson*, 513 U.S. 265 (1995); *Volt v. Stanford*, 489 U.S. 468 (1989).

353. The US Congress, however, can and has passed legislation limiting arbitration on behalf of special interest groups. See Motor Vehicle Franchise Contract Act, Sect. 11028, Pub. L. No. 107-273, 116 Stat. 1758 (enacted as 15 U.S.C. Sect. 1226), sometimes known as the Bono Bill in recognition of its original sponsor the late Sonny Bono.

354. 281 Kan. 655 (2006), 132 P.3d 898 (2006). To avoid reader confusion, it should be mentioned that "Credit" was the name of the individual borrower. See generally Christopher DRAHOZAL, "Jurisdiction of Arbitrators to Decide Their Own Jurisdiction", 17 World Arb. & Med. Rep. (September 2006) p. 296.

stating, "When the existence of the [arbitration] agreement is challenged, the issue must be settled by a court before the arbitrator may proceed." The assertion has no foundation in logic, policy or law.[355]

While it would have been outrageous for the bank to have the award confirmed without producing the arbitration clause, a court can always address this matter at the award-enforcement stage. Or, the question could be raised earlier, in the context of a motion to compel arbitration (by the bank) or to stay court proceedings (by the borrower). However, to require an arbitration to stop merely because arbitral jurisdiction has been challenged departs from the very fundamentals of sound arbitration law and practice.

h. The next step

Where these cases leave us for the future is not entirely certain. The decisions in *Howsam* and *Bazzle* (like the decision in *Pacificare* discussed earlier) are plausible. However, the presumptions about the parties' intent may not be self-evident. If a case is not eligible for arbitration later than six years following the broker's misbehavior, can one even speak of an "arbitrator" for an arbitration begun in the seventh year? If a contract prohibits arbitrators from awarding the two-thirds part of treble damages that most people consider punitive, can arbitrators give themselves this power merely by saying that these damages are really compensatory? If an agreement to arbitrate is intended to provide bilateral dispute resolution, can an arbitrator turn the proceedings into a multilateral process? Do the cases presume their own conclusions and imply that arbitrators can create authority simply by defining contract terms that accord with the desired scope of arbitral power?

The heart of the jurisdictional dilemma is that language, while often ambiguous, is not infinitely plastic. Some contract terms with a jurisdictional significance may well fall within the spectrum of matters the parties intended the arbitrator to interpret. Others, however, do not. Much depends on the precise context of the jurisdictional issues, which are increasingly (and unfortunately) called "arbitrability questions" in many decisions.[356]

To illustrate, the Second Circuit has held that an ICC arbitrator may address claims for costs incurred in a court action allegedly brought in breach of an arbitration clause.[357]

---

355. Had the court purported to apply a Kansas statute, the matter might have been less serious. The Federal Arbitration Act, however, provided the applicable procedural law.

356. American courts often use "arbitrability" interchangeably with "jurisdiction". This is regrettable, since it blurs useful distinctions between an arbitrator who may not hear a case because of the parties' drafting choice, and an arbitrator lacking power because non-waivable legal norms prohibit him to consider the disputed subject matter. It is true that when arbitrators lack jurisdiction, a dispute is not arbitrable. However, the term would be better reserved to instances where the subject matter of a dispute has been declared off limits by the relevant legal system. In this sense, antitrust and securities disputes were traditionally non-arbitrable in the United States, and employment and consumer controversies remain non-arbitrable in many parts of Europe, at least under pre-dispute arbitration agreements.

357. *Shaw Group v. Triplefine International Corp.*, 322 F. 3d 115 (2d Cir. 2003); *Stone & Webster v. Triplefine International Corp.*, 118 Fed. Appx. 546 (2d Cir. 2004). The arbitration clause at issue covered disputes "concerning or arising out of [the parties'] Agreement".

This is hardly remarkable. In reaching the conclusion that the parties bargained to arbitrate "questions of arbitrability",[358] the court simply noted that the parties had signed a broad arbitration clause, which would be given effect under the ICC Rules.[359]

Let us change the facts a bit, however, and return to our earlier scenario about the constitution of the arbitral tribunal by an improper appointing authority. Imagine that a contract provides for arbitration under the rules of the American Arbitration Association, but the claimant files its request for arbitration with the International Chamber of Commerce, which it perceives as likely to appoint an arbitrator predisposed to claimant's case. It is difficult to see how an ICC arbitrator could render a final and binding award, absent modification of the parties' agreement.[360]

Or, to invoke another example, let us envisage two merchants who agree to arbitrate disputes arising out of the sale of fruit. The arbitrators might rule on whether "fruit" was used in the botanical sense (the contents of any developed seed plant ovary) to include pecans as well as apples.[361] However, it is not at all evident that a court, when asked to enforce an award or compel arbitration, should accept an arbitrator's determination that "fruit" includes typewriters.

The matter would not be so serious if the arbitrators' jurisdictional decision was only preliminary, subject to a clearly understood right of post-award judicial review. Unfortunately, the recent Supreme Court decisions on arbitration do not make clear (at least to this author) that a second look by the judiciary is in all events guaranteed.

Much of the work in allocating tasks between courts and arbitrators will turn on characterization of the analytic task. One formulation might ask, "May persons who call themselves arbitrators determine their jurisdiction free from judicial review?" An affirmative answer would be conceptually problematic, implying that a piece of paper labeled "award" could be enforced without regard to the legitimate mission of the alleged arbitrator.

An alternate phraseology could pose the jurisdictional question differently: "By agreeing to arbitrate, did the parties intend to waive their right to have courts determine

---

358. *Ibid.* At 125.

359. In light of the Court's citation to Art. 6(2) of the ICC Rules, there may have been some confusion in the court about the difference between the ICC Court and the arbitrators themselves. The former has power only to make preliminary (prima facie) determinations of jurisdiction, while the in-depth decisions are reserved for the arbitrator.

360. The hypothetical is presented only by way of illustration, the author being well aware that the ICC's excellent personnel and efficient internal controls would make such an attempt at fraud highly unlikely.

361. In this connection, one remembers a late 19th century customs case in which the US Supreme Court held that in common parlance tomatoes were vegetables rather than fruit, and thus not free of import duty under a free list for "fruits", but taxed at 10 percent ad valorem under a tariff on "vegetables". See *Nix v. Hedden*, 149 U.S. 304 (1893). Justice Gray noted that "botanically speaking tomatoes are the fruit of a vine, just as are cucumbers, squashes, beans and peas". However, in a breathtaking culinary excursion that makes one hungry just to read it, he continued that "in the common language of the people, whether sellers or consumers of provisions, all these are vegetables which are grown in kitchen gardens and which, whether eaten cooked or raw, are, like potatoes, carrots, parsnips, turnips, beets, cauliflower, cabbage, celery and lettuce, usually served at dinner in, with or after the soup, fish, or meats which constitute the principal part of the repast, and not, like fruits generally, as dessert". *Ibid.*

a particular jurisdictional precondition to arbitration (such as time-bars) or a particular substantive question (such as liability for costs of litigation begun in breach of the arbitration agreement)?" Answering the latter question would require a factual inquiry into the parties' true intent. In some instances the consent may reveal itself only through an explicit agreement. In other circumstances, presumptions and inferences might suffice. On this matter, considerable analytical toil remains.

VI.   CONCLUSION: COSTS AND BENEFITS

The principle known as *Kompetenz-Kompetenz* addresses a very narrow issue, albeit one of critical importance. The question is not whether the arbitrator possesses authority to decide the merits of a particular matter, but *who* (judge or arbitrator) gets to answer that preliminary question.

Most legal systems seem to accept that arbitrators may rule on their own jurisdiction and continue the proceedings, provided no court of competent jurisdiction tells them to stop. Far less consensus exists on the effect that an arbitrator's jurisdictional ruling will have in court, when judges can be asked to vacate an award, to enjoin an arbitral proceeding or to hear a case notwithstanding an allegedly valid arbitration clause. For example, judges might be asked to vacate an award, or to declare an arbitration clause invalid before proceedings begin.

The various ways that different countries address the matter contain their own relative costs and benefits. In all events, two issues lie in most challenges to an arbitrator's jurisdiction: (i) the timing of judicial intervention to address questions related to arbitral jurisdiction; and (ii) the effect of any jurisdictional rulings that arbitrators might make.

The first inquiry concerns the moment for the judicial consideration of jurisdictional questions. Some point (or points) must be fixed in the arbitral process for courts to entertain motions concerning arbitral authority, with a view to preventing or to correcting an excess of jurisdiction. The second question relates to whether courts should ever defer, and if so in what circumstances, to arbitral determinations related to matters and parties subjected to arbitration. The analysis is one of contract, with a focus on the basics of party intent.

On the matter of timing, there is much to commend the French rule, which leaves most judicial intervention until after the award, when the arbitrator's decision is known. The "delayed review" principle limits opportunities for dilatory measures that might derail or sabotage an arbitration. Moreover, postponing jurisdictional motions may preserve judicial resources. Judges need not get involved if the case is settled or decided in a way acceptable to both sides. If the case does not settle, judges may receive the benefit of an arbitrator's discussion and findings on the jurisdictional questions, particularly for international cases where reasoned awards remain the norm.

The French rule has its cost, however. A person who never agreed to arbitrate may need to hedge bets by taking part in a bogus arbitration, at substantial cost of time and money. Herein lies the proverbial fly in the Gallic ointment: innocent respondents must wait until the end of proceedings to challenge even the most obvious jurisdictional defects.

While frivolous attacks on arbitral authority are sometimes used as a delaying tactic, unwarranted arbitrations also pose their own risk. Believing its chances better in arbitration than in court, a claimant playing hard ball might bring an arbitral proceeding with weak jurisdictional foundation, hoping for an easy win that will exert undue settlement pressure.

Out of fairness, a rapid and summary mechanism should exist to permit courts to halt proceedings when the arbitration clause is manifestly void or clearly against public policy.[362] Without some evidence of a valid arbitration agreement, the respondent's burden of costly hearings (a possible default award being the only alternative) usually outweighs any societal benefit from reducing dilatory tactics in other cases. An arbitration would go forward only if a court has been prima facie satisfied of the validity and application of the arbitration clause (no forgery or gun at the head during signing), subject to more extensive review at the award stage.[363]

Such a process could be combined with greater use of court-imposed sanctions (monetary penalties) to discourage frivolous jurisdictional challenges, an option increasingly considered by American judges frustrated with groundless motions to vacate awards.[364] No good reason exists why, as a matter of policy, a similar measure should not be available to moderate improper motions to compel litigation or to stay arbitration.

Addressing the second matter (judicial deference to arbitrators' rulings on their own authority) calls for considerable nuance and balance. In considering what to do with *Kompetenz-Kompetenz* clauses, legal systems must navigate between two extremes. One is a lack of judicial rigor in examining the validity of such agreements. The other is a blanket over-inclusive rejection of all such clauses, no matter how clearly the evidence might support their validity in a given factual context.

Alleged grants of jurisdictional power to arbitrators must be considered with caution. A danger always exists that judges lacking analytic rigor will be tempted to clear their dockets through sloppy interpretation of the parties' intent, thereby denying one side

---

362. The suggestion here is for something equivalent to the summary process (*examen sommaire/summarische Prüfung*) of a Swiss court when asked to appoint an arbitrator. See LDIP Art. 179(3).

363. For a somewhat contrasting view, see Pierre MAYER, *op. cit.*, fn. 2, at p. 346, suggesting that courts seized of a case prior to commencement of arbitration should address jurisdiction fully, not limiting the review to determining if the clause is "manifestly" void. *Ibid.*, paragraph 15. ("On se demandera s'il est très logique pour le droit français d'obliger le juge étatique, saisi d'une demande au fond par une partie au mépris d'une convention d'arbitrage, à se déclarer incompétent sans pouvoir constater, sauf si elle est 'manifeste', la nullité de la convention.") Professor Mayer takes a different view when the arbitration has already begun, expressing concern that the greater risk remains dilatory actions (*Ibid.*, at p. 347, para. 17).

364. *Dominion Video v. Echo Star Satellite*, 430 F. 3d 1269 (10th Cir. 2005) (sanctions imposed on party bringing baseless challenge to award confirmation); *Harbert International v. Hercules Steel Co.*, 441 F. 3d 905 (11th Cir. 2006) (motion to vacate for "manifest disregard of the law" led to stern warning that the court was "ready, willing and able" to impose sanctions on parties who "attempt to salvage arbitration losses through litigation that has no sound basis in the law applicable to arbitration awards".); *CUNA Mutual Insurance Society v. Office & Professional Employees Int'l Union*, 443 F. 3d 556 (7th Cir. 2006) (warning that courts will not permit "spinning out the arbitral process unconscionably through the filing of meritless suits and appeals".)

its day in court. Arbitrators should never be given jurisdiction on the basis of a mere contract recital (such as "the arbitrator has jurisdiction over all questions") without verifying the true consent of the party sought to be bound. Even the best of rules may be misunderstood. Recitation of a "pro-arbitration" mantra often leads to cloudy thinking. Such potential misapplication must be considered in balancing the costs and the benefits of any legal rule.

That being said, the concern that contracts will be misinterpreted need not lead to a public policy that bans all forms of jurisdictional clauses in arbitration. Legitimate bargains should not be trumped by fears of occasional abuse. From a commercial perspective, business managers may wish to reduce the prospect of judicial intervention (particularly for international transactions) by giving an arbitral tribunal the final say on a jurisdictional issue. Respecting such agreements furthers fundamental respect for the parties' legitimate expectations.

While not entirely free from doubt, the American cases are probably getting things more right than wrong. While exceptions exist, judges in the United States seem to be asking the correct question: what did the litigants actually agree to arbitrate? On public policy issues, of course, arbitrators can never be empowered to make binding determinations.

Judicial review will in all events involve examination of the validity of the initial agreement, allegedly granting the arbitrators power on questions related to their authority. Such agreements will be most plausible when related to jurisdictional matters such as the time limits, scope of procedural powers and range of issues submitted to arbitration.

When one side challenges the very existence of an arbitration clause, the arbitrators' authority does not always yield to routine presumptions. Many cases present their own peculiar facts and issues. Was the arbitration clause forged or signed with a gun at the head? Did the corporate officer who executed the contract have power to commit the company? With respect to such questions, arbitrators can make binding rulings only if the supervisory court has been satisfied of the parties' informed and explicit consent (normally in the form of a distinct second agreement) to submit the precise jurisdictional question to the arbitrator.

In all these lines of inquiry, legal maxims and phrases on arbitral jurisdiction can facilitate analysis by communicating general norms quickly. The expressions lose their value, however, if pressed into service with excessive formalism, or pursuant to the type of thoughtless mimicry that parrots perform. When lawyers invoke contract recitals divorced from context, much as wizards incant magic words, the result is a voodoo jurisprudence that has no place in a healthy legal framework for arbitration.

As in most areas of the law, the articulation of specific standards that work in practice will require thoughtful analysis by policy-makers and practitioners alike. The goal of such efforts remains an arbitral system that gives effect to the parties' legitimate expectations about what questions are subject to final and binding private adjudication.

APPENDIX

Jurisdiction in Practice: Selected Scenarios

1. A claim against a "nonsignatory" company[365] might be brought on the basis of an arbitration clause signed by a corporate affiliate, either offensively (to reach assets of the corporate parent) or defensively (to permit a parent corporation to avoid jury trial), on theories such as agency (express or implied), alter ego, or piercing the corporate veil.[366]

2. Assertions of arbitral jurisdiction might invoke principles of estoppel.[367]

---

365. The term "non-signatories" remains useful shorthand to describe persons whose relationship to the arbitration is unclear at first blush. The term can be misleading, however, in its implication that a duty to arbitrate must derive from signed documents. Better taxonomy might classify such cases as involving "un-mentioned" parties. Unsigned arbitration agreements can be valid, inter alia under New York Convention Art. II (exchanges of letters), as well as agreements subject to the procedural law of countries that dispense with a signature requirement, including England (Arbitration Act of 1996 Sect. 5) and the United States (FAA Sect. 2, which refers only to a "written provision"). See generally, James M. HOSKING, "Non-Signatories and International Arbitration in the United States: The Quest for Consent", 20 Arb. Int'l (2004) p. 289.

366. For theories used to bind "non-signatories" see *Thomson-CSF v. American Arbitration Association*, 64 F. 3d 773 (2d Cir. 1993). See also *Intergen v. Grina*, 344 F. 3d 134 (1st Cir. 2003), in which Judge Selya noted the "abecedarian tenet that a party cannot be forced to arbitrate if it has not agreed to do so". Unlike many other cases involving corporate affiliates (where either claimant or respondent will have agreed to arbitrate), *Intergen* involved litigation between two parent entities, neither of which had signed an arbitration clause. Compare *Bridas v. Turkmenistan*, 447 F. 3d 411 (5th Cir. 2006), finding that government manipulation of an oil company made it the state's alter ego. By contrast, in *Sarhank v. Oracle Corp.*, 404 F. 3d 657 (2d Cir. 2005) the Court of Appeals decided that a parent should not answer for the obligations of its subsidiary pursuant to an arbitration clause signed by the latter. Citing "customary expectations of experienced business persons" the court vacated a decision recognizing the Egyptian award and remanded the case for a finding on whether, as a matter of fact, the parent's actions or inactions had given the subsidiary apparent or actual authority to consent to arbitration on its behalf. For reasons not fully explained, the court assumed such determination would be made under "American contract law or the law of agency". Similarly, an English court rejected piercing the corporate veil in *Republic of Kazakhstan v. Istil Group*, 2006 WL 1020597 (2006), [2006] EWHC 448 (Comm.) QBD, applying the 1996 English Arbitration Act, Sect. 67, to vacate an award against Kazakhstan for lack of substantive jurisdiction. For a related problem involving the overlap between the Russian Federation and the Russian Government, see *Compagnie Noga v. Russian Federation*, 361 F. 3d 676 (2d Cir. 2004).

367. *JML Industries v. Stolt-Nielsen*, 387 F. 3d 263 (2d Cir. 2004). Charterers brought antitrust action against owners of "parcel tankers" used in chemical transport. Owners permitted to invoke so-called "ASBATANKVOY" arbitration clause (used in affreightment of liquefied products) contained in charter contracts signed by owners' subsidiaries, given intertwining of issues to be resolved in arbitration and issues in agreements containing arbitration clause; *Fluor Daniel Intercontinental v. General Electric Co.*, 1999 WL 637236 (S.D.N.Y., 20 August 1999), invoking estoppel principles to hold that signatories of arbitration clauses were estopped from refusing to arbitrate with GE entities that sought to arbitrate issues intertwined with the contracts containing the arbitration clause;. *In Re Vesta Insurance Group*, Supreme Court of Texas No. 04-0141 (17 March 2006) (dispute between insurance company and its agent; arbitration of tortious

3. A duty to arbitrate might be based on trade usage, absent an explicit agreement.[368]

4. Corporate affiliates might be joined to an arbitration under what has been called "group of comapnies" doctrine.[369]

5. An award might be rendered by an arbitral tribunal whose appointment contained irregularities.[370]

6. An employer might assert the right to arbitrate on the basis of an "exchange" of letters, contested by the employee.[371]

7. After an insurance company and its policyholder settle a dispute that had been subject to arbitration, they disagree on implementation of the settlement agreement. Whether the arbitrator has power to decide the subsequent quarrel will depend on the terms of the settlement's dispute resolution clause.[372]

8. If a dispute among law partners is submitted to arbitration, does the arbitrator have authority to declare forfeiture of the withdrawing partner's capital interest?[373]

---

interference claims between signatory to arbitration agreement and affiliates of another signatory).

368. See BGH, Decision of 3 December 1992, III ZR 30/91, discussed in 1993 *Deutsche Zeitschrift für Wirtschaftsrecht* p. 465 (commentary, Klaus Peter BERGER) where the *Bundesgerichtshof* said that a duty to arbitrate might be implied through custom in the sheepskin trade.

369. See *Isover St. Gobain v. Dow Chemical France et al.*, ICC Case 4131 (1982) in Sigvard JARVIN & Yves DERAINS, eds., *op. cit.*, fn. 152, upheld by the Paris *Cour d'appel*, 21 October 1983, 1984 Rev. arb. p. 98; English language extracts in *Yearbook* IX (1984) p. 132. English law has rejected the "group of companies" doctrine, and requires evidence of agency before joinder of related companies. See *Peterson Farms Inc. v. C&M Farming Ltd.*, [2004] EWHC 121, [2004] 1 Lloyd's Rep 603, 2004 WL 229138 (4 February 2004, Q.B. Div., Commercial Court).

370. See *Encyclopaedia Universalis S.A. v. Encyclopaedia Britannica*, 2003 WL 22881820 (S.D.N.Y., December 2003). The tribunal's presiding arbitrator had been appointed by the *Tribunal de commerce* in Luxembourg, as provided in the arbitration clause. However, this Luxembourg appointment was not preceded by an attempt to select a chairman by the party-nominated arbitrators, which was another requirement of the parties' agreement.

371. See *Dynamo v. Ovechkin*, 412 F. Supp 2d 24 (D.D.C. 2006), involving hockey prodigy Alexander Ovechkin who had played with the Dynamo Club in Moscow before signing with the Washington Capitals to play in the National Hockey League. In the United States, the federal district court refused to recognize an award by the Arbitration Committee of the Russian Ice Hockey Federation that prohibited Ovechkin from playing for the American team. No arbitration agreement resulted from the Russian Club's offer that failed to elicit any "matching letter" from the player.

372. For example, arbitrators with power to decide controversies arising from one specific transaction would not necessarily have authority to decide disputes arising from a prior or subsequent commercial relationship between the same parties.

373. See decision by Judge Mosk in *O'Flaherty v. Belgum*, 11 Cal. App. 4th 1004, 9 Cal. Rptr. 3d 286 (2004), holding that an arbitrator exceeded his authority (as granted in the partnership agreement) by declaring forfeiture of a withdrawing partner's capital account.

9. Does an arbitrator lack jurisdiction because the matter has already been decided by another arbitral tribunal?[374] When an arbitration clause gives rise to multiple arbitrations, will principles of res judicata and issue preclusion bar later arbitrators from deciding particular questions?[375]

10. A breach of contract action asserts recovery of punitive damages. The arbitrator's power to include a non-compensatory element in the award could depend on the terms of the parties' agreement,[376] the applicable law[377] or a combination of both as seen through the lens of the applicable institutional arbitration rules.[378] The same might be said of claims for compound interest or for an award denominated in a currency other than the one of the controverted transaction.[379]

11. If a court in Country X has already begun to hear a matter when an arbitration begins in Country Y, does the arbitral tribunal have the authority proceed? Or do notions of *lis pendens* require the work to be suspended?[380]

---

374. Determinations about res judicata and issue preclusion (what the French might call *force de chose jugée* and *opposabilité* and the Germans *Rechtskraft*) do not yield to facile analysis. In the real world, difficult factual nuances often arise with respect to (i) identity of parties and (ii) identity of action, both prerequisites to preclusion. On the one hand, a losing party should not be permitted to begin another arbitration in the hope of getting a better result. On the other hand, due process requires that one company should not be denied an opportunity to vindicate a claim simply because similar issues were litigated by another entity. Particularly difficult issues arise when the same arbitration clause gives rise to multiple proceedings, or when in the middle of an arbitration one party sells a business unit that might later find itself seeking to assert related claims.

375. For an example of multiple arbitrations arising from a single clause, see *Admart AG v. Stephen & Mary Birch Foundation*, 457 F. 3d 302 (3d Cir. 2006). A court in the United States was asked to enforce an award rendered ten years earlier in a matter where a second arbitral tribunal was deciding questions related to the same parties and the same dispute, left open by the prior award. In the initial arbitration, the buyer of an open air art exhibition was denied the right to rescind the purchase. The second tribunal was asked to ascertain alleged damage to the purchased art works, which damage would have reduced the price ultimately borne by the buyer. Determining damage, however, implicated an examination of the art work which the first award had purported to preclude, at least as a precondition to payment of the price.

376. See *Pacificare Health Systems v. Book*, 538 U.S. 401 (2002).

377. *Mastrobuono v. Shearson Lehman Hutton*, 514 U.S. 52 (1995), interpreting the New York state rule in *Garrity v. Lyle Stuart, Inc.*, 40 N.Y.2d 354 (1976).

378. The AAA International Arbitration Rules exclude punitive damages unless the applicable statute "requires" that the compensatory damages be increased in a specified manner. Arguably, adoption of the AAA International Rules might be deemed a waiver of the right to request punitive damages in jurisdictions that permit parties to enter into such exclusions. See, e.g., *Drywall Systems v. ZVI Construction*, 435 Mass 664 (2002) (relating to the consumer protection provisions of M.G.L. Ch. 93A Sect. 11), in which the court stated that "[p]arties who prefer to exclude multiple damage claims ... from arbitration may do so by the terms of their agreement to arbitrate, or they may elect to waive them entirely". *Ibid.* at p. 671, n. 5. In the instant case (a domestic construction dispute) no such waiver was found.

379. *Lesotho Highlands Development Authority v. Impreglio SpA* [2005] UKHL 43 (30 June 2005).

380. See *Fomento de Construcciones y Contrats S.A. v. Colon Container Terminal S.A.*, Swiss Tribunal fédéral, 14 May 2001 (*le Cour Civile*), BGE 127 III 279/ ATF 127 III 279; discussed supra.

12. Is an arbitrator deprived of authority because the stronger party, in order to maximize its litigation options,[381] has imposed an arbitration clause that binds one side only to arbitrate?[382] What role does "mutuality of remedy" play in arbitral jurisdiction?[383]

13. If arbitrators are asked to consolidate arbitration of claims arising from separate contracts or transactions, the power to do so may depend on what the parties' agreement or the applicable arbitration rules say on the matter.[384] A similar question may arise prior to the commencement of the proceedings, with courts asked to make a declaratory pronouncement about whether the arbitrators will have authority to consider the matter at all.[385] Sometimes arbitration rules will address the matter, at least in part,[386] but in most cases remain silent on the matter.[387]

---

381. From the perspective of litigation strategy, an institution would normally want to reserve an option either to elect arbitration or to go to court. A unilateral right permits significant flexibility with respect to hard-to-forecast elements such as whether extensive document discovery (available in court to a greater extent than in arbitration) will be beneficial in a particular dispute.

382. See *Circuit City v. Adams*, 279 F. 3d 889 (9th Cir. 2002) (arbitration clause "unconscionable" for "unilaterally" forcing employee to arbitrate). By contrast, when employees and consumers (rather than employers and manufacturers) benefit from a right to opt-out of arbitration (through signing a form within thirty days of being hired), arbitration obligations have been upheld. See *Circuit City v. Ahmed*, 283 F. 3d 1198 (9th Cir. 2002); *Circuit City v. Najd*, 294 F. 3d 1104 (9th Cir. 2002).

383. Some courts invoke the principle of "mutuality" (of remedy or of obligation) to invalidate arbitration agreements. The theory is that if both parties are not bound, then neither is bound. See *Hull v. Norcom, Inc.*, 750 F. 2d 1547 (11th Cir. 1985) (employer retained right to go to court). Other courts have enforced optional clauses. See *Pittalis v. Sherafettin* [1986] 1 QB 868, [1986] (landlord/tenant rent review); *Law Debenture Trust Corp. v. Elektrim*, [2005] 1 All E.R. 476; 2005 WL 1630790; *Sablosky v. Gordon*, 73 N.Y.2d 133, 138-139 (N.Y. 1989). American financial institutions have used unilateral clauses to enhance litigation flexibility and reduce the prospect of what they perceive as biased jury proceedings. See generally William W. PARK, "Arbitration in Banking and Finance", 17 Ann. Rev. Banking L. p. 213, pp. 251–253 (1998); William W. PARK, "Jurisdictional Issues in Financial Arbitration" in Klaus Peter BERGER, ed., *Festschrift für Otto Sandrock zum 70. Geburtstag* (2000) p. 745.

384. See *Shaw's Supermarkets v. United Food*, 321 F. 3d 251 (1st Cir. 2003), a union grievance arbitration (concerning whether union members should take leaves of absence when on a negotiation committee) in which arbitrators were given the right to consolidate three collective bargaining arbitrations brought by the same union.

385. See *Employers Insurance Company of Wausau v. Century Indemnity Company*, 2006 WL 851643 (7th Cir. 2006). Allstate Insurance and Employers Insurance had entered into reinsurance contracts with Century Indemnity, which requested a consolidated arbitration of its claims against Employers and Allstate, as well as several other companies. Although holding that the question of consolidation was for the arbitrators, the Court of Appeals also determined that each side would appoint only one arbitrator, thus giving a substantial practical nudge to consolidation. Had the Court ordered constitution of two or more tribunals, it would not have been self-evident which would have ceded its work to the other.

386. See LCIA Rules 22.1(h).

387. There may, of course, be institutional practices (ICC practice) or rules with respect to judicial consolidation. See *New England Energy v. Keystone Shipping Co.*, 855 F. 2d 1 (1st Cir. 1988) (allowing consolidation under Massachusetts law). Compare *United Kingdom v. Boeing*, 998 F. 2d 68 (2nd Cir. 1993) (consolidation denied).

14. May an arbitrator award attorneys' fees? Does the answer depend on the applicable law, the norms of the arbitral situs, arbitration rules, or some combination thereof?[388]

15. Related to consolidation, arbitrators in the United States sometimes face the question of whether they are authorized to direct "class action" proceedings for similar claims arising that would normally yield individual recoveries too small to make arbitration economically viable.[389]

16. Arbitration under investment treaties might raise the following jurisdictional issues.[390]

– A foreign investor might bring an arbitration claiming indirect expropriation by a country whose courts allegedly denied the investor a fair trial. In order for the arbitrators to hear the case, the alleged judicial misbehavior will need to fit within the definition of governmental "measures" covered by the relevant investment treaty.[391]

– A host state might bring a counterclaim against the foreign investor or a company related to the investor. Would the arbitral tribunal constituted to hear the claim have authority to hear the counterclaim as well? [392]

– There might be an issue related to the nationality of the claimant. Does the arbitral

---

388. See, e.g., *CIT Project Finance v. Credit Suisse First Boston*, 799 NYS2d 159, (2004), discussed supra, holding arbitrators to be without power to grant attorneys' fees notwithstanding Art. 31 of the AAA International Rules, which provides for "the reasonable costs for legal representation of a successful party". See also *PaineWebber v. Bybyk*, 81 F. 3d 1193 (2d Cir. 1996); *Shaw Group v. Triplefine Int'l Corp.*, 322 F. 3d 115 (2nd Cir. 2003); *Stone & Webster v. Triplefine International Corp.*, 118 Fed. Appx. 546 (2d Cir. 2004). For another aspect of the problem of attorneys' fees in arbitration, see Christopher R. DRAHOZAL, "Arbitration Costs and Contingent Fee Contracts", 59 Vand. L. Rev. (2006) p.729.

389. See *Green Tree Financial v. Bazzle* 539 U.S. 444 (2003) discussed supra. A recent Court of Appeals decision held that a ban on class actions would invalidate the arbitration agreement but for the possibility of severing the class action prohibition. See *Kristian v. Comcast Corp*, 2006 WL 1028758 (1st Cir. 2006), an action for antitrust violations under both state and federal law arising from customers' dispute with a cable television provider. Under what might best be called a public policy (consumer protection) analysis, the decision concluded that the validity of the ban on arbitrability of the class actions should be decided by courts rather than arbitrators. The court struck down and severed the ban, and only then permitted arbitration to proceed. See also *Discover Bank v. Superior Court*, 113 P. 3d 1100 (2005), declaring a class action waiver to be unconscionable and *Strand v. U.S. Bank N.A.*, 693 N.W.2d 918 (N.D. 2005), upholding such waivers.

390. See generally, Pierre LALIVE, *op. cit.*, fn. 143. Professor Lalive lists a half dozen categories for jurisdictional challenge in investor-state arbitration: nationality, the nature of an "investment", assignment, absence of prior "friendly negotiations", non-exhaustion of local remedies, and a fork in the road between a local and international forum.

391. *Loewen Group, Inc. v. U.S.A.*, ICSID Case No. ARB (AF)/98/3, Interim Award on Jurisdiction, 5 January 2001.

392. *Saluka Investments B.V. v. Czech Republic*, Decision on Jurisdiction (UNCITRAL Rules, Netherlands-Czech BIT, 7 May 2004), rejecting jurisdiction over counterclaim without deciding on the relationship between claimant Saluka and another company of the Japanese merchant banking group (Nomura) with which it was affiliated.

tribunal have jurisdiction to hear the claim when an investor possesses dual nationality, including citizenship in the host state?[393] What is the arbitrator's power when the surviving entity in an investor's reorganization is incorporated in the host state?[394]
– A host state might assert that the treaty's definition of "investment" excludes certain categories of property (contract rights to build a factory), or requires that the original investor continue to hold shares of a company whose property was expropriated (rather than sell in order to mitigate damages). Or there may be a question of whether the arbitrator's jurisdiction covers disputes in which the state acts as a contracting party.[395]
– A host state might assert that the treaty's jurisdiction does not cover tax claims.[396]

17. An arbitral tribunal is asked to decide a dispute between a consumer and a manufacturer in different countries. Two different arbitration statutes may be applicable. One expressly prohibits arbitration of consumer disputes. The other impliedly allows arbitration of cross-border contracts regardless of any consumer element. The arbitrators' power to hear the case will depend on which regime applies.[397]

18. Do arbitrators have authority to decide a dispute on the basis of an arbitration clause contained in Terms and Conditions of Sale appearing through a hyperlink on a manufacturers' website shopping page?[398]

---

393. Decision on Jurisdiction in the case of *Champion Trading Company, Ameritrade International Inc., James T. Wahba, John B. Wahba, Timothy T. Wahba v. Arab Republic of Egypt*, Case No. ICSID ARB/02/9 (21 October 2003). On nationality in investment arbitration, see generally, Robert WISNER and Nick GALLUS, "Nationality Requirements in Investor-State Arbitration", 5 J. World Investment and Trade (2004, no. 6) p. 927; Anthony SINCLAIR, "Nationality of Individual Investors in ICSID Arbitration", Int'l. Arb.L.Rev. (2004) p. 191. See also decision in *Wena Hotels v. Egypt*, Award (2000) reproduced 41 I.L.M.(2002) p. 896; Annulment Decision reproduced 41 I.L.M. (2002) p. 93. In *Sedelmayer v. Russia*, a tribunal constituted under the German-Russian BIT addressed the question of whether the corporate veil should be pierced when investor and owner had different nationalities.

394. *Loewen Group, Inc. and Raymond L. Loewen v. U.S.A.*, ICSID Case No. ARB (AF)/98/3, Final Award 26 June 2003.

395. Sophie LEMAIRE, *"Treaty Claims et Contract Claims: La Compétence du CIRDI à l'épreuve de la dualité de l'état"*, 2006 Rev. arb. (2006) p. 353.

396. See, e.g., *Ecuador v. Occidental Exploration and Production Co.* [2006] EWHC 345 (English High Court), 2006 WL 690585; UNCITRAL arbitration (LCIA Administered Case No. UN 3467), 1 July 2004 (Value Added Tax payments subject of investment dispute; taxpayer prevailed in arbitration). For a case in which the taxpayer did not prevail see *EnCana v. Ecuador*, UNCITRAL Arbitration (Final Award, 3 February 2006; dissenting opinion by Horacio Grigera Naón).

397. French *Cour de cassation*, 21 May 1997, *Meglio v. Société V2000*. Cass, 1e civ., 21 May 1997, Rev. arb. (1997) p. 537 (note GAILLARD); see also Cass, 1e civ., 21 May 1997, Rev. Crit. Dr. Int'l Privé (1998) p. 87 (note HEUZÉ). The *Cour de cassation* upheld the validity of an arbitration clause in an agreement for the purchase of a limited series Jaguar, finding that the contract implicated international commerce by virtue of a transfer of goods and funds between France and the United Kingdom.

398. See *Dell Computer Corp v. Union des Consommateurs & Olivier Dumoulin*, Appeal to Supreme Court of Canada, S.C.C. File 31067, Leave to Appeal, 19 January 2006 (Docket: 31067), 2006 CarswellQue 84, appeal from 2005 CarswellQue 3270, *Cour d'appel du Québec*, 2005.

19. Will a buyer of goods be bound to arbitrate on the basis of an arbitration clause in a contract between a manufacturer and a distributor?[399]

20. The parties to a contract provide for arbitration in a particular city, but under non-existent rules and without any identifiable appointing authority. To what extent may an arbitral institution in the chosen locale confer upon itself power to constitute a tribunal?[400]

21. Does an arbitrator lack jurisdiction because the arbitration clause lacks consideration?[401]

22. Arbitrators award monetary sanctions for one side's failure to comply with discovery orders. The award is challenged on the basis that the tribunal lacked authority to impose such a penalty.[402]

---

399. For an affirmative answer, see *International Paper Co. v. Schwabedissen Maschinen & Anlagen GMBH*, 206 F. 3d 411 (4th Cir. 2000), concerning sale of an industrial saw. When the buyer sought to enforce guarantees and warranties contained in the contract between the manufacturer of the saw and one of its distributors, the doctrine of equitable estoppel precluded the buyer's assertion that it was not bound by the arbitration clause in contract manufacturer – distributor agreement.

400. See *Marks 3-Zet-Ernst Marks GmbH v. Presstek, Inc.*, 455 F. 3d 7 (1st Cir. 2006), in which an arbitration clause between a German company and a Delaware corporation provided only for "arbitration in the Hague under the International Arbitration rules". The Permanent Court of Arbitration (PCA) in The Hague found no agreement to apply the UNCITRAL Arbitration Rules so as to permit the arbitration to go forward under its auspices. A request to compel arbitration made to a court in the United States was subsequently dismissed.

401. See *Douglass v. Pflueger Hawaii, Inc.*, 135 P. 3d 129 (Hawaii 2006), holding that an arbitration clause failed for lack of "bilateral consideration" when included in an employee handbook which the employer could change at will.

402. *Superadio Ltd. Partnership v. Winstar Radio Productions*, 446 Mass. 330, (2006), permitting arbitrators' imposition of sanctions for violation of discovery orders. In a case arising from an agency for sale of advertising on radio (each side accusing the other of failing to turn over advertising revenues), the court upheld the tribunal's interpretation on the AAA rules, which in Rule 23(c) authorize arbitrators "to resolve any disputes concerning the exchange of information". As a matter of contract interpretation, the arbitral power to award sanctions may or may not be misplaced. However, the court's analytic methodology seems sound, in its attempt to discern what authority the parties granted the arbitrator. For a contrasting perspective, see Philip J. O'NEILL, "The Arbitrator's Power to Award Monetary Sanctions for Discovery Abuse", 60 Dispute Res. J. (Nov. 2005/Jan. 2006) p. 60; "Update: Massachusetts Allows Arbitrators to Award $$ Sanctions to Remedy Discovery Abuse", 61 Dispute Res. J. (May-August 2006) p. 8. Mr. O'Neill suggests it might be best for American judges and arbitrators simply to look to institutional (AAA) interpretation of rules, rather than exercising independent judgment. Decided under the Massachusetts Arbitration Act rather than the FAA, *Superadio* also refused to vacate the award on the ground that one side's attorney was not admitted to practice in Massachusetts.

The Similarity of Aims in the American and French Legal Systems With Respect to Arbitrators' Powers to Determine Their Jurisdiction

*Virginie Colaiuta**

I. INTRODUCTION

As stated by William Park, the competence-competence principle "possesses a chameleon-like quality that changes color according to the national and institutional background of its application".[1] Among the various applications of this principle expounded by national legal systems, two different approaches have been identified in the American and the French legal systems.[2]

On the one hand, the American approach is said to be based on the contractual will of the parties,[3] focusing on the language of the arbitration agreement to find the source of the powers of the arbitrators to determine their own jurisdiction. On the other, the French approach is based on the status of the arbitrator, having a power created by law to render decisions binding at law (*fonction juridictionnelle*). This is said to be the source of the competence-competence principle in the French legal system.[4]

---

* Partner, Hughes Hubbard & Reed LLP, Paris; admitted to practice in Paris and New York.

1. William W. PARK, "The Arbitrator's Jurisdiction to Determine Jurisdiction", see this volume, pp. 55-153, at p. 56.

2. *Ibid.* at p. 80.

3. Alan Scott RAU, "The Culture of American Arbitration and the Lessons of ADR", 40 Texas Int. L. J., (2005) p. 449, p. 451.

4. The foundation of such a principle is based, according to some authors, on the presumed will of the parties to give arbitrators the power to decide on their jurisdiction. However, as arbitrators may decide on their jurisdiction even when the basis thereof does not subsist, that is, even in the event an arbitration agreement did not exist, the basis of such a principle may not be found in the will of the parties. The basis also cannot derive from the status of the arbitrator, as advocated by others, because such a status exists only to the extent that the parties have agreed to give such a status to the arbitrators by means of a valid arbitration agreement. For these reasons and because the competence-competence principle is a procedural principle, some suggest that its foundation should be based on the law of the seat of the arbitration.

Although these two approaches are seen as extremes,[5] I will suggest in this Commentary that, notwithstanding their theoretical difference, their aim is in fact very similar: that is, to reduce the role of courts in the determination of arbitral jurisdiction and to enhance the powers of arbitrators to decide upon their own jurisdiction.

In essence both these approaches are based on a fiction. The American contractual approach relies on the fiction that the *a posteriori* construction of the language of the arbitration agreement stipulated by the parties indicates the parties' acceptance that an arbitrator should decide whether or not he has jurisdiction over a dispute, and its extent. While the French approach is based on law, it relies on the presumption, or fiction, that the arbitrator derives his powers from the status he has, which can exist only if there is a valid and applicable arbitration agreement.

Despite having the same aim, the two regimes may vary in the process adopted to achieve their goal. Under the French system, court intervention is effectively barred until after the arbitrator has made his jurisdictional decision, but judicial review of that decision is permitted. Under the American regime, courts are permitted to test arbitral jurisdiction at any point in the proceedings, but a determination that the parties had agreed that the arbitrator should have the power to decide on his own jurisdiction may prevent any judicial control of his decision.

To understand the similarity of aims of the two different legal systems, it may be useful to analyze the major features of the French (Sect. II) and American (Sect. III) approaches.

II.   THE FRENCH APPROACH

The French application of the competence-competence principle is based on Arts. 1466 and 1458 of the French *Nouveau Code de Procédure civile* (NCPC). Art. 1466 states that:

> "If, before the arbitrator, one of the parties challenges the principle or scope of the arbitrator's jurisdiction, the arbitrator shall rule on the validity and scope of his jurisdiction."[6]

According to Art. 1458:

> "Where a dispute, submitted to an arbitral tribunal pursuant to an arbitration agreement, is brought before a court of law of the State, such court shall decline jurisdiction.
>
> If the arbitral tribunal has not yet been seized of the matter, the court shall also decline jurisdiction unless the arbitration agreement is manifestly void.

---

5. See William W. PARK, supra, at p. 80.
6. The original French version of Art. 1466 states that:

   "Si devant l'arbitre, l'une des parties conteste dans son principe ou son étendue le pouvoir juridictionnel de l'arbitre, il appartient à celui-ci de statuer sur la validité ou les limites de son investiture."

In neither case may the court decline jurisdiction on its own motion."[7]

The French legal system draws a distinction regarding the intervention of national courts in jurisdictional matters, according to whether or not an arbitral tribunal has been seized of the dispute.

Where the arbitral tribunal has yet to be constituted, any attempt to have recourse to a French court is effectively frustrated by the French arbitration statute, which requires national courts to declare their lack of jurisdiction unless the arbitration clause is "manifestly void".

The cases where the arbitration agreement was found "manifestly void" have been extremely rare and have corresponded to the circumstances of an arbitration agreement between corporations which were previously dissolved,[8] an arbitration agreement declared void in a res judicata decision,[9] and an arbitration agreement concerning a dispute clearly non-arbitrable under Art. 2060 of the French Civil Code.[10] Other situations where a manifest nullity of the arbitration agreement could be found are where there is no mutual consent by the parties to solve their dispute by arbitration or there is some patent vitiating defect, such as the lack of capacity of one of the parties to the arbitration agreement.

In addition to the manifest nullity, the French Court of Cassation has identified a further ground for French courts to determine the arbitrators' jurisdiction before the arbitral tribunal has been constituted; that is, when the arbitration agreement is "manifestly inapplicable".[11]

In considering the possibility for the national courts to rule on the arbitrators' jurisdiction, it seems that Art. 1458 of the French NCPC and the jurisprudence of the French Court of Cassation make a clear distinction between:

a. Whether the parties agreed to arbitrate *at all*; and,
b. The determination of the *scope* of the arbitration clause agreed to between the parties.

---

7. According to the original French version of Art. 1458:

> *"Lorsqu'un litige dont un tribunal arbitral est saisi en vertu d'une convention d'arbitrage est porté devant une juridiction de l'Etat, celle-ci doit se déclarer incompétente.*
> *Si le tribunal n'est pas encore saisi, la juridiction doit également se déclarer incompétente à moins que la convention d'arbitrage ne soit manifestement nulle.*
> *Dans les deux cas, la juridiction ne peut relever d'office son incompétence."*

8. Ch. KAPLAN and G. CUNIBERTI, Note, Cass. Civ. 1, 16 October 2001 no. 1555, JCP 274 (2002).

9. Ph. FOUCHARD, *"La coopération du Président du Tribunal de grande instance à l'arbitrage"*, Revue de l'arbitrage (1985) p. 1.

10. See Jerry SAINTE-ROSE, Note, Gazette du Palais, 16-17 August 2006, at p. 6 and E. GAILLARD, Note, Cass. Civ. 1, 26 June 2001 no. 1100, Revue de l'arbitrage (2001) p. 532.

11. The ground based on the manifest inapplicability is mentioned for the first time in the decision *Quarto Children's Book Ltd* rendered on 16 October 2001 by the Civil Chamber of the French Court of Cassation. For a severe criticism of the additional grounds conceived by the Court of Cassation, see Dominique COHEN, Note, Revue de l'arbitrage (2002) p. 919.

As shown below, the cases where manifest inapplicability of the arbitration agreement was found by French national courts mainly related to the scope of arbitration clauses. Some recent decisions of the French Court of Cassation have clarified the situations where an arbitration clause is manifestly inapplicable.

An initial decision dated 4 July 2006 related to two separate contracts (a supply contract and a pledge stipulated in order to guaranty the performance of the supply contract), signed by the same parties, which contained respectively an arbitration clause and a national jurisdiction clause. The Court of Cassation decided that the dispute arising out of the pledge, which contained a clause giving jurisdiction to national courts, did not fall within the jurisdiction of the arbitral tribunal constituted under the terms of the arbitration clause contained in the supply contract. In accordance with the intent of the parties, each contract had to be governed by the clause contained therein. The arbitration agreement specified in the supply contract was therefore manifestly inapplicable to the dispute relating to the pledge.[12]

Two weeks later, on 11 July 2006 the Court of Cassation handed down a second decision finding the manifest inapplicability of an arbitration clause[13] in relation to a maritime freight shipment case. In this case, booking notes contained arbitration clauses and set out that the latter would be annulled and replaced by the terms of bills of lading to be subsequently entered into by the parties. The bills of lading contained a clause which provided for the exclusive jurisdiction of the national courts of the country in which the freight forwarder was located. In determining the applicability of the arbitration agreement, the Court of Cassation held that "the arbitration clause, contained in the preliminary contracts which were the booking notes, had been replaced, through a new expression of the intent of the parties, by the terms of the bills of lading, in a way which meant that it had become manifestly inapplicable".[14]

Another example of manifest inapplicability may be found in a decision rendered on 13 June 2006 by the Commercial Chamber of the French Court of Cassation, where the Court referred to "evident" instead of "manifest" inapplicability with the possible intent to attenuate the "manifest" standard.[15] This case concerned an arbitration clause contained in multiple franchising agreements concluded between two corporations, Gemodis and Prodim. Following a bankruptcy proceeding commenced against the franchisee Gemodis, the receiver commenced commercial judicial proceedings against the franchisor Prodim claiming that the latter was liable for having irresponsibly increased the debts of the franchisee. Prodim alleged that French courts lacked jurisdiction over any dispute arising out of its franchising agreements with Gemodis because of the arbitration clauses contained therein. In its decision, the French Court of

---

12. Cass. Civ. 1, 4 July 2006, no. 05-11.591, no. 1127, *Société Champion supermarché France v. SA Recape.*

13. Cass. Civ. 1, 11 July 2006, no. 03-19.838, *SA PT Andhika Lines v. Axa Corporate solutions assurances.*

14. The original French version of the 11 July 2006 decision rendered by the French Court of Cassation stated as follows "*la clause compromissoire contenue aux avants-contrats qu'étaient les réservations de fret, avait été remplacée, par une nouvelle expression de la volonté des parties, par les stipulations des connaissements, de sorte qu'elle était de ce fait devenue manifestement inapplicable*" (Cass. Civ. 1, 11 July 2006, no. 03-19.838, *SA PT Andhika Lines*).

15. Cass. Com., 13 June 2006, no. 03-16.695, *Société Prodim v. GEMODIS.*

Cassation affirmed the decision of the Court of Appeal, which recognized the jurisdiction of French national courts on the basis that the arbitration clauses were applicable only to the relationships between the franchisee and the franchisor and not to the relationship between the franchisor and the receiver when the latter represented the creditors, as in the case at hand.

On the other hand, the mere fact that the dispute is based on non-contractual claims relating to a contract containing an arbitration clause is not sufficient for a French court to accept jurisdiction under Art. 1458 and deprive the arbitral tribunal of its power to initially determine its jurisdiction and the extent thereof.[16] In the absence of a finding that the arbitration clause is manifestly null or manifestly inapplicable the court must decline jurisdiction and refer the parties to arbitration. It is up to the arbitral tribunal to determine as an initial matter whether the scope of the arbitration clause is sufficiently broad to cover the non-contractual claims.

Accordingly, on 25 April 2006, the Court of Cassation annulled a decision whereby, before an arbitration procedure was commenced, a lower court had denied the arbitrators' jurisdiction over a tort claim on the basis that such a claim was not within the scope of the arbitration agreement.[17] The Court of Cassation annulled the lower court's decision on the basis that the only grounds which allow French national courts to rule on the arbitrators' jurisdiction before an arbitral tribunal is constituted are the manifest nullity or inapplicability of the arbitration clause, and the interpretation given by the court did show that the alleged nullity or inapplicability was manifest. Actually, the necessity of having to engage in an interpretation of the arbitration clause implied the fact that the nullity or inapplicability was not manifest.[18]

Although the cases mentioned above indicate that the French Court of Cassation is willing, at times, to uphold the inapplicability of an arbitration agreement, the limitation with which this exception is applied can be appreciated more completely when viewed in light of decisions where its application has been denied. In this respect, the decision of 18 December 2003[19] is worthy of note as the Court of Cassation censured a decision of the Court of Appeal which disregarded an agreement to arbitrate because the intention of the parties to resort to arbitration was not established, as the contract contained both an arbitration clause and a clause attributing jurisdiction to national courts. The Court of Cassation held that the Court of Appeal had failed to characterize

---

16. Cass. Civ. 1, 4 July 2006, Decision no. 1128, no. 05-17.460, *Prodim v. Epoux X.* See also Cass. Civ. 1, 25 April 2006, no. H 05-15.528, no. 693, *DMN Machinefabriek BV v. Tripette and Renaud* mentioned above upholding arbitrators' jurisdiction over a tort claim, and Cass. Civ. 1, 8 November 2005, no. 02-18.512 where the Court of Cassation approved the application of the principle of competence-competence in relation to an action involving claims of unfair competition.

17. Cass. Civ. 1, 25 April 2006, no. H 05-15.528, no. 693, *DMN Machinefabriek BV v. Tripette and Renaud.*

18. See for a similar analysis, Nicolas BOUCHE, *"L'inapplicabilité manifeste de la convention d'arbitrage"*, RJDA (December 2006) p. 1109.

19. Cass. Civ. 2, 18 December 2003, no. 1774, *La Chartreuse v. Cavagna.* Even though this decision related to a domestic arbitration, it remains relevant to the definition of when an arbitration may be found to be manifestly null or inapplicable for international arbitration proceedings.

either the nullity or the manifest inapplicability of the arbitration clause and had therefore violated the principle of competence-competence. It therefore appears that the attribution of contradictory jurisdiction will only operate to exclude the jurisdiction of arbitrators when the contradictory intention of the parties is "manifestly" evidenced in separate instruments (with different objects) entered into by the same parties.

Likewise, in a decision handed down shortly thereafter, the Court of Cassation refused to allow the intervention of French national courts in a dispute which provided for arbitration in London on the basis that "the insurers did not supply proof of the manifest nullity of the arbitration agreement".[20]

In a decision rendered on 7 June 2006, the French Court of Cassation has clarified how the "manifest" character of the nullity or inapplicability of the arbitration agreement is to be understood by stating that:

> "whereas the combination of the principles of validity and competence-competence prevents, as a result of their rationale, the French national judge from making a substantive and thorough analysis of the arbitration agreement regardless of where the arbitral tribunal is located or has its seat, the only grounds in view of which the judge may analyze the arbitration clause before he is asked to verify the existence or the validity of the clause in connection with a challenge of the arbitral award, are those of the manifest nullity or inapplicability of the clause".[21]

If the issue of manifest nullity or inapplicability is raised after the arbitral tribunal has been seized, it must then be determined by the arbitrators and not by national courts. This is the result of the application of the first sentence of Art. 1458 of the NCPC quoted above.

---

20. The original French version of the 11 July 2006 decision rendered by the French Court of Cassation stated as follows "*les assureurs n'apportent pas la preuve de la nullité manifeste de la convention d'arbitrage*". See Cass. Civ. 1, 11 July 2006, no. 05-18.681, *Generali France Assurances v. Universal Legend*.

21. The original French version of the 7 June 2006 decision rendered by the French Court of Cassation stated as follows

"*que la combinaison des principes de validité et de compétence-compétence interdit, par voie de conséquence, au juge étatique français de procéder à un examen substantiel et approfondi de la convention d'arbitrage, et ce, quel que soit le lieu où siège le tribunal arbitral, la seule limite dans laquelle le juge peut examiner la clause d'arbitrage avant qu'il ne soit amené à en contrôler l'existence ou la validité dans le cadre d'un recours contre la sentence, étant celle de sa nullité ou de son inapplicabilité manifeste*".

See Cass. Civ. 1, 7 June 2006, no. 03-12.034, *copropriété maritime Jules Verne*. See also Cass. Civ. 1, 8 November 2005, no. 02-18.512 and Cass. Civ. 1, 7 June 2006, no. 04-10.156, *Société à responsabilité limitée Daso*, which confirmed that according to the NCPC, where litigation is commenced before national courts, but recourse to an arbitral tribunal is indicated by virtue of an arbitration clause, the state court must declare that it lacks jurisdiction unless the clause is null or manifestly inapplicable.

Where an arbitral tribunal has been constituted in relation to a particular dispute, a French court must decline its jurisdiction over that dispute and has no power to rule on the arbitrator's jurisdiction except in respect of later actions brought for the execution or judicial review of an arbitral award. The Court of Cassation recently reaffirmed this principle holding, in the context of a dispute arising under a bill of lading providing for arbitration in London, that the *tribunal de commerce* of Bordeaux "did not have jurisdiction to hear and determine the action because, as a matter of priority, it was up to the arbitrator to determine, under the supervision of the judge in the annulment proceedings, the existence, the validity and the extent of the arbitration agreement".[22]

In this way the intervention of French national courts is postponed until after the rendering of the award on jurisdiction or on the merits.[23] At this stage, the review by French national courts of the jurisdictional decision is conducted de novo, that is, without any deference to the determination made by the arbitrators.[24]

In the French legal system, it is assumed that, by agreeing to have recourse to arbitration, the parties have taken the risk of having arbitrators define the limits of their jurisdiction, at least on a preliminary basis. Even if the arbitrators' jurisdictional findings may later be subject to review by national courts, arbitrators are given the initial opportunity to decide any jurisdictional matter. Further, by letting the arbitration procedure be conducted without the interference of national courts, arbitrators' jurisdictional decisions may become binding as the parties may lose their interest in challenging them, or the dispute may be rendered moot with respect to the arbitrator's jurisdiction or the merits. This could be the case, for instance, where a decision on the merits is rendered in favor of the respondent, who challenged the arbitrator's jurisdiction. Finally, by letting the arbitral procedure evolve, the parties may be encouraged to settle their dispute before any award is rendered.

In sum, the restrained intervention of French national courts allows the arbitral procedure to evolve preventing any dilatory actions and multiplication of parallel proceedings on the determination of the arbitrators' jurisdiction.

---

22. The original French version of the 11 July 2006 decision rendered by the French Court of Cassation stated as follows "*le tribunal de commerce de Bordeaux était incompétent pour connaître de la demande dès lors qu'il appartient à l'arbitre de statuer, par priorité, sous le contrôle du juge de l'annulation, sur l'existence, la validité et l'étendue de la convention d'arbitrage*". See Cass. Civ. 1, 11 July 2006, no. 05-18.681, *Generali France Assurances*.

23. Such jurisdictional review is provided by the terms of Art. 1502 of the NCPC, which provides that an arbitration award made abroad or in international matters may be set aside if "the arbitral tribunal decided the case in the absence of an arbitration agreement or on the basis of an agreement which was void or had expired" and if "the arbitral tribunal decided the case otherwise than in accordance with the terms of the mandate conferred on it". The same grounds are available under Art. 1504 of the NCPC to set aside in France an award made in France in connection with an international arbitration.

24. This was decided in the *SPP v. RAE* case by the Court of Appeal on 12 July 1984 (See B. GOLDMAN, Note, Journal de droit international (1985) p. 129), whose decision was later confirmed by the French Court of Cassation on 7 January 1987 (See Ph. LEBOULANGER, Note, Revue de l'arbitrage (1987) p. 469. See also Jean-Louis DÉVOLVÉ, Jean ROUCHE and Gerald H. POINTON, *French Arbitration Law and Practice* (Kluwer, The Hague 2003) p. 245.)

III.   THE AMERICAN APPROACH

While the US Federal Arbitration Act contains a general presumption that arbitrability should be decided by the court,[25] federal cases hold that the issue may be referred to the arbitrator if the arbitration agreement clearly shows that the parties intended that the question of arbitrability should be decided by the arbitrator. Unlike the case in France, a court in the United States need not decline to consider jurisdictional issues just because an arbitral tribunal has been seized of the matter. The intervention of American courts is allowed without limitation. Courts can intervene in respect of the jurisdiction of arbitrators at any moment of the arbitral procedure and in relation to any jurisdictional issue.

One reason put forward in support of such a liberal approach to court intervention is that national courts have, by default, jurisdiction over disputes, including disputes over whether the parties have agreed to derogate from court jurisdiction by entering into a valid and binding arbitration agreement.

However, American courts have found that the parties may specifically give the arbitrators the power to determine their own jurisdiction. When the arbitration clause contains language indicating the existence of such a specific agreement, arbitrators may then render binding jurisdictional decisions to the exclusion of the intervention of national courts.

In the United States, if the parties agreed to have jurisdictional matters determined by the arbitrators, it is permissible that a jurisdictional issue be converted into a question of fact or law, on which the arbitrators' decision is final.[26]

American courts do not accept that there is some implicit doctrine of competence-competence by which an arbitrator is presumed to have the power to determine his own jurisdiction, subject to review after the award has been rendered. They instead focus on

---

25. Sect. 3 of the Federal Arbitration Act provides that

> "If any suit or proceeding be brought in any of the courts of the United States upon any issue referable to arbitration under an agreement in writing for such arbitration, the court in which such suit is pending, *upon being satisfied that the issue involved in such suit or proceeding is referable to arbitration under such an agreement*, shall on application of one of the parties stay the trial of the action until such arbitration has been had in accordance with the terms of the agreement, providing the applicant for the stay is not in default in proceeding with such arbitration." (emphasis added)

> Art. 4 provides that a party may ask a federal court for an order compelling arbitration but "If the making of the arbitration agreement ... be in issue, the court shall proceed summarily to the trial thereof." In terms of review of awards rendered by arbitrators in which lack of jurisdiction is alleged Sect. 10(a)(4) of the FAA provides for a vacating and setting aside procedure "Where the arbitrators exceeded their powers..." and Sect. (11)(c) "Where the arbitrators have awarded upon a matter not submitted to them, unless it is a matter not affecting the merits of the decision upon the matter submitted."

26. See William W. PARK, supra, at p. 72. For a similar conclusion see also Alan RAU, supra, fn. 3, at p. 464. However, see footnote 69 in Professor Rau's article where it is stated that "it does not follow that *all* questions – including questions that implicate the very existence of consent to arbitrate – can thus be re-allocated to the arbitrators".

the contractual issue of whether the parties, through the language of their contract, agreed to give the arbitrators competence-competence powers.

However, the US Supreme Court made an important qualification to the ability of the parties to grant jurisdictional jurisdiction to arbitrators, stating that "Courts should not assume that the parties agreed to arbitrate arbitrability unless there is clear and unmistakable evidence that they did so."[27]

Subsequent cases, however, seem to have reduced any constraints imposed by the "clear and unmistakable evidence" standard and have found that the parties' agreement to arbitrate under most institutional arbitration rules, which provide that arbitrators shall determine jurisdictional questions, is sufficient.[28]

While on its face the *First Options dicta*, with its insistence on unmistakable evidence, seems to undercut the notion that American courts are inclining toward a generalized application of the competence-competence principle, the manner in which the principle has been adopted and applied by American courts in fact clearly demonstrates their willingness to find such evidence. There appears to be an ever increasing willingness of American courts, even those applying the "*dicta*", to find arbitrators fit to assess the scope of their own jurisdiction.

This increased willingness manifests itself in two ways. The first (and more obvious) way involves the interpretation of arbitration clauses to find that evidence merely suggestive of an intent to confer competence-competence powers to arbitrators is "clear and unmistakable". Through their interpretation of arbitration clauses, some courts, particularly those in the Second Circuit, have found "clear and unmistakable" evidence of an intent to grant arbitrators the power to determine their own jurisdiction, even in circumstances where the contracts contained broad, essentially "boilerplate" arbitration clauses. For example, in *PaineWebber Inc. v. Bybyk*[29] the court held that an agreement to arbitrate "*any and all*" controversies reflected the parties' intent to "arbitrate issues of arbitrability" and therefore to confer on the arbitrators the powers to determine their jurisdiction. In *Bell v. Cendant Corp.*,[30] an agreement providing for the arbitration of "any controversy arising in connection with or relating to this Agreement ... or any other matter or thing" satisfied the *First Options* "clear and unmistakable" standard. In *Rocket Jewelry Box, Inc. v. Quality Int'l Packaging Ltd.*,[31] the court held that "the phrase 'all of the issues' manifested and preserved in ... arbitration clauses [the parties'] 'clear and unmistakable' intent to arbitrate all issues, including arbitrability". While the above rulings represent a minority approach, they do suggest a healthy disregard for the

---

27. *First Options of Chicago, Inc. v. Kaplan*, 514 U.S. 938, 944 (1995), quoting *AT & T Technologies, Inc. v. Communications Workers*, 475 U.S. 643m 649 (1986).

28. See *Vladimir Poponin Ph.D. v. Virtual Pro Inc.*, no. C 06-4019 PJH, N.D. Calif. (2006).

29. *PaineWebber Inc. v. Bybyk*, 81 F.3d 1193, 1200 (2nd Cir. 1996).

30. *Bell v. Cendant Corp.*, 293 F.3d 563, 568 (2nd Cir. 2002).

31. *Rocket Jewelry Box, Inc. v. Quality Int'l Packaging Ltd.*, 2002 WL 987280 (13 May 2002 S.D.N.Y.).

Supreme Court's effort to create what is essentially a presumption against a finding that parties have conferred jurisdictional jurisdiction on an arbitrator.[32]

This suggestion derives further support in those cases finding the parties' incorporation of arbitration rules containing a competence-competence provision as clear and unmistakable evidence of an intent to grant arbitrators the authority to determine their authority.[33] While some courts have dissented,[34] this appears to have emerged as the majority approach.[35] For example, the court in *Shaw Group, Inc. v.*

---

32. The court's use of a broad arbitration clause as sufficiently clear evidence of an intent to grant arbitrators competence-competence powers is made all the more puzzling by *AT&T Technologies, Inc. v. Communications Workers of America*, 475 U.S. 643, 649, 651 (1986), a case on which the *First Options* dicta relies and in which the court determined that a broad arbitration clause did not represent a clear and unmistakable intent to remove arbitrability questions from the purview of the courts.

33. See, e.g., United Nations Commission on International Trade Law (UNCITRAL) Rules of Arbitration, Art. 21 ("The arbitral tribunal shall have the power to rule on objections that it has no jurisdiction, including any objections with respect to the existence or validity of the arbitration clause or of the separate arbitration agreement."). In addition, the rules of most preeminent arbitral bodies contain such a provision:

    – International Chamber of Commerce (ICC) Rules of Arbitration, Art. 6(2) ("[A]ny decision as to the jurisdiction of the Arbitral Tribunal shall be taken by the Arbitral Tribunal itself.");
    – International Centre for Settlement of Investment Disputes (ICSID), Rules of Procedure for Arbitration Proceedings, Rule 41(2) ("The Tribunal may on its own initiative consider, at any stage of the proceeding, whether the dispute or any ancillary claim before it is within the jurisdiction of the Centre and within its own competence.");
    – American Arbitration Association (AAA) International Arbitration Rules, Art. 15 ("The tribunal shall have the power to rule on its own jurisdiction, including any objections with respect to the existence, scope or validity of the arbitration agreement.");
    – AAA Commercial Arbitration Rules, Rule 7(a) ("The arbitrator shall have the power to rule on his or her own jurisdiction, including any objections with respect to the existence, scope or validity of the arbitration agreement.");
    – London Court of International Arbitration (LCIA), Rules of Arbitration, Art. 23.4 ("The Arbitral Tribunal shall have the power to rule on its own jurisdiction....").

34. See *Diesselhorst v. Munsey Building, L.L.L.P.*, 2005 WL 327532 *4 ("Simply by agreeing that any matters sent to arbitration would be governed by the AAA Rules, [the parties] did not clearly and unmistakably demonstrate an intent to have an arbitrator determine the question of arbitrability.") and *Martek Biosciences Corp. v. Zuccaro*, 2004 WL 2980741 *3 ("[T]he specification in the arbitration clause that the rules of JAMS apply to matters submitted to arbitration does not clearly and unmistakably demonstrate an intent to have an arbitrator of JAMS determine the question of arbitrability.").

35. See, e.g., *Shaw Group, Inc. v. Triplefine Int'l Corp.*, 322 F.3d 115, 118, 121-122 (2nd Cir. 2003) (determining that an agreement to arbitrate "all disputes ... concerning or arising out of" the container contract together with the agreement's adoption of the ICC Arbitration Rules satisfied the mandates of *First Options*); *Contec Corp. v. Remote Solution Co., Ltd.*, 298 F.3d 205, 211 (2nd Cir. 2005) (AAA rules); *Terminix Int'l Company, L.P. v. Palmer Ranch Ltd. Partnership*, 432 F.3d 1327, 1332 (11th Cir. 2005) (AAA rules); *Wal-Mart Stores, Inc. v. PT Multipolar Corp., P.T.*, 202 F.3d 280, 280 (UNCITRAL rules); *Book Depot Partnership v. American Book Co.*, 2005 WL 1513155 *3 and n. 3 (E.D. Tenn.) (AAA rules; gathering cases); *Johnson v. Polaris Sales, Inc.*, 257 F.Supp.2d 300, 309

Triplefine Int'l Corp.[36] held that an agreement to arbitrate "all disputes … concerning or arising out of" the contract, together with adoption of the ICC Rules of Arbitration, reflected sufficient intent to confer the power to determine jurisdiction on the arbitrators. Likewise, in a recent case rendered on 20 September 2006 the court held in *Vladimir Poponin Ph.D. v. Virtual Pro Inc.* that "the cases hold that where the parties' agreement to arbitrate includes an agreement to follow a particular set of arbitration rules – such as the ICC Rules – that provide for the arbitrator to decide arbitrability, the presumption that courts decide arbitrability falls away, and the issue is decided by the arbitrator".[37]

The emphasis given to the language of the arbitration agreement may be seen as a type of a legal artifice that allows the competence-competence principle to find its justification based on the will of the parties.

The second way American courts have encouraged the competence-competence principle is by simply redefining or restricting the meaning of "arbitrability".[38] In this instance, the drive has been led by no less than the Supreme Court, which effectively curtailed the types of questions that will fall under the "arbitrability" rubric in its recent trilogy: *Howsam v. Dean Witter Reynolds, Inc.*,[39] *Pacificare Health Systems, Inc. v. Book*[40] and *Green Tree Financial Corp. v. Bazzle.*[41]

In essence, the approach of the American courts, which amounted to "an adoption of the kompetenz-kompetenz doctrine on an ad hoc, contractual basis",[42] consistently appears to be favorable to the recognition of competence-competence powers to arbitrators.

The fact that broad language typically contained in arbitration clauses or institutional arbitration rules is found to be sufficient to attribute to arbitrators the powers to determine their own jurisdiction greatly reduces the situations where the competence-competence principle is not applied, thus undermining the practical difference between the American and the French legal system.

Even when the parties have clearly agreed to confer upon the arbitrators the power to decide on their own jurisdiction, a challenge to the existence of such an agreement before American national courts remains possible and the resulting judicial procedure arising from such a challenge may involve a jury. If the parties had in fact agreed on

---

(D. Maine 2003) (AAA rules); see also *Apollo Computer, Inc. v. Berg*, 886 F.2d 469, 473 (1st Cir. 1989) (ICC rules); *Daiei, Inc. v. United States Shoe Corp.*, 755 F.Supp. 299, 303 (D. Hawaii 1991) (ICC rules).

36. *Shaw Group, Inc. v. Triplefine Int'l Corp.*, 322 F.3d 115, 121-122 (2nd Cir. 2003).

37. *Vladimir Poponin Ph.D. v. Virtual Pro Inc.*, No. C 06-4019 PJH, N.D. Calif. (2006). See also supra text at fns. 33-35.

38. This phenomenon was recognized and discussed by Alan Scott RAU, "Everything You Really Need to Know About 'Separability' in Seventeen Simple Propositions", 14 Am. Rev. Int'l Arb. (2003, no. 1) pp. 100-109.

39. *Howsam v. Dean Witter Reynolds, Inc.*, 537 U.S. 79, 86 (2002).

40. *Pacificare Health Systems, Inc. v. Book*, 538 U.S. 401 (2003).

41. *Green Tree Financial Corp. v. Bazzle*, 539 U.S. 444 (2003).

42. Thomas E. CARBONNEAU, "Beyond Trilogies: A New Bill of Rights and Law Practice through the Contract of Arbitration", 6 Am. Rev. Int'l Arb. (1995) p. 1.

attributing a competence-competence power to the arbitrator, the judicial procedure will presumably ascertain the existence of the agreement and the binding character of the jurisdictional decisions rendered by the arbitrators.

Even though there are no cases to report for similar, parallel judicial and arbitral proceedings in France concerning the arbitrators' jurisdiction, if one party decides to commence a judicial proceeding before a French court after the arbitral tribunal has been constituted and despite the fact that according to Art. 1458 the French court is to decline its jurisdiction in favor of the arbitrator, the judicial proceeding will necessarily evolve and both parties will have to present their arguments before the French judge who eventually will conclude that he is not competent to rule on the dispute. Furthermore, if one considers that French courts may not raise ex officio their lack of jurisdiction under Art. 1458, if the defendant does not claim the jurisdiction of the arbitral tribunal over the dispute, the hypothetical and absurd situation of two parallel proceedings on the same dispute may take place: one before the French judge and one before the arbitrators.

Another difference between the systems – that the determination of jurisdiction by an arbitrator having competence-competence powers is binding and unreviewable in the United States while it would be reviewable in France – is in practice reduced. A reviewing court convinced that an arbitral tribunal had acted flagrantly outside of its jurisdiction is unlikely to conclude that the parties had intended to give the power to the tribunal to arbitrate arbitrability.

Moreover, the binding character of the jurisdictional decisions rendered by arbitrators to whom the competence-competence powers were attributed according to the American legal system is also open to discussion. It is in fact difficult to accept, under *any* system of law, that the principle of competence-competence can result in the arbitral tribunal having the "last word" on the issue of jurisdiction, unreviewable at the seat of arbitration. To be sure, in the terms of the contract one could waive and renounce any right to appeal, but this is not to say that courts will recognize such waiver. There may be a public policy whereby the state will wish to retain certain minimum grounds of review in relation to whether an arbitration award complies with the legal standards necessary for the state to enforce it. Accordingly, even where there is an agreement of the parties allocating the determination of the scope of the arbitration clause to the arbitrators, the jurisdictional decision may still be subject to limited court review, particularly where the issue is whether the parties had agreed to arbitrate at all.

As to this latter point, Alan Rau quite properly points out, in relation to the binding character of jurisdictional decisions of arbitrators rendered on the basis of a competence-competence agreement, that "it does not follow that *all* questions – including questions that implicate the very existence of consent to arbitrate – can thus be re-allocated to the arbitrators".[43]

Here too there may be a similarity between the French and the American system: it will be much more difficult to contest in court the determination by an arbitrator of the *scope* of the arbitration agreement under which he is seized than his determination of the *existence* of that agreement *at all*.

---

43. See footnote 69 in Professor RAU's article, supra, fn. 3.

IV.   CONCLUSION

Despite the different theoretical approaches followed by the French and the American legal systems, the outcome achieved by both legal systems is to enhance the power of arbitrators to determine their own jurisdiction.

In France, this is accomplished by restraining the intervention of national courts on the basis of the status of the arbitrator so that the arbitral procedure is allowed to evolve and the arbitrators are entitled to decide jurisdictional issues prior to any possible intervention by national courts. However, in extreme cases, where the nullity or inapplicability of the arbitration agreement is alleged to be manifest, national courts may intervene before the arbitral tribunal is constituted and may decide the issue.

In the United States, this is accomplished by preventing national courts from reviewing any jurisdictional findings of the arbitrators made as a result of an agreement where the parties have specifically agreed that arbitrators should decide arbitrability, thus providing the arbitrators with binding power in respect of their jurisdiction. As such a specific agreement may be found by the American courts in the language of boilerplate arbitration clauses, even if the national courts' intervention is not excluded or restrained, it is greatly discouraged.

The Effect of Arbitral Authority and the Timing of Judicial Review:
Japan's Approach Under its New Arbitration Law Based on the UNCITRAL Model Law

*Hiroyuki Tezuka**

I.   JAPAN'S NEW ARBITRATION LAW AND *KOMPETENZ-KOMPETENZ*

Japan has replaced its old arbitration law of 1890 (Law Concerning Procedure for General Pressing Notice and Arbitration Procedure, Law No. 29 of 1890, hereinafter the Old Law)[1] with an entirely new arbitration law (Law No. 138 of 2003, hereinafter the Arbitration Law), which was enacted in July 2003 and came into effect on 1 March 2004.[2] The Arbitration Law is based on the UNCITRAL Model Law on International Commercial Arbitration (hereinafter the Model Law).[3] Except for arbitrations involving consumer contracts and individual labor contracts, the Arbitration Law has essentially adopted, with respect to most issues, the same provisions as those under the Model

---

* Nishimura & Partners.

1. The provisions of the Old Law were originally contained in the old Japanese Civil Procedure Code of 1890, which was based on the 19th century German Civil Procedure Law. When the new Japanese Civil Procedure Code was enacted in 1996, provisions on procedures for general pressing notice and arbitration procedure were left untouched, and the old Civil Procedure Code (with only provisions on those two procedures remaining in existence therein) was renamed the "Law Concerning Procedure for General Pressing Notice and Arbitration Procedure."

2. A semi-official English translation of the Arbitration Law is available on the Japanese government's website. See Arbitration Law (Law No. 1238 of 2003), translated by the Arbitration Law Follow-up Research Group, available at <http://www.kantei.go.jp/foreign/policy/sihou/arbitrationlaw.pdf> (last accessed 17 May 2006).

3. For a brief overview of the Arbitration Law in English, see, e.g., Tatsuya NAKAMURA, *Salient Features of the New Japanese Arbitration Law Based Upon the UNCITRAL Model Law on International Commercial Arbitration*, JCAA NEWSLETTER, No. 17 (2004) at <http://www.jcaa.or.jp/e/arbitration-e/syuppan-e/newslet/news17.pdf> (last accessed 17 May 2006), and Hiroyuki TEZUKA, "Japan" in J. William ROWLEY, ed., *Arbitration World*, 2nd edn. (The European Lawyer 2006).

Law.[4] This is also true, to a large extent, with respect to the provisions regarding the arbitral tribunal's jurisdiction to determine its jurisdiction. The competence-competence or *Kompetenz-Kompetenz* of the arbitral tribunal and the separability of the arbitration agreement are recognized under the Arbitration Law basically in the same manner as under the Model Law.[5]

The Arbitration Law provides that "the arbitral tribunal may rule on assertions made in respect of the existence or validity of an arbitration agreement or its own jurisdiction"[6] (Art. 23(1)). A party must raise an objection to the tribunal's jurisdiction in a timely manner (i.e., "promptly") where the grounds for the assertion arise during the course of arbitral proceedings, or in other cases "before the time at which the first written statement on the substance of the dispute is submitted to the arbitral tribunal" (Art. 23(2)).[7]

In response to such a plea,

"the arbitral tribunal shall give ... (i) a preliminary independent ruling or an arbitral award, when it considers it has jurisdiction, or (ii) a ruling to terminate arbitral proceedings, when it considers it has no jurisdiction" (Art. 23(4)).

Where the arbitral tribunal gives a preliminary independent ruling that it has jurisdiction, the Arbitration Law provides that "any party may, within thirty days of receipt of such ruling, request the court to decide the matter" (Art. 23(5), first sentence).[8] The Arbitration Law also provides that, "while such a request is pending before the court, the arbitral tribunal may continue the arbitral proceedings and make an arbitral award" (Art. 23(5), second sentence).

In their commentary, members of the legislation team have explained that the purpose of the mechanism permitting the court's intervention under Art. 23(5) is to provide the parties with "a simple and prompt procedure" to obtain the court's ruling on the jurisdiction of the arbitral tribunal. The mechanism also helps to avoid the waste

---

4. In December 2003, a commentary on the Arbitration Law authored by members of the legislation team (the Arbitration Study Group within the Secretariat of the Office for Promotion of Judicial system Reform) in Japanese was first published. See *Chusai-Hou Commentary (the Arbitration Law Commentary)* (Shojihomu 2003). In November 2004, an English translation of this commentary was published. See Masaaki KONDO, et al., *Arbitration Law of Japan* (Shojihomu 2004).
5. In the process of the legislation of the Arbitration Law, Japan has taken account of arbitration laws of modern arbitration jurisdictions, especially the various enactments of the Model Law, including that of Germany.
6. The term "its own jurisdiction" is defined as the tribunal's "authority to conduct the arbitral proceedings and to make arbitral awards" (Arbitration Law, Art. 23(1)).
7. The arbitral tribunal, however, "may admit a later plea if it considers the delay justified" (Arbitration Law, Art. 23(2)).
8. In contrast, where the arbitral tribunal considers that it has no jurisdiction and has issued a ruling to terminate the arbitral proceedings, there is no recourse to challenge such ruling in national courts, which is the same as under the Model Law.

168

of time and costs incurred in the arbitral proceedings that could arise if the parties had to wait until the final award and then apply for the setting aside of such award.[9]

Thus, first, if the arbitral tribunal decides in its preliminary independent ruling pursuant to the first sentence of Art. 23(5) that it has jurisdiction, and the party disputing the jurisdiction has elected not to seek the court's ruling under the second sentence of Art. 23(5), the objecting party may wait for the final arbitral award and then ask that the arbitral award be set aside in the national court. In other words, the party's failure to challenge the arbitral tribunal's ruling under Art. 23(5) within the thirty-day period would not deprive that party of the right to request that the final arbitral award be set aside.

Secondly, the court's ruling that the arbitral tribunal has jurisdiction cannot be appealed, and it is interpreted that such ruling shall have no *res judicata* effect.[10] The objecting party may challenge the tribunal's jurisdiction at the time the arbitral award is sought to be enforced or set aside, and the court hearing the request for setting aside is not in any way bound by the court's previous ruling pursuant to the second sentence of Art. 23(5).[11]

As Professor William W. Park discusses in his Report, the concept of competence-competence, or the arbitrator's power to rule on jurisdiction, has at least three different aspects: (i) arbitrators need not stop the arbitral proceedings when a party raises a jurisdictional objection;[12] (ii) courts delay consideration of an arbitral tribunal's jurisdiction until after an award is made;[13] (iii) arbitrators decide on their own jurisdiction free from judicial review.[14]

Among those three aspects, the Japanese Arbitration Law clearly has recognized the arbitral tribunal's power to continue the arbitral proceedings despite a party's challenge of the tribunal's jurisdiction.

With regard to the second aspect, i.e., the timing of the national court's judicial review of the arbitral tribunal's jurisdiction, the Japanese approach is a kind of *hybrid* approach taken by the Model Law. Once the arbitral tribunal decides to rule

---

9. See KONDO, et al., *Arbitration Law of Japan*, supra, p. 104.

10. In contrast, a court's decision in the procedure to set aside an arbitral award shall have res judicata effect, in that its ruling on the issues as to whether there was any ground for setting aside the arbitral award will bind the parties in any subsequent proceedings.

11. See KONDO, et al., *Arbitration Law of Japan*, supra, p. 104. The authors further state that,

"the court in receipt of a request to set aside the arbitral award should independently hear and rule on whether or not [the arbitral tribunal's] jurisdiction exists. The content of the paragraph (5) ruling should not affect in any way the court's ruling on the setting aside of an arbitral award."

However, others argue that the objecting party's later challenge on the same grounds may be barred by estoppel. See, the Round-table Discussions in Koichi MIKI and Kazuhiko YAMAMOTO, co-eds., *Theories and Practices of New Arbitration Law (Shin Chusai-hou-no Riron-to Jitsumu)* (Jurist Zoukan, Yuhikaku April 2006) p. 189.

12. See this volume, p. 58.

13. *Ibid.*, p. 60.

14. *Ibid.*, p. 61.

affirmatively on its own jurisdiction in the form of a preliminary independent ruling under the first sentence of Art. 23(5), then a party has the right to file a request, within thirty days, that the court decide on the matter under the second sentence of Art. 23(5). However, if the arbitral tribunal decides simply to proceed with the arbitral proceedings and make the decision on its own jurisdiction in the form of the final arbitral award, the party disputing the jurisdiction will have to wait until the final award, and then ask that the award be set aside by the national court.[15]

There are debates as to whether or not the arbitral tribunal may issue a "preliminary" or "partial" arbitral *award* to decide solely on the jurisdictional issue, as distinguished from a "preliminary and independent *ruling*" under the first sentence of Art. 23(5).[16] It appears that the majority view considers that the arbitral tribunal can make such decision in the form of a preliminary or partial *award*.[17] If the arbitral tribunal's decision on its own jurisdiction can be made in the form of a preliminary or partial arbitral *award*, such award shall be subject to the procedures to set aside the award by the national court. The court's decision in such setting aside procedures shall be final and conclusive after the appeal to the High Court has been exhausted.[18]

In any event, under the Arbitration Law, the arbitral tribunal's decision regarding its own jurisdiction is not free from the court's review. As long as the challenging party has raised its objection to the tribunal's jurisdiction in a timely fashion, as required by Art.

---

15. See KONDO, et al., *Arbitration Law of Japan*, supra, at p. 103, which states that "in the case where the assertion that the arbitral tribunal has no jurisdiction is groundless, we can assume that this can be left by indicating the ruling in the arbitral award".

16. Prof. Tatsuya Nakamura, the director of International Arbitration Department of the Japan Commercial Arbitration Association, argued, in the Round-table Discussions (*Theories and Practices of New Arbitration Law*, supra, pp. 190-193), that the court's ruling on the party's challenge to the tribunal's ruling affirming its own jurisdiction should resolve the issue finally rather than only provisionally, citing various literature in other jurisdictions (including those based on the Model Law), e.g., Julian D.M. LEW, Loukas A. MISTELIS, Stefan M. KRÖL, *Comparative International Commercial Arbitration* (Kluwer Law International 2003) para. 14-25 ("If no challenge procedure is initiated within the period foreseen in the applicable law a preliminary award in favor of jurisdiction bars any later attack on the jurisdiction of the tribunal. Its res judicata effects also prevent parallel court proceedings in the country where the award is rendered."); Alan REDFERN and Martin HUNTER, *Law and Practice of International Commercial Arbitration*, 3rd edn. (Sweet & Maxwell 1999) para. 8-06 (the most current version is the 4th edition from Sweet & Maxwell (2004) and is cited here) ("If the tribunal takes the second course [i.e., dealing with a plea that the arbitral tribunal does not have jurisdiction as a 'preliminary question'], then its award, which will presumably be known as a 'partial award' or 'interim award' (or possibly as a 'preliminary award'), may be challenged in the competent court within 30 days of its notification. As may be seen from this example, important consequences flow from a ruling or decision of the arbitral tribunal that has the status of an award. The time-limit for challenge of the award will begin to run; and, once the final award has been made, it may be impossible for a party to challenge some element of that award if it follows from an earlier interim or partial award which was not challenged.").

17. See the Round-table Discussions in *Theories and Practices of New Arbitration Law*, supra, pp. 188-193.

18. An immediate appeal (*sokuji koukoku*) may be filed against the decision regarding the application for setting aside an arbitral award (Arbitration Law, Art. 44(8)). Such immediate appeal must be filed within two weeks from the notice of the District Court's decision (Arbitration Law, Art. 7).

23(2) of the Arbitration Law, the tribunal's affirmative decision on its own jurisdiction (i.e., either in the form of a preliminary and independent ruling under Art. 23(5) or in the form of the final or preliminary/partial award) is subject to the court's review (i.e., either in the procedure for the court's ruling under Art. 23(5) or in the procedure to set aside the arbitral award). While the court normally interprets the scope of arbitration clauses liberally so as to favor the parties' intention to resolve disputes outside of the court system,[19] the court's decision on the tribunal's jurisdiction in a ruling under Art. 23(5) of the Arbitration Law, or in the procedures to set aside an arbitral award, will be made independently from the tribunal's ruling.

The question then is, if the parties have agreed in the arbitration clause that the tribunal has the final power to decide on its own jurisdiction, and that the tribunal's decision on its own jurisdiction shall not be subject to the court's review, would such an agreement be effective and binding? This kind of agreement is called a *Kompetenz-Kompetenz* clause in Germany. As Professor Park explains in his Report, these types of clauses were once considered valid by the German court as long as such clauses in fact existed. However, the 1998 reforms to the German arbitration law have changed this and such change (i.e., the prohibition of such clauses) has been confirmed by a 2005 decision of the highest German court.[20] In Japan, there were debates under the Old Law as to whether or not such a clause was effective.[21] The debates still continue under the new Arbitration Law, but it appears that there are provisions of the Arbitration Law which would support the view that such a clause is not effective.[22]

---

19. For decisions in which courts liberally interpreted arbitration agreements under the Old Law, see, e.g., Takeshi KOJIMA, *Arbitration Law*, 59 Gendai-Houritsugaku-Zenshu (Seirin Shoin 2000) pp. 144-146. See, also, Hiroyuki TEZUKA, "Who is a Party — Case of the Nonsignatory, *Institutional Arbitration in Asia* (ICC/SIAC 2005), which discussed at p. 69 the decision of Nagoya District Court of 27 October 1995, Kaijiho Kenkyu 150- 33, in which the court held that under the rule of reason (*jori*), non-signatory individual defendants shall be bound by the arbitration agreement in a distributor agreement signed by the company, of which they were directors.

20. See this volume, p. 73, and fn. 71.

21. See, e.g., Takeshi KOJIMA and Takashi INOMATA, "Conflicts between Arbitral Proceedings and Court Proceedings" in *Issues on Contemporary Arbitration Law (Gendai-Chusai-Hou-no-Ronten)* (Yuhikaku 1998, pp. 292-294 (in Japanese), which argues that a *Kompetenz-Kompetenz* clause shall be considered effective as a second arbitration agreement on the jurisdictional issue, except where the grounds for challenge relate to violation of public policy.

22. See, the Round-table Discussions in *Theories and Practices of New Arbitration Law*, supra, pp. 197-199. While the members of the Round-table Discussions (mostly members of the legislation team) have different views, those who object to the validity of a *Kompetenz Kompetenz* clause argue that such clause is invalid because (i) it is inconsistent with Art. 23(5) of the Arbitration Law, which does not allow the parties to agree otherwise; (ii) Art. 44(1) of the Arbitration Law provides that the invalidity of the arbitration agreement and the tribunal's exceeding its power are grounds for setting aside an arbitral award and it is interpreted that the parties cannot agree to exclude such grounds for setting aside; and (iii) even if such clause is considered to be a second arbitration agreement, an arbitral award based on such second arbitration agreement shall be subject to the setting aside procedures in the courts.

II.   ACTION IN COURTS ON THE SUBJECT MATTER OF ARBITRATION AGREEMENT

Where there is an arbitration agreement that a party considers invalid or otherwise not properly covering the subject matter of the dispute, such party may elect to file an action in the court on this matter. If such action is filed with a Japanese court, the court shall, if the defendant so requests, "dismiss the action" unless it finds that the arbitration agreement is invalid or that the arbitral tribunal otherwise does not have jurisdiction (Arbitration Law, Art. 14(1)).[23] Art. 14(2) of the Arbitration Law specifically provides that the arbitral tribunal "may commence or continue arbitral proceedings and make an arbitral award even while the action referred to in the preceding paragraph is pending before the court". The Arbitration Law does not limit the application of Art. 14(1) to cases where the filing of an action in courts precedes the commencement of an arbitration.

Thus, where an arbitration is commenced and a party challenges the jurisdiction of the arbitral tribunal, but where the arbitral tribunal, believing it has jurisdiction, nevertheless has elected to issue neither (a) a preliminary and independent ruling under the first sentence of Art. 23(5) nor (b) a preliminary or partial arbitral award on the jurisdictional issue (electing instead to continue the arbitral proceedings so as to make its formal decision on the jurisdiction only in the final arbitral award), then the party who objects to the tribunal's jurisdiction may file an action on the same subject matter in the national court. This action may allege that the arbitration agreement is void, or the tribunal otherwise does not have jurisdiction in the dispute. In such a case, Art. 14(1) of the Arbitration Law applies, and, if the defendant requests that the court dismiss the action because of the arbitration agreement, the court shall do so unless it finds the arbitration agreement is invalid or the tribunal otherwise does not have jurisdiction.

Here, again, the arbitral tribunal does not have to stop the arbitral proceedings even where a party has filed an action in court challenging its jurisdiction and such action is pending. However, if such action is filed with a Japanese court, the court does not have to wait for the arbitral tribunal to make its determination on its own jurisdiction. Rather, the court shall decide on the defendant's request to dismiss the court action,

---

23. Art. 14(1) of the Arbitration Law provides as follows:

"A court before which an action is brought in respect of a civil dispute which is the subject of an arbitration agreement shall, if the defendant so requests, dismiss the action. Provided, this shall not apply in the following instances:

(i) when the arbitration agreement is null and void, cancelled, or for other reasons invalid;
(ii) when arbitration proceedings based on the arbitration agreement are inoperative or incapable of being performed; or
(iii) when the request is made by the defendant subsequent to the presentation of its statement in the oral hearing or in the preparations for argument proceedings on the substance [i.e., merits] of the disputes."

In contrast, the main text of Art. 8(1) of the Model Law provides that the court shall "refer the parties to arbitration" unless it finds that the arbitration agreement is null and void, etc.

which will raise as a preliminary procedural defense the existence of the allegedly valid arbitration agreement.

III. AN ACTION IN COURT FOR DECLARATION OF INVALIDITY OF ARBITRATION AGREEMENT

While the discussion above focuses on a court action that addresses the same subject matter as is covered by the arbitration agreement, we can distinguish from this an action for a declaration of the non-existence or invalidity of an arbitration agreement as such. There are debates as to whether or not such an action is categorically impermissible.[24] Those who argue against such actions point out that

(i) Art. 4 of the Arbitration Law provides that "with respect to arbitral proceedings, no court shall intervene except where so provided in this Law" and there is no provision in the Arbitration Law that allows such an action;
(ii) allowing such an action would seriously undermine Art. 23 of the Arbitration Law, which specifically provides for the framework of the court's remedy on the jurisdictional dispute; and
(iii) the validity of an arbitration agreement is only a procedural issue and not an issue on the merits, and an action for the court's declaration solely on such a procedural issue shall, as a matter of civil procedure law, categorically lack the legitimate interest in obtaining the court's declaration.

In this connection, it should be noted that the current German arbitration law, which is essentially based on the Model Law, has a specific provision that addresses this issue. Art. 1032(2) thereof provides that "prior to the constitution of the arbitral tribunal, an application may be made to the court to determine whether or not arbitration is admissible". Thus, under German law, it seems rather clear that once the arbitral tribunal has been constituted, an application cannot be made to the court to determine whether or not arbitration is admissible.[25]

In Japan, those who argue that an action for the court's declaration that the arbitration agreement is invalid, or otherwise not admissible, is not permissible point to the fact that Japanese Arbitration Law does not have a provision similar to Art. 1032(2) of the German law. As such, they argue, this is an indication that no such action

---

24. See the Round-table Discussions in *Theories and Practices of New Arbitration Law*, supra, pp. 23-26, pp. 193-197.
25. See Peter F. SCHLOSSER, "The New German Law on Arbitration: What is Capable of a Generalisation and what is not" in Takeshi KOJIMA, ed., *Theories and Practices of ADR II* (Chuo University Press 2005) p. 373, which states:

"[The] German legislator has decided that declaratory relief may be requested from the courts but that it also must be requested promptly. The courts may be addressed only as long as the arbitration tribunal is not definitively constituted."

is permissible under Japanese Arbitration Law either before or after the constitution of the arbitral tribunal.[26] Art. 4 of the Arbitration Law, like Art. 5 of the Model Law, provides that "with respect to arbitral proceedings, no court shall intervene except where so provided in the [Arbitration] Law". The fact that, unlike the Old Law, the Arbitration Law no longer has any provision that refers to the "actions for disallowance of arbitration" may also support such argument.[27] Others argue, however, that an action for a declaration that an arbitration agreement does not exist or is invalid is permissible so long as the prerequisite requirements of "legal interests" for obtaining such declaration are met.[28]

IV.   SEPARABILITY

The "separability" of an arbitration agreement was recognized under the Old Law by court precedents.[29] Now, however, the Arbitration Law clearly states in Art. 13(6) that "even if in a particular contract containing an arbitration agreement, any or all of the contractual provisions, excluding the arbitration agreement, are found to be null and void, cancelled or for other reasons invalid, the validity of the arbitration agreement shall not necessarily be affected." Thus, even where a party shows that there are grounds to invalidate the main agreement (such as rescission of the main agreement based upon alleged fraud), such a showing alone would not prevent the arbitral tribunal from proceeding with the arbitration and issuing an arbitral award. In such a ruling, the

---

26. See, Prof. Koichi MIKI's statement in the Round-table Discussions in *Theories and Practices of New Arbitration Law*, supra, pp. 23-24.

27. The Old Law referred to "actions for ... the disallowance of arbitration" in Art. 805, which was a provision setting forth which court shall have the competence to entertain such action, and which did not define the requirements for such actions. The Old Law, however, provided for the arbitrators' power to continue the arbitration procedure even where their jurisdiction was challenged. Art. 797 provided as follows: "The arbitrators may continue the arbitration procedure and make the award, even where a party asserts that the arbitration procedure is not permissible, or, in particular, that no legally valid arbitration agreement was concluded, that the arbitration agreement has no relation to the dispute to be decided, or that the arbitrators have no power to perform the office." In contrast, the Arbitration Law has no provision that refers to actions for disallowance of arbitration. With regard to actions for disallowance of arbitration under the Old Law, see, Hiroyuki TEZUKA, "Litigation Related to Arbitration" in Yasuhei TANIGUCHI, et al., *Complete Legal Forms Annotated* (1995).

28. See, e.g., Prof. Yoshimitsu AOYAMA's statement in the Round-table Discussions in *Theories and Practices of New Arbitration Law*, supra, p.25. Prof. Aoyama argued that whether an action for declaration of validity or invalidity of an arbitration agreement is permissible is an issue of the legal interests for obtaining a declaration by the courts generally, and Art. 4 of the Arbitration Law is irrelevant.

29. A Supreme Court judgment on 15 July 1975, MINSHU 29-6-1061, held that "while an arbitration agreement is executed by accompanying the main agreement, its validity shall be judged separately and independently from the main agreement, and that unless the parties have agreed otherwise, even where there is a defect in the formation of the main agreement, the validity of the arbitration agreement shall not necessarily be affected".

tribunal may determine that the main agreement is in fact invalid, but that the tribunal still has the jurisdiction to make that determination.

V. CONCLUSIONS

When Japan adopted the Model Law by introducing the new Arbitration Law, the legislators tried to adopt the Model Law in a straightforward way so as to make the Arbitration Law as compatible as possible with arbitration laws in other modern jurisdictions. The Arbitration Law has thereby succeeded both the pros and cons of the Model Law. On the issues of the arbitral tribunal's jurisdiction to determine on its own jurisdiction, the Arbitration Law has basically adopted the same provisions as in the Model Law. Thus, modern principles of *Kompetenz-Kompetenz* as reflected in the Model Law have similarly been adopted by the Arbitration Law. It is therefore relatively clear under the Arbitration Law that

(i) the arbitral tribunal does not need to stop the arbitral proceedings even where there is a challenge to its jurisdiction,

(ii) the court does not have to wait until the final award is issued in order for the court to intervene with respect to the issue of the tribunal's jurisdiction (i.e., the court may review the tribunal's affirmative ruling on its own jurisdiction, if a party challenges the tribunal's ruling within 30 days), and

(iii) the court has the final word on the issue of jurisdiction and the arbitral tribunal's determination on its jurisdiction is not free from the court's review.

The downside of the straightforward adoption of the Model Law is perhaps that on certain limited issues where the Model Law is relatively unclear or ambiguous, the Arbitration Law has inherited such ambiguities. They are:

(a) whether or not the arbitral tribunal's ruling on its jurisdiction as a "preliminary question" under Art. 16(3) of the Model Law must be or can be in the form of a preliminary/partial/interim award, and if such ruling is not in the form of a preliminary/partial/interim award, whether or not a party's failure to challenge such ruling would later bar the party from challenging the jurisdiction when the party seeks to set aside the final award; and

(b) whether or not an action or application for the court's declaration that the arbitration agreement is invalid or arbitration is otherwise impermissible may be filed with the court either before or after the tribunal is constituted.

A Brazilian View of the *Kompetenz-Kompetenz* Principle

*Paulo Cezar Aragão**

I.   A FUNDAMENTAL DISTINCTION

Professor William Park showed us in his Report, with the usual talent and thoroughness, the fundamental distinctions between the three variations of the principle by which arbitrators have the authority to rule on their own jurisdiction.[1]

First, the basic form of *Kompetenz-Kompetenz*, with its German origin, in which the arbitral tribunal would make a final ruling as to its jurisdiction (not subject to review by the courts). Second, a delayed judicial intervention whereby the courts refuse to examine the jurisdiction of an arbitral tribunal until such time as the arbitrators have ruled on the issue themselves (renamed by the French as *compétence-compétence*). The third model follows the binding determinations of the parties, in which the parties themselves decide who will have the final say.

Although the same principle is known in Portuguese as *competência-competência*, in our legal system, as in France and Germany itself,[2] the arbitrator has competence (*competência*) to decide on his own jurisdiction.[3] There is, however, a relevant issue to be mentioned in the use of the Portuguese terms for jurisdiction and competence, i.e., *jurisdição* and *competência*.

While, strictly and technically speaking, the former refers to the authority by which the state court system adjudicates a dispute in an enforceable and final way, the latter refers to which court, within the whole judicial system, has the authority to adjudicate a specific dispute. The difference is fundamental, since an arbitration agreement obviously withdraws the merits of a dispute from the state *jurisdiction* and not merely

---

* Partner, Barbosa, Müssnich & Aragão Advogados (Brazil). Former General Counsel of the Brazilian Securities and Exchange Commission. Vice-Chairman of the Arbitration Commission of the São Paulo Stock Exchange (BOVESPA).

1. See Sect. I of Professor William PARK's Report: "An Arbitrator's Jurisdiction to Determine Jurisdiction", this volume, pp. 55-153.

2. See *Fouchard, Gaillard, Goldman on International Commercial Arbitration*. (Kluwer Law International, The Hague 1999) p. 396.

3. For Brazilian case law see São Paulo Appellate Court, *Conflito de Competencia* (Jurisdiction Determination) no. 93.381-0/3-00 – Judge Regina Afonso Portes – 03.06.03

from a specific court within the judicial system.[4] However, to say in Portuguese that the arbitral tribunal has jurisdiction to determine its own jurisdiction would not be strictly correct.

A more appropriate way to express the concept would be to say that the arbitral tribunal has the authority to exclude the jurisdiction (*jurisdição*) of the court system. In effect, only the judicial system can be said to have jurisdiction, a point proven by the fact that the Brazilian arbitration law[5] never uses the word *jurisdição*.

II. SEPARABILITY

Nevertheless, the so-called *separability* and the *Kompentenz-Kompetenz* principles are clearly stated in Art. 8 of the Brazilian Arbitration Law,[6] which changed the traditional status of Brazil as one of the world's last remaining "islands of resistance" against arbitration, in the famous words of Professor René David. As a result of this change, Brazil has also recently adhered to the 1958 New York Convention.[7]

The *Kompetenz-Kompetenz* principle is seen in Brazil, as elsewhere, as a corollary of the *separability* principle. While the first deals with the *status* of the arbitrator (i.e., his capacity to adjudicate over the dispute) and to issues relating to the existence, validity and effectiveness (*eficácia*) of the arbitration agreement, the separability principle is understood by our legal commentators as an "isolation" of the arbitration clause vis-à-vis the agreement in which it has been included.

Under these principles of Brazilian law, an arbitration agreement is enforceable and may be the basis for an arbitration proceeding despite a party's challenge to the validity of the arbitration clause or even of the whole contract in which the arbitration clause is inserted.

This is seen in Brazil, as everywhere else, as a result of the acknowledgment by the judicial system and by the rules of civil procedure (which are enacted by the Federal Congress) of the parties' intention, in entering into an arbitration agreement, to exclude potential judicial adjudication of a dispute, due to the specific nature of the transaction or for any other reason.

---

4. Competence (*competência*) in Brazil refers to which of the courts within the judicial system will have jurisdiction in respect of a specific matter. See Art. 115 of the Brazilian Code of Civil Procedure.

5. Federal Law no. 9,307 of 23 September 1996, usually cited as Law 9,307/96.

6. Art. 8 of Law 9,307/96 reads as follows:

"An arbitration clause which forms part of a contract shall be treated as an agreement independent of the other terms of the contract. A decision that the contract is null and void shall not entail ipso jure the invalidity of the arbitration clause.

Sole paragraph: The arbitrator shall decide, at his own motion or on request by the parties, issues concerning the existence, validity and efficacy of the arbitration agreement and of the contract which contains the arbitration clause."

7. Enacted by Presidential Decree no. 4,311 dated 23 July 2002.

III.   TIMING AND EXTENT OF COURT INTERVENTION

Under Art. 8 of the Brazilian Arbitration Law, the state judicial system is prevented from ruling initially on the validity of the agreement and/or of the arbitration clause and will review or adjudicate the dispute, as the case may be, if and only if the arbitrator decides that he lacks jurisdiction or one of the parties eventually brings an annulment action under Art. 32 of the Law.[8] Clearly, then, in Brazil we follow the system where, absent a manifestly void agreement, intervention by the state courts is deferred to a subsequent stage, after the completion of the arbitration, when the courts may be asked to intervene as a result of an annulment lawsuit initiated by the aggrieved party.

However, because Brazil is a true full-fledged newcomer to the world of international commercial arbitration (notwithstanding a few scattered precedents of arbitration awards found in case law repertories of the last century), it is difficult to exclude the possibility of a request for the initial intervention by the state court system, through an injunction to restrain the arbitrators, under penalty of criminal contempt, from proceeding with arbitration. Recent court cases, in which governmental or government-controlled entities were involved, show that such a preliminary injunction may block an arbitration for a substantial time, even though the injunction was eventually quashed and the arbitration proceeded as originally agreed by the parties.

As Professor Park mentions, certain legal systems may distinguish between disputes as to the scope and validity of the arbitration clause, seen separately, and those related to the validity of the whole agreement in which the arbitration clause is inserted, with the former falling to the state court system, and the latter to the arbitral tribunal.[9]

In Brazil, however, no distinction is made between the grounds for challenging the arbitrability of a matter.

Arguments as to the invalidity of the arbitration clause as well as arguments as to the nullity of the agreement in which the arbitration clause is found must be submitted to the arbitrators. If the arbitrators find that the arbitration clause is valid, the arbitration will proceed until an award is granted by the arbitrators.[10] On the other hand, if the arbitral tribunal determines that it lacks jurisdiction, the tribunal should send the parties to the state court system.

The intervention *a posteriori* of the state courts results not only from Art. 8 of the Brazilian Arbitration Law, but also from Art. 20 thereof, which reads as follows:

---

8. Actions for annulment may be based on a number of jurisdictional defects: the arbitration agreement is null and void (Art. 32 under I), it was granted by someone who could not have served as an arbitrator(Art. 32 under II), it was rendered outside the limits established in the arbitration agreement (Art. 32 under IV), among others.

9. See Professor William Park's Report, supra, fn. 1.

10. See Art. 20, Second Paragraph:

"When the arguments are not accepted, the arbitration shall proceed normally, subject however to review of that decision by the competent judicial body, at the time a petition for setting aside the award is filed, as provided by Art. 33 of this Law."

"The party which intends to argue questions related to competence, bias or disqualification of the arbitrator or arbitrators, as well as the nullity, invalidity or inefficacy of the arbitration agreement, must do so at the first opportunity, after the initiation of the arbitration."

It is important to note that the *a posteriori* judicial review of the arbitration agreement is only applicable in those cases where the arbitration clause provides in an effective way for how the arbitration proceeding shall be initiated and conducted, or, as we say in Brazil, there is a full arbitration agreement.[11]

Since the arbitration is considered to have commenced upon the acceptance of the arbitrators of their function,[12] an agreement to arbitrate that provides for an effective nomination of the arbitrators is capable of commencing arbitration despite resistance by the other party. In this case, no judicial intervention is necessary to commence the proceeding.

On the other hand, when an arbitration agreement does not provide for the manner of commencing an arbitration proceeding, the other party may seek an order from the state courts to compel commencement of the arbitration. The procedure for doing so is set out in Arts. 6 and 7 of the Brazilian Arbitration Act:

"*Article 6.* In the absence of a provision as to the method of initiating the arbitration, the interested party shall serve the other party with a written notice by registered letter or by any other means which provides a record of delivery, calling for the other party to appear at a set date, time and place in order to sign the arbitration agreement.

Sole Paragraph: Where the party to whom notice is served fails to appear or refuses to sign the arbitration agreement, the other party can, pursuant to article 7 of this law, seek assistance from the Judicial Court which originally would have had jurisdiction to hear the case.

Article 7. Where there is an arbitration clause but one of the parties shows resistance as to the initiation of arbitration, the interested party may request a subpoena for the other party to appear in court in order to prepare the arbitration agreement with the judge designating a special hearing for such purpose."

---

11. See Pedro A. Batista MARTINS, "*O Poder Judiciário e Arbitragem: Quatro anos da Lei No. 9.307/96 (2ª Parte)*" [Judicial System and Arbitration: Four Years of Law no. 9,307 of 1996], *Revista Forense*, v. 358.

12. Art. 19 of the Brazilian Arbitration Act:

"An arbitral procedure is commenced when the appointment is accepted by the sole arbitrator or by the arbitrators, if several."

In this case, the specific performance of the arbitration agreement is conditional upon judicial verification of the existence, validity and effectiveness of the arbitration clause, as well as of the agreement in which the clause is found.

To render a decision that supplements the parties' agreement to arbitrate, the state court will necessarily have to analyze these preliminary issues. In such cases, when the arbitration agreement is dependent upon a ruling under Art. 7 of the Brazilian Arbitration Law, the application of the *Kompetenz- Kompetenz* principle may be restricted.

Recently, a new debate regarding the *Kompetenz-Kompetenz* principle and the New York Convention was raised in Brazil, as a result, on the one hand, of a lack of experience with international arbitration and, on the other hand, the recent coexistence of the domestic law and the international convention.

Indeed, Art. 8 of the Brazilian Arbitration Law refers to concepts similar to those found in Art. II of the New York Convention[13] with respect to the general rule that an arbitration agreement is sufficient to trigger an arbitration.

The New York Convention expressly limits, so to speak, the scope of the *Kompetenz-Kompetenz* principle in its Art. II(3), by giving jurisdiction to the state courts if "it finds that the agreement is null and void, inoperative or incapable of being performed".

Our law refers to the competence of the arbitral tribunal to rule on the "existence, validity and effectiveness of the arbitration clause". The issue, then, is when this residual authority of the court system shall be exercised.

Despite the clear rule under the Brazilian Arbitration Law, the arbitrators' competence was challenged in a complex case before the State Courts of Rio de Janeiro. The party challenging the arbitration agreement based its arguments on Art. II(3) of the New York Convention, arguing that the agreement was tainted by conflict of interest, fraud and simulation, and that as a result, the arbitration agreement was null and void and that the judicial courts had jurisdiction over the matter in dispute, setting aside the arbitration.

The lower court ruled that the *Kompetenz-Kompetenz* principle might be overcome when elements that would result in the invalidity of the entire agreement, and so necessarily of the arbitration clause as well, were present, such that the intention of the parties when executing the agreement was compromised. Based on Art. II(3) of the New York Convention (which, with all due respect, the lower court overstretched), the lower court held that the state courts could rule initially on the validity and operability of the arbitration agreement in cases where the will of the parties is being challenged. An appeal against this decision is still pending.

The lower court's decision seems contrary to both the New York Convention and Art. 8 of the Brazilian Arbitration Law, but since Brazilian courts are now passing through the same transition period that occurred in other countries during the second

---

13. Art. II(3) of the New York Convention reads as follows:

"The court of a Contracting State, when seized of an action in a matter in respect of which the parties have made an agreement within the meaning of this article, shall, at the request of one of the parties, refer the parties to arbitration, unless it finds that the said agreement is null and void, inoperative or incapable of being performed."

half of the last century, it may take the Brazilian court system a little while fully to accept the private restriction of its constitutional authority to adjudicate private disputes, as well as, specifically, to determine initially whether these disputes may or may not be arbitrated.

Another aspect of this transitional phase can be seen in the fact that complex commercial transactions that provide for arbitration are often the object of numerous judicial proceedings seeking interim measures to protect or safeguard rights. Sometimes these judicial proceedings enter into the merits of the transaction, which should be, in theory, subject to the jurisdiction of the arbitral tribunal.

Questions as to whether these judicial proceedings represent a waiver of the arbitration agreement have arisen in Brazil. In an annulment action before the São Paulo State Court, a party that had participated in arbitration argued that the award was null and void because the claimant had previously commenced a specific performance proceeding in the state courts of Sao Paulo,[14] and that the proceeding for specific performance represented a waiver of the arbitration agreement.

The São Paulo Appellate Court ruled that a waiver should be strictly construed and could only be inferred if the object of the judicial proceeding related to the entirety of the arbitration clause. Conversely, an action for the specific performance of a contractual arrangement could be interpreted as a change of the parties' intention to submit their disputes to arbitration. Based on Art. 20 of the Brazilian Arbitration Law, the court found that the waiver argument should have been presented to the arbitral tribunal, not the judicial court. In this case, therefore, the *Kompetenz-Kompetenz* principle was respected.

In summary, although Brazilian courts are still occasionally suffering from growing pains as they learn to deal with their deprivation of jurisdiction, it is fair to say that in Brazil we adopt the second of the models discussed by Professor Park, the French version of *compétence-compétence*, in which the courts will examine *a posteriori* the jurisdiction of the arbitral tribunal.

---

14. São Paulo Appellate Court. Interlocutory Appeal [*Agravo de Instrumento*] No. 416.598-4/0.

Working Group A

3. Control of Jurisdiction by Injunction Issued by National Courts

Control of Jurisdiction by Injunctions Issued by National Courts

*Dr. Julian D.M. Lew QC**

I.   INTRODUCTION

In recent years, there has been an increasing discussion and concern about national courts issuing orders preventing a party from initiating, continuing, participating in, or even co-operating with arbitration proceedings. Several cases have been reported where such injunctions were issued. In most of these cases the court issuing the "anti-suit" or more particularly "anti-arbitration" injunction, has been a court of the place of residence of the party requesting the injunction (often a State or a State-entity).[1] Indeed, it is often the respondent in the arbitration, "who runs to its own courts to get the kind of 'assistance' which it could not hope to get from a neutral court or tribunal".[2] Furthermore, the court issuing the injunction is either a court of the seat of arbitration or a court of the place of eventual enforcement of the award.[3]

---

* Arbitrator & Barrister, 20 Essex Street, Visiting Professor and Head of School of International Arbitration, Centre for Commercial Law Studies (CCLS), Queen Mary, University of London.

1. Sigvard JARVIN, Comment on ICC No. 4862, Partial Award, 1986 in Sigvard JARVIN, Yves DERAINS, Jean-Jacques ARNALDEZ, eds., *Collection of ICC Awards 1986-1990* (Deventer 1994) p. 517. For examples, see *Himpurna California Energy v. Republic of Indonesia*; *Salini Costruttori S.p.a. v. Ethiopia*; *HUBCO v. WAPDA* (for a discussion of these cases, see below, IV.1-IV.3, pp. 207-211). This observation is corroborated by informal information given to me by the General Counsel of the ICC, according to which the criterion that is the most frequently used to determine the national court having jurisdiction to grant the anti-arbitration injunction is the nationality of the respondent in the arbitral proceedings. Indeed, during the past ten years, approximately thirty-one cases involving anti-suit injunctions were brought to the attention of the ICC Court Secretariat. In twenty-five of these cases, the jurisdiction of the national court was based on the nationality of the respondent in the arbitration.

2. Jan PAULSSON, "Interference by National Courts" in Lawrence W. NEWMAN, Richard D. HILL, eds., *The Leading Arbitrators' Guide to International Arbitration* (New York 2004) p. 123.

3. Alan REDFERN and Martin HUNTER, *Law and Practice of International Commercial Arbitration*, 4th edn., (London 2004) p. 409, para. 7-33.

The extent of the problem of national courts' wrongful interference with the arbitration process in this way is unclear. Informal estimations given to me by some of the leading arbitration institutions suggest that cases of anti-arbitration injunctions remain relatively rare. Since 1996, the ICC Court Secretariat has been informed of thirty-one cases where requests for anti-arbitration injunctions were filed.[4] It is interesting to note that ten of these cases were filed in 2005 alone. Fortunately, the occurrence of anti-arbitration injunctions is still far less frequent in international arbitrations administered by other institutions. In the case of the LCIA I understand that during the past ten years, there have only been seven cases affected by an anti-arbitration injunction, three of which arose during the past five years. The ICDR does not presently record the occurrence of anti-arbitration injunctions in ICDR arbitrations. The Stockholm Chamber of Commerce has reported only one case involving an anti-arbitration injunction in the past five years, and in this case the request for injunction was withdrawn before the court took any decision. Finally, the Hong Kong International Arbitration Centre, WIPO, the Singapore International Arbitration Centre,[5] the Swiss Chamber of Commerce, the Austrian Federal Economic Chamber, as well as the Czech Arbitration Court, all have had no arbitrations affected by anti-arbitration injunctions.[6]

These figures are very small. However, anti-arbitration injunctions cause serious concerns for all those involved in the arbitration.[7] As pertinently described by Jan Paulsson

> "[t]he subversion of an arbitration agreement is a grave matter. Instead of a neutral forum, the victim suddenly finds itself confronted by a jurisdiction which will judge its conduct according to a very different yardstick. Without even mentioning the unmentionable (corruption and xenophobia), everything is suddenly stacked in favour of the other side: language, procedure, practical convenience, ability to use one's own lawyers, cultural affinities with the decision-maker ... and the list goes on".[8]

This is exactly what the selection of arbitration aimed to avoid.

---

4. It must be assumed that certain cases involving anti-arbitration injunctions were not brought to the attention of the ICC Court Secretariat. In twenty-seven out of the thirty-one reported cases, the request for the anti-arbitration injunction was filed by the respondent to the arbitral proceedings.

5. For a case involving anti-arbitration injunctions in Singapore see *Mitsui Engineering and Shipbuilding Co Ltd v. Easton Graham Rush and Another* [2004] 2 SLR 14; [2004] SGHC 26. In this case, the High Court of Singapore refused to grant an anti-arbitration injunction in order to stay an arbitration governed by the Singapore International Arbitration Act which has incorporated the UNCITRAL Model Law.

6. It is important to note that this information was provided unofficially and does not constitute definitive statements of these institutions. The information is however illustrative of the rare nature of this problem.

7. Julian D.M. LEW, "Anti-suit Injunctions Issued by National Courts – To Prevent Arbitration Proceedings", in Emmanuel GAILLARD, ed., *Anti-suit Injunctions in International Arbitration*, IAI Series on International Arbitration No. 2 (Bern 2005) p. 25.

8. J. PAULSSON, *op. cit.*, fn. 2, p. 124.

The effect of an anti-arbitration injunction is to destabilize the parties' dispute resolution environment. In many cases, anti-arbitration injunctions are sought to protect a weak party and perhaps as a tactical play to indicate the power available to the party seeking the injunction. The effect of the injunction is to undermine the efficacy and integrity of international arbitration. Hence, Judge Stephen Schwebel described anti-arbitration injunctions as "one of the gravest problems of contemporary international commercial arbitration".[9] In the absence of exceptional reasons, perhaps anti-arbitration injunctions should not exist at all.

Anti-arbitration injunctions are sought when the existence or validity of an arbitration agreement is called into question.[10] It is generally accepted that the court of the seat of the arbitration has supervisory jurisdiction. Namely, this court may stay an arbitration or set aside an award on jurisdiction if they consider that the arbitral tribunal does not have jurisdiction, e.g., there is no valid arbitration agreement. However, in accordance with the principle of competence-competence, national courts should normally allow the arbitral tribunal to consider the issue of its jurisdiction and the validity of the arbitration agreement in the first instance.

There may be situations in which the court of the seat of the arbitration considers it appropriate to intervene in the arbitration process in order to stop or at least stay the arbitration until it has decided the issue of arbitral jurisdiction itself. The obligation to stay court proceedings in favour of arbitration under Art. II of the New York Convention is subject to the arbitration agreement not being "null and void, inoperative or incapable of being performed". In this case, "[w]hen the intervening court is one at the seat of arbitration, it may be pointless, imprudent, or indeed unlawful for the arbitrators to proceed".[11]

The question of greater interest is whether national courts not situated in the country of the seat of the arbitration – and therefore not enjoying any supervisory jurisdiction – may also stop arbitration proceedings by granting anti-arbitration injunctions. Can these courts determine the issue of arbitral jurisdiction and impose that decision on an arbitral tribunal sitting in another country before it has had an opportunity to rule on the issue? Why would a national court wish to take such action? What is the national court's interest to do so? What is the source of the national court's jurisdiction over foreign arbitration proceedings, i.e., what is the legal basis for granting anti-arbitration injunctions? Most interesting, in many respects, is what actions should arbitrators take in the event of an anti-arbitration injunction? Should an arbitrator's personal interest under the law override his duty to the parties under the law and rules governing the arbitration?

These are some of the questions that the present report will seek to analyse. The primary focus will be on anti-arbitration injunctions issued by national courts not in the country of the seat of arbitration seeking to restrain the implementation, continuation or conclusion of arbitration proceedings. The aim is to decide whether, and if so when,

---

9. S.M. SCHWEBEL, "Anti-Suit Injunctions in International Arbitration – An Overview" in *Anti-suit Injunctions in International Arbitration*, *op. cit.*, fn. 7, p. 5.

10. S. JARVIN, *loc. cit.*, fn. 1.

11. J. PAULSSON, *op. cit.*, fn. 2, p. 114.

the granting of these anti-arbitration injunctions may be compatible with the system of international arbitration. Before answering these questions, the notion of "anti-arbitration injunction" must be clarified.

II. WHAT IS AN ANTI-ARBITRATION INJUNCTION AND WHAT IS IT MEANT TO DO?

An anti-suit injunction is a court order preventing a party from initiating or continuing with alternative proceedings abroad.[12] It is "a device, originally found in common law countries, whereby a court orders a party to refrain from bringing a claim before the courts of another State or before an arbitral tribunal or, if the party has already brought such a claim, orders that party to withdraw from, or to suspend, the proceedings".[13] Anti-suit injunctions have been designed to prevent vexatious or oppressive litigation abroad.[14] The aim of the injunction is to protect the jurisdiction of one court in respect of the same parties and the cause of action from interference by the exercise of a jurisdiction of another court abroad.[15]

In the context of international arbitration, anti-suit injunctions can be requested to protect or to prevent the jurisdiction of an arbitral tribunal.[16] In the first case, the injunction is granted by a national court in order to stay court proceedings brought in violation of an arbitration agreement. The aim of this first type of injunction would be to enforce an arbitration agreement between the parties. This is in accordance with the requirements of Art. II of the New York Convention and is found in many national laws. It also is clearly set out in Art. 8(1) of the UNCITRAL Model Law. This type of injunction is in support of the arbitration process.

In the second case, the injunction seeks to prevent arbitration proceedings in order to protect the jurisdiction of a State court over a given case. As this second type of injunction is specifically directed against the arbitration, it is more appropriately called an "anti-arbitration injunction".

Like anti-suit injunctions, anti-arbitration injunctions are made in personam. They may be directed against one or both parties to the arbitration, against the arbitral tribunal or a particular arbitrator, or against the arbitral institution itself.[17]

Anti-arbitration injunctions may have two purposes. Firstly, they may be granted in order to restrain the implementation, continuation or conclusion of arbitration proceedings. Secondly, they may seek to prevent actions for the enforcement of arbitral

---

12. J.D.M. LEW, *loc. cit.,* fn. 7.
13. Emmanuel GAILLARD, Introduction to *Anti-suit Injunctions in International Arbitration, op. cit.,* fn. 7, p. 1.
14. S.M. SCHWEBEL, *op. cit.,* fn. 9, p. 8.
15. S.M. SCHWEBEL, *ibid.*
16. J.D.M. LEW, *op. cit.,* fn. 7, p. 26.
17. J.D.M. LEW, *op. cit.,* fn. 7, p. 33.

awards.[18] Since the present report deals with the control of arbitration proceedings by injunctions issued by national courts, the primary focus will be on the first type of anti-arbitration injunctions.

III.   ANTI-ARBITRATION INJUNCTIONS IN THEORY

May a national court situated in a country other than the seat of the arbitration grant an anti-arbitration injunction in order to stop an arbitration abroad? In other words, may it decide the issue of arbitral jurisdiction and impose that decision on the arbitrators before they have had an opportunity to rule on the issue themselves?

At first sight, anti-arbitration injunctions do not raise the same criticism levelled at traditional anti-suit injunctions because they do not directly interfere with the jurisdiction of a sovereign State.[19] However, the legality of anti-arbitration injunctions remains in question as they appear to be incompatible with international arbitration law.[20]

Anti-arbitration injunctions most often arise when the existence or validity of an arbitration agreement is called into question – though this may be just the pretext to stop or destabilize the arbitration. In theory at least, it may be entirely justified for a party contesting the existence of a valid arbitration agreement to commence court actions before the court it considers to have jurisdiction, rather than to initiate arbitration proceedings and to wait for the arbitral tribunal to render an award which would then be challenged on grounds of lack of jurisdiction. The question which arises is whether it also would be justified for a party having signed an arbitration agreement to commence a court action in order to prevent arbitration proceedings from being initiated, continued or concluded. Essentially, in each instance the question is whether an anti-arbitration injunction can be justified by the facts of the particular case or whether it is being used by a party and its lawyer as a device to undermine, destabilize, delay or avoid an arbitration.[21]

There are two fundamental practical considerations as to how anti-arbitration injunctions are used in practice and whether there are circumstances in which anti-arbitration injunctions can be justified. First, what in theory are the powers of national

---

18. See, *e.g.*, *Oil & National Gas Commission Ltd v. Western Company of North America*, (1987) All India Rep SC 674; *KBC v. Pertamina* (Indonesian courts grant injunction in order to prevent KBC from starting enforcement proceedings before US courts under penalty of US$ 500,000 per day fine for any breach). On this case, see Emmanuel GAILLARD, "KBC v. Pertamina: Landmark Decision on Anti-Suit Injunctions", New York Law Journal, 2 October 2003.

19. J.D.M. LEW, *loc. cit.*, fn. 16; see also Sandrine CLAVEL, "*Anti-Suit Injunctions et arbitrage*", Revue de l'arbitrage, (2001, no. 4), p. 701.

20. S.M. SCHWEBEL, *op. cit.*, fn. 9, pp. 5 et seq. and pp. 9 et seq.; J.D.M. LEW, *loc. cit.*, fn. 16; S. CLAVEL, *loc. cit.* fn. 19; Emmanual GAILLARD, "*Il est interdit d'interdire: réflexions sur l'utilisation des anti-suit injunctions dans l'arbitrage commercial international*", Revue de l'arbitrage, (2004, no. 1), p. 47.

21. J.D.M. LEW, *op. cit.*, fn. 7, p. 27.

courts to grant anti-arbitration injunctions? Second, what are the various ways in which national courts can support – instead of hinder – foreign arbitration proceedings?

1. Anti-arbitration Injunctions in Domestic Law

Anti-suit injunctions originated in common law jurisdictions. However, in international arbitration, anti-suit injunctions have also been granted by courts in certain civil law countries. This paper reviews the circumstances in which courts from common law and civil law countries have exercised the power to grant anti-arbitration injunctions. The primary focus is on the legal systems in England, United States, Switzerland, France, Sweden and the UNCITRAL Model Law.

The principles used in considering the granting of anti-arbitration injunctions are similar to those used in anti-suit injunctions. Analogy with anti-suit injunctions can therefore be made in the absence of clear anti-arbitration jurisprudence.

a. England

Courts in England have a general power to grant injunctions. However, the basis for the granting of anti-arbitration injunctions in particular is not entirely clear.

Under the Arbitration Act 1996, a party who has taken no part in the arbitral proceedings, including participating in the constitution of the arbitral tribunal, can nevertheless apply to the courts for a declaration that the tribunal lacked jurisdiction. This request can be coupled with an injunction restraining the continuation of the arbitral proceedings.[22] The possibility to apply for such an injunction is only available to a person who has not participated in the arbitration.[23]

However, in *Welex AG v. Rosa Maritime Ltd* (*The Epsilon Rosa*),[24] the Court of Appeal held that, in accordance with Sect. 37(1) of the Supreme Court Act 1981 for England and Wales, the High Court has a general power to grant permanent anti-suit injunctions "... in all cases in which it appears to the court to be just and convenient to do so". This case concerned an appeal against the High Court's decision to grant an anti-suit injunction restraining Welex from proceeding with court proceedings in Poland brought in violation of an arbitration agreement. The Court of Appeal ruled that even if the Arbitration Act 1996 did not give an express power to the High Court to grant the injunction, such power could be derived from its general power under Sect. 37(1).

Even if the English courts' general power to grant injunctive relief includes anti-arbitration injunctions, they exercise this power only rarely. Indeed, the English courts take a very strict position regarding injunctions seeking to restrain arbitration proceedings. Only in exceptional circumstances and specifically only where it is clear

---

22. Sect. 72(1) Arbitration Act 1996.
23. MUSTILL and BOYD, *Commercial Arbitration*, 2nd edn., 2001 Companion (London 2001) p. 362. See also Andrew TWEEDDALE/ Keren TWEEDDALE, *Arbitration of Commercial Disputes*, (Oxford 2005) para. 24.65, p. 704.
24. [2003] EWCA Civ 938, [2003] 2 Lloyd's Report 509.

that the arbitration proceedings have been wrongly brought will an anti-arbitration injunction be granted.[25]

This position is illustrated by the case of *Compagnie Nouvelle France Navigation S.A. v. Compagnie Navale Afrique du Nord* (the *Oranie* and the *Tunisie*).[26] In this case, the Court of Appeal held that although, as a matter of principle, courts have the power to stay arbitration proceedings when the validity of the arbitration agreement is in question, this power should be exercised very carefully. Indeed, anti-arbitration injunctions should not be granted simply because the balance of convenience favours the injunction. According to Sellers LJ, the guiding principles for granting anti-arbitration injunctions are (1) that the stay must not cause injustice to the claimant in the arbitration, and (2) that the applicant for a stay must satisfy the court that the continuation of the arbitration would be oppressive or vexatious on him or an abuse of process of the court. In this case, the Court of Appeal decided that the conditions were not met and denied the granting of the anti-arbitration injunction.[27]

This approach was confirmed recently in *Weissfisch v. Julius, Weissfisch & Davis*.[28] In this case, an action was brought before the English High Court seeking (1) a declaration that the arbitration agreement providing for Swiss law and a Swiss arbitral seat was void and (2) an injunction restraining the sole arbitrator under the agreement from acting as arbitrator. The only real connection with England was the fact that the arbitrator was an English lawyer within the jurisdiction of the court.

The Court of Appeal rejected the request on essentially the same grounds as the High Court. These grounds were: (1) the arbitration agreement states expressly that disputes should be resolved by the sole arbitrator, with his seat in Switzerland and governed by Swiss law; (2) consequently, any issues as to the validity of the arbitration agreement must be resolved in Switzerland according to Swiss law; (3) this conclusion accords with the principles of international arbitration law set out in the New York Convention and recognized in the English Arbitration Act 1996; (4) an English court which restrains an arbitrator under an arbitration agreement with a seat in a foreign jurisdiction to which the parties unquestionably agreed would violate these principles; (5) exceptional circumstances may, nonetheless, justify the English court in taking such an action; (6) in the present case, no special circumstances were shown to exist.

---

25. David St. John SUTTON and Judith GILL, *Russel on Arbitration*, 32nd edn. (London 2003) p. 309, para. 7-031; Julian D.M. LEW, Loukas A. MISTELIS, Stefan M. KRÖLL, *Comparative International Commercial Arbitration* (The Hague, London, New York 2003), p. 363, para. 15-25. See also the case of the *"Ithaka"* [1939] 3 All. E. R. 630, in which Mackinnon LJ held that a party could not be granted an anti-arbitration injunction because parties must be bound by their agreement to arbitrate.

26. [1966] 1 Lloyd's Law Reports 477.

27. See also *Industry Chimiche Italia Centrale v. Alexander G. Tsavliris and Sons Maritime Co. (The Choco Star)* [1987] 1 Lloyd's Report 508, CA. In this case, the Court of Appeal decided not to grant an anti-arbitration injunction, even if the validity of the arbitration agreement was in question and even if the issues raised in the arbitration were less extensive than those raised in the court proceedings.

28. [2006] EWCA Civ 218 (available under <www.bailii.org/ew/cases/EWCA/Civ/2006/218.html>). On this case, see H.R. DUNDAS, "An Extraordinary Arbitration: Weissfisch v. Julius & Ors [2006] EWCA Civ 218", in 3 Transnational Dispute Resolution (2006, Issue 2).

The Court of Appeal did not specify the nature of these "exceptional circumstances" susceptible of justifying the granting of an anti-arbitration injunction, but referred this matter back to the High Court.

b. United States

It is well established that in the United States courts have a general power to grant anti-suit injunctions.[29] Before a court may grant an anti-suit injunction, three threshold requirements must be met: (1) the court issuing the injunction must have jurisdiction; (2) the parties to both proceedings must be the same; and (3) the decision in the action before the court issuing the injunction must dispose of the foreign court proceedings. Once these requirements have been met, the standard applied for issuing an anti-suit injunction varies depending on the court before which the injunction is sought.[30] There appear to be different approaches of the US Courts of Appeal.

The Courts of Appeal for the Second, Third, Sixth and District of Columbia Circuits apply a restrictive standard based on comity.[31] Accordingly, one court must not interfere with the jurisdiction of another court, even if the foreign court proceedings are oppressive or vexatious. In case of parallel proceedings, both proceedings may proceed until one court renders a final judgment which can be pled as a res judicata before the other court. Anti-suit injunctions should be granted rarely and only to protect the jurisdiction or a public policy of the US forum.

The Courts of Appeal for the Fifth, Seventh, and Ninth Circuits follow a liberal standard when considering the granting of anti-suit injunctions.[32] According to these courts, anti-suit injunctions may be granted if the foreign court proceedings "would frustrate a policy of the forum issuing the injunction, would be vexatious or oppressive, would threaten the issuing court's jurisdiction, and when adjudicating in separate actions would result in delay, inconvenience, expense, inconsistency or race to judgement".[33] Under this liberal standard, less importance is placed on comity. The most important criteria is whether the foreign proceedings are vexatious or oppressive. In this regard, the mere inconvenience of duplicative proceedings, namely the additional costs and delays involved, may suffice for granting the anti-suit injunction.[34]

---

29. *Kaepa, Inc. v. Achilles Corp.*, 76 F.3d 624, 626 (5th Cir. 1996).

30. On anti-suit injunctions in the United States, see generally John FELLAS, "Anti-Suit Injunctions – Litigating Across Borders", 3 Transnational Dispute Management (2006, Issue 1).

31. See, e.g., *Laker Airways Ltd v. Sabena, Belgian World Airlines*, 731 F.2d 909 (D.C. Cir. 1984); *Gau Shan Co v. Bankers Trust Co*, 956 F.2d 1349 (6th Cir. 1992); *China Trade*, 837 F.2d 34; *Compagnie Des Bauxites de Guinea v. Ins Co of N America*, 651 F.2d 877 (3rd Cir. 1981), cert. denied, 457 U.S. 1105 (1982); *Younis Bros & Co v. Cigna Worldwide Ins Co*, 167 F. Supp. 2d 743 (E.D. Pa. 2001); *Kirby v. Norfolk S Ry Co*, 71 F. Supp. 2d 1363, 1367 (N.D. Ga. 1999).

32. See, e.g., *Kaepa*, 76 F.3d 626-627 ; *Allendale Mut Ins Co v. Bull Data Sys, Inc*, 10 F.3d 425 (7th Cir. 1993); *Seattle Totems Hockey Club, Inc v. Nat'l Hockey League*, 652 F.2d 852 (9th Cir. 1981), cert. denied, 457 U.S. 1105 (1982).

33. J. FELLAS, *op. cit.*, fn. 30, p. 2.

34. Marco STACHER, "You Don't Want to Go There – Antisuit Injunctions in International Commercial Arbitration", 23 ASA Bulletin (2005, no. 4), p. 643.

The approach of the Court of Appeal for the First Circuit is somewhere in between the restrictive and the liberal standards.[35] Comity is an important criteria to be considered before granting an anti-suit injunction. However, an anti-suit injunction can be justified not only in the two situations contemplated by the courts following the restrictive approach, but also in other situations. The test is whether the anti-suit injunction can be justified in light of "the totality of the circumstances". According to the court

> "these include (but are by no means limited to) such things as: the nature of the two actions (i.e., whether they are merely parallel or whether the foreign action is more properly classified as interdictory); the posture of the proceedings in the two countries; the conduct of the parties (including their good faith or lack thereof); the importance of the policies at stake in the litigation; and, finally, the extent to which the foreign action has the potential to undermine the forum court's ability to reach a just and speedy result".[36]

US courts are reluctant to grant anti-arbitration injunctions. One of the few cases where a US court has granted an anti-arbitration injunction in order to stop an arbitration abroad was *General Electric Company v. Deutz AG*.[37] This case concerned a contract providing for ICC arbitration in London concluded between General Electric and a third company. Deutz subsequently joined in this agreement. A dispute arose and General Electric commenced court proceedings before a US court against Deutz alleging breach of contract. Deutz responded by requesting an order to compel General Electric to arbitration in conformity with the arbitration agreement. Deutz's request was denied on the ground that there was no arbitration agreement between Deutz and General Electric. Deutz nonetheless initiated an ICC arbitration. In response, General Electric requested an anti-arbitration injunction enjoining Deutz from proceeding with the ICC arbitration in London.

The Court granted the anti-arbitration injunction based on its general power to grant injunctive relief. It held that the principle of comity required it to distinguish between domestic and international arbitrations. It could not apply the rule, applicable in domestic arbitration, according to which a district court is obliged to enjoin arbitration if it concludes that the parties have not agreed to arbitrate. Rather, in order to respect the international nature of the arbitration, the court decided to follow the restrictive standard applicable in case of an anti-suit injunction against foreign court proceedings. It held that both situations for the granting of an anti-arbitration injunction under the restrictive standard existed. Firstly, the ICC arbitration commenced by Deutz threatened the jurisdiction of the US forum. Secondly, Deutz, by commencing arbitration proceedings, was evading strong US public policies. The court held that the preservation of the sanctity of the earlier judgment which denied the existence of an

---

35. *Quaak v. Klynveld Peat Marwick Goerdeler Bedrijfsrevisoren*, 361 F.3d 11 (1st Cir. 8 Mar. 2004). For an analysis of this case, see J. FELLAS, *op. cit.*, fn. 30, pp. 15 et seq.

36. 361 F.3d 19.

37. Published in 15 Mealey's International Arbitration Report (2000, no. 10) pp. C-1 et seq.

arbitration agreement between Deutz and General Electric was an important public policy of the United States.

From the above it follows that US courts have the power to grant anti-arbitration injunctions on the same legal basis and under the same conditions as those applicable to anti-suit injunctions directed against foreign court proceedings.

c. Switzerland

There are no provisions in Swiss law providing Swiss courts with a legal basis for the granting of anti-arbitration injunctions.[38]

Further, the granting of anti-arbitration injunctions by the Swiss courts seems to be incompatible with the Swiss legal system. Indeed, in the very recent decision in *Air (PTY) Ltd v. International Air Transport Association (IATA) and C SA in liquidation*,[39] the Court of First Instance of the Canton of Geneva ruled that anti-suit injunctions, including anti-arbitration injunctions, are contrary to the Swiss legal system.[40]

This is true for various reasons. Firstly, as will be shown in more detail below,[41] anti-arbitration injunctions violate the New York Convention to which Switzerland is a Contracting State. Secondly, even in cases where the New York Convention does not apply, the granting of anti-arbitration injunctions seems to be contrary to Swiss law. Indeed, in its decision cited above, the Geneva Court ruled that anti-arbitration injunctions contradict the principle of competence-competence, which is a well established principle in Swiss law. According to the court

> "[a]s a matter of Swiss law there is no such thing as a 'judicial tutelage' of the courts over arbitrators; quite to the contrary, Swiss law fully implements the principle of 'Kompetenz-Kompetenz' both in its positive effect ... and its negative effect.... The jurisdiction of a court to determine whether an arbitration agreement is valid – *which cannot in any event lead to an anti-suit injunction* – exists only when the arbitration agreement is relied upon as a defence before the court...". (Emphasis added)[42]

This conclusion is consistent with the decision of the Swiss Federal Tribunal in *Fomento de Construcciones y Contratas S.A. v. Colon Container Terminal S.A.*[43] There the Federal Tribunal held that in cases of parallel proceedings, arbitral tribunals with seat in Switzerland must apply the principles of lis pendens and res judicata in order to avoid

---

38. Jan-Michael AHRENS, Enforcing Arbitral Jurisdiction in Switzerland, Arbitration Seminar, London 2-3 June 2005, para. 5.

39. Case no. C/1043/2005-15SP, Republic and Canton of Geneva Judiciary, Court of First Instance, 2 May 2005 (an English translation of the decision is published in 23 ASA Bulletin (2005, no. 4) pp. 739 et seq.).

40. See 23 ASA Bulletin (2005, no. 4), pp. 739 et seq. at p. 747.

41. See infra, under V. pp. 217-218.

42. *Air (PTY) Ltd v. International Air Transport Association (IATA) and C SA in liquidation*, decision cited under fn. 39, p. 747.

43. DFT 127 III 279; on this argument see M. STACHER, *op. cit.*, fn. 34, pp. 650 et seq.

contradictory awards.[44] These principles do not empower Swiss courts or arbitral tribunals to prevent foreign courts from continuing with parallel proceedings and from rendering judgments. In accordance with these principles, contradictory judgments are avoided, not by preventing the rendering of foreign judgments, but by recognizing or enforcing such judgments.[45]

d. France

It appears to be generally possible for French courts to order a party not to continue proceedings brought before a foreign court.[46] However, concerning anti-arbitration injunctions in particular, the arguments against such injunctions in Swiss law seem to apply with even more force in French law. Indeed, the French New Code of Civil Procedure expressly mandates the negative effect of the competence-competence principle, and the French courts are very strict in its application.[47]

Art. 1458 of the NCCP, which applies to both domestic and international arbitrations, provides that

---

44. In the *Fomento* case the Swiss Federal Tribunal set aside an arbitral tribunal's award accepting jurisdiction, because the question of the validity of the arbitration agreement was still pending before the Panamanian courts which had been seized of an identical action prior to the commencement of the arbitral proceedings. According to the Federal Tribunal the arbitral tribunal should not have rendered an award on its jurisdiction but should have stayed the arbitral proceedings in favour of the Panamanian court proceedings. This decision is somewhat perverse to the normally positive pro-arbitration approach of the Swiss courts and may well be challenged at an appropriate time. A proposal for a modification of the Swiss Private International Law Act is currently before the Swiss Federal Parliament and is likely to be approved. According to this proposal an arbitral tribunal with seat in Switzerland may rule on its jurisdiction even if an identical action is already pending before another arbitral tribunal or a national court, unless the tribunal considers a stay of the arbitral proceedings appropriate. A report of the Swiss Federal Government in favour of this proposal, issued on 17 Feburary 2006, is available on the web under <http://www.admin.ch/ch/d/ff/2006/4677.pdf> (in German).

45. See Art. 27(2)(c) Swiss Private International Law Statute.

46. See, e.g., *Banque Worms v. Epoux Brachot et autres*, Cour de cassation (1er Ch. Civile), 19 November 2002, 2003.797, commented by G. KAIRALLAH; JCP, 2002 II 10201; Gazette du Palais, 25-26 June 2003, 29, commented by M-L NIBOYET.

47. On the negative effect of the competence-competence principle in French law, see generally Emmanuel GAILLARD and John SAVAGE, eds., *Fouchard Gaillard Goldman on International Commercial Arbitration*, (The Hague, Boston, London 1999) p. 407, paras. 661 et seq.; see also, *Société American Bureau of Shipping (ABS) v. Copropriété maritime Jules Vernes et autres (Cour de cassation* (1re Ch. Civile), 26 June 2001, Revue de l'arbitrage (2001, no. 3), pp. 529 et seq.) where the *Cour de cassation* ruled:

"*Seule la nullité manifeste de la convention d'arbitrage est de nature à faire obstacle à l'application du principe selon lequel il appartient à l'arbitre de statuer sur sa propre compétence, principe qui consacre la priorité de la compétence arbitrale pour statuer sur l'existence, la validité et l'étendue de la convention d'arbitrage.*"

"(1) [i]f a dispute pending before an arbitral tribunal on the basis of an arbitration agreement is brought before a State court, it shall declare itself incompetent.

(2) If the dispute is not yet before an arbitral tribunal, the State court shall also declare itself incompetent, unless the arbitration agreement is manifestly null and void.

(3) In neither case may the State court declare itself incompetent at its own motion."

The effect of Art. 1458 NCCP is to ensure that the arbitral tribunal is the first to decide the issue of its jurisdiction "prior to any court or other judicial authority".[48] The role of the courts is limited to the review of the arbitrator's award on jurisdiction at the annulment or enforcement stage.

It is interesting to note that at the time of the French international arbitration law reform in 1981, the adoption of the negative effect of the competence-competence principle was justified by two policy considerations. Firstly, the objective was to avoid delaying tactics by the parties. Secondly, the reform intended that all questions about the existence and validity of the arbitration agreement should be considered by the court of appeal of the place of arbitration. It was intended that no other court, in France or abroad, should have the power to rule on the existence or validity of the arbitration agreement at least before the arbitral tribunal has reached its own decision.[49]

Accordingly it would seem that French courts cannot grant anti-arbitration injunctions as they are contrary to French international arbitration law.

e.   Sweden

Swedish law does not recognize the negative effect of the competence-competence principle. Art. 2(1) of the Swedish Arbitration Act 1999 provides

"[t]he arbitrators may rule on their own jurisdiction to decide the dispute. *The aforesaid shall not prevent a court from determining such a question at the request of a party.* The arbitrators may continue the arbitral proceedings pending the determination by the court". (Emphasis added)

Hence, under Swedish law arbitral tribunals do not enjoy a priority over State courts in determining the issue of their jurisdiction. A party may request a court to render a declaratory judgment on the jurisdiction of the arbitral tribunal before the arbitrators have rendered an award on the issue.

This rule must be read in relation with Art. 2(2) which provides that the decision of an arbitral tribunal that it has jurisdiction is not binding. The arbitrators' acceptance of their jurisdiction is not expressed in the form of an award, but in the form of a decision, which is not final and binding either on the parties or on the arbitrators.[50] This would

---

48. P. FOUCHARD, E. GAILLARD, B. GOLDMAN, *op. cit.*, fn. 47, p. 401, para. 660.

49. On the policy considerations, see P. FOUCHARD, E. GAILLARD, B. GOLDMAN, *ibid.*, pp. 410 et seq., paras. 677 et seq.

50. See Sect. 27 Arbitration Act 1999 on the distinction between decision and award.

appear to mean that the arbitrators are free to reverse or amend their decision on jurisdiction at a later stage in the proceedings. It also means that a party dissatisfied with the arbitrators' decision can institute a court action during the continuation of the arbitration proceedings.[51]

The fact that Swedish law rejects the negative effect of the competence-competence doctrine suggests that Swedish courts may grant anti-arbitration injunctions or, at least, that the issuance of such injunctions is not contrary to the Swedish legal system. On the other hand, none of the rules contained in the Swedish Arbitration Act provide Swedish courts with a legal basis for the granting of anti-arbitration injunctions. By contrast, Art. 2(1) expressly empowers the arbitral tribunal to continue the arbitral proceedings pending the determination by the court of the arbitral jurisdiction. It would appear to be for the arbitrators – not to the courts – to decide whether to stay the arbitral proceedings awaiting the decision of the court or not. Hence the Swedish courts should not exercise the power to prevent the continuation of arbitration proceedings by issuing anti-arbitration injunctions.

This conclusion is in line with the philosophy underlying the Swedish Arbitration Act, which "is, and has always been, that of freedom of contract, trust in the arbitrators and recognition of the advantages of a single, privately administered dispute settlement mechanism".[52] It also reflects the general practice of Swedish courts not to interfere in the arbitration process.[53]

f.   UNCITRAL Model Law

The UNCITRAL Model Law does not specifically deal with either anti-suit or anti-arbitration injunctions. However, both the purport of Art. 5 of the Model Law and the intention of the Model Law itself suggest the preclusion of anti-arbitration injunctions.[54] Art. 5 states:

> "In matters governed by this Law, no court shall intervene except where so provided in this Law."

What matters are governed by the Model Law for the purposes of Art. 5 may depend on the law of the particular country which has adopted the Model Law. It has been suggested that these matters shall include all matters concerning "the assistance to the arbitral process" and the "control of the legality of the arbitral process".[55]

---

51. Kaj HOBÉR, "Arbitration Reform in Sweden", 17 Arbitration International (2001, no. 4) p. 358; Ulf FRANKE, "National Report Sweden in ICCA *International Handbook on Commercial Arbitration* (hereinafter *Handbook*) (Supplement 32, 2000) p. 15

52. K. HOBÉR, *op. cit.*, fn. 51, p. 351.

53. *Ibid.*

54. On the impact of Art. 5 Model Law on anti-suit injunctions, see generally Frédéric BACHAND, "The UNCITRAL Model Law's Take on Anti-Suit Injunctions", in *Anti-suit Injunctions in International Arbitration*, *op. cit.*, fn. 7, pp. 87 et seq.

55. F. BACHAND, *ibid.*, p. 100. See also Aron BROCHES, "Commentary on the UNCITRAL Model Law" in *Handbook*, (Supplement 11, 1990) *ad* Art. 5, para. 13.

Anti-arbitration injunctions clearly seek to control the legality of the arbitral process. This is true no matter whether the injunction is directed against the arbitrators or against the parties.[56] Even if the injunction is directed against the parties, it still directly interferes in the arbitral process.[57] In both cases it seeks to control the jurisdiction of the arbitral tribunal and thus the legality of the arbitration process. Hence, anti-arbitration injunctions must be considered matters governed by the Model Law for the purposes of Art. 5. Accordingly, national courts situated in a Model Law country may not rely on their domestic rules in order to grant anti-arbitration injunctions in those countries where there are separate arbitration regimes for domestic and international arbitration.

It is also worth noting that, according to Art. 1(2) Model Law, Art. 5 only applies if the injunction is granted by a court situated in the country of the seat of the arbitration. Therefore, it does not apply in the situation contemplated by the present report, where a national court grants an anti-arbitration injunction in order to prevent an arbitration abroad. Hence, the Model Law does not prohibit national courts from enjoining arbitration proceedings abroad.

However, there is a strong argument that an anti-arbitration injunction seeking to restrain an arbitration abroad is contrary to the system which the Model Law establishes of judicial control of the legality of the arbitration process only after an award has been rendered. This assertion is corroborated by the *travaux préparatoires*. There it was decided to limit possibilities for court interventions during the course of the arbitration in order to discourage delaying tactics. In its report on the work of its eighteenth session, UNCITRAL noted that "resort to intervention by a court during the arbitral proceedings was often used only as a delaying tactic and was more often a source of abuse of the arbitral proceedings than it was a protection against abuse".[58]

This supports the view that an anti-arbitration injunction, even if directed against an arbitration abroad, contradicts the non-interventionist system of the Model Law as it seeks to control the legality of the arbitration process before an award has been rendered. Further, the Model Law reserves the right to control the arbitration process to the courts of the seat of the arbitration. No national court situated outside the country of the seat of the arbitration should therefore seek to interfere or control the arbitration.

---

56. See however the decision of the Quebec Court of Appeal in *Lac d'amiante du Canada Ltée v. Lac d'amiante du Québec Ltée*, REJB 1999-15419, [1999] Q.J. (Quicklaw) No. 5438 (Qué. C.A.). In this case, an anti-arbitration injunction was rendered prohibiting one of the parties from pursuing an ICC arbitration in New York. The arbitrators admitted their jurisdiction over the claim. The anti-arbitration injunction was nevertheless upheld by the Court of Appeal of Quebec on the grounds that the injunction did not interfere with the arbitration proceedings, but was destined to stop an arbitration abusively brought by one of the parties and incompatible with an action already pending before a Quebec Court.

57. *Channel Tunnel Group Ltd. v. Balfour Beatty Construction Ltd.* [1993] A.C. 334, 364-365.

58. XVI *UNCITRAL Yearbook* 3, 11, para. 63 (1985) (available online under <www.uncitral.org/pdf/english/yearbooks/yb-1985-e/vol16-p3-46-e.pdf>).

g.   Other legal systems

Anti-arbitration injunctions may be granted under several other legal systems, mostly common law systems. This is the case, for example, in Australia, New Zealand, Malaysia, Nigeria, Israel, Indonesia and Pakistan.

In Australia, which has adopted the Model Law without any amendments, courts have granted anti-arbitration injunctions based on their general power to grant injunctive relief when this is considered appropriate.[59] Under Australian Law, in accordance with Art. 16 of the Model Law, an arbitral tribunal may rule on the issue of its own jurisdiction. However, the tribunal's decision is not considered to be binding and does not prevent a party from applying to the courts for an injunction restraining the arbitration.[60]

The Arbitration Act of New Zealand of 1996 is also based on the Model Law. It would seem that under this Act anti-arbitration injunctions may be granted in international arbitration, but only under very limited circumstances, namely if the parties agree to the application of the optional rules contained in the second schedule of the Act. These optional rules do not provide expressly for anti-arbitration injunctions. However, Sect. 4 of the optional rules appears to allow the High Court to rule on the arbitral tribunal's jurisdiction prior to the arbitral tribunal.[61] According to this provision, with the consent of the arbitral tribunal or the parties, the High Court has the jurisdiction to determine "any question of law arising in the course of the arbitration".

Under the Nigerian Arbitration and Conciliation Decree 1988, anti-arbitration injunctions seem to be available. The Decree implements the Model Law and does not contain any provision expressly providing the Nigerian courts with the power to grant anti-arbitration injunctions. However, according to one author

"[a]lthough it is provided in Sect. 12(1) of the Decree that an arbitral tribunal is competent to decide on a plea regarding its jurisdiction and in Sect. 12(4) that the ruling of the arbitral tribunal on any plea concerning its jurisdiction 'shall be final and binding', it is still possible for either party to take an action to the court.... Furthermore, it is possible for either party to bring an action in court to stop arbitral proceedings until the court rules on the issue brought before it."[62]

The Malaysian Arbitration Act 1980 expressly allows the High Court to grant an anti-arbitration injunction if it considers that the arbitrators are not impartial or if the dispute involves a question of fraud.[63] In these situations, the High Court may either revoke the

---

59. See, e.g., *Allstate Life Ins Co v Australia and New Zealand Banking Group*, Federal Court of Australia, 19 January 1996, unreported.

60. Michael C. PRYLES, "National Report Australia" in *Handbook* (Supplement 40, 2004) p. 22.

61. Tómas KENNEDY-GRANT, "National Report New Zealand" in *Handbook* (Supplement 25, 1998) p. 23.

62. Tinuade OYEKUNLE, "National Report The Federal Republic of Nigeria" in *Handbook* (Supplement 26, 1998) p. 15.

63. See Art. 3 and Art. 25 Malaysian Arbitration Act 1980.

authority of the arbitrators or grant an injunction restraining the parties or the arbitral tribunal from proceeding with the arbitration.

An express authorization for the granting of anti-arbitration injunctions is also contained in the Arbitration Act of Israel of 1968. According to Art. 18 of the Act

"[t]he filing of an application with the court in connection with an arbitration, whether by a party or by the arbitrator, shall not stay the arbitration proceedings *unless the court or the arbitrator so directs*". (Emphasis added)

The power of the Israeli courts to grant anti-arbitration injunctions can be explained by the fact that under Israeli law, the arbitral tribunal does not have the power to rule on its own jurisdiction, unless the parties specifically authorize it to do so. If the tribunal starts to rule on its jurisdiction in the absence of such an authorization, the parties may apply to the courts for an injunction against the arbitral tribunal.[64] However, such an injunction will only be granted if the court is convinced that the arbitration agreement is null and void.[65]

It would seem that for the same reason, namely the arbitral tribunal's lack of power to rule on its own jurisdiction, courts in Indonesia have the power to grant anti-arbitration injunctions. It is for the Indonesian courts, not the arbitrators, to rule on the existence or validity of an arbitration agreement.[66]

Finally, Pakistani courts can also grant anti-arbitration injunctions. Under the Arbitration Act of Pakistan of 1940, a court can revoke the authority of the arbitral tribunal[67] and can order that a given arbitration agreement shall cease to have any effect.[68] Like in Israel and Indonesia, the arbitral tribunal does not have the power to rule on its own jurisdiction.[69] Furthermore, according to the Arbitration Act 1940, the existence of an arbitration agreement does not oust the jurisdiction of the national courts and, therefore, a party to an arbitration agreement may nevertheless commence court proceedings. When court proceedings upon the whole of the subject matter of the arbitration have been commenced between all the parties to the arbitration and a notice thereof has been given to the arbitrators, the arbitration will be considered invalid unless a stay of court proceedings is granted.[70]

---

64. Smadar OTTOLENGHI, "National Report Israel" in *Handbook* (Supplement 2, 1984) p. 16.

65. *Mashiach v. Ravia*, L.A. 130/71, 25 (2) P.D. 572. On anti-arbitration injunctions in Israel, see Smadar OTTOLENGHI, *The Law of Arbitration in Israel* (The Hague, London, Boston 2001) pp. 295 and 297.

66. See generally Sudargo GAUTAMA, "National Report Indonesia" in *Handbook* (Supplement 26, 1998) p. 19.

67. Art. 5 Arbitration Act 1940.

68. See, e.g., Art. 12 Arbitration Act 1940.

69. Sect. 31 Arbitration Act 1940.

70. Sect. 35 Arbitration Act 1940. On arbitration in Pakistan, see generally Mahomed J. JAFFER, "National Report – Pakistan" in ICCA *Yearbook Commercial Arbitration* V (1980) (hereinafter *Yearbook*, pp. 119 et seq.

h.   Conclusion

In common law jurisdictions the power of national courts to grant anti-arbitration injunctions is well established. The arbitration laws of several common law countries provide a clear legal basis for the granting of such injunctions by national courts. The specific conditions for the granting of anti-arbitration injunctions vary from one jurisdiction to the other. Under both English and US law, it would seem that a court may only grant an anti-arbitration injunction to protect its jurisdiction against a foreign arbitration proceeding which it considers to be wrongly brought.

In civil law countries, anti-arbitration injunctions are generally not available. Swiss, French and Swedish law do not provide a legal basis for the granting of anti-arbitration injunctions. It would seem that anti-arbitration injunctions are in fact contrary to these legal systems.

Finally, although Art. 5 UNCITRAL Model Law only expressly prohibits national courts situated in the country of the seat of the arbitration from granting anti-arbitration injunctions, the effect is much more extensive. The aim and purpose of the Model Law effectively precludes anti-arbitration injunctions generally, reflecting accepted international arbitration law and practice.

2.   Support by National Courts of Arbitration Proceedings

Instead of granting injunctions to prevent or interfere with foreign arbitration proceedings, national courts may also support arbitrations abroad. Foreign arbitrations may be supported in several ways, aimed specifically to enforce or to support an arbitration agreement.

a.   Enforcement of arbitration agreements

National courts may enforce an arbitration agreement by issuing an anti-suit injunction destined to stay concurrent court proceedings brought in violation of the arbitration agreement. In practice, anti-suit injunctions supporting arbitration proceedings are more frequent than anti-arbitration injunctions.[71] However, anti-suit injunctions are not the only measure permitting the enforcement of arbitration agreements. In the United States, for example, courts may grant orders compelling the performance of arbitration agreements and ordering parties to submit to arbitration.

i.   Anti-suit injunctions in support of arbitration proceedings

The majority of English cases involving anti-suit injunctions in international arbitration concern injunctions ordering the stay of foreign court proceedings brought in violation of an arbitration agreement providing for arbitration in England.[72] The position taken

---

71. J.D.M. LEW, L.A. MISTELIS, S.M. KRÖLL, *op. cit.*, fn. 25, p. 364, para. 15-28.

72. Such an anti-suit injunction was granted in the very recent case of *Hewlett-Packard International Bank PLC v. Egypt Cyber Centre, National Telecommunication Company, Commercial International Investment Co SAE and Egyptian Networks Company SAE*. In this case, the English High Court granted an anti-suit injunction against respondents restraining them to pursue court actions in Egypt brought to prevent LCIA arbitration proceedings in London.

by the English courts in this matter is well illustrated in the case of *Aggeliki Charis Compania Maritima v. Pagnan* (*The Angelic Grace*). There, the Court of Appeal had to consider whether to grant a permanent injunction preventing a party to an arbitration in England from proceeding with a claim before the courts in Italy. The charter agreement clearly provided for arbitration in London. The charterer, Pagnan, argued that the particular claim before the court in Venice did not fall within the scope of the arbitration agreement. Furthermore, the High Court should not have granted an injunction that effectively pre-empted the decision of the Italian court on its own jurisdiction. The Court of Appeal held that

> "where an injunction is sought to restrain a party from proceeding in a foreign Court in breach of an arbitration agreement governed by English law, the English Courts feel no diffidence in granting the injunction, provided that it is sought promptly and before the foreign proceedings are too far advanced.... The justification for the grant of the injunctions in either case is without it the plaintiff will be deprived of its contractual rights in a situation in which damages are manifestly an inadequate remedy. The jurisdiction is, of course, discretionary and is not exercised as a matter of course...."[73]

In *The Angelic Grace*, the Court of Appeal made it clear that in cases concerning the enforcement of arbitration agreements, anti-suit injunctions may be granted more freely than in other cases involving injunctions in relation with foreign proceedings. According to Millet LJ

> "the time has come to lay aside the ritual incantation that this is a jurisdiction which should only be exercised sparingly and with great caution. [...] I cannot accept the proposition that any Court would be offended by the grant of an injunction to restrain a party from invoking a jurisdiction which he had promised not to invoke and which it was its own duty to decline".[74]

---

73. [1995] 1 Lloyd's Law Reports 87, 96.
74. [1995] 1 Lloyd's Law Reports 87, 96.

Although in subsequent case law the approach of the English courts has sometimes been more cautious,[75] the liberal approach set out in *The Angelic Grace* has continuously been confirmed.[76]

The position of US courts regarding anti-suit injunctions enforcing arbitration agreements is set out in *BHP Petroleum (Americas) Inc et al v. Walter F Baer Reinhold*. In this case, BHP Petroleum requested the US District Court of the Southern District of Texas to compel Baer to arbitration in Texas and to enjoin him from continuing with court proceedings in Ecuador. The court decided

> "that an injunction barring a foreign action was proper if the simultaneous prosecution of an action would result in 'inequitable hardship' and 'tend to frustrate and delay the speedy and efficient determination of the cause'. [...] The focus of the inquiry is whether there exists a need to prevent vexatious or oppressive litigation. In light of the strong federal policy favouring arbitration, the court finds that plaintiffs would be irreparably harmed if Baer were permitted to continue litigation in Ecuador while the same claims were being arbitrated. Therefore, the court grants plaintiffs' application for injunction."[77]

The position of the US courts is stricter than the position of the English courts. An important criteria for the granting of the injunction is "irreparable harm".[78] This requirement was defined recently by the United States District Court for the Southern District of New York in *ITABO v. CDEEE*. In this case, ITABO, a private company incorporated in the Dominican Republic, requested the court to compel CDEEE, a company owned by the Dominican Republic, to ICC arbitration in New York in

---

75. See, e.g., *Welex AG v. Rosa Maritime Ltd (The Epsilon Rosa)* [2003] 2 Lloyd's Report 509, [2003] All E. R. (D) 71 (July). In this case, the Court of Appeal held that "there is considerable debate as to whether the English courts should grant anti-suit injunctions where the Lugano or New York Conventions apply. Although the injunction acts in personam and is not directed at the foreign court this is not how it is always perceived." See also *Tonicstar Ltd v. American Home Assurance Co* ([2004] All E.R. (D) 400 (May 2004)), where the High Court ruled that "the remedy of an anti-suit injunction is discretionary and the Court must look at all the circumstances of the case and only make an order if the interests of justice so require".

76. See, e.g., *West Tankers Inv v. Ras Riunione Adriatica di Sicurta "The Front Comor"* [2005] EWHC 454 (Comm), [2005] 2 Lloyd's Rep. 257; *Through Transport Mutual Insurance Association (Eurasia) Ltd v. New India Assurance Co Ltd,* [2004] EWCA Civ 1598, [2005] 1 Lloyd's Rep. 67. This liberal approach has also been followed in a recent case involving not an arbitration agreement but an exclusive jurisdiction agreement: *OT Africa Line Ltd v. Magic Sportswear Corporation and others* ([2005] EWCA Civ 710; [2005] 2 Lloyd's Rep 170; [2006] 1 All ER (Comm) 32).

77. No H-97-879, *Yearbook* XXIII (1998) pp. 949-955 (US no. 249), 12 Mealey's International Arbitration Law Report I-1 (1997, no. 5), (USDC, Southern District of Texas, Houston Division, 28 April 1997). See also *Wal-Mart Stores, Inc v. PT Multipolar Corp et al, Yearbook* XXV (2000) p. 1085 at p. 1086 (US no.329) (9th Cir 1999).

78. *Paramedics Electromedicina Comercial Ltda v. GE Medical Systems Information Technologies Inc*, 2003 U.S. Dist. Lexis 26928, 4 June 2003. In this case the U.S. District Court of the Southern District of New York confirmed that "[i]rreparable harm is the single most important prerequisite for the issuance of a preliminary injunction".

conformity with the arbitration agreement contained in ITABO's bylaws. It also requested an anti-suit injunction to enjoin CDEEE from continuing with litigation in the Dominican courts. The court denied both requests. Concerning the anti-suit injunction, the court held that ITABO had not met the heavy burden of establishing irreparable harm. It defined this notion in the following terms:

> "[i]njunctive relief 'is an extraordinary and drastic remedy which should not be routinely granted'. Where necessary to prevent irreparable harm, 'a federal court may enjoin a party before it from pursuing litigation in a foreign forum'. Irreparable harm is injury that 'is likely and imminent, not remote or speculative, and [...] is not capable of being fully remedied by money damages'. The movant is required to establish not a mere possibility of irreparable harm, but that it is 'likely to suffer irreparable harm if equitable relief is denied'."[79]

In addition to irreparable harm, when deciding whether to grant an anti-suit injunction a court must also consider the stage of the foreign proceedings, as well as the expectation of the parties to litigate in that particular court.[80]

ii.   Court orders compelling the performance of arbitration agreements
In the United States, an arbitration agreement can be enforced by a court order forcing a reluctant party to go to arbitration. Indeed, Sects. 4, 206 and 303 of the Federal Arbitration Act (FAA) authorize US courts to compel a party to arbitrate, and a party that does not follow the court's order will be in contempt of court.[81]

Sect. 4 FAA "empowers a court to grant what amounts to an injunction requiring a party to arbitrate pursuant to its arbitration agreement".[82] According to this provision

> "[a] party aggrieved by the alleged failure, neglect, or refusal of another to arbitrate under a written agreement for arbitration may petition any United States district court which, save for such agreement, would have jurisdiction under Title 28, in a civil action or in admiralty of the subject matter of a suit arising out of the controversy between the parties, for an order directing that such an arbitration proceed in the manner provided for in such agreement. [...]".

Sect. 206 FAA implements Art. II of the New York Convention. Under this provision, a US court may compel a party to go to arbitration if (1) it has personal jurisdiction over the party; (2) it has subject matter jurisdiction; and (3) the venue in the compelling court is proper under the FAA or otherwise. This compelling power applies even if the agreed-upon seat of the arbitration is outside the United States. By contrast,

---

79. *Empresa Generadora de Electricidad ITABO SA ("ITABO") v. Corporacion Dominicana de Empresas Electricas Estatales ("CDEEE")* 2005 U.S. Dist. Lexis 14712, 18 July 2005.
80. J.D.M. LEW, L.A. MISTELIS, S.M. KRÖLL, *op. cit.*, fn. 25, p. 366, para. 15-32.
81. On court orders compelling the performance of arbitration agreement in U.S. law, see generally Gary B. BORN, *International Commercial Arbitration*, 2nd edn., (The Hague 2001) pp. 381 et seq.
82. G.B. BORN, *op. cit.*, fn. 81, p. 386.

Sect. 206 FAA does not apply if the parties have not agreed upon an arbitral seat or if this seat is situated in a State that is not a signatory to the New York Convention.[83]

In *Paramedics Electromedicina Comercial Ltda v. GE Medical Systems Information Technologies Inc,*[84] the District Court for the Southern District of New York granted a motion to compel the performance of an arbitration agreement on the basis of Sect. 4 FAA. In this case, a Brazilian company (Paramedics) and a US company (GE Medical Systems) concluded two agreements, both containing an arbitration clause providing for arbitration under the rules of the Inter-American Commercial Arbitration Commission in Miami. When a dispute arose, Paramedics brought suit before a Brazilian court notwithstanding the arbitration agreement. GE Medical Systems initiated arbitration proceedings. When Paramedics requested an anti-arbitration injunction from a New York court, GE Medical Systems moved the action to the United States District Court for the Southern District of New York requesting an order compelling arbitration and an anti-suit injunction enjoining Paramedics from continuing with the Brazilian court proceedings. The court rejected Paramedics' request for an anti-arbitration injunction against GE Medical Systems. At the same time, it granted both the motion to compel Paramedics to arbitration and the anti-suit injunction enjoining Paramedics from continuing with the Brazilian action. The court held that where it is established that an arbitration agreement exists and that one of the parties to this agreement is not in compliance with it, an order compelling arbitration without further proceedings may be issued.

3. *Support of Arbitration Agreement*

Instead of actively enforcing an arbitration agreement, most national courts take a passive role, giving effect to the arbitration agreement only indirectly. For instance, a court may simply stay an action brought before it in breach of an arbitration agreement instead of forcing a party either to go to arbitration or to stop a concurrent court proceeding. The court will not force the parties to arbitration. It is up to the claimant to initiate an arbitration.

The stay of court actions brought in breach of an arbitration agreement is an indirect but efficient means of ensuring the respect of an arbitration agreement. It forces the claimant to go to arbitration, because the latter will have no other forum in which to bring his claim.[85]

A stay of court action is provided for in Sect. 9 of the English Arbitration Act 1996. According to the first paragraph of this provision

---

83. Similarly, Sect. 303 FAA permits US courts to enforce arbitration agreements subject to the Inter-American Convention. Since, to date, there are only a few cases applying Sect. 303 FAA, cases applying Sect. 206 FAA may have an influence on the interpretation of Sect. 303 FAA.

84. Decision cited under fn. 78.

85. Jean-François POUDRET, Sébastien BESSON, *Droit comparé de l'arbitrage international* (Brussels, Paris, Zurich, Basel, Geneva 2002) p. 449, para. 497.

"[a] party to an arbitration agreement against whom legal proceedings are brought ... in respect of a matter which under the agreement is to be referred to arbitration may ... apply to the court in which the proceedings have been brought to stay the proceedings so far as they concern that matter".

Sect. 9 further provides in its fourth paragraph that "the court shall grant a stay unless satisfied that the arbitration agreement is null and void, inoperative, or incapable of being performed".[86] The obligation to stay proceedings under Sect. 9 applies even if the arbitral seat "is outside England, Wales or Northern Ireland or no seat has been designated or determined".[87] However, there is no power under the English Arbitration Act 1996 for the courts to order a party to participate in an arbitration.

A prominent example for a case where a court action was stayed in support of an arbitration agreement is the *Channel Tunnel* case. Eurotunnel (the owners of the tunnel) and Trans-Manche Link (a consortium of English and French companies) had concluded a contract for the construction of a tunnel under the English Channel between England and France. The contract provided for a "two stage" dispute resolution mechanism. First, any dispute between Eurotunnel and Trans-Manche Link should be brought before a Panel of Experts. Then, if either party disagreed with the Panel's decision, the dispute could be referred to ICC arbitration with its seat in Brussels. A dispute arose as to the amounts payable in respect of the works on the tunnel's cooling system. Trans-Manche Link threatened to suspend their work alleging a breach of contract by Eurotunnel. Eurotunnel brought an action in the English courts requesting an interim injunction to restrain Trans-Manche Link from suspending their works. Trans-Manche Link argued that the English courts did not have the power to order such an injunction. In addition, Trans-Manche Link requested a stay of the action brought by Eurotunnel in favor of the arbitration on the basis of the then governing Arbitration Act 1975. The case went to the House of Lords which decided to stay the proceedings in favor of arbitration. This decision was not based on Sect. 1 Arbitration Act 1975,[88] but rather on the court's inherent jurisdiction to stay proceedings brought before it in breach of an arbitration agreement.

---

86. See also Art. 8(1) UNCITRAL Model Law:

> "A court before which an action is brought in a matter which is subject of an arbitration shall, if a party so requests no later than when submitting his first statement on the substance of the dispute, refer the parties to arbitration unless it finds that the agreement is null and void, inoperative or incapable of being performed."

Unlike Art. 8 Model Law, Sect. 9 Arbitration Act 1996 does not instruct the court to "refer the parties to arbitration".

87. Sect. 2(2)(a) Arbitration Act 1996.

88. The House of Lords held that a "two stage" dispute resolution provision was not an "arbitration agreement" for the purposes of Sect. 1 Arbitration Act 1975. Therefore, it held that Sect. 1 Arbitration Act 1975 could not apply in the present case. This problem does not arise anymore under Sect. 9 Arbitration Act 1996. Indeed, according to para. 2 of this section "[a]n application may be made notwithstanding that the matter is to be referred to arbitration only after the exhaustion of other dispute resolution procedures".

IV.   ANTI-ARBITRATION INJUNCTIONS IN PRACTICE

I turn now to analyse how the power to grant anti-arbitration injunctions is used, or more properly abused, in practice. Indeed, in order to be able to determine whether the granting of anti-arbitration injunctions can ever be justified, it is important to consider not only how anti-arbitration injunctions are supposed to be used in theory, but also how they can be used in practice.

As discussed above, anti-arbitration injunctions are intended to protect the national court's jurisdiction against foreign arbitration proceedings which have been wrongly brought. Are anti-arbitration injunctions used in this manner in practice or are they tools used by parties and their lawyers to undermine, destabilize, delay or avoid an arbitration?

On reviewing past cases, it is clear that anti-arbitration injunctions are used primarily as a tactical tool to stop or delay the arbitration process.

1.   *Himpurna California Energy v. Republic of Indonesia*

The *Himpurna California Energy v. Republic of Indonesia* case is a spectacular example of an anti-arbitration injunction granted in order to stop an arbitral tribunal from rendering an award against a party to the arbitration.[89]

This case arose from various contracts relating to the exploitation of geothermal reserves, by which Bermudan corporations owned by US investors agreed to build and operate an electrical generation plant in Indonesia. The contracts provided for ad hoc arbitration with seat in Jakarta under the UNCITRAL Rules. Two different arbitration proceedings were subsequently initiated against the Republic of Indonesia.

After the first arbitral tribunal rendered an award against PLN, an Indonesian State owned electricity corporation, an Indonesian court granted an injunction ordering the suspension of the enforcement of the first award. The court also granted an anti-arbitration injunction against Himpurna in order to prevent the second arbitration from taking place. A penalty of US$1 million per day was imposed on any party who violated this injunction.

Despite this injunction, the arbitral tribunal continued the arbitration proceedings. The proceedings were held in The Hague, but the seat of the arbitration remained in Jakarta. After an attempt to obtain an anti-arbitration injunction in The Netherlands failed, the Indonesian arbitrator was prevented from participating in the hearings in The Hague and was forced to return to Indonesia. The truncated tribunal continued the proceedings and rendered an award against the Republic of Indonesia.

---

89. On this case see, e.g., Peter CORNELL, Arweb HANDLEY, "Himpurna and Hub: International Arbitration in Developing Countries", 15 Mealey's International Arbitration Report (2000, no. 9), pp. 39 et seq.; Jacques WERNER, "When Arbitration Becomes War – Some Reflections on the Frailty of the Arbitral Process in Cases Involving Authoritarian States", 17 Journal of International Arbitration (2000, no. 4), pp. 97 et seq.; H. Priyatna ABDURRASYID, "They Said I Was Going To Be Kidnapped", 18 Mealey's International Arbitration Report (2003, no. 6), pp. 29 et seq.

The arbitral tribunal based its decision to continue with the arbitration proceedings on several grounds. Applying international law,[90] the tribunal held that the Indonesian State had violated international public policy by first signing an arbitration agreement and then seeking to rely on the incompatibility of its obligation to arbitrate with its internal system, i.e. an anti-arbitration injunction issued by its courts. The tribunal stated in emphatic terms:

> "The present Arbitral Tribunal considers that it is a denial of justice for the courts of a State to prevent a foreign party from pursuing its remedies before a forum to the authority of which the State consented, and on the availability of which the foreigner relied in making investments explicitly envisaged by that state."[91]

Further, the tribunal justified its decision to continue with the arbitration on the grounds that the tribunal's authority comes from the parties' agreement to arbitrate. Its authority does not emanate from the legal order of the seat of the arbitration but rather from an international order.[92]

2. *Salini Costruttori S.p.a. v. Ethiopia*

The *Salini Costruttori S.p.a. v. Ethiopia* case is another example where the courts of the State party to the arbitration granted an injunction in order to stop arbitration proceedings which were taking an unfavorable turn for the State party.[93]

The dispute arose out of a FIDIC contract, supplemented by special conditions specifically negotiated by the parties. One of the general conditions contained an ICC arbitration clause providing for arbitration in Addis Ababa, and one of the special conditions contained an arbitration clause also providing for arbitration in Addis Ababa, but pursuant to the Ethiopian Civil Code. When the dispute arose, Salini initiated ICC arbitrations. Ethiopia objected to the jurisdiction of the arbitral tribunal.

After the tribunal had accepted its jurisdiction, it was decided that for reasons of practical convenience a hearing on the merits should be held in Paris, but that the arbitral seat should remain in Addis Ababa. Ethiopia requested the ICC Court to have all arbitrators removed from the tribunal. It alleged that the fact that the arbitrators had decided to hold a hearing in Paris and not in Addis Ababa clearly showed that they were biased. After the ICC Court rejected this request, Ethiopia brought an identical request

---

90. The arbitral tribunal held that international law was applicable because of the existence of an international arbitration agreement and the involvement of a State party.
91. *Himpurna California Energy Ltd v. Republic of Indonesia*, Interim Award, 26 September 1999, *Yearbook* XXV (2000), pp. 109-186, para. 184.
92. *Himpurna California Energy Ltd v. Republic of Indonesia*, decision cited under fn. 91, paras. 175 et seq.
93. Decision published in 21 ASA Bulletin (2003, no. 1) pp. 82 et seq. On this case see, e.g., Antonio CRIVELLARO, Note – Award of 7 December 2001 in Case No. 10623, 21 ASA Bulletin (2003, no. 1) pp. 60-81; Matthias SCHERER, Note – Award of 7 December 2001 in Case No. 10623, 21 ASA Bulletin (2003, no. 1) pp. 112-119; Frédéric BACHAND, "Must an ICC Tribunal Comply With an Anti-Suit Injunction Issued by the Courts of the Seat of Arbitration?", 20 Mealey's International Arbitration Report (2005, no. 3), pp. 47-52.

before the Ethiopian courts. Pending the decision on the issue, the Ethiopian courts granted two anti-arbitration injunctions, one directed against the arbitral tribunal and one against the claimant.

The ICC tribunal ruled that the injunctions had no bearing on the arbitral proceeding. It based its decision on three guiding principles of international arbitration, namely "the primary duty of the arbitral tribunal is owed to the parties", "the arbitral tribunal's duty to make every effort to render an enforceable award", and "a State or State entity cannot resort to the State's courts to frustrate an arbitration agreement".[94]

On the first principle, the tribunal held that

> "the primary source of the Tribunal's powers is the parties' agreement to arbitrate. An important consequence of this is the Tribunal has a duty vis à vis the parties to ensure that their arbitration agreement is not frustrated".[95]

In other words, since the primary duty of an international arbitral tribunal is owed to the parties, it is not bound by a court order which is inconsistent with the parties' agreement.[96] If the tribunal finds that the parties had agreed to resolve their disputes by arbitration, it must continue the arbitration in accordance with that agreement and make an award.[97] The fact that one party has changed its mind, for whatever reason, should not be allowed to derail the original agreement of the parties. Furthermore, the respect for party autonomy requires the tribunal to continue with the proceedings without any interruption because "[t]o wait for the decisions of the courts [...] would, in any event, be inconsistent with the Arbitral Tribunal's duty to render an award in due time".[98]

Concerning the second principle, the tribunal considered that its duty to render an enforceable award[99] did not oblige it to follow a court order contrary to the parties' arbitration agreement. Quite the contrary, it held that

> "the tribunal must follow its own judgment, even if that requires non-compliance with a court order. To conclude otherwise would entail a denial of justice and fairness to the parties and conflict with the legitimate expectations they created by entering into an arbitration agreement."[100]

The tribunal added that

---

94. See paras. 125 et seq., 140 et seq. and 156 et seq. of the decision cited under fn. 93.
95. *Salini Costruttori S.p.a. v. Ethiopia*, ICC No. 10623, Award of 7 December 2001, in 21 ASA Bulletin (2003, no. 1), para. 128.
96. F. BACHAND, *op. cit.*, fn. 93, p. 48.
97. F. BACHAND, *ibid.*, p. 49.
98. *Salini Costruttori S.p.a. v. Ethiopia*, cited under fn. 95, para. 139.
99. This principle is codified in Art. 35 of the ICC Rules which states that "[i]n all matters not expressly provided for in these Rules, the Court and the Arbitral Tribunal shall act in the spirit of these Rules and make every effort to make sure that the Award is enforceable at law".
100. *Salini Costruttori S.p.a. v. Ethiopia*, cited under fn. 95, paras. 142-143.

"[a]n arbitral tribunal should not go so far as to frustrate the arbitration agreement itself in the interests of ensuring enforceability. Such an outcome would be, to say the least, a paradox".[101]

Concerning the last principle, i.e. a State or State entity cannot resort to the State's courts to frustrate an arbitration agreement, it suffices to refer to the last paragraph of the tribunal's thorough analysis of the principle in which the tribunal sharply criticized Ethiopia's conduct of requesting anti-arbitration injunctions. The tribunal said that

"[f]or the avoidance of doubt, we do not mean to suggest that any application by a state party to its own courts, in their capacity as the courts of the seat in arbitral proceedings, would be objectionable. [...] The problem arises in this particular case from the fact that a state entity is resorting to the state's own courts in an illegitimate effort to renege upon the arbitration agreement. It is unacceptable for a state party to invoke its own law in an effort to avoid the effect of an arbitration agreement that it has freely entered into. For similar reasons, it is unacceptable for a state party to resort to its own courts for the same purpose."

3.   *The Hub Power Company Ltd (HUBCO) v. Water and Power Development Authority of Pakistan (WAPDA)*

HUBCO v. WAPDA is yet another example where a State party to an arbitration agreement successfully applied to the courts of its country for an order preventing an arbitration from proceeding.[102]

A tariff dispute arose out of a Power Purchase Agreement (PPA) concluded between HUBCO, a company incorporated in Pakistan, and WAPDA, a Pakistani State-owned company. Under the PPA, HUBCO was to develop an electricity-generating plant in Pakistan and to sell the output to WAPDA. The Government of Pakistan guaranteed WAPDA's obligations under the PPA and the World Bank provided further guarantees. Three amendments were subsequently made to the PPA providing for an increase in the amount payable by WAPDA to HUBCO, and for a transformation of the PPA from a Build-Operate-Transfer deal into a Build-Operate-Own deal.

When the dispute arose, HUBCO initiated an ICC arbitration in London in accordance with the arbitration agreement contained in the PPA. The method of calculating the price of electricity was the key issue to be determined by the arbitrators. Soon after, WAPDA wrote to HUBCO stating that it considered the three amendments to be illegal, fraudulent, collusive, without consideration, mala fide and designed to

---

101. *Ibid.*, para. 144.
102. Supreme Court of Pakistan, 20 June 2000, 16 Arbitration International (2000, no. 4), pp. 439 et seq.; 15 Mealey's International Arbitration Report (2000, no. 7), pp. A.1 et seq. (2000). On this case see, e.g., Louise BARRINGTON, "Hubco v. WAPDA: Pakistan Top Court Rejects International Arbitration", 11 American Review of International Arbitration (2000) pp. 385 et seq.; Nudrat B. MAJEED, "Commentary on the Hubco Judgment", 16 Arbitration International (2000, no. 4), pp. 431-438; Neil KAPLAN, Arbitration in Asia – Developments and Crises – Part 2, 19 Journal of International Arbitration (2002, no. 3) pp. 245-260.

cause wrongful loss to WAPDA and the Government of Pakistan with consequential wrongful gain to HUBCO. WAPDA also threatened to bring a lawsuit against HUBCO before the courts of Pakistan.

In response to this letter, HUBCO filed suit in the High Court of Sindh at Karachi seeking an injunction restraining WAPDA from seeking resolution of the dispute through any other means except through ICC arbitration. The injunction was granted. WAPDA then filed suit before the Lahore court asking for a permanent injunction restraining HUBCO from pursuing the arbitration. The Lahore court granted an interim injunction. A large number of further proceedings and appeals on the injunction followed. At one point, HUBCO agreed not to continue the arbitration proceedings, but then filed a second request for arbitration with the ICC.

The Supreme Court of Pakistan heard two appeals filed by HUBCO and WAPDA respectively. The HUBCO appeal concerned the injunctions preventing the first ICC arbitration, and the WAPDA appeal asked that HUBCO be restrained from invoking the arbitration clause in the PPA.

The Supreme Court held that the only question to be decided was whether the dispute was arbitrable. In a majority decision it ruled that the matters raised were not arbitrable as they involved matters of criminality. Thus, it decided that the injunctions must be continued and that HUBCO must bring its claim before the courts of Pakistan.[103]

The Supreme Court decision, interestingly, never questioned the validity of the PPA, and thus the existence of a valid arbitration agreement. Little understanding of the fundamental principles of international arbitration, i.e. separability and competence-competence, was shown and no relevant international arbitration case law was reviewed. It is generally considered that this was a political decision and a most unfortunate example of the courts being a pawn of the Government.[104]

In July of 2000, HUBCO filed a petition requesting the Supreme Court to revisit the case and to reverse its decision. However, before the Supreme Court rendered a decision on the issue, HUBCO and WAPDA announced that they had agreed to settle their dispute, thus rendering moot the question of review.

---

103. By contrast, Jehangiri J, in his dissenting opinion, concluded that the ICC arbitration clearly should have been allowed to proceed.

104. See N. KAPLAN, *op. cit.*, fn. 102, p. 252, where he said:

"The majority decision was six pages long, with no citation of authority. The claimants had put in a 100-page written submission with copious citation of local and English authority, which was not referred to once by the majority. The minority decision was forty-four pages long and cited a considerable amount of authority. An interesting feature of the hearing before the Supreme Court was that not only did uniformed generals attend every day, but they were so fascinated by the legal argument, that they could not restrain themselves from making their own submissions in the middle of the claimant's submissions. The state-owned electricity company was the second largest employer in Pakistan after the army and the generals told the court how important the case was and that an ICC award would inevitably be adverse to the electricity authority and that the award would, therefore, be adverse to Pakistan's national interests."

4.   *Société Générale de Surveillance SA v. Pakistan*

In *Société Générale de Surveillance SA (SGS) v. Pakistan*, the Pakistani Supreme Court issued an anti-arbitration injunction against SGS restraining it from "taking any step, action or measure to pursue or participate or to continue to pursue or participate" in an ICSID arbitration.[105]

The dispute between SGS and Pakistan arose out of a contract concluded in 1994 for the assessment of all custom duties payable on goods imported into Pakistan. The contract contained an arbitration clause providing for arbitration in Islamabad under the Pakistani Arbitration Act of 1940. In 1996, Pakistan terminated the contract and SGS accepted the termination reserving its legal rights. SGS then initiated court proceedings in Switzerland alleging wrongful termination of the contract. Further, it claimed that it could not rely on the arbitration clause in the contract because no fair trial could be expected in Pakistan. The Swiss courts denied SGS's request.

In 2000, Pakistan brought an action before the Pakistani courts seeking an order to enforce the arbitration agreement contained in the contract. In 2001, SGS initiated an ICSID arbitration on the basis of the Pakistan-Switzerland BIT.

On 3 July 2002, the Supreme Court of Pakistan decided that SGS was not allowed to proceed with the ICSID arbitration, primarily on the ground that neither the ICSID Convention nor the Pakistan-Switzerland BIT had been implemented into Pakistani law. Therefore, the BIT and the ICSID Convention could not be enforced as law and could not defeat the arbitration clause contained in the contract. The Supreme Court granted Pakistan's request to proceed with the arbitration under the Arbitration Act 1940 pursuant to the contract.

The ICSID tribunal decided to proceed with the arbitration notwithstanding the injunction, but one of the arbitrators, being a Pakistani national, resigned. The tribunal held that it was not bound by the Pakistani Supreme Court's decision and that, in accordance with Art. 41(1) of the ICSID Convention, it had the power to rule on its own jurisdiction. Further, the tribunal held that

> "the right to seek access to international adjudication must be respected and cannot be constrained by an order of a national court. Nor can a State plead its internal law in defence of an act that is inconsistent with its international obligations."[106]

---

105. *Société Générale de Surveillance SA (SGS) v. Federation of Pakistan*, Supreme Court of Pakistan (Appellate Jurisdition), 3 July 2002, Civil Appeal Nos. 459 & 460 of 2002, para. 84 (decision published in *Yearbook* XXVIII (2003) pp. 1312-1341(Pakistan no. W1)).

106. *Société Générale de Surveillance SA (SGS) v. Pakistan*, ICSID Case No. ARB/01/13, Procedural Order No. 2, in *Anti-Suit Injunctions in International Arbitration*, *op. cit.*, fn. 7, p. 220 (also published in 18 ICSID Review – Foreign Investment Law Journal (2003) pp. 293 et seq.).

5. *Companhia Paranaense de Energia (COPEL) v. UEG Araucária Ltda.*

COPEL v. UEGA is one of the few examples where an anti-arbitration injunction was granted by a court in a civil law country, namely Brazil.[107] The dispute arose out of a contract relating to the investment for the construction and operation of a power plant in Brazil. The contract provided for ICC arbitration in Paris.

UEGA, a private company, commenced ICC arbitration proceedings in Paris. COPEL, a Brazilian State-owned company, sought an injunction before the Paraná State Second Lower Treasury Court to stop UEGA from pursuing the arbitration and a declaration that the arbitration agreement was null and void. COPEL claimed that the dispute was not arbitrable, firstly, because, COPEL was a State-controlled company and, secondly, because the dispute involved matters of public interest which are inarbitrable under the Brazilian Arbitration Act. The Lower Treasury Court granted the anti-arbitration injunction against UEGA and imposed a daily penalty of approximately US$ 400,000 in case of violation of the injunction.

Without delay, UEGA filed an appeal on the injunction before the Paraná State Superior Court of Justice. Although the final decision on the merits of the appeal has not yet been rendered, UEGA was allowed to continue with the arbitration. The arbitral tribunal rendered a partial award accepting its jurisdiction.

The decision of the Superior Court of Justice was challenged twice by COPEL within the Superior Court. In the first decision, the fourth Civil Chamber of the Court upheld the decision allowing the continuation of the arbitration holding that a Brazilian State-controlled entity could agree to arbitration, and that to prevent UEGA from proceeding with the arbitration would violate its right to access to justice, because arbitration was the method of dispute resolution agreed upon by the parties.

The second challenge was brought by COPEL before the Special Chamber of the Paraná State Superior Court. This court also denied COPEL's request. However, it should be noted that the request was denied on procedural grounds only and, therefore, cannot be interpreted as a general rejection of anti-arbitration injunctions.[108]

6. *Lac d'Amiante du Canada Ltée et 2858-0702 Québec Inc v. Lac d'Amiante du Québec Ltée*

The *Lac d'Amiante* case is another example of an anti-arbitration injunction issued by a court in a civil law jurisdiction.[109]

This case concerned two Canadian companies, Lac d'Amiante du Québec (LAQ) and Lac d'Amiante du Canada (LAC), who were involved in a joint venture for the exploitation of asbestos sites in Quebec. Several court actions and arbitration

---

107. The information on the *COPEL v. UEGA* case was provided by Mr Mauricio Gomm FERREIRA DOS SANTOS who reported on this case in a paper prepared for the 4th Annual ICDR/AAA Meeting in Miami, 26-28 March 2006.

108. COPEL AND UEGA have recently reached an agreement and an award on agreed terms has been rendered. All court proceedings have also been terminated.

109. On this case, see generally note by Stewart R. SHACKLETON, in 13 International Arbitration Law Review (2000, Issue 1), pp. N-6 et seq.

proceedings were brought in order to resolve disputes arising from this joint venture. In 1992, LAQ commenced court actions in Montreal against LAC. In 1996, LAC commenced an ICC arbitration in New York against LAQ. A few weeks later, LAQ filed a second action against LAC, again before the courts of Montreal.

In 1997, LAQ informed the arbitral tribunal in the ICC arbitration that it intended to file a counterclaim in the New York arbitration relating to the same disputes that were already pending before the courts in Montreal. LAQ then filed a motion to stay the Montreal court actions commenced by itself against LAC pending the arbitral tribunal's decision on the counterclaim.

LAQ's motion to stay the court actions was denied. LAQ nevertheless maintained the counterclaim in the ICC arbitration. LAC contested the arbitral tribunal's jurisdiction over the counterclaim. When the arbitral tribunal decided that it had jurisdiction over the counterclaim, LAC sought an anti-arbitration injunction from the courts in Montreal to prevent LAQ from maintaining its counterclaim in the ICC arbitration.

The Quebec Superior Court granted the anti-arbitration injunction against LAQ on several grounds. It considered that LAQ had waived its right to arbitrate by commencing court actions and that the counterclaim was, in fact, not covered by the arbitration agreement.

The anti-arbitration injunction was upheld by the Quebec Court of Appeal, primarily on the grounds that the injunction would stop an arbitration which had been abusively brought by LAQ and which was incompatible with the actions already pending before the courts in Montreal. According to the court, the aim of the injunction was not to control the arbitration process, but rather to stop the abusive behavior of LAQ.[110]

7.   ICC No. 5294, 22 February 1988, Final Award

In ICC case 5294, a contract was concluded between a Danish company and an Egyptian employer for the construction of a cattle abattoir in Egypt. The contract provided for ICC arbitration in Zurich. The Danish company subsequently subcontracted some works to an Egyptian company. When a dispute arose between the Danish company and the Egyptian company, the Danish company initiated an ICC arbitration in Zurich. A sole arbitrator was appointed by the ICC.

The Egyptian party objected to the jurisdiction of the arbitrator. It informed the arbitrator that a court action had been introduced in Egypt requesting a declaration that the arbitration clause was invalid and a suspension of the arbitration proceedings pending the outcome of the Egyptian court proceedings. A couple of months later, the Egyptian

---

110. In the words of the Quebec Court of Appeal :

"*Le recours en injonction des intimées constitue une procédure destinée à arrêter des initiatives procédurales, abusives et incompatibles avec les demandes déjà présentées à Montréal pour des objets et des causes semblables. La demande de LAC vise le comportement même de la partie, non le contrôle de la décision des arbitres.*"

(decision available online under <www.mcgill.ca/files/arbitration/LacdAmiante.pdf >).

party informed the arbitrator that an anti-arbitration injunction had been granted by the Egyptian court.

The sole arbitrator decided to ignore the anti-arbitration injunction and accepted jurisdiction. He held:

> "No order of any Egyptian Court was actually ever notified or submitted to the arbitrator either directly or by either of the parties. This is, however, immaterial.... [C]ourt proceedings in Egypt did not and do not have any direct influence on the present arbitration proceedings, since Egyptian Courts would not have jurisdiction of either these proceedings or the arbitrator. They certainly do not have any influence on the arbitrator's jurisdiction in the present case."

8. Conclusion

As the review of these cases shows, lawyers have discovered anti-arbitration injunctions as a tactical device. Originally intended to render the administration of justice more efficient, anti-arbitration injunctions are used – or abused – in practice as a tactical tool to stop or delay arbitrations. Unfortunately, these examples are not isolated cases[111] and one can presume that the tactical use of anti-arbitration injunctions will increase in the future.

V.   ARE ANTI-ARBITRATION INJUNCTIONS EVER JUSTIFIED?

I now revert to the question initially raised, i.e. are anti-arbitration injunctions ever justified? Even if a domestic law gives its courts the power to grant anti-arbitration injunctions, is the exercise of this power appropriate?

Typically, a party may attempt to justify the use of an anti-arbitration injunction on the basis that it would be highly unreasonable, inefficient, and very costly to proceed with the arbitration only to have the award set aside at the end of a lengthy arbitral process and to then bring the claim anew before the competent national court. Rather, time and money will be saved by bringing this issue directly before the national court in the first instance.

Logically this argument is attractive. However, it ignores the nature and accepted practice of international arbitration and the accepted international law rules applicable to international arbitration. Anti-arbitration injunctions can rarely be justified; they are contrary to fundamental principles of international arbitration law, including the doctrines of competence-competence, separability, and party autonomy. They also

---

111. See also, Bangladesh High Court, Dhaka, Decision of 5 April 2000 regarding ICC No. 7934/CK, Manjurul BASIT, J, extracts in ASA Bulletin (2000, no. 4), pp. 821-829; *Hitachi Ltd v Rupali Polyester*, Supreme Court of Pakistan, 10 June 1998, *Yearbook* XXV(2000), pp. 443 et seq.; *Paramedics Electromedicina Comercial Ltda v. GE Medical Systems Information Technologies Inc*, decision cited under fn. 80; ICC No. 4862, Partial Award,1986, in Sigvard JARVIN, Yves DERAINS, Jean-Jacques ARNALDEZ, eds., *Collection of ICC Awards 1986-1990* (Deventer 1994) pp. 508 et seq., commentary by Sigvard JARVIN.

ignore the principle according to which judicial control of the legality of the arbitral process should only occur after an award has been rendered, either by a court of the arbitral seat or a court of the place of enforcement.

According to the principle of competence-competence, "[a]n international arbitral tribunal is the judge of its own competence".[112] In other words, the tribunal is empowered to decide on its own jurisdiction prior to a national court. Therefore, anti-arbitration injunctions intended to prevent the arbitral tribunal from exercising this power violate the competence-competence principle.[113] In the words of the late Professor Fouchard,

> "[t]he issuance of an anti-suit injunction based on a given court's understanding of the validity and scope of an arbitration agreement clearly negates the principle of competence-competence. For that reason alone, it should be avoided."[114]

The principle of separability recognizes that the arbitration clause remains effective notwithstanding the fact that there is a challenge to the existence or validity of the main agreement.[115] The arbitration agreement is autonomous from the main agreement in which it is contained. The granting of an anti-arbitration injunction may violate the principle of separability, because not infrequently, such injunctions are granted in response to a claim of the invalidity of the main contract.[116]

The anti-arbitration injunction being at variance with the principle of party autonomy was the driver of decision of the ICC tribunal in the *Salini* case. It refused to consider itself bound by an anti-arbitration injunction contrary the parties' agreement. As seen above, following the principle of party autonomy, the tribunal decided that since the parties' wish was to resolve their disputes by arbitration, it had no choice but to ignore the anti-arbitration injunction and to continue the arbitration in accordance with the parties' agreement.[117]

Finally, anti-arbitration injunctions also violate the general principle according to which the legality of the arbitral process may only be controlled after an award was made, either by the court of the seat of the arbitration or by the court of the place of enforcement. Again, this was stated very clearly by the *Salini* tribunal holding that

> "[t]he appropriate occasion for the courts of State X to consider the issue of jurisdiction is in the context of an action to set aside the Tribunal's award, after

---

112. S.M. SCHWEBEL, *op. cit.*, fn. 9, p. 15.

113. S.M. SCHWEBEL, *loc. cit.*, fn. 112. See also the *Salini* award (cited under fn. 97, para. 152), where the ICC tribunal held that "[i]t would be a clear breach of the fundamental principle of competence-competence if an international arbitral tribunal were obliged to stay its proceedings in deference to a court proceeding which had specifically been instituted to determine the question of the tribunal's jurisdiction".

114. Philippe FOUCHARD, Anti-Suit Injunctions in International Arbitration – What Remedies?" in *Anti-suit Injunctions in International Arbitration, op. cit.*, fn. 7, p. 155.

115. J.D.M. LEW, *op. cit.*, fn. 7, p. 38.

116. S.M. SCHWEBEL, *op. cit.*, fn. 9, p. 14.

117. See supra, IV.2. (pp. 208-210).

the Tribunal has determined its own jurisdiction. The courts cannot, in the meantime, pre-empt the Tribunal's decision on its own jurisdiction."[118]

These four principles are well established in international arbitration law. They may have their origins in one system or another, but they are fundamental to the mechanism and smooth working of international arbitration. Through wide acceptance, these principles are part of customary international law as it applies to international arbitration. These are today codified in the New York Convention, as well as in the UNCITRAL Model Law. They also exist in most modern arbitration legislation.

In the New York Convention, the relevant provisions are Arts. II, III, and V. According to Art. II New York Convention

"(1) Each Contracting State shall recognize an agreement in writing under which the parties undertake to submit to arbitration all or any differences which have arisen or which may arise between them in respect of a defined legal relationship, whether contractual or not, concerning a subject matter capable of settlement by arbitration.

....

(3) *The court of a Contracting State*, when seized of an action in a matter in respect of which the parties have made an agreement within the meaning of this article, *shall, at the request of one of the parties, refer the parties to arbitration*, unless it finds that the said agreement is null and void, inoperative or incapable of being performed." (Emphasis added)

Accordingly, under Art. II New York Convention, there is an obligation under public international law on all States that are party to that Convention to stay court proceedings in favour of arbitration. This provision suggests that if there is a valid arbitration clause, the courts should not be issuing injunctions to stop an arbitration.[119] Indeed, when a national court issues an anti-arbitration injunction, it blocks the arbitration process agreed upon by the parties instead of referring the parties to arbitration as required by Art. II New York Convention.[120] As has been pointed out by Judge Stephen Schwebel, it also

"fails anticipatorily to 'recognize arbitral awards as binding and enforce them', (Art. III) and it pre-emptively refuses recognition and enforcement on grounds that do not, or may not, fall within the bounds of Art. V of the New York Convention".[121]

---

118. *Salini Costruttori S.p.a. v. Ethiopia*, Award cited under fn. 95, para. 153.
119. J.D.M. LEW, *op. cit.*, fn. 7, p. 31.
120. S.M. SCHWEBEL, *op. cit.*, fn. 9, p. 10.
121. S.M. SCHWEBEL, *loc. cit.*, fn. 120.

The same arguments can be made for the incompatibility of anti-arbitration injunctions with the principles contained in Arts. 8[122] and 16[123] of the UNCITRAL Model Law, i.e. competence-competence, separability and party autonomy. Art. 34 of the Model Law contains the principle that the judicial control of the legality of the arbitral process may occur only after an award was made by an application for setting aside the award before the courts of the seat of the arbitration.

To date, the New York Convention has been ratified by 139 countries. By contrast, the UNCITRAL Model Law has been adopted by forty-nine countries. The principles reflected in the Model Law are generally accepted, even by countries that have not adopted it. Therefore, it can be said that the principles codified both in the New York Convention and in the Model Law constitute the law of international arbitration. Due to their wide recognition, they are part of customary international law and *lex mercatoria* as it applies to international arbitration.

It follows that national courts which grant anti-arbitration injunctions violate conventional and customary international law, international public policy and international arbitration law.[124] International arbitration law and practice does not allow national courts outside the country of the seat of the arbitration to intervene in the arbitration process by granting anti-arbitration injunctions. An anti-arbitration injunction which aims to stop or interfere with an arbitration taking place in another jurisdiction cannot be justified.

VI.   THE INJUNCTED ARBITRATOR OR TRIBUNAL

Finally, what should an arbitrator do when faced with an injunction from a court other than at the seat of arbitration, ordering that he personally and/or a tribunal in which he is a member, should stay its proceedings or otherwise not continue with the arbitration?

---

122. Art. 8 Model Law:

"(1) A court before which an action is brought in a matter which is the subject of an arbitration agreement shall, if a party so requests not later than when submitting his first statement on the substance of the dispute, refer the parties to arbitration unless it finds that the agreement is null and void, inoperative or incapable of being performed.
(2) Where an action referred to in paragraph (1) of this article has been brought, arbitral proceedings may nevertheless be commenced or continued, and an award may be made, while the issue is pending before the court."

123. Art. 16(1) Model Law:

"The arbitral tribunal may rule on its own jurisdiction, including any objections with respect to the existence or validity of the arbitration agreement. For that purpose, an arbitration clause which forms part of a contract shall be treated as an agreement independent of the other terms of the contract. A decision by the arbitral tribunal that the contract is null and void shall not entail ipso jure the invalidity of the arbitration clause."

124. S.M. SCHWEBEL, *op. cit.*, fn. 9, p. 5.

218

Should the arbitrator consider his duty to the parties and the arbitration agreement to override his own personal freedom and situation, especially as in some cases the penalty for breaching a court order may be fines or even imprisonment for contempt of court?

One possibility may be to simply ignore any injunction directed against the arbitration on the grounds that the court issuing the injunction does not have jurisdiction over the arbitration (only the court of the seat of arbitration does) and that such order violates the law and practice of international arbitration. This would be a bold action and may place the arbitrator or tribunal in a difficult predicament if any arbitrator visited the jurisdiction in question. However, the arbitrators must take a pragmatic and legal position if they are to comply with their duty to the parties under the applicable arbitration rules and law.

It is suggested the approach for arbitrators in the face of an anti-arbitration injunction will depend on the circumstances and vary from case to case. In each case, the arbitral tribunal and the individual arbitrators should examine carefully the various effects the injunction may have on the tribunal or one of its members, or on the parties. The arbitral tribunal's primary duty is owed to the parties. If it finds that the parties have agreed to resolve their dispute by arbitration, it must respect this agreement and make an award. Often the injunction will be against one of the parties, or at least a party and the arbitrators. The reaction of the parties to the anti-arbitration injunction may well take the decision-making responsibility away from the arbitrators, e.g., where the party subject to the anti-arbitration injunction considers it must respect and comply with it.

The arbitral tribunal also should consider that an award rendered notwithstanding an injunction might not be enforceable in the country where the injunction was issued. A tribunal has a duty to make every effort to render an enforceable award. Hence, if it decides to ignore the injunction, it must be sure that this will not endanger the enforceability of the award. On the other hand, if the problem is merely an enforceability issue, i.e. under the New York Convention, the tribunal may feel constrained to make an award and then allow the successful party to seek to enforce the award where it can, regardless of its effect in the country where the injunction seeking to stay or stop the arbitration was made.

VII.   CONCLUSION

It is now widely recognized, both in national laws, international arbitration practice and international law, that the validity of an arbitration agreement should be decided in the first place by the arbitral tribunal properly appointed. It is also widely accepted that no national court outside the country of the seat of the arbitration should determine the validity of the arbitration agreement prior to the decision of the arbitral tribunal.

Anti-arbitration injunctions rendered in order to prevent a foreign arbitral tribunal from determining its jurisdiction violate this international arbitration law and the accepted and expected practice of international arbitration. Therefore, even if some domestic laws empower their courts to grant anti-arbitration injunctions against arbitral tribunals abroad, this power should not be exercised.

According to the late Professor Fouchard, "[i]n an ideal world, state courts should refrain from issuing anti-suit injunctions in the context of international arbitration".[125] Professor Fouchard probably was correct in assuming that only "in an ideal world" will national courts refrain from issuing anti-arbitration injunctions. Given the possibility of using anti-arbitration injunctions as a tactical device and some national courts' tendency to protect their own interests at all costs, regrettably some national courts may continue to grant anti-arbitration injunctions in order to stop foreign arbitrations. However the courts are out of line with the law, practice and expectations in international arbitration.

---

125. P. FOUCHARD, *op. cit.,* fn. 114, p. 154.

Comments on Control of Jurisdiction by Injunctions Issued by National Courts

*José I. Astigarraga**

TABLE OF CONTENTS

I. INTRODUCTION

Julian Lew's excellent Report covers two aspects of court control of arbitral jurisdiction: one, injunctions in a secondary jurisdiction against arbitration, and the other, court injunctions in support of arbitration.

With respect to injunctions against arbitration, Julian Lew concludes that:

> [N]ational courts which grant anti-arbitration injunctions violate conventional and customary international law, international public policy and international arbitration law. International arbitration law and practice does not allow national courts outside the country of the seat of the arbitration to intervene in the arbitration process by granting anti-arbitration injunctions. An anti-arbitration injunction which aims to stop or interfere with an arbitration taking place in another jurisdiction cannot be justified."[1] (Footnote omitted.)

In his Commentary, Pierre Karrer, consistent with sentiments expressed by others as well, lucidly takes the premise a step further. He suggests that:

> "not only anti-arbitration injunctions by state courts should be prohibited, but also _all_ anti-arbitration injunctions by arbitral tribunals, and _all_ *anti-suit injunctions by arbitral tribunals and by state courts*. As Emmanuel Gaillard aptly put it some three years ago: It should be prohibited to enjoin."[2]

Were all arbitral and judicial decision makers of the caliber of Pierre Karrer, Emmanuel Gaillard and Julian Lew, I would agree.

But I work often in jurisdictions that do not have substantial jurisprudence or experience dealing with arbitration or the New York Convention. And so driven

---

* Astigarraga Davis, Miami, Florida.

1. "Control of Jurisdiction by Injunctions Issued by National Courts", this volume, pp. 185-220, at p. 218.
2. "Anti-Arbitration Injunctions – Theory and Practice", this volume, pp. 228-232, at p. 230. (Underlined emphasis in original; italicized emphasis added.)

primarily by practical reasons, I wish to make sure that the blanket notion that "it should be prohibited to enjoin" is understood to have its exceptions.

There's a sense in the arbitration community, I think, that we are seeing more and more anti-arbitration tactics. See, e.g., Michael Hwang's article, "Why Is There Still Resistance to Arbitration in Asia", in which he discusses arbitration guerrillas, arbitration atheists and arbitration agnostics.[3] And you see articles such as "Arbitral Terrorism" in Focus Europe.[4]

We're seeing cases such as the *Companhia Paranaense de Energia (COPEL) v. UEG Arancaria Ltd.*, (relating to anti-arbitration proceeding in Brazil) cited in Julian Lew's article, and *Four Seasons Hotels and Resorts, B.V. v. Consorcio Barr, S.A.*,[5] in which courts not having primary jurisdiction, that is, cases in which the arbitration is seated outside the national territory of the judicial forum, are attempting to control the jurisdiction of a foreign arbitration.

With that backdrop, I'd like to compare two cases in which injunctions were issued in support of arbitration.

To put this in context, let me explain that in the United States, the federal appellate courts disagree as to the proper test for issuance of an anti-suit injunction.

Under the liberal approach,[6] "an international anti-suit injunction is appropriate whenever there is a *duplication of parties and issues* and the court determines that the prosecution of simultaneous proceedings would *frustrate the speedy* and efficient determination of the case".[7]

The factors to be considered under the liberal approach include:

– Vexatiousness
– Duplication of expenses
– Waste of judicial resources
– Delay
– Inconvenience
– Race to judgment
– Inconsistent rulings

---

3. Michael Hwang, "Why Is There Still Resistance to Arbitration in Asia?" in Global Reflections on International Law, Commerce and Dispute Resolution, ICC Publishing, Publication 693, p. 401.

4. < http://www.americanlawyer.com/focuseurope/aterror.html> (Summer 2003).

5. 267 F.Supp.2d 1335, 1338 (S.D. Fla. 2003)(relating to court proceedings in Venezuela), *vacated*, 377 F.3d 1164 (11th Cir. 2004).

6. *Kaepa. Inc. v. Achilles Corp.*, 76 F.3d 624 (5th Cir. 1996); *Seattle Totems Hockey Club, Inc. v. Nat'l Hockey League*, 652 F.2d 852 (9th Cir. 1981); *Philips Med. Sys. Int'l v. Bruetman*; 8 F.3d 600 (7th Cir. 1993).

7. *Quaak v. Klynveld Peat Marwick Goerdeler Bedrijfsrevisoren*, 361 F.3d 11, 17 (1st Cir. 2004) (emphasis added).

Under the conservative approach,[8] "the critical questions anent the issuance of an international anti-suit injunction are whether the foreign action either *imperils jurisdiction* of the forum court or *threatens* some strong *national policy*".[9]

The third approach rejects both tests. It provides that:

> "The *gatekeeping inquiry* is ... whether parallel suits involve *the same* parties and issues.... If – and only if – this threshold condition is satisfied should the court proceed to consider all the *facts and circumstances* in order to decide whether an injunction is proper.
>
> (....)
>
> If, after giving due regard to the circumstances (including the salient interest in international comity), a court supportably finds that *equitable considerations preponderate in favor of relief*, it may issue an international anti-suit injunction."[10]

II. *PERTAMINA* AND *PARAMEDICAS*: A COMPARISON

The first case I'd like to compare is the well-known case of *Pertamina*.[11] To recap very generally: KBC entered into contracts with Pertamina to develop an energy project in Indonesia. The contracts provided for arbitration in Switzerland. The arbitrators entered an award against Pertamina and an affiliate for more than $260 million. Pertamina challenged the award in Swiss courts. During the pendency of the Swiss challenge, KBC brought an enforcement action in Texas federal court. After the Texas federal court granted judgment for enforcement of the award and Pertamina had lost its Swiss challenge to the award, Pertamina filed a suit challenging the award in Indonesia, and the Indonesian court eventually issued an injunction prohibiting KBC from enforcing the judgment on pain of a fine of $500,000 each day. The Texas court determined that KBC would "suffer irreparable harm if the Indonesian court issued an injunction to prevent KBC from 'enforcing or executing' the Judgment",[12] and granted the injunction to enjoin Pertamina from proceeding in Indonesia. Ultimately, the Texas judge entered multiple orders and held Pertamina in contempt of court, noting, among other things, that she slowed down the proceedings in order to allow time for Pertamina's Swiss court challenge to run its course based on the position that Pertamina had taken that Swiss arbitral law controlled and at a minimum implicitly that the Swiss courts were the competent forum.

---

8. See *China Trade & Dev. Corp. v. M.V. Choong Yong*, 837 F.2d 33 (2d Cir. 1987); *Stonington Partners, Inc. v. Lernout & Hauspie Speech Prods.*, 310 F.3d 118 (3d Cir. 2002); *Gau Shan Co. v. Bankers Trust Co.*, 956 F.2d 1349 (6th Cir. 1992); *Laker Airways Ltd. v. Sabena Belgian World Airlines*, 731 F.2d 909 (D.C. Cir. 1984).

9. *Quaak*, 361 F.3d at 18 (emphasis added).

10. *Ibid.* at 18-19 (emphasis added).

11. *Karaha Bodas Co., L.L.C. v. Perusahaan Pertambangan Minyak Dan Gas Bumi Negara*, 335 F.3d 357 (5th Cir. 2003).

12. *Ibid.* at 361.

The appellate court reversed the anti-suit injunction. It noted several points: The United States was not a primary jurisdiction under the New York Convention. The US court would not be bound by the annulment of the award in Indonesia, even if Indonesia were to be deemed a primary jurisdiction. Essentially, the appellate court concluded that the Indonesian proceedings did not really interfere with the US court's jurisdiction, judgment or enforcement of the award, since the US courts are free under the Convention to enforce the award even if the award has been annulled in a primary jurisdiction. It opined that as a secondary jurisdiction, it was not the burden of the US court to "protect KBC from all the legal hardships it might undergo" as a result of the foreign arbitration or deal.[13]

That's interesting because the Fifth Circuit adheres to the liberal standard that, for example, considers that vexatiousness can be a ground for an anti-suit injunction. But it found that the Indonesian proceedings could not be regarded as truly vexatious since multiple parallel proceedings are fully contemplated under the Convention.

This is consistent with cases Julian Lew has cited at p. 194 of his Report, such as *Fomento de Construcciones y Contratas S.A. v. Colon Container Terminal S.A.*[14] in which he notes that contradictory judgments in Switzerland are avoided not by preventing the rendering of the foreign judgment, but by refusing to enforce such judgments.

That's fine in so far as it goes. The US court was not a primary jurisdiction, and at the end of the day, what the US court was properly concerned with was the enforcement or not in the United States of the foreign award.

But that is very different from another case Julian Lew cites, *Paramedics Electromedicina Comercial Ltda v. GE Medical Systems Information Technologies Inc.,* at p. 205 of his paper. I was counsel for the arbitral claimant in that case. There, a US manufacturer had entered into distributorship and sales representation agreements with a Brazilian company. The contract provided for arbitration in the United States, governed by US law. The manufacturer initiated arbitration. The Brazilian company filed suit in Brazil asserting, among other things, that: the arbitral agreement was unenforceable; it was not bound to arbitrate; this contract for distribution of high-tech medical equipment was a contract of adhesion; and the arbitral tribunal, which included one of the leading international arbitrators as chair, and included a leading Brazilian arbitration expert as one of the coarbitrators, was not qualified to consider the Brazilian legal issues involved. The Brazilian company didn't just sue the manufacturer but also its affiliate that had not signed the agreement. It also sued in the United States, to obtain an anti-arbitration injunction, and we immediately countersued to obtain an anti-suit injunction against the prosecution of the Brazilian lawsuit. The first-instance court in the United States found that the Brazilian claims were arbitrable, and granted an injunction prohibiting the Brazilian company from prosecuting its lawsuit in Brazil and imposed a fine of $5,000 a day. The Brazilian company appealed.

Using the conservative analysis, the appellate court upheld the injunction, declaring:

---

13. *Ibid.* at 369 (citations omitted).
14. DFT 127 III 279.

"An anti-suit injunction against parallel litigation may be imposed only if: (A) the parties are the same in both matters, and (B) resolution of the case before the enjoining court is dispositive of the action to be enjoined. [Citation omitted.] Once past this threshold, courts are directed to consider a number of additional factors, including whether the foreign action threatens the jurisdiction or the strong public policies of the enjoining forum."[15]

On the requirement that the parties be the same, the appellate court ruled that "[t]he district court did not abuse its discretion in ruling that the parties to the two actions are thus sufficiently similar to satisfy the first threshold requirement of *China Trade*".[16] So even though the Brazilian company had tried to circumvent the arbitration by suing an affiliate, the court saw through that.

The second requirement was that the resolution of the case before the court be dispositive of the foreign proceeding. Here, the first instance court had ruled that the Brazilian claims were arbitrable, so the question under *China Trade* is whether the ruling on arbitrability is dispositive of the [Brazil] litigation, even though the underlying disputes are confided to the arbitral panel and will not be decided by the enjoining court. In short, the district court's judgment disposes of the [Brazil] action because the [Brazil] litigation concerns issues that, by virtue of the district court's judgment, are reserved to arbitration.[17]

So the two threshold requirements to qualify for an anti-suit arbitration were met.

The question then became whether the "additional factors" such as "whether the foreign action either *imperils jurisdiction* of the forum court or *threatens some strong national policy*"[18] were also present. The court held:

"The *federal policy* favoring the liberal enforcement of arbitration clauses (as discussed above) applies with particular force in international disputes. [Citation omitted.] The [Brazil] action, filed 31 days after [the manufacturer] filed [the] arbitration with the IACAC, was a tactic to evade arbitration.... An anti-suit injunction *may be needed to protect the court's jurisdiction* once a judgment has been rendered. The doctrine of res judicata, where applied, may obviate injunctive relief against re-litigation in a second forum; but a foreign court might not give res judicata effect to a United States judgment, particularly since United States courts 'may choose to give res judicata effect to foreign judgments on the basis of comity,' but 'are not obliged' to do so."[19]

---

15. *Paramedics Electromedicina Comercial, Ltda., v. GE Medical Systems Information Technologies, Inc.,* 369 F.3d 645, 652 (2d Cir. 2004).
16. *Ibid.* (emphasis added).
17. *Paramedics,* 369 F.3d at 653 (citation omitted).
18. *Quaak* 361 F.3d at 18 (emphasis added).
19. *Paramedics,* 369 F.3d at 654 (citations omitted) (emphasis added).

So, because of the strong US policy favoring enforcement of arbitral agreements and the need to protect the US court's judgment that the Brazil claims were arbitrable, the appellate court upheld the injunction.

The court did add that:

> "We need not decide categorically whether an attempt to sidestep arbitration is alone sufficient to support a foreign anti-suit injunction, because '[t]here is less justification for permitting a second action,' as here, 'after a prior court has reached a judgment on the same issues'."[20]

The Second Circuit thus upheld the injunction barring the Brazilian litigation.

I submit that was exactly the right result. Here you had:

– A court of primary jurisdiction;
– An arbitral tribunal that had ruled that the claims were arbitrable;
– A court that independently evaluated the arbitrability of the Brazilian claims and held they were arbitrable;
– A defiant party that unquestionably was subject to the court's jurisdiction;
– A lawsuit in Brazil that not only could yield an irreconcilable conflicting judgment, namely, that the claims were not arbitrable, but also, the prosecution of which in court was, by definition, in violation of the determination that the claims were not subject to litigation but had to be pursued in arbitration.

III. CONCLUSION

There are myriad examples of courts without primary jurisdiction that have countenanced court lawsuits in violation of arbitral clauses and, at a minimum, violative of the principle of *Kompetenz-Kompetenz*, without regard for Art. II of the New York Convention's instruction that parties should be referred to arbitration absent voidness and the other special conditions.

The aim of the Convention is to promote and protect the enforceability of arbitral agreements and awards. If under the national law, a court lacks the power to enjoin a recalcitrant party, then so be it. But the question is whether in those jurisdictions where courts do have that power, the Convention bars its exercise.

In *Pertamina*, the appellate court declared:

> "Although [the New York Convention] obligations limit the grounds upon which the court can refuse to enforce a foreign arbitral award, there is nothing in the Convention or implementing legislation that expressly limits the inherent authority of a federal court to grant injunctive relief with respect to a party over whom it has jurisdiction. Given the absence of an express provision, we discern

---

20. *Ibid.* (citations omitted).

no authority for holding that the New York Convention divests the [first instance] court of its inherent authority to issue an anti-suit injunction."[21]

In sum, I submit that in instances such as the ones I've described, such as where an arbitral tribunal has made a determination that a claim is arbitrable or a court in the primary jurisdiction has, itself, ruled that a claim is arbitrable, a court with primary jurisdiction does no violence to the Convention by ordering the defiant party to desist from foreign actions that would eviscerate or undermine the arbitration.[22]

---

21. *Karaha Bodas Co., L.L.C.*, 335 F.3d at 365.

22. The opinions expressed in this paper are those of the author and do not necessarily reflect the opinions of his firm, any of its members or any client of the firm.

Anti-arbitration Injunctions: Theory and Practice

*Pierre A. Karrer**

I.   ANTI-ARBITRATION INJUNCTIONS ISSUED BY ARBITRAL TRIBUNALS

I will take no issue at all with Julian Lew's case that the UNCITRAL Model Law and more generally the New York Convention and international arbitration law prohibits state courts from issuing anti-arbitration injunctions to arbitral tribunals outside their jurisdiction. This proposition made some three years ago by Judge Schwebel is now supported by Julian Lew's thorough research into various jurisdictions.[1]

On the contrary, let me venture from the I believe now *firm* ground of anti-arbitration injunctions by courts into the *related subjects* of cross-border anti-arbitration injunctions by arbitral tribunals and anti-suit injunctions by arbitral tribunals and courts.

I believe that the Model Law and the New York Convention's prohibition is well grounded in *even more general* jurisprudential thinking.

Can an arbitral tribunal issue an anti-arbitration injunction against another arbitral tribunal, possibly not yet formed? I have been asked to do that, but I have never done it. Why not?

This raises of course the question whether arbitral tribunals are bound by the New York Convention. I believe that they are, at the very least indirectly, where the state courts at the seat of the arbitration are bound by the New York Convention. Awards are subject to setting aside proceedings in the country of the seat before state courts. In the vast majority of jurisdictions, these can exercise an unfettered review of the arbitral tribunal's decision on its own jurisdiction. That decision raises the issue, I would have thought, whether a question may be considered de novo or must be left to another forum, the decision of which must be recognized. If that other forum is an arbitral tribunal, the New York Convention applies.

But admittedly, my own reluctance to issue an anti-arbitration injunction stemmed from a more general idea that cannot be derived directly from the New York Convention: The idea is that my arbitral tribunal is not any better than anybody else's arbitral tribunal. My arbitral tribunal is a creation of the parties' autonomy. Another arbitral tribunal may also be created by the parties' autonomy. We must live with this.

---

*   Dr.iur. (Zurich), LL.M. (Yale); FCI Arb; Honorary President, ASA Swiss Arbitration Association; Vice President, Stockholm Institute; Member, International Court of Arbitration of the ICC; Chairman, Swiss National Committee of the ICC.

1. "Control of Jurisdiction by Injunctions Issued by National Courts", this volume, pp. 185-220.

By having created another arbitral tribunal and having established its jurisdiction, possibly also only by an unconditional appearance before that arbitral tribunal, the parties may have countermanded an earlier exercise of their party autonomy. It will be for my arbitral tribunal to decide whether this is really so. Of course, I would hope to get it right, but I think we all should recognize that on occasion we may get it wrong; and in any event, some other arbitral tribunal, on any point, honestly may come to a different determination. We must also then recognize that in our world there is no way to avoid honest diverging decisions on the same point. Of course, within a given legal system, there are mechanisms that will *tend* to, but only tend to, lead to harmonization of decisions in each individual case and also between similar cases. However, in the wider world this is not so.

II.   ANTI-ARBITRATION INJUNCTIONS ISSUED BY COURTS

I accordingly reject the theory that you sometimes hear that a decision by a state court *inherently* deserves more weight than a decision by an arbitral tribunal. The New York Convention is based on the contrary philosophy. Indeed, if we try to see where international arbitral tribunals having their seat in a particular jurisdiction are positioned within the judicial system of that jurisdiction, we would have to say that international arbitral tribunals sit quite far up in the judicial system of a particular jurisdiction and operate in the relatively thin legal air that blows around the nostrils of the highest courts in any jurisdiction. A trial court has an intermediate appellate court and then yet another layer of courts, or more, breathing down its neck on most decisions that it takes. International arbitral tribunals feel the presence of state courts at the seat, but not quite that close and quite that often.

Another mechanical way of establishing a hierarchy between fora is the idea that once a case is pending before a particular forum, the other fora should, under *lis pendens*, decline jurisdiction over that same case between the same parties, or even beyond the narrow limits of technical *lis pendens*. This is a very reasonable criterion within the same jurisdiction where indeed a system *can* be designed, and *is* regularly designed, to avoid conflicting decisions.

However, between arbitral tribunals I do not believe that the temporal priority between claims should be relevant at all. It is for each forum to decide whether to accept jurisdiction. One forum's decision on its own jurisdiction cannot, internationally, be res judicata for another forum on the question of *that* forum's jurisdiction. There is no obligation to recognize another forum's acceptance of jurisdiction.

Julian Lew discusses the Swiss decisions. One by a lower Geneva Court flatly says that Swiss state courts *cannot,* issue anti-arbitration or anti-suit injunctions. This is good law, and I for one would not wish to change it.

The *other* decision is not on injunctions, but on *lis pendens,* and it is not good law in Switzerland. It is the decision of the Swiss Federal Supreme Court in *Fomento* that an arbitral tribunal must stay proceedings on its *own* jurisdiction pending a foreign state court's decision on *that* court's jurisdiction. In early 2007, the Swiss Federal PIL Statute will be amended and will expressly say the opposite.

In other words, all international arbitral tribunals should be put on an equal footing, regardless of whether they are arbitral tribunals in our own jurisdiction or in a foreign jurisdiction, and regardless of whether they were put in place earlier or later or issued their award earlier or later. The same should also hold true for state courts of different jurisdictions. Between sovereign nations, small or large, powerful or not, the principle of equality must prevail.

Some will say, and you will hear it this afternoon, "Let's be flexible: Good anti-arbitration injunctions and *good* anti-suit injunctions should be allowed, but *bad* injunctions should not." Not a good idea, I think. Nobody issuing an injunction will say that it is a bad one.

This leads me to say, well beyond what Julian Lew suggests, that not only anti-arbitration injunctions by state courts should be prohibited, but also *all* anti-arbitration injunctions by arbitral tribunals, and *all* anti-suit injunctions by arbitral tribunals and by state courts. As Emmanuel Gaillard aptly put it some three years ago: It should be prohibited to enjoin.

We can see that this is correct by remembering that one basic human right is that every person should have *access to justice*. Obviously, any anti-arbitration injunction and any anti-suit injunction curtails that right.

We can also see that the proposition must be right because if you accept that anti-suit injunctions or anti-arbitration injunctions could be proper at least in certain, exceptional cases, where would you stop? Should it then not also be proper to issue anti-anti-suit injunctions and anti-anti-anti-arbitration injunctions?

Far from promoting unity of decisions, an elusive goal to begin with, anti-arbitration and anti-suit injunctions lead to diverging decisions and to the fight between the various jurisdictions on recognition and enforcement. Rather than promote the peaceful resolution of disputes by arbitral tribunals whose decisions are then recognized and enforced, they promote battles in the state courts. This is exactly what the New York Convention sought to avoid.

Some will say, "the jurisdiction of sovereign nations is one thing, but if a party appears before me in my arbitral tribunal or in my court, surely I can tell *that party* what to do or not to do. Therefore, I can tell it not to start an arbitration before another arbitral tribunal or not to sue in a foreign court. In that case, I am not telling that other forum anything." But indirectly, that is what you are doing.

Others will say, "it may well be that I am not allowed to tell another arbitral tribunal or another court what to do, not even indirectly, but I *still* have jurisdiction over *my own* nationals or *my own residents*, and surely, I can tell them here *at home* what to do and not to do. If I tell them, for example, that they cannot leave the country to do bad things abroad, this surely is no infringement of another country's sovereignty."

We all have heard these clever ways of evading the question. But we are all sufficiently trained in the law to know that the law, including the law of nations, expects people and even courts or arbitral tribunals to act in good faith and not to play with words.

III.   MINIMIZING THE IMPACT OF ANTI-ARBITRATION INJUNCTIONS

Let me now add some remarks from the point of view of a party or a practicing arbitrator or an arbitral institution faced with the possibility of anti-arbitration injunctions from courts.

1.   What Can the Parties Do?

Parties can agree on a seat of arbitration in an arbitration-friendly country. Provide that none of the arbitrators shall have the nationality or be resident of the country of one of the parties. Structure the transaction in such a way that assets against which a possible arbitral award might be enforced are situated in a New York Convention country known for a faithful application of the New York Convention. Use an arbitral institution or an appointing authority of known independence, and in a country that is neither party's country.

Appoint an arbitrator with experience also with difficult countries and difficult co-arbitrators.

2.   What Can an Arbitrator Do?

Arbitrators can agree on a presiding arbitrator who is not only not a national or citizen of one of the parties (which many arbitration rules require anyway), but also not a *resident* of any of the countries of the parties. The fascination with nationality or citizenship strikes me as misguided in any case.

Provide in the Terms of Reference that meetings and hearings may take place outside the seat of the arbitration, and that the award need not be signed at the seat.

If the arbitration clause provides that all actions of the arbitral tribunal and all hearings must take place in a particular country, ask innocently why this is important. If the answer is, for convenience of the local party, suggest the possibility of an equally convenient and attractive place across the border. In my experience, people living in "difficult" countries may feel unable to make the suggestion themselves, but will gladly take up a suggestion to go elsewhere on official business. Build in sufficient time for their private agenda.

Avoid even more scrupulously than normally anything that may be construed as evidence of bias. For example, it is obvious that Terms of Reference will list as "parties" to the arbitration parties that do not wish not to participate in the arbitration, or will list as "issues" issues that will not be relevant if the arbitral tribunal decides in a particularly way on some logically earlier issues, or will reproduce the arguments of one party, as indeed Terms of Reference must do. Lace this liberally with caveats such as "without prejudice to the arbitral tribunal's decision on the point which the arbitral tribunal does not make today with the Terms of Reference, but that will make later, if necessary".

Repeat information, particularly about upcoming hearings, several times. Be prepared for the statement: "Oh, I never saw this. I never received this. This is totally new to me."

Generally, move fast. Provide for the possibility of telephone hearings. Obtain signatures of co-arbitrators on a Final Award and other decisions early. Provide that the chair's signature will be sufficient. Pre-sign a copy of the Final Award at the right place, but a few hours earlier than the officially announced time so that an anti-signing injunction arrives late.

Give a dissenting arbitrator from a "difficult" country ample opportunity to file a dissenting opinion; even help him or her with it.

To sum up: Above all, drive safely and defensively – Michael Hwang's advice – but drive as fast as possible.

Seize upon any ambiguity in an anti-suit injunction to find *wiggle room*.

If an anti-suit injunction is directed at a party and directs that party to withdraw its complaint, – a case I have seen, and not even from a "difficult" country – consider saying with a straight face: "Claimant notified us on such and such date that it was withdrawing the complaint, thereby obeying an injunction it had received from the ... court. The Arbitral Tribunal follows its own procedure, and under that procedure only those procedural actions are attributed to a party that reflect that party's free will. If a party acted under duress, its action will be disregarded. The complaint therefore remains as originally filed." What happened after that? Nothing.

Another example of "wiggling": A court issued an anti-suit injunction against an institution "and others", but did not specify who the "others" were. The arbitral tribunal said that it had no indication regarding who the "others" were. It presumed that whoever the "others" were, they were made aware of the court proceedings as required by the law of the country of the court that had issued the anti-suit injunction (a law no doubt implemented only selectively, but the arbitral tribunal would not say that, nor would anybody in the country concerned). Since neither the arbitral tribunal nor its members nor the counterparty appeared to have been involved in the state court proceedings, all these could be excluded from the "others" group, and therefore were not bound by the injunction.

Courts that issue anti-arbitration injunctions are often sloppy because they do not understand the process in the first place, or because doing exactly what your master tells you to do is not much of a challenge, and people in such situations will think about other things, such as where they can find that sausage that they have been looking for all week but the shelves were empty.

Arbitral Institutions should be aware that their arbitral tribunals may be truncated by surprise anti-arbitration measures – for example, one of the arbitrators may be prevented by an anti-suit injunction from traveling to the place of the hearing. In such cases, a replacement emergency arbitrator should stand by to be appointed quickly and step in to save the hearing date. This presupposes arbitration rules that do not foresee that any replacement arbitrator must be appointed in exactly the same way as the arbitrator who resigns or otherwise becomes incapable or unwilling to continue to fulfil his or her duties.

Working Group A

4. Protection of Jurisdiction by Injunctions Issued by Arbitral Tribunals

Anti-suit Injunctions Issued by Arbitrators

Emmanuel Gaillard*

I.   INTRODUCTION

It has become increasingly frequent in international arbitration for a recalcitrant party to attempt to disrupt the arbitral process by bringing the dispute covered by the arbitration agreement before national courts (ordinarily those of that party's own State) and seeking an "anti-suit injunction" from those courts. The nuisance introduced into international arbitration by this type of measure has been widely commented upon and criticized.[1] The fact that the mechanism of anti-suit injunctions—in this instance, anti-arbitration injunctions—originates from common law systems in no way means that the disruption of the arbitral process is specific to those systems. Courts in civil law countries such as Brazil or Venezuela have had recourse to this mechanism in the same way as courts in common law countries such as Pakistan, India or the United States.[2]

---

* Partner and head of the International Arbitration Group, Shearman & Sterling LLP; Professor of Law, University of Paris XII°; Member of ICCA.

1. On anti-suit injunctions in international arbitration, see Emmanuel GAILLARD, ed., *Anti-Suit Injunctions in International Arbitration, IAI Series on International Arbitration No. 2* (Juris Publishing 2005) (hereinafter *Anti-Suit Injunctions in International Arbitration*). See also the report by Julian LEW, "Control of Jurisdiction by Injunctions Issued by National Courts", this volume, pp. 185-220.

2. For the numerous examples of anti-suit injunctions issued by domestic courts against arbitral proceedings at the request of one of the parties, see *Anti Suit Injunctions in International Arbitration, op. cit.*, fn. 1; Emmanuel GAILLARD, *"Il est interdit d'interdire: Réflexions sur l'utilisation des anti-suit injunctions dans l'arbitrage commercial international"*, Rev. Arb. (2004) p. 47; "Reflections on the Use of Anti-Suit Injunctions in International Arbitration" in L.A. MISTELIS & D.M. LEW, eds., *Pervasive Problems in International Arbitration* (Kluwer 2006) p. 203. On the situation in Latin America, see Horacio A. GRIGERA NAÓN, "Competing Orders Between Courts of Law and Arbitral Tribunals: Latin American Experiences" in *Global Reflections on International Law, Commerce and Dispute Resolution, Liber Amicorum in Honour of Robert Briner* (ICC Publishing 2005) (hereinafter *Liber Amicorum in Honour of Robert Briner*) p. 335.

Although severe criticism has been expressed in relation to orders issued by domestic courts enjoining the parties, an arbitral institution or the arbitrators from proceeding with or participating in an arbitration, the frequency of the parties' recourse to anti-suit injunctions has not diminished in any manner. In reaction, in those jurisdictions most familiar with the mechanism of anti-suit injunctions, the question was raised as to the possibility for the courts to provide support to the arbitral process by enjoining the recalcitrant party from proceeding with its request for an anti-suit injunction, or prohibiting the party targeted by the injunction from complying with the first court's decision. This chain reaction results in anti-anti-suit injunctions whereby each State court prohibits a party either from proceeding with an arbitration or from pursuing its disruptive attempts against an arbitral proceeding. Neither situation, however, offers a suitable response to the extent that, in each case, the domestic court's injunction is based on the presumption that that court's view of the existence and validity of the arbitration agreement will have absolute extraterritorial effect.[3]

Although less often debated,[4] the question has arisen as to whether arbitrators, when they are confronted with a party's attempt to submit a dispute that is covered by an arbitration agreement to a domestic court – or another arbitral tribunal[5] – may issue an injunction to prohibit that party from escaping the arbitration agreement. In other words, may arbitrators issue anti-suit injunctions? Three situations are, in this respect, relevant: when a party starts a court action in relation to a dispute that is covered by an arbitration agreement; when the court seized decides that it has jurisdiction to hear the dispute; when the court, having decided that it has jurisdiction, enjoins the other party from initiating an arbitral proceeding or from pursuing an ongoing arbitral proceeding. In other words, the arbitral tribunal may be confronted with the introduction of a parallel court action or with an existing court action, and a possible anti-arbitration injunction issued by the court. In all these situations, the same outcome is sought, more or less successfully, by the recalcitrant party: disrupt or terminate the arbitral proceeding by submitting the dispute that is covered by the arbitration agreement to another court. What is the appropriate response in such cases? Must the arbitrators comply with anti-suit injunctions issued against them and stay the arbitral proceeding? Should they ignore anti-suit injunctions issued against them on the basis of the fundamental principle of competence-competence and the recognition of the existence

---

3. See Emmanuel GAILLARD, "The Misuse of Anti-Suit Injunctions", New York Law Journal (1 August 2002) pp. 3 and 7; "*KBC v. Pertamina*: Landmark Decision on Anti-Suit Injunction", New York Law Journal (2 October 2003) pp. 3 and 8.
4. See Laurent LÉVY, "Anti-suit Injunctions Issued by Arbitrators", in *Anti-Suit Injunctions in International Arbitration*, *op. cit.*, fn. 1, p. 115.
5. In practice, this question arises less frequently, for example when a dispute arises as to the respective scope of two distinct arbitration agreements (see, e.g., the example given by L. LÉVY in his article, *op. cit.*, fn. 4, p. 115) or, in investment arbitration, when a contractual claim is brought before the arbitral tribunal having jurisdiction over such claims and, at the same time, another claim is brought before the tribunal having jurisdiction on the basis of the investment protection treaty containing an umbrella clause for the violation of such clause. See also Kaj HOBÉR, "Parallel arbitration proceedings – Duties of the Arbitrators" in *Parallel State and Arbitral Procedures in International Arbitration* (ICC Publishing 2005) p. 243.

and validity of the arbitration agreement on the basis of which the arbitral tribunal has been constituted? Can, and should, the arbitrators issue anti-suit injunctions against a recalcitrant party? All these questions are addressed below through the examination of the arbitrators' jurisdiction to issue anti-suit injunctions (II), the widespread recognition of such jurisdiction in arbitral case law (III), the advisability of arbitral anti-suit injunctions (IV) and the legal regime of such measures (V).

II. THE ARBITRAL TRIBUNAL'S JURISDICTION TO ISSUE ANTI-SUIT INJUNCTIONS

Well-established principles of international arbitration law unquestionably provide the basis for the arbitrators' jurisdiction to issue anti-suit injunctions. These are the jurisdiction to sanction violations of the arbitration agreement and the power to take any measure necessary to avoid the aggravation of the dispute or to protect the effectiveness of the final award (1). Contrary views, which have denied arbitrators the power to issue anti-suit injunction, are unpersuasive (2).

1. The Legal Bases of the Arbitral Tribunal's Jurisdiction to Issue Anti-suit Injunctions

The notion that, in issuing anti-suit injunctions, arbitrators would make use of powers exclusively vested in State courts, echoes past debates over the power of the arbitrators to award punitive damages[6] or "*astreintes*".[7] Such power is deeply rooted in well recognized principles of international arbitration law, namely the arbitrators' jurisdiction to sanction all breaches of the arbitration agreement and the arbitrators' power to take any appropriate measures either to avoid the aggravation of the dispute or to ensure the effectiveness of their future award.

a.   Jurisdiction to sanction, by equivalent or in kind, violations of the arbitration agreement
The agreement by which two or more parties undertake to submit to international arbitration the disputes which may arise in relation to their contract unquestionably grants arbitrators the power to decide all questions related to the merits of the dispute brought before them.

However, the jurisdiction thus conferred to the arbitral tribunal by the arbitration agreement is not confined to the resolution of the merits of the dispute. The two main

---

6. M. Scott DONAHEY, "Punitive Damages in International Commercial Arbitration", 10 J. Int'l Arb. (1993, no. 3) p. 67; E. Allan FARNSWORTH, "Punitive Damages in Arbitration", 7 Arb. Int. (1991, no. 1) p. 3; for US case law, see *Mastrobuono v. Shearson Lehman Hutton, Inc.*, 514 U.S. 52 (1995), 10 Int'l Arb. Rep. (Mar. 1995) p. 3, and Rev. Arb. (1995) p. 295, commentary by Laurent NIDDAM, *ibid.*, p. 301.

7. See Laurent LÉVY, "*Les astreintes et l'arbitrage international en Suisse*", 19 ASA Bull. (2001, no. 1) p. 21. For the French case law, see *S.A. Otor Participations*, "*Emballage 48*", *Yves Bacques and Michèle Bouvier [together "the founders"] v. S.A.R.L. Carlyle (Luxembourg) Holdings 1 and S.A.R.L. Carlyle (Luxembourg) Holdings 2 [together, "Carlyle"]*, Paris Court of Appeal, 7 October 2004, reported by Denis BENSAUDE, "*S.A. Otor Participations v. S.A.R.L. Carlyle (Luxembourg) Holdings 1*: Interim Awards on Provisional Measures in International Arbitration", 22 J. Int'l Arb. (2005, no. 4) p. 357.

effects of the arbitration agreement are to oblige the parties to submit all disputes covered by the arbitration agreement to arbitration, and to confer jurisdiction on the arbitral tribunal to hear all disputes covered by the arbitration agreement. It is thus a fundamental principle of arbitration law that arbitrators have the power to rule on their own jurisdiction, a principle that is the corollary of the principle of the autonomy of the arbitration agreement. Under this latter principle, any claim that the contract containing the arbitration agreement is void or voidable has no impact on the arbitration agreement and the arbitrators' jurisdiction. Thus the principle of autonomy allows arbitrators to examine any challenges to their jurisdiction based on the alleged ineffectiveness of the disputed contract. The principle of competence-competence further allows the arbitrators to decide any challenge to the arbitration agreement itself.

The fundamental principles of international arbitration law thus allow any disputes related to the arbitration agreement to be decided by the arbitrators themselves, something that has been widely recognized in case law[8] and in domestic arbitration statutes or international arbitration rules.[9] They provide solid grounds to the arbitrators to decide such matters notwithstanding the parties' attempts to frustrate the arbitral process by escaping their contractual undertaking to arbitrate their dispute.

Against this background, the arbitrators' jurisdiction to decide disputes relating to the arbitration agreement contains, by definition, the jurisdiction to decide breaches of the obligation to arbitrate. It also contains the arbitrators' power to sanction any breaches that are ascertained on that basis.[10] Arbitral jurisdiction would, otherwise, be simply negated. By comparison, a significant body of case law has developed in national systems according to which submitting disputes that are covered by an arbitration agreement to the domestic courts, or refusing to perform the undertaking to arbitrate, amounts to breaches of the arbitration agreement.[11] Domestic courts have further ruled that damages can be awarded on that ground,[12] taking into account, for the quantification of the damages, the costs incurred by the party brought before a national court in the face of an arbitration agreement.

---

8. See generally Emmanuel GAILLARD, John SAVAGE, eds., *Fouchard Gaillard Goldman on International Commercial Arbitration* (Kluwer Law International 1999) (hereinafter *Fouchard Gaillard Goldman on International Commercial Arbitration*) paras. 388 et seq. and paras. 647 et seq.; Julian LEW, Loukas A. MISTELIS, Stefan KRÖLL, *Comparative International Commercial Arbitration* (Kluwer Law International 2001) pp. 390 et seq.; Jean-François POUDRET, Sébastien BESSON, *Droit comparé de l'arbitrage international* (Bruylant 2002) pp. 407 et seq.

9. See Art. 6(2) of the ICC Arbitration Rules; Art. 23.1 of the LCIA Arbitration Rules; Art. 21(1) of the UNCITRAL Arbitration Rules.

10. For a different view, see Laurent LÉVY, *op. cit.*, fn. 4, p. 120.

11. See, e.g., *Aggeliki Charis Compania Maritime S.A. v. Pagnan SPA*, [1995] 1 Lloyd's Law Rep. 87; *Shell International Petroleum Co. Ltd. v. Coral Oil Co. Ltd.*, [1999] 1 Lloyd's Law Rep. 72; *Through Transport Mutual Insurance Association (EURASIA) Ltd. v. New India Assurance Co. Ltd.*, [2005] 1 Lloyd's Law Rep. 67.

12. See, e.g., *Mantovani v. Carapelli S.p.A.*, [1980] 1 Lloyd's Law Rep. 375. See also Jane WESSEL, Sherri NOTH COHEN, "In Tune with Mantovani: The 'Novel' Case of Damages for Breach of an Arbitration Agreement", Int. A.L.R. (2001) p. 65.

Arbitral case law shows that arbitral tribunals have repeatedly recognized their power to award damages for the breach by a party of its undertaking to arbitrate its dispute, taking into account the costs incurred by the other party in domestic proceedings notwithstanding the arbitration agreement.[13] Such compensation is nothing more than the reparation, by equivalent, of the breach of the arbitration agreement. Ordinary rules of reparation, however, also provide for reparation in kind. In other words, arbitrators have the power to sanction a contractual breach either by an award of damages or by ordering specific performance, the recalcitrant party being ordered to cease such breach and take all necessary measures to restore the situation. In that context, anti-suit injunctions ordered by the arbitrators are in reality nothing more than an order given to the party acting in breach of the arbitration agreement to comply with its contractual undertaking to arbitrate the dispute it has submitted to domestic courts.[14]

b.   *Power to take any measure necessary to avoid the aggravation of the dispute or to protect the effectiveness of the award*
In deciding the dispute before them and assessing the question of whether or not they may order anti-suit injunctions, the arbitrators often refer to the principle according to which the parties must refrain from any conduct that may aggravate their dispute.[15]
Submission of the matters covered by an arbitration agreement to the domestic courts, or even the risk of such submission, constitutes a factor that may aggravate the dispute between the parties, and that may justify the issuance of an order addressed to the parties prohibiting such conduct.[16] Depending on the facts of each case, it is within the arbitrators' power, as recognized in international arbitration law, to decide whether a decision in the form of an anti-suit injunction directed to one or more parties is the appropriate measure designed to prohibit conduct which may aggravate the dispute.[17]
A further principle may justify the recourse by the arbitrators to anti-suit injunctions in the context of the protection of the arbitral process. It is an entrenched principle of

---

13. See, e.g., ICC Award No. 5946 (1990), ICCA *Yearbook Commercial Arbitration* XVI (1991) (hereinafter *Yearbook*) p. 97; ICC Award No. 8887 (April 1997), 11 ICC Bull. (2000, no. 2) p. 91; Final Award dated 13 July 1993, *Yearbook* XXII (1997) p. 197; Final Award dated 19 September 2003, *Yearbook* XXVIII (2003) p. 100.
14. For a review of the case law in this respect, see infra Part III.
15. See, e.g., ICC Award No. 3896 (dated 23 December 1982), 110 J.D.I. (1983) p. 914, commentary by Sigvard JARVIN, *ibid.*, p. 918 (English translation in Sigvard JARVIN, Yves DERAINS, eds., *Collection of ICC Arbitral Awards 1974-1985* (ICC Publishing/Kluwer 1990) p. 161); *Amco Asia Corporation and others v. Republic of Indonesia*, ICSID Case No. ARB/81/1, Decision on Request for Provisional Measures of 9 December 1983, 24 I.L.M. (1985) p. 365; ICC Case No. 10596, Interlocutory Award (2000), *Yearbook* XXX (2005) p. 66 ("the parties must refrain from any conduct (whether action or inaction) which may aggravate the dispute, and ... arbitrators sitting under the ICC Rules have the power to issue decisions prohibiting such conduct", *ibid.*, para. 17).
16. See, e.g., *Plama Consortium Limited v. Republic of Bulgaria*, ICSID Case No. ARB/03/24, Order dated 6 September 2005, para. 45 (published on the ICSID website).
17. For a review of the case law in this respect, see infra Part III.

international arbitration that arbitrators must render an award capable of being recognized and enforced.[18]

By submitting to a domestic court a matter that is covered by an arbitration agreement, and creating the risk of multiple, and possibly divergent, decisions on such matter (including on the question of the existence and the validity of the arbitration agreement), a party may not only breach the arbitration agreement but also undermine the effectiveness of the award to be rendered by the arbitrators. In that context, it is not questionable that the power to issue anti-suit injunctions is only one aspect of the arbitrators' power to take all necessary measures to protect the international effectiveness of their future award.[19]

2. *Analysis of Arguments Sometimes Raised to Deny Arbitrators the Power to Issue Anti-suit Injunctions*

The arbitrators' power to issue anti-suit injunctions is not unanimously recognized. Three types of criticism have been expressed in this respect, all of which have in common the meaning and scope of the principle that arbitrators have jurisdiction to decide their own jurisdiction.

Under a first view, it would be somehow improper for an arbitral tribunal to address injunctions to State courts. A second critical position is advanced on the basis that domestic courts, too, have competence-competence. Finally, it has been maintained that an arbitral tribunal that issues anti-suit injunctions would be a judge in its own cause. Each of these positions will be examined in turn.

---

18. See, e.g., Art. 35 of the ICC Arbitration Rules; Art. 32.2 of the LCIA Arbitration Rules. See also ICC Case No. 9593, Final Award (December 1998), 11 ICC Bull. (2000, no. 1) p. 105, at pp. 109-110 ("The Arbitral Tribunal urges both parties to refrain from taking any steps that may deprive of any purpose the Arbitral Tribunal's decision to be rendered following the hearing to be held on....").

19. See the recent decision by the High Court of Justice, Queen's Bench Division Commercial Court, *Republic of Ecuador v. Occidental Exploration & Production*, 2 March 2006, [2006] EWHC 345 (Comm). The High Court had to decide on the request for annulment of an award in which the arbitral tribunal held that it had jurisdiction and ordered the claimant to desist from carrying claims brought before the Ecuadorian courts on subject matters related to the arbitration. The Court refused to vacate the award under Sect. 68 of the 1996 Arbitration Act, considering that the arbitrators, who acted under the UNCITRAL Arbitration Rules, did not exceed their powers by ordering in their award that a party should refrain from pursuing national judicial actions connected to the subject matter of the BIT arbitration. The Court found that the justification on which the tribunal based its order (avoidance of the risk of double recovery by the investor) shows that the anti-suit injunctions were "consequential declarations that follow from the tribunal's decision that [the investor] is entitled to monetary compensation" (para. 125). Judge Aiksen further held that, "[i]n principle, it seems to me, the tribunal must have the power to make orders that are intended to give the proper effect to its primary order granting [the investor] monetary compensation" (para. 125) and that "[i]t is an order which is consequential to the order granting [the investor] monetary compensation, and is made so as to ensure that [the investor] does not obtain a double recovery" (para. 127).

a.   It is somehow improper for an arbitral tribunal to address injunctions to State courts
Some scholars have expressed the view that an arbitral tribunal should not issue anti-suit injunctions because such orders interfere with the State courts' jurisdiction or the parties' fundamental right of seeking relief before those courts:

> "... it is highly doubtful whether an arbitral tribunal should be allowed to tell another tribunal or a state court what to do, or whether it should be allowed to interfere indirectly with the working of another arbitral tribunal by ordering one of the parties what to do in the other arbitration or litigation".[20]

It has been suggested that, even when issuing an order to prohibit the parties from submitting their dispute to the State courts in order to protect the arbitral proceedings, "arbitrators must ensure that these measures do not violate a party's fundamental right of seeking relief before national courts".[21]

These views overlook the fact that, other than in relation to the right to seek interim measures for which jurisdiction remains vested in the State courts, the parties who enter into an arbitration agreement accept, by definition, to waive their right to resort to domestic courts for the settlement of their dispute. By entering into the arbitration agreement, the parties undertake to submit to arbitration any disputes covered by their agreement, thereby renouncing to have recourse to the courts of a given country for the settlement of the same disputes, the corollary principle being that such courts are prohibited from hearing such disputes and that, if seized of a matter covered by the arbitration agreement, they will be required, under the applicable rules, to refer the parties to arbitration.[22]

---

20. Pierre KARRER, "Interim Measures Issued by Arbitral Tribunals and the Courts: Less Theory, Please", in *International Arbitration and National Courts, The Never Ending Story*, ICCA Congress Series no. 10 (2001) (hereinafter *ICCA Congress Series no. 10*) p. 97, at p. 106. For a different view, see Horacio A. GRIGERA NAÓN, "Competing Orders Between Courts of Law and Arbitral Tribunals: Latin American Experiences", in *Liber Amicorum in Honour of Robert Briner, op. cit.*, fn. 2, p. 335, at p. 340. See also ICC Case No. 9593, Final Award (December 1998), *op. cit.*, fn. 18, p. 110, which is often referred to as establishing the principle of the arbitrators' refusal to issue anti-suit injunctions, although, in that case, the outcome was determined by the fact that the court proceedings were outside the scope of the arbitration agreement ("... [the tribunal] has no authority to interfere in State Court proceedings dealing with the compliance of prior judicial decisions rendered and thus outside the scope of the arbitration clause and its subject matter"). See also *Société Générale de Surveillance S.A. (SGS) v. Islamic Republic of Pakistan*, ICSID Case No. ARB/01/13, Procedural Order No. 2 dated 16 October 2002, 18 ICSID Review–FILJ (2003, no. 1) p. 293, at p. 301 (the tribunal rejected the request to enjoin the respondent State from "commencing or participating in all proceedings in the courts of Pakistan relating in any way to this arbitration in the future", on the basis that the request would have required to "enjoin a State from conducting the normal processes of criminal, administrative and civil justice within its own territory").
21. Laurent LÉVY, *op. cit.*, fn. 4, p. 123.
22. See, in particular, Art. 8 of the UNCITRAL Model Law, or Art. II(3) of the New York Convention (the court of a Contracting State, "when seized of an action in a matter in respect of which the parties have made an agreement within the meaning of this article, shall, at the request

The relevant question, therefore, is not a party's fundamental right to seek relief before national courts, but whether a valid arbitration agreement exists and whether the dispute is covered by such agreement, and who has jurisdiction to decide these questions. In that context, the answer is provided by the rules of international arbitration law concerning the interaction between arbitral tribunals and domestic courts: accepting the principle of competence-competence and the arbitrators' inherent power to determine their jurisdiction on the basis of the arbitration agreement entails the consequence that domestic courts should not, in parallel and with the same degree of scrutiny, rule on the same issue, at least at the outset of the arbitral process. In other words, when seized of the matter, the courts should limit, at that stage, their review to a prima facie determination that the agreement is not null and void, inoperative or incapable of being performed.

Recognizing the arbitrators' power of first determination of their jurisdiction by no means suggests that domestic courts relinquish their power to review the existence and validity of an arbitration agreement or that the parties lose any fundamental right in that respect. The acceptance by the national legal systems—by way of rules incorporated in arbitration statutes or in international conventions—that the courts refer the parties to arbitration simply means that the courts, when making a *prima facie* determination that there exists an arbitration agreement and that it is valid, leave it to the arbitrators to rule on the question and recover their power of full scrutiny at the end of the arbitral process, after the award is rendered by the arbitral tribunal. Under this rule, known as the negative effect of the rule of competence-competence, the arbitrators must be the *first* (as opposed to the *sole*) judges of their own jurisdiction and the courts' control is postponed to the stage of any action to enforce or to set aside the arbitral award rendered on the basis of the arbitration agreement. As a result, a court that is confronted with the question of the existence or validity of the arbitration agreement must refrain from hearing substantive arguments as to the arbitrators' jurisdiction until such time as the arbitrators themselves have had an opportunity to do so.[23] A fortiori, a court that is seized of a party's claim pertaining to the merits of a dispute covered by an arbitration agreement must refer the parties to arbitration or, at the very least, exercise self-restraint,[24] the parties having relinquished their right to seek relief before national courts upon entering into the arbitration agreement.

b.   Arbitral anti-suit injunctions deny the State courts' competence-competence
Somewhat related to the argument according to which arbitral tribunals are not in a position to address injunctions to State courts, a second type of reasoning lays emphasis

---

of one of the parties, refer the parties to arbitration, unless it finds that the said agreement is null and void, inoperative or incapable of being performed".).

23. On the notion of competence-competence generally, see *Fouchard Gaillard Goldman on International Commercial Arbitration*, op. cit., fn. 8, paras. 650 et seq.; on the negative effect of competence-competence and the prima facie review more particularly, see Emmanuel GAILLARD, *"La reconnaissance, en droit suisse, de la seconde moitié du principe d'effet négatif de la compétence-compétence"*, in *Liber Amicorum in honour of Robert Briner*, op. cit., fn. 2, p. 311.

24. On the notion of self-restraint, see the references at fns. 2 and 3.

on the co-existence between the jurisdiction of arbitral tribunals and that of State courts, each being entitled to equal recognition of its jurisdiction to rule on its own jurisdiction:

> "... Jurisdiction is something that is declared, not something that can be ordered. Declaring jurisdiction enables the arbitrator to rule on the merits of the dispute before him but does not comprise the power to exclude the jurisdiction of others.
> Confronted with existing or impending parallel proceedings with a similar subject matter, arbitrators may only rule on their own jurisdiction. If arbitrators affirm their jurisdiction, this may result in discouraging a party from referring the matter to a domestic court or another arbitral tribunal. Yet the arbitrators may not enjoin the party in this regard. Arbitrators may neither decide on the jurisdiction of a court (or that of another arbitral tribunal) nor, *a fortiori*, on the cogency of the case brought before such court (or arbitral tribunal). In other words, arbitrators should not enjoin the parties from bringing an action in a court (or another arbitral tribunal) on the sole ground that they retain jurisdiction whereas the court (or arbitral tribunal) does not."[25]

This view seems to be based on the premise that, in issuing anti-suit injunctions, arbitrators will decide the question of the State courts' jurisdiction in lieu of the State courts:

> "... Nevertheless, in deciding upon the jurisdiction of a court or another arbitral tribunal, arbitrators must respect the following basic principles:
> 1. Each court or arbitral tribunal has the power to decide on its own jurisdiction...."[26]

Such a position, however, discounts the fact that the dispute which is covered by the arbitration agreement is, by definition, excluded from the jurisdiction of the State courts. As recognized by the same authority, "[a]dmittedly, in upholding their jurisdiction, arbitrators implicitly declare that any other court or arbitral tribunal is prevented from ruling on the same subject matter. In due course, domestic courts, at least those of the seat of the arbitration, will have the last word in this respect."[27]

The recognition of the courts' competence-competence is therefore not at issue. Nor is there any doubt as to the fact that ordering a party to comply with its undertakings under the arbitration agreement does not result in negating the exercise of the courts' competence-competence. The question is rather one of the existence, validity and scope of the arbitration agreement, with a right of first determination by the arbitrators, the courts recovering their power of full scrutiny at the end of the arbitral process.

---

25. Laurent LÉVY, *op. cit.*, fn. 4, p. 120. See also Pierre KARRER, *op. cit.*, fn. 20, p. 106.
26. Laurent LÉVY, *op. cit.*, fn. 4, p. 117.
27. *Ibid.*

c.   The arbitral tribunal is a judge in its own cause when issuing anti-suit injunctions
A further view has been suggested according to which arbitrators issuing anti-suit injunctions should exercise utmost care so as to avoid such measures to be more harmful than the problem they are seeking to resolve, something that would occur when the measure "leads to the annulment of the award on the ground that the arbitral tribunal has been the judge in its own cause and, hence, lacked impartiality".[28]

The rationale behind this proposition is not convincing. This warning suggests that, because in deciding on their own jurisdiction arbitrators would be the judge in their own cause, they could not as a matter of principle be entrusted with the determination of their jurisdiction, something that fundamentally conflicts with the principle of competence-competence. Furthermore, an arbitral award would likely be set aside if rendered in the absence of an arbitration agreement or on the basis of an arbitration agreement that is void or has expired, or if the arbitral tribunal has ruled without complying with the mission conferred upon it. The issuance of an order to the parties to comply with their agreement to arbitrate, however, is merely a measure designed to protect the arbitrators' jurisdiction, be it in the presence of an existing and valid arbitration agreement or on the basis of a *prima facie* determination that there exists an arbitration agreement and that it is valid, until such time as the arbitrators have made a final determination, subject to the domestic courts' power of full scrutiny at the end of the arbitral process. Any other understanding would imply a fundamental distrust of the arbitral process and the arbitrators' ability to be entrusted with the mission of determining whether they have been established on the basis of an existing and valid arbitration agreement and reaching decisions that are fair and that protect the interests of society as well as those of the parties to the dispute.

III.   THE RECOGNITION OF THE ARBITRAL TRIBUNAL'S JURISDICTION TO ISSUE ANTI-SUIT INJUNCTIONS

The conclusion that arbitrators, as a matter of principle, have jurisdiction to issue anti-suit injunctions is consistent with, and confirmed by, international arbitration practice. Anti-suit injunctions have been issued in a significant number of ICSID and Iran-US arbitrations, as well as in international commercial arbitration proceedings (1). The Reports of the UNCITRAL Working Group on Arbitration concerning possible modifications of the UNCITRAL Model Law also confirm that the arbitrators' power to issue such injunctions is both widespread and legitimate (2).

1.   Arbitral Case Law

a.   ICSID
Requests addressed to ICSID tribunals to enjoin a party to refrain from initiating or continuing State court proceedings are far from being a recent trend. In fact, this issue was raised in the very first ICSID arbitration in 1972, *Holiday Inns S.A. and others v.*

---

28. Laurent LÉVY, *op. cit.*, fn. 4, p. 129.

Morocco.[29] The tribunal ordered both parties "to abstain from any measure incompatible with the upholding of the Contract and to make sure that the action already taken should not result in any consequences in the future which would go against such upholding". Regarding the risk that a party might raise questions before the Moroccan courts which were also before the arbitral tribunal, the tribunal held that "[i]n such a hypothetical situation the Moroccan tribunals should refrain from making decisions until the Arbitral Tribunal has decided these questions or, if the Tribunal had already decided them, the Moroccan tribunals should follow its opinion. Any other solution would, or might, put in issue the responsibility of the Moroccan State and would endanger the rule that international proceedings prevail over internal proceedings."[30]

In *Maritime International Nominees Establishment (MINE) v. Guinea*,[31] the parties entered into a contract under which a mixed company (Sotramar) was to be established in order to export Guinean bauxite from Guinea to Europe and North America. The contract contained an ICSID arbitration clause. The contract was never performed and a dispute arose between the parties as to which of them was responsible. Claiming that Guinea was refusing to participate in ICSID proceedings, MINE obtained an order from a US court compelling arbitration before the AAA. In the AAA arbitration, in which Guinea did not participate, an award was rendered in favor of MINE. Guinea then appeared in the US proceedings in which MINE moved to confirm the AAA award and sought the dismissal of the motion on the ground that the arbitral tribunal had lacked jurisdiction. MINE eventually filed a request for arbitration with ICSID, seeking both a finding that Guinea was liable and an award for damages. In the meantime, on the basis of the AAA award, MINE had obtained attachments on Guinean assets from Swiss and Belgian courts. Guinea asked the ICSID tribunal to order that the company dissolve all the attachments. The tribunal at first refused to grant the request as premature, because Guinea had not yet presented any defense in the State court proceedings, but the ICSID tribunal later issued an unreported order finding that, by initiating legal action to enforce the AAA award, MINE had breached both the requirement of exclusivity of ICSID arbitration (pursuant to Art. 26 of the Convention) and the ICSID arbitration agreement. Furthermore, the tribunal stated that these actions had harmed the respondent, and it therefore recommended that MINE:

> "immediately withdraw and permanently discontinue all pending litigation in national courts and it commence no new action ... [and] dissolve every existing attachment and that it seek no new remedy in any national court".[32]

---

29. *Holiday Inns S.A. and others v. Morocco*, ICSID Case No. ARB/72/1, reported by Pierre LALIVE, "The First 'World Bank' Arbitration (*Holiday Inns v. Morocco*) – Some Legal Problems", 51 British Yearbook of International Law (1980) p. 123, at p. 134. This commentary represents the only available source on this matter.

30. *Ibid.*, p. 137 and p. 160.

31. *Maritime International Nominees Establishment v. Republic of Guinea*, ICSID Case No. ARB/84/4, Award of 6 January 1988, 4 ICSID Rep. (1997) p. 59.

32. As reported in the Award dated 6 January 1988, *ibid.*, p. 69.

The tribunal also made it clear that, should MINE not comply with the recommendation, it would take this failure into account in its award.[33]

In *Ceskoslovenska Obchodni Banka (CSOB) v. Slovak Republic*, the dispute related to a "Collection Agreement" between CSOB, the Ministry of Finance of the Slovak Republic and the Ministry of Finance of the Czech Republic, which contained an ICSID arbitration clause. During the arbitration, a bankruptcy proceeding was initiated before the Bratislava Regional Court against the Slovak Collection Company. Although the Slovak Collection Company was not a party to the ICSID arbitration, CSOB argued that the arbitration and the bankruptcy case involved the same issues, namely "the nature and the extent of the Slovak Republic's obligations to fund the Slovak Collection Company and the validity and quantum of CSOB's claims against the Slovak Collection Company".[34]

For this reason, CSOB requested that the tribunal order "that Respondent take all necessary measures immediately to stay until the issuance of the final award in this arbitration the bankruptcy proceeding". After having rejected the request twice,[35] in January 1999, the tribunal recommended the suspension of the Slovakian bankruptcy proceedings, which dealt "with matters under consideration by the Tribunal in the instant arbitration", after the Regional Court had denied the claimant's application for a stay. It recommended that the national bankruptcy proceedings

> "be suspended to the extent that such proceedings might include determinations as to whether the Slovenska inkasni spol. s.r.o. [Slovak Collection Company] has a valid claim in the form of a right to receive funds from the Slovak Republic to cover its losses as contemplated in the Consolidation Agreement at issue in this arbitration".[36]

By Procedural Order No. 5 dated 1 March 2000, the tribunal not only reiterated its previous Order, but also recommended that the bankruptcy proceedings

---

33. MINE subsequently presented evidence that it had withdrawn the attachments and discontinued the litigation, as reported in the Award dated 6 January 1988, *ibid.*, p. 69. As a counterclaim, Guinea sought to recover the expenses and legal fees it had incurred both to reverse the US court's confirmation of the AAA award and to obtain the release of the attachments. The tribunal denied the former claim (since MINE had not attempted to avoid ICSID arbitration by seeking to compel arbitration and because Guinea was properly informed of all judicial and arbitral proceedings) and upheld the latter claim, awarding Guinea a sum for the costs and legal fees it incurred in connection with the attachments. It found that the actions brought by MINE before the national courts "were contrary to the exclusive jurisdiction granted ICSID in this proceedings".

34. *Ceskoslovenska Obchodni Banka (CSOB) v. Slovak Republic*, ICSID Case No. ARB/97/4, Procedural Order No. 2 dated 9 September 1998, p. 1 (published on the ICSID website).

35. The tribunal found no reason to assume that the Regional Court would not have suspended the proceedings if it had been informed of the pendency of an ICSID arbitration and of the legal rules applicable thereto (see Procedural Order No. 2, *op. cit.*, fn. 34, and Procedural Order No. 3 dated 5 November 1998, published on the ICSID website).

36. Procedural Order No. 4, dated 11 January 1999, p. 2 (published on the ICSID website).

"be suspended to the extent that such proceedings might include determinations as to whether the Slovenska inkasni spol. s.r.o. has made a loss resulting from the operating costs and the schedule of payments for the receivables assigned to it by Ceskoslovenska Obchodni Banka, A.S., including payment of interest, as contemplated in the Consolidation Agreement at issue in this arbitration".[37]

The tribunal requested the parties to bring the Order to the attention of the "appropriate judicial authorities of the Slovak Republic so that they may act accordingly".[38]

These orders are worthy of note for two reasons, as they show that anti-suit injunctions designed to protect the ongoing arbitral proceeding may be far-reaching. First, the parallel court proceedings in this case involved bankruptcy, a subject generally reserved for the exclusive jurisdiction of national courts. Second, the entity that was the focus of these bankruptcy proceedings was not a party to the arbitration in which the anti-suit injunctions were granted.

Société Générale de Surveillance S.A. (SGS) v. Islamic Republic of Pakistan[39] involved a contract for pre-shipment inspection services, entered into by SGS and the Government of Pakistan. The contract contained an arbitration clause, with Islamabad as the place of arbitration. A dispute arose between the parties under the contract. After having unsuccessfully brought an action before the Swiss courts, which declined jurisdiction, SGS filed a request for ICSID arbitration on the basis of the Swiss-Pakistani bilateral investment treaty (BIT), claiming that the respondent had breached its obligations under the BIT. Pending the ICSID decision on jurisdiction, Pakistan obtained from a Pakistani court an anti-suit injunction against the ICSID proceedings and an order stating that the dispute between the parties should be referred to a domestic arbitrator appointed by the court. SGS asked the ICSID tribunal to recommend that the respondent withdraw immediately from all State court proceedings (including an action to hold SGS in contempt of court) and refrain from commencing or participating in any such proceedings in the future.[40] Furthermore, the claimant requested a stay of the domestic arbitration until the ICSID tribunal had decided on its jurisdiction.[41]

---

37. Procedural Order No. 5, dated 1 March 2000, pp. 2-3 (published on the ICSID website).
38. *Ibid.*, p. 3.
39. ICSID Case No. ARB/01/13, *op. cit.*, fn. 20.
40. See Procedural Order No. 2 dated 16 October 2002, *op. cit.*, fn. 20, p. 293 ("immediately withdraw from and cause to be discontinued all proceedings in the courts of Pakistan relating in any way to this arbitration, including Pakistan's application for a stay of this arbitration and its application to have SGS held in contempt of court, and that the Respondent refrain from commencing or participating in any other such proceeding in the future".).
41. *Ibid.*, pp. 293-294 ("the Islamabad-based arbitration pending between SGS and Pakistan be stayed until such time, if any, as this Tribunal has issued an award declining jurisdiction over the present dispute, and that award is no longer capable of being interpreted, revised or annulled pursuant to the ICSID Convention".). The tribunal was also requested to order Pakistan to "take no action of any kind that might aggravate or further extend the dispute" submitted to it (*ibid.*, p. 294). The tribunal rejected this request, finding that no party had taken any measure that could aggravate the dispute.

Having noted that the Pakistani court's anti-suit injunction against the ICSID proceedings, while final, did not as a matter of international law bind the ICSID tribunal,[42] the arbitrators recommended that Pakistan take no action to have SGS held in contempt of court. The tribunal also recommended a stay of the Islamabad-based arbitral proceeding, considering that it would be "wasteful of resources for two proceedings relating to the same or substantially the same matter to unfold separately while the jurisdiction of one tribunal awaits determination".[43]

In *Tokios Tokelés v. Ukraine*,[44] the arbitral tribunal addressed the claimant's requests for anti-suit injunctions directed against national proceedings in two different orders.

In the first Order, the tribunal stated that all Ukrainian authorities had the legal obligation "to abstain from, and to suspend and discontinue, any proceedings before any domestic body, whether judicial or other, which might in any way jeopardize the principle of exclusivity of ICSID proceedings or aggravate the dispute before it".[45] This was because only the ICSID tribunal had jurisdiction to determine whether the BIT between Ukraine and Lithuania had been breached. The tribunal therefore issued an Order which was worded in broad terms:

> "Pending the resolution of the dispute now before the Tribunal, both parties shall refrain from, suspend and discontinue, any domestic proceedings, judicial or other, concerning Tokios Tokelés or its investment in Ukraine, namely Taki Spravy – including those noted in the request for provisional measures and in the Claimant's letter of June 24, 2003 – which might prejudice the rendering or implementation of an eventual decision or award of this Tribunal or aggravate the existing dispute."[46]

In a second Order,[47] the tribunal dismissed the claimant's request that the respondent be ordered to refrain from, suspend and discontinue criminal proceedings against the General Director of the claimant's subsidiaries in Ukraine, an arrest of their assets and a tax investigation initiated against them. The tribunal refused to take these measures, finding a lack of both necessity and urgency, which are essential requirements for the granting of a provisional measure. At the same time, the tribunal recognized that an ICSID tribunal has the power to order an anti-suit injunction even in relation to criminal proceedings or tax investigations. It specified that in order to direct a stay of national proceedings, it is not necessary that these proceedings satisfy the jurisdictional

---

42. *Ibid.*, p. 299.
43. *Ibid.*, p. 304. On the other hand, the tribunal refused to order the respondent to refrain, in the future, from commencing or participating in all proceedings relating in any way to the arbitration. It held that it could not "enjoin a State from conducting the normal processes of criminal, administrative and civil justice within its own territory" (*ibid.*, p. 301), since such a request was not sufficiently determined.
44. ICSID Case No. ARB/02/18.
45. Procedural Order No. 1 dated 1 July 2003, p. 3 (published on the ICSID website).
46. *Ibid.*, p. 4.
47. Procedural Order No. 3 dated 18 January 2005, 20 Int'l Arb. Rep. (Feb. 2005) C14.

requirements of Art. 25 of the Convention, but it is required that "the actions of the opposing party 'relate to the subject matter of the case before the tribunal and not to separate, unrelated issues or extraneous matters'".[48]

In *Plama Consortium Limited v. Republic of Bulgaria*,[49] the claimant requested that the tribunal order the respondent to discontinue all pending proceedings and refrain from bringing new actions before the Bulgarian courts and Bulgarian authorities relating to the arbitration, including: (i) insolvency proceedings against Nova Plama; (ii) execution actions commenced by the Agency for State Receivables to recover Nova Plama's tax debts, an action that, according to the claimant, would have aggravated the existing dispute; and (iii) the execution of the Commission on Protection of Competition's decision that Nova Plama had to reimburse an illegal State subsidy that it had received. The claimant also requested that Bulgaria be ordered to take "no action of any kind that might aggravate or further extend the dispute submitted to the Tribunal".[50]

The arbitral tribunal, composed of C. Salans, A. van den Berg and V.V. Veeder, refused to issue the anti-suit injunctions requested by the claimant. However, it is noteworthy that the request was rejected on the grounds that the requirements necessary for the issuance of an order had not been met, not on the grounds that the tribunal lacked the authority to take such a measure.

The tribunal dismissed the request on the grounds that it was not aimed at protecting "rights relating to the dispute" and that none of the Bulgarian proceedings could affect the issues involved in the arbitration since their outcomes have "no foreseeable effect on the Arbitral Tribunal's ability to make a determination of the issues in the arbitration".[51] Nevertheless, as a matter of principle, the tribunal stated that:

> "Provisional measures are appropriate to preserve the exclusivity of ICSID arbitration to the exclusion of local administrative or judicial remedies as prescribed in Art. 26 of the ICSID Convention. They are also appropriate to prevent parties from taking measures capable of having a prejudicial effect on the rendering or implementation of an eventual award or which might aggravate or extend the dispute or render its resolution more difficult."[52]

Furthermore, the tribunal provided the following guidance on the circumstances justifying ICSID tribunals to issue anti-suit injunctions against State court or administrative proceedings:

---

48. *Ibid.*, p. 6.
49. ICSID Case No. ARB/03/24, *op. cit.*, fn. 16.
50. Procedural Order dated 6 September 2005, *op. cit.*, fn. 16, p. 1.
51. *Ibid.*, p. 14. The tribunal also determined that the parties to the national proceedings and to the arbitration were different, and thus an order to stay the national proceedings would have had a prejudicial effect on third parties, who would therefore be deprived of their right to pursue their judicial remedies.
52. *Ibid.*, p. 12.

"The proceedings underway in Bulgaria may well, in a general sense, aggravate the dispute between the parties. However, the Tribunal considers that the right to non-aggravation of the dispute refers to actions which would make resolution of the dispute by the Tribunal more difficult. It is a right to maintenance of the *status quo*, when a change of circumstances threatens the ability of the Arbitral Tribunal to grant the relief which a party seeks and the capability of giving effect to the relief."[53]

On this basis, the tribunal found that none of the outcomes of the pending Bulgarian proceedings would likely affect the tribunal's ability to determine the issues raised in the ICSID arbitration.

b.   Iran-United States Claims Tribunal
In the same way, the Iran-United States Claims Tribunal (Iran-US Tribunal) has not hesitated to affirm its power to issue anti-suit injunctions when it has felt such measures to be appropriate in the context of the dispute before it.

The seminal decision in this respect is the award rendered in *E-Systems, Inc. v. The Islamic Republic of Iran, Bank Melli Iran*.[54] All subsequent decisions of the Iran-US Tribunal on this issue have referred to this case.

The claim brought by E-Systems against Iran and Bank Melli Iran related to a contract that the company had entered into with the Iranian Government for the modification of two Iranian military aircraft and their equipment. E-Systems was to install on the airplanes equipment to be supplied to it by the Government through suppliers in the United States. The claimant alleged that Iran had breached the contract by not paying the suppliers who were to deliver the necessary equipment, thereby causing E-Systems to interrupt its deliveries, and by not compensating E-Systems for the work it had performed. The claimant therefore terminated the contract and filed an action with the Iran-US Tribunal requesting, inter alia, compensation for the damages it had incurred as a result of such termination of the contract.

During the proceedings, Iran sought from the Public Court of Tehran an order requiring E-Systems to return the aircraft and to reimburse the damages Iran had incurred as a result of both the breach and the termination of the contract by E-Systems. The company filed with the Iran-US Tribunal a motion to compel the dismissal or stay of the Iranian proceedings. It alleged that the claims brought in the domestic lawsuits should have been brought as counterclaims before the Iran-US Tribunal, as they arose from the same contracts, transactions, and occurrences as the claim before the tribunal, and that Iran, by filing these lawsuits in a different forum, had violated "the overall intent and spirit of the Algiers Declarations", specifically their arbitration provisions. E-Systems requested that the tribunal order that the Government "immediately cause to be dismissed the claim filed with the Iranian Court" and that "there be no re-filing of the

---

53. *Ibid.*, p. 15.
54. Iran-US Tribunal, Award No. ITM 13-388-FT, Case No. 388, *E-Systems, Inc. v. The Islamic Republic of Iran, Bank Melli Iran*, 4 February 1983, 2 Iran-United States Claims Tribunal Rep. (1983) p. 51.

claim in Iran or any other forum so long as the Tribunal has pending before it a claim for relief by E-Systems regarding the subject matter as referred to in the instant case".[55]

The request was heard by the Full Tribunal. It found that the claim brought by Iran before the Iranian court would have been admissible as a counterclaim in the arbitral proceeding. However, the Tribunal concluded that the Algiers Declarations did not reveal an intent by Iran and the United States to provide exclusive jurisdiction over counterclaims to the Tribunal. Thus, the Tribunal held that "the Algiers Declarations leave the Government of Iran free to initiate claims before Iranian courts even where the claims had been admissible as counterclaims before the Tribunal". Nevertheless, the Tribunal went on to state that it

> "has an inherent power to issue such orders as may be necessary to conserve the respective rights of the Parties and to ensure that this Tribunal's jurisdiction and authority are made fully effective. Not only should it be said that the award to be rendered in this case by the Tribunal, which was established by inter-governmental agreement, will prevail over any decisions inconsistent with it rendered by Iranian or United States courts, but, in order to ensure the full effectiveness of the Tribunal's decisions, the Government of Iran should request that actions in the Iranian Court be stayed until proceedings in this Tribunal have been completed.
>
> For these reasons,
>
> the Tribunal requests the Government of Iran to move for a stay of the proceedings before the Public Court of Tehran until the proceedings in this case before the Tribunal have been completed."[56]

In his concurring opinion, Judge Holtzmann opined that the issuance of such an order was a means of protecting the Tribunal's jurisdiction and the integrity of its awards, since the claims before the Tribunal and the Iranian lawsuit involved the same issues relating to the same contract.[57]

c.   International commercial arbitration

The principle of confidentiality, which covers most arbitral awards and procedural orders in international commercial arbitration, makes it difficult to determine how often arbitrators have actually issued anti-suit injunctions in purely commercial matters. A review of reported cases, however, shows that, contrary to what one might assume, the issuance of such measures by arbitral tribunals is neither recent nor uncommon in international commercial arbitration.

---

55. *Ibid.*, p. 53.

56. *Ibid.*, p. 57.

57. He further observed that the power of an international tribunal to order a party to halt proceedings initiated in its national courts has been recognized by other international tribunals and can also be based on Art. 26 of the Iran-US Tribunal Rules, according to which the tribunal may issue interim protective measures (*ibid.*, pp. 59 et seq.).

The initiation by a party of parallel State court proceedings in violation of an arbitration agreement is an issue that arbitral tribunals have faced for some time. In such cases, the party relying on the arbitration agreement frequently complains of such a breach before the arbitral tribunal itself, requesting sometimes damages, sometimes a decision to enjoin the other party not to initiate or pursue the court proceedings in violation of the arbitration agreement.

As early as 1970, a sole arbitrator, Pierre Lalive, in ICC Case No. 1512, chose to continue the arbitral proceeding in the face of simultaneous national court proceedings, although, in appearance, he had not been requested to (and so did not) issue an anti-suit injunction. The dispute was between an Indian cement company and a Pakistani bank. It arose in connection with a guarantee agreement, containing an ICC arbitration clause, that the bank had offered to the cement company in relation to the obligations of a manufacturer to deliver a certain amount of cement to the cement company. When the manufacturer failed to deliver the cement, the cement company initiated ICC arbitration against the bank to enforce the guarantee. The arbitration took place in Geneva. In a second preliminary Award, dated 14 January 1970[58], the sole arbitrator addressed an argument by the Pakistani bank that the arbitrator lacked jurisdiction because the Pakistani cement manufacturer had brought an action (after the initiation of the arbitral proceeding) against the bank in a Pakistani court. In addition, the bank had brought suit against the Indian cement company and the Pakistani cement manufacturer in the High Court of West Pakistan, which then issued an injunction restraining the Indian cement company from pursuing the arbitration.

In upholding his jurisdiction, the sole arbitrator found that "the defendant's decision to institute the national lawsuits was another tactical move to gain time and to slow down the arbitration proceedings".[59] Noting that the parties had agreed to international arbitration outside Pakistan according to the ICC Rules, the arbitrator declared that there was a widely held principle that "once the parties have chosen a law to govern the arbitration proceedings, there is no room for the laws of the country of the parties". The arbitrator went on to state that:

> "[T]he ICC rules, expressly accepted by both parties, constitute the law governing the objection raised by the defendant.
> ... No support whatever can be found in the Rules for the contention that the admissibility or justification of the defendant's objection should be governed by the defendant's own law, that of Pakistan.
> It is indisputable also that the ICC Rules *exclude* any resort by one party to a judicial authority *pendente arbitratione* outside the narrow limits of Art. 13(5), a provision which ... has no application here."[60]

Thus, the arbitrator made clear that he would exercise jurisdiction despite the Pakistani court proceedings:

---

58. *Yearbook* V (1980) p. 170 at p. 174.
59. *Ibid.*, p. 175.
60. *Ibid.*, pp. 176-177.

"I have no alternative but to conclude, with regret, that the defendant has contravened its undertaking to arbitrate and violated the ICC Rules in instituting [proceedings] in the West Pakistan High Court. This course of action may well have been caused by a misunderstanding as to the exact legal position and an insufficient familiarity with the peculiar features of international arbitration. I would therefore venture to express the hope that this arbitration may now go on its normal course with the full cooperation of both parties."[61]

Subsequent decisions show that ICC tribunals have been willing to issue injunctions to parties in order to ensure that arbitral proceedings were able to follow their "normal course". In ICC Case No. 3896 of 1982,[62] the arbitral tribunal, composed of Pierre Lalive (President), Jacques Robert and Berthold Goldman, having its seat in Lausanne, had to settle a dispute brought by a French construction company against an Iranian Government agency. During the arbitration, the respondent instructed an Iranian bank to make a call under a performance guarantee given by a banking syndicate to secure the claimant's contractual obligations. The claimant asked the arbitral tribunal to issue, as interim relief, a declaration that the bank guarantee was invalid, that the respondent's attempt to call the guarantee was fraudulent, and that the respondent should suspend the call until a decision was reached on the merits of the dispute. Meanwhile, a national court issued an order prohibiting the guarantor from paying any sum until the arbitral tribunal had rendered a final decision on the merits. The respondent asked the tribunal to declare that the action in State court was abusive because it tended to obstruct the performance of the guarantee and to aggravate or extend the dispute. In response, the tribunal issued a Partial Award stating that

"it has the duty to recommend or propose to them measures which, in its view, are appropriate to prevent an aggravation of the dispute between the Parties.... From this point of view, the Tribunal must recall the well-established principle of international arbitration law ... according to which : The parties must abstain from any action likely to have a prejudicial effect on the execution of the forthcoming decision and, in general, to refrain from committing any act, whatever its nature, likely to aggravate or to prolong the dispute." [63]

It concluded:

---

61. *Ibid.*, p. 177.

62. ICC Award No. 3896, *op. cit.*, fn. 15.

63. *Ibid.* (*"il a le devoir de leur recommander ou proposer les mesures propres, à son avis, à prévenir une aggravation du litige entre les Parties.... De ce point de vue, le Tribunal tient à rappeler le principe bien établi en droit international de l'arbitrage commercial ... selon lequel: Les parties doivent s'abstenir de toute mesure susceptible d'avoir une répercussion préjudiciable à l'exécution de la décision à intervenir et, en général, ne laisser procéder à aucun acte, de quelque nature qu'il soit, susceptible d'aggraver ou d'étendre le différend."* (110 J.D.I. (1983) p. 917)).

"the Arbitral Tribunal considers that there exists, undeniably, the risk of the dispute before it becoming aggravated or magnified, and that the parties should, in the same spirit of goodwill that they have already demonstrated in signing the Terms of Reference, refrain from any action likely to widen or aggravate the dispute, or to complicate the task of the Tribunal or even to make more difficult, in one way or another, the observance of the final arbitral award".[64]

In ICC Case No. 5650,[65] the dispute related to a contract entered into by an African State, a US company and two other companies pursuant to which these companies were to "study and carry out the complete extension program" for a hotel. The contract provided for ICC arbitration as the means to settle any disputes. Before the initiation of the arbitration, the US company received a writ (*assignation en référé*) from three experts appointed by the courts of the African State in relation to a lawsuit between the African State and another company involved in the hotel program. The US company was informed that, in the lawsuit, some of the hotel's deficiencies were attributed to it. The US company responded that, since an ICC arbitration agreement covered disputes relating to the contract, the writ should be withdrawn. A month later, however, the State filed a Summons and Petition for damages in its own courts against the US company and the other companies. The US company then commenced an arbitration seeking a declaration that the respondent had breached the arbitration agreement by initiating the lawsuit and that this lawsuit should be terminated. During the arbitration, the respondent withdrew the lawsuit brought before its courts.

In his Final Award of 1989, the sole arbitrator, sitting in Lausanne, dismissed the argument that the writ (*assignation en référé*) had breached the arbitration agreement, since no judicial action was brought against the claimant at that time. However, the arbitrator declared that the subsequent Summons and Petition before the African court amounted to "a clear violation of Art. 8(5) of the ICC Arbitration Rules and consequently of" the arbitration agreement. The arbitrator seemed to approve of the use of anti-suit injunctions by arbitrators in such situations, stating: "According to the statements of the respondent, said violation is no more continuing, as the lawsuit against the claimant has been terminated. Should that not be the case, the claimant would be entitled to have the lawsuit terminated in favour of the arbitration proceedings pursuant to [the arbitration agreement]."[66]

In an arbitration conducted pursuant to the Arbitration Rules of the Zurich Chamber of Commerce, the arbitral tribunal, having its seat in Zurich, had to decide questions

---

64. *Ibid.*, p. 164 for the English translation (*"le Tribunal estime qu'il existe des risques indéniables d'aggravation ou d'augmentation du litige qui lui est soumis et que les Parties devraient, dans l'esprit de bonne volonté qu'elles ont déjà manifesté en signant l'Acte de Mission, s'abstenir de tout acte susceptible d'étendre ou d'aggraver le différend, de compliquer la tâche du Tribunal arbitral, voire même de rendre plus difficile, d'une manière ou d'une autre, l'exécution d'une éventuelle sentence arbitrale."* (110 J.D.I. (1983) p. 918)). Finally, the tribunal "proposed" that, in order to preserve the status quo, the claimant withdraw its allegations of fraud and the defendant withdraw its call under the guarantees, until the tribunal's decision on the merits.

65. *Yearbook* XVI (1991) p. 85.

66. *Ibid.*, p. 91.

relating to alleged breaches of contract in the contractual relations based on four different agreements. In parallel to the arbitration, a subsidiary of the claimant brought an action in the US against the respondent in relation to two other agreements concluded for the development and marketing of the same products, which did not provide for an arbitration clause. The respondent objected to the jurisdiction of the US court on the basis that these two agreements related to the four agreements being the subject of the exclusive arbitration pending in Zurich. The respondent later amended its response to make a counterclaim against the claimant's subsidiary as well as the claimant in the arbitration, seeking the production of documents from the claimant in the US proceeding on the basis of the four agreements being considered in the arbitration.

The claimant requested from the arbitral tribunal a preliminary injunction with respect to the pursuit, by the respondent, of any claims in relation to the agreements being the subject of the arbitration. The arbitral tribunal found that it had the power to order the requested measures, on the basis of Art. 28 of the International Arbitration Rules of the Zurich Chamber of Commerce, which allows for provisional or conservatory measures in accordance with Art. 183 of the Swiss Private International Law Statute, as well as the Zurich Civil Procedure which allows for protective measures in the event of irreparable harm or urgency. As to the appropriateness of the measures, the arbitral tribunal found that the measures requested seemed "appropriate in order to prevent imminent disadvantages to the petitioner", in particular in light of the fact that the production of documents in the US proceeding would have represented a "genuine danger" with respect to business secrets, to the benefit of the claimant's competitors and other third persons.

In a Resolution concerning provisional measures, the arbitral tribunal therefore ordered the respondent:

> "to refrain from submitting or pursuing any claim arising out of, or relating to the Agreements ... their breach, termination or invalidity by way of action, notice or any other manner against [the Claimant] to any authority or Court other than this contractually agreed Arbitration Tribunal.
>
> to refrain from disclosing to any third party or otherwise using any information (including but not limited to briefs, documents, testimonies, expert opinions etc.) which have been made available by [the Claimant] to this Arbitration Tribunal...
>
> "to refrain from submitting or pursuing any claim which it may allege to have under the Agreements before any other Court outside the jurisdiction of the Arbitration Tribunal...."[67]

It is worthy of note that the injunctions were made "under the penalty of referral of the respondent's officers to the criminal prosecution bodies for punishment (detention or fine) under Art. 292 of the Swiss penal code in case of disobedience".

---

67. Decision of the Arbitral Tribunal dated 20 September 1994, unpublished.

In an ICC arbitration held in Paris in 1994,[68] the arbitral tribunal was faced with a claim brought by two companies (of US and Monaco nationality) against two joint ventures (of Swiss and Monaco nationality) relating to a contract for the building and leasing of a hotel in Monaco. Despite the arbitration clause in the contract, the Monaco joint venture filed two legal actions with the *Tribunal de Grande Instance* in Monaco involving claims related to the contract. The tribunal found that the lawsuits violated the parties' agreement to arbitrate, or "at least" the ICC Rules. The Monaco joint venture had previously agreed to suspend these actions. Since the tribunal had now decided on its jurisdiction and on the merits of the dispute, the tribunal in its Final Award "invited" the Monaco joint venture to withdraw its court actions.

ICC Case No. 8887[69] involved a claim brought by an Italian company against a Turkish company relating to civil engineering works that the Italian company was to perform on a liquid petrochemical trans-shipment facility in Romania. After the initiation of the arbitration, the respondent sought from the Turkish courts a declaration that the claimant had no valid claim against it. In the meantime, appearing in the arbitral proceedings, the respondent contended that the sole arbitrator lacked jurisdiction. During the course of the proceedings, the sole arbitrator, sitting in Geneva, issued a procedural order requesting the respondent to refrain from pursuing the lawsuit in court. The respondent, however, did not abide by this injunction and continued to argue in the arbitration that the arbitration agreement was invalid and that the arbitration should be stayed under *lis pendens*, since the arbitration and the lawsuit involved the same parties and subject matter. In its Final Award of 1997, the sole arbitrator rejected both arguments, holding that in light of the arbitration clause, the Turkish courts were required by Art. II(3) of the New York Convention to refer the matter to arbitration. The sole arbitrator stated that:

> "I therefore find that the *lis pendens* objection is not admissible and that Defendant is in breach of its agreement to arbitrate. This breach not only raises jurisdictional issues but, as the agreement to arbitrate is a part of a binding contract between the parties, Defendant makes itself liable for damages which Claimant might suffer, provided such damages are in direct causation with the breach. Relief for such damages is specifically sought by Claimant in its request ... Claimant has alleged in these proceedings – without being contradicted – that, due to the breach, it had to retain counsel in Istanbul and instruct counsel in representing [it] in the Turkish proceedings. Obviously, the cost triggered by such proceedings has to be considered as damage in direct relation with the breach."[70]

In ICC Case No. 8307, the sole arbitrator, Pierre Tercier, sitting in Geneva, issued an Interim Award[71] on a request by party A and party C that party B be enjoined from

---

68. ICC Case No. 6998, Final Award of 1994, *Yearbook* XXI (1996) p. 54.
69. Excerpts published in 11 ICC Bull. (2000, no. 1) p. 91.
70. *Ibid.*, pp. 93-94.
71. The Interim Award dated 14 May 2001 is published as Annex 5 in *Anti-Suit Injunctions in International Arbitration*, *op. cit.*, fn. 1, p. 307.

pursuing the domestic judicial proceedings it had brought against the other two parties on "the same object of the dispute outlined in the Terms of Reference".[72] The arbitrator found that party B's actions in the domestic courts violated the binding arbitration clause between the parties, which granted exclusive jurisdiction to the arbitrator. He then concluded that he had the power to issue an anti-suit injunction:

> "... the agreement to arbitrate implies that the parties have renounced to submit to judicial courts the disputes envisaged by the arbitral clause. If a party despite this commence a judicial action when an arbitration is pending, it not only violates the rule according to which a dispute between the same parties over the same subject can be decided by one judge only, but also the binding arbitration clause....
>
> It is not contested that an arbitrator has the power to order the parties to comply with their contractual commitments. The agreement to arbitrate being one of them, its violation must be dealt with in the same manner when it is patent that the action initiated in a state court is outside the jurisdiction of such court and is therefore abusive. This is also a guarantee of the efficiency and credibility of international arbitration."[73]

The arbitrator therefore ordered party B to desist from pursuing its actions in the State courts. He added that, should the measures to enforce the anti-suit order be unsuccessful, the parties could seek in arbitration relief for any damages suffered as a consequence of the breach of the arbitration agreement.

An arbitral tribunal composed of Horacio Grigera Naón (Chairman), John Rooney and Emilio Pittier, constituted pursuant to the ICDR Arbitration Rules and having its seat in Miami (United States), was asked to settle a dispute arising from a contract for the operation and management of a hotel. The respondent, a corporation organized under the laws of Venezuela, contested the tribunal's jurisdiction, alleging, inter alia, the exclusive jurisdiction of the Venezuelan courts over disputes arising from the contract. During the arbitration, the respondent filed various claims with these courts. In response, the claimants, three companies incorporated under the laws of Venezuela, The Netherlands and Canada, requested the US courts to compel the respondent to arbitrate. They also asked the arbitral tribunal to issue an injunction to prohibit the

---

72. In order to rule on the applications, the sole arbitrator declared that, as requested by the parties, he had to examine the relations between the arbitral proceedings and domestic court proceedings. He concluded that the parties, the remedies requested, and the subject matters were primarily the same. Finally, he rejected the contention that the claims of the two proceedings would be different, asserting that both claims were grounded on the same facts, which were within the jurisdiction of the arbitrator.

73. *Ibid.*, paras. 9-10, pp. 313-314. In deciding whether to issue the measure, the arbitrator highlighted, inter alia, the risk of contradictory judgments, due to the similarity of the two proceedings, and the duplication of expenses and costs that the respondent de facto imposed on the claimant by bringing the action before national courts.

respondent from pursuing the domestic lawsuits. In an unpublished Partial Award of 10 October 2002, the tribunal held that it had jurisdiction[74] and stated that:

"by initiating certain legal actions in Venezuela, Respondent has disregarded the arbitration clauses set out in the Contracts and failed to honor its obligations thereunder. By upholding and asserting its jurisdiction under such arbitration clauses and finding that all claims under the Contracts, including those submitted in Claimant's arbitration request and those introduced by Respondent through its amended complaint ... before the Caracas Tenth Court of First Instance, Civil and Commercial Division ... the Arbitral Tribunal has signified that Respondent's introduction of such complaint and provisional relief obtained *inaudita parte* in the same case ... and on the same date ... in support of such complaint ... constitutes a breach of Respondent's obligations to arbitrate under [the arbitration clause]. The inevitable consequence of these findings by the Arbitral Tribunal is that Respondent must withdraw and desist from continuing legal action on the merits and supportive injunctive relief obtained from the Caracas Tenth Court of First Instance, Civil and Commercial Division, and refrain from initiating or re-instating similar actions, or applying for injunctive relief in support of such actions, from that and any other courts in Venezuela in connection with any, or all, of the Contracts."[75]

Finally, the tribunal ordered the respondent

"(i) [t]o desist and withdraw from the lawsuit ... initiated by Claimant against [Respondent] before the Caracas Tenth Court of First Instance, Civil and Commercial Division and injunctive relief applied for and obtained in such legal suit;
(ii) [t]o refrain from (a) re-introducing such claims in a new lawsuit, or reinstating such or similar lawsuit, before the Venezuelan courts; (b) applying for injunctive relief before the courts of Venezuela in connection with, or in support of, any such lawsuits or claims, or (c) submitting claims ... to the Venezuelan courts arising out or relating to the Contracts."[76]

In an arbitration that took place in Singapore under the UNCITRAL Rules between two Bangladesh companies, the claimant requested the arbitral tribunal, composed of Michael Lee (Chairman), Michael Pryles and Andrew Rogers, to issue an emergency measure to restrain the respondent from continuing an action it had brought before a national court aiming to obstruct the claimant's participation in the arbitration, and from commencing similar actions concerning issues within the tribunal's jurisdiction. At that time, the arbitral tribunal had not yet decided on its jurisdiction. After granting a temporary emergency restraining order on 31 January 2006, the tribunal heard the

---

74. Partial Award, 10 October 2002, para. 11 of the "Merits" section
75. *Ibid.*, para. 26.
76. *Ibid.*, para. A(2) of the dispositive part of the Award.

parties' arguments on the injunction. In an unreported interim Order of 8 February 2006, it ruled that under UNCITRAL Rules and Art. 12(1)(i) of the Singapore Arbitration Act[77], it had the power to issue the injunction. Finding that the requirements for the issuance of the order (prima facie jurisdiction, urgency, irreparable harm) had been met and that the measure was appropriate under the circumstances of the case,[78] the tribunal ordered that:

> "Respondent be restrained by itself, its servants and agents until further order of the Tribunal from arguing otherwise than before this Tribunal issues as to the Tribunal's jurisdiction and competence to determine all matters arising from the [request for arbitration]."

2. Findings of the UNCITRAL Working Group on Arbitration

The Reports of the UNCITRAL Working Group on Arbitration are another useful resource for assessing the extent to which the arbitrators' power to issue anti-suit injunctions is recognized and accepted in international arbitration.

Since March 2000, the Working Group has been dealing with the topic of interim measures of protection issued by arbitral tribunals and has been devising a mechanism for their enforcement,[79] as part of its mission to evaluate "in a universal forum ... the acceptability of ideas and proposals for the improvement of arbitration laws, rules and practices".[80] During its fortieth session, held in New York on 23-27 February 2004, the Working Group took up a new draft of Art. 17 of the UNCITRAL Model Law concerning the arbitrators' power to issue interim measures. After expressing the principle that, unless the parties have agreed otherwise, arbitral tribunals have the power to grant interim measures, the new draft provides at para. 2 that:

---

77. Art. 12 (Powers of arbitral tribunal) of the Singapore International Act of 2002 reads as follows:

> "Without prejudice to the powers set out in any other provision of this Act and in the Model Law, an arbitral tribunal shall have powers to make orders or give directions to any party for ...
> (i) an interim injunction or any other interim measure."

78. Inter alia, the arbitrator specified that:

> "Whilst the Tribunal has the greatest respect for [the national court seized of the claims] the Tribunal considers this to be a case where the claim made in the [national] proceedings and those made in this arbitration are sufficiently connected and that the Claimant may be deprived of its contractual right to have those claim decided by arbitration, the parties' chosen forum."

79. During its thirty-third session (Vienna, 20 November-1 December 2000), the Working Group agreed that a new Article (numbered as 17 *bis*) should be added to the UNCITRAL Model Law in order to regulate the enforcement of interim measures issued by arbitral tribunals.

80. "Report of the Working Group on Arbitration on the work of its fortieth session" (New York, 23-27 February 2004) UNCITRAL, 40th Sess., UN Doc. A/CN.9/547 (16 April 2004) para. 1.

"An interim measure of protection is any temporary measure, whether in the form of an award or in another form, by which, at any time prior to the issuance of the award by which the dispute is finally decided, the arbitral tribunal orders a party to:

"(a) Maintain or restore the status quo pending determination of the dispute;
  "(b) Take action that would prevent, or refrain from taking action that is likely to cause, current or imminent harm;
  "(c) Provide a [preliminary] means of [securing] [preserving] assets out of which a subsequent award may be satisfied; or
  "(d) Preserve evidence that may be relevant and material to the resolution of the dispute."

The Working Group discussed whether this paragraph, with the list of measures that may be issued by tribunals, should be interpreted to include the power to issue anti-suit injunctions, particularly in light of the wording of sub-para. (b). Although the discussion clearly showed that there were different positions, the majority of the Working Group agreed that modifying the wording of para. 2(b) of Art. 17 would be appropriate in order to clarify that arbitrators possess the power to issue this kind of injunction, taking into account, inter alia, that these measures were "becoming more common and served an important purpose in international trade".[81] Indeed, anti-suit injunctions are increasingly issued even by arbitral tribunals having their seat in countries which traditionally are not familiar with the use of anti-suit injunctions. Furthermore, given the unfamiliarity of some legal systems with these measures, the majority felt that the Model Law presented an opportunity to harmonize legal practices by expressly providing for their use. The Working Group stated that "[a]nti-suit injunctions [are] designed to protect the arbitral process and it [is] legitimate for arbitral tribunals to seek to protect their own process".[82] Finally, the Working Group took into account that the issuance of anti-suit injunctions by arbitrators seemed to have been implicitly accepted during the Working Group's previous session, particularly in cases in which the arbitration was to be governed by the UNCITRAL Arbitration Rules. The wording of the new draft Art. 17 was therefore modified for further consideration as follows:

"Take action that would prevent, or refrain from taking action that is likely to cause, current or imminent harm [or to prejudice the arbitral process itself]."

At its forty-third session (Vienna, 3-7 October 2005), the Working Group re-examined the issue in light of the UNCITRAL Commission's expectation that the Group would be able to present its proposal for the revision of Art. 17 of the Model Law for the adoption by the Commission at its session in 2006. The Working Group re-examined the wording of the Article as agreed upon during its previous session, and in particular the phrase "or to prejudice the arbitral process itself", with a view to clarifying

81. *Ibid.*, para. 77.
82. *Ibid.*, para. 77.

the arbitrators' power to issue anti-suit injunctions and other measures intended to prevent the obstruction and delay of the process.[83] In addition to the criticisms that had already been expressed at the previous session, another issue was raised concerning the appropriateness of dealing with anti-suit injunctions in articles on provisional measures. Some felt that such injunctions are not always of a provisional nature, and relate to the issue of the jurisdiction of the tribunal, "which [is] a matter not to be confused with the granting of an interim measure".[84] Against this background, in addition to the considerations raised during the previous session, it was noted that arbitral tribunals are "increasingly faced with tactics aimed at obstructing or undermining the arbitral process".[85] At the end of the session, the wording as elaborated in the previous session was retained, so that the new draft which was finally adopted enables the arbitrators to order a party to:

> "Take action that would prevent, or refrain from taking action that is likely to cause, current or imminent harm or to prejudice the arbitral process itself."

With the new draft of Art. 17 of the UNCITRAL Model Law, the Working Group has chosen to recognize the arbitrators' power to issue anti-suit injunctions in order to protect the integrity of the arbitral process against the parties' obstructive tactics. Since the mission of the Working Group is to foster consensus and harmonization in response to the needs of international practitioners, its work on Art. 17 provides another indication of the general acceptance that anti-suit injunctions may be issued by arbitrators.

IV. THE ADVISABILITY OF THE ISSUANCE OF ANTI-SUIT INJUNCTIONS BY ARBITRAL TRIBUNALS

The question of arbitral anti-suit injunctions is not restricted to the arbitrators' power to issue such measures. A further question is often raised, that of the advisability of such measures in the context of international arbitration. A first approach considers that anti-suit injunctions are never advisable. Another approach limits such measures to situations in which a party has committed a fraud or otherwise engaged in abusive behavior in order to revoke the arbitration agreement. In practice, the advisability of anti-suit injunctions by arbitrators can be assessed only on a case-by-case basis, depending on whether such measures provide the appropriate response to the parties' procedural behavior in the presence of an arbitration agreement.

---

83. "Report of the Working Group on Arbitration and Conciliation on the work of its forty-third session" (Vienna, 3-7 October 2005) UNCITRAL, 43rd Sess., UN Doc. A/CN.9/589 (12 October 2005).
84. *Ibid.*, para. 23.
85. *Ibid.*

1.   Are Anti-suit Injunctions Always Unadvisable?

The view has sometimes been expressed that anti-suit injunctions are, in all situations, unadvisable and illegitimate, irrespective of their purpose and the authority issuing them:

> "Anti-suit injunctions are not to be encouraged in any type of litigation. In the context of international arbitration, they constitute even more of a nuisance. This conclusion, which may seem somewhat abrupt, applies, in my opinion, regardless of the purpose of the anti-suit injunction and regardless of the authority that issues such injunction.... In all ... situations, anti-suit injunctions, are, in my view, illegitimate."[86]

This position is limited to the sole question of the legitimacy of anti-suit injunctions, including when they are issued by arbitrators. The rationale behind it is the negative impact that such measures may have on the arbitration, namely the aggravation of the dispute, the undermining of the procedure's environment, the dispersal of the dispute in different fora, or the retaliatory measures that may be taken in the form of anti-anti-suit injunctions by national courts in response to anti-suit injunctions issued by arbitral tribunals.[87]

The focal point, under this approach, is the danger of competing arbitral and judicial orders in parallel proceedings, such conflicting measures being considered as an extreme occurrence in almost every case. As a practical matter, however, it overlooks the genuine difficulty with which arbitrators may be confronted when a party, in the presence of an arbitration agreement, opts for disruptive tactics by bringing its dispute before domestic courts.

2.   Should the Issuance of Anti-suit Injunctions Be Limited to Situations in Which a Party Has Committed a Fraud or Otherwise Engaged in Abusive Behavior in Order to Revoke the Arbitration Agreement?

Under a second approach, arbitral anti-suit injunctions are inappropriate but could be conceived in limited cases where a party has engaged in abusive conduct:

---

86. Philippe FOUCHARD, "Anti-Suit Injunctions in International Arbitration: What Remedies?", in *Anti-Suit Injunctions in International Arbitration, op. cit.*, fn. 1, p. 153.

87. For an example of anti-anti-suit injunctions rendered after the termination of the arbitral proceeding, see *Karaha Bodas Company L.L.C. (KBC) v. Persusahaan Pertambangan Minyak Dan Gas Bumi Negara a.k.a. (Pertamina)*, Civil Action H01-0634 S.D. Texas, Houston Div., 17 Mealey's Int'l Arb. Rep. (June 2002) E1; United States District Court, Fifth Circuit, dated 18 June 2003, *Yearbook* XXVIII (2003) p. 945. For commentaries on this case, see E. GAILLARD, references at fns. 2 and 3. See also Michael E. SCHNEIDER, "Court Actions in Defence Against Anti-Suit Injunctions", in *Anti-Suit Injunctions in International Arbitration, op. cit.*, fn. 1, p. 41; Konstantinos D. KERAMEUS, "Anti-suit Injunctions in ICSID Arbitration", in *Anti-Suit Injunctions in International Arbitration, op. cit.*, fn. 1, p. 131, at p. 137.

"Arbitrators will have to ensure that the requested measures are urgent, aimed at preventing irreparable harm or necessary to facilitate the enforcement of the upcoming award....

In our opinion, in the absence of a clear basis and confirmed case law, arbitrators should only issue anti-suit injunctions when it comes to their attention that one of the parties has committed fraud or otherwise engaged in abusive behavior in order to revoke the arbitration agreement. This can be the case when there is an abusive petition for interim measures designed to paralyze the arbitration or of when there is an attempt to slow down the proceedings or to harm the interests of another party, as is well-illustrated by the *Turner v. Grovit* case."[88]

Thus, to the extent that arbitral anti-suit injunctions would be justified only in cases of fraud or abusive conduct, the presumption remains against the issuance of such measures. Further, under this view, even in such exceptional circumstances, utmost care should be exercised by arbitrators in issuing anti-suit injunctions "as the effect of these anti-suit injunctions may be more harmful than the problem they are seeking to resolve".[89]

The focal point, under this approach, is the nature of the parties' procedural conduct in resorting to domestic courts, the threshold for arbitral anti-suit injunctions being thus extremely high. The advisability of arbitral anti-suit injunctions, however, cannot solely depend on the characterization of the parties' procedural attitude. Depending on the circumstances of each case, arbitral anti-suit injunctions may be unadvisable notwithstanding a party's abusive conduct. Conversely, there may be situations in which the issuance of such measures is advisable where the recalcitrant party has committed no fraud or abuse of procedure.[90]

3.	Possible Factors to Take into Account for the Issuance of Anti-suit Injunctions by Arbitral Tribunals

The advisability of arbitral anti-suit injunctions is distinct from the question of the arbitrators' power to issue such measures. Recognizing that such measures are within the arbitrators' judicial power is not a reason to believe that, in every situation, the response to a recalcitrant party who submits the dispute covered by an arbitration agreement to the domestic courts or to another arbitral tribunal will be the issuance of

---

88. Laurent LÉVY, *op. cit.*, fn. 4, pp. 125-126.
89. *Ibid.*, pp. 128-129.
90. For examples of such situations, see supra, Part III.

an anti-suit injunction.[91] Different factors may be considered in order to determine whether such measures are, in fact, advisable.

The arbitrators may first take into account the effectiveness of their order in the case at hand. It may be argued, in this respect, that arbitral anti-suit injunctions are not an effective means of resolving the situation created by a recalcitrant party seeking relief before the domestic courts, to the extent that the arbitrators' order is not, in and of itself, enforceable before those courts. It may also be objected that the issuance of anti-suit injunctions by the arbitrators may cause, or be confined in, a chain of contradictory orders issued in parallel proceedings. On the other hand, an order issued by the arbitral tribunal to the parties to comply with the arbitration agreement reflects a power deriving from the arbitrators' judicial role, that can be exercised either by way of an order for specific performance or by equivalent, in the form of damages for the breach of the arbitration agreement.[92] Should a party to an arbitral proceeding breach its obligation to comply with the arbitration agreement, including after an order has been issued by the arbitrators, it may be sanctioned through monetary damages. As a result, the breach of an anti-suit injunction does not necessarily remain unsanctioned. The question of whether or not a party should be ordered to cease its disruptive conduct and comply with its previous undertakings is an issue that should be decided by the arbitrators alone in light of all of the circumstances of the case. In that context, a recalcitrant party's fraudulent conduct or abusive behavior is not, in and of itself, a triggering factor for the issuance of an anti-suit injunction, but it can be taken into account by the arbitral tribunal either for the issuance of such measures in the course of the arbitral proceeding or for the award of damages at the end of the arbitral process.

The arbitrators may also consider the desirability of anti-suit injunctions as a means to alert a recalcitrant party. The parties would indeed be expected to comply with their obligations under the arbitration agreement all the more that they have received a clear indication and have been cautioned by the arbitrators, including by way of an anti-suit injunction, against the possible consequences of breaching such obligations. Being nothing more than a prerogative within the arbitrators' judicial powers, anti-suit injunctions may thus have an edifying effect, that of reminding the parties of their voluntary acceptance of international arbitration for the resolution of their dispute, and protecting the integrity of the arbitral process.

As a practical matter, the issuance of anti-suit injunctions, as for any other judicial power conferred upon the arbitrators, must therefore be decided in light of the circumstances of each case. Such circumstances may include, but are not limited to,

---

91. For example, in *Himpurna California Energy Ltd. v. Republic of Indonesia*, the arbitral tribunal ruled that it was not appropriate for it to order Indonesia to cause its two wholly-owned and controlled entities, PLN and Pertamina, to withdraw their pending actions before the Indonesian courts, because it did not consider appropriate "to issue orders reactive to unilateral initiatives which may or may not be of any consequence" (Interim Award dated 26 September 1999, *Yearbook* XXV (2000) p. 112, at p. 119).

92. See supra, Part II.

whether or not the relief is necessary[93] or urgent,[94] or if a party would suffer an irreparable harm.[95]

V. THE LEGAL REGIME OF THE ISSUANCE OF ANTI-SUIT INJUNCTIONS BY ARBITRAL TRIBUNALS

1. Can an Arbitral Tribunal Issue an Anti-suit Injunction at any Stage of the Arbitral Proceeding?

Arbitral anti-suit injunctions being measures designed to protect the integrity of the arbitral process, they can presumably be issued at any stage of the arbitral proceeding. This assumption, however, begs the question of whether or not the arbitrators may issue anti-suit injunctions before they have ruled on their jurisdiction.

Before an arbitral tribunal has ruled on its own jurisdiction, it should be in a position to direct the parties not to act in any way that would jeopardize its prima facie jurisdiction until such time as it has formed its own judgment on its jurisdiction and established in a final manner whether it has been established on the basis of an existing and valid arbitration agreement and whether the scope of that agreement includes the dispute that has been brought before it. After such a determination has been made, the

---

93. For example, in *Yaung Chi Oo Trading PTE Ltd. v. Government of the Union of Myanmar,* ASEAN ID Case No. ARB/01/1, the tribunal refused to grant an anti-suit injunction arguing that the party did not demonstrate the necessity of such measure (Procedural Order No. 2 dated 27 February 2002, 8 ICSID Rep. (2005) p. 456 at p. 461). In *Ceskoslovenska Obchodni Banka (CSOB) v. Slovak Republic,* ICSID Case No. ARB/97/4, the tribunal's refusal to issue an injunction was justified by the fact that there were no reasons to assume that the national court would not stay the proceedings if duly informed of the existence of the ICSID proceeding (Procedural Orders No. 2 and 3 dated 9 September 1998 and 5 November 1998, *op. cit.,* fn. 35). In *Société Générale de Surveillance S.A. (SGS) v. Islamic Republic of Pakistan,* ICSID Case No. ARB/01/13, the tribunal's refusal to order the stay of the pending Pakistani proceedings was justified on the fact that those proceedings had already concluded (Procedural Order No. 2 dated 16 October 2002, *op. cit.,* fn. 20). In *Tokios Tokelés v. Ukraine,* ICSID Case No. ARB/02/18, the tribunal expressly stated that the "Claimant has failed to show that provisional measure is either necessary or urgent to protect those rights" (Procedural Order No. 3 dated 18 January 2005, *op. cit.,* fn. 47, paras. 12 and 18).
94. See, e.g., the order rendered in the Singapore arbitration quoted supra, fn. 78. In ICC case No. 11761 (2003) (unpublished, reported by Michael W. BÜHLER and Thomas H. WEBSTER, *Handbook of ICC Arbitration, Commentary, Precedents, Materials* (Sweet & Maxwell 2005) p. 294), the tribunal refused to grant the measure because it considered that the requesting party did not show that the measure was "essential to do justice between the parties" (because it did not seek immediate relief when the other party commenced the proceedings before the domestic courts, preferring to file an objection in those proceedings) and because of the stage reached in the national proceedings.
95. See, e.g., *Plama Consortium Limited v. Republic of Bulgaria,* ICSID Case No. ARB/03/24, Procedural Order dated 6 September 2005, *op. cit.,* fn. 16, para. 46. See also the case discussed in relation to the anti-suit injunction ordered by the arbitral tribunal in the arbitration conducted pursuant to the Arbitration Rules of the Zurich Chamber of Commerce, supra, fn. 67.

issuance of anti-suit injunctions is even less problematic.[96] Indeed, once it has been established that there is an arbitration agreement, that it is valid and that the dispute is within the scope of such agreement, there can be no doubt that a party's procedural conduct consisting in bringing the same dispute before domestic courts is in breach of the arbitration agreement and the tribunal's jurisdiction and can be sanctioned as such.

2. Should an Anti-suit Injunction Be Issued by Way of an Award or of a Procedural Order?

The form of an order enjoining the parties to comply with the arbitration agreement depends on various factors, among which the stage of the arbitral proceeding at which disruptive tactics may be employed (for example, whether or not the tribunal has ruled on its jurisdiction) or the type of measure decided (recommendation or binding order; specific performance or award of damages; measure of a temporary or permanent effect).[97]

Against this background, it may reasonably be argued that measures of a procedural nature may be addressed through procedural orders. Similarly, before a tribunal has ruled on its jurisdiction and established that it has been constituted on the basis of an existing and valid arbitration agreement, any measure designed to safeguard its prima facie jurisdiction would be taken in the form of a procedural order. The form of an award, which by definition has a permanent nature and finally binds the parties (with the corresponding protection offered by international conventions such as the New York Convention of 1958 on the Recognition and Enforcement of Foreign Arbitral Awards), would be more appropriate for measures designed to definitively sanction a party's disruptive conduct, such as an award of damages. The form of the decision is therefore a question to be decided on a case-by-case basis, depending on the circumstances of each case and the type of party conduct being sanctioned by the arbitral anti-suit injunction.

---

96. See Emmanuel GAILLARD, "Reflections on the Use of Anti-Suit Injunctions in International Arbitration", *op. cit.*, fn. 2, p. 214.
97. See, e.g., Michael W. BÜHLER and Thomas H. WEBSTER, *op. cit.*, fn. 94 (forming the view that a permanent injunction would necessarily be made through a final award).

A Claim for Monetary Relief for
Breach of Agreement to Arbitrate as a Supplement or Substitute to
an Anti-Suit Injunction

*Paul Friedland and Kate Brown**

I.   INTRODUCTION

When a respondent in an arbitration initiates litigation which the arbitration claimant believes violates the respondent's undertaking to arbitrate, the arbitration claimant's options include (i) an application for an anti-suit injunction, and (ii) a claim for monetary relief, whether for an award of damages or an indemnity against any judgment that might be rendered in the parallel litigation.

The remedy of monetary relief for breach of an arbitration agreement has received far less attention than anti-suit injunctions. Yet monetary relief addresses the same wrong as an anti-suit injunction, and offers a compensatory remedy that anti-suit injunctions do not. Monetary relief is also usually a simpler and in many circumstances more effective way of affirming arbitral jurisdiction, because it largely bypasses the vexing issues of efficacy and arbitral authority that make anti-suit injunctions by arbitrators so contested.

This article first summarizes the difficulties that beset applications to arbitrators for anti-suit injunctions, and then compares anti-suit injunctions by arbitrators to monetary relief for breach of arbitration agreements. We then examine the viability of claims for monetary relief in a range of factual scenarios.

---

*   The authors are lawyers in the White & Case International Arbitration Group (New York).

II.   ANTI-SUIT INJUNCTIONS BY INTERNATIONAL ARBITRATORS: COMPLEXITIES AND CONSTRAINTS

1.   *The Efficacy Problem: Difficulties of Enforcement Failing Voluntary Compliance*

If a party that is the object of an anti-suit injunction issued by arbitrators does not voluntarily comply, the arbitral injunction must, in order to have its intended effect, be enforced in the same jurisdiction where the parallel foreign litigation is being pursued. The prospect of court enforcement of an arbitrator-issued anti-suit injunction is therefore slight in many situations.[1]

Anti-suit injunctions are designed to protect the arbitral process and foster arbitral authority. But an order that is ignored and unenforceable will likely have the opposite of the intended effect: it may undermine the authority of the arbitrators.

2.   *Authority to Issue an Anti-suit Injunction, and the Wisdom of Doing So*

The authority of arbitrators to issue anti-suit injunctions is contested by prominent commentators.[2] Even if, as argued by Emmanuel Gaillard,[3] arbitrators are empowered to issue anti-suit injunctions, the fact remains that arbitrators are often, and understandably, unwilling to do so. There are several reasons for this reluctance.

---

1. Emmanuel GAILLARD, "Anti-Suit Injunctions Issued by Arbitrators", this volume, pp. 235-266, (hereinafter *Gaillard*) at IV.3., pp. 263-265; Laurent LEVY, "Anti-suit Injunctions Issued by Arbitrators" in Emmanuel GAILLARD, ed., *Anti-suit Injunctions in International Arbitration* (hereinafter *Levy*)(2005) p. 115 at p. 126 ("It is unnecessary to restate here the difficulties inherent to the enforcement of interim measures failing voluntary compliance...."). See also *ibid.* at p. 128 ("[S]uch a measure would not really be effective in an international context: if a party does not comply with an anti-suit injunction in a country other than the one where the seat of arbitration is located, it will not be punished unless this behavior ... is also punishable in the country in question."); Final Award of April 1997 in ICC Case No. 8887, 11 ICC ICArb. Bull. (2000, no. 1) p. 91 at p. 96 (contract provided for ICC arbitration in Switzerland and defendant commenced proceedings in the Turkish courts; although the tribunal requested defendant not to take further action in the Turkish courts, defendant pursued parallel proceedings); Emmanuel GAILLARD, "*Il est interdit d'interdire: reflexions sur l'utilization des anti-suit injunctions dans l'arbitrage commercial international*", Rev. Arb. (2004) p. 44 at p. 56 ("*Il est vrai que si une partie a choisi d'adopter une stratégie de rupture, la mesure n'aura vraisemblablement qu'un effet limité.*").
2. *Levy*, at p. 128 ("[F]irst, arbitrators should not take the risk of ordering a judge or other arbitrators how to behave. They are the arbitrators' equals and have no orders to receive. Second, jurisdiction is something that is declared, not something that can be ordered."); Pierre A. KARRER, "Interim Measures Issued by Arbitral Tribunals and the Courts: Less Theory Please" in Albert Jan van den BERG, ed., *International Arbitration and National Courts: The Never Ending Story*, ICCA Congress Series No. 10 (Kluwer Law Int'l 2001), p. 97 at p. 106 ("[I]t is highly doubtful whether an arbitral tribunal should be allowed to tell another arbitral tribunal or state court what to do, or whether it should be allowed to interfere indirectly with the workings of another arbitral tribunal by ordering one of the parties what to do in the other arbitration or litigation.... The principle should be that each arbitral tribunal should decide on its own jurisdiction.").
3. *Gaillard*, at II, pp. 237-244.

First, arbitrators do not wish to be seen to interfere with the jurisdiction of a state court.[4]

Second, as a consequence of the uncertainty regarding the authority of arbitrators to issue anti-suit injunctions, arbitrators are legitimately concerned that the ultimate arbitral award will be unenforceable in a foreign jurisdiction where anti-suit injunctions are not a recognized remedy, or are against public policy.[5]

Third, granting one party's application for an anti-suit injunction may trigger a retaliatory application by the other side, an anti-anti-suit injunction, resulting in conflicting orders in parallel proceedings, and associated delay and costs.[6]

Finally, arbitrators will (or should) consider the risk that an anti-suit injunction may prevent a party from exercising legitimate rights before national courts, including, for example, the right to use litigation to toll a limitations period.[7]

---

4. Unreported ICC Case, Procedural Order of November 2000 (refusing to issue an anti-suit injunction due to serious reservations about ruling on the jurisdiction of a state court, and the risk of issuing a decision which could deny a party access to a state court given the fundamental principle that each court and arbitral tribunal is to rule on its own jurisdiction), cited in *Levy*, at pp. 117, 119. See also Final Award of December 1998 in ICC Case No. 9593, 11 ICC ICArb. Bull. (2000, no. 1) p. 105 at p. 109 ("The tribunal stated in Procedural Order No. 2 that it has no authority to interfere with proceedings before State courts"); *SGS S.A. v. Islamic Republic of Pakistan* (ISCID Case No. ARB/01/13), Procedural Order No 2 of 16 October 2002, 18 ICSID Rev.–Foreign Inv. L.J. (2003, no. 1) p. 293, at p. 304 ("At the same time, the Tribunal is concerned that Pakistan not be effectively deprived of a forum for the hearing of its own claims relating to the ... Agreement").

5. [Greek Court of Appeals Maritime Cases Section] 2004 (Greece), Piraiki Nomologia 92 (the Greek Court of Appeals considered the validity of an anti-suit injunction issued by the English High Court in relation to a maritime arbitration in London, and held that orders enjoining a party from resorting to the courts are contrary to the Greek Constitution, which guarantees a right of access to courts); *Re the Enforcement of an English Anti-Suit Injunction*, I.L.Pr. (1997) p. 320 (OLG Dusseldorf) (the German court, asked to assist with service of an anti-suit injunction on a German citizen, declared that such an order would infringe the sovereignty of Germany and the jurisdiction of the German court, as well as deny the German litigant his right of free access to the courts); *Levy*, at p. 125 ("In addition, courts directly or indirectly concerned with the measure may chafe at such measures. In particular, they may refuse to enforce the arbitral award on their territory, on the grounds, for example, that the award violates public policy....").

6. *Gaillard*, at p. 262; Konstantinos D. KERAMEUS, "Anti-suit Injunctions in ICSID Arbitration" in Emmanuel GAILLARD, ed., *Anti-suit Injunctions in International Arbitration* (2005) *op. cit.*, fn. 1, p. 131 at p. 137 ("... anti-suit injunctions, once admitted, may well be a double-edged sword. Indeed, a judicial panel to which an anti-suit injunction has been addressed may reciprocate in a similar way. This would result in a judicial war by way of reciprocal anti-suit injunctions."); Sandrine CLAVEL, "Anti-suit injunctions et arbitrage", Rev. Arb. (2001) p. 669 at p. 673 ("*[C]es mesures ont, pour l'arbitrage un 'revers'. Elles peuvent être également exploitées contre l'arbitrage*").

7. *Levy*, at p. 123 ("[A]rbitrators must ensure that ... [the anti-suit injunction does] ... not violate a party's fundamental right of seeking relief before national courts...."). See also *ibid.*, at p. 125 ("First of all, there is a risk that the requested measures be ordered without the arbitrators having fully taken into account their impact. For example, prohibiting the initiation of proceedings before another court or arbitral tribunal may prevent a party from tolling a limitations period and may cause the loss of a party's rights."); (Unreported) ICC Case, Procedural Order of November 2000 (refusing to issue an anti-suit injunction, and noting that a request that the tribunal order a party to withdraw from the parallel proceedings with prejudice would finally determine the issue, and

3. Uncertainty as to Standard: Irreparable Harm or Abuse of Process?

Even if an arbitral tribunal decides that it is empowered to issue an anti-suit injunction, and that the possible inefficacy of the measure should not deter the tribunal, there is no consensus with respect to the standard for issuance of an anti-suit injunction.

Some commentators maintain that an anti-suit injunction should be granted only where it is necessary to prevent irreparable harm,[8] particularly where the anti-suit relief is treated as a type of provisional measure. Yet, in circumstances where the only harm suffered will be attorneys' fees and other costs associated with the parallel litigation, no such irreparable harm exists.[9] Other commentators suggest that anti-suit injunctions are appropriate only where a party's conduct in commencing the parallel proceedings constitutes an abuse of process.[10]

---

would not constitute a provisional or conservatory measure), cited in *Levy*, at pp. 117, 119.

8. *Levy*, at p. 125 ("Arbitrators will have to ensure that the requested measures are urgent, aimed at preventing irreparable harm or necessary to facilitate the enforcement of the upcoming award.").

9. Republic and Canton of Geneva Judiciary, Court of First Instance, Decision of 2 May 2005 (C/1043/2005-15SP), 23 ASA Bull. (2005, no. 4) p. 739 at pp. 746-747 (in an application for an injunction to stop an International Air Transport Association arbitration in Switzerland and enforce an anti-suit injunction issued by the English High Court, the Swiss Court ruled that the injunction was contrary to Swiss law, and that the court must be satisfied that refusing the injunction sought would cause a "serious injustice" to either party or irreparable harm, which was not present because the only damage would be attorney's fees in the arbitration and perhaps an advance on costs).

10. *Levy*, at p. 126 ("[I]n the absence of a clear legal basis and confirmed case law, arbitrators should only issue anti-suit injunctions when it comes to their attention that one of the parties has committed fraud or otherwise engaged in abusive behavior in order to revoke the arbitration agreement. This can be the case when there is an abusive petition for interim measures designed to paralyze the arbitration or of when there is an attempt to slow down the proceedings or to harm the interests of ... [the other] ... party...."); Sandrine CLAVEL, *op. cit.*, fn. 6 (noting that, in issuing an anti-suit injunction, English jurisprudence usually requires that the foreign proceedings were commenced with the object of defrauding the rights of the claimant in the English proceedings such that they are "vexatious or oppressive", and suggesting that an anti-suit injunction is not available for mere breach of a contractual obligation such as an arbitration clause); Jean R. STERNLIGHT, "Forum Shopping for Arbitration Decisions: Federal Courts' Use of Antisuit Injunctions Against State Courts", U. Pa. L. Rev. p. 91, at p. 127 (1998-1999, no. 147) (in the US domestic context) ("In deciding whether to issue an anti-suit injunction, federal courts should consider whether either party had engaged in bad faith or harassing litigation.").

III. CLAIM FOR MONETARY RELIEF AS A SUPPLEMENT OR AN ALTERNATIVE TO APPLICATION FOR ANTI-SUIT INJUNCTION

1. *Comparison to Anti-suit Relief*

a. *No (or reduced) uncertainty as to efficacy*

If, as a consequence of a respondent's commencement of litigation in breach of the arbitration agreement, the arbitral tribunal awards damages to the claimant to compensate for costs incurred in the parallel proceeding, and/or an indemnity against any future judgment in that proceeding, these remedies will presumably be part of the final award on the merits, and will be enforceable (or not) as any other part of the award. Unlike an anti-suit injunction, an award of monetary relief would not necessarily depend upon cooperation by courts and parties within the jurisdiction of the foreign litigation.

Because enforcement of an award of monetary relief can, thus, be had with less difficulty than enforcement of an anti-suit injunction, the threat of a final award of damages, or of an award of an indemnity, can have a dissuasive effect superior to that of an anti-suit injunction, and an award of monetary relief will have a compensatory effect which is incontestably superior to that of an anti-suit injunction.

b. *No question of arbitral authority, and procedural simplicity*

As arbitrators are plainly empowered to award monetary relief as between the parties, an award of damages and/or an indemnity for breach of an arbitration agreement raises no special issue of arbitral authority.

A claim for monetary relief also has the advantage of procedural simplicity. A claim for monetary relief for breach of an arbitration agreement would likely be considered in the ordinary course of the arbitration, together with other claims for breach. Nor should a claim for damages and/or an indemnity require an interim application before the arbitrators, although such claim would often be accompanied by some effort before a foreign court to try to stop the foreign litigation.[11] Because a claim for monetary relief would not take the form of an application for provisional measures, the uncertainties in applicable standard particular to applications for anti-suit injunctions are absent, although other uncertainties – arising from questions as to choice of law and the content of the applicable law – cannot be avoided, as discussed in the following section.

c. *Remaining uncertainty: what law governs a claim for monetary relief for breach of an arbitration agreement?*

In the few available examples of awards by arbitrators of monetary relief for breach of an arbitration agreement, there has been little or no discussion of either choice of law

---

11. See infra III.3.

or the content of the governing law.[12] This section offers a few observations on choice of law principles, a full discussion of the subject being beyond the scope of this article.

Where arbitral jurisdiction is treaty-based, the choice of law is not difficult: a breach of the undertaking to arbitrate should be assessed under treaty principles. While the authors are aware of no treaty law regarding claims for monetary relief for breach of an undertaking to arbitrate, the principles of damages usually applicable to treaty claims would logically apply.

The choice of law analysis is more challenging for international commercial contracts. Although a claim for monetary relief is a simpler alternative to an anti-suit injunction in several ways, not everything about the damages/indemnity remedy is simple. There are four options respecting the law governing a claim for breach of an arbitration clause in a commercial contract: first, the law (if any) chosen by the parties to govern the arbitration agreement; second, the law of the seat of arbitration (lex arbitri); third, "general principles of international arbitration law"[13] (which may not in fact differ from the law of the seat of the arbitration); and fourth, the law of the contract (lex contractus).

The first choice of law option – the law chosen by the parties – is rarely encountered because it is seldom that parties choose a law to govern their arbitration agreement.

The second and third choice of law options – the law of the seat of arbitration and "general principles of international law" – accept that the law governing the arbitration agreement is distinct from the law governing the rest of the contract. This distinction rests on the familiar notion of the autonomy of the arbitration clause, an autonomy that implies that the law governing the arbitration clause is independent of the *lex contractus*. This approach is attractive because it results in, for choice of law purposes, all claims arising from breach of an arbitration agreement, whether for an anti-suit injunction or

---

12. Final Award of April 1997 in ICC Case No. 8887, *op. cit.*, fn. 1 (arbitral tribunal sitting in Geneva awarded damages to claimant for defendant's breach of its agreement to arbitrate, ruling that "[t]he agreement to arbitrate is part of a binding contract between the parties, [and] Defendant makes itself liable for damages which Claimant might suffer, provided such damages are in direct causation with the breach."); Final Award of December 1998 in ICC Case No. 9593, *op. cit.*, fn. 4, p. 113 (damages available in principle; considered under contractual principles without reference to a governing law; situs was France and the parallel case was in the Ivory Coast); ICC Award No. 5946 (1990), ICCA *Yearbook Commercial Arbitration* XVI (1991) (hereinafter *Yearbook*), p. 97 at p. 112 (tribunal sitting in Geneva; N.Y. law applicable; referring to US law, tribunal awarded damages for the fees and costs of defending against a foreign litigation); See also SCC Final Award dated 13 July 1993, *Yearbook* XXII (1997), p. 197 at p. 210 (awarding claimant its costs and fees in the arbitration but not its costs and fees incurred defending against a foreign litigation notwithstanding that the foreign litigation was inconsistent with the arbitration agreement).

13. Emmanuel GAILLARD & John SAVAGE, eds., *Fouchard Gaillard Goldman on International Commercial Arbitration* (1999) p. 317 ("The French courts have developed particularly important substantive rules concerning arbitrability. These have been so often adopted in international conventions, in comparative law and in international arbitral practice that they now also constitute general principles of international arbitration law regularly applied by arbitrators, irrespective of the seat of the arbitration and the applicable law.").

monetary relief, being decided under the same law, as applications for anti-suit relief are also not governed by the lex contractus.

The forth option – the lex contractus – considers that a claim for monetary relief for breach of an arbitration agreement does not implicate the inherent powers of the arbitrators to rule on their own jurisdiction, and does not require reference to any powers derived from the arbitral rules. Rather, under this approach, a claim for monetary relief for breach of an arbitration agreement is seen as simply compensatory, as any other claim for damages for breach of a contractual obligation, and hence subject to the lex contractus.

2. Availability under National Laws

In practice, even if not required by a formal choice of law analysis, arbitrators and parties will want to have regard to national laws, whether for reassurance that a claim for monetary relief for breach of an arbitration agreement is a recognized cause of action or for guidance as to the standard for assessing such a claim.

If reference is had to national law, the paucity of cases considering claims of monetary relief for breach of an arbitration agreement is conspicuous. This paucity of authority arises from the circumstance that the scenarios in which a party would ask *a court* for an award of damages and/or an indemnity for breach of an arbitration agreement are few. Why this is so becomes evident upon consideration of the situation of the arbitration claimant who finds that the respondent has started litigation before a foreign court. The claimant's options are to ask the arbitrators for injunctive or monetary relief (in which case there will be no claim before a court for the same relief) or to go to the court and seek dismissal of the litigation. In the latter situation, the claimant may seek and obtain an order for costs from the foreign court (if costs are available in that jurisdiction), but an application for court costs is not a claim for monetary relief for breach of an arbitration agreement.

There are nonetheless some instances where courts have considered whether monetary relief is available for breach of an arbitration agreement. These cases are considered below.

a. Common law jurisdictions: monetary relief available
English courts have recognized the availability of damages and/or an indemnity for breach of a forum selection clause,[14] including an arbitration clause,[15] notwithstanding

---

14. *A/S D/S Svendborg af 1912 A/S Bodies Corporate trading in partnership as "Maersk Sealand" v. Akar*, [2003] EWHC 797 (Comm) (defendants' issuance of proceedings against claimant in Hong Kong and Guinea in breach of the forum selection clause entitled claimant to recover its reasonable expenses incurred in defending those proceedings); *Union Discount Co. Ltd v. Zoller* (Union Cal Ltd, Part 20 defendant) [2001] EWCA (Civ.) 1755, 2002 WLR 1517 (plaintiff successfully challenged New York proceedings commenced in breach of a jurisdiction clause, but was unable to recover legal costs under New York law, and sought to recover those costs by way of action in England for damages; English Court held that such costs could be recovered where the rules of the foreign forum permitted recovery of costs only in exceptional circumstances and the foreign court did not make any adjudication as to costs), *Donohue v. Armco Inc.*, [2001] U.K.H.L. 64, [2001] 1 Lloyd's

the supplementary right to seek a stay of the litigation commenced in breach of the clause.

In the United States, damages have been awarded for breach of a forum selection clause,[16] but not specifically for breach of an arbitration agreement. However, US courts have recognized that the legal principles applicable to an action for breach of a forum selection clause also govern claims for breach of an arbitration agreement,[17] and have found that damages may be an appropriate remedy for such breach.[18]

b.   Civil law jurisdictions: availability uncertain

In many civil law countries, the traditional view has been that forum selection clauses are procedural, not substantive, and do not give rise to a right to damages or an

---

Rep. 425 (House of Lords accepted that damages are available for breach of a jurisdiction clause, not only to recover any expenses incurred in defending the action, but also to recoup any greater liability in the foreign forum than would have been the case in England).

15. *Mantovani v. Carapelli S.p.A.*, [1980] 1 Lloyd's Law Rep. 375. See also Jane WESSEL & Sherri N. COHEN, "In Tune with *Mantovani*: The 'Novel' Case of Damages for Breach of an Arbitration Agreement", Int'l A.L.R. (2001) p. 65.

16. *Indosuez Intern. Finance, B.V. v. National Reserve Bank*, 304 A.D.2d 429 758 N.Y.S.2d 308 (N.Y. App. Div. 2003) (forum selection clause breached by proceedings in Russia; damages available, particularly in light of clear evidence of defendant's bad faith resort to foreign forum); *Allendale Mutual Insurance Co. v. Excess Insurance Co. Ltd.*, 922 F.Supp. 278, 285-287 (S.D.N.Y. 1998) (defendants' attempt to win a declaratory judgment in England in breach of a forum selection clause in favor of the United States was an opportunistic attempt to evade the forum clause, and defendants were liable for the expenses incurred by claimants defending the English action). See also *Ball v. Versar, Inc.*, 454 F.Supp.2d 783, 808-810 (S.D.Ind. 2006) (considering a claim that, by filing suit in federal district court in Pennsylvania, defendant breached the parties' forum selection clause in favor of the United States Court for the Southern District of Indiana). See generally Daniel S. TAN, "Enforcing International Arbitration Agreements in Federal Courts: Rethinking the Court's Remedial Powers", 47 Va. J. Int'l L. (Spring 2007), (summarizing US case law on damages and indemnity for breaches of forum selection and arbitration agreements).

17. *Paramedics Electromedicina Comercial LTDA v. GE Medical Systems Information Technologies, Inc.*, 369 F.3d 645 (2d Cir, 2004) (applying the test for granting anti-suit injunctions developed in relation to forum selection clauses to an arbitration clause).

18. *Payton v. Hurst*, 318 S.W.2d 726 (Ct of Civil Appeals, Texas 1958) ("Under the common law and well-settled case law of this state, appellant could not compel an arbitration under the facts in this case and is relegated to a suit for damages for any breach of the arbitration clauses."). See also, *Cunningham v. Prudential Prop. &Cas. Ins. Co.*, 340 Pa.Super.130 489 A2d-875 (1985) (automobile accident; insurer refused to arbitrate; ruled that "[w]e do not now decide that there can be no circumstances under which a party may be allowed to recover special damages because of another party's refusal to arbitrate.... It is difficult to comprehend in what manner a party can be damaged by another's failure to arbitrate when the former has available to him the means by which to compel arbitration."); *Shaw Group Inc. v. Triplefine Intern. Corp.*, 322 F.3d 115 (2d Cir. 2003) (holding that the arbitrability of a claim by the claimant in the arbitration for damages for breach of the parties' arbitration agreement, in an amount equal to attorneys' fees and costs incurred in opposing motions to stay the arbitration, were for the arbitrator to determine, not the court).

indemnity for their breach.[19] The authors have not, however, seen cases or commentary disavowing a right to such monetary relief.[20]

3.   *In Practice: Scenarios for Claims for Monetary Relief Before Arbitral Tribunals*

When the respondent in an arbitration commences a foreign proceeding which the claimant considers to violate the parties' arbitration agreement, the claimant will naturally consider its prospects before the foreign court, and the claimant's chances of prevailing on a claim before the arbitrators for monetary relief for breach of the arbitration agreement (whether damages or an indemnity against any judgment which might ultimately be rendered in the foreign proceedings) will be influenced by what the claimant has done, or not done, to pursue or protect its rights before the foreign court.

This section considers five scenarios of action or inaction by the arbitration claimant before a foreign court, with varying consequences for the claimant's prospects for recovery of damages or an indemnity from the arbitral tribunal. Assessment of the scenarios reveals, inter alia, the importance of an issue which remains unresolved in view of the limited precedent on point: whether the fact that the proceeding before the foreign court was commenced in breach of the agreement to arbitrate will be sufficient by itself to merit an award of damages and/or an indemnity against the respondent in the arbitration, or whether evidence of bad faith on the part of the respondent (or unfairness by the foreign court) will be required.

Common law authority suggests that an arbitration clause is effective as a contractual term, the breach of which is compensable in damages, without any additional requirement of bad faith.[21] But as noted above (III.*1.c.*), common law authority may not apply to a claim for monetary relief for breach of an arbitration agreement, even where the lex contractus is common law. In practice, it is likely that arbitrators will hesitate

---

19. See also, Otto SANDROCK, Speech at the German-American Lawyers' Association in Frankfurt (2004) (criticizing the majority view that the enforcement of arbitration and forum selection clauses is a procedural rather than substantive issue).

20. Republic and Canton of Geneva Judiciary, Court of First Instance, Decision of 2 May 2005 (C/1043/2005-15SP), 23 ASA Bull. (2005, no. 4) p. 739, at pp. 746-747 (application for injunction to stop an International Air Transport Association arbitration in Switzerland and enforce an anti-suit injunction issued by the English High Court, the Swiss Court ruled that the injunction was contrary to Swiss law; although there was no award on damages, the Court noted that "it is difficult for the petitioners to argue that the attorneys' fees to be paid in connection with the arbitration constitute a damage which is difficult to be made good..." thereby suggesting that damages may indeed be the appropriate remedy).

21. *A/S D/S Svendborg af 1912 A/S Bodies Corporate trading in partnership as "Maersk Sealand" v. Akar*, [2003] EWHC 797, 37 (Comm Ct) ("[D]efendants are in breach of that exclusive jurisdiction clause. In consequence of that breach, the claimants have suffered loss and damage consisting of the legal fees and other expenses they have incurred in investigating and defending those proceedings.... [T]he claimant is entitled to recover its reasonable expenses...."); *Union Discount Co. Ltd v. Zoller* (Union Cal Ltd, Part 20 defendant) [2001] EWCA (Civ) 1755, 2002 WLR 1517, 19 ("[R]elief is predicated on the assumption, not in issue before us, that the bringing of the New York proceedings itself constituted a breach of contract which has resulted in damages which are prima facie recoverable.").

to award damages or an indemnity unless the foreign proceeding was affected in some way by overreaching, bad faith or abuse of process.[22]

a.   Foreign proceeding unchallenged by arbitration claimant
Scenario 1 posits that the party seeking monetary relief from the arbitral tribunal has done nothing to challenge the foreign proceeding.

By failing to apply to dismiss the foreign litigation and thereby failing to give the foreign court a chance to rule on its own jurisdiction, the arbitration claimant in this scenario exposes itself to the arguments that it failed to mitigate its damage and that its claim for monetary relief calls upon the arbitrators to overstep their role vis-à-vis national courts. Whether these arguments would be persuasive depends upon the circumstances of the case.

If the arbitral tribunal is of the opinion that an application before the foreign court to dismiss the foreign litigation would have had little impact, the arbitration claimant's inaction before the foreign court should not deter an award of monetary relief (here, an indemnity against any judgment issued by the foreign court rather than litigation-related costs, which would be zero), or an anti-suit injunction.

Where there was no evidence of bad faith or overreaching by either the respondent party or the foreign court, and where the arbitrators could reasonably consider that an application before the foreign court to dismiss the foreign litigation would have been given due consideration and may have been successful, the arbitrators could well find that the arbitration claimant's inaction doomed its claim for monetary relief.[23] The comity principles that apply as between judiciaries do not apply directly to arbitrators. But similar considerations of prudence and deference would likely come to bear if the arbitrators had no reason to doubt the fairness of the foreign court proceeding. This is especially so in this scenario because the monetary relief that would be sought here would be an indemnity, rather than damages. Even in the situation where there is no evidence of bad faith or overreaching, however, the arbitrators should consider whether it is fair to impose upon the arbitration claimant the precondition of an appearance before the foreign court, as the obvious purpose of an arbitration agreement is to keep disputes away from the courts.

b.   Foreign proceeding challenged by arbitration claimant and foreign court does not rule on challenge
Scenario 2 assumes that the arbitration claimant has challenged the foreign proceeding, and that the foreign court has, due to delay or other dysfunction, not ruled upon the

---

22. See, e.g., *Union Discount Co. Ltd v. Zoller* (Union Cal Ltd, Part 20 defendant) [2001] EWCA (Civ) 1755, 2002 WLR 1517, 36 (discussing, without resolving, whether damages should be available where the foreign court considered the issue of damages and denied the application, or awarded damages to the defendant in an amount less than the defendant's costs).

23. *Union Discount Co. Ltd v. Zoller* (Union Cal Ltd, Part 20 defendant) [2001] EWCA (Civ) 1755, 2002 WLR 1517, 10 ("[A] party has failed to apply for costs which he would have got if he had asked for them, a subsequent claim for damages may be defeated; but that would be because in such a case his loss would be held to be due to his own fault or omission." (quoting *Berry v. BTC* [1962] 1 Q.B. 306, 321)).

challenge at the time that the arbitral tribunal considers the arbitration claimant's claim for monetary relief for breach of the arbitration agreement.

In this situation, there could be no argument that the claimant in the arbitration failed to mitigate its damages, and no argument that the foreign court's decision on jurisdiction should be respected. In *Svendborg*, the English High Court ruled that, by commencing and pursuing proceedings in Hong Kong and Guinea, the defendants had breached the forum selection clause in the parties' agreement, which provided for the exclusive jurisdiction of the English Courts. The High Court awarded the claimants damages equal to their legal fees and other expenses associated with the foreign litigation and an indemnity in respect of future costs and expenses incurred in the Hong Kong and Guinea proceedings.[24] The court stated: "It does not seem ... that the application of [the principle that the claimant can recover its expenses incurred in the foreign litigation commenced by the defendant in breach of an exclusive jurisdiction clause] is dependant upon the claimant showing that the relevant expenses are irrecoverable in the foreign proceedings...."[25] Moreover, any risk that the claimant in the arbitration might later bring a claim in the foreign proceeding for double recovery of its expenses can be addressed by an undertaking that such conduct will not occur.[26] While *Svendborg* is not authority for a claim subject to international law or to any law other than English law, its reasoning could fairly be applied by arbitrators who may, in this scenario, award to the arbitration claimant damages in the amount of the fees expended in the foreign litigation, perhaps conditioned on an undertaking by the arbitration claimant that it will not seek to recover those same costs before the foreign court.

An arbitral tribunal in this scenario would also consider whether to award an indemnity against a potential future judgment. Such a remedy, unlike an award of damages for the legal fees spent, would have the intended effect of unraveling the foreign proceeding, and the result achieved would resemble an anti-suit injunction. Before granting such relief, it is foreseeable that the arbitrators would look beyond the mere breach of the arbitration clause for evidence of bad faith conduct on the part of the arbitration respondent or unfairness by the foreign court.

c.   *Foreign proceeding challenged and foreign court dismisses proceeding without an award of costs because foreign law does not authorize such an award*

The third scenario transposes to the arbitration context the *Zoller* case decided by the Court of Appeal in England in 2002.[27] In that case, there was a forum selection clause in favor of the English courts, and the defendant commenced litigation in the New York courts. The Court of Appeal awarded damages, consisting of the costs and fees reasonably incurred by the plaintiff to obtain dismissal of the New York litigation. The Court of Appeal was careful to say in its ruling that its award was not inconsistent with

---

24. *A/S D/S Svendborg af 1912 A/S Bodies Corporate trading in partnership as "Maersk Sealand" v. Akar*, [2003] EWHC 797, 36-38 (Comm Ct).

25. *Ibid.*, at 37.

26. *Ibid.*

27. *Union Discount Co. Ltd v. Zoller* (Union Cal Ltd, Part 20 defendant) [2001] EWCA (Civ) 1755, 2002 WLR 1517.

the decision by the New York court, positing that the New York court might well have granted costs if so authorized by its law. The Court of Appeal also noted that "there is no reason of comity ... why [the parties' contractually elected forum] should enforce a foreign jurisdiction's policy [on costs] in preference to [its] own".[28] It is questionable that international arbitrators – unencumbered by any consideration of inter-judiciary comity – would be as concerned with the foreign court's policy on costs. Absent any authority to the contrary or additional circumstances, this is a scenario where an award of damages should be appropriate.

d.   *Foreign proceeding challenged and foreign court dismisses proceeding and either rejects the application for costs or awards costs in less than the full amount of costs/fees expended*
Scenario 4 assumes that the arbitration claimant has challenged the foreign proceeding and succeeded in its challenge, but without obtaining costs. The difference between this and the preceding scenario is that in scenario 3 the foreign law did not authorize an award of costs and in scenario 4 the foreign law permitted an award of costs but costs were nevertheless either not awarded or not awarded in full.

Where the foreign court dismisses the lawsuit brought in violation of the arbitration clause, but either rejects the arbitration claimant's application for costs or awards costs amounting to less than the sum expended, the issue is whether it is appropriate for the arbitrators to revisit the issue of costs, and award damages to cover the full amount of the arbitration claimant's expenses in the litigation. International arbitrators are not bound by considerations of judicial comity and, because the foreign court here will not have considered the costs issue in the form of a claim for damages for breach of the arbitration agreement, there is no issue of res judicata.[29] The arbitrators would likely seek to determine whether the foreign court here did in fact consider the issue of costs. If the foreign court did consider the issue of costs, the arbitrators will likely look for more than a mere breach of the arbitration clause, and make an assessment of the fairness of the court's decision.

e.   *Foreign proceeding challenged and foreign court denies the challenge to its jurisdiction*
This final scenario assumes that a challenge before the foreign court has been made and that the foreign court has rejected the challenge and maintained the litigation.

A claim for damages and/or an indemnity before the arbitral tribunal in this scenario would have at least three possible outcomes, each fact-specific.

Were the arbitrators to find that the foreign court's ruling was correct, the claim for monetary relief would be denied.

Were the arbitrators to find that the foreign court's ruling was incorrect but that the foreign judicial process was fair, and that the party that brought the foreign proceeding acted in good faith, the arbitrators would have the choice between awarding damages and perhaps an indemnity against any future judgment of the foreign court, effectively

---

28. *Ibid.*, at 23.

29. *Ibid.*, at 25 ("[W]here there is assumed to be an independent cause of action [for recovery of costs and expenses associated with the foreign proceeding] then ... what is being adjudicated upon on the second occasion is not the same point.").

unraveling the foreign judgment, or deciding that the claimant in the arbitration had an adequate and fair opportunity to raise its arguments before the foreign court and that conflicting parallel judgments on the issue should be avoided. Essentially, the question in this situation would be whether monetary relief should be awarded in every case where the proceedings before the foreign court are in breach of the agreement to arbitrate, or whether the standard is higher, requiring some bad faith conduct on the part of the arbitration respondent (or evidence of unfairness in the judicial process). While the mere breach standard is defensible under contact principles, arbitrators may in practice be reluctant to unravel a foreign judgment where there is no evidence of bad faith, overreaching or abuse of process.

The best case for an award of monetary relief would be a finding by the arbitrators that the foreign court was both incorrect and unfair, and that the party that brought the foreign litigation had acted in bad faith. In *Zoller*, the English Court of Appeal noted that the policy in favor of avoiding conflicting parallel judgments is not applicable where there is evidence of bad faith in the foreign proceedings.[30] The reasoning of the court in *Zoller* is persuasive in such situation. Where there is evidence of bad faith, overreaching or abuse of process in the foreign litigation, no deference to a foreign court is due and there should be little reluctance to award an indemnity against a future judgment, the purpose of which is effectively to unwind the foreign court ruling.[31]

IV.   OTHER ISSUES

1.   Preconditions to Claims for Monetary Relief?

a.   Challenge to the jurisdiction of the foreign court?
In many jurisdictions, there is a duty to mitigate any claim for damages. The arbitration claimant must therefore consider whether it should challenge the jurisdiction of the foreign court in order to protect itself against the argument that it allowed the foreign proceedings to proceed to judgment, without a challenge, and thus cannot later claim any expenses or an indemnity.

b.   Anti-suit application?
It is unlikely that an application for an anti-suit injunction before the arbitrators would be a prerequisite to a successful claim for monetary relief for breach of an arbitration agreement. In the *Zoller* case described above, involving a claim for damages for breach of a forum selection clause, the defendant contended that, by failing to seek an anti-suit injunction in England, and by choosing to apply in New York to have the New York proceedings dismissed, the claimant had failed to mitigate its costs incurred in the New

---

30. *Ibid.*, at 29-30 (the "unity of the law" argument "should not apply in malicious prosecution cases.").
31. *Indosuez Intern. Finance, B.V. v. National Reserve Bank*, 758 N.Y.S.2d 308, 310 (N.Y. App. Div. 2003) (holding that the grant of a permanent injunction against defendant's pursuit of foreign litigation was proper "in light of the clear evidence of defendant's harassing and bad faith foreign litigation".).

York proceedings. The court ruled that, even if this submission were correct, it would go to quantum of the damages, not the availability of the damages. "We confess that it seems to us unattractive for the New York claimant to submit that the English defendant should not have gone to New York to resist the proceedings which the New York claimant had, as a matter of choice, started there."[32]

2. Effect of Appearance in Competing Jurisdiction (Waiver)?

Before attempting to defend foreign proceedings brought in breach of an arbitration clause, the arbitration claimant should determine whether mounting a defense will prejudice the arbitral tribunal's jurisdiction to determine the dispute. If a party appears in the foreign court merely to contest its jurisdiction, it will not have submitted to its jurisdiction. However, if the arbitration claimant presents a defense on the merits in the foreign court, perhaps to satisfy a requirement for contesting the court's jurisdiction, it should consider whether it may need later to withdraw its defense on the merits to preserve the tribunal's jurisdiction, for example, if the foreign court rules against the challenge to its jurisdiction.[33]

3. Measure of Monetary Relief

It is logical that an award of damages for breach of an arbitration agreement should include the arbitration claimant's legal fees and costs associated with any anti-suit injunction application, and those associated with challenging jurisdiction in, and defending against, the foreign proceedings. The award could also include an indemnity against the judgment of the foreign court.[34]

---

32. *Union Discount Co. Ltd v. Zoller* (Union Cal Ltd, Part 20 defendant) [2001] EWCA (Civ) 1755, 2002 WLR 1517, 33.

33. Stuart DUTSON, "Breach of an Arbitration or Exclusive Jurisdiction Clause: the Legal Remedies if it Continues", 16 Arb. Int'l (2000, no. 1) p. 89, at pp. 97-98 (hereinafter *Dutson*).

34. Daniel S. TAN, "Damages for Breach of Forum Selection Clauses, Principled Remedies, and Control of International Civil Litigation", 40 Tex. Int'l L.J. (2005) p. 623, at p. 658 ("Compensating a party for costs and expenses incurred in defending wrongfully instituted proceedings is intrinsically compelling. However, as a matter of legal principle, it is hard to argue that only costs and expenses can be recovered, but no more."); Daniel S. TAN, "Anti-Suit Injunctions and the Vexing Problem of Comity", 45 Va.J. Int'l L. (2005) p. 283, at pp. 253-254 ("But the law of remedies tells us that damages need not be restricted [to costs and expenses incurred by the non-breaching party].... The courts may award full compensatory damages that completely indemnify the plaintiff."); *Dutson*, at pp. 98-99 (the amount of the judgment obtained from a competing court "patently fall[s] within the usual measure of damages and are not too remote in law."); *Donohue v. Armco Inc.*, [2001] U.K.H.L. 64, [2002] 1 Lloyd's Rep. 425, 437, 439, 443 (accepted in principle that damages were available for breach of a jurisdiction clause, not only to recover any expenses incurred in defending the action, but also potentially to recoup any greater liability in the foreign forum than would have been the case in England).

V. CONCLUSION

There has been a paucity of commentary on the subject of monetary relief for breach of an undertaking to arbitrate. The controversial subject of anti-suit injunctions has been far more attractive to commentators.

Compared to anti-suit relief by arbitrators, claims for monetary relief are more easily enforced and are simpler procedurally. As such, claims for monetary relief should be added to the repertoire of remedies available to arbitration claimants who face parallel litigation brought by arbitration respondents.

Where the ruling of a foreign court, directed at people or objects within its jurisdiction, causes irreparable harm and paralyzes the arbitral process, an anti-suit injunction is a necessary remedy. However, not all cases are so extreme and, even in extreme circumstances, a party may usefully supplement its application for anti-suit relief with a claim for damages to cover its attorneys' fees and costs incurred defending the foreign litigation, or arm itself with an indemnity against any judgment issued by the foreign court.

"Arbitral Lifelines":
The Protection of Jurisdiction by Arbitrators

*Toby T. Landau**

I.   INTRODUCTION

In the range of interim measures that parties might seek from arbitral tribunals, "anti-suit" injunctions – or orders restraining a party from commencing or pursuing proceedings before a national court or other forum – have long occupied an uncertain position. To many they are an oddity of the Anglo-American legal system with no relevance to international arbitration. To others, they are a menace and more often than not no more than a tactical sideshow with little practical importance.

In practice, at least in the field of non-treaty-based commercial arbitration, there is little precedent, and little experience. This is an area into which the majority of arbitrators seem unwilling to tread. The notion of interfering with a national court has been seen as beyond an arbitrator's authority and mandate. Indeed, as a matter of history, many international arbitration rules have hindered initiatives in this area by limiting interim measures to those that concern the "*subject matter*" of the dispute (e.g., Art 26 of the UNCITRAL Arbitration Rules (1976)), a requirement that has been interpreted as excluding measures to protect the arbitral process itself.

This reluctance, suspicion and timidity, however, sits uneasily with the increasing trend on the part of recalcitrant parties in international arbitration to deploy disruptive tactics – frequently before national courts. It is now a fact of life in the field of international arbitration that if, for whatever reason, a party decides to avoid an arbitration, there is every likelihood that it will try to commence competing proceedings before a national court (often its own local court), or worse still, to take positive action to obstruct the arbitral process by means of local challenge proceedings, or an anti-arbitration injunction. There is now a rich and troubling jurisprudence in this regard, with any number of international arbitrations and arbitrators that have been the subject of local court interference and restraints, secured in breach of an arbitration agreement. In the words of Judge Schwebel, this is:

---

* Essex Court Chambers; M.A., B.C.L. (Oxford); LL.M. (Harvard); FCIArb; CArb; Barrister-at-Law (London); also of the New York State Bar.

"...a timely and serious subject. The threats to and breaches of the efficacy, the integrity, and in some cases the very viability of international arbitration are profound."[1]

The result is something of a dislocation. The ability to withstand such attacks is a critical element in the success of the process, and often a key factor in the very choice of arbitration as opposed to national courts. Further, as Emmanuel Gaillard has demonstrated, international arbitrators are capable of insulating and protecting the arbitral process. And yet, there remains a fundamental reluctance to do so.

At the heart of the problem lies a tendency to analyze such interim measures through the prism of national court practice, and to impose on arbitrators the same constraints as may limit the powers of a judge. This approach, it is suggested, is now both outdated and analytically flawed. Fresh thinking is urgently required, in order to ensure that, in ever more troubled times, international arbitration continues to deliver the solutions for which it was designed.

This note urges a new approach by:

(a) testing the analogy between the interim measures of national courts and international arbitration;

(b) considering the nature of arbitrators' powers in this regard (as analyzed by Emmanuel Gaillard in his report); and

(c) suggesting factors that might delimit the proper use of such measures.

II.   COURT-ORDERED "ANTI-SUIT" RELIEF: A FALSE ANALOGY

1.   Court Orders

"Anti-suit" injunctions were, in their earliest form, creations of the English courts, and were developed as far back as the 1500s.[2] Initially, their application was limited to the allocation of jurisdiction as between competing domestic courts in domestic cases, and, in general, to prevent oppression or vexation. In particular, such orders were first issued by common law courts to prevent the expansive jurisdiction of ecclesiastical courts. Thereafter, they were used by the Court of Chancery to restrain parties from bringing

---

1. Stephen M. SCHWEBEL, "Anti-Suit Injunctions in International Arbitration: An Overview" in Emmanuel GAILLARD, ed., *Anti-Suit Injunctions in International Arbitration* (Juris Publishing, Inc.) p. 5.
2. See generally: David JOSEPH, *Jurisdiction and Arbitration Agreements and their Enforcement*, 1st edn., (Sweet & Maxwell 2005), Chapter 12, pp. 308-381; David W. RAACK, "A History of Injunctions in England Before 1700", 61 Ind.L.J. p. 539; Marco STACHER, "You Don't Want to Go There – Antisuit Injunctions in International Commercial Arbitration", 23 ASA Bulletin (2005, no. 4) at p. 640; George BERMANN, "The Use of Anit-Suit Injunctions in International Litigation", 28 Columbia Journal of Transnational Law (1990) p. 593; Trevor HARTLEY, "Comity and the Use of Antisuit Injunctions in International Litigation", 35 American Journal of Comparative Law (1987) p. 487.

suits in the common law courts. Gradually, their scope was extended to other courts, and then, from the early nineteenth century, competing proceedings in Scotland, Ireland and the British colonies, and finally, in more recent times, to proceedings before courts in the rest of the world. A broadly similar historical development took place in the United States.

Nowadays, this jurisdiction has developed into a sophisticated regime, designed to protect parties from oppressive and vexatious conduct, as well as to restrain breaches of choice of court and arbitration agreements.[3] Beyond the Courts of England and the United States, the jurisdiction to grant such measures has now been confirmed in, for example, New Zealand, Canada, Australia, India, Singapore, Malaysia, Bermuda, Pakistan, Fiji, Jersey, and many other common law countries.[4]

Although this is primarily a common law development, it is not in fact the sole preserve of common law courts. There is at least some (albeit limited) theoretical support for the view that courts in civil law jurisdictions may issue "anti-suit" injunctions, or equivalent measures, in the application of civil law doctrines such as "*abus de droit*", especially when parallel proceedings are brought in violation of a contractual arrangement.[5] Some civil law jurisdictions, indeed, have recognized such a power. By way of example, Joseph cites,[6] amongst others, the Courts of Quebec,[7] the French *Cour de Cassation*,[8] and the District Court of The Hague.[9]

2. Criticisms

And yet, despite the widespread use of this type of measure, in both common law and civil law jurisdictions, "anti-suit" injunctions issued by national court judges still attract substantial criticism, and remain highly controversial. The key points of concern may be summarized as follows:

---

3. This is obviously not the place to examine the precise nature of the jurisdiction to grant this form of relief, and the criteria that are applied. As to this, see, e.g., JOSEPH, *op. cit.*, fn. 2.

4. See the comparative survey in JOSEPH, *op. cit.*, fn. 2, at pp. 375-380. With respect to the United States, both JOSEPH and STACHER (*op. cit.*, fn. 2) note that differences in approach have developed across different circuits in the United States.

5. See, e.g., Yuval SHANY, *The Competing Jurisdictions of International Courts and Tribunals* (Oxford University Press 2003) at p. 161, who cites Dogauchi for the proposition that Japanese law may in theory support anti-suit injunctions, and Lenenbach for the proposition that Sect. 826 of the German Civil Code, prohibiting wilful conduct contrary to public policy, provides a proper basis for anti-suit injunctions in cases where initiation of foreign parallel proceedings may be deemed an unconscionable act.

6. *Op. cit.*, fn. 2.

7. See, e.g., *Johns-Manville Corp v. Dominion of Canada General Insurance Co*, [1991] Recueils de jurisprudence de Quebec 616 (CA); *Opron Inc v. Aero Systems Engineering*, 1999 CarswellQue 940; *Lac D'Amiante du Canada Ltd v. Lac D'Amiante du Quebec Ltd*, 1999 CarswellQue 3688.

8. See, e.g., *Banque Worms v. Epoux Brachot*, 19 Nov. 2002 Cass. Civ. 1re, noted by Muir WATT in [2003] C.L.J. 573.

9. See, e.g., *Medinol v. Cordis*, Judgment 5 August 2004, Cause no. KG 04/688.

(a) An "anti-suit" injunction is perceived as an unwarranted interference by a judge in the legal process of another jurisdiction. Despite the fact that such orders are addressed to an individual litigant rather than a foreign court, it is said that the effect is the same, and that, de facto, the measure deprives the sovereign courts of one state of their right to determine their own jurisdiction, and regulate their own process. As stated by Bachand, "anti-suit" injunctions are:

"... as serious and effective an interference with the judicial process of a foreign State as one can think of".[10]

(b) Similarly, "anti-suit" injunctions in effect pitch one national court judge against another. This in turn raises serious issues of sovereignty and international comity.
(c) An "anti-suit" injunction expresses a conclusion that the foreign forum has no jurisdiction. In issuing such an order, one national court judge is effectively ruling upon an issue that another national court judge would otherwise be entitled to consider. In substance, this pre-emption reflects a lack of trust or confidence by one judge with respect to the other. Once again, serious issues of sovereignty and international comity arise.
(d) Further, "anti-suit" injunctions, when addressed to litigants before foreign fora, effectively give extraterritorial effect to the determinations of a national court, where otherwise there may be no such effect, or no reciprocal recognition and enforcement.
(e) "Anti-suit" injunctions risk denying a party what might be a fundamental and/or constitutional right of access to a court.
(f) Given the concerns of sovereignty and international comity, "anti-suit" injunctions may be perceived as a provocation, and simply lead a foreign forum to protect itself by asserting its own sovereignty and issuing a corresponding measure (such as an "anti-anti-suit" injunction).
(g) Within regional jurisdiction and enforcement regimes, such as the Brussels Regulation (44/2001) in the EU, "anti-suit" injunctions are particularly controversial, since they bypass the agreed mechanisms for the allocation of jurisdiction as between the courts of different Member States, and, in particular, the ability of each court itself to apply the relevant compulsory jurisdiction rules. Hence, in the context of the Brussels Convention, the European Court of Justice (ECJ) has famously prohibited the issuance of "ant-suit" injunctions by the courts of one Member State, to restrain a party from proceeding before the courts of another Member State.[11] The ECJ emphasised that within the context of a regional regime such as this, the courts of each Member State have to trust the courts of all other Member States to apply the rules correctly. The

---

10. Frédéric BACHAND, "The UNCITRAL Model Law's Take on Anti-Suit Injunctions", in Emmanuel GAILLARD (ed.), *op cit.*, fn. 1, at p. 88.
11. *Turner v. Grovit*, Case C-195/02 [2004] ECR I-3565. See also *Gasser GmbH v. MISAT Srl*, Case C-116/02 [2003] ECR I-14693 (which decided that a court of a Member State on which exclusive jurisdiction has been conferred pursuant to Art. 23 cannot issue an injunction to restrain a party from prosecuting proceedings before a court of another Member State if that court was first seised of the dispute).

critical question as to whether a court of a Member State may grant an injunction against a person bound by an arbitration agreement to restrain him from proceeding in breach of that agreement in a court of another Member State remains undecided, and has recently been referred to the ECJ by the English House of Lords.[12]

This is not the place to evaluate the strength of these arguments. Rather, what is critical for present purposes is the fact that this Court-based jurisprudence, and the controversies and criticisms to which it has given rise, have directly infected the approach to "anti-suit" relief in the field of international arbitration.

In circumstances where many consider that judges should have no such power, there is a strong body of opinion that arbitrators should be equally restricted – for the same or analogous reasons.[13] Many have difficulty conceiving of a situation in which arbitral tribunals might have greater or different powers in this regard than national court judges. If a measure is inappropriate for a judge – as many believe is the case with "anti-suit" relief – so it must also be inappropriate for an arbitrator. Indeed, it is often said that a private tribunal is necessarily less well-placed than a judge to intrude upon a national and sovereign Court process.

Many civil lawyers disregard such measures, on the basis that they are unknown in civil law courts.[14] Even if, technically, such interim measures are available to an arbitral tribunal, it is a common view amongst both common and civil lawyers that they should not be granted, since it forms no part of an arbitrator's authority, mandate, or proper function to interfere in a national court process. As a practical reality, these are issues that are not always expressed in terms, but which, it is suggested, frequently infuse arbitrators' thinking in this area. When asked to restrain a party from proceeding before a national court, it takes a very robust arbitral tribunal to put aside all concerns as to interference with a national and sovereign legal process; interference with fundamental or constitutional rights; expressing disrespect for a national court judiciary; seeking extraterritorial effect for a jurisdiction determination; short-circuiting a Court's right to determine its own jurisdiction.

Further, it is frequently said (or thought) that such measures are futile in any event if rendered by an arbitral tribunal, since they are unlikely ever to be recognized or enforced.

Further still, it is considered by many that the New York Convention's mandate on Contracting States to enforce arbitration agreements and to stay or dismiss proceedings brought in breach thereof should suffice to address concerns in this area.

---

12. *West Tankers Inc. v. Ras Riunione Adriatica di Sicurta SPA ("the Front Comor")*, [2007] UKHL 4.

13. See, e.g., Laurent LÉVY, "Anti-suit Injunctions Issued by Arbitrators" in Emmanuel GAILLARD (ed.), *op. cit.*, fn. 1, pp. 115-119.

14. This point was frequently made in discussions within the UNCITRAL Arbitration Working Group, in the course of deliberations on the new Art. 17 of the UNCITRAL Model Law (powers of arbitrators to issue interim measures). These deliberations have now been concluded, and the scope of Art. 17 has now been expanded in order to include "anti-suit" injunctions and related measures.

3.   A Flawed Approach

It is submitted that this approach to "anti-suit" relief in the field of international arbitration is fundamentally flawed. National courts are in a completely different position to international arbitral tribunals, and the jurisprudence and experience of the former is an inappropriate model for the latter.

Most of the specific factors that impact upon national courts, and that have shaped the approach to this issue, have little or no relevance to international arbitration. In particular, national courts:

(a) are bound by a formal system of "international comity";
(b) must conduct themselves within sovereign limits, and with careful regard to, and respect for, the courts of other sovereign nations;
(c) generally have territorial limits upon their jurisdiction;
(d) operate within the confines of procedural codes/civil procedure rules that are far more rigid and limited than international arbitration rules;
(e) are often subject to specific doctrines as to the allocation of jurisdiction (such as, e.g., *forum non conveniens* and *lis alibi pendens*);
(f) in the case of the EU, operate within a self-contained regime on the allocation of jurisdiction as between Member States.

International arbitration, as primarily a creature of contract, is free of virtually all of these constraints. In the absence of these factors, many of the traditional criticisms of "anti-suit" relief fall away, or at the very least lose much of their force. This does not mean that international arbitrators are thereby free to intermeddle at will with national court processes, but it does suggest that the concerns expressed in the context of court orders must be treated with caution in the context of arbitration.

Further, there are a number of factors that are relevant in international arbitration, that strongly militate in favour of the availability of such relief, but that have little or no significance for national courts.

International arbitral tribunals are constituted precisely because parties have contracted *out* of national courts. In agreeing to arbitrate, they are undertaking not to pursue their claims before a court, and so the notion of an arbitral tribunal enforcing that agreement by restraining a party from proceeding before a national court is a natural consequence of the agreement. In so far as there may be doubts as to the arbitral tribunal's jurisdiction, the doctrine of *kompetenz-kompetenz* still endows the arbitral tribunal with the power to investigate its own jurisdiction, at least in the first instance.

Although there are many reasons why parties might prefer international arbitration to national courts as a system of dispute resolution, the truth is that in many areas of international commercial activity, international arbitration is the only viable option, or as once famously put, "the only game in town". National courts may be considered unfamiliar, inexperienced, unreliable, inefficient, partial, amenable to pressure, or simply hostile. The larger and more significant the transaction in question, the less appropriate, or more risky, a national court may be. And so, where a third country's courts cannot be agreed upon, international arbitration becomes an essential mechanism actively to *avoid* a particular court. Once again, some form of restraining measure would then appear a natural consequence of the agreement, if one party nevertheless seeks to pursue its claim before the court in question. In such circumstances, it may be no answer at all to expect the other party to appear before the (unfamiliar/inexperienced/unreliable/inefficient/partial/pliable/hostile) court, and challenge its jurisdiction. Not only might this be a futile exercise, it forces a party to engage precisely that forum from which it was agreed it would be insulated.

It is true that national courts that have been expressly chosen by parties (e.g., by a choice of court clause) may be in a similar position. However, such courts must still operate within the constraints and limitations set out above. In contrast, in choosing international arbitration, parties not only agree to avoid a particular court or courts, they also agree to do so by way of an international mechanism that is free from many constraints and limitations, and able to enforce the parties' expectations by diverse means.

The result, it is suggested, is that "anti-suit" forms of relief are in fact more appropriate in international arbitration than national courts. On any view, there are powerful reasons why arbitrators – and *not* national courts – ought to have control over the grant of such measures. As noted by Joseph:

> "The exercise of such powers diminishes the sense that one national court, in granting an injunction, has interfered with the jurisdiction of another. It might also in due course diminish the sense that the wide availability of the remedy in common-law jurisdictions has created an unequal playing field in international litigation. The availability of the remedy would then largely depend upon the terms of the parties' arbitration agreement."[15]

At the very least, this is an area that requires a fresh approach, divorced from the jurisprudence, and conceptual baggage, of national courts.

III. THE NATURE OF ARBITRATORS' POWERS TO GRANT RELIEF

In analyzing this area afresh, one must reconsider the type of measures that an arbitral tribunal might impose, and the juridical bases for the grant of such measures.

1. *Types of Measures*

One of the principal reasons why "anti-suit" relief in international arbitration has been so encumbered by the baggage of national courts, and so controversial, is terminology – and in particular the use of the phrase "*anti-suit injunction*". This is an entirely misleading term, both in court and (more so) in arbitration.

As for usage in courts, it was noted by Lord Hobhouse in *Turner v. Grovit*[16] that the term "*anti-suit injunction*" is problematic. As observed earlier, such injunctions restrain

---

15. *Op. cit.*, fn. 11, at p. 309.
16. [2002] 1 W.L.R. 107, 117, at para. 23.

parties from taking steps before a court. They are *"in personam"* (i.e., addressed to a defendant), and are neither directed at another court or judge, nor designed to stop the competing suit itself. As Joseph has pointed out,[17] such injunctions come in a variety of forms, many of which are not easily described as *"anti-suit"*: for example, an order restraining a party from enforcing a judgment or annulling an award; or making an application for an anti-suit injunction; or commencing or proceeding with an arbitration; or making a disclosure application in a foreign forum; or pursuing a third party by way of indemnity or contribution.

More significantly, the problem with using the term *"anti-suit"* in arbitration is that (a) it directly imports the jurisprudence – and thinking – of national courts and (b) it suggests that all that is in issue is an actual injunction restraining a party from commencing or continuing proceedings elsewhere. There is no reason at all why the powers of arbitrators should be limited in this way. On the contrary, if the purpose of such measures is to protect the arbitral process, and the parties' expectations, there are any number of measures that an arbitral tribunal might impose, short of an actual *"anti-suit injunction"* as this concept is understood in court. This is an area where arbitrators (unlike some judges) are free to act creatively. So, by way of random example only, an arbitral tribunal might:

(a) impose notification or reporting requirements upon a party, in order to ensure that full information is provided to the arbitral tribunal and all other parties with respect to each step taken before a different forum;
(b) require that the offending party provide information to the other forum in question, such as a letter or request from the arbitral tribunal;
(c) require the offending party to raise particular points before the other forum;
(d) impose conditions on each step that a party may take before the different forum (such as the making of an application to the arbitral tribunal, or the securing of the prior consent of the arbitral tribunal);
(e) impose a "recommendation" or declaration on an offending party, as opposed to a strict "order";
(f) impose costs penalties on the offending party;
(g) impose orders for limited periods of time (e.g., up until the completion of the arbitral tribunal's own enquiry into its own jurisdiction).

There are many other possibilities, short of the imposition of an actual overall restraint. Few of these other types of order attract the same criticisms as full-blooded, court-style *"anti-suit injunctions"*. Yet all such measures are best analyzed as aspects of the same procedural power.

To this end, in the recently introduced Art. 17(2)(b) of the UNCITRAL Model Law, a broad wording has been adopted that encompasses a range of different types of interim measure, including but not limited to *"anti-suit injunctions"*, but without any mention of *"anti-suit injunctions"* themselves. Hence interim measures are specified as including (inter alia) any measure by which a party is ordered to:

---

17. *Op. cit.*, fn. 2, pp. 309-310.

"Take action that would prevent, or refrain from taking action that is likely to cause, current or imminent harm or prejudice to the arbitral process itself."[18]

It is suggested, therefore, that if some other term is used, instead of an "*anti-suit injunction*" (such as, for example, a "*jurisdiction protection*" measure), much of the unhelpful court "baggage" will be jettisoned; resistance to such measures may well be diffused; and the way will be cleared for some fresh thinking in this area.

As set out below, this issue has an important bearing upon the analysis one may adopt to explain the juridical basis for such measures.

2.   *Juridical Bases*

In his excellent report, Emmanuel Gaillard advances two different bases for the grant of "anti-suit" relief by arbitrators: (1) the arbitral tribunal's jurisdiction to sanction violations of the arbitration agreement, and (2) the arbitral tribunal's power to take any measure necessary to avoid the aggravation of the dispute or to protect the effectiveness of the award.

The first of these bases represents a core element in Gaillard's approach. The principle of "*kompetenz-kompetenz*" allows the arbitrators to decide any challenge of the arbitration agreement itself, which by definition includes the jurisdiction to decide on breaches of the obligation to arbitrate – and the power to sanction such breaches by way of remedies for breach of contract (e.g., damages, specific performance or injunctions). Gaillard deploys this analysis to neutralize attacks on the exercise of the power, and in particular the criticism that "anti-suit" relief constitutes an undue interference with national courts. According to Gaillard, such orders cannot be seen as an undue interference, because:

> "the parties who enter into an arbitration agreement accept, by definition, to waive their right to resort to domestic courts for the settlement of their dispute." (p. 241)
> (....)
> The relevant question, therefore, is not a party's fundamental right to seek relief before national courts, but whether a valid arbitration agreement exists and whether the dispute is covered by the agreement, and who has jurisdiction to decide these questions. (p. 242)
> (....)
> In that context, the answer is provided by the rules of international arbitration law concerning the interaction between arbitrators and domestic courts.... Domestic courts should not, in parallel and with the same degree of scrutiny, rule on the same issue at least at the outset of the arbitral process. In other words ... the courts should limit, at that stage, their review to a prima facie determination

---

18. See the UNCITRAL 39th Commission Report, available at <www.uncitral.org>.

that the agreement is not null and void, inoperative or incapable of being performed. (p. 242)

(....)

As a result, a court that is confronted with the question of the existence or validity of the arbitration agreement must refrain from hearing substantive arguments as to the arbitrators' jurisdiction until such time as the arbitrators themselves have had an opportunity to do so." (p. 242)

This is obviously a powerful rationale for relief to protect jurisdiction. There are, however, a number of difficulties with this approach.

First, by characterizing this form of relief as simply a remedy for the breach of the arbitration agreement, the jurisdiction to grant such remedies and the type of order that may be available may depend upon the law governing the arbitration agreement. It is far from clear that every such law will allow the grant of injunctive relief as a remedy for breach, and even if it does so, it may well be with limitations. More importantly, even if injunctive relief is available, the other types of order or recommendation suggested above may be unavailable as a remedy for a breach of contract.

Second, whilst Gaillard's reasoning on "kompetenz-kompetenz" is impeccable, as a practical matter, it still remains aspirational in many jurisdictions. Regrettably, the notion that, pending the completion of the arbitral tribunal's own enquiry into its jurisdiction, courts must restrict their review to a *prima facie* enquiry, has yet to be adopted in many systems,[19] and until it is, the "undue interference" argument may persist (on the basis that the court in question, according to its own rules, is entitled to proceed further than simply a "*prima facie*" review).

Third, there is a timing problem with this approach. Once an arbitral tribunal has ruled on its own jurisdiction, for example in a partial award, and the "*kompetenz-kompetenz*" phase is over, the way may then be cleared for national courts to step in and review the arbitrators' jurisdiction. However, at this point, on this analysis, there would appear to be no justification for imposing any restraint upon a party from proceeding before a national court – notwithstanding that the arbitral proceedings may still have some way to go, and that the proceedings before the national court might entirely undermine them. Any such restraint would again be vulnerable to the "undue interference" complaint.

It is suggested that Gaillard's second rationale for this type of relief (the power to take any measure necessary to avoid the aggravation of the dispute or to protect the effectiveness of the award) avoids these difficulties.

Unlike the first basis, this second approach is not dependent upon the law that governs the arbitration agreement, and the remedies that may be available for breach of contract. Instead, it depends primarily upon the law governing the arbitral proceedings, which is likely to be far more flexible, allowing the arbitral tribunal a broad discretion

---

19. See, e.g., the different approaches in *Birse Construction Ltd v. St David Ltd (No. 1)* [2000] B.L.R. 57 & [1999] B.L.R. 194; *Al Naimi v. Islamic Press Agency* [2000] 1 Lloyd's Rep. 522; *Shin-Etsu Chemical Co. v. Aksh Optifibre* (2005) SCC 234 (Indian Supreme Court, including an analysis of different approaches in various jurisdictions worldwide).

with respect to the types of procedural measures it might impose, in order to safeguard the overall arbitral process and the parties' expectations. This, in turn, allows for creativity on the part of the arbitral tribunal.

Equally, as a practical matter, this second basis is safer, since it does not depend upon the "*prima facie*" approach to arbitral jurisdiction being adopted by the national courts in question.

Gaillard's second basis may also be justified by a further argument. It is well settled that when a domestic court acts, it acts as an organ of the State for whose actions that State is internationally responsible. As Judge Schwebel has explained, when a domestic court issues an injunction against an international arbitration, it acts in breach of the letter and spirit of the New York Convention 1958, as well as in violation of customary international law (denial of justice to an alien). Its acts might also amount to an arbitrary or tortuous confiscation of an alien's contractual rights.[20] There is now a developing body of jurisprudence that international arbitral tribunals may properly disregard such international law violations, and continue, notwithstanding restraining orders.[21] If an international arbitral tribunal can or indeed should disregard an anti-arbitration injunction rendered by a national court, it is only a small step in the analysis to say that such a tribunal ought also to be able to take proactive measures to protect itself and its process against such interference. Further, such measures (to stop or limit the interference of parallel proceedings) ought to be available even where no anti-arbitration injunction has actually been ordered, since the very existence of parallel proceedings will often effectively undermine the integrity of the arbitral process, and thereby violate international norms.

On this theory, arbitral tribunals ought to be free to implement measures to protect their own jurisdiction and the arbitral process, including restraining a party from proceeding before a national court, as part of their overall procedural powers and discretion.

As Joseph notes in his extremely valuable analysis,[22] there is high authority for the proposition that any international tribunal possesses an inherent jurisdiction to make such orders as are necessary to ensure the orderly and enforceable disposal of disputes over which it has jurisdiction,[23] and the principle underlying the grant of interim measures of protection has been described as a "general principle of law" within the meaning of Art. 38(1)(c) of the Statute of the International Court of Justice.

---

20. Judge Stephen SCHWEBEL, "Anti-Suit Injunctions in International Arbitration, An Overview", in Emanuel GAILLARD (ed.). *Op. cit.*, fn. 1, at pp. 9-10.
21. See e.g., F.A. MANN, "The Consequences of an International Wrong in International and National Law", 48 British Yearbook of International Law (1976-1977) 1 at p. 46; *Salini v. Ethiopia*, ICC Arbitration No. 10623/AER/ACS (Award of 7 December 2001) (Gaillard; Bernadini; Bunni) ASA Bulletin (2003, no. 1) at p. 59.
22. *Op. cit.*, fn. 2, at pp. 308-9.
23. Joseph cites, inter alia: *Nuclear Tests Case (Australia v. France)* 1974 I.C.J. 253, 259-260; *Case Concerning the Northern Cameroons (Cameroons v. UK) (Preliminary Objection)* 1963 I.C.J. 97, 103; *Anglo Iranian Oil Company Case (UK v. Iran)* 1951 I.C.J. 89, 93; *Electricity Company of Sofia v. Bulgaria*, 1939 P.C.I.J., series a/B, no. 79 at 199; COLLINS, "Provisional and Protective Measures in International Litigation", in *Essays in International Litigation and the Conflict of Laws*, pp 169-170.

Seen in this light, and given the totally different nature of a national court's standing and authority as compared to that of an international arbitral tribunal, the example of "anti-suit injunctions" issued by national court judges is of very limited assistance.

IV.   DELIMITING THE PROPER AMBIT OF SUCH MEASURES

Once one has swept away the "cobwebs" of national court practice, and focused upon the true nature of the measures in question, there remains the key question: When a party is pursuing its claim before a national court or other forum, in violation of the arbitration agreement, when is it appropriate for arbitral tribunals to grant relief to protect their own jurisdiction and process?

And it is here where more courage on the part of arbitrators is urged.

1.   The Paradigm Case

There is an increasingly important category of case where such measures are absolutely vital, and where nothing less will do. In this type of case, interim measures constitute, in effect, "lifelines", without which the entire arbitral process may be defeated. This category, it is suggested, defines the paradigm case, and is a useful starting point. Its components are as follows:

(a) A cross-border transaction, often (though not necessarily) of substantial size and complexity, and of political or economic sensitivity (such as a power plant or similar foreign investment).

(b) A choice of international arbitration primarily motivated by a desire to avoid an inexperienced/unreliable/inefficient/partial/pliable/hostile/local court – particularly if the transaction in question is the subject of local politics.

(c) A defendant who nevertheless approaches the local court, in breach of the arbitration agreement, and seeks an anti-arbitration injunction or some other interference with the arbitral process, or commences a challenge procedure.

(d) At least one of the participants in the arbitration being an entity subject to the jurisdiction of the local court in question (e.g., a local investment vehicle), such that it will be bound by any order of the local court, and such that the remedy of ignoring such a court order (e.g., as in *Salini v. Ethiopia* [24]) is of no assistance.

Wherever all of these components are present, an anti-arbitration injunction, or other interference by a local court – unless restrained – is likely to defeat the entire arbitration. As long as one of the parties is subject to the local court's jurisdiction (as is so often the case in foreign investment), it will have no choice but to engage with the national court process, and comply with the result (to avoid a contempt). Where the stakes are high, recalcitrant parties may deploy any number of tactics to shift the focus of the dispute away from the arbitration and into the court of their choosing. In such

---

24. *Op. cit.*, fn. 21.

cases, the award of damages by the arbitral tribunal for breach of the arbitration agreement is a wholly inadequate remedy. If the arbitration is defeated, the losses may be vast, and simply not compensable by damages. Indeed, the entire project may be threatened. An award of damages may never be enforced (particularly if the local court has justified its own intervention). Further, the impact of the local court process will rarely be quantifiable in damages in any event. Procedural safeguards, such as confidentiality, may have been lost; sensitive documents may have been ordered to be produced; individuals may have been subjected to local pressures; and the politics (and so economics) of the project may have been forever changed.

In such cases, it is also no answer to expect the local court to comply with its New York Convention obligations, or for the arbitral tribunal to proceed on the basis of respect and trust for a national judiciary – for the weaknesses of the local court system were precisely the reason why the arbitral tribunal was constituted in the first place.

With this combination of factors, the arbitral tribunal may be the one and only available source of help. Indeed, this is precisely the type of help for which the parties will have contracted in choosing international arbitration. An application for a measure to restrain a party from proceeding before the local court is, in effect, a plea for a final "lifeline" – and a refusal by the arbitral tribunal to throw it is then a dereliction of duty, which may compromise the whole arbitral process.

There are many – too many – recent examples of this paradigm case. By way of illustration, one may focus on one case in particular: *The Hub Power Company Ltd v. WAPDA*,[25] a widely reported major foreign investment in Pakistan, involving the construction and operation of one of the world's largest electricity-generating plants, located on the Hub river estuary. As required by local regulations, the foreign investors operated through a vehicle incorporated locally in Pakistan (Hubco). In August 1992, a Power Purchase Agreement (PPA) was concluded between Hubco and the Governmental entity responsible for water and power (WAPDA). The project was hugely significant in Pakistan in terms of both economics and politics. A Sovereign Guarantee was executed on behalf of the President of the Islamic Republic of Pakistan guaranteeing (inter alia) WAPDA's obligations under the PPA. Further guarantees were provided by the World Bank and other co-financiers. Perhaps unsurprisingly, the foreign investors insisted upon an arbitration agreement in the PPA, and the parties agreed to ICC arbitration in London, with a choice of English governing law.

In the years following signature of the PPA, a number of amending agreements were concluded between the parties, which coincided with a number of different governments that came and went. In 1994, during the term of office of Benazir Bhutto, one such amendment (Amendment No. 2) markedly increased the tariff for electricity payable by WAPDA to Hubco. This gave rise to a political storm locally, with widespread disquiet

---

25. *The Hub Power Company Ltd v. (1) WAPDA &(2) The Federation of Pakistan* Judgment of the Supreme Court of Pakistan, 14 June 2000 (Civil Appeal No. 1398 and 1399 of 1999) [2000] 16 *Arbitration International* 431; 15 Mealey's International Arbitration Report (2000, no. 7) at Sect. A.1 This case is cited because it is now very well known, and serves as a good illustration of the paradigm case. It should be noted, however, that the author acted as counsel. The description here draws only from materials in the public domain, and seeks to present an objective account.

at the cost of electricity, and doubts as to the justification for the whole project. On 5 November 1996, Bhutto was dismissed as Prime Minister, and a new government was elected in February 1997, with Nawaz Sharif as Prime Minister.

The tariff issue as between Hubco and WAPDA maintained an extremely important political dimension, with almost daily reporting in the Pakistan press. Hubco asserted its rights to receive the increased tariff. On 8 May 1998, a public interest Writ Petition was filed by an individual petitioner in the Lahore High Court in Pakistan, joining Hubco and WAPDA, challenging WAPDA's decision to enter into Amendment No. 2. It was alleged that Hubco had colluded with WAPDA and the then government in fixing what was described as an exorbitant tariff, and that the amendment was the product of bribes, kickbacks and other corrupt practices. During the course of these proceedings, WAPDA allied itself with the position of the Petitioner, seeking to avoid Amendment No. 2 – but *not* the underlying PPA containing the arbitration agreement – on the grounds that it was "illegal, fraudulent, collusive, without consideration, mala fide and designed to cause wrongful loss to WAPDA and the Government of Pakistan".

On 9 July 1998, Hubco referred this dispute to arbitration in accordance with the ICC Rules, and the provisions of the PPA. Both Hubco *and* WAPDA paid substantial advances on costs and nominated arbitrators, and the ICC duly constituted a Tribunal. On 16 January 1999, WAPDA filed a suit before the Senior Civil Judge in Lahore for an ex parte application that Hubco be permanently restrained from proceeding any further with the ICC proceedings. One of the primary grounds advanced was that the issue in dispute (allegations of bribery and corruption) was not arbitrable in an ICC proceeding in London, since it raised fundamental issues of public policy. The injunction was granted. Since Hubco is a Pakistan company, it was bound thereby.

There followed a large number of appeals and other court proceedings concerning this injunction, culminating in a month's argument before five judges in the Supreme Court of Pakistan in April 2000. Meanwhile, various members of the Hubco Board of Directors were the subject of preliminary criminal investigations, and were prevented from leaving the country by being placed on the Exit Control List (although no criminal charges were ever brought). By the time of the Supreme Court hearing, the Pakistan military had taken over the government. Ultimately, the Supreme Court upheld the injunction. Thereafter, Hubco was forced to pursue its claims in the domestic courts of Pakistan, and the ICC arbitration was rendered defunct.

In India, almost exactly the same scenario was replicated in the long-running dispute between Dabhol and the Government of Maharashtra/Government of India.[26] In that case, the parties had contracted for UNCIITRAL arbitration in London, yet the focus of the dispute soon shifted to the Indian courts, with multiple anti-arbitration injunctions, and challenge proceedings in India (both pre- and post- the 1996 Indian Arbitration and Conciliation Act), all of which ultimately bound the Claimant (Dabhol

---

26. For related aspects of this dispute, see the OPIC claim between GE/Bechtel (available at: <www.opic.gov/FOIA/Awards/2294171_1.pdf>) and the US Govt Claims under an Investment Incentive Agreement, 1997 (available at <www.opic.gov/foia/awards/GOI110804.pdf>). Again, by way of caution, it should be noted that the author acted as counsel in this dispute.

Power Company), it being a locally incorporated investment vehicle. Ultimately, every UNCITRAL arbitration that was commenced was ended prematurely by the action of the Indian Courts, and recourse was then sought under a Bilateral Investment Treaty.

The examples may be multiplied, and drawn from many areas of the World. All, however, share the same basic features.

The *Hubco* and *Dabhol* type of case is the classic instance in which an arbitral tribunal should do all that it can to protect its own process, and the parties' expectations. Interestingly, in each of these cases, applications were made to each of the arbitral tribunals for injunctions to restrain the commencement or continuation of actions in, respectively, Pakistan and India. And yet in each case, these applications were refused. Without embarking on a critique of each of the arbitral tribunal's reasoning, it is instructive to note that in each case, concerns were expressed (a) as to the power of an arbitral tribunal to grant such relief; (b) as to the possible adverse impact such an order might have in each country; and (c) as to the enforceability, and thus utility, of such orders.

Issue (a) has now been laid to rest by Emmanuel Gaillard's Report.

As to issues (b) and (c), experience shows that in many such cases, some form of restraint issued by an arbitral tribunal can be of immense help – even if it is not enforceable in terms.[27] It can counter arguments before local courts that the international arbitration is an ineffective forum, or that the arbitration can be disregarded without any difficulty. It can be a source of influence and deterrence on local judges. It can be a source of education for local courts on the norms of international arbitration. It can attract international and political attention. It can also act as a deterrent on the offending party, for in many such cases, that party will still pause before breaching an international arbitral tribunal's order. Given the range of possible measures, any adverse impact locally can be minimized by the way the order, or recommendation, is crafted.

Further, in many cases, such measures are the only option left, before the arbitration grinds to a halt.

Overall, such cases often involve a delicate but critical local situation, of which the arbitral tribunal may not be fully aware, or best placed to judge. If a claimant comes to an arbitral tribunal with a plea for such an order, then it should not be regarded as an exceptional measure, but rather a lifeline that, absent special circumstances, ought to be thrown. This, after all, is simply to provide one of the specific protections for which international arbitration was chosen in the first place. This, it is suggested, is a powerful ground to counter those that caution against the use of such measures.

---

27. In contrast to *Hubco*, mention may be made here of *SGS v. Pakistan* (2002) – the well known ICSID case arising out of a Swiss-Pakistan BIT. In that case, an anti-arbitration injunction was sought by the Government of Pakistan, and issued by the Pakistan Supreme Court. Subsequently, however, the ICSID Tribunal recommended interim measures to protect its own jurisdiction and process. Ultimately, the Pakistan Government decided to participate in the arbitration, rather than the Pakistan Courts.

2. Other Cases

Stepping away from the paradigm case, there exists a spectrum of situations, ranging all the way to those instances where an action before a local court is of no significance to the arbitration.

For example, no party may be technically bound by a local court action, and yet there may still be an adverse impact on the arbitration by virtue of the cost and distraction of a parallel proceeding, or the risk of inconsistent results. Alternatively, a local court may not be hostile or unreliable, but perfectly trustworthy, supportive, and efficient.

With each step further away from the paradigm case, there are likely to be less compelling reasons to issue such orders. However, the approach in each case should be flexible, pragmatic – and robust. Measures ought to be carefully crafted and imposed whenever there is a need to insulate the arbitral process from any adverse impact, or to safeguard the expectations of the parties.

In this way, international arbitration may continue as a viable and effective form of dispute resolution, in the face of ever increasing, and ever more ingenious, attacks.

Working Group A

5. Applicable Law – Consensus or Confusion?

Re-examining the Arbitration Agreement:
Applicable Law – Consensus or Confusion?

*Klaus Peter Berger**

I. INTRODUCTION

Arbitration is essentially an agreement to establish "private justice", e.g., private dispute resolution by a private tribunal.[1] This is why it is generally recognized today that arbitration agreements have a hybrid nature, comprising both procedural and contractual elements.[2] Leaving aside special scenarios such as arbitration under investment protection treaties[3] or free trade agreements, every arbitration requires an agreement by the parties. The English Commercial Court has explained the contractual character of arbitration as follows:

---

* LL.M.; University of Cologne, Germany.

1. *E. I. Du Pont De Nemours and Co. v. Rhodia Fiber and Resin Intermediates SAS*, Int'l Arb. Rep. (June 2001) p. 13 at pp. 15 et seq. (US Court of Appeals for the 3rd Circuit): "Arbitration is fundamentally a creature of contract, characterized by consent. As a matter of contract law, no party should be forced to arbitrate its claims unless that party has agreed to do so"; see also Reinhold GEIMER, in Richard ZÖLLER (ed.), *Zivilprozessordnung*, 25th edn. (Otto Schmidt Verlag 2005) Vor Sect. 1025, no. 4: "... nobody may be deprived of the state court system against his will".

2. See Julian D.M. LEW, Loukas A. MISTELIS, Stefan M. KRÖLL, *Comparative International Commercial Arbitration* (Kluwer Law International 2003) no. 5-23:

   "In spite of their apparent diametrically opposed views, the jurisdictional and contractual theories can be reconciled. Arbitration requires and depends upon elements from *both* the jurisdictional and the contractual viewpoints; it contains elements of *both* private and public law; it has procedural *and* contractual features. It is not surprising that a *compromise theory*, claiming arbitration to have a mixed or hybrid character should have been developed."

   (Emphasis added).

3. See Torsten LÖRCHER, *Neue Verfahren der Internationalen Streiterledigung in Wirtschaftssachen* (Peter Lang Verlag 1999) pp. 173 et seq.

"An arbitration clause in a commercial contract like the present one is an agreement inside an agreement. The parties make their commercial bargain, i.e. exchange promises in relation to the subject matter of the transaction, but in addition agree on a private tribunal to resolve any issues that may arise between them."[4]

Given that the arbitration agreement is "the gateway to arbitration",[5] one is struck by surprise to hear that the determination of the law applicable to that agreement is "certainly a more complex task than determining the law governing the [main] contract" and that in spite of these alleged difficulties, parties who negotiate and draft an arbitration agreement do not agree on the law applicable to the arbitration agreement but rather "rely on the future arbitrators' wisdom".[6] Surprise changes into sheer horror when one hears that, in his comment to Julian Lew's Report on "The Law Applicable to the Form and Substance of the Arbitration Clause", presented to the ICCA Congress in May 1998 in Paris, which celebrated forty years of application of the New York Convention, Marc Blessing identified, as a starting point for his analysis, no less than nine different potential conflict rules for determining the law applicable to the arbitration agreement.

Given that there is also the law applicable to the parties' capacity to conclude the arbitration agreement,[7] the law applicable to the arbitral procedure (*lex loci arbitri*), the law applicable to the arbitrator's contract (*receptum arbitri*),[8] the law applicable to the contract between the parties and the administering institution and the law applicable to the substance of the dispute,[9] one would be faced with fourteen conflict of laws issues in international arbitration. In light of this myriad of legal theories, Marc Blessing rightly asked the question: "Are we thus faced with a magnificent confusion?"[10]

Eight years later, this Report undertakes a fresh attempt to find out whether confusion still prevails or whether international doctrine and arbitration practice have finally reached a consensus on how to deal with applicable law issues related to an international agreement to arbitrate.

---

4. *Union of India v. McDonnell Douglas Corp.*, (1993) 2 Lloyd's L. Rep. 48, 50.
5. Thomas E. CARBONNEAU, *Cases and Materials on the Law and Practice of Arbitration*, 3rd edn. (Thomson-West 2005) p. 17.
6. Piero BERNARDINI, "Arbitration Clauses: Achieving Effectiveness in the Law Applicable to the Arbitration Clause" in *Improving the Efficiency of Arbitration Agreements and Awards, 40 Years of Application of the New York Convention*, ICCA Congress Series no. 9 (1999) (hereinafter *ICCA Congress Series no. 9*) pp. 197 and 199; see also Pierre LALIVE, Jean-Francois POUDRET, Claude REYMOND, *Le Droit de L'Arbitrage. Interne et International en Suisse* (Editions Payot 1989) Art. 178, no. 14 in fine.
7. See infra V.
8. See Klaus Peter BERGER, *International Economic Arbitration* (Kluwer 1993) p. 232.
9. See Alan REDFERN and Martin HUNTER, *Law and Practice of International Commercial Arbitration*, 4th edn. (Sweet & Maxwell 2004) no. 2-86.
10. Marc BLESSING, "The Law Applicable to the Arbitration Clause and Arbitrability" in *ICCA Congress Series no. 9*, p. 168 at pp. 169 et seq.

II. BASIC DISTINCTIONS

A major reason for the confusion which has prevailed over the past years in the area of the law applicable to the arbitration agreement stems from the fact that very often, basic distinctions between essential issues and elements relating to the validity of arbitration agreements are neglected, misunderstood or not distinctly perceived by arbitral tribunals.[11] In particular, there are various, often closely related factors which might affect the existence and validity of the arbitration agreement, all of which may be submitted to different laws.[12] Neglecting these vital distinctions has caused misleading and unproductive discussions creating more uncertainty instead of less confusion.

1. Form vs. Substance

A first and essential distinction relates to the difference between substance and form.[13] The former relates to the question whether there was a valid meeting of the minds of the parties with respect to dispute settlement through arbitration. The latter concerns special formal validity rules established to ensure that the parties are aware that by concluding the arbitration agreement, they oust the jurisdiction of the otherwise competent state courts. There is a hierarchy between both issues. The formal validity comes into play only if and to the extent that the parties have reached an agreement to arbitrate. As in general conflict of laws theory,[14] formal and substantive validity are subject to different conflict of laws approaches. This can, but must not necessarily mean that both issues are governed by different laws. Even though the distinction seems to be obvious and clear, state courts have sometimes not differentiated between the formal validity requirements governed by the New York Convention and the substantive validity requirements governed by domestic law, and have applied the latter to both requirements.[15]

There may also be other issues in dispute between the parties which relate to the validity of the arbitration agreement. Thus, the parties' capacity to arbitrate, sometimes called "subject arbitrability", may be in question. Also, a party's authority to represent another party in the conclusion of the arbitration agreement may be disputed. Finally, one party may challenge the objective "arbitrability" of all or certain claims that are in dispute. All these issues can be governed by different laws.

---

11. Horacio A. GRIGERA-NAÓN, "Choice-of-law Problems in International Commercial Arbitration", 289 Rec. Cours (2001), p. 13 at p. 41.

12. Julian D.M. LEW, Loukas A. MISTELIS, Stefan M. KRÖLL, *op. cit.*, fn. 2, no. 6-26.

13. See Julian D.M. LEW, "The Law Applicable to the Form and Substance of the Arbitration Clause" in *ICCA Congress Series no. 9*, p. 119.

14. See Arts. 3 et seq. and Art. 8 (substantive validity) and Art. 9 (formal validity) Rome Convention on the Law Applicable to Contractual Obligations.

15. See, e.g., Swiss Federal Tribunal, *Compagnie de Navigation de Transports SA v. MSC Mediterranean Shipping Company SA*, BGE 121 III 38; Italian Supreme Court in *Conceria G De Maio & F snc (Italy) v. EMAG AG (Switzerland)*, ICCA Yearbook Commercial Arbitration XXI (1996) (hereinafter *Yearbook*) p. 602; UN Doc. A/CN.9/WG.II/WP.139 (14 December 2005) pp. 18 et seq.

In any event, it would be wrong to say that we are dealing with "the *law*" applicable to the arbitration agreement. The above considerations as well as the following observations show that we are searching for "the laws" applicable to that agreement.

2. Arbitrability vs. / and Validity of the Arbitration Agreement

The arbitration agreement forms the basis of the tribunal's jurisdiction. American courts and legal doctrine are using the sweeping term "arbitrability" to cover all issues of jurisdiction. This term, however, can mean different things.[16] In Europe, its meaning is limited to "subject matter arbitrability". Subject matter arbitrability determines those types of issues which can or cannot be submitted to dispute settlement by arbitration.[17] If the subject matter of the dispute is non-arbitrable, the arbitration agreement is invalid and the tribunal has no jurisdiction to decide the dispute even if both parties want this.[18] The arbitrability issue, therefore, resolves the conflict between public policy and party autonomy.[19] However, American courts and legal doctrine extend this concept beyond the ambit of public policy to cover the validity (i.e., existence) and scope of the arbitration agreement ("contractual arbitrability"). From a conflict of laws perspective, this extended view is problematic because subject matter arbitrability and contractual arbitrability are subject to completely different conflict of laws approaches.

Today, all modern arbitration laws contain substantive rules of private international law which govern the subject matter arbitrability of claims that are in dispute in arbitrations which have their seat in that jurisdiction. Art. 177 Swiss Statute on Private International Law,[20] Sect. 1030(1) German Arbitration Act,[21] Sect. 1020(3) Dutch

---

16. See William W. PARK, "The Arbitrability Dicta in *First Options v. Kaplan*: What Sort of Kompetenz-Kompetenz Has Crossed the Atlantic?", 16 Arb. Int'l (1996) p. 137 at pp. 144 et seq.; Alan S. RAU, "The Culture of American Arbitration and the Lessons of ADR", 40 Texas Int'l L.J. (2005) p. 449 at p. 462 footnote 64: "Arbitrability is of course a much-abused and much-litigated concept ... I don't think we would lose much, though, if we were simply to refrain from using this and other 'unnecessary' and incoherent formulations."

17. Thomas E. CARBONNEAU, *op. cit.*, fn. 5, p. 17.

18. See for Swiss law Christoph MÜLLER, *International Arbitration – A Guide to the Complete Swiss Case Law (Unreported and Reported)* (Schulthess 2004) p. 19 with reference to the case law of the Swiss Federal Tribunal.

19. Julian D.M. LEW, Loukas A. MISTELIS, Stefan M. KRÖLL, *op. cit.*, fn. 2, no. 9-1 quoting Carbonneau and Janson who have stated that arbitrability "determines the point where the exercise of contractual freedom ends and the public mission of adjudication begins".

20. Art. 177(1) provides: "Any dispute involving an economic interest may be the subject matter of an arbitration."

21. Sect. 1030(1) German Arbitration Act provides that "any claim involving an economic interest (*vermögensrechtlicher Anspruch*) can be the subject of an arbitration agreement. An arbitration agreement concerning claims not involving an economic interest shall have legal effect to the extent that the parties are entitled to conclude a settlement on the issue in dispute."

Arbitration Act[22] or Sect. 1(1) Swedish Arbitration Act[23] contains such "*règles materielles*". These mandatory rules replace classical conflict of laws analysis. Due to the territoriality principle,[24] these substantive rules apply as soon as the seat of the arbitration is fixed in that country. The seat serves as the connecting factor for these rules when the question is to be determined by the tribunal itself. However, when this issue is to be determined by a court in a country other than that where the arbitration had its seat, e.g., in recognition and enforcement proceedings, that court will determine that issue according to its own law. This approach is confirmed by Art. V(2)(*a*) New York Convention and Art. 36(1)(b)(i) UNCITRAL Model Law on International Commercial Arbitration which provide that recognition and enforcement of the award may be refused if the subject matter of the dispute is not arbitrable under the law of the state where enforcement is sought. Thus, the legal determination of the objective arbitrability of the subject matter of the arbitration is only relative, i.e., limited to the viewpoint of the forum whose rules are applied. The significance of this problem is substantially reduced due to the worldwide trend in favor of arbitrability which has begun with the *Mitsubishi* decision of the US Supreme Court.[25]

The substantive validity of the arbitration agreement, i.e., the contractual arbitrability, however, is governed by the choice of law principles to be elaborated below.[26] Again, in spite of these different approaches both subject matter and contractual arbitrability may be governed by the same law. One must be aware of the fact that such a result does not follow from a uniform conflict of laws principle and that both kinds have to be distinguished from each other in terms of conflicts of laws methodology.

3.   *Arbitral Tribunals vs. Courts*

An often overlooked but vital distinction is that the issue of the existence and validity of the arbitration agreement may arise in different fora and at different stages of the proceedings.[27] A basic distinction must be made in this respect between arbitral tribunals and state courts.

Arbitral tribunals must determine the law applicable to the arbitration agreement whenever they have to ascertain the basis of their own jurisdiction. They are allowed to

---

22. Sect. 1020(3) Dutch Arbitration Act provides that the "arbitration agreement shall not serve to determine legal consequences of which the parties cannot freely dispose".
23. Sect. 1(1) provides that all disputes are arbitrable that "concern matters in respect of which the parties may reach a settlement".
24. See, e.g., Art. 1(2) Model Law which provides that "[t]he provisions of this Law, except articles 8, 9, 35 and 36, apply only if the place of arbitration is in the territory of this State".
25. *Mitsubishi Motors Corp. v. Soler Chrysler Plymouth Inc.*, 473 US 614 (1985); see generally L. Yves FORTIER, "Arbitrability of Disputes" in *Global Reflections on International Law, Commerce and Dispute Resolution; Liber Amicorum in honour of Robert Briner* (ICC Publishing 2005) p. 269 at p. 284. "Indeed, in the vast majority of cases, it could be said that arbitrability has become a 'non-issue'."
26. See infra III.
27. Julian D.M. LEW, Loukas A. MISTELIS, Stefan M. KRÖLL, *op. cit.*, fn. 2, no. 6-26.

do this under the generally accepted principle of *Kompetenz-Kompetenz*.[28] Such an examination of the existence, validity or scope of the arbitration agreement under the law applicable to it is required if one party challenges the jurisdiction of the tribunal for all or certain claims submitted to it or if one party requests arbitral interim relief which, as an annex to the tribunal's decision-making power,[29] requires the validity of the arbitration agreement as the basis of the tribunal's jurisdiction. However, the arbitral tribunal has no lex fori.[30] This means that the tribunal is under no legal obligation to have resort to the conflict of laws rules at the seat of the arbitration to determine the law applicable to the arbitration agreement. Due to the territoriality principle, arbitral tribunals are under an obligation to apply the arbitration law at the seat of the arbitration. However, only very few of these arbitration laws contain specific conflict rules for the determination of the law applicable to the arbitration agreement *by the arbitral tribunal*, the Swedish Act being a notable exception to this rule. Those conflict rules that deal with this issue are concerned with the determination of the applicable law *by the courts* in setting aside[31] and enforcement[32] proceedings.

Therefore, the tribunal must develop its own conflict rule(s) in order to determine the law applicable to the arbitration agreement. This, of course, entails the tribunal's right to draw inspiration from the conflict laws of domestic laws, including those in force at the seat of the arbitration, and from international uniform law instruments such as the New York Convention and the UNCITRAL Model Law.

The situation is different when the law applicable to the arbitration agreement is to be determined by state courts. This may be the case if a party is sued before a state court and invokes the existence of an arbitration agreement, if a party seeks interim relief or other measures of assistance from a state court under the applicable arbitration law in force at the seat of the arbitration or in another jurisdiction or in the post-award stage, if the losing party seeks to have the award set aside by the courts at the seat of the arbitration for lack of a valid arbitration agreement[33] or if the winning party seeks to have the award enforced at the seat of the arbitration[34] or in another jurisdiction.[35] Under German arbitration law, a German court may also have to determine the law applicable to the arbitration agreement if one party seeks a declaration as to the

---

28. See Art. 16 Model Law; Klaus Peter BERGER, *Private Dispute Resolution in International Business* (Kluwer Law International 2006) Vol. II (Handbook), no. 20-22 et seq.; *Sole Arbitrator Dupuy in Texaco Overseas Petroleum Co & California Asiatic Oil Co. (TOPCO) v. The Government of the Libyan Arab Republic*, Int'l L. Rep. (1979) 389, 405; see also *Christopher Brown v. Genossenschaft Österreichischer Waldbesitzer*, 1 Q.B. 8, 12 (1984); Court of Appeal of Bermuda, *Sojuznefteexport (SNE) (USSR) v. Joc Oil, Ltd.*, Yearbook XV (1990), pp. 384, 389.

29. Klaus Peter BERGER, *op. cit.*, fn. 28, Vol. II (Handbook), no. 20-22 et seq.

30. Alan REDFERN and Martin HUNTER, *op. cit.*, fn. 9, no. 2-80.

31. See Art. 34 Model Law; Sect. 1059 German Arbitration Act.

32. Art. 36 Model Law; Sect. 1060 German Arbitration Act.

33. Klaus Peter BERGER, *op. cit.*, fn. 8, p. 663.

34. Art. 35 Model Law, Sect. 1060 et seq. German Arbitration Act.

35. Art. 5 New York Convention on the Recognition and Enforcement of Foreign Arbitral Awards.

admissibility or non-admissibility of the arbitration proceedings prior to the constitution of the arbitral tribunal under Sect. 1032(2) German Arbitration Act.[36]

There are two major differences in these state court scenarios when compared with the determination of the law applicable to the arbitration agreement by arbitral tribunals. First, unlike arbitral tribunals,[37] state courts have a lex fori and they must apply the conflict of laws rules of that lex fori. This may lead to a forum-shopping effect, meaning that different laws are applied to the same arbitration agreement in different jurisdictions. Secondly, to avoid these forum shopping effects, state courts are under an obligation to apply conflict of laws rules contained in international uniform law instruments. The two most important instruments are the New York Convention and the 1961 European Convention. Both contain conflict of laws rules related to the law that determines the substantive validity of the arbitration agreement and formal validity rules in the form of directly applicable *règles materielles*.

4. Domestic Laws vs. International Uniform Laws

What has been said above about the determination of the law applicable to the arbitration agreement leads us directly to another distinction which has contributed a lot to the confusion in this area: the complex interplay between domestic laws and international uniform instruments. Given the freedom of international arbitrators in choice of law issues, it seems to be an open question which law a tribunal should apply to the formal or substantive validity of the arbitration agreement. Or should it apply the conflict rules or formal validity rules of the New York Convention even though the scope of this Convention is restricted to proceedings before state courts on the enforcement of arbitration agreements and foreign awards? A state court, on the other hand, can apply international uniform law in lieu of its own domestic law only if the state in which it sits has ratified the instrument and the problem with which the court is concerned in a given case falls within the scope of the instrument. Unfortunately, the latter question is not always clear. The European Convention defines its scope in a clear and unambiguous way. Art. I(1)(a) provides that the Convention applies to arbitration agreements concluded for the purpose of settling disputes arising from international trade between physical or legal persons having, when concluding the agreement, their habitual place of residence or their seat in different contracting states. Due to the drafting history of the New York Convention, there is no such clear rule with respect to the formal validity rule of Art. II New York Convention. However, it is generally recognized today that this rule applies whenever the arbitration agreement will probably lead to an award covered by the New York Convention pursuant to its Art. I, i.e., where the award will be made in a different contracting state irrespective of the country where the parties are resident.[38] Another source of confusion is the fact that the conflict

---

36. Sect. 1032(2) of the German Arbitration Act provides: "Prior to the constitution of the arbitral tribunal, an application may be made to the court to determine whether or not arbitration is admissible."

37. See supra text at fn. 30.

38. Julian D.M. LEW, Loukas A. MISTELIS, Stefan M. KRÖLL, fn. 2, no. 6-35.

rule related to the substantive validity of the arbitration agreement which is contained in Art. V(1)(a) New York Convention is concerned only with the enforcement of foreign arbitral awards, i.e., with the post-award stage. The same is true for conflict rules contained in domestic laws such as Arts. 34 and 36 UNCITRAL Model Law which deal only with the setting aside and the enforcement of awards. If a court has to determine the law applicable to the arbitration agreement in the pre-award phase, e.g., when determining the admissibility of the arbitration pursuant to Sect. 1031(2) German Arbitration Act, can it apply these conflict rules?

5.   *Submission Agreements vs. Arbitration Clauses*

Pursuant to Art. 7(1) UNCITRAL Model Law, Sect. 1029(2) German Arbitration Act and the provisions in most arbitration laws around the world, an arbitration agreement may be in the form of a separate agreement (separate arbitration agreement) or in the form of a clause in a contract (arbitration clause). A separate arbitration agreement may deal with future disputes arising out of a contract to which it is attached. However, it may also deal with an existing dispute which it submits to arbitration instead of dispute resolution before domestic courts. For these "submission agreements",[39] the qualification attached to them by the English Commercial Court quoted in the Introduction[40] – "an agreement inside an agreement" – does not apply. The submission agreement is a freestanding contract. This has important repercussions on conflict of laws analysis. It is a much debated question whether the law applicable to the main contract also applies to the arbitration clause contained therein.[41] For submission agreements, this question cannot arise. Typically, this contract contains nothing more than the arbitration agreement itself and a choice of law clause contained therein necessarily governs that agreement:

> "Where the agreement to arbitrate is set out in a specially drawn submission agreement, the parties should choose a law to govern that agreement and should set out their choice in an appropriate clause. This is what the parties would normally do in any other kind of international agreement; and in this respect a submission agreement is no different. If no express choice of law is made, and a question arises as to the law governing the submission agreement, the general principles as to the choice of law will apply...."[42]

6.   *Territoriality vs. Transnationalism*

The eternal conflict between territoriality and transnationalism is not limited to the determination of the law applicable to the substance of the dispute where the doctrine of the "new lex mercatoria" has provoked strong reactions from those who favor a more

---

39. See generally Julian D.M. LEW, *op. cit.,* fn. 13, pp. 117 et seq.
40. See supra text at fn. 4.
41. See infra III.3.
42. Alan REDFERN and Martin HUNTER, *op. cit.,* fn. 9, no. 2-93.

traditional, positivistic approach to conflict of laws in international arbitration.[43] The same conflict between territoriality and transnationalism exists with respect to the determination of the law applicable to the substantive validity of the arbitration agreement. The transnational approach to the substantive validity of international arbitration agreements is a particularity of French legal doctrine. Rather than relying on a classical, and by its very nature territorial, conflict of laws approach, French courts have developed a substantive rule of international arbitration law pursuant to which the arbitration agreement is not only independent from the main contract but which also provides that, subject only to mandatory provisions of French law and the French international *ordre public*, the existence and validity of the arbitration agreement "depends only on the common intention of the parties, without it being necessary to make reference to a national law".[44] This transnational approach had already been adopted by a three-member arbitral tribunal in the famous *Isover Saint Gobain* interim award in which the tribunal, apparently influenced by French arbitration doctrine[45] and decisions of the French *Cour de cassation* going back to 1975,[46] held that the tribunal had:

> "determine[d] the scope and effect of the arbitration clause in question, and thereby reach[ed] its decision regarding jurisdiction, by reference to the common intent of the parties to these proceedings, such as it appears from the circumstances that surround the conclusion and characterize the performance and later the termination of the contracts in which they appear ... [To ensure the enforceability of the award in France, the tribunal] will assure itself that the solution it adopts is compatible with international public policy, in particular, in France."[47]

In his 1998 ICCA Report, Julian Lew maintained the view that "[i]n reality, courts, arbitrators and parties today recognize that the arbitration clause is governed by the common intention of the parties, general principles and usages of international business".[48] In his comment to Julian Lew's Report, Marc Blessing argued that since the "strictly academic approach", which favors a traditional conflict of laws analysis, has

---

43. See, e.g., Klaus Peter BERGER, *The Creeping Codification of the Lex Mercatoria* (Kluwer Law International 1999) p. 32.

44. French *Cour de cassation*, decision of 20 December 1993, *Comité populaire de la municipalité de Khoms El Mergeb v. Dalico Contractors*, Clunet (Journal du Droit International)1994, p. 432; see also *Cour de cassation*, decision of 21 May 1997, *Renault v. V 2000 (formerly Jaguar France)*, Rev. d'Arb. (1997) p. 537; Emmanuel GAILLARD and John SAVAGE, *Fouchard Gaillard Goldman on International Commercial Arbitration* (Kluwer Law International 1999) (hereinafter *Fouchard Gaillard Goldman*) no. 435 et seq.

45. One of the arbitrators was Professor Berthold Goldman from France, the conceptual father of the modern lex mercatoria doctrine (the other arbitrators were Professor Pieter Sanders from the Netherlands and Professor Vasseur from France).

46. Paris Court of Appeals in *Menicucci v. Mahieux*, Rev. d'Arb. (1977) p. 147.

47. ICC Interim Award no. 4131, *Dow Chemical France et al. v. Isover Saint Gobain*, Yearbook IX (1984) p. 131 at p. 134.

48. Julian D.M. LEW, *op. cit.*, fn. 13, p. 123.

produced unsatisfactory answers and results, international arbitrators should indeed "go back to the parties and take the most determinative guidance from the intentions which the parties have expressed (either explicitly or implicitly and by their behavior), taking into account their fair and reasonable expectations and the kind of usage which may exist between them".[49]

Such a transnational approach certainly has the beauty of avoiding the uncertainties and idiosyncrasies connected with the application of a multiplicity of connecting factors and resulting domestic laws to international arbitration agreements.[50] Such an approach is particularly relevant in international arbitration, where practice and doctrine have always strived to escape the pitfalls of domestic laws. However, there are two reasons why such a transnational approach should not be adopted in this context. First, a "reasonable contract interpretation" as the essential source of guidance for the determination of the validity of the arbitration agreement does not necessarily require the abandonment of traditional conflict of laws analysis. As we will see below,[51] the notion of *in favorem validitatis* as the guiding principle for the interpretation of international arbitration agreements is part of almost any developed legal system. The French approach may thus be characterized as an unnecessary exaggeration of transnationalism. Piero Bernardini's comment to Julian Lew's Report at the 1998 ICCA conference is still valid today:

> "The French rule, with its extreme liberalism, may bring about results going beyond parties' expectations in view of the wide discretion left to the arbitrator in determining the parties' common intent, considering also the absence of any requirement of form of the arbitration clause in case of international arbitration."[52]

Secondly and more importantly, the need to ensure the validity and enforceability of the award will usually prevent international arbitrators from "transnationalizing" the arbitration agreement from which they derive their jurisdiction. If the award is attacked in setting aside proceedings before the courts at the seat of the arbitration or in recognition and enforcement proceedings for lack of a valid arbitration agreement, these courts will determine the validity of the agreement pursuant to the conflict of laws rules of their lex fori, whether they are derived from autonomous domestic law or unified law. These conflict of laws rules are based on the traditional conflict of laws approach. A purely transnational character is read into these rules in only very few jurisdictions. France is the exception, not the rule. It was (only) due to this extremely liberal and transnational approach of French law to the validity of international arbitration agreements that the arbitral tribunal in the *Isover Saint Gobain* award[53] could apply

---

49. Marc BLESSING, *op. cit.*, fn.10, p. 174.
50. Piero BERNARDINI, *op. cit.*, fn. 6, p. 202; *Fouchard Gaillard Goldman, op. cit.*, fn. 44, no. 441.
51. See infra II.7.
52. Piero BERNARDINI, *op. cit.*, fn. 6, p. 202.
53. ICC Interim Award no. 4131, *Dow Chemical France et al. v. Isover Saint Gobain*, *Yearbook IX* (1984) p. 131 at p. 134.

transnational principles to the substantive validity of the arbitration agreement without risking the refusal of enforcement of the award in France.[54] Not surprisingly, a survey of arbitral case law reveals "how important still are more traditional or conservative approaches to the determination of choice-of-law issues concerning international commercial arbitration".[55]

Here lies the basic difference between the transnationalization of substantive law and of the law applicable to the arbitration agreement. With respect to the former, a conflict with a traditional, territorial attitude of the courts is unlikely given that the well-known prohibition of a "*révision au fond*" of the arbitral tribunal's substantive decision prevents a full-fledged scrutiny of the tribunal's conflict of laws decisions. With respect to the latter, there are no such limitations of the courts' powers to examine *en detail* the tribunal's conflict of laws decision relating to the arbitration agreement. It is for this reason that arbitral tribunals that determine their jurisdiction based on the will of the parties and general arbitration practice make sure that the law of the seat of the arbitration does not conflict with such solutions.[56]

This view has recently been confirmed by the English High Court in its *Peterson Farms* judgment of 4 February 2004. In the award that was before the court, the tribunal had argued that the law applicable to the arbitration agreement may differ from the law applicable to both the substance of the contract[57] and to the arbitral proceedings themselves, i.e., the law of the seat.[58] It then decided the question whether other group entities of the claimant[59] were bound by the arbitration agreement and whether claimant could claim (the vast majority) of the alleged damages on their behalf by interpreting the arbitration agreement according to the common intent of the parties, without referring to any domestic law. The court set aside that part of the award for want of jurisdiction and argued:

> "There was ... no basis for the tribunal to apply any other law whether supposedly derived from the 'common intent of the parties' or not. The common intent was indeed expressed in the Agreement: that is both English [as the law of the seat of the arbitration which did not know the group of companies doctrine] and Arkansas [as the law chosen by the parties in the choice of law clause contained in the contract which likewise did not know the group of companies doctrine] law...The 'law' the tribunal derived from its approach was not the proper law of

54. William L. CRAIG, William PARK, Jan PAULSSON, *International Chamber of Commerce Arbitration*, 3rd edn. (Oceana Publ. 2000) para. 5.05.

55. Horacio A. GRIGERA-NAÓN, *op. cit.*, fn. 11, p. 95.

56. *Ibid.*, p. 57.

57. This assumption was justified, see infra III.3.

58. This assumption was not justified, see infra III.2.

59. See for a survey on the group of companies doctrine S.P. WOOLHOUSE, "Group of Companies Doctrine and English Arbitration Law", 20 Arb. Int'l (2004) pp. 435-443.

the agreement nor even the law of the chosen place of arbitration but, in effect, the group of companies doctrine itself."[60]

It may well be that the tribunal's approach of effectively de-localizing the law applicable to the arbitration agreement may have given rise to difficulties in enforcing the award had it not been challenged under Sect. 67 English Arbitration Act 1996.[61]

It was for these reasons that Julian Lew, even though in favor of a transnational approach towards the determination of the substantive validity of the arbitration agreement,[62] had to conclude his 1998 ICCA Report by stating that "the application of national laws prevails in this field".[63] This view is even more valid today. It goes without saying that this does not prevent an arbitral tribunal from attaching more persuasive force to its decision on jurisdiction by arguing that the solution reached on the basis of domestic law is compatible with a-national legal rules or "international arbitral practice".[64]

7.   Conflict Analysis and the "In Favorem" Rule

In most modern jurisdictions it is generally acknowledged that the principle of "*in favorem validitatis*" must be applied to international arbitration agreements. This pro-arbitration approach serves to enforce the common intention of the parties to have their dispute decided before an international arbitral tribunal:

> "An agreement to arbitrate before a specified tribunal is, in effect, a specialized kind of forum-selection clause.... The invalidation of such an agreement ... would not only allow the respondent to repudiate its solemn promise but would, as well, reflect a parochial concept that all disputes must be resolved under our laws and in our courts."[65]

The *in favorem* approach to arbitration agreements is also a consequence of today's arbitration-friendly climate which is based on the understanding that dispute settlement by international arbitral tribunals has the same value and standing as adjudication before

---

60. *Peterson Farms Inc. v. C&M Farming Ltd.*, [2004] 1 Lloyd's L. Rep. 603, 610; see also John P. GAFFNEY, "The Law Applicable to the Arbitration Agreement", Int'l. Arb. Rep. (June 2004) p. 1 at pp. 5 et seq.; see also *Amin Shipping Corporation v. Kuwait Insurance Co.*, [1983] 2 Lloyd's L. Rep. 365, 371 where the court held that under English law an arbitration agreement, like any other contract, must be governed by some system of private law.

61. John P. GAFFNEY, *op. cit.*, fn. 60, p. 1 at p. 7.

62. See text at fn. 48.

63. Julian D.M. LEW, *op. cit.*, fn. 13, p. 145.

64. Horacio A. GRIGERA-NAÓN, *op. cit.*, fn. 11, p. 94 with reference to unpublished arbitral awards.

65. *Scherk v. Alberto-Culver Co.*, 417 U.S. 506, 519 (1974).

domestic courts.[66] International arbitrators, therefore, show a natural tendency to respect the common intention of the parties as expressed in their agreement to arbitrate and tend to adopt a very liberal "pro-arbitration" approach in order to make sure that the will of the parties to arbitrate their disputes is not frustrated.

> "The arbitrators have from the [arbitration] clause and the pleadings of the parties decided that both parties desire a settlement of disputes outside state jurisdiction. *That wish, expressed by both parties, has essentially determined the attitude of the arbitrators vis-à-vis the clause inserted into the contract. They felt an obligation to help the parties realize such a wish.*"[67]

This *in favorem* rule has two important effects.

First, an arbitration agreement should be construed in good faith[68] and in a way that upholds its validity.[69] Julian Lew argued in his Report to the 1998 ICCA Congress that "the validity of the arbitration clause is presumed".[70] Others argue that "doubts about the intended scope of an agreement to arbitrate are [to be] resolved in favor of arbitration".[71] This means that a liberal way of construing arbitration agreements has to be pursued even in those cases where in general contract law the ambiguity could not be resolved through the application of traditional means of interpretation. However, one must stress that the *in favorem* rule relates to the interpretation of the arbitration agreement which is the way to determine its substantive validity. It goes too far to argue that under this rule "the *formal* and substantive validity of the arbitration clause is presumed".[72]

Second, in determining the law applicable to the arbitration agreement, the tribunal should seek a solution that upholds the validity of the arbitration agreement. This approach is known as "*favor negotii*" in general conflict of laws theory.[73] This *in favorem* approach with respect to the determination of the law applicable to the arbitration

---

66. Julian D.M. LEW, Loukas A. MISTELIS, Stefan M. KRÖLL, *op. cit.*, fn. 2, no. 7-61 with reference to the "pro-arbitration bias" expressed in such landmark decisions as *Mitsubishi Motors Corp. v. Soler Chrysler Plymouth Inc.*, 473 U.S. 614 (1985).

67. *Yugoslav Co. v. PDR Korea Co.*, Arbitration Court attached to the Chamber for Foreign Trade of the GDR, *Yearbook* VIII (1983) p. 129 at p. 131 (emphasis added).

68. See Decision on Jurisdiction, *Amco Asia Corp. et al. v. Republic of Indonesia*, ILM (1984), pp. 351, 359 et seq.: "… any convention, including conventions to arbitrate, should be construed in good faith, that is to say by taking into account the consequences of their commitments the parties may be considered as having reasonably and legitimately envisaged".

69. Alan REDFERN and Martin HUNTER, *op. cit.*, fn. 9, no. 3-38; William L. CRAIG, William PARK, Jan PAULSSON, *op. cit.*, fn. 54, pp. 86 et seq.

70. Julian D.M. LEW, *op. cit.*, fn. 13, p. 123.

71. *Kaplan v. First Options of Chicago, Inc.*, 19 F.3d 1503, 1512 (3rd Cir. 1994); see also *Moses H. Cone Memorial Hosp. v. Mercury Constr. Corp.*, 460 U.S. 1, 24 (1983).

72. Julian D.M. LEW, *op. cit.*, fn. 13, p. 123.

73. See Principle no. XV.2 of the Transnational Law Database at <www.tldb.de>; see also ICC Award no. 4145, *Yearbook* XII (1987) p. 97 at p. 100; ICC Award no. 4996, Clunet (1986) p. 1132 at p. 1134.

agreement[74] has been adopted by the Swiss legislature in Art. 178(2) Swiss Federal Statute of Private International Law. An identical rule is contained in Sect. 458 *bis* 1(3) Algerian Code of Civil Procedure.[75] Art. 178(2) provides that:

> "As regards its substance, an arbitration agreement shall be valid if it conforms *either* to the law chosen by the parties, *or* the law governing the subject matter of the dispute, in particular the law governing the main contract, or if it conforms to Swiss law."

The idea of alternative application of different laws to the substantive validity of the arbitration agreement has also been employed in a similar vein and with express reference to the legal concept of *in favorem validitatis* in Art. 4 of the Santiago de Compostela Resolution of the Institut de Droit International:

> "Where the validity of the agreement to arbitrate is challenged, the tribunal shall resolve the issue by applying one or more of the following: the law chosen by the parties, the law indicated by the system of private international law stipulated by the parties, general principles of public or private international law, general principles of international arbitration, or the law that would be applied by the courts of the territory in which the tribunal has its seat. In making this selection, the tribunal shall be guided by the principle *in favorem validitatis*."[76]

While the drafters of the Swiss provision acknowledge that this alternative conflict rule implements the *in favorem validitatis* principle, they also emphasize that in all cases and whatever the law applicable to the arbitration agreement is, it must always also meet the formal validity requirements established in Art. 178(1) Swiss Federal Statute of Private International Law, which in their view means that in many cases, the absence of a written text as required by Art. 178(1) will prevent the enforcement of the arbitration agreement even under the extremely liberal conflict of laws rules of Swiss arbitration law.[77]

---

74. Julian D.M. LEW, *op. cit.*, fn. 13, p. 139: "The mere fact that the choice lies between two systems of law, under one of which the arbitration agreement would be invalid, has been considered as a factor in favor of choosing the other."

75. *Fouchard Gaillard Goldman, op. cit.*, fn. 44, no. 448.

76. Resolution *"L'arbitrage entre Etats et entreprises étrangères"*, adopted at the 18th Session in Santiago de Compostela, 4-14 September, 1989, (5) ICSID Rev–FILJ (1990) p. 139 at p. 141; in Art. 5 of its previous Amsterdam Resolution, the Institute had advocated the mandatory application of the law of the seat, see Institute of International Law Yearbook 47-II, pp. 479 et seq.

77. Pierre LALIVE, Jean-Francois POUDRET, Claude REYMOND, *op. cit.*, fn. 6, Art. 178, no. 14 and 16.

III. THE LAW APPLICABLE TO SUBSTANTIVE VALIDITY

1. The General Consensus

It seems that with respect to the determination of the law governing the substantive validity of the arbitration agreement, there is a gross discrepancy between the amount of doctrinal writings and the need for clarification. Far from the nine theories listed by Marc Blessing in his comment to Julian Lew's 1998 ICCA Report the conflict rule contained in Art. V(1)(*a*) New York Convention reflects the modern view of a single conflict of laws rule for the determination of the law applicable to the arbitration agreement. It provides that enforcement of the arbitral award may be refused if:

> "[the arbitration] agreement is not valid under the law to which the parties have subjected it or, failing any indication thereon, under the law of the country where the award was made".

Pursuant to Art. 31(3) UNCITRAL Model Law, "[t]he award shall be deemed to have been made at th[e] place [of arbitration]". Contrary to the alternative Swiss conflict rule,[78] this conflict rule establishes a hierarchy between party autonomy, to which it attaches primary importance, and the law of the place (seat) of arbitration, which applies in those cases where the parties have not chosen the law applicable to the arbitration agreement.

The rationale behind the application of the law of the seat of the arbitration is the closest-connection or center-of-gravity test which, in itself, is a generally accepted principle of conflict of laws.[79] It is widely acknowledged today that an agreement to arbitrate is more closely connected with the law of the seat of the arbitration as the place of performance of the arbitration agreement than with any other country.[80] The close functional connection between the arbitration agreement and the arbitral procedure, which is reinforced if the parties include detailed procedural stipulations in the agreement to arbitrate, should then also lead to the application of this law to the arbitration clause.[81]

Thus, the choice of the seat by the parties, or on their behalf by the arbitral institution or the arbitral tribunal, functions as an indirect choice of law not only for the law

---

78. See supra II.7.
79. See Principle no. XV.1 of the Transnational Law Database at <www.tldb.de>.
80. Alan REDFERN and Martin HUNTER, *op. cit.*, fn. 9, no. 2-90; Julian D.M. LEW, Loukas A. MISTELIS, Stefan M. KRÖLL, *op. cit.*, fn. 2, no. 6-61; Piero BERNARDINI, *op. cit.*, fn. 6, p. 201; Albert V. DICEY and John H.C. MORRIS, *Dicey and Morris on the Conflict of Laws*, 13th edn. (Sweet & Maxwell 2000) p. 598.
81. See Albert Jan VAN DEN BERG, *The New York Convention of 1958* (Kluwer 1981) p. 849; Bernd VON HOFFMANN, *Internationale Handelsschiedsgerichtsbarkeit* (Metzner 1970) pp. 60 et seq.; German Federal Supreme Court BGHZ 55, 162, 164; Klaus Peter BERGER, *op. cit.*, fn. 8, p. 159.

applicable to the arbitration procedure[82] but also for the law applicable to the substantive validity of the arbitration agreement, and, as we have seen above,[83] for the law that determines the arbitrability of the claims raised and the formal validity of that agreement. In fact, this approach has been taken by some older French court decisions.[84] While from a practical perspective, the significance of the seat of the arbitration is reduced to a mere "formal legal domicile" (*formales Legaldomizil*) of the arbitration,[85] its significance for choice of law issues related to the arbitral procedure and the arbitration agreement cannot be emphasized enough. Also, since we are dealing here with one single connecting factor for a variety of legal issues, the seat of the arbitration has an important harmonizing effect on applicable law issues in international commercial arbitration.[86]

2. The Transnational Conflict Rule

It is fair to say that today, the conflict rule contained in Art. V(1)(*a*) New York Convention, Art. VI (a) and (b) European Convention, in Arts. 34(2)(a)(i) and 36(1)(a)(i) UNCITRAL Model Law, Sect. 1059(2)1.a) and 1060(2) German Arbitration Act, Art. 1073 Dutch Arbitration Act, and Sect. 48 Swedish Arbitration Act has developed into a truly transnational conflict rule for the determination of the law governing the substantive validity of the arbitration agreement.[87] This rule has been applied in numerous international arbitral awards,[88] is favored by international arbitral

---

82. See Gabrielle KAUFMANN-KOHLER, "Globalization of Arbitral Procedure", 36 Vand. J. Transnat'l L. (2003), p. 1313 at p. 1319:

    "Choice of the seat indirectly effects a choice of the law governing the arbitral procedure.... Rather than directly choosing the law that governs the arbitration, the parties select a seat in a given state and the arbitration law of that state will apply, by operation of law [i.e., due to the territorial theory]. The choice of a seat results in an indirect choice of law";

    see also Noah RUBINS, "The Arbitral Seat Is No Fiction: A Brief Reply to Tatsuya Nakamura's Commentary, 'The Place of Arbitration in International Arbitration, its Fictitious Nature and Lex Arbitri'", Int'l Arb. Rep. (January 2001) pp. 23 et seq.

83. See supra II.2.

84. *Fouchard Gaillard Goldman*, *op. cit.*, fn. 44, no. 430.

85. Klaus LIONNET and Annette LIONNET, *Handbuch der internationalen und nationalen Schiedsgerichtsbarkeit*, 3rd edn. (Boorberg 2005) p. 160; see also Klaus Peter BERGER, "'*Sitz des Schiedsgerichts' oder 'Sitz des Schiedsverfahrens'?*", RIW (1993), p. 8 at p. 10; Klaus Peter BERGER, *op. cit.*, fn. 28, Vol. II (Handbook), no. 16-66.

86. Klaus Peter BERGER, *ibid.*, no. 20-46.

87. See the decision of the Dutch District Court of The Hague, *Yearbook* XIX (1994) p. 703, where the court stated that this rule "can be considered as a general rule of private international law as a result of the broad international influence of the [New York] Convention...".

88. ICC Award no. 4145 (First Interim Award), *Yearbook* XII (1987), p. 97 at p. 99; ICC Award no. 6149, in Jean-Jacques ARNALDEZ, Yves DERAINS, Dominique HASCHER (eds.), *Collection of ICC Arbitral Awards 1991-1995*, (Kluwer 1997) p. 315 at p. 318: "... the only other rule of conflicts of laws whose application would seem appropriate would be the application of the law where the

doctrine[89] and has been accepted by domestic courts.[90] The significance and persuasive force of the New York Convention must lead international arbitrators to apply that conflict rule:

> "Given the fact that the law applicable to the arbitration clause is rarely the subject of a specific stipulation, it is hardly surprising to find that most national court decisions under the New York Convention have applied the law of the country where the award was rendered. What this means is that prudent ICC arbitrators, although free to decide on the validity of the arbitration clause without reference to a national law should also deem themselves bound, under Article 35's exhortation that they 'shall make every effort to make sure that the Award is enforceable at law', to take account of the law of the place of arbitration."[91]

In view of its transnational character, the rule applies irrespective of whether a tribunal or court deals with the question of the validity of the arbitration agreement in the pre-award stage or a court deals with this issue in the post-award stage in setting aside or enforcement proceedings.[92] This means that in practice the territorial connection of

---

arbitration takes place and where the award is rendered. This conclusion would be supported also by Art. V(1)(a) of the ... [1958 New York Convention]"; ICC Award no. 7154, *ibid.*, p. 555; ICC Award no. 6719, *ibid.*, p. 567; ICC Award no. 4472, in Sigvard JARVIN and Yves DERAINS (eds.), *Collection of ICC Arbitral Awards 1974-1985* (ICC Publishing 1990), p. 525; see also for a survey on arbitral and court case law Alan REDFERN and Martin HUNTER, *op. cit.*, fn. 9, no. 2-89.

89. Julian D.M. LEW, *op. cit.*, fn. 13, p. 142: "There is a strong line of authority in case law for the application of the law of the seat of arbitration, which complies with this provision [Art. V(1)(a)] of the New York Convention"; Julian D.M. LEW, Loukas A. MISTELIS, Stefan M. KRÖLL, *op. cit.*, fn. 2, no. 6-60; Stelios KOUSSOULIS, "*Zur Dogmatik des auf die Schiedsvereinbarung anwendbaren Rechts*" in *Festschrift P. Schlosser* (Mohr 2005) p. 415 at pp. 423 et seq.; Karl Heinz SCHWAB and Gerhard WALTER, *Schiedsgerichtsbarkeit*, 7th edn. (Verlag C.H. Beck 2005) p. 385; Jens-Peter LACHMANN, *Handbuch für die Schiedsgerichtspraxis*, 2nd edn. (Schmidt 2002) no. 196; *Fouchard Gaillard Goldman*, *op. cit.*, fn. 44, no. 429: "Where the parties have not chosen a law governing the arbitration, the seat of the arbitration is undoubtedly considered to be the most significant factor in the determination of the applicable law"; Gary BORN, *International Commercial Arbitration*, 2nd edn. (Kluwer Law International 2001) p. 111, note (d); Horacio A. GRIGERA-NAÓN, *op. cit.*, fn. 11, pp. 65 et seq; Klaus Peter BERGER, "Power of Arbitrators to Fill Gaps and Revise Contracts to Make Sense", 17 Arb. Int'l (2001) p. 389 at p. 392 ("hard and fast rule"); Alan REDFERN and Martin HUNTER, *op. cit.*, fn. 9, no. 2-87, 2-90; Klaus Peter BERGER, *op. cit.*, fn. 28 Vol. II (Handbook), no. 16-66; Pieter SANDERS, *Quo Vadis Arbitration?* (Kluwer Law International 1999) p. 330; cf. also UN Doc A/CN.9/WG.II/WP.49, para. 37 stating that a general conflict of laws rule applicable to the arbitration agreement should refer to the law chosen by the parties, or, failing such, to the law of the place of arbitration.

90. See, e.g., *XL Insurance Ltd v. Owens Corning* [2000] 2 Lloyd's L. Rep. p. 500 at p. 508: "... by stipulating for arbitration in London ... the parties ... by implication chose English law as the proper law of the arbitration clause".

91. William L. CRAIG, William PARK, Jan PAULSSON, *op. cit.*, fn. 54, para 5.05.

92. Julian D.M. LEW, Loukas A. MISTELIS, Stefan M. KRÖLL, *op. cit.*, fn. 2, no. 6-55.

the arbitration law to the law of the seat of the arbitration prevails over any attempts to transnationalize the arbitration clause.

3.   *The Relationship Between the Traditional Choice of Law Clause and the Arbitration Agreement*

The only question that is still disputed is whether the choice of law clause of the main contract also extends to the arbitration clause contained therein.[93] The prevailing view answers this question in the affirmative and reformulates the general conflict rule explained above by stating that:

> "... the real choice [today] – in the absence of any express or implied choice by the parties – appears to be [only] between the law of the seat and the law which governs the contract as a whole".[94]

Likewise, Julian Lew, in his 1998 ICCA Report, argued that "[i]n practice, one may wonder whether the proper law of the arbitration clause would be deemed to be other than *either the law of the main agreement in which it is contained, or the law of the seat of arbitration*".[95] This view has also been applied in a variety of arbitral awards.[96] It extends the parties' choice of law to the arbitration agreement included in the contract because it would be artificial to assume that the choice of law clause whose purpose is to fix the law for the whole contract does not cover the arbitration clause which is an integral part

---

93. See ICC Award no. 6149, *op. cit.*, fn. 88, p. 318:

"It may be disputed whether an arbitration agreement, as a matter of principle, is subject to the same proper law by which also the main contract is governed so that both, arbitration agreement and main contract, share the same proper law, or whether the proper law of the arbitration agreement has to be determined upon its own, i.e., irrespectively of the proper law of the main contract";

see also Manja EPPING, *Die Schiedsvereinbarung im internationalen privaten Rechtsverkehr nach der Reform des deutschen Schiedsverfahrensrechts* (Beck 1999) p. 52.

94. Alan REDFERN and Martin HUNTER, *op. cit.*, fn. 9, no. 2-87.

95. Julian D.M. LEW, *op. cit.*, fn. 13, p. 142 (emphasis added).

96. See, e.g., ICC Award no. 2626, in Sigvard JARVIN and Yves DERAINS (eds.), *op. cit.*, fn. 88, p. 316; ICC Award no. 3572, in Sigvard JARVIN, Yves DERAINS, Jean-Jacques ARNALDEZ (eds.), *Collection of ICC Arbitral Awards 1986-1990* (ICC Publishing SA 1994) p. 154; ICC Award no. 6379, in Jean-Jacques ARNALDEZ, Yves DERAINS, Dominique HASCHER (eds.), *op. cit.*, fn. 88, p. 134 at p. 141; ICC Award no. 6752, *ibid.*, p. 195 at p. 197; ICC Award no. 6840, *ibid.*, p. 467; ICC Award no. 5505, in Sigvard JARVIN, Yves DERAINS, Jean-Jacques ARNALDEZ (eds.) *Collection of ICC Arbitral Awards 1986-1990* (ICC Publishing SA 1994) *ibid.*, p. 142; cf. also Horacio A. GRIGERA-NAÓN, *op. cit.*, fn. 11, p. 64.

of that contract.[97] Also it is argued that due to the substantive nature of arbitration agreements, the law governing this agreement is to be determined by virtue of the principles of the "proper law" of the contract.[98] One exception from this rule is made for submission agreements concluded after the dispute has arisen. It is argued that since such agreements are physically separated from the main contract, there may be less reason to imply the same proper law as that applicable to the main contract.[99]

However, this view ignores the legal effects of the doctrine of separability. That doctrine separates the arbitration agreement legally from the main contract even if it is physically included in that contract,[100] and the particular character of an arbitration agreement involving both substantive and procedural aspects ascribes it a special character different in nature from the main contract.[101] Both aspects speak against an automatic extension of the standard choice of law clause to the arbitration agreement.[102] Craig, Park, Paulsson have rightly stated:

> "Even when a contract is expressly subject to a particular law, as by a stipulation for example that 'any difference arising hereunder shall be settled ... according to Belgian law', it is not certain that the validity, scope, and effects of the arbitration clause would be determined by reference to Belgian law.

---

97. See, e.g., ICC Award no. 2626, Clunet (1978) p. 981; no. 6379, *Yearbook* XVII (1992) p. 215; BGH, RIW (1976) p. 449; *Union of India v. McDonnell Douglas Corp*, supra, fn. 4; *Sonatrach Petroleum Corporation (BVI) v. Ferrell Internatinal Ltd*, [2002] 1 All ER (Comm) 627; Julian D.M. LEW, Loukas A. MISTELIS, Stefan M. KRÖLL, *op. cit.*, fn. 2, no. 6-59; Alan REDFERN and Martin HUNTER, *op. cit.*, fn. 9, no. 2-87; Yves DERAINS, ICC Court of Arb. Bull., vol. 6, pp. 16 et seq.; John P. GAFFNEY, *op. cit.*, fn. 60, p. 1 at p. 6.

98. See Julian D.M. LEW, *op. cit.*, fn. 13, p. 118.

99. Francis RUSSELL, *Russell on Arbitration*, 21st edn. (Sweet & Maxwell 1997) no. 2-094.

100. Julian D.M. LEW, Loukas A. MISTELIS, Stefan M. KRÖLL, *Comparative International Commercial Arbitration*, *op. cit.*, fn. 2, no. 6-9.

101. See Piero BERNARDINI, *op. cit.*, fn. 6, p. 201:

> "Even where the parties have chosen the law governing their contract it does not necessarily follow that this law applies to the arbitration clause, since the autonomy of the arbitration clause is an obstacle to reaching such a conclusion automatically;"

> see also the holding of the tribunal in the Peterson Farms arbitration, quoted in *Petersons Farms Inc. v. C&M*, supra, fn. 60, at p. 609: "A corollary to the separability doctrine is that the law applicable to the arbitration agreement may differ from the law applicable both to the substance of the contract ... and to the arbitral proceedings themselves."

102. See ICC Award no. 3380, Clunet (1981) p. 927; no. 4131, Clunet (1984) p. 899; no. 4381, Clunet (1986) p. 1102; no. 4504, Clunet (1986) p. 1118; no. 5065, Clunet (1987) p. 1039; Albert Jan VAN DEN BERG, *op. cit.*, fn. 81, p. 293; Peter SCHLOSSER, *Das Recht der privaten internationalen Schiedsgerichtsbarkeit*, 2nd edn. (Mohr 1989), no. 840; Marc BLESSING "*Das neue internationale Schiedsrecht der Schweiz – ein Fortschritt oder ein Rückschritt?*" in Karl-Heinz BÖCKSTIEGEL (ed.), *Die internationale Schiedsgerichtsbarkeit in der Schweiz (II)* (Carl Heymanns Verlag 1989) p. 13 at p. 40; Klaus Peter BERGER, *op. cit.*, fn. 8, p. 158; Dominique HASCHER in *Yearbook* XX (1995) p. 1027; Yves DERAINS, Clunet (1985) p. 980; Klaus LIONNET and Annette LIONNET, *op. cit.*, fn. 85, p. 131.

This is so because of the autonomy of the arbitration clause.... By referring to ICC arbitration, the parties have accepted that the arbitrators are to decide upon challenges to their jurisdiction and to the validity of the main contract. In so doing, ICC arbitrators need not apply the law applicable to the merits of the dispute."[103]

Also, even though both clauses are typically located at the very end of the contract, the parties rarely, if ever, consider the arbitration clause when negotiating the choice of law clause in the contract. Finally, extending the general choice of law clause to the arbitration agreement would be inconsistent with a stipulation in the arbitration clause that any dispute should be determined by an arbitral tribunal having its seat in a country different from the one whose law is to govern the substance of the dispute.[104]

Therefore, since the parties usually fail to include a special choice of law clause for the arbitration agreement into their contract[105] and absent any special indications hinting at a tacit choice of law for the arbitration agreement,[106] the second tier of the two-tier transnational conflict rule applies: the law of the seat of the arbitration should be applied to determine the substantive validity of the arbitration agreement. This principle was also acknowledged by the UN Working Group that drafted the UNCITRAL Model Law:

> "... to use the place of arbitration as a secondary criterion was beneficial in that it provided the parties with a degree of certainty which was lacking under [other suggested approaches, like the application of the law of the main contract]. There were also doubts as to whether in fact a trend could be discerned in favour of determining the question of the validity of the arbitration agreement according to the law of the main contract."[107]

This means that in most cases, the seat of the arbitration is transformed from a subsidiary[108] to the primary connecting factor for the determination of the law applicable to the arbitration agreement.[109]

Thus, rejecting the automatic extension of the choice of law clause to the arbitration agreement achieves harmonization of decisions between the law applicable to the arbitral procedure and the law applicable to the arbitration agreement. This approach takes account of the fact that the arbitration clause is a contract intended to achieve procedural

---

103. William L. CRAIG, William PARK, Jan PAULSSON, *op. cit.*, fn. 54, para. 5.05.

104. *XL Insurance v. Owens Corning*, supra, fn. 90, at p. 508.

105. Cf. fn. 4.

106. A tacit choice of the law applicable to the arbitration agreement may be assumed if the parties have agreed on institutional arbitration rules (e.g., commodity arbitration) which are clearly rooted in a domestic legal system, see the decision of the German Federal Supreme Court BGHZ 55, p. 162 at p. 164; Manja EPPING, *op. cit.*, fn. 93, p. 57.

107. UN Doc. A/40/17, para. 284.

108. See *Fouchard Gaillard Goldman*, *op. cit.*, fn. 44, no. 431 in fine.

109. Klaus LIONNET and Annette LIONNET, *op. cit.*, fn. 85, at pp. 131 et seq.

effects, i.e., the establishment of a system of private justice for the parties.[110] The smooth running of this procedural system requires harmonization of decisions between the arbitration agreement as the basis of this system and the procedure itself.[111] This is confirmed by the fact that there are no overwhelming party interests requiring a harmonization of the law applicable to the arbitration agreement and the law applicable to the main contract.[112]

4. Determining the Applicable Law When the Seat Has Not yet Been Fixed

It has been argued that the value of the seat of the arbitration as the connecting factor for the law applicable to the substantive validity of the arbitration agreement is relatively low.[113] While this view has been refuted above, it is still justified in cases where the seat has not (yet) been fixed by the parties or on their behalf by the arbitral institution or the arbitral tribunal. Indeed, English courts have sometimes taken the approach that in such a case, the law of the contract, which was English law, governs the arbitration agreement and have then applied certain sections of the previous English arbitration laws by regarding them as statutory implied terms in the arbitration agreement governed by English law, thereby qualifying these provisions of the Arbitration Act as a matter of substance.[114] This rather confusing approach has raised the question whether in cases where the arbitration has its seat in England, but the arbitration agreement is governed by a foreign law, the English courts might not be able to apply these provisions of the English Arbitration Act due to their substantive qualification.[115]

However, Art. VI(c) 1961 European Convention provides that in such cases, the courts shall determine the substantive validity of the arbitration agreement "by virtue of the rules of conflict of the court seized of the dispute". This rule merely repeats the obvious: the court will apply the conflict rule of its own lex fori, which will almost certainly be the closest-connection or center-of-gravity test.[116] Application of this objective conflict rule will in most cases lead to the application of the law of the main contract.[117]

It must be stressed that this approach is characterized by two issues. First, the application of the lex contractus to the arbitration agreement does not result from an extension of the parties' choice of law clause but from the application of the objective closest connection test. Second, if the seat of the arbitration is later fixed by the parties or by the arbitral institution or the arbitral tribunal, then the law of that seat applies to

---

110. See supra text at fn. 1.
111. Manja EPPING, *op. cit.*, fn. 93, pp. 55 et seq.; Peter SCHLOSSER, *op. cit.*, fn. 102, no. 264.
112. Manja EPPING, *op. cit.*, fn. 93, p. 56.
113. *Fouchard Gaillard Goldman, op. cit.*, fn. 44, no. 433.
114. Francis RUSSELL, *op. cit.*, fn. 99, no. 2-095; *International Tank and Pipe SAK v. Kuwait Aviation Fuelling Co. KSC* [1975] QB 224; *Mitsubishi Corporation v. Castletown Navigation Ltd., The Castle Alpha* [1989] 2 Lloyd's L. Rep. 383.
115. Francis RUSSELL, *op. cit.*, fn. 99.
116. See supra text at fn. 79.
117. Manja EPPING, *op. cit.*, fn. 93, p. 56.

the arbitration agreement. If this law is different from the law applicable to the main contract, then the subsequent choice of the seat leads to a change of the law applicable to the arbitration agreement (*Statutenwechsel*). Such a change is nothing unusual in conflicts doctrine and is provided for in Art. 3(2) Rome Convention on the Law Applicable to Contractual Obligations.[118] Also, this change of the applicable law is inherent in the general conflict rule which links the arbitration agreement to the law of the seat, given that there is no indication in the Conventions or the UNCITRAL Model Law or the domestic arbitration laws from which this rule is derived[119] that it shall apply only in cases where the seat of the arbitration has been fixed in advance by the parties.[120] Finally, the subsequent choice of the seat is always connected to the will of the parties, either directly or because the parties have delegated that power to the arbitral institution or the arbitral tribunal.[121]

5.   The Scope of the Law Applicable to the Substantive Validity

The law determined according to the conflict of laws rule explained above governs all issues that relate to the substantive validity of the arbitration agreement. This includes the conclusion of the arbitration agreement, i.e., the validity of offer and acceptance and the determination of the moment of conclusion of contract, as well as errors of consent such as fraud, error, coercion, undue force, etc., and the execution and termination of the arbitration agreement, e.g., duration, impossibility, the prerequisites and consequences of cancellation and the application of the rule *exceptio non adimpleti contractus*.[122] Finally, this law governs all questions that relate to the scope of the arbitration agreement, including the extension of the arbitration agreement to third parties.[123] Typically, this latter issue must be determined by applying the rules of contract interpretation of that law, including the principle of *in favorem validitatis* dealt with above.[124]

In certain circumstances, it can be difficult to ascertain whether a certain legal issue is to be determined under the law applicable to the substantive or the formal validity of the arbitration agreement. Thus, Art. 7(2) UNCITRAL Model Law provides that an arbitration clause contained in standard terms is formally valid only if "the reference in a contract to a document containing an arbitration clause constitutes an arbitration

---

118. Art. 3(2) Rome Convention provides: "The parties may at any time agree to subject the contract to a law other than that which previously governed it, whether as a result of an earlier choice under this Article or of other provisions of this Convention."
119. See supra fns. 87-90.
120. Manja EPPING, *op. cit.*, fn. 93, p. 56.
121. Piero BERNARDINI, *op. cit.*, fn. 6, p. 201.
122. Pierre LALIVE, Jean-Francois POUDRET, Claude REYMOND, *op. cit.*, fn. 6, Art. 178, no. 14; Manja EPPING, *op. cit.*, fn. 93, p. 39; Francis RUSSELL, *op. cit.*, fn. 99, no. 2-095; see also the English decisions *Dalmia Dairy Industries Ltd. v. National Bank of Pakistan* [1978] 2 Lloyd's L. Rep. 223; *Black-Clawson International Ltd v. Papierwerke Waldhof-Aschaffenburg AG* [1981] 2 Lloyd's L. Rep. 446.
123. Pierre LALIVE, Jean-Francois POUDRET, Claude REYMOND, *op. cit.*, fn. 6, Art. 178, no. 14.
124. See supra II.7.

agreement provided that the contract is in writing *and the reference is such as to make that clause part of the contract*". The first part of this provision is certainly a formal validity requirement. The situation is not so clear with respect to the second, highlighted passage of this provision. In this context one is frequently confronted with the observation that inclusion by reference of an arbitration clause contained in standard forms does not only concern the formal validity of the arbitration agreement but at the same time decides on the existence of the parties' consent to submit the dispute to arbitration.[125] It would not be correct to deduce from this observation a strong interaction of formal and substantive requirements, in a way that the formal requirements, construed restrictively, decide over the substantive consensus of both parties[126] or that the question of formal validity is decided solely on the basis of the substantive national law which governs the question of consent of the parties.[127] Confusing substantive and formal validity requirements does not do justice to the different functions of both kinds of rules and runs the risk of restricting the ways of including an arbitration clause by reference to an extent which is incompatible with the needs of modern commercial transactions.[128] Instead, the problem of inclusion by reference has to be tackled by taking into account the specificity of international commercial arbitration. The customs and usages of international trade and commerce and not the law of the seat decide over the question of whether "the reference was such as to make that clause part of the contract".[129] Based on these considerations, two rules have been developed by international doctrine. First, a specific reference to the arbitration clause contained in a set of standard terms is always sufficient to make that clause part of the contract. Second, in case of a global reference to a set of standard terms which contains an arbitration clause that is not specifically mentioned in the reference, the generally accepted view is that the formal validity rule is met if the other party is already in possession of the standard forms or if the other party is put in a position to check the reference, for example where the conditions are

---

125. Klaus Peter BERGER, *op. cit.*, fn. 8, p. 150.
126. See Albert Jan VAN DEN BERG, *op. cit.*, fn. 81, p. 177 (Compliance with formal validity requirements establishes a "strong presumption" for substantive validity).
127. Marc BLESSING, *op. cit.*, fn. 102, p. 12 at p. 39; Joachim H. GRANZOW, *Das UNCITRAL Modellgesetz über die internationale Handelsschiedsgerichtsbarkeit* (Florentz 1987) pp. 91 et seq.; Gabriele HUßLEIN-STICH, *Das UNCITRAL Modellgesetz über die internationale Handelsschiedsgerichtsbarkeit* (Heymanns 1990) p. 42.
128. See for a strict separation of formal and substantive validity rules Pierre LALIVE, Jean-Francois POUDRET, Claude REYMOND, *op. cit.*, fn. 6, Art. 178, no. 13, 20; ICC Award no. 4710, ASA Bulletin (1985) p. 65 at pp. 66 et seq.; see also Tadeusz SZURSKI, "Arbitration Agreement and Competence of the Arbitral Tribunal" in *UNCITRAL's Project for a Model Law on International Commercial Arbitration*, ICCA Congress Series no. 2 (1984) (hereinafter *ICCA Congress Series no. 2*) p. 62.
129. Philippe FOUCHARD, *"La Loi-type de la C.N.U.D.C.I. sur l'arbitrage commercial international"*, 114 Clunet (1987) p. 884; cf. also Howard M. HOLTZMANN and Joseph E. NEUHAUS, *A Guide to the UNCITRAL Model Law on International Commercial Arbitration* (Kluwer Law and Taxation Publishers 1989) p. 264; Manja EPPING, *op. cit.*, fn. 93, p. 144.

set out on the reverse side of the contract or attached to it or, alternatively, if dispute settlement through arbitration is customary in that particular business.[130]

IV.   THE LAW APPLICABLE TO FORMAL VALIDITY

1.   General Considerations

Almost every arbitration law contains formal validity requirements applicable to the arbitration agreement. The reason for these requirements is that the parties shall be made aware that by concluding the arbitration agreement they oust the jurisdiction of the domestic courts ("warning function"). Also, such "in writing" requirements serve to preserve the text of the arbitration agreement if the jurisdiction of the arbitral tribunal is disputed ("proof function").[131] Sometimes, one of these functions prevails. Thus, it is undisputed that the formal validity rule contained in Sect. 1021 Dutch Arbitration Act is a provision of proof which is reflected in the wording of that provision ("... shall be proven...").[132] From a practical perspective, these differences are immaterial for two reasons. First, courts seized of a matter relating to the arbitration may refuse to proceed if the party invoking the arbitration agreement cannot prove its existence just as the court would have to refuse to act if the arbitration agreement violates any substantive formal validity rules. Second, the competence of the tribunal may be established under all laws if the existence of an arbitration agreement is alleged by one party and not denied by the other.[133]

If a tribunal has to deal with the formal validity of the arbitration agreement, it must apply the formal validity rule contained in the lex loci arbitri. This very clear rule follows from the fact that, first, these formal validity rules must be qualified as substantive rules of private international law,[134] and that, second, the territorial connection of the arbitration to the arbitration law of the seat, which is so widely accepted today, necessarily leads to the conclusion that an arbitral tribunal sitting in that country must apply the mandatory formal validity rules contained in that law.[135] It is in view of this clear-cut rule that most international arbitration rules "ignore the formal validity issue".[136] It is also for that reason that the drafters of the UNCITRAL Model Law

---

130. Peter SCHLOSSER, op. cit., fn. 102, no. 379; Albert Jan VAN DEN BERG, "New York Convention of 1958 Consolidated Commentary Cases Reported in Volumes XIII (1988) – XIV (1989)", Yearbook XIV (1989) p. 552; Albert Jan VAN DEN BERG, op. cit., fn. 81, pp. 216 et seq.; French Cour de cassation, Société Bomar Oil NV v. E.T.A.P., Rev. d'Arb. (1990) pp. 134 et seq.

131. See Klaus Peter BERGER, op. cit., fn. 8, pp. 135 et seq.

132. See Albert Jan VAN DEN BERG, "Aan de Balie van het Scheidsgerecht", 4 Tijdschrift voor Arbitrage (1984) p. 179.

133. Art. 16 Model Law; Sect. 1040 German Arbitration Act.

134. Julian D.M. LEW, Loukas A. MISTELIS, Stefan M. KRÖLL, op. cit., fn. 2, no. 6-37.

135. Manja EPPING, op. cit., fn. 93, p. 55; see also Julian D.M. LEW, Loukas A. MISTELIS, Stefan M. KRÖLL, op. cit., fn. 2, no. 6-47: "The principle of territoriality enshrined in the Model Law is an argument in favour of relying on the place of arbitration."

136. Julian D.M. LEW, op. cit., fn. 13, p. 130.

stated that "the model law is intended to govern all international commercial arbitration agreements".[137]

What makes this very clear rule more complicated is the fact that one is confronted here with the interplay of domestic law and international uniform law described above[138] and more specifically, Art. II(2) New York Convention. Here one has to draw a distinction between the arbitration agreement being examined by the arbitral tribunal or by a state court.

2. Formal Validity Rule to be Applied by the Tribunal

In this context, it must first be noted that the uniform rules contained in the New York Convention are addressed to courts and not to arbitral tribunals. International arbitrators are therefore under no treaty obligation to apply the formal validity requirements of the Convention. However, they may feel a practical necessity to ensure compliance with the Convention if parties indicate possible enforcement fora and the arbitrators realize that the enforcement judge will apply the New York Convention.[139] For these purely practical reasons, the tribunal in ICC Award no. 5730, after having rejected the theory of the direct application of the New York Convention by international arbitrators, reasoned that it is nonetheless desirable that international arbitral tribunals do not "without serious reasons" depart from the formal validity rule laid down in Art. II(2) New York Convention in order to ensure that the tribunal will not judge its competence along criteria which are different from those that a judge would apply under Art. V New York Convention.[140] This practical approach follows from the arbitrators' "soft" obligation to render an enforceable award. However, the clear rule stated above and the international arbitrators' tendency to accept jurisdiction means that if the arbitration agreement is not in line with Art. II(2) of the Convention but meets the more lenient requirements of the formal validity rule of the law of the seat, then the tribunal must apply this rule[141] because it is under a *legal duty*, and not just a practical *"nobile officium"* obligation to do so,[142] due to the two principles outlined above.[143]

---

137. UN Doc. A/CN.9/264, para. 6.

138. See supra II.4.

139. Klaus Peter BERGER, *op. cit.*, fn. 8, p. 135; Julian D.M. LEW, Loukas A. MISTELIS, Stefan M. KRÖLL, *op. cit.*, fn. 2, no. 6-48.

140. ICC Award no. 5730, Clunet (1990) p. 1033.

141. Julian D.M. LEW, Loukas A. MISTELIS, Stefan M. KRÖLL, *op. cit.*, fn. 2, no. 6-49.

142. See Award of the Netherlands Tribunal for Metal Industry and Trade, *Yearbook* XI (1986) p. 185; ICC Award no. 6281, Clunet (1991) p. 1054; see also ad hoc award of Hamburg Commodity Exchange arbitration tribunal of 18 July 1986, *Yearbook* XVI (1991), p. 13 at p. 14; Award of the Hamburg Friendly Arbitration of 15 January 1976, in Kuno STRAATMANN and Peter ULMER (eds.), *Handelsrechtliche Schiedsgerichtspraxis*, vol. 2, (Verlag Dr. Otto Schmidt 1982) no. B 24 stating that the rule of Art II(2) New York Convention does not impose a rule of universal applicability.

143. See supra text at fns. 134, 135.

3. *Formal Validity Rule to be Applied by State Courts*

If a court is faced with the question of which formal validity rule applies to an arbitration agreement, the approach to be taken depends on where the seat of the arbitration is located.

a. *State courts in the country of the seat*

i. Art. II(2) New York Convention as a maximum form requirement
If the seat is located in the country where the court sits, the court will apply the formal validity requirements of Art. II(2) of the New York Convention if it is concerned with the enforcement of the arbitration agreement under Art. II, irrespective of whether the law at the seat contains stricter form requirements. The Convention sets a maximum standard and supersedes any stricter form requirements within its scope.[144]

ii. Art. II(2) New York Convention as a minimum form requirement?
If a party decides to profit from the "more favorable rights" provision in Art. VII(1) of the Convention, it may rely on a more lenient formal validity rule contained in the lex arbitri. In that case, however, enforcement of the arbitration agreement or the award is based on non-unified local law and not on the unified and widely tested and respected enforcement system of the New York Convention. It must be assumed that Art. II of the New York Convention provides not only a maximum, but also a minimum form requirement for the enforcement of arbitration agreements and awards under the Convention. The Convention is a self-contained regime and it would be contrary to the intention of its drafters if awards made on the basis of an agreement that did not comply with the Convention's formal validity requirement would nevertheless benefit from its regime. This means that a party is not allowed to combine the enforcement provisions of the Convention with the lenient form requirements of domestic law. Rather, a choice must be made to rely either on the New York Convention or on domestic law.[145] This can make a considerable difference in practice.[146]

iii. UNCITRAL's efforts to modernize Art. II(2) New York Convention and to promote the revised Art. 7(2) Model Law
The UNCITRAL Working Group on Arbitration, however, seems to assume that the New York Convention contains nothing to prevent the use of some of its provisions in conjunction with other more liberal form requirements of domestic laws,[147] a position

---

144. See Julian D.M. LEW, Loukas A. MISTELIS, Stefan M. KRÖLL, *op. cit.*, fn. 2 no. 6-39.
145. See Court of Appeal of Cologne of 16 December 1992, *Yearbook* XXI (1996), p. 535; UN Doc. A/CN.9/WG.II/WP.139 of 14 December 2005, p. 19.
146. Klaus Peter BERGER, *op. cit.*, fn. 8, p. 135; Julian D.M. LEW, Loukas A. MISTELIS, Stefan M. KRÖLL, *op. cit.*, fn. 2, no. 6-44; Pierre LALIVE, Jean-Francois POUDRET, Claude REYMOND, *op. cit.*, fn. 6, Art. 178, no. 7.
147. Doc. A/CN.9/WG.II/WP.139 of 14 December 2005, p. 20.

which is shared by some domestic courts.[148] Based on this approach, the Working Group has suggested a draft interpretative declaration regarding the interpretation of Art. VII(1) and Art. II(2) of the New York Convention. Such a non-binding instrument is regarded as a viable alternative to the promulgation of a binding amending protocol relating to Art. II(2) on which the Working Group has not been able to reach a consensus.[149]

With respect to the more favorable rights provision of the Convention the draft interpretative declaration recommends that:

"...article VII, paragraph (1), of the Convention should be applied to allow any interested party to avail itself of rights it may have, under the law or treaties of the country where the arbitration agreement is sought to be relied upon, to seek recognition of the validity of such arbitration agreement".[150]

Opening the Convention to the application of more lenient form requirements of domestic law, such as those based on the revised Art. 7(2) UNCITRAL Model Law,[151] is regarded as a means to promote the modernized form requirements of the Model Law.

At the same time, the Working Group seeks to create a "friendly bridge" between the new form requirement in Art. 7(2) Model Law and Art. II(2) New York Convention by promoting a liberal, flexible and broad approach to the interpretation of the form requirement of Art. II(2) of the Convention. Promoting a liberal interpretation of the form requirement instead of adapting the text of Art. II(2) itself to the requirements of modern trade avoids the potential damage that a change of the text of that provision could do to the complex and vulnerable enforcement mechanism established in the Convention as an instrument of international uniform law. Towards that end, the drafters of the interpretative declaration recommend:

---

148. Court of Appeal of Hamm of 2 November 1983, *Yearbook* XIV (1989) p. 629; Netherlands Court of First Instance of Rotterdam of 24 November 1994, *Isaac Glecer v. Moses Israel Glecer and Estera Glecer-Nottman*, *Yearbook* XXI (1996) p. 635.

149. UN Doc. A/CN.9/508, para. 42 et seq.; UN Doc. A/CN.9/WG.II/WP.139 of 14 December 2005, pp. 5 et seq.

150. UN Doc. A/CN.9/607 of 13 April 2006, p. 4; Doc. A/CN.9/WG.II/WP.139 of 14 December 2005, pp. 21 et seq.

151. The Working Group has drafted a revised text for Art. 7 Model Law, see UN Doc. A/CN.9/WG.II/WP.136 of 19 July 2005, p. 2; the draft contains the following sub-sections which take account of modern IT communication:

"(2) The arbitration agreement shall be in writing. 'Writing' means any form, including, without limitation, a data message, that provides a record of the arbitration agreement or is otherwise accessible so as to be useable for subsequent reference.
(3) 'Data message' means information generated, sent, received or stored by electronic, optical or similar means, including, but not limited to, electronic data interchange (EDI), electronic mail, telegram, telex or telecopy."

"... that article II, paragraph (2), of the Convention be applied *recognizing that the circumstances described therein are not exhaustive*".[152]

Together with the reference in the draft declaration to the modernized form requirement of Art. 7(2) Model Law and to the UNCITRAL Model Law on Electronic Commerce, the UNCITRAL Model Law on Electronic Signatures and the UN Convention on the Use of Electronic Communications in International Contracts, this recommendation is intended to ensure that state courts understand that the express reference to "letter or telegram" in Art. II(2) of the Convention does not prevent an interpretation which allows for the formally valid conclusion of an arbitration agreement through modern means of telecommunication.[153] The idea of using Art. 7(2) Model Law as an "interpretation tool"[154] to clarify the application of Art. II(2) of the Convention is in line with the Swiss Federal Tribunal's approach to modernize ("actualize") the outdated form requirement of Art. II(2) New York Convention by construing Art. II (2) New York Convention in light of Art. 7 UNCITRAL Model Law.[155] To speed up this process of modernizing the form requirement of the Convention, the Working Group also considers the promulgation of a non-binding commentary to be used by domestic courts as guidance in their application and interpretation of the form requirement of the New York Convention.[156]

Thus, UNCITRAL is taking a dual approach to the creation of harmonized and modernized formal validity rules for international arbitration agreements. The "friendly bridge" which it intends to build between the Model Law and the New York Convention is not a one-way street. The more favorable rights provision in Art. VII(1) of the Convention is seen as a catalyst for the adoption of the modernized form requirement of Art. 7(2) Model Law by domestic legislatures worldwide. At the same time, the modernized Art. 7(2) Model Law – provided that it is adopted by as many legislatures as possible – shall serve as a means for a more liberal interpretation of Art. II(2) of the Convention by domestic courts which is in line with modern trade practice.

---

152. UN Doc. A/CN.9/607 of 13 April 2006, p. 4; UN Doc. A/CN.9/592 of 27 February 2006, p. 28 (emphasis added).

153. UN Doc. A/CN.9/WG.II/WP.139 of 14 December 2005, pp. 14 et seq.; UN Doc. A/CN.9/607 of 13 April 2006, pp. 4 et seq.

154. UN Doc. A/CN.9/607 of 13 April 2006, p. 4.

155. See Swiss Federal Supreme Court in *Compagnie de Navigation et Transports SA v. MSC (Mediterranean Shipping Company)*, Yearbook XI (1986), p. 690; Albert Jan VAN DEN BERG, "The Application of the New York Convention by the Courts" in *ICCA Congress Series no. 9* (1999) p. 25 at p. 32:

"It may indeed be questioned whether the uniform rule of Art. II(2) of the Convention should be maintained in all its respects. As almost 40 years have elapsed since its drafting, it seems justified to bring its interpretation in accordance with views generally held in our times with respect to the conclusion of contracts that contain an arbitration clause."

156. UN Doc. A/CN.9/607 of 13 April 2006, p. 6.

b.   State courts in countries other than the country of the seat

If the seat of the arbitration is outside the country where the court sits, the court will apply the formal validity rule of Art. II(2) New York Convention in all cases covered by the Convention. In all other cases, the territoriality rule should direct the court to apply the formal validity requirement, to be qualified as "*règles materielles*", of the arbitration law in force at the seat of the arbitration. This would follow from a logical application of the two principles outlined above.[157] However, the policy judgments behind the formal validity rules of domestic law, especially their function to "protect" the parties from an unwilling derogation of the competence of the state courts, makes most domestic courts apply the formal validity rules of their own law because they do not (yet!) accept that this question should be decided by a law other than their own.[158] The courts adopt a similar approach to that of objective arbitrability where the enforcement courts are called upon to apply their own law instead of that of the seat of the arbitration.[159] One may state that this is the last bulwark of judicial skepticism and parochialism in the area of international commercial arbitration.

V.   THE LAW APPLICABLE TO THE PARTIES' CAPACITY TO ARBITRATE

1.   The General Conflict Rule

The parties' capacity to conclude the arbitration agreement ("subjective arbitrability") follows special conflict of laws considerations. Sect. 48(2) Swedish Arbitration Act provides that the general conflict rule for the determination of the law governing the substantive validity of the arbitration agreement "shall not apply to the issue of whether a party was authorized to enter into an arbitration agreement...".[160] This negative rule of the Swedish Act does not state which conflict rule applies to the issue of the parties' capacity to arbitrate. Likewise, Art. 1(2)(a) Rome Convention on the Law Applicable to Contractual Obligations provides that its conflict rules do not apply to "questions involving the status or legal capacity of natural persons...". Sect. 1059(2) no. 1a) German Arbitration Act is more specific. It provides that the award may be set aside if "a party to the arbitration agreement ... was under some incapacity *pursuant to the law applicable to him*". The *travaux préparatoires* for the German law state that Art. 34(2)(a)(i) UNCITRAL Model Law, which Sect. 1059(2) no. 1a) transforms into German law, does not contain such a rule and that the German legislature intended to close this gap by

---

157. See supra text at fns. 134, 135.
158. Julian D.M. LEW, Loukas A. MISTELIS, Stefan M. KRÖLL, *op. cit.*, fn. 2, no. 6-47 in fine; "Each state wants to determine for itself under which circumstances the jurisdiction of its courts can be excluded, i.e., whether or not a written agreement is required."
159. See supra II.2.
160. See Klaus Peter BERGER, *op. cit.*, fn. 8, p. 393.

adopting the rule contained in Art. V(1)(*a*) New York Convention and Art. VI(2) European Convention.[161]

Indeed, this approach reflects a general conflict rule which is accepted both in international commercial arbitration[162] and in general conflicts doctrine.[163] The problem remains that different connecting factors are considered relevant in the various jurisdictions to determine a party's capacity to enter into contractual relations. They include the party's nationality, place of business, domicile or residence, or place of incorporation. In international commercial arbitration, which involves commercial entities as parties to the arbitration agreement, these differences are rarely relevant.

2.   A State Party's Capacity to Arbitrate

It must be noted that in certain cases, the rules applicable to a party's capacity to enter into arbitration agreements may be superseded by substantive rules of private international law. This applies in particular to a state party's capacity to arbitrate. Sect. 177(2) Swiss Private International Law Statute provides that: "If a party to the arbitration agreement is a state or an enterprise or organisation controlled by it, it cannot rely on its own law in order to contest its capacity to be a party to an arbitration or the arbitrability of a dispute covered by the arbitration agreement." This provision confirms a general principle of international arbitral practice.[164] It has been confirmed

---

161. *Travaux préparatoires*, reprinted in Klaus Peter BERGER (ed.), *The New German Arbitration Law* (RWS Verlag Kommunikationsforum 1998) p. 288.
162. Tadeusz SZURSKI, *op. cit.*, fn. 128, p. 53 at p. 70; Julian D.M. LEW, Loukas A. MISTELIS, Stefan M. KRÖLL, *op. cit.*, fn. 2, no. 6-50; Pieter SANDERS, *op. cit.*, fn. 89, p. 187; Horacio A. GRIGERA-NAÓN, *op. cit.*, fn. 11, pp. 103 et seq.
163. Albert V. DICEY and John H.C. MORRIS, *op. cit.*, fn. 80, p. 1275, quoting from the Restatement of Conflicts of Laws:

     "If the state of a person's domicile has chosen to give him capacity to contract ... there can usually be little reason why the local law of some other state should be applied ... and to declare the contract invalid to the disappointment of the parties' expectations";

     Art. 7(1) German Introductory Law to the Civil Code which provides that a person's capacity to enter into contracts is governed by the law of the state to which that person belongs.
164. See, e.g., Ad hoc Award *Benteler v. Belgian State* 1 J.Int'l.Arb. (1984), pp. 184 et seq.; Ad hoc Award *Framatome et al v. Atomic Energy Organization of Iran*, Clunet (1984) pp. 58 et seq.; Interim Award of 14 January 1982 *Elf Aquitaine Iran v. National Iranian Oil Company*, Yearbook XI (1986) p. 97 at pp. 103 et seq.; ICC Award no. 3227, Clunet (1982) p. 971; ICC Award no. 2521, Clunet (1976) p. 997; ICC Award no. 4381, Clunet (1986) p. 1102; ICC Award no. 6162, Yearbook XVII (1992) p. 153 at p. 158; Jan PAULSSON, "May a State Invoke Its Internal Law to Repudiate Consent to International Commercial Arbitration: Reflections on the *Benteler v. Belgium* Preliminary Award", 2 Arb. Int'l (1986), pp. 90 et seq.; Horacio A. GRIGERA-NAÓN, *op. cit.*, fn. 11, p. 79; Claude REYMOND, "*Souveraineté de l'état et participation à l'arbitrage*", Rev. d'Arb 1985, p. 517 at pp. 527 et seq.; Philippe FOUCHARD, *L'arbitrage commercial international* (Dalloz 1965) p. 103; see also Court of First Instance of Tunis of 22 March 1976, *Société Tunesienne d'Électricité et de Gaz v. Société Entrepose*, Yearbook III (1978) p. 283; Tadeusz SZURSKI, *op. cit.*, fn. 128, p. 72.

in Art. 5 of the Santiago De Compostela Resolution of the Institut de Droit International.[165] The notion of sovereignty as developed in public international law and the confidence of the private party in the validity of the arbitration agreement concluded with the state or state-controlled party bind the state to the arbitration agreement which it cannot rescind unilaterally by invoking its internal law. This rule is a specification of the more general principle of *"non concedit venire contra factum proprium"*[166] which in itself, is a general principle of transnational law.[167]

Therefore, Art. 177(2) Swiss Private International Law Statute reflects a substantive rule of private international law (*règle materielle*) which incorporates a general principle of customary international law and transnational *ordre public* that supersedes any conflicting domestic law the application of which has been determined according to the special conflict of laws provision for the parties' subjective arbitrability.[168] It was for this reason that the German legislature, when enacting the 1998 German Arbitration Act, repealed the "Law on Arbitral Disposition of Private Disputes of the Empire and the States" which required the consent of the German Ministry of Finance as a prerequisite under German law for the validity of every arbitration agreement concluded by the German federal state or the federal government. The *traveaux préparatoires* of the Act state that this Law, which "served to protect the state as party to an arbitration against itself" appeared no longer timely, given the undisputed acceptance of arbitration as a means of dispute resolution equivalent to that before domestic courts.[169]

The same considerations apply to the cases in which a state or state-controlled entity does not invoke its internal laws but simply claims immunity from suit before the tribunal. It is generally accepted today[170] and was confirmed in the Santiago de

---

165. Text reprinted in 5 ICSID Rev–FILJ 1990, p. 141: "A state, a state enterprise, or a state entity cannot invoke incapacity to arbitrate in order to resist arbitration to which it has agreed."

166. *Benteler* Award, *op. cit.*, fn. 164, p. 190; Karl-Heinz BÖCKSTIEGEL, "Public Policy and Arbitrability" in *Comparative Arbitration Practice and Public Policy in Arbitration*, ICCA Congress Series no. 3 (1986) p. 177 at p. 203; Emmanuel GAILLARD, "A Foreign View of the New Swiss Law on International Arbitration", 4 Arb. Int'l (1988) p. 25 at p. 26.

167. See Principle I.7 CENTRAL Transnational Law database at <www.tldb.de> with further references from international doctrine and arbitral case law.

168. Pierre LALIVE, "*Ordre public transnational (ou réellement international) et arbitrage international*", Rev. d'Arb. 1986, pp. 344 et seq.; Jan PAULSSON, *op. cit.*, fn. 164, p. 81; see also Tadeusz SZURSKI, *op. cit.*, fn. 128, p. 72.

169. *Travaux préparatoires*, reprinted in Klaus Peter BERGER (ed.), *op. cit.*, fn. 161, pp. 180 et seq.

170. See, e.g., Karl-Heinz BÖCKSTIEGEL, *Der Staat als Vertragspartner ausländischer Privatunternehmen* (Athenäum 1971) p. 240; ICC Award no. 3493, *SPP (Middle East) Ltd., Southern Pacific Properties Ltd. v. Arab Republic of Egypt, The General Company for Tourism and Hotels (EGOTH)*, Yearbook IX (1984) p. 111 at p. 120 ("The Pyramids"); ICC Award no. 2321, *Solel Boneh International Ltd. and Water Resources Development International v. Republic of Uganda and National Housing and Construction Corporation of Uganda*, Yearbook I (1976) p. 133 at p. 135; Cour d'appel of Paris, *The Arab Republic of Egypt v. SPP Ltd., SPP (Middle East) Ltd.*, Yearbook X (1985) p. 113 at p. 118; ICC Award no. 3879, *Westland Helicopters Ltd. ("Westland") v. Arab Organization for Industrialization et al.*, ILM (1984) p. 1071 at p. 1089.

Compostela Resolution of the Institut de Droit International[171] that a state party, once having accepted arbitration in a contract as the sole conflict remedy, may not paralyze the proceedings by pleading sovereign immunity from suit. It is considered to have waived a plea of immunity from jurisdiction.[172]

VI.   THE LAW APPLICABLE TO A PARTY'S REPRESENTATION

A tribunal of the German Maritime Arbitration Association (GMAA) has held that the question whether a party was duly represented when it concluded the arbitration agreement should be governed by the generally accepted conflict rule contained in Art. V(1)(a) New York Convention.[173] However, it is also generally accepted today in conflicts doctrine that the question whether a party was duly represented is subject to independent connecting factors.[174] Again, Sect. 48(2) Swedish Arbitration Act provides that the general conflict rule for the determination of the law governing the substantive validity of the arbitration agreement "shall not apply to the issue of whether a party ... was duly represented". As in the case of subjective arbitrability,[175] the Swedish Act does not state which law shall apply to this question. The generally accepted rule today is that in the interest of protecting potential contract partners who are not able to know the details of the relationship between representative and principal, this issue should be governed by the law of the place where the contract was to be concluded by the representative for the party that has authorized him to act on its behalf vis-à-vis the other side.[176] This means that the *locus regit actum* rule applies here.[177]

VII.   CONCLUSION

This study has revealed that, leaving aside the complex relationship between domestic law and the New York Convention in the area of formal validity, there is today more consensus than confusion with respect to the law applicable to the arbitration agreement. The study has also revealed that the juridical seat of the arbitration plays a dominant role as a connecting factor for the determination of the law applicable to the

---

171. Art. 9, text reprinted in 5 ICSID Rev.–FILJ 1990, p. 141: "Denial of the tribunal's jurisdiction based on a State's sovereign status is not admissible in arbitration between a State, a state enterprise, or a state entity, on the one hand, and a foreign enterprise, on the other."

172. Pieter SANDERS, *op. cit.*, fn. 89, p. 207.

173. GMAA Award of 8 November 2005, <www.gmaa.de/gmitsp11.htm>, at p. 4.

174. Jan KROPHOLLER, *Internationales Privatrecht*, 5th edn. (Mohr Siebeck 2004), p. 300.

175. See supra text at fn. 160.

176. See, e.g., the German Federal Supreme Court BGH NJW 1990, p. 3088; BGHZ 128, p. 41 at p. 47; see also Albert V. DICEY and John H.C. MORRIS, *op. cit.*, fn. 80, p. 1255 (with respect to form); Klaus Peter BERGER, *op. cit.*, fn. 8, p. 393.

177. William L. CRAIG, William PARK, Jan PAULSSON, *op. cit.*, fn. 54, para. 5.03.

formal and substantive validity of the arbitration agreement.[178] This role does not follow from a procedural characterization of the arbitration agreement.[179] Rather, it is based on the intrinsic value of the seat as a clearly determinable connecting factor. The way in which the law of the seat becomes involved can be different. Its application may be due to the fact that the law of the seat contains a substantive rule of private international law which applies to all arbitrations having their seat in that country, as in the case of the formal validity requirements or objective arbitrability rules. It may also be due to the fact that the seat serves as a classical connecting factor of conflict of law provisions in effect at the seat or in other countries, as in the case of the determination of the law applicable to the substantive validity of the arbitration agreement.

Leaving aside these dogmatic differences, it must be noted that the law of the seat governs the following issues, three of which relate to the validity of the arbitration agreement:

1. The substantive validity of the arbitration agreement absent a choice of law;
2. The formal validity of the arbitration agreement if it is to be determined by the tribunal;
3. The objective arbitrability of the subject matter of the dispute;
4. The arbitral procedure.

This significance of the law of the seat has an important harmonizing effect on the determination of the law applicable to the validity of the arbitration agreement. It serves to avoid friction and contradictions that might arise if different laws apply to these issues. Harmonization of decisions created by the seat is important because the arbitration agreement constitutes the very basis of the tribunal's jurisdiction. This requires hard, fast, workable and generally accepted conflict rules in order to avoid further complications if the jurisdiction of the tribunal is contested by one side. This is also in line with the notion of party autonomy as one of the principal maxims of international commercial arbitration. The seat is typically chosen by the parties or by the tribunal or by the arbitral institution on their behalf. The choice of the seat thus becomes a direct or indirect choice of law by the parties with respect to the issues listed above.[180]

---

178. See also Horacio A. GRIGERA-NAÓN, *op. cit.*, fn. 11, p. 45 at p. 70: "(Arbitral practice) illustrates ... the prevailing influence of the law of the place of arbitration or lex arbitri on the determination of the applicable law to issues regarding the validity of the arbitration agreement...".

179. But see *Fouchard Gaillard Goldman*, *op. cit.*, fn. 44, para. 424, who argue that application of the law of the seat follows from a procedural characterization of the arbitration agreement.

180. See Alan REDFERN and Martin HUNTER, *op. cit.*, fn. 9, no. 2-90: "In choosing the law of the place of arbitration as the law governing the arbitration agreement, the court or tribunal may be seen as having decided to give effect to the parties' agreement"; see also Art. 3 1996 English Arbitration Act:

"In this Part 'the seat of the arbitration' means the juridical seat of the arbitration designated–
(a) by the parties to the arbitration agreement, or
(b) by any arbitral or other institution or person *vested by the parties with powers in that regard*, or

If the issue at stake relates to the personal status of a party or to the protection of the other party, the significance of the seat is overridden by other connecting factors which are better able to do justice to these policy considerations. This applies to:

5. The parties' capacity to arbitrate ("subjective arbitrability"), which is governed by the law of the country where the party has its residence, domicile or seat and
6. The issue of whether a party was duly represented when concluding the arbitration agreement, which is governed by the law of the state where the agent has concluded the arbitration agreement.

Thus, there are only three different connecting factors, the seat reigning most prominently among them, with respect to the determination of the law governing all aspects of the validity of international arbitration agreements for six different legal issues.

(c) by the arbitral tribunal *if so authorised by the parties*, or determined, in the absence of any such designation, having regard to the parties' agreement and all the relevant circumstances."

(emphasis added).

The Applicable Law to the Arbitration Agreement: A Comment on Professor Berger's Report

*Yasuhei Taniguchi**

TABLE OF CONTENTS

I. INTRODUCTION

As Professor Berger admits in his Report on the Applicable Law to the Arbitration Agreement, the scholarship of private international law looks very "esoteric" to a lay person like me. I have been working mainly in the fields of procedure and bankruptcy. Nevertheless, I would like to attempt to mention four brief points: The place (seat) of arbitration as the key (II); the subjective scope of the arbitration agreement and the "cross-filing clause" (III); the objective scope and method of interpretation of the contract as a part of applicable law (IV); and the due process aspect in the choice of law (V).

II. PLACE OF ARBITRATION

The concept of the place of arbitration has traditionally occupied an important position in the doctrines of arbitration law because in the modern sovereign state, the institution of arbitration exists under the sanction of state authority. Thus, Professor Berger emphasizes the "intrinsic value of the seat" of arbitration. With increasing a-nationalization of international commercial arbitration, the legitimacy of this basic approach has been doubted. Moreover, the place of arbitration can be and sometimes is merely fictitious. It is fictitious because the parties are allowed to designate any country as the place of arbitration without actually conducting any part of the arbitration in that country. Professor Berger advocates the theory that the law applicable to the arbitration agreement should be the law of the seat of arbitration. If such is the law, however, the parties are able to avoid the law of a certain country by choosing another country which has an arbitration law more favorable to them as the seat of arbitration.

The opposing theory advocates that the law applicable to the arbitration agreement should be primarily determined by the parties because the arbitration is an autonomous

---

* Of-counsel, Matsuo & Kosugi, Tokyo; Member of ICCA.

product of the parties. But a problem arises from the fact that the parties to an arbitration agreement do not usually include such an agreement although it is rather usual to include an agreement on the governing law of the merits of the main contract. On the other hand, the place of arbitration is often agreed or somehow fixed sooner or later. When there is no explicit agreement on the applicable law to the arbitration agreement itself, a question is whether an agreement should be inferred or even construed or whether some other standard must be relied upon.

It is difficult to say that an agreement on the law applicable to the arbitration agreement is not allowed because the New York Convention seems to recognize such an agreement (Art. V(1)(a)). If an agreement to that effect does not exist, it will be better to have a predetermined solid rule than to resort to an unpredictable search for the possible intention of the parties either by a judge or by an arbitrator. If such a principle is established, the parties to an arbitration agreement will choose a place of arbitration with that principle in mind.

Assuming that, absent a clear agreement of the parties, the place of arbitration is the solid basis for the law applicable to an arbitration agreement, the matters to be determined by such law can be various and disputable. The scope of the binding effect of an arbitration agreement is admittedly determined by the law applicable to the arbitration agreement. There are two aspects to this issue. They are the subjective scope: namely, the question who is bound by the agreement; and the objective scope: namely, what matter is bound to be subject to arbitration under the arbitration agreement.

III.   SUBJECTIVE SCOPE AND CROSS-FILING CLAUSE

The Japanese Supreme Court decided on this issue in an interesting case involving a "cross-filing arbitration clause". It is common in Japan and in Asia to agree to international arbitration in a peculiar way. Under this arrangement, the claimant must bring arbitration in the respondent's home country. My guess is that this type of agreement is used to deter both parties from initiating arbitration. Nobody likes to litigate on the respondent's home territory, especially when the respondent's legal system in general or arbitration system in particular is considered unfamiliar and unfavorable. Asian legal systems are not only different from each other but also unfamiliar to each other. Japanese lawyers know the American legal systems better than, say, the nearby Korean or Chinese legal systems. American lawyers do not know the Japanese legal system as Japanese lawyers know the American. In addition, physical distance also has a deterrent effect. Under this condition, such a cross-filing agreement is commonly included in standard contract forms. When I mentioned this practice in a conference in Europe, I understood that it was unknown in Europe, perhaps because of a lack of physical and psychological distance even across the Atlantic.[1]

---

1. Such an arbitration clause was dealt with in an American court decision reported in ICCA *Yearbook Commercial Arbitration* XXXI (2006) (hereinafter *Yearbook*) p. 1034.

In the above-mentioned Japanese Supreme Court case, a Japanese company concluded a contract with Ringling Brothers, an American circus company. In the contract, the latter agreed to stage certain circus performances in Japan. There was a cross-filing arbitration agreement for ICC arbitration either in Japan or in New York depending on who became the claimant. The circus performance allegedly did not live up to the standard agreed upon. The Japanese party sued the president of Ringling Brothers for fraud in the Japanese courts. The defendant president raised the arbitration agreement as defense. The first- and second-instance courts dismissed the action because of the arbitration agreement. The Japanese company appealed to the Supreme Court. It asserted that Japanese law was applicable to the arbitration agreement, according to which only the contracting parties, namely the plaintiff and Ringling Brothers were bound by the arbitration agreement, and, therefore, the non-party president could be sued in a competent court.

The Japanese Supreme Court upheld the decision below by holding that the applicable law to determine the scope of the binding effect of an arbitration agreement is the law of the place of arbitration which was, according to the court, New York. The court found that under the relevant New York law the president of a company is bound by an arbitration agreement concluded by his or her company, which is not the case under Japanese law. The decision was much discussed. Most commentators agreed with its conclusion but differed in their reasoning. Why the court found the place of arbitration to be New York is not clear because the arbitration had not yet begun and it could also have been Japan. It was true that the Japanese party took the initiative to commence a legal action but it was not arbitration. I wonder how an expert like Professor Berger resolves the issue.[2]

IV. OBJECTIVE SCOPE

The next question concerns the objective scope, that is, what kind of dispute must be subject to an arbitration agreement. Some time ago there was a dispute involving Nissan Motor Company in London. Nissan wanted to terminate a contract with Nissan UK, an independent United Kingdom company. There was an arbitration agreement for arbitration in Japan in the initial contract between the parties. The contract was revised several times as the business conditions changed. These later contracts did not include any arbitration agreement. Nissan UK sued Nissan in London for damages. Nissan pleaded the arbitration agreement in defense saying the later contracts should be interpreted as implying or adopting the arbitration agreement in the original contract. I was retained as expert for Nissan, and the High Court decided in favor of Nissan.

---

2. The above-mentioned American case (see previous footnote) involved a similar issue. According to the editor's explanation of facts, the American court held that it could not decide whether a non-signatory party to an arbitration agreement could compel arbitration of certain claims against it because the parties failed to address the issue of the law applicable to the determination of this issue. Moreover, although the party framed its motion to compel arbitration under federal law, the court held that state law governs the interpretation of arbitration clauses. See Yearbook XXXI (2006) at pp. 1037, 1044, 1046.

Arbitration in Tokyo with the Japan Commercial Arbitration Association ensued. I was asked to explain how a Japanese court would resolve the issue. But I wondered which law should govern the matter of interpretation of the arbitration agreement, UK law or Japanese law. Even if Japanese law applies as the law of the place of arbitration, it was to be interpreted by an English judge who cannot be free from his own legal training and legal culture. In that sense, the law of the forum seems to affect the outcome unavoidably. In that particular case, the English judge decided the case without paying any attention to my views on Japanese law.

V. DUE PROCESS

This leads us to the last issue, namely, the due process consideration in determining the applicable law. This argument is not limited to the applicable law to an arbitration agreement but is also valid, perhaps more so, in dealing with the law applicable to the substance of a dispute. The applicable law can be chosen by a court or by an arbitrator. Thus, the deciding authority, either a judge or an arbitrator, should not surprise the parties by his choice of law. A surprise may happen in respect of this issue in view of the existence of many conflicting views. The parties should be made fully aware of the law a court or an arbitrator is going to apply so that the parties can assert relevant facts and advance appropriate arguments. It is desirable and required of a judge or an arbitrator to inform the parties, at an appropriate procedural stage, of the law which is to be applied. Perhaps, an interim decision should be made on this point in order to give the parties a full opportunity to argue on the basis of the determined applicable law. In this respect, the Japanese *Ringling Brothers* case was unsatisfactory because the contents of the eventually applicable New York law were not given enough opportunity to be scrutinized in the lower court proceedings.

Working Group A

6. Jurisdiction
Over Non-signatories:
National Contract Law or
International Arbitral Practice?

Non-signatories in International Arbitration: Lessons from Thirty Years of Case Law

Bernard Hanotiau[*]

I. DEFINITION OF THE ISSUE AND DISTINCTION FROM OTHER CONNECTED ISSUES

1.   Non-signatories in International Arbitration: The Issue

Given the increasing number and complexity of commercial transactions and of national and international groups of companies and the fact that for financial, tax or other commercial reasons the individual(s) or company(ies) that has (have) signed the agreement and those that perform it are not always identical, international arbitrators and national courts are more and more often confronted with the issue whether an arbitration agreement concluded by one individual or company may be extended or imputed to other non-signatory individuals or companies or States as additional claimants or defendants.[1]

The issue may be more precisely defined as follows. One or more individuals or companies (or even a State) are formal parties to an arbitration agreement. If a dispute arises and an arbitration procedure is initiated, may an individual, a company or a State, which is not a formal party to the agreement, join the arbitration as an additional claimant or be joined as an additional defendant in the request for arbitration:[2]

– because even though it is not a formal signatory to the agreement, it is in fact a party, by application of the mechanism of representation or given the existence of a principal-agent relationship;

---

[*] Member of the Brussels and Paris bars, Professor, University of Louvain. Vice-Chairman, LCIA Court of Arbitration, the Institute of Transnational Arbitration (Dallas) and CEPANI (Brussels). Member, ICC International Arbitration Commission. Member of ICCA.

[1] On this issue, see Bernard HANOTIAU , *Complex Arbitrations – Multiparty, Multicontract, Multi-Issue and Class Actions* (hereinafter *Complex Arbitrations*), (Kluwer Law International 2006) in particular Chapter II and the bibliography.

[2] In contrast, the issue referred to as "Joinder" arises when an additional party wants to join in the course of the arbitration or a party to the arbitration wants to join a non-party thereto in the course of the procedure. See below, I.7.

– by application of the theory of apparent mandate or ostensible authority;
– because it is a third-party beneficiary or an assignee of the contract containing the clause or a member with the signatories of a general partnership or a community of rights and duties;
– as a result of the application of the theory of estoppel or the theory of alter ego;
– because it may be inferred from the circumstances of the case that the party concerned has consented to the arbitration agreement, at least impliedly, by its conduct in the negotiation and performance of the contract;
– because the fraudulent conduct of the party concerned justifies the extension, or if it is a company, justifies piercing the corporate veil?

Before addressing the issue, I would like to denounce the lack of rigor and the use of imprecise terminology in the doctrinal writings and even in the arbitral and judicial case law.

2.   Groups of Companies and Groups of Contracts

First, a clear methodological distinction – one that is not often made – should be made between the issues arising from the circumstance that the project at the centre of the dispute has been negotiated and performed by one or more companies that belong to a group, some of which are not signatories of the arbitration clause, and the issues arising from the fact that the dispute involves or concerns a variety of problems originating from, or in connection with, two or more agreements entered into by the same and/or different parties and which do not all contain the same – or at least compatible – arbitration clauses. In this second scenario, the fact that the parties to the contracts may belong to a group is a priori irrelevant, although it may in some cases help clarify or resolve the issues that arise from the existence of a group of contracts.[3]

In other words, the question of "extension" of the arbitration clause to non-signatory members of a group of companies, and the question whether and to what extent it is possible to bring into one arbitral proceeding all the parties that have participated in a single economic transaction through various agreements and to decide in the same proceeding all the issues arising from the latter, should be clearly distinguished and are indeed – in the main – the subject of distinct case law. In the first case, the issue is whether an arbitration clause contained in one contract may be "extended" to a company that did not sign the arbitration agreement. In the second case, there are two or more connected agreements and the issue of whether it is possible to join and decide together in one single set of proceedings all the disputes arising from these interrelated contracts arises because the parties thereto are not identical; or because the jurisdiction clauses in the various agreements are not identical or compatible or one or more contracts do

---

3. See, e.g., *Société Kis France v. Société Générale* (Paris Court of Appeal, 31 Oct. 1989) Rev. Arb. (1992) p. 90; ICCA *Yearbook Commercial Arbitration* XVI (1991) p. 145 , and text accompanying notes 285-289 in *Complex Arbitrations* and ICC Partial Award in Case No. 8910 of 1998, 127 J. Droit Int'l (2000) p. 1085, obs. D. HASCHER (Paris, French law) and text accompanying note 304.

not contain any jurisdiction or arbitration clause. Moreover, the problem may arise in two-party as well as in multiparty situations.

3.   "Extension" to Non-signatories Is a Misleading Concept

On the other hand, the widely used concept of "extension" of the arbitration clause to non-signatories is a misleading concept, and moreover, is probably wrong to a large extent since, in most cases, courts and arbitral tribunals still base their determination of the issue on the existence of a common intent of the parties and, therefore, on consent. The basic issue therefore remains: who is a party to the clause, or has adhered to it, or eventually is estopped from contending that it has not adhered to it. This is in other words a classical problem of contract law. The real issue therefore becomes whether in international arbitration, given its specific character and taking into consideration the usages of international trade, one should follow the same rules as are applicable to ordinary civil and commercial cases or adopt a more liberal approach; and in the latter case what approach should be adopted.[4]

4.   The So-called "Group of Companies" Doctrine

The issue of "extension" of the arbitration clause to non-signatories is sometimes "reduced" by commentators to the issue of "groups of companies", or by Courts to the issue whether the applicable law recognizes or not the existence of groups of companies or the so-called group of companies doctrine. This is an unfortunate "reduction" of the issue of "extension". First, even if it is true that *"irrespective of the distinct juridical identity of each of its members, a group of companies constitutes one and the same economic reality of which the Arbitral Tribunal should take account when it rules on its own jurisdiction ..."*,[5] it remains that the issue of "extension" of the arbitration clause to non-signatories not only arises in relation to companies (belonging or not to the same group) but also in relation to individuals or States. Second, I will emphasize in the conclusions that I have drawn from an analysis of the case law, that the existence of a group of companies is not *per se* a sufficient element to allow the "extension" to a non-signatory company of an arbitration agreement concluded by another member of the group. Third, to allow the "extension", in most cases courts and arbitral tribunals require the existence of consent or of a conduct amounting to consent. Express consent or conduct as an expression of implied consent – or as a substitute for consent – is still the basis on which most courts and arbitral tribunals reason to decide on the "extension". It is true that the factual existence of a group of companies gives a special dimension to the issue of conduct or consent. But the fact that the signatory and the non-signatory belong to the same group is only one factual element (*un indice*) to be taken into consideration to determine the existence of

---

4. "Extension" is a proper term to eventually describe the result of the analysis, but not the analysis process itself.
5. *Dow Chemical v. Isover Saint Gobain,* ICC Interim Award of 23 September 1982 in case no. 4131, 1 ICC Awards, at p. 464.

consent.[6] It is doubtful in this respect that the non-recognition by the applicable law of the legal existence of groups of companies should in most cases have a decisive impact on this determination. The problem is more factual than legal and this is unfortunately overlooked by a number of commentators, courts and tribunals.

In other words, it is probably better to avoid using the formula "group of companies doctrine" as the sole tool for legal reasoning in the determination of whether an arbitration clause should be extended to non-signatory companies of a group. Indeed, there is a risk that the formula will be used as a *shortcut permitting avoidance of rigorous legal reasoning,* to quickly agree without substantial factual or legal analysis, to the "extension" of the relevant arbitration clause to non-signatory companies of the group, in cases where such an "extension" is unwarranted; or to a refusal of "extension" in cases where it would be duly justified. In my view it is better to refer to the principles that have been applied by courts and arbitrators dealing with this issue in a great number of international disputes and apply them to the facts of the case. These principles are enunciated below by way of conclusion of my analysis of the case law.[7]

On the other hand, if one still wants to refer to the concept "group of companies doctrine" in the reasoning, it should at least be clear what this concept means and encompasses or in other words what principles among those referred to above are intrinsic, fundamental, to that theory. These principles are probably the following:

– the issue of consent to arbitration may take a special dimension when one (or more) company(ies) to a complex international transaction is (are) member(s) of a group of companies, given the nature of the relationships which exist between companies of such group;
– in particular, consent to arbitrate may sometimes be implied from the conduct of a company of the group – although it did not sign the relevant arbitration agreement – by reason of its "implication" in the negotiation and/or the performance and/or the termination of the agreement containing the arbitration clause and to which one or more members of its group are a party;[8]

---

6. As was pointed out by the sole arbitrator in ICC Case No. 11405 (unpublished, commented in *Complex Arbitrations* at no. 158), "[t]here is no general rule, in French international arbitration law, that would provide that non-signatory parties members of a same group of companies would be bound by an arbitration clause, whether always or in determined circumstances. What is relevant is whether all parties intended non-signatory parties to be bound by the arbitration clause. Not only the signatory parties, but also the non-signatory parties should have intended (or led the other parties to reasonably believe that they intended) to be bound by the arbitration clause... The legal literature confirms that what is relevant is whether the non-signatory parties were intended to be bound, rather than a general rule about a group of companies: '[c]learly, however, it is not so much the existence of a group that results in the various companies of the group being bound by the agreement signed by only one of them, but rather the fact that such was the true intention of the parties' (*Fouchard, Gaillard, Goldman on International Commercial Arbitration* (The Hague 1999) no. 500, p. 283)."
7. See below, III.2.
8. Whether one likes it or not, in a great number of legal systems, the parties' conduct at the time of negotiation of the contract or during its performance is evidence of the parties' intention and is often referred to by courts and arbitral tribunals to establish the true content of their agreement.

– on the other hand, the sole fact that a non-signatory company is part of a group of companies, one or more other members of which have signed the agreement containing the arbitration clause, is not per se a circumstance sufficient to permit the "extension" of the clause to the non-signatory.

5. Inadequate Qualifications

Courts and arbitral tribunals sometimes qualify an issue as one of jurisdiction of the arbitral tribunal over a non-signatory when the problem confronting the court is of a different nature. One illustration is the *Peterson Farms* case which ended in an English Commercial Court decision of 4 February 2004[9] in which the Court had to decide on a challenge under Sect. 67 of the 1966 English Arbitration Act of an award in which the tribunal had decided that it did have jurisdiction to consider and determine the damage claims of other entities within the claimant's group which were not parties to the arbitration. It is clear that the issue submitted to the Commercial Court was not a real issue of jurisdiction in relation to a group of companies. It was rather an issue of the extent of the damages that could be recovered by claimants, purchasers of live poultry which were subsequently sold to other group entities and to other purchasers. The real question with which the arbitrators and subsequently the Court were confronted was rather whether the purchasers, claimants in the arbitration, could also recover, beyond the damages they had suffered, the damages suffered by companies closely connected to them and to the contractual scheme. The issue was therefore not an issue of jurisdiction ratione personae but rather a classical issue of pass-through claim, which is not specific to groups of companies and does not necessarily have to be decided on the basis of the group of companies doctrine, as the Court did.

6. Inadequate Use of the Expression "Piercing the Corporate Veil"

The concept of "piercing the corporate veil" is often used, especially in the United States, as synonymous with "extending the arbitration clause to a non-signatory". This is totally wrong and inappropriate. Piercing the corporate veil means going behind the corporate veil of the company and holding its owners liable for the corporation's commitments. But this theory, in most legal systems, has a very limited scope of application. It will be applied only if the owners exercised complete control over the

---

9. *"Peterson" Farms Inc v. C&M Farming Ltd*, [2004] EWHC 121 (Comm). For an analysis of the decision, see *Complex Arbitrations*, at p. 462 and following. See also a.o. John LEADLEY and Liz WILLIAMS, "*Peterson Farms*: There is no group of Companies Doctrine in English Law, [2004] Int. A.L.R. 111, John P. GAFFNEY, "The Group of Companies Doctrine and the Law Applicable to the Arbitration Agreement", Mealey's International Arbitration Report, (2004) p. 47; Otto SANDROCK, "The Group of Companies Doctrine forms no part of English Law – *Ein bemerkenswertes Urteil der* Queen's Bench", 2005 IDR 51. See also in re. *Scaplake*, QB, [1978] 2 Lloyd's Rep. 380 and *Roussel-Uclaf v. Searle*, Ch. D., [1978] 1 Lloyd's Rep. 225.

corporation with respect to the transactions at issue and such control was used to commit a fraud or wrong that injured the party seeking to pierce the veil.[10]

7.   Distinction of the Non-signatory Issue from Joinder and Consolidation

The issue of "extension" of the arbitration clause to non-signatories should be clearly distinguished from the issues which are usually referred to as:

– joinder: that is, whether a non-party to the arbitration may intervene in the arbitration proceedings, once they have been initiated, or whether a party to the arbitration proceedings (Claimant on the one hand, Respondent on the other hand) may join a non-party during the arbitration;
– consolidation: that is, if multiple disputes that arise from, or in connection with, different contracts, must in the first place be the object of separate arbitration requests, can the arbitral proceedings subsequently be consolidated? It should however be pointed out that in the United States, the word consolidation has a broader meaning. It also overlaps to some extent the issues of group of contracts, i.e., the question of whether it is possible to bring into one "consolidated" arbitration proceeding all the disputes arising from various connected agreements. In this respect, it is not unusual for parties under these various contracts to petition a court in the United States to consolidate their disputes in advance in one arbitration procedure.

8.   Do the Issues of Extension to a State and to a Company Arise in the Same Terms?

This problem is complex and would deserve extensive development. I will limit myself in this article to a few basic remarks concerning arbitrations based on a contract. According to Fouchard, Gaillard and Goldman,[11] the problem of "extension" to the State of an arbitration agreement concluded by government entities does not arise in terms which are different from those of the extension of the scope of an arbitration clause within a group of companies (even if the issue may raise additional problems such as immunity from jurisdiction). In both cases, it is the intention of the parties that is the main criterion to determine the scope rationae personae of the arbitration clause. This is undoubtedly correct. But is it possible in relation to States, to apply the same reasoning to the problem as for groups of companies, when a court is asked to decide on the extension of the arbitration clause by application of theories such as *alter ego*, agency or third party beneficiary? Some authors have expressed serious doubts. In this respect it is worth citing Professor Roger Alford's critique of the decision of the United States Court of Appeals for the Fifth Circuit in *Bridas S.A.P.I.C. v. Government of*

---

10. In the same vein, one could also regret the sometimes abusive reference by counsel to the theory of alter ego.
11. P. 290 and following.

Turkmenistan[12] in which the Court considered unjustified and therefore invalidated the decision of an ICC Arbitral Tribunal to extend to the Government of Turkmenistan the arbitration clause contained in an agreement concluded by Bridas and entities owned by the Turkmen Government:

> "thus, the goal of such government instrumentalities is to create within the government structure a special enterprise that resembles a private corporate entity in form and purpose. Such entities often are created devoid of any traditional regulatory function, and specially established for the purpose of engaging in commercial activities. Thus, while the entity itself may resemble a private corporation, the motivation of the government in establishing the entity, and the relationship of that entity vis-à-vis its 'parent' are quite distinct. Bridas virtually ignored these distinctions, assuming that principles derived in the private sphere could be brought and applied in the government context. For example, in holding that the District Court erred in its alter-ego determination, the Court imposed a test for parent-subsidiary alter ego status that is far removed from the context of government instrumentalities. One cannot address, as the Court requires, whether the government of Turkmenistan is the alter ego of Turkmeneft based on the fact that the parent and subsidiary have 'common business departments' or 'consolidated financial statements' or 'common directors and officers' or 'common stock ownership'. In addition, the Court utilized traditional third-party beneficiary cases without addressing the special rules applicable to government contracts that may reflect public policies that afford rights to third parties to enforce the agreement. Likewise, in its analysis of agency, the Court utilized traditional notions of private agency to determine whether an 'agency relationship' existed between Turkmeneft and Turkmenistan. Yet government agencies and instrumentalities do not easily lend themselves to such private comparisons.... As difficult as it may be to develop a more accurate analysis of the circumstances under which a sovereign non-signatory should be bound by the signature of its instrumentality, Bridas certainly underscores the hazards of freely transposing criteria established in the private sector to government contracts."[13]

---

12. 345 F. 3d 347 (5th Cir. 2003) rehearing and rehearing en banc denied, 84 Fed. Appx 472 (5th Cir. 2003), cert. denied, 124 S.Ct. 1660, 158 L.Ed. 2d 357 (2004); "Binding Sovereign Non-Signatories", 19 Mealey's Intl. Arb. Rep. (2004, no. 3) p. 27; summary of the decision by C. LAMM, E. HELLBECK and A. KOVINA in 2004 Int'l A.L.R., N - 58.

13. Under United States law, the mere status of an entity as an agency or instrumentality of a foreign State is insufficient to subject the foreign State to suit for the agency or instrumentality's wrongdoings. US Courts generally look to the principal/agent relationship between a sovereign and a State-owned entity, or to abuses of the corporate form, such as where the State-owned entity is in fact an *alter ego* of the sovereign, or merely a corporate shell. Often this entails a fact-based inquiry into the level of control over the day-to-day operations of the instrumentality. US Courts also conduct a separate inquiry, namely whether principles of fairness and equity mandate that the State-owned entity's corporate form should be disregarded. Carolyn LAMM and Jocelyn AQUA, "Defining a Party – Who Is a Proper Party in an Arbitration Before the American

9. Procedure and Strategy

From a strictly procedural point of view, the issue of whether the arbitration clause signed by a company of the group should be extended to other companies of the same group – non-signatories – is an issue of jurisdiction that the parties sometimes ask the arbitral tribunal to decide in a partial award, in a preliminary phase of the arbitration. This is not always possible. The decision on jurisdiction often depends upon the facts of the case and therefore, on the evidence that will be submitted by the parties on the merits. On the other hand, it sometimes happens that the issue of "extension" will require the arbitrators to decide collateral procedural issues at an early stage of the arbitration, even before the signature of the terms of reference. For example, in ICC Case No. 13041 of 2004,[14] claimant had initiated the arbitration procedure against the party with which it had concluded a contract containing the arbitration clause, but also against other companies of the group. To support its case, claimant filed with its request for arbitration, a number of documents that had been exchanged between the parties, including the non-signatories, during settlement negotiations. Respondents immediately objected to the communication of these documents and asked the arbitral tribunal to order claimant to exclude them from its file. Extensive submissions were exchanged by the parties on this issue, before the signature of the terms of reference. After an oral hearing, the arbitral tribunal issued a procedural order on the issue of admissibility of the documents. The parties settled soon thereafter.

One should also consider why one wants to join non-signatory companies as additional claimants or respondents. The reasons are various and often pertain to strategy: for example, the real party in interest is not the company that signed the relevant agreement but rather a subsidiary or the parent company of the group; or the company that has signed the arbitration clause is insolvent while the other subsidiaries of the group or the parent company are not; or the victim of the damage resulting from a breach of contract or a tort committed by respondent, is not the company that signed the contract containing the arbitration clause with respondent but other companies of the group. Other parties invoke the fact that justice would not be well-administered if a specific, additional, non-signatory respondent could not be a party to the arbitration. One will immediately point out that this is not a good argument. However far one is ready to stretch the concept of consent (and it may go as far as considering certain specific conduct as a substitute for consent), one should not forget that consent is the fundamental pillar of international arbitration.

II. THE IMPACT OF THE REQUIREMENT THAT THE ARBITRATION CLAUSE BE IN WRITING

One will not dispute that an arbitration clause in writing is necessary to give jurisdiction to an arbitral tribunal. But by definition, if one wishes to join a non-signatory, it means that this particular company has not signed the arbitration clause. Can one say that there

---

Arbitration Association?", Int'l A.L.R. (2002) pp. 89 and 90 and references cited.
14. Unpublished.

is therefore no arbitration clause in writing in relation to this particular company and that therefore it may not be joined to the arbitration? The Swiss Federal Supreme Court, in its landmark decision of 16 October 2003,[15] had the opportunity to address this fundamental issue, which might be called the "formal" issue. It answered the question in the negative. The Court held that from the moment there is an arbitration clause, the issue of "extension" to a non-signatory may be considered. The fact that the clause or the contract containing the clause was not signed by the "non-signatory" is not a formal bar to the "extension".[16] In the words of the Swiss Federal Court:

> "this formal requirement (contained in Art. 178 al. 1 of the Swiss Law on Private International Law) only applies to the arbitration agreement itself, that is to the agreement ... by which the initial parties have reciprocally expressed their common will to submit the dispute to arbitration. As to the question of the subjective scope of an arbitration agreement formally valid under Art. 178 al. 1 – the issue is to determine which are the parties which are bound by the agreement and eventually determine if one or several third parties which are not mentioned therein nevertheless enter into its scope ratione personae –, it belongs to the merits and should consequently be decided in the light of Art. 178 al. 2 LDIP"[17]

(which provides that the arbitration agreement is valid, as to its substance, if it meets the conditions either of the law chosen by the parties, or the law governing the subject matter of the dispute, and in particular, the law applicable to the main agreement, or Swiss law).

In the United States too, it is accepted that even though there must be an agreement in writing to arbitrate, there is no requirement that this agreement be signed. Therefore, from the moment there is a written agreement, US Courts have held that a non-signatory may be considered in an appropriate case to have agreed to it or may be bound to submit to arbitration and that the ensuing award can be entitled to the protection of the New York Convention.[18]

---

15. *X. S.A.L., Y. S.A.L. and A v. Z, SARL* and ICC Arbitral Tribunal, DFT 129 III 727. The decision has been commented on by Laurent LÉVY and Blaise STUCKY in 2005 Int. A.L.R., N-5 and Rev. Arb. (2004) p. 695 at p. 707; Otto SANDROCK, *"Die Aufweichung einer Formvorschrift und anderes mehr"*, German Arb. J. (2005) p. 1; François KNOEPFLER and Philippe SCHWEIZER, *"Jurisprudence suisse en matière d'arbitrage international"*, Revue Suisse de Droit International et de Droit Européen (2005) p. 158 and Jean-François POUDRET, *"Un statut privilégié pour l'extension de l'arbitrage aux tiers"*, 22 ASA Bulletin (2004) p. 390. According to Poudret, the Federal Court gives a privileged status to the extension of the arbitration clause and therefore creates a discrimination between the initial parties and the non-signatory.

16. This principle is also often referred to in the US case law. See for example *McCarthy v. Azure*, 22 F. 3d 351, 355-56 (1st Cir. 1994).

17. DFT 129 III 736.

18. See, for example, *Fisser v. Int'l Bank*, 82 F. 2d 231 at 233 (2d Cir. 1960) and *Interocean Shipping Co. v. Nat'l Shipping and Trading Corp.*, 523 F. 2d 527 at 539 (2d Cir. 1975).

In France, when confronted with the objection that the non-signatory did not sign the arbitration agreement, arbitral tribunals have also from time to time held that the French law of international arbitration does not subordinate the validity of the arbitration provision to compliance with formal requirements.[19]

III.   ANALYSIS OF THE CASE LAW

There is no place in this limited article to analyze, case-by-case, all the court decisions and arbitral awards that have dealt with the issue of "extension" of the arbitration clause to non-signatories. This analysis has been done in other writings.[20] The reader is referred to them. I will limit my comments to an analysis of the fact patterns that may be encountered in the case law and to a presentation of the general conclusions that may be drawn from an analysis of thirty years of awards and court decisions.

1.   The Factual Schemes

The arbitral awards and court decisions in which tribunals have been confronted with the issue of "extension" of the arbitration clause to non-signatories may be subdivided into some twelve different fact patterns that may themselves be put into two groups: "extension" of the clause to one or several other defendants, and "extension" to one or several other claimants.

"Extension" to one or several non-signatories as additional defendants:
– to the parent company of the group;
– to a State;
– to one or more subsidiaries or one or more companies of the group that are not subsidiaries;
– to a sister corporation and an employee;
– to another company, unrelated to the signatory;
– to a director or general manager or CEO or to the owner of the group;
– to an individual, possibly a majority shareholder of the group, and another company within the group;

"Extension" to one or several non-signatories as additional claimants:
– to the parent company of the group;
– to a State;
– to an individual (possibly a majority shareholder of the group) and other companies within the group;

---

19. See for example ICC Award in Cases No. 7604 and 7610 of 1995, 125 J. Droit Int'l (Clunet) (1998) p. 1027 and 4 ICC Awards, p. 510 and note D.H.
20. In particular in *Complex Arbitrations*.

– to one or more subsidiaries or one or more companies within the group that are not subsidiaries;
– to a director and principal shareholder.

The various cases that fall within these categories are analyzed below.

2. Conclusions of the Analysis

It is very difficult to draw general conclusions from the above survey of the case law. The "extension" of the arbitration clause to other companies of the group – non-signatories – started in France, and still today, its courts and arbitrators are among the most innovative in the development of this jurisprudence. Swiss courts, on the other hand, initially appeared extremely reluctant to accept the "extension" of an arbitration clause to non-signatories, but the Swiss Federal Court has considerably relaxed its jurisprudence. On the other hand, the German approach still appears to be more restrictive[21] and this also seems to be the position in England, where the so-called group of companies doctrine is said to be inconsistent with the principle of privity of contract, the principle of the corporate veil and the treatment of derivative actions.[22] Moreover, the principles of lex mercatoria are not part of English law. The issue of who is party to the arbitration clause is therefore mainly viewed as an issue of consent, but "extension" may nevertheless be achieved by recourse to other theories such as agency, trust or piercing the corporate veil. The same theories are also applied in the United States, which to some extent appears to be one of the most liberal jurisdictions with respect to the "extension" of the arbitration clause to non-signatories.

Subject to these reservations, a first conclusion may be drawn from the awards and court decisions to the effect that the determination of whether an arbitral clause should be extended to other companies of the group or its directors or shareholders is "fact specific" and may differ depending upon the circumstances of the case.[23] As was expressed by the arbitral tribunal in its first interim award in ICC case no. 9517:[24]

> "... the question whether persons not named in an agreement can take advantage of an arbitration clause incorporated therein is a matter which must be decided on a case-to-case basis, requiring a close analysis of the circumstances in which the agreement was made, the corporate and practical relationship existing on one side and known to those on the other side of the bargain, the actual or presumed intention of the parties as regards rights of non-signatories to participate in the

21. According to POUDRET and BESSON, *Droit comparé de l'arbitrage international*, (L.G.D.J. 2002) p. 237, the German doctrine, according to Sandrock and Schlosser, rejects the theory of groups of companies and only admits in a very restrictive way the theory of piercing the corporate veil (*Durchgriff*). They point out that various authors like RAESCHKE-KESSLER and BERGER, consider that the German jurisprudence lies way behind the arbitral practice in this area.
22. See in particular the landmark decision *Peterson Farms Inc. v. C&M Farming Ltd.*, [2004] EWHC 121 (Comm.), fn. 9, above.
23. *Smith / Enron Cogeneration Ltd P'ship v. Smith Cogeneration Int'l, Inc.*, 198 F. 3d 88, 97 (2d Cir. 1999).
24. 30 November 1998, unpublished.

arbitration agreement, and the extent to which and the circumstances under which non-signatories subsequently became involved in the performance of the agreement and in the dispute arising from it".

A second conclusion is that arbitral tribunals do not always base their decision to extend the clause or not on a prior determination of the applicable law. Starting from the principle of autonomy of the arbitration clause, they sometimes feel free to determine their competence according to what they consider to be – on the basis of the facts of the case – the common intention of the parties, also taking into consideration the usages of international trade.

There seems on the other hand to be an agreement that the mere existence of a group of companies is not per se a sufficient element to allow the "extension" to a non-signatory of an arbitration agreement concluded by another member of the group.

In most cases, courts and tribunals require proof of the existence of an intention at least implicit of all the parties that the non-signatories be parties to the underlying contract and its arbitration clause.[25] Some courts however limit themselves to an awareness of the clause and the requirement that the additional claimant or defendant be concerned by the dispute. But the company concerned must always have played a role in the conclusion and the performance of the agreement and this has to be proved by the party requesting the "extension" of the clause.

The analysis of the arbitral awards also leads to the emergence of a rebuttable presumption that a parent company binds its subsidiaries[26] but that, on the other hand, only companies that have participated in the conclusion and performance of the agreement will be bound by the contract and the arbitration clause.

Various other elements equally play a role in the decision to extend the clause to a non-signatory:

– the fact that the other party has obviously entered into the agreement with a group as a whole and did not really care which companies would be involved in its performance, assuming that the determination of the signatory companies only concerned the details of performance of the contract;
– or the fact that all the companies concerned have participated in the rights and obligations of the contractual relationship (in what has sometimes been called "a total confusion").

---

25. However, in a recent decision, the Dutch Supreme Court decided that the "extension" could only take place if the will of the non-signatory to adhere to the arbitration agreement was clear and expressed without doubt, since it implied a waiver by the relevant individual or company of its constitutional right of access to the national court system. *Hoge Raad* (Civil Chamber) 20 January 2006, NJ 2006/77, JOL 2006, 40, RVDW 2006, 109. See, in contrast, the much more liberal approach of the Spanish Supreme Court in its 26 May 2005 decision, *ITSA v. Satcon & BBVA* (although the case did not properly address an issue of "extension" of the arbitration clause to a non-signatory but rather an issue of group of contracts).
26. See also K. BERGER, *The Creeping Codification of the Lex Mercatoria*, principle 50 at p. 300, and M. MUSTILL, "The New Lex Mercatoria", in *Liber Amicorum for Lord Wilberforce* (Clarendon Press 1987) principle No. 8, at p. 176.

The application of the theory of lifting the corporate veil is generally considered to be limited to cases of fraud, abuse of rights and violation of mandatory rules. It should moreover be pointed out that this theory is very often wrongly presented and applied by advocates. They invoke the theory to extend the arbitration clause, beyond the company whose corporate veil allegedly has to be lifted, to the owners of the company. In many legal systems, this is not correct: lifting the corporate veil means that the legal personality of the company is disputed and has to be lifted and that therefore the action should be directed only to its owners, those who stand "behind the corporate veil". In other words, it is often "the shareholders instead of the company" and not "the company plus the shareholders". Before raising such a theory one should therefore have in the first place a good understanding of basic principles of corporate law, which is not always the case.[27]

It is also admitted that the "extension" of the clause can never be considered a sanction of the conduct of the non-signatory.

Arbitral tribunals and courts have also emphasized the right to use a group structure as appropriate, but once a choice has been made, it must be fully assumed. In this respect, the use of a company vehicle for tax or other reasons is not per se an argument to justify lifting the corporate veil and extending the arbitration clause to the underlying shareholders.

It seems that at least in a great number of cases, a good test to decide whether an "extension" of the clause is appropriate is to determine whether the same solution would be justified if the situation were reversed. In other words, it is tentatively suggested that the principles used to determine the eventual "extension" of the clause to additional defendants should also be applied when the case concerns additional claimants and vice versa.[28]

Finally, it appears that in relation to the issue of "extension" of the clause to non-signatories, American case law is much more liberal than any in Europe, at least in some

---

27. As Professor Roger ALFORD rightly pointed out in "Binding Sovereign Non-Signatories", see above, fn. 12, "[i]n debating whether to 'pierce the corporate veil' or treat the principal as the alter ego of the subsidiary, the arbitration community often appears to have ignored the admonition of the Supreme Court, resorting to 'worn epithets' as a substitute for 'rigorous analysis'. Yet, as the Supreme Court has warned, '[m]etaphors in law are to be narrowly watched, for starting as devices to liberate thought, they end often by enslaving it'." (citing *First National City Bank v. Banco Para El Comercio Exterior ("Bancec")*, 462 U.S. 611, 623 (1983)).

28. Although, as it was rightly pointed out by the sole arbitrator in ICC case no. 11405 (unpublished, commented on in *Complex Arbitrations* at no. 158), "a distinction should be made between the case in which a claimant submits that it is a proper party to the arbitration ... and the case in which a respondent objects to the jurisdiction of an arbitral tribunal.... In the former case, the claimant non-signatory party expressly confirms that it intended to be bound by the arbitration clause. In the latter case, the respondent non-signatory party objects and submits to have never accepted the arbitration clause: it is then much harder for the claimant to extend the scope of the arbitration clause to the non-signatory party, as the claimant has to demonstrate the intent (or apparent intent) of the non-signatory party."

Circuits,[29] the paramount concern of the courts being the "federal policy favouring arbitration".

IV.   THE CHALLENGE OF AWARDS BY NON-SIGNATORIES

An arbitral award can be set aside in the State where it was made. National laws generally provide that such an application to set aside is available to the parties, either when the arbitral tribunal has not been validly constituted, or has exceeded its jurisdiction or powers, or where the principle of contradiction and of the rights of defence have not been respected, or in the event of a violation of international public policy.[30]

Similarly, the recognition or enforcement of the award can equally be refused, by virtue of Art. V of the New York Convention[31] on the following grounds:

(a) the party against whom the award is invoked was not given proper notice of the appointment of the arbitrator or of the arbitration proceedings or was otherwise unable to present his case;[32] or

(b) the award deals with a dispute not contemplated by or not falling within the terms of the submission to arbitration, or it contains decisions on matters beyond the scope of the submission to arbitration;[33] or

(c) the composition of the arbitral authority or the arbitral proceedings was not in accordance with the agreement of the parties, or, failing such agreement, was not in accordance with the laws of the country where the arbitration took place;[34] or

(d) the recognition or enforcement of the award would be contrary to the public policy of that country.[35]

---

29. Some Circuits are less liberal than others. See for example the decision of the Fifth Circuit in *Westmoreland v. Sadoux*, 299 F. 3d 462 (5th Cir. 2002) in which the Court refused the extension to a non-signatory. It pointed out that "... the courts must not offer contracts to arbitrate to parties who failed to negotiate them before trouble arrives. To do so frustrates the ability of persons to settle their affairs against a predictable backdrop of legal issues."

30. See for example Art. 1704 *Code Judicaire* in Belgium or Art. 1484 NCPC in France, or Art. 34(1) and (2)(a)(ii)(iii)(iv) and b(ii) of the UNCITRAL Model Law on International Commercial Arbitration.

31. Convention on the Recognition and Enforcement of Foreign Arbitral Awards, 10 June 1958. To illustrate the problems which might arise, see, i.a. the debate between S. JARVIN and A.J. VAN DEN BERG over the consolidation provisions of the Netherlands Arbitration Act 1986 in 3 Arb. Int'l (1987) p. 254 at p. 257.

32. Art. V(1)(*b*).

33. Art. V(1)(*c*).

34. Art. V(1)(*d*).

35. Art. V(2)(*b*).

National legislations concerning enforcement of arbitral awards generally provide for analogous grounds, in whole or in part.[36]

It is certain that the grounds cited above are such that would allow a party brought to arbitration proceedings (eventually consolidated) against its will[37] to lodge an application to set aside the award or to oppose its enforcement. Actions to set aside are quite frequent. On the other hand, decisions rendered in the context of enforcement proceedings are relatively rare. It remains that the risk of refusal of exequatur is a real one and should therefore encourage caution.

One example of a case where an award was refused enforcement against an individual who was not a party to the relevant arbitration agreement but was considered by the Court a party to the arbitral proceedings, is the decision of the Supreme Court of British Columbia in *Re. Javor v. Francoeur*.[38] An arbitration was carried out under the rules of the American Arbitration Association pursuant to an arbitration agreement dated 25 March 1995 entered into between the claimants Eddie Javor and Fusion-Crete, Inc., and the respondent Fusion-Crete Products Inc. Javor and Fusion-Crete Inc. filed the arbitration not only against respondent Fusion-Crete Products Inc., but also against respondent Luke Francoeur, who was not a party to the arbitration agreement. However, the arbitrator accepted jurisdiction over Francoeur considering that there was no separation between himself and the corporate respondent, thus he was the *alter ego* of Fusion-Crete Products Inc. The arbitrator did not decide that Francoeur was a party to the arbitration agreement but that he was a proper party to the arbitration proceedings. He found Francoeur "personally liable for any debts of the corporation that might ultimately be imposed in these proceedings...". He also found that Francoeur was liable jointly with the corporation to pay the costs of the arbitration.

Javor and Fusion-Crete Inc. sought an enforcement order against Francoeur under the provisions of either the Foreign Arbitral Awards Act or the International Commercial Arbitration Act. The Supreme Court of British Columbia refused enforcement of the award. It considered that enforcement could be ordered only if the conditions provided in either act were fulfilled. This was not the case here since an arbitration agreement is the common foundation upon which each of the two statutes rest. As Francoeur was not a party to the arbitration agreement but was only found by the arbitrator to be a proper party to the arbitration proceedings, petitioners could not have an award for costs against him enforced under the FAAA or the ICAA.

---

36. In Belgium, see Art. 1710(3) as well as 1723 of the *Code Judiciaire* of which para. 3 refers to the grounds to set aside set out in Art. 1704.

37. But, on the other hand, a non-signatory to an arbitration agreement, who initiated arbitration proceedings and signed the Terms of Reference prior to the arbitration, may not subsequently oppose the enforcement of an interim award of costs issued by the arbitrator after he has determined that he had no jurisdiction to entertain the proceedings because claimant was not a party to the written agreement containing the arbitration clause. He is bound by the award. The Terms of Reference are an arbitration agreement within the meaning of the New York Convention and the New Zeland International Arbitration Act 1974. *Commonwealth Development Corporation (United Kingdom) v. Austin John Montague*, Court of Appeal of the Supreme Court of Queensland, 17 April 2000, 27 June 2000, 2000 [QCA 252].

38. 2003 BCSC 350.

Another example of a case in which enforcement of a foreign award was refused, on the ground that one of the parties condemned by the arbitral tribunal was a non-signatory to the arbitration agreement, is the decision of the United States Court of Appeals for the Second Circuit in *Sarhank Group v. Oracle Corporation*.[39] Unfortunately, the decision is wrong, being based on a totally erroneous interpretation – which we have denounced several times[40] – of the term "arbitrability" referred to in Art. V(2) of the New York Convention. Art. V(2)(*a*) of the Convention, provides that a court may refuse to enforce a foreign award if the subject matter was not capable of settlement through arbitration. The "arbitrability" concept used in this article refers to a very restricted and shrinking core of disputes pertaining to public policy that legislators have reserved for the jurisdiction of their national courts (criminal law, family law...). In the history of the Convention, there have not been more than a few cases in which enforcement has been refused on the basis of Art. V (2)(*a*). In any case, this article has nothing to do with the stretched and unusual theory of arbitrability prevailing in the United States, which in other parts of the world is rather referred to as the determination of the scope ratione materiae and ratione personae of the arbitration agreement. In other words, enforcement may not be refused under Art. V (2)(a) of the New York Convention on the basis of the fact that one of the parties over which the arbitral tribunal accepted jurisdiction, did not sign the relevant arbitration agreement. This is however what the United States Courts of Appeals unfortunately did in the *Sarhank Group* decision.

An Egyptian corporation, Sarhank Group (Sarhank) had entered into an agency agreement with Oracle Systems Ltd. (Oracle Systems), under which Sarhank agreed to act as provider of Oracle products and services within Egypt. Oracle Systems is a wholly-owned subsidiary of Oracle Corporation (Oracle), a United States software manufacturer incorporated under the laws of Delaware. A few years later, a dispute arose between the contracting parties and Oracle Systems terminated the agreement. As a result, Sarhank commenced arbitration against both Oracle Systems and Oracle, the parent company. An arbitral tribunal was constituted under the auspices of the Cairo Regional Center for International Commercial Arbitration. Oracle argued that the tribunal lacked jurisdiction over it since it had not signed the agreement with Sarhank. The tribunal rejected the objection and affirmed its jurisdiction over Oracle on the basis that Oracle Corporation was a consolidated partner with Oracle Systems in the relation with Sarhank. The arbitral tribunal also decided that, as a matter of Egyptian law, despite their having separate legal personalities, subsidiary companies to one group of companies are deemed subject to the arbitration clause incorporated in the contract because contractual relations cannot take place without the consent of the parent company owning the trademark by and upon which transactions proceed.[41] In the arbitrators' view, a group of companies analysis was particularly appropriate since the agreement granted Oracle Systems a right to assign its rights and obligations to "an

---

39. 404 F. 3d 657 (2d Cir. 2005).

40. See for example B. HANOTIAU , *"L'arbitrabilité"*, in 296 *The Hague Academy of International Law, Collected Courses* (2003) p. 42.

41. At 662.

affiliated company" without Sarhank's consent. Finally, the tribunal rendered an award in favour of Sarhank jointly and severally against Oracle and Oracle Systems. The award was subsequently upheld by the Egyptian Court of Appeals and the Egyptian Court of Cassation.

Sarhank moved to enforce the award in the United States Federal Court on the basis of the New York Convention. On 8 October 2002, the United States District Court for the Southern District of New York confirmed the award and directed that judgment be entered accordingly. The District Court rejected Oracle's defenses that the arbitrators lacked authority to determine arbitrability and to impose liability on Oracle and that enforcement of the award would be contrary to American public policy. The decision was appealed. The Second Circuit refused enforcement on the basis of Art. V(2) of the Convention considering that

> "under American law, whether a party has consented to arbitrate is an issue to be decided by the Court in which enforcement of an award is sought. An agreement to arbitrate must be voluntarily made, and the Court decides, based on general principles of domestic contract law, whether the parties agreed to submit the issue of arbitrability to the arbitrators."[42]

The Court considered that it was for itself to determine whether the dispute was "arbitrable" in relation to Oracle. It considered that it was not, stating that "an American non-signatory cannot be bound to arbitrate in the absence of a full showing of facts supporting an articulable theory based on American contract law or American agency law".

As pointed out by two American commentators,[43] the Court could have based its decision not to enforce on other articles of the Convention. It could, for example, have formed a view that no arbitration agreement existed as between Sarhank and Oracle and that therefore, the arbitrators exceeded their authority. Alternatively, it might have concluded that the application of a group of companies analysis in this case offended United States public policy. But choosing the "arbitrability" exception was undoubtedly an erroneous decision.

On the other hand, in *Int'l Paper Co. v. Schwabedissen Maschinen & Anlagen GmbH,*[44] the United States Court of Appeals for the Fourth Circuit confirmed the enforcement of an award involving a non-signatory to the arbitration agreement. The main issue under Art. II(1) and V(1)(a) of the New York Convention was whether an award could be enforced against a predecessor-in-interest of one party when the predecessor was not a party to the arbitration agreement. The predecessor of International Paper Company, Westinghouse Electric Corporation, had agreed to buy an industrial saw manufactured by Schwabedissen Maschinen, through its United States distributor, Wood Systems

---

42. Citing the Supreme Court decision in *First Options v. Kaplan*, 514 US. 938, 943 (1995).

43. Barry H. GARFINKEL and David HERLIHY, "Looking for Law in All the Wrong Places: the Second Circuit's Decision in *Sarhank Group v. Oracle Corporation*", 20 Mealey's Intl. Arb. Rep. (2005, no. 6) p. 18. The two authors approve our conclusion.

44. 206 F. 3d 411 (4th Cir. 2000).

Incorporated. A purchase order was sent by Schwabedissen to Wood, without Westinghouse's signature. This purchase order included an ICC arbitration clause. In other words, the arbitration clause was included in a document that Westinghouse did not sign. A dispute arose between the parties and International Paper initiated arbitration against Schwabedissen. The arbitral tribunal held that there was no agreement between Schwabedissen and International Paper and therefore no basis for the arbitration. The arbitrators assessed costs against International Paper.

International Paper refused to comply with the award and Schwabedissen sought its enforcement in the United States District Court. The District Court granted Schwabedissen's motion to enforce the arbitral award. The Court of Appeals confirmed it. It pointed out that a party may be estopped from asserting that the lack of his signature on a written contract precludes enforcement of the contract's arbitration clause when he has consistently maintained that other provisions of the same contract should be enforced to benefit him or, in other words, when it receives a direct benefit from the contract. Quoting *Avila Group, Inc. v. Norma J. of California*,[45] the Court pointed out that "to allow [a plaintiff] to claim the benefit of the contract and simultaneously avoid its burdens would both disregard equity and contravene the purposes underlying enactment of the Arbitration Act".

V. CONCLUSION

The issue of "extension" of the arbitration clause to non-signatories would be easier to decide if it were approached by courts and commentators in a more rigorous way. Confusion with related issues, such as those arising from the existence of a group of contracts that do not all contain the same or compatible arbitration or jurisdiction clauses, the reference to inadequate qualifications, the inadequate use of expressions such as piercing the corporate veil or the unnecessary or arbitrary reference in some cases to the so-called group of companies doctrine, obscure the analysis and may even lead to totally unwarranted results.

On the other hand, there is not one unique answer to the issue with which we have dealt. Indeed, it is in the first place fact-specific. However, it results from a proper analysis of the case law that courts and arbitral tribunals generally follow the same scheme of reasoning. Their decisions are rarely based – and should not be based – on considerations such as equity or good administration of justice. The solution they reach is founded in most cases on classical contractual reasoning: the determination of who is a party to the arbitration clause, or who has adhered to it, or who eventually is estopped from contending that it has not adhered to it, such adhesion being based on the relevant individual's or company's consent, either express, or implied through its conduct in the negotiation, performance and termination of the agreement; or in a limited number of cases on classical theories of company law, such as piercing the corporate veil. The question may therefore be asked whether the non-signatory issue is not another "false problem".

---

45. 426 F. Supp. 537, 542 (S.D.N.Y. 1977).

Non-signatories in International Arbitration: An American Perspective

John M. Townsend*

I.   INTRODUCTION

Professor Hanotiau's thoughtful analysis of the swirl of cases relating to the involvement of non-signatories in arbitration proceedings focuses, properly, on consent as the essential element for determining when a person or entity that has not actually signed an agreement to arbitrate should be permitted to take advantage of such an agreement or, more rarely, compelled to comply with one.[1] Consent is also central to the American approach to this issue, although the complexity of the American approach has sometimes caused us to lose sight of its importance.

As Professor Hanotiau notes, the United States has made a disproportional contribution to the case law on this subject. There is an explanation for the volume of American case law, however, and understanding the explanation is central to putting the American cases in perspective. The explanation, in its simplest form, is that the American litigation system has a number of features that cause many parties to prefer to avoid it. Since an equal and opposite number prefer litigation in American courts to any system of alternative dispute resolution, the two views frequently clash.[2] The litany of the features that make American litigation a magnet to some and frightening to others will be familiar to practitioners of international arbitration: the trial of civil cases by juries, wide-ranging and intrusive discovery, the availability of contingent fees to encourage lawyers to bring cases, the availability of class actions to combine many small claims into one huge claim, and the ability to claim punitive damages (even if such damages are infrequently recovered).

---

* Partner and chair of the Arbitration and ADR Group, Hughes Hubbard & Reed LLP; Chair, Executive Committee, American Arbitration Association; Chair, Mediation Committee , International Bar Association. The author acknowledges with thanks the assistance of Nadine Gomes, associate, Hughes, Hubbard & Reed LLP.
1. Bernard HANOTIAU, "Non-Signatories in International Arbitration: Lessons from Thirty Years of Case Law", this volume, pp. 341-358.
2. Lord Denning's famous observation that "As a moth is drawn to the light, so is a litigant drawn to the United States," *Smith Kline & French Labs Ltd. v. Bloch* [1983] 1 WLR 730, was not made about American arbitration.

Many American companies are as fearful of these features as most foreign companies are, and this fear has contributed a good deal to the popularity of arbitration in the United States. One effect of this reaction, however, is that many American companies have attempted to use arbitration as a sort of talisman to ward off the most feared features of American litigation, especially in form contracts with their customers and employees. There is currently pending before our Supreme Court, for example, a petition for a writ of *certiorari* to review a decision of the Supreme Court of California holding that it is unconscionable to include in an arbitration agreement with consumers a waiver of the right to bring a class action.[3] This type of dispute, especially in the fields of consumer and employment litigation, is behind many of our reported cases, because our Supreme Court has held that the question of *who* may be bound to arbitrate is a decision to be made by the courts, not the arbitrators.[4]

II. BASES FOR REFERRAL TO ARBITRATION USED BY US COURTS: THREE CASES

1. InterGen v. Grina

It may be useful to use an actual case to illustrate how these forces can work in an international setting. The case of *InterGen N.V. v. Grina*, decided by the First Circuit Court of Appeals in 2003,[5] involved a dispute about the performance of a power plant built in England for a subsidiary of InterGen by a subsidiary of ALSTOM, pursuant to contracts between the subsidiaries that contained LCIA arbitration clauses. When negotiation to resolve the dispute broke down, the InterGen parent company sued several of the upstream ALSTOM holding companies (and one of their Massachusetts employees) in Massachusetts state court, alleging that "a pattern of false and deceptive statements" had induced InterGen to select ALSTOM equipment for the plant.[6] InterGen's reasons for wanting to assert its claims in an American court, rather than in an arbitration, are evident from the relief it sought: multiple damages under the Massachusetts Unfair Trade Practices Act, which permits a court to double or treble the actual damages awarded by a jury.[7]

ALSTOM removed the case to federal court, under a statute that provides for federal jurisdiction of cases related to an arbitration agreement "falling under the [New York] Convention",[8] and sought an order compelling arbitration of the dispute. InterGen objected that none of the parties on either side of the lawsuit — neither the plaintiff

---

3. *Parrish v. Cingular Wireless, LLC*, A105518, 2005 Cal. App. Unpub. LEXIS 9021 (Cal. Ct. App. 3 Oct. 2005), pet. for cert. pending sub nom. *Cingular Wireless LLC v. Mendoza*, No. 05-1119 (filed 3 Mar. 2006).

4. *First Options of Chicago v. Kaplan*, 115 S. Ct. 1920 (1995).

5. *InterGen N.V. v. Grina*, 344 F.3d 134 (1st Cir. 2003).

6. Complaint and Jury Demand, *InterGen N.V. v. Grina et al.*, No. A01-905 (Bristol County Super. Ct. 20 July 2001).

7. M.G.L.A. 93A Sect. 9.

8. 9 U.S.C. Sect. 205; *see* 344 F.3d at 140.

parent company nor the defendant holding companies – was a signatory to any of the project contracts that contained the agreements to arbitrate.[9] ALSTOM attempted to persuade the court that it was appropriate to compel the non-signatory plaintiff to arbitrate under almost every one of the theories recognized by American courts as a basis for ordering arbitration by or with non-signatories. Specifically, ALSTOM argued:

– That InterGen was bound by the arbitration agreement because it had pleaded that it stood in the shoes of the contracting subsidiary, so that it could be considered its successor or alter ego;[10]
– That InterGen should be required to arbitrate because it had asserted rights as a third party beneficiary of the contracts containing the arbitration clauses;[11]
– That InterGen should be estopped from denying its obligation to arbitrate, because the claims asserted were founded in and intertwined with the contracts containing the arbitration clauses;[12]
– That InterGen should be required to arbitrate, because the contracts containing the arbitration clauses were signed by its agent.[13]

ALSTOM also argued that InterGen's pleadings treated all the ALSTOM entities as a single whole, so that each of the ALSTOM entities should be entitled to claim the benefits of the agreements to arbitrate signed by the ALSTOM project subsidiaries.[14]

The District Court denied the motion to compel arbitration, because (in a sentence of which Professor Hanotiau would approve) "not all of the persons and entities" sought to be compelled "have manifested consent" to arbitration at the LCIA.[15] The First Circuit ultimately affirmed that order, although for different reasons than those articulated by the District Court.[16] In sending the case back to the District Court, the First Circuit

---

9. 344 F.3d at 140.
10. *Ibid.* at 148.
11. *Ibid.* at 146.
12. *Ibid.* at 145.
13. *Ibid.* at 147.
14. *Ibid.* at 145. The First Circuit never addressed whether ALSTOM could compel arbitration, because it found that InterGen was not obligated to arbitrate.
15. *InterGen N.V. v. Grina,* 2002 WL 32067127 (D. Mass. 6 Nov. 2002).
16. The District Court's opinion contained some notable reasoning:

"[U]nder the Constitution of the United States, I have no authority to compel proceedings in London. The Convention [on the Recognition and Enforcement of Foreign Arbitral Awards] cannot grant me that authority.
(....)
This court has available to it no means of enforcement of the kind of order defendants propose. For example, it is beyond genuine dispute that this court is without authority to order the United States Marshal for the District of Massachusetts to send a team of deputies to London to find and effect service on all interested persons and entities.
(....)
The record before me does not include any evidence that the London Court [of International Arbitration] is a private entity. Indeed, the record supports an inference that the London Court

recognized all the legal theories advanced by ALSTOM as valid bases for requiring arbitration of a dispute involving a non-signatory to an arbitration agreement: Judicial estoppel, equitable estoppel, third-party beneficiary, agency, and alter ego.[17] But, the court reasoned,

> "courts should be extremely cautious about forcing arbitration in 'situations in which the identity of the parties who have agreed to arbitrate is unclear'.... [N]o party to this case, plaintiff or defendant, is a signatory to any of the five agreements. Thus, if ALSTOM is to invoke any of the designated arbitration clauses against InterGen, it must somehow go beyond the four corners of the agreements themselves and show both that it is entitled to the agreements' benefits and that InterGen is obliged to shoulder their burdens."[18]

The court concluded that none of the arguments advanced by ALSTOM, all of which it recognized as valid legal theories, achieved that objective on the particular facts before it.[19]

2. International Paper

While I disagree with the *InterGen* court's conclusion (having represented the losing party), the *InterGen* opinion does represent a trend by American courts that should be reassuring to many. During the decade from roughly 1990 to 2000, American courts developed – one might even say invented – a number of solutions to the problems presented when one party to a commercial relationship seeks to avoid an arbitration clause to obtain a perceived advantage from resorting to the court system, or (more rarely) when another party seeks to take advantage of an arbitration agreement to which it is not a party.[20] The courts did so applying what the Fourth Circuit described as "well-established common law principles [which] dictate that in an appropriate case a nonsignatory can enforce, or be bound by, an arbitration provision within a contract executed by other parties".[21] Four of these theories – agency, incorporation by reference, third party beneficiary, and assumption by conduct – were relatively

---

is a governmental entity. Thus it could not be free to proceed independently, as the AAA does."

Ibid. at *2.

17. 344 F.3d at 144-150.

18. 344 F.3d at 143, quoting *McCarthy v. Azure*, 22 F3d 351, 355 (1st Cir. 1994).

19. *Ibid.* at 150.

20. E.g., *McBro Planning & Dev. Co. v. Triangle Elec. Constr. Co.*, 741 F.2d 342 (11th Cir. 1984); *J.J. Ryan & Sons, Inc. v. Rhone-Poulenc Textile, S.A.* 863 F.2d 315 (Cir. 1988); *Pritzker v. Merrill Lynch, Pierce, Fenner & Smith, Inc.*, 7 F.3d 1110 (3rd Cir. 1993); *Sunkist Soft Drinks, Inc. v. Sunkist Growers, Inc.*, 10 F.3d 753 (11th Cir. 1993); *Thomson-CSF, S.A. v. American Arbitration Association*, 64 F.3d 773 (2nd Cir. 1995); *Bel-Ray Co. v. Chemrite (PTY) Ltd.*, 181 F.3d 435 (3rd Cir. 1999); *Smith / Enron Cogeneration Ltd. v. Smith Cogeneration Int'l, Inc.*, 198 F.3d 88 (2d Cir.1999); *Int'l Paper Co. v. Schwabedissen Maschinen & Anlagen, GmbH*, 206 F.3d 411 (4th Cir. 2000).

21. *Int'l Paper Co.*, 206 F.3d at 416-417.

uncontroversial, if occasionally difficult to apply. Two others – alter ego and equitable estoppel – caused a good deal more trouble, because of the element of misconduct or sharp practice that is explicit in the first theory and that tends to be applied in practice in the second.[22]

The doctrine of equitable estoppel, especially, has given rise to considerable confusion, and to a corresponding amount of anxiety. It was explained by the Fourth Circuit as follows:

> "Equitable estoppel precludes a party from asserting rights 'he otherwise would have had against another' when his own conduct renders assertion of those rights contrary to equity. In the arbitration context, the doctrine recognizes that a party may be estopped from asserting that the lack of his signature on a written contract precludes enforcement of the contract's arbitration clause when he has consistently maintained that other provisions of the same contract should be enforced to benefit him."[23]

The decision of the Fourth Circuit in *International Paper*, from which this passage is quoted, is probably the high water mark of the willingness of American courts to require non-parties to arbitrate. That case involved the purchase by an American company of a piece of equipment made in Germany, and sold by the German company to a distributor under a contract that contained both warranties and an arbitration clause, and resold by the distributor to an American purchaser. By the time the purchaser (which was not a signatory to the contract) realized that the equipment didn't work, the distributor was bankrupt, so the purchaser sued the manufacturer in an American court for breach of the warranty. The Court of Appeals held that, when the purchaser invoked the warranties, it estopped itself from refusing to arbitrate under the arbitration agreement in the same contract.[24] The case was therefore ordered to arbitration.

Since about 2000, when *International Paper* was decided, our courts have become increasingly cautious about requiring non-signatories to arbitrate, as illustrated by the *InterGen* decision. This appears to have occurred even in commercial settings where there was no question about a consumer or an employee needing special protection. This caution was most clearly expressed by our Second Circuit Court of Appeals, in a case in which an investor (a foreign company) commenced an arbitration against both its broker, with whom it had a contract containing an arbitration clause, and the manager of the investment fund that had performed badly.[25] The fund manager was an affiliate of the broker's, but was not a signatory to any contract containing an agreement to arbitrate. The Second Circuit held that the fund manager was not obligated to arbitrate the investor's claim.[26] The court explained:

---

22. *See ARW Exploration Corp. v. Aguirre*, 45 F.3d 1455, 1460-1461 (10th Cir. 1995).
23. *Int'l Paper Co.*, 206 F.3d at 417-418.
24. *Ibid.* at 418.
25. *Merrill Lynch Investment Managers v. Optibase, Ltd.*, 337 F.3d 125 (2d Cir. 2003).
26. *Ibid.* at 131-132.

"[I]t matters whether the party resisting arbitration is a signatory or not. '[A] court should be wary of imposing a contractual duty to arbitrate on a non-contracting party.' Thus, a willing non-signatory seeking to arbitrate with a signatory that is unwilling may do so under what has been called an 'alternative estoppel theory,' which takes into account 'the relationships of persons, wrongs, and issues.' But a willing signatory (such as [the investor]) seeking to arbitrate with a non-signatory that is unwilling (such as [the fund manager]) must establish at least one of the five theories described in Thomson-CSF."[27]

Although non-Americans may not recognize all the "five theories" referred to as adequate bases for arbitration, they will certainly recognize the Second Circuit's statement as a manifestation of concern for the kind of consent that Professor Hanotiau would like the courts to focus on.[28]

3. Comer v. Micor, Inc.

The Ninth Circuit, in a very recent decision, made the same distinction between whether the party to be compelled to arbitrate was a signatory or a non-signatory.[29] In Comer v. Micor, Inc., the Ninth Circuit refused to apply the theory of equitable estoppel to compel an investor to arbitrate statutory claims that he sought to bring in court against an investment fund manager. The fund manager argued that the investor was required to arbitrate by arbitration clauses in the agreements between the fund manager and the trustee of the investor's retirement plans, to which the investor was not a party. This case thus arose in a context resembling the consumer and employment cases previously mentioned – a dispute between an individual and a corporation. The court did not rely on that circumstance, however, but on the absence of any agreement on the part of the investor to arbitrate. The Ninth Circuit went on to refuse to apply the doctrine of equitable estoppel, because there was "no evidence that [the investor] 'knowingly exploited the agreement[s] containing the arbitration clause[s] despite never having signed the agreement'…. Nor did he do so by bringing this lawsuit, which he bases entirely on [the statute]."[30]

---

27. Ibid. at 131 (citations omitted), quoting Smith/Enron Cogeneration Ltd. v. Smith Cogeneration Int'l, Inc., 198 F.3d 88, 97 (2d Cir.1999); Thomson-CSF, S.A. v. American Arbitration Association, 64 F.3d 773, 779 (2nd Cir. 1995); and Choctaw Generation Ltd. P'ship v. Am. Home Assur. Co., 271 F.3d 403, 406 (2d Cir. 2001).

28. Professor Hanotiau correctly identifies the Second Circuit's decision in Sarhank Group v. Oracle Corp., 404 F.3d 657 (2d Cir. 2005), as having gone too far in that direction. That case should be seen as an example of overreaching extraterritoriality, rather than as an appropriate application of the rules governing when a non-signatory may or may not be required to arbitrate.

29. Comer v. Micor, Inc.,436 F.3d 1098 (9th Cir. 2006).

30. Ibid. at 1102.

Our courts will still require signatories to arbitrate with non-signatories in appropriate circumstances.[31] The Eighth Circuit, for example, last year required a franchisor to arbitrate tort claims that it sought to bring in court against executives of the franchisee company that was the party to the contract with the franchisor that contained the arbitration clause.[32] The court explained that "[a] non signatory can enforce an arbitration clause against a signatory to the agreement ... when 'the relationship between the signatory and nonsignatory defendants is sufficiently close that only by permitting the nonsignatory to invoke arbitration may evisceration of the underlying arbitration agreement between the parties be avoided.'"[33] The court stressed in doing so that permitting the individuals to move the suit out of court and into arbitration was proper, because the franchisor "must rely on the written agreement" in making its claims against the non-signatory executives'".[34]

III. CONCLUSION

The forces that generate dozens of American court decisions a year concerning whether non-signatories may compel arbitration or be compelled to arbitrate continue to operate in the United States. The dramatic procedural differences between litigation and arbitration, and the higher-stakes nature of those differences, continue to fuel a desire on the part of many parties to be in a system other than the one that the underlying contracts may have specified, and our courts continue to be required to decide who (as opposed to what) may be required to go to arbitration.

While the basic rules of law have not changed, there does appear to be a trend over the last five or six years toward applying those rules differently, depending upon whether the party to be compelled has signed an arbitration agreement or not. If the party has agreed to arbitrate with anyone, our courts have continued to be willing to expand that agreement to embrace others. But they have been increasingly reluctant to use any of the theories available to force a party that has never agreed to arbitrate at all to do so.[35] Our decisions may not call the governing principle consent, but that would be as good a name for it as any.

---

31. Some relatively non-controversial ones involve assumption by conduct, *Trippe Manufacturing Co. v. Niles Audio Corp.*, 401 F.3d 529 (3rd Cir. 2005); and incorporation by reference, *Keytrade USA, Inc. v. Ain Temouchant M/V in rem*, 404 F.3d 891 (5th Cir. 2005).

32. *CD Partners, LLC v. Grizzle*, 424 F.3d 795 (8th Cir. 2005).

33. *Ibid.* at 798.

34. *Ibid.*

35. *E.g. Zurich American Insurance Co. v. Watts Industries, Inc.*, 417 F.3d 682, 688 (7th Cir. 2005) (agency theory found insufficient to require non-signatory to arbitrate).

Non-signatories in ICC Arbitration

*Anne Marie Whitesell**

I. INTRODUCTION

Whether or not a person or an entity should participate in an arbitration turns above all on the question of consent. The purpose of this article is to discuss the determination of consent in ICC arbitration. The article begins with a discussion of the relevant provisions of the ICC Rules of Arbitration (the ICC Rules).[1] This is followed by a brief look at how those provisions have been applied by the ICC International Court of Arbitration (the Court) in a number of cases. A final section is devoted to how certain arbitral tribunals have dealt with questions of non-signatories in ICC awards after receiving the file from the Court.

II. RELEVANT PROVISIONS OF THE ICC RULES

Art. 6 of the ICC Rules is entitled "Effect of the Arbitration Agreement". It provides the basis for the Court and the arbitral tribunal to determine their jurisdiction. Under Art. 6(2), "[i]f the Respondent does not file an Answer … or if any party raises one or more pleas concerning the existence, validity or scope of the arbitration agreement, the Court may decide, without prejudice to the admissibility or merits of the plea or pleas, that the arbitration shall proceed if it is prima facie satisfied that an arbitration agreement under the Rules may exist".

There are several important elements to highlight in this wording. First of all, the Court carries out an Art. 6(2) analysis only if the respondent does not file an Answer or a plea is raised concerning the existence, validity or scope of the arbitration agreement. Cases involving non-signatories may therefore go forward without the application of Art. 6(2) if all parties are participating in the proceedings and no objection has been raised. Also, Art. 6(2) refers to a plea by *any* party, which means that the

---

* Secretary General, ICC International Court of Arbitration, Paris, France. This publication represents the personal views of the author and should not be interpreted as binding upon the ICC or the ICC International Court of Arbitration.

1. Rules of Arbitration in force as from 1 January 1998, ICC Publication 838.

provision is not restricted to respondents only, but may be applied by the Court to both claimants and respondents.[2]

Secondly, the purpose of the Court's prima facie analysis is to determine whether an arbitration agreement under the ICC Rules *may* exist, not whether it *does* exist. The Court's decision is based on the information provided by the parties: no separate investigation is carried out by the Court itself.

What does the Court look for when deciding whether a case shall proceed? It first of all seeks to determine whether an arbitration agreement under the ICC Rules may exist. This may be necessary, for example, when it has been argued that an agreement does not exist; that there is no written evidence of an agreement; that a draft agreement, although initialled, was never signed; or that there was merely an exchange of documents but no signed agreement.[3] The Court also looks to ensure that, prima facie, an agreement under the ICC Rules may exist as concerns the entities that have been named in the matter.

The Court will make its decision on a case-by-case basis. If it decides that the arbitration shall take place, then, according to Art. 6(2), "any decision as to the jurisdiction of the Arbitral Tribunal shall be taken by the Arbitral Tribunal itself". If, on the other hand, the Court is not satisfied that an arbitration agreement under the ICC Rules may exist, "the parties shall be notified that the arbitration cannot proceed. In such case, any party retains the right to ask any court having jurisdiction whether or not there is a binding arbitration agreement".[4]

III.   APPLICATION OF ART. 6(2) BY THE COURT

Before going any further, it may be useful to clarify some points of terminology. When the Court decides that a matter shall proceed after a prima facie analysis pursuant to Art. 6(2), this is referred to as a *positive 6(2) decision*. When the Court decides that a matter shall not proceed or that a party shall not remain in the proceedings, this is called a *negative 6(2) decision*. Sometimes, the Court will decide to let a matter go forward with only some, but not all, of the parties originally named; in this case it is said to take a *partially negative 6(2) decision*.

To give an initial idea of the way in which Art. 6(2) is applied, it is instructive to look at recent statistics.[5] In 2003, the Court took a negative 6(2) decision in fifteen cases, eleven of which concerned a non-signatory. In the same year, the Court took a positive 6(2) decision in 194 cases. Of course, not all of those decisions involved non-signatories.

---

2. It may be noted that the Court's practice has evolved over the years. In the past it was traditional for the Court not to make negative Art. 6(2) (or its equivalent in previous versions of the ICC Rules) decisions for claimants.
3. The Court may also be required to decide, on a prima facie basis, whether the parties' intention may have been to refer the matter to the ICC rather than to another forum. However, this form of Art. 6(2) analysis is not directly relevant to the present discussion of non-signatories.
4. Art. 6(2) of the ICC Rules.
5. The references in this paragraph to negative 6(2) decisions also include partially negative 6(2) decisions.

In 2004, there were only four negative 6(2) decisions. Interestingly, three of the four cases concerned non-signatory issues. In that year there were 175 positive 6(2) decisions, again not all concerning non-signatories. Finally, in 2005, the Court took a negative 6(2) decision in eight cases, four of which concerned non-signatories. The number of positive 6(2) decisions made that year was 203. In 2005, the total number of new cases submitted to the Court was 445, which means that it carried out an Art. 6(2) analysis in 47 percent of the cases it considered.[6] This high percentage confirms the significant role that Art. 6(2) plays in ICC proceedings.

Let us now turn to some recent examples of Art. 6(2) decisions taken by the Court relating to non-signatories.[7]

1. Positive Art. 6(2) Decisions

Before allowing a case to proceed with a non-signatory, the Court will generally look for prima facie evidence that the party in question participated in the negotiation, performance or termination of the agreement containing the arbitration clause. Each case is treated individually and the Court's decision will depend on the specific circumstances. The arguments presented in support of a non-signatory being considered a party to the proceedings often refer to the doctrines of agency, assignment, company succession, group of companies or *alter ego*.

Case 1

A Request for Arbitration was introduced by three claimants against several respondents. Claimant 1 was a consortium. Claimants 2 and 3 were members of Claimant 1. The contract containing the arbitration agreement was signed only by the consortium. The question at issue was whether signature by the consortium was also binding on its members. The Court decided to let the arbitration proceed with all three claimants, leaving the issue to the arbitral tribunal.

Case 2

A Request for Arbitration was introduced by three claimants against three respondents. The agreement upon which they relied was signed by only two of the respondents. Jurisdictional objections were raised with respect to Respondent 2.

The agreement stated that the reference to each party "shall unless it be repugnant to the meaning or context thereof, be deemed to mean and include [the party's] successors and permitted assigns". The claimants alleged that as part of an increase in capital, Respondent 2 was allocated shares to which Respondent 1 was entitled. The question therefore was whether Respondent 2 acquired the shares as a permitted assignee of Respondent 1, in which case, under the above-mentioned provision, it would become a party to the agreement. The Court decided to send this question to the arbitrators.

---

6. As compared with 38 percent in 2004 and 44 percent in 2003.
7. As mentioned above, such Art. 6(2) decisions are taken only if respondent has not filed an Answer or a plea has been raised concerning the existence, validity or scope of the arbitration agreement.

Case 3

The contract at issue stated that it could not be assigned without the parties' consent. A Request for Arbitration was introduced against the respondent, which was not a signatory to the contract. The claimant alleged that the contract had been assigned to the respondent and that, even though the claimant had not formally given its consent, the assignment had taken place by operation of law. Also, the claimant alleged that it had implicitly given its consent by corresponding with the respondent after the latter had taken over the signatory's operations. The Court decided that it should be for the arbitral tribunal to decide whether the assignment was valid under the contract or applicable law.

Case 4

The claimant filed a Request for Arbitration against two respondents. The respondents objected that Respondent 2, an individual, could not be a party to the proceedings as he had not signed the underlying agreement on his own behalf, but as managing director of Respondent 1. The claimant alleged that Respondent 2 was personally liable for several key obligations under the agreement, including an obligation to transfer shares which he held as owner of Respondent 1. In addition, the agreement made references to Respondent 2 personally. The Court's prima facie analysis revealed indications that Respondent 2's involvement went beyond that of simply being the managing director of Respondent 1. The Court therefore made a positive 6(2) decision and sent the case to the arbitrators with both respondents.

Case 5

The respondent raised a jurisdictional objection, contending that the claimant was not a proper party to the contract containing the arbitration agreement since it had not signed the contract. The original signatory had been split into two independent corporations as part of a restructuring operation. One of those two corporations was the claimant, which alleged that it had succeeded to all of the signatory's rights and obligations under the contract. It claimed that the transfer had been notified and accepted by the respondent and provided documents evidencing such notification and the restructuring. The Court decided to submit the matter to the arbitral tribunal.

Case 6

The respondent objected to arbitral jurisdiction on the grounds that it was not the party that had signed the agreement upon which the Request for Arbitration was based. The claimant argued that the respondent came into existence as a result of a change of corporate form and submitted an excerpt from a commercial registry showing this. It also alleged that the agreement had been terminated by the respondent and not by the original signatory. The Court made a positive 6(2) decision.

Case 7

The claimant filed a Request for Arbitration against two respondents based on related contracts. The contracts had been signed by claimant and Respondent 1. The respondents objected to jurisdiction over Respondent 2. The claimant alleged that under the group of companies doctrine the arbitration should be set in motion against both respondents, as Respondent 1 was a wholly owned subsidiary of Respondent 2, the project was conceived by Respondent 2, Respondent 2 had drafted and negotiated the contracts, the contracts required that all related documentation be sent to both respondents, Respondent 2's General Conditions were an integral part of the contracts, and the performance of the contracts was directed and supervised by Respondent 2. The Court found that the documents submitted provided sufficient prima facie evidence that Respondent 2 had played a substantial role in the negotiation and performance of the contracts. It therefore sent the matter to the arbitral tribunal with both respondents.

2.   Negative Art. 6(2) Decisions

In the following cases, the Court was not "*prima facie* satisfied that an arbitration agreement under the Rules may exist" for certain of the parties named in the Request for Arbitration. These examples demonstrate that, where non-signatories are concerned, the number of partially negative 6(2) decisions made by the Court seems to exceed the number of negative 6(2) decisions pursuant to which the case does not proceed at all.

Case 1
Claimant 1 and the respondent entered into a distribution agreement. Subsequently, Claimant 1 and Claimant 2 entered into an agreement pursuant to which Claimant 2 acquired Claimant 1's assets and trademarks with respect to certain products. When the Request for Arbitration was introduced by both claimants, the respondent objected to the participation of Claimant 2, since it had not signed the agreement. The claimants responded that Claimant 2 was subject to the arbitration clause since the place of arbitration was in California and Claimant 2 would have been allowed to be joined as a third party in court proceedings under California civil procedure. The claimants did not respond to factual allegations made by the respondent arguing against Claimant 2 being a party to the arbitration. The Court was not prima facie satisfied that an arbitration agreement might exist with respect to Claimant 2 and therefore set the case in motion only between Claimant 1 and the respondent.

Case 2
The claimant introduced a Request for Arbitration against three respondents. Respondent 1 had signed the agreement. Respondents 2 and 3 were the managing directors of Respondent 1. The claimant argued that Respondents 2 and 3 should be included as parties to the arbitration on the grounds that they had authority to direct the activities of Respondent 1 and under New York law, in their capacity as managing directors, they were liable for all unlawful acts of Respondent 1. The respondents answered that under New York law an individual cannot be compelled to arbitration in the absence of an express agreement to arbitrate.

The agreement that served as the basis for the Request did not confer any rights or obligations on any officers of the parties. Moreover, it specified that "nothing contained herein shall confer or is intended to confer any rights of any kind upon any third party". Respondents 2 and 3 were not referred to in any way in the agreement. Also, the claimant did not assert that Respondents 2 and 3 ever acted beyond their roles as managing directors. The Court decided that the matter would proceed only between the claimant and Respondent 1.

Case 3

The claimants introduced a Request for Arbitration against three respondents. The respondents objected, claiming that Respondent 2 did not exist. The claimants did not deny this and failed to provide any evidence as to why Respondent 2 should be maintained in the proceedings. The Court took a negative 6(2) decision with regard to Respondent 2.

Case 4

The claimant filed a Request for Arbitration against two respondents. Only Respondent 1 had signed the agreement. Respondent 2 objected to being included in the proceeding. The claimant alleged that Respondent 1 was a subsidiary of Respondent 2. There was no other reference to Respondent 2 in the Request. Nor was there any evidence that Respondent 2 was involved in the negotiation, execution or performance of the contract. The Court decided that the matter would not proceed with respect to Respondent 2.

Case 5

A Request for Arbitration was introduced against two respondents based on two related contracts. Respondent 1 had signed both contracts. Respondent 2 had not signed either of the two contracts, but had signed a third agreement which did not contain an ICC arbitration clause. Respondent 2 objected to being a party to the arbitration. The Court considered that, prima facie, Respondent 2 had not taken part in the negotiation, execution, performance or termination of the first two contracts and thus decided that the matter would not proceed against Respondent 2.

Case 6

An arbitration was started against two respondents based on an agreement that had not been signed by Respondent 2. However, Respondent 2 had executed a guaranty with the claimant under the terms of which Respondent 2 undertook to guarantee payment of any award that would be rendered between the claimant and Respondent 1. Respondents both objected to Respondent 2 being included in the proceedings. Unlike cases in which there is a performance guarantee covering an agreement containing an arbitration clause, where the Court has decided that the guarantor may sometimes be deemed to have agreed to arbitrate the claims, the payment guarantee for an award was here not considered to justify pulling Respondent 2 into the proceedings.

Case 7

A Request for Arbitration was introduced against several respondents, including a non-signatory State party, whose only role had been to provide financing for operations that were the subject of the contract at issue. Following an objection from the State party, the Court took a negative 6(2) decision as regards that party.

3. *Decisions by ICC Arbitral Tribunals Concerning Non-Signatories After a Positive 6(2) Decision by the Court*

As previously stated, once the Court has decided that an arbitration shall proceed on the basis of Art. 6(2), "any decision as to the jurisdiction of the Arbitral Tribunal shall be taken by the Arbitral Tribunal itself".[8] The following examples present both positive and negative decisions by arbitral tribunals concerning their jurisdiction over non-signatories following a positive 6(2) decision by the Court.

Case 1
A Request for Arbitration was introduced by two partners in a joint venture. The respondent objected on the grounds that the contract had been signed by the joint venture and the respondent, not by the two claimants. The claimants responded that under the applicable law the joint venture was an ordinary partnership, without legal personality. As a consequence, all relations with the joint venture were actually with its partners. The Court sent the matter to the arbitral tribunal with a positive 6(2) decision.

The arbitral tribunal found that as the joint venture did not have legal personality, only its partners could initiate arbitration proceedings, but not the joint venture itself. The legal relationship was therefore between respondent and Claimants 1 and 2, and the joint venture served merely as a contractual framework for the execution and performance of the contractual undertakings made by the two partners. Thus, the arbitral tribunal held that it had jurisdiction over the two claimants.

Case 2
The claimant introduced a Request for Arbitration on the basis of an agreement that mentioned three parties on the first page, but was only signed by the claimant and one of the two named respondents. After a positive 6(2) decision by the Court, the arbitral tribunal rendered an award in which it found that it had jurisdiction over both respondents. The arbitrators based their holding on a Swiss Federal Supreme Court decision which was said to allow exceptions to the principle that an arbitration clause can only bind all parties if it is signed by each of them. Given the references to Respondent 2 in the agreement and the parties' behaviour following the signing of the agreement, the arbitral tribunal found that it also had jurisdiction over Respondent 2.

Case 3
In a case involving two claimants and one respondent, Claimant 1 had entered into an agreement with the respondent for the design, supply and set-up of a plant. The claimants alleged that Claimant 2 was a member of the same group of companies as Claimant 1 and that it had been tacitly agreed that Claimant 2 was also a party to the contract because it delivered the materials necessary for the project. The claimants pointed out that when the contract was concluded, the identity of the contracting party was highly confused. They alleged that the respondent had full knowledge of the joint efforts made by both claimants in fulfilling the contract. The respondent claimed that

---

8. Art. 6(2) of the ICC Rules.

there was no arbitration agreement between Claimant 2 and the respondent as Claimant 2 had not signed the contract. The respondent further argued that the deliveries made by Claimant 2 were not sufficient to include it in the arbitration. The Court allowed the matter to go forward with both claimants.

In a partial award, the arbitral tribunal held that Claimant 2 was not a party to the arbitration agreement or a proper party to the proceedings because it had not signed the contract and was merely a subcontractor of Claimant 1. That status did not make it a party to the contract. Nor did the arbitrators find any evidence of an agency relationship. After the partial award, the matter therefore proceeded only between Claimant 1 and the respondent.

Case 4

The claimant filed a Request for Arbitration against several respondents based on the group of companies doctrine. The Court found that, prima facie, there was a sufficient basis for sending the matter to the arbitrators.

The arbitral tribunal rendered a partial award in which it recognized that international arbitration may allow jurisdiction over non-signatories. However, the arbitrators specified that rather than permitting an automatic application of the group of companies doctrine, international arbitration calls for a case-by-case analysis based on the intention of the parties. Given the circumstances in this particular case, the arbitral tribunal found that it did not have jurisdiction over the parent company.

IV.   CONCLUSION

As international business transactions become increasingly complex, it is clear that situations involving non-signatories will continue to present many interesting issues for international arbitration, on both a theoretical and a practical level. As pointed out above, the questions that arise in each case are very fact-specific. It is therefore extremely important that discussions of these questions are not reduced to unfounded generalizations that pit one legal culture against another or lead to inaccurate comparisons between different arbitration forums.[9]

Art. 6(2) of the ICC Rules provides procedural protection for non-signatories so that they will not be pulled into an ICC arbitration unless there is a prima facie basis for doing so. This protection applies between parties, but it also allows parties to be protected from overenthusiastic arbitrators who might be tempted to find unwarranted jurisdiction. The screening done by the Court may also save parties from having to apply to a State court for a decision on whether their arbitration can and should proceed.

It is clear that in borderline cases the Court will usually take a positive 6(2) decision, leaving the matter to the arbitral tribunal. This is as it should be, since the Court, as an

---

9. For example, due to certain misconceptions, it has been asserted that certain types of institutional arbitration are "dangerous" because they allow arbitrations to take place on the basis of the group of companies doctrine.

administrative body, does not have the same powers to hear and evaluate evidence as an arbitral tribunal.

Despite the changing nature and growing complexity of international business transactions, the disputes arising out of such transactions continue to raise the fundamental questions of consent and intent to arbitrate. These core concepts remain key to international arbitration as it applies to non-signatories. Back to basics, *retour à l'essentiel*, we must preserve these roots in order to allow arbitration to flourish.

Non-signatories in International Arbitration: Some Thoughts from Canada

Babak Barin[*]

TABLE OF CONTENTS

I. INTRODUCTION

In a country where large and complex commercial transactions are precipitously becoming the norm, the oft-misunderstood issue of whether an arbitration agreement concluded between two or more parties may be (to use the words of Professor Bernard Hanotiau) "extended or imputed"[1] to a third-party individual, company or state that has *not* signed the agreement will no doubt become the gravamen of increasing disputes. When raised, among the questions that will have to be answered by arbitral tribunals and courts alike are: Who is a party to the arbitration clause? Who has adhered to it? And who is estopped from contending that it has not adhered to it?

Examining the issue from a transnational perspective, Professor Hanotiau points out that the widely used concept of "extension" of the arbitration clause to non-signatories is a misleading one because in most instances, courts and arbitral tribunals have based their decisions on the common intention of the parties or consent.[2] According to Professor Hanotiau, in international arbitration, the real issue is whether "given its specific character and taking into consideration the usages of international trade, one should follow the same rules as are applicable to ordinary civil and commercial cases or adopt a more liberal approach...".[3]

In his paper on the American perspective on the same issue, John Townsend makes two points. First he notes, consent too is "central to the American approach ... although the complexity of the American approach has sometimes caused [people] to lose sight

---

* Partner and head of the Arbitration and ADR Group, Woods LLP; Chair of the Board of Directors of ICCA Montreal 2006 Organizing Committee Inc.; Admitted to practice law in Quebec, Ontario, Alberta and England & Wales.

1. Bernard HANOTIAU, "Non-Signatories in International Arbitration: Lessons from Thirty Years of Case Law", this volume, pp. 341-358
2. *Ibid.*
3. *Ibid.*

of its importance". Second he contends, "the question of *who* may be bound to arbitrate is a decision to be made by the courts, not arbitrators".[4] In support of this last assertion, John Townsend cites the famous United States Supreme Court decision of *First Options of Chicago v. Kaplan.*

The situation in Canada is both similar and dissimilar to the country with which it has the largest geographical contact and financial relationship. As in the United States, "consent" has played an important role before civil and common law courts in this country agreeing to or refusing to "extend" arbitration agreements to non-signatories. Unlike in the United States, Canada's Supreme Court has not yet had the occasion to decide on whether the question of "*who* may be bound to arbitrate" is a decision for courts or arbitrators.

II. REFERRAL TO ARBITRATION AND THE PRIMACY OF THE AUTONOMY OF THE PARTIES: TWO CASES

1. Dell Computer Corporation

In the fall of 2006, Canada's Supreme Court will have a unique opportunity to offer its views on this issue in a consumer class action setting. In *Dell Computer Corporation* v. *Union des consommateurs,*[5] the class representative, Olivier Dumoulin, and a Quebec consumer agency lodged an action after consumers attempted to buy a computer from Dell's internet website when the website contained a pricing error. Dell's website displayed a notice that all sales were subject to the customer agreement or to Dell's standard terms of sale. The standard terms contained an arbitration clause providing that any dispute arising from the online purchase was to be resolved exclusively by arbitration administered by the US National Arbitration Forum (NAF) headquartered in Minneapolis.

Dell moved to dismiss the class action, arguing among other things that based on the Supreme Court's own decision in *Zodiak International Productions Inc. v. The Polish People's Republic,*[6] the arbitration clause barred court proceedings due to an absence of ratione materiae jurisdiction. According to Dell, the mere presence of an undertaking to arbitrate sufficed to bar the action in the Superior Court. At first instance, the Quebec Superior Court refused to dismiss the action and granted certification, holding that the arbitration clause was inconsistent with Art. 3149 (CCQ)[7] that gives a Quebec court

---

4. John M. TOWNSEND, "Non-Signatories in International Arbitration: An American Perspective", this volume, pp. 359-365.

5. [2005] R.J.Q. 1448 (C.A.) [*Dell*].

6. [1983] 1 S.C.R. 529 [*Zodiak*].

7. Art. 3149 Civil Code of Quebec (CCQ) states:

> "A Quebec authority also has jurisdiction to hear an action involving a consumer contract or a contract of employment if the consumer or worker has his domicile or residence in Quebec; the waiver of such jurisdiction by the consumer or worker may not be set up against him."

jurisdiction to hear an action involving a consumer contract despite any waiver of jurisdiction by the consumer.

The Court of Appeal unanimously dismissed Dell's appeal but disagreed with the reasons of the trial judge. The Court of Appeal found that the NAF's Code of Procedure provided for the arbitration to be held in Quebec, and that any arbitral award could be enforced or annulled in Quebec pursuant to the CCP. The court rejected the plaintiff's argument that the arbitration clause was inconsistent with the intent of Quebec's *Consumer Protection Act*: the legislature would have had to expressly indicate that consumer disputes could not be arbitrated, and it had not done so. The court also noted that the legislature had recognized the validity of both arbitration and class actions as dispute resolution mechanisms and noted, significantly, that there was no specific reference to one procedural vehicle having precedence over the other.

The Court of Appeal, however, characterized the arbitration clause as an external contract which, according to the Court, was not adequately brought to the attention of the representative plaintiff.[8] The arbitration clause therefore was found to be null under the *Civil Code*. By arriving at the decision it did, the Court of Appeal implicitly indicated that the question of who may be bound to arbitrate is a decision to be made by the courts and not the arbitrators. Whether this is right or wrong is a policy issue which will ultimately have to be ruled on by Canada's highest court.

In *Dell*, the Supreme Court will also have to reconcile its own findings in *Zodiak* and *GreCon Dimter Inc. v. JR Normand Inc.*[9]

2. GreCon Dimter

What is fascinating about *GreCon Dimter* is that it did not reach the Supreme Court as an international arbitration case. The dispute in fact concerned a forum selection clause. The Supreme Court deliberately chose to interpret Art. 940.1 CCP (which is the equivalent of Art. 8(1) of the UNCITRAL Model Law on International Commercial Arbitration[10] (Model Law) or Art. II(3) of the *Convention on the Recognition and Enforcement of Foreign Arbitral Awards*, more commonly referred to as the 1958 New York Convention (New York Convention), even though it was never asked by the parties to

---

8. Art. 1435 CCQ, states:

  "An external clause referred to in a contract is binding on the parties. In a consumer contract or a contract of adhesion, however, an external clause is null if, at the time of formation of the contract, it was not expressly brought to the attention of the consumer or adhering party, unless the other party proves that the consumer or adhering party otherwise knew of it."

9. [2005] 2 R.C.S. 401 (*GreCon Dimter*).

10. *Model Law on International Commercial Arbitration*, UNCITRAL, UN Doc. A/40/17 Annex 1 (1985), 24 ILM 1302. The *Explanatory note by the UNCITRAL secretariat on the Model Law on International Commercial Arbitration* depicts this document as "a sound and promising basis for the desired harmonization and improvement of national laws. It covers all stages of the arbitral process from the arbitration agreement to the recognition and enforcement of the arbitral award and reflects a worldwide consensus on the principles and important issues of international arbitration practice."

do so. In *Grecon Dimter*, a German manufacturer's failure to deliver certain equipment to a Quebec supplier caused the partial non-performance of the supplier's obligations to a customer operating a business in Quebec. The customer initiated an action in damages against the supplier in the Quebec Superior Court. The supplier based its claim in warranty. The German manufacturer moved to dismiss the action on the basis of a choice of forum clause in the contract according to which the German court had jurisdiction. The Supreme Court allowed the appeal of the German manufacturer and dismissed the action in warranty of the supplier based principally on "the recognition of the primacy of the autonomy of the parties". According to the Supreme Court of Canada:

> "Recognizing this primacy leaves considerable room for freedom of contract, subject to the limits imposed by the law or by the rules of public order.... It can be seen that the fundamental structure of the Civil Code is consistent with *the primacy of the autonomy of the parties as regards both the determination of whether a court has jurisdiction and the recognition of foreign judgments*.... Recognition of the principle also goes hand in hand with the legislature's tendency toward recognizing the existence and legitimacy of the private justice system, which is often consensual and is parallel to the state's judicial system. One example of this is Art. 2638 C.C.Q., which defines the arbitration agreement...."

(Emphasis added.)

The Supreme Court then concluded:

> "[b]oth the purpose of the New York Convention and the case law dealing with Art. II(3) confirm the position that the enforcement of an arbitration agreement cannot be precluded by procedural rules relating to actions in warranty. First, the purpose of the New York Convention is to facilitate the enforcement of arbitration agreements by ensuring that effect is given to the parties' *express* intention to seek arbitration....The interpreter must therefore encourage arbitration clauses, and facilitate their enforcement.... The cases decided in other countries have tended to favour recourse to arbitration by limiting opportunities for departing from the autonomy of the parties.... The same trend can be observed in decisions of the courts of the common law provinces involving Art. 8 of the [Model Law], which recognize that a judge is obliged to apply a valid arbitration agreement.... Finally, in Quebec, the application of Art. 940.1 C.C.P. is mandatory where the requirements are met. A court has no choice but to apply it...."

(Emphasis added.)

The Supreme Court's remarks in *GreCon Dimter* raise a number of important questions in both common law and civil law Canada. These questions have relevance to the non-signatory issue which is the focus of this paper. First, who is the "interpreter" referred to by the Supreme Court of Canada, who must "encourage arbitration"? If that person is a judge of a first instance court in a Canadian province, then how is he or she supposed to determine what constitutes a "valid arbitration agreement"? Is the "*mere presence*" of an arbitration agreement enough? If not, is the judge obliged to deal with the issue of "consent to arbitration" in order to determine its validity? What does "having an arbitration agreement" referred to in Art. 940.1 CCP, Art. 8(1) of the Model Law and Art. II(3) of the New York Convention really mean in Canada? How is a court of first instance in Canada supposed to determine that an arbitration agreement is null and/or void, or inoperative or incapable of being performed? Is there a public policy that requires the court to refer parties to arbitration where there is a doubt?

While Canada awaits a decision from its Supreme Court on some or all of the above questions, a quick glance at certain key past decisions from both the common law provinces and Quebec may be instructive. In looking at these decisions, one must be mindful of Professor Hanotiau's observation with respect to the plethora of international cases that he has to date examined on this topic. As observed by Professor Hanotiau, it appears in Canada that it is very difficult to draw any general conclusions concerning the issue of the extension of arbitration clauses to non-signatories from existing Canadian case law. As in the United States, what appears to be a common thread among the Canadian cases which have to date examined the non-signatory issue, is that "the determination of whether an [arbitration agreement] should be extended to other companies of the group or its directors or shareholders is fact specific and may differ depending upon the circumstances of the case".[11]

III. ARBITRATION LAW OF CANADA

No study of Canada's position on any arbitration law issue can begin without a basic understanding of this country's constitutional and arbitration law mosaic. Canada is a federal state comprising ten provinces and three territories. The basis for the division of powers between the provinces' legislatures and the Parliament of Canada is the *Constitution Act, 1867*.[12] While commercial arbitration is not expressly contemplated in the distribution of powers within the Constitution, it is, except for certain narrow purposes, a matter for the jurisdiction of the provincial legislatures.[13] One must also note Canada's *Commercial Arbitration Act*, R.S.C. 1985, c. 16. It essentially incorporates the Model Law. This statute applies to both domestic and international commercial arbitration matters where at least one of the parties to the arbitration is Her Majesty in right of Canada, a departmental corporation or a Crown corporation. The Act also applies in relation to maritime or admiralty matters.

---

11. *Smith/Enron Cogeneration Ltd P'ship v. Smith Cogeneration Int'l, Inc.*, 198 F. 3d 88, 97 (2d Cir. 1999).

12. Babak BARIN et al, *The Osler Guide to Commercial Arbitration in Canada* (The Netherlands, Kluwer Law International 2006).

13. Marc LALONDE, "National Report Canada" in ICCA *International Handbook on Commercial Arbitration* (Kluwer Law International Suppl. 42, November 2004) at p. 1.

In 1986, shortly after the Model Law was adopted, Canada became the first country in the world to enact legislation based on the Model Law.[14] The federal government itself led the way, and the provinces followed in step. Unlike the federal government and to mark a clear distinction between domestic and international arbitration, the Canadian common law provinces promulgated two arbitration statutes. One incorporates the Model Law for international matters, and the other conforms to the modern Model Law approach for domestic disputes.[15] The content of these two statutes, however, are markedly different.

Unlike the common law provinces, the Province of Quebec decided to legislate in a single statue both domestic and international arbitration *taking place in Quebec* in one document – the Quebec *Code of Civil Procedure*[16] (CCP).[17] In a rather typical civilian way, it also continues to treat the more substantive law provisions in the Quebec *Civil Code* (CCQ). Hence, while the CCP deals with the conduct of arbitrations and also covers the recognition and enforcement of domestic and foreign arbitral awards, the CCQ identifies the criteria for the validity of arbitration agreements. In this latter regard, (with the exception of questions of public order and certain matters such as the status of persons)[18], the CCP permits parties to submit any dispute to arbitration, and for them to define the arbitrator's terms of reference.[19]

Moreover, in order to make it clear that it was truly distinct from the other nine, the Province Quebec decided to explicitly state in the CCP that when it came to international and extra-provincial (which Quebec considers to be the same as international) matters, the CCP was to simply "take into consideration" the Model Law.[20]

---

14. Babak BARIN and Eva GAZUREK, "Enforcement and Annulment of Arbitral Awards in Quebec – *Vive la différence!*" 64 R. du B. (2004) p. 383 See also: Babak BARIN, "Provisional Remedies in Domestic Arbitrations: Time perhaps for a fresh look in Quebec?" 64 R. du B. (2004) p. 137.

15. Note that for the purposes of the common law province's domestic statutes, extra-provincial arbitration is considered to be domestic.

16. Code of Civil Procedure, R.S.Q. chapter C-25 – Book VII, Title I.

17. See *A. Bianchi S.R.L v. Bilumen Lighting Ltd,* [1990] R.J.Q. 1681.

18. See Art. 2639 CCQ which reads:

"Disputes over the status and capacity of persons, family matters or other matters of public order may not be submitted to arbitration.
   An arbitration agreement may not be opposed on the ground that the rules applicable to settlement of the dispute are in the nature of rules of public order."

19. *Desputeaux v. Éditions Chouette (1987) inc.*, [2003] 1 S.C.R. 178 [*Desputeaux*].

20. See Art. 940.6 CCP which states:

"Where matters of extra-provincial or international trade are at issue in an arbitration, the interpretation of this Title, where applicable, *shall take into* consideration:
   (1) the *Model Law on International Commercial Arbitration* as adopted by the United Nations Commission on International Trade Law on 21 June 1985;
   (2) the Report of the United Nations Commission on International Trade Law on the work of its eighteenth session held in Vienna from the third to the twenty-first day of June 1985;

Enticed by the opportunities available to Canadian business through the expanding Pacific Rim economies, British Columbia legislators led the effort to sponsor the federal-provincial agreements that allowed the adoption of the New York Convention. Unlike its rather quick adoption of the Model Law, in May of 1986, Canada was one of the last developed Western countries to accede to the New York Convention. In light of the division of powers between the federal and provincial governments, the federal government[21] and the nine common law provinces once again enacted their own respective statutes implementing the New York Convention.[22] To make its unique character known again, the Province of Quebec in Art. 948 CCP [23]declared:

> "This Title applies to an arbitration award made outside Quebec whether or not it has been ratified by a competent authority.
> *The interpretation of this Title shall take into account, where applicable,* the Convention on the Recognition and Enforcement of Foreign Arbitral Awards as adopted by the United Nations Conference on International Commercial Arbitration at New York on 10 June 1958."

(Emphasis added.)

In Quebec, unlike elsewhere in Canada[24], an award rendered outside of the province (including in another province) in civil and commercial matters is considered to be a foreign award and is subject to Arts. 948 to 951.2 CCP. This essentially reproduces the provisions of the New York Convention. In order for an arbitration award to be executory as a judgment in Quebec, it must be homologated.[25]

---

(3) the Analytical Commentary on the draft text of model law on international commercial arbitration contained in the report of the Secretary-General to the eighteenth session of the United Nations Commission on International Trade Law."

(Emphasis added)

21. *An Act to implement the United Nations Convention on the Recognition and Enforcement of Foreign Arbitral Awards*, R.S.C., 1985, c.16 (2nd Supp.).
22. With the coming into force of the Ontario *International Commercial Arbitration Act*, R.S.O. 1990, c. I.9 (OICAA), and in particular, Arts. 34, 35 and 36 of the Model Law incorporated therein, the province of Ontario has since repealed its *Foreign Arbitral Awards Act*, S.O. 1986, c.25. By contrast, British Columbia has two statutes, one implementing the Model Law and the other the New York Convention. Most of the other common law provinces, e.g. Alberta, have included the New York Convention and the Model Law in the same.
23. Book VII, Title II (Of Recognition and Execution of Arbitration Awards Made outside Quebec).
24. In Ontario, for example, Art. 1(3) of the Model Law which was incorporated in the OICAA states that an arbitration is "international" if the parties to an arbitration agreement had, at the time of the conclusion of that agreement, their places of business in different "states". Sect. 1(7) of the enacting portion of the OICAA explicitly states that "different States" means different countries.
25. Art. 946.6 and 951.2 CCP.

IV.   SAMPLE CASES FROM COMMON LAW CANADA

Kaverit Steel & Crane Ltd. v. Kone Corp.[26] is the most widely cited Canadian common law decision to examine the issue of the "extension" of an arbitration agreement to non-signatories. In that case, Kone Corporation, a Finnish manufacturer of industrial cranes, entered into license and distributorship agreements with Kaverit Steel, an Alberta corporation. The distributorship agreement granted Kaverit the exclusive right to manufacture and sell materials designed or manufactured by Kone. Kaverit, its parent company and a number of shareholders of the parent company later initiated an action in the Alberta Court of Queen's Bench alleging, inter alia, that Kone was directly or through its subsidiaries competing with Kaverit in Western Canada and was consequently in breach of the exclusive distributorship agreement. Kone, along with its three wholly owned subsidiaries, sought a stay of the proceedings on the grounds that the dispute should be referred to arbitration. The plaintiffs responded by saying that the Alberta *International Commercial Arbitration Act*, R.S.A. 2000, I-5 precluded arbitration since the parties to the arbitration clause did not include all of the litigants. They also argued that there was no arbitration agreement to which all parties were bound by consent. The arbitration clause found in both the licensing and distributorship agreements read as follows:

> "Any dispute arising out of or in connection with this agreement shall be finally settled without recourse to the courts, in accordance with the Rules of Conciliation and Arbitration of the International Chamber of Commerce by one or more arbitrators designated in conformity with those Rules. The arbitrator or arbitrators designated shall have the power to rule on their own competence and on the validity of the agreement to submit to arbitration. The place of arbitration shall be Stockholm, Sweden."

At first instance, the Alberta Court of Queen's Bench unfortunately saw the nub of the issue in dispute to be as follows: Has the plaintiff, "by its Statement of Claim, proliferated the issues and thereby the parties with the result that the arbitration provision is frustrated. If so the plaintiff's action should not deprive the defendant of the stay. On the other hand, if litigants in this action, who are not party to the arbitration provision and who are not consenting to it, have raised legitimate causes of action which are not connected to the main issue of breach of contract such that all matters should be tried in the same proceedings, then the arbitration provision is, in the words of the statute, inoperative or incapable of being performed. Since arbitration is consensual in nature persons not party to the agreement cannot be compelled to submit to the method of dispute resolution."

The court then dismissed the defendants' application for a stay on the basis that the parties to the action and who were not subject to the arbitration clause had raised legitimate causes which all should be decided in the same proceedings. According to the court, a decision by an arbitrator on the proper interpretation of the contract was not

---

26. (1992), 85 Alta. L.R. (2d) 287 (C.A.) [*Kaverit Steel*].

likely to be conclusive on the issues raised by all parties. Although the court did not exactly say so, it wrongly based itself on principles of efficacy and convenience to keep the parties away from what they may have bargained for.

On appeal, the Alberta Court of Appeal[27] disagreed with the decision of the Alberta Court of Queen's Bench. In a rather dismissive short paragraph it said: "With respect, the nub of the case is not whether the plaintiff raised "legitimate" causes that cannot go to arbitration. On the contrary, the agreement to arbitrate should be honoured and enforced whether or not the plaintiff displayed great imagination in the pleadings." The court then went on to say:

> "The power to grant or withhold a reference under the International Commercial Arbitration Act is very limited.…The Act directs me to hold [the parties] to their bargain. Sect. 2(1) of the International Commercial Arbitration Act makes the [New York Convention] part of the law of Alberta. It says that the Convention 'applies in the Province'. The Convention Art. II, Sect. 3 provides.… In modern commercial disputes, it is almost inevitable that many parties will be involved and very unlikely that parties will have an identical submission. The problem of multiple parties, which drove the decision of the [first instance] judge here, will exist in almost every case. There is no question that proliferation of litigation is a possibility … the Convention cannot reasonably be taken as having abandoned any attempt at arbitration when this problem arises."

Finally, and without much rigorous reasoning, the Alberta Court of Appeal concluded:

> "… the proviso about 'null and void, inoperative, and capable of being enforced' simply preserves the rule in *Heyman v. Darwins* Ltd.… The arbitrator cannot decide whether the submission is valid. Its validity and enforceability must be pronounced upon before the referring court can enforce it by a reference and stay. It is not valid if it, or the contract in which it is found, is, by operation of domestic law in the referring tribunal, either void or unenforceable. The proviso is an echo of the law about void contracts ('null and void'), unenforceable contracts ('inoperative'), and frustrated contracts ('incapable of being enforced').…"

In *Kaverit Steel*, the court also made two interesting statements. First, it stated that "[a]ssociated and connected parties like subsidiaries, shareholders, directors, employees,

---

27. The application for leave to appeal to the Supreme Court of Canada in *Kaverit Steel* was dismissed without reasons. It is rather unfortunate that the Supreme Court decided not to hear this case. Perhaps the court was then of the view that there was no national issue involved or that the case which was brought before it was appropriately decided based on its rather specific facts. As mentioned before, in hearing the case of *Dell* above, the Supreme Court will no doubt have an opportunity to address the issues relating to validity and enforceability of arbitration agreements referred to but not rigorously analyzed in *Kaverit Steel* and other cases.

agents and the like might be required to join an arbitration in one of three ways: by the governing law, by the submission itself, to the extent the parties to the contract can bind other parties, or by the later agreement of the other parties". Second, the court observed that "forcing ... subsidiaries to partake in the arbitration may well be sensible and practical", but that decision "is for the parties or the Legislature, not for [the court]".

What is interesting about *Kaverit Steel* is that in its passing analysis of the governing law, the Alberta Court of Appeal rejected the application of the English case, *Roussel-Uclaf v. G.D. Searle (U.K.)*[28] to support the claim that associated parties can be brought to arbitration over their objection. According to the court, "[i]n that case ... the English statute under review provided a reference of all those claiming 'through or under' a party to the submission". The Alberta *International Commercial Arbitration Act,*[29] simply did not. According to the court "Alberta, like the United Kingdom, could have sent to arbitration claims by or against those who claim through or under an agreement containing a submission. It has not, and perhaps this is to be regretted."

Another frequently cited decision is the British Columbia Supreme Court in *Javor v. Francoeur*.[30] Eddie Javor and Fusion-Crete Products Inc. were involved in an American Arbitration Association arbitration which took place in California. During the course of the arbitration, the arbitrator found that there was no separation between the corporate respondent Fusion-Crete Products Inc. and the individual respondent Francoeur. More specifically, the arbitrator determined that Francoeur was the *alter ego* of Fusion-Crete Products Inc. Javor brought an application to have this award enforced by the British Columbia Supreme Court pursuant to the *Foreign Arbitral Awards Act,* R.S.B.C. 1996, Chapter 154 [FAAA] and the *International Commercial Arbitration Act*, R.S.B.C. 1996, Chapter 233 [ICAA]. Francoeur argued that the personal liability of a company representative had to be decided by a court of law and that the award could not be enforced against him in his personal capacity. He also argued that the legislation regarding enforcement of foreign arbitration awards did not apply to non-parties to the arbitration agreement like himself.

The British Columbia Supreme Court dismissed Javor's application on the basis that Francoeur was not a party to the arbitration agreement and the claim against Francoeur for personal liability could not have been the subject of arbitration in British Columbia. The British Columbia Court of Appeal subsequently agreed with the British Columbia Supreme Court's decision without much comment.[31] According to the British Columbia Supreme Court, it was the intention of the FAAA and the ICAA to limit enforcement of arbitration awards to the parties to the arbitration agreement. Hence, since Francoeur was neither a named party to the arbitration agreement nor a signatory to it in his personal capacity, he could not be subjected to the enforcement provisions of the FAAA or the ICAA.

In order to arrive at this last conclusion, the British Columbia Supreme Court first examined the ICAA, saying that it addressed the issue squarely: "party means a party to

---

28. [1978] 1 L.L.R. 225 (Ch.).
29. R.S.A. 2000, c. I-5 [*Javor*].
30. (2003), 13 B.C.L.R. (4th) 195.
31. (2004) 25 B.C.L.R. 114.

an arbitration agreement ... and that the arbitration agreement ... must be in writing ... and is deemed in writing ... if it is contained in a document signed by the parties. As is the case here ... an arbitration agreement may be in the form of an arbitration clause in a contract...." The court then went on to reject Javor's argument that since the FAAA contained no definition of party, it must be given a broader interpretation. According to the court, the definition of "party" as used in the FAAA did *not* differ materially from the one found in the ICCA. The FAAA, the court remarked,

> "is based upon ... an agreement in writing under which the parties undertake to submit to arbitration. It is a contractual obligation and the parties are those to the agreement in writing, not persons procedurally added involuntarily as parties during arbitration."

What is rather surprising about *Javor* is that neither the British Columbia Supreme Court nor the Court of Appeal picked up on the comment made by the Alberta Court of Appeal in *Kaverit Steel* concerning how regretful it was in that case that Alberta law did not permit "claims by or against those who *claim through or under* an agreement containing a submission". As specifically referred to in the British Columbia Supreme Court decision itself, under the ICAA (unlike its Albertan counterpart), a "party" means "a party to an arbitration agreement and *includes a person claiming through or under a party*".

What is also rather disappointing about *Javor* is the British Columbia Supreme Court's determination (subsequently picked up in a cursory way by Saunders J.A. of the Court of Appeal) that the issue of Francoeur's personal liability could not properly have been the subject of arbitration under the British Columbia domestic *Commercial Arbitration Act*[32] and *Domestic Commercial Arbitration Rules of Procedure*,[33] because in British Columbia "the jurisdiction of arbitrators derives from statute and is confined to a jurisdiction over parties to arbitration agreements". Both the British Columbia Supreme Court and the Court of Appeal must have somehow overlooked the fact that the issues in *Javor* were subject to the British Columbia international arbitration statute and not the domestic one.

In *Pan Liberty Navigation Co. et al v. World Link (H.K.) Resources Ltd.*,[34] two shipowners, Pan Liberty and Blue Arctic, chartered ships to a corporation referred to as "World Link (HK)". When World Link (HK) failed to pay the hire, the owners brought arbitration proceedings in England, in accordance with the charterparties. The contracts required the parties to resolve any dispute arising out of or in connection with the charterparties through arbitration. The arbitrator made a final award in favour of each owner. The owners were unsuccessful in enforcing the awards, and they came to the conclusion that the defaulting charterer was a shell corporation used to obtain the benefit of the charters without paying for them and that it was carrying on business under similar names in Hong Kong. The owners learned that a ship under charter to World Link (HK) was due to arrive in British Columbia and brought an action to obtain a Mareva injunction against

---

32. R.S.C.B. 1996, c. 55, Sect. 22.
33. Sects. 2 and 20.
34. (2005) 253 D.L.R. (4th) 46 [*Pan Liberty*].

the ship's fuel and bunkers. They alleged that the defaulting charterer and various related companies deliberately set out to defraud them. The owners obtained the injunction. World Link (HK) then applied for and was granted an order that, upon paying a specified sum of money into court as security, the injunction would be lifted. World Link (HK) then moved for a stay pursuant to the federal *Commercial Arbitration Act*, R.S.C. 1985, c. 17 (2nd Supp.), requiring the owners to take steps in England before the arbitrator or the English courts to determine whether the World Link (HK) and possibly other defendants were to be included in the arbitral award. The chambers judge in British Columbia dismissed the motion, holding that because the action was an enforcement action it was not a matter properly brought through arbitration.

On appeal, the British Columbia Court of Appeal disagreed. It decided that the matter was one that fell within the arbitration provisions of the charterparties because the real issue was whether the respondent company was the defaulting charterer. According to the court, this was a dispute that fell under the charterparties. Moreover, the question of whether the English arbitrator had delivered a final award and still retained jurisdiction could only be determined by the arbitrator and by applying English law. Finally, since the application for stay had been brought under Art. 8(1) of the *Commercial Arbitration Act*, public policy required the court to defer to the arbitrator and hold the parties to their contract in which they agreed to resolve their differences by arbitration. This is what the court had to say:

> Having concluded that the issues raised by the British Columbia action fall outside the arbitration provisions of the charter agreements, the chambers judge made no reference to the application to stay having been brought under article 8(1) of the schedule to the *Commercial Arbitration Act*, R.S.C. 1985, c. 17 (2nd Supp.). That legislation applies because this is a matter falling within the federal power over navigation and shipping (a point not in dispute). Article 8(1) states:
>
> > '8(1) A court before which an action is brought in a matter which is the subject of an arbitration agreement shall, if a party so requests not later than when submitting his first statement on the substance of the dispute, refer the parties to arbitration unless it finds that the agreement is null and void, inoperative or incapable of being performed.'
>
> The leading authority in this Province with respect to article 8(1) is the decision of this Court in *Prince George (City) v. McElhanney Engineering Services Ltd.* (1995), 9 B.C.L.R. (3d) 368 (C.A.). In defining the approach to be taken by a court called upon to apply that article, Cumming J.A., for the Court, at para. 36, adopted this passage from the reasons of Mr. Justice Campbell in *Boart Sweden AB v. NYA Stromnes AB* (1988), 41 B.L.R. 295 (Ont. H.C.) at 302-303:
>
> > 'Public policy carries me to the consideration which I conclude is paramount having regard to the facts of this case, and that is the very strong public policy of this jurisdiction that where parties have agreed by contract that they will have the arbitrators decide their claims, instead of resorting to the Courts, the parties should be held to their contract....

To deal with all these matters in a single proceeding in Ontario instead of deferring to the arbitral process in respect of part of the action and temporarily staying the other parts of the action, would violate that strong public policy.

It would also fail to give effect to the change in the law of international arbitration which, with the advent of art. 8 of the Model Law and the removal of the earlier wide ambit of discretion, gives the Courts a clear direction to defer to the arbitrators even more than under the previous law of international arbitration.

I conclude that nothing in the nullity provisions of art. 8 prevents this Court from giving effect to the clear policy of deference set out in the article.

To conclude otherwise would drive a hole through the article by encouraging litigants to bring actions on matters related to but not embraced by the arbitration and then say that everything had to be consolidated in Court, thus defeating the policy of deference to the arbitrators.'

In my respectful view, for a British Columbia court to conclude on the facts of this case that it is open to these plaintiffs to pursue this action would fall directly within the evil described in the last paragraph of the passage quoted by Cumming J.A. Clearly, the question between these parties is, in the words of paragraph 17 of the charter party, a "dispute arising out of or in connection with this Charter Party". It is governed by English law and is to be referred to arbitration in London. There is a curious anomaly in the facts of this case in that each of the respondent owners, although a party to the respective charter party, contends that the dispute does not arise out of the charter party, whereas the appellant, which contends that it is not a party to the charter party, contends that the dispute arises under the charter party. The dispute is, however, as to whether the present appellant, although not named in the charter party, is nevertheless the charterer. That is clearly a dispute under the charter party.

A decision of this Court which is more directly in point on its facts, although it does not arise under the Commercial Arbitration Act, is *Gulf Canada Resources Ltd. v. Arochem International Ltd.* (1992), 66 B.C.L.R. (2d) 113 (C.A.). That appeal was from a decision of a chambers judge granting a stay of proceedings pursuant to s. 8 of the International Commercial Arbitration Act, S.B.C. 1986, c. 14, which is not materially different from Art. 8(1) of the federal Act. It reads, in part:

'*Stay of legal proceedings*
8. (1) Where a party to an arbitration agreement commences legal proceedings in a court against another party to the agreement in respect of a matter agreed to be submitted to arbitration, a party to the legal proceedings may, before or after entering an appearance and before delivery of any pleadings or taking any other step in the proceedings, apply to that court to stay the proceedings.

(2) In an application under subsection (1), the court shall make an order staying the legal proceedings unless it determines that the arbitration agreement is null and void, inoperative or incapable of being performed.'

The facts and the essence of the decision are conveniently set out in the headnote, which reads:

'The plaintiff made a contract with one or both of the defendants for the sale of 375,000 barrels of crude oil. The contract contained an arbitration clause. Before the time for delivery, the price fell by $10 a barrel and the defendants refused to take delivery under the terms of the contract. The plaintiff wrote to the defendants, advising that it accepted their repudiation. Both defendants replied, stating that one of them was not a party to the contract. The plaintiff sued for damages. The defendants obtained a stay under Sect. 8 of the International Commercial Arbitration Act. The plaintiff appealed.

Held - Appeal dismissed.

In order to obtain a stay of proceedings, it is not enough to point to an arbitration agreement and assert that the parties are parties to the agreement and that the dispute is within its terms. The court continues to have some residual jurisdiction. Thus, if the court concludes that one of the parties named in the legal proceedings is not a party to the arbitration agreement, or if the alleged dispute does not come within the terms of the agreement, or if the application is out of time, the application should not be granted. But it is not for the court, on a stay application, to reach any final determination as to the scope of the arbitration agreement or whether a particular party to the legal proceedings is a party to the agreement. Those are matters within the jurisdiction of the arbitral tribunal. Only where it is clear that the dispute falls outside the agreement, or that a party is not a party to it, or that the application is out of time, should the court make a final determination. In this case, the fact that the defendants had not performed the contract at all did not mean that the issue between the parties was not in relation to the "performance" of the contract as that term was used in the agreement. Whether the dispute fell within the agreement and whether both defendants were parties to it would fall to be determined in the arbitration....'

Counsel for the respondents submits that the authorities to which I have referred do not apply because here there has been a final award from which it follows that the jurisdiction of the arbitrator is exhausted. He also points to the element of fraudulent conduct asserted by the plaintiffs as taking the matter outside the scope of arbitration. The essence of the plaintiffs' case is, however, that, by whatever means, the owners were persuaded to enter into a charter party, either with a non-existent party or with one that was not the true charterer. In any event, having regard to the general policy of the law in this area, I would not presume to define the scope of the arbitrator's authority. This action has served and continues to serve the purpose of securing the plaintiffs' claim in a very effective way. The issue now is whether the appellant is the party indebted to the owners under the charter party. To that extent, the appellant properly seeks to be treated as a party so that the issue can be resolved in the appropriate arena."

In *Gulf Canada Resources Ltd. v. Arochem International Ltd. et al*[35] cited above, despite the explicit wording of Art. 8(1) of the Model Law, the British Columbia Court of Appeal held that the court had a *residual discretion* to reject a stay of legal proceeding, where, inter alia, it was clear that one of the parties named in the legal proceedings was not a party to the arbitration agreement. Despite this unfounded statement, the Court held that because it was not clear that Arochem International Inc. was a party to the arbitration agreement, the matter fell within the jurisdiction of the arbitral tribunal for determination.

In *BMW Investments Ltd. v. Saskerco Products Inc.*,[36] the Saskatchewan Court of Appeal rightfully took issue with the decision of the British Columbia Court of Appeal in *Gulf Canada* and stated:

> "In Canadian international arbitration matters, there does not appear to be a consistent approach taken by courts with regard to stay orders given the presence of third parties. In *Gulf Canada Resources Limited v. Arochem International Limited* (1992), 66 B.C.L.R. 113, the British Columbia Court of Appeal interpreted that province's ICAA to mean the court retained the residual jurisdiction to refuse a stay in certain circumstances. In the end, however, the Court ordered that all actions be stayed: unless the case for a stay is very clear, the Court stated that all questions should be resolved in arbitration. With respect, I find it difficult to see the basis for judicial discretion in the Gulf Canada case, given the wording of the legislation and the fact that a valid arbitration agreement was found: section 8 of the ICAA, S.B.C. 1986, c.14 states that legal proceedings 'shall' be stayed pending arbitration.
>
> In my opinion, a better approach is that taken by the Ontario High Court in *Boart*, supra. In spite of the presence of parties in the litigation who were not parties to the arbitration agreement, the court demonstrated a sound understanding of international arbitration by issuing a two-part stay order. The court ordered that litigation with regard to matters within the arbitration agreement (and between the principal parties) be stayed pending arbitration. With regard to related matters not directly within the arbitration agreement (specifically, torts that were alleged by both a principal party and a third party against one of the principal parties), the court ordered a stay of proceedings for the estimated time it would take to complete the arbitration (4 months).
>
> In making this order, the court relied on both the contractual intention of the principal parties and the need to be flexible in accommodating the interests of third parties [at (1988) 41 B.L.R. 295 at 303]:
>
> > 'To deal with all these matters in a single proceeding in Ontario instead of deferring to the arbitral process in respect of part of the action and temporarily staying the other parts of the action, would violate that strong public policy [of international commercial arbitration].

---

35. (1992), 66 B.C.L.R. (2d) 113 (C.A.) [*Gulf Canada*].
36. [1994] S.J. No. 69 (C.A.).

It would also fail to give effect to the change in the law of international arbitration which, with the advent of art. 8 of the Model Law and the removal of the earlier wide ambit of discretion, gives the Courts a clear direction to defer to the arbitrators even more than under the previous law of international arbitration.

I conclude that nothing in the nullity provisions of art. 8 prevents this Court from giving effect to the clear policy of deference set out in the article.

To conclude otherwise would drive a hole through the article by encouraging litigants to bring actions on matters related to but not embraced by the arbitration and then say that everything had to be consolidated in Court, thus defeating the policy of deference to the arbitrators.'"

In *Hi-Seas Marine Ltd. v. Boelman*,[37] the British Columbia Supreme Court considered whether Boelman, who was not a party to the arbitration agreement (being the Vessel Management Agreement), between Hi-Seas Marine and Trinav Shipping, but who was the *alter ego* of Trinav Shipping, could have an arbitration award enforced against him. On the basis of the British Columbia Court of Appeal decision in *Pan Liberty*, Boelman argued that Hi-Seas was obligated to make Boelman a party to the arbitration by reason of the claims advanced against him arising out the Vessel Management Agreement, and that in failing to do so it was now barred from maintaining this action. Carrying through with the legal proceedings would constitute an abuse of process by allowing for the use of the results of the arbitration as the foundation of an award alleging personal liability for corporate acts.

Hi-Seas argued that based on the British Columbia Court of Appeal's decision in *Javor*, Boelman could not have been joined as a party to the arbitration because he was not a signatory to the Vessel Management Agreement so that the claims against him had to be reserved to judicial determination. Hi-Seas also argued that in any event, Boelman was estopped from asserting the position now advanced by reason of the positions he had taken before in the arbitration on the same issue.

While the British Columbia Supreme Court noted the apparent contradiction in the *Pan Liberty* and *Javor* cases, given the conduct of the parties in the arbitration process and the conduct of the arbitration itself, it decided that it would be "unfair" to bar the court proceedings because of the arbitration. The court concluded:

"(1) It is apparent that neither the parties nor the Arbitration Panel turned their minds to whether the Arbitration was brought pursuant to the provisions of the British Columbia *International Commercial Arbitration Act*, R.S.B.C. 1996, c. 233 [*ICAA*], due to the dispute being one between a foreign corporation and a British Columbia corporation relating to matters arising largely in Mexico; or, pursuant to the Canadian *Commercial Arbitration Act*, R.S.C. 1985 (2nd Supp.), c. 17 [*Arbitration Code*], due to the subject matter of the dispute being 'in relation to maritime or admiralty matters' and thus within federal rather than provincial jurisdiction.

---

37. [2006] B.C.J. No. 655 [*Hi-Seas*].

(2) While the provisions of the two enactments are similar, they differ in some respects concerning jurisdiction over non-parties to an agreement to arbitrate. Under s. 2(1) of the *ICAA* a 'party' is defined as meaning 'a party to an arbitration agreement *and includes a person claiming through or under a party*'. There is no such expansive definition under the *Arbitration Code*.

(3) A close reading of Hi-Seas' Answer to Trinav's Reply and Counterclaim in the Arbitration leads to the conclusion that while the subject matter of the claims now advanced by Hi-Seas against Boelman in these proceedings was addressed in the Arbitration pleadings, there was no specific claim for relief against Boelman in any personal capacity arising from the allegations made.

(4) While represented by legal counsel, (who is not counsel in this litigation), Boelman formally asserted, both before the Arbitration Panel and in the Petition filed in this Court, that the Arbitration Panel had no personal jurisdiction over him. Boelman is now estopped from advancing his present argument to the opposite effect."

It is striking to what extent the discussions in the above cases implicitly reaffirm the principle of the primacy of the autonomy of the parties referred to in *Grecon Dimter* when making a determination as to whether a third party is a party to the arbitration agreement. These discussions also highlight how inappropriate equity concerns and arguments based on the good administration of justice are when used as criteria for "extending" arbitration clauses to non-signatories. If courts are uncertain as to whether the party to the legal proceeding is a party to the arbitration, they must defer the matter to the arbitrator. As it was most eloquently stated by Justice Campbell in *Boart Sweden*, there is a very strong public policy "that where parties have agreed by contract that they will have the arbitrators decide their claims, instead of resorting to Courts, [that] the parties [...] be held to their contract".[38] Consequently, the autonomy of the parties should take precedence over the exercising of any judicial discretion or the application of equity in international arbitration.

V.   SAMPLE CASES FROM QUEBEC

Condominiums Mont St-Sauveur Inc. v. Constructions Serge Sauvé Ltée,[39] is the most-referred-to arbitration decision in the Province of Quebec. In *Condominiums Mont St-Sauveur*, the appellant owner had contracted with the respondent general contractor for the construction of condominiums to be built according to the plans devised by the co-defendant architects. The contract between the owners and the general contractor contained an arbitration clause, while the one binding the architects did not. The appellant commenced an action before the Quebec Superior Court against both the general contractor and the architects for defects in construction and design. The respondent lodged a declinatory exception motion to refer the parties to arbitration

---

38. 41 B.L.R. 295 at para. 10.
39. [1990] R.J.Q. 2783 (C.A.) [*Condominiums Mont St-Sauveur*].

pursuant to the arbitration agreement. The first instance court granted the respondent's motion and referred the parties to arbitration.

The Quebec Court of Appeal dismissed the owner's appeal based on the Supreme Court of Canada's decision in *Zodiak*[40] and referred the matter to arbitration. In doing so, the court observed:

> "Finally, there remains the appellant's argument that the architects are not bound by the arbitration clause so that they would have to be sued in the ordinary courts while the claim against the builder would be decided by arbitration. In the result, appellant could not pursue joint and several claims against the two debtors in the same action. That may be so, but it is difficult to see how appellant can be heard to complain about the effect of contractual arrangements it has, itself, put in place."

While one commentator has expressed the view that it appears from the Court of Appeal decision in *Condominiums Mont St-Sauveur* that the Court of Appeal referred both the general contractor and the architects to arbitration,[41] that view was obviously not shared by one of the three Court of Appeal judges[42] in *Decarel Inc. v. Concordia Project Management Ltd.*[43] In *Decarel*, Concordia Project Management Ltd. and Decarel Inc. entered into a joint-venture contract for work relating to the Casino in Montreal. Chiniara and Salico were the principal shareholders and managers of Decarel, who then negotiated and signed the contract for the corporate defendant. Things then turned sour and Concordia alleged that Decarel was with the help of others delaying the work that was the object of the contract. As a result, Concordia brought an action for both contractual and extra-contractual damages against Decarel, Chiniara and Salico collectively. Subsequently, however, Concordia decided to invoke and rely upon the arbitration clause found in the joint-venture contract and pursuant to Art. 940.1 CCP asked the Quebec Superior Court to refer all three parties to arbitration. The Superior Court decided that Chiniara and Salico were so intricately involved in this matter that they had to join the corporate defendant in arbitration.

In a split decision, the Quebec Court of appeal decided to pierce the corporate veil of the corporate defendant Decarel, in order to extend to Chiniara and Salico the arbitration clause concluded between their company and Concordia. According to the court, the circumstances of that case required that everyone interested in the matter find themselves before an arbitral tribunal so as to avoid rendering the litigation among the parties absurd.

---

40. See fn. 6 supra.
41. Sabine THUILLEAUX, *L'arbitrage commercial au Québec: Droit interne, droit international privé* (Cowansville, Yvon Blais 1991) at p. 55.
42. See the in part dissenting decision of Justice Chamberland.
43. [1996] R.D.J. 484 (C.A.) [*Decarel*].

In arriving at its decision, the majority[44] in *Decarel* referred to that Court's own previous judgments in *Watson Computer Products Inc. v. 136067 Canada Inc.*,[45] and *Guns N' Roses Missouri Storm Inc. v. Productions Musicales Donald K. Donald Inc.*[46] in order to reach the conclusion that every case had to be decided on a "case by case" basis. In *Guns N' Roses*, the respondent Donald K. Donald became the subject of a class action suit for damages after the lead singer of the band represented by the appellant prematurely and abruptly ended a concert. The respondent in turn instituted an action in warranty against Guns N' Roses pursuant to Arts. 71 and 216 CCP which gives the court seized of the principal action the jurisdiction to hear any incidental actions in warranty.[47] The defendant in warranty presented a declinatory exception motion to the Superior Court raising the existence of an arbitration clause. The motion was dismissed in first instance. The Court of Appeal upheld the lower court's decision, stating:

> "I do not wish to suggest that the mere initiation of a suit by a third party will permit a party to an arbitration clause to defeat the purpose and intention of the clause by exercising warranty proceedings. There will doubtless be cases where the parties should be referred to arbitration, notwithstanding the existence of a suit by a third party. *Much will depend on the nature of the claims and the circumstances of each case.*
>
> But in this case, taking the facts alleged to be true, the sole reason for the premature collapse of the concert, and the near riot that followed it, was the conduct of the lead singer of Guns N' Roses. The whole cause of action alleged in the principal action was the misconduct of Axl Rose that took place in the Guns N' Roses performance. The sole issue in the warranty action, as in the principal action, is the misconduct that took place during the Guns N' Roses performance. It would be *manifestly unfair* to compel Donald K. Donald to face a refund claim before the Superior Court on behalf of 54,000 ticket holders when Guns N' Roses was the sole cause of the claim."

(Emphasis added)

It is interesting to note that while the Quebec Court of Appeal in *Decarel* cited the "manifestly unfair" criteria referred to in *Guns N' Roses*, it decided not to necessarily adopt it on the basis of the particular circumstances of that case. It is also interesting to note that the decision of the Court in *Decarel* was a notable departure from its earlier

---

44. Justice Chamberland of the Quebec Court of Appeal dissented in part, stating that in his view, it was a mistake to refer to arbitration two individuals who were not parties to an arbitration clause. Justice Chamberland then went on to say, that the action commenced by the respondents against Chinlara and Salico alleges personal responsibility against the two individuals and as such it ought to be decided by the Superior Court, even though the corporate defendant itself has accepted that the litigation concerning it be submitted to arbitration.

45. [1987] R.D.J. 326 (C.A.) [*Watson*].

46. [1994] R.J.Q. 1183 (C.A.) [*Guns N' Roses*].

47. Art. 3139 CCQ sets out the rule applicable to private international law situations. It provides: "Where a Quebec authority has jurisdiction to rule on the principal demand, it also has jurisdiction to rule on an incidental or cross demand."

decision in *Watson Computer Products Inc. v. 136067 Canada Inc.*,[48] where it had decided in favour of keeping claims against both a party and non party before the courts notwithstanding the existence of a valid arbitration clause, on the basis that the plaintiff was pursuing the defendants in joint and several liability and could only do so before the ordinary courts.

Another Quebec decision which requires a quick comment is the decision of the Quebec Court of Appeal in *Dominion Bridge Corp. v. Knai*.[49] It dismissed the plaintiff's argument that the claims against the defendant should go to arbitration, and that any decision rendered by the tribunal should be binding against the co-defendant wife. Finally in *Societe Asbestos Ltd. v. Lacroix*[50] the Quebec Court of Appeal decided that the arbitration clause contained in a collective bargaining agreement did not extend to the employer. In *Societe Asbestos*, the Appellant employer, Societe Asbestos Ltd., was also the administrator of a retirement pension fund which in 1985 had decided to transfer these funds to an investment fund. In February of 2002, the respondent, Lacroix, lodged a motion for authorization of a class action against the appellant, on the basis of the mismanagement of the pension fund. The Appellant brought a declinatory exception motion, arguing that the Quebec Superior Court lacked the jurisdiction ratione materiae to adjudicate the Respondent's claims. The Appellant argued that the class action had to be dismissed because there was an arbitration clause in the collective bargaining agreement.

In essentially reviewing the jurisprudence cited above, the Quebec Court of Appeal reiterated the principle set out in *Decarel* that every case had to be decided based on its own facts. The Court remarked that while in the past, the Court of Appeal had previously examined situations were arbitration clauses may be extended to non-signatories, there was still no established legal principle to speak of on this issue. According to the court, caution must be exercised in these circumstances as above all, the relationship between the parties is a contractual one.

The most recent Quebec Superior Court decision dealing with the effect of an arbitration clause on third parties is *3879607 Canada inc. v. Hôtel Cadim (Godin) inc.*[51] In 2002, three parties, Cadim inc. (Cadim), Daniel Langlois (Langlois) and a group of restaurant operators (the Buena Note Group) entered into a venture for the construction, ownership and operation of a hotel in Montreal. The parties incorporated and used a number of different affiliated companies to act as co-owners, lenders, and property manager. Hôtel Cadim (Godin) inc. (Hôtel Cadim), a wholly-owned subsidiary of Cadim, Hôtel Incognita Inc. (Incognita), a wholly-owned subsidiary of Langlois, and 3979607 Canada Inc. (Canada Inc.), a wholly-owned subsidiary of the Buena Note Group, became the co-owners (the co-owners) of the property and signed a co-ownership agreement containing an arbitration clause with respect to disputes between the co-owners.

---

48. [1987] R.D.J. 326 (C.A.).
49. [1998] R.J.Q. 321 [*Dominion Bridge*].
50. [2004] J.Q. no 9410 [*Société Asbestos*].
51. J.E. 2006-1791.

Gestion Hôtel Godin Inc. (Gestion), a wholly owned subsidiary of the Buena Note Group, became the manager of the property and signed a management agreement with the co-owners, which also contained an arbitration clause. Canada Inc. contracted a loan from Carente Inc. (Carente), a wholly owned subsidiary of Cadim, and Investissements Daniel Langlois Inc. (IDL), a wholly owned subsidiary of Daniel Langlois, pursuant to a loan agreement which did not contain an arbitration clause. The management agreement, loan agreement and co-ownership agreement contained cross-default provisions in the case of defaults by Gestion and Canada inc., respectively as manager, co-owner and borrower.

Following the construction of the hotel, the parties' application for an alcohol permit with the *Régie des alcools des courses et des jeux* was denied and, as a result, alleging various defaults under the management agreement by Gestion, the co-owners representing Cadim and Langlois terminated the management agreement with Gestion. Canada Inc. was also formally put in default under the co-ownership agreement and under the loan agreement.

Plaintiffs, Gestion and Canada Inc. commenced arbitration proceedings against Hôtel Cadim and Incognita, as defendants, and impleaded the lenders, Carente and IDL. Among other things, Gestion and Canada Inc. asked the arbitral tribunal to invalidate the termination of the management agreement and the notices of default under the co-ownership and loan agreements, and requested in the alternative, that the tribunal annul all of the agreements relating to the project. Hôtel Cadim and Incognita of course contested the tribunal's jurisdiction to render the orders sought. Despite the rather narrow wording of the arbitration clause, the tribunal concluded that it had jurisdiction to hear Gestion and Canada Inc.'s case.

Despite the very narrow language of the arbitration clause, which stated that "all claims *between the co-owners* arising out of the co-ownership agreement" was to be submitted to arbitration, the arbitral tribunal's award on jurisdiction was upheld by the Quebec Superior Court. In adopting an unduly liberal attitude and relying on the cases of *Condominiums Mont Saint-Sauveur* and *Société Asbestos*, the Court held that the arbitration clause contained in the *co-ownership agreement* was to be interpreted broadly so as to cover the dispute relating to the termination of the *management agreement*, despite the fact that the property manager, Gestion, was a separate corporate entity and not party to the co-ownership agreement. The Court also held that the arbitral tribunal had the jurisdiction, under that same arbitration clause, to annul the agreements relating to the project, including the loan agreement, which did not contain an arbitration provision, and in spite of the fact that neither of the lenders were parties to the co-ownership or the management agreement.

In reaching its conclusion, the Court appears to have given particular consideration to the fact that the parties and the various agreements were inter-connected. The Court specifically referred to the fact that the two lenders, Carente and IDL, were affiliates of the co-owners and were controlled by the same persons, namely, Cadim and Langlois. The Court also mentions that amendments to the co-ownership agreement were subject to the approval of the lenders, that the loan agreement made reference to the co-ownership agreement, and that the lenders were therefore aware of the arbitration clause in the co-ownership agreement. The Court also noted that Canada Inc., in the loan agreement, undertook to abide by the terms of the management agreement and that

Gestion, in the management agreement, undertook to abide by the terms of the co-ownership agreement.

VI. CONCLUSION

There may be policy reasons for extending the ambit of an international arbitration to individuals and companies which were not themselves parties to the agreement that gave rise to the arbitration. We are all familiar with those policy reasons, and the debates that can surround them.

The focus of this paper, however, has been the criteria used to determine, and the identity of the decision-maker who determines, whether or not a non-party can be compelled to become involved in an international arbitration. These questions, The Questions, are at the heart of the paper. Having framed this issue, and having then provided a primer in Canadian constitutional law, I have briefly summarized for you the state of Canadian arbitration law (both civil and common law) on point.

Canada is of course a country with two founding peoples, two official languages, and two legal systems. My summary has revealed that both the common and the civil law regimes are equally incomplete in their answers to The Questions. As a Canadian who has become quite familiar with differences between our two traditions, I find that there is a sort of ironic (almost perverse) pleasure in the unity that they both exhibit on this issue.

Fortunately, the Supreme Court of Canada is the ultimate appellate court for both the civil and the common law courts in this country. If, as and when it examines The Questions, we will then clearly have a true Canadian perspective.

Working Group A

7. Treaties as Agreements to Arbitrate

Treaties as Offers to Arbitration – Some Issues

*Gabrielle Kaufmann-Kohler**

The following contributions, which were all presented during one session, deal with investment treaty arbitration. This is a topic of major interest in international arbitration today, as investment arbitration is booming, numerous rules in investment treaty arbitration are still unsettled and the law is evolving rapidly.

The session, entitled "Treaties as agreements to arbitrate", focused on jurisdiction in treaty arbitration. It is actually more fitting to speak of "treaties as *offers* to arbitrate". Indeed, treaties contain unilateral offers to arbitrate extended by host states to all those who invest in their territories. These offers, and the jurisdiction that results from the acceptance of the offer, were addressed from *four different perspectives* in the following Reports.

The *first Report,* by Meg Kinnear,[1] looks at the *law governing treaties,* including the law governing the dispute resolution clause embodied in the treaties. The governing law obviously includes the rules applicable to the interpretation of the treaty and the dispute resolution clause.

Although investment arbitration is modeled on commercial arbitration, the two mechanisms differ in many respects. The interpretation of the dispute resolution clause is one area in which the difference is particularly apparent. In commercial arbitration, both the parties that negotiated the arbitration agreement are parties to the arbitration. Consequently, in the proceedings, it is relatively easy to establish their intent when the arbitration clause was concluded. In investment arbitration, however, the dispute resolution clause was negotiated by the two contracting states, one of which is not a party to the arbitration. How can this imbalance be resolved? This is one of the questions that was addressed in Meg Kinnear's contribution.

The *second perspective* is the *scope of the arbitration clause* as it relates to the *parties.* This was the subject of Peter Turner's presentation.[2] Once the issue of the applicable law is resolved, other issues remain. To whom is the offer directed? Which investors benefit from the offer to arbitrate? Are minority or indirect shareholders beneficiaries of the arbitration offer? How is nationality defined? At what point in time must it be established? These are just a few of the topics covered by Peter Turner.

The *third Report* also examines the *scope of the offer to arbitrate,* but this time from the viewpoint of the *subject matter* covered by the offer. These issues are addressed in Guido Tawil's Report.[3] First and foremost, the topic hinges on the distinction between treaty and contract claims. Although this distinction is well established in ICSID case law, many issues are still unresolved. How should the distinction be made? What is the

---

*   Professor, University of Geneva; Member of the Geneva Bar; Honorary President of the Swiss Arbitration Association (ASA); Member of ICCA.
1. See this volume, pp. 401-443.
2. See this volume, pp. 444-491.
3. See this volume, pp. 492-544.

relevant test? Is the distinction overcome by a broad dispute resolution clause pursuant to which "all disputes with respect to investments" may be subject to arbitration? Does this wording include contract claims in addition to treaty claims (contract claims being "with respect to investments")? Is the distinction overcome by an umbrella clause in a treaty?

Once the scope of the dispute resolution clause incorporated in a treaty has been determined, one needs to reflect on the possible *interaction of the dispute resolution regimes* established by the treaty and other dispute resolution regimes, mainly the one established under the contract. Such interaction is the *fourth perspective* addressed in this series of contributions on investment arbitration. It is dealt with in Mark Friedman's Report.[4]

Generally, projects giving rise to investments involve contracts. The contract may have an arbitration clause of its own or a "choice of court" clause. What effect, if any, do these contract dispute resolution clauses have on the investor's rights to arbitrate under the treaty? The answer may depend on a number of variables, including for instance the existence of a "fork in the road" clause in the treaty.

Finally, as a *bouquet final,* the series of contributions ends with Brigitte Stern's critical and most helpful *comments on all four aspects*.

There is no doubt that the reader will find in the following contributions helpful guidance for better understanding the intricate issues raised by jurisdiction under investment treaties. Similarly, there is no doubt that the law on these issues is in flux and that the final answers are still evolving.

---

4. See this volume, pp. 545-568.

Treaties as Agreements to Arbitrate:
International Law as the Governing Law

*Meg Kinnear**

I.   INTRODUCTION

A fundamental difference between arbitration pursuant to a treaty and private commercial arbitration is the use of public international law as the governing law. International law is usually the governing or substantive law of the treaty, in whole or part. This imports obligations from the recognized sources of international law, particularly the treaty itself, at customary international law, and in arbitral awards. In turn, customary international rules codified in the Vienna Convention on the Law of Treaties (VCLT)[1] ensure proper interpretation of the governing law of the treaty.

This paper addresses how international law is selected as the governing law of the treaty and the respective roles played by international and domestic law. It concludes by considering some recent decisions of arbitral tribunals applying the two most important aspects of international law: Art. 38 of the Statute of the International Court of Justice (ICJ)[2] and Arts. 31 and 32 of the VCLT, and by considering the role of State Parties to a treaty in interpretation of that treaty.

---

*   General Counsel and Director-General, Trade Law Bureau, Departments of Justice and Foreign Affairs & International Trade Canada.
The views expressed in this Report are solely those of the author in her personal capacity and do not necessarily represent the formal or informal views of the Government of Canada. The author would like to thank Robin Hansen, Tim Radcliffe, Lori Di Pierdomenico and Carolyn Bertrand for their assistance, as well as Andrea Bjorklund and John Hannaford for their very helpful comments on this Report.
1. 8 I.L.M. p. 679, 1155 U.N.T.S. 331 (1969) (entered into force 27 January 1980) (hereinafter VCLT).
2. Statute of the International Court of Justice, annexed to Charter of the United Nations, 59 Stat. 1031, T.S. No. 993, 3 Bevans 1153 (1945) (entered into force 24 October 1945) pursuant to Art. 92 (hereinafter ICJ Statute).

II.   CHOICE OF LAW: WHEN IS INTERNATIONAL LAW THE GOVERNING LAW OF THE TREATY?

Arbitration is based on respect for party autonomy: the parties negotiate any law or combination of laws as the substantive law governing their relationship,[3] and tribunals apply this selection. In the case of an investment agreement or a State contract, the parties generally stipulate the governing law of their contract or adopt procedural rules for arbitration that determine the governing law in default of an express choice by the parties.[4]

The selection of governing law in an investment treaty occurs in a slightly different manner. Bilateral and multilateral investment treaties[5] make a standing offer of arbitration to any covered investor who feels aggrieved by conduct of a State Party to the treaty. However, the governing law of the treaty is negotiated by the State Parties, well before the disputing investor is even identified as such. When the investor accepts the offer to arbitrate under the BIT, often by initiating an arbitration, it must also accept the choice of law negotiated by the State Parties.[6] The choice of law by the State Parties

---

3. Giorgio SACERDOTI, "Investment Arbitration under ICSID and UNCITRAL Rules: Prerequisites, Applicable Law, Review of Awards", 19 ICSID Rev.–F.I.L.J. (2004) p. 1 at p. 16 (hereinafter SACERDOTI); Emmanuel GAILLARD and Yas BANIFATEMI, "The Meaning of 'and' in Article 42(1), Second Sentence, of the Washington Convention: The Role of International Law in the ICSID Choice of Law Process", 18 ICSID Rev.–F.I.L.J. (2003) pp. 375-411 at p. 375 (hereinafter GAILLARD); Ibrahim F.I. SHIHATA and Antonio R. PARRA, "Applicable Substantive Law in Disputes Between States and Private Foreign Parties: The Case of Arbitration under the ICSID Convention", 9 ICSID Rev.–F.I.L.J. (1994) p. 183 at p. 188 (hereinafter SHIHATA); Christoph SCHREUER, *The ICSID Convention: A Commentary* (Cambridge University Press 2001) p. 558 (hereinafter SCHREUER).

4. Historically it was assumed that only contracts between States could be governed by international law and that a contract between a State and a private entity was governed by municipal law alone: see *Case Concerning the Payment of Various Serbian Loans Issued in France*, PCIJ Ser. A/20 (1929). The corollary was that international law applied only to transactions between States, usually in the context of a treaty. In the last century this assumption has been reversed to such an extent that a recent text on investment concludes: "... not only must disputes arising out of foreign private investments be settled by international arbitration: they must also be resolved on the basis of international law. No distinction is to be drawn in this regard between investments under a contract and investments based on a unilateral act of the host State." See R. Doak BISHOP, James CRAWFORD, and W. Michael REISMAN, *Foreign Investment Disputes* (Kluwer Law International 2006) p. 661 (hereinafter BISHOP). For consideration of the relationship between contract and treaty claims in investment treaty arbitrations, see the Report by Guido S. TAWIL, this volume, pp. 492-544.

5. Bilateral investment treaties (BITs) and multilateral investment treaties (MITs) are collectively referred to in this Report as BITs.

6. See Jan PAULSSON, "Arbitration Without Privity", 10 ICSID Rev–F.I.L.J. (1995) p. 232; SACERDOTI, *op. cit.*, fn. 3, pp. 7, 18; Antonio PARRA, "Applicable Substantive Law in ICSID Arbitrations Initiated Under Investment Treaties", 16 ICSID Rev.–F.I.L.J. (2001) p. 20 at pp. 21-24 (hereinafter PARRA); *Goetz v. Republic of Burundi* (Case No. ARB/95/3), Award (embodying the Parties' Settlement Agreement), 10 February 1999, 6 ICSID Rep. (2004) p. 5, paras. 94-96 (hereinafter *Goetz*); *Asian Agricultural Products Ltd. v. Sri Lanka* (Case No. ARB/87/3), Award, 27 June 1990, 4 ICSID Rep. (1997) p. 250 at p. 256, paras. 18-19 (hereinafter *Asian Agricultural*

preempts any choice of law that the disputing parties to the arbitration might have made.[7]

It seems logical to assume that States would invariably select public international law as the governing law of the treaty – and often they do.[8] However, one cannot assume that international law applies automatically to treaty arbitration or that it is the only law governing a treaty dispute. Usually international law is one of several sets of rules selected to govern a treaty-based dispute. That selection arises in one of three ways: (1) through an express choice of law clause in the treaty; (2) by operation of gap-filling rules; or (3) by implication.

1. Express Choice of Law Clause

International law is often the governing law because the choice of law clause in the treaty expressly mandates application of international law.[9] The choice of international law as the governing law of the treaty is compatible with the formal definition of a treaty in the VCLT, which is "an international agreement concluded between States in written form and *governed by international law...*".[10]

There are various formulations of choice of law clauses that expressly elect international law. Recent investment treaties of Canada,[11] Mexico[12] and the United

---

Products).

7. SACERDOTI, *op. cit.*, fn. 3, p. 15.

8. While unusual, a treaty may direct that only municipal law govern the treaty. For example, Art. 11(1), Agreement between the Swiss Confederation and the Republic of India for the Promotion and Protection of Investments, 4 April 1997, R.O. 2002 2037 (entered into force 16 February 2000) states: "Applicable Laws: All investments shall, subject to this Agreement, be governed by the laws in force in the territory of the Contracting Party in which such investments are made."

9. Gaillard and Banifatemi list twenty-eight countries whose BITs usually or sometimes require the dispute to be decided in accordance with international law. These include BITs of Argentina, Canada, Chile, China, France, The Netherlands, and Poland; see GAILLARD, *op. cit.*, fn. 3, p. 377.

10. VCLT, *op. cit.*, fn. 1, Art. 2(1)(*a*) [emphasis added]. See also PARRA, *op. cit.*, fn. 6, pp. 21-22.

11. See also:

– Art. XIII(7), Agreement Between the Government of Canada and the Government of the Republic of Trinidad and Tobago for the Reciprocal Promotion and Protection of Foreign Investment, 11 September 1995, available online at <www.dfait-maeci.gc.ca/tna-nac/documents/FIPA/TRINIDAD-TOBAGO-E.PDF> (last accessed 26 June 2006);
– Art. XIII(7), Agreement Between the Government of Canada and the Government of the Republic of Ecuador for the Reciprocal Promotion and Protection of Foreign Investment, 29 April 1996, available online at <www.dfait-maeci.gc.ca/tna-nac/documents/FIPA/ECUADOR-E.PDF> (last accessed 26 June 2006);
– Art. XIII(7), Agreement Between the Government of Canada and the Government of the Republic of Panama for the Reciprocal Promotion and Protection of Foreign Investment, 12 September 1996, available online at <www.dfait-maeci.gc.ca/tna-nac/documents/FIPA/PANAMA-E.PDF> (last accessed 26 June 2006);
– Art. XIII(7), Agreement Between the Government of Canada and the Government of the Kingdom of Thailand for the Reciprocal Promotion and Protection of Foreign Investment, 17

States[13] elect the treaty and international law as the governing law. For example, Art. 1131 of the North American Free Trade Agreement (NAFTA), entitled "Governing Law", provides that: "A Tribunal established under this Section shall decide the issues in dispute in accordance with the Agreement and applicable rules of international law."[14] Similarly, the Energy Charter Treaty states, "A tribunal ... shall decide the issues in dispute in accordance with this Treaty and applicable rules and principles of international law."[15] Art. 40(1) of the 2003 Canadian model foreign investment protection agreement is identical to Art. 1131 of NAFTA.[16] In the same vein, the "Governing Law" clause of the US Model BIT of 2004 states, "... when a claim is submitted under Article 24(1)(a)(i) (A) [claim by an investor] or Article 24(1)(b)(i)(A)

January 1997, available online at <www.dfait-maeci.gc.ca/tna-nac/documents/FIPA/THAILAND-E.PDF> (last accessed 26 June 2006).

12. This formula is found in most of the numerous investment treaties entered into by Mexico. See, e.g., Arts. 17-20, Cartagena Free Trade Agreement: Treaty on Free Trade between the Republic of Columbia, the Republic of Venezuela and the United Mexican States, 13 June 1994 (entered into force 1 January 1995).

13. US BITs before 2001 have no express governing law clause. Later US BITs refer to international law as the governing law. See, e.g., Art. VII(1), Treaty of the United States with the Czech and Slovak Federal Republic concerning the Reciprocal Encouragement and Protection of Investment, 22 October 1991 (entered into force 19 December 1992), available online at <www.unctad.org/sections/dite/iia/docs/bits/czech_us.pdf> (last accessed 27 June 2006), applying "the applicable rules of international law".

14. North American Free Trade Agreement between the Government of Canada, the Government of Mexico and the Government of the United States, 17 December 1992, Can. T.S. 1994 No. 2, 32 I.L.M. p. 289 (entered into force 1 January 1994) (hereinafter NAFTA). In *International Thunderbird*, Mexico noted that Art. 1131, NAFTA was more limited than many other applicable law provisions as it did not refer to the internal law of a NAFTA Party: *International Thunderbird Gaming Corp. v. The United Mexican States*, UNCITRAL, Award, 26 January 2006, para. 88 (hereinafter *Thunderbird*). Other examples of this formula include: Art. 9(6) of the Agreement between the Government of France and the Government of the United Mexican States on the Reciprocal Promotion and Protection of Investments, 12 November 1998, 2129 U.N.T.S. 175, 249 J.O. 5761 (entered into force 12 October 2000): "A tribunal established under this Article shall decide by a majority of votes the dispute in accordance with this Agreement and applicable rules and principles of international law."; Art. 9(6), Draft Republic of Austria Model BIT, cited in Rudolf DOLZER and Margrete STEVENS, *Bilateral Investment Treaties* (Martinus Nijhoff Publishers 1995) p. 167 (hereinafter DOLZER): "The arbitral tribunal shall reach its decision in virtue of this present Agreement and pursuant to the generally recognised rules of international law."

15. Art. 26(6), Energy Charter Treaty, 17 December 1994, 34 I.L.M., p. 400 (entered into force 16 April 1998) (hereinafter ECT).

16. Canadian Model Agreement for the Promotion and Protection of Investments, available online at <www.dfait-maeci.gc.ca/tna-nac/documents/2004-FIPA-model-en.pdf> (last accessed 26 June 2006) (hereinafter Canadian Model FIPA).

[claim by an investor on behalf of an investment], the tribunal shall decide the issues in dispute in accordance with this Treaty and applicable rules of international law".[17]

One might consider that the combination of the treaty and international law as the governing law would be the optimal choice. It is simple, clear and avoids any preference being given to the municipal law of either State Party. Nor does it resort to the alternative of incorporating the municipal law of a third State, which may be unfamiliar to both disputing parties or have little connection to the transactions governed by the treaty. Excluding municipal law as a governing law also ensures that no State can avoid treaty liability simply by amending its domestic law in a manner that prejudices the claimant.

Despite these virtues, many commentators suggest that it is preferable for the governing law clause in a treaty to refer to both international law and a specified municipal law. Schreuer suggests the combination of international and domestic law is preferable because international law may lack the clarity and detail required to address technical facts and complex legal obligations.[18] This is especially true where the treaty breach might arise in the context of a contractual agreement or involve the application of complex commercial law concepts. International law does not have fully developed laws of contract or commercial codes similar to those found in the municipal legislation of most countries. Nor has international law developed detailed rules governing corporations and other commercial actors.[19] In short, international law alone may not address a commercial dispute with sufficient precision.

In practice, most express clauses in treaties list international law as one of several types of governing law. In these cases international law is chosen as the applicable law in conjunction with one or more of the following: (1) the provisions of the relevant treaty; (2) the municipal law of the disputing State Party (with or without a reference to its conflict of law rules); (3) the domestic law of a neutral third State; (4) general

---

17. Art. 30(1), 2004 US Model BIT, available online at <www.ustr.gov/assets/Trade_Sectors/ Investment/Model_BIT/asset_upload_file847_6897.pdf> (last accessed 26 June 2006) (hereinafter 2004 US Model BIT). Art. 30(2) provides that the governing law for disputes arising out of investment authorizations or investment agreements are "the rules of law specified in the pertinent investment authorization or investment agreement, or as the disputing parties may otherwise agree, or, if the rules of law have not been specified or otherwise agreed, the law of the respondent, including its rules on the conflict of laws, and such rules of international law as may be applicable". This is a more complex provision, which recognizes that certain commercial transactions may be grounded in municipal law or specific agreements of the parties to the agreement, and that international law alone might not adequately address the subjects covered by those agreements.

18. SCHREUER, *op. cit.*, fn. 3, pp. 563-564.

19. Case Concerning *Barcelona Traction, Light and Power Company, Limited* (Belgium v. Spain), Second Phase, Judgment of 5 February 1970, 1970 ICJ Rep. 3, in particular paras. 46-47 commenting on the contemporary undeveloped state of international investment law. See also Stephen J. TOOPE, *Mixed International Arbitration* (Grotius Publications Limited 1990) p. 78 and generally at pp. 75-90 for discussion of the application of international law to State contracts (hereinafter TOOPE). Cf., Prosper WEIL, "The State, The Foreign Investor, and International Law: The No Longer Stormy Relationship of a Ménage À Trois", 15 ICSID Rev.–F.I.L.J. (2000) p. 401 at pp. 412-413 (hereinafter WEIL).

principles of law; (5) any specific agreement entered into relating to the treaty; or (6) trade usage.[20] The combination seen most frequently is the treaty, the municipal law of the host Party, any specific agreements relating to the treaty, and the rules of international law.[21] For example, the Colonia Protocol of the Mercosur Group provides that "[t]he arbitral tribunal shall decide the issues in dispute in accordance with the provisions of this Protocol, the law of the Contracting Party that is a party to this dispute, including its rules on conflict of laws, the terms of any specific agreements concluded in relation to the investment, as well as the relevant principles of international law".[22] A more flexible variation on this model lists the treaty, municipal

---

20. BISHOP, *op. cit.*, fn. 4, pp. 660-661; Lucy REED, Jan PAULSSON, and Nigel BLACKABY, *Guide to ICSID Arbitration* (Kluwer Law International 2005) p. 46 (hereinafter REED); GAILLARD, *op. cit.*, fn. 3, pp. 376-379, see BITs listed therein at footnotes 7-12 for examples of treaties with these particular clauses.

21. BISHOP, *op. cit.*, fn. 4, p. 660. See, e.g.,

– the Korea-Argentina BIT which directs an arbitral tribunal to decide disputes in accordance with "the provisions of this Agreement and the laws of the Contracting Party involved in the dispute, including its rules on conflict of law, the terms of any specific agreement concluded in relation to such an investment and the relevant principles of international law";
– Art. 8, Agreement between the Government of the Republic of Korea and the Government of the Republic of Argentina on the Promotion and Protection of Investments, 17 May 1994, 2111 U.N.T.S. 3 (entered into force 24 September 1996), available online at <www.unctad.org/sections/dite/iia/docs/bits/argentina_korea.pdf> (last accessed 29 June 2006);
–Art. 8(7), Agreement between the Government of the Republic of China and the Government of the Socialist Republic of Vietnam concerning the Encouragement and Reciprocal Protection of Investments, 2 December 1992, available online at <www.unctad.org/sections/dite/iia/docs/bits/china_vietnam.pdf> (last accessed 27 June 2006): "The tribunal shall adjudicate in accordance with the law of the Contracting State to the dispute accepting the investment including its rules on the conflict of laws, the provisions of this Agreement as well as the generally recognized principles of international law accepted by both Contracting States.";
– Art. 10(5), *Accord entre l'Union économique belgo-luxembourgeoise et la République d'Afrique du Sud concernant l'éncouragement et la protection réciproque des investissements*, 14 August 1998, 72 Bel. Mon. 10724 (entered into force 14 March 2003);
– Art. 13(6), Agreement between the Government of Australia and the Government of the Argentine Republic on the Promotion and Protection of Investments, 23 August 1995 (entered into force 11 January 1997), available online at <www.unctad.org/sections/dite/iia/docs/bits/argentina_australia.pdf> (last accessed 27 June 2006);
– Art. 8, *Accord entre le Gouvernement de la Confederation Suisse et le Gouvernement de la République démocratique socialiste de Sri Lanka concernant l'éncouragement et la protection réciproque des investissements*, 23 September 1981, R.O. 1982 772, (entered into force 12 February 1982), available online at <www.unctad.org/sections/dite/iia/docs/bits/switzerland_srilanka_fr.pdf> (last accessed 27 June 2006);
– Art. 8(6), Agreement between the Czech Republic and the Oriental Republic of Uruguay for the Promotion and Protection of Investments, 26 September 1996, available online at <www.unctad.org/sections/dite/iia/docs/bits/czech_uruguay.pdf> (last accessed 27 June 2006).

22. GAILLARD, *op. cit.*, fn. 3, p. 376.

law, and international law as the governing law and allows the tribunal to decide a dispute *ex aequo et bono*.[23]

The governing law clause applied by the Iran-US Claims Tribunal represents the "high-water mark" of flexible governing law clauses. Art. V of the Algiers Claims Settlement Declaration[24] stipulates as follows:

> "The Tribunal shall decide all cases on the basis of respect for law, applying such choice of law rules and principles of commercial and international law as the Tribunal determines to be applicable, taking into account relevant usages of the trade, contract provisions and changed circumstances."

As acknowledged by the Claims Tribunal, "It is difficult to conceive of a choice of law provision that would give the Tribunal greater freedom in determining case by case the law relevant to the issues before it."[25]

---

23. See, e.g.,

    – Art. 10(7), Agreement on Encouragement and Reciprocal Protection of Investments between the Kingdom of the Netherlands and the Czech and Slovak Federal Republic, 29 April 1991 (entered into force 1 October 1992), available online at <www.unctad.org/sections/dite/iia/docs/bits/czech_netherlands.pdf> (last accessed 27 June 2006), which provides that: "The tribunal shall decide on the basis of the present Agreement and other relevant Agreements between the two Contracting Parties, the general principles of international law, as well as such general rules of law as the tribunal deems applicable. The foregoing provisions shall not prejudice the power of the tribunal to decide the dispute *ex aequo et bono* if the Parties so agree." (hereinafter Netherlands-Czech BIT);
    – Art. 13(5), Agreement on Encouragement and Reciprocal Protection of Investments between the Kingdom of the Netherlands and the Republic of Bolivia, 10 March 1992, (entered into force 1 November 1994), available online at <www.unctad.org/sections/dite/iia/docs/bits/netherlands_bolivia.pdf> (last accessed 27 June 2006), states: "The tribunal shall decide on the basis of respect for the law, including in particular the present Agreement and any other relevant agreement between the Contracting Parties as well as the generally recognized rules and principles of International Law. Before the tribunal decides, it may at any stage of the proceedings propose to the Parties that the dispute be settled amicably. The foregoing provisions shall not prejudice the power of the tribunal to decide the dispute *ex aequo et bono* if the Parties so agree." (hereinafter Netherlands-Bolivia BIT).

24. Art. V, Declaration of the Government of the Democratic and Popular Republic of Algeria concerning the Settlement of Claims by the Government of the United States of America and the Government of the Islamic Republic of Iran (Algiers Claims Settlement Declaration), 20 I.L.M. (1981) p. 257.

25. *CMI International, Inc. v. Iran* (1983) 4 Iran-U.S. C.T.R. (Award No. 99-245-2) p. 263 at pp. 267-268 (hereinafter *CMI*). This provision was intended to address the concerns of the United States and Iran that it would be difficult to identify relevant Iranian and American law and domestic choice of law provisions, much less to achieve consensus on these. Hence, the article is extremely open-ended. See George H. ALDRICH, *The Jurisprudence of the Iran-United States Claims Tribunal* (Oxford 1996) p. 156 (hereinafter ALDRICH); David C. CARON, Lee M. CAPLAN, and Matti PELLONPAA, *The UNCITRAL Arbitration Rules: A Commentary* (Oxford University Press 2006) pp. 138-139 (hereinafter CARON).

2.   Gap-filling Provisions on Governing Law

Numerous treaties fail to state a governing law.[26] Treaties in this category are often older treaties; those concluded more recently tend to state the governing law expressly.[27] For example, American BITs before 2001 did not include a choice of law clause. Nor are choice of law provisions usually found in Swiss or Dutch BITs.[28] Gaillard and Banifatemi summarize that:

> "The majority of BITs entered into by countries such as the United States, the United Kingdom, France or Germany do not contain a clause on applicable law regarding investment disputes between one of the contracting States and the investors of the other contracting State. As of October 6, 2003, none of the 38 BITs entered into between the United States, and which are in force, contain a clause on the applicable law; such a clause can be found in only 12 of 77 BITs concluded by France (and in force), in only 6 out of 85 BITs concluded by the United Kingdom (and in force) and in only 8 out of the 62 available BITs concluded by Germany (and in force)."[29]

If no governing law is stated in the treaty, the arbitrator usually turns to "gap-filling" provisions in the arbitral rules adopted by the treaty. Invariably these provisions reiterate the overriding preference of arbitration to respect any selection of governing law by the parties. However, they recognize that parties do not always include an express choice of law clause. In this case such provisions establish a method to determine the governing law or alternatively they stipulate directly the governing law in default of an express choice by the parties.[30] All of the major arbitral rules have gap-filling provisions.

a.   Art. 33 of the UNCITRAL Rules

Art. 33(1) of the UNCITRAL Rules requires the tribunal to select governing law on the basis of the conflict of law rules it considers applicable.[31] It provides:

---

26. GAILLARD, op. cit., fn. 3, p. 379; see, e.g., The Government of the Republic of the Philippines and the Government of the Republic of Finland on the Promotion and Protection of Investments, 25 March 1998 (entered into force 16 April 1999) available online at <www.unctad.org/sections/dite/iia/docs/bits/finland_philippines.pdf> (last accessed 27 June 2006); Federal Republic of Germany Model BIT, February 1992, cited in DOLZER, op. cit., fn. 14, p. 187; Hong Kong Model BIT, cited in DOLZER, op. cit., fn. 14, p. 200.

27. BISHOP, op. cit., fn. 4, p. 660.

28. SACERDOTI, op. cit., fn. 3, therein at footnote 33.

29. GAILLARD, op. cit., fn. 3, p. 379.

30. Ibid., pp. 375-376.

31. CARON, op. cit., fn. 25, p. 131. See also Methanex Corp. v. US, Final Award of the Tribunal on Jurisdiction and Merits, 3 August 2005, Part II, Ch. B, paras. 7-9 (hereinafter Methanex Award on Jurisdiction).

"The arbitral tribunal shall apply the law designated by the parties as applicable to the substance of the dispute. Failing such designation by the parties, the arbitral tribunal shall apply the law determined by the conflict of laws rules which it considers applicable."[32]

UNCITRAL tribunals applying Art. 33 most frequently refer to the conflict rules of the place of arbitration selected by the disputing parties. While Art. 33 of the UNCITRAL Rules is "typical of private law",[33] it does not prevent international law from being selected as the governing law. Art. 33 also gives significant discretion to a tribunal to apply other conflict of law rules as it deems most appropriate. This might include selecting the conflict of law rules of one or both States associated with the dispute, of a third State having a substantial connection to the dispute, or applying the general principles of private international law.[34] The author is unaware of cases discussing Art. 33(1) in a BIT context; however there are examples of Art. 33 being used in a contract arbitration to import domestic and international law.[35]

---

32. Art. 33, UNCITRAL Arbitration Rules, Resolution 31/98 adopted by the UNGA on 15 December 1976, ICCA *Yearbook Commercial Arbitration* II (1977) (hereinafter *Yearbook*) p. 161.

33. SACERDOTI, *op. cit.*, fn. 3, p. 17.

34. CARON, *op. cit.*, fn. 25, pp. 121-164.

35. See, e.g., *Himpurna California Energy Ltd. (Bermuda) v. PT (Persero) Perusahaan Listruik Negara (Indonesia)*, Final Award, 4 May 1999, *Yearbook* XXV (2000) pp. 13-108 at paras. 34-41 (hereinafter *Himpurna*). In this case, the tribunal refers to a specific governing law clause in a contract ("This Contract shall be governed by the laws and regulations of the Republic of Indonesia"), in addition to the concept of party autonomy which "is central to international arbitration". In establishing Indonesian Law as the substantive law for the arbitration, the tribunal viewed the respondent's reference in its Closing Brief "that it is 'convenient' to refer to international practice with respect to matters 'where Indonesian law is less detailed'" as evidence of a common position between the parties, which is further consonant with (Art. 33) of the UNCITRAL Rules, "of a connection with discrete points where international precedents appear useful". Contrast with *Karaha Bodas Company LLC (Cayman Islands) v. Persuahaan Pertambangan Minyak Dan Gas Bumi Negara a.k.a. Pertamina (Indonesia)*, 355 Federal Reporter (3d) (5th Cir. 2003), p. 357 et. seq. distinguishing *Himpurna* to establish Swiss Law, the law of the forum in this case, as governing the dispute. There is also a large body of law concerning selection of applicable law under Art. V of the Algiers Claims Settlement Declaration, which is loosely based on Art. 33(1) of the UNCITRAL Rules. See, e.g., *Pepsico, Inc. v. Iran*, 13 Iran-U.S. C.T.R. (1986) at p. 26 (Award No. 260-18-1) upholding a choice of law clause specifying New York Law; *Questch, Inc. v. Iran*, 9 Iran-U.S. C.T.R (1985) p. 107 at p. 124 (Award No. 191-59-1). But see, e.g., *Mobile Oil Iran, Inc. v. Iran*, 16 U.S-C.T.R. (1987) p. 3 at p. 27 (Award No. 311-74/76/81/150-3); *CMI*, *op. cit.*, fn. 25, pp. 267-268. In these cases, for instance, the tribunals rejected the parties' choice of US or Iranian law, noting, instead, that international arbitrations having a semi-governmental character and involving government bodies should not be decided on the basis of the national laws of either party.

b.   Art. 42(1) of the ICSID Convention

Art. 42(1) of the *ICSID Convention* also addresses the choice of applicable law in default of selection by the parties.[36] Similar to Art. 33 of the UNCITRAL Rules, Art. 42(1) of the ICSID Convention addresses the parties' failure to elect a governing law by devising a process for its selection by the tribunal, and not simply by designating a particular law to govern the substance of the dispute.[37] Art. 42(1) provides:

> "The Tribunal shall decide a dispute in accordance with such rules of law as may be agreed by the parties. In the absence of such agreement, the Tribunal shall apply the law of the Contracting State party to the dispute (including its rules on the conflict of laws) and such rules of international law as may be applicable.[38]

As a result, Art. 42(1) makes both domestic and international law relevant to a BIT dispute where the parties have not elected the governing law.

Art. 42(1) represents a compromise between two almost irreconcilable positions advanced at the drafting of the ICSID Convention. On the one hand, capital-exporting States maintained that investment transactions should be governed by international law as it alone provided sufficient neutrality and sophistication. On the other hand, host States advocated the application of domestic law to ensure their ability to protect against exploitation of natural resources and to be consistent with domestic conflict of law norms.[39] The compromise fashioned by the ICSID drafters was to direct tribunals to apply the law of the contracting State, including its conflict of law rules, and such rules of international law as may be applicable.

Art. 42(1) of the ICSID Convention and its negotiating history have garnered significant comment in arbitral awards.[40] These comments evidence significantly

---

36. Art. 42(1) applies to the merits of the dispute and not to jurisdiction, which is governed by the Treaty and Art. 25 of the Convention on the Settlement of Investment Disputes between States and Nationals of Other States, Washington, 18 March 1965, (entered into force 14 October 1966) (hereinafter ICSID Convention): *Camuzzi International S.A. v. The Argentine Republic*, (Case No. ARB/03/2), Decision on Objection to Jurisdiction, 11 May 2005, paras. 17, 57.

37. Domenico DI PIETRO, "Applicable Law Under Article 42 of the ICSID Convention – The Case of *Amco v. Indonesia*" in Todd WEILER, ed., *International Investment Law and Arbitration: Leading Cases from the ICSID, NAFTA, Bilateral Treaties and Customary International Law* (Cameron May 2005) p. 235 (hereinafter DI PIETRO). See also SHIHATA, *op. cit.*, fn. 3, pp.191-195; GAILLARD, *op. cit.*, fn. 3, pp. 382-388; W. Michael REISMAN, "The Regime for Lacunae in the ICSID Choice of Law Provision and the Question of Its Threshold", 15 ICSID Rev.–F.I.L.J. (2000) p. 362 (hereinafter REISMAN).

38. Art. 42(1), ICSID Convention, *op. cit.*, fn. 36.

39. DI PIETRO, *op. cit.*, fn. 37, pp. 234-235, 249-253; SCHREUER, *op. cit.*, fn. 3, p. 553; Gaillard and Banifatemi note that despite the entrenched positions in this debate, the application of the rules of international law are not necessarily always in the investor's favour: GAILLARD, *op. cit.*, fn. 3, pp. 380-381. See also PARRA, *op. cit.*, fn. 6; Georges R. DELAUME, "The Proper Law of State Contracts Revisited", 12 ICSID Rev.– F.I.L.J. (1997) p. 1 (hereinafter DELAUME).

40. See generally: BISHOP, *op. cit.*, fn. 4, pp. 632-661; REED, *op. cit.*, fn. 20, pp. 29-31, 46-48; SCHREUER, *op. cit.*, fn. 3, pp. 549-631; K.V.S.K. NATHAN, *ICSID Convention* (Juris Publishing 2000) pp. 70-73; DI PIETRO, *op. cit.*, fn. 37, pp. 223-279; GAILLARD, *op. cit.*, fn. 3, pp. 375-

divergent views on the extent to which international law can be the governing law of the treaty under Art. 42(1) of the Convention. Three main approaches to this article have emerged.[41] The first approach gives international law a minimal role, suggesting that international law can be used only to supplement municipal law where the latter has a clear lacuna or to correct municipal law where it is inconsistent with international law (the "supplemental and corrective" approach). Under this approach, a treaty interpreter ascertains governing law in a sequential fashion, first looking to municipal law and only drawing on international law if there are real deficiencies in the municipal law or if that law cannot co-exist with international law. As explained by Gaillard and Banifatemi:

> "The triggering factor of the applicability of international law is therefore, not that its rules may be applicable *per se*, but the existence of *lacunae* or possible inconsistencies. Under this methodology, international law is viewed through the hypothetical gaps of national laws or through the inadequacies of such laws vis-à-vis international law and not as an independent body of law to which the arbitral tribunal has free access."[42]

The approach allowing international law only a supplemental and corrective role was first advanced in *Klockner v. Cameroon*,[43] where the tribunal based its decision on general principles of law recognized by civilized nations, rather than on Cameroonian law. The ICSID Annulment Committee reviewing the tribunal award concluded that this approach was erroneous, as the principles of international law have a:

> "... dual role, that is *complementary* (in the case of a 'lacuna' in the law of the State), or *corrective*, should the State's law not conform on all points to the principles of international law. *In both cases*, the arbitrators may have recourse to the 'principles of international law' only after having inquired into and established the content of the law of the State party to the dispute (which cannot be reduced to *one* principle, even a basic one) and *after* having applied the relevant rules of the State's law. Art. 42(1) therefore clearly does not allow the arbitrator to base his decision *solely* on the 'rules' or 'principles of international law'."[44]

---

411 (2003); REISMAN, *op. cit.*, fn. 37.

41. The article by Gaillard and Banifatemi identifies and discusses the three approaches to Art. 42(1) in detail: GAILLARD, *op. cit.*, fn. 3, pp. 380-411. See also *Goetz*, *op. cit.*, fn. 6, paras. 97-99.

42. GAILLARD, *op. cit.*, fn. 3, p. 389.

43. *Klöckner Industrie-Anlagen GmbH et al. v. United Republic of Cameroon and Société Camerounaise des Engrais, S.A.*, (Case No. ARB/81/2), Decision on Annulment, 3 May 1985, 2 ICSID Rep. (1994) p. 95 at p. 119 (hereinafter *Klöckner*). For a critique of this thesis, see GAILLARD, *op. cit.*, fn. 3, pp. 395-399.

44. *Klöckner*, *op. cit.*, fn. 43, p. 122, para. 70 (italics in original).

This approach has been reiterated in various cases, including *AGIP SpA v. Republic of the Congo*,[45] *Amco v. Republic of Indonesia*,[46] *LETCO v. Liberia*,[47] and *Southern Pacific Properties (Middle East) Ltd v. Arab Republic of Egypt*.[48]

The second approach to the relationship of international and domestic law under Art. 42(1) of the ICSID Convention modifies the "supplemental and corrective" approach. It has been advanced primarily by Reisman, in his consideration of what constitutes a true "lacuna" for the purposes of Art. 42(1). Pursuant to this approach, international law applies only in those rare cases where failure to apply international law would violate peremptory international law norms.[49] The fact that municipal law addresses a topic differently than would international law or that municipal law intentionally does not address a topic would not justify resort to international law.[50] Rather, "a veritable collision" between municipal and international law is required to justify applying the latter.[51] This approach also leaves little room for international law as the governing law of the treaty, as it will be unusual to find a true lacuna justifying resort to international law.

The third approach attributes a full role to international law and views international law as available to arbitrators without first considering, and rejecting, municipal law. For example, Gaillard and Banifatemi take the position that Art. 42(1) of the ICSID Convention makes both international and national law relevant, and the only real issue is what their respective roles should be.[52] This view appears to have been adopted in

---

45. *AGIP SpA v. Government of the People's Republic of the Congo*, (Case No. ARB/77/1), Award, 30 November 1979, 1 ICSID Rep., p. 305 at pp. 323-324, paras. 82-88.

46. *Amco Asia Corp. v. Republic of Indonesia*, (Case No. ARB/81/1), Award, Decision on Application for Annulment, 16 May 1986, 1 ICSID Rep. (1993) p. 509 at pp. 514-517, paras. 18-28. Note, however, that while not expressly disagreeing with the Annulment Committee, the tribunal on the resubmitted case appeared sceptical of the "supplementary and corrective" approach. That tribunal called the approach a "distinction without a difference" and noted its task was to test every claim first against Indonesian law and then against international law: *Amco Asia Corp. v. Republic of Indonesia*, (Case No. ARB/81/1), Award on Resubmitted Case, 31 May 1990, 1 ICSID Rep. (1993) p. 568 at pp. 579-580, paras. 37-40. This view was further commented upon by the Annulment Committee on the resubmitted case, which found that the tribunal's application of domestic and international law was satisfactory in the circumstances and did not justify annulment. However, the Annulment Committee did note that the tribunal "may have overstated the extent to which international law is generally applicable in the framework of an ICSID arbitration" and that the statement that international law is fully applicable "may amount to reading out of Article 42(1) the carefully drafted and very definite reference to the application of host-state law". *Amco Asia Corp. v. Republic of Indonesia*, (Case No. ARB/81/1), Decision on Annulment, 3 December 1992, 9 ICSID Rep. (2006) p. 9 at pp. 39-42, paras. 7.19-7.24.

47. *Liberian Eastern Timber Corp. (LETCO) v. Liberia*, (Case No. ARB/83/2), Award, 31 March 1986, 2 ICSID Rep. (1994) p. 342 at pp. 358-359.

48. *Southern Pacific Properties (Middle East) Ltd v. Arab Republic of Egypt*, (Case No. ARB/84/3), Award, 20 May 1992, 3 ICSID Rep. (1995) p. 188 at pp. 206-209, paras. 74-85.

49. REISMAN, *op. cit.*, fn. 37, p. 368.

50. *Ibid.*, p. 371.

51. *Ibid.*, pp. 375-377.

52. GAILLARD, *op. cit.*, fn. 3, p. 380.

virtually all recent arbitrations considering Art. 42(1). For example, in *CMS Gas Transmission Company v. The Argentine Republic* the tribunal noted the historical debate on interpretation of Art. 42 but concluded that:

> "... a more pragmatic and less doctrinaire approach has emerged allowing for the application of both domestic law and international law if the specific facts of the dispute so justifies. It is no longer the case of one prevailing over the other and excluding it altogether. Rather, both sources have a role to play."[53]

Similarly, the award of the annulment panel in *Wena* rejected the "supplemental and corrective" and the "collision" approaches to Art. 42(1) and found that Art. 42(1) did not draw a sharp distinction between the role of international and domestic law as the law applicable to the dispute. Rather, that provision gave significant discretion to tribunals to select either domestic or international law. The panel held:

> "The sense and meaning of the negotiations leading to the second sentence of Art. 42(1) allowed for both legal orders to have a role. The law of the host State can indeed be justified. So too international law can be applied by itself if the appropriate rule is found in this other ambit."[54]

The *Santa Elena* tribunal[55] went even further, and gave international law precedence if there was a conflict between domestic and international law. It stated, "to the extent that there may be any inconsistency between the two bodies of law, the rules of public international law must prevail".[56] This conclusion was based on the policy concern that application of domestic law alone would deprive the investor of international law protections in relation to takings of property, and would frustrate the purpose of the ICSID Convention.

c.   *Art. 54(1) of the ICSID Additional Facility Rules*
A third gap-filling provision is Art. 54(1) of the ICSID Additional Facility Rules. It provides:

---

53. *CMS Gas Transmission Company v. The Argentine Republic*, (Case No. ARB/01/8), Award, 12 May 2005, para. 116, and generally at paras. 115-123 (hereinafter *CMS*). The use of domestic and international law as the governing law is one of the grounds upon which Argentina has brought an application to annul the tribunal award: *CMS Gas Transmission Company v. The Argentine Republic*, (Case No. ARB/01/8), Application for Annulment, 8 September 2005, paras. 46-54.

54. *Wena Hotels Ltd. v. Arab Republic of Egypt*, (Case No. ARB/98/4), Decision on Application for Annulment, 5 February 2002, 41 I.L.M. (2002) p. 933, para. 40 (hereinafter *Wena Annulment*). See also: GAILLARD, *op. cit.*, fn. 3, pp. 403-411; *Goetz, op. cit.*, fn. 6, paras. 97-100.

55. *Compania del Desarrollo de Santa Elena, S.A. v. Republic of Costa Rica*, (Case No. ARB/96/1), Award, 17 February 2000, 15 ICSID Rev.–F.I.L.J. (2000) p. 169, paras. 64-65 (hereinafter *Compania del Desarrollo*).

56. *Ibid.*, paras. 60-67.

"The Tribunal shall apply the rules of law designated by the parties as applicable to the substance of the dispute. Failing such designation by the parties, the Tribunal shall apply (a) the law determined by the conflict of law rules which it considers applicable and (b) such rules of international law as the Tribunal considers applicable."

Art. 54(1) of the ICSID Additional Facility Rules combines the UNCITRAL Rules and ICSID Convention approaches. Like Art. 33(1) of the UNCITRAL Rules, Art. 54(1) gives the tribunal discretion to select governing law by applying appropriate conflict of law rules. On the other hand, similar to Art. 42(1) of the ICSID Convention, Art. 54(1) of the ICSID Additional Facility Rules also allows the tribunal to apply such rules of international law as it considers applicable. There appear to be no cases discussing Art. 54(1).

2. Implied Choice of International Law

The most controversial method of incorporating international law as the governing law in a treaty is by implication, based on the conduct and relationship of the parties and the circumstances surrounding the arbitration.[57] The case usually cited as an example of implying the governing law is *Asian Agricultural Products Ltd. v. Sri Lanka*.[58] The disputing parties in *Asian Agricultural Products* had not agreed on an applicable law prior to the claimant establishing its business in Sri Lanka. As a result, the tribunal had to determine the law governing a dispute under the relevant BIT. In this instance, the majority of the tribunal held that the Sri Lanka-United Kingdom BIT contained the governing law and that the disputing parties effectively had elected the BIT as the primary source of applicable legal rules. This election was based on the conduct of the disputing parties during the arbitration, and in particular their reference to the terms of the treaty in their arbitral submissions.[59] Unfortunately the majority's analysis concluding that there was an implied election of the BIT is not detailed, and it is hard to understand the basis for implying a governing law of the treaty. Further, from a systemic perspective, it is difficult to accept that the governing law might not be ascertained until after the submission to arbitration and might vary depending on the conduct of particular disputing parties to an arbitration. The dissenting arbitrator rejected the idea that applicable law could be selected by implication based on the conduct of the disputing parties. In his view, Art. 42(1) of the ICSID Convention was applicable and hence Sri

---

57. SCHREUER, *op. cit.*, fn. 3, pp. 573-581; DI PIETRO, *op. cit.*, fn. 37, pp. 248-249. See *Ceskoslovenska Obchodni Banka A.S. v. The Slovak Republic*, (Case No. ARB/97/4), Award, 29 December 2004, para. 58 et. seq. for discussion of international law being implied as the applicable law in a contract dispute.

58. *Asian Agricultural Products*, *op. cit.*, fn. 6, paras. 20-24. The *TOPCO* case has also been cited as an example of implied choice of law but it arises in the context of a contract, not a treaty: *Texaco Overseas Petroleum Company and California Asiatic Oil Company v. Government of the Libyan Arab Republic*, Award, 19 January 1977, 17 I.L.M. (1978) p. 1 (hereinafter *Texaco*); see also DELAUME, *op. cit.*, fn. 39, pp. 6-7.

59. *Asian Agricultural Products*, *op. cit.*, fn. 6, pp. 256-257.

Lankan law should have been the main source of applicable law coupled with such rules of international law as may be applicable.[60]

III. HIERARCHY OF APPLICATION – CHOICE OF LAW

Where several laws might govern the treaty, the obvious question is how to determine which law to apply and how to resolve conflicts between two or more potentially applicable laws. In other words, what is the hierarchy of application among the possible governing laws? This question has arisen more frequently in the last twenty-five years,[61] likely due to the increased number of BITs and resultant BIT arbitrations[62] in this period. Early cases on this question usually arose in arbitrations concerning a State contract or an investment agreement and almost invariably applied municipal law. On the other hand, recent cases arise more frequently in the treaty context and usually select international law as the governing law.

Several trends are discernable in recent BIT arbitrations dealing with the governing law of a treaty. In particular: (1) the Agreement will always be applied first, and perhaps exclusively; (2) there is a strong bias in favour of applying international law where a choice of law is given; and (3) the role of municipal law is often limited to establishing background facts to the arbitration rather than acting as a governing law.

1. Preference for Application of the Treaty

The architecture and content of most BITs is relatively similar, although not identical. The basic obligations are relatively few: investors are entitled to national treatment, the minimum standard of treatment, most-favoured-nation treatment, and not to be expropriated without compensation.[63] In addition, a variety of other treaty obligations such as prohibitions on performance measures may be included and some BITs contain umbrella clauses or fork-in-the-road provisions. In turn, investment treaty arbitration is building a fairly stable jurisprudence based on these common obligations. Gaillard calls this the "standardization" of investment dispute settlement.[64] This phenomenon is

---

60. *Ibid.*, pp. 298-299. For critiques of this approach see DI PIETRO, *op. cit.*, fn. 37, pp. 248-249; SCHREUER, *op. cit.*, fn. 3, pp. 576-581.
61. The number of BITs has grown steadily: they numbered 385 by 1989 and 2,265 by 2003, encompassing 176 countries. See UNCTAD, "Quantitative Data on Bilteral Investment Treaties and Double Taxation Treaties", available online at <www.unctad.org/Templates/WebFlyer. asp?intItemID=3150&lang=1> (last accessed 30 June 2006).
62. See SACERDOTI, *op. cit.*, fn. 3, p. 5 and therein at footnote 9; DELAUME, *op. cit.*, fn. 39, p. 5; *Arabian-American Oil Co. v. Saudi Arabia*, 27 I.L.R. (1958) p. 117, *Texaco, op. cit.*, fn. 58; *Liamco v. Libya*, 20 I.L.M. (1981) p. 78.
63. Every NAFTA Chapter 11 award to date has been based on Arts. 1102 (national treatment), 1105 (minimum standard of treatment) or 1110 (expropriation), despite the presence of other obligations and pleadings that have invoked other obligations such as most-favoured-nation and performance requirements.
64. GAILLARD, *op. cit.*, fn. 3, p. 379 and therein at footnote 18.

enhanced by numerous claims arising out of a single event, for example the Argentine peso crisis cases before ICSID or the challenges to US trade remedy action on Canadian softwood under NAFTA Chapter 11.

In virtually all awards where these obligations are at issue, the treaty provisions are applied automatically and tribunals rarely question what the applicable law should be.[65] These treaty obligations are international law obligations, based either on customary international law (for example the minimum standard of treatment or expropriation) or the treaty (national and most-favoured-nation treatment). By their very nature, they are governed by international law. As noted by Sacerdoti, "The breach of treaty provisions is obviously a matter of international law; the existence of any such breach has to be determined by application of its rules and principles."[66]

This is not to assert that the meaning of these obligations is without controversy; to the contrary, vigourous debate concerning the meaning of particular obligations at international law and the extent to which differences in the wording of an obligation narrow its scope is common in treaty arbitration.[67] Nonetheless, the obligations in BITs are certainly similar to one another and awards addressing similar obligations have been the best source of guidance to tribunals. For example, minimum standard of treatment clauses refer to an obligation known only to international law and call for the application of customary international law to understand the content of the obligation. In *Saluka v. The Czech Republic,* the tribunal acknowledged that general standards such as "fairness" and "equity" "represent principles that cannot be reduced to precise statements of rules". Nonetheless, the tribunal noted that it was bound to decide the dispute on the basis of law, including the treaty. As it stated:

> "Even though Art. 3 [fair and equitable treatment] obviously leaves room for judgment and appreciation by the Tribunal, it does not set out totally subjective standards which would allow the Tribunal to substitute, with regard to the Czech Republic's conduct to be assessed in the present case, its judgment on the choice of solutions for the Czech Republic....The standards formulated in Art. 3 of the Treaty, vague as they may be, are susceptible of specification through judicial practice and do in fact have sufficient legal content to allow the case to be decided on the basis of law. Over the last years a number of awards have dealt with such standards yielding a fair amount of practice that sheds light on their legal meaning."[68]

---

65. *Methanex* Award on Jurisdiction, *op. cit.*, fn. 31, p. 19 at para. 37. See also, therein, Ch. D. "How Is International Law Interpreted?".

66. SACERDOTI, *op. cit.*, fn. 3, pp. 16-17.

67. See, e.g., the vigorous debate in the NAFTA Chapter 11 context about the meaning of the minimum standard obligation, and in particular the word "including" in Art. 1105: Christoph SCHREUER, "Diversity and Harmonization of Treaty Interpretation in Investment Arbitration", 3 Transnational Dispute Management (2006) pp. 7-8 (hereinafter SCHREUER, "Diversity"). The same point is made with respect to umbrella clauses by the tribunal in *Noble Ventures, Inc. v. Romania*, (Case No. ARB/01/11), Award, 12 October 2005, para. 50 (hereinafter *Noble Ventures*).

68. *Saluka Investments BV (The Netherlands) v. The Czech Republic*, UNCITRAL/Permanent Court of Arbitration, Partial Award, 17 March 2006, p. 284 (hereinafter *Saluka Investments*).

Another example of a treaty obligation derived from customary international law is expropriation. While many domestic systems of law have legislative and constitutional provisions governing expropriation, the inclusion of an expropriation provision in a treaty is invariably seen as a reference to the body of awards and writings of publicists defining expropriation at international law. For example, cases decided by the Iran-US Claims Tribunal on expropriation were invariably dealt with in accordance with international law, notwithstanding the flexible choice of law provisions available to that Tribunal.[69] In the *Mobil Oil* case, the Iran-US Claims Tribunal determined that "the lawfulness of an expropriation must be judged by reference to international law. This holds true even when the expropriation is of contractual rights."[70] Similarly, ICSID and NAFTA cases on expropriation also apply that concept as it is known at international law and based on numerous arbitral awards interpreting the meaning of expropriation at international law.

2.   Bias in Favour of International Law

Where tribunals actually address the choice of law to govern a treaty, they usually apply international law rather than any other potentially applicable law. The reasoning leading to this conclusion is often unclear. Many tribunals simply assume that international law applies simply because the dispute arises out of a BIT and do not harmonize this with the choice of law clause applicable to the treaty.[71] Few tribunals have been explicit in how they approach, prioritize, and apply particular sets of laws. As noted by Reed, Paulsson, and Blackaby: "[I]n practice, Tribunals in BIT arbitrations generally apply the substantive provisions of the relevant treaty itself and other sources of international law rather than national law."[72] Prosper Weil concludes likewise that:

> "... cases are noteworthy illustrations of the trend – which can only grow stronger – toward ICSID arbitration governed by international law by virtue of the fact that the BIT implicitly or explicitly provides that disputes must be settled not only on the basis of the provisions of the treaty itself, but also, and more generally, on the basis of the principles and rules of international law".[73]

Case law developed by the Iran-US Claims Tribunal interpreting Art. V of the Claims Settlement Declaration is equally unsatisfying in terms of identifying a structured approach to selection among a menu of possibly applicable laws. The Iran-US Claims Tribunal chose applicable law based on the facts of each case. Their choice of law was dictated by a variety of considerations including the relevant provisions in applicable contracts, trade usage, the nationality of the disputing parties, or where the wrong

---

69. ALDRICH, *op. cit.*, fn. 25, pp. 156-157.

70. *Mobil Oil Iran, Inc. v. Iran*, (1985) Iran-U.S. C.T.R. 313 at para. 73.

71. *MTD Equity Sdn Bhd & MTD Chile S.A. v. Republic of Chile*, (Case No. ARB/01/7), Award, 25 May 2004, para. 87 (hereinafter *MTD Equity*).

72. REED, *op. cit.*, fn. 20, pp. 46-47. See also WEIL, *op. cit.*, fn. 19.

73. WEIL, *op. cit.*, fn. 19, p. 47.

occurred and the damage was suffered.[74] Cases construing Art. V give little guidance as to how to select the governing law from among several possibilities because it is so idiosyncratic. As Aldrich observes, "it is impossible to define any coherent set of choice of law rules followed by the Tribunal".[75] Even so, the Iran-US Claims Tribunal also tended to prefer the choice of international law where it was available. Aldrich concluded that:

> "whenever the Tribunal could find relevant rules of public international law, it tended to turn to them. The Tribunal employed such rules in the analysis of several categories of issues: expropriations, issues involving treaty interpretation, dual nationality, expulsion of aliens and foreign currency exchange."[76]

The Iran-US Claims Tribunal exercised the governing law provision in a creative and varied manner, selecting applicable law based on a variety of factors. Among these factors were the location of the subject of the claim, the location of the execution of the contract, the nationality of the disputing parties, equity, and "all relevant circumstances". In turn, this resulted in the tribunal applying not just international law and the domestic laws of Iran and the United States, but also, for example, such diverse sources of law as general principles of law, the Treaty of Amity, the International Monetary Fund Agreement, and Swiss law.[77]

Several recent BIT cases have addressed the choice of international law as the governing law in detail. The latest of these is *CME v. The Czech Republic* case.[78] The applicable law clause in *CME* instructed the tribunal to decide the case on the basis of law, "taking into account in particular though not exclusively" the law of the respondent State, the Agreement, and other relevant agreements between the Contracting Parties, special agreements relating to the investment and the general principles of international

---

74. For discussion of cases applying this provision see: G. HANESSIAN, "General Principles of Law in the Iran-U.S. Claims Tribunal", 27 Columbia J. of Transnational Law (1989) p. 309; J. WESTBERG, "The Applicable Law Issue in International Business Transactions with Government Parties – Rulings of the Iran-United States Claims Tribunal", ICSID Rev.– F.I.L.J. (1987) p. 473.

75. ALDRICH, *op. cit.*, fn. 25, at p. 156.

76. *Ibid.*, p. 157.

77. *Ibid.*, pp. 156-170; See also CARON, *op. cit.*, fn. 25, pp. 138-139.

78. *The Czech Republic v. CME*, UNCITRAL Partial Award, 13 September 2001, available online at <http://ita.law.uvic.ca/documents/CME-2001PartialAward.pdf> (last accessed 29 June 2006, hereinafter *CME* Partial Award) where the tribunal applies international law, in spite of the Respondent's argument that Czech law, as the law of the host state, should take precedence; *CME v. The Czech Republic*, UNCITRAL Final Award, 14 March 2003, available online at <http://ita.law.uvic.ca/documents/CME-2003-Final_001.pdf> (last accessed 29 June 2006, hereinafter *CME* Final Award), where the Tribunal establishes that all four sources of law cited in the Netherlands-Czech BIT rank equally, as confirmed by a Common Position released by the Parties to the BIT; *The Czech Republic v. CME*, Svea Court of Appeal, Review of Tribunal Decision, 15 May 2003, available online at <http://ita.law.uvic.ca/documents/CME2003-SveaCourtofAppeal_000.pdf> (last accessed 29 June 2006, hereinafter *CME* Svea Appeal), where the Court confirms that the Tribunal in the *CME* Partial Award was under no obligation to apply Czech law over any other source of law provided in the Netherlands-Czech BIT.

law.[79] The tribunal found that this wording did not create a ranking or order of precedence among the various sources. Further, the tribunal stated that a decision based on well-recognized international law precedents is decided on the basis of the law, and that reference to domestic law is not mandatory.[80]

The Swedish Court of Appeal in *CME v. The Czech Republic* took this same view. It found that the claims arising under the Netherlands-Czech Republic BIT could have been evaluated according to a variety of laws including international and domestic law of the State concerned. However, the treaty did not state an order of precedence and hence it was sufficient to clarify whether the tribunal applied any of the sources of law listed in the governing law clause. At the same time, the Court of Appeal intimated a preference for international law:

> "The wording that the arbitral tribunal shall 'take into account in particular although not exclusively' must be interpreted such that the arbitrators may also use sources of law other than those listed. The four sources of law are not numbered, nor are they otherwise marked in such a manner that governing law in the relevant contracting state should be primarily applied and general principles of law applied thereafter. The un-numbered list almost gives the impression that contracting states have left to the arbitrator the determination, on a case by case basis, as to which sources of law shall be applied. If the case concerns an alleged violation of the Investment Protection Treaty, it might be relevant first of all to apply international law, in light of the Investment Protection Treaty's purpose of affording protection to foreign investors by prescribing norms in accordance with international law."[81]

In *Wena Hotels*, the BIT did not stipulate the governing law and so this task was left to the tribunal. The tribunal found that international law governed the dispute because a violation of a BIT was alleged, and international law directed that the treaty itself be considered the primary source of applicable law. However, it also noted that the treaty was "terse" and that Egyptian law was relied on by the disputing parties to address issues not dealt with in the BIT.[82] Despite this apparent openness to relying on Egyptian law where the BIT did not speak to an issue, and the fact that the BIT in this case did not provide a limitation period, the tribunal refused to apply Egyptian law on time bars. Rather, it held that applying domestic limitations law would collide with the fundamental international law norm that municipal statutes of limitations do not bar claims before an international tribunal. Further, the tribunal found that the intent of the BIT was not to rush parties into arbitration, and hence it did not apply any limitation.[83] The Annulment Committee agreed that the tribunal's use of the treaty and international

---

79. Netherlands-Czech BIT, *op. cit.*, fn. 23, Art. 8(6).
80. *CME* Final Award, *op. cit.*, fn. 78, pp. 396-413.
81. *CME* Svea Appeal, *op. cit.*, fn. 78.
82. *Wena Hotels Limited v. Arab Republic of Egypt*, (Case No. ARB/98/4), Award, 8 December 2000, 41 I.L.M. (2002) p. 896 at paras. 78-79 (hereinafter *Wena* Award).
83. *Ibid.*, paras. 106-109.

law was not in derogation of Egyptian law or policy and was not a ground for annulment.[84]

In *Goetz v. Republic of Burundi*, Art. 8(5) of the applicable BIT contained the familiar choice of law clause: the governing law consisted of the domestic law of the host State, including its conflict of law rules, the treaty, specific agreements with respect to the investment and generally accepted rules and principles of international law. The tribunal noted that in the circumstances the only relevant rules of international law were contained in the treaty, and hence applied those rules.[85] A similar governing law clause in the Venezuelan-Netherlands BIT listing domestic law, the BIT and related agreements, special agreements between the parties and general principles of international law was considered in *Fedax v. Venezuela*. The tribunal held that all these sources of law noted in the applicable law clause had an effect on its decision, although it is hard to see how these sources had an impact from a reading of the decision.[86]

Using international law as the governing law does not just provide a tool to interpret the substantive obligations. It also imports more general concepts developed at international law. Often these are accepted as being customary international law and have been codified in texts such as the International Law Commission's "Draft Articles on State Responsibility".[87] For example, the rules of attribution which make a State responsible for the conduct of a person or entity exercising governmental authority is part of the law applicable to a treaty.[88] In the *Vivendi* annulment decision, the tribunal applied these rules, noting that Argentina was responsible for the acts of its constituent units under international law rules, whereas it would not have been responsible in domestic law for conduct of the sub-national. As it stated:

> "Each of these claims will be determined by reference to its own proper or applicable law – in the case of the BIT, by international law; in the case of the Concession Contract, by the proper law of Tucuman. For example, in the case of a claim based on a treaty, international law rules of attribution apply, with the result that the state of Argentina is internationally responsible for the acts of its provincial authorities. By contrast, the state of Argentina is not liable for the performance of contracts entered into by Tucuman, which possesses separate legal personality under its own law and is responsible for the performance of its own contracts."[89]

---

84. *Wena* Annulment, *op. cit.*, fn. 54, paras. 37-46.

85. *Goetz, op. cit.*, fn. 6, para. 94 et seq.

86. *Fedax N.V. v. The Republic of Venezuela*, (Case No. ARB/96/3), Award, 9 March 1998, para. 30.

87. *Noble Ventures, op. cit.*, fn. 67, para. 69.

88. *Ibid.*, paras. 68-84. See also: *Generation Ukraine Inc. v. Ukraine*, (Case No. ARB/00/9), Final Award, 16 September 2003, paras. 10.2-10.7; *The Loewen Group Inc. v. United States*, (Case No. ARB(AF)/98/3), Award on Jurisdiction, 5 January 2001, para. 53 (hereinafter *Loewen*).

89. *Compania de Aguas del Aconquija S.A. et Conpagnie Generale des Eaux (Vivendi Universal) v. Argentine Republic*, (Case No. ARB/97/3), Decision on Annulment, 3 July 2002, para. 96. See also *Eureko B.V. v. Republic of Poland*, Partial Award, 19 August 2005, paras. 115-134 applying international rules of attribution of responsibility for acts on behalf of the State.

Similarly, in *Feldman v. Mexico*, the tribunal considered whether an American citizen with permanent residence in Mexico could claim against Mexico under NAFTA Chapter 11 as an investor of the other State Party. The tribunal found that Feldman had standing to arbitrate as an American citizen based on the fact that citizenship rather than residence was the main connecting factor between a state and an individual under general international law. Having determined the result at public international law, the tribunal affirmed that this position was consistent with NAFTA definitions of a "national" of a Party. Similarly, in *Middle East Cement*, the tribunal applied a duty to mitigate damages as part of the rules of international law.[90] In *Metalclad* the finding of a NAFTA tribunal that transparency had become a part of customary international law governing the minimum standard of treatment was overturned on an application to set aside.[91] In short, while tribunals recognize the choices available to them under most governing law clauses, they tend to apply international law first and foremost.

In fact, the grasp of international law on treaty arbitration is so strong that it has been applied even when the governing law clause in the treaty does not include international law.[92] Various ICSID tribunals have applied international law in the face of an express choice of law clause that does not include international law.[93] From a principled perspective, the omission of international law from a governing law provision should be seen as an affirmative choice by the parties not to apply international law, and is contrary to the overriding principle that the autonomy of the parties, including their selection of applicable law, must be respected.[94] Nonetheless, the majority of writers believe that tribunals retain an inherent power to apply international law to a treaty despite the parties' failure to elect that law as the applicable law. In the ICSID context, Schreuer concludes that "the practice of ICSID tribunals, the overwhelming weight of writers and important policy considerations all indicate that there is at least some place for international law even in the presence of an agreement on choice of law which does not incorporate it".[95] These writers base their argument primarily on the policy rationale that it would be extraordinary for an investor to be able to discard the very protections ICSID was intended to safeguard. As expressed by Schreuer:

"The complete exclusion of standards of international law as a consequence of an agreed choice of law pointing towards a domestic legal system would indeed lead to some extraordinary consequences. It would mean that an ICSID tribunal would have to uphold discriminatory and arbitrary action by the host State, breaches of

---

90. *Middle East Cement Shipping & Handling Co. S.A. v. Arab Republic of Egypt*, (Case No. ARB/99/6), Award, 12 April 2002, 7 ICSID Rep. (2005) p. 177 at p. 205, para. 167.

91. *Metalclad Corp v. United Mexican States*, (Case No. ARB(AF)/97/1), Award, 30 April 2000, para. 70; set aside by *Mexico v. Metalclad Corp.*, Reasons for Judgment, 2 May 2001, 2001 BCSC 664 (B.C.S.C.), paras. 68-70.

92. This question has arisen in various ICSID arbitrations and raises questions concerning the meaning of the first clause of ICSID Art. 42(1), which directs a tribunal to decide a dispute "in accordance with such rules of law as may be agreed by the parties".

93. SCHREUER, *op. cit.*, fn. 3, p. 586.

94. *Ibid.*, p. 585.

95. *Ibid.*, p. 586.

its undertakings which are evidently in bad faith or amount to a denial of justice as long as they conform to the applicable domestic law, which is most likely going to be that of the host State."[96]

3.   Role of Municipal Law

The only role for municipal law in a BIT arbitration that tribunals agree upon is to establish relevant background facts. For example, in an expropriation case municipal law could be considered to determine who held title or if the claimant had been dispossessed, but what constitutes expropriation for purposes of establishing liability under the treaty will be resolved by the application of international law.[97] In most treaty arbitrations municipal law will simply be described as part of the salient facts.[98] As noted in a claim under the Energy Charter Treaty:

> "... two fundamental principles are important. The first principle is that for the purposes of an international law claim, domestic law and governmental measures are essentially matters of fact or evidence. The second fundamental principle concerning the relationship between international law and domestic law is that a state cannot invoke its municipal law as a reason for not fulfilling its international obligations."[99]

Municipal law generally will not be applied as the governing law,[100] even when the governing law clause purports to make that possible.

Given the tendency to apply international law almost exclusively in BIT arbitration, the question is whether there is any role for municipal law as the governing law in a treaty arbitration. Some commentators do not think there is such a role. They take the position that a breach of a treaty is decided solely and simply in accordance with international law. For example, according to Sacerdoti, even if an express choice of law clause in a BIT offers municipal and other laws as options for the governing law,

---

96. *Ibid.*, p. 588, and generally at pp. 585-590. See also DI PIETRO, *op. cit.*, fn. 37, pp. 241-246.

97. Ian BROWNLIE, *Principles of Public International Law*, 6th edn. (Oxford University Press 2003) pp. 36-41 (hereinafter BROWNLIE). See also: *Saluka Investments, op. cit.*, fn. 68, pp. 442-444; *Thunderbird, op. cit.*, fn. 14, pp. 123-127; *ADF Group Inc. v. United States*, (Case No. ARB(AF)/00/1), Final Award, 9 January 2003, para. 42 (hereinafter *ADF*); *Loewen, op. cit.*, fn. 88, para. 134.

98. See, e.g., *MTD Equity, op. cit.*, fn. 71, para. 204; *Southern Pacific Properties (Middle East) Ltd. v. Arab Republic of Egypt*, (Case No. ARB/84/3), Decision on Jurisdiction, 27 November 1985, 3 ICSID Rep. (1995) p. 112 at pp. 140-143, paras. 55-61. See also SACERDOTI, *op. cit.*, fn. 3, pp. 22-24.

99. *Petrobart Limited v. The Kyrgyz Republic*, Stockholm Chamber of Commerce, Arbitral Award, 29 March 2005, p. 23.

100. Some would argue that umbrella clauses in effect elevate municipal law into international law. See discussion of differing views in *El Paso Energy International Company v. The Argentine Republic*, (Case No. ARB/03/15), Decision on Jurisdiction, 27 April 2006, paras. 71-82 (hereinafter *El Paso*).

international law still is the only choice available in a BIT arbitration. Sacerdoti views the express reference to municipal or non-international law in an express choice of law clause in a BIT as an option only for disputes stemming from those cases where the BIT also governs disputes concerning investment contracts between the State and the investor, and not as a viable option for a BIT dispute. This then gives relevance and meaning to the choice of law clause offering municipal and international law.[101]

While this explanation is plausible, it is not made express by any choice of law clauses in BITs that offer domestic and municipal law. These clauses are stated to be broadly applicable to disputes under the BIT and are not differentiated according to the type of dispute. Further, if this was the intent of the Parties, one would expect them to make this express distinction in the governing law clause. For example, the applicable law clause in the 2004 US Model BIT makes such a clear distinction. Art. 30(2) therein provides that the governing law for disputes arising out of investment authorizations or investment agreements are

> "the rules of law specified in the pertinent investment authorization or investment agreement, or as the disputing parties may otherwise agree, or, if the rules of law have not been specified or otherwise agreed, the law of the respondent, including its rules on the conflict of laws, and such rules of international law as may be applicable".[102]

This is a more complex provision than found in most BITs, which recognizes that certain commercial transactions may be grounded in municipal law or specific agreements of the parties to the agreement, and that international law alone might not adequately address the subjects covered by those agreements.

Tribunals appear reluctant to apply municipal law, even when the treaty incorporates municipal law as a governing law. For example, in *Aguas del Tunari*, Art. 2 of the Netherlands-Bolivia BIT provided that each Party would protect investments in its territory by nationals of the other Party and would admit such investments subject to its domestic laws and regulations. The tribunal read the reference to domestic laws and regulations as a limited reference to the details of how each Party would fulfill the treaty obligation to protect investments. It refused to apply Bolivian law or to allow the reference to Bolivian law to import aspects of domestic law that would result in Bolivian courts having exclusive jurisdiction over disputes under the BIT and thereby defeat the jurisdictional provisions of ICSID.[103] Similarly, in *Feldman v. Mexico*, the tribunal noted that decisions of Mexican courts concerning the entitlement of the investor to tax rebates which he claimed under NAFTA Art. 1110 had been expropriated should not

---

101. SACERDOTI, *op. cit.*, fn. 3, pp. 21-22.

102. 2004 US Model BIT, *op. cit.*, fn. 17. See also Art. 30(2), Treaty between the United States of America and the Republic of Uruguay Concerning the Encouragement and Reciprocal Protection of Investment, 25 October 2004, available online at <www.bilaterals.org/IMG/pdf/US-Uruguay_BIT.pdf> (last accessed 27 June 2006).

103. *Aguas del Tunari, S.A. v. Republic of Bolivia*, (Case No. ARB/02/3), Decision on Respondent's Objections to Jurisdiction, 21 October 2005, paras. 139-155 (hereinafter *Aguas del Tunari*).

be given significant weight precisely because they applied Mexican law, whereas a NAFTA tribunal must apply the Agreement and international law.[104]

Numerous tribunals have avoided making a finding as to whether international or domestic law took precedence by relying on the similarity of a host State's domestic law with international law or the fact that domestic law has itself incorporated international law to justify using international law as the governing law. For example, in *Wena v. Egypt*, the tribunal noted that the Egyptian Constitution gave ratified treaties the force of law, terming this "a kind of *renvoi* to international law by the very law of the host State".[105] As a result, it found that applying the relevant BIT and interpreting it through international law was consistent with domestic legal norms in the host State.[106] In *SPP (Middle East) Ltd. v. Arab Republic of Egypt*, the ICC tribunal considering the contract at issue noted that the applicable law was Egyptian domestic law but that international law principles such as *pacta sunt servanda* and "just compensation for expropriatory measures" were compatible with the Egyptian legal system.[107] In *Benvenuti & Bonfant v. The Republic of the Congo*, the tribunal held that the Congolese Constitution and international law both affirmed the requirement of compensation for nationalized property.[108]

A few tribunals take the view that both international and domestic law have a role to play in a BIT dispute. One of the first ICSID tribunals to consider the respective roles of international and national law when a governing law clause allowed application of both sets of laws was *Goetz v. Republic of Burundi*. The tribunal commented that:

> "The bilateral investment protection treaty ... determines the applicable law.... [T]he fairly common reference, within the 'choice of law' clauses inserted in treaties for the protection of investments, to the provisions of the treaty itself – and, more broadly, to the rules and principles of international law – has caused, after a certain reversal both in practice and in the case-law, a remarkable return to the area of legal relations between States and foreign investors for international law. This internationalisation of investment relationships – whether they be contractual or otherwise – has certainly not led to a radical 'denationalisation' of the legal relations springing from international investment, to the point that the domestic law of the host State would be deprived of all relevance or application in the interests of an exclusive role for international law. It merely signifies that these relations relate at once – in parallel, one might say – to the sovereign

---

104. *Feldman v. United Mexican States*, (Case No. ARB(AF)/99/1), Award, 16 December 2002, para. 84.

105. *Wena* Annulment, *op. cit.*, fn. 54, para. 42.

106. *Ibid.*, paras. 43-45. See also *Goetz, op. cit.*, fn. 6, para. 96; *Compania del Desarrollo, op. cit.*, fn. 55, para. 64.

107. *SPP (Middle East) Ltd. v. Arab Republic of Egypt*, ICC Arbitration No. 3493, 11 March 1983, 3 ICSID Rep. (1995) p. 46 at pp. 63-67.

108. *Benvenuti & Bonfant v. The Republic of the Congo*, 15 August 1980, (Case No. ARB/77/2), 1 ICSID Rep. (1993) p. 357.

supremacy of the host State in domestic law and to the international undertakings to which it has subscribed."[109]

Of course, application of domestic, as opposed to international, law could lead to very different results.[110] In fact, it can make the difference between winning or losing an arbitration. For example, in *CMS Gas*, the tribunal considered whether there was any valid excuse under Argentine law for not complying with the terms of the contractual and legal arrangements Argentina had entered into. It found that the state of necessity was not recognized by Argentine law and hence was not an excuse for failure to perform contractual obligations in this case.[111] The tribunal then considered whether there was a defence of necessity at international law under either the BIT at issue or customary international law. While it found that necessity was a defence known to international law, it found that the circumstances for invoking the defence were not present in this case.[112] It also found that the defence of emergency provided by the Treaty text did not justify non-performance in the circumstances.[113]

4. Basis for Inclination Toward International Law

In practice, arbitrators usually apply international law where it is one of several potential governing laws of a treaty, often in preference to other systems of law which facially appear to have been given equal standing in the express choice of law clause in the treaty. It is not always obvious why international law should be applied in preference to other sources of law stated as equal sources in the governing law clause.

One may speculate on several pragmatic reasons for this inclination toward international law as the governing law of a treaty. First, most BIT claims are based on familiar treaty provisions, many of which derive from customary international law. Tribunals often apply these without even questioning the effect of the applicable law clause in the treaty. Second, international law is likely attractive to a tribunal because it is more neutral than applying the domestic law of the State of either disputing party. At the same time, the choice of international law seems more logical than picking the municipal law of a third party (unless it has some real and substantial connection to the treaty). Third, the choice of international law prevents the State Party to the treaty from making unilateral changes in domestic law that might prejudice the non-State party relying on the treaty.[114] Fourth, international law has developed significantly in the last century, especially in commercial and investment issues, and is a more nimble and sophisticated instrument than it was even twenty-five years ago. In particular, there is

---

109 *Goetz, op. cit.*, fn. 6, para. 69; see generally paras. 63-69. Despite this pronouncement, the *Goetz* tribunal determined that in the circumstances of that case, the governing law was found entirely in the BIT.

110. GAILLARD, *op. cit.*, fn. 3, pp. 380-381.

111. *CMS, op. cit.*, fn. 53, paras. 200-227.

112. *Ibid.*, paras. 304-331.

113. *Ibid.*, paras. 332-382.

114. SCHREUER, *op. cit.*, fn. 3, p. 562; TOOPE, *op. cit.*, fn. 19.

a growing body of arbitral decisions, books and articles on international economic law and international investment law that reflects the development of this area.[115] Fifth, it may be that treaty arbitrators are more comfortable applying international law than a given national law. These arbitrators are usually selected on the basis of their knowledge of, and facility with, international law and might be expected to "default" to international law where given the choice. As the volume and sophistication of the corpus of international law grows, this comfort level is likely to grow. Finally, the preference for international law by arbitrators ensures that the treaty provides some protection against conduct that breaches international law yet is acceptable under the domestic law of a Party to the treaty.[116]

IV.   SOURCES OF INTERNATIONAL LAW

The applicable rules of international law include Art. 38 of the Statute of the ICJ[117] and Arts. 31 and 32 of the VCLT.[118] Art. 38 of the Statute of the ICJ directs the court to the formal sources of international law. Although Art. 38 is a direction to the ICJ, it is generally accepted as an authoritative statement of the sources of international law for any entity applying international law.[119] The sources listed in Art. 38(1)(a) to (c) are of equal and primary importance in determining the content of an international obligation. On the other hand, judicial decisions and teachings of publicists are a subsidiary means of interpretation.[120] Several observations can be made about each of the sources in Art. 38 and their application in treaty arbitration.

(1) Conventions: While international conventions do not take precedence in the ICJ list of sources, most observers would agree that "treaties and treaty-making are gradually

---

115. *Suez, Sociedad General de Aguas de Barcelona S.A. v. Argentine Republic*, (Case No. ARB/03/17), Decision on Jurisdiction, 16 May 2006, para. 50 (hereinafter *Suez*).

116. SCHREUER, *op. cit.*, fn. 3, p. 568.

117. ICJ Statute, *op. cit.*, fn. 2, Art. 38(1) states:

"The Court, whose function is to decide in accordance with international law such disputes as are submitted to it, shall apply:
(a) international conventions, whether general or particular, establishing rules expressly recognized by the contesting States;
(b) international custom, as evidence of a general practice accepted as law;
(c) the general principles of law recognized by civilized nations; subject to the provisions of Article 59, judicial decisions and the teachings of the most highly qualified publicists of the various nations, as subsidiary means for the determination of rules of law."

118. *Thunderbird, op. cit.*, fn. 14, para. 89-91.

119. David J. BEDERMAN, *International Law Frameworks* (Foundation Press 2001) p. 12 (hereinafter BEDERMAN); BROWNLIE, *op. cit.*, fn. 97, pp. 3-4. See also, e.g., *Thunderbird, op. cit.*, fn. 14, para. 90.

120. BEDERMAN, *op. cit.*, fn. 119, p. 12.

becoming the dominant source of rules for international conduct".[121] In BIT disputes, arbitrators refer first and foremost to the words of the treaty in question.

(2) International Custom: Customary international law is a significant source of international law in arbitration. Academic literature and arbitral awards suggest that the proponent of a customary international rule must prove that the rule is followed by States as a general practice (the objective element) and the rule has been accepted as law by States out of a sense of legal obligation (the subjective or *opinio juris* element).[122] While customary international law is often relied on in treaty arbitration, tribunals rarely go through a methodical, two-step analysis to satisfy themselves that the subjective and objective elements are present. This may be attributable to the difficulty of proving custom, in particular proving the *opinio juris* element required to establish customary international law.[123] It also reflects the fact that tribunals tend to rely significantly on case law to interpret international law rather than doing a classic analysis of whether a rule has become customary international law and the content of such a rule.[124]

(3) General Principles of Law: Art. 38(1)(c) citing "general practice accepted as law" refers to practices in municipal law, and in effect enables a domestic practice to be elevated to an international rule. However, this requires proof that the world's major legal cultures share the same rule.[125] The burden of proving that a general practice has been so extensively accepted that it has become a general principle of law is onerous, and requires a survey of relevant practice in the main legal systems of the world. General principles of law are less frequently relied on as a source of law in treaty arbitration, perhaps because the burden of proof is onerous. Where arbitrators rely on

---

121. *Ibid.*, p. 25; BROWNLIE, *op. cit.*, fn. 97, pp. 12-15. Note also that treaty obligations prevail over rules of customary international law except where the customary international law rules are of a peremptory character: *AES Corporation v. The Argentine Republic*, (Case No. ARB/02/17), Decision on Jurisdiction, 26 April 2005, para. 23 (hereinafter *AES*). See also VCLT, *op. cit.*, fn. 1, Art. 53.

122. BEDERMAN, *op. cit.*, fn. 119, pp. 15-24; BROWNLIE, *op. cit.*, fn. 97, pp. 6-12.

123. As noted by Judge Tanaka in the *North Sea Continental Shelf* Cases 1969 ICJ Rep. 3 (20 February 1969):

"To decide whether these two factors [usage and *opinio juris*] in the formative process of a customary law exist or not, is a delicate and difficult matter ... so far as .. *opinio juris sive necessitates* is concerned, it is extremely difficult to get evidence of its existence in concrete cases."

See also Dissenting Opinion of Judge ad hoc Sørensen stating:

"In view of the manner in which international relations are conducted, there may be numerous cases in which it is practically impossible for one government to produce conclusive evidence of the motives which have prompted the action and policy of other governments."

124. In *Mondev*, the tribunal noted the two-step analysis that is required to establish a customary international law obligation but decided it was not required in the circumstances: *Mondev International Ltd. v. United States*, (Case No. ARB(AF)/99/2), 11 October 1992, paras. 110-113.

125. BEDERMAN, *op. cit.*, fn. 119, pp. 12-13; BROWNLIE, *op. cit.*, fn. 97, pp. 15-19.

such principles, they are usually explained in vague terms and the extensive proof of practice in different legal cultures is rarely undertaken.[126]

(4) Judicial Decisions and Writings: Judicial decisions and writings of publicists are relegated to secondary status under Art. 38.[127] It is commonly acknowledged that there is no doctrine of binding precedent or *stare decisis* in international law. This is also the position in treaty arbitration: most treaties or their procedural rules expressly state that panel awards bind only the immediate parties to the award.[128] In practice, however, BIT tribunal awards now have an influence in treaty arbitration that is reminiscent of *stare decisis* in common law legal systems. Although arbitrators acknowledge that their decisions are not precedential, they generally look to previous relevant decisions and strive for uniformity, or, if that is impossible, at least for a rationale for taking a different path.[129]

Jurisprudence from similar treaties can also be a relevant source. For example, in *Methanex*, the tribunal noted that the direction to construe principles of international law in NAFTA Art. 1131 did not give it jurisdiction to decide General Agreement on Tariffs and Trade (GATT) or WTO breaches, but that it could derive guidance from the interpretation of phrases in the GATT or WTO Agreements which were similar to those in the obligations at issue under NAFTA Chapter 11. At the same time, a tribunal relying on jurisprudence under a similar treaty provision must be cautious that the interpretation is appropriate having regard to the potentially different contexts, object and purpose, practice of the parties and *travaux*. In *Methanex*, the GATT and WTO addressed like products, whereas NAFTA Art. 1102 addressed treatment of investments in like circumstances. The tribunal recognized that the NAFTA parties had been careful in differentiating use of terms such as like products, like goods, and like circumstances. As a result, cases concerning like products or goods could not be used to construe

---

126. BEDERMAN, *op. cit.*, fn. 119, pp. 13-14.

127. This is reinforced by Art. 59 of the ICJ Statute, *op. cit.*, fn. 2, which states: "The decision of the Court has no binding force except between the parties and in respect of that particular case."

128. See, e.g., NAFTA Art. 1136(1) which states: "An Award made by a Tribunal shall have no binding force except between the disputing parties and in respect of the particular case." Similarly, Art. 53 of the ICSID Convention, *op. cit.*, fn. 36 states: "the award shall be binding on the parties and shall not be subject to any appeal...". Art. 52(4) of the ICSID Additional Facility Arbitration Rules is to the same effect. See also Christopher S. GIBSON, "Precedent in Investor-State Arbitration", Paper presented to "Conference on The Iran-United States Claims Tribunal at 25: The Cases Everyone Needs to Know for Investor-State and International Arbitration", 29 March 2006, Washington, DC; *AES, op. cit.*, fn. 121, paras. 23, 27-33.

129. SCHREUER, "Diversity", *op. cit.*, fn. 67, pp. 10-15. See, e.g., *Suez, op. cit.*, fn. 115, para. 26 (other ICSID decisions involving Argentine measures are "not binding" ... but "nonetheless instructive"); *Bayindir Insaat Turizm Ticaret Ve Sanayi A.S. v. Islamic Republic of Pakistan*, (Case No. ARB/03/29), Decision on Jurisdiction, 14 November 2005, para. 76 ("not bound by earlier decisions, but will certainly carefully consider such decisions whenever appropriate") (hereinafter *Bayindir*); *Wena Hotels Ltd. v. Arab Republic of Egypt*, (Case No. ARB/98/4), Decision on Application for Interpretation, 31 October 2005, paras. 73-91, relying on ICJ and PCIJ because no previous ICSID decisions dealt with the relevant issue; *Gas Natural SDG S.A. v. The Argentine Republic*, (Case No. ARB/03/10), Decision of the Tribunal on Preliminary Questions of Jurisdiction, 17 June 2005, para. 37.

treatment in like circumstances. Consistent with the VCLT, the terms of the treaty were the best indicator of the drafter's intent, and could not be overridden by similar but nonetheless different terms in other treaties.[130]

Case law can be expected to continue to be a key source of reference for tribunals as they respond to a desire for consistency and certainty in the various awards.[131] One may speculate as to why case law has become so important in treaty arbitration. First, arbitrators appear to recognize that treaty arbitrations often occur in the context of public policy and can have an impact on government policy and practice. These arbitrations often have wider ramifications than private commercial or contractual disputes. This makes decisions in past cases and similar facts that much more relevant. Second, the increased transparency and availability of treaty awards has likely contributed to increased use of other awards. Third, the increase in the number of awards has made tribunals and States more aware of the potential for discrepancy between tribunals; consideration of past awards is one way to avoid inconsistent awards. This concern is felt particularly by States which must ensure that they comply with treaty obligations as interpreted by tribunals. The importance of a predictable and consistent jurisprudence for States is illustrated by two innovations in the 2004 US Model BIT. The Model BIT requires new investment agreements to provide for interim review of decisions, similar to the interim review procedure of the WTO. The aim of such review is to catch and correct errors before a panel report is released publicly. Another tool to ensure predictable jurisprudence in the 2004 US Model BIT is the requirement for the BIT parties to consider creating a bilateral appellate facility or submitting to review under an appellate facility in a multilateral treaty if available.[132]

V.   HOW IS INTERNATIONAL LAW INTERPRETED?

1.   General Rules

Where international law is the governing law of the treaty, it is interpreted in accordance with relevant principles of treaty interpretation. The mantra of treaty

---

130. *Methanex* Award on Jurisdiction, *op. cit.*, fn. 31, paras. 29-38.

131. Schreuer identifies four particular issues where investment jurisprudence has been inconsistent: consent to "all disputes" being arbitrated; umbrella clauses; observance of cooling off periods before institution of proceedings; and whether MFN obligations apply to dispute settlement: SCHREUER, "Diversity", *op. cit.*, fn. 67, pp. 15-18.

132. Andrea J. MENAKER, "Benefiting from Experience: Developments in the United States' Most Recent Investment Agreements", 12 U.C. Davis J. Int'l L. & Pol'y (2006) p. 121 at p. 128. See also SCHREUER, "Diversity", *op. cit.*, fn. 67, pp. 20-23. Another method sometimes suggested to enhance the development of a consistent jurisprudence is a mechanism to refer preliminary questions to a tribunal authorized for this purpose: SCHREUER, "Diversity", *op. cit.*, fn. 67, pp. 23-24 and sources cited therein.

interpretation is Arts. 31[133] and 32 of the VCLT.[134] These provisions codify customary international law on treaty interpretation.[135]

The three main elements (text, context, and object and purpose) in Art. 31 must be considered in an integrated way, and not as a hierarchy.[136] As noted in *Aguas del Tunari*:

> "Interpretation under Article 31 of the Vienna Convention is a process of progressive encirclement where the interpreter starts under the general rule with (1) the ordinary meaning of the terms of the treaty, (2) in their context and (3) in light of the treaty's object and purpose, and by cycling through this three step inquiry iteratively closes in upon proper interpretation.... [T]he Vienna Convention does not privilege any one of these three aspects of the interpretation method."[137]

---

133. Art. 31 of the VCLT states the general rule of interpretation:

"(1) A treaty shall be interpreted in good faith in accordance with the ordinary meaning to be given to the terms of the treaty in their context and in the light of its object and purpose.
(2) The context for the purpose of the interpretation of a treaty shall comprise, in addition to the text, including its preamble and annexes:
(*a*) any agreement relating to the treaty which was made between all the parties in connexion with the conclusion of the treaty;
(*b*) any instrument which was made by one or more parties in connexion with the conclusion of the treaty and accepted by the other parties as an instrument related to the treaty.
(3) There shall be taken into account, together with the context:
(*a*) Any subsequent agreement between the parties regarding the interpretation of the treaty or the application of its provisions;
(*b*) Any subsequent practice in the application of the treaty which establishes the agreement of the parties regarding its interpretation;
(*c*) Any relevant rules of international law applicable in the relations between the parties.
(4) A special meaning shall be given to a term if it is established that the parties so intended."

134. See also SCHREUER, "Diversity", *op. cit.*, fn. 67, pp. 1-2, and cases cited therein.

135. Anthony AUST, *Modern Treaty Law and Practice* (Cambridge University Press 2000) pp. 184-185 (hereinafter AUST). See also *Ethyl Corp. v. Canada*, Award on Jurisdiction, 24 June 1998, para. 51. As noted by the WTO Appellate Body, Art. 31(1) has attained become of a rule of customary or general international law ... [and] is not to be read in clinical isolation from public international law: *United States – Standards for Reformulated and Conventional Gasoline*, WT/DS2/AB/R, 29 April 1996, p. 3 at p. 16. See also: *Canfor Corp. v. United States and Terminal Forest Products Ltd. v. United States*, UNCITRAL, Decision on Preliminary Question, 6 June 2006, para. 177 (hereinafter *Canfor* Preliminary Question); *Saluka Investments*, *op. cit.*, fn. 68, para. 63; *Aguas del Tunari*, *op. cit.*, fn. 103, para. 88.

136. BEDERMAN, *op. cit.*, fn. 119, pp. 34-36; I.M. SINCLAIR, *The Vienna Convention on the Law of Treaties* (Manchester University Press 1973) pp. 70-76 (hereinafter SINCLAIR); AUST, *op. cit.*, fn. 135, pp. 184-196.

137. *Aguas del Tunari*, *op. cit.*, fn. 103, para. 91.

Invariably treaty arbitrators commence their interpretive analysis by citing Art. 31 of the VCLT and a review of the text of the provision being interpreted. Review of the text often involves resort to dictionary meanings of a term being interpreted.[138] It may also involve reference to legal dictionaries where a legal term of art is being construed.[139] Sometimes the treaty text appears so clear that the tribunal does not continue its interpretive analysis to consider context or object and purpose.[140]

Where a treaty provision is based on a customary international law obligation, the specific words of the treaty and the rules of treaty interpretation remain relevant to determining the content of the international law obligation. As noted by the tribunal in *Aguas del Tunari*:

> "The Vienna Convention's directive to look to the ordinary meaning of a word in its context and in light of the object and purpose of the treaty is intended ... (1) to find the intent of the parties in the specific instrument, (2) to respect the possibility that the parties have used the instrument to address issues of mutual concern in innovative ways, and (3) to not forcibly conform the specific aims of a treaty to general assumptions about the intent of states, assumptions which necessarily are based on assessments of past practice."[141]

Similarly, a treaty obligation may be stated in different treaties and not have the exact same meaning. For example, the obligation to accord national treatment exists in various chapters of NAFTA and the GATT. However, it is expressed slightly differently in each context and must be interpreted in light of the specific wording of the provisions. This was pointed out in *Methanex v. United States* in a discussion comparing the scope of national treatment under Art. 1102 of the investment chapter of NAFTA and Art. III of the market access chapter of the GATT. Citing the MOX Plant and OSPAR cases before the International Tribunal for the Law of the Sea, the *Methanex* tribunal concluded:

> "... the application of international law rules on interpretation of treaties to identical or similar provisions of different treaties may not yield the same result, having regard to, inter alia, differences in the respective contexts, objects and purposes, subsequent practice of parties and travaux preparatoires."[142]

The second step in treaty interpretation is to consider context. The context of a treaty is derived from a variety of sources, including the preamble, other relevant

---

138. *Ibid.*, para. 227 concerning meaning of "controlled".

139. *Ibid.*, paras. 230-234.

140. See, e.g., *Suez, op. cit.*, fn. 115, paras. 53-59; *The Republic of Ecuador v. Occidental Exploration & Production Co.*, High Court of Justice, Queen's Bench Division Commercial Court, Case 04/656, 2 March 2006, paras. 90-102; *Thunderbird, op. cit.*, fn. 14, para. 175.

141. *Aguas del Tunari, op. cit.*, fn. 103, para. 91.

142. *Methanex* Award on Jurisdiction, *op. cit.*, fn. 31, para. 16.

provisions and annexes to the treaty,[143] other relevant agreements, and practices and relevant rules of international law. In the *Canfor* consolidation case, a NAFTA Chapter 11 tribunal put special emphasis on the architecture of the treaty as a whole. It noted that interpretation of the investment chapter could not be made without considering the general principles and exceptions throughout the text of the free trade agreement, and that it would be a mistake to consider each chapter as if it were "made in a separate negotiation by a separate negotiating committee".[144] When considering other international agreements, tribunals can be expected to look to subsequent agreements modifying the treaty at issue, side letters signed at the time of the treaty, and the like.[145] BIT tribunals have also been willing to look to a wider variety of relevant agreements. For example, in the *Myers* case, the tribunal considered whether a Canadian export ban on the transportation of toxic waste violated Chapter 11 of NAFTA. In so doing the tribunal took note of international treaties concerning the movement of hazardous waste binding Canada and the United States.[146]

The final aspect is consideration of the object and purpose of the treaty. Again, tribunals may look to the treaty text, including its title and preamble, to discern the object and purpose of the provisions.[147] While the objectives of a treaty can help clarify the meaning of a provision, they cannot override or supercede the provision.[148] This is especially true when the object and purpose is derived from preambular text and statements of objectives in a treaty which are often cast at an abstract and hortatory level.

Often, the object and purpose is clear from a reading of the text or simple common sense. For example, in *International Thunderbird*, the tribunal construed the consent and waiver provisions of NAFTA by reference to their purpose of preventing a party from pursuing concurrent domestic and international remedies, avoiding conflicting outcomes and ensuring against double recovery.[149]

Preambles and statements of objectives in a treaty also elucidate the objects and purposes. In the case of investor-State arbitration, reference to preambular language can favour investors. This is because preambles invariably identify protection of investors as an object of the treaty. In *SGS v. Philippines* the tribunal found that it was "legitimate to resolve uncertainties in its interpretation [of the BIT] so as to favour the protection of covered investments" based on the preambular statement that the intent of the treaty

---

143. *Saluka Investments*, *op. cit.*, fn. 68, para. 298.

144. *Canfor* Preliminary Question, *op. cit.*, fn. 135, para. 183, and generally paras. 178-187. See, to the same effect, *ADF*, *op. cit.*, fn. 97, para. 147.

145. See below for discussion of the NAFTA Free Trade Commission Art. 1131(2) interpretation and the VCLT.

146. *S.D. Myers Inc. v. Canada*, Partial Award, 13 November 2000, paras. 204-221.

147. *Saluka Investments*, *op. cit.*, fn. 68, para. 299; *EnCana Corp. v. Republic of Ecuador*, UNCITRAL/LCIA, Award, 3 February 2006, para. 117; *Aguas del Tunari*, *op. cit.*, fn. 103, para. 241.

148. *Canfor* Preliminary Question, *op. cit.*, fn. 135, para. 179. See also *ADF*, *op. cit.*, fn. 97, para. 147.

149. *Thunderbird*, *op. cit.*, fn. 14, para. 118; see also *Bayindir*, *op. cit.*, fn. 129, paras. 97-102 concerning the object and purpose of the requirement to give notice of a claim.

was to create and maintain favourable conditions for investments.[150] Other arbitrations have explicitly rejected this view.[151] Likewise, tribunals have rejected an approach that resolves differences in favour of State sovereignty. For example, in *Methanex v. United States*, the tribunal rejected the argument of the United States that ambiguity in jurisdictional clauses should be resolved in favour of the State.[152] The better view is that only the approach of the VCLT should apply, and there is no need to layer on presumptions.[153] The tribunal in *Aguas del Tunari* made this point clearly:

"... the Vienna Convention represents a move away from the canons of interpretation previously common in treaty interpretation and which erroneously persist in various international decisions today. For example, the Vienna Convention does not mention the canon that treaties are to be construed narrowly, a canon that presumes States can not have intended to restrict their range of action. Rather than cataloguing such canons (which at best may be said to reflect a *general pattern*), the Vienna Convention directs the interpreter to focus upon the *specific case* which may, or may not, be representative of such general pattern."[154]

In *Saluka v. The Czech Republic*, the tribunal noted the balanced nature of the preamble to the BIT of The Netherlands and Czech Republic at issue in that case. In so doing it recognized the mischief that can result by focussing solely on the object of investor protection:

"This is a more subtle and balanced statement of the Treaty's aims than is sometimes appreciated. The protection of foreign investments is not the sole aim of the Treaty, but rather a necessary element alongside the overall aim of encouraging foreign investment and extending and intensifying the parties' economic relations. That in turn calls for a balanced approach to the interpretation of the Treaty's substantive provisions for the protection of

---

150. *SGS v. Philippines*, (Case No. ARB/02/6), Decision on Objection to Jurisdiction, 29 January 2004, para. 116.

151. *Canfor* Preliminary Question, *op. cit.*, fn. 135, para. 197; *Noble Ventures*, *op. cit.*, fn. 67, para. 52 ("it is not permissible, as is too often done regarding BITs, to interpret clauses exclusively in favour of investors"); *Fireman's Fund Insurance Company v. United Mexican States*, (Case No. ARB(AF)/02/01), Decision on the Preliminary Question, 17 July 2003, para. 64; *Siemens A.G. v. The Republic of Argentina*, (Case No. ARB/02/8), Decision on Jurisdiction, 3 August 2004. See also SCHREUER, "Diversity", *op. cit.*, fn. 67, p.3.

152. *Methanex* Award on Jurisdiction, *op. cit.*, fn. 31.

153. SCHREUER, "Diversity", *op. cit.*, fn. 67, pp. 5-6. See, e.g., *Suez*, *op. cit.*, fn. 115, para. 59.

154. *Aguas del Tunari*, *op. cit.*, fn. 103, para. 91 (italics in original). See also *Methanex v. United States*, Preliminary Award, para. 105, available online at <http://teaching.law.cornell.edu/faculty/drwcasebook/docs/Methanex%20Preliminary%20Award.pdf> (last accessed 29 June 2006): "... the provisions of Chapter 11 [of NAFTA] should be interpreted in good faith in accordance with their ordinary meaning ... without any one-sided doctrinal advantage built into their text to disadvantage procedurally an investor seeking arbitral relief".

investments, since an interpretation which exaggerates the protection to be accorded to foreign investments may serve to dissuade host States from admitting foreign investments and so undermine the overall aim of extending and intensifying the parties' mutual economic relations."[155]

Similarly, the tribunal in *El Paso v. The Argentine Republic* opted in favour of an interpretation that balanced the interests of investors and States. It noted:

"... a balanced interpretation is needed, taking into account both State sovereignty and a State's responsibility to create an adapted and evolutionary framework for the development of economic activities, and the necessity to protect foreign investment and its continuing flow".[156]

Art. 32 of the VCLT[157] governs use of supplementary sources for interpretive purposes. Tribunals that resort to supplementary means of interpretation look to a variety of sources. For example, to assist in defining "control" in the Netherlands-Bolivia BIT, the tribunal in *Aguas del Tunari* considered the negotiating history of the BIT, jurisprudence on Art. 25(2) of the ICSID Convention, holdings of other tribunals concerning "control" and the general BIT practice of Bolivia and the Netherlands.[158]

Art. 32 clearly requires that supplementary sources not be considered other than to confirm the meaning of the provision as construed under Art. 31, or to determine the meaning when the interpretation according to Art. 31 leaves the meaning ambiguous or obscure or leads to a manifestly absurd or unreasonable result. Unfortunately most arbitral decisions do not follow this approach rigorously, and there is a tendency either not to explain why resort to supplemental means is needed or to approach Arts. 31 and 32 almost as a package rather than as two sequential steps.[159]

The lack of rigour in resorting to supplementary means is seen especially in the debate concerning use of *travaux preparatoires*. *Travaux* consist of documents generated in the course of negotiating the treaty which had a formative effect on the final draft of

---

155. *Saluka Investments*, *op. cit.*, fn. 68, para. 300.

156. *El Paso*, *op. cit.*, fn. 100, para. 70.

157. Art. 32, entitled "Supplementary means of interpretation", states:

"Recourse may be had to supplementary means of interpretation, including the preparatory work of the treaty and the circumstances of its conclusion, in order to confirm the meaning resulting from the application of article 31, or to determine the meaning when the interpretation according to article 31:
(*a*) leaves the meaning ambiguous or obscure; or
(*b*) leads to a result which is manifestly absurd or unreasonable."

158. *Aguas del Tunari*, *op. cit.*, fn. 103, paras. 266-323.

159. BEDERMAN, *op. cit.*, fn. 119, p. 35; SINCLAIR, *op. cit.*, fn. 136, pp. 71-73; SCHREUER, "Diversity", *op. cit.*, fn. 67, p. 2.

the treaty.[160] There is widespread concern about the reliability of *travaux* and the extent to which they should be viewed as indicative of the intent of a Party. Aust warns that, "Travaux must therefore always be approached with care. Their investigation is time-consuming, and their usefulness often marginal and very seldom decisive."[161] This concern is legitimate: for example, rolling drafts of treaty text and related materials are often incomplete and may represent no more than the state of the text at the end of any given day. Additionally, some States do not keep such records (or keep them poorly), which ultimately disadvantages the party seeking to rely on the archives of that State.[162] Despite these frailties, many tribunals rely on *travaux* in the same manner as a primary source. As noted by Bederman, "use of travaux has become a constant feature of interpretive disputes over treaties."[163] Frequently one finds awards that simply draw conclusions based on the treaty at issue and *travaux* of the treaty. They do not analyse why recourse to a secondary source is needed or consider the reliability of the *travaux* presented to them.[164] Schreuer attributes this practice to the mere availability of *travaux* – that tribunals will resort to preparatory work if it is offered to them.[165]

Professor Wälde expressed concern about the use of *travaux* in the context of the ECT, noting that commercial arbitrators may not be inclined to apply international law rules strictly:

"As many arbitrators appointed in ECT and BIT cases have rather a commercial than an international law background, the legal significance, but also the practical utility of following the Vienna Convention interpretation guidelines materially need to be emphasized. The Convention gives clear priority to the literal ('plain') meaning, the legal context and the identifiable (Preamble of the ECT, 1994 European Energy Charter) purpose. It relegates the '*travaux*' to a secondary position. There are no official '*travaux preparatoires*'; there are collections of – always fragmented – files with the ECT Secretariat, the IEA and probably some of the larger countries that participated. Recollections of the – probably over 300 in total – participants of the negotiations, including more significant players – are not reliable, often contradictory and of limited value. If one examines the *travaux* on a particular issue, one is struck by unresolved contradictions, by not followed

---

160. D.P. O'CONNELL, *International Law*, 2nd edn. (Stevens & Sons 1970) p. 262; AUST, *op. cit.*, fn. 137, p. 198; Sir Robert JENNINGS and Sir Arthur WATTS, eds., *Oppenheim's International Law*, 9th edn. (Longman Group UK Ltd. 1992) p. 1277. On the definition of *travaux*, see also *Canfor Corp. (Canada) v. United States*, UNCITRAL, Procedural Order No. 5, 28 May 2004, para. 2 (hereinafter *Canfor* Procedural Order); c.f. *Methanex* Award on Jurisdiction, *op. cit.*, fn. 31, Part II, Ch. H, para. 1-21.

161. AUST, *op. cit.*, fn. 135, p. 199.

162. Detlev F. VAGTS, "Treaty Interpretation and the New American Ways of Law Reading", 4 E.J.I.L. (1993) p. 472 at p. 485.

163. BEDERMAN, *op. cit.*, fn. 119, p. 35.

164. See Lord McNAIR, *Law of Treaties* (1961) pp. 410-423 noting that resort to *travaux* should not become a main basis of interpretation and "should only be admitted when it affords evidence of the common intention of both or all parties" (at p. 423).

165. SCHREUER ,"Diversity", *op. cit.*, fn. 67, p. 9.

up statements by delegates and by the fact that the interpretative issues now arising were rarely clearly identified during the negotiation and drafting process. The wisdom of the Vienna Convention's relegation of the *travaux* to a tertiary role is fully confirmed by any work on the *travaux* of the ECT."[166]

The tribunal in *Methanex* approached *travaux* in a manner consistent with Art. 32 of the VCLT. In that case, the investor had requested production of *travaux* relevant to four articles of NAFTA. The tribunal refused to order production of these documents, noting that Art. 32 allowed limited resort to supplementary text only in the specific circumstances in Art. 32(a) and (b). Hence, it concluded:

> "... pursuant to Article 32, recourse may be had to supplementary means of interpretation only in the limited circumstances there specified. Other than that, the approach of the Vienna Convention is that the text of the treaty is deemed to be the authentic expression of the intentions of the parties; and its elucidation, rather than wide-ranging searches for the supposed intentions of the parties, is the proper object of interpretation."[167]

The tribunal cited the failure of Methanex to explain why the interpretation based on Art. 31 of the VCLT led to an ambiguous or obscure result or was manifestly absurd or unreasonable, and hence the conditions triggering resort to supplementary means were not met.[168] The tribunal noted its sympathy with the position of an investor who did not have access to *travaux* and hence could not explain why they might be relevant or useful. However, this inequality was irrelevant where a claimant failed to address why resort to supplementary means was needed. In this respect, the investor and the State were on equal footing, as both could address the criteria in Art. 31. As noted by the tribunal:

> "In these circumstances, there is no inequality of arms as between the Disputing Parties in this arbitration under Article 31 and the relevant provisions of NAFTA The point of Article 31 is that both Disputing Parties are equally obliged to construe the ordinary meaning of the text."[169]

The *Methanex* tribunal noted in particular that even were the test for reliance on supplementary sources under Art. 31 to have been met, it would not have ordered production of documents that had not been shared between the negotiating Parties at the time of negotiations. It held that one could not reliably search for the intent of the

---

166. Thomas W. WÄLDE, "Investment Arbitration Under the Energy Charter Treaty: An Overview of Selected Key Issues Based on Recent Litigation Experience" in Norbert HORN, ed., *Arbitrating Foreign Investment Disputes* (Kluwer Law International 2004) p. 193 at p. 198. At footnote 6, Professor Wälde cites the *SGS v. Pakistan* arbitration as a further example of arbitrators paying lip service to the VCLT "before engaging in quite subjective decision-making on what the content of the Treaty should be rather than what its plain meaning explicitly suggests".

167. *Methanex* Award on Jurisdiction, *op. cit.*, fn. 31, para. 22.

168. *Ibid.*, Ch. H, paras. 1-21.

169. *Ibid.*, para. 20. See also paras. 21-26.

Parties through documents that had never even been shared or discussed among the negotiators.[170]

2.   Role of State Parties in Interpretation

A recent trend in investor-State arbitration is for State Parties to address interpretation of the treaty in a capacity additional to their role as a disputing party. Some question whether this is appropriate and whether it disturbs the level playing field of the arbitration. In fact, this role is not novel: Art. 31(3) of the VCLT has always recognized that a subsequent agreement of the Parties regarding interpretation or application of a treaty forms part of the relevant context for interpretive purposes.[171]

It is suggested that such interpretation is appropriate given the systemic role of a State in treaty arbitration. Although an investor obtains a right to arbitrate alleged treaty breaches that caused it loss or harm, it has no long-term interest in the treaty or the inter-State relationship governed by the treaty.[172] The arbitration is a "one-off" event for the investor and hence it may take positions that win the day but have no systemic viability. By contrast, State Parties to the treaty have a long-term, continuing, and multi-faceted interest in the treaty. Only the State Parties take on obligations under the treaty. They alone must ensure that their measures (and those of sub-national entities) comply with the treaty obligations. These obligations must be factored into the design of domestic policies and legislation to comply with the treaty and avoid arbitration. If the State fails to comply with the treaty, it may be sued; if it loses, it is responsible for remedial action, usually the payment of significant damages.

Some commentators argue that States will abuse their interpretive authority and develop interpretations solely to ensure victory in individual arbitrations. As Schreuer notes:

> "Unilateral assertions of the disputing State party, on the meaning of a treaty's provisions, made in the process of ongoing proceedings are of limited value. Such a statement will be perceived as self-serving since it is probably determined by the desire to influence the tribunal's decision in favour of the State offering the interpretation."[173]

---

170. *Ibid.*, para. 25 and therein at footnote 18. See also *Canfor* Procedural Order, *op. cit.*, fn. 160, para. 19 ordering disclosure of memoranda shared between the Parties but not of internal US documents which were held not to reflect the common negotiating intent of the NAFTA Parties. For cases distinguishing the application of VCLT Arts. 31 and 32, see, e.g., *Enron Corporation & Ponderosa Assets L.P. v. The Argentine Republic*, (Case No. ARB/01/3), 2 August 2004, para. 32.

171. See, e.g., *Methanex* Award on Jurisdiction, *op. cit.*, fn. 31, para. 18.

172. There is a significant debate in investment arbitration literature about whether to characterize the ability of the individual investor to initiate arbitration as a direct or derivative right: see, e.g., Zachary DOUGLAS, "The Hybrid Foundations of Investment Treaty Arbitration", 74 BYIL, p. 151 at pp. 152-189 and sources cited therein. Regardless of how one characterizes the investor's right, it is undeniable that investors and States have different perspectives on the interpretation of the treaty offering arbitration.

173. SCHREUER, "Diversity", *op. cit.*, fn. 67, p. 18.

This perspective incorrectly assumes that the disputing State has only defensive interests in the treaty arbitration and will invariably advance a restrictive and technical interpretation of the obligations to win the day. It ignores the fact that a State's interest in an investment treaty is not monolithic. In fact, the primary goal of entering an investment treaty is not to participate in arbitration, but rather to obtain benefits for citizens when they interact with the other treaty Party. The State Parties have a significant interest in ensuring an interpretation of the treaty that will promote foreign direct investment in their territory and will protect the investments of their nationals when they operate in the territory of the other treaty Party. The State also wants a reasonable and consistent interpretation of obligations so that it can ensure government operations comply with treaty undertakings and avoid litigation. These considerations justify an enhanced interpretive role for the State Parties in treaty arbitration which is not available to private claimants.[174]

a.   Interpretive statements by the disputing State

Two recent interpretations by States defending investor-State claims have fueled the debate concerning such statements. In *CME v. The Czech Republic*,[175] the Czech-Netherlands BIT allowed the State Parties to consult at any time to resolve an issue concerning application or interpretation of the treaty. After receipt of an unfavourable partial award in *CME*, the Czech government approached the Netherlands government with a view to drafting common interpretations on various issues arising out of their BIT, including the question of the appropriate applicable law that had been raised in *CME*. The two governments met and signed formal minutes recording their interpretation on 1 July 2002. The Czech government filed the minutes with the tribunal, taking the position that they were binding and required the tribunal to revise its partial award. The tribunal took note of the minutes and indeed, agreed with the Czech Republic that "[T]he common positions, representing the interpretations and

---

174. The trend appears to be to maintain and enhance the capacity of Treaty Parties to play a role in interpretation of the obligations. For example, the 2004 US Model BIT, *op. cit.*, fn. 17, Art. 30(3) states,

"A joint decision of the Parties, each acting through its representative designated for purposes of this Article, declaring their interpretation of a provision of this Treaty, shall be binding on a tribunal, and any decision or award issued by a tribunal must be consistent with that joint decision."

Art. 40(2) of the Canadian Model FIPA, *op. cit.*, fn. 16 is to the same effect.

175. *CME* Final Award, *op. cit.*, fn. 78 at paras. 87-93. See also commentary on interpretation by contracting parties in *CME* in Martin HUNTER and Alexei BARBUK, "Procedural Aspects of Non-disputing Party Interventions in Chapter ii Arbitrations", in Todd WEILER, ed., *NAFTA Investment Law and Arbitration: Past Issues, Current Practice, Future Prospects* (Transnational Publishers Inc. 2004) pp. 156-157 (hereinafter HUNTER); and Richard H. KREINDLER, "The Law Applicable to International Investment Disputes", in Norbert HORN, ed., *Arbitrating Foreign Investment Disputes* (Kluwer Law International 2004) p. 411.

application of the Treaty agreed between its contracting parties, are conclusive and binding on the Tribunal."[176]

The second interpretation was issued pursuant to NAFTA Art. 1131 which institutionalizes the right of the NAFTA Parties to issue binding interpretations of the Agreement. Art. 1131(2) of NAFTA provides: "An interpretation by the Free Trade Commission of a provision of this Agreement shall be binding on a Tribunal established under this Section."[177] The Free Trade Commission (FTC) has used this power once, in issuing a binding interpretation of Art. 1105 on 31 July 2001. The interpretation stated that the minimum standard of treatment in Art. 1105 was the customary international law minimum standard of treatment of aliens and that a breach of another provision of NAFTA or another Agreement did not establish a breach of Art. 1105. Although such interpretations were authorized by the treaty, the issuance of the 2001 interpretation was critiqued by many.[178] Schreuer noted:

> "As the example of the July 2001 interpretation of the FTC under NAFTA demonstrates, the home States of disputing investors are less interested in interpretations favourable to their nationals in pending disputes than in interpretations that favour State respondents generally. It is obvious that a mechanism whereby a party to a dispute is able to influence the outcome of judicial proceedings, by issuing official interpretations to the detriment of the other party, is incompatible with principles of a fair procedure and is hence undesirable."[179]

Schreuer's view was shared by most investors litigating NAFTA Art. 1105 claims at the time the FTC issued its interpretation. All of these investors assumed the interpretation was directed at, and intended to defeat, their specific Art. 1105 claim.[180] While there is no ideal time to issue an interpretive statement as cases are always pending, this should not cause States to refrain from issuing statements which bring clarity to interpretation of the treaty. The Art. 1105 interpretation appears to have

---

176. *CME* Final Award, *op. cit.*, fn. 78 at paras. 216-217.
177. NAFTA Art. 1131 interpretations are binding on tribunals. This should be contrasted with subsequent agreements of the Parties under Art. 31(3) of the VCLT which become part of the interpretive context but are not necessarily binding. See KINNEAR, BJORKLUND, and HANNAFORD, "Investment Disputes Under NAFTA: An Annotated Guide to NAFTA Chapter 11", pp. 1131-27 to 1131-36 for a review of NAFTA Chapter 11 cases discussing Art. 1131 (hereinafter KINNEAR).
178. See, e.g., *Methanex Corp. v. United States*, Expert Opinion of Robert Jennings, Exhibit C, Resubmitted (Second) Amended Statement of Claim, 5 November 2002, available online at <http://NAFTAclaims.com/Disputes/USA/Methanex/MethanexResubAmendStateClaimAppend.pdf> (last accessed 29 June 2006).
179. SCHREUER, "Diversity", *op. cit.*, fn. 67, p. 20 and generally pp. 19-20.
180. *Methanex* Award on Jurisdiction, *op. cit.*, fn. 31, paras. 11-14 and Part IV, Ch. C, para. 18; *Methanex Corp. v. United States*, Rejoinder of United States, 23 April 2004, available online at <http://NAFTAclaims.com/Disputes/USA/Methanex/MethanexUSrejoinderMerits.pdf> (last accessed 29 June 2006) para. 186.

created certainty and predictability where previous jurisprudence was chaotic and contradictory.[181] Use of interpretive statements in this fashion is a positive step for claimants and respondents in investor-State arbitration. In any event, investors who elect investor-State arbitration under NAFTA consent to the possibility of an interpretation when they trigger Chapter 11 arbitration. The *Methanex* tribunal stressed this consideration in its discussion of Art. 1131:

> "The purport of Art. 1131(2) is clear beyond peradventure (and any investor contemplating an investment in reliance on NAFTA must be deemed to be aware of it). Even assuming that the FTC interpretation was a far-reaching substantive change (which the Tribunal believes not to be so with respect to the issue relating to this case), Methanex cites no authority for its argument that far-reaching changes in a treaty must be accomplished only by formal amendment rather than by some form of agreement between all of the parties.... Nor is Art. 1131(2) improper under general principles of law or international constitutional principles. If a legislature, having enacted a statute, feels that the courts implementing it have misconstrued the legislature's intention, it is perfectly proper for the legislature to clarify its intention. In a democratic and representative system in which legislation expresses the will of the people, legislative clarification in this sort of case would appear to be obligatory, The Tribunal sees no reason why the same analysis should not apply to international law."[182]

b. Interpretive statements by the non-disputing State

A related debate concerns the proper role of the non-disputing State Party in an on-going arbitration. This arises in investor-State cases where the State whose measure is not at issue[183] wants to address the tribunal concerning the proper interpretation of the treaty. It is suggested that this is also a legitimate role for the non-disputing State, when one recalls the systemic interest of all State Parties to the treaty, whether specifically implicated in an arbitration or not. The non-disputing State can have a useful perspective which will assist the tribunal in interpreting the treaty obligations correctly and restraining overly ambitious or idiosyncratic interpretations advanced by either disputing party. There are few examples of this type of statement other than under the NAFTA.[184]

---

181. See the discussion of Art. 1105 case law and the effects of the Art. 1105 interpretation in KINNEAR, *op. cit.*, fn. 177, pp. 1105-18 to 1105-43.

182. *Methanex* Award on Jurisdiction, *op. cit.*, fn. 31, Part IV, Ch. C, paras. 20, 22.

183. In the case of a bilateral treaty, this would refer to the State of the investor/investment. In the case of a multilateral treaty, this could refer to the State of the investor/investment or to a State of a different nationality than the investor/investment.

184. In *Aguas del Tunari*, the claim against Bolivia was made under the Netherlands-Bolivia BIT. During the hearing both disputing parties referred to three inconsistent statements concerning interpretation of the BIT made by Government Ministers in the Parliament of the Netherlands. The Legal Advisor of the Netherlands confirmed that the statements given by Government Members may not have been correct. As a result, the tribunal found that the statements did not constitute an agreement of the State Parties on interpretation and could not even be seen as

The NAFTA has institutionalized the role of the non-disputing State Party in arbitration. Art. 1128 allows the Parties to make submissions to a tribunal on a question of interpretation of the Agreement. It is complemented by Arts. 1127 and 1129, which require the disputing State to provide the other State Parties with copies of all pleadings, evidence tendered to the tribunal, and the written argument of the disputing parties. This enables the State Parties to assess whether there is a systemic interest at play upon which they wish to intervene. Non-disputing NAFTA State Parties also generally attend arbitration hearings so that they can assess whether they wish to make submissions.[185]

More than seventy submissions have been filed under Art. 1128 of NAFTA (roughly seventeen of these were filed in the *Pope & Talbot v. Canada* case alone). The majority of these submissions were filed in the early days of Chapter 11 interpretation; and fewer have been filed in the last few years, likely reflecting the fact that a relatively cohesive Chapter 11 jurisprudence has emerged over time. Most of the Art. 1128 submissions have been consistent with one another and the position of the disputing State, although the NAFTA Parties have differed on some issues. For example, in *Methanex v. Mexico*, Canada and the United States filed Art. 1128 submissions suggesting that tribunals had the authority to accept *amicus* submissions in Chapter 11 arbitrations. Mexico and the investor disagreed with this position. Ultimately the tribunal held that Art. 15 of the UNCITRAL Arbitration Rules authorized *amicus* submissions.

Provisions similar to NAFTA Art. 1128 are found in US free trade agreements with Chile, Singapore, Central America-Dominican Republic, and Morocco.[186] Art. 35 of the 2003 Canadian Model FIPA allows non-disputing Parties to intervene on interpretation of the Agreement and expressly allows such Parties to attend hearings regardless of whether they make submissions.

Commentators are also sceptical about the participation of a non-disputing State in treaty arbitration.[187] In their view, treaty Parties will band together against the investor and undue weight will be placed on the shared interpretation of the State Parties. It should not be surprising that non-disputing States who negotiated the treaty usually share the disputing State's interpretation of the Agreement. This is positive in that it prevents opportunistic interpretations that might seem logical in a single case but are less appropriate when applied to other situations. One might also suggest that to the

---

relevant or as a basis for a general interpretive position on the application of the BIT: *Aguas del Tunari, op. cit.*, fn. 103, paras. 45-49 and 249-263.

185. In the early days of Chapter 11 there was some debate as to whether a non-disputing State Party had the right to be physically present at hearings. The practice universally adopted now is that they are invited to attend hearings; usually they are invited to make written submissions by a specified date if they wish to address interpretation of the Agreement, although in rare cases they may be asked to make oral submission. For further consideration of Art. 1128 see KINNEAR, *op. cit.*, fn. 177, pp. 1127-1 to 1129-3.

186. Cited in OECD, *Transparency and Third Party Participation in Investor-State Dispute Settlement Procedures*, Working Paper on International Investment, No. 2005/1, April 2005 at 5. See also Mark KANTOR, "The New Draft Model U.S. BIT: Noteworthy Developments", 21 J. Int'l Arb. (2004) p. 383 at p. 387.

187. See, e.g., Todd WEILER, "The Ethyl Arbitration: First of its Kind and a Harbinger of Things to Come", 11 Am. Rev. Int'l Arb. (2000) p. 187 at p. 199.

extent a disputing party is concerned that the disputing State would take an idiosyncratic interpretation aimed solely at "winning the day",[188] participation by non-disputing States would be welcome check on any such inclination. As noted by counsel for Metalclad on reflection at the end of that proceeding:

> "A Party's right to intervene may be a mixed blessing for a claimant. NAFTA Parties are unlikely to endorse interpretations and theories of recovery that enlarge their own exposure to claims. Their involvement in the process is nonetheless to be welcomed. During the seminal stages of NAFTA investment jurisprudence, Party submissions that agree on an interpretive point will presumably be helpful to the tribunal. And such submissions may provide an important check on fanciful theories of recovery or treaty interpretations proffered by only one NAFTA Party."[189]

Some NAFTA Parties have even suggested that consensus on a point of interpretation through Art. 1128 submissions should be seen as authoritative within the meaning of Art. 31(3) (b) of the VCLT.[190] While no tribunal has found such consensus to constitute a practice establishing agreement of the parties regarding interpretation, there is no doubt that the unanimous views of the three Parties to the treaty should be persuasive to a tribunal.

Of course, while such participation might not be usual in private commercial arbitration, it is the norm in State to State dispute settlement. For example, NAFTA Art. 2013 allows a State Party that is not a disputing Party to attend hearings and make oral and written submissions. Similarly, Art. 10 of the WTO Dispute Settlement Understanding[191] requires panels to fully take into account the interests of non-disputing members during the panel process and such non-disputing members are entitled to make submissions to the panel where they have a "substantial interest" in the matter before the panel.

VI.   CONCLUSION

There is a very strong preference for international law to be applied as the governing law of treaties, either because it is expressly stated to govern by the State Parties to the treaty or because tribunals find it is the appropriate substantive law in the circumstances of the case. Even where municipal law is stated to be a possible governing law, tribunals

---

188. The author suggests that this is unlikely given the long term interests of the State in interpretation of the treaty, but it has been a concern of some counsel for investors.

189. Clyde C. PEARCE and Jack COE Jr., "Arbitration under NAFTA Chapter Eleven: Some Pragmatic Reflections upon the First Case Filed Against Mexico", 23 Hastings Int'l & Comp. L. Rev. (2000) p. 311 at p. 338.

190. See submissions of Mexico in *Methanex v. Mexico*, cited in HUNTER, *op. cit.*, fn. 175, pp. 157-160.

191. *Understanding on Rules and Procedures Governing the Settlement of Disputes, Marrakesh Agreement Establishing the World Trade Organization*, Annex 2, 1869 U.N.T.S. 401, 33 I.L.M. (1994) p. 1226.

rarely refer to municipal law other than to set the facts upon which the treaty violation will be assessed. So common is resort to international law that tribunals rarely question the analytical basis for applying it beyond the mere fact that the breach is based on an international treaty. As a result, while laws other than international law may govern treaty interpretation from a theoretical perspective, in practice international law has gained an overwhelming role as the governing law of treaties.

Issues of Scope: Parties, Ownership and Control

*Peter J. Turner**

I.   INTRODUCTION

The study of investment-treaty arbitration has to date mainly focused on the substantive rights granted by those treaties, but the question of who is protected by them is of at least equal interest.

Even though treaties are concluded between states, a characteristic feature of investment treaties is that they confer the right on legal and natural persons (who are not traditionally thought of as subjects of international law) with the nationality one of the contracting states to benefit from the treaty and issue proceedings against the other state.[1] As arbitration without privity[2] between states and investors under investment treaties becomes more widespread, there are conflicting tendencies regarding the scope of the classes of persons who qualify as "investors" under a given treaty and thus have standing to bring a claim.

The tendency among states who are respondents to investment-treaty claims (and those who see themselves as potential respondents) is naturally to seek to narrow these classes as far as possible, while investors (who might formerly have been pleased just to discover that they benefited from the protection of a treaty after a dispute had arisen) now actively seek to bring themselves within the ambit of such treaties from the outset, for example, by routing their investment through a country that has concluded a BIT with the host state. This gives rise to a natural tension about who can claim, which in

---

* Partner, International Arbitration and Public International Law Groups, Freshfields Bruckhaus Deringer, Paris.

    The author acknowledges with thanks the very considerable help received in the preparation of this Report from his Freshfields colleagues Georgios Petrochilos in Paris and Anne Hoffmann and Alice Goodenough in London.

1. For a fuller discussion of the hybrid nature of investment treaties, see Zachary DOUGLAS, "The Hybrid Foundations of Investment Treaty Arbitration", 74 British Year Book of International Law (2003) p. 151. For the concept of subjects of international law, see the *Reparations* case *(Reparation for Injuries Suffered in the Service of the United Nations (Advisory Opinion)* ICJ Reports (1949) p. 174 at p. 178.
2. First so called in Jan PAULSSON, "Arbitration without Privity", 10 ICSID Review–FILJ (1995) p. 232.

turn, it is submitted in this Report, has led to the development of an "investment law of nationality" that clearly derives from, but equally clearly now differs from, the rules of customary international law as developed in the law of diplomatic protection, whether before the Permanent Court of International Justice and the International Court of Justice themselves or before ad hoc claims commissions or under lump-sum settlement agreements.

It now seems to be generally accepted that, while it must be acknowledged that modern investment-treaty practice has developed out of, and is still to an extent influenced by, the law of diplomatic protection, investment-treaty arbitration should now be regarded as being distinct from the rules and practice of interstate dispute resolution in the realm of diplomatic protection. Nonetheless, investment treaties are international treaties like any other and are thus of course to be interpreted in accordance with customary international law, including the law of diplomatic protection.[3] In the absence of a specific provision in the treaty, as *lex specialis*, it may indeed be the case that, even in the context of investment-treaty arbitration, the rules of customary international law will govern matters such as the nationality of claims. This was, indeed, the rationale of the tribunal in the *Loewen* case (which will be discussed further below), in a much-remarked decision on the application (and, more importantly, scope) of the continuous-nationality rule in the context of a NAFTA arbitration.[4] The arbitral tribunal in that case noted that the continuous-nationality rule was not dealt with in NAFTA as the *lex specialis*, and said:

> "It is that silence in the Treaty that requires the application of customary international law to resolve the question of the need for continuous national identity."[5]

This indeed echoes the opinion of the International Court of Justice in the *ELSI* case (which will also be discussed below), to the effect that the rule of exhaustion of local remedies, as an important rule of international law, could not be regarded as having been "tacitly dispensed with" in a bilateral treaty (in the given case, the treaty of Friendship, Commerce and Navigation between the USA and Italy).[6]

The ICSID Convention[7] provides specific and comprehensive rules on the nationality of claims in its Art. 25, and investment treaties also, with varying degrees of precision,

---

3. See in general Art. 31 of the Convention on the Law of Treaties (Vienna, 22 May 1969) (1980 1155 UNTS 331 (the Vienna Convention). See also a paper by Christoph SCHREUER given at the Investment Treaty Forum of the British Institute of International Comparative Law on 6 February 2006. See also Duncan FRENCH, "Treaty Interpretation and the Incorporation of Extraneous Legal Rights" 55 ICLQ (2006) p. 281.

4. *Loewen Group, Inc. and Raymond L. Loewen v. United States of America*, ICSID Case No. ARB(AF)/98/3, Award dated 26 June 2003, 7 ICSID Reports, p. 442.

5. *Ibid.*, para. 226.

6. Case concerning *Elettronica Sicula S.p.A. (ELSI) (United States of America v. Italy)* ICJ Reports (1989) p. 15 at p. 42.

7. Convention on the Settlement of Investment Disputes between States and Nationals of Other States (Washington, 18 March 1965) 575 UNTS 159.

specify the requirements that the contracting states wished to see apply to determine the standing of claimants thereunder. It has not, to the author's knowledge, been suggested by ICSID tribunals or commentators that the detailed rules on nationality in the ICSID Convention should be displaced or overridden by any rules of customary international law. The *Loewen* tribunal, indeed, expressly disavowed ICSID case law in deciding as it did on the importation of rules of customary law into the NAFTA context, where the treaty itself was silent.[8] The question that remains, therefore, is the extent to which either (a) the ICSID Convention, and practice under it, affects the treatment of the nationality of claims in cases decided other than under the ICSID Rules, by having contributed to a general "investment-treaty" law of nationality of claims, or (b) such a generalized investment-treaty law of nationality has arisen by a combination of ICSID and non-ICSID cases alike. It is in this context that the practice of the Iran-US Claims Tribunal is instructive. In the *Dual Nationality* case,[9] the tribunal rejected the application of the rule of customary international law that prevented a state from espousing a claim on behalf of a dual national who also held the nationality of the respondent state, as this would go against the object and purpose of the Algiers Accords.

Interestingly, in that and subsequent cases, the Iran-US Claims Tribunal did have recourse to the customary international law concept of effective nationality, in determining whether a claimant with dual US-Iranian nationality was to be regarded as predominantly American or Iranian. The place of the effective-nationality rule in investment-treaty practice is also controversial, and is dealt with below.

In the end, the best evidence that investment-treaty practice, whether ICSID or not, is distinct from the international law used in cases of diplomatic protection is probably that almost all investment-treaty tribunals have rejected the wholesale importation of customary international law rules derived from diplomatic protection practice. This is also recognized as a reality by the International Law Commission (ILC) in its work as codifier of international law. As early as 1988, the ILC noted that bilateral investment treaties and the ICSID Convention "created a legal framework outside the traditional area of diplomatic protection".[10]

The International Law Association (ILA) addressed the issue of the interrelationship of investment treaties and diplomatic protection at its conference in New Delhi in 2002. Professor Kokott highlighted the popularity of investment treaties as a means of resolving investment disputes, and their differences from diplomatic protection. She said in her interim report:

> "There is no need to go so far as to say that diplomatic protection and the rules governing the protection of foreign investment exclude each other. However, the result might well appear disappointing from the perspective of someone who wants to argue that diplomatic protection should play a strong role in today's law of foreign investment. The analysis of the BIT regime as well as multilateral

---

8. *Loewen v. USA, op. cit.*, fn. 4, para. 235.

9. Case A/18 5 Iran-US Claims Tribunal Reports 251 (1984).

10. ILC Report to the General Assembly, UN Doc. A/53/10 (1998), para 66. The ILC's current work on diplomatic protection is considered further below.

approaches has shown that diplomatic protection does not play a major role among the available means of dispute resolution. Generally speaking, the agreements, both bilateral and multilateral, prefer alternative dispute resolution procedures and allow investors to access international arbitration bodies. This way gives them standing under international law and circumvents diplomatic protection. This report shows that this development offers a number of advantages, compared to the need to resort to a home State's willingness (or ability) to exercise diplomatic protection.

There appears to be a very strong sentiment of distrust towards diplomatic protection – as regards its political uncertainties, its discretionary nature and its ability to protect foreign shareholders under the ICJ's doctrine. What is the consequence? There appear to be two different options. One of them might be a call for a change of the rules governing diplomatic protection with the aim of meeting the demands of investors. However, this option does not seem to be realistic because it neglects the existence of a network of bilateral agreements, accompanied by multilateral agreements. Sooner or later, a successor of the Multilateral Agreement on Investment will come into existence. Based on these considerations, a second option is more realistic: to accept that, in the context of foreign investment, the traditional law of diplomatic protection has been to a large extent replaced by a number of treaty-based dispute settlement procedures".[11]

Although both the ILC and the ILA seem to be talking only about the dispute resolution mechanism represented by the network of bilateral and multilateral investment treaties now in existence when they say that there is a new "legal framework", in the words of the ILC, or that diplomatic protection is distrusted, as Kokott says, it is clear that the law of investment protection cannot be looked at only through the prism of customary international law.[12]

---

11. Juliane KOKOTT, "The Role of Diplomatic Protection in the Field of the Protection of Foreign Investment", International Law Association, *Report of the Seventieth Conference, New Delhi* (2002) pp. 276-277.

12. The debate as to the role to be played by international law in a discussion of the standing of investors under investment treaties is part of the wider discussion about the rights conferred by investment treaties and, in particular, whether they are the rights of the investor or of the contracting state. This is important in the context of the renunciation of claims, and in particular whether this can be done by an investor before a conflict with the host state arises. The English Court of Appeal has held, in the case of *Occidental Exploration and Production Co. v. Republic of Ecuador* [2005] EWCA Civ. 1116, that the protections conferred by investment treaties are owed to investors directly. Thus, those rights, being the investors', are theirs to use or renounce. This gives rise to the possibility that investors can, and states will insist that they do, waive any investment-treaty rights before (or at the time of) making an investment. This would seem to eviscerate the protections negotiated by the contracting states, with the consequence that if (a) investors are required to (and validly can) waive their rights, then (b) the countries that insist on such waivers will, in practice, be treated as applying the late (un)lamented Calvo Clause in their investment policies, with the result that they will lose whatever benefits in the attraction of foreign investment that are thought to come with having concluded bilateral investment treaties. Although

Nonetheless, as investment treaties are still creatures of international law, and the questions that they pose are still to be resolved within the scope of international law, it is still essential for any analysis of the specific investment-treaty regime to look at the current state of customary international law, with a view to determining its viability and appropriateness in the investment-treaty context.

The topic of nationality of claims is naturally divided into investors who are legal persons and those who are natural persons. These two broad themes will thus be looked at in turn, before dealing with the question of continuous nationality, which is equally applicable to both of them.

II.   THE NATIONALITY OF LEGAL PERSONS AS CLAIMANTS UNDER INVESTMENT TREATIES

In line with the discussion of the role of international law in investment-treaty practice, this Report first looks at the nationality of legal persons as protected "aliens" in customary international law before embarking on an analysis of the different tests employed by investment treaties.

1.   *Customary International Law*

In the context of the nationality of legal persons, whose claim is espoused by their state of nationality in the law of diplomatic protection, the seminal case is the *Barcelona Traction* case.[13]

The International Court of Justice had to consider an application by Belgium espousing a claim of Belgian nationals. The Belgian nationals were the majority shareholders in a Canadian-incorporated company whose assets comprised Spanish subsidiaries (including the Barcelona Traction Co.) that supplied the major part of Catalonia's electricity. During the Spanish Civil War and under Franco's rule, the Spanish government made the transfer of foreign currency from Spain to service company bonds illegal. This had the effect that Barcelona Traction Co. was unable to service its debt owed to foreign lenders under its bond issues. The company's share price dropped dramatically. A public auction was held to sell the company's interest in

---

this is rather off the track of the present Report, it is submitted that this cannot have been the intention of the contracting parties to investment treaties, whose object and purpose is the attraction of foreign investment as well as protection, and that the rights conferred by such treaties on investors should better be regarded as contingent procedural rights, perfected upon the starting of an arbitration. This would still allow (as it must) the investor to settle a claim once brought, while preserving the single most valuable right given by investment treaties to investors, namely the right to bring an arbitration directly against the host state. The two possible ways of looking at the issue were discussed in DOUGLAS, *op. cit.*, fn. 1, at pp. 181-184.

13. *Case Concerning the Barcelona Traction, Light and Power Company, Limited (Belgium v. Spain)* (1973) 46 International Law Reports, p. 2.

its Spanish subsidiaries. They were bought by Spanish nationals far below even the pure asset value of the subsidiary companies.[14]

With Canada reluctant to pursue the Barcelona Traction Co.'s interests, Belgium espoused the claim on behalf of its nationals, shareholders in the company, before the International Court of Justice, on the basis that they had suffered loss by virtue of the Spanish government's (allegedly spoliatory) actions. The Court was faced with the question whether Belgium had standing to bring the case on behalf of the Belgian shareholders, when it was Barcelona Traction Co., the Canadian-incorporated company, which had had to sell the shares in its subsidiaries at an undervalue and, therefore, had suffered the direct loss.

The Court held that as a matter of customary international law the nationality of legal persons is determined by their country of incorporation and that, absent extraordinary circumstances, a claim of the company could only be espoused by the country of incorporation. The Court reasoned that international law had to recognize institutions of municipal law according to which shareholders' rights were not synonymous with the company's rights. Furthermore, the Court stated that allowing states to bring claims on behalf of shareholders in addition to claims espoused on behalf of companies themselves would create confusion and insecurity in international relations where these claims were espoused and brought by different states.[15]

Therefore, Belgium could not bring the claim, as the Belgian shareholders could not exercise the rights of the company on behalf of the company (or at least those of the company's rights that the Court considered Belgium to be pursuing). This solution has been described by a commentator as "unworkable".[16] It is indeed likely that states will feel less inclined to take up the cudgels on behalf of companies that are incorporated in their territory but which have no other economic links with them, than for those whose economic interests are really damaged by the host state's conduct, which would include the interests of shareholders.[17] This is reflected in the United Kingdom's rules for the exercise of diplomatic protection on behalf of legal persons, which provide that "[I]n determining whether to exercise its right of protection, Her Majesty's Government may consider whether the company has in fact a real and substantial connection with the United Kingdom".[18]

---

14. For an excellent general discussion of the *Barcelona Traction* case, see the article by John BROOKS in the *New Yorker*, now reprinted in 2 TDM (2006).

15. An exception, the Court opined, may be where the company had ceased to exist or the state in which the company was incorporated was incapable of pursuing the claim on behalf of the company.

Whether or not one could argue that the *ELSI* case overruled *Barcelona Traction*, as to which, see infra, the rule in the latter is far from dead: see the judgment of the European Court of Human Rights in *Agrotexim and others v. Greece* No. 14807/89, Series A, No. 330, 24 October 1995 (1996) EHRR 250.

16. Stanley METZGER, "Nationality of Corporate Investment under Investment Guarantee Schemes – The Relevance of Barcelona Traction", 65 AJIL (1971) p. 532 at p. 541.

17. A fact recognized in the dissenting opinion of Judge Gross in the *Barcelona Traction* case itself.

18. Reproduced at 37 ICLQ (1988) p. 1006 at 1007.

This leads to the following question: when the International Court of Justice did not allow Belgium to bring the case against Spain, did it merely refuse to recognize that Belgium could bring a Canadian company's claim or did it also deny the possibility of claiming for loss of investment as a shareholder?[19] In other words, would the Court have decided differently if Belgium had asked for compensation of the loss of shareholder value rather than the disability to transfer money abroad?

The Court stated that

> "[a] distinction must be drawn between an injury in respect of a right and an injury in respect of a simple interest (e.g., financial losses as the result of the situation of the company). The legal issue in the present case was whether it was legitimate to identify an attack on company rights, resulting in damage to shareholders, with the violation of their direct rights....
>
> Only in the event of the legal demise of a company are the shareholders deprived of the possibility of a remedy available through the company, and only in that event could an independent right of action for them and their Government arise."[20]

This passage seems to indicate that the Court would not have accepted a claim on behalf of the shareholders for a loss of the value of their shareholding.

However, the Court also said that

> "[t]he Court has noted from the Application ... that the Belgian Government did not base its claim on an infringement of the direct rights of the shareholders. Thus it is not open to the Court to go beyond the claim as formulated by the Belgian Government and it will not pursue its examination of this point any further."[21]

This passage may allow one to say that the *Barcelona Traction* case establishes the principle in customary international law that a company is a national of the state in which it is incorporated, but at least does not preclude shareholders of the company from bringing a claim in respect of their own loss *qua* shareholders (at the very least if such loss flows from measures directed at their rights as such).[22]

Assuming that the International Court of Justice in the *Barcelona Traction* case did, however, require claims to be brought by the injured company itself and not by

---

19. F.A. MANN, in his case-note on the *ELSI* case ("Note and Comment: Foreign Investment in the International Court of Justice: The ELSI Case", 86 AJIL (1992) p. 92), suggests that the Court did not answer the latter question, which was the crux of the matter. But the application to the ICJ may of course have been formulated in such a way as not to require or lead to such an answer.

20. *Barcelona Traction, op. cit.,* fn. 13, p. 9.

21. *Ibid.,* p. 211.

22. Vaughan LOWE, "Shareholders' Rights to Control and Manage: From Barcelona Traction to ELSI", *Liber Amicorum Judge Shigeru Oda,* p. 269 at p. 275.

shareholders, another decision by a Chamber of the Court is often cited as having overturned the *Barcelona Traction* case, namely the *ELSI* case.[23]

The Court was concerned with the espousal of a claim by the US shareholders of ELSI by the US government against Italy. The shareholders had invested in ELSI, an Italian company, and eventually held 99.16 per cent in it. When fate turned against ELSI, the American shareholders sought to sell the remaining assets in the company to recover some of their investment. The Italian state, however, became interested in ELSI as there were strong public concerns (related to high local unemployment) about ELSI's impending dissolution. Some of ELSI's major assets were subsequently requisitioned and sold at public auction for a fraction of their actual value.

The International Court of Justice allowed the United States of America to bring a claim against Italy on behalf of its nationals, although they were only shareholders in an Italian company. The claim was based on a breach of the 1948 Treaty of Friendship, Commerce and Navigation (FCN) between the USA and Italy, which treaty, as with other FCN treaties, can be considered to be a forerunner of modern investment treaties and which, in this case, included provisions about activities of corporations in the other contracting party and the protection of property (although not, of course, a direct right of action by an investor against the host state).

The Court accepted jurisdiction to hear the claim despite the fact that the direct loss had been sustained by the Italian company rather than the shareholders, thus seeming to mirror precisely the situation in the *Barcelona Traction* case. This judgment and the separate opinion of Judge Oda have fuelled the debate on the question whether *Barcelona Traction* has in fact been overruled.

Given the relative desuetude into which pure diplomatic protection claims have fallen (no doubt mainly due to the proliferation of investment treaties giving a direct right of arbitration against the host state), this is a fairly academic question these days (assuming one regards *ELSI* as being relevant only to diplomatic protection). Nevertheless, it is in the opinion of the present author at least premature to regard the *Barcelona Traction* case as having been overruled buy the *ELSI* case. The latter was based on the specific breach of the FCN Treaty between Italy and the United States. It could thus be distinguished on that ground alone. Furthermore, as discussed above, the Chamber of the Court in *ELSI* itself, although unrelated to the current question, cautioned against assuming that an "important principle of customary international law should ... have been tacitly dispensed with, in the absence of any words making clear an intention to do so".[24] On the assumption that the *Barcelona Traction* case represents "an important principle of customary international law", this passage would suggest that, as the Court did not explicitly state that it aimed to overturn the rule in *Barcelona Traction*, it did not want to do so (and did not, in fact, do so).

In negotiating investment treaties, states can decide freely what test they wish to apply as to the nationality of investors, and thus claims, and have in fact, more often than not, chosen the place of incorporation test for the nationality of a legal person bringing a claim. They have avoided the trap presented by the *Barcelona Traction* case by

---

23. *Op. cit.*, fn. 6.
24. *ELSI*, *op. cit.*, fn. 6, para. 51 (referring, as noted above, to prior exhaustion of domestic remedies).

a combination of inserting an "ownership or control" test to establish nationality and including shareholdings in the categories of investments in respect of which an investor can bring a claim, thus ensuring that the jurisdiction to hear claims by or on behalf of shareholders for their own losses as established by the *ELSI* case is also available for claimants under modern BITs.

2. The Investment Treaty Regime

Before delving into more detail on the approaches chosen by states in individual investment agreements, it is instructive to look at the ICSID Convention. The ICSID Convention – amongst other things – set up an institution and administrative and procedural framework for resolving international investment disputes. About twenty investment laws and over 900 investment agreements include dispute resolution mechanisms according to the Convention.[25] The provisions on jurisdiction of the Convention form an "outer limit"[26] for those investment agreements referring to ICSID dispute resolution. The relevant article of the Convention states in relevant parts:

> "'National of another Contracting State' means:
> (a) ....
> (b) any juridical person which had the nationality of a Contracting State other than the State party to the dispute on the date on which the parties consented to submit such dispute to conciliation or arbitration and any juridical person which had the nationality of the Contracting State party to the dispute on that date and which, because of foreign control, the parties have agreed should be treated as a national of another Contracting State for the purposes of this Convention."[27]

Thus, the Convention does not limit states to a particular test, but requires them to define nationality in arbitration agreements with investors, whether in contracts or (more relevantly in the present context) in investment treaties (or national inward-investment legislation).[28]

Two different approaches can be found in investment treaties. In a typical investment treaty, the nationality of a company is determined by either (a) the place of incorporation or seat of the legal entity, or (b) the country of ownership or control of the legal person. It should be noted that some agreements apply a combination of some or all of these elements, an example of which is the 1995 Swiss model BIT. The relevant passage of Art. 1(1) reads:

---

25. See <www.worldbank.org/icsid/about/about.htm> (last accessed 29 March 2006).

26. Aron BROCHES "The Convention on the Settlement of Investment Disputes between States and Nationals of Other States", 136 Recueil des Cours de l'Académie de Droit International (1972-II) p. 331 at pp. 350-360, as cited in *Tokios Tokelés v. Ukraine*, ICSID Case No. ARB/02/18, Decision on Jurisdiction, dated 29 April 2004, para. 25, 16 World Trade and Arbitration Materials (2004, no. 4) p. 75.

27. Art. 25(2).

28. Christoph SCHREUER, *The ICSID Convention: a Commentary* (Cambridge 2001) para. 481.

"The term 'investor' refers with regard to either Contracting Party to…

(b) legal entities, including companies, corporations, business associations, and other organisations, which are constituted or otherwise duly organised under the law of that Contracting Party and have their seat, together with real economic activities, in the territory of that same Contracting Party;

(c) legal entities under the law of any country which are, directly or indirectly, controlled by nationals of that Contracting Party or by legal entities having their seat, together with real economic activities, in the territory of that Contracting Party."[29]

It should further be noted that there might be a substantial further difference between the adoption of a pure "place-of-incorporation" test and one based on the location of a company's seat, or *siège social*.

a.   Place of incorporation or seat

The place-of-incorporation test is chosen by many investment treaties, indeed probably the majority. For example, the Energy Charter Treaty, in Art. 1(7)(a)(ii), defines an "investor" as "a company or other organization organized in accordance with the law applicable in that Contracting Party".[30]

Domestically, the place-of-incorporation principle dominates in the company laws of the United States, the United Kingdom and the Netherlands[31] and, thus, the model BITs of these countries incorporate this test.[32]

Other investment agreements, however, look to the effective seat of the legal person. An example of this approach is contained in the 1991 German model BIT, whose Art. 1(4)(a) states that a company for purposes of the agreement is any legal person "having its seat in the territory of the Federal Republic of Germany".[33]

---

29. Further examples include: Convention Establishing the Inter-Arab Investment Guarantee Corporation, Art. 17(1) (combining the test of statutory seat and ownership); ASEAN Agreement for the Promotion and Protection of Investments, Art. I(2) (combining the place-of-incorporation test with the control test).

30. It should be noted, however, that the "Decisions with Respect to the Energy Charter Treaty" states that even though the investor is not registered in a Contracting Party to an energy investment treaty it may nevertheless rely on most favoured nation treatment if the investment has its registered office, central administration or principal place of business in the Contracting Party or, if it only has its registered office in the Contracting Party, has an effective and continuous link with the economy of one of the parties to the relevant energy investment treaty.

31. Carsten EBENROTH, Karlheinz BOUJONG and Detlev JOOST, *Handelsgesetzbuch – Anhang Handelsregisteranmeldungen mit Auslandsbezug* (Vahlen 2001) para. 7.

32. 2004 United States model BIT, definition of "enterprise"; 1991 United Kingdom model BIT, Art. 1(d)(i); Netherlands model BIT ("Agreement on Encouragement and Reciprocal Protection of Investments between _____ and the Kingdom of the Netherlands (No. 135)"), Art. 1(b)(ii).

33. See also: 1995 Swiss model BIT, Art. 1(1)(b), as cited above.

The seat of a company can be found where it is incorporated *and* has its effective centre of administration.[34] It should not be confused with the statutory seat, which is the registered office of a company. The aim of adopting the company-seat test in domestic law is both to prevent companies from avoiding regulation merely by incorporating in a state favourable to companies (the so-called "Delaware-Effect") and to allocate companies to the state most interested (in economic terms) in governing it. A state will be interested in governing a company if its directors, shareholders, employees, beneficiaries and creditors are located within its borders. The state in which all these interested parties can be found is, according to the theory, the state where the company has its effective centre of administration.[35] The company-seat principle is mainly used in continental European countries such as Germany, Belgium, France, Luxembourg, Austria, Portugal and Spain[36] (although it is interesting to note that this does not always lead those countries to adopt it as the test for the nationality of a legal person in its investment treaties, a good example being the German model BIT quoted above).

A further refinement of the company-seat principle in investment treaties (which derives from a perceived need to avoid so-called "treaty-shopping") is the addition in some treaties of an explicit "economic connection" requirement, which is additional to either the place of incorporation or the company seat, as the case may be. An alternative example of the former (place of incorporation plus economic links) is the Greek model BIT. Art. 1(3) provides that investors are "legal persons ... which are constituted or otherwise duly organised under the laws of that Contracting Party and have their effective economic activities in the territory of that same Contracting Party". Although this test does not refer to the effective centre of administration, it does require a closer connection with the country of its incorporation through effective economic activities than would a place of incorporation test alone.

A digression: A brief digression is perhaps useful at this point to consider other areas in which the allocation of a legal person to a particular state may be important, for example, European Community legislation, conflict of laws and international tax treaties.

European Community legislation makes use of the company-seat principle. So, for example, certain provisions of Directive 2000/12/EC of 20 March 2000, relating to the taking up and pursuit of the business of credit institutions, are applicable to companies that have their head offices in the Community. These provisions are not, however, concerned with the nationality of a company.

---

34. This can cause problems if the company has its seat and its place of incorporation in different jurisdictions. Some countries have fall-back provisions that treat the place of the seat as the place of incorporation and do not in those cases require formal incorporation. In other countries, the company might lose its legal personality and limitation of liability for its members in such circumstances.
35. Peter KINDLER, *Münchener Kommentar zum BGB – Internationales Handels- und Gesellschaftsrecht* (Beck Online 2006) paras. 400-401.
36. EBENROTH *et al.*, *op. cit.*, fn. 31, para. 6.

Similarly, in the realm of conflict of laws, the Brussels Regulation[37] (which has replaced the Brussels Convention), which (among other things) regulates the international jurisdiction of courts within the European Community, focuses on the domicile of a legal person rather than its nationality. It provides that a company:

"is domiciled at the place where it has its:
(a) statutory seat, or
(b) central administration, or
(c) principal place of business".

It should be noted, however, that according to the most recent line of cases decided by the European Court of Justice, the company-seat principle cannot be applied to infringe a company's right to freedom of establishment embedded in Arts. 43 and 48 of the EC Treaty.[38] An illustrative example is the *Überseering* case, discussed below.

Überseering B.V. (Überseering) was a company incorporated under the laws of the Netherlands and initially managed from the Netherlands. Subsequently, the company was bought by two persons domiciled in Germany and thereafter managed from Germany. When Überseering issued proceedings against a German construction company for breach of contract, the respondent claimed that Überseering did not have standing to bring the claim. The respondent argued that, since the company had relocated its seat to Germany, but had not complied with German municipal law to incorporate a company to gain legal personality, the company could not be party to legal proceedings for lack of legal personality.

The European Court of Justice held that the company-seat principle could not work to override and invalidate the fundamental right to freedom of establishment as promulgated in the EC Treaty. Thus, the company had legal personality and could bring the claim.

In the realm of conflict of laws, but with wider geographic importance, is the recently signed Convention on Choice of Court Agreements, which is yet to be ratified by many states. The Convention regulates the jurisdiction of courts of the signatory states in the event that an agreement contains an exclusive choice of court agreement. It focuses on the residence rather than the nationality of legal persons and provides that a legal person:

"shall be considered resident in the State:
(a) where it has its statutory seat;
(b) under whose laws it was incorporated or formed;

---

37. Council Regulation (EC) No 44/2001 of 22 December 2000 on jurisdiction and the recognition and enforcement of judgments in civil and commercial matters, [2001] OJ L 12/1, Art. 60(1).
38. See generally Case C-212/97 *Centros Ltd. v. Erhvervs- og Selskabsstyrelsen*, [1999] ECR I-01459; Case C–208/00 *Überseering B. V. v. Nordic Construction Company Baumanagement GmbH (NCC)*, [2002] ECR 2002 I-09919; Case C-167/01 *Kamer van Koophandel en Fabrieken voor Amsterdam v. Inspire Art Ltd.*, [2003] ECR 2003 I-10155.

(c) where it has its central administration; or

(d) where it has its principal place of business".[39]

Double-taxation conventions also need to allocate legal persons to specific states. The OECD's model tax convention states that nationals of a state are "any legal persons, partnership or association deriving its status as such from the laws in force in that Contracting State".[40] However, the core obligations under the model convention turn on the residence of the tax-paying entities and the concept of nationality mainly plays a role in the provisions about non-discrimination.[41]

In summary, while this brief overview of international agreements in fields other than investment protection shows that they also refer to the place-of-incorporation and company-seat principles, this may be of limited relevance to the investment-treaty context as these agreements mainly deal with the domicile or residence of companies. Jurisprudence under such other international agreements may nonetheless be helpful in establishing what, in a given state's municipal company law, is meant by "seat", but it may not be of greater interest than that.

b.   Ownership and control

As noted above, one of the ways in which states have sought to overcome the limitations placed in the way of espousal of claims by the *Barcelona Traction* case is by the inclusion of an "ownership or control" test in their investment treaties to establish the nationality of an investor.

Many countries require or encourage foreign investment to be made via a local investment vehicle.[42] As such a locally incorporated company would not qualify under either of the place-of-incorporation or the company-seat tests as a foreign investor, many foreign investments would not be protected by an investment treaty. As noted above, the "outer limit" of Art. 25(2)(b) of the ICSID Convention states that a national of another contracting state is not only "any juridical person which had the nationality of a contracting state other than the state party to the dispute" but also "any juridical person which had the nationality of the Contracting State party to the dispute on that date and which, because of foreign control, the parties agreed should be treated as a national of another Contracting State".[43] Thus, the Convention specifically allows states to agree that companies, even though incorporated in the host state, are to be treated as nationals of the other contracting party to the investment treaty (or investment agreement) if they are controlled by nationals of that other state.

---

39. Convention on Choice of Court Agreements (The Hague, 30 June 2005) Art. 4(2).

40. OECD Model Convention with Respect to Taxes on Income and Capital, Art. 3(1)(g)(ii).

41. *Ibid.*, Art. 24.

42. See Christoph SCHREUER, "Shareholder Protection in International Investment Law", 23 May 2005, pp. 3-4, <www.univie.ac.at/intlaw/text01.html> (last accessed 22 March 2006).

43. Similarly, Art. 1117 of NAFTA states that "[a]n investor of a Party, on behalf of an enterprise of another Party that is a juridical person that the investor *owns or controls* directly or indirectly, may submit to arbitration under this Section a claim...." (emphasis added).

i.   Companies incorporated in the host state

An example of an investment treaty implementing this provision is the BIT between the United Kingdom and Chile. For purposes of application of the dispute-resolution mechanism, the treaty (as with all United Kingdom BITs) provides that "any legal person which is constituted in accordance with the legislation of one Contracting Party, and in which, before a dispute arises, the majority of shares are owned by investors of the other Contracting Party, shall be treated, in accordance with Article 25(2)(b) of the Washington Convention, as a legal person of the other Contracting Party".[44]

Another example of an investment agreement looking to the country of control of a legal person is the Netherlands-Bolivia BIT, Art. 1(b)iii of which states that "nationals" also comprise "legal persons controlled directly or indirectly, by nationals of that Contracting Party, but constituted in accordance with the law of the other Contracting Party". In *Aguas del Tunari*,[45] the respondent state argued that the Bolivian claimant could not rely on the Netherlands-Bolivia BIT because it was not effectively or actually controlled by Dutch investors. The question for the ICSID tribunal was what constituted "control" within the meaning of the BIT.

Aguas del Tunari S.A. was a Bolivian company that entered into a concession agreement with the Bolivian Water and Electricity Superintendencies to provide a regular volume of drinkable water of a certain quality for the city of Cochabamba in exchange for a negotiated return on its investment. The ownership structure of Aguas del Tunari S.A. was as follows: four Bolivian companies owned five per cent, a Uruguayan company owned twenty-five per cent and a Luxembourg company owned the remaining fifty-five per cent. This Luxembourg company was a wholly owned subsidiary of a Dutch company (International Water (Tunari) B.V.) which in turn was wholly owned by another Dutch company (International Water Holdings B.V.). This last was co-owned by yet another Dutch company (Baywater Holdings B.V.) and Edison S.p.A., a large Italian energy company. Baywater Holdings B.V., the highest Dutch company in the ownership chain, was in turn a wholly-owned subsidiary of Bechtel Holdings Inc., a US-incorporated engineering and construction company. From an economic perspective, Edison and Bechtel, neither of them Dutch, were the ultimate owners of Aguas del Tunari.

The respondent state argued that, in order to find "control", there must be more than ownership and potential control, namely actual and effective control. Here, the ultimate control was exercised by Bechtel, a US company, and not by the various intermediate Dutch companies, which were merely shell companies. Bolivia claimed that the tribunal

---

44. Art. 7(4). In addition, the United Kingdom-Chile BIT defines "Investor" with respect to legal persons as "any corporations, firms or associations incorporated or constituted under the law in force in the territory of the Contracting Party and having their registered office, central administration or principal place of business in that territory".

45. *Aguas del Tunari SA v. Republic of Bolivia*, ICSID Case No. ARB/02/3, Decision on Respondent's Objection to Jurisdiction dated 21 October 2005, available at <http://ita.law.uvic.ca/documents/AguasdelTunari-jurisdiction-eng_000.pdf> (last accessed 29 April 2006).

therefore did not have jurisdiction to hear the claim under the Netherlands-Bolivia BIT.[46]

The tribunal had to decide the meaning of "controlled directly or indirectly" as stated in Art. 1(b)iii of the Netherlands-Bolivia BIT. After noting that on a literal interpretation "control" did not "necessarily entail[] a degree of active exercise of powers or discretion",[47] but was in the context of the treaty more akin to "ownership",[48] the tribunal came to the conclusion that both one hundred per cent parent companies of the Luxembourg company with the fifty-five per cent interest in the claimant (i.e., International Water (Tunari) B.V. and International Water Holdings B.V.) controlled the Bolivian company for the purposes of the Netherlands-Bolivia BIT.

In more abstract terms, the tribunal decided that:

— a company can "control" an investment SPV even if itself is controlled by another company incorporated elsewhere; and
— fifty-five per cent ownership suffices to establish control even though a seventy-five per cent majority may be required for certain corporate acts.

ii.   Companies incorporated in a third state
The examples discussed so far allow foreign nationals to rely on an investment treaty if they are nationals of one contracting party and have invested in the host state via a company incorporated in the latter state. The Sweden-Bolivia BIT of 1990 seems to go one stage further in allowing a legal entity incorporated in a *third state* to claim the benefits of the treaty if an investor of either contracting party has major interests in that entity.[49] The Swedish 2002 model BIT confirms this policy: it provides that an investor of a contracting party can be "any legal person not organised under the law of that Contracting Party but controlled by an investor [who is either a natural person of the Contracting Party or a legal person organised in accordance with the law applicable in that Contracting Party]" (Art. 1(2)(c) in conjunction with sub-paras. (a) and (b) of Art. 1(2)).[50]

It should be noted that these provisions take the Swedish investment treaties outside the jurisdiction of ICSID, as the Convention only contemplates companies incorporated in the host State to be treated as foreign, but not companies incorporated elsewhere. Thus, the Sweden-Bolivia BIT refers to dispute resolution according to the UNCITRAL rules.[51] The Swedish model BIT includes as possible dispute resolution mechanisms according the ICSID Rules, the ICSID Additional Facility Rules and the UNCITRAL Rules, at the investor's choice.[52] A claimant that was a company incorporated in a third state would obviously have to opt for arbitration under the UNCITRAL Rules.

---

46. *Ibid.*, paras. 206-209.
47. *Ibid.*, para. 234.
48. *Ibid.*, paras. 242-243.
49. Art. 1(3)(b).
50. See also 1995 Swiss model BIT, Art. 1(1)(c), as cited above.
51. Sweden-Bolivia BIT, Art. 8(2).
52. 2002 model BIT, Art. 8(2).

Outlandish as this example may seem, however, it could be argued that it does no more than make apparent what already happens under an investment treaty that allows indirect investors to claim. To take an example, if a Dutch investor in Bolivia made his investment through a company incorporated in (for the sake of argument) the British Virgin Islands, the Dutch investor would still be entitled to claim as the treaty allows for investments to be held indirectly.[53] It is fair to say that the notion of such an "indirect" investment is controversial, not least because it could be argued that the investment could be seen as the shares in the investment vehicle, and thus not in the host state at all but in the state of incorporation of the investment vehicle. Clearly, such an objection could be overcome by suitable wording in the treaty concerned, allowing indirect investment, but in the absence of an explicit recognition of indirect investments, one could see such an argument being raised.

A further potential difficulty with the model of the indirect investor is that it gives rise to a discussion about the damages that the indirect investor can be said to have suffered. If damage is done to an investment held several layers below that of the qualifying investor under the treaty, how is the damage to the ultimate investor to be determined? It could be said that the Swedish practice is more honest in that it allows the same claims to be brought but recognizes where the real economic interest is and thus allows damages to be awarded that correspond to the harm done to that interest.

c.   *Investment treaty arbitral practice*

How are these differing treaty standards applied in practice by arbitral tribunals? At least two issues need to be examined in order to have an idea of how provisions will be interpreted by arbitral tribunals. The first is how tribunals have treated a pure place-of-incorporation test; the second is the question, touched upon above, of claims by shareholders of locally incorporated companies in the host state.

i.   Applying the place-of-incorporation test

The examples provided show that specific provisions in investment agreements together with their wide interpretation by tribunals have added to the general rule of the place-of-incorporation test allowing shareholders to claim on behalf of companies. It should not, however, be overlooked that most investment agreements also allow companies merely organized under the laws of the contracting states to benefit from the agreements. One may query whether the requirement of control exercised by nationals of the home state has led tribunals to modify the formalistic approach to the place-of-incorporation test. An extreme example in which the tribunal has not accepted that the place-of-incorporation test has been modified by the addition of the control test is an award rendered in connection with the Lithuania-Ukraine BIT, *Tokios Tokelés v. Ukraine*.[54] This case will be discussed further below.

What is an arbitral tribunal to do when a claimant satisfies the place-of-incorporation test specified in the relevant treaty but where the economic interests behind the claimant

---

53. Whether express inclusion of the word "indirect" is needed in order to allow such an investor to bring a claim is discussed further below.

54. *Tokios Tokelés v. Ukraine*, op. cit, fn. 26.

are clearly not located in the same country? Should a tribunal seek to modify the clear words of the treaty – which are to be taken as reflecting the wishes of the contracting parties – to craft, in other words, a less formalistic approach? On the other hand, should the fact that investment treaty drafting differs so widely, sometimes adopting the place-of-incorporation test, sometimes the company-seat (*siège social*) test and sometimes adding a test of economic connection to one or other of the preceding, lead tribunals to respect the wishes of the contracting parties for the particular formulation that they have adopted?

It is clear from investment-treaty jurisprudence that arbitral tribunals will give effect to a bare place-of-incorporation test, whatever the links, or lack of them, with the state of incorporation may be. This is perhaps a guide to the question of how to interpret the company-seat principle, discussed above. The two cases that are discussed below in this connection, *Tokios Tokelés v. Ukraine*[55] and *Saluka Investments v. Czech Republic*,[56] show how arguments as to economic reality (such as it can be ascertained, which may not be very well in all or at least some cases) have failed to deflect tribunals from applying the test that the contracting parties have set out in their treaties.

In *Tokios Tokelés*, which may fairly be seen as the most extreme example (to date) of the genre, the claimant company was incorporated in Lithuania, before that country had entered into its BIT with Ukraine, and subsequently brought a claim against Ukraine under that treaty. The treaty specified the place-of-incorporation test in addition to the control test to determine the nationality of a legal person.[57]

The respondent state argued that the arbitral tribunal should not allow the claim for lack of standing. As the Lithuanian company was ninety-nine per cent-owned by Ukrainian nationals, had no substantial business activities in Lithuania, since the investment treaty itself included not only the place-of-incorporation test, but also the control test, the respondent state argued that the claimant did not qualify as an investor. Ukraine argued that the both the object and purpose of the ICSID Convention and the particular treaty in question as well as investment-treaty case law compelled the tribunal to pierce the corporate veil and look beyond the mere formality of where the claimant company was incorporated.

The ICSID tribunal held by a majority of the two party-appointed arbitrators (the president, Professor Prosper Weil, dissenting) that the only relevant consideration was whether the claimant was incorporated under the laws of Lithuania. Piercing of the corporate veil was only justified where fraud or malfeasance was involved, or where it was necessary to protect third persons such as creditors or purchasers or to prevent the evasion of legal requirements or obligations. None of these exceptions applied here as the tribunal relied on the fact that the company had been incorporated before the BIT was entered into. The tribunal followed the *Barcelona Traction* case closely and did not

---

55. *Ibid.*
56. *Saluka Investments B.V. v. The Czech Republic*, arbitration conducted under UNCITRAL rules administered by the Permanent Court of Arbitration according to the Netherlands-Czech Republic BIT, Partial Award of 17 March 2006, available on the website of the Permanent Court of Arbitration, <www.pca-cpa.org/ENGLISH/RPC/#Saluka> (last accessed 15 April 2006).
57. Art. 1(2)(b) and (c).

consider the rule that it established under customary international law to have changed. According to this decision, the place-of-incorporation and control tests have to be seen as two separate tests and no requirement of a further nexus is imposed on a company that is incorporated in the other contracting party, in the absence, of course, of an explicit further requirement in the treaty.

In his dissenting opinion, Professor Prosper Weil felt compelled by the object and purpose of the ICSID Convention to deny Tokios Tokelés the right to claim as a Lithuanian national.[58] Professor Weil felt that the ICSID mechanism and remedy were not meant for investments made in a state by its own citizens with domestic capital through the channel of a foreign entity, whether pre-existing or created for that purpose.[59] He explicitly stated that he did not intend to pierce the corporate veil as suggested by the *Barcelona Traction* case.[60] In the instant case, where (in his view) there was no "foreign" investment at all (but only Ukrainian investment made via another state, in this case Lithuania), Professor Weil argued that the ICSID Convention was not meant to apply.[61] He wrote further:

> "Insofar as business law and issues of business liability are involved, there is no reason for denying effect to the corporate structure chosen by the economic agents. When it comes to mechanisms and procedures involving States and implying, therefore, issues of public international law, economic and political reality is to prevail over legal structure, so much that the application of the basic principles and rules of public international law should not be frustrated by legal concepts and rules prevailing in the relations between private economic and juridical players."[62]

This passage goes directly contrary to the reasoning in the *Barcelona Traction* case where the International Court of Justice held that deference had to be paid to municipal law even where the matter was to be decided between states under international law. In applying the place-of-incorporation test, in the absence of special circumstances allowing the corporate veil to be pierced, municipal law does not look beyond the company to the shareholders, but only to the company itself.

Professor Weil's argument is interesting. Art. 31(1) of the Vienna Convention on the Law of Treaties[63] requires that a treaty be interpreted:

> "in good faith in accordance with the ordinary meaning to be given to the terms of the treaty in their context and in the light of its object and purpose".

---

58. *Ibid.*, para. 19.
59. *Ibid.*
60. *Ibid.*, para. 21.
61. *Ibid.*, para. 27.
62. *Ibid.*, para. 24.
63. Vienna Convention, *op. cit.*, fn. 3.

It is clear that the purpose of investment treaties and the ICSID Convention is to encourage foreign investment. Professor Weil's reasoning questions whether an investment that ultimately comes from nationals of the host state can be regarded as foreign, and he came to the conclusion that it cannot.

In reality, this is a completely circular argument. The nationality of an investment is determined by the treaty itself. The treaty in question (the Lithuania-Ukraine BIT) has defined it as the place of incorporation of an investor who is a legal person. There is no need to go further, and indeed to do so would do damage not only to the wording of the treaty concerned but would also raise a number of other questions, such as where an investment made by a widely held multinational company such as BP or ExxonMobil actually "comes from". Even if Professor Weil's principle is to be restricted to the peculiar facts of the given case, where the investment (allegedly) came from nationals of, and within, Ukraine itself, the counter-argument would be that the investment might still never have been made in the absence of the treaty, which guarantees investors' rights to a higher standard than the law of the host state.[64] If countries such as Ukraine can encourage the return of capital that has fled and would otherwise remain abroad, that can hardly be said to deny the purpose of a treaty for the promotion and encouragement of investment. This argument holds good for any challenge to the place-of-incorporation test generally. The purpose of investment treaties being to attract investment as well as protect it, if a state can attract more investment by allowing investors who would not make an investment in the absence of an investment treaty to make the investment through a shell company in a state with which the host state does have such a treaty, this can only be regarded as the fulfilment of the purpose of the treaty in question.

An UNCITRAL tribunal arrived at the same conclusion as *Tokios Tokelés* as to the validity of the place-of-incorporation test in *Saluka Investments v. Czech Republic*. Saluka, a Dutch company, held a 46.16 per cent interest in IPB, a Czech bank. Saluka brought an arbitration against the Czech Republic under the Netherlands-Czech Republic BIT, arguing that the treatment by the Czech Republic of IPB, which Saluka alleged (and the tribunal found) had led to the forced administration of IPB in the course of which all of IPB's assets were sold to a competitor, was wrongful. The Czech Republic argued that the Dutch company had no standing to bring the claim, as the real investor into the Czech Republic was an English-registered company, Nomura Europe plc, a subsidiary of the Japanese investment bank, which had caused Saluka to be established as a special purpose vehicle to hold the shares in IPB bought originally by Nomura. The Czech Republic argued that Nomura and Saluka were so closely linked that the real party with

---

64. Although it must be recognized in the actual case that the claimant company had been incorporated since before the date of the treaty, and indeed there could be a possible argument of "treaty-shopping" and thus abuse of the investment treaty regime (by analogy with the concept of effective nationality in dealing with natural persons) if the investment vehicle had been established with the sole aim of acquiring rights under the treaty to invest in one's own country. In the author's view, if the use of brass-plate companies incorporated in order to come within a particular treaty and have its protections encourages investment, it is wholly in line with the purpose and object of the treaty and should not be seen as an abuse. By definition, if the treaty allows (say) brass-plate companies to bring a claim, there can be no abuse.

the interest in the shareholding was the English company. Saluka, according to the Czech Republic, was merely a shell company with no real economic interest in the shares in IPB. Thus, the Czech Republic argued, Saluka was not a bona fide investor in the Czech Republic (by which it seems to have meant that Saluka was not to be regarded as a genuine Dutch investor entitled to the protections given to Dutch investors by the Czech Republic under the Netherlands-Czech Republic BIT).

The arbitral tribunal rejected these arguments. The key to deciding the issue was the terms of the treaty that defined investor to include "legal persons constituted under the law of one of the Contracting Parties".[65] The tribunal considered the disadvantages of the mere formalistic test, especially the danger for "treaty-shopping", but felt bound by the contracting parties' choice of definition of investor.[66]

Since *Saluka* is based on a treaty which does not incorporate the control test, *Tokio Taxales* remains the best evidence of a jurisdictional decision based on a treaty which included both the place-of-incorporation and control tests, but where the tribunal nevertheless refused to commingle the two.

ii.   Applying the company-seat test
This is at present a theoretical discussion, as, to the author's knowledge, there has not yet been a decision under an investment treaty applying the company-seat test that has clearly set out the requirements of such a test in deciding whether or not a particular claimant qualifies as an investor.

It is interesting nonetheless to speculate, given the "treaty-shopping" concern about applying the strict language of the place-of-incorporation test in the Netherlands-Czech Republic BIT that seems to have been felt by the tribunal in *Saluka v. Czech Republic*.

It is of course very common for companies, for perfectly legitimate reasons, to incorporate special purpose vehicles to hold their investments. This can be done in a number of ways. One is the setting-up of a wholly-owned subsidiary in a tax-friendly jurisdiction. This subsidiary may exist only on paper and have no management at all in the country of its incorporation. Would it satisfy the company-seat test? As this principle allocates companies to the state where they are incorporated and have their effective center of administration, it is suggested that, in this example, it would not be satisfied.

A further way in which a special-purpose vehicle is incorporated is to keep it entirely separate from the "parent", which, in fact, is not the parent at all but is merely linked to the special-purpose company by contract. The special-purpose company is then independent, has local shareholders and management (even if these are just trust companies who do the same for thousands of other similar companies) and is not controlled from abroad in the sense meant by the ACCEDE Convention and many BITs. Its activities are nonetheless very closely controlled by the company that caused it to come into existence, albeit solely as a matter of contract. Does this kind of legal entity satisfy the company-seat test? It is hard indeed to say that it does not, even if it may not have been what the framers of the test originally had in mind. The fact is that the company in question would be managed (even if it did not need very much

---

65. Netherlands-Czech Republic BIT, Art. 1(b)ii.
66. *Saluka, op. cit.,* fn. 56, para. 240-241.

management) from within the state of its incorporation. The contractual limits on such management should be seen as irrelevant to the legal test of where the company has its seat.

But the question is even less simple than these examples may suggest. Where is the effective administration of an operating subsidiary of a large multinational group? What degree of autonomy will be recognized or required? If a company operates in a local market but is one hundred per cent owned by a parent located abroad, where is its effective center of administration? It is clear that control and center of administration are two different concepts. In *SOABI v. Senegal* the ICSID tribunal said:

> "[a]s a general rule, States apply either the head office or the place of incorporation test. By contrast, neither the nationality of the company's shareholders nor foreign control, other than over capital, normally govern the nationality of a company...."[67]

To open the question up even further, how would an investment-treaty tribunal apply a control test if the parent itself was quoted on more than one stock market and widely held?

The main criticism of the place-of-incorporation test is that it is formalistic and allows investors to take advantage of an investment treaty in a country with which they have no real economic link (and to which they make, in all likelihood, little economic contribution), thus leading to the dangers identified by the *Saluka* tribunal of "treaty-shopping".[68] If the treaty adopts the company-seat principle, it is perhaps natural to assume that there should at least be some activity in the contracting state. If the special-purpose company is just a shell, it is likely (although not at all impossible) that it has its center of administration elsewhere. On the other hand, if this is allowed by the state of incorporation, what concern can it be to other states? In the end, though, if a company is incorporated in a contracting state, and is at least ostensibly (whatever the underlying economic realities and contractual limits on the company's freedom of action) managed from that state, there should be a presumption, perhaps rebuttable, that its effective center of administration is there also. Any decision is therefore likely to turn on the facts of the particular case.

iii. Claims as shareholder

Where the discussion above has been of claims by shareholders to bring what is effectively a derivative action on behalf of the company enabling shareholders to claim damages for losses sustained by the company, investment treaties also (in all cases of which the present author is aware) include shares (in companies incorporated in the host state) as protected qualifying investments. This allows shareholders of companies incorporated in the host state to claim for loss of shareholder value if the locally

---

67. *Société Ouest Africaine de Bétons Industriels v. State of Senegal*, ICSID Case No. ARB/82/1, Decision on Jurisdiction dated 1 August 1984, 2 ICSID Reports, p. 164 at p. 180.

68. *Saluka v. Czech Republic, op. cit.*, fn. 56, paras. 240-241.

incorporated company has been mistreated by the host state and the investment treaty does not allow the shareholder to claim for the company's own losses.

An example of an investment treaty that incorporates a very narrow definition of legal entities protected under it is the United States-Estonia BIT. It states that a company is "any kind of corporation, company, association, partnership, or other organisation, legally constituted under applicable laws and regulations of a Party" and "each Party reserves the right to deny any company the advantages of this Treaty if nationals of any third country control such company and, in the case of a company of the other Party, that company has no substantial business activities in the territory of the other Party or is controlled by nationals of a third country with which the denying Party does not maintain normal economic relations".[69] "Investment dispute" is defined as "a dispute between a Party and a national or company of the other Party...".[70]

The treaty, however, defines investments to include "a company or shares of stock or other interests in a company or interests in the assets thereof".[71]

This provision was applied in *Alex Genin v. Estonia*:[72] Mr. Genin, Eastern Credit and Baltoil sought relief from Estonia for revoking a licence in favour of EPB, an Estonian bank of which the three claimants were the principal shareholders. Baltoil, an Estonian company, was wholly owned by Eastern Credit, a US company, which in turn was wholly owned by Mr. Genin, a US national. The ICSID tribunal had to decide whether to allow Eastern Credit and Mr. Genin to pursue the claim even though the revoked licence was not directly in their favour, but in favour of EPB, the locally incorporated company.

The tribunal held that Mr. Genin and Eastern Credit were entitled to claim under the treaty because the treaty defined investments to include shares. Thus, Mr Genin and Eastern Credit did not bring claims on behalf of EPB, but rather in order to protect their own rights as shareholders of an Estonian company. The protected right potentially violated by the Estonian government was not EPB's right to a licence, but the effect the revocation of the licence had on the value of the shareholdings in that company held by the US nationals entitled to bring the claim.

This position is of course to be contrasted with the discussion above of the *Barcelona Traction* case and the *ELSI* case. The conclusion to be drawn is that investment-treaty law derogates from customary international law by virtue of the particular definitions contained in the relevant investment treaty as the *lex specialis*, although the question of proving a causal link between the investment and the damage suffered is not always simple in such cases.

Investment-treaty arbitral tribunals have usually been careful not to express a view on the tension created in public international law by the seemingly conflicting decisions in the *Barcelona Traction* and *ELSI* cases as to whether claims can be made in customary international law for the harm suffered by shareholders of locally incorporated

---

69. Art. 1(1)(b) and (2).

70. Art. 6(1).

71. Art. 1(1)(a)(ii).

72. *Alex Genin, Eastern Credit Limited and A.S. Baltoil v. The Republic of Estonia*, ICSID Case No. ARB/99/2, Award dated 25 June 2001, 6 ICSID Reports, p. 236.

companies.[73] Commentators have been less cautious. It has been suggested that the advent and proliferation of bilateral investment treaties that generally allow shareholders to claim in their own right[74] has changed customary international law.[75] The counter-argument to this is that investment treaties must be distinguished from customary international law. Investment treaties explicitly protect investment in the form of shares. This reflects the argument that the *ELSI* case should be distinguished from the *Barcelona Traction* case, as the claim brought by the United States in *ELSI* was based on a breach of the specific terms of the FCN Treaty between the USA and Italy.

In summary, arguments can be found to support the view that *Barcelona Traction* does not require *all* company-related claims to be made by companies directly (either on its proper reading or because it has been overturned) and arguments can be found to support the opposite. Tribunals constituted under investment treaties have chosen the safest option in deciding according to the black letter of the particular treaty as the *lex specialis*. Since such treaties typically include shares as a qualifying investment, shareholder claims are correspondingly common.

Such a discussion does not, however, decide the thorny questions of whether minority and/or indirect shareholders should qualify as investors.

iv.   Indirect and minority shareholdings

It is obviously very common that indirect shareholders, i.e., shareholders of intermediate companies interposed between the claimant and the investment, seek to enforce their rights as investors against the host state. This was the situation, of course, in *Aguas del Tunari*, discussed above, in which the ICSID tribunal allowed the claim to be brought because of the indirect Dutch shareholding, even though an interposed Luxembourg company was between the Dutch shareholders and the locally-incorporated Bolivian company. Since the underlying BIT stated that it applied to "legal persons controlled directly *or indirectly*, by nationals of that Contracting Party, but constituted in accordance with the law of the other Contracting Party"[76] (emphasis added), the companies higher in the corporate chain could bring the claim on behalf of the local company.

However, where claims are brought by shareholders relying on a definition of investment including shares, thus bringing claims *as shareholders* as opposed to derivative

---

73. See, e.g., *Azurix Corp. v. The Argentine Republic*, ICSID Case No. ARB/01/12, Decision on Jurisdiction, dated 8 December 2003, para. 72, 43 ILM (2004) p. 262. On the other hand, the NAFTA tribunal in *GAMI Investments, Inc. v. United Mexican States*, UNCITRAL arbitration, Final Award dated 15 November 2004, available at <www.investmentclaims.com/decisions/GAMI-Mexico-FinalAward-15Nov2004.pdf> (last accessed 30 April 2006), seemed to imply at para. 30 that *ELSI* had indeed overruled the *Barcelona Traction* case.

74. See discussion of claims as shareholders below.

75. Francisco ORREGO VICUÑA, "The Changing Law of Nationality of Claims, International", ILA Report (2000) p. 28 at p. 42; I. LAIRD, "A Community of Destiny – The *Barcelona Traction* case and the Development of Shareholder Rights to Bring Investment Claims" in Todd WEILER, ed., *International Investment Law and Arbitration: leading cases from the ICSID, NAFTA, bilateral treaties and customary international law* (Cameron May 2005) pp. 85-86.

76. See above.

claims made *on behalf of* the company, the interposition of an intermediary company has engaged tribunals' attention.

In *Siemens v. Argentina*,[77] the underlying BIT between Germany and Argentina determined a company's nationality according to the company-seat principle. Investments were defined to include shares and other forms of interests in legal entities.[78] The claim was brought by Siemens A.G., which wholly owned SNI A.G., both German companies, which in turn wholly owned SITS S.A., an Argentinian company, alleging that Argentina had wrongfully terminated a contract with SITS.

The respondent state argued that Siemens could not bring the claim, as it was SNI's and not Siemens' interest in SITS that had allegedly been violated. Indirect claims could only be brought, Argentina argued, if there was express authorization to do so in the treaty.[79]

The ICSID tribunal refused to accept the respondent state's submission that Siemens was not entitled to bring the claim. The tribunal pointed out that there were two separate issues involved: first, whether a shareholder's indirect investment via an interposed company was protected under the treaty and, secondly, whether the shareholder may claim damage suffered by a company in which it holds shares. The tribunal came to the conclusion that:

(a) the treaty did support indirect investments as neither a literal nor systematic interpretation of the treaty demanded a different outcome; and
(b) the shareholder was allowed to bring proceedings for a wrong inflicted upon an indirect subsidiary.

With respect to the former, the tribunal referred to the treaty and stated that:

> "the plain meaning of [Art. 1(1)(b) of the treaty] is that shares held by a German shareholder are protected under the Treaty. The Treaty does not require that there be no interposed companies between the investment and the ultimate owner of the company."[80]

With respect to the second finding, Argentina sought to convince the tribunal that case law showed that arbitral tribunals only found standing of indirect investors where treaties explicitly said so. To support this proposition, Argentina referred to *Maffezini v. Spain*,[81] where the tribunal heard the claim of an individual, who was the majority

---

77. *Siemens A.G. v. The Argentine Republic*, ICSID Case No. ARB/02/8, Decision on Jurisdiction dated 3 August 2004, 44 ILM (2005) p. 138.

78. Germany-Argentina BIT, Art. 1(1)(b) (free translation from the German by the author).

79. *Siemens, op. cit.*, fn. 77, para. 125.

80. *Ibid.*, para. 137.

81. *Emilio Agustin Maffezini v. Kingdom of Spain*, ICSID Case No. ARB/97/7, Decision on Jurisdiction dated 25 January 2000, 5 ICSID Reports, p. 396.

shareholder in a local company; *AMT v. Congo*,[82] where the claimant was a company with a direct shareholding in the local investment vehicle; and *AAPL v. Sri Lanka*,[83] where the tribunal heard an indirect claim, but where the underlying UK-Sri Lankan BIT (which was extended to the territory of Hong Kong under Art. 11 of the treaty by agreement dated 14 January 1981) explicitly referred to Art. 25(2)(b) of the ICSID Convention, which (as discussed above) allows claims to be brought on behalf of local companies if controlled by nationals of the other contracting party.[84]

The tribunal did not accept that the cases cited by the respondent compelled the conclusion that an indirect shareholder could not bring the claim arising under an investment dispute himself. None of the cases actually dealt with this point but showed that tribunals were generally in favour of allowing shareholder claims.

The ICSID tribunal in the NAFTA case of *Waste Management, Inc. v. United Mexican States*[85] came to a similar conclusion:

> "Chapter 11 of NAFTA spells out in detail and with evident care the conditions for commencing arbitrations under its provisions. In particular it distinguishes between claims brought by an investor of another Party in its own right and claims brought by an investor on behalf of a local enterprise. The relevant provisions cover the full range of possibilities, including direct and indirect control and ownership.... There is no hint of any concern that investments are held through companies or enterprises of non-NAFTA States, if the beneficial ownership at relevant times is with a NAFTA investor."[86]

As to minority shareholdings, a minority shareholding in this context means a shareholding that does not control the company (which may of course beg the question of what is meant by "control" in different contexts under the *lex societatis*, but that is most definitely outside the scope of this Report). Minority shareholders (in this sense) cannot rely on Art. 25(2)(b) of the ICSID Convention, as they do not control the locally incorporated company.[87] Minority shareholders thus have to rely on the inclusion of shares as part of the definition of qualifying investments in the investment treaty concerned and claim for loss of shareholder value rather than for loss on behalf of the company.

It is widely recognized that minority shareholders have the right to bring proceedings in such circumstances. In *AAPL v. Sri Lanka*,[88] the tribunal heard a claim brought by a

---

82. *American Manufacturing & Trading v. Democratic Republic of the Congo*, ICSID Case No. ARB/93/1, Award dated 21 February 1997, 5 ICSID Reports, p. 14.

83. *Asian Agricultural Products Ltd v. Democratic Socialist Republic of Sri Lanka*, ICSID Case No. ARB/87/3, Final Award dated 27 June 1990, 4 ICSID Reports, p. 245.

84. See United Kingdom-Sri Lanka BIT, Art. 8(2).

85. *Waste Management, Inc. v. United Mexican States*, ICSID Case No. ARB(AF)/00/3, Award dated 30 April 2004, 43 ILM (2004) p. 967.

86. *Ibid.*, para. 80.

87. *Ibid.*, p. 5.

88. *AAPL v. Sri Lanka, op. cit.*, fn. 83.

shareholder holding forty-eight per cent of the ordinary shares of the Sri Lankan investment company. The fact that the foreign investor only held a minority stake in the company was not even raised. The tribunal pointed out that it was important to distinguish between the assets of the company and the interests of the shareholder.

> "The undisputed 'investments' effected since 1985 by AAPL in Sri Lanka are in the form of acquiring shares in Serendib Company, which has been incorporated in Sri Lanka under the domestic companies law.
> Accordingly, the Treaty protection provides no direct coverage with regard to Serendib's physical assets as such … or to the intangible assets of Serendib if any.… The scope of the international law protection granted to the foreign investor in the present case is limited to a single item: the value of his share-holding in the joint-venture entity (Serendib Company)."[89]

In *CMS v. Argentina*,[90] the respondent state argued that the fact that the claimant only held a 29.42 per cent stake in the Argentinian company that had allegedly been harmed by Argentina's conduct mean that the tribunal should decline jurisdiction.[91] The tribunal rejected this argument and said that it

> "finds no bar in current international law to the concept of allowing claims by shareholders independently from those of the corporation concerned, not even if those shareholders are minority or non-controlling shareholders".[92]

The same was true in *Saluka Investments v. Czech Republic*, in which the fact that Saluka only held a minority of shares in the bank that the Czech Republic was found to have treated unfairly and inequitably was not raised as part of the Czech Republic's jurisdictional objections, which were focused on the alleged lack of connection between Saluka and the Netherlands and its own alleged lack of interest in the shares it held in the Czech bank.[93]

---

89. *Ibid.*, para. 87.

90. *CMS Gas Transmission Company v. Republic of Argentina*, ICSID Case No. ARB/01/8, Decision of the Tribunal on Objections to Jurisdiction dated 17 July 2003, 7 ICSID Reports, p. 492.

91. *Ibid*, paras. 46 and 58-59.

92. *Ibid.*, para. 48.

93. *Op. cit.*, supra. Other examples of cases where tribunals have found jurisdiction over minority shareholders' claims are: *Compañia de Aguas del Aconquija, S.A. & Compagnie Générale des Eaux v. Argentine Republic* (the *Vivendi case*), ICSID Case No. ARB/97/3, Decision on Annulment dated 3 July 2002, para. 50, 6 ICSID Reports, p. 340; *Champion Trading Co. and Others v. Arab Republic of Egypt*, ICSID Case No. ARB/02/9, Decision on Jurisdiction dated 21 October 2003, para. 3.4.2 (indirect minority shareholding of natural persons), 19 ICSID Review–FILJ (2004) p. 275; *GAMI Investments, Inc. v. United Mexican States*, NAFTA proceedings under UNCITRAL rules, Final Award dated 15 November 2004, paras. 33, 37, 44 ILM (2005) p. 545; *LG&E Energy Corp & Others. v. Argentine Republic*, ICSID Case No. ARB/02/1, Decision of the Arbitral Tribunal on Objections to Jurisdiction dated 30 April 2004, para. 50, available at <http://ita.law.uvic.ca/documents/LGEDecisionJurisdiction-English.pdf> (last accessed 30 April 2006); *LANCO International Inc v.*

Causation: As has already been mentioned, tribunals have to consider that the damages suffered by the investing company are different from the damages suffered by shareholders in this company as well as the damages suffered by the shareholder in an interposed company. In addition, tribunals need to deal with the phenomenon of several claims being brought about the same basic facts (whether different claims under different treaties or diverse claims brought in different fora) and states will not necessarily know to whom they owe duties, and under which treaty or treaties, as they may not be able to detect the ultimate shareholder of a company.[94]

The most notorious example of such issues is that provided by the parallel cases brought by CME Czech Republic B.V., a Dutch company, and Ronald Lauder, an American individual, against the Czech Republic. Mr. Lauder held interests in several investment vehicles that in turn held (at varying times and in varying amounts) interests in a Czech company. This Czech company operated a television station under a licence granted to one of its other shareholders, a Czech investor. When the relationship with the Czech investor broke down, with the consequence that his companies lost their interest in the Czech television station, much litigation ensued, both in the Czech Republic and elsewhere, in arbitration and litigation. Among this multi-faceted litigation were two claims under investment treaties, one brought under the United States-Czech Republic BIT by Mr. Lauder himself,[95] the other brought by one of the companies in which he had an interest (and which in turn held an interest in the Czech company), CME Czech Republic, this time under of the Netherlands-Czech Republic BIT.[96] The Czech Republic refused offers by Mr. Lauder and CME to consolidate the two arbitrations.

The Czech Republic argued that the tribunal in *Lauder* did not have jurisdiction to hear the claim as the same dispute had been submitted to litigation in state courts and was subject to other arbitral proceedings and that the same remedies were sought in these other fora.[97]

The tribunal disagreed with these arguments, finding that the other proceedings were initiated by different claimants, concerned different disputes and were based on different causes of action. The tribunal recognized, however, that, if CME recovered any loss in the other investment treaty arbitration, the tribunal would take it into account if they were to award any damages in the *Lauder* proceedings.[98] Eventually, the tribunal did not award any damages for lack of causation between the breach of the treaty as found by the tribunal and the loss.

Argentine Republic, ICSID Case No. ARB/97/6, Decision on Jurisdiction dated 8 December 1998, para. 10, 5 ICSID Reports, p. 367.

94. The International Court of Justice identified this problem in the *Barcelona Traction* case.

95. *Ronald S. Lauder v. The Czech Republic,* arbitration conducted under UNCITRAL rules according to the United States-Czech Republic BIT, Final Award dated 3 September 2001, 9 ICSID Reports, p. 62.

96. *CME Czech Republic B.V. v. The Czech Republic,* arbitration conducted under UNCITRAL rules according to the Netherlands-Czech Republic BIT, Partial Award dated 13 September 2001, 9 ICSID Reports, p. 121.

97. *Lauder, op. cit.,* fn. 95, paras. 168-169.

98. *Ibid.,* para. 172.

The tribunal in the parallel arbitration brought by CME was faced with a similar argument on jurisdiction by the respondent state. It in its turn found it had jurisdiction to hear the claim and stated that:

> "[t]here is no abuse of the Treaty regime by Mr. Lauder in bringing virtually identical claims under two separate Treaties.... This has the consequence that there will be two awards on the same subject which may be consistent with each other or may differ."[99]

With respect to the assessment of damages, it was pointed out that Mr. Lauder might not be able to recover the whole loss in the *Lauder* proceedings, as "it is brought on behalf of only a single controlling ultimate shareholder of CME".

The result was, in fact, two differing awards, as the tribunal in *CME* found on the same facts that the Netherlands-Czech Republic BIT had been breached and awarded damages in the amount of US$ 269,814,000. In the award on damages, the tribunal dismissed the respondent's argument that it should take account of the *Lauder* award. Even though the tribunal recognized that Mr. Lauder was the ultimate interest holder, it went on to say:

> "[t]he two arbitrations are based on differing bilateral investment treaties, which grant comparable investment protection, which, however, is not identical. Both arbitrations deal with the Media Council's interference with the same investment in the Czech Republic. However, the Tribunal cannot judge whether the facts submitted to the two tribunals for decision are identical and it may well be that facts and circumstances presented to this Tribunal have been presented quite differently to the London Tribunal [i.e., the *Lauder* Tribunal]."[100]

It is suggested that, even though states cannot know exactly which duties are owed in respect of which shareholders of a particular company, the issue may not be serious in practice because, first, investment agreements often afford often more or less the same substantive protection and, secondly, most-favoured-nation clauses may even out any differences. Furthermore, these cases should not be used to argue against allowing claims of indirect shareholders. As a respected commentator has said, "the problem could have been dealt with satisfactorily through a consolidation of the two cases or a flexible application of the principles of *lis pendens* and *res judicata*".[101] While the *Lauder/CME* saga has attracted much comment, it is unlikely that tribunals (and parties) will be faced with quite the same dilemma on very many future occasions.[102]

---

99. *CME v. Czech Republic, op. cit.,* fn. 96, para. 412.

100. *Ibid.,* para. 432.

101. SCHREUER "Shareholder Protection", *op. cit.,* fn. 42, p. 14.

102. Although it is of course commonplace in investment-treaty arbitration that there may be claims brought by the locally incorporated company and the foreign investor in different *fora*, as recognized by those tribunals that have been called upon to consider the distinction between contract and treaty claims, the most recent example being *Bayindir Insaat Turizm Ticaret Ve Sanayi*

III.   THE NATIONALITY OF NATURAL PERSONS AS CLAIMANTS UNDER INVESTMENT
       TREATIES

Since most investment treaty claims have been brought (and will no doubt continue to
be brought) by legal persons, the question of the nationality of claims brought by natural
persons is less often encountered, but presents issues every bit as complex as those
looked at under the previous heading. Again, customary international law will be
examined first, before turning to the few investment treaty arbitral decisions that have
dealt with this issue to date.

1.   Customary International Law

It has traditionally been the case that the right to grant and withdraw nationality over
individuals is part of a state's reserved domain. Neither international tribunals nor other
states can set aside grants of nationality.

The classic statement is probably that of the Permanent Court of International
Justice, which in 1923 said in the *Tunis and Morocco Nationality Decrees* case that. "in the
present state of international law, questions of nationality are, in the opinion of the
Court, in principle within the reserved domain".[103] In other words, it was a matter in
respect of which international law did not restrict a state's rights to make rules as it
thought fit. This principle was restated in Art. 1 of the Hague Convention on Certain
Questions Relating to the Conflict of Nationality Laws (1930)[104] and in the *Nottebohm*
case.[105] It has been endorsed more recently by the 1997 European Convention on
Nationality.[106]

The question before tribunals has therefore been whether, and to what extent, a state
can refuse to recognize the opposability of the nationality of a given claimant.

Thus, it can be seen that the sovereign right of a state to grant nationality on whom
it pleases is restricted in two important ways when it comes to the opposability of that
nationality to another state. First, an international tribunal arguably has the power to
determine whether an individual has met the criteria for nationality under the domestic
law of the state whose nationality he holds (or claims to hold) – at least when it is
manifest that the applicable domestic law has been wrongly applied. Secondly, the grant
of nationality may have been exercised in circumstances that mean that the resulting
grant need not be recognized by the respondent state. In neither case is the international
tribunal capable of invalidating the grant of nationality as a matter of the granting state's

---

A.S. v. Islamic Republic of Pakistan, ICSID Case No. ARB/03/29, Decision on Jurisdiction dated
14 November 2005, para. 148, available at <http://ita.law.uvic.ca/documents/Bayindr-jurisdiction.pdf> (last accessed 30 April 2006).

103. *Nationality Decrees in Tunis and Morocco,* PCIJ Reports, Series B, No. 4, p. 24.

104. Convention on Certain Questions relating to the Conflict of Nationality Laws (The Hague, 12
April 1930), (1937) 179 LNTS 89. The Convention is anyway to be treated carefully as a source
of international law: only twenty-two states are currently parties to it, eight of them as successors
to the United Kingdom on attaining independence.

105. *Nottebohm (Liechtenstein v. Guatemala)* ICJ Reports 4, 1955.

106. ETS No. 166, Art. 3.

domestic law (or even for other purposes, such as the right to travel on a given passport). It simply restricts the opposability of that nationality as the basis for claims as against another state.

a.   *The Nottebohm case and effective nationality*

In the *Nottebohm* case, the International Court of Justice recognized the sovereign prerogative of a state to grant nationality, but also accepted that this did not require all states to recognize that grant of nationality in all situations. In particular, nationality did not have to be recognized by other states if it was not "real and effective". A state granting nationality is not entitled to have that nationality recognized by another state unless nationality is based on an individual's "genuine connection" with the granting state.

The facts of *Nottebohm*, which are in many respects extreme and most unlikely to be repeated, deserve a short exposition. Mr. Nottebohm was originally of German nationality and had moved to Guatemala in 1905. In 1939 he travelled to Liechtenstein to visit his brother and obtained Liechtenstein nationality "in exceptional circumstances of speed and accommodation" (as the Court found) only to enable him to substitute for his status as a national of a belligerent state that of the subject of a neutral state. He returned to Guatemala in 1940 and remained there until he was deported to the United States of America in 1943 as a German national and thus enemy alien. He then tried to rely on his Liechtenstein nationality to support a diplomatic protection claim against Guatemala. The Court held that in these circumstances, Liechtenstein could not assert Mr. Nottebohm's nationality against Guatemala, where Mr. Nottebohm had settled his life, family and interests for thirty-four years. In its judgment, the Court relied on:

> "[t]he practice of certain States which refrain from exercising protection in favour of a naturalized person when the latter has in fact, by his prolonged absence, severed his links with what is no longer for him anything but his nominal country".[107]

In practice, given Mr. Nottebohm's overwhelming links to Guatemala, and the "extremely tenuous" ties he had with Liechtenstein, Guatemala was to be treated as the equivalent of his national state. In those circumstances, the Court could be said to be following its previous jurisprudence to the effect that a state should not exercise diplomatic protection on behalf of one of its nationals against a state that regards him as its own national.[108]

---

107. *Nottebohm, op. cit.*, fn. 105, at p. 22

108. See, e.g., Reporters' Note 1 to Sect. 211 of the *Restatement (Third) of Foreign Relations Law of the United States* (1987), which reads:

"It is not clear from the opinion [of the ICJ in *Nottebohm*] whether a third country would have been entitled to ignore Liechtenstein's naturalization of Nottebohm, since the court stressed the comparative ties of Nottebohm to Liechtenstein and to Guatemala. Nothing in this case suggests that a state may refuse to give effect to a nationality acquired at birth, regardless of how few other links the individual had at birth or maintained later."

It is in any event suggested that the true state of international law is more accurately represented by the Draft Convention on Diplomatic Protection of the ILC, of which Art. 6(1) states that:

> "Any State of which a dual or multiple national is a national may exercise diplomatic protection in respect of that national against a State of which that individual is not a national."[109]

This restates the rule of customary international law that a claim cannot be brought against a state of which the individual whose claim is being espoused is also a national, and which can be seen to be the underlying justification for the decision in the *Nottebohm* case.

In any event, the requirement of demonstrating effective nationality would be very onerous in the modern world. Considerations cited in *Nottebohm* included the individual's attachments to the state through tradition, establishment, interests, activities, family ties and intentions for the near future. Property, taxation and marriage are other relevant considerations.

The ILC's adoption of the article set out above recognized the need for a change from the strict principles of *Nottebohm*. The ILC thus specifically excluded the test of effectiveness from nationality requirements in its report on diplomatic protection, stating:

> "if the genuine link requirement proposed by *Nottebohm* was strictly applied it would exclude millions of persons from the benefit of diplomatic protection as in today's world of economic globalization and migration there are millions of persons who have drifted away from the State of nationality and made their lives in States whose nationality they never acquire or have acquired nationality by birth or descent from States with which they have a tenuous connection".[110]

Amerasinghe adds:

"[T]here is a distinction between diplomatic protection and jurisdiction for the purposes of the [ICSID] Convention.... [E]ven if the *Nottebohm Case* were to be used as an applicable precedent, it is arguable that an effective link is relevant to negating the existence of nationality only in the particular circumstances of that case, or at any rate, in very limited circumstances."

C.F. AMERASINGHE, "The Jurisdiction of the International Center for Settlement of Investment Disputes", 19 Indian Journal of International Law (1979) p. 166 at p. 203.

109. Art. 6(1) of the Draft Convention on Diplomatic Protection (2004 draft), UN Doc. A/CN.4/L.647 (24 May 2004). All subsequent references in this Report to the ILC's Draft Convention are to this draft unless otherwise specified.

110. "Report of the International Law Commission on the work of its fifty-fourth session" (2002) (UN Doc. A/57/10) Chap. V, p. 176.

This restriction was supported by the United Nations General Assembly's Sixth Committee for similar reasons.[111] *Nottebohm* principles are, however, still usefully applied in cases of dual or multiple nationality where the claim is against a state of nationality: this is reflected by Art. 7 of the Draft Convention, which, as discussed immediately below, requires the nationality of the claimant state to be "predominant".

b.   Dual and multiple nationality

i.   Where the claimant is a national of the host state as well as of the espousing state
The ILC Draft Convention states at Art. 7:

> "A State of nationality may not exercise diplomatic protection in respect of a person against a State of which that person is also a national unless the nationality of the former State is predominant, both at the time of the injury and at the date of the official presentation of the claim."

The last phrase, referring to the times at which the nationality has to be held (the implications of which for the continuous-nationality rule are discussed below), was not present in the 2002 draft of the Convention, but otherwise the article remains unchanged. The ILC cited a number of authorities in support of the proposition that claims could be asserted even against the state of nationality on behalf of a dual or multiple national.[112] In contrast, the General Assembly's Sixth Committee expressed concern at the problems involved in determining the predominance of one nationality over another and the lack of criteria given for making such a judgment.[113] The Committee suggested an additional paragraph explaining that "predominant" meant "the nationality with which the person had the strongest effective link". An alternative suggestion was to replace "predominant nationality" with "effective nationality", which would bring us back to the considerations set out in the *Nottebohm* case. In the end, as just noted, no such additional qualification has been retained by the ILC.

The Iran-US Claims Tribunal had adopted this reasoning in holding that claims could proceed in situations where the dominant and effective nationality of the individual was that of the state exercising diplomatic protection.[114]

ii.   Where the claimant is a national of a third state as well as of the espousing state
This is the situation referred to in the *Third Restatement* in its comments on (or criticisms of) the *Nottebohm* case.[115] In general, it is has been held by international tribunals that the

---

111. UN Doc. A/CN.4/529 (2003) para. 25.

112. In particular the *Mergé* claim (1955) 22 International Law Reports, p. 455.

113. Supra, para. 28. The General Assembly has not yet adopted the ILC Draft Convention although it has issued resolutions commending its work in the area of diplomatic protection and recommending comments from governments.

114. See, e.g., *Esphahanian v. Bank Tejarat* (1983) 22 Iran-US Claims Tribunal Reports, p. 166 and the *Dual Nationality* case, *op. cit.*, fn. 9.

115. *Op. cit.*, fn. 108.

opposability of nationality of a dual or multiple national cannot be rejected by a third state. In the *Salem* case, Egypt objected to a claim brought on behalf of a United States national on the grounds that he ought to be regarded as a national of Persia. The tribunal found that Mr. Salem was indeed a Persian national as well as a national of the United States, but held that:

> "In a case of dual nationality a third power is not entitled to contest the claim of one of the two powers whose national is interested in the case by referring to the nationality of the other power."[116]

The arbitral tribunal's reasoning in *Salem* was endorsed by the ILC in its report and has become Art. 6(1) of the Draft Convention.

This reasoning corresponds to state practice in diplomatic protection. The United Kingdom will consider espousing the cause of a dual national holding British nationality and that of a third state without any examination of questions of effective nationality.[117]

iii.   Other circumstances in which nationality might not be recognized
For the sake of completeness, it should be mentioned that there may be other circumstances in which a state's grant of nationality might not be recognized, unlikely as these may be in practice.

Art. 4 of the ILC Draft Convention defines nationality as that acquired by: "Birth, descent, succession of States, naturalization, or in any other manner, *not inconsistent with international law*". (Emphasis added.)

It would thus be open to a respondent state to challenge a claim on behalf of an injured foreign individual who has acquired nationality in a manner contrary to international law. For example, grants of nationality must be exercised in accordance with human rights requirements. A grant of nationality to men in more favourable circumstances than women would be invalid for contravening Art. 9(1) of the Convention on the Elimination of All Forms of Discrimination against Women, which states: "States parties shall grant women equal rights to men to acquire, change or retain their nationality." No doubt other examples can be conceived of (such as the Baltic states' claim to be able to espouse the claims of ethnic Russians living in their territories but not holding their citizenships).

c.   *Loss of nationality*
As with the grant of nationality, the withdrawal of nationality is also left up to the state and the general rules are therefore largely the same as those set out above. Nationality is commonly lost through release, deprivation, expiration, renunciation, and substitution.[118] There seems no reason to believe that tribunals would not examine potentially abusive withdrawals of nationality (such situations in the past being the case

---

116. *Salem* claim, 2 Reports of International Arbitral Awards (1932) p. 1184 at p. 1188.

117. United Kingdom Rules Applying to International Claims, *op. cit.*, fn. 18, Rules I and II.

118. Robert JENNINGS and Arthur WATTS, eds., *Oppenheim's International Law*, 9th edn. (Longman 1996) vol. 1, Sect. 391.

of Jews in National Socialist Germany and dissidents in the Soviet Union), but this seems unlikely to arise in cases of diplomatic protection since, by definition, if an individual has lost the nationality of his state, in whatever circumstances, the state will not espouse his claim (although another state might, for humanitarian reasons). The ILC did not examine this issue in its 2002 Report on Diplomatic Protection.

d.   Stateless persons
Both the ILA and the ILC have considered exceptions to the nationality rule. The ILA discusses two departures under international law.[119] The first concerns claims made on humanitarian grounds. Nationals of a respondent state have had their claims successfully brought by an unconnected state in situations of gross human rights violations.[120] Secondly, the rules of the United Nations Compensation Commission state that a government may submit claims on behalf of its nationals and, at its discretion, on behalf of other persons resident in its territory.[121]

Art. 8 of the ILC's Draft Convention on Diplomatic Protection sets out a much broader exception. It says that a state may exercise diplomatic protection in respect of a stateless person (or a refugee) who, at the time of injury and at the date of the official presentation of the claim, is lawfully and habitually resident in that state. The ILC does not attempt to define statelessness and instead relied on the customary international law definition of "stateless" enshrined in the Convention Relating to the Status of Stateless Persons of 1954. Art. 1 of that Convention defines a stateless person "as a person who is not considered as a national by any State under the operation of its law". The phrase "lawful and habitual residence" is taken from the 1997 European Convention on Nationality.[122] The ILC noted that this set a fairly high threshold but justified it on the basis that it equated to the test of effectiveness for nationality claims. Given the unlikelihood of this being an issue for investment-treaty arbitration, the question of stateless persons will not be considered further in this Report.

---

119. INTERNATIONAL LAW ASSOCIATION, London Conference (2000) "First Report" at II,I, pp. 33-34.

120. The *"I'm Alone"* case, (1935) 3 RIAA 1609; and *Letelier and Moffitt*, 31 ILM (1992) pp.7-18. In this case Commissioner Francisco Orrego Vicuña, in his Separate Concurrent Opinion, stated: "the Chilean nationality or dual nationality of some of the persons protected by the US Government was not raised as a bar to the disposition of the corresponding claims". The ILA points out that *Letelier* was a sitting member of the Chilean Congress, but it was also the case that Chile had attempted to revoke his Chilean nationality the week before he was murdered.

121. UNCC, Provisional Rules for Claims Procedure, 1992, Art. 5(1)(a).

122. Art. 6(4)(g). On the meaning of "habitual residence" see Resolution (72) 1 on the standardization of the legal concept of "residence", adopted by the Committee of Ministers of the Council of Europe on 18 January 1972. Rule No. 9 in the annex to that resolution stipulates that: "In determining whether a residence is habitual, account is to be taken of the duration and the continuity of the residence as well as of other factors of a personal or professional nature which point to durable ties between the person and his residence."

e.   Summary

While international law has always recognized that the grant of nationality is in a state's reserved domain, it is nonetheless the case that tribunals will, and do (hence the wealth of authority in the area, only a very little of which has been referred to above) examine whether an individual's nationality is opposable to the respondent state. This sometimes depends upon the terms of a particular treaty (such was the case of the Italian-United States Conciliation Commission, which made several well-known decisions in the field of nationality, including *Mergé*,[123] *Flegenheimer*[124] and *Stankovic*[125]) and the Iran-US Claims Tribunal), and sometimes on general principles of international law.

The major principle that emerges from these cases is that of the non-opposability of a nationality against a state that also considers the individual to be its national, although this was derogated from in favour of a pure effective-nationality test by the Iran-US Claims Tribunal.[126] Furthermore, it seems as if the very existence of a nationality can be looked at as a matter of fact[127] and where there is a suggestion of a nationality's having been obtained in bad faith, for example, for the purposes of bringing the claim.[128] The alternative line of authority is more restrictive in its approach; the only bases for examining grants of nationality are cases of fraud or similar "manifest grounds". The Iran-US Claims Tribunal stuck closely to this line of reasoning in several decisions.[129] Tribunals have therefore given themselves maximum flexibility while still respecting state sovereignty.

---

123. *Mergé* claim, *op. cit.*, fn. 112.

124. *Flegenheimer* claim (1958-I) 25 International Law Reports, p. 91.

125. *Stankovic* claim (1963) 40 International Law Reports, p. 153.

126. In the *Dual Nationality* case, *op. cit.*, fn. 9, as noted in the Introduction above, the Tribunal rejected Iran's claim that the Tribunal could not exercise jurisdiction over claims by dual US-Iranian nationals because the object and purpose of the Algiers Accords was not to "extend diplomatic protection in the normal sense". The rules of customary international law did not therefore prevent such dual nationals from bringing a claim.

127. *Flegenheimer* claim, *op. cit.*, fn. 124.

128. The practice of the United Nations Compensation Commission is instructive in this regard. Its Governing Council limited its mandate to exclude claims by Iraqi nationals "who do not have the *bona fide* nationality of any other state". This excluded "an Iraqi dual national [who] had acquired his or her second nationality mainly or solely for the purpose of becoming eligible to claim compensation...".

    GOVERNING COUNCIL OF THE UNCC, "Criteria for Expediting Processing of Urgent Claims", 2 August 1991, UN Doc. S/AC.26/1991/1 (1991) para 17; "Report and Recommendations of the UNCC Panel of Commissioners concerning the Sixth Instalment of Category 'A' Claims", 16 October 1996, UN Doc. S/AC.26/1996/3 (1996) paras. 29-30; "Report and Recommendations of the UNCC Panel of Commissioners concerning the Sixth Instalment of Category 'C' Claims", 2 July 1998, UN Doc. S/AC.26/1998/6 (1998) para. 14.

129. See, e.g., *Nemazee v. Iran* (Partial Award, 1990), 25 Iran-US Claims Tribunal Reports, p. 153 at p. 157, note 5; and *Khosravi v. Iran* (1996) 32 Iran-US Claims Tribunal Reports, p. 73.

2. The Investment Treaty Regime

As has been seen above in the context of the nationality of claims brought under investment treaties by legal persons, the law of diplomatic protection and investment treaty law are not one and the same. As noted above, in 1988 the ILC noted that investment treaties and the ICSID Convention "created a legal framework outside the traditional area of diplomatic protection".[130] It is a subject to which we shall return in the section of this Report dealing with continuous nationality, but again the starting point is the specific rules established for the nationality of claims by the ICSID Convention (if applicable in a particular case) and the individual treaties themselves.

Art. 25(2)(a) of the ICSID Convention requires that an individual claimant have the nationality of a contracting state to the Convention on particular dates (which will be looked at again in the context of continuous nationality) so long as he or she does not also hold the nationality of the respondent state. It is thus for the investment treaties or national laws to spell out any further requirements. Nearly all investment treaties define a national as someone who has the nationality of one of the contracting parties in accordance with its laws. UNCTAD argues that the silence of investment treaties on the need for a genuine link means that no such link is needed at all.[131]

The alternative argument is that silence cannot be interpreted as a departure from the traditional international law requirement of effective nationality. The difficulty that this argument presents is that, while most investment treaties do not require any economic or other link with the country of nationality, some expressly do impose such a requirement, which would be unnecessary if it were to be implied as a matter of customary international law.[132] For example, Art. 1(2) of the Italy-Algeria BIT requires that individual investors have *"le center principal de leurs intérêts économiques sur le territoire de leur État respectif, au sens de la législation ou de la réglementation de ce dernier"*. The UNCTAD report gives another example from a multilateral investment agreement. Art. 3(1) of the Treaty Establishing the Caribbean Community Agreement on the Harmonisation of Fiscal Incentives to Industry provides that "national" means:

> "a person who is a citizen of any Member State and includes a person who has a connection with such a State of a kind which entitles him to be regarded as belonging to or, if it be so expressed, as being a native resident of the State for the purpose of such laws thereof relating to immigration as are for the time being, in force".

---

130. "ILC Report to the General Assembly", UN Doc. A/53/10 (1988) para. 66, *op. cit.*, fn. 10.
131. UNCTAD, "International Investment Agreements: Key Issues", vol. I Chap. 3. Scope and Definitions, at 127.
132. As an illustration of this point, Greek BITS vary considerably in their definition of "investor". Since these provisions would seem to have been specifically negotiated by the parties in each case, it is likely that they would also have included effective nationality, or a genuine link requirement, had they wished. See in particular, the Greece-Lithuania BIT Art. 1(3).

A different sort of express restriction is provided by the Germany-Israel BIT, which at Art. 1(3)(b) defines nationality for Israel as: "Israeli nationals being permanent residents of the State of Israel", thus adding residence as a requirement, rather than economic ties as in the Italy-Algeria example.

The only available argument in reply is that it is not for states to decide whether the principle of effective nationality is or is not incorporated into a treaty. A tribunal ruling on nationality can apply the principle of effective nationality where the relevant treaty is silent because it is a principle of international law that states cannot contract out of.

On balance, this seems unlikely for two reasons.

First, as has been seen, the ILC appears to have concluded that the doctrine of effective nationality does not (as a matter of customary international law) prevent a state from espousing a claim on behalf of a dual national, if that national does not hold the nationality of the respondent state, although it would still need to be established that the home state's nationality was predominant if the dual national did hold the nationality of the respondent state. This severely weakens the rigour of the effective-nationality rule as expressed in *Nottebohm*. Secondly, the drafting history of the ICSID Convention shows that the concept of effective nationality was rejected as a requirement,[133] which would seem to imply that it was seen by the contracting states to the Convention as an option and not as a necessity. The drafting history also shows that the Convention is not intended to exclude claims by dual nationals if their second nationality is not that of the respondent state.[134] The drafters of the Convention further considered whether certificates of nationality furnished by contracting states should be conclusive as to the existence of nationality, and rejected that idea as well.

Thus, the ICSID Convention leaves it to states to define nationality as they wish in their investment treaties, but also enables tribunals constituted under those treaties to consider all of the evidence available (which might of course include certificates of nationality, where a state's practice is to issue them) to decide whether a given claimant is or is not, as a matter of fact, a national of a contracting state.

In practice, investment treaty case law as to the nationality of individuals is limited to two cases, *Soufraki v. The United Arab Emirates*[135] and *Champion Trading v. Egypt.*[136]

---

133. It had been proposed by the Guatemalan delegate, no doubt influenced by his country's success in *Nottebohm*. See LEGAL COMMITTEE ON SETTLEMENT OF INVESTMENT DISPUTES, Working Group II, "Interim Report on Article 30(iii)", Doc. SID/LC/20 (30 November 1964), reprinted in ICSID, *Documents Concerning the Origin and Formulation of the Convention (ICSID History)* (1968) vol. II, p. 876 at p. 876, para. 2. There is no further trace of this suggestion in the subsequent negotiating record.

134. Aron BROCHES, 136 *Recueil des Cours de l'Académie de Droit International* (1972), vol. II, p. 331 at pp. 357-358.

135. *Hussein Nuaman Soufraki v. United Arab Emirates*, ICSID Case No. ARB/02/7, Award dated 7 July 2004, available at <http://ita.law.uvic.ca/documents/Soufraki_000.pdf> (last accessed 26 April 2006). The claimant has initiated annulment proceedings under the ICSID Convention, still underway as at the date of this Report, as can be seen from the ICSID website at <www.worldbank.org/icsid/cases/pending.htm> (last accessed 29 April 2006).

136. *Champion Trading & Others v. Arab Republic of Egypt*, op. cit., fn. 93.

a.   The Soufraki case

The *Soufraki* case has, as do many cases of this nature, somewhat peculiar facts. Mr. Soufraki entered into a concession contract with the Dubai Department of Ports and Customs in 2000, which he signed in his individual capacity and expressly as a Canadian national. He subsequently brought an ICSID arbitration against the United Arab Emirates under the Italy-United Arab Emirates BIT. The respondent state challenged Mr. Soufraki's capacity to do so on two grounds: first, that as a dual national his effective nationality was Canadian and not Italian, and secondly that he was not, as a matter of Italian law, an Italian national at all as he had automatically lost that nationality on gaining Canadian citizenship and had not subsequently regained it. Mr. Soufraki produced, in support of his Italian nationality, two Italian passports, five certificates of nationality issued by the competent Italian authorities and a letter from the Italian Ministry of Foreign Affairs supporting his right to bring a claim under Italy's BIT with the United Arab Emirates as an Italian citizen.

The relevant provision of the Italy-United Arab Emirates BIT was Art. 1(3), which defined an individual investor of a contracting party as a "natural person holding the nationality of that State in accordance with its law". Mr. Soufraki was, or claimed to be, a national of both Italy and Canada. He was not a national of the United Arab Emirates and there was no allegation that he had obtained Italian nationality in a manner akin to bad faith (i.e., expressly to enable him to commence proceedings against the United Arab Emirates). The question was whether the tribunal could look behind the certificates of nationality to determine whether Mr Soufraki was, in fact, a national of Italy "in accordance with its laws".

The ICSID tribunal held that it could look behind the certificates of nationality and other documentation produced by Mr. Soufraki. It found that they could have been issued by the Italian authorities without knowledge of the loss of nationality occasioned by Mr. Soufraki's having obtained a second nationality and without knowledge of whether Mr Soufraki had subsequently regained that nationality. It thus examined the factual evidence before it as to whether Mr. Soufraki had fulfilled the conditions laid down by Italian law to regain a lost nationality, and found that he had not, and thus was not an Italian national for the purposes of the investment treaty concerned. The tribunal thus permitted itself to correct, as it were, the Italian authorities' mis-assessment of Mr. Soufraki's position.

The tribunal did not thus have to consider the applicability of effective nationality to investment treaty practice. It is suggested that in light of the discussion of the difference between such practice and diplomatic protection law, and of the drafting history of the ICSID Convention, such a concept (even to the extent it survives in diplomatic protection at all) is not applicable to investment treaty arbitration.

This leaves us with the effect of the decision that the ICSID tribunal in *Soufraki* did take. At first sight, it seems to have been a wholly reasonable decision. Tribunals have surely got the ability to examine the evidence to see whether a claimant fulfils the definition of investor under the relevant treaty and the ICSID Convention, and the *Soufraki* tribunal can be said to have done no more than that. On the other hand, the tribunal was concerned that the Italian authorities might have issued Mr. Soufraki's certificates of nationality on the basis of incomplete information. In so doing, however, the tribunal has supposed that the Italian authorities, had they been in possession of what

481

the tribunal believed were the true facts, would have decided the question in a different manner. By pre-empting the Italian authorities' decision, the tribunal has eroded the exclusive right of Italy to determine the grant or loss of its own nationality. Since this was not a case of fraud it seems that the *Soufraki* case can be seen as an additional limitation on the sovereign right to grant nationality.

b.   The Champion Trading case

Champion Trading was brought by two legal and three natural persons as claimants. The natural persons held dual US-Egyptian nationality and Egypt argued that the tribunal did not have jurisdiction on the basis of Art. 25(2)(a) of the ICSID Convention. In a curious contrast to the *Soufraki* case, the individual claimants actually asked the tribunal (which had Yves Fortier as a common member with the *Soufraki* tribunal) to apply the effective nationality test to determine that their US nationality was the one to be regarded for the purposes of the claim as their effective nationality and thus entitled them to bring the claim against their other national state.

The ICSID tribunal refused to apply the rule in the *Nottebohm* case to the case. The individual claimants had actually used their Egyptian nationality in making their investment in Egypt and the tribunal found that this made them dual nationals within the meaning of the ICSID Convention and thus precluded them from bringing a claim against Egypt. The tribunal recognized that there might be circumstances in which, for example, through the application of the *jus sanguinis* through many generations, the holding of the nationality of the respondent state would make the strict application of the terms of Art. 25(2)(a) of the ICSID Convention manifestly absurd and unreasonable,[137] but this was not one of them, as it involved the claims of sons born of an Egyptian father.

While the decisions in *Soufraki* and *Champion Trading* still leave open the question of the applicability of the effective nationality principle to investment treaty arbitration, in the sense that it was not applied because both tribunals decided the cases on other grounds, the better view is that the tribunals implicitly rejected it as the ICSID Convention and the BIT read together provide a full code for the resolution of disputes as to the nationality of a natural person under an investment treaty.[138]

c.   Evidence, the burden of proof and challenges

What constitutes proof of nationality will depend on the facts that need to be proved in each given case. As a matter of customary international law, a number of guidelines have been established. These provide some help also in considering what an investment treaty tribunal might wish to see by way of evidence of nationality.

For example, in cases of naturalization, the best evidence is the original certificate of naturalization or a copy of the record of proceedings in which nationality was

---

137. Under Art. 32(b) of the Vienna Convention.

138. It should be noted that Prof. Schreuer takes a different view. He says that, when determining nationality, an international tribunal is entitled to question a claim of nationality in "cases of ineffective nationality lacking a genuine link between the State and the individual". He cites the *Nottebohm* case as authority. See SCHREUER, *The ICSID Convention: A Commentary, op. cit.*, fn. 28, p. 267, para. 429.

conferred.[139] In cases where nationality is conferred upon birth, then a valid birth certificate should be sufficient evidence of that conferral. In certain circumstances, so-called "primary" evidence, such as a birth or naturalization certificate, may not be available, in which case "secondary" material may then need to be relied upon. One commentator argues that, before secondary evidence can be relied upon, sufficient proof must be established that the primary evidence is not available.[140] The same commentator also recognizes that there is no inclusive definition of what will amount to secondary evidence.[141] It seems that what is sufficient will depend to a certain extent on the factors surrounding the case. For example, the ILC Report on Diplomatic Protection recognizes that in developing countries where primary evidence, such as birth certificates, may not be available, "residence could provide proof of nationality although it may not constitute a basis for nationality".[142]

In the end, of course, these rules do no more than establish what can be used, not what is necessary, nor what is always to be accepted. As has been seen, the drafters of the ICSID Convention declined to accept certificates of nationality as irrefutable proof of nationality, but the ICSID tribunal in the *Soufraki* case accepted them as part of the evidence it had to consider. The *Soufraki* tribunal cited Professor Schreuer in support of their conclusion:

> "A certificate of nationality will be treated as part of the 'documents or other evidence' to be examined by a tribunal in accordance with Art. 43. Such a certificate will be given its appropriate weight but does not preclude a decision at variance with its contents."[143]

The tribunal nonetheless, of course, rejected Mr. Soufraki's claim that he was an Italian national for the purposes of the Italy-United Arab Emirates BIT. This is despite the fact that such certificates would have been conclusive as a matter of Italian domestic law.

As to burden of proof, the International Court of Justice in *Avena* accepted that the initial burden of proof in demonstrating nationality lay with the claimant, in that case Mexico. Once Mexico had met this burden, by providing birth certificates and declarations from the individuals on whose behalf it was pursuing the claim that they had not obtained US nationality, the burden shifted to the respondent, which then had to demonstrate that this was not the case. If the relevant evidence was not available to the United States, because it was in the possession of Mexico, then the United States had to

---

139. JENNINGS and WATTS, eds., *Oppenheim's International Law*, op. cit., fn. 118, vol. 1, Sect. 381, p. 866.

140. Dui waid SANDIFER, *Evidence Before International Tribunals* (University Press of Virginia, Charlottesville 1975) p. 221.

141. *Ibid.*, pp. 222-223 for a discussion of different types of "secondary" evidence that have been accepted by tribunals.

142. "Report of the International Law Commission on the work of its fifty-fourth session", *op. cit.*, fn. 110, p. 175.

143. *Soufraki v. United Arab Emirates*, op. cit., fn. 135, para. 63, citing SCHREUER, *The ICSID Convention: A Commentary*, op. cit., fn. 28, p. 268, para. 433.

prove that the evidence was requested with sufficient specificity, and that the Mexican authorities declined or failed to respond to those requests.[144]

In investment-treaty arbitral practice, neither the *Soufraki* nor the *Champion Trading* tribunals addressed the point in quite the same detail as the International Court of Justice in *Avena*, but it seems tolerably clear from the manner in which they went about their findings that, in practice, the burden was first on the party challenging the jurisdiction of the tribunal to make out a *prima facie* case and then for the claimants to rebut it.

Turning to challenge, it has been seen that, in customary international law and also in investment treaty practice, evidence of nationality can be challenged on the basis of fraud or "manifest error".[145] In the end, tribunals have to decide on their own jurisdiction and are thus faced with a stark choice. Either, in the absence of fraud or "manifest error", they accept as conclusive the primary evidence that a claimant furnishes, or they conduct some kind of examination. Since an examination of, at least, an allegation of manifest error will lead them to examine the circumstances of a claimant's acquisition, loss or retention of nationality, in practice this must lead them to have the jurisdiction to decide that nationality does not exist for the purposes of a given treaty. In other words, as is the case in customary international law, one has to accept that a state does not have the last word (and can thus be said not to be wholly sovereign) in deciding questions of nationality in order to give international tribunals the tools they need to do their job.

IV.   ASSIGNMENT AND CONTINUOUS NATIONALITY

The last issue to be discussed is the question of when the relevant nationality must be held. This question is relevant both to legal and natural persons, and customary international law will again be looked at before turning to investment treaty practice.

1.   Customary International Law

The continuous-nationality rule under customary international law is stated by the learned editors of *Oppenheim's International Law* to be as follows:

> "[f]rom the time of occurrence of the injury until the making of the award the claim must continuously and without interruption have belonged to a person or to a series of persons (a) having the nationality of the state by whom it is put forward, and (b) not having the nationality of the state against whom it is put forward".[146]

---

144. *Avena and other Mexican Nationals (Mexico v. United States of America)* (2004).

145. See, e.g., *Salem, op. cit.,* fn. 116; *Flegenheimer, op. cit.,* fn. 124; and the decisions of the Iran-US Claims Tribunal in *Nemazee* and *Khosravi, op. cit.,* fn. 129.

146. JENNINGS and WATTS, eds., *Oppenheim's International Law, op. cit.,* fn. 118, vol. 1, pp. 512-513.

The principle is derived from the fiction that a wrong done to a national of a state is an injury to the state itself.[147] Thus, the injured person must have been a national of the claimant state at the time of the injury. In addition, the rule as set out in *Oppenheim* requires that the injured alien still be a national of the claimant state at the time the claim is brought *and* at the time the award is rendered.

A consequence of this principle is that a claim can only be transferred or assigned to individuals of the same nationality as the espousing state.[148]

A main reason for the proposition that the injured alien must have been a national of the espousing state at the time of the injury has been stated to be that it prevents nationals from abusing diplomatic protection by choosing a nationality with high leverage vis-à-vis the respondent state after an injury has been inflicted. Similarly, the rule prevented states from acquiring non-nationals' claims for the purpose of putting political pressure on other states.[149]

The rule, however, is not as settled as may perhaps be inferred from the above.

Although it is not contested that the national must be of the espousing state's nationality at the time of the injury,[150] there is (to put it mildly) more controversy regarding the time until which continuous nationality of the claim is required (the *dies ad quem*).[151] More generally, the main points raised by the opposition to the principle of continuous nationality are:

– If the underlying reason for diplomatic protection is that an injury to the alien is at the same time an injury to the alien's state, the change of nationality of the particular alien cannot change the state's vested claim (which vests upon the injury).[152]

– In addition, examining the rationale for the rule, there is no reason why the national should have to be continuously of the nationality of the claimant state. It is conceivable, albeit somewhat theoretical, that the individual is of the claimant state's nationality at the time of the injury, then acquires another state's nationality and then becomes a national of the claimant state again.[153]

---

147. See *Mavrommatis Palestine Concessions*, PCIJ Series A, No. 2 (1924) 12. See also John DUGARD "First report on diplomatic protection", International Law Commission, Addendum, UN Doc. A/CN.4/506/Add1 (2000) p. 2.

148. DUGARD, "First report", *op. cit.*, fn. 147, p. 12; ORREGO VICUÑA, *op. cit.*, fn. 75.

149. DUGARD, "First report", *op. cit.*, fn. 147, p. 3. An additional, somewhat more technical argument is that the claim of diplomatic protection can only be brought once all local remedies are exhausted. This, however, will only occur some time after the actual injury. Therefore, the national has to be a national of the state up until this time. (See Maurice MENDELSON "The Runaway Train: the 'Continuous Nationality Rule' in the *Panevezys-Saldutiskis Railway* case to *Loowen*", in WEILER, ed., *International Investment Law and Arbitration: leading cases from the ICSID, NAFTA, bilateral treaties and customary international law, op. cit.*, fn. 75).

150. DUGARD, "First report", *op. cit.*, fn. 147, p. 12.

151. *Ibid.*, p. 10; Jan PAULSSON "Loewen v. United States, ICSID Additional Facility Case No. ARB/AF/98/3 – Continuous Nationality in Loewen", 20 Arbitration International (2004) p. 213 at p. 213; MENDELSON, *op. cit.*, fn. 149, p. 106.

152. DUGARD, "First report", *op. cit.*, fn. 147, p. 13.

153. *Ibid.*, p. 10; MENDELSON, *op. cit.*, fn. 149, p. 109.

– Further, the rule seems obviously unfair where a national loses his nationality involuntarily, for example, through marriage, adoption or state succession.[154]

It is submitted that the main policy reason for the continuous-nationality rule (namely to prevent abuse of diplomatic protection) can be realized by the concepts of effective nationality and, especially, good faith. Where the injured alien has changed his nationality or assigned his claim to a national of a third state, respondent states could in all likelihood argue that the lack of a genuine link between the national and the espousing state deprived the claimant state of standing.[155] Similarly, a tribunal could find that it had no jurisdiction to hear a claim by a state on behalf of an individual who obtained that state's nationality only in order to bring the claim, as is discussed more fully above.

These considerations led Professor John Dugard, the ILC's Special Rapporteur, to propose in his "First report on diplomatic protection" a new regime of international law eliminating the concept of continuous nationality.[156] The state of the original nationality of the injured alien at the time of the injury may espouse the claim. If, however, a state has not begun an action by the time the injured alien has changed his nationality, the new state of nationality of the injured alien may bring the claim if the change in nationality was bona fide. The same approach was suggested for the transfer or assignment of the claim.

This proposal was not accepted by the ILC. The relevant article finally adopted on first reading by the Commission to form part of the Draft Convention on Diplomatic Protection in its fifty-sixth session in 2004 reads as follows:

> "1. A State is entitled to exercise diplomatic protection in respect of a person who was its national at the time of the injury and is a national at the date of the official presentation of the claim.
>
> 2. Notwithstanding paragraph 1, a State may exercise diplomatic protection in respect of a person who is a national at the date of the official presentation of the claim but was not a national at the time of the injury, provided that the person has lost his or her former nationality and has acquired, for a reason unrelated to the bringing of the claim, the nationality of that State in a manner not inconsistent with international law.
>
> 3. Diplomatic protection shall not be exercised by the present State of nationality in respect of a person against a former State of nationality of that person for an injury incurred when that person was a national of the former State of nationality and not of the present State of nationality."[157]

---

154. DUGARD, "First report", *op. cit.*, fn. 147, p. 14.

155. *Ibid.*, p. 15.

156. *Ibid.*, p. 15.

157. UN Doc. A/CN.4/L.647 Art. 5. See also Art. 7 on claims against a state of nationality, as discussed above. The General Assembly has not yet adopted any of the draft articles, but has encouraged governments to convey their views to the ILC (see General Assembly Resolutions 59/41 and 60/22).

On any view, it is notable that there is no reference to the date of the award (as opposed to the date of the presentation of the claim) as the *dies ad quem*.

Commentators have been less concerned with the application of the continuous-nationality rule with respect to companies.[158] Under the place-of-incorporation test, a company would first have to dissolve and then reorganize under the laws of a new state should it wish to change its nationality.[159] The possibility of a transfer or assignment of a claim from one company to another has nevertheless led the ILC to propose a draft article which requires the company to be of the nationality of the espousing state at the time of the injury as well as at the time of the presentation of the claim.[160]

2.   The Investment Treaty Regime

The promoters of a revision or abandonment of the continuous-nationality rule stress that the individual's role in the realm of international law has changed since the promulgation of the rule.[161]

The ICSID Convention, as the "outer limit" of investment agreements incorporating its dispute resolution mechanism,[162] does not require nationality to be established at the time of the injury. It does, however, state that the nationality of the claimant must be that of the contracting state – in the case of a natural person – "... on the date on which the parties consented to submit such dispute to conciliation or arbitration as well as on the date on which the request [to arbitrate] was registered... "[163] and – in the case of legal persons – "... on the date on which the parties consented to submit such dispute to conciliation or arbitration...".[164]

---

158. John DUGARD, "Fourth report on diplomatic protection", UN Doc. A/CN.4/530 (2003) p. 39.

159. It is perhaps less difficult to change a company's effective center of business administration. The concept of good faith may help a tribunal faced with a situation where the company has changed its seat to a more powerful home state to bring proceedings. However, this problem has been applied to argue for the adoption of the place of incorporation test as opposed to the company-seat principle by the ILC's Special Rapporteur (see DUGARD, "Fourth report", *op. cit.*, fn. 158, p. 40).

160. Draft Article 10 (UN Doc. A/CN.4/L.647 (2004)) adopted at first reading reads as follows:

"1. A State is entitled to exercise diplomatic protection in respect of a corporation which was its national at the time of the injury and is its national at the date of the official presentation of the claim.

2. Notwithstanding paragraph 1, a State continues to be entitled to exercise diplomatic protection in respect of a corporation which was its national at the time of the injury and which, as the result of the injury, has ceased to exist according to the law of that State."

There is again no reference to the need to maintain nationality until the date of the award.

161. DUGARD "First report", *op. cit.*, fn. 147, p. 14; ORREGO VICUÑA, *op. cit.*, fn. 75, p. 30; MENDELSON, *op. cit.*, fn. 149, p. 123.

162. BROCHES, as cited in *Tokio Taxales v. Ukraine*, *op. cit.*, fn. 26, para. 25.

163. ICSID Convention, Art. 25 (2)(a).

164. ICSID Convention, Art. 25 (2)(b).

The dates for natural persons and legal persons differ: natural persons must be of the other contracting state's nationality both on the date of submission, i.e., usually the date of the agreement including the arbitration clause or the date the person accepts the respondent state's offer to arbitrate expressed in an investment treaty by filing a claim with ICSID, and on the date at which the request is registered at the Center. Thus, the Convention resolves the dispute prevalent in customary international law as to what time the relevant nationality must be held (*dies ad quem*) in favour of the date of the registration of the claim. There is no need to maintain the nationality after this date in the course of the proceedings.

Perhaps due to the difficulties in changing a company's nationality through dissolution and reorganization,[165] the Convention requires legal persons only to be of the relevant nationality at a single date, namely the time of the consent to arbitrate. Again, any change in the legal person's nationality after this date is immaterial.[166]

In *Banro American Resources v. Democratic Republic of Congo*,[167] the tribunal was faced with a situation where an agreement to submit to ICSID arbitration (albeit by contract, not pursuant to the terms of an investment treaty) was entered into by the respondent state and a Canadian national. Canada, however, is not a signatory to the ICSID Convention, so that a Canadian national does not fall within the ambit of the ICSID Convention, since the claimant in an ICSID arbitration must be a national *of another contracting state*.[168] The tribunal considered whether the Canadian national could assign its contractual right to claim before an ICSID tribunal to an American subsidiary, through which the investment in the Congo was held. The United States of America is a party to the ICSID Convention. In this particular case, the American subsidiary had not, however, entered into an arbitration agreement submitting to arbitration under the ICSID Rules with the Congo.

The tribunal found that allowing the American subsidiary to sue would be tantamount to allowing investors to benefit both from enforcing their rights before an ICSID tribunal and applying to a non-contracting state (in this case, Canada) to exercise diplomatic protection. Thus, an assignment of contractual right should not be possible in those circumstances and the tribunal declined jurisdiction.

Another decision concerned with the question of continuous nationality (but outside the scope of the ICSID Convention) is *EnCana v. Ecuador*.[169] The claimant held its investment in Ecuador indirectly through an investment vehicle incorporated in Ecuador. When the claimant sold its interest in this Ecuadorian company to a Chinese investor after proceedings had commenced, the respondent state argued that EnCana's claim

---

165. MENDELSON, *op. cit.*, fn. 149, p. 128l.

166. SCHREUER, *The ICSID Convention: A Commentary*, *op. cit.*, fn. 28, para. 493.

167. *Banro American Resources Inc. and Société Aurifère du Kivu et du Maniema S.A.R.L. v. The Democratic Republic of the Congo*, ICSID Case No. ARB/98/7, Award dated 1 September 2000, 17 ICSID Review–FILJ (2003) p. 382.

168. As required by Art. 25(1) of the ICSID Convention.

169. *EnCana Corporation v. Republic of Ecuador*, proceedings under the UNCITRAL Rules under the Canada-Ecuador BIT administered by the London Court of International Arbitration, Award dated 3 February 2006, available at <http://ita.law.uvic.ca/documents/EncanaAwardEnglish.pdf> (last accessed 30 April 2006).

could not longer be sustained, as nationality was no longer continuous. The tribunal dismissed this contention. It based its decision on two arguments.

First, EnCana claimed on its own behalf and not on behalf of the investment company. The underlying BIT protected investments of "any kind ... owned or controlled either directly, or indirectly through an investor of a third State".[170] Secondly, the tribunal found that the investment company need not be in the ownership of the claimant during the course of the proceedings. The case talks, however, not about the nationality of the claimant but rather about the nationality of the underlying investment. The tribunal stated that:

> "it is accordingly unnecessary to deal with the question whether and how far international law rules in the field of diplomatic protection such as the rule of continuous nationality apply to direct claims by investors under BITS, and if they do, to identify the *terminus ad quem* for the purposes of that rule".[171]

It is submitted that this analysis leaves the continuous-nationality rule in investment treaty arbitration dead and buried. In summary, tribunals will have regard to the black letter of the underlying treaty rather than importing customary international law rules on continuous nationality.

This discussion may seem to have ignored the "elephant in the room" that is the *Loewen* case.[172] It is suggested that *Loewen* is unlikely to represent a precedent in future investment treaty arbitration, and that its application in customary international law will be similarly limited. Nonetheless, for completeness, a brief discussion is in order.

Loewen was a case under NAFTA. Arts. 1116 and 1117 of NAFTA only refer to the need for nationality to be maintained up until submission of the claim. The tribunal found, however, in an echo of the argument discussed above that effective nationality is to be read into investment treaties that do not otherwise mention it, that silence on the issue of nationality at the time of the resolution of the claim did not exclude the rules of customary international law, but rather led to their application. The tribunal recognized that the continuing-nationality rule was of less importance today, where individuals were claiming in their own right, but it also noted that where the rule had been relaxed, BITs and other treaties had included specific rules to that effect. Since NAFTA did not contain anything more specific, the tribunal felt that the relaxation of the continuous-nationality rule could not be inferred.[173]

The decision is to be criticized on at least three grounds. First, in reading silence on a topic as important as this as inadvertent and not a positive statement that the absence of a concept means it does not apply, the award does considerable violence to the agreement of the NAFTA parties. Secondly, even less excusably, it ignores the ILC's

---

170. Canada-Ecuador BIT, Art. I(g).

171. *EnCana v. Ecuador, op. cit.*, fn. 169, para. 128.

172. *Loewen v. USA, op. cit.*, fn. 4. The decision has been roundly criticized both by other investment-treaty arbitral tribunals (e.g., *EnCana v. Ecuador, op. cit.*, fn. 169, para. 128) and commentators (e.g., MENDELSON, *op. cit.*, fn. 149, p. 148; PAULSSON, *op. cit.*, fn. 151, p. 214).

173. *Loewen v. USA, op. cit.*, fn. 4, paras. 225-230.

detailed discussion and codification of the state of customary international law on the subject of the continuous-nationality rule as discussed above. Thirdly, it ignores the entirety of the discussion of the role of customary international law of the nationality of claims in investment-treaty arbitration, in non-ICSID as much as in ICSID practice, as has been set out above. For these reasons, it is suggested that the case is to be treated as an aberration.

V.   CONCLUSION

The conclusions of this Report can be summarized in the ten points below:

1. While investment treaties, like all international treaties, are to be interpreted in accordance with international law, the investment-treaty regime is now distinct from the diplomatic protection regime in customary international law, and in this respect the treatment of the nationality of claims is no exception.

2. The nationality requirements for investors to have standing to bring a claim under an investment treaty are thus exclusively to be found in the applicable treaty or (as in the case of a claim under the ICSID Rules) treaties, but, in interpreting those rules, customary international law and existing jurisprudence are and will continue to be of great relevance.

3. Silence in an investment treaty on a particular rule of customary international law will not therefore automatically be taken to mean that that rule is to be imported into the dispute.

4. It is thus up to contracting states to define the nationality requirements they wish to impose on investors. In the case of legal persons, this can be the imposition of the place-of-incorporation or company-seat tests. For natural persons, the almost universal formulation is that an investor must have the nationality of the contracting state in accordance with its (municipal) laws.

5. It is open to contracting states to establish more stringent conditions, requiring, for example, a real economic interest in the contracting state to be established by an investor holding its nationality, or indeed to relax them, for example in enabling non-nationals to bring claims if they are habitually resident in the contracting state.

6. Arbitral tribunals in investment-treaty cases have upheld the pure place-of-incorporation test in relation to legal persons as investors, thus allowing an investor to make his investment through a vehicle incorporated in a state benefiting from an investment treaty with the host state.

7. It is clear that minority and indirect shareholders can qualify as investors under investment treaties and can bring claims in respect of damage to their shareholdings, so long as the wording of the treaty in question allows, or does not forbid, this.

8. This gives rise nonetheless to a number of issues, including (a) whether an indirect shareholding in a company incorporated other than in the home or host states can be regarded as an investment in the host state in the absence of express wording in the treaty to that effect, and (b) how to calculate the loss of an indirect investor, especially when his investment is in shares in a company that may be several layers above the final

investment in the host state and which has directly suffered the loss for which redress is sought.

9. In claims brought by natural persons, unless (a) the claim is brought by a dual national holding the nationality of the host state (in a non-ICSID case) or (b) there is an express mention in the investment treaty concerned, the effective nationality rule has no application in investment-treaty arbitration.

10. The continuous-nationality rule (whatever its scope may be in customary international law) is not a requirement in investment treaty practice unless it is so specified in the treaty concerned.

The Distinction Between Contract Claims and Treaty Claims: An Overview

*Guido Santiago Tawil**

I. INTRODUCTION

The distinction between contract claims and treaty claims has certainly become one of the most highly debated issues in investment treaty arbitration.

Does the case brought to arbitration involve a treaty claim or a contractual one? This is one of the questions that arbitrators are more frequently asked to examine in those investment disputes that involve an investment-related contract. Both arbitrators and counsel are well aware of how the decision adopted in this respect can impact the outcome of the case.[1]

Nonetheless, and as will be discussed later in this Report under current case law, the distinction between contract claims and treaty claims does not necessarily mean that international tribunals will not have jurisdiction to deal with claims arising under a contract.[2] This is the starting point of relevant discussions on the scope of protection

---

* Partner, M. & M. Bomchil, Buenos Aires, Argentina; Member of ICCA.
The author would like to acknowledge the assistance of Ignacio J. Minorini Lima in the preparation of this report.

1. The distinction between contract claims and treaty claims is far from trivial. Denial of the existence of a treaty claim or a treaty breach related to a contract breach may divest the tribunal of jurisdiction or leave the case without merits. Further, in many cases, the relevance of dispute settlement clauses in contracts, the triggering of the so-called treaty's fork in the road clauses and the State's international responsibility could depend on the answers to such question. We will not address these issues in this Report as they will be developed in other Reports.

2. Christoph SCHREUER, "Investment Treaty Arbitration and Jurisdiction over Contract Claims – the *Vivendi I* Case Considered" in Todd WEILER, ed., *International Investment Law and Arbitration: Leading Cases from the ICSID, NAFTA, Bilateral Treaties and Customary International Law* (Cameron May 2005) p. 281 at p. 295.

that investment treaties provide to contracts and the extent to which international tribunals should enter in the discussion of contractual related issues.

We will not deal in this Report with all the matters related to this topic. We will only describe the main issues under debate and discuss the principles and answers provided by arbitral decisions and scholarly writings. The issues that will be addressed are:

(i) How may a treaty claim be distinguished from a contract claim? May the same set of facts trigger both a contract claim and a treaty claim?

(ii) How should jurisdiction be established when the respondent alleges that the claimant has put forward a mere contractual claim outside the scope of the tribunal's competence?

(iii) How does the different wording of the treaty's dispute settlement clause impact on the jurisdiction of tribunals called to deal with mere contractual claims?

(iv) When does a contract breach amount to a treaty breach?

(v) What is the role and effect on these issues of the treaty's so-called umbrella clauses?

II. THE RELATIONSHIP BETWEEN CONTRACT CLAIMS AND TREATY CLAIMS

Although distinguishing contract claims and treaty claims could be rather simple in theory, it has become increasingly difficult in practice, in particular, when the tribunal has been called to deal with complex disputes. A distinction based on five criteria has been proposed to differentiate them:[3]

(i) *The source of the right*: a treaty claim bases its cause of action in a treaty while a contract claim finds its cause of action in a contract.

(ii) *The content of the right*: while treaty rights are drafted in general terms and defined by international law, contract rights are specifically drafted for each investment and defined by the domestic law of the host State.

(iii) *The parties to the claim*: the parties to a treaty dispute are always a qualifying investor under the treaty and the host State. By contrast, the parties to a contract claim are those parties that executed the contract (which could include or not the parties to the treaty dispute).

(iv) *Applicable law*: treaty claims are governed by the provisions of the very same treaty, the host State's domestic law and general principles of international law. Contract claims are generally governed by the host State's domestic law.

(v) *The host State's responsibility*: a treaty claim finally proven to be a treaty breach will imply the host State's international liability, while a contract breach will involve the State contractual party's responsibility under municipal law.

---

3. Bernardo M. CREMADES and David J.A. CAIRNS, "*La seguridad jurídica de las inversiones extranjeras: la protección contractual y de los tratados*" in *La seguridad jurídica y las inversiones extranjeras en América Latina. El caso argentino*, Real Instituto Elcano de Estudios Internacionales y Estratégicos de Madrid, Working Document (DT) No. 2/2004, at <www.realinstitutoelcano.org/documentos/77/DT-2-2004-E.pdf> (last visited 27 March 2006).

Overlaps between a treaty claim and a contract claim may arise in certain cases, particularly when an umbrella clause is involved.[4] This will not be the case when applying the first criterion as treaty rights could never arise from a contract.[5] Thus, the distinction between a treaty claim and a contractual one will primarily focus on the cause of action that the dispute involves.[6] While a treaty claim asserts a treaty breach, a contract claim alleges a contract breach.

The distinction becomes more difficult in those cases in which treaty claims find their root in contracts that have served as the claimant's investment under the treaty or the instrument for channeling it. This happens all the time. As explained in *SGS v. Philippines*,

> "by definition, investments are characteristically entered into by means of contracts or other agreements with the host State and the local investment partner (or if these are different entities, with both of them)".[7]

Investments and contracts are thus closely related. But that should not change the nature of a treaty claim. If its cause of action is a treaty, the tribunal's jurisdiction to entertain treaty breach claims should be affirmed, even in those cases in which the claim finds its root in a contract.[8]

As explained by Alexandrov,[9] this is confirmed by the fact that:

(i) the taking of foreign investor's contractual rights entails an expropriation or a measure tantamount to expropriation;[10]

---

4. *Ibid.*

5. *Ibid.*

6. Alejandro ESCOBAR, "Contractual Claims, Courts and Bilateral Investment Treaties" in *Third Investment Treaty Forum Conference* (10 September 2004), British Institute of International and Comparative Law, 2 TDM (August 2005, no. 4) p. 40.

7. *SGS Société Générale de Surveillance S.A. v. Republic of the Philippines* (ICSID Case No. ARB/02/6), Decision on Jurisdiction (29 January 2004), para. 132(d), at <http://ita.law.uvic.ca/documents/SGSvPhil-final_001.pdf> (last visited 21 March 2006).

8. Stanimir A. ALEXANDROV, "Breaches of Contract and Breaches of Treaty. The Jurisdiction of Treaty-based Arbitration Tribunals to Decide Breach of Contract Claims in *SGS v. Pakistan* and *SGS v. Philippines*", 5 The Journal of World Investment and Trade (2004) p. 555 at p. 559. See also, Javier DÍEZ-HOCHLEITNER, "*El arbitraje internacional como cauce de protección de los inversores extranjeros en los APPRIS*", Actualidad Jurídica Uría y Menéndez (November 2005) p. 49 at p. 61.

9. ALEXANDROV, "Breaches of Contract and Breaches of Treaty. The Jurisdiction of Treaty-based Arbitration Tribunals to Decide Breach of Contract Claims in *SGS v. Pakistan* and *SGS v. Philippines*", *op. cit.*, fn. 8, pp. 559-561.

10. See Christoph SCHREUER, "The Concept of Expropriation under the ETC and Other Investment Protection Treaties", 2 TDM (November 2005, no. 5) paras. 50-64; August REINISCH, "Expropriation", 2 TDM (November 2005, no. 5) pp. 3-11. International practice has held that government assurances and undertakings create "acquired rights" for investors. In the *Rudloff Case*, for example, Commissioner Bainbridge assimilated the taking of tangible property to the one involving intangible property: "The taking away or destruction of rights acquired, transmitted, and defined by a contract is as much a wrong, entitling the sufferer to redress, as the taking away or

(ii) the breach of contractual commitments may amount to the violation of the fair and equitable treatment standard;[11] and
(iii) the wide definition of investments under most treaties explicitly or implicitly covers contracts.[12]

Several decisions have dealt with the distinction between contract and treaty claims, its relative independent nature and how a treaty-based tribunal should determine whether a treaty breach has taken place.

---

destruction of tangible property." (*Rudloff Case*, Interlocutory Decision (1903), 9 *Reports of Int'l Arbitral Awards* (hereinafter RIAA) (1959) p. 244 at p. 250). Similarly, in the *Norwegian Shipowners Claims* and *Certain German Interests in Polish Upper Silesia (Chorzów Factory)* cases, it was held that not only tangible rights but also contractual rights may be expropriated (*Norwegian Shipowners' Claims (Norway v. United States)*, Award (13 October 1922), 1 RIAA p. 307 at pp. 318-325; *Case Concerning Certain German Interest in Polish Upper Silesia (Germany v. Poland)*, Judgment No. 7 (25 May 1926), 1 World Court Reports (1934) p. 510). As well, the tribunal in *Saudi Arabia v. Aramco*, a case concerning oil concession rights, reasoned:

"By reason of its very sovereignty within its territorial domain, the State possesses the legal power to grant rights which it forbids itself to withdraw before the end of the Concession, with the reservation of the Clauses of the Concession Agreement relating to its revocation.... Such rights have the character of acquired rights."

(*Saudi Arabia v. Arabian American Oil Company (Aramco)*, Award (23 August 1958), 27 Int'l Law Reports (1963) p. 117 at p. 168). Property rights that could be expropriated may include contractual rights and the right to complete a project that is the object of a contract or agreement signed by the government with the investor or a controlled subsidiary, such as it happened in *Starrett Housing Corp.* The Iran-United States Claims Tribunal in *Starrett Housing Corporation v. The Government of the Islamic Republic of Iran* stated:

"There is nothing unique in the Claimants' position in this regard. They rely on precedents in international law in which cases measures of expropriation or taking, primarily aimed at physical property, have been deemed to comprise also rights of a contractual nature closely related to the physical property.... The Tribunal holds that the property interest taken by the Government of Iran must be deemed to comprise the physical property as well as the right to manage the Project and to complete the construction in accordance with the Basic Project Agreement and related agreements, and to deliver the apartments and collect the proceeds of the sales as provided in the Apartment Purchase Agreements."

(*Starrett Housing Corporation v. The Government of the Islamic Republic of Iran* (Case No. 24), Interlocutory Award No. 314-24-1 (19 December 1983), 4 IRAN-U.S. C.T.R. p. 122 at pp. 156-157).
11. See Christoph SCHREUER, "Fair and Equitable Treatment in Arbitral Practice", 6 The Journal of World Investment & Trade (2005) p. 357 at pp. 374-380.
12. See *Azurix Corp. v. The Argentine Republic* (ICSID Case No. ARB/01/12), Decision on Jurisdiction (8 December 2003), para. 62, at <http://ita.law.uvic.ca/documents/Azurix-Jurisdiction.pdf> (last visited 21 March 2006), where the tribunal stated that "a concession contract ... qualifies as an investment for purposes of the BIT given the wide meaning conferred upon this term in the BIT that includes 'any right conferred by law or contract'".

The well known *Aguas del Aconquija v. Argentina* case,[13] also known as the *Vivendi* case, is probably the most cited one.

In order to assess its jurisdiction, the tribunal addressed the distinction between contract and treaty claims.[14] Even though it affirmed its jurisdiction on the basis of a treaty claim, it observed that the underlying facts of the dispute were closely linked to the performance of the concession contract. In the tribunal's view, as the forum selection clause of the concession contract assigned the task of interpreting and applying that agreement to local courts, the tribunal could not determine which actions of the Province of Tucumán – a political subdivision of Argentina which was a party to the concession contract – were taken in exercise of its sovereign authority and which in the exercise of its rights as a party to the concession contract.[15] The tribunal asserted:

> "[T]he Tribunal holds that, because of the crucial connection in this case between the terms of the Concession Contract and these alleged violations of the BIT, the Argentine Republic cannot be held liable unless and until Claimants have, as Article 16.4 of the Concession Contract requires, asserted their rights in proceedings before the contentious administrative courts of Tucumán and have been denied their rights, either procedurally or substantively.
> (....)
> In this case, however, the obligation to resort to the local courts is compelled by the express terms of Article 16.4 of the private contract between Claimants and the Province of Tucumán and the impossibility, on the facts of the instant case, of separating potential breaches of contract claims from BIT violations without interpreting and applying the Concession Contract, a task that the contract assigns expressly to the local courts."[16]

Based on that reasoning, the tribunal dismissed the claim. The ad hoc Committee appointed in Vivendi's annulment proceedings adopted the opposite view. While acknowledging that a treaty cause of action may raise contractual issues, it affirmed that

---

13. *Compañía de Aguas del Aconquija, S.A. & Compagnie Générale des Eaux, v. Argentine Republic* (Case No. ARB/97/3), Award (21 November 2000), 16 ICSID Review–Foreign Investment Law Journal (2001, no. 2) p. 643 (also called *Vivendi I*); and Decision on Annulment (3 July 2002), 19 ICSID Review–Foreign Investment Law Journal (2004, no. 1) p. 89 (also known as *Vivendi II*). See also "Improving the System of Investor-State Dispute Settlement: an Overview" in *Making the Most of International Investment Agreements: a Common Agenda*, Symposium co-organized by ICSID, OECD and UNCTAD (12 December 2005) Paris, pp. 25-26.

14. *Compañía de Aguas del Aconquija, S.A. & Compagnie Générale des Eaux, v. Argentine Republic* (Case No. ARB/97/3), Award (21 November 2000), *op. cit.*, fn. 13, at para. 53 ("In this case the claims filed by CGE against Respondent are based on violation by the Argentine Republic of the BIT through acts or omissions of that government and acts of the Tucumán authorities that Claimants assert should be attributed to the central government. ... those claims are not based on the Concession Contract but allege a cause of action under the BIT").

15. *Ibid.*, para. 79.

16. *Ibid.*, paras. 78 and 81.

such fact should not undermine the tribunal's powers to apply the treaty.[17] In those cases, the tribunal remains competent to analyze the contractual disputed issues in order to rule on the treaty claims brought by the claimants. Even though a contract claim and a treaty claim may be based on similar or identical facts, they rely on fundamentally different legal bases and are assessed according to different standards.

In the ad hoc Committee's words:

> "As to the relation between breach of contract and breach of treaty in the present case, it must be stressed that Articles 3 and 5 of the BIT do not relate directly to breach of a municipal contract. Rather they set an independent standard. A state may breach a treaty without breaching a contract, and vice versa, and this is certainly true of these provisions of the BIT. The point is made clear in Article 3 of the ILC Articles, which is entitled 'Characterization of an act of a State as internationally wrongful':
>
> 'The characterization of an act of a State as internationally wrongful is governed by international law. Such characterization is not affected by the characterization of the same act as lawful by internal law.'
>
> In accordance with this general principle (which is undoubtedly declaratory of general international law), whether there has been a breach of the BIT and whether there has been a breach of contract are different questions. Each of these claims will be determined by reference to its own proper or applicable law – in the case of the BIT, by international law; in the case of the Concession Contract, by the proper law of the contract, in other words, the law of Tucumán...."[18]

Therefore, the ad hoc Committee distinguished between (i) pure contract breaches that do not amount to treaty breaches, (ii) treaty breaches that do not amount to contract breaches, and (iii) treaty breaches that entail at the same time contract breaches.[19]

---

17. *Compañía de Aguas del Aconquija S.A. and Vivendi Universal (formerly Compagnie Générale Des Eaux) v. Argentine Republic* (ICSID Case No. ARB/97/3), Decision on Annulment (3 July 2002), *op. cit.*, fn. 13, paras. 60, 101-102.

18. *Ibid.*, paras. 95-96.

19. On a similar approach, see *Salini v. Morocco*. It concerned a BIT dispute focusing on the amount payable under a construction contract. In order to determine its jurisdiction, the tribunal considered the difference between claims based on the treaty and on the contract. Even though the tribunal's finding will be matter of further analysis below, it asserted that it had "jurisdiction in relation to breaches of contract that would constitute, at the same time, a violation of the Bilateral Treaty by the State" (*Salini Costrutorri S.p.A. and Italstrade S.p.A. v. Kingdom of Morocco* (ICSID Case No. ARB/00/4), Decision on Jurisdiction (23 July 2001), para. 62, at <http://ita.law.uvic.ca/documents/Salini-English.pdf> (last visited 21 March 2006)).

As explained by Gaillard, *Vivendi* founds its rationale "… solely on the distinction between the separate causes of action based on the contract, taken in isolation, and on the treaty, even where it encapsulates in turn a violation based on the contract".[20]

The reasoning of the ad hoc Committee in *Vivendi* was followed in several ICSID decisions, such as *CMS v. Argentina*,[21] *Azurix v. Argentina*,[22] *SGS v. Pakistan*,[23] *PSEG v. Turkey*,[24] *Enron v. Argentina*,[25] *AES v. Argentina*,[26] *Impregilo v. Pakistan*,[27] *Siemens v.*

---

20. Emmanuel GAILLARD, "Vivendi and Bilateral Investment Treaty Arbitrations", 6 February 2003 N.Y.L.J. at p. 3.

21. *CMS Gas Transmission Company v. The Argentine Republic* (ICSID Case No. ARB/01/8), Decision on Jurisdiction (17 July 2003), paras. 72, 76 and 80, at <http://ita.law.uvic.ca/documents/cms-argentina_000.pdf> (last visited 21 March 2006).

22. *Azurix Corp. v. the Argentine Republic* (ICSID Case No. ARB/01/12), Decision on Jurisdiction (8 December 2003), *op. cit.*, fn. 12. When analyzing the scope of the contractually agreed dispute settlement provisions, the tribunal asserted that "The point is that the rights under the Concession Agreement and under the BIT are not the same…." (*Ibid.*, para. 81).

23. *SGS Société Générale de Surveillance S.A. v. Islamic Republic of Pakistan* (ICSID Case No. ARB/01/13), Decision on Jurisdiction (6 August 2003), at <http://ita.law.uvic.ca/documents/SGSvPakistan-decision_000.pdf> (last visited 21 March 2006). The tribunal held: "As a matter of general principle, the same set of facts can give rise to different claims grounded on differing legal orders: the municipal and the international legal orders." (*Ibid.*, para. 147).

24. *PSEG Global Inc., The North American Coal Corporation, and Konya Ilgin Elektrik Üretim ve Ticaret Limited Sirketi v. Republic of Turkey* (ICSID Case No. ARB/02/5), Decision on Jurisdiction (4 June 2004) at <http://ita.law.uvic.ca/documents/psegdecision.pdf> (last visited 21 March 2006). Pursuant to the distinction based on the different causes of action, the tribunal held that: "… contract based disputes are different from treaty based disputes and arise out of separate causes of action. Treaty based disputes can always be submitted to international arbitration from this point of view." (*Ibid.*, para. 158).

25. *Enron Corporation and Ponderosa Assets L.P. v. The Argentine Republic* (ICSID Case No. ARB/01/3), Decision on Jurisdiction (14 January 2004), para. 91, at <http://ita.law.uvic.ca/documents/Enron-Jurisdiction.pdf> (last visited 21 March 2006); *Enron Corporation and Ponderosa Assets L.P. v. The Argentine Republic* (ICSID Case No. ARB/01/3), Decision on Jurisdiction (Ancillary Claim) (2 August 2004), paras. 49 and 51, at <http://ita.law.uvic.ca/documents/Enron-DecisiononJurisdiction-FINAL-English.pdf> (last visited 21 March 2006).

26. *AES Corporation v. The Argentine Republic* (ICSID Case No. ARB/02/17), Decision on Jurisdiction (26 April 2005), at <http://ita.law.uvic.ca/documents/AES-Argentina-Jurisdiction_001.pdf.> (last visited 21 March 2006). The tribunal affirmed: "In other terms, the present Tribunal has jurisdiction over any alleged breach by Argentina of its obligations under the US-Argentina BIT. As such, it has no jurisdiction over any breach of the concession contracts binding upon the companies controlled by AES and the Argentine public authorities under administrative Argentine law, unless such breach would at the same time result in a violation by the host State of its obligations towards the US private investors under the BIT." (*Ibid.*, para. 94).

27. *Impregilo S.p.A. v. Islamic Republic of Pakistan* (ICSID Case No. ARB/03/3), Decision on Jurisdiction (22 April 2005), at <www.investmentclaims.com/decisions/Impregilo-Pakistan-Jurisdiction-22Apr2005.pdf> (last visited 21 March 2006). After quoting the *Vivendi* annulment decision, the tribunal found that "The fact that Article 9 of the BIT does not endow the Tribunal with jurisdiction to consider Impregilo's Contract Claims does not imply that the Tribunal has no jurisdiction to consider Treaty Claims against Pakistan which at the same time could constitute breaches of the Contracts." (*Ibid.*, para. 219).

Argentina,[28] Sempra v. Argentina,[29] Camuzzi v. Argentina,[30] Eureko v. Poland,[31] Aguas del Tunari v. Bolivia,[32] Bayindir v. Pakistan[33] and Suez v. Argentina,[34] among others.

In the words of the Bayindir tribunal, the principle set out by the Annulment Committee in Vivendi "is well established".[35] Following its rationale, the tribunal concluded that: "... when the investor has a right under both the contract and the treaty,

---

28. In Siemens v. Argentina, the respondent argued that "Siemens is submitting to the Tribunal a dispute related to contractual rights of a third party that does not qualify as an investor or as an investment." (Siemens A.G. v. the Argentine Republic (ICSID Case No. ARB/02/8), Decision on Jurisdiction (3 August 2004), para. 174, at <http://ita.law.uvic.ca/documents/SiemensJurisdiction-English-3August2004.pdf> (last visited 21 March 2006)). By contrast, Siemens sustained that the claim brought before the tribunal was a claim under the BIT and not under the contract (Ibid., paras. 177-178). The tribunal concluded: "The Tribunal has already found that Siemens qualifies as an investor and that the dispute arises directly from an investment for purposes of the jurisdiction of the Tribunal under the Treaty and the Convention.... Arbitral tribunals have found that a dispute arising out of a contract may give rise to a claim under a bilateral investment treaty. The dispute as formulated by the Claimant is a dispute under the Treaty." (Ibid., para. 180).

29. Sempra Energy International v. The Argentine Republic (ICSID Case No. ARB/02/16), Decision on Objections to Jurisdiction (11 May 2005), at <http://ita.law.uvic.ca/documents/semprajurisdiction.pdf> (last visited 21 March 2006). The tribunal asserted that: ".... A claim can have a purely contractual origin and refer to a right that does not qualify as an investment, in which case there will be no jurisdiction, as was the case in Joy; but it can also originate solely in the violation of a provision of the treaty independently from domestic law or, as is more frequently the case, originate in a violation of a contractual obligation that at the same time amounts to a violation of the guarantees of the treaty. In these other cases there will be no obstacle to the exercise of jurisdiction." (Ibid., para. 95).

30. Camuzzi International S.A. v. Argentine Republic (ICSID Case No. ARB/03/7), Decision on Objections to Jurisdiction (10 June 2005), paras. 61-62 at <http://ita.law.uvic.ca/documents/Camuzzi2jurisdiction.pdf> (last visited 21 March 2006).

31. Eureko B.V. v. Republic of Poland, Partial Award (19 August 2005), at <http://ita.law.uvic.ca/documents/Eureko-PartialAwardandDissentingOpinion.pdf>. The tribunal assessed: "It is clear to this tribunal that the decision of the ad hoc Committee in Vivendi, as applied to the facts of the case now before this Tribunal, authorizes, and indeed requires, this Tribunal to consider whether the acts of which Eureko complains, whether or not also breaches of the SPA and the First Addendum, constitute breaches of the Treaty." (Ibid., para. 112).

32. Aguas del Tunari S.A. v. Republic of Bolivia (ICSID Case No. ARB/02/3), Decision on Respondent's Objections to Jurisdiction (21 October 2005), at <http://ita.law.uvic.ca/documents/AguasdelTunari-jurisdiction-eng_000.pdf> (last visited 21 March 2006). The tribunal affirmed: "The circumstance that a claim under the Concession against the Water Superintendency and a claim under the BIT against Bolivia could both point to the same set of facts should not blur the legal distinction between the two types of claims. It is often the case that one set of facts may give rise to disputes under different laws in different fora." (Ibid., para. 114).

33. Bayindir Insaat Turizm Ticaret Ve Sanayi A.S. v. Islamic Republic of Pakistan (ICSID Case No. ARB/03/29), Decision on Jurisdiction (14 November 2005), para. 148, at <http://ita.law.uvic.ca/documents/Bayindr-jurisdiction.pdf> (last visited 21 March 2006).

34. Suez, Sociedad de Aguas de Barcelona S.A., and InterAguas Servicios Integrales del Agua S.A. v. The Argentine Republic (ICSID Case No. ARB/03/17), Decision on Jurisdiction (16 May 2006), <http://ita.law.uvic.ca/documents/Suez-Jurisdiction.pdf> (last visited 12 June 2006), para. 43.

35. Ibid.

499

it has a self-standing right to pursue the remedy accorded by the treaty. The very fact that the amount claimed under the treaty is the same as the amount that could be claimed (or was claimed) under the contract does not affect such self-standing right".[36]

This "well established" principle was in theory reaffirmed in SGS v. Philippines.[37] The dispute dealt with the payment of outstanding invoices under a comprehensive import supervision service agreement. The tribunal held that it had jurisdiction over SGS's claims for violation of the fair and equitable treatment standard and the umbrella clause, despite the fact that no question of a treaty breach independent of a contract breach had been raised.[38]

However, in a split decision,[39] the tribunal ordered the stay of the proceedings until the contractually agreed forum determined the amount due under the agreement.[40] In the tribunal's words, "being an unresolved dispute as to the amount payable [under the contract], for the Tribunal to decide on the claim in isolation from a decision by the chosen forum under the CISS Agreement is inappropriate and premature".[41]

The tribunal's decision slightly differed from the approach undertaken in the Vivendi I.[42] It has raised some concern based on its resemblance with such decision and the practical difficulties that it poses in order to differentiate its rationale from the requirement to exhaust local remedies.[43]

To date, the approach taken in SGS v. Philippines has not been followed by other arbitral panels. Further, both the Impregilo and Bayindir tribunals explicitly refused to follow the conclusion handed down in that case and denied the stay of proceedings until the contractually agreed dispute settlement forums had determined the contractual issues at stake.[44]

---

36. Ibid., para. 167.
37. SGS Société Générale de Surveillance S.A. v. Republic of the Philippines (ICSID Case No. ARB/02/6), Decision on Jurisdiction (29 January 2004), op. cit., fn. 7. We will not deal with this case in depth since it is closely related to the issue of contractually agreed forum clauses, which will be addressed in another Report.
38. Ibid., para. 177(a).
39. With the dissent of Professor Crivellaro.
40. SGS Société Générale de Surveillance S.A. v. Republic of the Philippines (ICSID Case No. ARB/02/6), Decision on Jurisdiction (29 January 2004), op. cit., fn. 7, para. 177(c).
41. Ibid., para. 162. The tribunal asserted that: "Thus the question is not whether the Tribunal has jurisdiction: unless otherwise expressly provided, treaty jurisdiction is not abrogated by contract. The question is whether a party should be allowed to rely on a contract as the basis of its claim when the contract itself refers that claim exclusively to another forum." (Ibid., para. 154).
42. The SGS tribunal did not reject claimant's claims, but stayed proceedings until domestic courts established the content of the contractual obligations.
43. See Christoph SCHREUER, "Calvo's Grandchildren: The Return of Local Remedies in Investment Arbitration", 4 The Law and Practice of International Courts and Tribunals (2005) p. 1 at p. 11.
44. Impregilo S.p.A. v. Republic of Pakistan (ICSID Case No. ARB/03/3), Decision on Jurisdiction (22 Apri 2005), op. cit., fn. 27, paras. 289-290 ("The Tribunal considers that, whilst arguably justified in some situations, a stay of proceedings would be inappropriate here, for a number of reasons. Firstly, such a stay, if anything, would confuse the essential distinction between the Treaty Claims and the Contract Claims as set out above. Since the two enquiries are fundamentally different (albeit with some overlap), it is not obvious that the contractual dispute resolution mechanisms

Despite decisions such as *Vivendi I* and *SGS v. Philippines*, the general trend in BIT arbitration seems to be that tribunals have jurisdiction over all treaty claims, including those that involve questions related closely or even exclusively to a contract.

Nonetheless, the relatively independent nature of contract claims and treaty claims raises questions not yet settled. Tribunals have not provided an uncontested answer as to how they should determine their own jurisdiction when the respondent challenges the nature of the claimant's claim; under what particular circumstances tribunals may have jurisdiction even on pure contract claims and where to draw the line between a "mere" contract breach and a treaty breach. We will address these issues in turn.

III. THE FINDING OF A TREATY CLAIM AT THE JURISDICTIONAL STAGE

In most investment disputes involving contracts, respondents raise the argument that, on their face, claims have no basis in the treaty, but merely find a cause of action under the underlying contract. Based on such approach, they challenge the tribunal's jurisdiction and request the arbitral panel to declare that it has no jurisdiction to entertain the claim. This is of one of the most frequently debated issues during the jurisdictional phase.[45]

---

in a case of this sort will be undermined in any substantial sense by the determination of separate and distinct Treaty Claims. Indeed, this is all the more so in a case such as the present, where (unlike *SGS v. Philippines*) the parties to these proceedings (Impregilo and Pakistan) are different from the parties to the contract arbitration proceedings (GBC and WAPDA). Further, if a stay was ordered, as Pakistan has sought, it is unclear for how long this should be maintained; what precise events might trigger its cessation; and what attitude this Tribunal ought then to take on a resumed hearing to any proceedings or findings that may have occurred in the interim in Lahore.") (*Ibid*, paras. 289-290). *Bayindir Insaat Turizm Ticaret Ve Sanayi A.S. v. Islamic Republic of Pakistan* (ICSID Case No. ARB/03/29), Decision on Jurisdiction (14 November 2005), *op. cit.*, fn. 33, paras. 264-273 ("In the Tribunal's view its jurisdiction under the BIT allows it – if this should prove necessary – to resolve any underlying contract issue as a preliminary question. Exactly like the arbitral tribunal sitting in Pakistan, this Tribunal should proceed with the merits of the case. This is an inevitable consequence of the principle of the distinct nature of treaty and contract claims. The Tribunal is aware that this system implies an intrinsic risk of contradictory decisions or double recovery. In this respect, in *Camuzzi v. Argentina* – a case where it was explicitly held that 'the claim was [...] founded on both the contract and the Treaty' – the tribunal noted that 'this is an issue belonging to the merits of the dispute' and for which 'international law and decisions offer numerous mechanisms for preventing the possibility of double recovery'.") (*Ibid.*, para. 270).

45. As noted above, several related discussions on jurisdiction stem from this core argument, such as the relevance of any contractual forum-selection clause, the eventual triggering of fork in the road clauses, etc. In fact, respondents frequently contend that whenever a forum-selection clause agreed by the parties to the contract requires any dispute to be submitted to local courts, the claimant is not entitled to bring claims to any court or tribunal other than that agreed in that instrument. Something similar happens with the fork in the road issue when the claimant has previously filed a breach of contract claim before local courts. Almost automatically, respondents will object to the arbitral tribunal's jurisdiction by arguing that having submitted the dispute before local courts, it could not be filed later on before an arbitral tribunal.

The predominant view is that the tribunal is not empowered to determine during the jurisdictional phase whether there has been indeed a violation of the treaty and not a mere contractual breach. That task belongs to the merits stage.

At the time of deciding this type of issue, the tribunal is called to address objections to jurisdiction which are closely related to the merits of the case, without engaging in prejudgment. On the other hand, general assertions such as that the claim is a treaty claim rather than a contractual one, without a full discussion on the merits of the case, can only be admitted on a provisional basis.

To confront this type of situation, case law has developed a useful test by requesting tribunals to conduct a preliminary analysis of the treaty obligations invoked by the claimant and assess whether the facts alleged by it are prima facie capable of constituting a violation of such obligations.[46]

Simply put, and for purposes of jurisdiction, the tribunal must accept the facts invoked by the claimant as if they were correct and determine on that basis whether, if proven true, they could amount to a breach of the treaty. Thus, for purposes of jurisdiction, the characterization of the dispute as arising from a contract or from the treaty depends strongly on how the claims have been put forward by the claimant.

Initially developed by the International Court of Justice (ICJ), this standard was later adopted in investment treaty arbitrations.[47] Even though it did not involve a BIT, the decision rendered in *Amco v. Indonesia*[48] constitutes a clear example of application of the prima facie test in an ICSID arbitration.

The respondent objected to ICSID jurisdiction on the basis that the claim entailed a lease dispute between two private parties. In contrast, claimants argued that, in fact, the Indonesian Government had deprived them of their investment in an armed military action. The tribunal applied the prima facie test and denied Indonesia's defense in the following words:

> "The Tribunal is of the view that in order for it to make a judgment at this time as to the substantial nature of the dispute before it, it must look firstly and only at the claim itself as presented to ICSID and the Tribunal in the Claimant's Request for Arbitration. If on its face (that is, if there is no manifest or obvious misdescription or error in the characterization of the dispute by the Claimants) the claim is one 'arising directly out of an investment', then this Tribunal would have jurisdiction to hear such claims. In other words, the Tribunal must not attempt at this stage to examine the claim itself in any detail, but the Tribunal must only be satisfied that prima facie the claim, as stated by the Claimants when

---

46. As explained by Professor Schreuer, the practice on this point is not uniform. While some scholars believe that the claim's characterization must be undertaken by reference to the claimant's pleadings, others maintain that the tribunal should look behind the claim to determine whether it is plausible. See SCHREUER, "Investment Treaty Arbitration and Jurisdiction over Contract Claims – the *Vivendi I* Case Considered", *op. cit.*, fn. 2.

47. See *Impregilo S.p.A. v. Republic of Pakistan* (ICSID Case No. ARB/03/3), Decision on Jurisdiction (22 April 2005), *op. cit.*, fn. 27, paras. 238-240.

48. *Amco Asia Corporation and Others v. the Republic of Indonesia* (ICSID Case No. ARB/81/1), Decision on Jurisdiction (25 September 1983), 1 ICSID Reports, p. 389.

initiating this arbitration, is within the jurisdictional mandate of ICSID arbitration, and consequently of this Tribunal."[49]

Several decisions followed a similar trend in order to rule on jurisdiction. *Wena Hotels v. Egypt*,[50] *Maffezini v. Spain*,[51] *Vivendi v. Argentina*,[52] *Salini v. Morocco*,[53] *Methanex v. United States*,[54] *UPS v. Canada*,[55] *CMS v. Argentina*,[56] *SGS v. Pakistan*,[57] *Azurix v. Argentina*,[58] *SGS*

---

49. *Ibid.*, p. 405.

50. *Wena Hotels Limited v. Arab Republic of Egypt* (ICSID Case No. ARB/98/4), Decision on Jurisdiction (25 May 1999), 41 ILM (2002) p. 881 at p. 890.

51. *Emilio Agustín Maffezini v. Kingdom of Spain* (ICSID Case No. ARB/97/7), Decision of the Tribunal on Objections to Jurisdiction (25 January 2000), 16 ICSID Review–Foreign Investment Law Journal (2001) p. 212. The tribunal applied the prima facie test to rule on the claimant's standing and asserted that "at this stage of the proceedings, however, it is enough for him to demonstrate that, if true, his allegations would give him standing to bring this case in his personal capacity" (*Ibid.*, para. 69).

52. *Compañía de Aguas del Aconquija, S.A. & Compagnie Générale des Eaux, v. Argentine Republic* (Case No. ARB/97/3), Award (21 November 2000), *op. cit.*, fn. 13. The tribunal applied the prima facie test as evidenced by the phrase "as formulated": "…. In this case the claims filed by CGE against Respondent are based on violations by the Argentine Republic of the BIT through acts or omissions of that government and acts of the Tucumán authorities that Claimants assert should be attributed to the central government. As formulated, these claims against the Argentine Republic are not subject to the jurisdiction of the contentious administrative tribunals of Tucumán, if only because, ex hypothesi, those claims are not based on the Concession Contract but allege a cause of action under the BIT." (*Ibid.*, para. 53). The ad hoc Committee confirmed the tribunal's approach on this point (*Compañía de Aguas del Aconquija, S.A. & Compagnie Générale des Eaux v. Argentine Republic* (ICSID Case No. ARB/97/3), Decision on Annulment (3 July 2002), *op. cit.*, fn. 13, para. 74).

53. *Salini Costruttori S.p.A. and Italstrade S.p.A. v. Kingdom of Morocco* (ICSID Case No. ARB/00/4), Decision on Jurisdiction (23 July 2001), *op. cit.*, fn. 19. The tribunal held that "The Italian companies have expressly specified in their Request for Arbitration that 'the claims submitted to the present arbitration […] also include claims addressed directly to the Government of Morocco and which relate to the infringement of the Contractor's rights as a foreign investor according to the international regulation of foreign investments (the so-called "treaty claims")' …. The Tribunal declares that it has jurisdiction over the Italian companies' claims, as they are formulated…." (*Ibid.*, paras. 62 and 64).

54. *Methanex Corp. v. United States of America* (UNCITRAL case), Preliminary Award on Jurisdiction and Admissibility (7 August 2002), at <www.investmentclaims.com/decisions/Methanex-US-1stPartialAward-7Aug2002.pdf> (last visited 7 March 2006). The tribunal referred to the ICJ's *Oil Platforms* case in which in order to decide its jurisdiction to hear the case, the ICJ "… interpreted each treaty provision as to which breach was alleged by the claimant (Iran), so as to establish whether the facts alleged by Iran were capable of leading to a breach of the provision: '… the Parties differ on the question whether the dispute between the two States with respect to the lawfulness of the actions carried out by the United States against the Iranian oil platforms is a dispute "as to the interpretation or application" of the Treaty of 1955. In order to answer that question, the Court cannot limit itself to noting that one of the Parties maintains that such a dispute exists, and the other denies it. It must ascertain whether the violations of the Treaty of 1955 pleaded by Iran do or do not fall within the provisions of the Treaty and whether, as a consequence, the dispute is one which the Court has jurisdiction ratione materiae to entertain, pursuant to Article XXI, paragraph 2.' (ICJ Reports 1996 (II), p. 810, paragraph 16). In her separate opinion, Judge Higgins explains the reasoning behind the ICJ's approach: 'The only way

503

v. Philippines,[59] *Saluka v. The Czech Republic,*[60] *Siemens v. Argentina,*[61] *Salini v. Jordan,*[62]

in which, in the present case, it can be determined whether the claims of Iran are sufficiently plausibly based upon the 1955 Treaty is to accept pro tem the facts as alleged by Iran to be true and in that light to interpret Articles I, IV and X for jurisdictional purposes, that is to say, to see if on the basis of Iran's claims of fact there could occur a violation of one or more of them.'" (*Ibid.,* paras. 117-118).

55. *United Parcel Service of America Inc. v. Government of Canada* (UNCITRAL case), Award on Jurisdiction (22 November 2002), at <http://naftaclaims.com/Disputes/Canada/UPS/UPSAwardOnJurisdiction.pdf> (last visited 7 March 2006). The tribunal described the prima facie test as the one in which "the Tribunal must conduct a prima facie analysis of the NAFTA obligations, which UPS seeks to invoke, and determine whether the facts alleged are capable of constituting a violation of these obligations" (*Ibid.,* para. 33).

56. *CMS Gas Transmission Company v. The Argentine Republic* (ICSID Case No. ARB/01/8), Decision on Jurisdiction (17 July 2003), *op. cit.,* fn. 21, paras. 35, 69, 109.

57. *SGS Société Générale de Surveillance S.A. v. Islamic Republic of Pakistan* (ICSID Case No. ARB/01/13), Decision on Jurisdiction (6 August 2003), *op. cit.,* fn. 23. The tribunal asserted: "At this stage of the proceedings, the Tribunal has, as a practical matter, a limited ability to scrutinize the claims as formulated by the Claimant. Some cases suggest that the Tribunal need not uncritically accept those claims at face value, but we consider that if the facts asserted by the Claimant are capable of being regarded as alleged breaches of the BIT, consistently with the practice of ICSID tribunals, the Claimant should be able to have them considered on their merits. We conclude that, at this jurisdiction phase, it is for the Claimant to characterize the claims as it sees fit. We do not exclude the possibility that there may arise a situation where a tribunal may find it necessary at the very beginning to look behind the claimant's factual claims, but this is not such a case." (*Ibid.,* para. 145).

58. *Azurix v. Argentine Republic* (ICSID Case No. ARB/01/12), Decision on Jurisdiction (8 December 2003), *op. cit.,* fn. 12. The tribunal held that "... for purposes of determining its jurisdiction, the Tribunal should consider whether the dispute, as it has been presented by the Claimant, is prima facie a dispute arising under the BIT. The investment dispute which the Claimant has put before this Tribunal invokes obligations owed by the Respondent to Claimant under the BIT and it is based on a different cause of action from a claim under the Contract Documents. Even if the dispute as presented by the Claimant may involve the interpretation or analysis of facts related to performance under the Concession Agreement, the Tribunal considers that, to the extent that such issues are relevant to a breach of the obligations of the Respondent under the BIT, they cannot per se transform the dispute under the BIT into a contractual dispute." (*Ibid.,* para. 76).

59. *SGS Société Générale de Surveillance S.A. v. Republic of the Philippines* (ICSID Case No. ARB/02/6), Decision on Jurisdiction (29 January 2004), *op. cit.,* fn. 7. The tribunal asserted: "The test for jurisdiction is an objective one and its resolution may require the definitive interpretation of the treaty provision which is relied on. On the other hand, as the Tribunal in *SGS v. Pakistan* stressed, it is for the Claimant to formulate its case. Provided the facts as alleged by the Claimant and as appearing from the initial pleadings fairly raise questions of breach of one or more provisions of the BIT, the Tribunal has jurisdiction to determine the claim." (*Ibid.,* para. 157).

60. *Saluka Investments B. V. v. The Czech Republic* (UNCITRAL case), Decision on Jurisdiction (7 May 2004), at <http://ita.law.uvic.ca/documents/Saluka-DecisiononJurisdiction-counterclaim.pdf> (last visited 7 March 2006). After quoting the relevant statement of *Amco v. Indonesia,* the tribunal – dealing with jurisdictional objections raised by the claimant in connection with a counter-claim submitted by the respondent – held: "In the context of the present arbitration the Tribunal is thus required to have regard to the counterclaim as formally presented in the relevant paragraphs of the Respondent's Counter-Memorial, and to be satisfied prima facie that the counterclaim as so presented is within the Tribunal's jurisdiction under the Treaty. Where particular matters are

Impregilo v. Pakistan,[63] *El Paso v. Argentina,*[64] among other cases, have effectively applied this standard in order to decide on the nature of the dispute.

The way this standard has been applied varies from case to case, since tribunals do not construe it in an identical way. While in some cases the tribunal's jurisdiction appears crystal clear, others require a deeper analysis so as to ascertain whether jurisdiction can be affirmed. Thus, the degree of scrutiny of the claims is not uniform.

For instance, in *SGS v. Pakistan*, the tribunal described the standard as one in which the tribunal at the jurisdictional phase should accept the characterization of the claim as the claimant sees fit. However, after noting that "if the facts asserted by the Claimant are capable of being regarded as alleged breaches of the BIT, the Claimant should be able

---

disputed, the Tribunal must for purposes of determining its jurisdiction look at them objectively, in their terms as pleaded, and consider whether there is at least a reasonable possibility that they could be determined, after subsequent proceedings on the merits, in the Respondent's favour." (*Ibid.*, para. 36).

61. *Siemens A.G. v. the Argentine Republic* (ICSID Case No. ARB/02/8), Decision on Jurisdiction (3 August 2004), *op. cit.*, fn. 28, para. 174.

62. *Salini Costruttori S.p.A. and Italstrade S.p.A. v. The Hashemite Kingdom of Jordan* (ICSID Case No. ARB/02/13), Decision on Jurisdiction (29 November 2004), 20 ICSID Review–Foreign Investment Law Journal (2005, no. 1) p. 148. The arbitration panel stated that "... the Claimants are free to present facts they rely upon and claims they advance in the way they think appropriate. It is up to the Claimants to characterize these claims as they see fit, and, in particular, to identify the contractual and/or Treaty provisions, which, according to them, have been violated. When considering its jurisdiction to entertain those claims, the Tribunal must not address the merits of the claims, but it must satisfy itself that it has jurisdiction over the dispute, as presented.... [T]he Tribunal will accordingly seek to determine whether the facts alleged by the Claimants in this case, if established, are capable of coming within those provisions of the BIT which have been invoked." (*Ibid.*, paras. 136-137, 151; see also, in general, paras. 136-151).

63. *Impregilo S.p.A. v. Islamic Republic of Pakistan* (ICSID Case No. ARB/03/3), Decision on Jurisdiction (22 April 2005), *op. cit.*, fn. 27, paras. 237-254. The tribunal held: "When considering its jurisdiction to entertain the Treaty Claims, the Tribunal considers that it must not make findings on the merits of those claims, which have yet to be argued, but rather must satisfy itself that it has jurisdiction over the dispute, as presented by the Claimant." (para. 237). After referring to the existing case law on the matter, it concluded: "The present Tribunal is in full agreement with the approach evident in this jurisprudence. It reflects two complementary concerns: to ensure that courts and tribunals are not flooded with claims which have no chance of success, or may even be of an abusive nature; and equally to ensure that, in considering issues of jurisdiction, courts and tribunals do not go into the merits of cases without sufficient prior debate. In conformity with this jurisprudence, the Tribunal has considered whether the facts as alleged by the Claimant in this case, if established, are capable of coming within those provisions of the BIT which have been invoked." (*Ibid.*, para. 254).

64. *El Paso Energy International Company v. The Argentine Republic* (ICSID Case No. ARB/03/15), Decision on Jurisdiction (27 April 2006), at <www.iisd.org/pdf/2006/itn_elpaso_decision.pdf> <www.worldbank.org/icsid/cases/ARB0315-DOJ-E.pdf> (last visited 12 June 2006). The Tribunal expressed that: "... as long as they are not frivolous or abusive the claims made in the present case must be taken as they are by the Tribunal whose only task it is, in the jurisdictional phase of the proceedings, to determine if those claims, as formulated, fit into the jurisdictional frame drawn by the relevant treaty instrument or instruments...." (*Ibid.*, para. 45).

to have them considered on their merits",[65] it did not discard situations in which "the tribunal may find it necessary at the very beginning to look behind the claimant's factual claims".[66]

Slightly different, in *SGS v. Philippines*, the tribunal put forward the standard in a narrower way by asserting that "... it is not enough for the Claimant to assert the existence of a dispute as to fair treatment or expropriation"[67] and later expressed that the jurisdictional test of objective nature "... may require the definitive interpretation of the treaty provision which is relied on".[68]

The *SGS v. Philippines* decision slightly departed from the prima facie test by asserting that the tribunal may *definitively* interpret the treaty provisions. This seems to be an unusual construction of the test as such interpretation seems to be proper only for the merits of the case. As it has been generally understood, the prima facie test just allows during the jurisdictional phase to discard absurd claims, those in which the facts asserted by the claimant fall manifestly outside the provisions invoked.

However, even asserting different approaches, investment arbitration panels have generally abided by the principle that, absent an obvious misdescription of the case, tribunals should consider the facts as alleged by the claimant and determine whether, if proven, they are prima facie capable of falling within the BIT provisions invoked.

In carrying out these tasks, tribunals should act with particular care. The jurisdictional phase should not be turned into a merits stage, thus preventing claimant from fully presenting and arguing its case. Due process is at stake and arbitration panels should be extremely cautious when denying jurisdiction based on the alleged lack of a treaty claim. On the other hand, they should exclude obviously nonsensical cases in order to preclude pointless claims from moving further and preventing parties and arbitrators from incurring unnecessary costs and wasting time and resources. Nonetheless, if any serious doubt arises on the plausibility of claimant's claim, tribunals should affirm their jurisdiction. The merits stage and not the jurisdictional one is the appropriate phase to assess the facts of the case and the scope of the treaty provisions, and to determine whether a breach of the treaty has taken place.

---

65. *SGS Société Générale de Surveillance S.A. v. Islamic Republic of Pakistan* (ICSID Case No. ARB/01/13), Decision on Jurisdiction (6 August 2003), *op. cit.*, fn. 23, para. 145.

66. *Ibid.*

67. *SGS Société Générale de Surveillance S.A. v. Republic of the Philippines* (ICSID Case No. ARB/02/6), Decision on Jurisdiction (29 January 2004), *op. cit.*, fn. 7, para. 157.

68. *Ibid.*

While recent decisions as *Bayindir v. Pakistan*[69] ratify the importance that most arbitral tribunals give to the prima facie test, others such as the one rendered in *Joy Mining v. Egypt*[70] evidence that such test could be subject to exceptions.

The dispute arose out of a contract for the provision of specific equipment to be applied to phosphate mining activity, executed between Joy Mining, a British company, and the General Organization for Industrial and Mining Projects of the Arab Republic of Egypt (IMC). Letters of guarantee were supplied by Joy Mining for each of the contract's stages. During execution, certain disagreements appeared regarding technical aspects related to the commissioning and performance tests of the equipment. Even though Joy Mining was paid the full purchase price of the equipment pursuant to the contract provisions, the guarantees were not released by IMC, who argued that they had to remain in place until the equipment commissioning and testing was satisfactorily carried out.

Joy Mining instituted ICSID proceedings under the United Kingdom-Egypt BIT, claiming that the contract was an investment protected by the treaty and that the decisions by IMC and Egypt of not releasing those guarantees were in violation of it.

The tribunal acknowledged that the prima facie test was a useful rule for jurisdictional decisions. Nonetheless, the panel held that it should yield to the specific circumstances of each case. The tribunal found that in cases where the parties have substantial divergent views about the meaning of the dispute in the light of a contract and the treaty, it would not be appropriate for it to rely only on the assumption that the contentions presented by the claimant are correct. In such cases, the views expressed

---

69. *Bayindir Insaat Turizm Ticaret Ve Sanayi A.S. v. Islamic Republic of Pakistan* (ICSID Case No. ARB/03/29), Decision on Jurisdiction (14 November 2005), *op. cit.*, fn. 33, paras. 195-197 ("The Tribunal notes that the approach has been followed by several international arbitration tribunals deciding jurisdictional objections by a respondent state against a claimant investor, including *Methanex v. USA*, *SGS v. Philippines*, *Salini v. Jordan*, *Siemens v. Argentina* and *Plama v. Bulgaria*. In the last of these cases, the tribunal held that 'if on the facts alleged by the Claimant, the Respondent's actions might violate the [BIT], then the Tribunal has jurisdiction to determine exactly what the facts are and see whether they do sustain a violation of that Treaty'. Likewise, the tribunal in *Impregilo* considered that 'it must not make findings on the merits of those claims, which have yet to be argued, but rather must satisfy itself that it has jurisdiction over the dispute, as presented by the Claimant'. The Tribunal is in agreement with this approach, which strikes a helpful balance between the need 'to ensure that courts and tribunals are not flooded with claims which have no chance of success or may even be of an abusive nature' on the one side, and the necessity 'to ensure that, in considering issues of jurisdiction, courts and tribunals do not go into the merits of cases without sufficient prior debate' on the other. Accordingly, the Tribunal's first task is to determine the meaning and scope of the provisions which Bayindir invokes as conferring jurisdiction and to assess whether the facts alleged by Bayindir fall within those provisions or are capable, if proved, of constituting breaches of the obligations they refer to. In performing this task, the Tribunal will apply a *prima facie* standard, both to the determination of the meaning and scope of the BIT provisions and to the assessment whether the facts alleged may constitute breaches. If the result is affirmative, jurisdiction will be established, but the existence of breaches will remain to be litigated on the merits.")

70. *Joy Mining Machinery Limited v. Arab Republic of Egypt* (ICSID Case No. ARB/03/11), Award on Jurisdiction (6 August 2004), at <www.investmentclaims.com/decisions/JoyMining-Egypt-Jurisdiction-30Jul2004.pdf> (last visited 21 March 2006).

by the respondent should be weighed so as to reach a decision on jurisdiction.[71] Following that criterion, the tribunal concluded that the lack of release of the guarantee could not be considered a treaty violation.[72]

The *Joy Mining* case never reached the merits phase. The claim was dismissed without the claimant even submitting its Memorial on the Merits prior to the jurisdictional objections filed by Egypt.

Some criticism has been raised on whether the *Joy Mining* tribunal went too far and determined the pure contractual nature of the dispute and the absence of a treaty breach at a premature phase of the arbitration.[73]

From a different perspective, it could be argued that in *Joy Mining* the prima facie test was not totally overlooked, but applied to a certain extent since the tribunal asserted that "not even the prima facie test would be met"[74] in the case at hand. It could be sustained that the arbitral panel found an obvious misdescription or error in the characterization of the dispute by the claimant, an exception already noted in *Amco v. Indonesia*.[75]

A question that could still be raised is whether the tribunal may uncover the gross mischaracterization of the claim through the contentions made by the respondent or, in order to turn down the case, such misdescription must appear so patent that there should be no need to examine the respondent's views.[76]

---

71. *Ibid.*, para. 30. The same reasoning had been put forward in *PSEG Global Inc., The North American Coal Corporation, and Konya Ilgin Elektrik Üretim ve Ticaret Limited Sirketi v. Republic of Turkey* ((ICSID Case No. ARB/02/5), Decision on Jurisdiction (4 June 2004), *op. cit.*, fn. 24, paras. 64-65), but with no major practical effect in the decision reached.

72. *Joy Mining Machinery Limited v. Arab Republic of Egypt* (ICSID Case No. ARB/03/11), Award on Jurisdiction (6 August 2004), *op. cit.*, fn. 70, para. 78 ("... a bank guarantee is clearly a commercial element of the Contract. The Claimant's arguments to the effect that the non-release of the guarantee constitutes a violation of the Treaty are difficult to accept. In fact, the argument is not sustainable that a nationalization has taken place or that measures equivalent to an expropriation have been adopted by the Egyptian Government. Not only is there no taking of property involved in this matter, either directly or indirectly, but the guarantee is to be released as soon as the disputed performance under the Contract is settled. It is hardly possible to expropriate a contingent liability. Although normally a specific finding to this effect would pertain to the merits, in this case not even the prima facie test would be met. The same holds true in respect of the argument concerning the free transfer of funds and fair and equitable treatment and full protection and security.")

73. See SCHREUER, "Investment Treaty Arbitration and Jurisdiction over Contract Claims – the *Vivendi I* Case Considered", *op. cit.*, fn. 2, p. 319.

74. *Joy Mining Machinery Limited v. Arab Republic of Egypt* (ICSID Case No. ARB/03/11), Award on Jurisdiction (6 August 2004), *op. cit.*, fn. 70, para. 78.

75. *Amco Asia Corporation and Others v. the Republic of Indonesia* (ICSID Case No. ARB/81/1), Decision on Jurisdiction (25 September 1983), *op. cit.*, fn. 48, p. 405.

76. Those who support the latter view would state that if manifest, the mischaracterization of the claim must appear on its face to the tribunal and there would be no need to investigate further. By contrast, if one should look into the respondent's contentions, the issue would lack any manifest character and, since at the jurisdictional phase the tribunal is unable to assess the facts and the content of rights under dispute, there is no other way than to prima facie rely – for jurisdictional purposes only – on the characterization made by the claimant.

In general, the prima facie test has been considered a valuable tool in order to address this type of question. Claimant should be provided with enough opportunity to present its case and justify its treaty claims. If after doing so, the absence of a treaty claim leaves no doubt, the tribunal should declare its lack of jurisdiction at a preliminary phase providing well-grounded reasons to support the claim's dismissal at that early stage.[77]

Further discussions concerning how far international tribunals should enter into merits issues at preliminary stages will probably be triggered by the recent amendments to the ICSID Arbitration Rules, which entered into force as from 10 April 2006.

Under the old rules, there were two stages at which claims could be summarily dismissed prior to the merits phase.[78]

As a first threshold, every request for arbitration is required to go through the screening performed by ICSID in order to be registered. This screening power is of limited nature and should be primarily conducted based on the information provided by the claimant in its request. The analysis carried out by ICSID is extremely preliminary and registration shall be denied only when the dispute manifestly falls outside ICSID jurisdiction.[79]

The Secretary General's decision to register a request for arbitration and, thus, to institute the proceedings, does not bind the tribunal. The ICSID Convention reaffirms the *Kompetenz-Kompetenz* principle[80] by asserting that the tribunal is the judge of its own competence and, consequently, the respondent remains free to file objections to the panel's jurisdiction.[81] This generally takes place at the jurisdictional stage of the

---

77. SCHREUER, "Investment Treaty Arbitration and Jurisdiction over Contract Claims – the *Vivendi I* Case Considered", *op. cit.*, fn. 2, pp. 322-323.

78. This description is merely illustrative based on how arbitration proceedings develop in practice, since from a strict legal standpoint ICSID tribunals are empowered to consider on their own initiative "... at any stage of the proceeding, whether the dispute or any ancillary claim before it is within the jurisdiction of the Centre and within its own competence" (Rule 41(2) of ICSID Arbitration Rules).

79. According to Art. 36(3) of the ICSID Convention, "The Secretary-General shall register the request unless he finds, on the basis of the information contained in the request, that the dispute is manifestly outside the jurisdiction of the Centre. He shall forthwith notify the parties of registration or refusal to register." In this path, Rule 6(1) of ICSID Institution Rules provides: "The Secretary-General shall, subject to Rule 5(1)(b), as soon as possible, either: ... (b) if he finds, on the basis of the information contained in the request, that the dispute is manifestly outside the jurisdiction of the Centre, notify the parties of his refusal to register the request and of the reasons therefor."

80. See Emmanuel GAILLARD and John SAVAGE, *Fouchard, Gaillard, Goldman on International Commercial Arbitration* (Kluwer Law International 1999) pp. 394-401; Alan REDFERN and Martin HUNTER, *Law and Practice of International Commercial Arbitration*, 3rd edn. (Sweet & Maxwell 1999) pp. 264-267; Mauro RUBINO-SAMMARTANO, *International Arbitration. Law and Practice*, 2nd edn. (Kluwer Law International 2001) pp. 584-586.

81. ICSID Convention, Art. 41(1) and (2). As explained by Professor Schreuer, "a decision by the Secretary-General to register a request for arbitration does not in any way bind the tribunal in its determination of its own competence or the Centre's jurisdiction in accordance with Art. 41. A respondent remains free to raise jurisdictional objections and a tribunal remains free to decline jurisdiction even if the Secretary-General has found that the dispute is not manifestly outside the Centre's jurisdiction." (Christoph SCHREUER, *The ICSID Convention: A Commentary* (Cambridge

proceedings, where most tribunals apply the prima facie test described above in order to assess their jurisdiction.

The recent amendments to the ICSID Arbitration Rules seem to have introduced a new intermediate stage, at which a party may request the dismissal of a claim by alleging that it is manifestly without legal merit. Arbitration Rule 41(5) now reads:

> "Unless the parties have agreed to another expedited procedure for making preliminary objections, a party may, no later than 30 days after the constitution of the Tribunal, and in any event before the first session of the Tribunal, file an objection that a claim is manifestly without legal merit. The party shall specify as precisely as possible the basis for the objection. The Tribunal, after giving the parties the opportunity to present their observations on the objection, shall, at its first session or promptly thereafter, notify the parties of its decision on the objection. The decision of the Tribunal shall be without prejudice to the right of a party to file an objection pursuant to paragraph (1) or to object, in the course of the proceeding, that a claim lacks legal merit."

The reasons behind this amendment are explained by the Discussion Paper on Possible Improvements of the Legal Framework for ICSID Arbitration and the Working Paper on Suggested Changes to the ICSID Rules and Regulations, issued by the ICSID Secretariat in October 2004 and May 2005 respectively. ICSID practice revealed that the Secretary-General screening power "… does not extend to the merits of the dispute or to cases where jurisdiction is merely doubtful but not manifestly lacking".[82] Therefore, in order to address concerns towards the limited scope of such screening power, it was considered useful to introduce a special procedure under which tribunals could dismiss all or part of the claim on an expedited basis at an early stage and without prejudice to the objections that the respondent may further raise in case its request was rejected.[83]

It is an open question how ICSID tribunals will apply this new provision. They are explicitly empowered to examine at this new preliminary stage whether a claim

---

University Press 2001) Art. 36, para. 59).

82. ICSID Secretariat, "Possible Improvements of the Framework for ICSID Arbitration" (Discussion Paper, 22 October 2004), para. 9, at <www.worldbank.org/icsid/highlights/improve-arb.pdf> (last visited 21 March 2006).

83. The Discussion Paper stated: "It might in this context be useful to make clear in the ICSID and Additional Facility Arbitration Rules, by provisions establishing a special procedure for the purpose, that the tribunal may at an early stage of the case be asked on an expedited basis to dismiss all or part of the claim. Such provisions could specify that a request for such a dismissal would be without prejudice to the further objections a party might make, if the request were denied. The provisions would be helpful in reassuring parties that consider the screening power of the Secretary-General to be too limited, especially insofar as it does not extend to the merits of the dispute. The provisions could be introduced by amending ICSID Arbitration Rule 41 and Article 45 of the Additional Facility Arbitration Rules, which deal with preliminary objections to jurisdiction." (*Ibid.*, para. 10). See also ICSID Secretariat, "Suggested Changes to the ICSID Rules and Regulations" (Working Paper, 12 May 2005), pp. 8-9, at <www.worldbank.org/icsid/highlights/052405-sgmanual.pdf> (last visited 21 March 2006).

manifestly lacks legal merit. Will they employ the prima facie test or another one at this early stage? Will tribunals change their analysis at the jurisdictional stage or keep on applying the prima facie test?

IV. THE WORDING OF TREATIES' DISPUTE SETTLEMENT CLAUSES AND THEIR IMPACT ON THE TRIBUNAL'S JURISDICTION

Tribunals have in general established that disputes should be decided under the specific treaty provisions governing the case. Therefore, looking into the particular wording of the treaty under which the claimant has instituted the arbitral proceedings is the first thing that tribunals should do.

Dispute settlement clauses have a relevant role to play in this context. They draw up the boundaries of the tribunal's jurisdiction, delimiting which kind of claims they could or could not entertain.

Subject matter jurisdiction of treaty-based tribunals differs substantially. It may be established in broad or narrow terms, admitting all investment disputes or, by contrast, only those claims asserting a treaty violation.[84] No uniform position has been reached on how such dispute settlement clauses should be construed.[85]

Some authors believe that, depending on how treaty dispute settlement clauses are drafted, the distinction between contractual and treaty claims may become to a certain extent irrelevant. In their view, treaty clauses broadly drafted in order to encompass all disputes concerning an investment would enable tribunals to address and decide on mere contractual disputes even if no violation of the treaty's substantial standards of treatment (fair and equitable treatment, non-discriminatory or arbitrary measures, expropriation, etc.) took place.[86]

---

84. "Improving the System of Investor-State Dispute Settlement: An Overview", *op. cit.*, fn. 13, para. 94.

85. "International Investment Agreements: Key Issues" (New York and Geneva 2004), United Nations Conference on Trade and Development, vol. II, p. 6. On these matters, see the divergent positions adopted by Professors Schreuer and Gaillard (SCHREUER, "Investment Treaty Arbitration and Jurisdiction over Contract Claims – the *Vivendi I* Case Considered", *op. cit.*, fn. 2, pp. 296-299; SCHREUER, "Calvo's Grandchildren: The Return of Local Remedies in Investment Arbitration", *op. cit.*, fn. 43, pp. 11-12; Emmanuel GAILLARD, "Treaty-Based Jurisdiction: Broad Dispute Resolution Clauses", in 10 June 2005 N.Y.L.J. p. 3 (col. 1); Emmanuel GAILLARD, "Investment Treaty Arbitration and Jurisdiction over Contract Claims – the SGS Cases Considered" in Todd WEILER, ed., *International Investment Law and Arbitration: Leading Cases from the ICSID, NAFTA, Bilateral Treaties and Customary International Law*, *op. cit.*, fn. 2, p. 325 at p. 334).

86. As explained by Professor Schreuer, "where a BIT provides for investor/State arbitration in respect of all investment disputes rather than disputes concerning violations of the BIT, the tribunal is competent even for pure contract claims" (SCHREUER, "Investment Treaty Arbitration and Jurisdiction over Contract Claims – the *Vivendi I* Case Considered", *op. cit.*, fn. 2, p. 296). Broadly drafted clauses could become a useful tool to overcome the negative consequences that stem from the conceptual distinction between treaty and contract claims. In this path, Professor Schreuer points out that the need to dissect cases into contract claims and treaty claims to be dealt

511

Dispute settlement clauses such as the one existing in the Lebanon and Italy BIT comprising "... disputes regarding investments between a Contracting Party and an investor of the other Contracting Party..."[87] would allow tribunals to entertain contractual claims involving such parties, even if they did not amount to a treaty violation. In this view, as long as the claimant is able, inter alia, to prove (i) that it is a qualifying investor under the treaty that holds a qualifying investment and (ii) the relationship between the dispute and the investment, no relevant obstacles would appear to the tribunal's jurisdiction. Since, in general, State contracts qualify as protected investments under treaties, claimants would have no difficulties in establishing that even mere contractual breach claims entail disputes concerning a qualifying investment.

The panorama changes if the governing dispute settlement clause provides no room for the submission of pure contract claims. For instance, the United Kingdom-Venezuela BIT provides that disputes between a contracting party and a national or company of the other contracting party must concern an obligation under the BIT.[88] Therefore, absent an umbrella clause,[89] such kind of clauses would set aside pure contract claims from the scope of the tribunal's jurisdiction.

This position is challenged by those who sustain that if BITs create substantive standards of protection under international law, dispute resolution clauses of those BITs should be understood to establish a neutral forum to deal with alleged violations of those standards. Professor Gaillard seems to favor this position by stating that if no specific wording indicates the contrary, it would be odd to construe a treaty as creating a forum to entertain claims other than violations of that same treaty.[90] Absent an umbrella clause, they propose to limit treaty-based tribunals' jurisdiction to treaty claims and

---

with by separate fora leads to claim splitting and has the potential of leading to parallel proceedings. This would be uneconomical and contrary to the goal of reaching final and comprehensive resolutions of disputes. As Professor Schreuer concludes, "if competing competences exist, it makes more sense to have the entire dispute heard by one forum, preferably the one with the most comprehensive jurisdiction. If the terms of reference in the BIT are broad enough to include contract claims in addition to treaty claims the international tribunal would be the one with the broadest jurisdiction." (SCHREUER, "Calvo's Grandchildren: The Return of Local Remedies in Investment Arbitration", *op. cit.*, fn. 43, p. 12). As it has been accurately noted to us while drafting this Report, if the host State's judicial system is not independent from political directives, domestic proceedings could be promoted by the host State, based on the same set of facts, in order to counteract and frustrate the international ones. This could undermine the procedural protection granted to the foreign investor in treaties. For instance, the host State or a third party instructed by it may seek to "compensate" the amount awarded to the investor under the treaty arbitration through a claim for breach of contract against the investor before local courts.

87. Italy-Lebanese Republic BIT, Art. 7.

88. United Kingdom-Venezuela BIT, Art. 8.

89. As will be explained in Sect. VI below, if the treaty contains an umbrella clause, as the United Kingdom-Venezuela BIT does in its Art. 2, in principle a pure contractual claim could be heard by the tribunal as a treaty claim pursuant to that clause.

90. GAILLARD, "Treaty-Based Jurisdiction: Broad Dispute Resolution Clauses", *op. cit.*, fn. 85, p. 6.

reserve mere contractual claims to the applicable contractually agreed dispute settlement forum.[91]

Both positions have been reflected in case law. In *Salini v. Morocco*, the dispute settlement clause of the Italy-Morocco BIT encompassed all disputes or differences between a Contracting Party and an investor of the other Contracting Party, including disputes related to the amount of compensation due in the event of expropriation, nationalization or a similar measure, between a Contracting Party and an investor of the other Contracting Party concerning an investment of said investor in the territory of the first Contracting Party.[92] Based on this broad provision, the tribunal concluded that its jurisdiction not only comprised treaty claims, but also mere contractual claims that did not necessarily amount to a treaty breach.[93]

---

91. *Ibid.* See also GAILLARD, "Investment Treaty Arbitration and Jurisdiction over Contract Claims – the SGS Cases Considered", *op. cit.*, fn. 85, p. 336.

92. *"Tutte le controversie o divergenze insorte tra una Parte Contraente e gli investitori dell'altra, incluse quelle sull'importo ed il pagamento degli indennizzi in caso di espropriazione, nazionalizzazione o analoghe misure, in relazione ad un investimento di tale investitore sul territorio della prima Parte Contraente...."*

93. *Salini Costruttori S.p.A. and Italstrade S.p.A. v. Kingdom of Morocco* (ICSID Case No. ARB/00/4), Decision on Jurisdiction (23 July 2001), *op. cit.*, fn. 19. The tribunal held: "The terms of article 8 are very general. The reference to expropriation and nationalization measures, which are matters coming under the unilateral will of a State, cannot be interpreted to exclude a claim based in contract from the scope of application of this Article.... Article 8 compels the State to respect the jurisdiction offer in relation to violations of the Bilateral Treaty and any breach of a contract that binds the State directly." (*Ibid.*, paras. 59 and 61). In case of contract claims, the tribunal held that the jurisdiction offer was only applicable to contracts executed by the State directly. The tribunal ruled that "the jurisdiction offer contained in Article 8 does not, however, extend to breaches of a contract to which an entity other than the State is a named party" (*ibid.*, paras. 60-61). For those reasons, the tribunal declared that "it has jurisdiction over the Italian companies' claims, as they are formulated, but specifies that it does not have jurisdiction over mere breaches of the contract concluded between the Italian companies and ADM [a State entity] that do not simultaneously constitute a violation of the Bilateral Treaty" (*ibid.*, para. 64). See also SCHREUER, "Investment Treaty Arbitration and Jurisdiction over Contract Claims – the *Vivendi I* Case Considered", *op. cit.*, fn. 2, p. 297.
In *Impregilo v. Pakistan*, the tribunal reached a similar conclusion. Even though it declared its jurisdiction to entertain mere contractual claims based on the dispute settlement clause of the applicable BIT, it declined jurisdiction in the specific case at hand pursuant to a restricted construction of its ratione personae jurisdiction. Art. 9 of the Italy-Pakistan BIT referred to "Any disputes arising between a Contracting Party and the investors of the other, including disputes relating to compensation for expropriation, nationalization, requisition or similar measures, and disputes relating to the amount of the relevant payments...."
Based on this provision, the tribunal concluded that "Article 9 of the BIT covers only 'disputes arising between a Contracting Party and the investors of the other'. As is clear from its own terms, the scope of application of this provision is limited to disputes between the entities or persons concerned." (*Impregilo S.p.A. v. Islamic Republic of Pakistan* (ICSID Case No. ARB/02/17), Decision on Jurisdiction (26 April 2005), *op. cit.*, fn. 27, para. 211). The tribunal then applied the analysis made in *Salini* and stated that "This analysis applies in terms to Article 9 of the BIT between Italy and Pakistan. In the Tribunal's view, the jurisdiction offer in this BIT does not extend to breaches of a contract to which an entity other than the State is a named Party. Indeed, had the intention been to extend each Contracting Party's jurisdiction offer in this way, the language of Article 9

As noted by Professor Schreuer, a similar approach was adopted by the ad hoc

---

would have been so crafted.... Given that the Contracts at issue were concluded between the Claimant and WAPDA, and not between the Claimant and Pakistan; that under the law of Pakistan, which governs both the Contracts and the status and capacity of WAPDA for the purposes of the Contracts, WAPDA is a legal entity distinct from the State of Pakistan; and given that Article 9 of the BIT does not cover breaches of contracts concluded by such an entity, it must follow that this Tribunal has no jurisdiction under the BIT to entertain Impregilo's claims based on alleged breaches of the Contracts." (*Ibid.*, paras. 214 and 216).

The tribunal further supported its finding on the analytical distinction between contract claims and treaty claims and the different rules of attribution that govern responsibility under the BIT and domestic law contracts: "In this respect, the Tribunal has noted in Section IV.A above that the legal personality of WAPDA is distinct from that of the State of Pakistan, and that the Contracts were concluded by that authority rather than the State itself. As a consequence, the Tribunal has declined to exercise jurisdiction over the Contract Claims presented by Impregilo. In contrast, under public international law (i.e. as will apply to an alleged breach of treaty), a State may be held responsible for the acts of local public authorities or public institutions under its authority. The different rules evidence the fact that the overlap or coincidence of treaty and contract claims does not mean that the exercise of determining each will also be the same."

In *Salini v. Jordan*, claimants alleged that the dispute settlement clause of the applicable BIT – Art. 9 of the Italy-Jordan BIT– was broadly drafted so as to cover "not only disputes relating to alleged violations of a provision of the BIT, but any dispute which may arise between a State Party and an investor of the other Party, including disputes concerning alleged violations of the Contract" (*Salini Costruttori S.p.A. and Italstrade S.p.A. v. The Hashemite Kingdom of Jordan* (ICSID Case No. ARB/02/13), Decision on Jurisdiction (29 November 2004), *op. cit.*, fn. 62, para. 98). Claimants highlighted the fact that Art. 9(1) referred to any disputes that may arise "on investments". However, the tribunal did not decide on the matter. It found that the contract was executed between claimants and a State entity with different personality to that of Jordan and therefore Art. 9(2) of the BIT was to be applied to contractual claims which read as follows: "[i]n case the investor and an entity of the Contracting Parties have stipulated an investment Agreement, the procedure foreseen in such investment agreement shall apply" (*Ibid.*, paras. 70-96).

However, *obiter dictum*, the arbitration panel noted in connection with the relevance of the way in which dispute settlement provisions are drafted that "... ICSID Tribunals have taken divergent positions on this matter in cases of alleged breaches of contracts entered into between a foreign investor and a State Party to a BIT.... Now, one may doubt whether Articles 9(1) and 9(3) also cover breaches of a contract concluded in name between an investor and an entity other than a State Party, and the Tribunal observes that several ICSID tribunals have already handed down decisions against such extensions of jurisdiction (see *Salini Costruttori and Italstrade v. Kingdom of Morocco*, case No. ARB/00/06, decision of 23 July 2001 on jurisdiction, paras. 60 to 62; *Consortium RFCC v. Kingdom of Morocco*, case No. ARB/00/06, Decision of 22 December 2003 on jurisdiction, paras. 67 to 69).... However, the Tribunal will not be required to decide on whether Articles 9(1) and 9(3), taken in isolation, could cover the contractual disputes at issue in this instance. In fact, Article 9(2) of the BIT makes it obligatory to refer such disputes to the dispute settlement mechanisms provided for in the contracts and, where such disputes are concerned, excludes recourse to the procedure set forth in Article 9(3) for such disputes (see para. 60 above)." (*Ibid.*, paras. 100-101).

As noted by Gaffney, notwithstanding the fact that it avoided taking a decision on the issue, the tribunal seemed not to support the extension of its jurisdiction to entertain pure contractual claims based on the wording of the dispute settlement clauses (John P. GAFFNEY, "Case Summary: *Salini Costruttori S.p.A. and Italstrade S.p.A. -v- The Hashemite Kingdom of Jordan* (ICSID Case No. ARB/02/13)", 2 TDM (January 2005, no. 1) Sect. 5(a)).

514

Committee in the *Vivendi* case.[94] The Argentina-France BIT dispute settlement clause embraces "all disputes relating to investments". In contrast to other instruments, such as Art. 1116 of the NAFTA that only applies to claims for breaches of certain NAFTA specific provisions, the ad hoc Committee found that Art. 8 of the applicable BIT did not require the investor to allege a BIT breach, but only that the dispute related to an investment.[95]

This reasoning leads to two different consequences. First, such broadly worded clauses enhance the tribunal's jurisdiction since they allow arbitral panels to entertain contractual claims in investment disputes under BITs. However, on the other hand, they could raise jurisdictional hurdles through the application, for instance, of eventual fork in the road clauses contained in the same BIT, as implied by the ad hoc Committee.[96] In case the investor has previously filed pure contract claims before national courts, which qualify under the dispute settlement clause of the BIT as a "dispute relating to investments", such filing could be regarded as having triggered the fork in the road clause, preventing those mere contractual claims from being submitted to arbitration.[97]

The decision in *SGS v. Philippines* – a dispute under the Swiss-Philippines BIT– supports the view that broadly drafted clauses such as those that make reference to

---

94. SCHREUER, "Investment Treaty Arbitration and Jurisdiction over Contract Claims – the *Vivendi I* Case Considered", *op. cit.*, fn. 2, p. 297.

95. As explained by the ad hoc Committee: "Article 8 deals generally with disputes 'relating to investments made under this Agreement between one Contracting Party and an investor of the other Contracting Party'. It is those disputes which may be submitted, at the investor's option, either to national or international adjudication. Article 8 does not use a narrower formulation, requiring that the investor's claim allege a breach of the BIT itself. Read literally, the requirements for arbitral jurisdiction in Article 8 do not necessitate that the Claimant allege a breach of the BIT itself: it is sufficient that the dispute relate to an investment made under the BIT. This may be contrasted, for example, with Article 11 of the BIT, which refers to disputes 'concerning the interpretation or application of this Agreement', or with Article 1116 of the NAFTA, which provides that an investor may submit to arbitration under Chapter 11 'a claim that another Party has breached an obligation under' specified provisions of that Chapter. Consequently, if a claim brought before a national court concerns a 'dispute relating to investments made under this Agreement' within the meaning of Article 8(1), then Article 8(2) will apply. In the Committee's view, a claim by CAA against the Province of Tucumán for breach of the Concession Contract, brought before the contentious administrative courts of Tucumán, would prima facie fall within Article 8(2) and constitute a 'final' choice of forum and jurisdiction, if that claim was coextensive with a dispute relating to investments made under the BIT." (*Compañía de Aguas del Aconquija S.A. and Vivendi Universal (formerly Compagnie Générale Des Eaux)* (ICSID Case No. ARB/97/3), Decision on Annulment (3 July 2002), *op. cit.*, fn. 13, para. 55).

96. *Ibid.*

97. Under current case law, fork in the road clauses will not necessarily preclude claimant's treaty claims even if they are related to contractual issues. In order to trigger such clauses, identity of parties and causes of action concerning the disputes filed before the domestic courts and the arbitral tribunal is required. As explained by Professor Schreuer, "the dispute before domestic courts or administrative tribunals must be identical with the dispute in the international proceeding" (Christoph SCHREUER, "Travelling the BIT Route. Of Waiting Periods, Umbrella Clauses and Forks in the Road", 5 The Journal of World Investment and Trade (2004) p. 231 at p. 248).

"disputes with respect to investments" allow all investment disputes – including those arising from contracts – to be submitted to arbitration.[98] In that case, the tribunal provided a list of reasons which justify why contract claims could be entertained by arbitral tribunals under this kind of dispute settlement clause: (i) arbitral panels to which the investment dispute can be submitted have the competence to apply the law of the host State, including its law of contract, (ii) if the States parties to the BIT had intended to limit investor-State arbitration to claims concerning breaches of the BIT substantive standards, they would have said so expressly, (iii) drawing technical distinctions between causes of action arising under the BIT and those arising under the investment agreement is capable of giving rise to overlapping proceedings and jurisdictional uncertainty, and (iv) investments are characteristically entered into by means of contracts or other agreements with the host State and the local investment partner (or if these are different entities, with both of them).

A different conclusion was reached in *SGS v. Pakistan*, where the tribunal did not give much weight to the way the BIT's dispute settlement clause was drafted. Based on Art. 9 of the Swiss-Pakistan BIT, which provided for "disputes with respect to investments", the claimant argued that the tribunal had jurisdiction over claims grounded solely on the contract which did not include any element of, or amount to, violation of a substantive BIT standard even if the tribunal did not accept that the BIT's umbrella clause elevated its contractual claims into BIT claims.

In its finding on jurisdiction, the tribunal recognized that disputes arising from claims grounded on alleged violations of the BIT, and disputes arising from claims based wholly on supposed violations of a contract, can both be described as "disputes with respect to investments", the phrase used in Art. 9 of the BIT. Nonetheless, it concluded that such article only described the factual subject matter of the disputes, but did not relate to the legal basis or cause of action of the claims.[99] In the tribunal's words, "from that description alone, without more, we believe that no implication necessarily arises that both BIT and purely contract claims are intended to be covered by the Contracting Parties in Art. 9".[100]

---

98. The *SGS v. Philippines* tribunal held that "Article VIII of the BIT provides for settlement of 'disputes with respect to investments between a Contracting Party and an investor of the other Contracting Party'.... Prima facie, Article VIII is an entirely general provision, allowing for submission of all investment disputes by the investor against the host State. The term 'disputes with respect to investments' (*différents relatifs à des investissements* in the French text) is not limited by reference to the legal classification of the claim that is made. A dispute about an alleged expropriation contrary to Article VI of the BIT would be a 'dispute with respect to investments'; so too would a dispute arising from an investment contract such as the CISS Agreement." (*SGS Société Générale de Surveillance S.A. v. Republic of the Philippines* (ICSID Case No. ARB/02/6), Decision on Jurisdiction (29 January 2004), *op. cit.*, fn. 7, para. 132(d).

99. *SGS Société Générale de Surveillance S.A. v. Islamic Republic of Pakistan* (ICSID Case No. ARB/01/13), Decision on Jurisdiction (6 August 2003), *op. cit.*, fn. 23, para. 161.

100. *Ibid.*

According to those who suggest a broader construction, the tribunal established limitations not existing in the text, nor evident from the treaty's negotiating history.[101] The tribunal seems to have sought to restrict treaty-based arbitration to treaty claims only, excluding pure contractual ones, so as to avoid an overlap with dispute settlement clauses in contracts that provide contractual disputes to be submitted before local courts. This line of thought stems from the proposition explicitly challenged by Professor Crivellaro in his dissenting opinion in *SGS v. Philippines*[102] that different dispute settlement forums cannot coexist and one necessarily should take precedence over the other.

The tribunal in *LESI-Dipenta v. Algeria*[103] equally decided not to bind itself to the phrasing of the dispute settlement clause. Although Art. 8 of the Italy-Algeria BIT referred to "any dispute related to an investment between a Contracting State and an investor from the other Contracting State",[104] the tribunal decided to exclude mere contractual claims from its jurisdiction.

Even though the clause seems to admit any claim related to an investment – pure treaty claims, treaty claims that at the same time entail contract claims and mere

---

101. See *Tokios Tokeles v. Ukraine* (ICSID Case No. ARB/02/18), Decision on Jurisdiction (29 April 2004), para. 52, at <www.worldbank.org/icsid/cases/tokios-decision.pdf> (last visited 21 March 2006). In a footnote to that paragraph, the tribunal asserted that: "In this case [*SGS v. Pakistan*], a Swiss company asserted claims against the Government of Pakistan for breach of contract and for breach of the BIT between the Swiss Confederation and Pakistan. Article 9 of that BIT provides for ICSID arbitration of 'disputes with respect to investments…'.*Id.* at para. 149. The provision does not in any manner restrict the scope of such disputes. Although the tribunal recognized that BIT claims and contract claims 'can both be described as "disputes with respect to investment"', it nonetheless decided—without support from the text or evidence of the parties' intent—to exclude contract claims from the scope of 'disputes' that could be submitted to ICSID arbitration. *Id.*, paras. 161-62."

102. See Professor Crivellaro's dissenting opinion in *SGS Société Générale de Surveillance S.A. v. Republic of the Philippines* (ICSID Case No. ARB/02/6), Decision on Jurisdiction (29 January 2004), *op. cit.*, fn. 7, para. 132(d). ("The question is whether the BIT dispute clause 'overrides' or 'replaces' the contract dispute clause. I wonder whether this way of defining the question is the correct way. In the reality, neither one of the two provisions 'overrides' or 'replaces' the other. They both survive and coexist…. It is my understanding that the most significant advantage which, in practice, is granted by a BIT to foreign investors is, precisely, the right to select, amongst the alternative forums made available by the BIT, the forum that the investor deems the most suitable *to him after* that the elements of fact or law of the dispute have become clear. A BIT can certainly limit the investor's freedom of choice, for instance providing that a forum which has already been agreed in a past investment agreement remains the 'exclusive' forum for disputes arising from that investment agreement. Such a limitation is not uncommon in BITs practice. However, it is not provided in the BIT here in question.").

103. *Consorzio Groupement L.E.S.I. – DIPENTA v. Democratic and Popular Republic of Algeria* (ICSID Case No. ARB/03/08), Award (10 January 2005), at <http://ita.law.uvic.ca/documents/dipentav.algeria.pdf> (last visited 21 March 2006).

104. "*Ogni controversia relativa ad investimenti, tra uno degli Stati Contraenti ed un Investitore dell'altro Stato Contraente….*"

contract claims – the tribunal concluded that Algeria's consent was limited to measures which would constitute a breach of the BIT's substantive provisions.[105]

The tribunal held that

> "... the consent is not granted, extensively, to all rights and claims that could be related to an investment. It is required that the measures taken amount to a breach of the Bilateral Agreement – meaning that they are unjustified or discriminatory – in law or in fact. Thus, that is not necessarily the case of any contract breach."[106]

The tribunal also concluded that the applicable treaty did not contain an umbrella clause which would have evidenced the intention of the contracting parties to submit pure contractual claims to treaty-based arbitration.[107]

The existing case law seems to confirm that treaty-based tribunals have predominantly affirmed their jurisdiction to entertain contractual claims based on broadly drafted dispute settlement provisions. Nonetheless, those same tribunals have avoided to recognize their own jurisdiction to deal with contractual claims in the cases at hand, based on other grounds (i.e., a strict construction of ratione personae jurisdiction; stay of proceedings due to a contractual dispute resolution provision in the underlying contract; etc.).[108]

V. WHERE TO DRAW THE LINE BETWEEN A "MERE" CONTRACT BREACH AND A TREATY BREACH?

In those cases where the tribunals find that, under the applicable treaty, they are not competent to hear pure contract claims, but only treaty claims, they should then assess at the merits stage whether the State's measures breach the treaty's substantive standards of treatment. That leads to the question of when a contract breach constitutes a violation of the treaty standards of fair and equitable treatment, full protection and security, non-discrimination and protection against expropriation, among others.

In general, investment treaties have not been intended to set up a regime under which a massive amount of disputes arising out of ordinary commercial transactions involving foreign investors and governments should be submitted to international arbitration.[109]

---

105. *Consorzio Groupement L.E.S.I. – DIPENTA v. Democratic and Popular Republic of Algeria* (ICSID Case No. ARB/03/08), Award (10 January 2005), *op. cit.*, fn. 103, paras. 25-26.

106. *Ibid.*, para. 25(i) (Free translation from the French text). See also GAILLARD, "Treaty-Based Jurisdiction: Broad Dispute Resolution Clauses", *op. cit.*, fn. 85, p. 6.

107. *Ibid.*, para. 25(ii).

108. GAILLARD, "Treaty-Based Jurisdiction: Broad Dispute Resolution Clauses", *op. cit.*, fn. 85, p. 6.

109. *Robert Azinian, Kenneth Davitian, & Ellen Baca v. The United Mexican States* (ICSID Case No. ARB (AF) /97/2), Award (1 November 1999), para. 83, at <http://naftaclaims.com/Disputes/Mexico/Azinian/AzinianFinalAward.pdf> (last visited 21 March 2006).

It appears that a treaty breach should require something more than a simple breach of contract. As explained by the *Vivendi* ad hoc Committee, "[a] treaty cause of action is not the same as a contractual cause of action; it requires a clear showing of conduct which is in the circumstances contrary to the relevant treaty standard".[110] Not every breach of contract amounts to a discriminatory treatment, an expropriation or the violation of the full protection and security standard.

In some cases, the distinction between one and the other is relatively simple: a non-substantive contract breach such as the lack of payment of an isolated invoice owed under a contract could rarely amount to a treaty breach. However, that task becomes increasingly hard when the tribunal should face borderline cases, such as a persistent breach by an State of its contractual obligations that heavily impairs the investor's legitimate expectations.

Even though this Report is not aimed at examining the treaties' general standards of treatment and the way they could be distinguished from simple contract breaches, a brief reference will be made to the fair and equitable treatment standard as it has been occasionally construed so as to also protect contractual undertakings.

It has been generally accepted that the fair and equitable treatment standard cannot be summarized precisely. In applying it to specific situations, some tribunals have found that measures undertaken by the States against the investor's legitimate expectations violate the fair and equitable standard.[111] Based on that line of precedents, Professor

---

110. *Compañía de Aguas del Aconquija, S.A. & Compagnie Générale des Eaux v. Argentine Republic* (ICSID Case No. ARB/97/3), Decision on Annulment (3 July 2002), *op. cit.*, fn. 13, para. 113).

111. An analysis of those cases can be found in SCHREUER, "Fair and Equitable Treatment in Arbitral Practice", *op. cit.*, fn. 11, at pp. 374-380. *Tecmed v. Mexico* has endorsed that the fair and equitable treatment "... in light of the good faith principle established by international law, requires the Contracting Parties to provide to international investments treatment that does not affect the basic expectations that were taken into account by the foreign investor to make the investment. The foreign investor expects the host State to act in a consistent manner, free from ambiguity and totally transparently in its relations with the foreign investor, so that it may know beforehand any and all rules and regulations that will govern its investments, as well as the goals of the relevant policies and administrative practices or directives, to be able to plan its investment and comply with such regulations. Any and all State actions conforming to such criteria should relate not only to the guidelines, directives or requirements issued, or the resolutions approved thereunder, but also to the goals underlying such regulations. The foreign investor also expects the host State to act consistently, i.e. without arbitrarily revoking any preexisting decisions or permits issued by the State that were relied upon by the investor to assume its commitments as well as to plan and launch its commercial and business activities. The investor also expects the State to use the legal instruments that govern the actions of the investor or the investment in conformity with the function usually assigned to such instruments, and not to deprive the investor of its investment without the required compensation. In fact, failure by the host State to comply with such pattern of conduct with respect to the foreign investor or its investments affects the investor's ability to measure the treatment and protection awarded by the host State and to determine whether the actions of the host State conform to the fair and equitable treatment principle. Therefore, compliance by the host State with such pattern of conduct is closely related to the above-mentioned principle, to the actual chances of enforcing such principle, and to excluding the possibility that state action be characterized as arbitrary...." (*Técnicas Medioambientales Tecmed S. A. v. The United Mexican States* (ICSID Case No. ARB (AF)/00/2), Award (29 May 2003), 43 ILM

Schreuer has raised the question whether "… it [can] be said that non-performance of a contract between the investor and the host State or one of its territorial subdivisions or entities is contrary to the investor's legitimate expectations and hence a violation of the fair and equitable treatment standard?".[112] If (i) the fair and equitable treatment provision protects the investor's legitimate expectations, (ii) contracts are entered into so as to be complied with by the parties and, (iii) the State's compliance with contracts constitutes a basic expectation of any investor, a contract breach could be considered as a breach of the fair and equitable treatment provision and, therefore, of the treaty.

There is, however, not enough case law on the application of the fair and equitable treatment standard to contract claims, in order to draw a general criterion. Both in *Mondev v. United States*[113] and *SGS v. Philippines*[114] the tribunals asserted that a breach of contract *may* amount to a breach of the fair and equitable treatment standard. But they did not elaborate under which circumstances this may actually happen.

It seems reasonable to require something more than a simple contract breach to deem the fair and equitable treatment standard violated. Otherwise, it could operate in fact as a second umbrella clause turning redundant provisions of that nature existing in several BITs. Moreover, contracting parties probably would not have incorporated umbrella clauses into BITs if they had regarded contractual commitments as already embraced by the fair and equitable treatment standard.

This takes us back to the initial question: when should a contract breach also be considered a breach of the treaty's fair and equitable treatment standard? The answer will depend on the particular circumstances of the case.[115] As held by the UNCITRAL tribunal in *CME v. Czech Republic*,

---

133 (2004) para. 154). In Vasciannie's words: "… the balance of considerations having some bearing on fairness and equity as between investors and States turns essentially on ways in which State action or inaction may undermine the economic expectations, profitability and survival of individual investments" (Stephen VASCIANNIE, "The Fair and Equitable Treatment Standard in International Investment Law and Practice", 70 The Brit. Y.B. Int'l Law 1999 (2000) p. 99, at pp. 146-147). As Paulsson states, tribunals that are asked to determine if a State's measures violate the fair and equitable treatment standard may need to examine "the impact of the measure on the reasonable investment-backed expectations of the investor; and whether the state is attempting to avoid investment-backed expectations that the state created or reinforced through its own acts". (Jan PAULSSON, "Investment Protection Provisions in Treaties", *Investment Protection/La protection de L'Investissement*, ICC Institute of World Business Law (2000) p. 19 at p. 22).

112. SCHREUER, "Fair and Equitable Treatment in Arbitral Practice", *op. cit.*, fn. 11, p. 379.

113. *Mondev International Ltd. v. United States of America* (ICSID Case No. ARB(AF)/99/2), Award (11 October 2002), paras. 98 and 134, at <http://ita.law.uvic.ca/documents/Mondev-Final.pdf.> (last visited 21 March 2006). See also SCHREUER, "Fair and Equitable Treatment in Arbitral Practice", *op. cit.*, fn. 11, pp. 379-380.

114. *SGS Société Générale de Surveillance S.A. v. Republic of the Philippines* (ICSID Case No. ARB/02/6), Decision on Jurisdiction (29 January 2004), *op. cit.*, fn. 7, para. 162. See also SCHREUER, "Fair and Equitable Treatment in Arbitral Practice", *op. cit.*, fn. 11, p. 380.

115. SCHREUER, "Fair and Equitable Treatment in Arbitral Practice", *op. cit.*, fn. 11, p. 380.

"Whether conduct is fair and equitable depends on the factual context of the State's actions, including factors such as the undertakings made to the investor and the actions the investor took in reliance on those undertakings. This requirement can thus prohibit conduct that might be permissible in some circumstances but appears unfair and inequitable in the context of a particular dispute."[116]

To establish a unique standard distinguishing between a contract breach and a fair and equitable treatment violation that could be universally applicable to all cases under any circumstances seems, at this stage, an extremely difficult task.

Nonetheless, and assuming that "a judgment of what is fair and equitable cannot be reached in the abstract",[117] it is still possible to propose some guidelines in order to distinguish a pure contract breach from a violation of that standard.

From a rather quantitative standpoint, the contractual breach should appear before the eyes of an impartial party as a State conduct that violates the investor's legitimate expectations and has a relevant impact on the investor's ability to recoup its investment and obtain a reasonable profit from it.

Following the analysis of fair and equitable treatment in arbitral practice recently carried out by Professor Schreuer, a contract breach – and, thus, a violation of the investor's legitimate expectations – will surpass the threshold required to become a treaty breach, when the State's measure (i) constituted a "wilful disregard of due process of law, an act which shocks, or at least surprises, a sense of judicial propriety", (ii) could be regarded as improper and discreditable, (iii) involved discrimination, or (iv) could be characterized as arbitrary, idiosyncratic, unjust, lacking good faith or lacking of due process and proportionality.[118]

From a qualitative perspective, it seems useful to refer back briefly to some general concepts.

The most widely accepted criterion for distinguishing between a simple contract breach and the expropriation of contract rights consists in establishing the role in which the State has acted, whether it has done so in its commercial or sovereign capacity.[119]

---

116. *CME Czech Republic B. V. v. The Czech Republic* (UNCITRAL case), Partial Award (13 September 2001), para. 157, at <http://ita.law.uvic.ca/documents/CME-2001PartialAward.pdf> (last visited 21 March 2006).

117. *Mondev International Ltd. v. United States of America* (ICSID Case No. ARB(AF)/99/2), Award (11 October 2002), *op. cit.*, fn. 113, para. 118. See SCHREUER, "Fair and Equitable Treatment in Arbitral Practice", *op. cit.*, fn. 11, p. 364.

118. SCHREUER, "Fair and Equitable Treatment in Arbitral Practice", *op. cit.*, fn. 11, p. 373.

119. SCHREUER, "The Concept of Expropriation under the ECT and other Investment Protection Treaties", *op. cit.*, fn. 10, p. 25.

Professors Schreuer[120] and Reinisch[121] recall the *Jalapa Railroad* case in which such criterion was elaborated.[122]

The prevailing view under general international law is that a breach of contract does not necessarily give rise to a State's international responsibility. As noted by Judge Schwebel:

> "... [T]here is more than doctrinal authority in support of the conclusion that, while mere breach by a State of a contract with an alien (whose proper law is not international law) is not a violation of international law, a 'non-commercial' act of a State contrary to such a contract may be. That is to say, the breach of such a contract by a State in ordinary commercial intercourse is not, in the predominant view, a violation of international law, but the use of the sovereign authority of a State, contrary to the expectations of the parties, to abrogate or violate a contract with an alien, is a violation of international law."[123]

---

120. *Ibid.*

121. August REINISCH, "Expropriation", *op. cit.*, fn. 10.

122. As described by Professor Reinisch, "In that case the American-Mexican Claims Commission regarded a legislative decree declaring a clause in a contract between the state and the investor to be void as expropriatory act. It held: 'In the circumstances, the issue for determination is whether the breach of contract alleged to have resulted from the nullification of clause twelfth of the contract was an ordinary one involving no international responsibility or whether said breach was effected arbitrarily by means of a governmental power illegal under international law [...] the 1931 decree of the same Legislature, [...] was clearly not an ordinary breach of contract. Here the Government of Veracruz stepped out of the role of contracting party and sought to escape vital obligations under its contract by exercising its superior.'" (*Ibid.*, Sect. 3).

123. Stephen M. SCHWEBEL, *Justice in International Law. Selected Writings of Stephen M. Schwebel*, (Cambridge University Press 1994) pp. 431-432. Judge Schwebel further states: "Examples of repudiation or breach by a State of a contract with an alien for governmental rather than commercial reasons are not unusual. The salient illustration is the repudiation by a State of a contract with an alien in the course of nationalization of an industry or the taking of the particular interest of the alien. Where the State does not pay damages that compensate for the breach of the alien's contractual rights, such a breach of contract certainly gives rise to responsibility under international law. Indeed, when the State employs its legislative or administrative or executive authority as only a State can employ governmental authority to undo the fundamental expectation on the basis of which parties characteristically contract – performance, not non-performance – then it engages its international responsibility. It is recognized that this conclusion is the opposite of an approach which is currently accepted in some quarters, namely, that if a State employs its governmental authority in order to promote the national welfare in a manner which overrides the contractual rights of an alien, the international responsibility of the State is not incurred. It is believed that that approach is in error, not only for the legal reasons set out above, but because the alien, by definition, is not part of the national public whose welfare the State promotes. He is a sojourner in the community ruled by the State and, if it casts him or his rights out, then the State is obligated in equity as well as under international law to repair the resultant situation, whether by payment of compensation, restitution, or specific performance of its contract." (*Ibid.*, p. 435). UNCTAD has expressed in this regard that a breach caused by an act taken in a government capacity amounts to a violation of international law ("International Investment Agreements: Key Issues", *op. cit.*, fn. 85, p. 3). For a more restrictive position, see Ian BROWNLIE, *Principles of Public International Law*, 5th edn. (Oxford University Press 1998) pp.

In *Waste Management v. Mexico*, the tribunal identified certain situations that would amount to a taking of contractual rights:

(i) cases where a whole enterprise is terminated or frustrated because its functioning is simply halted by decree or executive act, usually accompanied by other conduct;
(ii) cases where there has been an acknowledged taking of property, and associated contractual rights are affected in consequence (including all associated contractual and other incorporeal rights, unless these are severable and retain their value in the hands of the claimant notwithstanding the seizure of the related property); and
(iii) cases where the only right affected is incorporeal.[124]

Concerning the third type of case, it elaborated further on the basis of the nature of the State's conduct:

> "In such cases, simply to assert that 'property rights are created under and by virtue of a contract' is not sufficient. The mere non-performance of a contractual obligation is not to be equated with a taking of property, nor (unless accompanied by other elements) is it tantamount to expropriation. Any private party can fail to perform its contracts, whereas nationalization and expropriation are inherently governmental acts, as is envisaged by the use of the term 'measure' in Article 1110(1). It is true that, having regard to the inclusive definition of 'measure', one could envisage conduct tantamount to an expropriation which consisted of acts and omissions not specifically or exclusively governmental. All the same, the normal response by an investor faced with a breach of contract by its governmental counter-party (the breach not taking the form of an exercise of governmental prerogative, such as a legislative decree) is to sue in the appropriate court to remedy the breach."[125]

549-553.

124. *Waste Management, Inc. v. United Mexican States* (ICSID Case No. ARB(AF)/00/3), Final Award (30 April 2004), paras. 172-174, at <http://ita.law.uvic.ca/documents/laudo_ingles.pdf> (last visited 21 March 2006).

125. *Ibid.*, para. 174. Some clarifications should be made with respect to the tribunal's assertion that "... the normal response by an investor faced with a breach of contract by its governmental counter-party (the breach not taking the form of an exercise of governmental prerogative, such as a legislative decree) is to sue in the appropriate court to remedy the breach". If the State's conduct amounts to a pure contractual breach, which does not reach to the level of a treaty breach – and the dispute settlement provision of the applicable treaty does not embrace pure contractual disputes, as is the case of the NAFTA – the investor would have only the remedies available for a contract breach before local courts. This is quite different, however, than to say that in order to consider the treaty standards violated, the investor should first have had recourse to domestic courts so as to show that a reasonable effort to obtain correction has been made, as has been asserted – among others – in *Waste Management v. Mexico* regarding the breach of the NAFTA's fair and equitable standard provision (*Ibid.*, 116) and *Generation Ukraine v. Ukraine* (*Generation Ukraine, Inc. v. Ukraine* (ICSID Case No. ARB/00/9), Award (16 September 2003), para. 20.30, at <http://ita.law.uvic.ca/documents/GenerationUkraine_000.pdf> (last visited 28 March 2006)), with respect to the determination of an expropriation under the applicable BIT.

This distinction between a State's governmental and commercial acts has been applied in some cases in order to differentiate a treaty breach from a contract breach, particularly concerning the standard of fair and equitable treatment. From this angle, the *Joy Mining* tribunal held:

> "... a basic general distinction can be made between commercial aspects of a dispute and other aspects involving the existence of some form of State interference with the operation of the contract involved".[126]

A similar approach was adopted in *Salini v. Jordan* in order to distinguish a breach of the fair and equitable standard from a contract breach:

> "Therefore, not any breach of an investment contract could be regarded as a breach of a BIT. In the words of the Arbitral Tribunal in *Consortium RFCC v. Kingdom of Morocco*, a breach of the substantive provisions of a bilateral investment treaty can certainly result from a breach of contract, without a possible breach of the contract constituting, ipso jure and by itself, a breach of the Treaty. (See para. 48 of the Award).
>
> In fact, the State, or its emanation, may have behaved as ordinary cocontractants having a difference of approach, in fact or in law, with the investor. In order that the alleged breach of contract may constitute unfair or inequitable treatment within the meaning of the bilateral agreement, it must be the result of behaviour going beyond that which an ordinary contracting party could adopt. Only the State, in the exercise of its sovereign authority (*puissance publique*), and not as a contracting party, has assumed obligations under the bilateral agreement. (*ibid*, para. 51). In other words, an investment protection treaty cannot be used to compensate an investor deceived by the financial results of the operation undertaken, unless he proves that his deception was a consequence of the behaviour of the receiving State acting in breach of the obligations which it had assumed under the treaty. (*ibid*, para. 108)".[127]

In this regard, see SCHREUER, "Calvo's Grandchildren: The Return of Local Remedies in Investment Arbitration", *op. cit.*, fn. 43, pp. 13-16.

126. *Joy Mining Machinery Limited v. Arab Republic of Egypt* (ICSID Case No. ARB/03/1), Award on Jurisdiction (6 August 2004), *op. cit.*, fn. 70, para. 72.

127. *Salini Costruttori S.p.A. and Italstrade S.p.A. v. Hashemite Kingdom of Jordan* (ICSID Case No. ARB/02/13), Decision on Jurisdiction (29 November 2004), *op. cit.*, fn. 62, paras. 154-155.

An identical view was adopted by the tribunal in *Impregilo v. Pakistan*.[128] It further sustained that, in the merits phase, claimant would have to evidence that the contract breach was committed by the State in the exercise of sovereign powers.[129]

As noted by Happ and Rubins, these cases would show the growing support obtained by the idea that a sovereign act is needed as opposed to a commercial one in order to consider a contract breach as a treaty breach.[130]

Even though the nature of the State's acts is both a useful approach to determine an expropriation case under international law and a helpful guidance to assess other treaty breaches, it should not be established as a unique and inflexible threshold that the claimant must necessarily surpass, even less at the jurisdictional phase. This would set aside all cases in which the State, in its commercial capacity, takes an abusive attitude towards foreign investors, disregarding any respect for basic principles of law. Investment treaties contain broader protective provisions than those set out under general international law and the threshold of expropriation cannot be equated to that required for considering the fair and equitable treatment standard violated.

It is certainly useful, although not conclusive, to examine in each case whether the contract breach has been caused by the State acting in its commercial role as a party to the contract or in its sovereign capacity. This may serve not in order to exclude the violation of the fair and equitable standard in all cases that the State has conducted itself in its commercial capacity, but to require a higher threshold in those cases and a lower one in those instances in which the State carries out its measures as a sovereign body.

If the State adopted the measures in its sovereign capacity, the breach could not be equated, in principle, to an ordinary non-compliance of contract and, therefore, absent exculpatory circumstances, one could easily conclude that the State has committed a violation of the fair and equitable treatment standard by acting against the investor's legitimate expectations.

---

128. The tribunal held: "... the fact that a breach may give rise to a contract claim does not mean that it cannot also – and separately – give rise to a treaty claim. Even if the two perfectly coincide, they remain analytically distinct, and necessarily require different enquiries.... In fact, the State or its emanation, may have behaved as an ordinary contracting party having a difference of approach, in fact or in law, with the investor. In order that the alleged breach of contract may constitute a violation of the BIT, it must be the result of behaviour going beyond that which an ordinary contracting party could adopt. Only the State in the exercise of its sovereign authority ('*puissance publique*'), and not as a contracting party, may breach the obligations assumed under the BIT. In other words, the investment protection treaty only provides a remedy to the investor where the investor proves that the alleged damages were a consequence of the behavior of the Host State acting in breach of the obligations it had assumed under the treaty." (*Impregilo S.p.A. v. Islamic Republic of Pakistan* (ICSID Case No. ARB/03/3), Decision on Jurisdiction (22 April 2005), *op. cit.*, fn. 27, paras. 258-260).

129. The tribunal sustained: "In the Tribunal's view, if it is assumed pro tem that Impregilo can establish the facts upon which it relies, it is possible, at least in theory, that Impregilo might establish breaches of the BIT in this regard. Whether or not this is so will depend upon: ... (b) Whether Impregilo is able to meet the threshold for treaty claims outlined above, i.e. activity beyond that of an ordinary contracting party ('*puissance publique*')." (*Ibid.*, para. 266).

130. Richard HAPP and Noah RUBINS, "Awards and Decisions of ICSID Tribunals in 2004", 47 German Yearbook of International Law (2004) p. 878 at p. 921.

On the contrary, if the State's conduct is shown to be a commercial act, the tribunal would be prone to consider the fair and equitable treatment standard not violated if it does not find aggravating circumstances showing a significant arbitrary behavior on the State's side, pursuant to the threshold described above. The latter assertion encounters some basis in an *obiter dictum* in the *Waste Management v. Mexico* case, which concerning expropriation, held that "one could envisage conduct tantamount to an expropriation which consisted of acts and omissions not specifically or exclusively governmental".[131]

While case law and scholars have not drawn a precise limit between a contract breach and a treaty breach such as the violation of the fair and equitable treatment standard, the criterion that looks into the capacity in which the State incurs in its non-compliance with a contract would serve – together with the quantitative approach – as a useful factor, albeit neither exclusive nor determining, to assess whether the State should be held internationally responsible.[132]

It is probably too much to require that a State's measure be of a governmental nature in order to consider that a treaty breach has taken place, as implied in *Joy Mining*, *Salini v. Jordan* and *Impregilo v. Pakistan*. This last proposition appears to narrow the protection provided to foreign investors under treaties.

The issue is currently under debate and some uncertainty remains on how case law will evolve. It will also depend on the meaning that tribunals attribute to the umbrella clause.

VI.   THE ROLE AND EFFECT OF UMBRELLA CLAUSES

Several treaties contain specific clauses aimed at providing investors with further assurance that the obligations and commitments assumed by the host State towards them will be honored.

---

131. *Waste Management, Inc. v. United Mexican States* (ICSID Case No. ARB(AF)/00/3), Final Award (30 April 2004), *op. cit.*, fn. 124, para. 174.

132. A related question in which legislation, case law and scholars are far from reaching some consensus consists in the criteria to apply so as to distinguish a commercial act from a governmental one. This issue has been largely discussed in the field of State immunity. See, among others, Christoph SCHREUER, *State Immunity. Some Recent Developments* (Grotius 1988) pp. 10-43. BROWNLIE, *Principles of Public International Law, op. cit.*, fn. 123, pp. 329-335; Peter MALANCZUK, *Akehurst's Modern Introduction to International Law*, 7th edn. (Routledge 1997) pp.121-123; Thomas BUERGENTHAL and Sean D. MURPHY, *Public International Law*, 3rd edn. (West Group 2002) pp. 239-241; Antonio REMIRO BROTÓNS, Rosa M. RIQUELME CORTADO, Javier DÍEZ-HOCHLEITNER, Esperanza ORIHUELA CALTAYUD and Luis PÉREZ-PRAT DURBÁN, *Derecho Internacional* (McGraw-Hill 1997) pp. 799-813. When elaborating his position towards the umbrella clause, Professor Wälde mentions a number of indicators that can help to qualify an act as governmental (Thomas W. WÄLDE, "The 'Umbrella' (or Sanctity of Contract/Pacta Sunt Servanda) Clause in Investment Arbitration: A Comment on Original Intentions and Recent Cases", 1 TDM (October 2004, no. 4) p. 86). He further recognizes, however, the difficulties to assess whether a State's act is governmental or commercial (*Ibid.*, p. 81).

Clauses of this kind are generally referred to as "umbrella clauses", and are occasionally also called "pacta sunt servanda", "mirror effect", "elevator", "parallel effect" and "sanctity of contract" clauses.[133]

According to a study carried out by Anthony Sinclair, the origin of umbrella clauses goes back to the 1950s, based on suggestions made by Sir Eli Lauterpacht to draft treaties assuring parallel protection so that a breach of contract would also be considered a breach of treaty.[134]

The *Abs-Shawcross* Draft Convention on Investment Abroad of 1959[135] contained an umbrella clause in its Art. II that read as follows:

> "Each Party shall at all times ensure the observance of any undertakings which it may have given in relation to investments made by nationals of any other Party."[136]

Following the understanding of the *Abs-Shawcross* Draft Convention, the OECD Draft Convention on the Protection of Foreign Property of 1967 contained a provision which, under the title of "Observance of Undertakings", held:

> "Each Party shall at all times ensure the observance of undertakings given by it in relation to property of nationals of any other Party."[137]

---

133. "Improving the System of Investor-State Dispute Settlement: An Overview", *op. cit.*, fn. 13, p. 30.

134. Anthony SINCLAIR, "The Origins of the Umbrella Clause in the International Law of Investment Protection", 20 Arbitration International (2004, no. 4) p. 411, at pp. 414-418. See also "Improving the System of Investor-State Dispute Settlement: An Overview", *op. cit.*, fn. 13, pp. 31-33.

135. The Draft Convention was a private initiative by Hermann Abs – then Chairman of Deutsche Bank – and Lord Hartley Shawcross – former British Attorney-General and by then a Director of the Shell Petroleum Company.

136. SINCLAIR, "The Origins of the Umbrella Clause in the International Law of Investment Protection", *op. cit.*, fn. 134, p. 421. As explained by this author: "the reference to 'any undertakings' was intended to dispel any doubt that the Abs-Shawcross Draft Convention would confer protection on, inter alia, contractual undertakings entered into between states and foreign private investors, and the vast majority of commentators at the time agreed that this was what was intended. It was also widely believed that the clause was intended to encompass unilateral and general promises such as undertakings contained in legislation on the basis of which foreign investor makes an investment." (Anthony SINCLAIR, "Contractual Claims, Courts and Bilateral Investment Treaties", in *Third Investment Treaty Forum Conference* (10 September 2004), British Institute of International and Comparative Law, 2 TDM (August 2005, no. 4) p. 38).

137. SINCLAIR, "The Origins of the Umbrella Clause in the International Law of Investment Protection", *op. cit.*, fn. 134, p. 427. Concerning this draft, Sinclair notes that "There is no suggestion in the preparatory work for the OECD Draft (or the Abs-Shawcross Draft) or the commentaries thereon, that the undertakings referred to in the umbrella clause should be limited only to other international obligations. To limit the scope of the umbrella clause only to a host state's other obligations arising in international law would add nothing to the existing state of international law. The consistent understanding of commentators and drafters alike is that while the umbrella clause probably did cover international obligations, the focus of the umbrella clause

The OECD Draft Convention was recommended to OECD Member States in 1967. Although it never attracted consensus,[138] it served as a model to forthcoming bilateral investment treaties.[139]

The first bilateral investment treaty, the Germany-Pakistan BIT, included an umbrella clause within its provisions.[140] Umbrella clauses have been included in approximately 40 percent of the more than 2,000 bilateral investment treaties in force today.[141] While several multilateral and regional treaties such as the Energy Charter Treaty contain umbrella clauses,[142] others such as NAFTA have not incorporated them.[143]

The predominant view is that umbrella clauses elevate contractual commitments into international ones. However, scholars and arbitral practice have not reached yet a consensus on their precise meaning and scope, and how and when such elevation takes place.[144]

Treaty-based tribunals had not ruled on umbrella clauses until recent years. Decisions are still too few to set a clear trend and the issue remains highly unsettled.[145]

---

was contractual obligations and unilateral commitments accepted by the host state with regard to foreign property." *Ibid.*, p. 429

138. SINCLAIR, "Contractual Claims, Courts and Bilateral Investment Treaties" in *Third Investment Treaty Forum Conference* (10 September 2004), *op. cit.*, fn. 136, p. 39.

139. *Ibid.*

140. Art. 7 of the Germany-Pakistan BIT provided: "Either Party shall observe any other obligation it may have entered into with regard to investments by nationals or companies of the other party." Many other treaties such as the Argentina-United States BIT currently in force seem to have followed its wording.

141. Vlad ZOLIA, "Effect and Purpose of 'Umbrella Clauses' in Bilateral Investment Treaties: Unresolved Issues", 2 TDM (November 2005, no. 5) p. 1, footnote 2.

142. Art. 10(1) of the Energy Charter Treaty provides: "Each Contracting Party shall observe any obligations it has entered into with an Investor or an Investment of an Investor of any other Contracting Party."

143. See *Waste Management, Inc. v. United Mexican States* (ICSID Case No. ARB(AF)/00/3, Final Award (30 April 2004), *op. cit.*, fn. 124, para. 73 ("... unlike many bilateral and regional investment treaties.... NAFTA Chapter 11 does not give jurisdiction in respect of breaches of investment contracts such as the Concession Agreement. Nor does it contain an 'umbrella clause' committing the host State to comply with its contractual commitments. This does not mean that the Tribunal lacks jurisdiction to take note of or interpret the contract. But such jurisdiction is incidental in character, and it is always necessary for a claimant to assert as its cause of action a claim founded in one of the substantive provisions of NAFTA referred to in Articles 1116 and 1117.").

144. "International Investment Agreements: Key Issues" (New York and Geneva 2004), United Nations Conference on Trade and Development, vol. II, p. 7.

145. See Bernardo CREMADES, "Investor Protection and Legal Security in International Arbitration", p. 1, at <http://findarticles.com/p/articles/mi_qa3923/is_200505/ai_n14717721> (last visited 26 March 2006) and "Disputes Arising Out of Foreign Direct Investment in Latin America. A New Look at the Calvo Doctrine and Other Jurisdictional Issues", Dispute Resolution Journal (May-June 2004) pp. 78-84 and p. 15 (endnotes).

The first case that dealt with umbrella clauses, in rather an indirect way, was *Fedax v. Venezuela* in 1998.[146] The dispute arose out of the non-payment of promissory notes issued by the Government of Venezuela. Fedax submitted its claim before an ICSID tribunal under the dispute settlement clause contained in the Venezuela-Netherlands BIT, which provided for the submission of "disputes between one Contracting Party and a national of the other Contracting Party concerning an obligation of the former under this Agreement in relation to an investment of the latter".[147] The tribunal's jurisdiction did not extend to contractual claims and it was only established for "... determining whether there is a breach by the Contracting Party concerned of its obligations under this Agreement, whether such breach of obligations has caused damages to the national concerned, and, if such is the case, the amount of compensation".[148]

Nonetheless, in its Art. 3(4), the BIT contained an umbrella clause, which read: "Each Contracting Party shall observe any obligation it may have entered into with regard to the treatment of investments of nationals of the other Contracting Party...".

Avoiding specific references to how the umbrella clause operated, the tribunal enforced it by ordering the Government of Venezuela to abide by its commitments.[149]

It was not until 2003 that an ICSID tribunal discussed in more detail the meaning and effect of an umbrella clause. In *SGS v. Pakistan,*[150] the dispute arose out of a pre-shipment inspection agreement entered into between SGS and Pakistan, which during its execution triggered claims by both parties. While Pakistan initiated an arbitration in its territory on the basis of the dispute settlement clause in the contract, SGS instituted ICSID arbitration under the Switzerland-Pakistan BIT.

SGS argued that, among other provisions, Pakistan had breached the BIT's umbrella clause[151] by failing to guarantee the observance of its contractual commitments under the PSI Agreement.

---

146. *Fedax N.V. v. The Republic of Venezuela* (ICSID Case No. ARB/96/3), Award (9 March 1998), 37 I.L.M. (1998) p. 1391. See also SCHREUER, "Travelling the BIT Route – Of Waiting Periods, Umbrella Clauses and Forks in the Road", *op. cit.*, fn. 97, pp. 251-252.

147. Venezuela-Netherlands BIT, Art. 9(1).

148. *Ibid.*, Art. 9(3).

149. *Fedax N.V. v. The Republic of Venezuela* (ICSID Case No. ARB/96/3), Award (9 March 1998), *op. cit.*, fn. 146, para. 29. The tribunal ruled that it "... is fully satisfied that the purchase by Fedax N.V. of the promissory notes subject matter of the request for arbitration meets the requirement of an investment both under the Convention and the Agreement, It follows that the Republic of Venezuela is under the obligation to honor precisely the terms and conditions governing such investment, laid down mainly in *Article 3 of the Agreement*, as well as to honor the specific payments established in the promissory notes issued, and the Tribunal so finds in the terms of Article 9(3) of the Agreement...."

150. *SGS Société Générale de Surveillance S.A. v. Islamic Republic of Pakistan* (ICSID Case No. ARB/01/13), Decision on Jurisdiction (6 August 2003), *op. cit.*, fn. 23.

151. Art. 11 of the Pakistan-Switzerland BIT provided: "Either Contracting Party shall constantly guarantee the observance of the commitments it has entered into with respect to the investments of the investors of the other Contracting Party."

Pakistan challenged ICSID jurisdiction on the basis, among other grounds, that all of SGS's claims were entirely contractual in nature.[152] SGS alleged that its claims were BIT claims and further that "the inclusion of an 'umbrella clause' such as Article 11 of the BIT has the effect of elevating a simple breach of contract claim to a treaty claim under international law".[153]

The tribunal rejected SGS's construction by affirming that

> "as a matter of textuality therefore, the scope of Article 11 of the BIT, while consisting in its entirety of only one sentence, appears susceptible of almost indefinite expansion. The text itself of Article 11 does not purport to state that breaches of contract alleged by an investor in relation to a contract it has concluded with a State (widely considered to be a matter of municipal rather than international law) are automatically 'elevated' to the level of breaches of international treaty law. Thus, it appears to us that while the Claimant has sought to spell out the consequences or inferences it would draw from Article 11, the Article itself does not set forth those consequences."[154]

The tribunal added that if it was to adopt the interpretation provided by the claimant, clear and convincing evidence should have been provided to the tribunal by SGS.[155] It also emphasized the broad consequences that accepting the claimant's view would entail: an unlimited number of State contracts as well as other municipal law instruments would be incorporated by reference under the BIT; the BIT substantial standards of treatment would be rendered superfluous since a simple contract breach would suffice to consider the treaty violated; and the investor may, at will, nullify any freely negotiated dispute settlement clause in a State contract since it will be always free to choose between the contract forum and arbitration under the BIT.[156]

To sustain its reading, the tribunal also relied on the location of the umbrella clause (Art. 11) among the BIT provisions. It held that it was not placed together with the substantive obligations undertaken in Arts. 3 to 7. This led the tribunal to conclude that the umbrella clause was not intended to be a first order standard obligation and constitute a substantive obligation like those set out in Arts. 3 to 7.[157]

The tribunal thus concluded that "Article 11 of the BIT would have to be considerably more specifically worded before it can reasonably be read in the extraordinarily expansive manner submitted by the Claimant."[158] The arbitral panel also justified its conclusion by stating that it did not leave the umbrella clause devoid of any effect. In its view, the umbrella clause would serve, for instance, as "... an implied affirmative

---

152. *SGS Société Générale de Surveillance S.A. v. Islamic Republic of Pakistan* (ICSID Case No. ARB/01/13), Decision on Jurisdiction (6 August 2003), *op. cit.*, fn. 23, para. 43.
153. *Ibid.*, para. 98.
154. *Ibid.*, para. 166.
155. *Ibid.*, para. 167.
156. *Ibid.*, para. 168.
157. *Ibid.*, paras. 169-170.
158. *Ibid.*, para. 171.

commitment to enact implementing rules and regulations necessary or appropriate to give effect to a contractual or statutory undertaking in favor of investors of another Contracting Party that would otherwise be a dead letter".[159] Furthermore, it held that the violation of a State contract could constitute a breach of the BIT's umbrella clause under exceptional circumstances, such as the State's failure to abide by a contractually agreed dispute settlement provision.[160]

The tribunal itself clarified, however, that the criteria adopted were strictly and only applicable to this case. Being ICSID precedents case specific in their analysis, the tribunal did not close the door to the fact that States may agree under a treaty that all contract breaches will amount to treaty breaches. It just found that there was no evidence that such had been the case under Art. 11 of the Switzerland-Pakistan BIT.[161]

The SGS v. Pakistan decision has been subject to strong criticism.[162] The tribunal claimed that it would approach the analysis of the BIT umbrella clause following the Vienna Convention on the Law of Treaties, thus looking into its ordinary meaning in its context and in the light of the treaty's object and purpose.[163] At the end, however, it seemed to have favored an implied rather than an express meaning of the umbrella clause.[164]

The Government of Switzerland expressed its concern on the construction made by the SGS v. Pakistan tribunal of the BIT umbrella clause. In a letter addressed to ICSID's Deputy Secretary-General dated 1 October 2003, Switzerland asserted that it was:

"... alarmed about the very narrow interpretation given to the meaning of Article 11 by the [ICSID] Tribunal, which not only runs counter to the intention of Switzerland when concluding the Treaty but is quite evidently neither supported

---

159. *Ibid.*, para. 172.

160. *Ibid.* The tribunal added that: "The modes by which a Contracting Party may 'constantly guarantee the observance of' its contractual or statutory or administrative municipal law commitments with respect to investments are not necessarily exhausted by the instant transubstantiation of contract claims into BIT claims posited by the Claimant." (*Ibid.*)

161. *Ibid.*, para. 173.

162. See SCHREUER, "Travelling the BIT Route – Of Waiting Periods, Umbrella Clauses and Forks in the Road", *op. cit.*, fn. 97, pp. 252-254; Thomas W. WÄLDE, "Energy Charter Treaty-based Investment Arbitration", 5 The Journal of World Investment and Trade (2004) p. 373 at pp. 392-393 (2004); ALEXANDROV, "Breaches of Contract and Breaches of Treaty. The Jurisdiction of Treaty-based Arbitration Tribunals to Decide Breach of Contract Claims in *SGS v. Pakistan* and *SGS v. Philippines*", *op. cit.*, fn. 8, pp. 569-572. Summing up the predominant view on the decision, Alexandrov commented that: "The *SGS v. Pakistan* Tribunal ignored the ample authorities interpreting the umbrella clause for what it is: a substantive treaty obligation requiring States to observe contractual and other commitments entered into with foreign investors." (*Ibid.*, p. 572).

163. *SGS Société Générale de Surveillance S.A. v. Islamic Republic of Pakistan* (ICSID Case No. ARB/01/13), Decision on Jurisdiction (6 August 2003), *op. cit.*, fn. 23, para. 164.

164. See Nick GALLUS, "When is a Contract Breach a Treaty Breach? The Scope of International Investment Protection Treaty Obligations Observance Clauses", 2005 App. News 0510, p. 6.

by the meaning of similar articles in BITs concluded by other countries nor by academic comments on such provisions".[165]

A few months after the *SGS v. Pakistan* decision, another ICSID tribunal was asked to rule on the umbrella clause of the Swiss-Philippines BIT. The dispute involved the same claimant. This time the respondent was the Philippines.[166] As in *SGS v. Pakistan*, the case pertained to the payment of outstanding debts. The umbrella clause included as Art. X(2) of the applicable BIT read:

> "Each Contracting Party shall observe any obligation it has assumed with regard to specific investments in its territory by investors of the other Contracting Party."

In constructing this clause, the tribunal in *SGS v. Philippines* noted that:

> "... Article X(2) makes it a breach of the BIT for the host State to fail to observe binding commitments, including contractual commitments, which it has assumed with regard to specific investments. But it does not convert the issue of the extent or content of such obligations into an issue of international law. That issue (in the present case, the issue of how much is payable for services provided under the CISS Agreement) is still governed by the investment agreement."[167]

Regarding the finding made by the *SGS v. Pakistan* tribunal, it qualified it as a highly restrictive interpretation of the umbrella clause[168] and held that:

> "Not only are the reasons given by the Tribunal in *SGS v. Pakistan* unconvincing: the Tribunal failed to give any clear meaning to the 'umbrella clause'."[169]

Following these two decisions, other tribunals have also addressed the issue.

Even though it found that it lacked jurisdiction based on the absence of a qualifying investment under the United Kingdom-Egypt BIT, the *Joy Mining* tribunal further based its ruling on the contractual nature of all claimant's claims. As regards to the effect of the BIT umbrella clause under its Art. 2(2),[170] it asserted:

---

165. Quoted by ALEXANDROV ("Breaches of Contract and Breaches of Treaty. The Jurisdiction of Treaty-based Arbitration Tribunals to Decide Breach of Contract Claims in *SGS v. Pakistan* and *SGS v. Philippines*", *op. cit.*, fn. 8, at pp. 570-571).

166. *SGS Société Générale de Surveillance S.A. v. Republic of the Philippines* (ICSID Case No. ARB/02/6), Decision on Jurisdiction (29 January 2004), *op. cit.*, fn. 7.

167. *Ibid.*, para. 128.

168. *Ibid.*, para. 120.

169. *Ibid.*, para. 125.

170. Art. 2(2) of the UK-Egypt BIT provides: "Each Contracting Party shall observe any obligation it may have entered into with regard to investments of nationals or companies of the other Contracting Party."

"... it could not be held that an umbrella clause inserted in the Treaty, and not very prominently, could have the effect of transforming all contract disputes into investment disputes under the Treaty, unless of course there would be a clear violation of the Treaty rights and obligations or a violation of contract rights of such a magnitude as to trigger the Treaty protection, which is not the case. The connection between the Contract and the Treaty is the missing link that prevents any such effect. This might be perfectly different in other cases where that link is found to exist, but certainly it is not the case here."[171]

So, up to August 2004, ICSID precedents had provided four different constructions of umbrella clauses. *Fedax v. Venezuela* applied the umbrella clause, without much elaboration, to a plain non-payment of promissory notes, a breach that on its face did not qualify as a sovereign act. *SGS v. Pakistan* rejected the proposition that such a clause automatically elevates contractual claims into treaty claims. On the opposite side, albeit based on a differently phrased clause, *SGS v. Philippines* found that through the application of the umbrella clause, a lack of compliance with contractual commitments can amount to a BIT breach,[172] a similar finding to that reached in *Fedax v. Venezuela*. And finally, *Joy Mining v. Egypt* ruled that umbrella clauses may elevate contractual claims into treaty claims inasmuch as the contract violation is of such a magnitude as to trigger the Treaty's protection.[173]

To a certain extent, this last construction could be seen as devoiding the umbrella clause of an autonomous content. A breach of other treaty standards or international obligations would be required in order to trigger the application of the umbrella clause.

According to Zolia, it is not clear if the threshold mentioned *in Joy Mining* in order to consider the umbrella clause violated is self-contained in treaties or in the clause itself. As well, the tribunal failed to clarify whether that threshold is similar to the one held under the customary international law minimum standard of treatment of aliens.[174]

In *Salini v. Jordan* the dispute was governed by the Italy-Jordan BIT. Claimants sustained that Arts. 2(4), 2(5) and 11(2) of the treaty created an umbrella clause, which obliged the respondent to guarantee compliance with investment contracts within the framework of the treaty.[175]

---

171. *Joy Mining Machinery Limited v. the Arab Republic of Egypt* (ICSID Case No. ARB/03/1), Award on Jurisdiction (6 August 2004), *op. cit.*, fn. 70, para. 81.

172. Notwithstanding so, the tribunal held that the issue of the extent or content of such commitments remained as a matter of contract law (*SGS Société Générale de Surveillance S.A. v. Republic of the Philippines* (ICSID Case No. ARB/02/6), Decision on Jurisdiction (29 January 2004), *op. cit.*, fn. 7, para. 128).

173. See ZOLIA, "Effect and Purpose of 'Umbrella Clauses' in Bilateral Investment Treaties: Unresolved Issues", *op. cit.*, fn. 141, p. 39.

174. *Ibid.*, p. 46.

175. *Salini Costruttori S.p.A. and Italstrade S.p.A. v. The Hashemite Kingdom of Jordan* (ICSID Case No. ARB/02/13), Decision on Jurisdiction (29 November 2004), *op. cit.*, fn. 62, para. 37.

The tribunal found that no umbrella clause was embodied in the applicable BIT[176] and, therefore, asserted that the obligations allegedly breached remained purely contractual in nature.[177]

The tribunal did not elaborate further as it had no need to do so. But if the *obiter dictum* above is read *a contrario sensu*, it could be concluded that an umbrella clause would have transformed contractual obligations into treaty ones.[178]

In *Eureko v. Poland*, the tribunal admitted that the umbrella clause established in Art. 3(5) of the Netherlands-Poland BIT protected the investor against the State's breach of any obligations undertaken with regard to investments. Even though the case appeared to deal with State's sovereign measures, the tribunal did not restrict the operation of the clause to the nature of the contract breach.[179]

---

176. *Ibid.*, paras. 126-130.

177. *Ibid.*, para. 127 ("Of course, each State Party to the BIT between Italy and Jordan remains bound by its contractual obligations. However, this undertaking was not reiterated in the BIT. Therefore, these obligations remain purely contractual in nature and any disputes regarding the said obligations must be resolved in accordance with the dispute settlement procedures foreseen in the contract. Contrary to what the Claimants argue, this is not at all an absurd solution: the States Parties to the BIT are still bound by their treaty obligations as well as their contract obligations, but the dispute settlement procedures in each case are different.").

178. In a similar path, Gaffney has affirmed that the tribunal's decision "... indicates a willingness on the part of that Tribunal to consider the extension of its jurisdiction to purely contractual claims on the basis of an 'umbrella clause' by which the relevant State party commits itself to observe its contractual obligations or to guarantee the observance of such commitments" (GAFFNEY, "Case Summary: *Salini Costruttori S.p.A. and Italstrade S.p.A. v. The Hashemite Kingdom of Jordan* (ICSID Case No. ARB/02/13), *op. cit.*, fn. 93, Sect. 5(b)).

179. The tribunal held: "Article 3.5 of the Treaty provides that each Contracting Party 'shall observe any obligations it may have entered into with regard to investments of investors of the other Contracting Party'. (A clause of such substance is often called 'the umbrella clause'. Thus, insofar as the Government of Poland has entered into obligations vis-à-vis Eureko with regard to the latter's investments, and insofar as the Tribunal has found that the Respondent has acted in breach of those obligations, it stands, prima facie, in violation of Article 3.5 of the Treaty.... The plain meaning – the 'ordinary meaning' – of a provision prescribing that a State 'shall observe any obligations it may have entered into' with regard to certain foreign investments is not obscure. The phrase, 'shall observe' is imperative and categorical. 'Any' obligations is capacious; it means not only obligations of a certain type, but 'any' – that is to say, all – obligations entered into with regard to investments of investors of the other Contracting Party.... It follows that the effect of Article 3.5 in this proceeding cannot be overlooked, or equated with the Treaty's provisions for fair and equitable treatment, national treatment, most-favored-nation treatment, deprivation of investments, and full protection and security. On the contrary, Article 3.5 must be interpreted to mean something in itself. The immediate, operative effects of Article 3.5 are two. The first is that Eureko's contractual arrangements with the Government of Poland are subject to the jurisdiction of the Tribunal, a conclusion that reinforces the jurisdictional conclusions earlier reached in this Award. The second is that breaches by Poland of its obligations under the SPA and its First Addendum, as read together, that are not breaches of Articles 3.1 and 5 of the Treaty nevertheless may be breaches of Article 3.5 of the Treaty, since they transgress Poland's Treaty commitment to 'observe any obligations it may have entered into' with regard to Eureko's investments." (*Eureko B. V. v. Republic of Poland*, Partial Award (19 August 2005), *op. cit.*, fn. 31, paras. 244, 246, 249 and 250). See also GALLUS, "When is a Contract Breach a Treaty Breach?

In *LESI-DIPENTA v. Algeria*, the tribunal only made side statements regarding umbrella clauses in BITs. Even though it did not elaborate on the issue, the tribunal's statements seem to indicate a broad construction of the clause's scope.[180]

In *Noble Ventures v. Romania*, the tribunal dealt with the umbrella clause existing in the United States-Romania BIT.[181] The dispute arose out of a privatization agreement concerning the acquisition, management, operation and disposition of a substantial steel mill and other assets, Combinatul Siderurgic Resita, located in Resita, Romania.

The tribunal observed that such a clause should be read pursuant to the rules of treaty interpretation set out by the Vienna Convention on the Law of Treaties and taking into account the principle of effectiveness.[182] Based on a plain reading of the umbrella clause, the tribunal concluded that the provision was intended to create obligations beyond those specified in other BIT provisions and the employment of the notion "entered into" indicated that the clause was making reference to contractual obligations and not general commitments, for example, by way of legislative acts. The tribunal added that such provision "... would be very much an empty base unless understood as referring to contracts".[183]

The Scope of International Investment Protection Treaty Obligations Observance Clauses", *op. cit.*, fn. 164, p. 12.

The dissenting opinion in that case expressed a different view. According to it, a broad construction of umbrella clauses could cause prejudicial consequences to the development of foreign investment and undermine the principle by which all parties to commercial contracts should benefit from equal legal protection no matter their nationality. In his opinion, Profesor Rakski sustained: "It is worth to note that by opening a wide door to foreign parties to commercial contracts concluded with a State-owned company to switch their contractual disputes from normal jurisdiction of international commercial arbitration tribunals or state courts to BIT Tribunals, the majority of this Tribunal has created a potentially dangerous precedent capable of producing negative effects on the further development of foreign capital participation in privatizations of State-owned companies. At the same time, this decision may lead to undermine the fundamental principles upon which both national and international laws on contracts have been based: equal legal protection of all parties to commercial contracts irrespective of their nationality. The Tribunal's decision may lead to create a privileged class of foreign parties to commercial contract who may easily transform their contractual disputes with State-owned companies into BIT disputes. This way, jurisdiction clauses agreed by the parties submitting all contractual disputes between the parties to an international arbitration tribunal or a state court may be easily frustrated by a foreign contracting party...." (*Eureko B.V. v. Republic of Poland*, Dissenting Opinion by Professor Jerzy Rajski (19 August 2005), *op. cit.*, fn. 31, para. 11).

180. Although the Italy-Algeria BIT does not contain an umbrella clause the *LESI-DIPENTA v. Algeria* tribunal asserted that: "the effect of such clauses is to transform the violations of the State's contractual commitments into violations of the treaty umbrella clause and by this to give jurisdiction to the tribunal over the matter...". (*Consorzio Groupement L.E.S.I. – DIPENTA v. Democratic and Popular Republic of Algeria* (ICSID Case No. ARB/03/08), Award (10 January 2005), *op. cit.*, fn. 103, para. 25(ii)).

181. Art. II(2)(c) of the United States-Romania BIT reads: "Each Party shall observe any obligation it may have entered into with regard to investments."

182. *Noble Ventures, Inc. v. Romania* (ICSID Case No. ARB/01/11), Award (12 October 2005), para. 50, at <http://ita.law.uvic.ca/documents/Noble.pdf> (last visited 25 March 2006).

183. *Ibid.*, para. 51.

The tribunal further noted the extraordinary character of this kind of clause which "introduces an exception to the general separation of State obligations under municipal and international law"[184] and, thus, to the established general rules of law.[185] Therefore, quoting the *ELSI* case,[186] it affirmed that given its exceptional nature, "the identification of a provision as an 'umbrella clause' can as a consequence proceed only from a strict, if not indeed restrictive, interpretation of its terms and, more generally, in accordance with the well-known customary rules codified under Article 31 of the Vienna Convention of the Law of Treaties".[187]

In the particular case at hand, the tribunal decided that the provision of Art. II(2)(c) of the United States-Romania BIT qualified as a real umbrella clause, which tends to assimilate contractual obligations to treaty ones.[188] However, the tribunal dismissed claimant's claims on the basis, inter alia, that no legally binding obligation existed on the part of Romania and that the claimant failed to bring sufficient evidence on the contract breach.

Thus, even though Romania had alleged that umbrella clauses were aimed at creating a treaty obligation to protect investors against the exercise of sovereign powers which interfered with contractual obligations and other binding obligations in relation to investments,[189] the tribunal considered unnecessary to express any definitive conclusion as to whether the umbrella clause "... of the BIT perfectly assimilates to breach of the BIT any breach by the host State of any contractual obligation as determined by its municipal law or whether the expression 'any obligation', despite its apparent breadth, must be understood to be subject to some limitation in the light of the nature and objects of the BIT".[190] In fact, the tribunal's conclusions were not to be affected in any way by the decision that it may have taken on that question.

Nonetheless, the method of interpretation adopted by the tribunal and the emphasis put on the clause's wording, in particular to the fact that the provision embodied "any obligation", seem to indicate that the panel would probably not have limited the operation of the clause to breaches of governmental nature only.[191]

---

184. *Ibid.*, para. 55.

185. *Ibid.*, para. 55.

186. The tribunal quoted the following paragraph from the *ELSI* case: "an important principle of international law should not be held to have been tacitly dispensed with by international agreement, in the absence of words making clear an intention to do so" (*Case concerning the Elettronica Sicula S.p.A. (ELSI) (United States of America v. Italy)*, Judgment (20 July 1989), ICJ Reports (1989) p. 15 at p. 42).

187. *Noble Ventures, Inc. v. Romania* (ICSID Case No. ARB/01/11), Award (12 October 2005), *op. cit.*, fn. 182, para. 55.

188. *Ibid.*, para. 60.

189. *Ibid.*, para. 45.

190. *Ibid.*, para. 61.

191. For instance, the tribunal held that "... where the acts of a governmental agency are to be attributed to the State for the purposes of applying an umbrella clause, such as Art. II(2)(c) of the BIT, breaches of a contract into which the State has entered are capable of constituting a breach of international law by virtue of the breach of the umbrella clause" (*Ibid.*, para. 85). As well, it asserted "For reasons already stated, a breach of the SPA is, as a matter of law, capable of

More recently, in *El Paso v. Argentina*, the tribunal addressed the scope of umbrella clauses, bearing in mind previous decisions on the matter and the consequences that a broad interpretation could entail.[192] Sympathizing with *SGS v. Pakistan* and adopting the distinction made in *Joy Mining v. Egypt* between governmental and commercial State acts, the tribunal found that the protection of the applicable umbrella clause would only be triggered by breaches to contracts of a governmental nature, setting aside those concerning ordinary commercial agreements.[193]

The tribunal grounded its finding on a joint construction of the umbrella clause (Art. II(2)(c)) and Art. VII(1) of the Argentina-United States BIT, which provides that an investment dispute arises out or relates to, inter alia, an investment agreement. The arbitration panel defined this last notion as "... an agreement in which the State appears as a sovereign"[194] and, therefore, excluded from the scope of protection of the umbrella clause those contracts in which the State enters into acting as a merchant.[195] The tribunal seemed to have concluded that umbrella clauses, such as the one contained in the Argentina-United States BIT, only cover State contracts in which some *"clauses*

---

constituting a breach, attributable to the Respondent, of the BIT by reason of the inclusion in the BIT of Article II(2)(c), and, in the judgment of the Tribunal, whatever, if any, limitation is to be placed on the meaning of 'obligation' where that expression is used in Article II(2)(c) of the BIT (cf. paragraph 61 above), a breach that is attributable to the Respondent of Article 7.4.2 of the SPA would constitute a breach by the Respondent of Article II(2)(c) of the BIT." (*Ibid.*, para. 136). The tribunal also affirmed: "In conclusion with regard to the issue of alleged breach of Article 7.4.2 of the SPA, the Claimant's claim fails not because a proved breach would not have constituted a breach of the BIT, i.e. Article II(2)(c) of the BIT...." (*Ibid.*, para. 158). It also expressed: "If a settlement was indeed concluded, a claim for breach of the settlement would be included under the umbrella clause contained in Art. II(2)(c) of the BIT because the text of the alleged settlement provided inter alia for modifications of the SPA." (*Ibid.*, para. 198).

192. *El Paso Energy International Company v. The Argentine Republic* (ICSID Case No. ARB/03/15), Decision on Jurisdiction (27 April 2006), *op. cit.*, fn. 64 , paras. 66-88.

193. The Tribunal asserted that "In this Tribunal's view, it is necessary to distinguish the State as a merchant from the State as a sovereign.... The view that it is essentially from the State as a sovereign that the foreign investors have to be protected through the availability of international arbitration is confirmed, in the Tribunal's opinion, by the language in the new 2004 US Model BIT, which clearly elevates only the contract claims stemming from an investment agreement stricto sensu, that, is an agreement in which the State appears as a sovereign, and not all contracts signed with the State or one of its entities to the level of treaty claims, as results from its Article 24(1)(a). In view of the necessity to distinguish the State as a merchant, especially when it acts through instrumentalities, from the State as a sovereign, the Tribunal considers that the 'umbrella clause' in the Argentine-US BIT ... can be interpreted in the light of Article VII (1), which clearly includes among the investment disputes under the Treaty all disputes resulting from a violation of a commitment given by the State as a sovereign State, either through an agreement, an authorization, or the BIT.... Interpreted in this way, the umbrella clause in Article II of the BIT, read in conjunction with Article VII, will not extend the Treaty protection to breaches of an ordinary commercial contract entered into by the State or a State-owned entity, but will cover additional investment protections contractually agreed by the State as a sovereign – such as a stabilization clause – inserted in an investment agreement." (*Ibid.*, paras. 79-81).

194. *Ibid.*, para. 80.

195. *Ibid.*, paras. 79-81.

exorbitantes du droit commun" are inserted and provide no shelter to the State's pure commercial contracts.[196]

One additional consideration should be made in framing the tribunal's approach in *El Paso*. Despite its restrictive view on the umbrella clause, the panel clarified that such view did not imply that it lacked jurisdiction to deal with contractual issues if the measures adopted by the State violated treaty rights. While the tribunal rejected that pure contractual claims could be entertained under the scope of the umbrella clause, on the other hand, it confirmed that the arbitral tribunal has jurisdiction over all claims, even those relating to contracts, when it is called to rule on whether State measures breached the applicable treaty.[197]

This overview of cases shows that ICSID decisions have evidenced different approaches concerning the scope and operation of umbrella clauses.

One of the main discussions that still remains in connection with the application of umbrella clauses as arises from *Fedax, SGS v. Philippines, Joy Mining, Salini v. Jordan, Eureko* and *El Paso* is whether those provisions transmute all contract breaches into treaty breaches or just some kinds of contractual violations, i.e., those that involve measures of governmental nature or relate to contracts which the State entered into in its sovereign capacity.

The same debate is reproduced in scholarly writings. Some authors have expressed themselves in favor of the latter. This is the case, for instance, of Professor Wälde, who notes that, in their origin, umbrella clauses were proposed as a reaction to nationalizations and breaches of concession contracts, in which the State exercised its sovereign powers[198] and were based on the assumption that States and not investors would enforce them before arbitral institutions.[199] In his words, "... the clause could be argued to acquire a much wider scope than was ever intended for it by the original inventors of BITs and framers of the sanctity of contract clause. The simple addition of direct investor arbitration and the widening concept of 'investment' has suddenly put teeth into investment treaty disciplines which were not envisaged when the clause was born."[200]

On the grounds of the original intention of drafters, Wälde comes to the conclusion that the key question is the exercise of governmental powers or reliance on governmental prerogatives. If the dispute constitutes a normal contract dispute, the BIT

---

196. *Ibid.*, para. 77.

197. *Ibid.*, para. 84 (".... There is no doubt that if the State interferes with contractual rights by a unilateral act, whether these rights stem from a contract entered into by a foreign investor with a private party, a State autonomuos entity or the State itself, in such a way that the State's action can be analysed as a violation of the standards of protection embodied in a BIT, the treaty-based arbitration tribunal has jurisdiction over all the claims of the foreign investor, including the claims arising from a violation of its contractual rights. Moreover, Article II, read in conjunction with Article VII(1), also considers as treaty claims the breaches of an investment agreement between Argentina and a national or company of the United States".).

198. WÄLDE, "The 'Umbrella' (or Sanctity of Contract/Pacta Sunt Servanda) Clause in Investment Arbitration: A Comment on Original Intentions and Recent Cases", *op. cit.*, fn. 132, pp. 14-15.

199. *Ibid.*, pp. 15-16.

200. *Ibid.*, p. 21.

and the umbrella clause would have no role to play. On the contrary, in case the dispute involves the State's abusive interference relying on government powers and privileges, the umbrella clause would be operative.[201]

In this view, the umbrella clause would act as a clarifying provision of the status of customary international law, which requires the involvement of governmental powers or a governmental abuse to consider a breach of contract as a violation of international law.[202] In Wälde's opinion, this view would

> "... do justice to the original intention of the *pacta sunt servanda* clause in investment treaties, and to the continuing intention of investment treaties to discipline government conduct which abuses its powers in respect to contractual relationships of foreign investors, but not to get involved in normal commercial conduct just because there is involvement of a state and a foreign company".[203]

The predominant opinion among the authors seems to be, however, that umbrella clauses cover investment-related contracts and protect the investor from any contractual breaches, whatever the nature of the State measures in the particular case.[204] This

---

201. *Ibid.*, p. 85.
202. *Ibid.*, p. 21.
203. *Ibid.*, p. 86.
204. Writing on State contracts as early as 1969, Prosper Weil affirmed that "There is, in fact, no particular difficulty when there is an 'umbrella treaty' between the contracting State and the State of the other contracting party, which turns the obligation to perform the contract into an international obligation of the contracting State vis-à-vis the State of the other contracting party. The intervention of the umbrella treaty transforms contractual obligations into international obligations thereby ensuring, as it has already been stated, 'the intangibility of contract under threat of violating the treaty'; any non-performance of the contract, even if it is legal under the national law of the contracting State, gives rise to the international liability of the latter vis-à-vis the national State of the other contracting party." (Prosper WEIL, *"Problèmes relatifs aux contrats passés entre un Etat et un particulier"*, 128 Recueil des Cours (1969) p. 95 at p. 130 (translation from ALEXANDROV, "Breaches of Contract and Breaches of Treaty. The Jurisdiction of Treaty-based Arbitration Tribunals to Decide Breach of Contract Claims in *SGS v. Pakistan* and *SGS v. Philippines"*, *op. cit.*, fn. 8, pp. 566-567 and SCHREUER, "Travelling the BIT Route–Of Waiting Periods, Umbrella Clauses and Forks in the Road", *op. cit.*, fn. 97, pp. 250-251)).
    Mann asserts that even a variation in the terms of the State's undertakings amounts to a treaty breach under an umbrella clause: "This is a provision of particular importance in that it protects the investor against any interference with his contractual rights, whether it results from a mere breach of contract or a legislative or administrative act, and independently of the question whether or no[t] such interference amounts to expropriation. The variation of the terms of a contract or license by legislative measures, the termination of the contract or the failure to perform any of its terms, for instance, by non-payment, the dissolution of the local company with which the investor may have contracted and the transfer of its assets (with or without the liabilities) – these and similar acts the treaties render wrongful.... What is assumed is that the State has entered into a particular commitment which imposes obligations. Such obligations may arise from contract with the State or from the terms of the license granted by it. It may be express or implied, it may be in writing or oral. But it must be clearly ascertainable as an obligation of the State itself arising from its own commitments." (F.A. MANN, "British Treaties

seems to be the view, among others, of Schreuer,[205] Gaillard,[206] Alexandrov[207] and Zolia.[208]

For those supporting this view, umbrella clauses should be analyzed according to their ordinary meaning and in the light of the object and purpose of the treaty,[209] the wide

---

for the Promotion and Protection of Investments", 52 The Brit. Y.B. Int´l Law 1981 (1982) p. 241 at p. 246).

Dolzer and Stevens express as well that umbrella clauses throw light to international law by providing protection against simple breaches of contracts or by administrative or legislative acts: "These provisions seek to ensure that each Party to the treaty will respect specific undertakings towards nationals of the other Party. The provision is of particular importance because it protects the investor's contractual rights against any interference which might be caused by either a simple breach of contract or by administrative or legislative acts, and because it is not entirely clear under general international law whether such measures constitute breaches of an international obligation." (Rudolph DOLZER and Margrete STEVENS, *Bilateral Investment Treaties* (Martinus Nijhoff Publishers 1995) pp. 81-82).

Based on the German model BIT, Karl notes that this provision transforms responsibility incurred under a contract towards a private investor into international responsibility: "Article 8(2) of the model agreement provides that the contracting parties shall observe any other obligation they have assumed with regard to the investment. This relates particularly to investment contracts between the investor and the host country which often contain very detailed rules. The protection of such contracts is now a standard clause in bilateral investment agreements. Sometimes, countries are reluctant to accept this provision which transforms responsibility incurred towards a private investor under a contract into international responsibility." (Joachim KARL, "The Promotion and Protection of German Foreign Investment Abroad", 11 ICSID Review–Foreign Investment Law Journal (1996) p. 1 at p. 23).

205. SCHREUER, "Travelling the BIT Route. Of Waiting Periods, Umbrella Clauses and Forks in the Road", *op. cit.*, fn. 97, pp. 250-251 ("Clauses of this kind have been added to some BITs to provide additional protection to investors beyond the traditional international standards. They are often referred to as umbrella clauses because they put contractual commitments under the BIT's protective umbrella. They add the compliance with investment contracts, or other undertakings of the host State, to the BIT's substantive standards. In this way, a violation of such a contract becomes a violation of the BIT.... Under the regime of such an umbrella clause, any violation of a contract thus covered becomes a violation of the BIT.").

206. GAILLARD, "Investment Treaty Arbitration and Jurisdiction over Contract Claims – the SGS Cases Considered", *op. cit.*, fn. 85, p. 345.

207. ALEXANDROV, "Breaches of Contract and Breaches of Treaty. The Jurisdiction of Treaty-based Arbitration Tribunals to Decide Breach of Contract Claims in *SGS v. Pakistan* and *SGS v. Philippines*", *op. cit.*, fn. 8, pp. 565-566 ("... States may wish to agree in an investment treaty to consider all contractual breaches, or breaches of other obligations undertaken by the State with respect to foreign investors, as treaty breaches. Typically, they do so in the form of an 'umbrella clause' or an 'observance of undertakings clause' providing that the host State must observe any commitments that it has undertaken with respect to the foreign investor.").

208. ZOLIA, "Effect and Purpose of 'Umbrella Clauses' in Bilateral Investment Treaties: Unresolved Issues", *op. cit.*, fn. 141, p. 35.

209. The Vienna Convention distinguishes between principal means of interpretation – enumerated in Art. 31– and "supplementary means of interpretation", which are to be used only to confirm the meaning resulting from the application of Art. 31 or when the application of Art. 31 fails to yield a clear meaning. The first rule under Art. 31 is that "[a] treaty shall be interpreted in good faith in accordance with the ordinary meaning to be given to the terms of the treaty in their

definition of investment under modern investment treaties, and the availability of investor-State arbitration.

That was the approach followed by the tribunals in *Eureko* and *Noble Ventures*. They entered into the analysis of the ordinary meaning of the clause and concluded that "the plain meaning – the 'ordinary meaning' – of a provision prescribing that a State 'shall observe any obligations it may have entered into' with regard to certain foreign investments is not obscure. The phrase, 'shall observe' is imperative and categorical. 'Any' obligations is capacious; it means not only obligations of a certain type, but 'any' – that is to say, all – obligations entered into with regard to investments of investors of the other Contracting Party."[210]

As noted in *Eureko*, an umbrella clause should be interpreted to mean something in itself and cannot be equated to the rest of the substantive standards of treatment.[211] If investors are already protected against a State's sovereign measures that impair their investment-related contracts under general international law and other BIT provisions, umbrella clauses would add nothing, but just reinforce what it is already said in the

---

context and in the light of its object and purpose". Under this rule, "the text [of the treaty] must be presumed to be the authentic expression of the parties; and in consequence the starting point of interpretation is the elucidation of the meaning of the text, not to investigate ab initio the intentions of the parties". Sir Humphrey WALDOCK, Special Rapporteur, "Third Report on the Law of Treaties", 2 Y.B. INT'L. COMM'N (1964) p. 5 at p. 56, U.N. Doc. A/CN.4/167 and Add.1-3. As the ICJ explained, "[T]he first duty of a tribunal which is called upon to interpret and apply the provisions of a treaty, is to endeavour to give effect to them in their natural and ordinary meaning in the context in which they occur. If the relevant words in their natural and ordinary meaning make sense in their context, that is an end of the matter." (*Opinion on the Competence of the General Assembly in the Admission of a State to the United Nations*, ICJ Reports 1950, p. 8). One may say that the intention of the parties to the treaty may evidence that the meaning of the clause is different from the one that arises out of its literal construction. Even if such possibility was accepted, however, the party that attributes a distinct meaning to a treaty provision has the burden of proof. And such proof should mainly be based on the common intention expressed by the parties during the negotiation of the particular treaty that governs the dispute.

210. *Eureko B.V. v. Republic of Poland*, Partial Award (19 August 2005), *op. cit.*, fn. 31, para. 246. In *Noble Ventures v. Turkey*, the tribunal observed that "With regard to Art. II (2)(c) of the bilateral investment treaty which is of relevance in the present case, it has to be observed that there are differences between the wording of the clause and the clauses in the other cases. Therefore, it is necessary, first, to interpret Art. II (2)(c) regardless of the other cases. In doing so, reference has to be made to Arts. 31 et seq. of the Vienna Convention on the Law of Treaties which reflect the customary international law concerning treaty interpretation. Accordingly, treaties have to be interpreted in good faith in accordance with the ordinary meaning to be given to the terms of the treaty in their context and in the light of the object and purpose of the Treaty, while recourse may be had to supplementary means of interpretation, including the preparatory work and the circumstances of its conclusion, only in order to confirm the meaning resulting from the application of the aforementioned methods of interpretation. Reference should also be made to the principle of effectiveness (*effet utile*), which, too plays an important role in interpreting treaties." (*Noble Ventures, Inc. v. Romania* (ICSID Case No. ARB/01/11), Award (12 October 2005), *op. cit.*, fn. 182, para. 50).

211. *Eureko B.V. v. Republic of Poland*, Partial Award (19 August 2005), *op. cit.*, fn. 31, para. 249.

remaining BIT standards. That approach would deprive umbrella clauses of any effective meaning, contradicting general rules of interpretation.

Referring to this issue, Zolia notes that:

> "Breaches of contract that are motivated by non-commercial considerations create international state responsibility even in the absence of an 'umbrella clause'. Therefore, as a matter of logic, 'umbrella clauses' should offer a broader protection against all breaches, whether governmental or not.... Interpreting the 'umbrella clause' as applying only to governmental acts / commitments in all circumstances would leave the investor without treaty protection in case of intolerable commercial behavior (whether in bad faith or abusive)."[212]

Umbrella clauses were drafted in order to provide investors with further protection.[213] This is in line with the object and purpose of investment treaties, i.e., to promote foreign investments and protect foreign investors.[214] As noted in *Noble Ventures*:

> "The object and purpose rule also supports such an interpretation. While it is not permissible, as is too often done regarding BITs, to interpret clauses exclusively in favour of investors, here such an interpretation is justified. Considering, as pointed out above, that any other interpretation would deprive Art. II (2)(c) of practical content, reference has necessarily to be made to the principle of effectiveness, also applied by other Tribunals in interpreting BIT provisions (see *SGS v. Philippines*, para. 116 and *Salini v. Jordan*, para. 95). An interpretation to the contrary would deprive the investor of any internationally secured legal remedy in respect of investment contracts that it has entered into with the host State. While it is not the purpose of investment treaties per se to remedy such problems, a clause that is readily capable of being interpreted in this way and which would otherwise be deprived of practical applicability is naturally to be understood as protecting investors also with regard to contracts with the host

---

212. ZOLIA, "Effect and Purpose of 'Umbrella Clauses' in Bilateral Investment Treaties: Unresolved Issues", *op. cit.*, fn. 141, pp. 34-35.

213. ALEXANDROV, "Breaches of Contract and Breaches of Treaty. The Jurisdiction of Treaty-based Arbitration Tribunals to Decide Breach of Contract Claims in *SGS v. Pakistan* and *SGS v. Philippines*", *op. cit.*, fn. 8, at p. 566 ("... an umbrella clause in a treaty intends to achieve more than what is already the norm under customary international law").

214. Regarding the role of the treaty's object and purpose in the interpretation of treaties, the tribunal in *Siemens v. Argentina* held: "The Tribunal shall be guided by the purpose of the Treaty as expressed in its title and preamble. It is a treaty 'to protect' and 'to promote' investments. The preamble provides that the parties have agreed to the provisions of the Treaty for the purpose of creating favorable conditions for the investments of nationals or companies of one of the two States in the territory of the other State. Both parties recognize that the promotion and protection of these investments by a treaty may stimulate private economic initiative and increase the well-being of the peoples of both countries. The intention of the parties is clear. It is to create favorable conditions for investments and to stimulate private initiative." (*Siemens A.G. v. the Argentine Republic* (ICSID Case No. ARB/02/8), Decision on Jurisdiction (3 August 2004), *op. cit.*, fn. 28, para. 81).

State generally in so far as the contract was entered into with regard to an investment."[215]

It is true that, as noted by Gallus, the restriction of umbrella clauses' scope to sovereign breaches lies in policy[216] and that the protection of pure contractual breaches under umbrella clauses may potentially promote the submission by investors of a high number of contractual disputes before international arbitration tribunals.[217]

However, this should not create a problem in itself, unless investors begin to file claims for trivial disputes.[218] This is not likely to happen and in those unusual cases that trivial disputes have effectively been filed, the existence of umbrella clauses has not been the exclusive basis of such filings.

The truth is that international State contracts involve relevant investments, which require for their success a close relationship and collaboration between the investor and the host State. Both parties are, in most cases, interested in the contract's development and, save a relevant breach, the parties to the contract will not be willing to trigger litigation, which could frustrate such relationship and affect the proper execution of the contract. For this reason, most of the contract-related investment disputes involve terminal conflicts and are only filed when no other legal or practical solution is available. In addition, international arbitration costs have increased significantly during the years and should discourage, in most cases, the filing of trivial disputes.[219]

To conclude, even though different positions have been adopted concerning the scope and effect of umbrella clauses, the trend leans toward construing them as including commitments assumed by host States under investment-related contracts. Some ambiguity still remains as whether they protect investors against any kind of contract breaches, whether governmental or not. However, the case law examined above seems to indicate the predominance of the broader view.

VII.   CONCLUSIONS

Throughout this report, we have summarily addressed the distinction between contract and treaty claims, the tribunals' approach to it at the jurisdictional phase, the relevance of the treaty's dispute settlement clauses, the unsettled discussion on when a contract breach amounts to a treaty breach and, finally, the scope and effect of the so-called umbrella clauses.

---

215. *Noble Ventures, Inc. v. Romania* (ICSID Case No. ARB/01/11), Award (12 October 2005), *op. cit.*, fn. 182, para. 52.

216. GALLUS, "When is a Contract Breach a Treaty Breach? The Scope of International Investment Protection Treaty Obligations Observance Clauses", *op. cit.*, fn. 164, p. 12.

217. *Ibid.*, p. 1.

218. SCHREUER, "Travelling the BIT Route–Of Waiting Periods, Umbrella Clauses and Forks in the Road", *op. cit.*, fn. 97, p. 255.

219. ZOLIA, "Effect and Purpose of 'Umbrella Clauses' in Bilateral Investment Treaties: Unresolved Issues", *op. cit.*, fn. 141, p. 48.

As in any other field of law, there are no conclusive or strict standards to be universally applied in every situation. We have seen, however, that scholars and arbitral practice have developed useful principles in order to delineate the jurisdiction of treaty-based tribunals based on the nature of the claims that they can be called to entertain. Despite the unavoidable disagreements that will always exist, the prevailing view is summarized below:

First, the cause of action is the central tenet to distinguish a contract claim from a treaty claim. A contract claim alleges a breach of a contract while a treaty claim invokes a breach of the treaty.

Second, even though not every breach of contract is a treaty breach, and vice versa, identical facts could give rise to both a contract and a treaty claim.

Third, even in those cases in which the tribunal has no jurisdiction to hear contract claims, the tribunal still remains competent to interpret a contract so as to rule on a treaty claim.

Fourth, at the jurisdictional phase of the proceedings, the tribunal should determine the nature of the claimant's claims by conducting a preliminary analysis of the treaty obligations invoked by the claimant and assess whether the facts alleged by it are capable prima facie of constituting a violation of such obligations.

Fifth, most tribunals have been inclined to hold that the way in which dispute settlement clauses in treaties are drafted define the tribunal's jurisdiction. If they are broadly drafted to encompass all disputes related to investments, the tribunal will have, in principle, jurisdiction over purely contractual claims.

Sixth, there seems to be a growing trend to consider that in order for a contract breach to amount to a breach of the treaty's substantive standards of treatment – other than the umbrella clause – the Government must have conducted itself in its governmental capacity.

Seventh, umbrella clauses elevate contractual commitments into treaty obligations.

Eighth, under the operation of an umbrella clause – and subject to its particular wording in each treaty – any contract breach amounts to a treaty breach, despite the character of the State's measure or the nature of the contract, whether governmental or not.

Treaties as Agreements to Arbitrate – Related Dispute Resolution Regimes: Parallel Proceedings in BIT Arbitration

*Mark Friedman**

I. INTRODUCTION

The prospect of multiple proceedings concerning the same event has long been an issue in international litigation and arbitration. Imperfectly defined and partially overlapping jurisdictional mandates in various fora present risks of duplicative proceedings, inconsistent judgments and even double recovery. This concern has also emerged in investment treaty arbitration. Investment treaty disputes have grown explosively over the last decade, and many of those disputes have featured some form of multiple proceedings arising out of the same basic set of facts. Investment treaties have no uniform approach to dealing with the prospect of parallel proceedings. Some treaties are silent on the subject. Some treaties provide "fork in the road" provisions that appear to require an election of a forum. Some treaties preserve the pursuit or exhaustion of local remedies rule as a precondition to commencing treaty arbitration. Other treaties require waiver of potentially competing claims.

Running through each of these approaches is an overarching question about the balance between investor rights and efficiency. Should investors be required to defer or even abandon potentially meritorious claims to reduce the prospect of multiple proceedings? Viewing the approaches within this framework may help explain decisions in recent treaty arbitration awards, and inform views about where the balance should lie.

---

* Partner, Debevoise & Plimpton LLP.
   The author wishes to thank his Debevoise colleagues Jed Coleman, Yulia Andreeva and Blaise Stucki for their assistance in preparing this paper.
   © 2006 Mark Friedman and Debevoise & Plimpton LLP.

II. PARALLEL PROCEEDINGS IN BIT CASES

Multiple proceedings in investment treaty disputes have now become commonplace. We were able to locate and review awards in seventy-eight completed ICSID cases, and we found evidence of parallel proceedings in forty-one percent of them.[1]

A familiar fact pattern involves a foreign investor who owns shares in a company incorporated in the host State. The local company sues in the host State's courts on contract or administrative claims, which are typically governed by the host State's own law. The foreign investor subsequently commences arbitration under the BIT. Take for example *Enron Corp. and Ponderosa Assets LP v. The Argentine Republic*. The claimants were US shareholders in an Argentine company called Transportadora de Gas del Sur Sociedad Anonima, or TGS. In 2001 the claimants asserted an initial BIT claim challenging assessment of stamp taxes by Argentine provinces through which TGS transported gas. In 2003, the claimants asserted a further BIT claim challenging Argentina's refusal to adjust TGS's tariffs in accordance with the US Producer Price Index (PPI) and enactment of a law nullifying calculation of tariffs in US dollars. Apparently TGS had domestically "appealed the PPI measures" and "submitted to administrative courts other aspects of the dispute".[2]

The tribunal was able to consolidate the two sets of BIT claims. It did so by finding that the second BIT claim was "ancillary" to the first pursuant to Art. 46 of the ICSID Convention.[3] However, no similar procedural opportunity existed to combine the foreign investors' BIT claims with TGS's Argentine court and administrative proceedings. Accordingly, although they at least in substantial part arose out of the same set of operative facts, the BIT claims and the Argentine law claims continued on their separate paths.

A less typical but equally well known example of multiple proceedings are the twin arbitrations brought by CME and Ronald Lauder against the Czech Republic.[4] Ronald Lauder was the controlling shareholder of a publicly listed Bermudan company, CME, Ltd. A CME, Ltd. indirect subsidiary, CME Czech Republic BV (CME), operated a successful television station in the Czech Republic. Lauder and CME each claimed that the Czech Republic's Media Council had caused the loss of that station and left it in the hands of CME's former local business partner. Lauder asserted claims under the US-Czech BIT. CME asserted claims under the Netherlands-Czech BIT. (At the same time, CME had commenced an ICC arbitration against the local business partner, and the Czech company in which CME owned stock had commenced various suits before Czech courts.)

The result was that two BIT arbitrations, involving substantially overlapping facts, proceeded simultaneously. As ad hoc arbitrations under the UNCITRAL Rules, and being pursued by different claimants with claims arising out of different treaties, there

---

1. Table on file with author.
2. *Enron Corp. and Ponderosa Assets LP v. The Argentine Republic*, ICSID No. ARB/01/3, Decision on Jurisdiction (Ancillary Claim) at 23 (2 August 2004).
3. *Ibid.* at 3.
4. The author was counsel to the claimants in these disputes.

was no fixed procedure for consolidating the cases. The Czech Republic rejected the claimants' various proposals to join the two cases by one means or another, including formal consolidation, appointing the same tribunal to hear both cases, agreeing to treat the findings in one case as binding in the other, and the like. "This has the consequence that there will be two awards on the same subject which may be consistent with each other or may differ."[5]

Another kind of parallelism common to BIT arbitration is where parallel issues are considered by more than one tribunal. The SGS cases are just one example of this kind of parallelism. SGS is a Swiss company that commenced two arbitrations, one against Pakistan and one against the Philippines. Each case featured a BIT with a so-called "umbrella" clause. This is a clause in which the host State generally agrees to "observe commitments" made to foreign investors. SGS contended that this clause meant that contract claims became BIT claims, and hence that SGS could pursue contract claims in an arbitration brought pursuant to the dispute settlement mechanism set forth in the BIT.

These disputes, which proceeded roughly simultaneously, arose out of different contracts and featured different respondents. They did not involve the same facts. But they both presented the same question of law: what is the effect of an umbrella clause? The two tribunals that decided those cases reached different conclusions. The Pakistan tribunal concluded that the umbrella clause (or at least the one at issue in that case) did not empower a BIT tribunal to decide contract claims.[6] The Philippines tribunal concluded that the umbrella clause (or at least the one at issue in that case) did empower a BIT tribunal to decide contract claims, but only after those claims had been addressed by the dispute settlement mechanism set forth in the contract at issue.[7] The Philippines tribunal rendered its decision less than six months after the Pakistan tribunal and suggested that the cases were distinguishable due to differences in the wording of the umbrella clauses presented in the two cases.[8] However, many observers consider no material distinction to exist between the clauses at issue in those cases and consequently that there was a genuine and substantive difference of view between the two tribunals.[9]

These examples portray three different manifestations of parallel proceedings in BIT cases: parallel BIT arbitration and national court proceedings; parallel BIT arbitrations under several treaties; and parallel proceedings involving more or less the same legal issue. It is easy to imagine other constellations of parallel proceedings as well. I have chosen these examples to illustrate how to speak of "parallel proceedings" is actually to

---

5. *CME v. Czech Republic*, Partial Award at 412 (13 September 2001).
6. *SGS Société Générale de Surveillance S.A. v. Islamic Republic of Pakistan*, ICSID No. ARB/01/13, Decision on Jurisdiction at 190 (6 August 2003).
7. *SGS Société Générale de Surveillance S.A. v. Islamic Republic of the Philippines*, ICSID No. ARB/02/6, Decision on Jurisdiction at 169 (29 January 2004).
8. *Ibid.* at 119.
9. See, e.g., Judith GILL, 2 TDM (April 2005, no. 2); Christoph SCHREUER, "Traveling the BIT Route: of Waiting Periods, Umbrella Clauses and Forks in the Road", 5 The Journal of World Investment and Trade (2005) p. 231 at p. 254.

touch upon a subject that is not only complex, but also highly varied in the way it manifests itself in real life.

In the balance of this Report I will endeavour to explore some of the ways that BITs attempt to deal with the prospect of parallel proceedings. If those attempts are measured against the range of situations that might give rise to parallel proceedings, one cannot help but be struck that BITs actually purport to address remarkably few of those situations, and even where they do, they seem to have proven largely ineffective. At the same time, one might conclude that this is the right result, and that efforts aggressively to curb multiple proceedings would have undesirable consequences outweighing any benefit associated with them.

III.   MEANS BY WHICH INVESTMENT TREATIES ADDRESS MULTIPLE PROCEEDINGS

A widespread global web of BITs now exists. They tend to be broadly similar in the basic substantive rights they provide, and there seems to be an evolving and coalescing sense of the meaning of those rights. Yet the BITs display considerable variation in some of the procedural mechanisms they contain. Some of those procedural mechanisms appear to be directed at the multiple proceedings issue. Additionally, there are some doctrinal attempts to address multiple proceedings that are not anchored to any particular BIT.

1.   Fork in the Road Provisions

The BIT provision that most obviously attempts to address parallel proceedings is the fork in the road. This clause in effect requires the investor to elect the forum in which he or she will pursue a claim. It provides that the investor may submit the dispute to either national courts in the host State or to international arbitration – but not to both. Such provisions have, however, had little practical effect.

a.   Current interpretation of fork provisions

Fork provisions may be phrased differently in different treaties. However, their basic elements are similar. For example, Art. VII(2) of the United States-Argentina BIT (at issue in *CMS Gas Transmission Co v. Argentina* and other cases) provides:

> "If the dispute cannot be settled amicably, the national or company concerned may choose to submit the dispute for resolution:
> (a) to the courts or administrative tribunals of the Party that is party to the dispute; or
> (b) in accordance with any applicable, previously agreed dispute-settlement procedures; or
> (c) in accordance with the terms of paragraph 3 [which offers 'binding arbitration']."[10]

---

10. Available at <www.unctad.org/sections/dite/iia/docs/bits/argentina_us.pdf>.

Art. 26 of the Energy Charter Treaty contains a nearly identical fork in the road clause.[11] Art. 8 of the France-Argentina BIT provides that if the dispute cannot be resolved amicably it

"shall, at the request of the investor, be submitted:
– Either to the domestic courts of the Contracting Party involved in the dispute;
– Or to international arbitration under the conditions described in paragraph 3 below".[12]

The clause further makes clear that once the investor "has submitted the dispute" to either forum "the choice of one or the other of these procedures is final".[13] The Netherlands-Turkey BIT contains a more unusually phrased fork clause:

"The investor concerned may choose to submit the dispute ... for settlement by arbitration ... provided that in case the investor concerned has brought the dispute before the courts of justice of the Contracting Country that is a party to the dispute, [] there has not been rendered a final award."[14]

On their face, such fork in the road clauses appear to address and prohibit multiple proceedings. They require that the dispute be resolved either in national courts or by international arbitration.

In practice, however, these clauses have been toothless. As others have observed, it appears that despite the existence of considerable parallel litigation not a single State has successfully invoked a fork in the road defense to a BIT claim.[15] That is because arbitral tribunals have consistently held that a "dispute" is defined by (a) the parties to it, (b) the claims asserted in it, and (c) its subject matter. These elements are the "triple identity" criteria borrowed from the doctrines developed largely in municipal law of *lis pendens* and *res judicata*. If an arbitration and a national court litigation are not identical in all three respects, then tribunals have found that commencement of the court case has not triggered the fork in the road.

For example, *Azurix Corp. v. Argentina* involved a claim under the United States-Argentina BIT.[16] Azurix was a company incorporated in Delaware in the United States. It created subsidiaries, which in turn incorporated Azurix Buenos Aires SA (ABA) to hold a thirty-year concession contract to provide potable water and sewage disposal services to the Province of Buenos Aries. The Province terminated the concession

---

11. Available at <www.encharter.org//upload/9/12052067451575115819204971474343532131 935190860213f2543v3.pdf>.

12. Available at <www.unctad.org/sections/dite/iia/docs/bits/france_argentina_fr.pdf>.

13. *Ibid.*

14. Available at <www.unctad.org/sections/dite/iia/docs/bits/netherlands_turkey.pdf>.

15. See Peter TURNER, 2 TDM (August 2005, no. 4) at 20.

16. *Azurix Corp. v. Argentina Republic*, ICSID No. ARB/01/12, Decision on Jurisdiction at 88-89 (8 December 2003).

agreement, and ABA lodged more than a dozen administrative appeals and sued the Province in the provincial Court of Justice.

Yet when Azurix also asserted a BIT claim in its own name, the tribunal constituted to hear that case brushed aside Argentina's jurisdictional challenge based on the fork in the road clause. The tribunal made express the connection it drew between the BIT's fork clause and the *lis pendens* doctrine. In explaining its reasoning it cited a 1980 ICSID case, *Benevenuti & Bonfant Ltd. v. Congo*,[17] and said:

> "In one of the first cases that an ICSID tribunal had to decide on the existence of a pending suit and its relevance to the ICSID proceedings, the tribunal 'declared that there could only be a case of *lis pendens* where there was identity of the parties, object and cause of action in the proceedings pending before both tribunals'.
>
> This line of reasoning has been consistently followed by arbitral tribunals in cases involving claims under BITs...."[18]

The tribunal's reference to *Benevenuti* is intriguing because that was not a fork in the road case or even an investment treaty case. It was predicated on an ICSID arbitration clause in a contract for a plastic bottle manufacturing operation, and the award contains no real exploration of the *lis pendens* rule, its applicability to international arbitration, or the source of authority for it. Yet the *Azurix* tribunal applied these *lis pendens* principles to interpret a treaty-based fork in the road provision. It noted that the parties to the BIT arbitration – Azurix and Argentina – were not parties to the court case between ABA and the Province, and that the contract claims asserted in the local proceedings differed from the BIT claims asserted in the BIT arbitration. The tribunal consequently held that the fork in the road had not been taken.[19]

The *Azurix* tribunal also relied in part on the decision in *CMS Gas Transmission Co. v. Argentina*. That case also arose under the United States-Argentina BIT. In that case, too, the locally incorporated entity (called TGN) sought to avail itself of local court and administrative remedies and at the same time a TGN shareholder (CMS) asserted BIT claims. The tribunal dismissed the fork in the road challenge. It reasoned:

> "[A]s contractual claims are different from treaty claims even if there had been or there currently was a recourse to the local courts for breach of contract, this would not have prevented submission of the treaty claims to arbitration. This Tribunal is persuaded that with even more reason this view applies to the instant dispute, since no submission has been made by CMS to local courts and since, even if TGN had done so – which is not the case – this would not result in

---

17. *Benevenuti & Bonfant Ltd. v. The Government of the People's Republic of the Congo*, 21 ILM (1982) p. 740.

18. *Azurix Corp.*, *op. cit.*, fn. 16 at 88-89.

19. *Ibid.*

triggering the 'fork in the road' provision against CMS. *Both the parties and the causes of action under separate instruments are different.*"[20]

The consequence of such decisions is that the fork in the road has little practical application in many cases. As in *Azurix* and *CMS*, it is often the case that national proceedings are commenced by locally incorporated entities, and BIT arbitrations are commenced by direct or indirect foreign shareholders in those entities. Even if the foreign investor were itself to participate in the national court proceedings, the respondent is often a State subdivision, department or instrumentality, not the State itself. And the claims asserted in national proceedings are often predicated on a contract, regulation or national law, whereas the claims in a BIT arbitration are usually predicated on international law rights the BIT confers. Indeed, it seems unlikely that investors would assert BIT-conferred international law rights in national courts, even if those courts had jurisdiction over such claims.

b. *Identifying the "claim"*
As we have seen, decisions regarding fork in the road clauses in *Azurix*, *CMS* and other cases rest on defining the "dispute" by reference to the time-honoured triple identity test – parties, claim and object. One of those three elements – the claim – deserves special comment because it has been the subject of particularly intense interest.

i. BIT tribunals' efforts to define discrete claims
In the last few years much jurisprudential ink has been devoted to distinguishing "treaty claims" from "contract claims". There are now a considerable number of arbitral decisions available on this topic. For example, in *Lauder v. Czech Republic* the tribunal rejected an argument that the multiplicity of proceedings by Mr. Lauder and "entities he controls" was an abuse of process. It pointed out that the BIT arbitration was "the only forum with jurisdiction to hear Mr. Lauder's claims based on the Treaty". Although other proceedings were underway, "no possibility exists that any other court or arbitral tribunal can render a decision similar to or inconsistent with the award which will be issued by this Arbitral Tribunal, i.e. that the Czech Republic breached or did not breach the [US-Czech] Treaty...". It elaborated with respect to the *CME v. Czech Republic* treaty arbitration that was proceeding in parallel:

> "Only this Arbitral Tribunal can decide whether the Czech Republic breached the Treaty towards Mr. Lauder, and only the arbitral tribunal in the parallel Stockholm Proceedings can decide whether the Czech Republic breached the Dutch/Czech bilateral investment treaty in relation to CME. As a result, CME has neither a better – nor a worse – claim in the parallel arbitration proceedings than Mr. Lauder's claims in the present arbitration proceedings. *It only has a different claim.*"[21]

---

20. *CMS Gas Transportation Company v. Argentine Republic*, ICSID No. ARB/01/8, Decision on Jurisdiction at 80 (17 July 2003).
21. *Ronald S. Lauder v. The Czech Republic*, Final Award at 117 (3 September 2001) (emphasis added).

The idea expressed was that claims arising under different sources of law – either under a different treaty or under national law – were different claims. On this view each treaty is *res inter alios acta*, each source of law its own master.[22] The tribunal in the CME case elaborated on this point in its quantum award. Citing three older international law precedents it held:

> "[T]he fact that one tribunal is competent to resolve the dispute brought before it does not necessarily affect the authority of another tribunal, constituted under a different agreement, to resolve a dispute – *even if it were the 'same' dispute*."[23]

Other tribunals have applied these concepts in cases involving assertion of national-law claims (often based on contract or administrative law) and international law BIT claims. A leading case in this regard is the *Vivendi* annulment decision, in which the tribunal stated: "A treaty cause of action is not the same as a contractual cause of action; it requires a clear showing of conduct which is in the circumstances contrary to the relevant treaty standard."[24] The tribunal in *PSEG Global Inc. v. Turkey* followed this holding, pointing out that recent cases had established that "contract based disputes are different from treaty based disputes and arise out of separate causes of action. Treaty based disputes can always be submitted to international arbitration from this point of view."[25] In *Lanco v. Argentina* the tribunal applied this distinction to find that an exclusive dispute resolution provision in a contract did not bar commencement of a BIT arbitration that arose out of that contract.[26] The recent case *Bayindir v. Pakistan* said this distinction between treaty claims and contract claims was "now well established", so much so that Pakistan did not contest the point in principle.[27] These cases tend to look to the source of authority on which the case is to be decided rather than the underlying facts. That is, if the tribunal's rule of decision will be supplied by the BIT – that a State measure is expropriatory or discriminatory or unfair and inequitable – it is considered a BIT claim. This is true even if the measure is in whole or in part an alleged breach or revocation of a contract, license or other national law instrument. This is not entirely surprising given that BITs typically define "investments" under the BIT to include contracts, licenses or other national law instruments. The United States-Argentina BIT, for example, has a customarily broad definition of "investment" as "every kind of investment" including without limitation "any right conferred by law or contract, and any licenses and permits pursuant to law". So if a State revokes an investor's license to

---

22. See Giorgio SACERDOTI, *"Czech Republic v. CME* – Expert Opinion of Professor Sacerdoti", 2 TDM (November 2005, no. 5) at 126.

23. *CME Czech Republic BV v. The Czech Republic*, Final Award at 435 (14 March 2003) (emphasis added).

24. *Compañia de Aguas del Aconquija S.A. and Vivendi Universal v. Argentine Republic*, ICSID No. ARB/97/3, Decision on Annulment Proceeding at 113 (3 July 2002).

25. *PSEG Global Inc. v. Republic of Turkey*, ICSID No. ARB/02/5, Decision on Jurisdiction at 158 (4 June 2004).

26. *Lanco International, Inc. v. Argentine Republic*, ICSID No. ARB/97/6, Award (8 December 1998).

27. *Bayindir Insaat Turizm Ticaret Ve Sanayi A.S. v. Islamic Republic of Pakistan*, ICSID No. ARB/03/29, Decision on Jurisdiction at 148 (14 November 2005).

engage in certain activity within that State and thereby deprives the investor of that "investment", the license revocation is subject to evaluation under the substantive standards of treatment set forth in the BIT. That would be the case even if the license revocation were also amenable to challenge in domestic court or administrative proceedings under national law.

ii.   Intersection with fork clauses

As the Report by Guido Santiago Tawil probes the definitional boundary between treaty claims and contract claims,[28] I will not explore the precise contours of that boundary in greater depth here. However, we should not simply abandon the topic altogether. For the BIT claim/contract claim jurisprudence may bear on the application of fork in the road provisions in two ways.

First, some BITs define "dispute" broadly to encompass both international law and contract claims, suggesting the prospect that assertion of some of those claims could be submission of "the dispute" to one or the other forum and hence trigger the fork provision. For example, the investor-State dispute resolution article of the United States-Argentina BIT says that

> "an investment dispute is a dispute ... arising out of or relating to
> (a) an investment agreement between that Party and such national or company;
> (b) an investment authorization granted by that Party's foreign investment authority ... to such national or company; or
> (c) an alleged breach of any right conferred or created by this Treaty with respect to an investment".[29]

This language provokes the interesting question of whether pursuit of non-BIT claims in domestic proceedings could amount to an election of forum for fork in the road purposes and thereby deprive an investor of an international arbitration forum to pursue international law claims. To consider this question, assume that the State entered into a contract with the foreign investor by which it agreed to license certain operations of the foreign investor in the State, the State then revoked the license, and the investor protested the license revocation in the State's courts or administrative tribunals. He protests based solely on alleged breach of the contract, the licensing regime, administrative procedure or some other national law basis, without reference to any of the BIT-conferred international law rights. Has the investor made an election of forum under a fork in the road provision?

The dispute appears to be one "arising out of or relating to" an "investment agreement". That appears to make it an "investment dispute" within the definition of the BIT. As we have already seen, Art. VII(2) of the BIT goes on to employ this very definition in its fork in the road clause: it says that if an "investment dispute" arises, the national may choose to submit "the dispute" either to international arbitration, or to national courts or administrative tribunals. The fork in the road jurisprudence

---

28. See this volume, pp. 492-544.
29. Art. VII(1).

predicated on the triple identity test would say that the national court or administrative proceeding (based on national law rights) was not the same "dispute" as the investment treaty arbitration (based on international law rights), because the "claims" were different. Does the United States-Argentina BIT's definition of "the dispute" – an expansive definition that includes claims based on both national and international law rights – supplant the triple identity test?

It appears that the answer to this question is at present not entirely settled in arbitral jurisprudence. The issue has been considered in some form in at least two BIT cases.

In *Vivendi v. Argentina*, a French company, CGE, operated in Argentina through an Argentine project company, CAA. CAA had a contract with the Province of Tucumán. That contract has an exclusive jurisdiction clause referring disputes to the administrative courts of Tucumán. When Tucumán repudiated the contract, CGE and CAA commenced an ICSID arbitration. (Although CAA was an Argentine company, it was nevertheless considered an "investor" under the France-Argentina BIT, which defined an "investor" to include both a body corporate with the nationality of one of the Contracting Parties, and "[a]ny body corporate effectively controlled, directly or indirectly", by a corporate entity with the nationality of one of the Contracting Parties.) The original ICSID tribunal decided that the dispute was so integrally tied to and dependent upon contract issues that it should be handled through domestic proceedings, and concluded it had no jurisdiction.[30]

The case was then considered by an ICSID annulment committee. The thrust of the annulment committee's much quoted award was that a BIT tribunal cannot disregard its duty to decide a dispute arising under the BIT even if doing so involves consideration, interpretation and findings with respect to a contract that is or forms part of the investment. So part of the annulment committee's job was to explain the breadth of a BIT tribunal's jurisdiction, and how that jurisdiction extended even to matters touching on contracts when those matters also formed part of the BIT claim itself.

Against this background the annulment committee addressed the fork in the road clause. It said that the "disputes" which could be submitted at the investor's election to either national courts or international arbitration were the "disputes" referenced by the BIT. That is, disputes "relating to investments made under [the BIT]". The tribunal observed that this language did not use a "narrower formulation" that would require "that the investor's claims allege a breach of the BIT itself". Instead, it was "sufficient that the dispute relate to an investment made under the BIT". Since any dispute "relating to investments made under the BIT" was a "dispute" within the meaning of the BIT, a claim in local courts that related to investments made under the BIT was one of the "disputes" referenced in the fork in the road clause. The tribunal concluded:

> "Consequently, if a claim brought before a national court concerns a 'dispute relating to investments made under this Agreement' within the meaning of Article 8(1), then Article 8(2) [the fork clause] will apply. In the Committee's view, a claim by CAA against the Province of Tucumán for breach of the

---

30. *Compañia de Aguas del Aconquija S.A. and Vivendi Universal v. Argentine Republic*, ICSID No. ARB/97/3, Award (21 November 2000).

Concession Contract, brought before the contentious administrative courts of Tucumán, would *prima facie* fall within Article 8(2) and constitute a 'final' choice of forum and jurisdiction, if that claim was coextensive with a dispute relating to investments made under the BIT."[31]

By this language the tribunal appeared to be saying that if CAA brought a domestic law claim against the Province of Tucumán, that would *prima facie* bar its ability to assert an international law claim against Argentina under the BIT. Such a conclusion is actually in some tension with the evident distinction the tribunal recognized between international law BIT claims and national law contract claims:

"In accordance with this general principle (which is undoubtedly declaratory of general international law), whether there has been a breach of the BIT and whether there has been a breach of contract are different questions. *Each of these claims* will be determined by reference to its own proper or applicable law...."[32]

The tension is so significant that one might reasonably wonder whether the last clause in the above quoted text at fn. 31 – "if that claim was coextensive with a dispute relating to investments made under the BIT" – was intended to recognize that if the disputes were not "coextensive", in the sense that different claims were asserted in national court from those asserted in BIT arbitration, the fork provision would not apply. However, the tribunal later appeared to undercut any such interpretation. It explained that the claimants' decision not to pursue claims in local courts "carried risks" for them:

"Having declined to challenge the various factual components of its treaty cause of action before the administrative courts of Tucumán, instead choosing to commence ICSID arbitration – *and having thereby, in the Committee's view, taken the "fork in the road"under* Article 8(4) [sic] – CAA took the risk of a tribunal holding that the acts complained of neither individually nor collective rose to the level of a breach of the BIT. In that event, *it would have lost both its treaty claim and its contract claim.*"[33]

The committee did not expressly state how it would view the reverse situation, namely whether if CAA had commenced proceedings in local courts it would also have taken the fork and foregone any right to BIT arbitration. But that seems to be the implication. The committee appears to have read the fork clause to require a choice of forum with respect to the underlying facts – what it called "the various factual components of [*Vivendi's*] treaty cause of action" – rather than with respect to the cause of action itself.

This reasoning in the *Vivendi* case was the product of a somewhat unusual context. There the claimants were trying to explain why a BIT tribunal should have jurisdiction

---

31. *Compañía de Aguas del Aconquija S.A. and Vivendi Universal v. Argentine Republic, op. cit.*, fn. 24 at 55.
32. *Ibid.* at 96.
33. *Ibid.* at 113 (emphasis added).

despite the substantial contract issues in the case. One of their arguments was that if they submitted the contract claims to local courts they would be forever denied the ability to seek redress in BIT arbitration or to assert their international law rights. They accordingly argued for a broad reading of the fork in the road clause. This is unusual because typically investor claimants in BIT cases will urge a narrow construction of such a clause.

The *Vivendi* case illustrates how a broad definition of the "dispute" – typically considered a pro-investor BIT provision – may have a perverse consequence of dramatically expanding the breadth of an otherwise innocuous fork in the road provision. However, one might wonder whether an expansive and inclusive provision authorizing arbitration is really intended to accomplish such a result. After all, it is equally consistent with the language of these United States BITs simply to understand them as conferring the right to commence BIT arbitration when any one of several kinds of "disputes" arises. If one of those disputes is submitted to national courts, it is not clear why that should represent a bar to asserting another of those disputes to BIT arbitration. Under the triple identity test, those disputes would remain distinct; they are not the same dispute.

Following similar reasoning, the *Occidental v. Ecuador* tribunal appears to have come to a different conclusion than the *Vivendi* annulment committee.[34] Like the United States-Argentina BIT already discussed, the United States-Ecuador BIT at issue in that case defines "investment dispute" as a dispute arising out of or relating to any of three sources of legal rights: (a) an investment agreement, (b) an investment authorization or (c) rights conferred by the BIT.[35]

In that case the Ecuadorian tax administration denied VAT refunds on the grounds that VAT was already being reimbursed to Occidental through its participation percentage under an oil and gas participation contract. Occidental filed claims against the Ecuadorian tax administration for the VAT refunds in the Ecuadorian courts on the basis that VAT was not being reimbursed through the participation contract. Occidental subsequently sought reimbursement of the same VAT refunds from the BIT tribunal on the grounds that denying those VAT refunds constituted a breach of the BIT.

Ecuador argued before the BIT tribunal that Occidental had submitted the same dispute "relating to" the participation contract, which the tribunal accepted was an "investment agreement" within the meaning of the BIT, to both the Ecuadorian courts and the BIT tribunal. Occidental replied that even if the two disputes did "relate to" the same investment agreement, in the Ecuadorian courts it had relied solely on Ecuadorian law, whereas in the BIT arbitration it relied on the BIT.[36]

The BIT tribunal accepted Occidental's view. It acknowledged that to some extent the two disputes both involved the same investment agreement. But it then went on to find against Ecuador, giving significant weight to the different nature of the claims asserted in the respective proceedings:

---

34. The author's law firm represented Occidental in this case.
35. Art. VI. Available at <www.unctad.org/sections/dite/iia/docs/bits/us_ecuador.pdf>.
36. *Occidental Exploration and Production Company v. The Republic of Ecuador*, LCIA No. UN3467, Final Award at 41 (1 July 2004).

"But the fact is that this dispute, its contractual aspects aside, involves a number of issues arising from the legislation of Ecuador, the Andean Community legal order and international law, including of course the question of rights under the Treaty. This explains the fact that the Claimant is *addressing different questions* to different mechanisms of dispute resolution.

The Tribunal is persuaded in this context by the Claimant's interpretation of Article II (3)(b) of the Treaty, which in its second sentence allows for submission to arbitration of arbitrary and discriminatory measures even if the claimant has resorted to the courts or administrative tribunals of the Respondent seeking a review of such measures."[37]

According to the BIT tribunal, this conclusion "cannot be taken to mean that the death knell has sounded for the 'fork in the road' provisions of bilateral investment treaties" because "the functions of domestic mechanisms and international arbitration are different".[38]

The second intersection between the fork in the road jurisprudence and the treaty claims/contract claims divide appears in cases involving so-called "umbrella clauses". These clauses typically provide that a host State will observe all its commitments to investors.[39] Some investors and scholars have contended that these clauses give BIT tribunals jurisdiction to decide claims sounding purely in contract.[40] They contend that a contract is a "commitment" the State has made to the investor, and the State's failure to abide by it is consequently within the scope of the BIT.

Tribunals have somewhat famously not yet settled on a single view of what these clauses mean. In *SGS v. Pakistan* the tribunal essentially rejected outright the proposition that such clauses conferred jurisdiction over contract claims.[41] This conclusion has not won widespread support.[42] In *SGS v. Philippines* the tribunal held that the clauses did confer jurisdiction, but that the tribunal could only ensure enforcement of the entire contract including any dispute resolution clause it contained. Accordingly, in that case the tribunal stayed the BIT arbitration and instructed the parties to follow the dispute resolution procedures set out in the contract.[43] This holding has also attracted criticism.[44]

---

37. *Ibid.* at 48-49 (emphasis added).
38. *Ibid.* at 50.
39. See, e.g., Art. III(4) of the Netherlands-Belize BIT ("Each Contracting State shall observe any obligation it may have entered into with regard to investments of nationals of the other Contracting State.") Available at <www.unctad.org/sections/dite/iia/docs/bits/netherlands_belize.pdf>.
40. See, e.g., Christoph SCHREUER, *op. cit.*, fn. 9 at 250.
41. *Op. cit.*, fn. 6 at 165.
42. See, e.g., Christoph SCHREUER, *op. cit.*, fn. 9 at 255.
43. *Op cit.*, fn. 7 at 175.
44. See, e.g., Thomas WÄLDE, "The 'Umbrella' (or Sanctity of Contract/Pacta sunt Servanda) Clause in Investment Arbitration: A Comment on Original Intentions and Recent Cases", 1 TDM (October 2004, no. 4) at 70 to 80.

There are several grounds from which to argue that an umbrella clause empowers (and, some would say, obligates) a BIT tribunal to address contract claims regardless of the presence or absence of a dispute resolution clause in the contract. Some contend that arbitration clauses are typically separable or autonomous from the substantive rights in a contract, and hence requiring the State to observe its contractual commitments does not require preserving contractual dispute resolution clauses. Others contend that when an investor accepts the State's outstanding offer of BIT arbitration, a new agreement regarding dispute resolution arises and supplants the one in the contract itself. As the tribunal observed in *Lanco,* the agreement between an investor and a State to arbitrate under a BIT arises not when the BIT enters into force, but when the investor accepts the State's standing offer of BIT arbitration.[45] This view draws from municipal law the notions that a contract can be modified by the parties to it, and that a later agreement on the same subject as an earlier one controls with respect to that subject.

Again, these issues are explored in greater depth in the Report by Guido Tawil.[46] What is important for present purposes is that umbrella clause cases present a different context for considering fork in the road issues. It is one thing where substantially the same set of facts give rise both to treaty claims and contract claims. In that circumstance the notion that there may be a difference in "claims" for triple identity purposes – even if the facts are the same, and even if interpretation or non-performance of the contract is relevant to the treaty arbitration – has some force. However, it may be something else when the very same contract claim, governed by the same national law, is asserted in both national courts and in BIT arbitration under an umbrella clause. In such a circumstance, it appears the triple identity criteria would be satisfied and a fork in the road provision would apply.

2. Exhaustion Clauses

Another way that some BITs attempt to limit parallel proceedings is by clauses requiring exhaustion or at least pursuit of local remedies prior to commencement of a BIT arbitration. These clauses are in a sense the antithesis of fork in the road clauses – instead of requiring the dispute be brought in one place, they contemplate the prospect that it can be brought in two places so long as a certain order is followed. These clauses have by and large likewise proven ineffective at curbing parallel proceedings.

True exhaustion clauses have proven ineffective in large part because they appear to be so rare. Professor Schreuer has observed that they are characteristic of "older" BITs.[47] Examples of them do not abound. Elimination of a requirement to pursue local remedies for international law rights is widely considered to be one of the great innovations of modern international investment law. It is some testament to how unpopular an exhaustion requirement is today that, although Art. 26 of the ICSID Convention permits

---

45. *Op. cit.*, fn. 26, at 33.
46. See this volume, pp. 492-544.
47. Christoph SCHREUER, "Calvo's Grandchildren: The Return of Local Remedies in Investment Arbitration", 4 The Law and Practice of International Courts and Tribunals (January 2005, no. 1) p. 2.

States to reserve the right to impose such a requirement, only a single State has recently done so under the means provided for by the Convention.[48]

More often BITs require "that efforts be made in domestic courts to resolve the dispute for a certain period of time".[49] These BITs contain "opt out" provisions requiring that if no decision has been rendered by a local court within a certain time limit (e.g., twelve months (Switzerland-Sri Lanka BIT, Art. 9(2)); eighteen months (Spain-Argentina BIT, Art. 10(2)), or two years (France-Morocco BIT, Art. 10)) arbitration may nevertheless be instituted. For example, Art. 8(1) of the United Kingdom-Egypt BIT says that a dispute can be submitted to international arbitration if "agreement cannot be reached within three months between the parties to this dispute through pursuit of local remedies, through conciliation or otherwise".[50] Art. 10(2) and (3) of the Germany-Argentina BIT provide that if no settlement is reached within six months from the date at which the dispute arose, either party can submit it to local courts. Then, if (a) there is no court decision on the merits within eighteen months, (b) there is a court decision on the merits within that period but the dispute continues or (c) by agreement of the parties, either party can submit the dispute to ICSID or UNCITRAL arbitration.

These clauses have proven to be ineffective and even puzzling. It is not entirely clear what these clauses actually mean in practice. If the triple identity test were applied to these clauses as it is to fork in the road clauses, then to exhaust local remedies the investor would presumably have to submit his international law claims to national courts in the State accused of violating international law rights. That is because if he did not do so he could be said not to have presented the same dispute to the local courts; his international law BIT claims might never have been exhausted.[51] Assuming the investor did present his international law claims to a national court and the dispute was pursued through to a final judgment in that national court system, what would the proper subject of any subsequent arbitration be? Can the entire case be retried, or does the arbitration tribunal play a more limited role of ensuring that the national court process did not result in a denial of justice? Would the national court judgment be *res judicata*, despite the familiar rule that international tribunals are typically not bound by decisions of national courts?

---

48. On 16 January 2003, Guatemala notified the Centre that "the Republic of Guatemala will require the exhaustion of local administrative remedies as a condition of its consent to arbitration under the Convention". See NOTIFICATIONS CONCERNING CLASSES OF DISPUTES CONSIDERED SUITABLE OR UNSUITABLE FOR SUBMISSION TO THE CENTRE, available at <www.worldbank.org/icsid/pubs/icsid-8/icsid-8-d.htm>. In addition to a reservation under the ICSID Convention, "this demand may be made (i) in a bilateral investment treaty that offers submission to ICSID arbitration, (ii) in domestic legislation, or (iii) in a direct investment agreement that contains an ICSID clause". *Lanco, op. cit.*, fn. 26 at 39.

49. Christoph SCHREUER, *op. cit.*, fn. 9, p. 231 at p. 239.

50. Available at <www.unctad.org/sections/dite/iia/docs/bits/egypt_uk.pdf>.

51. But see *Case Concerning Elettronica Sicula S.P.A. ("ELSI")*, ICJ, Judgment of 20 July 1989 at 48-63 (local remedies exhausted under United States-Italy Treaty of Friendship, Commerce and Navigation when US companies pursued claims in Italian courts but had not cited treaty provisions).

The emerging BIT jurisprudence for the most part has found ways to render these quasi-exhaustion clauses largely irrelevant. Such was the case in *Gas Natural SDG, S.A. v. Argentina*, which was decided under the Spain-Argentina BIT. The tribunal disagreed with Argentina's argument that the eighteen-month period provided for in Art. X(3) of the BIT constitutes a requirement of exhaustion of local remedies from which no derogation is permitted and observed that:

> "[U]nder that provision it would be possible to have recourse to arbitration even if there were a decision in the case by the national courts, and *a fortiori* if no final decision had been rendered in the national courts. Accordingly, the 18-month provision does not come within the concept of prior exhaustion of local remedies as understood in international law. Furthermore, Article 26 of the ICSID Convention provides expressly that a state may require the exhaustion of local administrative or judicial remedies as a condition of consent to arbitration under the Convention, and this condition is not expressed in the BIT."[52]

A similar outcome was reached earlier in *Siemens A.G. v. Argentina*, in which Argentina argued that Art. 10(2) of the Argentina-Germany BIT is a "moderate" version of the exhaustion of local remedies rule and that that rule may not be tacitly waived. The tribunal concurred with the respondent that the contracting parties had intended to give the local tribunals an opportunity to decide a dispute first before it would be submitted to international arbitration. However, it then held:

> "This does not mean that this provision requires the exhaustion of local remedies as this rule has been understood under international law. Article 10(2) does not require a prior final decision of the courts of the Respondent. It does not even require a prior decision of a court at any level. It simply requires the passing of time or the persistence of the dispute after a decision by a court. Then, even if this decision is one subject to appeal, the requirement of Article 10(2) would have been fulfilled. For these reasons, the Tribunal considers that Article 10(2) is not comparable to the local remedies rule and the issue of a tacit waiver of a rule of international law does not arise."[53]

The tribunal in *Maffezini v. Spain* exemplifies the most negative treatment of such local remedies clauses, holding that the eighteen-month "opt out" provision of the Spain-Argentina BIT differs from the exhaustion of local remedies and "speaks merely of a decision on the merits, which respondent admits does not even have to be a final or non-appealable decision under Spanish law...".[54] Moreover, in the tribunal's opinion, this provision could be bypassed by a "most favored nation" clause.[55]

---

52. *Gas Natural SDG, S.A. v. Argentina*, ICSID No. ARB/03/10, Award on Jurisdiction at 30 (17 June 2005).

53. *Siemens v. Argentina*, ICSID No. ARB/02/8, Decision on Jurisdiction at 104 (3 August 2004).

54. *Maffezini v. Spain*, ICSID No. ARB/97/7, Decision on Jurisdiction at 28 (25 January 2000).

55. *Ibid.* at 38 et seq.

Hence, exhaustion provisions have likewise proven ineffective in ending multiple proceedings. At most, they create a procedural detour before a dispute may proceed to international arbitration.

3.   Alternative Approaches

As we have seen, the application of clauses attempting to control parallel disputes turns significantly on how a "dispute" is defined. In recent BIT cases, the "dispute" has typically been defined by the triple identity test developed through jurisprudence about the related doctrines of res judicata and lis pendens. However, the triple identity test is not the only approach to preclusion doctrines, and indeed some treaties take a different approach that does not depend on the nature of the claim asserted.

a.   The triple identity test approach used in the fork cases
The triple identity test, and the preclusion doctrines in whose service it labours, has an impressive pedigree. The res judicata principle can be traced back through the centuries to Roman Law and even to more ancient writings. One author has discerned the doctrine in the writings of Sophocles dating back to around 450 BC.[56] In a 1916 decision on appeal from India, the Privy Council noted that the principle of res judicata is recorded in the Hindu writings of Katyayana, who lived in India around 200 BC.[57] In AD 529 the Eastern Roman Emperor Justinian I included the doctrine in his first draft of the Roman Civil Code (the *Corpus Juris Civilis*).[58] And around AD 1600, the famous English jurist Sir Edward Coke considered the concept of res judicata estoppel to be of such "uncontrollable credit and verity" that no party may presume to impeach it.[59] Coke's legal texts were exported to English colonies and first found their way to what is now the United States of America in 1620 aboard the Mayflower.[60]

The doctrine of *res judicata*, or more fully, *res judicata pro veritate accipitur*, is based on two policy considerations, one public, the other private. The first is that it is in the interest of the community that there be final and conclusive judicial decisions (*interest republicae ut sit finis litium*), and the second is the right of the individual to be protected from multiple suits regarding the same subject (*nemo debet bis vexari pro una et eadem causa*). Or, as simply put by the House of Lords, "the doctrine of res judicata estoppel ... is one founded on considerations of justice and good sense".[61]

---

56. See BARNETT, *Res Judicata, Estoppel and Foreign Judgments* (Oxford University Press 2001) p. 8, citing an extract from the play *The Ajax*, by the Greek playwright Sophocles.
57. *Sheoparson Singh v. Ramnandan Singh* (1916) LR 43 Ind App 91, 98.
58. The Code was the first of its kind, bringing together and simplifying the writings of the most prominent Roman jurists. The Code was updated a number of times in subsequent years and is said to have ultimately ensured the survival of Roman Law by providing one readily accessible body of law. It formed the basis of much continental European law, passing to the West in the twelfth century.
59. See SPENCER BOWER, TURNER and HANDLEY, *Res Judicata* (Butterworths 1996) p. 1.
60. <http://en.wikipedia.org/wiki/Edward_Coke>.
61. *New Brunswick Rly Co v. British and French Trust Corporation Ltd* [1939] AC 1, at 19-20.

While the common law concept of *res judicata* has been said to stem from its civil law counterpart, and some English cases go so far as to say that the English common law doctrine of *res judicata* is "entirely consistent with ... the rule of the Civil Law",[62] there are some important differences in articulation and application of the doctrine. Of particular significance to the issue at hand is that the civil law jurisdictions tend to require triple identity – parties, grounds and subject matter – whereas common law jurisdictions tend to require only double identity – of parties and subject matter. Additionally, common law jurisdictions tend to extend preclusion not just to the parties to an action, but also to others in some form of "privity" with those parties.[63]

Consequently in common law courts parties should assert all causes of action that might arise from the underlying facts for they will not get a second bite at the apple to pursue additional causes of action. Once there has been a suit arising out of a set of facts and it proceeds to final judgment, those parties will be barred from bringing another suit. Under the civil law's triple identity rule, however, if a particular legal ground was not raised in an initial suit, it may be possible to pursue it in a subsequent action even between the same parties.[64] Although it may considerably oversimplify a complex issue, in general the common law approach is more transaction focused and the civil approach more claim focused.

International law has tended to follow the civil law approach requiring triple identity.[65] For example, Judge Jessup of the International Court of Justice noted in his dissenting opinion in *The South-West Africa Case*:

> "Judge Anzilotti [in *Factory at Chorzow*], in what has been called 'the classic enunciation of the law' (Rosenne, op. cit., p. 624) listed as the essentials for the application of the *res judicata* principle, identity of parties, identity of cause and identity of object in the subsequent proceedings – 'persona, petitum, causa petendi'."[66]

The ILA's interim report on *res judicata* found:

---

62. *New Brunswick Rly Co v. British and French Trust Corporation Ltd* [1939] AC 1 (Maugham LC); *Nelson v. Couch* (1863) 15 CB(NS) 99, 108 (Willes J).

63. INTERNATIONAL LAW ASSOCIATION, *Interim Report: "Res Judicata" and Arbitration* (December 2004) (hereinafter *ILA Interim Report*) pp. 6-18.

64. *Ibid.*, p. 16 ("Identity of the 'same grounds' or '*causa petendi*' also requires that the legal basis for the claim should be identical in both proceedings. Consequently, later proceedings may be brought and the case can be relitigated if a party chooses to take a second shot and attempts to bring its case based on a different cause of action.")

65. See, e.g., *Compañía de Aguas del Aconquija S.A. and Vivendi Universal v. Argentine Republic, op. cit.*, fn. 30; *Alex Genin, Eastern Credit Limited, Inc and AS Baltoil v. The Republic of Estonia*, ICSID No. ARB/99/2, Award (25 June 2001); *Ronald S. Lauder v. The Czech Republic*, Final Award, 3 September 2001 (available at <www.investmentclaims.com/oa1.html>).

66. *Ethiopia v. South Africa, Liberia v. South Africa* 1966 ICJ 6 (citing Interpretation of Judgments Nos. 7 and 8 (*Factory at Chorzow*), Judgment No. 11, 1927, P.C.I.J., Series A, No. 13, pp. 23-27).

"Broadly speaking, there are four preconditions for the doctrine of *res judicata* to apply in international law, namely proceedings must: (i) have been conducted before courts or tribunals in the international legal order; (ii) involve the same relief; (iii) involve the same grounds: and (iv) be between the same parties."[67]

That civilian and international law background appears to have been the background against which modern BITs have generally been interpreted, at least to the extent they have involved questions about fork in the road provisions or more general notions of *res judicata* or *lis pendens*.

b. *Transaction-based approaches*
Some modern treaties, however, take an alternative approach. They focus not on the nature of the claims asserted in different jurisdictions, but rather on the measure being challenged. This approach has also been espoused more broadly.

i. Treaties containing a transaction approach
The most prominent treaty-based example of a transaction-based approach is probably NAFTA Art. 1121, which states:

"A disputing investor may submit a claim under Article 1116 to arbitration only if:
(....)
b) the investor and, where the claim is for loss or damage to an interest in an enterprise of another Party that is a juridical person that the investor owns or controls directly or indirectly, the enterprise, waive their right to initiate or continue before any administrative tribunal or court under the law of any Party, or other dispute settlement procedures, any proceedings with respect to the measure of the disputing Party that is alleged to be a breach referred to in Article 1116, except for proceedings of injunctive, declaratory or other extraordinary relief, not involving the payment of damages, before an administrative tribunal or court under the law of the disputing Party."[68]

The US and Canadian model BITs contain similar or identical language.[69]
This is different from the typical fork in the road clause in several important respects. First, it does not contain an irrevocable election at the outset. An investor presumably could commence a court action without compromising her right later to pursue a NAFTA claim. Instead, the requirement is that at the time of commencing the NAFTA claim other litigation concerning the measure must be waived. Second, it turns entirely on the measure being challenged. In triple identity language (loosely interpreted), it is concerned only with the "object" of each proceeding, not with the claims asserted. It to

---

67. *ILA Interim Report*, p. 19.
68. Available at <www.nafta-sec-alena.org/DefaultSite/index_e.aspx?DetailID=160>.
69. United States Model BIT Art. 26(2); Canada Model BIT Art. 26(1)(e).

some extent also dispenses with the requirement of identity of parties by extending the waiver requirement to enterprises the investor "owns or controls directly or indirectly".

The difference between NAFTA 1121 and a typical fork in the road clause was illustrated in *Waste Management, Inc. v. United Mexican States*. In that case Waste Management (on behalf of itself and its subsidiary Acaverde S.A. de C.V.) commenced an ICSID arbitration against Mexico under NAFTA. Along with its notice of institution or arbitration proceedings, the claimant submitted the following waiver:

> "Additionally, Claimants hereby waive their right to initiate or continue before any administrative tribunal or court under the law of any NAFTA Party, or other dispute settlement procedures, any proceedings with respect to the measures taken by Respondent that are alleged to be a breach of NAFTA Chapter Eleven and applicable rules of international law, except for proceedings of injunctive, declaratory, or other extraordinary relief, not involving the payment of damages. This waiver does not apply, however, to any dispute settlement proceedings *involving allegations that Respondent has violated duties imposed by other sources of law, including the municipal law of Mexico.*"[70]

The ICSID Secretariat questioned whether this complied with Art. 1121. The claimant thereafter asserted in several letters that it intended to waive claims as to the extent Art. 1121 required but that it considered that the waiver "does not apply to any dispute settlement proceedings involving allegations that Respondent has violated duties imposed by sources of law other than Chapter Eleven of NAFTA, including the municipal law of Mexico".[71] In other words, it maintained that since claims in national courts or administrative proceedings would be predicated on national law, they were not within the scope of claims that had to be waived under Article 1121. By this time Acaverde was simultaneously pursuing two lawsuits and an arbitration against State-owned entities or political subdivisions. A tribunal was constituted and heard Mexico's jurisdictional challenge. The tribunal said it was "clear" that the Article 1121 waiver calls for "a show of intent" to waive the right to initiate or continue "any proceedings whatsoever before other courts or tribunals with respect to the measure allegedly in breach of the NAFTA provisions".[72] The tribunal considered the claimant's argument that the waiver should be limited only to proceedings that expressly invoked the failure to comply with international law obligations set forth in NAFTA. It concluded that interpretation was unsustainable because "the same measure may give rise to different types of claims"; the other proceedings "directly affect the arbitration in that their object consists of measures also alleged ... to be breaches of the NAFTA"; and "when both legal actions have a legal basis derived from the same measures, they can no longer continue simultaneously in light of the imminent risk that the Claimant may obtain the double benefit in its claim for damages. This is precisely what NAFTA Article 1121 seeks to

---

70. *Waste Management, Inc. v. United Mexican States*, Award on Jurisdiction, at 94 (2 June 2000) (emphasis removed and added).
71. *Ibid.*, para. 4.
72. *Ibid.*, para. 24.

avoid."[73] Accordingly, the tribunal (in a split decision and over a lengthy dissent) dismissed the arbitration, despite the fact that its scope was not entirely coextensive with the scope of the other proceedings.

Art. 26 of the ICSID Convention is arguably a similar provision. It provides: "Consent of the parties to arbitration under this Convention shall, unless otherwise stated, be deemed consent to such arbitration to the exclusion of any other remedy." Professor Schreuer, in his treatise on ICSID arbitration, without explanation likens this provision to NAFTA 1121.[74] It is, however, not entirely clear whether Art. 26 is really as expansive as NAFTA 1121. Art. 26 does not speak of the "measure" challenged in an ICSID arbitration. Instead, it speaks only of "remedy". The text does not answer the question whether it should be understood as any other remedy with respect to the same measure (a NAFTA-like approach), or any other remedy with respect to the same claim (a triple identity approach). In the *Lanco* case the tribunal said that Art. 26 means that once the parties submit to ICSID jurisdiction they "lose their right to seek to settle *the dispute* in any other forum".[75] If "the dispute" is interpreted in this context the same way it is interpreted in the fork in the road cases – namely, as the dispute based on the BIT itself rather than as any dispute based on the same set of underlying facts – then Art. 26 would be distinctly unlike NAFTA 1121.

ii.   Doctrinal developments

Many and perhaps most BITs contain none of the clauses described so far in this paper. They are simply silent on the topic of other proceedings. For example, the Netherlands-Czech BIT at issue in the *CME* case contained no fork in the road, exhaustion requirement or waiver language.

Is there any law that regulates multiple proceedings in such a circumstance? It is not clear that there is. As mentioned, domestic legal systems commonly recognize *res judicata* and *lis pendens* in one form or another. However, it is an open question how and to what extent these rules apply in the context of BIT arbitration. For example, during the *CME* case the governments of The Netherlands and Czech Republic (at the Czech Republic's request) conferred regarding the meaning of certain aspects of the BIT. They issued joint minutes of those consultations, which said in relevant part:

> "The two delegations agree that, although it might be undesirable that investors submit the same subject matter to different arbitral tribunals under different Investment Protection Agreements, the Czech-Dutch investment Agreement does not deal with this situation....
>
> The delegation of the Netherlands believes that neither written nor unwritten international law at present deals with this question. The Czech delegation indicated that there are rules available in international law, based on fundamental principles, which deal with the question referred to....

---

73. *Ibid.*, para. 27.
74. Christoph SCHREUER, *The ICSID Convention: A Commentary* (2001) p. 368.
75. *Op. cit.*, fn. 26, para. 36.

On the issue of different tribunals dealing with supposedly identical cases, the Netherlands delegation believes that it cannot be maintained that there are always identical cases when a legal dispute is submitted to international arbitration under different Investment Protection Treaties and/or by different investors. The provisions of Investment Protection Treaties may be controlled by the same economic entity, are not necessarily the same claims and difference in legal personality has been recognised by tribunals (see, e.g., the ICJ Barcelona Traction cases)."[76]

The conceptual challenge is that there was no particular relationship between the two regimes established by the two treaties involved in the BIT cases. Within a national legal system there is authority to impose overarching rules of law that subordinate one claim (made later in time) to another (made earlier in time). In international law, however, there is arguably no similar overarching rule of law. Each treaty exists on the same plane, and need not be subordinated to another. This at least was the view expressed by Professor Giorgio Sacerdoti in his expert opinion submitted in the *CME* case during the challenge proceedings in the Svea Court in Stockholm.[77]

At the same time, there are calls in the international arbitration and international law communities for rethinking the preclusion doctrines in international arbitration, including BIT arbitration. The International Law Association's Commercial Arbitration Committee has been studying the applicability of *res judicata* and *lis pendens* to international arbitration since 2002. It is due to make a final report on *res judicata* and an interim report on *lis pendens* at its annual meeting this year to be held in Toronto immediately following the ICCA Congress. The ILA's December 2004 interim report on *res judicata* observed that "[a] number of commentators favour an approach that looks at the underlying nature of a dispute and not at its formal classification", a clear challenge to strict application of the triple identity rule.[78] For example, in a 2004 paper, Professor August Reinisch argued that a more "economic approach" should be taken and "realistic attitude" adopted.[79] He contends that some cases (such as *Amco Asia v. Indonesia*) have adopted approaches that pierce through corporate forms to get at the "reality" of a dispute, and that a corollary of this approach must be a similar widening of the concepts of *res judicata* and *lis pendens* in order to avoid multiplicity of actions.

Putting aside for a moment views on the risks and benefits of such a proposal, it raises an interesting meta question: what is the relevance of revised thinking about *res judicata* and *lis pendens*? There is not likely to be a multilateral convention on these topics, and

---

76. On file with author.
77. Giorgio SACERDOTI, *op. cit.*, fn. 22; see also *CME v. Czech Republic*, Case No. T8735-01, Svea Court of Appeal (2002) ("The mere fact that the arbitrations were initiated under different investment treaties which were entered into between different states ... militates against these legal principles [*res judicata* and *lis pendens*] being applicable at all") (available at <www.investmentclaims.com/oa1.html>).
78. *ILA Interim Report*, p. 20.
79. August REINISCH, "The Use and Limits of *Res Judicata* and *Lis Pendens* as Procedural Tools to Avoid Conflicting Dispute Settlement Outcomes", 3 The Journal of World Investment and Trade, p. 37 at p. 74.

it will likely remain the case that there is no single universally accepted standard for defining and applying these concepts. Should tribunals considering fork in the road clauses begin to revise the so far consistent jurisprudence to reflect a "reality" based approach?

IV. CONCLUSIONS

At present treaties provide very few effective means of addressing the risk or consequences of parallel proceedings. Many are simply silent on the subject. None deals with what is perhaps the most fundamentally challenging kind of parallelism, which involves SGS-like situations in which multiple tribunals provide different interpretations of nearly identical treaty provisions.

The most direct approach reflected in a significant number of treaties is the fork in the road clause. That clause, however, has been rendered almost meaningless in practice. That is because it requires an election about the forum in which to submit a "dispute", and (following the traditional triple identity test) tribunals have consistently considered suits asserting contract or State law claims to be different "disputes" than BIT arbitrations asserting international law claims. Hence commencement of State court suits does not constitute an election with respect to the "dispute".

This approach may be subject to erosion in the future. NAFTA Art. 1121 contains a different and broader forum selection provision. It allows an investor to pursue national law claims prior to commencing a BIT arbitration, but then requires her (and any corporate entities she controls directly or indirectly) to waive rights to pursue any proceedings with respect to the challenged State "measure" regardless of the grounds asserted or capable of assertion in each proceeding. Such an approach may become more common as it is now included in the United States and Canadian Model BITs.

NAFTA 1121-style provisions are likely to be much more effective than fork in the road clauses at preventing parallel proceedings. However, there is reason to wonder whether the price paid for that benefit is simply too high. A NAFTA 1121-style transactional approach, which focuses on the underlying facts (what some call the "reality" of the dispute) or on the State "measure" being challenged, to the exclusion of the legal basis of the claims asserted, may force investors to sacrifice entirely valid legal claims as the price for BIT arbitration.

To illustrate, let us return to the example suggested earlier of a license revocation that the investor contends breaches both a specific contract with the State and international law rights the BIT conferred. Under a transactional approach the investor can bring only one action, either in BIT arbitration or national court. If he goes to national court, he is frankly unlikely to have a meaningful hearing on his international law claims (assuming the national court even has jurisdiction to hear such claims). If he goes to BIT arbitration, he is unlikely to have any hearing on his contract claims, unless the BIT has an umbrella clause that the tribunal is prepared to apply more broadly than happened in either of the SGS cases.

This kind of forced choice – requiring sacrifice not just of forum but (at least as a practical matter) of substantive rights – seems wrong. BITs are supposed to provide remedies in addition to those provided by contract or national law, not in place of them.

Such an example illustrates a significant shortcoming with a transactional approach to preclusion in BIT arbitration: it may not be right for the context. Broad applications of preclusion doctrines work within a unified legal system with coordinate courts, each of which has equally broad competence and jurisdiction. In such a setting, rules compelling parties to centralize all claims into a single proceeding make sense. But the reality of BIT arbitration is very different. BIT tribunals and national courts or administrative bodies are not the same; they have considerably different competencies and jurisdictional mandates.

The choice forced by NAFTA 1121 (and the US and Canadian Model BITs) in particular is of course not quite so stark. Those treaties actually permit the investor to pursue domestic remedies prior to commencing BIT arbitration. But they do require the choice to be made at some point. There are many circumstances when it might make sense for an investor — and even for the respondent State — not to force this choice. For example, the United States Model BIT also contains a limitations period, which bars commencement of BIT arbitration "if more than three years have elapsed from the date on which the claimant first acquired, or should have first acquired, knowledge of the breach ... and knowledge that the claimant ... has incurred loss or damage".[80] It is entirely conceivable that significant domestic proceedings could still be pending three years after the alleged breach, and in that circumstance the investor would be forced to abandon them if she wanted to commence BIT arbitration. Although many lament the existence of parallel proceedings, sometimes they are necessary and important.

Recognizing this reality, as much of the current BIT jurisprudence does at least implicitly, may mean that parallel proceedings continue to feature in BIT cases. But that seems like a reasonable price to pay to ensure that investors need not sacrifice significant legal rights in the name of efficiency. As the *Bayindir* tribunal commented when it announced it was going to proceed with the BIT arbitration and decide contract issues as necessary despite the fact there was another arbitration tribunal seized of the contract claims:

> "This is an inevitable consequence of the principle of the distinct nature of treaty and contract claims. The Tribunal is aware that this system implies an intrinsic risk of contradictory decisions or double recovery."[81]

The tribunal then noted that the potentially adverse consequences of such "intrinsic risks" were really questions to be addressed as part of the merits of the case "and for which 'international law and decisions offer numerous mechanisms for preventing the possibility of double recovery'".[82] That would seem the better way to balance rights and efficiency than through jurisdictional provisions or doctrines that effectively bar assertion of potentially valid and valuable claims.

---

80. United States Model BIT Art. 26(1).

81. *Op. cit.*, fn. 27 at 270.

82. *Ibid.* (quoting *Camuzzi International S.A. v. The Argentine Republic*, ICSID No. ARB/03/2, Decisions on Objections to Jurisdiction at 91 (11 May 2005)).

Treaties as Agreements to Arbitrate: Comments

Brigitte Stern[*]

I. INTRODUCTION

A first comment I would like to make concerns the title of this section which I am not sure covers adequately the topics developed by the four Rapporteurs. In my view, if a treaty can be considered as an agreement to arbitrate, then this agreement to arbitrate is necessarily an agreement between the parties to the treaty, in other words between States, or indeed possibly marginally between States and international organizations or between international organizations. In other words, *a treaty as an agreement to arbitrate is an agreement between subjects of public international law*, and as such can only give rise to arbitrations under public international law. An old example of such a treaty as an agreement to arbitrate is the Washington Convention of 1871 – adopted to settle the claims of the United States against the United Kingdom, for the latter's breach of the rules of neutrality as it had helped the Confederacy against the North – under which the famous *Alabama* arbitration took place.

This is indeed not the topic here. I think a more correct title could have been "Treaties as instruments of consent of States to accept arbitration with nationals of other States". Of course this title – although more accurate – is certainly less elegant than the title given to this section, but my introductory remark was simply intended to focus on our real topic. While dealing with semantics, for the sake of precision it should be noted that I will use the expression "investment treaties" to refer to treaties for the promotion and protection of international investments, whether bilateral or multilateral.

In fact, the thematic line that runs through the four very interesting Reports in this section, is the impact on "traditional" arbitration – based on an arbitration clause inserted in a contract (*clause compromissoire*) or in an arbitration agreement (*compromis d'arbitrage*) – of the development of arbitration based on treaties for the protection of international investments, whether bilateral treaties, the BITs, or multilateral treaties. In other words, how does treaty-based arbitration impact on contract-based arbitration?

[*] Professor at the University of Paris I, Panthéon-Sorbonne; Adjunct Professor at the Graduate Institute for International Studies, Geneva; Director of the CERDIN, Centre d'étude et de recherche en droit international de Paris I.

In order to answer such a broad question, a two-step approach is necessary: first to analyze these treaties *in themselves* and then to analyze the arbitration process based on these treaties *in their context*, that is, in relation to and in interaction with the arbitration process based on contracts.

The first set of questions will then naturally be to define *the scope of these treaties* embodying a reference to international arbitration: what type of dispute do they encompass? Is there a difference between the treaties having a broad definition of an investment dispute and the others? What is the meaning of the so-called umbrella clauses? Are there difficulties of articulation between claims based on a treaty and claims based on a contract; can they contradict; are they redundant or complementary; do they imply the same or a different approach towards matters such as the definition of the claim; and how is the applicable law determined?

The second set of questions, then, concerns *the relation of the treaties to other means of investment dispute settlement*, the interaction and possible conflicts or at least difficulties raised by the possible coexistence of treaty-based arbitration procedures and contract-based arbitration or jurisdictional procedures.

All these questions have been covered by the four Reports in this section.

The treaties as such have been analyzed first:

– Meg Kinnear has focused on "International Law as the Governing Law" and has set forth the sources of international law, as well discussing the important question of the interpretation of international law as embodied in the investment treaties;[1]
– Peter Turner, for his part, has looked into the definition of the legal and natural persons to whom the investment treaties confer rights in his Report entitled "Issues of Scope: Parties, Ownership and Control".[2]

In other words, the two first Reports looked at the applicable law and the beneficiaries under the investment treaties. Then, the treaties were replaced in the general context of investment dispute settlement, and the focus shifted to the coordination or non-coordination between the disputes litigated under the treaties and other disputes:

– Guido Tawil's Report addressed "The Distinction between Contract Claims and Treaty Claims: an Overview",[3] which we all know is a difficult and controversial issue;
– and last but not least, Mark Friedman looked into the possible ways to solve contradictions between the different available procedures in his Report entitled "Related Dispute Resolution Regimes: Parallel Proceedings in BIT Arbitration".[4]

Concerning the substance of what has been said, it may be that one way to look at our topic is to question some of the things that are considered as given, but that might not be as evident as they look at first sight. It seems that, in the domain of international

---

1. See this volume, pp. 401-443.
2. See this volume, pp. 444-491.
3. See this volume, pp. 492-544.
4. See this volume, pp. 545-568.

arbitration, once a statement is made by an arbitral tribunal – composed, it goes without saying, of eminent arbitrators – it is generally taken as the truth, not questioned anymore and then repeated and repeated by other arbitral tribunals. I will of course not be able to comment on every and all of the sometimes very exciting points made by the four Rapporteurs for this section, but will just pick up a few issues on which I thought it would be interesting to focus the discussion.

My comments will be on three points:

— Problems of interpretation of international law as applied to treaty-based arbitration;
— Treatment of nationality of legal persons in investment treaty regimes;
— Problems of definition and articulation of contract claims and treaty claims.

II.   INTERPRETATION OF INTERNATIONAL LAW IN TREATY-BASED ARBITRATION

Two questions raised by Meg Kinnear are in my view quite interesting, the first question being whether interpretation of an investment treaty should favour the investor, the second being the weight that should be given by arbitrators to an interpretation of an investment treaty given by a State party to such treaty.

1.   Should the Interpretation of Investment Treaties Favour the Investors?

The first question is whether the interpretation of an investment treaty should favour the investor as sometimes stated by the investor, because as underlined by Meg Kinnear the provisions of the preamble "invariably identify protection of investors as the object of the treaty". This interpretation in favour of the investor has sometimes been accepted by arbitral tribunals, like the ICSID tribunal in the case of *SGS v. Philippines*, where it stated:

> "The BIT is a treaty for the promotion and reciprocal protection of investments. According to the preamble it is intended 'to create and maintain favourable conditions for investments by investors of one Contracting Party in the territory of the other'. It is legitimate to resolve uncertainties in its interpretation so as to favour the protection of covered investments."[5]

The opposite approach to interpretation has been put forward by the United States in the *Methanex* case, where it contended that

> "a doctrine of restrictive interpretation should be applied in investor-state disputes. In other words, wherever there is any ambiguity in clauses granting jurisdiction over disputes between states and private persons, such ambiguity is always to be resolved in favour of maintaining state sovereignty."[6]

---

5. *SGS v. Philippines*, Award on Jurisdiction, 29 January 2004, para. 116.
6. Partial Award on Jurisdiction, 7 August 2002, para. 103.

However, I would suggest that neither of these two approaches is to be retained and therefore I agree on that point with Meg Kinnear, when she states that

> "[c]onsidering investor protection as *the* object of the treaty can result in an incorrect interpretation if it is not also balanced with what is also usually stated: that such treaties promote foreign direct investment in the host State".

This was indeed the position adopted by the arbitral tribunal in *Methanex*, where it stated that the interpretation suggested by the United States could not prevail. In the tribunal's own words,

> "the provisions of Chapter 11 ... should be interpreted in good faith in accordance with their ordinary meaning (in accordance with Article 31(1) of the Vienna Convention), without any one-sided doctrinal advantage built into their text to disadvantage procedurally an investor seeking arbitral relief".[7]

I personally fully agree with this analysis and consider that a balanced interpretation is needed, taking into account both the State's sovereignty and its responsibility to create an adapted and evolutionary framework for the development of economic activities and the necessity to protect foreign investment and its continuing flow.

2. *What Weight Should an Arbitral Tribunal Give to the Parties' Interpretation of an Investment Treaty?*

The second question is the role played by the interpretation of international law given by a State party to an investment treaty. I think that in order to evaluate the admissibility of such interpretation, one has to distinguish clearly – and that might extend Meg Kinnear's text – between a unilateral interpretation and a common interpretation, and when speaking of unilateral interpretation between an interpretation given by the State party to the arbitration or an interpretation given by another State party.

As far as a unilateral interpretation of the law by a State party to an arbitration is concerned, whether it is in fact its own national law or the international rules embodied in the treaty as applicable to an arbitration case, such interpretation has naturally no binding force on the tribunal. This was, for example, stated quite clearly in the *Pyramids* case by the ICSID tribunal in its second decision on jurisdiction: according to the tribunal "[w]hile Egypt's interpretation of its own legislation is unquestionably entitled to considerable weight, it cannot control the Tribunal's decision".[8] The same would be true for an interpretation of an investment treaty.

As far as unilateral interpretation of the international rules embodied in an investment treaty by a State non-party to the arbitration is concerned, there is no reason to give to the State's interpretation a special weight, as its interpretation is *res inter alios*

---

7. *Ibid.*, para. 105.
8. *Southern Pacific Properties Ltd. v. Arab Republic of Egypt*, ICSID Case No. ARB/84/3, Decision on Jurisdiction, Award of 14 April 1988, ICCA *Yearbook Commercial Arbitration* XVI (1991) para. 38.

acta, being subject to the general relativism of international law, according to which one State's interpretation has no reason to prevail over another State's interpretation. But I predict that the time is not far away when a State party to an investment treaty, having some interest in the interpretation to be given to a provision of that treaty, will ask to submit an *amicus curiae*, and now that they are accepted in ICSID arbitration, I see no legal basis on which this could be refused. It can be noted that not much time elapsed between the time when the Appellate Body of the WTO accepted *amicus curiae* from NGOs and other private parties and the time when it accepted the same from a State party to the WTO – Morocco – in the *Sardines* case.[9]

Whatever the means of presentation of a unilateral interpretation by one or the other State party to the investment treaty, such interpretation does not bind the tribunal.

The analysis is quite different if one speaks about a common interpretation of a disposition of a treaty by the two or more parties to the treaty. According to Art. 31 of the Vienna Convention on the law of treaties it is well known that

> "[t]he context for the purpose of the interpretation of a treaty shall comprise, in addition to the text, including its preamble and annexes:
>
> "(a) any subsequent agreement between the parties regarding the interpretation of the treaty or the application of its provisions;
> (b) any subsequent practice in the application of the treaty which establishes the agreement of the parties regarding its interpretation…".

In other words, it is absolutely acceptable from a legal point of view that the parties to a treaty give their common interpretation of the treaty although from a due process point of view it can, as in the *Lauder* case with the interpretation given by the Netherlands and the Czech Republic on applicable law and other relevant issues, in the words of Meg Kinnear, be "portrayed as a way for a State Party to influence the outcome of a tribunal award". And we know that this is indeed what happened as the tribunal, after having rendered a partial award in *CME v. The Czech Republic*, accepted the common interpretation given by the two States parties of the governing BIT, stating in its final award that "[t]he common positions, representing the interpretations and application of the Treaty agreed between its contracting parties, are conclusive and binding on the Tribunal".[10]

This general rule of interpretation has been expressly stated in Art. 1131 of NAFTA, where the interpretation was entrusted to the Free Trade Commission, composed of Representatives of the States parties having a ministerial rank, as well as in the new US Model BIT of 2004 which provides in Art. 30(3):

---

9. *European Communities - Trade Description of Sardines*, case DS 231, Panel Report, 24 May 2002; Report of the Appellate Body, 26 September 2002; Mutually Agreed Solution, 29 July 2003.

10. *CME Czech Republic B.V. (The Netherlands) v. The Czech Republic*, Final Award, 14 March 2003 (UNCITRAL Arbitration Tribunal) paras. 216-217.

"A joint decision of the Parties, each acting through its representative designated for purposes of this Article, declaring their interpretation of a provision of this Treaty, shall be binding on a tribunal, and any decision or award issued by a tribunal must be consistent with that joint decision."

It is well known that in the context of NAFTA, early arbitral tribunals gave different interpretations of the "fair and equitable" provision of the NAFTA text. In order to clarify the interpretation of Art. 1105(1), the NAFTA Free Trade Commission (FTC) issued a binding interpretation on 21 July 2001, according to which:

"1. Article 1105 (1) prescribes the customary international law minimum standard of treatment of aliens as the minimum standard of treatment to be afforded to investments of investors of another Party.

2. The concepts of 'fair and equitable treatment' and 'full protection and security' do not require treatment in addition to or beyond that which is required by the customary international law minimum standard of treatment of aliens.

3. A determination that there has been a breach of another provision of the NAFTA, or of a separate international agreement, does not establish that there has been a breach of Article 1105 (1)."

This interpretation has thereafter been applied by NAFTA tribunals.

III.   TREATMENT OF LEGAL PERSONS IN INVESTMENT TREATY REGIMES

The point of departure of my reflections on this topic is the introductory statement of Peter Turner, according to which we can observe

"the development of an 'investment law of nationality' that clearly derives from, but equally clearly now differs from, the rules of customary international law as developed in the law of diplomatic protection".

His Report very convincingly shows this development, first as far as legal persons are concerned, second as far as natural persons are concerned.[11] I shall concentrate my comments on the problems raised by legal persons and here I see of course – this is not very inventive – two interesting issues, the first being the determination of a company's nationality, the second being the extent to which shareholders are entitled to claim for damage done to their company.

---

11. I am not going to deal with the second part of the topic, which is at the heart of the *Soufraki* Annulment Committee, of which I am a member.

1.   Determination of a Company's Nationality

It is well known that on the question of the nationality of a company, general international law as expressed in the seminal case of *Barcelona Traction*, has adopted a formal approach when stating that

> "[t]he traditional rule attributes the right to diplomatic protection of a corporate entity to the State under the laws of which it is incorporated and in whose territory it has its registered office".[12]

It is also not open to debate that investment treaties have sometimes – even quite often – followed that pattern, but also that some investment treaties have to a certain extent taken into consideration the effective economic links, either in order to restrict the offer to arbitrate or in order to expand it.

The most obvious example of an extension of the offer to arbitrate to companies whose nationality would not allow them to benefit from an ICSID arbitration is naturally Art. 25(b) of the Washington Convention, which is well known.[13] In other instances, BITs have adopted provisions allowing a party to deny the benefits of the agreement to investors that have no "substantial business activities" in their putative home country, reflecting the intent of the agreements to protect only bona fide transnational investments between the home country and the host country.[14]

This is a manner in which a contracting State party to an investment treaty can expressly guard itself against "treaty shopping". Or, even more drastically, some BITs have only offered arbitration to companies being both registered in the Contracting State and having real economic links with it through business activities in its territory or control by its nationals: an example of such a provision can be found in Art. I(2) of the ASEAN Agreement of 1987 on investment protection according to which

> "[t]he term 'company' of a Contracting Party shall mean a corporation, partnership or other business association, incorporated or constituted under the

---

12. *Case Concerning the Barcelona Traction, Light and Power Company, Limited (Belgium v. Spain)*, *ICJ Rep.* 1970, para. 70.

13. "'National of another Contracting State' means:

(....)

(b) any juridical person which had the nationality of a Contracting State other than the State party to the dispute on the date on which the parties consented to submit such dispute to conciliation or arbitration and any juridical person which had the nationality of the Contracting State party to the dispute on that date and which, because of foreign control, the parties have agreed should be treated as a national of another Contracting State for the purposes of this Convention."

14. An example of this can be found in the Argentine-US BIT of 1994, in Art. I(2):

"Each Party reserves the right to deny to any company of the other Party the advantages of this Treaty if (a) nationals of any third country or nationals of such Party, control such company and the company has no substantial business activities in the territory of the other Party...".

laws in force in the territory of any Contracting Party wherein the place of effective management is situated".

Another example is Art. VII of the Algiers Declaration:[15]

"For the purposes of this agreement:
1. A 'national' of Iran or of the United States, as the case may be, means (a) a natural person who is a citizen of Iran or the United States; and (b) a corporation or other legal entity which is organized under the laws of Iran or the United States or any of its states or territories, the District of Columbia or the Commonwealth of Puerto Rico, if, collectively, natural persons who are citizens of such country hold, directly or indirectly, an interest in such corporation or entity equivalent to fifty per cent or more of its capital stock."

In other words, it is not open to discussion that conventional law as embodied in investment treaties can modify the international customary rule according to which a company has the nationality of its State of incorporation. The "nationality for arbitration purposes" can be defined differently than in public international law, in a more encompassing or more restrictive manner. This being said on the nationality of companies, to me the most interesting problem in this context of treaty-based arbitration is the one raised by the right to claim of the shareholders. This brings me to the second question.

2. Shareholders' Right to Claim

It is common knowledge that in general international law, as stated in the *Barcelona Traction* case, the rights of the shareholders and the rights of the company are clearly distinguished and the shareholders are only considered to have a right to assert (through the diplomatic protection of their State, if so granted) if one of their own rights was violated (such as the right to a dividend).

The question of the rights of shareholders is not really answered in the Washington Convention, although it seems that the intention of the drafters was to protect the foreign majority shareholders in a local company, in giving *jus standi* to that company through Art. 25(b), mentioned above. So, it might be concluded that, in the Washington Convention, on its face, the minority and indirect shareholders did not seem to be protected.

But, as for nationality criteria, the extent to which shareholders can be protected can differ in conventional international law and customary international law. And indeed, the answer is quite different in the BITs, the great majority of which today have accepted to protect both minority shareholders and indirect shareholders, the result being theoretically that a share representing one per cent of the capital of a company, owned through twenty or more layers of companies, is protected. The question is thus raised

---

15. The Algiers Accords which ended the hostage crisis between Iran and the United States, 19 January 1981.

for an ICSID tribunal whether there is no limit. It might safely be recalled that one limit might be the definition of investment itself, as stemming from ICSID case law, with its three or four elements – depending on the decisions – to define an investment: contributions of capital or other resources, certain duration, taking of risk and participation to the development of the country, this last element being not considered as relevant by all decisions.

Another question about which it would be interesting to think, is whether some other limits should be found. I would also like to cite here the decision by an ICSID tribunal presided over by Francisco Vicuña, which can give us some food for thought:

> "This Tribunal must accordingly conclude that under the provisions of the Bilateral Investment Treaty, broad as they are, claims made by investors that are not in the majority or in control of the affected corporation when claiming for violations of their rights under such treaty are admissible."[16]

But he added an interesting *caveat* a few paragraphs later:

> "The Tribunal notes that while investors can claim in their own right under the provisions of the treaty, there is indeed a need to establish a cut-off point beyond which claims would not be permissible as they would have only a remote connection to the affected company."[17]

In summary, it is clear that investment treaties have adopted a broad approach to the concepts of "investors", and tribunals have increased the number of persons, notably legal persons, who can initiate claims arising under an investment treaty dispute. Even if my main reaction is to consider it a good thing as it follows the objectives of investment treaties to increase the protection of the investors, it does so not without raising certain procedural issues, notably the risks of a multiplicity of fora and of treaty shopping.

The risk of a multiplicity of claims has been illustrated in the *Lauder* case, and should probably be dealt with when giving more thought to procedures of consolidation.

Another way to limit the multiplicity of fora is to insert a provision in the relevant treaty providing that the shareholders can only act if the company cannot, and I would think that this might be a welcomed development in BITs. An example of such a solution can be found in Art. VII(2) of the Algiers Declaration:

> "2. 'Claims of nationals' of Iran or the United States, as the case may be, means claims owned continuously, from the date on which the claim arose to the date on which this agreement enters into force, by nationals of that state, including claims that are owned indirectly by such nationals through ownership of capital stock or other proprietary interests in juridical persons, provided that the ownership interests of such nationals, collectively, were sufficient at the time the

---

16. *Enron v. Argentina*, Decision on Jurisdiction, 14 January 2003, para. 49.
17. *Ibid.*, para. 52.

claim arose to control the corporation or other entity, and provided, further, that the corporation or other entity is not itself entitled to bring a claim under the terms of this agreement. Claims referred to the Arbitral Tribunal shall, as of the date of filing of such claims with the Tribunal, be considered excluded from the jurisdiction of the courts of Iran, or of the United States, or of any other court."

These are some of the quick thoughts that have been stimulated by Peter Turner's Report.

IV.   PROBLEMS OF DEFINITION AND CO-EXISTENCE OF CONTRACT CLAIMS AND TREATY CLAIMS

To start my comment on these points, I will first mention that I agree one hundred per cent with Guido Tawil when he says that "[t]he distinction between contract claims and treaty claims has certainly become one of the most highly debated issues in investment treaty arbitration". And I am sure the debate will go on.

I will concentrate on some of the many aspects that have been addressed by the two Rapporteurs who dealt with these questions: the distinction contract claim/treaty claim as elaborated by ICSID case law, the umbrella clause, and the different ways to deal with parallel proceedings, which was the central topic of Mark Friedman.

1.   The Deceptively Simple Distinction Between Treaty Claims and Contract Claims

Without entering into details, it can be asserted that the distinction rests essentially on the applicable law. As stated by the *ad hoc* annulment Committee[18] in *Vivendi I*:

> "A state may breach a treaty without breaching a contract, and vice versa.... Each of these claims will be determined by reference to its own proper or applicable law – in the case of the BIT, by international law; in the case of the Concession Contract, by the proper law of the contract, in other words, the law of Tucumán...."[19]

In other words, as it results from today's case law, a contract claim and a treaty claim can be based exactly on *the same factual situation*. But the situation is qualified differently with regard to two different legal orders, international law and national law; a contract

---

18. May I note that I do not share Guido Tawil's analysis of the first decision in *Compañía de Aguas del Aconquija S.A. & Compagnie Générale des Eaux, v. Argentine Republic,* Case No. ARB/97/3, Award, 21 November 2000, saying that the Tribunal "dismissed" the contract claims. In fact, it merely stated that they were so intermingled that it could not decide on any concession claims until the local tribunals have decided these issues.

19. *Compañía de Aguas del Aconquija S.A. and Vivendi Universal (formerly Compagnie Générale Des Eaux) v. Argentine Republic,* ICSID Case No. ARB/97/3, Decision on Annulment, 3 July 2002, paras. 95-96.

claim and a treaty claim can also ask for *the same remedy*, as decided in *Bayindir*, where the Tribunal concluded that:

"... when the investor has a right under both the contract and the treaty, it has a self-standing right to pursue the remedy accorded by the treaty. The very fact that the amount claimed under the treaty is the same as the amount that could be claimed (or was claimed) under the contract does not affect such self-standing right."[20]

Although Guido Tawil mentioned five criteria to distinguish the two types of claim – (i) the source of the right; (ii) the content of the right; (iii) the parties to the claim; (iv) applicable law and (v) the host State's responsibility – I wonder if the heart of the distinction is not just the way the investor qualifies its claim either under international law or national law. In fact, in his concluding remarks, where he stated that "the cause of action is the central tenet to distinguish a contract claim from a treaty claim. A contract claim alleges a breach of a contract while a treaty claim invokes a breach of the treaty," he seems to have arrived at the same conclusion. The idea that the distinction rests merely on the legal qualification as far as applicable law is concerned can also be found in Mark Friedman's paper.

Here, I would like to reflect a little more on that distinction which at first sight seems simple and convincing. Mark Friedman wrote that the choice of law in case of a treaty claim is simple: it is international law. In fact, it is not so simple. It is not open to discussion that acceptance by an investor of an offer by a State to arbitrate in a treaty in which there is an implied or express choice of law means that the investor agrees with this choice of law.

A first branch of our questioning could be: is it certain that treaty claims only involve international law? Indeed it appears that there are two types of choice of law provisions in investment treaties.

One type of provision on applicable law follows the disposition of Art. 1131 of NAFTA, referring exclusively to public international law:

"A Tribunal established under this Section shall decide the issues in dispute in accordance with the Agreement and applicable rules of international law."

The same type of clause exists in the US Model BIT of 2004 (in its Art. 30(1)), the Energy Charter (in its Art. 26(6)) and many other treaties mentioned by Meg Kinnear in her presentation.

A second type of provision on applicable law is more encompassing and refers to different sources of law emanating from different legal orders.

An example cited by Christoph Schreuer[21] is Art. 10 of the Argentine-Netherlands BIT of 1992 stating:

---

20. *Bayindir Insaat Turizm Ticaret Ve Sanayi A.S. v. Islamic Republic of Pakistan*, ICSID Case No. ARB/03/29, Decision on Jurisdiction, 14 November 2005, para. 148.
21. *The ICSID Convention. A Commentary* (Cambridge University Press 2001) p. 582.

"The arbitral tribunal addressed in accordance with paragraph (5) of this article shall decide on the basis of the law of the Contracting Party which is a party to the dispute (including its rules on the conflict of law), the provisions of the present Agreement, special Agreements concluded in relation to the investment concerned as well as such rules of international law as may be applicable."

The same type of clause is found in the Algiers Accords of 1981, whose Art. V provides:

"The Tribunal shall decide all cases on the basis of respect for law, applying such choice of law rules and principles of commercial and international law as the Tribunal determines to be applicable, taking into account relevant usages of the trade, contract provisions and changed circumstance."

Other examples of these all-encompassing provisions are the ones that can be found in the Colonia Investment Protocol of Mercosur (in its Art. 9(5)) and in several bilateral treaties mentioned by Meg Kinnear.

Now, if it is really a specificity of the treaty-based claim that it is a claim based on international law, we are faced here with a problem if the choice of law is broader and not restricted to international law. I am of course not going to solve it, I just wanted to raise it.

But there is a second branch to this inquiry: is it certain that contract claims only apply national law? It suffices here to recall how the ICSID tribunal has interpreted the reference to national law in its decision on the merits in the *SPP v. Egypt* case, also called the *Pyramids* case: in this case, the question of the interpretation of the two sentences of Art. 42 of the Washington Convention[22] was discussed between the parties: Egypt considered the first sentence had to be applied as there was an agreement between the parties to apply Egyptian law, while according to the claimant, it was not the first sentence but the second sentence of Art. 42(1) which should be applied so that "the Tribunal should apply the 'law of the Contracting State party ... and such rules of international law as may be applicable'" (para. 77). The parties had chosen Egyptian law but the tribunal considered that even when national law is to be applied this results *in fine* in the application of international law, as it is included in national law or supplements it in case of lacunae:

"In the Tribunal's view, the Parties disagreement as to the manner in which Article 42 is to be applied has very little, if any, practical significance ... even accepting the Respondent's view that the Parties have implicitly agreed to apply

---

22. Art. 42(1):

"The Tribunal shall decide a dispute in accordance with such rules of law as may be agreed by the parties. In the absence of such agreement, the Tribunal shall apply the law of the Contracting State party to the dispute (including its rules on the conflict of laws) and such rules of international law as may be applicable."

Egyptian law, such an agreement cannot entirely exclude the direct applicability of international law in certain situations. The law of ARE, like all municipal legal systems, is not complete or exhaustive, and where a lacunae occurs it cannot be said that there is agreement as to the application of a rule of law, which *ex hypothesis*, does not exist. In such case, it must be said that there is 'absence of agreement' and, consequently, the second sentence of Art. 42(1) would come into play.... When municipal law contains a lacunae, or international law is violated by the exclusive application of municipal law, the Tribunal is bound in accordance with Art. 42, to apply directly the relevant principles and rules of international law."[23]

I think this could be a first point for discussion. It can, in passing, be noted that this opens the gates wide to ICSID arbitration for foreign investors, as they are the ones that can choose how to present their claims, and as ICSID tribunals have at the jurisdictional level considered that they should accept the facts invoked by the claimant as if they were correct and determine on that basis whether, if proven true, they could amount to a breach of the treaty. While the predominant view is thus that the tribunal is not empowered to determine during the jurisdictional phase whether there has been indeed a violation of the treaty and not a mere contractual breach, case law has developed a useful test by requesting tribunals to conduct a preliminary analysis of the treaty obligations invoked by the claimant and assess whether the facts alleged by it are prima facie capable of constituting a violation of such obligations. The liberty of the claimant to qualify a claim as a treaty claim together with the prima facie test for jurisdiction used by arbitration tribunals indeed opens the doors to treaty-based arbitration, even if of course, the true qualification will be reviewed at the merits level, and purely contractual claims not entertained.

2. Umbrella Clauses

Another highly debated question – Guido Tawil said "the issue remains highly unsettled" – is of course the scope of the so-called umbrella clause, but linked to that question is also the question of the meaning of certain very broad definitions of investment disputes in investment treaties.

Indeed, I suggest, in order to try to clarify the matter for the debate, that in fact two types of clauses have been used in order to transform any contractual breach into a treaty breach.

The first type of clause consists of a *broad dispute resolution clause in a BIT* providing that "all disputes" concerning investments between a contracting party and an investor of the other contracting party can be submitted to international arbitration.

As explained by Guido Tawil,

---

23. Award and Dissenting Opinion of 20 May 1992, 8 ICSID Rev.–FILJ (1993) p. 328, paras. 78, 80 and 84.

"[s]ome authors believe that, depending on how treaty dispute settlement clauses are drafted, the distinction between contractual and treaty claims may become to a certain extent irrelevant. In their view, treaty clauses broadly drafted in order to encompass all disputes concerning an investment would enable tribunals to address and decide on mere contractual disputes even if no violation of the treaty's substantial standards of treatment (fair and equitable treatment, non-discriminatory or arbitrary measures, expropriation, etc.) took place.[24]
(....)
However, it would be strange 'to construe a treaty as creating a forum to entertain claims other than violations of that same treaty'."[25]

In a series of decisions,[26] ICSID tribunals have asserted that, according to these provisions, they have no jurisdiction on purely contractual claims, whether they rest on a contract with the State or one of its entities, but they have jurisdiction over claims for the interference by the State with contract rights, if this interference results from a measure taken by the State as a sovereign and amounts to a breach of the standards of protection of the foreign investments provided for in the BIT. An example of this position is the decision in *Impregilo S.p.A. v. Islamic Republic of Pakistan*:

"a Host State acting as a contracting party does not 'interfere' with a contract; it 'performs' it. If it performs the contract badly, this will not result in a breach of the provisions of the Treaty relating to expropriation or nationalisation, unless it be proved that the State or its emanation has gone beyond its role as a mere party to the contract, and has exercised the specific functions of a sovereign authority" (para. 278).

"... it is the Tribunal's view that only measures taken by Pakistan in the exercise of its sovereign power ('*puissance publique*'), and not decisions taken in the implementation or performance of the Contracts, may be considered as measures having an effect equivalent to expropriation." (para. 282)

So, on this point, I do not agree with Guido Tawil's analysis when he states that, for example, in *Salini v. Morocco*, "the tribunal concluded that its jurisdiction not only comprised treaty claims, but also mere contractual claims that did not necessarily

---

24. "As explained by Professor Schreuer, 'where a BIT provides for investor/State arbitration in respect of all investment disputes rather than disputes concerning violations of the BIT, the tribunal is competent even for pure contract claims'. Christoph SCHREUER, 'Investment Treaty Arbitration and Jurisdiction over Contract Claims – the *Vivendi I* Case Considered' in Todd WEILER[, *International Investment Law and Arbitration: Leading Cases from the ICSID, Nafta, Bilateral Treaties and Customary International Law* (London, Cameron May 2005) ... at p. 296...."

25. "Emmanuel GAILLARD, "Treaty-Based Jurisdiction: Broad Dispute Resolution Clauses", 6 October 2005 N.Y.L.J. 3, at p. 6."

26. *Salini Costruttori S.p.A. & Italstrade S.p.A. v. Kingdom of Morocco*, Decision on Jurisdiction, 23 July 2001; *Consortium R.F.C.C. v. Royaume du Maroc*, Decision on Jurisdiction, 16 July 2001; *Impregilo S.p.A. v. Islamic Republic of Pakistan*, Decision on Jurisdiction, 22 April 2005.

amount to a treaty breach",[27] and therefore also not with his more general summary of ICSID case law, which according to him "seems to confirm that treaty-based tribunals have predominantly affirmed their jurisdiction to entertain contractual claims based on broadly drafted dispute settlement provisions". I think here some clarification should be given. It is true that some tribunals have considered that they can deal with breaches of contracts, but only if the contract is signed directly with the State. For contracts signed with a State entity, they have not excluded dealing with claims arising out of a contract, but, in my understanding, *only if such "contract" claims amount to treaty claims*, i.e., that can be analyzed as a violation of the treaty's standards.

But another type of clause has been said to transform automatically all contract claims into treaty claims, and it is for that type of clause that the qualification of "umbrella clause" has been used. This brings us to the topic of the role and effect of the umbrella clause.

On that question also, there is an ongoing debate as divergent positions have been adopted by different ICSID tribunals. Umbrella clauses are not always drafted in the same manner and some decisions insist on the variations in the drafting in order to explain a different analysis. I personally am not convinced that the clauses analyzed so far really should receive different interpretations. The broadest clauses read like the one contained in the relevant clause in the United States-Argentina BIT, which provides:

> "Each Party shall observe any obligation it may have entered into with regard to investments."

It is probably true, as noted by Guido Tawil, that "[t]he predominant view is that umbrella clauses elevate contractual commitments into international ones". But he adds "[h]owever, scholars and arbitral practice have not reached yet a consensus on their precise meaning and scope".

The debate is not simple. It is true that if such a clause is considered as *not elevating* all contractual breaches into treaty breaches, it does not have a very far reaching meaning; conversely, it is equally true, that if one considers it is *elevating* any obligation of the State to the level of treaty obligations, this might render the whole Treaty completely useless: indeed, if this interpretation were to be followed – to the effect that the violation of any obligation of a State, and not only of any contractual obligation, with respect to investment is a violation of the BIT, whatever the source of the obligation and whatever the seriousness of the breach – it could be sufficient to have a so-called "umbrella clause" and a dispute settlement mechanism, and no other articles setting standards of protection of foreign investments in any BIT! It would also necessarily imply that any commitment of the State in respect to investments, even the most minor ones, would be transformed into treaty claims. This fear has been articulated by

---

27. The exact wording of the Tribunal's decision is quite unambiguous: "However the Arbitral Tribunal retains jurisdiction in relation to breaches of contracts that would constitute, at the same time a violation of the Bilateral Treaty by the State." *Salini Costruttori S.p.A. & Italstrade S.p.A. v. Kingdom of Morocco*, Decision on Jurisdiction, 23 July 2001, para. 63.

Christoph Schreuer, who has described what some of the practical consequences of a broad interpretation of the umbrella clauses could be:

> "Problems could ... arise if investors were to start using umbrella clauses for trivial disputes. It cannot be the function of an umbrella clause to turn every minor disagreement on a detail of a contract performance into an issue for which international arbitration is available. For example, a small delay in a payment due to the investor and interest accruing from the delay would hardly justify arbitration under a BIT. Equally a lease dispute with the host State that is peripherical to the investment will not be an appropriate basis for the institution of arbitral proceedings. It is to be hoped that investors will invoke the umbrella clauses with appropriate restraint."[28]

Maybe one way to try to have a clearer picture of the problem is to recall what the stakes really are, in other words to look at a systemic perspective. The central problem is to protect the investors from the sovereign State's interference with its investment, and this is why through different schemes, it has been endeavoured to give the investors an international remedy in these types of cases. In other words, everybody would agree that the investor should be protected on the international level by recourse to international arbitration against the State as a sovereign that can infringe on its rights, but there is no compelling reason that the same investor should not assert its commercial claims in the realm of the State's legal order.

So maybe the solution to this intricate problem is still ahead of us, with the idea that the investors really want to be protected on the international level from interferences from the State's discretionary power: this is exactly why the investment arbitration is provided for. I just mention here the new US model BIT, in its Art. 24(1)(a) in which it is said that an investment dispute is a claim by an investor that the State has breached:

> "(A) an obligation under Articles 3 through 10,
> (B) an investment authorization, or
> (C) an investment agreement...".

And from the definition given in Art. 1 of an "investment agreement", it is quite clear that *not every contract* entered into by a State or one of its entities can be qualified as such, but only an agreement in which the State enters through *one of its authorities*, and which is moreover entered into for the *fulfilment of the public goals* of the State, linked with its economic sovereignty: natural resources, basic services to the public or general infrastructure:

> "'investment agreement' means a written agreement between *a national authority of a Party* and a covered investment or an investor of the other Party, on which the covered investment or the investor relies in establishing or acquiring a covered

---

28. "Travelling the BIT Route. Of Waiting Periods, Umbrella Clauses and Forks in the Road", 5 J. of World Inv. & Trade (April 2004, no. 2) p. 255.

investment other than the written agreement itself, that grants rights to the covered investment or investor:
(a) with respect to *natural resources* that a national authority controls, such as for their exploration, extraction, refining, transportation, distribution, or sale;
(b) to supply *services to the public* on behalf of the Party, such as power generation or distribution, water treatment or distribution, or telecommunications; or
(c) to undertake *infrastructure projects*, such as the construction of roads, bridges, canals, dams, or pipelines, that are not for the exclusive or predominant use and benefit of the government."

This is quite in line with the old trend on internationalization of State contracts in the eighties.

However, as long as there is a distinction between contract claims and treaty claims, there might be overlaps.

3.   Coexistence of Dispute Settlement Mechanisms

The distinction of contract claims and treaty claims raises in fact such difficult issues because of its legal consequences, that is, mainly because at first sight these two types of claims are not answerable to the same dispute settlement procedures: the treaty claim can benefit from the offer to arbitrate included in the investment treaty, while the contract claim should utilize the applicable contractually agreed dispute settlement forum. As stated by Mark Friedman, in his introductory remarks,

> "[i]mperfectly defined and partially overlapping jurisdictional mandates in various fora present risks of duplicative proceedings, inconsistent judgments and even double recovery. This concern has also emerged in investment treaty arbitration. Investment treaty disputes have grown explosively over the last decade, and many of those disputes have featured some form of multiple proceedings arising out of the same basic set of facts."

In fact there are different methods to deal with a possible duplication, which have been very clearly explained and presented by Mark Friedman. After having given several recent examples of parallel proceedings in BIT cases – I was very impressed by the figure he provided of evidence of parallel proceedings in forty-one per cent of seventy-eight reviewed ICSID cases – Mark Friedman reviewed the different means established in investment treaties in order to avoid parallel proceedings. The different configurations of parallel proceedings encountered were:

– company/subsidiary, which could imply several layers of companies, each being a shareholder in its subsidiary, some acting at the international level, the subsidiary at the national level (many of the Argentine cases);
– individual shareholder/company under different BIT (*Lauder* case);
– company/in different States under different BIT (*SGS* cases).

585

Naturally, what comes immediately to mind when one speaks of avoiding parallel proceedings is what has come to be known as the "fork in the road" provision. Everybody knows that this means that when at a crossroads one chooses one path or another, as provided for in these types of clauses, and that one's choice is final; one cannot come back. The fork in the road provision "provides that the investor may submit the dispute to either national courts in the host state or to international arbitration – but not to both" – and that this choice is final. But as aptly shown by Mark Friedman, the current interpretation given by ICSID tribunals to what is a contract claim and what is a treaty claim renders the provision of no practical effect; they have been rendered "toothless", with the result that "not a single state has successfully invoked a fork in the road defence to a BIT claim". Why is this so? It has already been mentioned that the same facts can give rise to different claims if they are given different legal qualifications. This is exactly what happens here. Each time ICSID tribunals have been faced with fork in the road provisions, they have applied triple identity criteria to decide whether or not it was, for example, the same claim in arbitration and in the national courts. According to Mark Friedman, the three elements of a claim to take into consideration are: "(a) the parties to it, (b) the claims asserted in it, and (c) its subject matter". The ICSID tribunals refer to the "identity of the parties, object and cause of action in the proceedings pending before both tribunals": obviously the cause of action is never the same, as it is asserted under international law in the international proceeding and under national law before the national courts, as explained, for example, in *Azurix*:

> "As contractual claims are different from treaty claims even if there had been or there currently was a recourse to the local courts for breach of contract, this would not have prevented submission of the treaty claims to arbitration.... Both the parties and the causes of action under separate instruments are different."[29]

In other words, as long as the same claim can be christened by two different names, according to the place where the investor wants to pursue its claim, the fork in the road provisions will be of no avail to avoid parallel proceeding on the national and the international planes; as long as the same dispute can give rise to different claims, a contract claim under national law and a treaty claim under international law, the fork in the road provision will not have any practical effect. Mark Friedman seems to welcome this interpretation; I wonder if an interpretation the result of which is to deprive a provision of any *effet utile* is a good interpretation.

Mark Friedman then raises a fascinating question, assuming that through a broadly designed definition of investment disputes, the contract disputes are included in the realm of the investment treaty. To put it in his own words, "[d]oes the ... BIT's definition of 'the dispute' – an expansive definition that includes claims based on both national and international law rights – supplant the triple identity test?". Said differently, the question raised here is whether if one considers that a contract claim is dealt with by the investment treaty, through a broad definition of investment disputes, couldn't it

---

29. *Azurix Corp. v. Argentina Republic*, ICSID Case No. ARB/01/12, Decision on Jurisdiction, 8 December 2003.

be said then that if the investor starts a case in the local court, this could then trigger the fork in the road provision, as the same contract claim can be pursued in national courts and in international arbitration? I leave that very subtle question open but I am very grateful to Mark Friedman for having raised it. Although not always crystal clear, the *Vivendi I* annulment decision gives according to Mark Friedman a positive answer to that question – with which I understand he is not fully in agreement – and thus "illustrates how a broad definition of the 'dispute' – typically considered a pro-investor BIT provision – may have a perverse consequence of dramatically expanding the breadth of an otherwise innocuous fork in the road provision". According to Mark Friedman the reasoning is not exactly the same if the contract claim has been transformed in a treaty claim through an umbrella clause: so here we do not have the same contract claim that can be asserted in a national or an international forum, we have the same dispute that can be considered as a remaining contract claim or as having been transformed in a treaty claim: in this case – again if I understood him well – he thinks that the fork in the road provision should apply.

Many other interesting questions were raised by Mark Friedman. Although I I will not be able to deal with them, I just mention them for the record.

In order to introduce some order in the proceedings that can follow an interference by a State with a foreign investment, some BITs have also introduced more or less broad provisions for exhaustion of local remedies. As stated by Mark Friedman,

> "[a]nother way that some BITs attempt to limit parallel proceedings is by clauses requiring exhaustion or at least pursuit of local remedies prior to commencement of a BIT arbitration. These clauses are in a sense the antithesis of fork in the road clauses – instead of requiring the dispute be brought in one place, they contemplate the prospect that it can be brought in two places so long as a certain order is followed."

But the result is the same as with the fork in the road provision: "[t]hese clauses have by and large likewise proven ineffective at curbing parallel proceedings".

The general principle of *res judicata* and some specific provisions in treaties such as Art. 1121 of NAFTA[30] (and in the new United States model BIT) also tend to avoid parallel proceedings with the existing risk of conflicting decisions or double recovery. Also, the ILA's December 2004 interim report on *res judicata* observed that "[a] number

---

30. A disputing investor may submit a claim under Art. 1116 to arbitration only if:

"b) the investor and, where the claim is for loss or damage to an interest in an enterprise of another Party that is a juridical person that the investor owns or controls directly or indirectly, the enterprise, waive their right to initiate or continue before any administrative tribunal or court under the law of any Party, or other dispute settlement procedures, any proceedings with respect to the measure of the disputing Party that is alleged to be a breach referred to in Article 1116, except for proceedings of injunctive, declaratory or other extraordinary relief, not involving the payment of damages, before an administrative tribunal or court under the law of the disputing Party."

of commentators favour an approach that looks at the underlying nature of a dispute and not at its formal classification", a clear challenge to strict application of the triple identity rule.[31]

However, at the end of the day, Mark Friedman suggests, and I would be ready to go along with him, that rather than providing procedural jurisdictional bars to potentially valid and valuable claims, on the basis of their qualification as one or another type claim, it should be the task of the arbitral tribunals to decide on the different claims at the merits stage and in doing this to deal with all the claims on which they have jurisdiction while avoiding double recovery. This seems quite a reasonable position, which is based on confidence in the good judgment of international arbitrators, a statement with which I am sure we all agree.

---

31. ILA Committee of Res Judicata (Berlin Conference 2004) Interim Report at 20.

Note
General Editor

As noted in the Preface to this Volume, the Working Group B sessions were in a variety of formats: Panels with a Reporter with Commentators who were asked to provide written papers, and Roundtables. Participants in the Roundtables were not required to prepare publishable papers in preparation for their session. However, a number of them did so, and we are pleased to be able to include them in this Volume. In addition, we are fortunate to be able to include, in one case, a Summary of the discussion at the Roundtable on Oral Evidence, accompanied by Notes from the Moderator, Johnny Veeder.

Working Group B

1. Round Table on Document Production

Five Fundamental Things About Document Production, and a Question

James H. Carter[*]

Before discussing the five fundamental things we know about document production, I should note two assumptions that I believe are relevant to this subject and that I think now are common ground among many international arbitration practitioners. One of these is that historic civil versus common law lines are blurring. Document production in arbitration is a topic that can be discussed, rather than an issue over which civil and common lawyers necessarily will disagree fundamentally.

The other preliminary assumption is that, at least in an international arbitration occurring in the United States, document production by the parties typically will be extensive, and it does follow a systematic approach: party request, followed by a process of objection/negotiation, and then arbitrator rulings (sometimes delegated to the chairman alone) on matters remaining in dispute, resulting in definition of the universe of materials to be produced.

With that background, what are the five fundamental things we know about document production?

Firstly, document production can be extremely useful to the parties and arbitrators. For a party, production of documents from the files of the opposing party can fill in factual holes in a case and provide materials that will serve as a check on witness recollections. For the arbitrators, document discovery typically provides the factual nexus within which agreements in dispute may be interpreted.

But, secondly, document production is inherently subject to tactical abuse. There will always be pressure by counsel for "more" production, and costs can be enormous. The danger of abuse is manageable if there is an "equality of arms" between the two sides, so that each is at risk and knows its own temptation to overreach is likely to provoke heated combat and perhaps a response in kind. But where there is inequality, there may be occasion for the "strong" party to disadvantage its opponent by outspending it; and, conversely, the "weak" party may exert pressure by demanding extensive document production from its opponent in a situation where the stronger party has virtually all of the documents and the weaker party is not subject to any risk of parallel production.

Thirdly, we know that the problems involved with document production soon will metastasize as a result of electronic record keeping. This already has become a major problem in document discovery in US litigation, with hundreds of thousands of E-mails and other electronic documents available for search in a typical commercial dispute. Inevitably, there is a question of who pays for such an extensive review process.

Fourthly, we know that arbitrators generally hate to deal with document production issues. There is a natural dislike for immersion in the swamp of document details, particularly because ruling on these disputes is hard to do at an early stage of an

[*] Sullivan & Cromwell, New York.

593

arbitration, often before the arbitrators can fully appreciate the issues. As a result, there are timing questions, with some believing that document production is best dealt with at the very beginning of a case and others arguing that the issues will be more manageable if addressed after detailed pleadings or even initial witness statements are completed. There is also an underlying fear that wide document production will result in a huge volume of documents to be dealt with at the hearing, increasing costs to all; but in practice, such fears often are not borne out because parties can reduce the documents truly needed to "mini bundles".

Finally, however, we know that tools do exist for coping with the problems of document production. Primary among these of course are the IBA Rules of Evidence, which contemplate that each party will produce documents it relies on in support of its case and also contemplate limited US-style requests for production, objections and arbitrator rulings.[1] The IBA Rules include precatory wording of reasonableness, but it is left for individual arbitrators to interpret how this cautionary principle should be applied.[2]

To summarize, then, the five fundamental things we know about document production are that it is:

– useful
– subject to abuse
– about to metastasize
– highly distasteful to arbitrators, but
– manageable to some extent with existing guidelines.

The question, therefore, is whether the world (or, at least, the world outside the United States) wants or needs new rules, guidelines or procedures, or whether what exists is adequate. There are possibilities for additional procedures. One would be a process of voluntary disclosure, such as is followed in American federal courts, whereby each party at an early stage voluntarily discloses from its files certain categories of materials, including copies of or descriptions of documents or categories of documents on which it may rely.[3] Or, arbitral institutions and parties could develop what Professor Park has described as "procedure heavy" arbitration rules, allowing expressly for relatively broad document production more typical of US litigation.[4] These of course would be optional, for parties to elect or not. Or, drafters could develop additional, more detailed sets of guidelines, perhaps adding specific details to the IBA Rules, or expanding upon the concept of required initial disclosure, or providing for "discovery masters".

This undoubtedly will be a subject for increasing discussion in the international arbitration community, if only because the realities of electronic document production

---

1. IBA Rules on the Taking of Evidence in International Commercial Arbitration (1999) Art. 3, available at <www.ibanet.org> (IBA Rules).
2. Art. 3(3) provides only for requests for "a narrow and specific requested category of documents".
3. Federal Rules of Civil Procedure, Rule 26(a).
4. William W. PARK, "The 2002 Freshfields Lecture – Arbitration's Protean Nature: The Value of Rules and the Risks of Discretion", 19 Arb. Int'l (2003, no. 3) p. 279 at pp. 289-290.

will force the issue. My own preliminary assessment is that working within existing parameters, such as those of the IBA Rules, offers a better prospect than new sets of rules; but this is a subject on which I expect further debate.

Document Production in Chinese International Arbitration Proceedings

*Jingzhou Tao**

I. INTRODUCTION

In China, arbitration has always been popular, and for a long time was (and still is in certain areas) a compulsory way of resolving disputes. Although it used to be in the hands of different local commissions subject to government control, over the last decade China has substantially reviewed its arbitration laws, bringing them more and more in line with international standards.

Although the revision of laws and arbitration rules is the indispensable first step to modernizing and increasing the competitiveness of Chinese arbitration practice, it may not be sufficient to create uniform and competitive arbitration practice in China per se. Indeed, according to the growing number of international arbitration proceedings, one of the challenges that Chinese arbitration still faces concerns the question of how arbitration commissions and arbitral tribunals will deal with problems arising from cultural and legal diversity of the parties involved, especially in respect to the way to conduct arbitration procedures. This challenge is of course not unique to China, but exists in all other countries with broad international arbitration practice, where arbitrators, counsel and parties come from different cultural and legal backgrounds.

In this respect, one issue which has recently given rise to animated discussion is the question of document production in international arbitration. Be it in court proceedings or in international arbitration, documents are often regarded as the most reliable type of evidence. However, according to their legal backgrounds parties and arbitrators have very different approaches concerning the handling of the evidence-gathering process and in particular the handling of the production of documents. Parties originating from a common law background will usually expect the tribunal to proceed to a wide "discovery", whereas parties originating from civil law systems will usually expect such

---

* Managing Partner, DLA Piper, Beijing; Avocat à la Cour de Paris; FCIArb; Adjunct Professor, Peking University Law School.

The author gratefully acknowledges the assistance in the preparation of this paper of his DLA Piper colleagues Clarisse von Wunschheim, Yi Kang and Edward Hillier.

document production to be very limited. How should an arbitral tribunal deal with such contradictory interests and traditions?

How far are arbitral tribunals entitled to order a party to produce certain documents? Under what circumstances and conditions should the arbitral tribunal order such document production? What are the consequences of the refusal by one party to comply with such an order?

These questions have been dealt with in a series of recent studies.[1] The aim of the present article is to give a brief overview of the global trend as to document production in international arbitration and compare it to the actual situation in China, while suggesting some guidelines for arbitrators and parties.

II.   THE POWER OF THE ARBITRAL TRIBUNAL TO ORDER DOCUMENT PRODUCTION

1.   The Starting Point: The Procedural Law Applicable to the Arbitration

As part of the evidence-gathering process, the issue of document production is in principle subject to the law applicable to the procedure.[2]

According to Art. 19(1) of the 1985 UNCITRAL Model Law on International Commercial Arbitration (UNCITRAL Model Law):

"(1) Subject to the provisions of this Law, the parties are free to agree on the procedure to be followed by the arbitral tribunal in conducting the proceedings.

(2) Failing such agreement, the arbitral tribunal may, subject to the provisions of this Law, conduct the arbitration in such manner as it considers appropriate. The power conferred upon the arbitral tribunal includes the power to determine the admissibility, relevance, materiality and weight of any evidence."

---

1. Peter R. GRIFFIN, "Recent Trends in the Conduct of International Arbitration – Discovery Procedures and Witness Hearings", 17 J. Int'l Arb. (2000, no. 2) p. 19 et seq.; Thomas WEBSTER, "Obtaining Documents from Adverse Parties in International Arbitration", 17 Arb. Int'l (2001, no. 1) p. 41 et seq.; Hilmar RAESCHKE-KESSLER, "The Production of Documents in International Arbitration – A Commentary on Article 3 of the New IBA Rules of Evidence", 18 Arb. Int'l (2002, no. 4) p. 411 et seq.; Gabrielle KAUFMANN-KOHLER and Philippe BÄRTSCH, "Discovery in International Arbitration: How Much Is too Much?", SchiedsVZ (2004, no. 1) p. 13 et seq.; Tan Chuan THYE and John CHOONG, "Disclosure of Documents in Singapore International Arbitrations: Time for a Reassessment?", 1 Asian International Arbitration Journal (2005, no. 1) p. 49 et seq.; Michael POLKINGHORNE, "The Withholding of Documentary Evidence in International Arbitration: Remedies for Dealing with Uncooperative Parties", 2 Transnational Dispute Management (November 2005, no. 5) p. 1 et seq.

2. However, as may not be unusual in international contracts, a party may have a contractual, i.e., a substantive right to the documents, namely when a contract provides for exchange of information between the parties. In such case, the obligation to produce documents constitutes a contractual obligation and is thus subject to the law applicable to the substance. In this respect, cf. Thomas WEBSTER, *op. cit.*, fn. 1, p. 41 et seq.

This article contemplates the primacy of party autonomy in respect to the determination of the law applicable to the procedure, and failing an agreement of the parties in this respect, the subsidiary competence of the arbitral tribunal to determine the applicable rules.

The UNCITRAL Model Law has served and continues to serve as the basis for numerous national arbitration laws,[3] and most modern arbitration laws[4] and arbitration rules provide for the same principles. This is the case with Art. 15 of the Rules of Arbitration of the International Chamber of Commerce (ICC Rules), Art. 20 of the Rules of the Arbitration Institute of the Stockholm Chamber of Commerce (SCC Rules), Art. 17 of the International Arbitration Rules of the Singapore International Arbitration Center (SIAC Rules), Art. 14 of the Rules of Arbitration of the London Court of International Arbitration (LCIA Rules); Art. 24 of the International Arbitration Rules of the German Institution for Arbitration (DIS Rules), etc.

However, regardless of whether the parties or the arbitral tribunal determine the procedure to be followed, their freedom to do so is not unlimited. In any case, the procedure followed has to comply with certain principles of due process, such as the principle of equal treatment of the parties and their right to be heard, the latter being of particular importance as regards the submission of evidence.[5] Those principles will usually be stated in the arbitration law itself, establishing the limit of the parties' autonomy and of the arbitral tribunal's power. A violation of such principles may constitute grounds to challenge the award or, at least, to hinder its enforcement (see below IV.*2.b*).

Thus, the global practice as to the law applicable to the procedure can be summarized as follows:

(i) primacy of party autonomy as to the procedural rules to be followed,
(ii) subsidiary determination by the arbitrators, *and*
(iii) observation of minimum standards of due process as determined by the law of arbitration.

Applied to the question of document production, these principles mean that an arbitral tribunal may have the power to order production of documents when:

(i) the parties have expressly bestowed this power on the arbitral tribunal, *or*

---

3. For an updated and detailed list of all signatory countries to the UNCITRAL Model Law, cf. <www.uncitral.org/uncitral/en/uncitral_texts/arbitration/1985Model_arbitration_status.ht ml>.
4. Cf., e.g., Art. 182(2) of the Swiss Private International Law Statute (PILS), Art. 1494 of the French New Code of Civil Procedure. Cf. in this respect Philippe FOUCHARD, Emmanuel GAILLARD and Berthold GOLDMAN, *On International Commercial Arbitration*, Emmanuel GAILLARD and John SAVAGE, eds. (1999) no. 1200.
5. Cf. Art. 18 UNCITRAL Model Law.

(ii) the parties have indirectly bestowed this power on the arbitral tribunal by choosing procedural rules, for instance the rules of an arbitration institution, which provide for a document-production mechanism, *or*

(iii) in the absence of consent between the parties in this respect, the arbitral tribunal decides that document production shall take place, *and*

(iv) the mechanism for document production does not violate any compulsory provision of the applicable law of arbitration.

2.   *International Practice*

In practice, it is rare for the parties to address the issue of document production in their arbitration agreement[6] and few arbitration laws provide for rules in this respect.[7] Most of the time, the parties will merely refer to a set of institutional or ad hoc arbitration rules, which will determine the conduct of the arbitration, including the evidence-gathering process.

The solutions provided for by commonly used arbitration rules as to the production of documents can be classified in three main categories:

(i) arbitration rules which do not mention the production of documents;

(ii) arbitration rules which expressly mention the power of the arbitral tribunal to order production of documents, but are silent on the procedure to be followed;

(iii) arbitration rules which do mention not only the possibility of document production, but also provide a detailed set of rules.

Whereas, for instance, the SCC Rules do not expressly mention the possibility of document production, most arbitration rules do – at least briefly – state the arbitral tribunal's power to order such production of documents, such as Art. 20(1) ICC Rules, Art. 24(3) UNCITRAL Arbitration Rules, Art. 24(3) Swiss Rules of International Arbitration (Swiss Rules), Art. 19(3) International Arbitration Rules of the American Arbitration Association (AAA's International Rules), Art. 25(h) SIAC Rules, Art. 22(e) LCIA Rules, Art. 27.2 DIS Rules, etc.

Actually, nowadays the power of the arbitral tribunal to order production of documents is very well established and there is hardly an arbitration without a request for it. As a consequence of their general authority to determine the procedure failing agreement between the parties, arbitral tribunals usually have no hesitation assuming the power to order document production, irrespective of whether or not such power is

---

6. Providing for a rule on document production in the arbitration agreement itself may offer a great advantage as to the predictability of the applicable rules; however, it may in some situations prematurely limit the parties' options, especially in complex international agreements.

7. Cf., for instance, Art. 1460 of the French New Code of Civil Procedure, according to which "[i]f a party possesses an element of proof, the arbitrator may require also that he produce it". Similar provisions are to be found in Sect. 7 of the US Federal Arbitration Act, Sect. 34 of the English Arbitration Act of 1996, and Art. 12(1) of the Singapore International Arbitration Act. In this respect, cf. Thomas WEBSTER, *op. cit.*, fn. 1, p. 46 et seq.

expressly granted by the competent national legislation, the applicable arbitration rules or the parties' agreement.[8]

3. Where Does China Stand?

As demonstrated above, most arbitration laws and arbitration institution rules give the arbitral tribunal the power to proceed to document production. Does the same principle apply to Chinese arbitral tribunals?[9]

a. Limited party autonomy as to the choice of the procedural rules

Although China has not adopted the UNCITRAL Model Law and the Chinese Arbitration Law of 1994 seems to be silent in this regard, it is admitted that the principle of party autonomy also applies to the choice of the procedural rules to be followed by the arbitral tribunal. However, this is a very recent development in Chinese international arbitration.[10]

The main Chinese arbitration institution that deals with "foreign-related", i.e., international arbitrations is the Chinese International Economic and Trade Arbitration Commission (CIETAC).[11] Prior to 1998, all disputes submitted to CIETAC for arbitration were conducted under the CIETAC Rules. In 1998, CIETAC amended its Rules to provide that where the parties agree to submit their dispute to CIETAC for arbitration, CIETAC's Rules apply, unless the parties have agreed otherwise, in which case, subject to the consent of the arbitration commission, the agreement of the parties will prevail. Undoubtedly, the requirement that CIETAC's consent had first to be obtained substantially limited the autonomy of the parties and effectively permitted CIETAC to deny the use of other rules without having to furnish any reasons for its decision.[12] The revision of the CIETAC Rules in 2000 failed to correct this iniquity. However, the last revision of the CIETAC Rules in 2005 finally remedied this situation. The new Art. 4(2) CIETAC Rules now expressly provides that:

> ".... Where the parties have agreed on the application of other arbitration rules, or any modification of these Rules [i.e., the CIETAC Rules], the parties'

---

8. Cf. Charles N. BROWER and Jeremy K. SHARPE, "Determining the Extent of Discovery and Dealing with Requests for Discovery: Perspectives from the Common Law" in Lawrence W. NEWMAN and Richard D. HILL, eds., *The Leading Arbitrators' Guide to International Arbitration* (Juris Publishing, Inc. and Staempfli Publishers Ltd. 2004) p. 310; Gabrielle KAUFMANN-KOHLER and Philippe BÄRTSCH, *op. cit.*, fn. 1, p. 15.

9. "Chinese arbitral tribunal" shall mean any arbitral tribunal ruling on an arbitration having its seat within the People's Republic of China.

10. "Chinese international arbitration" shall mean any foreign-related arbitration (in the sense of Chapter VII of the Chinese Arbitration Law) conducted by an arbitral tribunal having its seat within the People's Republic of China.

11. Unless the dispute is of a maritime nature, in which case the dispute will most likely be dealt with by the Chinese Maritime Arbitration Commission (CMAC).

12. Jingzhou TAO, *Arbitration Law and Practice in China* (Kluwer Law International 2004) p. 103.

agreement shall prevail except where such agreement is inoperative or in conflict with a mandatory provision of the law of the place of arbitration."

Thus, the application of the rules chosen by the parties no longer depends on the consent of CIETAC, which no longer has discretionary power in this respect.[13] Full effect is given to the parties' chosen arbitration rules, except where such an agreement is inoperative or in conflict with the lex arbitri.

However, if the parties choose the rules of an arbitration institution other than CIETAC, they are not totally free to submit their arbitration to a foreign arbitration institution. Although the Chinese arbitration law does not expressly prohibit submitting an arbitration to a foreign arbitration institution, Art. 16 of that law requires that a specific arbitration commission be expressly designated in the arbitration agreement, otherwise the agreement is invalid.[14] Of course, foreign arbitral institutions, such as the International Chamber of Commerce, the London Court of International Arbitration or the Stockholm Chamber of Commerce are never called "commissions", and their recommended arbitration clauses merely refer to the names of their rules, not specifically to their institution. So they are an invalid choice under Chinese arbitration law and the courts in China can refuse to enforce such arbitration clauses.

This issue gave rise to a famous case in 2004. The Supreme People's Court of China instructed a lower court in Jiangsu province to refuse to recognize an arbitration clause that read "Arbitration: ICC Rules, Shanghai shall apply." The reasoning of the Supreme People's Court was that the clause in question failed to specify any arbitration institution by name, and only mentioned that the "ICC Rules" would apply, in Shanghai. So there was a lack of a designated arbitration commission. Obviously, this decision will create a real obstacle for foreign arbitral institutions selecting China as the seat for arbitration.[15]

Although China has finally recognized the principle of party autonomy as to the choice of the procedural rules to be followed by the arbitral tribunal, the parties are not free yet to submit an arbitration seated in China to a foreign arbitration institution. In most cases, international arbitrations conducted in China will be submitted to the CIETAC.

Under a CIETAC arbitration the arbitral tribunal may have the power to order the production of document, when:

(i) the parties have expressly provided for it; *or*

---

13. Michael MOSER and Peter YUEN, "The New CIETAC Arbitration Rules", 21 Arb. Int'l (2005, no. 3) p. 394.

14. As a consequence of this requirement, ad hoc arbitration is not possible in China. However, an arbitral award resulting from ad hoc arbitration conducted abroad will be recognized and enforced in China according to the New York Convention.

15. For other cases involving the ICC, cf. Robert BRINER, "Arbitration in China Seen from the Viewpoint of the International Court of Arbitration of the International Chamber of Commerce" in *New Horizons in International Commercial Arbitration and Beyond*, ICCA Congress Series no. 12 (2004) p. 21 et seq.

(ii) the CIETAC Rules or other arbitration rules chosen by the parties provide for such a mechanism; *and*

(iii) such a mechanism is not in conflict with any mandatory provision of the Chinese Arbitration Law of 1994.

b.   The arbitral tribunal's power to order document production

Although the Chinese Arbitration Law mentions in its Art. 43(2) that "the arbitration tribunal may, as it considers necessary, collect evidence on its own", it contains no specific rules as to the production of documents.

According to the CIETAC Rules Art. 36 and following, document production is permitted. Although Art. 36(1) of the CIETAC Rules first states that "[e]ach party shall have the burden of proving the facts relied on to support its claim, defense or counterclaim", it further provides that "[t]he arbitral tribunal may specify a time period for the parties to produce evidence and the parties shall produce evidence within the specified time period...". Moreover, according to Art. 37(1) "[t]he arbitral tribunal may, on its own initiative, undertake investigations and collect evidence as it considers necessary". Finally Art. 38 provides that the arbitral tribunal has the right to appoint experts and appraisers for clarification on specific issues and that it "has the power to request the parties to deliver or produce to the expert or appraiser any relevant materials, documents, or property and goods for checking, inspection and/or appraisal".

Thus, arbitral tribunals established under the CIETAC Rules in principle have the power to order production of documents. In fact, historically, arbitral tribunals proceeding under the rules of the CIETAC have had ample powers in terms of the discovery of evidence, according to the strong inquisitorial tradition of the Chinese legal system.[16]

As for the case where parties to an international arbitration in China have chosen to apply other arbitration rules according to Art. 4(2) of the CIETAC Rules, the power of the arbitral tribunal shall be determined in accordance with such rules (cf. above II.2).

III.   THE SCOPE OF DOCUMENT PRODUCTION

1.   The Problem

Even when competent national legislation, arbitration rules or the parties do provide for the power of the arbitrators to order production of documents, they almost all fail to establish detailed guidelines as to the scope and conditions of the production of documents. This has led to delicate situations, when arbitration proceedings involve parties, counsel and arbitrators from different legal and cultural backgrounds.

---

16. Andrew SHIELDS, "China's Two-Pronged Approach to International Arbitration: New Rules and New Law", 15 J. Int'l Arb. (1998, no. 2) p. 76.

It is generally admitted that international arbitration practice does not allow a document-production mechanism as wide as the American concept of "discovery",[17] unless the parties have agreed on it. It is also generally recognized that there is no pretrial discovery procedure in international arbitration, nor may a document production concern an unlimited number or category of documents (so-called "fishing expeditions"). However, if the arbitration community agrees that there should be a certain level of document discovery and that the common law and civil law approaches should converge, there is as yet no consensus on the exact scope of document production.[18] Since the decision on the scope of document production lies within the discretionary power of the arbitral tribunal and "adopting a flexible approach does not mean an absence of parameters",[19] in designing the most appropriate document-production approach, arbitrators will have to take into account diverse factors such as the cultural and legal background of the parties and counsel involved, the amount in dispute, the more factual or legal nature of the issues in dispute, the volume and type of documents readily available, etc.

In deciding on matters of document production, the arbitral tribunal has to seek a balance between (1) an efficient and economic manner of taking evidence and (2) the real need for further document production in order to establish the truth. In fulfilling this task, the arbitral tribunal should always take special care to respect the principle of equal treatment of the parties and each party's right to fully present its case.

2. *The Global Trend: The IBA Rules on the Taking of Evidence*

An attempt to converge common law and civil law procedures and establish guidelines as to what should be acceptable in international arbitration has been developed by the International Bar Association (IBA) and is illustrated in the 1999 IBA Rules on the Taking of Evidence in International Commercial Arbitration (IBA Rules on Evidence), which set out a hybrid approach to evidence in general, and to document production in particular. Although the IBA Rules on Evidence only apply when adopted by the parties, they should not be totally ignored by an arbitral tribunal faced with the problem of document production. These rules have received a very positive response from practitioners around the world and have revealed themselves to be very practical. Thus, they may be considered as general guidelines for arbitrators.[20]

---

17. W. Laurence CRAIG, William W. PARK and Jan PAULSSON, *International Chamber of Commerce Arbitration*, 2nd edn. (ICC Publishing SA 1990) p. 410; Tan Chuan THYE and John CHOONG, *op. cit.*, fn. 1, p. 59; Thomas H. WEBSTER, *op. cit.*, fn. 1, p. 42 and reference quoted therein; Gabrielle KAUFMANN-KOHLER and Philippe BÄRTSCH, *op. cit.*, fn. 1, p. 17; Charles N. BROWER and Jeremy K. SHARPE, *op. cit.*, fn. 8, p. 309.

18. For a comparison of the different approaches, cf. Mauro RUBINO-SAMMARTANO, *International Arbitration, Law and Practice*, 2nd edn. (Kluwer Law International 2001) pp. 670-679.

19. Tan Chuan THYE and John CHOONG, *op. cit.*, fn. 1, p. 66.

20. Cf. comments of Michael POLKINGHORNE, *op. cit.*, fn. 1, p. 2; Peter R. GRIFFIN, *op. cit.*, fn. 1, p. 21; Tan Chuan THYE and John CHOONG, *op. cit.*, fn. 1, p. 63 et seq.; Gabrielle KAUFMANN-KOHLER and Philippe BÄRTSCH, *op. cit.*, fn. 1, p. 18; Hilmar RAESCHKE-KESSLER, *op. cit.*, fn. 1, p. 411 et seq.

The IBA Rules on Evidence clearly affirm the arbitral tribunal's power to order the production of documents, while subjecting this power to certain formal and substantial conditions.[21]

The production of documents may take place under different circumstances, depending upon who is requesting document production and who is the producing party. According to the situation at stake, the formal and material requirements for the production of documents will vary.

a. Production of documents available to one party

In principle, each party to an arbitration has the burden of proving the facts relied on to support its claim.[22] Thus, it rests on each party to submit all documents it considers to be relevant with its statement.

This rule is widespread in international arbitration and there are no fundamental differences between civil law countries and common law countries with regard to the production of documents available to a party, except those of a practical kind concerning the time of submission and the treatment of presented evidence.[23] These practical questions will usually be dealt with in the arbitration rules, or in absence of specific rules in this respect, by the arbitral tribunal itself.

b. Production of documents in possession of the opposing party

In case a party wants to use certain documents as evidence, but cannot produce them on its own because they are in the possession of the opposing party, it may under certain circumstances request the arbitral tribunal to order the opposing party to produce these documents.

The exact circumstances will firstly depend on the legal background of the arbitrators, counsel and parties involved, but here again the IBA Rules on Evidence attempt to converge practices in order to find a generally acceptable compromise as to when and how an arbitral tribunal shall order production of documents.

According to Art. 3(6) of the IBA Rules on Evidence, the arbitral tribunal will order a party to produce documents if the "Request to Produce" fulfils all the requirements set in Art. 3(3) IBA Rules on Evidence and none of the reasons for objection set forth in Art. 9(2) IBA Rules on Evidence apply.

i. The "Request to Produce"

Art. 3(3) IBA Rules on Evidence provides that:

"3. A Request to Produce shall contain:
(a) (i) a description of a requested document sufficient to identify it, or (ii) a description in sufficient detail (including subject matter) of a narrow and specific requested category of documents that are reasonably believed to exist;

---

21. Art. 3 in connection with Art. 9 IBA Rules on Evidence.
22. Art. 23(1) UNCITRAL Model Law.
23. Hilmar RAESCHKE-KESSLER, *op. cit.*, fn. 2, p. 412.

(b) a description of how the documents requested are relevant and material to the outcome of the case; and

(c) a statement that the documents requested are not in the possession, custody or control of the requesting Party, and of the reason why that Party assumes the documents requested to be in the possession, custody or control of the other Party."

According to the IBA Rules on Evidence, a request to produce may only concern identifiable documents or a specific category of documents, which are reasonably believed to be in custody of the party to whom the order to produce is to be addressed and which are "relevant and material to the outcome of the case".

The requirement of "relevance" refers to the content of the requested documents, which must relate to procedural or substantive allegations made by either party. In this respect, the requesting party must sufficiently show:[24]

(i) that based on their content, the requested documents may serve to support its allegations or, conversely, may be needed to repudiate allegations made by the other party; and further

(ii) that those allegations – if proven right or wrong – may determine the outcome of the case.

"Materiality" means that the document is needed to allow complete consideration of the legal issues presented to the tribunal.[25] Hence, if the document is sought to establish a fact which the tribunal already considers proven, it may refuse the request as lacking materiality.

ii.   The objections of the opposing party

Before deciding on whether to grant or refuse the Request to Produce, the arbitral tribunal shall give the party to whom the request is addressed a time limit in order to raise objections to some or all of the documents requested.[26] This requirement derives from the principle of equal treatment of the parties and the right of each party to fully present its case.

As to the nature and content of objections which can be raised by the party to which the request to produce is addressed, Art. 9(2) IBA Rules on Evidence provides useful guidelines:

"The Arbitral Tribunal shall, at the request of a Party or on its own motion, exclude from evidence or production any document, statement, oral testimony or inspection for any of the following reasons:

(a) lack of sufficient relevance or materiality;

---

24. Cf. Hilmar RAESCHKE-KESSLER, *op. cit.*, fn. 1, pp. 419 and 427.

25. *Ibid.*, p. 419.

26. Art. 3(5) IBA Rules on Evidence.

(b) legal impediment or privilege under the legal or ethical rules determined by the Arbitral Tribunal to be applicable;
(c) unreasonable burden to produce the requested evidence;
(d) loss or destruction of the document that has been reasonably shown to have occurred;
(e) grounds of commercial or technical confidentiality that the Arbitral Tribunal determines to be compelling;
(f) grounds of special political or institutional sensitivity (including evidence that has been classified as secret by a government or a public international institution) that the Arbitral Tribunal determines to be compelling; or
(g) considerations of fairness or equality of the Parties that the Arbitral Tribunal determines to be compelling."

Art. 9(2) IBA Rules on Evidence aims at finding a balance between the need for efficient and economic conduct of the arbitration and the establishment of all the relevant facts, while trying to ensure at all points the equal and fair treatment of both parties. The objections listed in Art. 9(2) IBA Rules on Evidence are not meant to be exhaustive, as shown by Art. 9(2)(g), according to which the arbitral tribunal may refuse a request to produce documents based on further considerations of fairness or equality.

iii.   Confidentiality and privileged matters
In practice, objections raised by parties in international arbitration most often concern issues of confidentiality and privilege. A privilege is a legally recognized right not to disclose certain information and/or documents, even when compelled to do so by a court.

Most arbitration laws and rules do not even mention privilege. Those which do[27] usually fail to set guidelines as to which principle of privilege should apply. This is not surprising taking into account the complexity of the issue.

First of all, there are different kinds of privilege: professional privilege, such as attorney-client privilege, medical privilege, journalistic privilege, protection of business secrets, protection of sensitive governmental information, etc. Secondly, the nature and scope of privilege strongly varies across jurisdictional boundaries. What is privileged? What is the scope of the privilege? Who does the privilege belong to? The answers to these questions vary significantly and there is no single international code of commonly accepted principles.[28] The most vivid example of problematic privilege is probably the attorney-client privilege.

In common law jurisdictions the attorney-client privilege is a rule of discovery or evidence (i.e., a matter of substance), the privilege belongs to the client and covers communication between the client and his lawyer, including in-house counsel. In civil law jurisdictions, the attorney-client privilege, as well as all other professional privileges, are a matter of criminal law and professional ethics (i.e., a matter of procedure). The

---

27. Art. 20(7) ICC Rules, Art. 20(6) AAA International Rules.
28. Cf. Michelle SINDLER and Tina WÜSTEMANN, "Privileges Across Borders in Arbitration: Multi-jurisdictional Nightmare or a Storm in a Teacup?", 23 ASA Bulletin (2005, no. 4) p. 611.

privilege belongs to the lawyer, it covers not only communication between client and lawyer, but also between lawyers themselves. It does not apply, however, to in-house counsel. Furthermore, there is no uniform practice within civil law countries and the approach to the problem varies significantly.

Imagine a case involving parties and counsel from different countries, common law and civil law.[29] Which law should apply to the privilege of which party, and which counsel? Should the arbitral tribunal apply the law chosen by the parties, the lex fori, or another law? Should the same law apply to both parties or should each party be treated according to the law of its own country or place of residence?

As this series of questions shows, the problem with privilege is not so much the specific solution chosen at the end of the day by the arbitral tribunal, but the inability to predict that solution at the time of conclusion of the arbitration agreement. This uncertainty can be dangerous for parties and counsel, who rely on the rules of privilege they are familiar with, but are suddenly confronted with the application of different rules of privilege.

Therefore, there is an acute need for a solution allowing the parties to predict which rules of privilege will apply. Several suggestions have been made in this respect:

1. The contractual approach: Making express provision on the question of the law applicable to the privilege in the arbitration agreement has been suggested. This solution might however be problematic in countries where the privilege belongs to the lawyer and is a matter of criminal law and professional ethics. It is doubtful whether the parties may disregard such privilege by choosing another set of privilege rules.

2. Establishing an international standard: Some authors have suggested instituting a global privilege standard for international arbitration[30] and some institutions have already developed a code of conduct for lawyers.[31] However, if regional harmonization is possible, it is difficult to see how a universal standard could be established and enforced, namely because privilege is linked to considerations of ethical and professional conduct and responsibility.[32]

3. The cumulative approach: Depending on the jurisdictions, privilege may be considered as a matter of procedure or substance. It probably carries elements of both.[33] Thus, submitting privilege both to the law of the arbitration and to the law with the closest relationship to the evidence, and applying the one offering the widest protection in case of conflict, has been suggested.[34]

---

29. For an example of such case, cf. Javier H. RUBINSTEIN and Britton B. GUERRINA, "The Attorney-Client Privilege and International Arbitration", 18 J Int'l Arb. (2001, no. 6) p. 587 et seq.
30. Cf. Michelle SINDLER and Tina WÜSTEMANN, *op. cit.*, fn. 28, p. 599 and footnote 35.
31. Such as the "Code for Conduct for Lawyers in the European Union" or the Rules of the American Law Institute.
32. Michelle SINDLER and Tina WÜSTEMANN, *op. cit.*, fn. 28, p. 625.
33. Gabrielle KAUFMANN-KOHLER and Philippe BÄRTSCH, *op. cit.*, fn. 1, p. 19.
34. Michelle SINDLER and Tina WÜSTEMANN, *op. cit.*, fn. 28, p. 624.

4. The alternative approach or "Most-Favoured-Nation-Principle" approach: To achieve the greatest degree of predictability, some authors propose that the arbitral tribunal acknowledges the privilege generally enjoyed by each party in its home jurisdiction and selects the law that affords the broadest protection to privileged information. Moreover, if the law of any of the jurisdictions prohibits disclosure of certain categories of information because of ethical restrictions placed on a party's counsel, such categories of documents are immune from disclosure for both parties.[35]

In any case, the requirement of equal treatment demands that the same rules of privilege apply to both parties. In practice, arbitrators will tend to apply a common sense approach to questions of privilege and seek a workable solution.

In practice, besides the question of the law applicable to privilege, another difficulty lies in determining whether the documents requested are in fact covered by the alleged privilege.

The party asserting a privilege bears the burden of establishing its application to a particular communication. The arbitral tribunal will need to balance the claimed privilege with the need for evidence. In this respect it might be necessary to review the content of the document to decide whether it is or is not covered by the privilege. There are two ways to deal with such a situation:

1. "Private Inspection" by the arbitral tribunal: The arbitral tribunal can review the requested documents without the party requesting the documents having access to them. The arbitral tribunal will then decide whether these documents are covered by the privilege. This approach is however problematic, because it does not under all circumstances completely protect the legitimate interests regarding secrecy, confidentiality and equal treatment of the other party.[36]

2. Inspection by a neutral expert: The arbitral tribunal can also appoint a neutral expert who will review the document and decide on whether it should be privileged or subject to some other confidential duty.[37] If the expert considers the objection of confidentiality/privilege legitimate, he will inform the arbitral tribunal, which will reject the request for production or otherwise provide for sufficient measures to protect the confidentiality of the document at stake.[38] In case the expert considers the objection not to be legitimate, he will transfer the documents to the arbitral tribunal, who will then decide on the request and in principle forward the documents to the requesting party.[39]

---

35. Javier H. RUBINSTEIN and Britton B. GUERRINA, *op. cit.*, fn. 29, p. 598. With a slightly different approach, Michelle SINDLER and Tina WÜSTEMANN, *op. cit.*, fn. 28, p. 625.
36. Gabrielle KAUFMANN-KOHLER and Philippe BÄRTSCH, *op. cit.*, fn.1, p. 20; Hilmar RAESCHKE-KESSLER, *op. cit.*, fn. 1, p. 424.
37. See Art. 3(7) IBA Rules on Evidence.
38. Art. 3(12) IBA Rules on Evidence.
39. Hilmar RAESCHKE-KESSLER, *op. cit.*, fn. 1, p. 424 et seq.

In any case, the arbitral tribunal may only proceed to a private inspection or inspection by an expert if it is convinced that the content of the documents may be "relevant and material" to the outcome of the case.

c.   *Production of documents in possession of a third party*
When documents a party wants to introduce as evidence in the arbitration proceedings are neither in possession of the requesting party itself nor the opposing party, but in possession of a third person not party to the arbitration, the question arises whether the party requesting the production of such documents can file such a request with the arbitral tribunal and whether the arbitral tribunal may order the third party to produce such documents.

Since the power of the arbitral tribunal to rule on the dispute and to conduct the arbitration proceedings is always defined by, and thereby also limited to, the scope of the arbitration, the arbitral tribunal has no jurisdictional power towards a third party and may not order such party to produce any document.

However, it is widely admitted that within the scope of its duty to "establish the facts by all appropriate means", the arbitral tribunal may take further steps of a more or less formal nature. First of all, the arbitral tribunal shall be entitled to address an informal request to the third party, inviting the latter to submit the requested documents.[40] The arbitral tribunal shall however only proceed with such measures if it considers the requested documents to be "relevant and material to the outcome of the case". Usually, arbitral tribunals are very reluctant to invite third parties to produce a document.

In case the third party does not provide the documents of its own free will, the only means left for the arbitral tribunal is to approach the competent state courts for assistance in taking evidence, if such assistance is provided for by the applicable local law (see below IV.*2.a*).

d.   *Production of documents on request of the arbitral tribunal*
Most arbitration laws and rules provide for a supplementary power of the arbitral tribunal to require the parties, at anytime during the arbitral proceedings, to submit additional evidence.[41] According to the principle that the arbitral tribunal should establish the facts by all appropriate means,[42] the arbitral tribunal may exercise this power on its own initiative.

Thus, if the arbitral tribunal considers that the documents submitted by either party are not sufficiently conclusive or relevant, it may order a party to submit supplementary evidence.

However, according to the tendency of counsel to submerge the arbitral tribunal in floods of documents, it is rare that an arbitral tribunal will request additional documents from a party. This may nevertheless be the case in relation to the intervention of experts. When the arbitral tribunal appoints an expert in order to clarify specific issues, it may

---

40. Cf. Art. 3(8) IBA Rules on Evidence.
41. Art. 20(5) ICC Arbitration Rules, Art. 24(3) Swiss Rules, Art. 25(g) SIAC Rules, Art. 22.1(e) LCIA Rules, Art. 24(3) UNCITRAL Arbitration Rules, etc.
42. Art. 20 ICC Arbitration Rules.

require the parties to submit to the expert all documents he or she judges relevant to decide on the issue at stake.[43]

3. Where Does China Stand?

a. The problem

The way to conduct arbitration and the rules which will apply to specific procedural matters will firstly depend on the background of the parties and the composition of the arbitral tribunal. One may therefore think that the mere fact that an arbitration takes place in China will not per se have a determining impact on the arbitration procedure, but that it will ultimately depend on the parties, counsel and arbitrators involved in the arbitration. This is only true in theory; in practice the situation is different.

Even before the revision of the CIETAC Rules in 2005, the parties could appoint foreign arbitrators listed on the CIETAC panel. Since 2005, parties may appoint arbitrators from outside CIETAC's list, if both parties agree to do so and if CIETAC endorses the appointment.[44] Although this opens up the scope of choice, the necessity of the parties' common agreement and CIETAC's "veto" still scare the parties from opting for this possibility. In practice, a Chinese arbitral tribunal will most often be composed of at least one or two Chinese arbitrators.

Moreover, the principle of "free representation" is not fully guaranteed under Chinese arbitration. According to "Order No. 73" promulgated by the Ministry of Justice in 2002,[45] which regulates foreign law firms, foreign lawyers are prohibited from issuing opinions or comments on the application of the Chinese law and on facts somehow related to Chinese law as a counsel in arbitration proceedings. Although the Ministry of Justice modified Order No. 73 in June 2004 by deleting the prohibition of foreign law firms and foreign lawyers from issuing opinions or comments on facts related to Chinese law, in fact as soon as an arbitration is subject to Chinese law, foreign lawyers are not allowed to issue any opinions or comments as counsel in the arbitration.[46]

These restrictions leave little doubt that the conduct of the arbitration will be (strongly) influenced by Chinese legal practice. Therefore, it may be interesting to analyze how Chinese law deals with document production and how a Chinese arbitrator will usually rule when faced with a request for document production.

---

43. Cf., e.g., Art. 27(2) UNCITRAL Arbitration Rules, Art. 21.1(b) LCIA Rules, Art. 27(2) Swiss Rules, Art. 24 SIAC Rules, Art. 6(3) IBA Rules on Evidence, etc.
44. Art. 21(2) CIETAC Rules.
45. "Rules of the Ministry of Justice for the Implementation of the Administrative Regulations on the Representative Offices of Foreign Law Firms in China".
46. For more details, see Jingzhou TAO, "How arbitration friendly is China?", 1 Global Arbitration Review (2006, no. 3) p. 11.

b. The legal basis for document production under Chinese law

i. Document production in Chinese court litigation

The main relevant provisions concerning the evidence-gathering process are set out in Chap. VI of the Chinese Civil Procedure Law at Art. 63 et seq.

The principle is that each party has to bear the burden of proving the facts it relies on.[47] However, according to the inquisitorial tradition of Chinese legal institutions, the court is given broad and robust powers to investigate and collect evidence, namely when the parties and their representatives cannot collect the evidence because of objective reasons or simply when the court deems it necessary for the hearing.[48] Art. 65 further states that "[t]he People's Court has the right to acquire evidence from the relevant units and individuals, and they shall not refuse it".

In December 2001, the Supreme People's Court promulgated its "Several Provisions of the Supreme People's Court on the Evidence for Civil Actions" (Provisions on Evidence),[49] which comprehensively outline the rules of evidence to be used in civil lawsuits before the People's Court.

These provisions endorse the same principle, that each party has the burden to prove the allegations it relies on and even provides that "[w]here any party cannot produce evidence or the evidence produced cannot support the facts on which the allegations are based, the party concerned that bears the burden of proof shall bear the unfavorable consequences".[50] Nevertheless, Art. 3(2) provides that "any party who cannot independently collect evidence due to objective reasons may request the People's Court to collect after investigation". Similarly, Art. 17(3) provides for various circumstances under which the parties concerned and their counsel may petition the People's Court to investigate upon and collect evidential material that is not accessible by the parties concerned and their counsel.

Although this procedure is not called "document production", but "collection of evidence by the court" based on a "petition" by a party, nothing indicates that a request for document production may not be the object of such a petition for collection of evidence. It appears thus, that Chinese courts have the authority to order document production.

---

47. Art. 64 ab initio Civil Procedure Law.
48. "[E]vidences deemed as necessary by the people's court for hearing the case" refer to (1) facts that may injure the interest of the state, the public interest of the society or the lawful interest of other people, and (2) procedural matters that have nothing to do with the substantial dispute (cf. Art. 15 of the Several Provisions of the Supreme People's Court on the Evidence for Civil Actions of December 2001). See, e.g., the *Xunyi Company v. Ruishen Company* case, in which the Intermediate People's Court of Shanghai decided to collect evidence from another case upon its power. This procedure was supported by the Higher People's Court of Shanghai in its decision dated 1 September 2003.
49. Dated 21 December 2001, adopted by the 1201st Session of the Judicial Committee of the Supreme People's Court on 6 December 2001, and effective from 1 April 2002.
50. Arts. 2 and 5 Provisions on Evidence.

ii.   Document production in Chinese arbitration

The main relevant provisions concerning evidence are set out in Arts. 43 to 46 of the Chinese Arbitration Law. According to Art. 43:

> "Parties shall provide evidence in support of their own arguments.
>   The arbitral tribunal may, as it considers necessary, collect evidence on its own."

Art. 44 deals with the arbitral tribunal's power to appoint an expert, Art. 45 provides for the right of each party to examine the evidence presented during the hearing, and Art. 46 provides a mechanism for preservation of evidence. There is no provision dealing directly with document production.

More detailed rules of evidence are set out in Arts. 36 to 39 of the CIETAC Rules: Art. 36 contemplates the principle that each party has the burden of proving the facts relied on to support its claim; Art. 37 provides the arbitral tribunal with the power to undertake investigations and collect evidence on its own initiative and as it considers necessary, Art. 38 governs the appointment by the arbitral tribunal of an expert or appraiser and expressly confers the power "to request the parties to deliver or produce to the expert or appraiser any relevant materials, documents ..." on the arbitral tribunal; Art. 39 regulates the examination of the evidence.

Thus, neither the Arbitration Law nor the CIETAC Rules expressly deals with the issue of document production. However, both contemplate the principle that the arbitral tribunal may, as it considers necessary, collect evidence on its own. Moreover, Art. 38 CIETAC Rules confers on the arbitral tribunal the power to order a party to produce documents to an expert or appraiser. If the arbitral tribunal is entitled to do so on its own initiative, there is no valid reason to deprive it of such power in case the production of documents is requested by a party.

As a consequence, document production is to be considered as an admissible evidence-gathering process in Chinese arbitration. The question is more under what circumstances a Chinese arbitral tribunal may be inclined to directly order or grant a party's request for document production.

c.   The practice of document production in Chinese arbitration

Whilst the Provisions on Evidence do not directly apply to arbitration in China, it is widely expected that they will ultimately be formally incorporated into the next revision of the Chinese Arbitration Law.[51] Therefore, it is to be expected that the same principles of evidence-gathering, including the provisions on document production will apply *mutis mutandis* to Chinese arbitration.

As to the IBA Rules on Evidence, as stated above (see above III.2), they do not apply automatically, but only if the parties have provided for their applicability. In practice, it is rare that the parties reach an agreement regarding the application of the IBA Rules on Evidence in their arbitration agreement. Nevertheless, the Chinese arbitration

---

51. Jingzhou TAO, *op. cit.*, fn. 12, p. 113.

community has begun to refer to the IBA Rules on Evidence when dealing with matters of evidence in the arbitral proceedings, especially when international practitioners are involved in Chinese arbitration.[52]

i.   In general

The production of documents available to one party will hardly ever be a problem. According to the very well-established principle that each party has the burden of proving the facts it relies on, each party will automatically submit all documents in support of its allegations or in contradiction to the other party's allegations. If the parties do not submit their evidence on their own initiative, the arbitral tribunal may invite the parties to do so within a fixed time limit.

As to the production of documents which a party wants to use as evidence for its submissions but cannot produce on its own because they are in the possession of the opposing party, two main possibilities enter into account:

(i) a Chinese arbitral tribunal may, in accordance with international practice, take the IBA Rules on Evidence as a guideline to decide on the request, or
(ii) as is highly likely, a Chinese arbitral tribunal will also – or even only – take the Chinese Provisions on Evidence into account and in particular its provisions on evidence production.

According to Art. 17 Provisions on Evidence, a party may file a request for evidence collection with the court if it cannot collect the evidence due to "objective reasons". In such cases, the requesting party has to submit a written application,[53] which specifies:

(i) the basic information regarding the evidence, such as the name of the person investigated and the place where the evidence is supposed to be located;
(ii) the contents of the evidence to be collected;
(iii) the reasons why the evidence needs to be collected by the People's Court; and
(iv) the facts to be proven.

Implementing the Provisions on Evidence in an arbitration procedure might be problematic, since most arbitrators, especially Chinese arbitrators, are reluctant to issue such rulings. In practice, the arbitral tribunals do sometimes issue orders requesting a party to produce evidence at the demand of the other party, if the tribunal deems such a request as reasonable and considers the requested documents to be relevant and material to the outcome of the case and thus helpful in establishing the facts. However, it is generally to be expected that Chinese arbitrators will handle requests for document production in a restrictive way.

As to the production of documents which the party wants to use as evidence for its submissions but cannot produce on its own because they are in the possession of a third

---

52. The CIETAC Arbitration Institute of Arbitration Study has translated the IBA Rules on Evidence into Chinese.
53. Art. 18 Provisions on Evidence.

party, the principle is the same as in international practice: the Chinese arbitral tribunal has no competence to order a third party to produce a document. Chinese arbitral tribunals will also usually refrain from addressing any kind of informal request to a third party.

As already seen before, a Chinese arbitral tribunal may also order the production of documents on its own initiative according to Art. 43 of the Arbitration Law. It can do so, by analogy to Art. 3 of the Provisions on Evidence, when a party "cannot independently collect evidence due to objective reasons" and the arbitral tribunal considers it necessary to further investigate and collect evidence. A typical case in which a Chinese arbitral tribunal will order the production of documents concerns disputes between Joint Ventures partners, where it is necessary to proceed to an audit of the accounts of the Joint Venture company. In such cases, a Chinese arbitral tribunal will request each party to provide for all necessary accounting documents.

ii.   Privileged matters and confidentiality issues
Art. 66 of the Chinese Civil Procedural Law provides that:

> "The evidence shall be displayed and cross-examined by the litigants at the court. Evidence involving state secrets, commercial secrets and personal secrets shall be kept confidential. Where it is necessary to display such evidence, it shall not be done in public hearing."

As a matter of fact, confidentiality matters are not unfamiliar to the Chinese legal system. The situation is however slightly different regarding "privileges". Art. 66 only mentions "secrets" and not "privilege". In fact, privilege is not widespread in the Chinese legal system. There is, for instance, no specific attorney-client privilege under Chinese law. The Chinese Law on Lawyers of 1997 (promulgated in 2001) and the thereto related "Behaviour Criteria for the Practice of Lawyers (for Trial Implementation)" (Behaviour Criteria) in force since 2005 only provide for a general duty of confidentiality. Art. 33 of the Chinese Law on Lawyers provides that "[a] lawyer shall keep confidential secrets of the State and commercial secrets of the parties concerned that he comes to know during his practice activities and shall not divulge the private affairs of the parties concerned", and Art. 9 of the Behaviour Criteria states that "[l]awyers shall keep state secrets, commercial secrets of the clients and the privacy of individuals". There is no privilege entitling a lawyer not to divulge information relating to his client or the case when asked to do so by a court.

At first sight, it seems that according to Art. 66 of the Chinese Civil Procedure Law evidence shall be displayed, except when it involves state secrets, commercial secrets and personal secrets. However, Art. 66 does not state that that evidence shall not be produced, it only states that that evidence "shall be kept confidential". Further, Art. 17 of the Provisions on Evidence provides that the court may investigate and collect as evidence "material that concern state secrets, commercial secrets or personal privacy".

Thus, the court is allowed to proceed to a "private inspection" of the relevant documents and decide whether such documents are covered by a duty of confidentiality or secrecy and should be kept confidential. In this respect it is interesting to note that the wordings of Art. 17 of the Provisions on Evidence and Art. 9 of the Behaviour Criteria are the same, showing that the existence of a professional confidentiality duty in respect to state secrets, commercial secrets or personal privacy, may not hinder the People's Court to collect relating material.

By analogy with Art. 17 Provisions on Evidence, a Chinese arbitral tribunal may also proceed to a private inspection of relevant documents. However, this procedure is problematic for the same reasons mentioned before (see above III.2.b.i). It is therefore recommended that private inspections are avoided by designating a neutral expert, who decides on the confidential nature of the documents at stake in analogy to Art. 3(7) IBA Rules on Evidence. This solution is however not provided for in the Chinese Arbitration Law, nor in the CIETAC Rules and Chinese arbitrators may therefore feel reluctant to do so. In any case, in order to avoid any risks of challenge of the award, it is important that the arbitral tribunal addresses this issue with the parties before ordering the production of documents to a neutral expert.

IV. THE CONSEQUENCES OF NON-COMPLIANCE WITH AN ORDER FOR DOCUMENT PRODUCTION

1. *The Starting Point: The Form of the Order*

In case the arbitral tribunal considers the requested documents to be relevant and material to the outcome of the case, and the party to whom the request to produce is addressed has failed to raise convincing objections, the arbitral tribunal will order the latter to proceed to the production of the requested documents.

In so far as the production of documents relates to the evidence-gathering procedure, it has a purely procedural nature and should therefore be the object of a "Procedural Order".

Some authors assert however that an order to produce documents may also be the object of an "Interim Award". This will be the case if the obligation to produce documents is derived from the contract itself and thus constitutes a contractual, i.e., substantive obligation. But some authors go further and argue in favour of "interim awards", when the production of documents is the very issue of the dispute, irrespective of the substantive or procedural nature.[54]

2. *International Practice*

a. *The non-enforceability of procedural orders*
In case the addressee of the procedural order refuses to comply with such an order, the question arises whether a party may seek its enforcement.

The principle is that procedural orders are not enforceable as such in cross-border arbitration, as the New York Convention only applies to "final arbitral awards", meaning

---

54. Cf. Thomas H. WEBSTER, *op. cit.*, fn.1, p. 41 et seq. and the *Publicis* case mentioned therein.

awards which finally rule on a substantive matter of the dispute, and not procedural orders.

However, in 2000 in the *Publicis* case, the US Court of Appeals for the Seventh Circuit had to decide on the enforceability of a decision of an arbitral tribunal, which only ruled on the production of documents but which was rendered in the form of an award. The US Court admitted the enforceability of such an "award" under the New York Convention on the grounds that the award was sufficiently final as to the issue of production.[55] This means that if the issue of document production is "suitably critical"[56] to the case, the enforcement of an order to produce documents is not excluded and should therefore be rendered in the form of an award. However, the enforceability of such an order will eventually depend on the interpretation of the New York Convention by competent state courts.

The question whether a procedural order is enforceable in the State where it was rendered is subject to the relevant procedural laws of this State. But, it is not usually the case.

Nevertheless, some national laws provide for the possibility for the arbitral tribunal (or the parties) to request the assistance of the state courts in taking evidence.[57] However, this assistance remains limited in practice as the competence of the courts and the available measures are determined by the applicable procedural laws of the state where the measures are sought.[58]

b.   Other remedies against non-compliance by a party

By submitting themselves to arbitration, the parties have an obligation to comply with certain requirements of due process, including "aiding in the presentation of the whole truth to the arbitrators".[59]

Although procedural orders may not be enforceable, the arbitral tribunal may take the non-cooperation of a party into account when appreciating and evaluating the evidence and has in this respect different remedies at its disposal. These remedies derive from the arbitral tribunal's power to establish the facts of the case by all appropriate means and determine the admissibility, relevance, materiality and weight of any evidence:[60]

1. *Adverse inference*: It is largely recognized by international practice and doctrine that arbitral tribunals may draw an adverse inference from a party's unjustified non-compliance with an order to produce documents.[61] However, this remedy may not

---

55. Thomas H. WEBSTER, *op. cit.*, fn. 1, p. 42.

56. Michael POLKINGHORNE, *op. cit.*, fn. 1, p. 8.

57. Cf. Art. 27 UNCITRAL Model Law, Art. 184 PILS, Art. 1782 of the US Judicial Code, Sects. 43 and 44 of the English Arbitration Act. For more details cf. Peter R. GRIFFIN, *op. cit.*, fn. 1, p. 23 et seq. and Mauro RUBINO-SAMMARTANO, *op. cit.*, fn. 18, p. 395 et seq.

58. The 1970 Hague Convention on the Taking of Evidence Abroad in Civil or Commercial Matters is inapplicable to international arbitrations.

59. Michael POLKINGHORNE, *op. cit.*, fn. 1, p. 3.

60. Art. 19(2) UNCITRAL Model Law.

61. Cf. Art. 9(4) IBA Rules on Evidence.

always be satisfactory, especially when the requested documents are needed by a party to sustain its claim and the other party bases its defence on the absence of such documentary proof. A mere inference against the non-producing party may not suffice to sustain a claim for which no evidence exists.[62]

2. *Shifting the burden of proof*: When an adverse inference does not seem to be the appropriate means to deal with a party's unjustified non-compliance with an order to produce documents, the arbitral tribunal may also consider shifting the burden of proof. Shifting the burden of proof is particularly appropriate when the non-complying party controlling the evidence specifically relies on the absence of the evidence in support of its case.[63]

3. "*Astreintes*": It is contested whether the arbitral tribunal has the power to render subpoenal decisions, i.e., to impose sanctions on a party in the case of non-compliance with the order, as for example monetary penalties payable to the party in whose favour an order was issued. Such sanctions are well established in French arbitration and are termed *astreintes*,[64] in particular in connection with provisional measures. They are also known under the Federal Arbitration Act (Sect. 7) as "subpoenas".[65] Part of the doctrine asserts that the arbitral tribunal has this power, if it has been entitled to do so by the party, be it expressly or tacitly.[66] However, it remains doubtful whether arbitral tribunals should be given such a quasi-judiciary power.

4. *Challenge / non-enforcement of the award*: While a party not complying with the arbitral tribunal's order to produce documents may not face immediate consequences, an award rendered in its favour could – under certain circumstances – be challenged in court or

---

62. W. Laurence CRAIG, William W. PARK and Jan PAULSSON, *op. cit.*, fn. 17, p. 456; Gabrielle KAUFMANN-KOHLER and Philippe BÄRTSCH, *op. cit.*, fn. 1, p. 21; Charles N. BROWER and Jeremy K. SHARPE, *op. cit.*, fn. 8, p. 342 et seq.

63. Michael POLKINGHORNE, *op. cit.*, fn. 1, p. 6.

64. Cf., e.g., the *Otor* decision rendered by the Paris Court of Appeal on 7 October 2004, quoted in Denis BENSAUDE, "S.A. Otor Participations v. S.A.R.L. Carlyle (Luxembourg) Holdings 1: Interim Awards on Provisional Measures in International Arbitration", 22 J. Int'l Arb. (2005, no. 4) pp. 357-362.

65. Cf. *Stolt-Nielsen SA, Stolt-Nielsen Transportation Group Ltd (SNTG), Stolt-Nielsen Transportation Group, BV and Stolt-Nielsen Transportation Group, Inc v. Celanese AG, Celanese, Ltd, and Millenium Petrochemicals, Inc; Celanese Chemicals Europe GMBH, Celanese Pte, Ltd., Grupo Celanese SA, and Corporativos Celanese S de RL de CV; Odfjell ASA, Odfjell USA, Inc, Odfjell Seachem AS, Jo Tankers*, Case No 04-6373-CV, US Court of Appeals for the Second Circuit (21 November 2005). In this case, the arbitral tribunal issued subpoenas ordering non-parties to the arbitration to appear at the hearing and bring documents with them. The Court of Appeals for the Second Circuit confirmed the arbitral tribunal's authority under Sect. 7 of the Federal Arbitration Act to issue such subpoena orders.

66. Laurent LÉVY, "*Les astreintes et l'arbitrage international en Suisse*", 19 Bull. ASA (2001, no. 1) p. 21; Pierre MAYER, "*Imperium de l'arbitre et mesures provisoires*", in *Etudes de procédure et d'arbitrage en l'honneur de Jean-François Poudret* (Lausanne 1999) p. 442. See also Arts. 16 and 18(2) of the Arbitration Rules of the European Court of Arbitration, which allow the arbitral tribunal to apply fines for delay in compliance with an order.

prevented from being enforced.[67] According to Art. V of the New York Convention, recognition and enforcement of the award may be refused when the party against whom the award is invoked was unable to present its case or if the award violates public policy, for example, in cases of fraudulent withholding of evidence by the party to whom a request to produce was addressed.[68] Similar factors may also justify the challenge of the award before national state courts.[69] In any case, it is necessary for the party requesting the review of the award to demonstrate that the evidence in question would have been decisive for the outcome of the case and would probably have lead to a different conclusion.[70]

3. Where Does China Stand?

a. In general

Although the Arbitration Law does not expressly mention the feature of "procedural orders", it is largely admitted that a Chinese arbitral tribunal is entitled to issue orders regulating the procedure and without dealing with the merits of the case. This is, for example, illustrated in Art. 29(5) of the CIETAC Rules, which empowers the arbitral tribunal to issue "procedural directions". Are these procedural orders by a Chinese arbitral tribunal enforceable before Chinese courts?

A distinction has to be drawn between foreign arbitration and internal arbitration.

In foreign arbitration, the New York Convention applies and it does not provide for the enforcement of procedural orders (cf. above IV.2.a). Even if the foreign arbitral tribunal issues an order to produce documents in the form of an award, it is highly unlikely that the Chinese courts will interpret the New York Convention in a similar way to the US Court of Appeals for the Seventh Circuit in the *Publicis* case. Chinese courts are already reluctant to enforce awards which finally rule on a substantive matter of the dispute, so it is unlikely that Chinese courts will adopt a more favourable approach concerning awards on document production.

In internal Chinese arbitration, the enforcement of awards rendered by a Chinese arbitral tribunal is not subject to the New York Convention. The relevant rules are to be found in the national legislation, i.e., the Arbitration Law. As concerns foreign-related arbitrations, the Arbitration Law only mentions the enforcement of "awards" and refers in this respect to Art. 260 of the Civil Procedure Law.[71] Art. 260 allows the People's Court to refuse the enforcement of an "award rendered by a People's Republic

---

67. One may also consider the possibility of a revision by the arbitral tribunal itself (cf. Michael POLKINGHORNE, *op. cit.*, fn. 1, p. 12), although it may be difficult to reconstitute the former arbitral tribunal once the award has been rendered.

68. Michael POLKINGHORNE, *op. cit.*, fn. 1, p. 12.

69. In *National Casualty Company v. First State Insurance Group*, Case No. 05-1505, US Court of Appeals for the First Circuit (2 December 2005), it was judged that although the arbitral tribunal rendered an award favourable to the party refusing to produce documents, it was not enough per se to justify the challenge of the award.

70. Michael POLKINGHORNE, *op. cit.*, fn. 1, p. 13 and decisions quoted therein at footnote 54.

71. Art. 70 et seq. of the Arbitration Law.

of China arbitration institution handling foreign-related arbitration disputes" in cases such as the invalidity or absence of an arbitration clause, invalid or irregular constitution of the arbitral tribunal, instances where the tribunal acts either in excess of the scope of the arbitration agreement or the authority of the arbitration institution, etc. The wording of Art. 260 and the circumstances for non-enforcement listed therein indicate that Art. 260 is meant to apply to arbitral awards only, i.e., to decisions which put an end to all or part of the substantive claims, and not to procedural orders.

The enforceability of procedural orders by the Chinese courts is not ensured or safeguarded by any legal provision.[72] Art. Procedural orders are thus not directly enforceable in China. The question is left whether the arbitral tribunal may require the support of the Chinese courts in the taking of evidence.

b.   Intervention of state courts
According to Art. 68 of the Chinese Arbitration Law, a party may apply before the arbitration commission (not the arbitral tribunal) for preservation of the evidence, and the arbitration commission shall then further submit this application to the Intermediate People's Court in the place where the evidence is located. This principle is contemplated in Art. 18 of the CIETAC Rules, according to which "when a party applies for the protection of evidence, the CIETAC shall forward the party's application for a ruling to the competent court at the place where the evidence is located". Similar power is given to the courts in court proceedings.[73]

Besides this power to grant preservative measures, Chinese legislation makes no mention of any other mechanism in which an arbitral tribunal or arbitration commission may request the state courts' support in the taking of evidence.

Under Art. 68 of the Chinese Arbitration Law the possibility of an arbitral tribunal requiring the assistance of the People's Court in collecting documents from a party is not excluded. But, in the light of the lack of a pro-arbitration bias in the local courts in China, it is highly likely that such a request would be rejected on the grounds that it lacks any legal basis, although this attitude may change with time.

c.   What remedies are available to a Chinese arbitral tribunal?
Despite the lack of enforceability of procedural orders, a Chinese arbitral tribunal has remedies similar to those available in international arbitration at its disposal:

1. *Adverse inference*: Art. 75 Provisions on Evidence provides that "where there is evidence to prove that a party possesses the evidence but refuses to provide it without good reason and if the other party claims that the evidence is unfavourable to the possessor of the evidence, it may be deduced that the claim stands". Thus, Chinese courts, and *mutis mutandis* arbitral tribunals, are allowed to draw adverse inferences from the refusal of a party to produce evidence.

---

72. Houzhi TANG and Shengchang WANG, "National Report PR China" in Jan Paulsson, ed., ICCA
    International Handbook on Commercial Arbitration, Suppl. 25 (1998) p. 29.
73. See Art. 74 Civil Procedure Law and Art. 23 et seq. Provisions on Evidence.

2. *Shifting the burden of proof*: Shifting the burden of proof is actually just the continuation of the principle of adverse inference and has been used by Chinese courts in the past. Chinese arbitral tribunals should be entitled to use the means of shifting the burden of proof, when the non-compliant party who controls the evidence specifically relies on the absence of the evidence in support of its case and would not be affected by a mere adverse inference.

3. *"Astreintes"*: Chinese arbitral tribunals have no power to render subpoenal decisions, this power being exclusively reserved to the courts and deriving from their exclusive *imperium*.

4. *Challenge/non-enforcement of the award*: According to Arts. 70 and 71 of the Chinese Arbitration Law in connection with Art. 260 Civil Procedure Law, an award may be set aside or its enforcement may be disallowed when the party against whom the enforcement is sought or the party who seeks to challenge the award was not able to fully present its case due to reasons for which it is not responsible[74] or when the award is contrary to social and public interest. Based on these grounds, if a party refuses to comply with an order to produce, but the arbitral tribunal nonetheless renders an award favourable to that party, the other party may – according to the circumstances – request to set aside the award or impede its enforcement.

In certain cases, after accepting the People's Court application made by a party to set aside the People's Court may suspend the setting aside proceedings and will refer the case back to the arbitration tribunal in order for it to re-arbitrate the matter. This will be the case when a request to challenge the award is filed based on the grounds that (1) the evidence on which the award is based is forged, or (2) a party has withheld evidence which is sufficient to affect the impartiality of the arbitration.[75] Thus, if a party has fraudulently withheld evidence and thereby affected the impartiality of the award, for example, by refusing to produce certain documents, the People's Court will suspend the challenge proceedings and the arbitral tribunal will be entitled to re-arbitrate the case based on the new view of the evidential situation.

V. CONCLUSION

Chinese arbitral tribunals have the power to order production of documents, be it on their own initiative or at the request of a party, and they regularly do so. As is the case in international arbitration, although decisions of arbitral tribunals concerning document

---

74. See, e.g., the Decision of the Intermediate Court of Shenzhen dated 27 April 1997 concerning the Application by Yue Shang Developing Co. Ltd for the Revocation of the Arbitral Award Rendered by CIETAC. In this case, the court rejected a request to challenge the award based on the ground that the arbitration commission had denied one party's request to collect evidence and thus did not give to such party the opportunity to fully state its case. The court judged that although a party may ask the arbitral commission to collect evidence, the latter had the right to decide whether or not do so and its refusal in the specific case did not per se violate the arbitration rules.

75. See the Judicial Interpretations of the Supreme People's Court on Certain Issues Relating to the Application of the Arbitration Law dated 4 April 2006 (Draft for Approval) Art. 21.

production are not enforceable in China, the arbitral tribunals make use of other remedies, such as adverse inference or shifting the burden of proof, to force a party to comply with the order. To this extent, the production of documents in Chinese arbitration proceedings is similar to international practice.

However, Chinese and international practice differ when it comes to the scope of and framework for document production. Because of the lack of specific rules on evidence-gathering in arbitration, Chinese arbitrators often feel reluctant to depart from general principles applicable before state courts. Although the IBA Rules on Evidence are not unknown in China, they have not yet been assimilated by the Chinese arbitration community. The mechanism for document production in Chinese arbitration is still strongly influenced by national procedural laws and subject to restrictive conditions. Chinese arbitrators are all the more reticent to use "new" ways of conducting arbitration, as Chinese courts often lack the necessary pro-arbitration bias to endorse "untraditional" methods.

In the light of the frequent changes in Chinese legislation, it is to be hoped that the liberalization trend which characterizes the latest revisions of the Arbitration Law will go on and that the Chinese arbitration community will continue to draw inspiration from international arbitration practice. However, the development of arbitration practice in China also depends on the attitude of the state courts and their approach towards arbitration, especially with regard to procedural issues. In order to increase the efficiency and the competitiveness of arbitration in China, it is essential that state courts are involved in this process and start supporting arbitration commissions and tribunals more actively, especially with respect to uncooperative parties.

621

The Use of an Expert to Handle Document Production: IBA Rules on the Taking of Evidence (Art. 3(7))

Hans van Houtte[*]

I. INTRODUCTION

In Anglo-American court litigation, parties have to submit all documents – whether favorable or harmful – "up front" in the proceedings. It is then for the other side in a "discovery" action to request the production or disclosure of documents that are relevant but not yet submitted.

In the civil law tradition, there is no "up front" production of documents at the beginning of the proceedings. Only when the successive briefs are exchanged will each party submit the documents, favorable for its argument. Nevertheless even in civil law proceedings, there is some room for a limited discovery: a party may request the court to order the other side to submit a specific document that the former does not have but that would be relevant for its argument.[1]

II. DOCUMENT PRODUCTION IN ARBITRATION

Document production and discovery of evidence is likewise a common feature in arbitration proceedings conducted under the common law. Moreover, they have become part of arbitration proceedings with parties both from the common law as well as the civil law traditions. But even in pure civil law arbitrations, for example, when all parties as well as the seat of arbitration are established in Continental Europe, up-front document production and discovery have become part of the game.

However, in many arbitrations, up-front document-production and discovery requests often are delicate, time consuming and cumbersome. Indeed, parties frequently

---

[*] FCIArb.; LL.M. Harvard; Professor, University of Leuven, Belgium; Vice-President, CEPANI.

1. See, e.g., on the similarities and differences between the common law "discovery" and the civil law court-ordered production of a specific document: P. Van LEYNSEELE and M. DAL, "Pour un modèle belge de la procedure de 'discovery'", Journal des Tribunaux (1997) p. 225.

use production- and discovery-requests to "show their teeth" and impress the opposing side. They try to demonstrate their firmness and aggression by being very demanding or intransigent. But also without parties flexing their muscles, the evidence that should be produced may run into a few thousand pages of documents. Discovery and document production become even more complicated when some parties to the arbitration are not fully familiar with such practices and their rules.

Discovery requests for document production are required to comply with a few conditions. It is essential that the party, who requests the production of documents specifies in a narrow manner the categories and describes in sufficient detail the prospective content of the documents he requests to be produced. As the IBA Rules on the Taking of Evidence in International Commercial Arbitration (hereafter the IBA Rules) indicate, the request to produce should either contain "a description of the requested document sufficient to identify it or a description in sufficient detail (including subject matter) of a narrow and specific requested category of documents".[2] Moreover the request should indicate how the requested documents "are relevant and material for the outcome of the case" and that their production should not impose an unreasonable burden upon the other side.[3]

III. DIFFICULTIES WITH DOCUMENT PRODUCTION

However, it will not always be clear whether specific documents fall within the description. Moreover, documents might only vaguely or remotely cover the subject matter covered by the description so that parties may wrangle whether such documents have to be submitted or not. Parties may also bicker whether the documents are relevant and material to the outcome of the case or whether they are too cumbersome to produce, for example, because the documents are dispersed over the enterprise or – if they are in electronic form and have already been deleted from the computer – very hard to retrieve from the server.

Furthermore, as also confirmed by the IBA Rules, a party may argue that documents should not be submitted because they are covered by legal privilege,[4] because they would be confidential for commercial or technical reasons[5] or because they are politically too sensitive or are classified as state secrets.[6] The arbitrators can only decide on these exemptions after having examined the documents themselves. A document-by-document examination to see whether each document is covered by privilege or

---

2. IBA Rules, Art. 3(3)(a).
3. IBA Rules, Arts. 3(3)(b) and 9.
4. E.g., letters from legal counsel, internal documents that gather information to be passed on to legal counsel as a basis for the latter's legal opinion or communications received as copies by legal counsel.
5. E.g., because they mention the amount for which the claimant was willing to settle the case or because they contain confidential technical data or – if in electronic form and deleted – trade secrets unrelated to the present dispute.
6. IBA Rules, Art. 9(2).

confidentiality would consume dozens of billable hours, an extremely tedious and costly exercise especially when it has to be carried out by the full arbitral tribunal.

Furthermore, documents that contain confidential information may need some editing. Again, the redaction and sanitizing of documents can be a continuous source of quarrels between the parties and take much time from the tribunal.

As the IBA Rules confirm, the arbitral tribunal should consult the parties when one of them objects to the production of a document. The idea is that the tribunal should solve the matter "in a timely fashion". But this is not easy to do, especially when the objections are numerous and delicate. Indeed, the parties need to be given sufficient time to submit their views on the matter; the arbitrators have to examine the issues; a date for a hearing that the arbitrators and the parties are able to attend may have to be found. When the objections are many and delicate, the loss of time will be even more substantial.

Finally, the exclusion of confidential or privileged documents often boils down to a "Catch 22" situation. Indeed, the parties and arbitrators have to read a document to assess whether it is indeed confidential or privileged. However, once read, it is very unlikely that the parties and arbitrators will forget its content and will be able to erase from their memory what they read. It is noteworthy that "in (such) exceptional circumstances" and because "the propriety of an objection can only be determined by review of the document" the tribunal is allowed by the IBA Rules to "appoint an independent and impartial expert ... to review any such document and to report on the objection".[7] Likewise the WIPO Arbitration Rules allow the tribunal to appoint a document-production expert – named a "confidentiality advisor" – to decide on the confidentiality of evidence:

> "In exceptional circumstances, in lieu of itself determining whether the information is to be classified as confidential and of such nature that the absence of special measures of protection in the proceedings would be likely to cause serious harm to the party invoking its confidentiality, the Tribunal may, at the request of a party or on its own motion and after consultation with the parties, designate a confidentiality advisor who will determine whether the information is to be so classified, and , if so, decide under which conditions and to whom it may in part or in whole be disclosed...."[8]

However, as this paper will discuss, the arbitral tribunal may appoint an expert for many more facets of the discovery and production of documents. The modalities of the expert's intervention depend on the context in which he has to operate.

---

7. IBA Rules, Art. 3(7).
8. WIPO Arbitration Rules, Art. 52(d).

IV.   POSSIBLE TASKS FOR A DOCUMENT-PRODUCTION EXPERT

As indicated above, document production within arbitration proceedings may give rise to several difficulties. A document-production expert can help the tribunal and the parties in several ways to solve these.

How useful and varied the tasks of a document-production expert may be, is illustrated by the practice of some US courts to appoint a "special discovery master" to alleviate the document production. Such "special discovery master" is said to allow transferring twice as much information, data or documents in half the time and at half the expense.[9]

The document-production expert may visit a party's premises and examine whether the solicited documents are indeed not available or whether it would be too burdensome to produce them. He also may render an opinion on whether some documents fall within the category of evidence to be produced and are relevant for the case.

He may monitor and supervise a party in the selection of documents to be produced. He may even himself select the documents to be submitted. When the documents are in the hands of a third party, such selection by an independent expert may even be the only way out. Indeed, for instance, not the party itself but an independent expert may get access to documents related to a production branch that has since then been taken over by a company that does not want a competitor to browse through its papers.

The most common task for a document-production expert – and the only one mentioned in the IBA and the WIPO Rules –[10] would consist of reviewing documents to ascertain whether they are privileged. It is also the task most frequently assigned to the "special discovery master" by US courts.[11] The expert could also redact the documents when parts of them are privileged or confidential.[12]

Whenever the parties disagree on the production of a document, the production expert could try to settle the matter. He may orchestrate and even actively participate in negotiations about the manner in which a sensitive document should be produced. For

---

9. James B. LYNCH, "Evolving the Use of ADR Programs for early resolution of disputes", The Advocate (Idaho, November 2004) p. 9.

10. IBA Rules, Art. 3(7):

"In exceptional circumstances, if the propriety of an objection can only be determined by review of the document, the Arbitral Tribunal may determine that it should not review the document. In that event, the Arbitral Tribunal may, after consultation with the Parties, appoint an independent and impartial expert, bound to confidentiality, to review any such document and to report on the objection. To the extent that the objection is upheld by the Arbitral Tribunal, the expert shall not disclose to the Arbitral Tribunal and to the other Parties the contents of the document reviewed."

See also WIPO Rules, Art. 52(d) quoted at fn 8.

11. See Wayne D. BRAZIL, "Special Masters in the Pretrial Development of Big Cases: Potential and Problems" in W.D. BRAZIL, et al., eds., *Managing Complex Litigation: A Practical Guide to the Use of Special Masters* (American Bar Foundation, Chicago 1983) p. 1 at p. 9; see, e.g., *United States v. Stewart* (S.D.N.Y. 11 June 2002).

12. See, e.g., *Diversified Group Inc. v. Daugerdas*, 304 F.Supp. 2d 507, 510 (S.D.N.Y. 2003).

instance, he could try to bring the parties to accept that access to a confidential document will only be given to outside counsel and not to the in-house lawyers; or he could elaborate a confidentiality agreement for the parties to sign before exchanging documents.

The production expert may thus mediate, he may volunteer his opinion or he may decide, depending on the context and his task. He also may merely monitor the production process and report to the arbitral tribunal how the parties behave. Besides, when document production has become infected with acrimony and distrust, the expert's monitoring alone may already have a tempering effect on the parties and make them behave in an orderly manner.

The costs of a document-production expert have to be covered by the parties. An appointment would only be justified when a document-production expert would sufficiently facilitate the production process. When the tribunal believes that this will be the case, it may give an expert these tasks which would optimize the document production. As a US Court of Appeals stated in *First Iowa Hydro Electric Co-op v. Iowa-Illinois Gas & Electric Co.*:

> "After careful reflection the court is satisfied that the magnitude of the case, the complexity of the anticipated discovery problems, the sheer volume of documents to be reviewed, many of which are subject to claims of privilege, the number of witnesses to be deposed, the need for a speedy processing of all discovery problems ... all favor of using a special master to supervise discovery."[13]

However it is often difficult to predict whether the involvement of a production expert would be worth the expenses and an extra procedural layer. Sometimes smaller cases have the toughest discovery issues.

V.   CAN ARBITRATORS APPOINT A DOCUMENT-PRODUCTION EXPERT?

As a general rule, document production – like the other stages of the arbitral process – has to be organized and supervised by the arbitral tribunal. As discussed above, a document-production expert generally monitors the document-production process and makes suggestions. Occasionally he also may be given the task to decide. May the arbitrators delegate to a non-arbitrator the monitoring and even some decision-making with regard to document production?

The most extreme situation, i.e., the delegation of the decision-making, will be discussed first. Here again, the US Supreme Court can be of guidance. In an 1889 decision on the role of a "special master" it stated:

---

13. 245 F2d 613 at 620.

"[The Court] cannot, *of its own motion, or upon the request of one party*, abdicate its duty to determine by its own judgment the controversy presented and devolve that duty upon any of its officers." (Emphasis added.)[14]

From this quote it results that the US Supreme Courts impliedly accepted that the fullest delegation would be possible when both parties would have agreed upon the appointment of a special master.

If the parties agree on the appointment of the expert and on his or her powers, their consent appears a sufficient basis for referring the decisions on document production to the expert. That already had been confirmed by the US Supreme Court one-and-a-half centuries ago in the much stricter context of court litigation.[15]

This principle that continues to guide the US courts in their appointment of a "special master" is also relevant for arbitrators. A document-production expert can only actually decide when both parties agree to it.

Some may take offence at the thought that arbitrators, even with regard to a limited matter such as document production, may delegate their decision-making – be it with the consent of both parties – and be bound by the opinion of a non-arbitrator. However, parties who can agree in an arbitration clause that their dispute will be settled by arbitrators and not by the state court, a fortiori also can agree that a limited and preliminary aspect of this dispute settlement – i.e., the document production – will be carried out by an expert: "*qui peut le plus, peut le moins*". Besides, even when a production expert may decide on the document production, the arbitrators retain their core task, the decision on the merits. The arbitrators do not abdicate their judicial function.[16] Of course, the expert's decisions should be limited to document production and should not encroach upon the decision-making on the merits. The main bulk of the settlement has to remain with the tribunal.[17]

The parties may have agreed in advance, for instance in an arbitration clause, that a production expert may actually decide issues of document production. However, it is more likely that they would agree to give him decision-making powers when the arbitration proceedings have started. The parties will then have a better view on the nature of the problems that arise and may agree on the exact scope of the decision-making powers and on whom they will entrust this task.

---

14. *Kimberly v. Arms*, 129 U.S. 512 (1889) 524.

15. *Heckers v. Fowler*, 69 U.S. (2 Wall) (1864); see also Irving R. KAUFMAN, "Masters in the Federal Courts: Rule 53", 58 Columbia. L. Rev. (1958) p. 452 at p. 459 and Wayne D. BRAZIL, "Authority to Refer Discovery Tasks to Special Masters: Limitations on Existing Sources and the Need for a New Federal Rule?" in W.D. BRAZIL, et al., eds., *op. cit.*, fn. 11, p. 305 at pp. 312-313.

16. See Mark A. FELLOWS and Roger S. HAYDOCK, "'Federal Court Special Masters'; A vital Resource in the Era of Complex Litigation", 31 William Mitchel Law Review (2004-2005) p. 1269 at p. 1276.

17. *United States v. Hooker Chemical & Plastics Corp.*, 123 F.R.D. 62 (W./D.N.Y. 1988); cited by Shira A. SCHEINDLIN, "The evolution and impact of the new federal rules governing special masters", Federal Lawyer (February 2004) p. 34 at p. 36.

The appointment of a production expert who cannot decide matters, but merely has to offer his suggestions or has to monitor the production process does not require the consent of both parties. An arbitral tribunal can appoint an expert whenever it deems it necessary. This is, for instance, explicitly confirmed by many arbitration rules.[18] The objection of one party would not rule out such appointment. Only when all parties agree that no such expert should be appointed, no appointment would be possible.[19]

VI.   THE EXPERT'S PROFILE

The document-production expert should be a person in whom the arbitrators and the parties have confidence. Indeed, when both parties do not value the expert's opinion they will overload the tribunal with production incidents and objections. The expert will then be nothing but an additional and costly layer in the arbitration process.

The expert should in all events be impartial and independent. He should be subject to the same conflict-of-interest standards as the arbitrators. Before accepting the appointment, he should likewise submit a statement of independence, as an arbitrator does. The expert should also be familiar with the kind of business of the parties and the type of dispute so that he will be able to see the relevance of the evidence. Moreover, he should be acquainted with the rules of privilege and confidentiality. Most important, however, he should have a practical mind, be able to conciliate opposing views and be available on short notice to solve urgent issues, examine documents on site, etc.

VII.   THE EXPERT'S TERMS OF REFERENCE

As a rule, tribunal-appointed experts have to submit their findings to the parties and the tribunal and are frequently examined by the parties at the hearing. However, when a production expert would be examined and cross-examined about his selection and redaction of documents, much of the purpose of his involvement would be lost. Indeed, when the expert has to reveal to the arbitrators and the parties the existence and content of a privileged document or justify why he redacted parts of it, the essential benefit of his intervention – to keep this information secret – would have disappeared. It is for that reason that the confidentiality expert will not be subject to cross-examination by the parties.[20]

---

18. The arbitrators may appoint an expert: UNCITRAL Rules, Art. 27(1) ; For the AAA, see, e.g., the Commercial Arbitration and Mediation Center for the Americas, Art. 24 and the International Dispute Resolution Procedure, Art. 22. They may do so after consultation with the parties; IBA Rules on the Taking of Evidence, Art. 3(7); ICC Rules, Art. 20(4); Swiss Arbitration Rules, Art. 27(1); WIPO Arbitration Rules, Art. 55.
19. See also LCIA Rules, Art. 21.
20. The IBA Working Party that drafted the IBA Rules indicated that the document-production expert "would not necessarily need to be appointed pursuant to the terms of Article 6 of the IBA Rules of Evidence". ("Commentary on the New IBA Rules of Evidence in International Commercial Arbitration", 2 Business Lawyer International (2000) p. 14 at p. 21).

The terms of reference accepted by the tribunal as well as by all parties, should also indicate that the document-production expert can examine the documents, submitted by one party, without having to submit these documents to the other party. In fact, even in court proceedings such ex parte approach is not unusual in matters where confidentiality is at stake. For instance, also state courts allow experts to investigate possible patent infringements in the respondent's premises in the absence of the claimant.[21]

In order to keep confidential documents from the tribunal, the expert's terms of reference can also specify that the expert – at least in a first stage – has not to submit to the tribunal documents that he has discarded because of privilege as well as non-redacted documents, which have to be edited.

Furthermore, the terms of reference should also contain a confidentiality undertaking that the document-production expert signs and that the arbitrators and parties endorse.[22] This undertaking generally would have two aspects: First, it may confirm that the expert will not reveal the existence or content of documents, submitted to him, to outsiders to the arbitration process.[23] Second, it may forbid the expert to reveal confidential or privileged information in documents obtained from one party, to the other parties.

Finally, the tribunal and the parties have also to specify in the expert's terms of reference whether the latter's decisions are final or can be reconsidered by the tribunal at the request of one of the parties. However, in the event the expert's determinations are reviewed by the arbitral tribunal, the tribunal should – as a matter of policy – use some restraint. If the expert's views were to be overturned too easily, experts would be of no great use. The US Supreme Court stated already more than a century ago with regard to the "special masters" that the expert's determination should be considered "presumptively correct" and only be set aside on showing of "a manifest error in the consideration given to the evidence or in the application of the law, but not otherwise".[24] However, whenever the expert would err on the legal side, his legal errors should be corrected without hesitation.[25] The same guideline should inspire arbitrators when they have to assess the decisions of the production expert.

This implies, inter alia, that the document-production expert does not have to be present at the hearing and cross-examined by the parties (Art. 6(5) and (6)).

21. See, e.g., for Belgium: Code Judiciaire, Art. 1484 indicates that as a general rule the parties cannot be present when the expert carries out his examination; they only can be present with a special authorization from the court.

22. See WIPO Arbitration Rules, Art. 52(d) in fine.

23. See IBA Rules, Art. 3(7); WIPO Rules, Art. 52(d).

24. Kimberly v. Arms, 129 U.S. at 524.

25. See for US court analogies: Cademartori v. Marine Midland Trust Co., 18 F.R.D. 277 (S.D.N.Y.) 1955); Pollin v. Dun & Bradstreet, Inc., 634 F.2d 1319 (10th Cir. 1980).

Working Group B

2. Round Table on Fact Testimony

Managing Fact Evidence in International Arbitration

Laurent Lévy* and Lucy Reed**

I.   INTRODUCTION

A great number of books and articles have studied the evolution of arbitral procedural rules and practices over the last thirty years.[1]

Nonetheless, the legal and regulatory framework remains rather scant on the gathering and use of evidence. Statutes either do not address the issue of witness testimony or are limited to the very essentials, especially the provision of court assistance to secure the attendance of witnesses. Otherwise, in the words of the English Arbitration Act:

> "It shall be for the tribunal to decide all procedural and evidential matters, subject to the right of the parties to agree on any matter.... Procedural and evidential matters include ... whether to apply strict rules of evidence (or any other rules) as to the admissibility, relevance or weight of any material (oral, written or

---

*   *Docteur en droit*, Paris; Attorney at the Geneva Bar; Partner, Schellenberg Wittmer.

** Attorney at the New York and District of Columbia Bars; Partner, Freshfields Bruckhaus Deringer LLP (New York).

1. See W.W. PARK, *Arbitration of International Business Disputes, Studies in Law and Practice*, (Oxford University Press 2006) (hereinafter *Arbitration of International Business Disputes*) p. 45 et seq. Oral evidence, witness statements, conduct of hearings, the differences between the traditional common law and civil law approaches are the subject of numerous articles, conferences, etc. Rather than supplying a bibliography which would be redundant, we refer you to the extensive bibliography included in V.V. VEEDER and Laurent LÉVY, *Arbitration and Oral Evidence*, (ICC Publishing 2005) and to the following recent articles: B. HANOTIAU, "The Conduct of the Hearings" in L. NEWMAN and R. HILL eds., *The Leading Arbitrators' Guide to International Arbitration*, (Juris Publishing 2004), Chapter 16; A.J. VAN DEN BERG, "Organizing an International Arbitration Practice Pointers", *ibid.*, p. 163. S. ELSING and J. TOWNSEND, "Bridging the Common Law-Civil Law Divide in Arbitration", 18 Arbitration International (2002) p. 59, various contributions in K.H. BÖCKSTIEGEL, Carl HEYMANNS KG, *Liber Amicorum*, 2001, esp. A. BAUM, "Reconciling Anglo-Saxon and Civil Law Procedure: The Path to a Procedural *Lex Arbitrations*", p. 21 and D. RIVKIN, "21st Century Arbitration Worthy of Its Name", p. 661.

other) sought to be tendered on any matters of fact or opinion, and the time, manner and form in which such material should be exchanged and presented, whether and to what extent the tribunal should itself take the initiative in ascertaining the facts and the law; whether and to what extent there should be oral or written evidence or submissions."[2] *Nordo.*

Most arbitral rules elaborate on the taking of evidence, especially of oral evidence. The ICC Rules (Art. 20(2) and (6)) and the LCIA Rules (Art. 19) grant each party a right to be heard orally by the arbitrators; the ICC leaves it to the tribunal's discretion to manage the hearing ("The Arbitral Tribunal shall be in full charge of the hearings," Art. 21(3) ICC Rules) and the LCIA reserves the arbitrators' discretion on its guidelines (Art. 20 LCIA Rules).

There seems to be consensus that there are only two mandatory requirements, namely that, first, the arbitrators treat all parties equally and, second, provide an opportunity to be heard (equality of the parties, "principle of contradictory proceeding", "fairness of the trial", "due process"). Subject to these cardinal principles, and absent different arrangements by the parties, the arbitrators' discretion will rule. The courts will in principle not exercise any control over the proceedings beyond ensuring respect of such principles; the failure to follow other rules, such as do exist, will not invalidate an award or thwart its enforcement. For instance, the Swiss Federal Tribunal decided:

> "It should be underlined that procedural public policy will constitute only a simple exclusion provision, namely that it will merely have a protective function and will not generate any positive rules. This is because the legislature did not desire that procedural public policy should be extensively interpreted and that there should arise a code of arbitral procedure to which the procedure, as freely selected by the parties should be subjected."[3]

However, many authors have pointed to the emergence of relevant "soft law", namely norms originating privately which purport either to provide some guidance to arbitrators and parties or to collect the best practices of international arbitration.[4] There is a hot debate about the usefulness of such guidelines or collections of usages. Some authors support the idea, for example in Voser's article entitled "Harmonization by Promulgating Rules of Best International Practice in International Arbitration".[5] Others

---

2. English Arbitration Act 1996, Art. 34.2, lit. f,g,h.

3. Swiss Federal Tribunal, 30 December 1994, R. and U. v. W., 1 ASA Bull (1995) p. 217, 221.

4. IBA Rules on the Taking of Evidence in International Commercial Arbitration, 1 June 1999, available at <www.camera-arbitrale.com/upload/file/1234/617497/FILENAME/IBA% 20Rules%20on%20Taking%20of%20Evidence%201999.pdf> (last accessed 27 July 2006); UNCITRAL, UNCITRAL Notes on Organizing Arbitral Proceedings, available at <www. uncitral.org/pdf/english/texts/arbitration/arb-notes/arb-notes-e.pdf> (hereinafter "UNCITRAL Notes") (last accessed 27 July 2006).

5. N. VOSER, *Zeitschrift für Schiedsverfahren* (2005) p. 113; *Arbitration of International Business Disputes, op. cit.*, fn. 1; "The 2002 Freshfields Lecture Arbitration's Protean Nature: The Value of Rules and the Risk of Discretion", 19 Arb. Int. (2003) p. 279.

such as Lalive, deplore la *"fureur réglementaire"* and stress the need to preserve party autonomy and arbitrator discretion. For instance, in the preface to his book entitled *Procedural Law in International Arbitration*, Petrochilos writes:

> "This book sets out to explore the considerations that determine the applicable procedural law and rules in international arbitration, both before national courts and arbitral tribunals. However, only in part does this book set out the actual rules of procedure that may or should apply in such an arbitration. Indeed, it is one of the principal theses conveyed in the following pages that the parties participating in an international arbitration should be free to establish the rules of procedure that suit the particular circumstances of their case. Their liberty to do so is, accordingly, discussed extensively."[6]

Given the abundant literature, it is unnecessary to repeat here the advantages of harmonization. Suffice it to underline that harmonization will foster predictability – while reducing flexibility. Tellingly, arbitrators and counsel tend to want some of both: increasingly, parties and arbitral tribunals adopt the IBA Rules of Evidence, but as guidelines only, thus preserving the arbitrators' control of the proceedings.

The issue we address here is whether there is a further need for harmonization with respect, specifically, to fact testimony. As a first question, what are the main areas of witness testimony that would benefit from harmonization (II)? As a second question, is there a need for guidelines to achieve harmonization (III)? As a third question, absent specific guidelines, is there more the international arbitration community could do to maximize predictability (IV)?

II.   POSSIBLE ISSUES CALLING FOR HARMONIZATION OF RULES AND PRACTICES WITH RESPECT TO FACT TESTIMONY

1.   Pre-hearing Period

It has become customary for the parties to conduct a rather heavy pre-hearing fact-finding phase. The arbitrators supervise this from their vantage point, often by means of terms of reference or a preliminary conference. More often than not, at great time and cost, the parties will exchange two sets of written memorials and supporting evidence.

In addition to evidentiary documents, the parties typically produce testimonial evidence in the form of "witness statements". The IBA Rules (Art. 4(4) to 4(9)) acknowledge this practice and provide for the preparation and submission of witness statements. However, they leave certain questions open:

---

6. G. PETROCHILOS, *Procedural Law In International Arbitration*, (Oxford University Press 2004) initial paragraph of the Preface.

a. At what stage should witness statements be prepared and exchanged? The practice will vary: the witness statements will either accompany the memorials or be produced subsequently before the evidentiary hearing.
b. As a consequence, there is (or should be) no more debate as to whether counsel and the parties themselves may meet with the actual or potential witnesses. Otherwise, it would be quite impracticable to obtain witness statements. It could be argued that the scope and subject matter of such meetings are still subject to debate: May counsel "coach" the witness? May they "prep" the witness? Those questions are of course important. However, such importance should not be overemphasized. At the end of the day, the question boils down to whether the focus should be on counsel practice and rules of conduct (disciplinary rules) or on ensuring truthful witness statements.

Nowadays, the question is more or less settled that no witness will be allowed to testify if he or she has not submitted a written statement. The arbitrators retain their discretion to depart from such rule, for instance in order to permit the examination of third-party witnesses or recalcitrant witnesses. Sometimes, to placate a recalcitrant witness, the arbitrators will organize examination by way of video conferencing.

Conversely, should a written statement be mandatorily excluded if the witness fails to appear at the oral hearing? All will depend upon the circumstances and how "extraordinary" they may be, so that a uniform rule would not satisfy any need for enhanced predictability.

The IBA Rules do not make clear whether a party that has produced a witness statement may call such a witness for direct oral testimony if the other party waives cross-examination. Nor do the IBA Rules permit or exclude "witness depositions". Such depositions are most unusual in international arbitration practice, which is well recognized.

The IBA Rules do not consider the possibility that the witness will attach exhibits to his or her witness statement. Is the possibility of attaching documents an open issue in international arbitration practice? We submit it is not: the witness may attach such documents provided it is not a party's last-ditch attempt to produce a document outside of the time limit.

The IBA Rules, rightfully, do not cover these or other such questions. It was not inadvertence on the part of the members of the Working Party but rather a reasonable desire not to go into the "special circumstances" of each case.

2. Hearing

Evidentiary hearings are a most onerous part of arbitration, measured by time and expense. Seen from the Continental arbitrators' perspective, the hearing is probably second only to drafting of the awards in terms of time consumption; from the Anglo-Saxon arbitrators' perspective, it might be first. However, with remarkable regularity, unless both parties find it unnecessary, the arbitrators will hear a series of witnesses.[7] Indeed, there is a trend to limit hearing time almost exclusively to witness testimony, curtailing opening argument and saving closing argument for written post-hearing submissions.

One may wonder why, after heavy briefing (two rounds of written memorials, production (voluntary or ordered) of batches of documents, witness statements, expert reports, etc.), counsel and arbitrators alike wish to conduct an oral hearing. Obviously, one should not underestimate tradition: it is well known that common lawyers rely on witnesses. Some parties (and counsel) may (in despair?) hope for serendipity, meaning that their case will improve in the course of a hearing. If nothing else, it is certainly true that, even after a strong written phase of fact finding, only live witnesses will bring to life what, for the arbitrators, has been so far only a pile of paper.

It is possible to explore the different purposes that witness testimony serves by posing several questions:

a. To what extent is each witness credible in person and, thus, how reliable is his or her witness statement?
b. Would certain witnesses be in a position to clarify and elaborate facts that are the subject matter of the witness statements or even further facts?

---

7. It is a common rule that an arbitral tribunal should not decide a case solely on the basis of documents submitted by the parties unless both parties agree (ICC Rules, Art. 20(6)). However, this is not the point in issue: in principle, arbitral tribunals may in their discretion decide whether they wish to hear witnesses (ICC Rules, Art. 20(3)). As an example, on 7 January 2004, the Swiss Federal Tribunal confirmed that the parties' procedural rights (and thus the limit to arbitrator discretion) are exclusively the right to be heard and to be treated equally. Thus, the Swiss Federal Tribunal would not sanction (i.e., not annul an award) because arbitrators did not order the examination of witnesses (albeit a party supplied a witness statement):

"The cornerstone in the argument of the appellant is found in a published decision of the Swiss Federal Tribunal (ATF 124 V 90 consid. 5b). According to the appellant, and on the basis of this precedent, which should also be applicable to witness statements, it should be established that article 182 al. 3 PILA protects the right of a party to ask questions or to have questions put to the witnesses, in particular to the author of a witness statement. This would be done orally or in writing. It is doubtful that the decision, on which the appellant relied, and which was rendered in the field of social security, can be cited as is in international arbitration. However that may be, one cannot infer the right of a party to demand the oral examination of the author of a written statement. The topical passage in the above-mentioned decision refers only to the right of a party to acquaint itself with the written statement of a witness and its right to be in a position 'to ask additional questions or to have additional questions put to the witness'."

(Swiss Federal Tribunal, 7 January 2004, at 4.2.2.1 p. 8, 22 Bul. ASA (2004, no. 3) p. 592, esp. p. 600).
   Furthermore, the right of the parties to participate in the administration of the testimonial evidence, within the limits set by the above-mentioned precedent (cf. consid. 4.1), and to express an opinion on its result is uncontested. The appellant affirmed peremptorily that the Arbitral Tribunal did not grant it this right (ch. 213 in fine). This simple affirmation does not suffice to establish the validity of the grievance that it raises on this point.

c. Would certain witnesses assist in authenticating and interpreting certain documents in the record? Possibly, if allowed, could they supply and comment on further documents, not (yet) in the record?

d. Would the examination of witnesses enable counsel to identify which issues engage the arbitrators' attention and, thus, are especially relevant? Will the same examination permit counsel to check the arbitrators' knowledge of the file and their "learning curve" and so make necessary emphasis?

It is obvious that, traditionally at least, common lawyers and Continental lawyers would answer these questions differently. What is nowadays more relevant is, first, whether there can be common answers and, second, what can be done to improve the efficiency of witness examination (in terms of fact finding, time and expenses)?

Again, the IBA Rules (Arts. 4 and 8) offer some guidelines. However, there are still many open issues, reflecting (healthy) differences in practice and training. Some of the main ones are mentioned below:

a. What is the sequence? The default rule seems to be that the claimant will first present its witnesses, followed by the respondent's. However, arbitral tribunals not infrequently hear witnesses grouped by the subject matter of their testimony or in an order serving some practical constraint (availability of the witnesses, common language of some witnesses, etc.).

b. Should witnesses be heard separately or confronted? Is fact witness conferencing prevalent?[8] May a witness take advantage of the assistance of counsel?

c. Should the arbitrators question the witnesses themselves or should they leave it to counsel? Or both? More precisely, who should go first and who should do most of the questioning? It is obvious that, in the end, the arbitrators are in the best position to determine which topics are most relevant for their decision. However, it is just as obvious that, at the stage of the hearing, counsel (usually) have a better grasp of the facts and documents and can be more efficient. It is necessary for counsel to know in advance how this will play out, and avoid having the arbitrators arbitrarily exercise the generally accepted rule ("The Arbitral Tribunal may ask questions to a witness at any time." IBA Rules Art. 8(2)).

d. Will there be any direct examination or will the witness statements stand in lieu of direct examination? Will at least a short direct examination be allowed to "relax the witness?"

e. Will questions be allowed outside of the subjects addressed in the witness statements? The question is still very much open with respect to cross-examination.

f. Will leading questions be permitted? On direct as well as cross?[9]

---

8. Wolfgang PETER, "Witness conferencing revisited" in *Arbitral Procedure at the Dawn of the New Millennium*, (Bruylant Brussels 2005); Alain HIRSCH, "L'interrogatoire collectif des témoins", in *Liber Amicorum Guy Horsmans*, (Bruylant, Brussels 2004); IBA Rules, Art. 8.2.

9. The IBA Rules of Evidence provide: "Questions to a witness during direct and redirect testimony may not be unreasonably leading" (IBA Rules, Art. 8.1).

g. Will hearsay evidence be allowed? There is no absolute answer.[10]

h. Should witnesses be sequestered during breaks? Excluded from the hearings when other witnesses testify? Do the same roles apply for "party witnesses"?

i. May a witness read from his or her own documents, in or not in the record, and how?

III.   IN THE ABSENCE OF HARMONY, IS THERE A NEED FOR DETAILED GUIDELINES?

As appears from the foregoing, there are many questions. There may be basic harmony – the goal is to find the truth – but many differences exist as to elements of fact testimony.

However, we submit that detailed guidelines would not bring satisfactory answers, given that such questions should remain open in general and may be answered in specific arbitrations efficiently and at minimal expense.

It is not a coincidence that modern arbitration statutes include scarce procedural rules in general and with respect to examination of witnesses in particular. The same is true of arbitration rules. International arbitration is a complex arena: it involves various governing laws and sophisticated actors operating in every field of the world economy. Arbitrators develop their own preferences based on experience.

As already mentioned, the IBA Rules have contributed to fill gaps. Likewise, UNCITRAL has published its Notes on Organizing Arbitral Proceedings and the Chartered Institute of Arbitrators its guidelines.[11] Professor Park refers to such procedural guidelines as "soft law", in distinction to the "harder norms" imposed by arbitration statutes and treaties as well as the procedural framework adopted by the parties through choice of arbitration rules.[12] One could argue that such soft law is warranted if, as in other areas, it codifies existing usages. However, there simply are not many detailed common procedural usages in international arbitration. This is why such guidelines are very general.

"Best practices" may be elusive. They pose a significant risk of thwarting flexibility without any actual benefit. Is it really opportune to label as "best practice" what has evolved and become obvious over the years? For instance, that the arbitrators arrange for the taking of a verbatim transcript of testimony rather than dictate summaries as was once popular on Continental Europe? Or that the arbitrators admonish the witnesses, request them to speak the truth and advise them of possible sanctions otherwise, rather than administer oaths as used to be the norm?

Uniformity is certainly not in itself a goal: otherwise, one could imagine a computer programme bringing all the answers to all the procedural questions without any need

---

10. One of the main (not the only) reasons to prohibit hearsay evidence is to avoid an indirect examination of persons not permitted to appear as witnesses. As virtually anyone may be a witness in international arbitration, this justification does not apply.

11. "UNCITRAL Notes", *op. cit.*, fn. 4; Guidelines, Chartered Institute of Arbitrators, available at <www.arbitrators.org>.

12. *Arbitration of International Business Disputes*, *op. cit.*, fn. 1, p. 46.

for human intervention. Will the parties exchange messages through an *ad hoc* pre-existing website?

It may be for good reasons that "the Arbitral Tribunal shall at all times have complete control over the Evidentiary Hearing" (IBA Rules Art. 8(1), Art. 21(3) ICC Rules). There is easy consensus that expert case management is of the essence in international arbitration.

IV. PREDICTABILITY, AS WELL AS FLEXIBILITY, IS IMPORTANT IN ARBITRATION

1. The Benefits of Predictability

If more harmonization in witness testimony methodology is not desirable, the same cannot be said for more predictability. Flexibility plus predictability will advance the goals of equality and due process. Predictability is not an abstract exercise. Very rarely do the parties need actual procedural predictability prior to their dispute. More often than not, arbitration agreements contain no specific procedural rules.[13] At most, they refer to some arbitration rules, which may be more detailed than others on procedure.

The need for predictability arises at the beginning of the arbitration proceedings. At that time, it will be the arbitrators' (and counsel's) duty to bring forth clarifications with the necessary specificity.

From this vantage point, no two arbitrations will be alike. The answers to the above-mentioned questions will be different, and should remain different, depending on the circumstances. Moreover, the moment at which the answers must be found will also differ from one arbitration to another.

We submit that arbitrators should generally be proactive in managing procedure, rather than react to interlocutory procedural motions: in a defensive posture, the arbitrators must decide in favour of one of the parties and against the other, which may (wrongfully) appear as unequal treatment.

It does not follow that arbitrators must hand down an early procedural order detailing all the procedural rules possibly applicable to a specific arbitration. Most arbitrators do have template procedural orders detailing procedural rules, including how to handle fact witnesses, but they discuss these matters with the parties and endeavour to adjust them to the specific arbitration. Selecting the right way and the right time (and deciding on the extent of the procedural order or orders) is for the experienced arbitrator to decide. For instance, if all the counsel are well versed in international arbitration and originate from similar backgrounds, there is no need for early detailed intervention. When the arbitrators meet with the parties, for instance to execute the Terms of Reference in ICC proceedings, they may begin discussing procedure in order to adopt, ideally by consent, more detailed rules. A procedural hearing after the first round of written submissions is very often a good moment. At that time, the arbitrators

---

13. P. FRIEDLAND, *Arbitration Clauses for International Contracts*, (Juris Publishing, New York 2000), p. 64 ("It is usually prudent to await a dispute before trying to set a procedure for the presentation of evidence.").

are able to ascertain the main facts and legal issues and should be in a better position to assess the magnitude, relevance and materiality of certain testimony. With experienced arbitrators and counsel, such meetings will make a final pre-hearing conference superfluous or, at least, easily manageable by way of a telephone conference.

Adopting very detailed guidelines will not help and should not be the goal. Quite to the contrary, excessively detailed procedural rules may cause difficulties of their own, namely inevitable squabbles with respect to the applicability and proper construction of such rules, and an unintended form of US "motions practice".

2.   *Proposed Notes on Organizing Fact Testimony in Advance of Hearing*

Although initial preliminary hearings and Terms of Reference sessions can help to put the tribunal and parties on the same procedural page, all too often evidentiary hearings open with major misunderstandings between counsel for the parties (and sometimes the arbitrators) as to how fact witnesses should be presented. For example, as noted above, a US litigator representing the respondent may not appreciate that the time spent cross-examining claimant's witnesses counts against his or her own time, and be amazed to be told by the chairman at the end of the day that there is no time remaining for his or her witnesses. Similarly, the same US litigator may not appreciate that the time his or her own witnesses spend answering tribunal questions may count against respondent's time. Counsel may make presumptions about when their witnesses will be required and not have them available if other witnesses finish early.

Such misunderstandings lead, at best, to surprise and confusion and, at worst, to doubts as to due process. Time is always wasted: the tribunal can spend hours at the opening of the hearing and at the end of each session explaining what is happening and mediating between the parties.

One way to avoid this situation would be for the tribunal (full or just the chairman, after consulting with the others) to conduct a special procedural prehearing conference (presumably by telephone) with counsel a short time before the evidentiary hearing. The goal would be to ensure that both sides fully understand what each other plans to do and what the tribunal expects them to do. The goal would not be to force the same procedure on both sides, if they do not agree, but to elicit the preconceptions and plans that each side's counsel has for the fact evidence. All will at least be on the same page when the hearing opens.

The efficiency of the conference would be maximized if, in addition to requiring absolutely final witness lists, the tribunal would invest the time to send out to counsel in advance a list of questions concerning basic issues of fact evidence, taking common and civil law practices into account (as relevant to the case). This list would be analogous to the UNCITRAL Notes on Organizing Arbitral Proceedings, which include an outline and more detailed notes. A possible outline of questions is set out below.

Proposed Draft:
"Notes on Organizing Fact Testimony in Advance of Evidentiary Hearing in International Commercial Arbitration"

A. IBA Rules

Do you agree with basic principles in Art. 8 of the IBA Rules (arbitrator control, normal order of witnesses and questions, affirmation, scope of tribunal questions)? If so, scope of conference can be abbreviated. (Note: This focuses counsel new to international arbitration on the IBA Rules.)

B. Why? Underlying Purposes for Fact Witnesses

1. What is your perception as to the main purpose of fact testimony? To test the credibility of witness statements? Or to maximize fact-finding? Or both?
2. Would you welcome the tribunal indicating in advance what fact testimony it most wants to hear? If so, by witness or by issue? If not, why not?

C. Who? Details as to the Witnesses

1. Subject to the time allowed (see below), what witnesses do you intend to present?
2. Are there witness statements filed for all? Critical amendments to be made?
3. Order of priority? Comfortable that they are not duplicative?
4. Are there witnesses from the other side you require?
5. Do you have witnesses you wish to call even if the other side indicates it does not want to cross-examine them?
6. Does any witness require a formal order or subpoena?
7. Do you anticipate bringing witnesses for possible rebuttal? If so, why do you anticipate a need for rebuttal?

D. When? Scheduling and Order Issues

1. In what order do you intend to present the witnesses? All of claimant's witnesses followed by all of respondent's? Or claimant-respondent by issue? Or a combination?
2. Are all your witnesses available?
3. Any special scheduling requests?
4. Do you have an estimate, however rough, of how much time each witness should take?

E. How and What? Method and Scope of Testimony

1. Do you agree that the tribunal, specifically the chairman, shall be the umpire for all questioning?

2. Any special requirements/expectations for affirmations/oaths? Any Islamic witnesses?

3. Witness preparation: What are your expectations/intentions in relation to preparing your witnesses to testify? How much time do you intend to spend in cross-examination exploring the scope of preparation? How much preparation is likely to lead you to lodge an objection?

4. Sequestration of witnesses? Both before and after testimony? Special rules for party representatives?

5. Progression: Do you anticipate each witness going through direct, cross, redirect? Recross?

6. Progression: Do you anticipate limiting opening direct to thirty minutes, to affirm the witness statement and "relax" the witness?

7. Timing: Do you prefer the tribunal to use the "chess clock" or "guillotine" timing system?

8. Timing: Does time spent on cross come out of the time "account" of the sponsoring side or the crossing side? How about time spent on tribunal questions (asking and answering)?

9. Style: Do you anticipate using leading questions on direct as well as cross?

10. Style: On cross, do you intend to use a relatively aggressive US approach or a more conversational approach (subject to the chairman's control)?

11. Scope: Do you intend to limit direct and cross-questions to subjects covered in the witness statement? To object if the other side goes beyond those subjects? What are your expectations as to the scope of the arbitrators' questions?

12. Privilege: What are your expectations as to privilege/confidentiality for witness testimony?

13. Objections: Do you anticipate making objections on relevance? Hearsay? Privilege/confidentiality? Repetitiveness? Delaying tactics?

14. Objections: How would you envision making objections? How do you envision the tribunal should respond and rule on objections?

15. Use of documents: when you question a witness about a document, do you intend to refer him/her to an agreed hearing bundle or will you use loose copies (with copies for all)? Do you anticipate spending substantial witness time on documents, to focus the tribunal on the record?

16. Visual aids: do you intend to use new charts/maps/etc. with witnesses? If so, have copies available, as no surprises will be allowed.

17. Are you open to witness conferencing? If so, for which issues or witnesses?

The checklist above is just a starting point. It should prove especially useful for new arbitrators. Experienced arbitrators would be expected to add and delete questions, depending on the background and experience of the parties and counsel involved, the number and identity of the witnesses, and the sheer magnitude of the evidentiary record. As with the UNCITRAL Guidelines, it would be useful only if it remains a "living" document.

V.   CONCLUSION

Adopting formal guidelines (beyond possibly adjusting the IBA Rules occasionally to include a practice that has been firmly established or to dispel uncertainty) is unnecessary and counterproductive:

Unnecessary, given that open and early discussion between the arbitrators and the parties and counsel normally clears the way. There is no point, for instance, in deciding as a firm rule that the equal time allocation between the parties must be "chess clock" controlled or that equality means exactly the same number of minutes: it will simply depend upon the circumstances and the participants in the arbitration.

Counterproductive, because such guidelines will create new problems without solving others. After all, is it really the wish of the parties and their counsel to foster uniformity? Some leading arbitrators are known to have a hands-on approach, some to leave it to counsel to direct the proceedings and to intervene only in case of standoff: it would be "procrustean" and wasteful of talent and skill to adjust all arbitrations to the same yardstick. Exhaustive lists of "default rules" may look commendable but turn out to be counterproductive, leading to long debates at the outset of arbitration in order to opt in or opt out issue by issue. They may also lead to "expectation gaps" if they are not addressed early enough. At worst, nonobservance may create opportunities for unwarranted challenges of awards.

To prove the point with actual recent experience, the Swiss Rules of International Arbitration (January 2004) updated the 1979 UNCITRAL Rules: altogether, the Swiss Rules brought forth only two additions concerning witnesses, namely (i) "Any person may be a witness [...]" (Art. 25(2)) and (ii) "It shall not be improper for a party, its officers, employees, legal advisors or counsel to interview witnesses, potential witnesses or expert witnesses" (Art. 25(6)). Thus, wisely, the drafters thought it advisable to put down in black and white only essential and uncontested practices, leaving it to the users – arbitrators and counsel – to decide on the best presentation of fact testimony on a case-by-case basis.

Having taken the firm view that extensive harmonization of procedural rules for witness testimony would not serve the interests of parties wishing to resort to international commercial arbitration, we nonetheless believe that greater predictability would advance both due process and efficiency. To this end, arbitrators may wish to be more proactive in eliciting the different expectations and intentions of parties and counsel (especially inexperienced ones), in order to avoid surprises and delays in hearing testimony. A possible tool is the Proposed Notes on Organizing Fact Testimony in Advance of Evidentiary Hearing in International Commercial Arbitration, set forth above.

The Oral Presentation of Fact Witnesses in International Commercial Arbitration

Bernardo M. Cremades[*]

I.   INTRODUCTION

The oral presentation of fact witnesses in an international arbitration involves the personal interaction of witnesses, counsel and arbitrators. This personal and human interaction distinguishes the oral hearing from other forms of the presentation of evidence, such as the submission of documentary evidence, expert reports, or written witness statements. This session raises the questions of the presentation of fact witnesses as a matter of effective advocacy, and whether this phase of the arbitral process might be improved by the development of guidelines on questioning and cross-examination.

The effective oral presentation of fact witnesses forms part of a more general inquiry into the effective presentation of evidence, which in turn depends on the distinctive features of international arbitration and is not capable of a single or abstract answer. The first part of this article identifies certain features of international arbitration and the presentation of evidence that have an impact on the effective conduct of oral hearings. In the second part I explain why I consider that the professionalism of advocates and arbitrators is a better guarantee of effective oral hearing than the development of further guidelines or rules for oral hearings and questioning.

II.   FLEXIBILITY AND COMPROMISE IN INTERNATIONAL ARBITRATION

The following characteristics of international arbitration affect oral hearings:

1.   Party Autonomy

International arbitration is a jurisdiction created by the agreement of the parties and the arbitral tribunal must respect the procedural agreements of the parties. If the parties agree on an entirely written procedure then, as a matter of general principle, the arbitral tribunal should dispense with any oral hearing.

---

[*]   Senior Partner, B. Cremades y Asociados, Madrid; President, Spanish Court of Arbitration; member, Institute of World Business Law of the International Chamber of Commerce; Member of ICCA.

2. Multiple Procedural Traditions

International arbitration involves parties from different jurisdictions, and therefore in many cases accustomed to distinct procedural traditions relating to the presentation of evidence. The members of the arbitral tribunal, and particularly its chairman, might be accustomed to procedural practices distinct from either of the parties' counsel. There have been an attempt to harmonize different procedure traditions and to reflect contemporary international practice in the IBA Rules on the Taking of Evidence in International Commercial Arbitration.[1]

If the parties are unable to agree on the procedure, then: (i) in an institutional arbitration a skeleton procedure will be defined in the applicable rules; (ii) the arbitral tribunal might adapt a procedure based upon applicable law (most probably the law of the seat); (iii) the arbitral tribunal might design its own procedure based on the submissions of the parties, and its own evaluation of the necessities of the case. The practice today is for international arbitral tribunals to eschew fixing a procedure based on applicable law, and to design a procedure based on the submissions of the parties, its own perception of the case and the applicable institutional rules (if any).

3. Due Process

An arbitral tribunal must determine the procedure in accordance with its general duty, invariably required by arbitration statutes and institutional rules, to act fairly and impartially and ensure that each party has a reasonable opportunity to present its case.

4. The Subject Matter and the Participants

Arbitration is a quintessentially private form of dispute resolution. Justice must be done and seen to be done only to the parties. There is no public or social purpose to be served by the oral presentation and testing of evidence in international arbitration. "The less the subject matter is of social interest, or importance, the less necessary it is to preserve orality.... Arbitrations are private ... so there is no social need to allow any more orality than efficiency requires."[2]

The subject matter of international arbitration is international commerce or investment. All of the participants, including the members of the tribunal, counsel, witnesses and parties, are usually business people or professionals of some character. They are accustomed to reading, analyzing and digesting substantial quantities of written material, and their time is often at a premium. Another feature of the participants in international arbitration is that they often have diverse first languages.

---

1. See IBA WORKING PARTY, "Commentary on the New IBA Rules of Evidence in International Commercial Arbitration", Business Law International (2000) pp. 14-34.
2. Lord WILBERFORCE, "Written Briefs and Oral Advocacy", 5 Arbitration International (1989) pp. 348-351 at p. 349.

5. *Geographical Dispersion*

In international arbitration the parties, their counsel, the arbitrators, witnesses and the seat might be dispersed in various different countries. A procedure that minimizes the frequency of displacements, with its consequent scheduling complications is likely to be more efficient, and so significant where cost and speed are relevant considerations in the choice of procedure for the arbitration. From these premises, international arbitral procedure has developed a characteristic nature of compromise. Arbitral tribunals tend to avoid replicating a particular juridical tradition in all its procedural detail. Due process encourages compromise, because to adopt and strictly apply a procedure with which one party was fully accustomed and the other ignorant gives one party the advantage of familiarity, might influence the evidence presented to and accepted by the arbitral tribunal, and so raise doubts about the fairness of the arbitration.

Compromise tends firstly to take the form of a "procedural *tronc comun*", by accepting basic procedural features familiar to both parties; secondly, by the selective choice and marriage of features from multiple systems; and thirdly, by the avoidance of over-specification in order to maintain flexibility and allow each party a certain freedom in its presentation of proofs. Accordingly, *flexibility and compromise* between juridical traditions are the hallmarks of international arbitral procedure today.

A specific form of this compromise which has by now become substantially generalized is the practice of receiving evidence-in-chief by way of written brief, with little or no direct examination of witnesses. The important functions of the oral hearing are therefore cross-examination, the opportunity for counsel to make oral submissions to the tribunal, and for the tribunal to question counsel and witnesses about specific issues. The preparation and professionalism of an arbitral tribunal mean that cross-examination should be limited by counsel to only the most important issues. It should also be conducted strictly to inform the tribunal; theatrical cross-examination or attempts to humiliate a witness should be avoided. There should be a clear relationship between the cross-examination of counsel and the oral submissions made by counsel. Counsel knows well in advance from written briefs the evidence-in-chief of the witness, and should be able to prepare both the cross-examination and the oral submissions on common themes. Cross-examination is most effectively conducted where the tribunal, counsel and witness all speak the same language and there is no intervention of translators. The presence of translators in international arbitration is a further reason to limit cross-examination to the strictly necessary.

In my view, the present practice in respect of oral hearings in international arbitration functions efficiently. For parties that require further specificity the IBA Rules on the Taking of Evidence in International Commercial Arbitration are available. Art. 4 (Witnesses of Fact) is a good statement of the contemporary practice in relation to the provision of written witness statements. Art. 8 (Evidentiary Hearing) confirms the power of the arbitral tribunal to exclude questions that are "irrelevant, immaterial, burdensome, duplicative", or privileged, confidential or unfair. It also confirms that questions "to a witness during direct and redirect testimony may not be unreasonably leading". The IBA Rules go far enough in setting guidelines for the questioning of witnesses, and to go any further would cease to be an exercise in harmonization and become simply the replication in international arbitration of particular common law rules. Oral hearings and particularly the oral examination of witnesses are much more part of the common law than the continental system, and any more detailed guidelines are likely to reflect common law practices, and probably common law practices developed in other contexts (such as for public trials, lay witnesses and even for the presence of a jury).

I do not see any value in attempting to further formalize the procedure for oral hearings. The present practices will no doubt be further refined by experience over time, but does not require rules or guidelines.

III.   ADVOCACY, DISCRETION AND RULES

Advocacy is a sophisticated skill, applying accumulated legal knowledge and forensic experiences to the facts and circumstances of a particular dispute. The enormous documentary evidence and many potential witnesses and a relatively short hearing time make selection and presentation of evidence – distillation of the case – the core skill of the advocate in international arbitration. A rambling examination or cross-examination of a witness is not only unconvincing to the arbitral tribunal, but also dissipates the valuable and limited forensic resource of time.

Effective advocacy requires advocates to choose their material and use their time wisely. The effective advocate has a discretion in the choice of fact witnesses, the choice of topics for questioning, and also the mode of questioning. In the private, full professionalized arbitration hearing room there is no need for further rules or guidelines on the questioning of witnesses. Abusive questioning of witnesses carries its own sanction: it does not convince and it wastes valuable time.

The further particularization of hearing rules in international arbitration would not serve any useful purpose. Rules and guidelines are always a means to an end, not an end in themselves. I do not consider there is any problem in international arbitration relating to the presentation of evidence through fact witnesses. There is no interest that needs to be protected. There is no public gallery or jury to protect from being scandalized or manipulated by counsel. The parties or their four or five witnesses do not require protection because, as I have said, the tribunal will not be convinced by leading, overbearing or humiliating questioning by counsel, and witnesses' own counsel can object to the mode of questioning if necessary. In any event, international arbitration rarely depends, as a criminal trial might, on the oral testimony of one or more witnesses; instead oral testimony is limited by and constantly tested against a substantial documentary record, as well as the oral testimony of other witnesses. Accordingly, the efficient questioning of fact witnesses is best achieved through the professionalism of advocates and arbitrators, rather than through rules or guidelines.

Rules and guidelines might also impose additional costs. They might lead to subtle procedural discussions. They would replicate in arbitration the procedures of state courts, and potentially reduce the flexibility of arbitration that is one of its strengths and attractions to commercial parties. Arbitration users would not be served by more specific rules and guidelines. Rules or guidelines might introduce expectations of procedural uniformity and conformity, and so reduce the willingness to customize procedure for the particular characteristics of the case and witnesses by, for example, direct questioning of witnesses by the arbitral tribunal, the confrontation of witnesses, or witness conferencing.[3]

In conclusion, I consider that the proposal to introduce further guidelines for the questioning and cross-examination of witnesses in international commercial arbitrations is a good demonstration of the limits of rules. There are many matters in arbitration best left to the professionalism and discretion of advocates and arbitrators, and the conduct of an oral hearing is an example. The successful conduct of an arbitration requires a minimum procedural framework of rules, and the framework provisions of a modern arbitration law (such as the UNCITRAL Model Law) and modern institutional rules contain sufficient rules.

If the parties want more specificity, they have available the IBA Rules on the Taking of Evidence in International Commercial Arbitration. The success of arbitral procedure depends upon the parties or counsel reaching agreement on the more detailed aspects of the procedure, or the arbitral tribunal imposing further individualized guidelines in the form of procedural orders after consultation with the parties. This means that counsel and the tribunal have considerable discretion and rules are not fixed in advance, but this is an advantage because counsel and arbitrators are well qualified to exercise this discretion wisely, and for the benefit of the parties and the success of arbitration.

The successful procedural management of an arbitration, including the hearing of witnesses, requires not a priori rules or guidelines, but professional decisions by individual counsel and arbitrators.

---

3. On the technique of witness conferencing, see Wolfgang PETER, "Witness Conferencing Revisited" in *Arbitral Procedure at the Dawn of the New Millennium: Reports of the International Colloquium of CEPANI*, 15 October 2004 (Bruylant) at pp. 157-171.

The Role of Witness Statements in International Commercial Arbitration

Michael Hwang S.C.* and Andrew Chin**

I. INTRODUCTION

Witness statements are very commonly used in international commercial arbitrations nowadays,[1] although they are not commonly used in arbitrations conducted in the civil jurisdictions of Asia, such as China.[2]

The International Bar Association Rules on Taking of Evidence in International Commercial Arbitration (IBA Rules),[3] the UNCITRAL Arbitration Rules (UNCITRAL Rules)[4] and the London Court of International Arbitration Rules of Arbitration[5] (LCIA Rules) provide explicitly for the taking of witness statements.

Although the ICC Rules on Arbitration (ICC Rules) do not explicitly provide for the taking of witness statements,[6] Derains and Schwartz observe that witness statements are widely used in ICC arbitrations:

---

* Barrister and Chartered Arbitrator, Singapore; Vice President, ICC International Court of Arbitration; Member, LCIA; Former Vice Chair, Committee D, IBA; Deputy Chief Justice, Dubai International Financial Centre. Vice President of ICCA.

** Associate, Michael Hwang S.C., Singapore.

1. See Alan REDFERN and Martin HUNTER, *Law and Practice of International Commercial Arbitration*, 4th edn. (Sweet & Maxwell 2004) at para. 6-85 and Laurent LEVY, "Concluding Remarks" in Laurent LEVY and V.V. VEEDER, eds., *Arbitration and Oral Evidence* (ICC Publishing S.A. 2005) at pp. 143-148.

2. See comment by Michael MOSER in 21 Arbitration International (2005, no. 4) p. 583 at p. 588

3. See Rule 4(4)-4(8), available at <www.ibanet.org/images/downloads/IBA%20rules%20on %20the%20taking%20of%20Evidence.pdf> (last accessed 27 June 2006).

4. See Art. 25(5), available at <www.uncitral.org/pdf/english/texts/arbitration/arb-rules/arb-rules.pdf> (last accessed 27 June 2006).

5. See Art. 20.3-20.6, available at <www.lcia.org/ARB_folder/arb_english_main.htm> (last accessed 27 June 2006), available at <www.iccwbo.org/court/english/arbitration/pdf_documents/rules/rules_arb_english.pdf> (last accessed 27 June 2006).

6. See Art. 20(1) of the ICC Rules, which gives the arbitral tribunal the power to establish the facts of the case by all appropriate means.

"In order to save hearing time ... it has become commonplace in ICC arbitrations for parties to present the direct testimony of witnesses either wholly or partly by means of written witnesses statements. But if this is done, the witnesses are nevertheless generally required to be made available at the hearing for questioning. If a witness does not appear without a valid reason, the weight of his witness statement will be considerably reduced and it may even be stricken from the record."[7]

In this paper, the role of witness statements in international arbitrations will be discussed, and some suggestions offered on the preparation of witness statements.

II. USES OF WITNESS STATEMENTS

The Working Party which prepared the IBA Rules[8] describes the role which witness statements play in international commercial arbitrations:

"If Witness Statements are used, the evidence that a witness plans to give orally at the hearing is known in advance. The other party thus can better prepare its own examination of the witness and select the issues and witnesses it will present. The Tribunal is also in a better position to follow and put questions to these witnesses. Witness Statements may in this way reduce the length of oral hearings. For instance, they may be considered as the 'evidence in chief' ('direct evidence'), so that extensive explanation by the witness becomes superfluous and examination by the other party can start immediately. In order to save on hearing time and expenses, very often the Arbitral Tribunal and the parties can also agree that witnesses whose statement is not contested by the opposing party do not have to be present at the hearing. Of course, the drafting of a Witness Statement requires contacts between the witness and the party that is presenting him."[9]

As observed by the IBA Working Party, witness statements are used to replace the oral examination in chief of the witnesses. This brings about substantial savings of time during the hearing. This is particularly important for international commercial arbitrations, where the arbitrators, parties and their witnesses may come from various jurisdictions, as it is the international aspect of international commercial arbitration which contributes significantly to the costs of the arbitration.

In addition, the provision of witness statements from both parties before the evidentiary hearing will allow the arbitral tribunal to focus its attention on the key points

---

7. Yves DERAINS and Eric A. SCHWARTZ, *A Guide to the ICC Rules of Arbitration*, 2nd edn. (Kluwer Law International 2005) pp. 276-277.
8. The IBA Rules were prepared by the Working Party appointed by the Arbitration Committee of the International Bar Association.
9. See "Commentary on the New IBA Rules of Evidence" by the Working Party, published in Business Law International (2000) pp. 14-34.

of contention between the witnesses, leading to greater efficiency in the fact finding process during the evidentiary hearing.

Witness statements are particularly helpful in putting across the testimony of witnesses who are not fluent in the language of the arbitration more effectively to the arbitral tribunal. This ensures that the key points of what the witness is trying to put across in his evidence is not confused or lost simply because the witness is unable to communicate effectively through an interpreter. However, witness statements carry the obvious danger that the contents of the witness statement may not correctly reflect what the witness may want to say.

III.   ABUSES OF WITNESS STATEMENTS

Notwithstanding the benefits of witness statements, commentators have observed that witness statements are often used as a mouthpiece for the lawyers to make their pleadings. As observed by V.V. Veeder Q.C.:

> "The practice of taking factual witness statements requires urgent reform. Increasingly, many international arbitrators pay little credence to written witness statements on any contentious issue, unless independently corroborated by other reliable evidence. It is perhaps surprising that many sophisticated practitioners have not yet understood that their massive efforts at reshaping the testimony of their client's factual witnesses is not only ineffective but often counter-productive. Most arbitrators have been or remain practitioners, and they can usually detect the 'wood-shedding' of a witness."[10]

Unfortunately, this has become such a common practice in the international arbitration community that no one finds it surprising any more. As Anne Veronique Schlaepfer notes:

> "It is also accepted that witnesses usually do not write their statements themselves. The practice of having the last page of the statement only containing the date and the signature of the witness (in different characters from the other pages of the document) does not seem to surprise anyone anymore."[11]

V.V. Veeder Q.C. further observes that such practices "[diminish] the statement's probative value and increases the need for oral cross-examination".[12]

The utility of witness statements would be grossly diminished if the arbitral tribunal cannot have the basic assurance that the witness statement contains what the witness

---

10. Taken from the 2001 Goff Lecture, published in 18 Arbitration International (2002, no. 4) pp. 431-451.
11. Anne Veronique SCHLAEPFER, "Witness Statements" in LEVY and VEEDER, *op. cit.*, fn. 1, p. 68.
12. *Op. cit.*, fn. 10.

actually wants to say. The arbitral tribunal will have the unenviable task of identifying the parts of the witness statement which have been tailored by counsel to suit his case or to attack the opposing party's case.

In England, witness statements filed in court will have to be accompanied with a statement of truth signed by either the witness or his legal representative.[13] The form of the statement of truth is as follows: "I believe that the facts stated in this witness statement are true."

If a witness statement is not accompanied by a statement of truth, then the court has the discretion not to admit the witness statement. This is a worthwhile direction to impose in arbitration, possibly coupled with a statement as to whether the witness has been assisted by anyone in the preparation of his statement, as well as the nature and extent of that assistance, so that everyone will know how spontaneous the statement actually is.

IV.   POINTS OF INTEREST

1.   *How Should an Arbitral Tribunal Treat Testimony Given During Supplemental Examination in Chief by Counsel if It Expands on Material Given in the Witness Statement?*

There is no rule in international commercial arbitration that bars a party from orally examining its own witnesses by way of supplemental examination in chief even after witness statements have been submitted. But there is an inherent danger in that a witness, after having read the opposing party's witness statements, may be tempted to tailor his own witness statement by introducing new material into the record. This causes difficulties for opposing counsel as they might be caught by surprise and thus unable effectively to cross-examine the witness.

A tactic which has been used by some counsel to surprise opposing counsel is to insert only broad and conclusory statements into the witness statement, and introduce more detailed evidence through the witness by way of cross-examination or re-examination. This practice serves to reduce the intensity of cross-examination by opposing counsel, as he cannot effectively cross-examine the witness on the new material raised, not having been forewarned of it. If new evidence is orally introduced in re-examination, unless the cross-examiner can persuade the tribunal to allow him a second round of cross-examination, he may not even be able to cross-examine on the new material at all.[14] Of course, according to traditional common law rules of evidence, re-examination should only deal with matters raised in cross-examination, but, since the strict rules of evidence do not apply in arbitration, anything could happen in practice, particularly if the arbitrator is not an experienced common law litigator.

---

13. See English Civil Procedure Rules, Part 22 and the accompanying Practice Direction available at <www.dca.gov.uk/civil/procrules_fin/contents/parts/part22.htm> (last accessed 27 June 2006).
14. See comments given by David LANE, 21 Arbitration International (2005, no. 4) p. 561 at p. 579.

An arbitral tribunal has the discretion to reject such new evidence given by the witness, but it is likely to be confronted with an argument by counsel that there has been a breach of a party's right to have a full opportunity to present its case before the arbitral tribunal under Art. 18 of the UNCITRAL Model Law. However, the brief text of Art. 18 of the UNCITRAL Model Law does not take us very far, as standards of procedural fairness differ between jurisdictions. This difficulty is highlighted by V.V. Veeder Q.C.:

> "For the parties to an international commercial arbitration, justice should be the paramount objective; and procedural fairness by their legal representatives is subsumed in that single objective. But the practice of international arbitration is not so simple, certainly not for the parties' professional lawyers coming from different jurisdictions to a still different place of arbitration."[15]

It is generally accepted that there is no unlimited right for a party to present its case. As long as the procedural rules are applied fairly between the parties, there should not be any ground for argument that a party has been denied a full opportunity to present its case. In this regard, Holtzmann and Neuhaus provide an insight into the legislative history behind Art. 18 UNCITRAL Model Law:

> "The terms of Article 18 were modelled on Article 15(1) of the UNCITRAL Arbitration Rules. The Commission Report provides no authoritative guidelines to interpreting the terms 'treated with equality' and 'full opportunity of presenting his case'; nor do the reports of the Working Group. It is submitted that this may be because the delegates considered that the terms were so well understood in all legal systems that comment was unnecessary and that detailed definitions might limit the flexible and broad approach needed to assure fairness in the wide variety of circumstances that might be encountered in international arbitration. It is also submitted that the terms 'equality' and 'full opportunity' are to be interpreted reasonably in regulating the procedural aspects of the arbitration. *While, on the one hand, the arbitral tribunal must provide reasonable opportunities to each party, this does not mean that it must sacrifice all efficiency in order to accommodate unreasonable procedural demands by a party. For example, as the Secretariat noted, the provision does not entitle a party to obstruct the proceedings by dilatory tactics, such as by offering objections, amendments or evidence on the eve of the award. An early draft that would have required that each of the parties be given a full opportunity to present his case 'at any stage of the proceedings' was rejected precisely because it was feared that it might be relied upon to prolong the proceedings unnecessarily.*"[16] (emphasis added)

---

15. *Op. cit.*, fn. 10, p. 431.
16. See Howard M. HOLTZMANN and Joseph E. NEUHAUS, *A Guide to the UNCITRAL Model Law on International Commercial Arbitration: Legislative History and Commentary* (Kluwer Law International 1989) pp. 551-552

In my view, a witness should not be allowed to add to the matters contained in his witness statement subject to four exceptions:[17]

(a) the witness wishes to correct an error or ambiguity in his witness statement or affidavit;
(b) the witness wishes to elaborate on some relatively small detail in his witness statement or affidavit;
(c) the witness wishes to respond to matters raised in the opposing party's witness statement which he had not seen at the time when his own witness statement was filed;
(d) the witness wishes to give evidence about relevant facts which have occurred since the date of his witness statement.

In Singapore, the practice of arbitrators in international commercial arbitrations is to regard the witness statement as his complete testimony in chief. Singaporean arbitrators trained in our court system are reluctant to allow expansion of the contents in the witness statement by a witness during the evidentiary hearing unless one of the four exceptions stated above apply.

In other words, as a general rule of thumb, the arbitral tribunal should not allow opposing counsel to be taken by surprise[18] by matters that a witness may state during supplemental examination in chief, subject to the four exceptions.

2.   Should Witness Statements Be Exchanged Simultaneously or Sequentially?

The IBA Working Party summarized the advantages of simultaneous and sequential submission of witness statements in this way:

> "Simultaneous exchanges cause less delay and lead to more disclosure and equality between parties. There is also less tailoring of statements to neutralize statements received from the other party. On the other hand, consecutive exchanges allow parties to focus better on the relevant points, which makes the statements more efficient. In order to combine the advantages of simultaneous and consecutive exchanges the Arbitral Tribunal may organize two rounds of simultaneous exchanges. In the second round, only information contained in the other party's statements, submitted in the first round, should be addressed."[19]

---

17. See my chapter in Doak BISHOP, ed., *The Art of Advocacy in International Arbitration* (Juris Publishing Inc. 2004) p. 423.
18. The element of surprise was taken into account by the Singapore High Court in the case of *Lee Kuan Yew v. Vinocur* [1995] 3 SLR 477 where the judge held that the plaintiff's witnesses were allowed to supplement their affidavits of evidence in chief because the oral evidence to be given was nothing more than an amplification of the evidence given in their witness affidavits. Although this case dealt with court proceedings, the views of the judge could be applied in the context of international commercial arbitration.
19. *Op. cit.*, fn. 9.

In my standard directions for witness statements (see below), I normally make provision for two rounds of simultaneous exchange of witness statements, with the second round of witness statements to deal only with matters raised in the first round of witness statements.

3.   *How Should Arbitral Tribunals Draft Their Procedural Orders in Relation to Witness Statements?*

Special care must be taken by the arbitral tribunal when giving directions on witness statements. If this is not done properly, a possible consequence is that counsel on one side may have filed witness statements which give away the party's case in full (whether as a result of misunderstanding of the terms of the direction or otherwise) while counsel for the opposing side may file only skeletal witness statements, with the full witness testimony to follow during the evidentiary hearing. The result is that the party which has exposed its case in full will be tactically disadvantaged against the party who has only filed skeletal witness statements.

Two sample directions dealing with witness statements which I often use in the international commercial arbitrations that I am involved with are set out below:

> "(a) Parties are to prepare statements of evidence in chief (*in numbered paragraphs*) containing the *full evidence in chief* of all witnesses of fact upon whom they propose to rely. Photographs of the witnesses should be attached to their respective witness statements if possible. *All documents* intended to be referred to in the evidence in chief of the witnesses must be attached to the statements of evidence in chief and copies provided with the statements of evidence in chief if not previously provided to the Tribunal. Statements of evidence in chief are to be filed and exchanged by [insert date]. Parties are at liberty to file further statements of evidence in chief (either of the same witnesses or of new witnesses) *only in response to the original statements*. Responsive statements are to be exchanged by [insert date].
>
> (b) All witnesses who have given statements of evidence in chief are to attend for cross examination, if requested by the other Party. If a witness so requested does not attend then, on good cause shown, the Tribunal may accept the statement and decide what weight, if any, to attach to it. Each Party is to give the other Party notice whether any of the other Party's witnesses are not required to appear for cross examination not later than [insert date]. If any witness requested to attend cannot attend, notice of non-attendance must be given at the earliest possible opportunity to the other Party." (important parts italicized)

A few important points to note from the two sample directions:

(a) *in numbered paragraphs* — numbering of paragraphs is important as it allows for easy referencing by the arbitral tribunal and the parties;
(b) *full evidence in chief* — this is to prevent skeletal statements with witnesses wanting to amplify their written statements with detailed oral testimony at the hearing. The test of

656

whether new oral evidence should be allowed at the hearing should be whether opposing counsel will be required to spend extra time in preparing supplementary cross-examination on the oral evidence;

(c) *all documents* – if the witness has something to say about a document, that document should be either attached to his statement or in a bundle of documents which is available at the time the statement is filed;

(d) *only in response to the original statements* – unless the arbitral tribunal limits the scope of the responsive witness statements, this could lead to further surprises if one party decides to put in new evidence in the responsive witness statement. One of the consequences of this type of order (which is not always appreciated) is that, if the opposing party chooses not to cross-examine the witness, the party who called the witness cannot be allowed to supplement the witness's statement by way of oral testimony, subject to the four exceptions set out above.

In addition, the attachment of a statement of truth to every witness statement as mandated by the English Civil Procedural Rules (see above) should be encouraged.

V.   POINTERS ON PREPARATION OF WITNESS STATEMENTS

The following pointers will, we hope, help counsel to achieve what Robert S. Rifkind describes as the four objectives to meet in preparing witnesses:

"– *First*, the witness must be put at ease and made to feel comfortable with the task at hand.
– *Second*, the witness must be given an understanding of the process in which he is to participate and how his part of the story fits into the overall picture.
– *Third*, the witness must be intimately engaged in a dialogue that results in an outline of the questions and answers that will comprise his direct testimony.
– *Fourth*, the witness must be prepared in detail, so far as humanly possible, for every difficulty that he will face on cross examination."[20]

Although the comments above by Robert S. Rifkind apply to the role of counsel in preparation for oral examination in chief, they apply equally to the preparation of witness statements.

1.   *Attachment of an Executive Summary*

An executive summary of each witness statement should be provided so as to allow the arbitrators to focus on the main points on which a witness is expected to testify. This is especially important where a witness is providing testimony on technical matters, as the arbitrator may get lost in the myriad of detail. Furthermore, an executive summary

---

20. Robert S. RIFKIND, "Practices of the Horseshed: The Preparation of Witnesses by Counsel in America" in LEVY and VEEDER, *op. cit.*, fn. 1, p. 57.

serves to refresh the memory of the arbitral tribunal where the evidentiary hearing may stretch over many weeks.

2. Use of the Witness's Own Words Insofar as Possible

As far as possible, counsel should ensure that the witness's own words are used in the witness statement. This will avoid embarrassment to the witness during cross-examination when the witness is confronted with his own statement which he may not understand if drafted by counsel. In addition, the arbitral tribunal may tend to see a witness as more credible if the witness statement is in the witness's own words, in contrast to a witness statement that has been elegantly drafted by counsel. Legalistic words like "peruse" and "I verily believe" should be avoided at all costs.

On this point, Gerald Aksen offers this piece of advice:

> "Finally, in most of my arbitrations, I advise counsel at the beginning that if we are going to have witness statements, each witness should prepare the first draft by himself. Counsel can put the witness's testimony into a more logical order and line up the legal arguments."[21]

3. Use of Cross-referencing Between Witness Statements

Very often, witnesses testifying on the same issue have a tendency to repeat the same facts in their testimony during examination in chief. Witness statements offer witnesses the opportunity to cross-refer to each other's witness statements, so that any facts which have already been the subject of testimony by one witness need not be repeated by the other. This enables substantial saving of time and simplifies matters for the arbitral tribunal, as the arbitral tribunal need not review the same material again.

4. Use of Large Projector Screens to Take the Witness Through His Witness Statement

Counsel should go through the first draft of the witness statement with the witness by flashing the statement onto a large projector screen. This has the psychological effect of focusing the witness's attention on the words of his witness statement, and serves to prepare him to defend every word in his witness statement when cross-examined (when the same technique may be used by opposing counsel).

5. Demarcate Between the Witness's Testimony of Fact and Opinion

Witness statements very often contain, not only a witness's testimony of fact, but his opinions on why the opposing party's case is misconceived. This may arise from counsel's desire to give the arbitral tribunal the words from the 'horse's mouth' by putting everything a witness wishes to say into his witness statement. However, while

---

21. See 21 Arbitration International (2005, no. 4) p. 589.

the strict rules of evidence do not apply to arbitrations, it is a rule of common sense that a lay witness should only be giving factual evidence and not his opinions unless he is an expert.

Recently, I sat as arbitrator in an ICC arbitration where the claimant buyer was suing the respondent seller for damages arising out of equipment which did not meet the contractual specifications. The claimant alleged that the respondent was responsible for the faulty design of the equipment. The respondent responded by saying that the failure of the equipment to meet the contractual specifications was due to the claimant failing to maintain the equipment properly and failing to provide the correct conditions for operation of the equipment. In addition, the claimant alleged that the respondent had made fraudulent misrepresentations which induced the claimant to enter into the contract. The witness statements by the respondent's in-house experts (who were ostensibly held out as factual witnesses) contained testimony both of fact and opinion on why the equipment failed to meet the contractual specifications and why the respondent felt it was justified in making the alleged misrepresentations. The tribunal gave a direction that the respondent's in-house experts should avoid giving opinions on matters that would be dealt with by external experts unless the in-house experts' opinions were necessary to explain their own contemporaneous actions, for example, to show that in-house experts did not have a fraudulent state of mind at the relevant time when they made various representations concerning the equipment. The rationale for this direction was to prevent an unreasonable burden being placed on the claimant to have to cross-examine all of the respondent's in-house experts on technical issues.

6. *Highlight Portions of the Witness Statement Which Are Based on Hearsay*

A practice has arisen whereby some counsel select one witness as their key witness who will testify to all the facts on which their case is based, regardless of the personal knowledge of the witness of those facts. If this is done, the portions of the witness statement that are based on hearsay should be highlighted and the witness should further state the source of his information. Unless the arbitral tribunal and opposing counsel have notice of the hearsay portions in the witness statement, the key witness would lose his credibility unnecessarily if he is perceived to be pretending to have first-hand knowledge of the matters in his witness statement but is eventually unable to withstand cross-examination on those matters of which he has no personal knowledge. The practice of highlighting the hearsay portions of the witness statement helps to preserve the credibility of the key witness, and signals to the cross-examiner that he should save his cross-examination on the hearsay matters for those witnesses who have first-hand knowledge of those matters. Counsel cannot also assume that, even if hearsay evidence is not struck out (as it might be in court), it will be relied on by the tribunal, since the rule against hearsay is based on common sense that it is normally less reliable than first-hand evidence, and counsel should always aim to get witnesses with such first-hand evidence except where the facts are not crucial or controversial.

7. *Exhibit Documentary Evidence as Appendix or Extract*

If a witness wishes to rely on a particular document to support his point, this document should either be exhibited as an appendix or sufficiently extracted in the body of the witness statement. It is very tiring for members of the arbitral tribunal to dig into cartons of bundles of documents to obtain the relevant document, apart from increasing the time taken for the hearing.

8. *Use of Paragraph Numbering*

This is a basic but important practical point. The use of paragraph numbering enables counsel to quickly refer the witness to passages in his witness statement during cross-examination. This practice will lead to savings of time and should be insisted on by the tribunal.

VI.   CONCLUSION

Witness statements are indispensable tools in modern arbitrations to save time and make advance preparations for the hearing more efficient. However, they must be crafted with care and propriety if they are to fulfil their intended purpose of accurately and fairly setting out the witness's testimony.

Working Group B

3. Evidentiary Privileges

Evidentiary Privileges in International Arbitration

*Henri Alvarez**

I. INTRODUCTION

Surprisingly, the question of evidentiary privileges and their nature, scope and application have only recently begun to attract significant interest.[1] This is perhaps due to the fact that these privileges have generally been considered as evidentiary rules which are procedural in character and therefore included within the broad discretion accorded to arbitrators in respect of procedural matters in international arbitration. As is generally recognized, absent an express choice of procedural law or rules by the parties, arbitrators in international arbitration are not required to apply national rules of civil procedure or evidence, subject only to limited public policy requirements of the law of

---

* Partner, Fasken, Martineau DuMoulin LLP. The author gratefully acknowledges the assistance of Tina Cicchetti and Beta Gustafson in the preparation of this paper.

1. The substantial recent works on the topic include the following: Robert H. SMIT and Audley SHEPPARD, "Evidentiary Privileges in International Arbitration", 5 Arbitration and ADR (December 2000, no. 3) (Newsletter of Committee D of the International Bar Association Section on Business Law) p. 12; Richard M. MOSK and Tom GINSBERG, "Evidentiary Privileges in International Arbitration", 50 Int'l and Comp. L.Q. (2001) p. 345; Javier H. RUBINSTEIN and Britton B. GUERRINA, "The Attorney-Client Privilege and International Arbitration", 18 J. Int'l Arb. (2001) p. 587; Norah GALLAGHER, "Legal Privilege in International Arbitration", Int'l A.L.R. (2003) p. 45; Bernhard F. MEYER-HAUSER, *"Das Anwalt Geheimnis und Schiedsgericht"*, (Schulthess, Zurich 2004); Michelle SINDLER and Tina WÜSTEMANN, "Privilege Across Borders in Arbitration: Multi-jurisdictional Nightmare or a Storm in a Teacup?", 23 ASA Bulletin (December 2005, no. 4,) p. 610; Fabian VON SCHLABRENDORFF and Audley SHEPPARD, "Conflict of Legal Privileges in International Arbitration: An Attempt to Find a Holistic Solution" in Gerald AKSEN, et al., eds., *Global Reflections on International Law, Commerce and Dispute Resolution, Liber Amicorum in Honour of Robert Briner* (ICC Publishing, Paris 2005); Klaus P. BERGER, "Evidentiary Privileges – Best Practice Standards versus/and Arbitral Discretion", Conference Materials, ASA Conference, Zurich, 27 January 2006, published in 22 Arb. International (2006, no. 4) pp. 501-520 (subsequent page citations are to Conference Materials version). Other sources are set out in the Selected Bibliography below, pp. 699-704.

the place of arbitration.[2] Typically, subject to a contrary agreement of the parties, the conduct of an arbitration, including the admissibility and weight of evidence, is left to the discretion of the arbitral tribunal which is usually subject only to the general requirements of fair and equal treatment of the parties and the mandatory rules or public policy of the State in which the arbitration has its seat. For a number of possible reasons, including the increasing number and complexity of international disputes and arbitrations and the recent reconsideration of certain aspects of national law relating to privilege and related areas,[3] the topic of evidentiary privileges is attracting increasing attention. This has given rise to a welcome opportunity to reconsider the nature of evidentiary privileges and their application in international arbitration. This closer scrutiny reveals that the question is deserving of greater attention than it has received in the past and that the general solution of simply deferring to the discretion of the arbitral tribunal when the issues relating to privileges arise may not be entirely satisfactory.

As evidentiary privileges generally reflect the public policy of the legal system that adopts them,[4] failure to apply these privileges may give rise to a basis for the challenge of an arbitral award or resistance to recognition and enforcement of an award.[5] Further, since privileges are intended to exclude otherwise relevant evidence, they may affect an arbitral tribunal's fundamental task of establishing the facts of a dispute. Depending on how the arbitral tribunal determines the law or rule applicable to evidentiary privileges and how it applies that standard, the result may be the unequal or unfair treatment of one of the parties to the arbitration. Despite this potential impact of evidentiary privileges, there is very little authority or guidance on how international arbitrators should proceed in dealing with a claim of privilege.[6] As a result, arbitrators and parties alike may be faced with novel and often complex questions when the issue of the application of privileges arises.

A number of reasons have been suggested as to why the legal issues related to privileges and their application in international arbitration are as varied and complex as they are: the nature and concept of evidentiary privileges is different in civil and common law; there are essential differences in the qualification of privileges as substantive or procedural matters in common and civil law; and there are no established conflict of laws rules for the determination of the law applicable to privileges in

---

2. Jean-François POUDRET and Sebastien BESSON, *Droit comparé de l'arbitrage international* (Geneva 2002), no. 642; Emmanuel GAILLARD and John SAVAGE, eds., *Fouchard, Gaillard, Goldman on International Commercial Arbitration* (The Hague 1999), no. 1266.

3. SINDLER and WÜSTEMANN, *op. cit.*, fn. 1, pp. 610-612.

4. MOSK and GINSBERG, *op. cit.*, fn. 1, p. 352; Jean-Claude ROYER, *La Preuve Civil*, 3rd edn. (Éditions Yvon Blais 2003) pp. 890-891; John SOPINKA, Sidney L. LEDERMAN, Alan W. BRYANT, *The Law of Evidence in Canada*, 2nd edn. (Butterworths 1992) pp. 713-714.

5. As discussed below, in certain circumstances, the failure to consider or apply rules of privilege at the place of arbitration may also give rise to applications to stay or otherwise interfere with the arbitral process during the proceedings.

6. See BERGER, *op. cit.*, fn. 1, p. 2 and the sources cited there.

international arbitration.[7] To these reasons must be added the largely unexplored aspect of the application of ethical rules: many privileges are intimately linked to codes of professional conduct and ethics which apply to lawyers. These ethical rules are many and varied and their application, whether by an arbitral tribunal, professional bodies or the courts, may have unexpected and far-reaching consequences on the conduct of the arbitration as it relates to the production, admission and assessment of evidence and, ultimately, the award and its enforcement.

Despite these complexities, it appears to be broadly accepted that claims of privilege must be taken seriously and considered by an arbitral tribunal when they are raised by a party. The potential effect of disregarding a rule of a public policy nature compels this approach. Further, the need for predictability and the perception that parties rely on privileges and, therefore, have legitimate expectations as to the application of certain privileges, require the arbitral tribunal to consider claims of privilege in order to avoid unfair surprises and to accord equal treatment to the parties.[8] This need for predictability and concern for the legitimate expectations of the parties gives rise to the increasingly familiar debate over the need for uniform rules, guidelines or "best practices" on the choice and application of rules governing evidentiary privileges versus ad hoc decision-making by the arbitral tribunal in the exercise of its broad discretion.

II. THE NATURE OF EVIDENTIARY PRIVILEGES

1. Definition

Evidentiary privileges are based on a legally recognized right, and in some cases the obligation, to withhold certain documentary or testimonial evidence from a legal proceeding.[9] Unlike other rules of evidence which are intended to exclude evidence because of its inherent unreliability or lack of probative value, which are concerns related to the adversarial method of ascertaining the truth, the exclusionary rule of privilege is based on social values, external to the trial process.[10] Although the evidence is relevant, probative and reliable, privilege permits, and in certain cases requires, that it be excluded because of overriding social interests.[11]

---

7. See BERGER, *op. cit.*, fn. 1, p. 2. These reasons are generally discussed in the sources cited at fn. 1 above. This is without considering other legal systems which may not recognize the notion of privilege as articulated in the common or civil law.

8. See BERGER, *op. cit.*, fn.1, pp. 2-3 and the sources cited there; VON SCHLABRENDORFF and SHEPPARD, *op. cit.*, fn. 1, pp. 765-767.

9. MOSK and GINSBERG, *op. cit.*, fn. 1, p. 346. Also, see generally: SOPINKA, LEDERMAN and BRYANT, *op. cit.*, fn. 4, pp. 709-852; ROYER, *op. cit.*, fn. 4, pp. 811-983.

10. SOPINKA, LEDERMAN and BRYANT, *op. cit.*, fn. 4, p. 713.

11. SOPINKA, LEDERMAN and BRYANT, *ibid.*, p. 713. See also James H. CARTER, "The Attorney-Client Privilege and Arbitration", ADR Currents (Winter 1996-1997) at p. 16 where the author states as follows:

"Legal privileges, however, are grounded on rights. Privileges such as those protecting attorney-

Although the exclusionary rule of privilege flows from a different concept and is articulated differently than in common law, civil law recognizes the same underlying principle of exclusion to protect important societal values.[12] The civil law principle of professional confidentiality (*secret professionnel*) has been defined as follows:

> *"Le secret professionnel a une double finalité, soit celle de protéger la confidentialité des rapports entre un professionnel et son client à l'égard du public en général, soit celle d'assurer la non-divulgation en justice des informations confidentielles confiées par un client à un professionnel. Entendu dans le premier sens, ce secret est un devoir de discrétion qui s'impose au professionnel. Celui-ci ne peut généralement pas divulguer à des tiers les confidences de son client. Cette obligation peut découler d'une loi, d'un règlement et même de la seule existence d'un rapport contractuel. Sa violation expose le contrevenant à des sanctions. Entendu dans le deuxième sens, le secret professionnel est le droit ou l'obligation d'une personne de ne pas divulguer devant un tribunal des renseignements confidentiels qui lui ont été révélés dans l'exercice de ses fonctions. Il s'agit d'une immunité ou d'un privilège qui restreint la recevabilité de la preuve et qui est un obstacle à la découverte de la vérité. Le devoir de discrétion du professionnel est plus étendu que son immunité judiciaire. En common law, la confidentialité des communications entre l'avocat et son client a donné naissance à un privilège protégeant la divulgation en justice de certaines, mais non de toutes les communications confidentielles....*
>
> *La reconnaissance ou non du secret professionnel est étroitement liée aux valeurs fondamentales d'une société."*[13]

Most commentators on the notion of privilege note the underlying conflict or tension between two competing policies. The first is the promotion of the administration of justice which requires that all relevant, reliable evidence relating to the facts and issues to be determined be placed before the relevant adjudicator so that it can fully and properly consider and decide the merits of a dispute. The second is the social interest in preserving and encouraging particular relationships whose viability is based on confidential communications. For example, the relationship between a lawyer and his client is protected by a privilege which serves a public policy goal of candid

---

client, doctor-patient, husband-wife, priest-penitent and other types of communications are based on public policies intended to encourage and protect communications in situations where the law deems the freedom to engage in them more important than a party's right to intrude on them for purposes of discovery and use in litigation or arbitration. This is an area of law quite different from evidentiary rules intended to protect jurors. There is no reason why respect for privileges or the scope of privileges should be different in arbitration."

12. ROYER, *op. cit.*, fn. 4, pp. 11-12:

"En droit de la preuve, le privilège et la faculté ou, le cas échéant, l'obligation d'un témoin de ne pas divulguer en justice certaines information.... L'existence et l'étendue des communications privilégiées varient en fonction des régimes politiques et des valeurs sur lesquelles ils reposent."

13. *Ibid.*, pp. 889-890.

communication between clients and their lawyers which is deemed essential to the proper functioning of the legal system. Given the important policies in play, the rules governing privilege can be expected to vary from State to State as well as over time within a State as the public policy of its legal system evolves. Further, the law or rules governing privilege, whether contained in statutes, case law or both, can be expected to be detailed, complex and subject to exceptions.

The range of areas in which privileges have been recognized is broad, including, amongst others, the following categories: professional privileges (including attorney-client and the broad range of professional confidences recognized in civil law jurisdictions), the privilege against self-incrimination, spousal communications, clergy-penitent privilege, settlement discussions and Crown privilege.[14] These broad categories of privilege are implemented in a variety of different ways in different legal systems. The number, nature, scope and effect of evidentiary privileges as implemented may vary dramatically from country to country.[15]

2. The Public Policy Nature of Evidentiary Privileges

Evidentiary privileges are often described as important, fundamental rights. For example, in common law jurisdictions, solicitor-client or "legal privilege"[16] has been described as follows:

> "Solicitor-client privilege is part of and fundamental to the Canadian legal system. While its historical roots are a rule of evidence, it has evolved into a fundamental and substantive rule of law.
> (....)
> The importance of solicitor-client privilege to both the legal system and society as a whole assists in determining whether and in what circumstances the privilege should yield to an individual's right to make full answer and defence. The law is complex. Lawyers have a unique role. Free and candid communication between

---

14. See generally SOPINKA, LEDERMAN and BRYANT, *op. cit.*, fn. 4; ROYER, *op. cit.*, fn. 4. See also, Colin TAPPER, *Cross and Tapper on Evidence* (9th edn.) c. 10 and MOSK and GINSBERG, *op. cit.*, fn. 1. This list is by no means exhaustive. Further, various new categories of privilege may emerge such as, for example, the protection of "whistle-blowers" in the United States and elsewhere.

15. See, for example: SMIT and SHEPPARD, *op. cit.*, fn. 1, p. 12; VON SCHLABRENDORFF and SHEPARD, *op. cit.*, fn. 1; *Lex Mundi*, "In-House Council and the Attorney-Client Privilege", 2004 (updated, 15 September 2005); John FISH, "Regulated Legal Professionals and Professional Privilege Within the European Union, the European Economic Area and Switzerland and Certain Other European Jurisdictions", a report prepared for the Council of the Bars and Law Societies of the European Union (CCBE, February 2004).

16. The privilege relating to communications between a lawyer and his clients is referred to by different terms depending on the legal jurisdiction in question. These terms include attorney-client privilege, solicitor-client privilege, attorney work product privilege and solicitor's brief privilege, amongst others. For the sake of convenience we adopt the term used by von Schlabrendorff and Sheppard, "legal privileges" to refer to these and the privilege covered by the notion of *secret professionnel* in civil law insofar as it relates to communications between a lawyer and his client.

the lawyer and the client protects the legal rights of the citizen. It is essential for the lawyer to know all of the facts of the client's position. The existence of a fundamental right to privilege between the two encourages disclosure within the confines of the relationship. The danger in eroding solicitor-client privilege is the potential to stifle communication between the lawyer and the client. The need to protect the privilege determines its immunity to attack."

R. v. McClure, [2001] 1 SCR 445 (Supreme Court of Canada).[17]

"Legal professional privilege is thus more than an ordinary rule of evidence, limited in its application to the facts of a particular case. It is a fundamental condition on which the administration of justice as a whole rests."

R. v. Derby Magistrates' Court, [1995] 4 All ER 526 (House of Lords).[18]

"[The purpose of professional privilege is] to encourage full and frank communication between attorneys and their clients and thereby promote broader public interests in the observance of law and administration of justice. The privilege recognizes that sound legal advice or advocacy serves public ends and that such advice or advocacy depends upon the lawyer being fully informed by the client."

---

17. At paras. 17 and 33. In its judgment, the Supreme Court of Canada goes on as follows:

"Despite its importance, solicitor-client privilege is not absolute. It is subject to exceptions in certain circumstances. *Jones, supra,* examined whether the privilege should be displaced in the interest of protecting the safety of the public.

Just as no right is absolute so too the privilege, even that between solicitor and client, is subject to clearly defined exceptions. The decision to exclude evidence that would be both relevant and of substantial probative value because it is protected by the solicitor-client privilege represents a policy decision. It is based upon the importance to our legal system in general of the solicitor-client privilege. In certain circumstances, however, other societal values must prevail.

However, solicitor-client privilege must be as close to absolute as possible to ensure public confidence and retain relevance. As such, it will only yield in certain clearly defined circumstances, and does not involve a balancing of interests on a case-by-case basis."

18. These reasons were approved by the House of Lords in the recent decision in *Three Rivers District Council & Ors v. Governor & Company of The Bank of England (No. 10),* [2003] 3 WLR 1274 (HL). For our purposes, the opinion of Lord Scott of Foscote is of particular interest. In his opinion, at paras. 31-33, he refers to the fundamental importance of legal professional privilege in other common law jurisdictions. At para. 25 of his opinion he states that if a communication or document qualifies for legal professional privilege, the privilege is absolute and cannot be overridden by some supposedly greater public interest. In this respect, Lord Scott of Foscote disagrees with the Supreme Court of Canada and notes that it is the only other common law jurisdiction which permits the setting aside of legal professional privilege if a sufficiently compelling public interest for doing so, such as public safety, can be shown. See also the sources cited by VON SCHLABRENDORFF and SHEPPARD, *op. cit.,* fn. 1, pp. 746-748.

Upjohn Co. v. *United States* (1981), 449 US 383 (US Supreme Court).[19]

In civil law jurisdictions, where the concept of obligatory document disclosure does not exist as it does in common law jurisdictions, the notion of privilege or exemption from disclosure has developed differently. In many jurisdictions, the broad notion of *secret professionnel* protects communications between professionals, including lawyers, and their clients from disclosure and imposes an obligation of secrecy. Generally, lawyers are subject to strict obligations to preserve confidential professional information. Breach of this obligation may give rise to serious criminal penalties and/or disciplinary proceedings.[20] The importance attributed to professional confidences is reflected in the fact that these are protected explicitly in the civil and criminal laws of many civil law countries.[21] Despite these general similarities, however, the specific regime in respect of professional confidentiality and the exemption from disclosure of protected information in legal proceedings can vary substantially.

In Quebec, the concept of professional secrecy has been expressly recognized in the Charter of Human Rights and Freedoms:

> "Every person has a right to non-disclosure of confidential information.
>
> No person bound to professional secrecy by law and no priest or other minister of religion may, even in judicial proceedings, disclose confidential information revealed to him by reason of his position or profession, unless he is authorized to do so by the person who confided such information to him or by an express provision of law.
>
> The tribunal must, *ex officio*, ensure that professional secrecy is respected."[22]

---

19. This passage was quoted in the House of Lords decision in *Three Rivers District Council*. According to SMIT and SHEPPARD, *op. cit.*, fn. 1, the privilege is absolute insofar as it protects attorney-client communications from disclosure regardless of any countervailing interests in disclosure. Only limited, very specific exceptions apply. At US law, the attorney-client privilege serves two policies. In addition to the confidentiality it affords to encourage clients to make truthful and complete disclosure to their lawyers, it is also said to serve the purpose of voluntary compliance with the law by enabling a lawyer to provide frank advice about what the law requires.

20. See VON SCHLABRENDORFF and SHEPPARD, *op. cit.*, fn. 1, pp. 751-755, for the situation in Germany and France and an interesting discussion of why the question of privilege as it is known in the common law does not arise under the civil law in countries such as Germany.

21. For example, in Germany and France. See VON SCHLABRENDORFF and SHEPPARD, *op. cit.*, fn. 1, pp. 751-755; ROYER, *op. cit.*, fn. 4, pp. 893-895.

22. The French text reads as follows:

"*Chacun a droit au respect du secret professionnel.*

Toute personne tenue par la loi au secret professionnel et tout prêtre ou autre ministre du culte ne peuvent, même en justice, divulguer les renseignements confidentiels qui leur ont été révélés en raison de leur état ou profession, à moins qu'ils n'y soient autorisés par celui qui leur a fait ces confidences ou par une disposition expresse de la loi.

Le tribunal doit, d'office, assurer le respect du secret professionnel."

This obligation is also covered by a separate law, the *Code des Professions*, LRQ, c. C-26 which

Although articulated differently in its different member States (particularly between the United Kingdom and the other member States), the law of the European Union recognizes the existence of a general legal privilege between clients and independent lawyers. In *AM&S Europe Ltd. v. Commission of the European Communities*, the European Court of Justice held that although the scope and the criteria for applying it varied, a common principle existed amongst the member States with respect to the confidentiality of written communications between lawyer and client provided that such communications are made for the purposes and in the interests of the client's rights of defence and that they emanate from independent lawyers.[23] In the more recent decision in *Akzo Nobel Chemicals Ltd. and Akros Chemicals Ltd. v. Commission of the European Communities*,[24] the President of the Court of First Instance of the European Communities again recognized that the principle of confidentiality or privilege of written communications between lawyer and client is a general principle common to the EU member States. In doing so, the Court recognized the importance and complexities related to the issue of privilege raised in the case and reserved these for the court when it ruled on the merits of the main application.[25] Further, Arts. 6 and 8 of the European Convention on Human Rights have been interpreted as protecting confidential communications between lawyers and their clients.[26]

---

requires the adoption of professional codes of conduct which contain provisions to protect confidential professional information obtained in the course of rendering professional services. Since professional codes of conduct are approved by order in council or regulation, which are considered to be equivalent to "law" for the purposes of the *Charter of Human Rights and Freedoms*, the scope of application of the obligation and privilege contained in Art. 9 of the Charter is very broad. Although the scope of privilege or immunity from disclosure is narrower than the general duty of confidentiality, the potential scope of privilege remains broad and is considered as a fundamental right: see ROYER, pp. 909-911. See also *Descôteaux v. Mierzwinski*, [1982] 1 SCR 860 where the Supreme Court of Canada reviews the nature of professional secrecy and privilege at Quebec and Canadian law and concludes that the privilege attaching to confidentiality protects a fundamental right which gives rise to both a rule of evidence and a substantive rule. Court decisions from Quebec, particularly those which reach the Supreme Court of Canada, reflect an interesting blend of common and civil law elements relating to privilege.

23. 1982 E. Comm. Ct. J. Rep, 1575 (Case 115/79); [1983] 1 Q.B. 878 at pp. 949-950.

24. [2003] ECR II – 4771; available online at <http://curia.eu.int>; *Akzo Nobel Chemicals Ltd. and Akcros Chemicals Ltd. v. Commission*, Joined Cases T-125/03 R and T-253/03 R [2003] ECR II-4771; *Akzo Nobel Chemicals Ltd. and Akcros Chemicals Ltd.*, Case C-7/04 P(R) Order of the President of the European Court of Justice, 27 September 2004), available at <www.practicallaw.com> (last accessed 22 January 2006); SINDLER and WÜSTEMANN, *op. cit.*, fn. 1, pp. 628-629. The Court did not recognize the same protection or privileges in respect of communications with in-house counsel or with non-European lawyers. Von Schlabrendorff and Sheppard point out that this was despite the fact that the communications in question would likely have been held privileged in proceedings in England where the company being investigated in anti-trust proceedings was located: See VON SCHLABRENDORFF and SHEPPARD, *op. cit.*, fn. 1, pp. 755-756.

25. *Ibid.*

26. VON SCHLABRENDORFF and SHEPPARD, *op. cit.*, fn. 1, p. 755 and the sources cited there.

Certain international conventions and instruments also recognize, in general terms, certain privileges and the ability of a person to invoke them in order to refuse to provide evidence.[27]

A number of transnational initiatives have also recognized the widespread acceptance of certain privileges. These include the IBA Rules on the Taking of Evidence in International Commercial Arbitration (the IBA Rules) and the Principles of Transnational Civil Procedure, adopted by the American Law Institute and UNIDROIT.[28] Further, the rules of certain arbitral institutions make specific reference to privilege.[29]

Most commentators on the question of privilege in international arbitration have noted the importance accorded to the notion of privilege or professional confidentiality in those systems which recognize these principles and note the breadth of their general acceptance despite variations in their articulation and implementation at a detailed level.[30] This has led certain authors to suggest that evidentiary privileges are of an international public policy nature and that they may, in fact, constitute transnational public policy.[31]

---

27. See VON SCHLABRENDORFF and SHEPPARD, *op. cit.*, fn. 1, p. 762, where they refer to the 1970 Hague Convention on the Taking of Evidence Abroad in Civil and Commercial Matters whose Art. 11 permits a person to refuse to give evidence to the extent he has a privilege or duty to refuse to give evidence in response to a Letter of Request under either the law of the State of execution or the State of origin. The authors also refer to the 1975 Inter-American Convention on the Taking of Evidence Abroad, Art. 12, and EC Regulation 1206/2001. See also MOSK and GINSBERG, *op. cit.*, fn. 1, who note that national laws relevant to international civil and criminal litigation often reflect the same approach as the Hague Convention: a witness from whom evidence is sought may invoke a wide range of privileges available in either relevant State. The authors note that the approach of the courts dealing with requests for the taking of evidence differs in that some courts are required to defer to applicable foreign privilege while others are not.

28. The IBA Rules on the Taking of Evidence in International Commercial Arbitration are available at <www.ibanet.org> and the Principles of Transnational Procedure are available at <www.unidroit.org/english/principles/civilprocedure/ali-unidroitprinciples-e.pdf>. The relevant portions of these are noted below.
    See also the further comments of VON SCHLABRENDORFF and SHEPPARD, *op. cit.*, fn. 1, pp. 760-761, in respect of the Principles of Transnational Civil Procedure.

29. See the AAA International Arbitration Rules, Art. 20.6; the Rules of the Commercial Arbitration and Mediation Centre for the Americas (CAMCA), Art. 22(6); the International Institute for Conflict Prevention and Resolution Rules for Non-Administered Arbitration, Rule 12.2; the Zurich Rules of Arbitration, Art. 38. We return to these and the transnational solutions referred to above later.

30. See, for example, the sources cited at fn. 1.

31. See MOSK and GINSBERG, *op. cit.*, fn. 1, pp. 380-381. However, beyond a general recognition of some form of privilege or confidentiality in respect of certain communications, particularly those between a lawyer and his clients, it is hard to identify with any precision what the rule or principle of transnational public policy is. While there does not yet appear to be a comprehensive survey of the treatment of evidentiary privileges on a broad comparative basis, those studies which do exist reveal a great variation in the articulation and implementation of evidentiary privileges, their application, exceptions and waiver. For example, a review of the *Lex Mundi* Multi-Jurisdictional Survey, *op. cit.*, fn. 15, reveals that the notion of legal privilege is not a well-

3. The Diversity of National Rules Governing Evidentiary Privileges

As indicated previously, the range of evidentiary privileges recognized in different legal systems is broad and includes many different categories which are implemented in a variety of different methods. These include statutory provisions,[32] case law and codes of professional conduct.[33] Further, the categories of evidentiary privileges are not fixed or closed. For example, in Canada the Supreme Court has specifically recognized that the common law permits the development of new categories of privilege and the application of privilege in new situations where reason, experience and application of the principles that underlie the traditionally recognized privileges so dictate.[34]

Despite general similarities of approach between legal systems, such as the common and civil laws, detailed examination of national laws and rules reveals significant differences between often complex, detailed rules and their application. The same is true between national laws within the same general legal system.[35] This situation should

---

established principle in jurisdictions such as the People's Republic of China and Taiwan and a number of developing States, whereas it is highly developed and detailed in a number of common law jurisdictions and many civil law jurisdictions.

32. These statutes can vary broadly in nature from,e.g., the Quebec Charter of Human Rights and Freedoms, quoted above, to provisions of national civil codes or civil procedure codes and specific statutes on evidence which, in common-law jurisdictions, supplement the case law on privileges.

33. These may be adopted pursuant to an international instrument such as European Directive 98/5EC of 16 February 1998 or pursuant to national laws such as the Quebec *Code Des Professions*, LRQ, c. C-26, referred to above. These codes of conduct may also be multi-national in nature, such as the Code of Conduct for Lawyers in the European Union (hereinafter the CCBE Code). Further, as discussed below, the codes of professional conduct or ethics of bar associations may be considered and enforced by the courts in certain areas such as legal privilege.

34. *M(A) v. Ryan*, [1997] 1 SCR 157 as quoted in SOPINKA, LEDERMAN and BRYANT, *op. cit.*, fn. 4, p. 724. For example, a form of statutory privilege for counsellors of sexual assault victims has been developed in a number of jurisdictions, including California and Canada. See also MOSK and GINSBERG, *op. cit.*, fn. 1, pp. 349-367. On the other hand, governmental attempts to address terrorism, money laundering and corruption have led to legislation in a number of countries which have restricted, with varying degrees of success, certain aspects of traditionally recognized privileges.

35. For example, the common law approach reflects an adversarial system with non-voluntary disclosure requirements which are tempered by privilege, which includes legal advice and documents prepared in the context of litigation and attorney work product. In civil law jurisdictions, on the other hand, there is generally no non-voluntary disclosure in civil proceedings, and as a result, questions of privilege do not arise in the same manner. Rather, the approach is a more general one of confidentiality or professional secrecy. See VON SCHLABRENDORFF and SHEPPARD, *op. cit.*, fn. 1, pp. 745-746. While with respect to certain documents and information immunity from disclosure may be common to both systems (for example, communications with and documents of external lawyers), others may not (for example, communication with, and documents of, in-house counsel are protected in common law jurisdictions, but not, generally speaking, in civil law jurisdictions). Where similarity does exist between the two legal systems, the applicable principles and rules may vary significantly and their application in specific cases may yield very different results. The same is true with respect to national laws within the common and civil law systems. Most commentators on the topic of privilege offer a variety of examples of such differences. See, for example, VON

come as no surprise given the important public policy goals evidentiary privileges reflect.

Given the diversity of national rules on privileges, conflicts between potentially applicable rules in an international arbitration are easy to imagine. Among examples used by recent commentators are the following:

- In an arbitration based in Switzerland, a US multinational company pursues a claim against a German multinational company for breach of an agreement governed by English law. Each requests production of documents. Among the documents requested are communications between management and in-house counsel and reports prepared by an outside consulting firm and taxation advice prepared by the company's accountants. Also included in the requests are notes prepared by employees of the company to external lawyers for advice on the transaction with the other party.[36]

- In an arbitration an English party asks the managing director of the opposing party about the advice he received from his German lawyers concerning the matter in dispute.

- In an arbitration a US party is asked to disclose all communications with its in-house lawyers based in France concerning the matter in dispute.[37]

- A French company and an English company are involved in an ICC arbitration with its seat in Paris, concerning the English company's shares in the Argentine subsidiary of the French company. The contract in dispute is governed by New York law. The tribunal orders limited document discovery concerning the reasons for which the Argentine company launched a particular product at a particular time. The English company then demands production of documents reflecting the advice from the French company's general counsel and the French and Argentine company's outside counsel to the president of the Argentine company on the decision to launch the product in dispute. The English company argues that general counsel's advice is not privileged under French law and that advice received from outside counsel is not privileged, as far as a shareholder is concerned, under New York law.

  The Argentine company counters that an order applying French law to the question of privilege and requiring it to produce the French general counsel's documents would violate the principle that parties must be treated fairly and equally since the tribunal had already agreed to apply English law to the question of privilege in respect of the English company's general counsel and excluded certain documents on that basis.

SCHLABRENDORFF and SHEPPARD, *ibid.*, pp. 746-755; SINDLER and WÜSTEMANN, *op. cit.*, fn. 1, pp. 614-618 and the other sources cited at fn. 1.

36. See SINDLER and WÜSTEMANN, *op. cit.*, fn. 1, p. 618.

37. See VON SCHLABRENDORFF and SHEPPARD, *op. cit.*, fn. 1, p. 757.

In respect of the advice of outside counsel, the French company argues that the notion that shareholders are entitled to disregard privilege in disputes with the companies they hold as shareholders is a procedural rule which could not have been imported with a choice of law in the contract. Rather, French law, the procedural law of the place of arbitration, governs and the documents are privileged.

At the same time, the English company claims privilege over critical documents reflecting the notes of its own general counsel, a qualified New York lawyer, taken during a meeting with the French company. The French company argues that at English law, notes taken at a meeting between multiple parties are not privileged. The English company argues that the notes, taken in New York by a New York lawyer, are subject to New York law and covered by privilege.[38]

These types of scenarios are not unusual in international commercial arbitration. One might also consider other scenarios which arise relatively frequently in large infrastructure projects, where one or both of the parties involved is a consortium composed of various members from different countries. These projects also often involve the performance of certain parts of the project, such as engineering and design, in one country, procurement of materials and equipment from a variety of countries and performance in yet another country. Legal advice in respect of these different aspects of the project may be sought from and provided in different countries by lawyers (including in-house counsel) qualified in different jurisdictions. The potential for the application of different privilege rules and the dilemma of identifying the appropriate criterion for choosing between competing rules is apparent in these and the other scenarios referred to above.

These issues may arise with respect to the full range of evidentiary privileges briefly described above. However, the most likely privileges or aspects of confidentiality to

---

38. See Alexander A. YANOS, "Problems Arising From the Interplay of Common Law and Civil Law in International Arbitration: Defining the Scope of the Attorney-Client Privilege" (2006), 3 Transnational Dispute Management (April 2006, Issue 2) (available at <http://transnational-dispute-management.com). This scenario is quoted only in part and has been slightly modified for present purposes. One of the interesting aspects of this example is that privilege in respect of in-house counsel could fall to be determined under the laws of England, the United States, Argentina or France. While communications with in-house counsel may be privileged in the first three laws, privilege is not available under French law. In English and US law, in which there are broad, non-voluntary discovery requirements, relatively broad legal privilege, which belongs to the client, is available. In Argentine and French law where document discovery is narrow and may be obtained only through the court, the scope of privilege or immunity from disclosure is narrower than in the United States and England. In both Argentina and France the principle of professional secrecy or privilege is a professional and ethical obligation of the lawyer and its breach is subject to criminal sanctions. Further, the privilege cannot be waived by the client. In France the privilege applies to members of the bar (*avocats*) only. In Argentina, privilege is available with respect to communications with in-house counsel.

arise in an international arbitration are legal privilege,[39] settlement privilege,[40] business or trade secrets privilege[41] and crown privilege or state secrecy.[42] For present purposes, we will focus on legal privilege, which has attracted the most attention to date, as an example of the issues that the broad category of evidentiary privileges may raise in international arbitration.

The great diversity of national rules (including the lack of any rules) on legal privilege presents the possibility of unequal and unfair treatment of the parties in an arbitration, depending on how the arbitral tribunal identifies and applies the applicable rule or rules. For example, a decision by an arbitral tribunal to apply the rules of the place where a document was created may result in the granting or denying of privilege, and hence immunity or protection from disclosure, on the formal grounds of the location of the lawyer giving the legal advice. As a result, privilege could be granted to the confidential

---

39. As defined above at fn. 16. This relates to communications made between a legal advisor and his client for the purpose of obtaining or giving legal advice and in relation to contemplated or existing litigation. For our purposes, this includes communications with in-house counsel.

40. This relates to information and documents prepared for settlement negotiations between the parties and the discussion or negotiations, including settlement offers, between the parties. See on this topic Jason A. FRY "Without Prejudice and Confidential Communications in International Arbitration: When Does Procedural Flexibility Erode Public Policy?", Int'l A. L. R. (1998) p. 209. It has been suggested that this form of privilege constitutes a transnational principle of privilege: BERGER, op. cit., fn. 1, pp. 13-14. While there does appear to be fairly broad recognition of the public policy basis for encouraging settlement of disputes and, therefore shielding offers of settlement and settlement negotiations between the parties from production in evidence, the nature and scope of the exclusion varies. For example, such materials may be discoverable, depending on the circumstances, if they are relevant to the subject matter in dispute and will lead to the discovery of admissible evidence or are relevant to the settling parties' interest or prejudice or will be used for impeachment purposes in certain US jurisdictions. Further, there are a number of competing theories as to the basis for the exclusion of settlement negotiations including that these may be unreliable or irrelevant. See SOPINKA, LEDERMAN and BRYANT, op. cit., fn. 4, pp. 808-809 quoting from *Wigmore on Evidence*. Certainly, information or documents emanating from settlement negotiations are irrelevant to the issues to be determined by the arbitral tribunal and are often tendered for collateral purposes.

41. This is often referred to as a commercial confidentiality and is usually addressed by imposing certain conditions on how the information is handled and who has access to it. Usually it does not have the effect of completely excluding the protected information from evidence.

42. This is a complex form of privilege or immunity which may have many sources and vary significantly from State to State. See, for example, SOPINKA, LEDERMAN and BRYANT, op. cit., fn. 4, c. 15; MOSK and GINSBERG, op. cit., fn. 1, pp. 363-367. For an interesting decision on an aspect of crown privilege in the context of an investor-State arbitration, see the decision of the tribunal in *Pope & Talbot Inc. and the Government of Canada* dated 6 September 2000 and Procedural Order no. 10 in *S.D. Myers Inc. and the Government of Canada*, both rendered in arbitrations pursuant to Chapter 11 of the NAFTA and available at <www.dfait-maeci.gc.ca/tna-nac/dsp/sdm_archive-en.asp> and <www.dfait-maeci.gc.ca/tna-nac/dsp/pope_archive-en.asp>. See also Procedural Order No. 2 of the tribunal in *Biwater Gauff (Tanzania) Ltd. v. United Republic in Tanzania*, ICSID Case No. ARB/05/22, available at: <http://ita.law.uvic.ca>. The Tribunal in that case distinguishes between the general notion of "public interest immunity" at Tanzanian law and privilege. In its analysis, the tribunal notes the importance of equal treatment of the parties.

documents of one party, but not the other, depending on the applicable rules of the place where the advice was given. Alternatively, although some degree of privilege may be available pursuant to the rules applicable where each of the parties received the legal advice, the scope of protection might well be different. For example, rules in different countries vary on who holds the privilege (the lawyer or the client), how privilege must be invoked and how it may be lost by a waiver. The same types of considerations will apply if the tribunal decides to apply the rules of the country in which the lawyer giving the advice is qualified.

Perhaps the most striking example is that of in-house counsel who fall within the scope of legal practitioners for the purpose of legal privilege in most common law jurisdictions, but not in many civil law countries.[43] If the arbitral tribunal chooses a third or "neutral" law to govern the question of privilege, it runs the risk of failing to consider or apply rules which may be considered of a public policy nature. This may give rise to a challenge to the award or resistance to its enforcement depending on the place of arbitration or of enforcement of the award. This may be on the basis of an alleged failure to treat the parties fairly and equally and, hence a breach of due process, generally regarded as an element of international procedural public policy, or more broadly on the basis of failure to apply a rule of public policy. Further, the material law and ethical obligations applicable to counsel in their home jurisdictions will normally continue to apply in international arbitrations wherever these may take place. These rules, which may include criminal or regulatory sanctions, may well affect counsel's conduct of a case as well as her ability to comply with procedural orders of the tribunal. We return to these questions below in IV. In any event, failure to treat the parties equally and fairly will likely be seen, at a minimum, as arbitrary by one of the parties and result in disruption and loss of confidence in the process.

III. CHOICE OF LAW ISSUES

Although arbitrators are generally considered to be dispensed from applying national rules of evidence or civil procedure, it appears broadly accepted that parties do not automatically waive their right to invoke evidentiary privileges when they choose to arbitrate.[44] As discussed below, most commentators agree that, for a variety of reasons, claims of privileges must be considered and, in appropriate cases, a degree of protection or immunity from disclosure must be afforded. The primary reason for this appears to be the increasing recognition that rules of privilege are more than merely procedural in nature and, in fact, are substantive rules which reflect public policy. The difficulty is

---

43. See, amongst other sources: VON SCHLABRENDORFF and SHEPPARD, *op. cit.*, fn. 1; BERGER, *op. cit.*, fn. 1, pp. 4-5; William W. PARK, "Procedural Evolution in Business Arbitration: Three Studies in Change" (reprinted from William W. PARK, *Arbitration of International Business Disputes: Studies in Law and Practice* (Oxford University Press 2006) pp. 59-60. See also the sources set out in the Selected Bibliography (this volume, pp. 699-704) on this widely commented and difficult issue.

44. SINDLER and WÜSTEMANN, *op. cit.*, fn. 1; GALLAGHER, *op. cit.*, fn. 1, p. 45; RUBINSTEIN and GUERRINA, *op. cit.*, fn. 1, pp. 593-595.

determining which rules should apply in international arbitrations where there is no automatically applicable lex fori and the nature of the transactions involved usually gives rise to a number of potentially applicable rules.

The question of the law applicable to the administration of evidence is notoriously complex and difficult in private international law.[45] The question is even more difficult in international arbitration where very little, if any, guidance is given although a growing number of sources refer to the need to consider and apply applicable legal or ethical rules governing privilege. The primary sources which address the question of privilege in international arbitration in this regard are set out below.

1. National Laws

Most modern arbitration laws on international arbitration provide broad discretion to the arbitral tribunal in the taking and assessment of evidence, subject to a general duty to give the parties at least a reasonable opportunity of presenting their cases and to treat them fairly. While national laws usually contain general choice of law provisions with respect to the merits of the dispute, they do not address the question of applicable procedural law nor the law applicable to evidentiary privileges. However, a number of laws specifically empower the arbitral tribunal in their discretion to determine the admissibility and assessment of evidence. The specific adoption of such a rule suggests that the arbitral tribunal is empowered to exercise its discretion independently and to apply a law different than the law applicable to the contract or the merits of the dispute.[46] As a result, national arbitration laws provide little, if any, guidance on the issue of the law applicable to evidentiary privileges that might be raised in the course of an international arbitration.

Further, there is relatively little guidance to be obtained from national laws on the question of the law applicable to evidentiary privileges in civil proceedings more generally.[47] This is a complex question, subject to considerable uncertainty and exceptions, which has received a variety of different solutions in conflict of laws analysis in different countries.[48] For example, in Belgium it appears that obligations of professional secrecy or privilege attract the application of the law of the place where the professional who enjoys the privileges practices.[49] This situation may be contrasted with that in England where an English court has held that the lex fori governs the question of the admissibility of a document over which privilege has been claimed. In the United States, it appears that in international cases courts will generally apply the standard of

---

45. POUDRET and BESSON, *op. cit.*, fn. 2, p. 581 and the sources cited there.

46. For example, Art. 19(2) of the UNCITRAL Model Law, and other laws such as the England Arbitration Act 1996, Sect. 34(2)(f) which is even more detailed, specifically empower the arbitral tribunal in this regard. This provision and the power it confers appear to be separate and independent from Art. 28 of the Model Law which deals with the law applicable to the merits of the dispute. This raises interesting questions in view of the mixed procedural and substantive nature of rules of privilege.

47. SMIT and SHEPPARD, *op. cit.*, fn. 1, p. 12.

48. SMIT and SHEPPARD, *op. cit.*, fn. 1.

49. See the commentary by P. HOLLANDER in SMIT and SHEPPARD, *op. cit.*, fn. 1, p. 14.

the "most significant context/relationship" but will also consider factors such as comity, the interest of foreign States in the United States, contacts between the communication or document in question and the United States, and other factors.[50]

2. *Arbitral Rules*

Arbitral rules generally provide that in the absence of a contrary agreement of the parties the arbitral tribunal has broad discretion over the admissibility and assessment of evidence and over the conduct of the procedure more generally. Very few rules deal specifically with the question of evidentiary privileges. Those few sets of rules which do address privileges require the arbitral tribunal to take into account, and in one case apply, applicable principles of legal privileges.

American Arbitration Association International Arbitration Rules provide:

> *"Article 20(6)*
> The Tribunal shall determine the admissibility, relevance, materiality and weight of the evidence offered by any party. The Tribunal shall take into account applicable principles of legal privilege, such as those involving the confidentiality of communications between a lawyer and client."[51]

The Commercial Arbitration Mediation Center for the Americas Arbitration Rules provide:

---

50. SMIT and SHEPPARD, *op. cit.*, fn. 1, pp. 24-26. SMIT notes that the two most widely cited US Restatements of the Law that deal with choice of law with respect to privileges adopt different approaches. See the discussion at p. 25 on this point as well as the discussion of American case law indicating that US courts have confirmed that privileges apply in arbitration. This appears to have led to the more specific treatment of privilege in the International Arbitration Rules of the American Arbitration Association and the CPR Rules for Non-Administered Arbitration of International Disputes. The situation is similarly complex in Canadian law. In Canadian common law jurisdictions, the existence and scope of a privilege are generally governed by the lex fori, the law of the place where the trial or inquiry takes place. However, this may be subject to exceptions. In Quebec, evidence is governed by the law applicable to the merits of the dispute, subject to the application of rules more favourable to the establishment or administration of evidence. With respect to privilege arising in international cases, a Quebec court is likely to apply the local lex fori when an objection is based on a privilege existing outside Quebec, but not recognized in Quebec law. Generally, Quebec law favours the application of the law most favourable to the admission of evidence. However, Art. 3079 of the Quebec Civil Code permits the application of the mandatory provision of foreign law where legitimate and manifestly preponderant interests so require. This provision has been interpreted restrictively where its effect would be to limit the admissibility of evidence. See ROYER, *op. cit.*, fn. 4, no. 1044 and the interesting decision in *Banque Paribas (Suisse) S.A. c. Wightman*, J.E. 97 – 3006 (CA) in which the application of Swiss law on banking secrecy was rejected.
51. Amended and effective 1 July 2003. The same provision is contained in the Commercial Arbitration Rules of the American Arbitration Association, amended and effective 1 July 2003, Art. R-31(c).

"Article 22(6)
The admissibility, relevance, materiality and weight of the evidence offered by any party shall be determined by the Tribunal, provided that the Tribunal shall consider applicable principles of legal privileges."[52]

The International Institute for Conflict Prevention and Resolution, International Rules for Non-administered Arbitration state:

"Rule 12.2.
If either party so requests or the Tribunal so directs, a hearing shall be held for the presentation of evidence and oral argument. Testimony may be presented in written and/or oral form as a Tribunal may determine is appropriate. The Tribunal is not required to apply the rules of evidence used in judicial proceedings. The Tribunal shall determine the applicability of any privilege or immunity and the admissibility, relevance, materiality and weight of the evidence offered."[53]

Evidentiary privileges do not appear to be specifically addressed in other current institutional rules.[54]

Two international instruments of a private nature have also addressed the question of evidentiary privileges. The IBA Rules provide that an arbitral tribunal may exclude

---

52. Effective 15 March 1996.
53. Revised and Effective 15 June 2005. The commentary on Rule 12 provides, in relevant part, as follows:

"The Tribunal need not apply rules of evidence used in judicial proceedings. Rule 12.2 provides that the Tribunal shall determine the applicability of any privilege or immunity. That protection is intended to apply to pre-hearing disclosure as well as to evidence at the hearings."

The CPR's Rules for Non-Administered Arbitration (also revised and effective 15 June 2005) provide in relevant part as follows:

"12.2 .... The Tribunal is not required to apply the rules of evidence used in judicial proceedings, *provided, however, that the Tribunal shall apply the lawyer-client privilege and the work product immunity.* The Tribunal shall determine the applicability of any privilege or immunity and the admissibility, relevance, materiality and weight of the evidence offered." [emphasis added]

Rule 1.1 and the General Commentary on these rules indicate that they apply unless the parties specifically agree to the application of the International Rules. As a result, although the rule contained in Rule 12.2 of these rules appears to address internal or domestic arbitrations, it could apply in international arbitrations where the parties choose the CPR Rules for Non-Administered Arbitration but do not specify the International Rules.
54. Art. 38 of the International Arbitration Rules of the Zurich Chamber of Commerce (adopted in 1989) provided that a witness could refuse to testify against himself or if his testimony would infringe official or professional secrecy protected by criminal law. However, that rule has now been superseded by the new Swiss Rules of International Arbitration. See BERGER, *op. cit.*, fn. 1, p. 6.

from evidence or production or inspection material subject to privilege. Art. 9(2) provides in relevant part as follows:

> "*Article 9 — Admissibility and Assessment of Evidence.*
> (....)
> (2) The Arbitral Tribunal shall, at the request of a party or on its own motion, exclude from evidence or production any document, statement, oral testimony or inspection for any of the following reasons:
> (a) lack of sufficient relevance or materiality;
> (b) legal impediment or privilege under the legal or ethical rules determined by the arbitral tribunal to be applicable...
>
> (f) grounds of special political or institutional sensitivity (including evidence that has been classified as secret by a government or public international institution) and that the Arbitral Tribunal determines to be compelling; or
> (g) considerations of fairness or equality of the parties that the arbitral tribunal determines to be compelling."

The commentary to the IBA Rules indicates that the Working Party saw that the potential application of privileges was important, but that it had not addressed the question of the appropriate applicable law.[55] Interestingly, the commentary to the IBA Rules links the question of privilege and considerations of fairness or equality in its comments on Art. 9(2)(g) of the rules:

> "[D]ocuments that might be considered to be privileged within one national legal system may not be considered to be privileged within another. If the situation were to create an unfairness, the arbitral tribunal may exclude production of the technically non-privileged documents pursuant to this provision."[56]

---

55. See the Commentary to the IBA Rules on the taking of the evidence, [2000] Business Law International, 14 and 33, and the Comments of VON SCHLABRENDORFF and SHEPPARD, *op. cit.*, fn. 1, pp. 759-760.

56. [2000] Business Law International 14 at p. 34 and VON SCHLABRENDORFF and SHEPPARD, *op. cit.*, fn. 1, pp. 759-760, where they conclude that while the IBA Working Group considered that legal privileges should be recognized in international arbitration, some re-adjustment may be necessary to ensure "equality of arms" or equal treatment of the parties. See also Hilmar RAESCHKE-KESSLER, "The Production of Documents in International Arbitration – A Commentary on Article 3 of the New IBA Rules of Evidence", 18 Arbitration International (2002) p. 411 at pp. 428-429, who uses the example of in-house counsel to illustrate the inequality or unfairness which may arise from differences in rules on privilege. In comparing US and German Rules, the author states as follows:

"If the Arbitral Tribunal were to issue an order against the German party to produce documents prepared by its in-house counsel, while refusing a similar order against the American party based on the objection of an existing legal privilege, this would result in a considerable imbalance regarding the rights of each party to request the production of internal documents. It is the sole purpose of Art. 9, Sect. 2(g) to eliminate this imbalance.

The principles of Transnational Civil Procedure prepared by the American Law Institute (ALI) and the International Institute for the Unification of Private Law (UNIDROIT) deal with the question of evidentiary privileges and immunities in somewhat more detail.[57] The ALI-UNIDROIT Principles provide, in relevant part, as follows:

> "*16. Access to Information and Evidence*
> 16.1 Generally the court and each party should have access to relevant and non-privileged evidence, including testimony of parties and witnesses, expert testimony, documents, and evidence derived from inspection of things, entry upon land, or, under appropriate circumstances, from physical or mental examination of a person. The parties should have the right to submit statements that are accorded evidentiary effect.
>
> (....)
> *18. Evidentiary Privileges and Immunities*
> 18.1 Effect should be given to privileges, immunities, and similar protections of a party or non-party concerning disclosure of evidence or other information."[58]

One party will only be able to ask for the production of internal documents of the other party as far as itself is required to produce documents of the same type, when referring to Art. 9, Sect. 2(b) for its own protection. Art. 9, Sect. 2(g) suggests especially to parties from a civil law background that they should – for their own protection – be informed about the extent of the legal privilege of the American side well in advance, in order to be able to use the objection in Art. 9, Sect. 2(g) effectively."

57. See, the ALI-UNIDROIT Principles of Transnational Civil Procedure, adopted by the ALI in May 2004 and UNIDROIT in April, 2004, [2004] Uniform Law Review p. 758. Although they address civil procedure, the Principles state that they are equally applicable to international arbitration, except to the extent of being incompatible with arbitration proceedings. In this regard, the Principles give as examples the principles related to jurisdiction, publicity of proceedings and appeal.
58. Available at <www.unidroit.org/english/principles/civilprocedure/ali-unidroitprinciples-e.pdf>. The commentary on these articles provides, in part, as follows:

"P-18A All legal systems recognize various privileges and immunities against being compelled to give evidence, such as protection from self-incrimination, confidentiality of professional communication, rights of privacy, and privileges of a spouse or family member. Privileges protect important interests, but they can impair establishment of the facts. The conceptual and technical bases of these protections differ from one system to another, as do the legal consequences of giving them recognition. In applying such rules choice-of-law problems may be presented.
P-18B The weight accorded to various privileges differs from one legal system to another and the significance of the claim of privilege may vary according to the context in specific litigation. These factors are relevant when the court considers drawing adverse inferences from the party's failure to produce evidence.
P-18C Principles 18.2 and 18.3 reflect a distinction between direct and indirect sanctions. Direct sanctions include fines, *astreintes*, contempt of court, or imprisonment. Indirect sanctions include

3.   International Conventions and Instruments

At least two international conventions specifically deal with the question of privilege. The 1970 Hague Convention on the Taking of Evidence Abroad in Civil and Commercial Matters deals with privilege in the context of letters of request. Art. 11 of that Convention provides, in relevant part, as follows:

"In the execution of a Letter of Request the person concerned may refuse to give evidence in so far as he has a privilege or duty to refuse to give the evidence

(a) under the law of the State of execution; or
(b) under the law of the State of origin, and a privilege or duty has been specified in the Letter, or, at the instance of the requested authority, has been otherwise confirmed to that authority by the requesting authority.

A Contracting State may declare that, in addition, it will respect privileges and duties existing under the law of States other than the State of origin and the State of execution, to the extent specified in that declaration."

The Inter American Convention on the Taking of Evidence Abroad contains similar provisions:

"*Article 12*
A person called to give evidence in the State of destination pursuant to a letter rogatory may refuse to do so when he invokes impediment, exception or duty to refuse to testify:

(a) under the law of the State of destination; or
(b) under the law of the State of origin, if the invoked impediment exception or duty to refuse has been specified in the letter rogatory or has been confirmed by the requesting authority at the instance of the court of destination."

---

drawing adverse inferences, judgment by default, and dismissal of claims or defences. A court has discretionary authority to impose indirect sanctions on a party claiming a privilege, but a court ordinarily should not impose direct sanctions on a party or nonparty who refuses to disclose information protected by a privilege. A similar balancing approach may apply when blocking statutes hinder full cooperation by a party or nonparty.

P-18D In some systems, the court cannot recognize the privilege sua sponte but may only respond to the initiative of a party benefited by the privilege. The court should give effect to any procedural requirement of the forum that an evidentiary privilege or immunity be expressly claimed. According to such requirements, a privilege or immunity not properly claimed in a timely manner may be considered waived."

See also the further comments of VON SCHLABRENDORFF and SHEPPARD, *op. cit.*, fn. 1, pp. 760-761 in respect of the Principles of Transnational Civil Procedure.

EC Regulation 1206/2001 contains a similar provision:

> "*Article 14. Refusal to execute*
> 1. A request for the hearing of a person shall not be executed when the person concerned claims the right to refuse to give evidence or to be prohibited from giving evidence,
>
> (a) under the law of the Member State of the requested court; or
> (b) under the law of the Member State of the requesting court, and such right has been specified in the request, or, if need be, at the instance of the requested court, has been confirmed by the requesting court."

References to protection of privileges may also be found in international instruments such as the Rome Statute of the International Criminal Court.[59]

These international instruments recognize evidentiary privileges in certain circumstances and permit persons to take advantage of the best available privileges.[60] However, they give little indication of how to determine the applicable law in the case of a conflict of privileges, particularly in an international arbitration.

4.   How Should an Arbitral Tribunal Determine the Applicable Law?

Given that national laws, institutional rules and international instruments all give the arbitral tribunal broad discretion and little guidance on how to determine the law applicable to privileges, how should an arbitral tribunal determine the applicable law? In situations where the parties have failed to make a specific agreement with respect to applicable law and the tribunal is left to determine which law should apply, a tribunal usually commences the analysis with the goal of identifying the intention of the parties. This may be difficult where the parties have not addressed the specific question of the applicable rules of privilege and each have their own, different, legitimate expectations based on their national laws and practice.

Unlike a State court faced with the same question in an international litigation scenario, the tribunal has no automatically applicable *lex fori*. While it is accepted that privileges may be of a public policy nature, the tribunal does not have the mandate to uphold any one State's public policy. The tribunal's mandate does, however, include the duty to render an award that is likely to be enforced and it is this goal, together with the requirement to treat the parties fairly, that leads tribunals to engage in a considered analysis of the relevant factors when faced with this question. Like other choice of law questions, the analysis begins with the question of whether privileges are procedural or substantive in nature. This question has been commonly answered by stating that privileges have both procedural and substantive characteristics. This revelation then

---

59. See Art. 69(5) and the reference in MOSK and GINSBERG, *op. cit.*, fn. 1, p. 379.
60. See VON SCHLABRENDORFF and SHEPPARD, *op. cit.*, fn. 1, p. 762, who refer to this approach as the "most favourable privilege approach".

leads the tribunal to a number of possible approaches, each of which seeks to determine the law with the "closest connection" with the problem at hand.

When a national law applies, questions of procedure in international arbitration are usually determined through resort to the law of the place of arbitration or the *lex arbitri*. Thus, a determination that privileges are procedural in nature leads to the conclusion that the tribunal only needs to grant the privileges if the parties have agreed to the application of a particular procedural law or if the procedural law of the forum requires their application in arbitration.[61] Because privileges relate to the taking of evidence, they have a procedural element to them. In most civil law jurisdictions, the notion of *secret professionnel* is founded in professional ethics and carries sanctions for breach in the criminal law.[62] Privileges, in these systems, are likely to be considered to be a matter of procedure.[63]

Issues of substantive law in international arbitration are resolved through the application of the law of the contract, which is usually agreed by the parties or in the absence of such agreement, determined by the tribunal. Therefore, the classification of privileges as substantive in nature requires the tribunal to apply the law of the contract to determine the relevant rules to the assertion of privileges.[64] In common law jurisdictions, courts have classified privileges as substantive in nature.[65] If privileges are considered to be substantive, the usual result of the application of the law of the contract results in a search for the law with the closest connection to the evidence at issue. However, as noted previously, many laws specifically provide that the arbitral tribunal has the discretion to determine evidentiary questions in its discretion, suggesting that the tribunal may apply a different law or exercise its discretion independently.

In reality, privileges are both procedural and substantive in nature.[66]

In addition to the obvious choices of the *lex arbitri* or the law governing the agreement or merits of the dispute, some commentators have suggested that certain privileges might be seen to be general principles of international law.[67]

In the absence of a specific agreement between the parties as to which law will apply to privileges, it is questionable whether parties – by having selected a place of arbitration or a law to govern their contract – can be seen to have intended those laws to apply to privileges.[68] Privileges are seen to have a much more personal nature, that is related to the parties or their counsel, than other questions of procedural or substantive law.

---

61. MOSK and GINSBERG, *op. cit.*, fn. 1, pp. 376-377.
62. SINDLER and WÜSTEMANN, *op. cit.*, fn. 1, pp. 615-616.
63. SINDLER and WÜSTEMANN, *ibid.*, fn. 1, pp. 615-616; MOSK and GINSBERG, *op. cit.*, fn. 1, p. 368.
64. MOSK and GINSBERG, *op. cit.*, fn. 1, p. 377.
65. SINDLER and WÜSTEMANN, *op. cit.*, fn. 1, p. 616; MOSK and GINSBERG, *op. cit.*, fn. 1, p. 368.
66. VON SCHLABRENDORFF and SHEPPARD, *op. cit.*, fn. 1, p. 764.
67. MOSK and GINSBERG, *op. cit.*, fn. 1, pp. 378-379; Gabrielle KAUFMANN-KOHLER and Philippe BÄRTSCH, "Discovery in International Arbitration: How Much is Too Much?", SchiedsVZ (2004, no. 1) p. 19.
68. VON SCHLABRENDORFF and SHEPPARD, *op. cit.*, fn. 1, p. 770; BERGER, *op. cit.*, fn. 1, p. 11.

Recognizing this, commentators have suggested a number of alternative methods for determining which law should apply to privileges, which are all potentially available given the discretion afforded arbitrators with respect to these questions. One option is for the tribunal to choose the one law that has the closest connection to the evidence or privilege in issue and some have argued that this is the correct approach.[69] It is said that this approach is most likely to give effect to the legitimate expectations of the parties.[70] However, this approach also has disadvantages, including the fact that it could result in multiple laws applying to resolve the issue of privileges within one arbitration and the possibility of unfair treatment of the parties if one party's evidence is most closely connected to a law that is less protective than the law most closely connected to the other party's evidence.

It has been argued that the "closest connection" or "centre of gravity" test has developed into a transnational rule of conflict of laws, which must be applied to evidentiary privileges in international arbitration.[71] While some commentators would like to see a predictable rule emerge, for example the law of the place where the solicitor-client relationship has its predominant effects[72] or the law of the place where the solicitor has her professional domicile,[73] most commentators advocate some form of cumulative approach, where a number of different possible applicable laws are examined to determine whether the particular privilege claimed is recognized under each law.[74] The solution is relatively straightforward if all of the possible applicable laws would recognize the privilege claimed.[75] The practical question then becomes one of whether the particular evidence sought to be protected actually falls within the claimed privilege.[76] The situation is less clear if the cumulative analysis results in the determination that the privilege is recognized by some systems and not others. If the possible applicable laws are in conflict, the tribunal must choose the law that will apply.

Under a cumulative analysis, many laws (in addition to the law of the place of arbitration and the law that applies to the merits of the dispute) may be reviewed to determine the result of their application. These include: the law of the place where a document or witness is located; the law of the place where the document was sent; the law of the domicile of the party claiming privilege; the law of the professional domicile of the lawyer or the applicable rules of professional ethics. Depending on the type of evidence at issue, e.g., a document or a witness, each of these options can have a greater or lesser degree of relevance.

In an attempt to reconcile the need to treat the parties fairly with maintaining the legitimate expectations of the parties with respect to evidentiary privileges, it has been

---

69. MOSK and GINSBERG, *op. cit.*, fn. 1, p. 382; VON SCHLABRENDORFF and SHEPPARD, *op. cit.*, fn. 1, p. 768.

70. MOSK and GINSBERG, *op. cit.*, fn. 1, p. 382.

71. BERGER, *op. cit.*, fn. 1, p. 12.

72. BERGER, *ibid.*, pp. 12-13.

73. VON SCHLABRENDORFF and SHEPPARD, *op. cit.*, fn. 1, p. 771.

74. See, for example, KAUFMANN-KOHLER and BÄRTSCH, *op. cit.*, fn. 67, p. 19.

75. VON SCHLABRENDORFF and SHEPPARD, *op. cit.*, fn. 1, p. 769.

76. KAUFMANN-KOHLER and BÄRTSCH, *op. cit.*, fn. 67, p. 20.

suggested that arbitrators should take a "most favourable privilege approach".[77] This approach recommends that the tribunal apply the laws of each party's home jurisdiction and choose the law that accords the widest protection.[78] The wider protection would then apply equally to each party. This is arguably the most prudent approach in that it is the most likely to result in the equal treatment of the parties and avoid challenges to the award by meeting the legitimate expectations of all of the parties in respect of privileges.[79] One acknowledged shortcoming of this solution is the possibility that it might promote forum shopping.[80] Another shortcoming of greater concern is that applying the most favourable privilege rule may favour the exclusion of relevant evidence over the other fundamental aspect of a tribunal's mandate: the establishment of all of the facts of a case and the need to permit a party a fair opportunity of presenting its case. In order to offset this concern, arbitrators will need to adopt a healthy degree of scepticism and practicality when assessing privilege claims.

The corollary to the most favourable privilege approach is the "least favourable privilege approach". This standard would also establish formal equality between the parties but would adopt the lowest standard of protection and tend to compel the admission of evidence rather than its exclusion.[81] However, this approach runs the clear risk of being unfair to a party who is entitled to broader privilege protection under the law most closely connected to its communications with counsel and who expected protection pursuant to that law.[82]

Another option is the application of a general principle of international law or some form of transnational standard of privilege. This alternative has the appeal of offering a neutral standard which does not reflect the public policy of any particular national legal system. National privilege rules are the product of the particular nature and detailed procedural provisions of a legal system and the particular approach taken to balancing competing interests. For example, at a very general level, compulsory production of all relevant documents in an adversarial, common law system in which counsel are seen as officers of the court has resulted in the development of a complex system of rules

---

77. VON SCHLABRENDORFF and SHEPPARD, *op. cit.*, fn. 1, p. 773.

78. RUBINSTEIN and GUERRINA, *op. cit.*, fn. 1, p. 598.

79. See VON SCHLABRENDORFF and SHEPPARD, *op. cit.*, fn. 1, p. 773. However, as the authors acknowledge, it may not always be easy to determine which is, in fact, the most favourable privilege rule. Further, the concept of the "legitimate expectations" of a party cannot mean that the rule of privilege offering the broadest coverage will always apply. Parties from jurisdictions with more limited protection of privilege, for example in jurisdictions where communications with in-house counsel are not protected, will have no expectation that certain information or documents will be protected and may, in fact, expect to obtain the same types of documents from the opposing party in the event an arbitration arises.

80. RUBINSTEIN and GUERRINA, *op. cit.*, fn. 1, p. 599, VON SCHLABRENDORFF and SHEPPARD, *op. cit.*, fn. 1, p. 771.

81. See BERGER, *op. cit.*, fn. 1, p. 18.

82. BERGER, *ibid.*, gives as examples the situation where a party is deprived of the legitimate expectation that documents in the possession of its in-house counsel could be excluded under this rule. He also notes that the application of this rule would be harsh where the effect was to exclude the application of the principle of professional secrecy, thus subjecting counsel to sanctions if he does not comply with his obligations of secrecy.

686

governing privilege which is owned by the client. It is particularly difficult to justify plucking this type of procedural or evidentiary rule out of a national legal system and applying it in an international arbitration, especially where these rules will be applied to a party whose legal system has a completely different approach to privilege. The problem with the transnational approach is that there are no general principles or transnational standards of privilege which provide much guidance. The most that can be said is that privileges are more than merely procedural in nature and must be considered when raised in good faith in order to ensure the fair and equal treatment of the parties and the enforceability of the arbitral award. Even if one accepts the view of certain authors that in the area of legal privilege transnational or general principles have emerged,[83] the fact that some very general aspects of privilege are broadly recognized is not likely to give much guidance to arbitral tribunals or parties with respect to the specific issues which arise from differences in potentially applicable privilege rules. Although more can and should be done to further develop these basic notions, most commentators accept that the development of transnational rules at this time is not very realistic.[84]

IV. HOW LEGAL PRIVILEGE CAN AFFECT AN INTERNATIONAL ARBITRATION

The primary concern relating to evidentiary privileges in an international arbitration is that inequality of treatment and unfairness may result if the arbitral tribunal does not apply the same privilege standards to both parties. If different privilege standards apply to the production of documents and information or the admissibility of evidence, a party's ability to present its case (whether in asserting a claim or defending against it) may be affected and fundamental due process violated. This may give grounds for a challenge of the award or resistance against its enforcement.[85]

Further, the substantive aspect of privilege which reflects public policy of the adopting State raises the concern that failure to consider or apply specific privilege rules may rise to the level of a breach of public policy. While evidentiary privileges also clearly fall within procedure and the taking and assessment of evidence, over which arbitral tribunals have broad discretion,[86] due to the substantive public policy aspect of privilege rules the concern remains that failure to consider the application of a privilege rule that otherwise purports to apply may give rise to a challenge or resistance to

---

83. See KAUFMANN-KOHLER, *op. cit.*, fn. 67, p. 8; MOSK and GINSBERG, *op. cit.*, fn. 1, pp. 378-381.

84. See BERGER, *op. cit.*, fn. 2, p. 13 and the various sources cited there.

85. These could fall under a number of grounds accepted in the New York Convention and many arbitration laws: a party was unable to present its case, the arbitral procedure was not in accordance with the agreement of the parties, or the award is contrary to the public policy of the state in which the arbitration was held or in which enforcement is sought.

86. See POUDRET and BESSON, *op. cit.*, fn. 2, pp. 582-583, who note that a number of laws specifically include within an arbitral tribunal's broad power to conduct the arbitration as it considers appropriate, the power to determine the admissibility, relevance, materiality and weight of any evidence; BERGER, *op. cit.*, fn. 2, pp. 14-15.

enforcement of an award. For example, New York courts appear to expect arbitral tribunals to apply rules of privilege and the failure to apply privilege rules properly has been raised as a ground for potential annulment of an award.[87] As discussed below, ethical rules (which include privilege) and their application may also give rise to court intervention during the arbitral process in certain jurisdictions.

Finally, even if the failure to apply a particular privilege rule does not amount to a breach of the public policy of a particular State or another ground for challenge of the award, ad hoc decisions by an arbitral tribunal may appear arbitrary and give rise to uncertainty and inconsistency which may affect the conduct of the arbitration and the confidence the parties have in the procedure.[88]

It is also important to recall that in many countries privilege rules are contained in codes of professional conduct and ethical standards. The application of these rules is not normally restricted to the country in which a lawyer is professionally qualified but, rather, tend to follow a lawyer when he performs legal services outside of his home State. These rules may affect a lawyer's approach to a case, his conduct throughout the case and his or her ability to comply with orders and directions of the arbitral tribunal. For example, the rules governing professional secrecy or privilege in a lawyer's code of professional conduct, pursuant to which he normally practices, will inform his view of what documents are available as part of document production, which documents he may request and produce and what obligations, if any, apply to privileged documents of the other party. In addition, lawyers practicing in other States are often also required to abide by local ethical rules.[89]

To date, ethical standards for counsel and their applicability in international arbitration has received relatively little attention.[90] Ethical rules may affect a number of

---

87. James H. CARTER, "The Attorney-Client Privilege and Arbitration", 2 ADR Currents (1996/97) p. 1 at p. 15; Gary B. BORN, *International Commercial Arbitration*, 2nd edn. (Kluwer Law International 2001), pp. 489-490. Interestingly, Born notes that privilege issues are often factual in nature and that courts tend to be deferential under the Federal Arbitration Act in reviewing an arbitrator's factual determinations in respect of claims for privilege.

88. On this topic, see PARK, *op. cit.*, fn. 43, pp. 60-61; William W. PARK, "The 2002 Freshfields Lecture – Arbitration's Protean Nature: The Value of Rules and the Risks of Discretion" 19 Arb. Int'l (2003) p. 279.

89. See, for example, Directive 98/5/EC, Art. 6; Van Vechten VEEDER, "The Lawyer's Duty to Arbitrate in Good Faith: The 2001 Goff Lecture", 18 Arb. Int'l (2001) p. 431 at pp. 432-433; the CCBE Code of Conduct for Lawyers in the European Union, especially Arts. 2.3, 2.4, 3.2, 4.1-4.5, 5.3 and 5.5. Art. 4.5 makes it clear that rules governing a lawyer's relations with the courts also apply to his relations with arbitrators. Art. 4.1 states that a lawyer must comply with the rules of conduct applied before a court or tribunal. In New York state, the courts have held that local law applies to the issue of disqualification of counsel for ethical reasons in an arbitration taking place in that state since New York has the stronger interest in the conduct of counsel in a New York forum. See *Tekni-Plex, Inc. v. Meyner and Landis*, 220 A.D. 2d 326, discussed below at fn. 92.

90. Among the few articles on this topic see: Jan PAULSSON, "Standards of Conduct for Counsel in International Arbitration", 3 Am. Rev. of Int'l Arb. (1992) p. 214; VEEDER, *op. cit.*, fn. 89, note 3; Peter C. THOMAS, "Disqualifying Lawyers in Arbitrations: Do the Arbitrators Play any Proper Role?", 1 Am. Rev. Int'l Arb. (1990) p. 562 ; Catherine A. ROGERS, "Fit and Function in Legal

aspects of counsel's conduct in an arbitration and, in turn, the arbitral procedure. For example, ethical rules may apply to and affect conflicts of interest by counsel, contact by counsel for one party with opposing counsel's client or employees of the client, and the treatment and handling of privileged documents. These examples of ethical obligations have given rise to disputes in the course of litigation and, in certain cases, with respect to arbitrations conducted in the United States and elsewhere.[91] In New York state, the courts have intervened to stay arbitral proceedings in order to deal with applications by one of the parties that counsel for the opposing party should be disqualified on ethical grounds.[92]

Ethics: Developing a Code of Conduct for International Arbitration", 23 Mich. J. Int'l L. (2002) p. 241; Catherine A. ROGERS, "Context and Institutional Structure in Attorney Regulation: Constructing an Enforcement Regime for International Arbitration", 39 Stanf. J. Int'l L. (2003) p. 1.

91. For example, different arbitral tribunals have reached opposite conclusions depending on whether or not specific ethical standards were applicable. In one ICC arbitration, the arbitral tribunal declined to apply the code of ethics of a bar association "in the context of an international arbitration proceeding" where an application was made to disqualify counsel for the respondents where that counsel had previously provided to one of the claimants advice relating to the investment in dispute in the arbitration. One of the defences raised by the respondents related directly to advice previously given by their counsel to one of the claimants. That claimant applied to have counsel for the respondents disqualified on the basis of the provisions of the civil and criminal codes as well as the conflicts of interest provisions of the code of ethics of the home State of the respondents and of their counsel. The tribunal found that the request to exclude counsel was not within the scope of the arbitration clause and should be the subject of separate, domestic proceedings. In addition, among other grounds, the tribunal expressed doubts as to the application of the code of ethics of a domestic private bar association in the proceedings before it. On the other hand, in a different case sited in New York, another arbitral tribunal had little hesitation in applying the local code of ethics in dismissing an application to exclude counsel. See Horacio GRIGERA NAÓN, "Choice of Law Problems in International Commercial Arbitration", 289 Collected Courses of The Hague Academy of International Law (2001) at pp. 157-161.

92. See *Bidermann Industries Licensing Inc. v. Avmar N.V.*, N.Y.L.J., 26 October 1990, at p. 23 (Sup. Ct. N.Y. Co., 22 October 1990), aff'd. 570 N.Y.S. 2d 33 (1st Dept. 1991). In that case, counsel for the claimants sought to disqualify counsel for the respondents on the basis of a conflict of interest arising from counsel for the respondents' previous representation of one of the claimants in the arbitration. The respondents applied to the courts for a stay of the arbitration on the basis that it was against New York public policy to allow the arbitral tribunal to decide the ethical obligations of counsel. The court stayed the arbitration on the basis that a question of disqualification of counsel involved "an important interest of the public at large" and that "... the regulation of attorneys, and determinations as to whether clients should be deprived of counsel of their choice as a result of professional responsibilities and ethical obligations, implicate fundamental public interests and policies which should be reserved for the courts and should not be subject to arbitration". This decision was upheld on appeal. See Peter C. THOMAS, "Disqualifying Lawyers in Arbitrations: Do the Arbitrators Play Any Proper Role?", Am. Rev. Int'l Arb. (1991) p. 562 at pp. 565-566. The author presents a strong critique of the *Bidermann* decision and develops a convincing argument that an application for disqualification of counsel for a conflict of interest (or other breach of an ethical obligation) relating to matters arising as between the parties to the arbitration should be decided by the arbitral tribunal in order to ensure the fairness of the proceeding. In Thomas's view, arbitrators are empowered, directly and indirectly, to regulate the conduct of lawyers. In his view, the New York Code of Professional Responsibility, which

A good example of where ethical rules can affect the integrity and fairness of a proceeding is the treatment and use of privileged documents of the opposing party when these are disclosed inadvertently or obtained outside the document production process. This question has received substantial attention in the courts in a number of common law jurisdictions. In these cases, the courts have held that failure to follow applicable ethical rules on how privileged documents of the opposing party must be handled when disclosed inadvertently or obtained outside the discovery process may affect the integrity and fairness of the proceedings as well as the administration of justice. A number of decisions have led to the exclusion from evidence of privileged documents, the disqualification of counsel and, in extreme cases, dismissal of the case of a party who has participated in the improper obtention and use of privileged documents and information.[93]

---

provides that lawyers are obliged to act ethically in arbitrations, as well as in court proceedings, directly empowers arbitrators to deal with the conduct of counsel (at pp 576-577). See also, *Tekni-Plex Inc. v. Meyner and Landis*, 220 A.D. 2d 326 (Sup. Ct. N.Y., A.D., 24 October 1995) in which the court upheld a lower court decision to disqualify a law firm from representing a party in an arbitration under the auspices of the American Arbitration Association on the basis of a conflict of interest. In its decision, the court held that New York law, as the law of the forum, applied to the question of the conflict of interest and disqualification.

93. In the United States, see for example: *In re Beiny*, 517 N.Y.S.2d 474 (App. Div. 1st Dep't 1987) (counsel disqualified for improperly obtaining and using privileged documents; all privileged documents excluded from evidence; *Fayemi v. Hambretch & Quist*, 174 F.R.D. 319 (S.D.N.Y. 1997) (improperly obtained confidential information was excluded from evidence, further sanctions withheld because of other party's own misconduct); *Lipin v. Bender*, 644 N.E.2d 1300 (N.Y. 1994) (case dismissed with prejudice where plaintiff copies and reads privileged documents); *Sgambellone v. Wheatley*, 630 N.Y.S.2d 835 (Sup. Ct. Schenectady County 1995) (counsel improperly obtained privileged medical records – records excluded from evidence, fine imposed upon counsel but no disqualification in light of the nature of the information and stage of the proceedings); *Stephen Slesinger, Inc. v. Walt Disney Co.*, No. BC022365, 2004 WL 612818 (Cal. Super. Ct. 29 Mar. 2004) (plaintiff engages private investigator to secretly acquire privileged and confidential documents, many of which were so labelled. Plaintiff's agent trespassed on defendant's property to search through trash and obtain the documents. Plaintiff and its lawyers circulated the documents and reviewed them in detail. Plaintiff's case dismissed with prejuduice.); *Herrera v. Clipper Group*, Nos. 97-CIV-560, 97-CIV-561, 1998 WL 229499 (S.D.N.Y. 6 May 1998) (plaintiff improperly obtained confidential/privileged documents outside discovery process with knowledge of counsel – claimant required to pay costs but counsel not disqualified; non-privileged information admitted); *MMR/Wallace Power & Industrial, Inc. v. Thames Associates*, 764 F. Supp. 712 (D. Comm. 1991) ("... if court concludes that counsel's violation of ethical standards threatens to affect integrity of the adversarial process, it should take appropriate measures, including disqualification, to eliminate such taint. Counsel's contact with confidential former employee of opposing party yielded privileged information regarding trial preparation and strategy". – counsel disqualified); *Maldonado v. New Jersey*, Civ. A. No. 03-4703, 2004 WL 2904898 (D.N.J. 15 Dec. 2004) (plaintiff obtains critical privileged internal memorandum of defendant in unexplained manner – counsel do not observe "cease, notify and return" requirement of rules of professional conduct and review document. Counsel disqualified). In these cases, the primary focus of the court's attention was the effect of the impugned conduct on the fairness and integrity of the proceedings and the prejudice to the other party, rather than the breach of an ethical rule in and of itself. A number of courts have distinguished between these cases and their jurisdiction in disciplinary proceedings brought

Experience indicates that the same types of issues can and do arise in international arbitration.[94]

When these issues arise in an arbitration, the arbitral tribunal must address them as part of its jurisdiction over the proceedings and its duty to ensure the fair and equal treatment of the parties. The focus of an arbitral tribunal's enquiry and determination must be the fairness and integrity of the process before it. While it may not be part of a tribunal's mandate to apply ethical rules contained in codes of professional conduct and similar instruments and to sanction counsel for any infringements, this does not mean that these rules are irrelevant to a tribunal's determination of privilege issues. As mentioned previously, in many countries rules of privilege or professional secrecy are

---

by bar associations for breach of ethical rules. For similar Canadian cases see: *National Bank Financial Ltd. v. Daniel Potter*, 2005 NSSC 113 ("The underlying importance of confidentiality of solicitor-client communications is no less important in the civil law context than in the criminal law context. Once counsel become aware of the fact that they have communications between solicitor and client or should reasonably expect that they are in possession of such communication they should stop viewing the documents. Notice should be given to all potential privilege holders so as to afford them a reasonable opportunity to assert privilege." Counsel removed for failing to abide by this requirement. Privileged documents excluded from evidence.); *Nova Growth Corp. v. Kapinski*, [2001] O.J. No. 5993; *Celanese Canada Inc. v. Murray Demoltion Corp.*, 2006 SCC 36 where the Supreme Court of Canada held, in the context of the execution of an *Anton Piller* order, that the protection of solicitor-client confidences is a matter of high importance and that a violation of privilege need not be the result of "egregious" misconduct in order to give rise to disqualification of counsel. As counsel who had obtained privileged documents of the opposing party had not discharged the onus of showing that no use of privileged information would occur, they were disqualified. For English cases see, for example: *Ablitt v. Mills & Reeve*, The Times, 25 October 1995; *English and American Insurance Co. Ltd. & Ors v. Herbert Smith & Co.*, New Law Journal, 13 February 1987 at p. 148; *Ridehalgh v. Horsefield*, [1994] Ch. 205, [1994] 3 All. E.R. 848.

94. Anecdotal evidence indicates that parties do attempt to use documents or information which the opposing party considers to be confidential or privileged. The best example may be the use of documents or information exchanged in the course of settlement negotiations between the parties. There appears to be a relatively broad consensus that these are covered by a form of "settlement privilege" and are usually excluded from evidence. See, for example, BERGER, *op. cit.*, fn.1, at pp. 13-14. In addition, these documents and information are often viewed as irrelevant (or of marginal relevance) to the issues the arbitral tribunal must decide. Another example is where one party obtains privileged or confidential internal documents of the other party through inadvertent disclosure of that party or through allegedly improper means including by way of theft, trespass or inappropriate contact with employees of that party. In certain cases, the manner in which the privileged or confidential documents were obtained remains unexplained and the tribunal may be faced with the difficult task of making a finding in that respect. A number of these scenarios are addressed in the cases cited at fn. 93, particularly in the abundant US case law. An example in investor-State arbitration is the decision in *Methanex Corporation and the United States* where the tribunal was required to address the admissibility of documents alleged to have been illegally obtained, including by way of trespass to obtain confidential documents from the trash of an agent of one of the parties. See Part II, c. 1, "The USA's Application for the Exclusion of Certain of Methanex's Evidence". In its decision, the tribunal decided that certain documentation was procured unlawfully and that it would be inappropriate to permit the introduction of that evidence in violation of a general duty of good faith incumbent on all who participate in international arbitration: See Part II, c. 1, paras. 58-59. The tribunal's final award is available at <http://ita.law.uvic.ca/documents/MethanexFinalAward.pdf>.

contained in rules of professional conduct and codes of ethics. Further, ethical rules governing the conduct of counsel are generally intended to ensure the interests of justice and that certain standards of integrity and fairness are met. As a result, they may serve to inform the standard of procedural fairness a tribunal applies in an international arbitration. This may be particularly so where the ethical standard, for example with respect to the handling of privileged documents of the other party, is shared by counsel representing both parties as it will likely form part of the common expectations of the parties and their counsel. However, these ethical obligations will also be relevant where different ethical standards apply to counsel and the tribunal is required to establish a standard which will treat the parties equally and fairly.

Legal privilege is most likely to arise in an arbitration during the course of document production or in the process of admission and assessment of the evidence. An arbitral tribunal's handling of these issues during these phases of the procedure may give rise to court intervention during the arbitral process or to a challenge of the award or resistance against enforcement after the award has been rendered.

a. Document production

Privilege is an accepted basis for resisting the production of a document or information in document production. This is recognized, for example, in Art. 9(2)(b) of the IBA Rules on the Taking of Evidence. Depending on the circumstances of the arbitration, including the identity of the parties, their counsel and the members of the arbitral tribunal, the question of privilege or immunity from disclosure due to the principle of *secret professionnel* may never arise. This may be because there are no relevant documents which would be subject to protection or both parties and their counsel are from civil law jurisdictions and they do not consider the production of documents necessary or relevant. On the other hand, in an arbitration between parties from common law jurisdictions or between parties represented by common law counsel, counsel may share a common approach to document production and exchange substantial document production requests and detailed privilege logs listing documents in respect of which they claim privilege. In either situation, the parties' or counsels' expectations may be similar and disputes in respect of privilege or immunity from disclosure may not arise or, if they do, the applicable principles may be the same or similar and the tribunal will have little difficulty in determining the applicable rule and applying it to the disputed facts.

The potential for difficulty increases where the parties have different expectations in respect of privilege and rely upon different rules. The tribunal may then be faced with choosing the applicable rule to determine an objection to the production of a relevant document. As discussed previously, the tribunal will have a number of potential choices and will have to bear in mind the need to treat the parties equally and fairly. The tribunal will also have to bear in mind that there may be a number of document production requests emanating from both sides and that the question of privilege may also arise later in the proceedings during the presentation of documentary evidence or during the course of the hearing and that consistency in its decisions will be important. Failure to consider and, if appropriate, apply an applicable privilege rule at the document production stage of the proceedings may give rise to a challenge to the award or resistance against its enforcement at a later stage. If the tribunal refuses to consider or apply a privilege rule, the party resisting production may refuse to produce the document in any event, which may give rise to the drawing of an adverse inference or an apprehension that an adverse inference has been drawn, and give rise to a challenge on that basis. Alternatively, the resisting party may feel compelled to disclose the document or information which it alleges to be privileged and later challenge the award on the basis of that coerced disclosure.

On the other hand, if the tribunal applies the rule of privilege and exempts the document or information from disclosure, it must consider whether the claim of privilege is made in good faith and whether privilege properly applies. Otherwise, a party could use privilege as an excuse for improperly withholding relevant documents. If this were to occur and is discovered, it could give rise to a challenge to the award depending on the nature of the documents withheld and whether their withholding resulted in a substantial injustice.[95]

Another aspect of privilege which may arise during the course of document production is how counsel should treat privileged documents of the opposing party which may come into their possession during the course of document collection and production. In a number of common law jurisdictions, codes of professional conduct or similar ethical rules require that a lawyer who comes into possession of materials that on their face appear to be subject to solicitor-client privilege under circumstances where it is clear that they were not intended for the receiving lawyer, should refrain from examining the materials, notify the sending lawyer and abide by the instructions of the lawyer who sent them. Any dispute as to the use of the documents and their admissibility in evidence must then be referred to the court or relevant tribunal. The same rules apply to a lawyer whose client produces documents that appear on their face to be legally protected and where the lawyer knows that the documents have not been produced in the discovery process.[96] Courts in those jurisdictions which have dealt with this duty have found that a breach of the ethical obligations to treat privileged documents in a certain manner may fundamentally affect the fairness and integrity of the proceedings.[97] In a number of cases, the courts have either disqualified counsel or gone so far as to dismiss a party's claim or defence for breach of this duty. Similar conduct in the context of an arbitration could also affect the fundamental integrity and fairness of the proceedings and, if discovered, require the tribunal to address the issue and take

---

95. On this issue, see the English Commercial Court's decision in *Profilati Italia S.r.L. v. Paine Webber Inc.*, [2001] 1 Lloyd's Rep. 715 at 720 where the court suggested that where an important document which ought to have been disclosed is deliberately withheld and as a result the party withholding the document has obtained an award in its favour, the court may consider that the award was procured in a manner contrary to public policy and subject to annulment. See also VEEDER, *op. cit.*, fn. 89, at pp. 442-443 where the author refers to this case and suggests that deliberate withholding of a material document may constitute bad faith and a breach of the duty to arbitrate in good faith. Veeder suggests that this case is an example of where the English court has broadened the public policy exception in Sect. 68(2)(g) of the Arbitration Act 1996.

96. These rules are discussed in a number of the decisions cited above at fn. 93.

97. Such effect is not limited to the admission of the documents in evidence, but has been interpreted to include the simple acquisition of the privileged information and its use in cross-examination or to formulate strategy.

appropriate steps to protect or re-establish the fairness of the proceedings. Alternatively, the issue may be raised before the courts, either during the course of the arbitral proceedings or by way of a challenge to the award or resistance against enforcement.[98]

While these issues involving improper handling of privileged documents (or, possibly, other breaches of ethical obligations such as avoiding conflicts of interest in breach of a lawyer's duty of loyalty to his client) are exceptional, they serve to illustrate the relationship between ethical rules and procedural fairness and their possible impact in an international arbitration. They also show that national courts have dealt with these issues in terms of fundamental procedural fairness and public policy and have treated breaches of ethical obligations which affect the fairness of proceedings very seriously. In these circumstances, arbitral tribunals and counsel must have regard for these issues.

Further, even if inequality in the application of rules of privilege or breach of related ethical obligations do not rise to the level of challenging the validity of the award, an understanding of the applicable rules from the outset of an arbitration will do much to contribute to the efficiency of the process and the satisfaction of the parties. In so far as document production is concerned, it will assist in allowing counsel and the tribunal to identify the scope of document production requests, permissible objections and how to claim and deal with privilege.

b. Admission and assessment of evidence

The issues discussed with respect to privilege and the production of documents generally apply with respect to the admission and assessment of evidence. Often, the issues relevant to document production will not become apparent until the stage at which evidence is tendered by the parties or witnesses are examined at a hearing. This may often come as a surprise and disrupt the hearing.

c. Court intervention

The primary basis for involvement by the courts in relation to issues of privilege in an international arbitration is a challenge on the basis of a breach of the tribunal's duty to treat the parties equally and fairly. This situation could arise if the tribunal failed to apply the same rule of privilege to both parties such that they were treated unequally. Alternatively, the application of the same rule of privilege might result in unfairness to one party where it prevented that party from relying on a more favourable or broader rule of privilege which it had legitimately expected to apply with the result that, in the reviewing court's view, the party was denied basic procedural fairness.

The other possibility is that the failure to apply a specific privilege rule may be seen as a breach of public policy by the courts at the place of arbitration or by the courts at the place of enforcement of the award. To date, there do not appear to have been any reported cases dealing with challenges on this specific point.

---

98. In this regard, see the decisions cited at fn. 92 above where the New York courts stayed arbitration proceedings in order to deal with applications to disqualify counsel for breach of ethical obligations relating to conflicts of interest.

In either case, the broad discretion given to arbitrators in national laws and institutional rules to conduct the arbitral proceedings as they deem appropriate in the absence of agreement of the parties, including the admissibility and assessment of evidence, would require clear proof that the arbitral tribunal failed to consider applicable privilege rules which resulted in unfairness to a party such that it affected the award. In most cases, this will be a difficult standard to meet. However, the possibility of a challenge on either basis cannot be discounted.

Court intervention or involvement in respect of a privilege issue which arises in an arbitration is most likely by way of a challenge to the arbitral award or resistance to its enforcement. While court intervention is possible during the course of the arbitration, as demonstrated by the New York cases referred to previously,[99] this is not likely in those jurisdictions which have adopted the UNCITRAL Model Law or provisions on court intervention similar to those of the Model Law. Under the Model Law, court intervention is excluded except where specifically provided in the law and there is no specific provision for intervention during the course of the proceedings to deal with evidentiary rulings. Rather, Art. 19(2) provides that in the absence of agreement by the parties on the procedure to be followed, the tribunal has the discretion to conduct the arbitration in such manner as it considers appropriate, including the power to determine the admissibility, relevance, materiality and weight of any evidence.

V.   ARE HARMONIZED RULES THE ANSWER?

Uncertainty surrounding precisely how to deal with the complex notion of evidentiary privileges in a given case has given rise to the familiar debate over the need for uniform rules, guidelines or harmonized standards.[100] Certain authors favour further harmonization of privilege rules,[101] the further development of transnational rules[102] or

---

99. See the *Bidermann* and *Tekni-Plex* cases referred to in fn. 92 above. In view of the continuing favourable approach to arbitration adopted by US courts since these cases, one has to wonder whether these cases would be decided in the same way today. Surely the conduct of counsel and its effects on the arbitral proceeding must be dealt with, in the first place, by the arbitral tribunal whose duty is to ensure the integrity and fairness of the proceedings. The tribunal's decision can be reviewed after the award is rendered by way of a challenge to the award or resistance to enforcement. Application of ethical rules as such and discipline should remain a matter for the relevant professional body or the courts where they form part of the regime for the enforcement of ethical codes and the discipline of counsel. On the interesting, much broader and challenging topic of ethical rules for counsel in international arbitration see ROGERS, *op. cit.* and THOMAS, *op. cit.*, both at fn. 90.

100. For a good outline of this debate at the broader level of the IBA Rules of Evidence see Pierre-Yves GUNTER, "Transnational Rules on the Taking of Evidence" in Emmanuel GAILLARD (ed.), *Towards a Uniform International Arbitration Law* (Juris 2005), pp. 129-161.

101. Nathalie VOSER, "Harmonization by Promulgating Rules of Best International Practice in International Arbitration" 3 SchiedsVZ (2005) p. 113 at p. 118.

102. MOSK and GINSBERG, *op. cit.*, fn. 1, pp. 380-383; KAUFMANN-KOHLER, *op. cit.*, fn. 67, p. 21.

an autonomous set of privilege rules[103] in international arbitration. Others, noting the general guidelines or consensus which have been achieved to date and the dangers of unlimited rule-making, conclude that there is no need for further harmonization.[104] Yet others could be expected to argue that guidelines are not helpful and that maximum arbitral discretion and flexibility should be preserved. Unsurprisingly, each of these positions has merit and the challenge will be to find the appropriate balance between predictability and flexibility.

Despite general recognition of the substantive nature of privilege and its importance and some common aspects of the protection afforded by privilege, it cannot be said that an autonomous or harmonized set of rules of privilege have emerged nor are such rules feasible in the short term. While useful general principles are beginning to emerge, notions of privilege are too deeply embedded in national legal systems and policy and too detailed in nature to permit significant progress in the development of more detailed rules in the near term. While there is much to be said for an autonomous set of privilege rules in international arbitration, provided sufficient arbitral discretion and flexibility is maintained, this will require moving away from the national law context in which existing notions of privilege or professional secrecy have been developed. Rules of privilege as we know them have been developed within national legal systems and reflect the public policy of those systems, such as, for example, criminal or competition law concerns. When parties choose arbitration, they opt for an alternative to national legal systems and their methods of civil procedure and evidence. The context in which international arbitrators apply notions of privilege in a commercial dispute is quite different from that of national courts. Arbitral tribunals must focus primarily on the parties and ensuring that their dispute is resolved fairly in the specific circumstances of each case. Autonomous privilege rules will have to reflect this perspective and be sufficiently flexible to accommodate the diversity of international arbitration. Further, the successful development of any such rules will require movement away from the notion of the "legitimate expectations" of a party based on its national rules of privilege towards the common expectations of the parties as to what constitutes fair treatment in an international arbitration.

In order to achieve sufficient acceptance, any harmonized set of rules will have to be general in nature. This is particularly so in the case of privilege given the highly fact-intensive or specific nature of the circumstances in which privilege issues in international arbitration are likely to arise. The scenarios described earlier in this paper amply demonstrate this. Detailed harmonized privilege rules are unlikely to address the myriad scenarios in which privilege can emerge as an issue in an international transaction and

---

103. VON SCHLABRENDORFF and SHEPPARD, *op. cit.*, fn. 1, p. 774.

104. BERGER, *op. cit.*, fn. 1, pp. 18-19. The author finds that a "pragmatic consensus" has been achieved in respect of four key points: 1. privilege issues must be qualified as substantive law issues; 2. the parties' standard choice of law clause in the contract usually does not extend to the issue of evidentiary privileges; 3. in determining the law applicable to a certain privilege issue, the tribunal shall apply the law of the jurisdiction with which the relevant communication is most closely connected, i.e., the law where the party has its place of business; and 4. the tribunal may exclude evidence from both sides which is privileged under the law of one party but not under the law of the other based on compelling considerations of fairness or equality.

are unlikely to be workable in practice.[105] As a result, any harmonized rules eventually developed will have to remain general and flexible in nature and arbitral discretion will continue to play an important role.

General, flexible guidelines combined with arbitral discretion are likely to be sufficient to handle most privilege issues satisfactorily. Although the question of privilege can be challenging, it does not arise in every case. Further, privilege issues can often be avoided or reduced by taking a practical approach. In this respect, it is important to recall that privilege applies to relevant evidence which would otherwise be admissible. Documents or information in respect of which privilege is claimed are often irrelevant or immaterial and can thus be excluded from evidence on that basis. Further, a cumulative approach to the possible privilege rules which could apply in any given situation may identify sufficient commonality to resolve the privilege issue without having to apply one rule to the exclusion of others. Finally, a healthily sceptical approach to claims of privilege may help eliminate frivolous claims, particularly if this approach is made known early in the proceedings and applied consistently by the tribunal.

Predictability as to the applicable privilege regime within an arbitration can be enhanced by early consideration and discussion of the question at the outset of the proceedings. Early consideration of the nature of the case, the parties involved and the background and experience of their counsel will often provide useful guidance as to the nature of the privilege issues, if any, likely to arise. In light of these considerations, the tribunal, or a party, may raise the question of the applicable rules of privilege for discussion. While this may not prove useful or necessary in all cases, early consideration of the topic of privilege may well lead to agreement between the parties, particularly if the issue is raised before document production commences or, depending on the procedure adopted, a party files its first submission on the merits. This may lead to a general agreement on the applicable privilege rules. If this is not possible, early discussion between the tribunal and the parties may yield agreement on the procedure for handling claims of privilege. For example, the parties may agree on how and when claims for privilege must be asserted, the particularity with which documents over which privilege is claimed must be identified and whether the tribunal should conduct in camera review of documents in respect of which privilege is claimed or whether some other procedure should be adopted. In the absence of agreement between the parties on these points, the tribunal should consider the utility of providing directions in an early procedural order. If issues are identified and settled early in the procedure, many of the issues which arise from a conflict of privilege rules and culture can be avoided or reduced.

Given the great diversity of privilege regimes and the variety of situations and disputes which may arise in international arbitration, general guidelines and the types of procedural steps outlined above may not effectively address all of the thorny privilege issues which may arise in an arbitration. Difficult, unique cases will always remain.

---

105. SINDLER and WÜSTEMANN, *op. cit.*, fn. 1, p. 637. For example, the question of legal qualification of in-house counsel, currency of their bar membership in one or more jurisdictions and the determination of the place at which advice was provided would likely prove a formidable challenge to settling on a uniform rule.

These can best be resolved in the flexible manner which is one of the hallmarks of international arbitration: the exercise of arbitral discretion guided by the principle of equal and fair treatment of the parties.

Selected Bibliography

A.   *Evidentiary Privilege in the Conduct of International Arbitration*

1.   George BURN and Zara SKELTON, "The Problem with Legal Privilege in International Arbitration", 72 Arbitration (2006, no. 2) at p. 124.

2.   J.A. FRY, "Without Prejudice and Confidential Communications in International Arbitration [When Does Procedural Flexibility Erode Public Policy?]", Int'l A.L.R. (1998) p. 209.

3.   Norah GALLAGHER, "Legal Privilege in International Arbitration", Int'l A.L.R. (2003) p. 45.

4.   Allison M. HILL, "A Problem of Privilege: In-House Counsel and the Attorney-Client Privilege in the United States and the European Community", 27 Case W. Res. J. Int'l L. (1995) 145.

5.   Gabrielle KAUFMANN-KOHLER, "Globalization of Arbitral Procedure", 36 Vand. J. Transnat'l L. (2003) p. 1313.

6.   Gabrielle KAUFMANN-KOHLER and Philippe BÄRTSCH, "Discovery In International Arbitration: How Much Is Too Much?", SchiedsVZ (January 2004) p. 17.

7.   Richard M. MOSK and Tom GINSBERG, "Evidentiary Privileges in International Arbitration", 50 Int'l and Comp. L. Q. (2001) p. 345.

8.   Javier H. RUBINSTEIN and Britton B. GUERRINA, "The Attorney-Client Privilege and International Arbitration", 18 J. Int'l Arb. (2001) p. 587.

9.   Michelle SINDLER and Tina WÜSTEMANN, "Privilege Across Borders in Arbitration: Multi-jurisdictional Nightmare or a Storm in a Teacup?", 23 ASA Bulletin (December 2005, no. 4) p. 610.

10.   Detlev F. VAGTS, "Notes and Comments The International Legal Profession: A Need For More Governance", 90 Am. J. Int'l L. (1996) p. 250.

11.   Fabian VON SCHLABRENDORFF and Audley SHEPPARD, "Conflict of Legal Privileges in International Arbitration: An Attempt to Find a Holistic Solution", in Gerald AKSEN, et al., eds. *Global Reflections on International Law, Commerce and Dispute Resolution* (International Chamber of Commerce, Paris 2005).

12.   Alexander A. YANOS, "Problems Arising from the Interplay of Common Law and Civil Law in International Arbitration: Defining the Scope of the Attorney-

Client Privilege", Slide Presentation of 15 and 17 November 2005, published in 3 Transnational Dispute Management, (April 2006, Issue 2) <www.transnational-dispute-management.com>.

B.   *"Solicitor-Client" Privilege Generally*

13.   Geoffrey C. HAZARD Jr., "An Historical Perspective on the Attorney-Client Privilege", 66 Cal. L. Rev. (1978) p. 1061.

14.   J.-L. BAUDOUIN, *Secret professionnel et droit au secret dans le droit de la preuve*, (L.G.D.J., Paris 1965).

15.   Ronald D. MANES & Michael P. SILVER, *Solicitor-Client Privilege in Canadian Law* (Butterworths, Toronto 2001).

16.   Peter BURCKHARDT, "Legal Professional Secrecy and Privilege in Switzerland" in International Litigation News October (2004) (International Bar Association, Newsletter of the International Litigation Committee of the Section on Business Law) p. 33, available at: International Bar Association <www.ibanet.org> (last accessed January 2006).

17.   Osvaldo J. MARZORATI, "Privilege and Professional Secrecy: The Civil Law Model" (Paper presented to the International Bar Association, Dispute Resolution Section, 2005) (unpublished).

18.   M. McKERRY, "Bridging Ethical Borders: International Legal Ethics With an Islamic Perspective", 35 Tex. Int'l L. J. (2000) p. 289.

19.   PLC Global Counsel, "Privilege: A World Tour", (December 2004/January 2005), available at: <www.practicallaw.com/aboutglobal> (last accessed January 2006).

20.   Hilmar RAESCHKE-KESSLER, "The Production of Documents in International Arbitration – A Commentary on Article 3 of the New IBA Rules of Evidence", 18 Arbitration International (2002) p. 411.

21.   Robert H. SMIT and Audley SHEPPARD, "Evidentiary Privileges in International Arbitration" in 5 Arbitration and ADR (December 2000, no. 3) (Newsletter of Committee D of the International Bar Association Section on Business Law) p. 12 available at: International Bar Association <www.ibanet.org> (last accessed January 2006).

Canada

22. John SOPINKA, et al., *The Law of Evidence in Canada*, 2nd edn. (Butterworths, Toronto 1999).

23. John SOPINKA, et al., *The Law of Evidence in Canada*, Second Edition Supplement, (Butterworths, Toronto 2004).

24. *Smith v. Jones*, [1999] 1 S.C.R. 455.

Quebec

25. Jean-Claude ROYER, *La preuve civile*, 3rd edn. (Yvon Blais, Cowansville 2003).

26. *Banque Paribas (Suisse) S.A. v. Wightman*, (21 January 1997) Montreal 500-09-002739-969, J.E. 97-306 (C.A.).

27. *Frenette v. Metropolitan Life Insurance Co.*, [1992] 1 S.C.R. 647.

28. *Foster Wheeler Power Co. Societe intermunicipale de gestion et d'elimination des dechets (SIGED) inc.*, [2004] 1 S.C.R. 456.

C.   *Privilege and In-House Counsel*

29. Practical Law Company, "A Guide to In-House Legal Privilege", Cross-border Quarterly (January – March 2006) available at: <www.practicallaw.com> (last accessed 27 January 2006).

30. European Company Lawyers Association, "The Case for In-House Legal Privilege in EC Law", available at: <www.ecla.org> (last accessed 2 February 2006).

31. European Company Lawyers Association, "In-House Legal Privilege Needed with Modernization of EC Competition Law: August 2003 Position Paper", available at: <www.ecla.org> (last accessed 2 February 2006).

32. European Company Lawyers Association, "In-House Legal Privilege Needed with Modernization of EC Competition Law: December 2000 Position Paper", available at: <www.ecla.org> (last accessed 2 February 2006).

33. "In-House Counsel and the Attorney-Client Privilege", a *Lex Mundi* Multi-Jurisdictional Survey, available at <www.lexmundi.com>, updated to 15 September 2005.

34. John FISH, "Regulated Legal Professionals and Professional Privilege Within the European Union, the European Economic Area and Switzerland, and Certain

701

Other European Jurisdictions" (Report presented to the Council of the Bars and Law Societies of the European Union, February 2004) available at <www.ccbe.org/doc/En/fish_report_en.pdf> (last accessed 8 February 2006).

35. Diana GOOD, et al., "Privilege: The In-House View" (February 2005) available at: <www.practicallaw.com> (last accessed 27 January 2006).

36. Jettie VAN CAENEGEM, "Update on legal privilege for in-house counsel in Europe" (Lecture presented to the IBA International Corporate Counsel Conference February 2002) available at: <www.practicallaw.com> (last accessed 10 January 2006).

D. *Recent Caselaw*

37. *AM&S Europe Ltd. v. Commission of the European Communities* (1982), [1983] 1 Q.B. 878. (Excerpt).

38. Katie BRADFORD, et al., "Legal Advice Privilege: Here To Stay" Case Comment on *Three Rivers District Counsel and others (respondents) v. Governor and Company of the Bank of England (appellants)*, [2004] UKHL 48, available at: <www.practicallaw.com> (last accessed 27 January 2006).

39. Michael POLONSKY and Lorraine DESAI, "Recent Developments in the English Law of Legal Professional Privilege", Case Comment on *Three Rivers District Counsel and others v. Governor and Company of the Bank of England (No 5)*, [2003] EWCA Civ 474; *Three Rivers District Counsel and others v. Governor and Company of the Bank of England (No 10)*, [2004] EWCA Civ 218; *United States of America v. Philip Morris Inc. and others*, [2004] EWCA. Civ 330; International Litigation News October 2004 (International Bar Association, Newsletter of the International Litigation Committee of the Section on Business Law) available at: International Bar Association <www.ibanet.org> (last accessed January 2006).

40. *Three Rivers District Counsel and others (respondents) v. Governor and Company of the Bank of England (appellants)*, [2004] UKHL 48.

41. *Three Rivers District Counsel and others v. Governor and Company of the Bank of England (No 5)*, [2003] EWCA Civ 474.

42. *Three Rivers District Counsel and others v. Governor and Company of the Bank of England (No 10)*, [2004] EWCA Civ 218.

43. *United States of America v. Philip Morris Inc. and others*, [2004] EWCA Civ 330.

44. Gavin MURPHY, "CFI Signals Possible Extension of Professional Privilege to In-House Lawyers", Case Comment on *Akzo Nobel Chemicals Ltd. and Akcros Chemicals*

Ltd. v. Commission, Joined Cases T-125 T-125/03 R and T-253/03 R, available at:<www.globalcompetitionforum.org/regions/n_america/canada/LPP%20a nd%20Akzo% 20edit%201.0%20(changes%20integrated)2.pdf> (last accessed 1 February 2006).

45.   "ECJ annuls CFI interim relief order in legal privilege case", Case Summary on *Commission v. Akzo Nobel Chemicals Ltd. and Akcros Chemicals Ltd.*, Case C-7/04 P(R), available at: <www.practicallaw.com> (last accessed 27 January 2006).

46.   *Akzo Nobel Chemicals Ltd. and Akcros Chemicals Ltd. v. Commission*, Joined Cases T-125/03 R and T-253/03 R [2003] ECR II-4771.

47.   *Akzo Nobel Chemicals Ltd. and Akcros Chemicals Ltd.*, Case C-7/04 P(R) Order of the President of the European Court of Justice, 27 September 2004, available at <http://curia.europa.eu> (last accessed 22 January 2006).

48.   Geoff HEALY, "Current Developments Australia: Application of Attorney/Client Privilege to Communications with Non-Australian Lawyer" Case Comment on *Kennedy v. Wallace*, [2004] FCAFC 337, International Litigation News (October 2004) (International Bar Association, Newsletter of the International Litigation Committee of the Section on Business Law) available at: <www.ibanet.org> (last accessed January 2006).

49,   *Kennedy v. Wallace*, [2004] FCAFC 337.

50.   *Pratt Holdings Pty Ltd. v. Commissioner of Taxation*, [2004] FCAFC 122.

51.   *Vance v. Air Marshall McCormack*, [2004] ACTSC 78.

E.   *Ethical Considerations*

52.   Sheila BLOCK, "Ethics in International Proceedings" in International Litigation News October 2004 (International Bar Association, Newsletter of the International Litigation Committee of the Section on Business Law) p. 15 available at: <www.ibanet.org> (last accessed January 2006)

53.   Ronald A. BRAND, "Professional Responsibility in a Transnational Transaction Practice", 17 J.L. & Com. (1997-1998) p. 301.

54.   Mary C. DALY, "The Dichotomy Between Standards and Rules: A New Way of Understanding the Differences in Perceptions of Lawyer Codes of Conduct by US and Foreign Lawyers", 32 V and. J. Transnat'l L. (1999) p. 1117.

55. Catherine A. ROGERS, "Context and Institutional Structure in Attorney Regulation: Constructing an Enforcement Regime for International Arbitration", 39 Stan. J. of Int'l L. (2003) p. 1.

56. Catherine A. ROGERS, "Fit and Function in Legal Ethics: Developing a Code of Conduct for International Arbitration", 23 Mich. J. Int'l L. (2002) p. 341.

57. Peter C. THOMAS, "Disqualifying Lawyers In Arbitrations: Do the Arbitrators Play Any Proper Role?" 1 American Review of International Arbitration (1990, no. 4) p. 562.

58. John TOULMIN, "A Worldwide Common Code of Professional Ethics?" 15 Fordham Int'l L.J. (1991-1992) p. 673.

59. Jan PAULSSON, "Standards of Conduct for Counsel in International Arbitration", 3 American Review of International Arbitration (1992) p. 214.

60. Van Vechten VEEDER, "The 2001 Goff Lecture: The Lawyer's Duty to Arbitrate in Good Faith", 18 Arbitration International (2002, no. 4) p. 431.

61. *National Bank Financial Ltd. v. Daniel Potter*, 2005 NSSC 113 (CanLII).

62. *Nova Growth Corp. v. Kepinski*, [2001] O.J. No. 5993 (Ont. S.C.J.) (QL).

63. *Celanese Canada Inc., et al. v. Murray Demolition Corp., et al.* (2004), 244 D.L.R. (4th) 33, 73 O.R. (3d) 64 (C.A.), 2006 SCC 36.

Evidentiary Privileges in International Arbitration

*Matthieu de Boisséson**

I.   INTRODUCTION

The question of evidentiary privilege is one of the crucial questions in international arbitration today, due to the growth of international disputes and the increased need of a predictable and accessible arbitration procedure.

As Michelle Sindler and Tina Wüstemann have recently explained, "Much has been achieved but 'privilege' is one of the particularly delicate areas where there are no settled rules, and parties, counsel and tribunals are left to their own devices."[1]

In this Commentary, the term "evidentiary privilege" will mainly refer to the attorney-client privilege, which establishes the entitlement of a party to arbitration to withhold disclosure or production of evidence on the grounds that communications between a client and his lawyer have a special status. Therefore, all other communications that may be considered as privileged on other grounds (such as fiscal confidentiality or State secrecy) will not be specifically analyzed here, even though certain of these privileges, such as that of State secrecy, may be appreciated by arbitrators in the same manner as the attorney-client privilege.

The problem at issue is to determine solutions in order to resolve conflicts of privileges in international arbitration. This can be illustrated as follows: Which privilege rules should an arbitral tribunal apply when both parties have different nationality and ask for the disclosure of communications and documents from different lawyers based in different countries? Evidentiary privilege, which limits the obligation to disclose certain documents or information, is particularly delicate in international arbitration, because of the great diversity in the modes of taking evidence and the specificity of the arbitral proceedings (II). However, some arbitration solutions shall be proposed in order to resolve conflicts of privileges (III).

---

*   Partner, Darrois Villey Maillot Brochier.
1. M. SINDLER and T. WÜSTEMANN, "Privilege Across Borders in Arbitration: Multi-jurisdictional Nightmare or a Storm in a Teacup?", 23 ASA Bulletin (2005, no. 4) pp. 610-639.

II.   THE SPECIFICITY OF EVIDENTIARY PRIVILEGE IN INTERNATIONAL ARBITRATION

Privilege determinations in international arbitration are particularly complex because there are no established rules that govern these determinations in international law (*1*) and because different countries have very different conceptions regarding the nature and the extent of the attorney-client privilege (*2*).

1.   Rules Established by Arbitral Institutions

International law provides little institutional guidance to arbitral tribunals concerning evidentiary privileges (*a*). The increasing need for an internationally harmonized approach is not being met at the moment (*b*).

a.   A lack of international rules of arbitration related to evidentiary privileges
The rules of the major international arbitration institutions and international bodies do not provide assistance in determining how issues of privilege should be handled in international arbitration.

   Neither the ICC Rules of Arbitration nor the UNCITRAL Arbitration Rules directly refer to evidentiary privileges.[2]

   In particular, the fact that the ICC Rules make no specific provision on the power of the arbitral tribunal to compel production of documents can be illustrated by the ICC arbitral tribunal's order dated 7 January 1997 (in ICC Case no. 6401).

   In this arbitration, the tribunal was faced with the question of whether it should request (or permit the requesting party to request) an order from a national court in Switzerland compelling persons who were not parties to the arbitration to produce certain documents. In order to decide this question, the tribunal considered that it first needed to examine whether a request for production of the requested documents would be admissible under the applicable national law. Therefore, the tribunal examined the request on the sole ground of Art. 184 of the Swiss Federal Act on Private International Law.[3] As part of this examination, the arbitral tribunal had to take into consideration

---

2. There are other sets of rules which, by way of exception, refer to legal privileges: the AAA International Arbitration Rules (Arts. 16.1, 19.3 and 20.6) and the International Institute for Conflict Prevention and Resolution Rules for Non-administered Arbitration (Art. 12.2).
3. Art. 184 of the Swiss Federal Act on Private International Law, related to the "taking of evidence", provides that:

"1. The arbitral tribunal shall take evidence.
2. If the assistance of the judicial or administrative authorities of the State is needed to take evidence, the arbitral tribunal or, with the consent of the arbitral tribunal, a party may request the assistance of the judge at the seat of the arbitral tribunal who shall apply his own law."

To this extent, that arbitral tribunal held that:

"(3) .... With regard to the particular issue of obtaining the evidence, Art. 184(1) of the Act, as quoted above, specifically provides that the Arbitral Tribunal shall itself take the evidence. But, whereas Art. 184(2) provides for the assistance of the State Courts, it specifies that this assistance

applicable Swiss legal principles, notably those related to the duty of confidentiality imposed on professionals.[4]

Most rules of arbitration procedure recognize that an arbitral tribunal may determine procedural issues, but they do not indicate whether or not a tribunal must respect evidentiary privileges. Even where privileges are mentioned, such rules often do not specify how and when an arbitral tribunal should apply them. For example, the IBA Rules on the Taking of Evidence in International Commercial Arbitration provide that an arbitral tribunal may exclude any document from evidence or production on grounds of legal impediment or privilege (Art. 9(2)(b)),[5] but they do not go on to state which laws should apply or which tribunal should go about making that determination.[6]

Also, the Hague Convention on the Taking of Evidence Abroad in Civil or Commercial Matters, dated 18 March 1970, even if not applicable to arbitration, recognizes the right to claim evidentiary privileges by establishing a cooperation system

---

is governed by the proper law of such Courts. It follows that when examining whether it may require such assistance, the Arbitral Tribunal has to examine whether and to what extent the proper law of the Court of the seat of the Tribunal allows the request submitted by a party."

4. ".... (7) It should further be mentioned that Swiss law and practice impose a duty of confidentiality to the members of certain professions, that authorizes them to refuse to testify. It is generally accepted that the same duty authorizes them to refuse to produce documents. The violation of such duty of confidentiality is considered as a crime and made punishable under Art. 321 of the Swiss Criminal Code. This provision lists the professionals who are under a legal duty to keep confidential the information obtained in their professional capacity; this list includes members of the Bar and statutory auditors of companies. With regard to statutory auditors, their duty of confidentiality is inscribed at Art. 730 of the Swiss Code of Obligations.

It is generally admitted that a further and wider circle of professionals are authorized to respect a duty of professional confidentiality, even if the breach of such duty is not treated as a crime under Art. 321 of the Swiss Criminal Code. Thus, it is generally accepted that chartered accountants (even when not acting as statutory auditors) have a contractual duty of confidentiality towards their clients (Jean-Jacques Schwaab, *Devoir de discretion et obligation de témoigner et de produire des pieces (Etude de droit federal et de procedure vaudoise), thèse,* Lausanne, 1976, pp. 119-124). Thus, the Code of Civil Procedure of the Canton of Vaud, which is of particular importance in this matter since all but one of the individuals mentioned in the Request are residents of the Canton of Vaud and under the jurisdiction of its Courts, provides as follows (Art. 200): 'The Court may authorize the witness not to disclose confidential industrial or commercial information, or confidential facts concerning private life. The Court assesses each case in consideration of the importance of the evidence and of the interest of the confidentiality for the witness.'"

5. Art. 9(2)(b) of the IBA Rules on the Taking of Evidence in International Commercial Arbitration reads:

"The Arbitral Tribunal shall, at the request of a Party or on its own motion, exclude from evidence or production any document, statement, oral testimony or inspection for any of the following reasons: ... b) legal impediment or privilege under the legal or ethical rules determined by the Arbitral Tribunal to be applicable."

6. The IBA Working Group considers that legal privileges should be recognized in international arbitration, but that some equitable readjustment might be necessary to ensure "*equality of arms*": thus, it contemplates that an arbitral tribunal can order a measure of discovery.

between States, which does not refer specifically to arbitration procedure: it simply provides that a judicial authority of a Contracting State may, in accordance with the law of that State, request the competent authority of another Contracting State, by means of a Letter of Request, to obtain evidence.[7] This Letter of Request will be executed with respect to Art. 11 of the Hague Convention, which states that

> "In the execution of a Letter of Request the person concerned may refuse to give evidence in so far as he has a privilege or duty to refuse to give the evidence a) under the law of the State of execution, or b) under the law of the State of origin, and the privilege or duty has been specified in the Letter, or, at the instance of the requested authority, has been otherwise confirmed to that authority by the requesting authority."

Art. 11 also provides that

> "A Contracting State may declare that, in addition, it will respect privileges and duties existing under the law of States other than the State of origin and the State of execution, to the extent specified in that declaration."

b. The absence of a harmonized set of rules

The establishment of internationally harmonized rules could reinforce predictability and equality of arms for parties in international arbitration. The international arbitration bar could develop a set of principles defining the nature and scope of the attorney-client privileges.

Still, at the present time, there is no single international code of commonly accepted principles even though all professional privileges have the same object: to encourage communication between professionals and those with whom they have a professional relationship.

Such an attempt was made under the Principles of Transnational Civil Procedure, adopted by the American Law Institute and UNIDROIT.[8] Art. 18 on "Evidentiary Privileges and Immunities" allows a court to respect applicable evidentiary privileges, which may vary from jurisdiction to jurisdiction. Although many recommendations were made on this issue, most of them were not adopted.

This shows that achieving an autonomous set of privilege rules in international arbitration remains extremely difficult.

In this regard, it can be interesting to refer to the Council of Bars and Law Societies of Europe, which, as the representative of the legal profession in Europe, adopted a "Statement of Position on Lawyers' Secrecy and Confidentiality and Their Importance for a Democratic Society that Follows the System of Justice" in February 2001, and reaffirmed it in December 2004.

---

7. See EC Regulation 1206/2001 containing similar provisions.
8. It should be noted that preliminary remarks attached to these Principles directly state that "these Principles are equally applicable to international arbitration".

Through this Statement, the Council required "the lawyer to be treated in any other EEC country, as far as professional secrecy is concerned, the same way as the national lawyer, with reservation that in the State where professional secrecy is requested, the conditions to practice the profession are not incompatible with the ones applicable in the country". That means that the attorney-client privilege applicable in a European country is to be protected in the same manner in any other European country as if the lawyer of the first country were one of the second country.

The notion of confidentiality, as mentioned by the Council of Bars and Law Societies of Europe, has an extremely wide scope. The Code of Conduct for Lawyers in the European Union gives, indeed, in its Art. 2.3, a particularly broad definition:

"2.3.1. It is of the essence of a lawyer's function that he should be told by his client things which the client would not tell to others, and that he should be the recipient of other information on a basis of confidence. Without the certainty of confidentiality there cannot be trust. Confidentiality is therefore a primary and fundamental right and duty of the lawyer.

The lawyer's obligation of confidentiality serves the interest of the administration of justice as well as the interest of the client. It is therefore entitled to special protection by the State.

2.3.2. A lawyer shall respect the confidentiality of all information that becomes known to him in the course of his professional activity.

2.3.3. The obligation of confidentiality is not limited in time.

2.3.4. A lawyer shall require his associates and staff and anyone engaged by him in the course of providing professional services to observe the same obligation of confidentiality."

Such Statement, and the broad sense attributed to the attorney-client privilege by the Code of Conduct, may be seen as a trend toward harmonization of the rules related to confidentiality, at least in Europe.

2. National Rules on Attorney-Client Privilege

International arbitration involves parties, lawyers and arbitrators from diverse legal and cultural traditions. Arbitral tribunals will most often comprise arbitrators from multiple jurisdictions and legal traditions different from those of the parties and of their counsel. The problem is that even though there are similarities between most legal systems (a), different jurisdictions have different concepts as to the nature and scope of privileges (b).

a. Similarities between legal systems

The communications between lawyers and their clients are considered as confidential information – and protected as such – in common law and civil law jurisdictions. It should also be noted that the confidentiality of communications with external counsel is recognized in both legal systems.

Each legal system establishes a set of rules applicable to privileges. Most national laws (except Germany)[9] have general provisions related to the production of documents or privileges in arbitration. For example, Art. 1460 of the French New Code of Civil Procedure provides that an arbitral tribunal may order a party to produce evidence, but there is no mention of the defence of legal privileges.

Therefore, most systems acknowledge that privilege cannot be relied on as a blanket defence to disclosure, but must be considered on a case-by-case basis. According to this principle, the establishment of a general set of rules on legal privileges may not be sufficient to take each case into consideration.

b.   Differences between common law and civil law jurisdictions
A first main difference between the two legal systems lies in the concept of non-voluntary document disclosure: such disclosure is an obligation under English and American law, whereas German and French civil procedure are based on the fact that no litigant is required to provide weapons for his opponent's case.[10]

A second main difference is the nature of the attorney-client privilege, which is different in common law countries and civil law countries.

In common law countries, the attorney-client privilege (in the United States) or the legal professional privilege (in England) is considered as a rule of evidence, designed to encourage forthright communications between attorneys and their clients by ensuring that the content of such communications will not be introduced as evidence in legal proceedings.

In civil law countries, the attorney-client privilege is treated as a "professional secret", considered at the same time as a duty of the attorney and a matter of public policy. For example, in France the law on the *secret professionnel* is established in the French penal code.

3.   Interference of Public Policy Issues: State Secrets Approach

A comparison of the rules established by arbitral institutions and the national rules on attorney-client privilege shows a great variation in the treatment and implementation of evidentiary privileges. One of the difficult questions to be solved is that of the arbitral tribunal's reaction in case a party asserts that the disclosure of certain documents would breach public policy rules.

It seems difficult to determine a general rule of transnational public policy on evidentiary privileges. Even though some commentators recommend that legal privileges, particularly the communications between a lawyer and his client, constitute international public policy, there does not seem to be a general recognition of such privilege in all legal systems. In the absence of transnational public policy related to

---

9. V. FISCHER-ZERNIN and A. JUNKER, "Between Scylla and Charybdis: Fact Gathering in German Arbitration", 4 Journal of International Arbitration (1987, no. 2) pp. 9-34.

10. For a comparative analysis of the French and English notion of professional secrecy: see D. LE GRAND DE BELLEROCHE, *"L'avocat français et le solicitor anglais: le secret professionnel dans une dimension européenne"*, Petites Affiches (25 March 2005, no. 60) p. 3.

evidentiary privileges, the arbitral tribunal should concentrate on national public policy, on a case-to-case basis.

Therefore, should an arbitral tribunal automatically exclude the production of documents that fall under the scope of a national public policy? In some cases, it could be asserted that the refusal to produce certain documents could be justified on the basis that such documents are protected under the public policy of a country. Let's focus our attention on cases in which State secrets are at stake. Considering the importance of protecting State secrets, such a claim should allow the arbitral tribunal to reject demands to produce documents, even more easily than when attorney-client privileges are concerned.

a. Disclosure of documents

In a pending arbitration, in which a private company and a State are involved, the arbitral tribunal decided, in a procedural order unpublished and confidential, that it could not order the production of the requested documents in light of the legal impediments under the law of the State party to the arbitration. To rule on this issue, the arbitral tribunal did not deal with the question of confidentiality and concentrated on the question of whether the State party to the arbitration was in a position to produce the requested documents without violation of its own laws protecting military secrecy. The tribunal held in particular that the State and the persons acting on behalf of the State would run the risk of criminal sanctions and were therefore prevented from producing the requested documents. Such a decision is particularly interesting as it would enable a party, whose national law would prohibit the disclosure of specific and protected information or documents, to claim that, due to this prohibition, it is prevented from disclosing such documents.

On the contrary, in the NAFTA arbitration *Pope and Talbot Inc. v. the Government of Canada*, in which Canada refused to produce certain documents on the ground that they related to *Cabinet confidence* (State secrets), the arbitral tribunal, through its procedural order No. 11 dated 6 September 2000, analyzed the national provisions at stake and held that Canada did not "have domestic law that would permit or require them to withhold documents from Chapter 11 tribunals without any justification beyond a simple certification that they are some kind of state secret". Therefore, Canada was asked to justify or to "offer reasons why in conformity with a general law relating to State secrets those particular documents or any of them should be withheld".

b. Admissibility and enforcement of an arbitration

Art. 35 of the ICC Rules of Arbitration provides that "the Arbitral Tribunal shall … make every effort to make sure that the Award is enforceable at law".

Should an award contain references and information on State secrets, a party could claim that such award constitutes a breach of international public policy.

However, the refusal to produce documents on the basis of State secrets does not necessarily mean that arbitrators lack jurisdiction to rule on the issue at stake. In another pending arbitration award, the arbitral tribunal had to determine whether a case could be submitted to arbitration if national defence secrets were at stake. Since the parties had decided to submit this case to the arbitral tribunal on the basis of an arbitration agreement without mentioning any condition related to State secret information, the arbitral tribunal held, in an award unpublished and confidential, that the difficulty for a party to produce certain documents has no impact on the arbitration procedure and should be dealt with as a simple issue of evidence.

A problem could also arise if an arbitral tribunal did not recognize a privilege which, in the country of enforcement, was considered as a fundamental substantive right: disregarding such obligation could be ruled a breach of the public policy of that country. However, in practice, national judges have not yet refused to enforce an award on that ground.

This analysis of State secrets cases provides interesting solutions that could be applied to attorney-client privilege. We could conclude that public policy cannot automatically justify a refusal to produce documents: parties are expected to justify in each case the reasons why such document cannot be disclosed.

4.   Conclusion

This overview of the law on evidentiary privileges shows that international arbitral tribunals cannot expect much consistent guidance from international and national sources. This uncertainty has far-reaching consequences for the parties and counsel facing the prospect of international arbitration.

At the same time, as reflected in the overview, parties and their counsel from different countries and different legal systems likely have conducted their affairs with very different understandings and expectations about the nature of attorney-client privilege and about the ability of any adversary to obtain non-voluntary disclosure of documents in the event that a dispute goes to arbitration.

Therefore, arbitral tribunals must create their own rules for determining which legal privileges should apply in any given case and should be mindful of the different understanding and expectations of the parties bearing on the issue. We shall address some recommendations for legal privilege determination in international arbitration.

III.   RECOMMENDATIONS FOR RESOLVING CONFLICTS OF PRIVILEGES

Questions of conflicts of privileges can affect an international arbitration on different grounds (equality of treatment of the parties, ethical considerations, etc.) at different steps of the arbitration procedure (admission of evidence, enforcement of awards, etc.). How evidence is produced, its admissibility and assessment determine both the conduct and the result of the arbitration. Therefore, the determination of applicable privileges is extremely important.

This means that the choices made by arbitrators have practical effects that cannot be underestimated. For example, concerning the enforceability of awards, a problem could arise if an arbitral tribunal did not recognize a privilege which, in the country of enforcement, was considered as a matter of public policy. The disregard of this privilege could also be interpreted as a breach of due process.

Some commentators have suggested that to provide some certainty and to relieve the arbitrators from having to make such choices, privileges should be addressed in the arbitration clause. In keeping with the voluntary nature of arbitration, a contractual solution provides the parties with the most flexibility, allowing them to adapt the privilege rules to their particular concerns and needs. However, in practice, a standard arbitration clause is often used by contracting parties, with no reference to the issue of privileges.

Commentators have proposed a variety of approaches that may be taken by arbitrators to resolve conflicts of privilege in the absence of the parties' having settled such matters in the text of their arbitration clause. It seems to me that the most sensible approach is for the arbitrators to first apply the "closest connection test"[11] (1) and then, in case there is a still a conflict, to adopt the most favourable privilege approach (2).

1.   Choice-of-law Approach

The choice of law applicable to the administration of privileges remains complex, as a variety of "connecting factors" can be used by arbitrators to determine it. According to the prevalent practice as reflected in almost all leading institutional arbitration rules, arbitrators are granted wide discretion[12] in the method for selecting the appropriate applicable law.

The first possibility offered to arbitrators is to apply the *lex arbitri* or the law of the place of arbitration (*lex fori*) as being most closely connected to issues of privilege. Such approach would enable the application of the same privilege rules to all parties. However, it cannot be assumed that the parties' original choice of the place of arbitration was in any way influenced by legal privilege rules.

An appropriate connecting factor in many cases involving potential application of attorney-client privilege will be the law applicable at the lawyer's professional domicile. Taking into account that privilege rules in many countries are formulated as rules of professional ethics, it appears reasonable in respect of any given document to apply the same rules of privilege to the lawyer and to the client.

In many cases, the various mentioned factors will all lead to the same result and will provide an easily identifiable and predictable solution. But reliable answers must also be found in cases where the connecting factors do not coincide. Therefore, arbitrators must seek means to resolve conflicts of privileges.

2.   The "Most Favourable Privilege" Approach

In cases where there is a conflict, the choice-of-law method will lead to a situation in which different rules of privilege apply to different parties. The most favourable privilege approach appears to be the most appropriate method in order to determine which rules of legal privilege should apply in a particular case.

---

11. F. VON SCHLABRENDORFF and A. SHEPPARD, "Conflict of Legal Privileges in International Arbitration: An Attempt to Find a Holistic Solution", in Gerald AKSEN, et al., eds., *Global Reflections on International Law, Commerce and Dispute Resolution, Liber Amicorum in Honour of Robert Briner* (ICC Publishing, Paris 2005).

12. Art. 20(1) of the ICC Rules provides that the "Arbitral Tribunal shall proceed within as short a time as possible to establish the facts of the case by all appropriate means."

This approach allows any party to an international arbitration to claim the same privileges that are available to any other party. Objections must be raised on a case-by-case basis and the privilege must be claimed with respect to each specific communication at issue. Therefore, proportionality is of fundamental importance, and, to this extent, privilege is not to be regarded as an absolute rule.

In short, this is a common-sense approach according to which arbitrators resolve conflicting issues. The most favourable privilege approach simply implies that the parties should be treated equally and that the confidentiality of lawyers' communications and documents should generally be respected.

Indeed, adequate weight should be given to the expectations of the parties. Parties that agree to resolve a dispute by arbitration should be treated by the arbitral tribunal in a fair and reasonable manner. Communications that were privileged when made should remain privileged. The most favourable privilege approach tends to assure that the law and rules applied by the tribunal will be reasonably certain and predictable.

The arbitral tribunal should also take into consideration the equality of the parties, considered as one of the most important factors to which an arbitral tribunal must have regard when adopting and implementing any procedural rules. There is no need to give further details on the wide recognition of this principle. International arbitrators should adopt an approach that allows any party to the arbitration to claim the same legal privileges as are available to any other party.

The party claiming that a specific document is considered under national law as legally privileged must be able to justify its position. Indeed, in several cases, courts decided to protect the equality between the parties by asking the party objecting that a document should be considered as privileged, to give some justification as to the reasons why such document should not be disclosed.

An example can be found in the ICSID arbitration *ADF Inc. v. United States*, in which a general objection had been entered by the respondent that the documents required for production were "protected from disclosure by applicable law, including without limitation, documents protected by the attorney-client and government deliberative and pre-decisional privileges".

In its decision dated 9 January 2003, the arbitral tribunal ruled that such question was a matter for future determination and, in order to determine the applicability of the privileges adverted to, required the respondent to provide the tribunal with specific information:

– the respondent was asked to specify the documents in respect of which one or more privileges were claimed and the nature and scope of the particular privilege claimed;
– the respondent was also asked to show the applicability of such privilege at stake.

Another example may be recalled: the above-mentioned NAFTA arbitration *Pope and Talbot Inc. v. the Government of Canada* in which the tribunal had to decide whether Canada could refuse to produce certain documents on the ground of solicitor-client privilege.

In this case, the arbitral tribunal opted for a selective approach in order to determine which documents might be considered as privileged. The arbitral tribunal held in particular that:

> "The Tribunal accepts, in general, the contention by Canada that solicitor-client privilege extends to communication for the purpose of giving or seeking legal advice (*Smith v. Jones* 1999 ISCR 455; *Solosky v. Canada* 1980 ISCR 821; *Descôteaux v. Mierzwinski* 1982 ISCR 860). It rejects the contention on behalf of the Investor that the privilege is confined to legal advice given in contemplation of litigation."

In accordance with this consideration, the arbitral tribunal considered that Canada's claim for privilege should be accepted, to the extent that the documents at stake concerned legal advice. As a result, the tribunal accepted that, on this basis, some documents should not be produced and, at the same time, also decided in favour of the disclosure of several other documents which did "not appear to be confined to the provision of legal advice".

It should be noted that in the same arbitration, Canada also refused to produce other documents on the ground of Sect. 39 of the Canada Evidence Act, which Canada considered "creates an absolute prohibition on the disclosure of documents which are or contain Cabinet confidences".[13]

The decision of the arbitral tribunal on this issue is interesting in several respects.

The arbitral tribunal considered that the Canada Evidence Act was not applicable and held that

> "The Tribunal is not 'a court, person or body with jurisdiction to compel the production of information'. It is operating under the UNCITRAL Rules. While Art. 24(3) of those rules empowers to 'require the parties to produce documents, exhibits or other evidence', there is no power to compel that production. Indeed, Art. 28(3) characterises this requirement to produce as an invitation."[14]

---

13. Sect. 39 of the Canada Evidence Act provides, in its para. 1, that:

"Where a minister of the Crown or the Clerk of the Privy Council objects to the disclosure of information before a court, person or body with jurisdiction to compel the production of information by certifying in writing that the information constitutes a confidence of the Queen's Privy Council for Canada, disclosure of the information shall be refused without examination or hearing of the information by the Court, person or body."

14. Art. 28(3) of the UNICTRAL Rules states that:

"If one of the parties, duly invited to produce documentary evidence, fails to do so within the established period of time, without showing sufficient cause for such failure, the arbitral tribunal may make the award on the evidence before it."

The arbitral tribunal then acknowledged that the protection of State secrets may justify a refusal to produce documents[15] but only with respect to the equality of the parties. It stated that:

> "In the specific context of a NAFTA arbitration where the parties have agreed to operate by UNCITRAL Rules, it is an overriding principle (Art. 15) that the parties be treated with equality. The other NAFTA Parties do not, so far as the Tribunal has been made aware, have domestic law that would permit or require them to withhold documents from Chapter 11 tribunals without any justification beyond a simple certification that they are some kind of state secret. In these circumstances, Canada, if it could simply rely on Sect. 39, might be in an unfairly advantaged position under Chapter 11 by comparison with the United States and Mexico."

Since the tribunal had no means of knowing what sort of material was being withheld, it asked Canada to identify the documents and to justify the reason why such documents cannot be disclosed.

IV.   CONCLUSION

Increased application of the "most favourable privilege" approach should provide a greater predictability in international arbitration. It will also compensate the current absence of an internationally harmonized set of rules for privileges in international arbitration. It might also be more efficient than an autonomous set of rules in international law, because of its ability to take into consideration the specificity of each case.

---

15. "It is not in dispute that a ground that may justify refusal of a party to produce documents to an international arbitral tribunal may be the protection of state secrets."

Working Group B

4. Arbitral Provisional Measures: The Actual Practice

Introduction

*Fali S. Nariman**

The topic of this Section is in a global context. And we who earn our daily bread in international arbitration know what it is to live in a truly Global World. You may be surprised to hear, that this Global World has a Global Heaven and the other-place as well!

Globalization Heaven has been described as a place "where you have an American salary, live in a British house, eat Chinese food, and have an Indian wife". And the other place: Globalization Hell is "where you have an American wife, eat British food, have a Chinese house, and get an Indian salary"!

But on a serious note, let me begin by saying what this session is not: it is not about UNCITRAL's deliberations on the working text of Art. 17 *bis*. The reason is that Arbitral Provisional Measures defy textual analysis: in this particular area, the words of the statute are simply not enough.

It is not what the book says, but what arbitral tribunals actually do: the emphasis in this topic is on the Actual Practice.

Of course as we all know, urgency is a sine qua non for any interim measures.

But after that, it depends not so much on the complexities of the case at hand but on the arbitral tribunal's perception of the possibility of harmful effect. Most arbitrators play safe: "Don't alter the status quo," they say. But let us hear what is the actual practice – from Kaj Hobér, Jose Maria Abascal, Neil Kaplan and Marc Blessing[1] – each of whom are constantly and vigorously arbitrating.

They live, read and talk arbitration: when they are not talking to their wives (and when their wives are not looking, to their girl friends!) they are talking about arbitration! And they are here to talk to you about the difficult and often tricky business of interim measures and share with you their vast experience as counsel for parties in arbitral proceedings and as arbitrators.

To arrive at a decision after fully hearing a case is not too difficult – but with only a sketchy outline, an Arbitral Tribunal at the commencement of the proceeding is pretty much left on its own in deciding when to grant or when not to grant interim measures: it is always a little bit like playing that old card game known as "blind rummy". And it is here that the experienced arbitrator scores; he or she senses his or her way around the problem.

So I invite Kaj Hobér and the three speakers after him to share their rich experiences with us.

Kaj has twenty-five minutes, and the rest twelve minutes each. And my mandate is to be ruthless with time so as to leave twenty-nine to thirty minutes for comments and

---

* Honorary President of ICCA.

1. See pp. 721-750, pp. 751-767 and pp.768-776, respectively, for Kaj Hober's Report and José Maria Abascal's and Neil Kaplan's Comments. Marc Blessing's Comments are not reproduced in this volume.

questions from the floor, not much, but that's all that is provided for. At meetings like this the rule is: as long as everything worth saying gets said, it does not matter whether everyone has had a chance to speak!

I will not introduce the Speakers – they are far too praise-worthy for introduction. And as each of them has grown older in the world of international arbitration, there is just no amount of praise that they cannot possibly absorb – un-introduced!

Interim Measures by Arbitrators

*Kaj Hobér**

I.   INTRODUCTION

As we all know arbitration is nowadays the preferred dispute settlement mechanism for international commercial disputes. One of the advantages of arbitration is that it is quick, as a rule much quicker than court litigation. This notwithstanding, few international arbitrations are concluded in less than a year. This means that in many cases there will be a need to protect the parties' rights before a final award has been rendered, i.e., there is a need for interim measures of protection. Thirty or forty years ago this does not seem to have been much of a problem. If the arbitrator, or the arbitral tribunal, was of the view that one of the parties should do or refrain from doing something, the tribunal would say so and that was that. The parties having agreed to arbitration and appointed arbitrators – thereby entrusting them with decision-making power – usually accepted the authority and decisions of the arbitrators, complied with them and tried to apply the arbitration agreement in good faith.

During the last twenty to twenty-five years much has changed in the world of arbitration. It is probably fair to say that arbitration has become more aggressive, partly explained by the ever-increasing amounts at stake. Counsel represent their clients in a more one-sided, partisan way than before. This development has created new demands on modern international commercial arbitration. One element of this development is the growing need for interim protection. This is partly due to the globalization of the world economy in general and to the ease and speed with which assets can be transferred from one jurisdiction to another, in particular.[1]

---

* Mannheimer Swartling, Stockholm; Board Member, Arbitration Institute of the Stockholm Chamber of Commerce.

1. See, e.g., BESSON, *Arbitrage Internationale et measures provisoires* (1998) pp. 43-44. A study carried out by the AAA indicated that the number of requests for interim measures in international commercial arbitrations was nearly double the number of such requests in domestic arbitration; see NAIMARK-KEER, "Analysis of UNCITRAL, Questionnaires on Interim Relief", Mealey's International Arbitration Report (2001) p. 23 at p. 26.

It is against this background one must understand the initiative of UNCITRAL to establish a Working Group on Arbitration and Conciliation, inter alia, for the purpose of analyzing the question of interim measures.

The Working Group has now prepared draft legislative provisions on interim measures and interim orders to be implemented as amendments to Art. 17 of the UNCITRAL Model Law on International Commercial Arbitration.[2]

It is not the purpose of this Report to discuss and analyze the proposals of the Working Group. This has been done by many commentators in many different fora. Rather, the purpose of this report is to try to find out how arbitrators de facto approach and handle various issues relating to interim measures in international commercial arbitration. With a view to finding this out, a questionnaire was sent to forty-five leading international arbitrators.[3] Thirty-three of them responded. In 1982 Dr. Ottoarndt Glossner wrote an article entitled "Sociological Aspects of International Commercial Arbitration".[4] This was one of the first articles devoted to the sociological aspects of international arbitration. Dr. Glossner explains, by way of introduction, that he wants to provoke further thought, research and study of the human and sociological factors in international arbitration.[5] Over the years, however, not much work has been done in this direction. On the whole, there is very little empirical research being done in the field of international arbitration.[6]

Much of the previous debate on interim measures has consequently been based on anecdotal information rather than on empirical data. The questionnaire is a modest attempt to somewhat remedy this situation. The focus of the survey is thus the actual conduct of arbitrators, leaving aside most of the theoretical problems.[7]

The focus on actual conduct notwithstanding, it is helpful, by way of introduction and background to review, however briefly, the legal and institutional framework with

---

2. See Report of the Working Group on Arbitration and Conciliation on the work of its forty fourth session (New York, 23-27 January 2006).

3. The Questionnaire and the aggregated responses to the questions are presented in Annex I, pp. 742-746.

4. It was published in SCHULTSZ and VAN DEN BERG, eds., *The Art of Arbitration, Liber Amicorum Pieter Sanders* (1982).

5. *Ibid.*, p. 143.

6. One recent exception is the report "International Arbitration: Corporate Attitudes and Practices 2006", published in 2006 by the School of International Arbitration, Queen Mary College, University of London and PricewaterhouseCoopers; available at <www.pwc.com/ arbitrationstudy>.

7. This does not mean, of course, that the theoretical aspects are unimportant – far from it. This is illustrated, inter alia, by the reports of the UNCITRAL Working Group on Arbitration. The theoretical aspects are also subjected to scholarly analysis, inter alia, in the following publications: BÖTSCH, ed., *Provisional Remedies in International Commercial Arbitration – A Practitioner's Handbook* (1994); BESSON, *op. cit.*, fn. 1; SCHEEF, *Das einstweilige Rechtsschutz und die Stellung der Schiedsrichter bei dem Abschluss von Schiedsvergleichen nach deutschem und englischem Recht* (2001); LEW, MISTELIS, KRÖLL, *Comparative International Commercial Arbitration* (2003); YESILIRMAK, *Provisional Measures in International Commercial Arbitration* (2005); and MISTELIS and LEW, eds., *Pervasive Problems in International Arbitration* (2006).

respect to interim measures in international arbitration. Thereafter I shall turn to the results of the survey.

II.   THE LEGAL AND INSTITUTIONAL FRAMEWORK

1.   *The Authority of Arbitral Tribunals to Order Interim Security Measures*

a.   National arbitration legislation

Many modern arbitration acts are based on the UNCITRAL Model Law, albeit to varying degrees. The Model Law addresses the question of interim measures in Art. 17.
   Art. 17 of the current Model Law provides the following:

> "Unless otherwise agreed by the parties, the arbitral tribunal may, at the request of a party, order any party to take such interim measure of protection as the arbitral tribunal may consider necessary in respect of the subject-matter of the dispute. The arbitral tribunal may require any party to provide appropriate security in connection with such measure."

This provision gives the arbitral tribunal broad authority to order interim measures. The authority is not limited to certain measures, and it is in the tribunal's discretion to determine whether interim measures are appropriate and necessary given the circumstances of the individual case. The broad authority of the tribunal is limited, however, by the reference to a measure "in respect of the subject matter of the dispute".
   As previously mentioned, UNCITRAL's Working Group II (Arbitration) is discussing possible amendments to Art. 17 of the Model Law.[8] The proposed revisions aim at providing more detailed provisions as to (i) what kind of measures arbitrators may grant, (ii) the conditions which must be satisfied, (iii) the procedure to be applied, (iv) security, (v) disclosure of new circumstances, (vi) costs and damages and (vii) recognition and enforcement.[9]
   In *Canada* commercial arbitration is, save for limited federal powers, a matter in the exclusive jurisdiction of the provincial legislatures.[10] All provinces and territories except Quebec, i.e., all common law provinces, have adopted the UNCITRAL Model Law.[11] Under Art. 17 of the Model Law an arbitral tribunal may, at the request of a party, order any party to take such interim measure of protection as the arbitral tribunal may consider necessary in respect of the subject-matter of the dispute. Enforcement of interim awards is governed by the same rules that apply to regular awards. In Quebec,

---

8. See fn. 2, supra.

9. The proposal of the Working Group is reproduced as Annex II, pp. 747-750.

10. See LALONDE, "National Report Canada" in ICCA *Handbook on Commercial Arbitration* (hereinafter *Handbook*) p. 1.

11. *Ibid.*, p. 2.

Art. 940.4 of the Code of Civil Procedure states that the authority to order provisional interim measures lies with a judge, or a tribunal (as opposed to an arbitral tribunal).[12]

In *China* only the People's Court may order interim measures. Arbitrators and arbitral institutions can not do so (see Art. 258 of the Civil Procedure Law, Art. 28 of the Arbitration Act and Art. 17 of the CIETAC Arbitration Rules).[13]

Under Sect. 38 of the *English* Arbitration Act of 1996 an arbitral tribunal may give directions in relation to any property which is the subject of the arbitration proceedings or as to which any question arises in the proceedings and which is owned by or is in the possession of a party to the proceedings. However, unless otherwise agreed in writing, the tribunal may not order provisional payment of money or disposition of property.[14] The power of the tribunal thus significantly depends on the agreement of the parties.

Also in *France* an arbitral tribunal has the authority to issue decisions on interim measures. Such decisions may be rendered in the form of interim awards, which may be enforced immediately and separately from any award on the merits. Under Art. 1479 of the Code of Civil Procedure an arbitral tribunal may declare interim awards provisionally enforceable.[15]

In *Germany*, the arbitration act is based on the Model Law. Thus, under Sect. 1041 of the Code of Civil Procedure the arbitrators may, at the request of a party, order such interim or preventive measures as they consider necessary in respect of the subject matter of the dispute. A court may, at the request of a party, permit the execution of such tribunal's order. The court may also amend the order if necessary for the enforcement of the measure.[16]

Under the laws of *The Netherlands* certain interim measures of protection, such as for example, an order for the sale of perishable goods or for establishing a bank guarantee, may, at the request of a party, be ordered by the arbitrators. The measure may be given in the form of an order or interim award. Such orders and interim awards are not enforceable through Dutch courts. Under Art. 1051 of the Code of Civil Procedure the parties may agree to empower the arbitral tribunal, or its chairman, to render an award for provisional relief in summary proceedings. Awards resulting from such summary proceedings may be enforced or set aside as any other arbitral award. Conservative attachment of assets of a debtor or of a debt owed by a third party to the debtor, which is a type of interim measure frequently used in practice, can only be granted by state courts.[17]

According to Art. 17 of the law of the *Russian Federation* on international commercial arbitration arbitrators may, at the request of a party and unless otherwise agreed, order a party to take such interim measures as the arbitrators deem necessary. This provision is based on Art. 17 of the Model Law.[18]

---

12. *Ibid.*, p. 24.
13. See HOUZHI and SHENGCHANG, "National Report China P.R." in *Handbook*, pp. 26-27.
14. See VEEDER, "National Report England" in *Handbook*, p. 42.
15. See DERAINS and GOODMAN-EVERARD, "National Report France" in *Handbook*, p. 33.
16. See BÖCKSTIEGEL, "National Report Germany" in *Handbook*, pp. 17-18.
17. See VAN DEN BERG, "National Report the Netherlands" in *Handbook*, pp. 18-19.
18. See full text of the law in "Russian Federation (Annex I)" in *Handbook*, pp. 5.

Also in *Singapore*, an arbitral tribunal is empowered to order interim measures in accordance with Sect. 12 of the International Arbitration Act. Such orders may, by leave of court, be made enforceable as orders of the court.[19]

In *Sweden*, under Sect. 25 of the Arbitration Act, arbitrators are empowered to grant interim measures to secure claims being tried by an arbitral tribunal. Such orders by the arbitrators are not enforceable in Sweden.[20]

Under *Swiss* law on international arbitration, Art. 183(1) of Chapter 12 of the Private International Law Act, (PILA), arbitrators may, upon request of a party, grant interim measures. If the party does not comply the arbitrators may seek the assistance of a court for enforcement.[21]

The Federal Arbitration Act of the *United States* does not contain any provision empowering arbitrators to grant interim measures. However, although the United States Supreme Court has not ruled on the issue, courts in the United States typically enforce interim measures ordered by arbitrators. The courts have reasoned that in case an interim award of equitable relief is based on a finding of irreparable harm, the award will only have meaning if the parties are able to enforce it at the time it is made. Moreover, the Uniform Arbitration Act of 2000, adopted by many states, provides for enforcement of interim awards.[22]

b. Rules of arbitration institutions

The authority and powers of arbitrators are based on the arbitration agreement concluded by the parties; so too with respect to the power to grant interim measures, mostly exercised by incorporating rules of arbitration institutions in the arbitration clause. As the following brief survey will show, most international arbitration institutions today provide for the possibility of interim measures ordered by arbitral tribunals.[23] It is noteworthy, however, that these rules vary considerably in their scope and level of detail.

---

19. See HWANG, BOO and LAI, "National Report Singapore" in *Handbook*.
20. See FRANKE, "National Report Sweden" in *Handbook*, pp. 12-13.
21. See BRINER, "National Report Switzerland" in *Handbook*, p. 23.
22. See HOLTZMANN and DONOVAN, "National Report United States" in *Handbook*, pp. 43-46. See also RIVKIN and DONOVAN in *Arbitration World, Jurisdictional Comparisons*, 2nd edn., pp. 395-396 and 404.
23. Some arbitration institutions provide a complementary mechanism in the form of so-called emergency interim measures which are issued before an arbitral tribunal has been constituted. Such measures may, for example, be issued by the head of an arbitration institution, see, e.g., Sect. 1(b) of the 1995 Arbitration Rules of the International Commercial Arbitration Court at the Chamber of Commerce and Industry of the Russian Federation, Art. 12(1) of the 2002 Arbitration Rules of the Arbitration Court at the Economic Chamber of Commerce of the Czech Republic and Art. R37 of the 1994 Procedural Rules of the Court of Arbitration for Sport. This category of emergency interim measures also includes the ICC Pre-Arbitral Referee Procedures and the WIPO Emergency Relief Rules. The rules on emergency measures have been introduced in an attempt to overcome one of the limitations of the arbitrators' powers in this area, *viz.*, that arbitrators cannot take decisions until and unless they have been duly appointed and the tribunal duly constituted. This limitation is of course one reason why parties seek interim measures in state courts.

i.   The AAA and ICDR Arbitration Rules

Under both the Commercial Arbitration Rules of the AAA and the ICDR Arbitration Rules an arbitral tribunal may order interim measures (Arts. 34 and 21, respectively). Art. 21 of the ICDR Rules provides the following:

> "1. At the request of any party, the tribunal may take whatever interim measures it deems necessary, including injunctive relief and measures for the protection of property.
> 2. Such interim measures may take the form of an interim award, and the tribunal may require security for the costs of such measures.
> 3. A request for interim measures addressed by a party to a judicial authority shall not be deemed incompatible with the agreement to arbitrate or a waiver of the right to arbitrate.
> 4. The tribunal may in its discretion apportion costs associated with applications for interim relief in any interim award or in the final award."

The AAA Rules are supplemented by "Optional Rules for Emergency Measures of Protection". These Rules are only applicable where the parties by special agreement or in their arbitration agreement have adopted them. The Optional Rules provide for a special fast-track procedure with a single "Emergency Arbitrator" empowered to try applications for interim measures.

ii.   The CIETAC Arbitration Rules

As previously mentioned,[24] under Chinese law neither the arbitrators nor an arbitration institution, such as CIETAC, have the authority to grant interim measures. Under Art. 17 of the CIETAC Arbitration Rules, CIETAC shall forward a party's application for the preservation of property to the competent court at the place where the party against whom the measure is sought is domiciled, or where the property is located. A similar provision is found in Art. 18 of the Rules according to which CIETAC shall forward a request for protection of evidence to a competent court where the evidence is located.

iii.   The ICC Rules

Art. 23 of the ICC Rules contains the following provisions on conservatory and interim measures.

> "1. Unless the parties have otherwise agreed, as soon as the file has been transmitted to it, the Arbitral Tribunal may, at the request of a party, order any interim or conservatory measure it deems appropriate. The Arbitral Tribunal may make the granting of any such measure subject to appropriate security being furnished by the requesting party. Any such measure shall take the form of an order, giving reasons, or of an Award, as the Arbitral Tribunal considers appropriate.

---

24. See p. 724, supra.

2. Before the file is transmitted to the Arbitral Tribunal, and in appropriate circumstances even thereafter, the parties may apply to any competent judicial authority for interim or conservatory measures. The application of a party to a judicial authority for such measures or for the implementation of any such measures ordered by an Arbitral Tribunal shall not be deemed to be an infringement or a waiver of the arbitration agreement and shall not affect the relevant powers reserved to the Arbitral Tribunal. Any such application and any measures taken by the judicial authority must be notified without delay to the Secretariat. The Secretariat shall inform the Arbitral Tribunal thereof."

By contrast, the 1988 ICC Rules did not have any provision explicitly authorizing arbitrators to order interim relief. Interestingly enough, however, such authority was implied. The underlying rationale was that by entering into an arbitration agreement the parties have given the tribunal the powers necessary to resolve the dispute, including the authority to order interim relief for safeguarding rights of the parties, if the tribunal so deems necessary.[25]

iv.   The ICSID Arbitration Rules
Pursuant to Rule 39 of the ICSID Arbitration Rules a party may, at any time after the institution of the proceedings, request the tribunal to *recommend* provisional measures for the preservation of the right of a party. The tribunal may also recommend provisional measures *on its own initiative* or recommend measures other than those specified in a request. Rule 39 reads as follows.

"1. At any time after the institution of the proceeding, a party may request that provisional measures for the preservation of its rights be recommended by the Tribunal. The request shall specify the rights to be preserved, the measures the recommendation of which is requested, and the circumstances that require such measures.

2. The Tribunal shall give priority to the consideration of a request made pursuant to paragraph 1.

3. The Tribunal may also recommend provisional measures on its own initiative or recommend measures other than those specified in a request. It may at any time modify or revoke its recommendations.

4. The Tribunal shall only recommend provisional measures, or modify or revoke its recommendations, after giving each party an opportunity of presenting its observations.

5. If a party makes a request pursuant to paragraph (1) before the constitution of the Tribunal, the Secretary-General shall, on the application of either party, fix time limits for the parties to present observations on the request, so that the request and observations may be considered by the Tribunal promptly upon its constitution.

---

25. Cf., e.g., BERGER, *International Economic Arbitration* (1993) p. 331 et seq.

6. Nothing in this Rule shall prevent the parties, provided that they have so stipulated in the agreement recording their consent, from requesting any judicial or other authority to order provisional measures, prior to or after the institution of the proceeding, for the preservation of their respective rights and interests."

It is thus not possible for an ICSID tribunal to issue orders for interim protection, but it is limited to recommendations. It is possible that the economic pressure that could be exercised by the World Bank was deemed to be sufficient.

v.   The Swiss Rules of International Arbitration
Art. 26 of the Swiss Rules of International Arbitration stipulates that the tribunal may, at the request of a party, order interim measures. Such order may be issued in the form of an interim award. Art. 26 reads as follows:

"1. At the request of either party, the arbitral tribunal may take any interim measures it deems necessary or appropriate.
2. Such interim measure may be established in the form of an interim award. The arbitral tribunal shall be entitled to order the provision of appropriate security.
3. A request for interim measures addressed by any other party to a judicial authority shall not be deemed incompatible with the agreement to arbitrate, or as a waiver of that agreement.
4. The arbitral tribunal shall have discretion to apportion the costs relating to a request for interim measures in the interim award or in the final award."

This provision is again a good illustration of the broad power given to arbitral tribunals under the rules of many arbitration institutions.

vi.   The LCIA Rules
Art. 25 of the LCIA Rules sets forth the most detailed institutional rules on interim measures. Pursuant to this provision the tribunal may, at the request of a party, and unless otherwise agreed in writing, order interim and conservatory measures as follows:

"25.1
The Arbitral Tribunal shall have the power, unless otherwise agreed by the parties in writing, on the application of any party:

(a) to order any respondent party to a claim or counterclaim to provide security for all or part of the amount in dispute, by way of deposit or bank guarantee or in any other manner and upon such terms as the Arbitral Tribunal considers appropriate. Such terms may include the provision by the claiming or counterclaiming party of a cross-indemnity, itself secured in such manner as the Arbitral Tribunal considers appropriate, for any costs or losses incurred by such respondent in providing security. The amount of any costs and losses payable under such cross-indemnity may be determined by the Arbitral Tribunal in one or more awards;

(b) to order the preservation, storage, sale or other disposal of any property or thing under the control of any party and relating to the subject matter of the arbitration; and

(c) to order on a provisional basis, subject to final determination in an award, any relief which the Arbitral Tribunal would have power to grant in an award, including a provisional order for the payment of money or the disposition of property as between any parties.

25.2

The Arbitral Tribunal shall have the power, upon the application of a party, to order any claiming or counterclaiming party to provide security for the legal or other costs of any other party by way of deposit or bank guarantee or in any other manner and upon such terms as the Arbitral Tribunal considers appropriate. Such terms may include the provision by that other party of a cross-indemnity, itself secured in such manner as the Arbitral Tribunal considers appropriate, for any costs and losses incurred by such claimant or counterclaimant in providing security. The amount of any costs and losses payable under such cross-indemnity may be determined by the Arbitral Tribunal in one or more awards. In the event that a claiming or counterclaiming party does not comply with any order to provide security, the Arbitral Tribunal may stay that party's claims or counterclaims or dismiss them in an award.

25.3

The power of the Arbitral Tribunal under Article 25.1 shall not prejudice howsoever any party's right to apply to any state court or other judicial authority for interim or conservatory measures before the formation of the Arbitral Tribunal and, in exceptional cases, thereafter. Any application and any order for such measures after the formation of the Arbitral Tribunal shall be promptly communicated by the applicant to the Arbitral Tribunal and all other parties. However, by agreeing to arbitration under these Rules, the parties shall be taken to have agreed not to apply to any state court or other judicial authority for any order for security for its legal or other costs available from the Arbitral Tribunal under Article 25.2."

Art. 25 thus gives arbitral tribunals an overriding authority to grant interim relief and sets forth general rules therefor. In addition it has a rather detailed provision on security for costs.

vii.   The SCC Rules

The rules on interim measures set out in the SCC Rules are similar to those in the Swedish Arbitration Act.[26] Art. 31 of the SCC Rules states the following:

---

26. See p. 725, supra.

"1. Unless the parties have agreed otherwise, the Arbitral Tribunal may, during the course of the proceedings and at the request of a party, order a specific performance by the opposing party for the purpose of securing the claim which is to be tried by the Arbitral Tribunal. The Arbitral Tribunal may order the requesting party to provide reasonable security for damage which may be inflicted on the opposing party as a result of the specific performance in question.

2. A request addressed by a party to a judicial authority for interim measures shall not be deemed to be incompatible with the arbitration agreement or these Rules."

The SCC Rules have recently been revised. The new rules entered into force on 1 January 2007.[27]

Under Art. 26 of the UNCITRAL Rules, which have served as a model for many of the above-mentioned institutional rules, the tribunal may, at the request of a party, order any interim measure as it finds appropriate. The provision reads:

"1. At the request of either party, the arbitral tribunal may take any interim measure it deems necessary in respect of the subject-matter of the dispute, including measures for the conservation of the goods forming the subject-matter in dispute, such as ordering their deposit with a third person or the sale of perishable goods.

2. Such interim measure may be established in the form of an interim award. The arbitral tribunal shall be entitled to require security for the costs of such measures.

3. A request for interim measures addressed by any party to a judicial authority shall not be deemed incompatible with the agreement to arbitrate, or as a waiver of that agreement."

2. Requirements for Granting Interim Measures

Approximately two decades ago, it was still an open question if arbitral tribunals had the authority to grant interim measures. It follows from the foregoing sections, that this threshold issue has now been resolved in favour of such authority. Most national arbitration acts and institutional rules confirm this. Most national acts and rules say

---

27. Following the ICCA Montreal Congress in 2006 the SCC has issued its revised Rules (available at <www.sccinstitute.com>). Art. 32 of the revised SCC Rules provides as follows:

"(1) The Arbitral Tribunal may, at the request of a party, grant any interim measure it deems appropriate.
(2) The Arbitral Tribunal may order the party requesting an interim measure to provide appropriate security in connection with the measure.
(3) An interim measure may take the form of an order or an award.
(4) A request for interim measures made by a party to a judicial authority is not incompatible with the arbitration agreement or with these Rules."

preciously little, however, about the standards for granting interim measures. When this aspect is addressed, broad discretion is usually given to the arbitrators. The standards are usually described only in terms of "appropriate" and "necessary" without giving further details.[28] This, of course, provides for maximum flexibility and adaptability of the arbitral process. Each dispute is different and must be resolved on its own facts. On the other hand, such an approach is not conducive to consistency and predictability, aspects which become more important as the need for and importance of interim protection continues to grow.[29]

3. Enforcement of Interim Measures

Arbitrators generally lack the power to enforce decisions on interim measures. Also, they do not generally have the power to impose penalties for non-compliance with orders, unless such procedure has been agreed by the parties, or is possible under the applicable law.[30]

When enforcement is sought, it is therefore necessary to request the assistance of state courts. In many countries, including Sweden, decisions on interim measures rendered by arbitrators are not enforceable since they are not final.[31] In some modern arbitration acts provisions have been included allowing for court enforcement of interim measures ordered by an arbitral tribunal. This is the case in Germany, for example, where Sect. 1041(2) of the ZPO provides:

> "The court may, at the request of a party, permit enforcement of a measure ... unless application for a corresponding interim measure has already been made to a court. It may recast such an order, if necessary, for the purpose of enforcing the measure."

Similar provisions are found in Switzerland and Hong Kong.[32]

Such orders, while enforceable in the jurisdiction where rendered, are not *internationally* enforceable. That is why this aspect has been the focus of much of the work of the UNCITRAL Working Group on Arbitration.

---

28. Cf., e.g., LEW, MISTELIS, KRÖLL, *op. cit.*, fn. 7, 602–603.
29. Even though there are different views as to the statistical frequency of interim measures issued by arbitral tribunals, there is little dispute about the growing importance and need for interim protection in international arbitration, See, e.g., YESILIRMAK, *op. cit.*, fn. 7, pp. 12-16, 162-166.
30. See, e.g., Art. 1056 of the Code of Civil Procedure of The Netherlands, which provides that an arbitral tribunal has the power to impose penalties for non-compliance, in cases when a court of law has such power.
31. For a general discussion of this problem, see BESSON, *op. cit.*, fn. 1, p. 285 et seq.
32. Art. 183(2) of the Swiss PIL and Sect. 2GG of the Hong Kong Arbitration Ordinance; See also pp. 723-725 supra.

III.   THE QUESTIONNAIRE

At the beginning of 2006 a questionnaire, (the Questionnaire) was distributed to 45 experienced international arbitrators from the following jurisdictions: Belgium, Canada, Finland, France, Germany, New Zealand, Russian Federation, Spain, Sweden, Switzerland, The Netherlands, United Kingdom and United States. Thirty-three arbitrators (approximately 70 per cent) responded to the Questionnaire.

As explained above, the main purpose of the Questionnaire was to find out how international arbitrators de facto handle interim measures in their practice given the above legal and institutional framework.

Even though the selection of arbitrators was completely discretionary and unscientific, it is believed that the 45 arbitrators who received the Questionnaire are reasonably representative of arbitrator conduct in international commercial arbitration. Needless to say, it would theoretically have been possible to include more questions and more detailed questions in the survey. Experience shows, however, that the more detailed questions you have, the less is the likelihood that the questionnaire will be answered and returned. The Questionnaire as sent out, is thus the result of a pragmatic balancing act where the *Leitmotif* has been that the best must not become the enemy of the good.

In the following I shall discuss and comment on the responses to the Questionnaire.[33]

1.   Frequency and Types of Interim Measures

Questions Nos. 1-4 in the Questionnaire relate to the *frequency* and *types* of measures requested by parties and ordered by arbitrators:

"1. How many times have you as an arbitrator experienced that a party has requested the Tribunal to order an interim measure?

2. Out of the requests referred to in 1, how many have been for an order

(A) To maintain or restore the status quo pending determination of the dispute?
(B) To take action that would prevent, or refrain from taking action that is likely to cause, current or imminent harm or prejudice to the arbitral process itself?
(C) To provide means of preserving assets out of which a subsequent award may be satisfied?
(D) To preserve evidence that may be important and relevant to the resolution of the dispute? and
(E) Other type of interim measure?

3. Under which arbitration rules have you ordered interim measures, if any?

4. How many times have you ordered interim measures on basis of an express provision in the arbitration agreement?"

---

33. See Annex I, pp. 742-746.

As regards the *frequency* of requests for interim measures generally (*Question 1*) it appeared that a large majority (27 of 32) of the arbitrators had experience of such requests. Twenty of 32 had experienced this up to 20 times. Seven arbitrators answered that they had encountered such requests more than 20 times. Given the vast experience of the arbitrators in question who responded, it is probably correct to assume that today, requests for interim measures are not very frequent from a statistical point of view but are still made on a regular basis. One very experienced arbitrator specifically noted that his experience of interim measures, "while significant regarding court-ordered provisional measures in arbitration, is very limited with respect to arbitrators themselves". However, another arbitrator noted an increasing trend as regards cases where interim measures are sought and probably also in the number of cases where such measures are granted.

As mentioned above, many or most national laws do not provide for enforcement of arbitrator's decisions on interim measures. Furthermore, under many national laws it currently might not be possible to obtain ex parte orders from arbitrators. Without this possibility and given the lack of enforceability, it is perhaps not surprising that parties do not go to the arbitral tribunal on a regular basis to ask for interim measures. They go to court instead.

As regards the *types* of interim measures requested (*Question 2*), measures aiming at maintaining or restoring the status quo pending determination of the dispute are the most frequent ones.[34] Alternatives B (*"to take action that would prevent, or refrain from taking action that is likely to cause, current or imminent harm or prejudice to the arbitral process itself"*), and D (*"to preserve evidence that may be important and relevant to the resolution of the dispute"*) are also quite common.[35] These three types of measures are perhaps the ones most closely linked to the arbitral process itself. It is therefore not surprising that parties may find it worthwhile to request decisions on such measures from the arbitrators.

Measures referred to in Question 2, alternative C (*"to provide means of preserving assets out of which a subsequent award may be satisfied"*) appear somewhat less common.[36]

Alternative E (other types of interim measure) is the least frequent alternative with only 9 answers with relative frequency between 5 and 60 per cent.

---

34. Twenty-six arbitrators listed this alternative, with 10 to 100 per cent relative frequency. This type of measure is provided for in Art. 17(2)(a) of the Working Group Draft which reads:

 "An interim measure is any temporary measure, whether in the form of an award or in another form, by which, at any time prior to the issuance of the award by which the dispute is finally decided, the arbitral tribunal orders a party to:
 (a) Maintain or restore the *status quo* pending determination of the dispute."

35. Twenty arbitrators listed these alternatives, with 5 to 100 per cent relative frequency. These two types of measures are found in Art. 17(2)(b) and (d) of the Working Group Draft. This provision reads: "(b) Take action that would prevent or refrain from taking action that is likely to cause, current or imminent harm or prejudice to the arbitral process itself" and "(d) Preserve evidence that may be relevant and material to the resolution of the dispute."

36. Seventeen arbitrators listed this with 5 to 20 per cent relative frequency. Cf. Art. 17(2)(c) of the Working Group Draft, which reads: "(c) Provide a means of preserving assets out of which a subsequent award may be satisfied."

Based on the results of the survey, it would thus appear that Art. 17(2) of the Working Group Draft reasonably accurately reflects reality in that it lists the types of interim measures most commonly requested.

One would perhaps have expected that alternative C (preserving assets), such as attachment of property, would have been the most frequently sought interim measure. However, given the fact that such orders issued by tribunals are usually not enforceable – and certainly not internationally enforceable – such interim measures are probably more commonly sought in court.

As regards the *frequency* of interim measures ordered under various *arbitration rules* (*Question 3*) the following may be noted. The ICC and the UNCITRAL Rules were clearly the most frequently applied rules with 25 and 23 responses, respectively. This is not surprising because these sets of rules are perhaps the most frequently used rules in international commercial arbitration. The AAA/ICDR, ICSID, and LCIA Rules, and rules under "other institutions" received 5-8 answers each. Ad hoc arbitration yielded 11 answers. Further, not surprisingly, considering that Chinese law does not empower arbitrators to grant interim measures, no one had ordered interim measures under the CIETAC Rules. Nor had anyone ordered interim measures under the SCC Rules. Swedish parties and counsel rarely seek interim measures from arbitrators. The explanation is that such orders cannot be enforced in Sweden. Instead court assistance is sought, which normally is very effective.

With respect to the frequency of interim measures ordered under an express provision in the arbitration agreement – as opposed to a reference to institutional rules providing for interim measures to be decided by the arbitrators – such measures seem to be rather unusual. Twenty-four arbitrators responded that they had never experienced this. Seven arbitrators had some experience (1-10 times), and 1 answered "more than 10". From this, one could draw the conclusion that it is not realistic to expect parties to clarify in their agreement – through any express provisions – the authority of the arbitrators in this regard. Rather, there seems to be a need for this issue to be addressed and provided for in national arbitration legislation, or in institutional rules.

2. *Standards for Granting Interim Measures*[37]

Questions Nos. 5-12 and 15 relate to the standards for granting interim measures, i.e., the conditions which must be satisfied before an arbitral tribunal is prepared to grant an interim measure.

> "5. In your view, should the party requesting an interim measure be required to show that there is a possibility to succeed on the merits of the claim?
>
> 6. If your answer to question 5 is in the affirmative, what approximate degree of possibility would you require as a minimum?

---

37. Cf. Art. 17 *bis* of the Working Group Proposal, reproduced in Annex II of this Report at p. 747.

7. In your view, should the party requesting an interim measure be required to show that harm not adequately reparable is likely to result if the measure is not ordered?

8. If your answer to question 7 is in the affirmative, would you require the requesting party to show that such harm outweighs the harm that is likely to result to the party against whom the measure will be directed?

9. In your view, should the party requesting an interim measure be required to show that there is urgency, which necessitates the grant of the interim measure sought?

10. Would you deny a request for an interim measure if the request necessitates examination of the merits of the case, beyond a prima facie review?

11. Would you deny a request for an interim measure if the granting thereof would in fact operate to grant the final relief sought?

12. Would you deny a request for an interim measure when it is unlikely that the measure sought is capable of being carried out?

(....)

15. Would you deny a request for an interim measure if the party against whom the measure is sought declares or undertakes in good faith that it does not intend to infringe the right in question?"

As regards the condition that a party requesting an interim measure be required to show that there is a *possibility to succeed* on the merits of the claim (*Questions 5-6*)[38] a large majority of the arbitrators (over 85 per cent), agreed with this. Not surprisingly, for most arbitrators, this is a fundamental prerequisite for ordering interim measures for most arbitrators.

Although the arbitrators who participated in the survey had different views on what "possibility to succeed" actually means (*Question 6*), it appeared that a majority did not require the degree of "possibility to succeed" to be more than likely, i.e., over 50 per cent.[39] This is perhaps a bit surprising, but seems reasonable since it is usually very difficult to assess the outcome of a dispute when a request for interim measures is made, which normally would be at the initial stages of the proceedings. To put it differently, and in more general terms: the requesting party must establish prima facie that he has a case. It goes without saying, however, that this is a limited test which must not involve prejudging the merits of the case.[40]

Art. 17 *bis* (1)(a) of the Working Group Draft proposes that the requesting party shall satisfy the arbitral tribunal that (i) *"harm not adequately reparable by an award of damages is*

---

38. Cf., Art. 17 *bis* (1)(b) of the Working Group Proposal.

39. Ten arbitrators responded 25-50 per cent possibility, 6 responded 51-75 per cent, 5 less than 25 per cent, and 1 more than 75 per cent. One arbitrator responded that "it depends, in particular which measure is requested and of the harm that may be caused if the measure is not granted". Another arbitrator stated that "[a]s a general rule I try to avoid making precise predictions about the outcome and merely state that the claim to which the application relates has a reasonable chance of success".

40. Cf. Art. 17 *bis* (1)(b) in fine.

likely to result if the measure is not ordered",[41] and (ii) *"such harm substantially outweighs the harm that is likely to result to the party against whom the measure is directed if the measure is granted"*. These two conditions correspond to Questions Nos. 7-8 in the Questionnaire.

Thirty arbitrators agreed with condition (i) referred to above (Question 7).[42] Thus, clearly an important factor to be considered by a party requesting the measure.

With respect to the *proportionality* of the measure referred to in (ii) above (Question 8) most, but, in my view surprisingly not all, arbitrators (26 "yes" and five "no" answers), would require that the requesting party show such proportionality in accordance with Art. 17 *bis* (a) of the Working Group Draft.

As regards the *urgency* of the measure (*Question 9*), a large majority of the arbitrators (26) agreed with this condition. It would thus seem that urgency is an essential requirement for granting interim measures. In this context it may be noted that urgency is not an explicit, independent requirement under Art. 17 of the Working Group Draft.

It is submitted, however, that the urgency requirement is covered by Art. 17 *bis* (1)(a) of the working Group's draft. Urgency is in fact a *sine qua non* for interim measures: it is the urgency that necessitates interim protection. Otherwise, one could await the final award on the merits. The question remains, however, to define urgency – when is it urgent and when is it not? It is unavoidable that this will vary from case to case depending, inter alia, on the nationality, nature and organizational structure of the parties and the nature and complexity of the dispute.

Responses to Questions Nos. 10[43] and 11[44] show that most arbitrators would sometimes, depending on the circumstances, or always, deny a request for interim measure if it would involve *examination of the merits* beyond a prima facie review, or if a ruling in this respect would in fact result in a final determination of the dispute. The reason for this is of course that arbitrators want to avoid – as they should – determining de facto the dispute on the merits at an early stage of the proceedings before both parties have been given a reasonable opportunity to present their cases.

With respect to Question No. 12 a large majority[45] would sometimes, depending on the circumstances, deny a request for an interim measure when it is *unlikely* that the measure sought is *capable of being carried out*. This is perhaps a rather surprising result. I would have expected that no arbitrator would not order an interim measure when it is unlikely that the measure is capable of being carried out. On the other hand the majority's answers in fact display significant hesitation towards granting interim

---

41. Under common law this is usually referred to as a "risk of irreparable harm or prejudice".

42. One arbitrator disagreed and another arbitrator stated that it depends on the nature of the measure, specifically noting that "[t]here is no such requirement when it comes to preserving evidence".

43. Only 1 arbitrator answered "never" to this question. Twenty-three answered "sometimes depending on the circumstances", 7 "always" and 1 "mostly".

44. Four arbitrators answered "never" to this question. Sixteen stated "sometimes depending on the circumstances, whereas 11 answered "always".

45. Twenty-five of the arbitrators answered "sometimes depending on the circumstances". Four arbitrators answered "always" and 3 "never".

measures in such circumstances.[46] Generally speaking, arbitrators are not inclined to spend time and energy – and most likely delay the arbitration – when it is unlikely that the measure sought can be carried out. Under certain arbitration rules this may also result from the arbitrator's duty to take into account the enforceability of the award.[47]

A large majority of the arbitrators would also consider, depending on the circumstances, denying a request for interim measures if the party against whom the measure is sought declares or *undertakes in good faith* that it does *not* intend *to infringe* the right in question (*Question 15*).[48] Interestingly, and perhaps somewhat surprisingly, many of the arbitrators in the survey are prepared, as a substitute for an interim measure, to accept a declaration or undertaking from the party against whom the measure is sought, at least in certain circumstances. One important factor must of course be the previous conduct of the party against whom the measure is sought, both prior to and during the arbitration.

3. Security

Questions Nos. 13 and 14 relate to security:

> "13. Do you require the party requesting an interim measure to provide security for damages which the measure may result in?
>
> 14. Would you deny a request for an interim measure if the requesting party has failed to provide security for damages which the measure may result in?"

The answers to Questions Nos. 13[49] and 14[50] show that security is commonly requested from the party asking for the measure, and that failure to provide such security would sometimes, or always, result in the arbitrator denying a request for interim measure. This rather expected result underlines the practical importance of providing security for damages which the measure may result in. The rationale for security is simply to safeguard the interests of the party against whom the measure is sought, should the measure prove to be unjustified. Given the fact that an interim measure is always based on a prima *facie* evaluation of the dispute, there is always a risk that the final outcome will turn out to be different. Against this background the

---

46. Also, maybe, lawyers have a slight tendency of automatically answering "sometimes depending on the circumstances" irrespective of the question!

47. See, e.g., Art. 35 of the ICC Arbitration Rules.

48. Twenty-eight of the arbitrators responded "sometimes depending on the circumstances". Three answered "always" and 1 "never".

49. Sixteen of the arbitrators responded "mostly" to this question and 5 answered "always". One arbitrator answered "never" and 6 "seldom".

50. All respondents answered "always/mostly" (7) or "sometimes depending on the circumstances" (23). No one answered "never".

provision of security is often a practical and convenient way for arbitrators to resolve this dilemma.[51]

4. Form of the Decision

Questions Nos. 16-18 deal with the issue of form of the decision on interim measures:

> "16. In your experience, in what form are decisions on interim measures rendered?
>
> 17. In your experience, is the form of a decision with respect to an interim measure dependent on the applicable law?
>
> 18. In your experience, would a temporal element be included in a decision with respect to an interim measure, such as for example 'during the course of the proceedings', or 'until the final award on the merits', or for a certain period of time?"

Decisions on interim measures are normally issued as orders, in some cases as awards and occasionally in the form of a recommendation (*Question 16*). [52] As regards the latter, this variant probably comes from ICSID arbitrations, where in Rule 39 of the ICSID Arbitration Rules the term "recommendation" is used.[53] The questionnaire did not include any question on the definition of award and order, respectively. This notwithstanding, it is reasonable to assume that most arbitrators would understand an award as the final resolution of the dispute on the merits, whereas an order aims to deal with a specific issue on a provisional basis. If an award is rendered in the form of an award it may potentially be enforceable under the New York Convention. An order, on the other hand, is generally considered not to be so enforceable. In the final analysis this will be for the courts of the country where enforcement is sought to decide. The draft of the UNCITRAL Working Group defines an interim measure as "any temporary measure, whether in the form of an award or in any other form by which, at any time prior to the issuance of the award by which the dispute is finally decided".[54]

With respect to the question whether the form of the decision is dependent on the applicable law (*Question 17*) the views are diverging.[55] The most common answers are, as expected, that the form depends on either the law of the place of arbitration or the

---

51. Art. 17(1) of the UNCITRAL Working Group Proposal stipulates that an arbitral tribunal "may require" the requesting party to provide "appropriate security in connection with the measure". It is thus not a mandatory requirement, but is left to the discretion of the tribunal.

52. Twenty-seven of the arbitrators answered that such decisions are made in the form of an order. Ten stated that awards are issued. Quite a few answered both order and award. Four respondents added "recommendation" to their response. No one answered "other form".

53. See pp. 727-728, supra.

54. Art. 17(2).

55. Sixteen arbitrators chose the alternative "yes, it depends on the law of the place of arbitration". Ten answered that it depends on the law of the country where enforcement is likely to be sought. Nine stated "no", and 4 answered that it depends on the law applicable to the arbitration agreement. Quite a few arbitrators chose more than one answer.

law of the country where enforcement is likely to be sought. It is noteworthy that several arbitrators indicated that they would not make the form of the decision dependent on any law.

By contrast, *all* the arbitrators agreed that a temporal element, such as "during the course of the proceedings" or "until the award on the merits", would always or sometimes, depending on the circumstances, be included in a decision on an interim measure.[56] This is not surprising having regard to the provisional character of most interim measures.

5. Compliance and Enforcement

Questions Nos. 19 and 20 concern compliance with and enforcement of an interim measure:

> "19. In your experience, has the party against whom the order has been directed voluntarily complied therewith?

> 20. How many times have you experienced that a party has sought to enforce, through courts or government authorities, interim measures ordered by you as an arbitrator?"

Responses to *Question No. 19*[57] show that arbitrators who have issued decisions on interim measures have encouraging experiences with the parties' willingness to voluntarily comply with the decision.[58] This may suggest that the need to make decisions on interim measures internationally enforceable is perhaps not so urgent. On the other hand, it may very well be that the answers reflect situations where the requesting party has put forward a request because he believed that the other party would in fact be willing to comply voluntarily. Also, it cannot be ruled out – and in fact it is probably very likely – that parties in need of an enforceable interim measure prefer to go to court.

A majority of the arbitrators[59] had never experienced that a party had sought to enforce, through court or government authorities, interim measures ordered by the arbitrators (*Question 20*). If we read the answers to this question in conjunction with the answers to Question No. 19, it suggests that there has been little need to go to court because the party against whom the measure was directed has always or mostly/partly

---

56. Most arbitrators (20) stated that such decision would always include a temporal element, whereas quite a few (12) answered "sometimes depending on the circumstances". No one answered "never".

57. All answering arbitrators stated "mostly/partly" (18) or "always" (ten).

58. This result seems to correspond to the results of other surveys. In a survey done by the AAA it was said that in 45 out of 50 cases (national as well as international) the parties voluntarily complied with the arbitrators' decisions on interim measures, See NAIMARK-KEER, *op. cit.*, fn. 1, p. 26.

59. To Question No. 20, 24 arbitrators answered that they had never experienced this. Two answered that they had experienced this 1 time, 1 stated 4 times, and 3 5-10 times. No one answered 10 times or more.

voluntarily complied therewith. Another possible explanation, however, may be that it is difficult to enforce a decision on interim measures and, therefore, that attempts to do so are simply avoided.

In this context it is important to keep in mind that the need for enforceability of an interim measure varies with the type of interim measure. If the interim measure aims at facilitating the enforcement of a subsequent award, the need for efficient enforcement of the measure is significant, if not absolute. On the other hand, if the interim measure concerns the preservation of evidence, there is much less need for enforcement. The primary sanction available to the requesting party is to ask the tribunal to draw negative inferences from non-compliance with the order for the interim measure. In addition, most arbitrators would probably be prepared to hold the non-complying party responsible for costs and/or damages resulting from the non-compliance.

IV.   FINAL REMARKS

As mentioned in the foregoing, the statistical basis of the survey is quite limited. One must not therefore draw too far-reaching conclusions from it. On the other hand, 33 leading international arbitrators have responded to the questions, which should give us some idea of how arbitrators in fact deal with issues of interim measures.

The survey shows that arbitrators do from time to time issue decisions on interim measures. It also shows that it is not a very frequent occurrence today, but that interim measures are issued on a regular basis. In all likelihood this is partly due to the fact that parties go to court to obtain enforceable interim measures.

As regards the standards for the granting of interim measures it would seem that some common ground has been achieved. This is encouraging. In particular since this element is lacking in national legislation and in institutional rules. This common ground by and large corresponds to the draft prepared by the UNCITRAL Working Group. This is a good starting point for achieving uniformity and thereby also predictability. Judging from the responses to the questionnaire a majority of arbitrators appears to agree *that*

(a) the party who requests an interim measure must show that there is a possibility to succeed on the merits,

(b) the degree of such possibility does not need to exceed 50 per cent,

(c) the party requesting an interim measure must show that harm not adequately reparable is likely to result if the measure is not ordered,

(d) the requesting party must show that such harm outweighs the harm that is likely to result to the party against whom the measure will be directed,

(e) the requesting party must show that there is urgency,

(f) arbitrators should aim at avoiding examining the merits of the case when deciding on interim measures,

(g) arbitrators should aim at avoiding a final determination of the dispute through a decision on interim measures,

and that

(h) the requesting party should in most cases be requested to provide security for damages which the measure may result in, lacking which the request may be denied.

ANNEX I

Interim Measures in Arbitration Questionnaire

Name

1. **How many times have you as an arbitrator experienced that a party has requested the Tribunal to order an interim measure?**

   0 ☐   5 -10 ☐   10-20 ☐   More than 20 ☐

   15%   **44%**   **19%**   **22%**

2. **Out of the requests referred to in 1, how many have been for an order:**

A. To maintain or restore the status quo pending determination of the dispute?   ☐ % **28%**

B. To take action that would prevent, or refrain from taking action that is likely to cause, current or imminent harm or prejudice to the arbitral process itself?   ☐ % **22%**

C. To provide means of preserving assets out of which a subsequent award may be satisfied?   ☐ % **18%**

D. To preserve evidence that may be important and relevant to the resolution of the dispute?   ☐ % **22%**

E. Other type of interim measure   ☐ % **10%**

3. **Under which arbitration rules have you ordered interim measures, if any?**

   UNCITRAL ☐   ICC ☐   AAA/ICDR ☐   ICSID ☐   LCIA ☐

   26%   **28%**   **8%**   **6%**   **9%**

SCC ☐   CIETAC ☐   Other Institutional Rules ☐   Ad hoc ☐

1%   0%   9%   13%

4. How many times have you ordered interim measures on basis of an express provision in the arbitration agreement?

    0 ☐ (<5)   5 -10 ☐   More than 10 ☐

    88%   9%   3%

5. In your view, should the party requesting an interim measure be required to show that there is a possibility to succeed on the merits of the claim?

    Yes ☐   No ☐

    88%   12%

6. If your answer to question 5 is in the affirmative, what approximate degree of possibility would you require as a minimum?

    Less than 25 % ☐   25-50 % ☐   51-75 % ☐   More than 75 % ☐

                23%   45%   27%   5%

7. In your view, should the party requesting an interim measure be required to show that harm not adequately reparable is likely to result if the measure is not ordered?

    Yes ☐   No ☐

    97%   3%

8. If your answer to question 7 is in the affirmative, would you require the requesting party to show that such harm outweighs the harm that

743

is likely to result to the party against whom the measure will be directed?

Yes ☐   No ☐

   84%   16%

9. In your view, should the party requesting an interim measure be required to show that there is urgency, which necessitates the grant of the interim measure sought?

Yes ☐   No ☐

   87%   13%

10. Would you deny a request for an interim measure if the request necessitates examination of the merits of the case, beyond a prima facie review?

Always ☐   Sometimes depending on the circumstances ☐   Never ☐

   23%   74%   3%

11. Would you deny a request for an interim measure if the granting thereof would in fact operate to grant the final relief sought?

Always ☐   Sometimes depending on the circumstances ☐   Never ☐

   35%   52%   13%

12. Would you deny a request for an interim measure when it is unlikely that the measure sought is capable of being carried out?

Always ☐   Sometimes depending on the circumstances ☐   Never ☐

   13%   78%   9%

13. **Do you require the party requesting an interim measure to provide security for damages which the measure may result in?**

Never ☐	Seldom ☐	Mostly ☐	Always ☐
4%	21%	57%	18%

14. **Would you deny a request for an interim measure if the requesting party has failed to provide security for damages which the measure may result in?**

Always ☐	Sometimes depending on the circumstances ☐	Never ☐
23% (incl. "mostly")	77%	0%

15. **Would you deny a request for an interim measure if the party against whom the measure is sought declares or undertakes in good faith that it does not intend to infringe the right in question?**

Always ☐	Sometimes depending on the circumstances ☐	Never ☐
9%	88%	3%

16. **In your experience, in what form are decisions on interim measures rendered?**

Order ☐	Award ☐	Recommendation ☐	Other form ☐
66%	24%	10%	0%

17. **In your experience, is the form of a decision with respect to an interim measure dependent on the applicable law?**

No ☐ 23%

Yes, it depends on the law of the place of arbitration ☐ 41%

Yes, it depends on the law applicable to the arbitration agreement   ☐   **10%**

Yes, it depends on the law of the country where enforcement of the award or the interim measure is likely to be sought   ☐   **26%**

18. **In your experience, would a temporal element be included in a decision with respect to an interim measure, such as for example "during the course of the proceedings", or "until the final award on the merits", or for a certain period of time?**

Always ☐   Sometimes depending on the circumstances ☐   Never ☐

   62%   **38%**   **0%**

19. **In your experience, has the party against whom the order has been directed voluntarily complied therewith?**

Never ☐   Seldom ☐   Mostly/Partly ☐   Always ☐

   0%   **0%**   **64%**   **36%**

20. **How many times have you experienced that a party has sought to enforce, through courts or government authorities, interim measures ordered by you as an arbitrator?**

0 ☐ (<5)   5 -10 ☐   More than 10 ☐

   90%   **10%**   **0%**

ANNEX II

Revised Legislative Provisions on Interim Measures and Preliminary Orders[1]

CHAPTER IV BIS. INTERIM MEASURES AND PRELIMINARY ORDERS

Section 1—Interim measures

Article 17—Power of arbitral tribunal to order interim measures
(1) Unless otherwise agreed by the parties, the arbitral tribunal may, at the request of a party, grant interim measures.

(2) An interim measure is any temporary measure, whether in the form of an award or in another form, by which, at any time prior to the issuance of the award by which the dispute is finally decided, the arbitral tribunal orders a party to:

(a) Maintain or restore the status quo pending determination of the dispute;
(b) Take action that would prevent, or refrain from taking action that is likely to cause, current or imminent harm or prejudice to the arbitral process itself;
(c) Provide a means of preserving assets out of which a subsequent award may be satisfied; or
(d) Preserve evidence that may be relevant and material to the resolution of the dispute.

Article 17 bis—Conditions for granting interim measures
(1) The party requesting an interim measure under article 17 (2)(a), (b) and (c) shall satisfy the arbitral tribunal that:

(a) Harm not adequately reparable by an award of damages is likely to result if the measure is not ordered, and such harm substantially outweighs the harm that is likely to result to the party against whom the measure is directed if the measure is granted; and
(b) There is a reasonable possibility that the requesting party will succeed on the merits of the claim, provided that any determination on this possibility shall not affect the discretion of the arbitral tribunal in making any subsequent determination.

(2) With regard to a request for an interim measure under article 17 (2)(d), the requirements in paragraphs (1)(a) and (b) of this article shall apply only to the extent the arbitral tribunal considers appropriate.

---

1. *Note General Editor.* The final text of the Revised Articles of the UNCITRAL Model Law on International Commercial Arbitration as adopted by the Commission at its 39th session, 19 June-7 July 2006 is available at <www.uncitral.org/uncitral/en/uncitral_texts/arbitration/1985 Model_arbitration.html>.

Section 2—Preliminary orders

Article 17 ter—Applications for preliminary orders and conditions for granting preliminary orders
(1) Unless otherwise agreed by the parties, a party may, without notice to any other party, make a request for an interim measure together with an application for a preliminary order directing a party not to frustrate the purpose of the interim measure requested.

(2) The arbitral tribunal may grant a preliminary order provided it considers that prior disclosure of the request for the interim measure to the party against whom it is directed risks frustrating the purpose of the measure.

(3) The conditions defined under article 17 bis apply to any preliminary order, provided that the harm to be assessed under article 17 bis, paragraph (1)(a), is the harm likely to result from the order being granted or not.

Article 17 quater—Specific regime for preliminary orders
(1) Immediately after the arbitral tribunal has made a determination in respect of an application for a preliminary order, the arbitral tribunal shall give notice to all parties of the request for the interim measure, the application for the preliminary order, the preliminary order, if any, and all other communications, including by indicating the content of any oral communication, between any party and the arbitral tribunal in relation thereto.

(2) At the same time, the arbitral tribunal shall give an opportunity to any party against whom a preliminary order is directed to present its case at the earliest practicable time.

(3) The arbitral tribunal shall decide promptly on any objection to the preliminary order.

(4) A preliminary order shall expire after twenty days from the date on which it was issued by the arbitral tribunal. However, the arbitral tribunal may issue an interim measure adopting or modifying the preliminary order, after the party against whom the preliminary order is directed has been given notice and an opportunity to present its case.

(5) A preliminary order shall be binding on the parties but shall not be subject to enforcement by a court. Such a preliminary order does not constitute an award.

Section 3—Provisions applicable to interim measures and preliminary orders

Article 17 quinquies—Modification, suspension, termination
The arbitral tribunal may modify, suspend or terminate an interim measure or a preliminary order it has granted, upon application of any party or, in exceptional circumstances and upon prior notice to the parties, on the arbitral tribunal's own initiative.

Article 17 sexies—Provision of security
(1) The arbitral tribunal may require the party requesting an interim measure to provide appropriate security in connection with the measure.

(2) The arbitral tribunal shall require the party applying for a preliminary order to provide security in connection with the order unless the arbitral tribunal considers it inappropriate or unnecessary to do so.

Article 17 septies—Disclosure
(1) The party requesting an interim measure shall promptly disclose any material change in the circumstances on the basis of which the measure was requested or granted.

(2) The party applying for a preliminary order shall disclose to the arbitral tribunal all circumstances that are likely to be relevant to the arbitral tribunal's determination whether to grant or maintain the order, and such obligation shall continue until the party against whom the order has been requested has had an opportunity to present its case. Thereafter, the applying party shall have the same disclosure obligation with respect to the preliminary order that a requesting party has with respect to an interim measure under paragraph (1) of this article.

Article 17 octies—Costs and damages
The party requesting an interim measure or applying for a preliminary order shall be liable for any costs and damages caused by the measure or the order to any party if the arbitral tribunal later determines that, in the circumstances, the measure or the order should not have been granted. The arbitral tribunal may award such costs and damages at any point during the proceedings.

Section 4—Recognition and enforcement of interim measures

Article 17 novies—Recognition and enforcement
(1) An interim measure issued by an arbitral tribunal shall be recognized as binding and, unless otherwise provided by the arbitral tribunal, enforced upon application to the competent court, irrespective of the country in which it was issued, subject to the provisions of article 17 decies.

(2) The party who is seeking or has obtained recognition or enforcement of an interim measure shall promptly inform the court of any termination, suspension or modification of that interim measure.

(3) The court of the State where recognition or enforcement is sought may, if it considers it proper, order the requesting party to provide appropriate security if the arbitral tribunal has not already made a determination with respect to security or where such a decision is necessary to protect the rights of third parties.

Article 17 decies—Grounds for refusing recognition or enforcement*
(1) Recognition or enforcement of an interim measure may be refused only:

---

* The conditions set forth in article 17 decies are intended to limit the number of circumstances in which the court may refuse to enforce an interim measure. It would not be contrary to the level of harmonization sought to be achieved by these model provisions if a State were to adopt fewer circumstances in which enforcement may be refused.

(a) at the request of the party against whom it is invoked if the court is satisfied that:

(i) such refusal is warranted on the grounds set forth in article 36, paragraphs (1) (a)(i), (ii), (iii) or (iv); or
(ii) the arbitral tribunal's decision with respect to the provision of security in connection with the interim measure issued by the arbitral tribunal has not been complied with; or
(iii) the interim measure has been terminated or suspended by the arbitral tribunal or, where so empowered, by the court of the State in which the arbitration takes place or under the law of which that interim measure was granted; or

(b) if the court finds that:

(i) the interim measure is incompatible with the powers conferred upon the court unless the court decides to reformulate the interim measure to the extent necessary to adapt it to its own powers and procedures for the purposes of enforcing that interim measure and without modifying its substance; or
(ii) any of the grounds set forth in article 36, paragraphs (1)(b)(i) or (ii) apply to the recognition and enforcement of the interim measure.

(2) Any determination made by the court on any ground in paragraph (1) of this article shall be effective only for the purposes of the application to recognize and enforce the interim measure. The court where recognition or enforcement is sought shall not, in making that determination, undertake a review of the substance of the interim measure.

Section 5—Court-ordered interim measures

Article 17 undecies—Court-ordered interim measures
The court shall have the same power of issuing interim measures for the purposes of and in relation to arbitration proceedings whose place is in the country of the court or in another country as it has for the purposes of and in relation to proceedings in the courts and shall exercise that power in accordance with its own rules and procedures insofar as these are relevant to the specific features of an international arbitration.

The Art of Interim Measures

José Maria Abascal*

I.   INTERIM RELIEF: AN ART

Notwithstanding that arbitration is subject to legal provisions and rules, arbitration is an art, and interim measures on arbitration are part of that art. Furthermore, if there is a subject appropriate as evidence of the nature of arbitration as an art, it is interim measures. Indeed, dealing with interim measures, either in court or in arbitration, causes serious problems for judges and arbitrators.

In most instances, parties request interim measures which are closely connected with the merits of the dispute. Many times the main problem that the tribunal faces is whether granting the measure may amount to disposing of the subject matter of the dispute. This risk must be balanced against the potential damage that may result if the measure is denied. Naturally, parties frequently seek to obtain prompt decisions that will assure their positions and, if possible, give them strong leverage in bargaining. Most of the time the lack of substantial or sufficient knowledge when deciding on interim relief calls for skillful and prudent assessment of the circumstances known at that moment. Furthermore, some arbitral institutions, such as the International Court of Arbitration of the International Chamber of Commerce (ICC), the International Centre for Dispute Resolution (ICDR), and the London Court of International Arbitration (LCIA), have rules for appointing pre-trial referees, emergency arbitrators or for the expedited formation of the arbitral tribunal, with the sole purpose of empowering them to issue interim measures before the arbitral tribunal is constituted or with very little information.[1]

On the other hand, arbitrators must give the parties full (in ICC Rules Art. 15(2), reasonable) opportunity to present their cases. Strict application of that principle would lead to the conclusion that it is legally impossible to grant interim relief in any case. But the opposite also may be true: to deny an interim measure may amount to depriving a party of its right to be heard because the actions or omissions of its counterparty may

---

*   Counsel, advisor and arbitrator; Chairman of the UNCITRAL Working Group on Arbitration and Conciliation.
1.   ICC Rules for a Pre-Arbitral Referee Procedure. ICDR Rules Art. 37. Also see LCIA Rules Art. 9 on the expedited formation of the Arbitral Tribunal.

751

in fact dispose of the object of the dispute or cause irreparable harm before an award is rendered.

There are no boilerplate solutions; the basis for wise solutions is not to be found in definite dispositions, rules or principles, but indeed it is an art. The foundations of such art are in the will of the parties and the inherent power of the arbitrators. Some law provisions are needed for the sake of certainty: for example, to expressly empower the arbitrators to grant interim relief, define it, lay down minimum conditions that need to be satisfied; to address particular situations as in the case of ex parte measures; to provide some consequences and court enforcement.

Extensive court experience and now actual practice in arbitration show that interim measures are unavoidable. The increasing use of arbitration in international disputes, and its lawyerization, has increased the resort to interim measures. As arbitration is an alternative method to litigation, it is natural that interim measures are also needed. The mere fact that UNCITRAL recently amended its Model Law on International Commercial Arbitration (the UML) with the addition of a new chapter on interim measures is evidence of the increasing resort to interim measures and their relevance.[2] The debate within and outside UNCITRAL as well as the numerous events and papers devoted to the project also demonstrate the importance of this phenomenon.[3]

I was asked to address the issue of interim measures as they are in actual practice. The directions I received were clear: no debate on the then Draft of the UNCITRAL project, and I will make my best efforts to comply. But it cannot be ignored that the UML is now amended; nor can we ignore the importance and relevance of UNCITRAL texts in arbitration even for the purposes of interpretation; consequently, I will make references to some of the new provisions.

---

2. At its 39th Session, on 7 July 2006, the Commission amended the UML; inter alia, formally adopted Chapter IV A on Interim Measures and Provisional Orders. The final text of the Revised Articles of the UNCITRAL Model Law on International Commercial Arbitration as adopted by the Commission at its 39th Session, 19 June-7 July 2006 is available at <www.uncitral.org/uncitral/en/uncitral-texts/arbitration/1985Model_arbitration.html>; see also Appendix II of Kaj Hobér's Report, this volume, pp. 000-000. The quotations in this paper correspond to this text.

3. The debates of the Working Group are in the following reports: A/CN.9/485, 33rd session Vienna, 20 November-1 December 2000, paras. 78-106; A/CN.9/487, 34th session, New York, 21 May-1 June 2001, paras. 64-87; A/CN.9/508, 36th session, New York, 4-8 March 2002, paras. 51-94; A/CN.9/523, 37th session, Vienna, 7-11 October, paras. 15-80; A/CN.9/524, 38th session, New York, 12-16 May 2003, paras. 16-78; A/CN.9/545, 39th session, Vienna, 10-14 November 2003, paras. 19-104; A/CN.9/547, 40th session, New York, 23-27 February 2004, paras. 12-116; A/CN.9/569, 41st session, Vienna, 13-17 Sept. 2004, paras. 12-72; A/CN.9/573, 42nd session, New York, 10-14 January 2005, paras. 11-95; A/CN.9/589, 43rd session, Vienna, 3-7 Oct 2005, paras. 11-106; A/CN.9/592, 44th session, New York, 23-27 Jan 2006, paras. 12-45. In each of these reports appears the reference to the Secretariat Working Papers considered, which are of the utmost importance.

II.   THE SOURCES

1.   Scarce Case Law

The first problem is the practical impossibility to deal "scientifically" with interim relief in actual law and practice in international arbitration due to the absence of available or published case law. Little has been published. Under these circumstances a commentator cannot make a thorough analysis of the needs, problems and solutions as experienced in practice. Nobody doubts that interim measures in arbitration are normally requested, granted and executed; but the real decisions are rarely published. We only know of a handful of cases, mainly in the form of awards, and a few that have been reported because parties have sought enforcement, or the decisions were contested in courts. There is little or no hard information on interim measures granted in the form of procedural orders or in any other form.

Several reasons justify the scarcity of published decisions. The main one is the confidential nature of arbitration, and the fact that in most cases parties comply voluntarily with the orders of arbitrators. Cases become public when taken to court by parties seeking court enforcement or annulment. As there is no uniform system for enforcement of arbitration orders, parties usually resort to courts when interim measures were given in the form of awards, and not when given in the form of orders.

The absence of data is not absolute. For instance, there is a report on interim measures by the ICC International Court of Arbitration, and the ICC deserves a note of praise. But even this report has limited coverage: only twenty-three cases in awards between 1991 and 1999 in arbitrations under ICC Rules. There is no data on interim measures rendered as procedural orders. As Julian D.M. Lew acknowledged, twenty-three cases are far from representative of international trends and needs.[4]

There are other sources. The most complete one I found are the decisions of the Iran-US Claims Tribunal. But, certainly, the specific nature of this tribunal may limit its consideration as representative of a universal trend in international commercial arbitration. Often the Tribunal was favorable to granting the interim relief, as Brower and Brueschke state,

> "[D]ue to the large number and complexity of its cases, coupled with the Tribunal's liberal practice of extending filing deadlines, often many years pass before the Tribunal can conduct a hearing in any particular case. Furthermore, the deliberative process commencing after the hearing is often arduous and

---

4. Julian D.M. LEW, "Commentary on Interim and Conservatory Measures in ICC Arbitration Cases", 11 ICC International Court of Arbitration Bulletin,(Spring 2000, no. 1) pp. 23-30; Ali YESILIRMAK, "Interim and Conservatory Measures in ICC Practice", 11 ICC International Court of Arbitration Bulletin,(Spring 2000, no. 1) pp. 31-36; "Extracts from ICC Awards referring to Interim and Conservatory Measures", 11 ICC International Court of Arbitration Bulletin,(Spring 2000, no. 1) pp. 37-116.

protracted. As a result of these time consuming practices, the Tribunal has been very active in granting requests for interim measures where warranted."[5]

Another important difference is that in the case of the Iran-US Claims Tribunal, the enforcement of pecuniary awards had a strong guarantee of payment. Also, contrary to what happens in international arbitration, the frequency of non-compliance with interim measures issued by this Tribunal is high because the majority of the interim measures issued by the Tribunal were orders to Iran to stay parallel court proceedings; and it is reported that Iran did not always comply.

On the other hand, in support of the importance of the decisions of the Iran-US Claims Tribunal, is the fact that the Tribunal applies the UNCITRAL Arbitration Rules, and the experience of the members of the Tribunal, many of them renowned arbitrators. The main decisions of the Tribunal are reported in the *Yearbook Commercial Arbitration* as well as other sources.[6]

It is desirable that other arbitral institutions publish their experience on interim relief. The subject matter and form of orders granting or denying interim measures, by nature, are not to be published. Arbitral institutions have the information and — taking care not to betray the trust in the confidentiality of arbitration proceedings — may issue needed, interesting and informative publications. Among other examples on different subjects, for instance, is the useful report, by Dominique Hascher, on ICC decisions on the challenge and confirmation of arbitrators.[7] Recently, the LCIA decided to publish the reasons supporting decisions on challenges to arbitrators. Why not do something similar with interim measures?

2.   Rules and Legislation

Legal provisions are scarce; and not very enlightening. Interim relief is contemplated in many domestic statutes and most rules. But these do little more than empower arbitral tribunals to grant interim measures, and give a general definition of their scope and the option to request them from domestic courts or arbitral tribunals. As Kaj Hobér's Report states, old Art. 17 UML, and arbitration rules in general are interpreted as giving the arbitrators a general power to grant interim relief to preserve the subject

---

5. Charles N. BROWER and Jason D. BRUESCHKE, *The Iran-United States Claims Tribunal*, (Kluwer Law International 1998); passages and opinions quoted in pp. 216 and 238. See also David CARON, Lee M. CAPLAN and Matti PELLONPÄÄ, *The UNCITRAL Arbitration Rules*, (Oxford University Press 2006) with a chapter on interim measures and the experience of the Iran-Us Claims Tribunal, pp. 532-560.

6. For instance, BROWER and. BRUESCHKE, Chapter 6: Interim Measures of Protection, pp. 216-241, and CARON, CAPLAN AND PELLONPÄÄ.

7. "ICC Practice in Relation to the Appointment, Confirmation, Challenge and Replacement of Arbitrators", 6 ICC International Court of Arbitration Bulletin (1995, no. 2).

matter of the dispute. However, it appears that even now, under some national laws, only the domestic courts have the power to grant interim relief.[8]

Kaj Hobér reports an accurate description of the situation, and I would only add the list of the jurisdictions that have adopted legislation based on the UML, as published by UNCITRAL at the date of finishing this paper.[9] The importance of the list is that it must be assumed that in those countries Art. 9[10] and old Art. 17 UML[11] apply.[12]

Nevertheless, other than Art. 9 and old Art. 17 of the UML, and its wide acceptance, there is a broad legal lacuna regarding: (i) the power of national courts to issue interim measures in support of arbitrations held in places outside the jurisdiction of the requested court; (ii) the definition of interim measures that may be issued by courts in support of arbitrations held within or outside the territorial jurisdiction of the requested court, and (iii) the collaboration between courts of different jurisdictions on the enforcement of interim measures.

3. Commentary

While there is some commentary, there is not so much. The commentary sometimes tends to be repetitive and reflects either orthodox assertions or the personal opinions

---

8. For instance, the Greek Code of Civil Procedure (Art. 889) and the Italian Code of Civil Procedure (Art. 818), as reported by Alan REDFERN, "Interim Measures" in Lawrence W. NEWMAN and Richard D. HILL, eds., *The Leading Arbitrators' Guide to International Arbitration* (Juris Publishing, Inc., 2004) p. 226.

9. <www.uncitral.org> Texts & Status.

10. "Art. 9. Arbitration agreement and interim measures by court. It is not incompatible with an arbitration agreement for a party to request, before or during arbitral proceedings, from a court an interim measures of protection and for a court to grant such a measure."

11. "Art. 17. Power of arbitral tribunal to order interim measures. Unless otherwise agreed by the parties, the arbitral tribunal may, at the request of a party, order any party to take such interim measure of protection as the tribunal may consider necessary in respect of the subject-matter of the dispute. The arbitral tribunal may require any party to provide appropriate security in connection with such measure."

12. The jurisdictions are as follows.

Australia, Austria, Azerbaijan, Bahrain, Bangladesh, Belarus, Bulgaria, Canada, Chile, in China: Hong Kong Special Administrative Region, Macau Special Administrative Region; Croatia, Cyprus, Denmark, Egypt, Germany, Greece, Guatemala, Hungary, India, Iran (Islamic Republic of), Ireland, Japan, Jordan, Kenya, Lithuania, Madagascar, Malta, Mexico, New Zealand, Nicaragua, Nigeria, Norway, Oman, Paraguay, Peru, the Philippines, Poland, Republic of Korea, Russian Federation, Singapore, Spain, Sri Lanka, Thailand, Tunisia, Turkey, Ukraine, within the United Kingdom of Great Britain and Northern Ireland: Scotland; in Bermuda, overseas territory of the United Kingdom of Great Britain and Northern Ireland; within the United States of America: California, Connecticut, Illinois, Louisiana, Oregon and Texas; Zambia, and Zimbabwe.

and experiences of the author. All these sources are very useful, but they are not enough.[13]

The UNCITRAL *travaux preparatoires*
The experience of the UNCITRAL Working Group on International Arbitration and Conciliation (UWG) confirms the lack of hard data. The preparatory works of the draft UNCITRAL provisions on interim measures rely more on anecdotes than statutes, rules or case law. Indeed, the working papers prepared by the Secretariat, the proposals and debates, before and during the sessions of the UWG, were based on legal provisions on interim measures issued by courts, available written commentary, opinions and statements of participants. During the working sessions the actual experiences as related by participants, either representing countries or international organizations, were comments along the line of *"there was a case in which..."*.

The UNCITRAL Secretariat hardly referred to actual cases at all in the working papers offered to the UWG. It relied mostly on information from the arbitration rules of relevant institutions and domestic legal provisions in force in several countries. Indeed the legal provisions quoted most often were domestic provisions for court-ordered interim measures. Also, when the Secretariat requested information on enforced provisions and experiences in court-ordered interim measures from delegations, observers and interested international organizations, the feedback received was scarce.

The extensive and exhaustive debate that took place outside the UWG shows the same experience. For instance, on the two occasions ICCA dealt with the subject (during the 2002 and 2004 Congresses), mostly in relation to the then ongoing work of the UWG, there were written reports, commentary and debate; but the sources used were the same as those mentioned above, and the authors rarely provided new actual hard data.[14]

III.   COURT-ORDERED AND ARBITRATOR-ORDERED INTERIM MEASURES

1.   *As a Source of Law. Similitudes and Differences*

The lack of data and the similarities with court-ordered interim relief compel law-makers, arbitrators and commentators to turn for reference to the law, usages and practices on interim measures issued and enforced by courts in civil or commercial

---

13. It is impossible to list all the commentary published. All *de rigueur* treatises deal with the subject. In addition to the ones already quoted, it is worthwhile to mention the comprehensive work of Ali YESILIMARK, *Provisional Measures in International Commercial Arbitration*, (Kluwer Law 2005).
14. See *International Commercial Arbitration: Important Contemporary Questions*, ICCA Congress series no. 11 (Kluwer 2003) and *New Horizons in International Commercial Arbitration and Beyond*, ICCA Congress series no. 12 (Kluwer 2005).

litigation. However, while there are undeniable similarities that justify the reference, there are also profound differences.

One difference arises from the territorial origin and scope of application of the domestic statutes. National laws on procedure are made to solve domestic disputes before domestic courts. There is a wide range of different legal traditions and variations within each of them. Domestic laws are also modeled on the organization and legal structure of the domestic judiciary in which they apply. But the real reason for the flexibility of laws and rules on arbitration is not to defeat the legitimate expectations of the parties. These expectations are natural and create misunderstandings and conflicts between participants from different legal traditions. The purpose of flexibility in arbitration is to allow the parties and arbitrators, through dialogue, to arrange proceedings that are fair to all. It would be inconsistent with the needs of international arbitration to approach interim measures following various domestic methods.

For instance, in the drafting of the UML, care was taken to allow the maximum scope for party autonomy, only providing a minimum of supplemental provisions to fill the lacunae of the agreements, and almost no mandatory provisions. That way the legal framework permitting the accommodation of different legal traditions provides the international community with a balanced minimum of certainty and a maximum of flexibility. The making of arbitration rules, especially the international ones, followed the same approach.

The only analogy between court-ordered and arbitrator-ordered interim measures, is the need to give or deny an order that may affect relevant parts of the dispute, and to do so before giving the parties their day in court, when the decision-maker does not have the necessary data to make an informed decision. Other than that, the differences and legal obstacles, in court litigation and international arbitration, are quite substantial.

When parties agree to arbitrate, it is evidence of their desire to avoid courts. There are many reasons for this; parties fear alien procedural laws and forum practices and mainly wish: (i) to resort to an international tribunal and to avoid the courts of each other's country; (ii) to avoid forum shopping and conflicts of jurisdictions; (iii) to have the right to appoint the arbitrators or to participate in their appointment; (iv) to rely on the flexibility of the rules agreed in contrast to the rigidity of procedural laws; and (v) to avoid delays and costs.

Those characteristics of international arbitration which direct the conditions for the making of legal provisions and rules are completely different than the ones considered domestically in making the law of civil proceedings.

2. The Options: Courts or Arbitrators

Parties may seek interim relief before domestic courts or arbitrators. Parties often resort to courts due to the urgency of the relief needed and the absence of the arbitral tribunal. Indeed, it takes time to constitute an arbitral tribunal. But when the parties agree to arbitrate it is because they wish to exclude, to the maximum extent possible, court intervention. Under strict logic, resorting to courts may be understood as a breach of the arbitration agreement. Consequently, when a party resorts to domestic courts and there is an arbitration agreement, the other parties may ask the court to refer the requesting parties to arbitration; if the defendants do not oppose the arbitration agreement, it is deemed waived. Not long ago, one issue was whether those alternatives apply to requests for interim measures.

To solve this dilemma, Art. 9 UML, provides that it is not incompatible with an arbitration agreement for a party to request from a court, before or during arbitral proceedings, an interim measure of protection and for a court to grant such measure. Most relevant laws of commercial arbitration and rules follow that approach. But some rules restrict the right of the parties to seek interim measures from courts once the arbitrators are in place; for example, LCIA Rules Art. 25.3, although it allows the resort to courts in exceptional circumstances, and ICC Rules Art. 23.2, which permits resort to courts only in appropriate circumstances. There are some old cases in which US courts considered that requesting interim relief before domestic courts was incompatible with an agreement to arbitrate; although the cases are old, Redfern "still considers prudent to make this clear in the relevant rules of arbitration".[15]

There are also substantial legal and practical obstacles in resorting to national courts. Courts can only enforce interim measures within their territorial jurisdiction; in order to enforce an interim measure abroad the collaboration of a competent court is needed. Unfortunately, there are no uniform legal provisions, or international conventions, on court assistance or collaboration in enforcing interim measures granted by foreign courts. Thus, there will be little or no practical use in asking a court of the place of arbitration for an interim measure that probably will need to be enforced by courts elsewhere.

In that scenario, the logical action will be to look for the interim measure of protection in the place in which it can be enforced. But, again, reliance on a court not situated in the place of arbitration, may have problems. The place of arbitration in most cases is a neutral one. When the seat is in the place of business of one of the parties, the other parties may be reluctant to apply to a court seated in the place of business of their counterpart. Also, there is no uniform legal provision empowering courts seated outside the place of arbitration to grant interim measures in support of a foreign arbitration. Furthermore, there is no uniform legal definition of interim measures to be granted by courts in support of arbitration, and the relief that the requesting party is interested in may not be available from the national courts addressed.

Under the scenario discussed above, the preferred choice will be to rely on the arbitral tribunal. But that alternative is not exempt from serious obstacles.

Interim measures issued by arbitrators are binding only to the parties to the dispute, while courts have the power to bind third parties; for instance, a freezing of funds in a bank account may be addressed only to the party holding funds in the bank, but not to the bank which is not subject to the arbitration agreement. However, in certain jurisdictions the party that requested the measure may use the order to obtain from a competent domestic court an order ordering the bank to freeze the funds.

Freezing of assets is not the only case. For example, it is not uncommon that disputes on shareholders agreements are submitted to arbitration. While in principle there are

---

15. REDFERN, *op. cit.*, fn. 8, p. 224, footnote 10. See also CARON, CAPLAN AND PELLONPÄÄ, *op. cit.*, fn. 5, p. 543, footnote 72.

no issues of arbitrability regarding disputes between shareholders, it is doubtful that corporate governance disputes, which may affect the rights of third parties, can be submitted to arbitration. Thus, an interim measure that may affect the rights of third parties is of dubious legal value.

Arbitrators' interim measures quite often are voluntarily executed by the parties. Parties, in general, do not wish to contradict the arbitrators and prefer not to lose credibility with them. The fact that arbitrators have the last word is compelling; but not in some exceptional cases of bad faith or insolvent parties, whose intention is not to perform an unfavorable award. In many instances, courts may not have such compelling power, because the judgments of the court that issues an interim measure may be subject to appeal.

IV.   SOME PRACTICAL CONSIDERATIONS

In what follows I will address, some fundamental issues that may be considered when requesting, granting or denying interim relief. Included are some of the questions put by Kaj Hobér in his survey to which I respond from a different perspective.

1.   Jurisdiction

Arbitrators should exercise special care in ascertaining their jurisdiction before deciding on an application for interim relief. On many occasions the parties may have accepted the arbitrators' jurisdiction, but not in all cases. There are several scenarios: (i) an emergency or pre-trial arbitrator has been appointed; (ii) simultaneously with the request for arbitration an application for interim relief is made – it may even be made ex parte, the tribunal is appointed but the affected party has not had the opportunity to contest the jurisdiction; and (iii) the jurisdiction has been challenged.

The question is whether arbitrators, before granting the petition should expressly decide that they have jurisdiction, or whether a prima facie decision will suffice. Having a definite ruling on jurisdiction will avoid the embarrassing situation of a tribunal that granted interim relief and later found that it did not have jurisdiction. But to require an express decision may pose difficulties when a proper decision requires a substantive hearing, and the lapse of time risks jeopardizing the effectiveness of the measure if granted.

The Iran-US Claims Tribunal, for instance, has decided cases when it only appeared that it had jurisdiction. In many cases, the points at issue were requests to order a party to stay parallel court proceedings – for instance, when a claim was made before the Tribunal and the defendant filed a counterclaim in the courts.[16]

As usual in arbitration, it is for the arbitrators to ponder the circumstances of the case and to exercise their art. Even in dubious but urgent cases the decision may be

---

16. BROWER and. BRUESCHKE, *op. cit.*, fn. 5, pp. 218-221.

accompanied by a statement from the arbitrators that in the circumstances, it appears that there is jurisdiction.

2. Extent of the Interim Relief

Many rules recognize the power of arbitrators to take any interim measures they deem necessary in respect of the subject matter of the dispute (UNCITRAL Rules Art. 26(1)). Others are broader, and provide that the arbitrators may take whatever interim measures they deem necessary (ICDR Rules, Art. 21), or consider appropriate (ICC Rules, Art. 23(1)), or that they deem "necessary or appropriate" (Swiss Rules Art. 26(1)). Although it does not seem as controversial today, it must be noted that even when the laws and rules do not provide such a power it has been considered as part of "the relevant powers reserved to the arbitrators",[17] or of their power to protect "the effectiveness of the Tribunal's jurisdiction and authority", or of the inherent powers of the arbitrators.[18]

The UML offers concrete guidance and limits. Art. 17(2) provides a comprehensive, but restricted list. Considering the importance it will have in the future, it is worthwhile to quote it. It read as follows:

> "(2) An interim measure is any temporary measure, whether in the form of an award or in another form, by which, at any time prior to the issuance of the award by which the dispute is finally decided, the arbitral tribunal orders a party to:
> (a) Maintain or restore the status quo pending determination of the dispute;
> (b) Take action that would prevent, or refrain from taking action that is likely to cause, current or imminent harm or prejudice to the arbitral process itself;
> (c) Provide a means of preserving assets out of which a subsequent award may be satisfied; or
> (d) Preserve evidence that may be relevant and material to the resolution of the dispute."

3. Preserving the Status Quo

It is commonplace to refer to interim measures as needed to maintain or restore the status quo pending determination of the dispute. This statement is easier to express than to apply; what does status quo mean? There is no universally recognized, and applied, legal concept. If one resorts to plain language one may find that status quo is something like the existing condition or state of affairs. Is it so simple in arbitration? I have my reservations. The variety of disputes in international arbitration is endless, thus the status quo is equally varied; and there could not be a unique standard or solution. In

---

17. Yves DERAINS and Eric A. SCHWARTZ, *A Guide to the ICC Rules Of Arbitration*, 2nd edn. (Kluwer Law International 2005) p. 295.
18. BROWER and BRUESCHKE, *op. cit.*, fn. 5, p. 217.

other words, preserving the status quo may justify the interim relief in some cases; but in others what is needed is to modify the status quo.

For instance, in disputes over perishable goods, or goods in danger of losing their value, relief may be granted to modify the status quo; only in this way would the subject matter of the dispute be preserved. Indeed, in these cases, instead of preserving the goods, the aim is to preserve their value. Something similar happens when a party is requested to suspend parallel court, or arbitral, proceedings, allegedly initiated in violation of an arbitration agreement. As court proceedings naturally are ongoing and in constant evolution, ordering a party to stay them, would also amount to modifying rather than preserving the status quo.

Other cases are dubious. For instance, a licence agreement was terminated by the licensor on the allegation of breach of contract by the licensee, and that the licensee's actions and omissions were causing loss of market share to the products sold under the licence. The agreement authorized the licensor to terminate the contract without the need of an arbitral or court determination. The licensor alleged that it was necessary to grant an immediate license to a third party to stop the loss of market share. The defendant requested the arbitral tribunal to order the licensor to abstain from contracting with a third party. What was the real status quo in this case?

Finally, there are clear cases: for instance, in an arbitration between two shareholders, in which each one claimed that it was entitled to acquire the ownership of the shares of stock owned by the other party, one of them requested an interim measure directing its counterpart to deposit its shares in a trust, thus avoiding the possibility of the other party selling the stock. The arbitral tribunal directed "both parties" to deposit their shares in a trust, and ruled that the shares would be delivered as finally decided by the arbitral tribunal. By the way, this interim measure had the added advantage of avoiding further court proceedings for enforcement because the trustee delivered the stock to the wining party.[19]

It is common that arbitrators order one of the parties not to suspend partial payments, while ordering the other to guarantee with a letter of credit the payments received; or not to pursue collection claims of a bond to the issuer, on condition that the counterparty maintains the bond. In one such case, the arbitrators only allowed the claimant to start or continue proceedings if needed in order to preserve its rights: i.e., to avoid prescription.

4. Protecting the Arbitral Process

It is common to ask for interim measures ordering the affected party to take action that would prevent, or refrain from taking action that is likely to cause, current or imminent harm or prejudice to the arbitral process itself (UML 17 (2)(b)). These requests are similar to court-ordered anti-suit injunctions. In the UWG the main argument opposing anti-suit injunctions issued by arbitral tribunals is that they entitle private arbitrators to create an obstacle to the right of the parties to resort to courts. The reply given was that

---

19. This Case No. 8879, which the author knows by hindsight, is reported in 11 ICC International Court of Arbitration Bulletin (Spring 2000, no. 1) pp. 84-91.

the arbitral tribunal has power to order a party to perform the agreement to arbitrate without binding the competent courts.

Experience shows that anti-suit injunctions are needed in international arbitration. Increasing litigation practices that create obstacles to the peaceful and orderly evolution of the proceedings are the cause of the increasing number of requests for anti-suit injunctions. This need is demonstrated, for example, by the experience of the Iran-US Claims Tribunal, where the most common type of interim relief granted, was to "stay proceedings before other fora".[20]

The following case is another good example of one that justifies injunctions. The parties had a dispute over a contract to build, operate and administer a hotel in a certain country. The parties had agreed to arbitrate in a neutral site. The owner of the hotel started court proceedings in its country, seeking not only to annul the agreement to arbitrate, but also to obtain a domestic court judgment on the merits. The courts of the owner's county annulled the arbitration agreement in an interim measure ordered by a domestic court, and ordered the hotel operator not to continue and to terminate the arbitration abroad. The arbitrator appointed by the hotel owner was also ordered to stop serving as such. Meanwhile, the hotel operator had commenced arbitration in the agreed seat and obtained from the arbitral tribunal an award upholding the validity of the agreement to arbitrate and ordering the owner to terminate court actions in its country. The hotel operator moved to confirm the award and to compel the hotel owner to perform it before a court of the place of arbitration.

Another very interesting example arose out of a dispute between two shareholders in a subsidiary of one of the parties. One of the shareholders, also the parent company, complained that the other shareholder was using its corporate rights to obstruct systematically any action to promote the subsidiary; it therefore claimed the termination and liquidation of the venture. The parent company was also financing the operation of the subsidiary and was an important creditor of it. If the parent company claimed payment of the overdue sums owed to it by the subsidiary, the latter was legally bankrupt. The parent company sent a letter to the defendant shareholder requesting the infusion of fresh capital; failure to do so, the parent company warned the other party, would lead it to claim its credits and file insolvency proceedings in court against the subsidiary. The defendant requested the arbitral tribunal to enjoin the claimant from filing insolvency proceedings. Bankruptcy of the subsidiary would cause the demise of the subsidiary and would practically end the arbitration itself.

In a very interesting decision, the arbitral tribunal ruled that it could not enjoin the claimant from filing insolvency proceedings and exercising its rights of creditor against a third party to the arbitration. But the arbitral tribunal recommended that the claimant use its rights as creditor in good faith and with prudence, in order not to damage the subject matter of the arbitration.

---

20. BROWER and BRUESCHKE, *op. cit.*, fn. 5, p. 229.

5. Preservation of Evidence

Interim relief to preserve evidence may be granted, for example, to preserve some goods and be able to verify their conformity with the ones agreed in the contract or with the samples; or to preserve parts or scrap from construction sites to verify the quality of the construction works; or, in order to preserve books and records, not to erase electronic data and similar conduct.

In many cases, the issue of relief for preserving evidence may not be quite as controversial. Sometimes the issue of the costs of preserving evidence may arise; who bears storage and maintenance costs? In others the relief may cause damage to a party, and even to third parties. For instance, in a recent dispute over a construction contract terminated by the owner, the builder asked the arbitrators to order the owner not to continue the work until the experts could determine the amount and quality of work performed. The request was denied. To interrupt a construction program for such a long time was not justified, and there were other means to reasonably ascertain what the petitioner was looking for.

6. The Alleged Urgency

The need to show that the relief requested is urgent is considered by some as a requisite for granting it. This opinion misses the point. Yes, in many cases there is urgency, but to determine what is "urgent" is complicated and difficult. What the requesting party must show is the actual risk that a party may do something that would cause damage before the relevant issue is finally awarded. The damage may be to the arbitral proceeding itself, to the resolution of the dispute or may even place the enforceability of the award at risk. When dealing with an ex parte request, what the arbitrators must consider is whether the prior disclosure of the application to the affected party risks frustrating the purpose of the measure – not the urgency.

7. Ex Parte

In recent years there was a heated debate on ex parte relief. The debate was engendered by the UWG's Draft on interim measures. The question was finally settled in UNCITRAL and the UML contemplates them under the name of "Provisional Orders" (Art. 17 ter). I am not going to comment on the UNCITRAL text, but I will make a few comments regarding actual practice.

One of the main arguments against ex parte interim measures was that they were not legally possible in arbitration. That was not the opinion of the Iran-US Claims Tribunal, where "[I]n some instances the situation may be so urgent that the Tribunal is required to act immediately, without even asking the views of the party against which measures are to be issued." In some of those situations, the Tribunal's preferred course of action was to issue orders that could be named "temporary restraining measures", granted by the Tribunal "pending further determination of a request for interim measures". For instance, in a case in which "the Claimant stated that it has been summoned to appear before a court in Tehran in a case involving the same contract", the Tribunal requested "[R]espondent to move for a stay of the proceedings before the Tehran Court until such a time as the Tribunal can render its decision on Claimant's request". There were other similar cases, for instance, an order to stay an arbitration filed before the ICC. What makes the precedents of the Iran-US Claims Tribunal more important is the fact that they were made applying the UNCITRAL Rules.[21]

Similar practices were confirmed in the UWG. Arbitrators, before granting an interim measure, must give the parties a fair hearing. But giving a fair hearing takes time and on many occasions a quick decision is needed. What happens in real life? During the deliberations of the UWG, it was noted that often arbitrators, realizing the urgency to take some preventive action before the hearing, direct the party yet to be heard to stop or to take some action immediately needed. However, it was argued that in those cases, when the arbitrators made their determination, the affected party had been informed of the request, which does not mean that that party was "heard". In other words, to grant temporary relief when the affected party was notified of the request, but not given the opportunity to defend its case, is nothing other than granting a disguised ex parte interim measure.

8.   *Prima Facie Possibility*

Usually it is said that to grant interim relief, the applicant must have a reasonable opportunity to succeed in the merits (UML Art. 17 bis, (1) (b)). This is another standard which is easier to enunciate than to find in the particulars of a case. Scientifically and philosophically it is practically impossible to demonstrate that something will not happen; i.e., that the applicant will not succeed. Consequently, the standard cannot be anything but a practical, or common sense, assessment of the possibility of success. There is no way to establish a valid general standard, and only the art of the arbitrators will permit them to make a reasonable guess. On the other hand, arbitrators at the early stages of the arbitral proceedings, by definition, will have little or no knowledge of the case – especially emergency arbitrators or pre-arbitral referees. One cannot require much more than a prima facie opinion on the reasonableness or feasibility of the claim. In many cases, perhaps the only possibility is an assessment that the claim is not, prima facie, dismissible.

---

21. BROWER and BRUESCHKE, *op. cit.*, fn. 5, pp. 223-226. Among others quoted by those authors, *Component Builders, Inc*, Case No. 395, in 8 Iran-U.S. Cl. Trib. Rep 5; *Teledyne Industries Incorporated*, Case No. 10812, in 3 Iran-U.S. Cl. Trib. Rep 336; *Reading and Bates*, Interim Award No. ITM- 21-28-1, in 2 Iran-U.S. Cl. Trib. Rep 401; *Areonutronic Overseas Services*, Interim Award No. ITM 44-158-1, in 7 Iran-U.S. Cl. Trib. Rep 217; *Ford Aerospace and Communications Corporation*, Interim Award No. ITM 16-93-2, in 2 Iran-U.S. Cl. Trib. Rep 281; *Shipside Packing Company, Inc.*, Interim Award No. ITM 27-11875-1, in 3 Iran-U.S. Cl. Trib. Rep 331; *Accord RCA Global Communications Disc, Inc.*, Interim Award No. ITM 29-160-1, in 4 Iran-U.S. Cl. Trib. Rep 5, 8; *Rockwell International Systems*, Interim Award No. ITM 17-430-1, in 2 Iran-U.S. Cl. Trib. Rep 310, 310-11. Similarly, CARON, CAPLAN AND PELLONPÄÄ, *op. cit.*, fn. 5, p. 542, also quote the Iran-US Claims Tribunal and consider that it is possible to grant ex parte "temporary restraining orders", when the arbitral tribunal may not wish to issue a final decision until the other party has commented on the request made by its opponent.

In any event, arbitrators must exercise extreme care in showing that in granting the interim measure they are not prejudging the merits of the case (UML Art. 17 *bis*, (1) (b)).

9. Interim Measures and Public Policy

Sometimes interim measures are sought that go against public policy in the place of enforcement. For instance, in disputes between shareholders I have seen requests made to the arbitrators to appoint a third-party administrator, regardless of what the applicable mandatory company law – for instance, in one case, Mexican law – provides. Obviously such an interim measure will not be enforceable in the legal domicile of the corporation, especially when the corporation itself is not a party to the arbitration. In such circumstances the arbitrators cannot do more than direct the controlling shareholders to take action in order to appoint a designated person as an administrator or comptroller; or to the veto-empowered minority of shareholders, not to oppose compliance with the order. Even in such a case, care must be taken. It is possible that the shareholders, in following the arbitrators' directions, may violate or ignore the applicable company law, and incur liabilities toward third parties.

10. The Balance of Possible Harm

This is another common condition. One author points out that the interim measure should be "necessary," not "desirable" or "recommendable". Art. 17 *bis*, (1)(a) UML provides a good standard requiring that the harm that is likely to result if the measure is not ordered may not be adequately reparable by an award of damages, and may substantially outweigh the harm that is likely to result to the party against whom the measure is directed if the measure is granted.

I see no reason to require a "substantial" difference in the measure of the balance of the damages in deciding whether granting or denying the relief; this is a difficult standard for the applicant. It may suffice that the harm caused by not ordering the measure outweighs the harm that may be done to the party against whom the measure is directed.

In many legal systems damages are always reparable by a monetary award; thus, there is no irreparable harm. In some *common law* systems the notion of irreparable harm is harm that cannot readily be compensated by an award of damages. Thus, the importance of giving a flexible interpretation to the requirement that the damages may not be "adequately" reparable is of great importance.[22] Examples of this are when considering the unique nature of the assets or property threatened: for instance, a work of art.

Regarding damages, interesting considerations arise when dealing with large and complex cases, which require long preparation. When it is evident that the final decision of the case will come years later, it may be prudent to consider the possibility of a balanced relief in order to avoid the damages caused by the delay or the uncertainty.

---

22. CARON, CAPLAN and PELLONPÄÄ, *op. cit.*, fn. 5, pp. 536-537 and footnote 24.

11. Disposing of the Case in an Interim Measure

Another issue is when granting the interim measure would in fact give a party the final relief sought. In those cases interim relief must be denied. Also, when granting the measure may tip the balance between the parties and give the requesting party a strong bargaining position. This is a very delicate area, because in many instances aggressive litigators try to get interim measures for the purpose of forcing a rapid, but advantageous, settlement of the dispute.

12. Feasibility of Enforcement

The fact that it is unlikely that the measure sought is capable of being carried out must not prevent an arbitrator from granting it. The legal possibility of enforcement remains. Also, failure to perform an order will produce the legal consequences of a breach of contract.[23] Finally, arbitrators must keep in mind the power they have to make adverse inferences and to award damages.

13. Form and Reasons

Rules, commentary and some laws on arbitration, allow interim measures to be made in the form of an award or any other form.[24] The obvious advantage is that the measure may be enforced in courts under the provisions of the New York Convention or in UML countries or countries that follow a similar approach.

Making an interim measure in the form of an award may have problems. Not all courts in the world accept that an interim measure containing a non-final decision, notwithstanding its name, is an enforceable award. A party thinking that it has a gun, may find out later that its weapon is charged with wet powder. The other inconvenience is that under some rules, for example the ICC Rules, making an award takes much more time than issuing an order. At least in one case under the ICC Rules, the arbitrators announced the interim measure as an order, informing the parties that, as requested and agreed, they will give to it the final form of an award.[25] Was that device not defrauding the ICC scrutiny of awards rule?

It is generally understood that interim measures must be made in writing, and with reasons. How extensive the reasons should be is a difficult question to answer. On the one hand, it is fair and advisable to give plenty of reasons in order to convince the parties and encourage them to perform; but on the other hand, giving too many reasons may provide food for further litigation. When the interim measure is going to be granted in an award, parties may agree that the award be made without reasons.

---

23. *Ibid.*, p. 541.
24. UML Art. 17(2), ICC Art. 23(1), ICDR Art. 21(2), Swiss Rules Art. 26(2), UAR Art. 26(2).
25. ICC Case No. 8879, quoted above, fn. 19.

V.   CONCLUSION

Considering all the problems discussed, one cannot but conclude that dealing with interim relief is an art. It is against this background that the UML legal provisions may be of real help to the international arbitration community. They are a complete set of directions, but drafted in general terms that will allow prudence, flexibility, and good case law to develop.

Interim Measures – A Practical Experience

Neil Kaplan CBE, QC[*]

I.   INTRODUCTION

When account is taken of the amount of debate that has been generated by the topic of interim measures over the last two to three years one could be forgiven for thinking that an international arbitrator's daily diet consists of dealing with anti-suit injunctions, Mareva injunctions, orders for preservation of and inspection of the subject matter of the dispute, applications to retain the status quo and applications for security for the claim or for costs. This view is bolstered by the fact that at almost all arbitration conferences, seminars and courses being held, virtually weekly, around the world the topic of interim measures is on the menu.

I have been asked to approach this session not from an esoteric or academic viewpoint but from the perspective of a full-time international arbitrator with over twenty years of experience. In order to ensure that my experience has not been atypical I have consulted with some equally experienced arbitrators as well as with some of the arbitral institutions. The majority of this commentary was written before I had the advantage of reading Kaj Hobér's excellent Report[1] upon which I will make some comments at the end.

II.   EXPEDITED PROCEDURES

If an injunction is required it is usually required at about the time that the arbitration is about to commence. It takes some time to constitute a tribunal on any basis and sometimes the need for urgent relief is required at that time. This problem can lead to the application for relief being made to a national court pending the constitution of the tribunal. Most national courts will consider granting relief in aid of an arbitration before the tribunal is constituted. However, once constituted, some courts will say that it is a

---

[*] Former Judge of the High Court, Hong Kong; Chairman, Hong Kong International Arbitration Centre 1991-2004; Past President, Chartered Institute of Arbitrators; Member of ICCA.
1. See this volume, pp. 721-750.

matter for the tribunal especially in the light of the expanded powers given to arbitrators under modern legislation and rules.[2]

However, some think that the need to seek relief at any stage from a national court is antithetical to international arbitration. Thus some institutions have drafted procedures to ensure that if there are any urgent applications prior to the constitution of the tribunal they will be dealt with by an arbitrator appointed urgently and for that specific purpose. Other institutions have an expedited appointment procedure to ensure the swift appointment of the tribunal in cases of exceptional urgency. By this means the tribunal is appointed shortly after the request and can then go on to deal with the urgent application for an interim measure.

1. International Chamber of Commerce (ICC)

The ICC has Rules for a Pre-Arbitral Referee Procedure which came into force on 1 January 1990. The Introduction to these Rules sets out their purpose quite succinctly as follows:

> "During the course of many contracts, especially those made for long-term transactions, problems can arise which require an urgent response. It is frequently not possible to obtain in the time required a final decision from an arbitral tribunal or from a court.
>
> Accordingly, the International Chamber of Commerce (ICC) has set out the following Rules for a Pre-Arbitral Referee Procedure in order to enable parties that have so agreed to have rapid recourse to a person (called a 'Referee') empowered to make an order designed to meet the urgent problem in issue, including the power to order the preservation or recording of evidence. The order should therefore provide a temporary resolution of the dispute and may lay the foundations for its final settlement either by agreement or otherwise.
>
> Use of the Pre-Arbitral Referee Procedure does not usurp the jurisdiction of any entity (whether arbitral tribunal or national court) that is ultimately responsible for deciding the merits of any underlying dispute."

Since 1990 there have been seven cases under the Pre-Arbitral Referee Procedure. Two in 2001, two in 2002, one in 2003 and two in 2005. Obviously in each case the parties had specifically incorporated this procedure into their contract because it is predicated on consent. All of these appointments were made within thirty days. The parties

---

2. See *The Lady Muriel* [1995] HKCA 123 and Sect. 2GC of the Hong Kong Arbitration Ordinance which provides where relevant as follows:

> "(6) The Court or a judge of the Court may decline to make an order under this section in relation to a matter referred to in subsection (1) on the ground that –
> (a) the matter is currently the subject of arbitration proceedings; and
> (b) the Court or the judge considers it more appropriate for the matter to be dealt with by the relevant arbitral tribunal."

involved in these cases came from France, Switzerland, Congo, Portugal, The Netherlands, USA, Italy, Spain and Algeria.

The appointees in these cases are from Switzerland, Brazil, Belgium and USA.

It may well be that next time the ICC Rules are amended the Pre-Arbitral Referee Procedure may be incorporated into the Rules.[3]

2.   *London Court of International Arbitration (LCIA)*

This eventuality is covered by LCIA Rule 9 which provides as follows:

> "9.1 In exceptional urgency, on or after the commencement of the arbitration, any party may apply to the LCIA Court for the expedited formation of the Arbitral Tribunal, including the appointment of any replacement arbitrator under Articles 10 and 11 of these Rules.
>
> 9.2 Such an application shall be made in writing to the LCIA Court, copied to all other parties to the arbitration; and it shall set out the specific grounds for exceptional urgency in the formation of the Arbitral Tribunal.
>
> 9.3 The LCIA Court may, in its complete discretion, abridge or curtail any time-limit under these Rules for the formation of the Arbitral Tribunal, including service of the Response and of any matters or documents adjudged to be missing from the Request. The LCIA Court shall not be entitled to abridge or curtail any other time-limit."

In 2005 the LCIA Court received seven applications under Art. 9 and granted six. In most of these cases the Art. 9 application was made at the same time as the filing of the Request for Arbitration. The time to the appointment of the tribunals in these cases from the date of receipt of the Request for Arbitration was fourteen days, five days, twenty-five days, six days, five days and eighteen days the average being twelve days.[4]

III.   INSTITUTIONAL EXPERIENCE WITH INTERIM MEASURES

1.   *Singapore International Arbitration Centre (SIAC)*

SIAC dealt with 182 new cases during the period between January 2004 and February 2006 and noted six applications for interim relief. One was an anti-suit injunction which was granted and the others were for security for costs or security for the claim.[5]

---

3. I am grateful to Emmanuel Jolivet of the ICC for providing this information. See also Ali YESILIRMAK, *Provisional Measures in International Commercial Arbitration* (Kluwer 2005).
4. I am grateful to Mathew Sillett, Deputy Registrar of LCIA for providing these statistics.
5. These statistics were given by Sabiha Shiraz,counsel and Senior Assistant Registrar of SIAC at the joint ICC/HKIAC seminar in Hong Kong on 27 March 2006.

2. Stockholm Chamber of Commerce (SCC)

SCC did not keep records of interim relief applications however it is thought that there are a very few, possibly only one per year.

However, in 2001 an SCC tribunal ordered a respondent "to refrain from any disposition with regard to the equipment delivered under the contract, as a result of which the equipment would be sold, leased, conveyed or otherwise transferred to a third party".

In 2002 another SCC tribunal ordered a respondent "not to dispose of, or otherwise diminish its interest in the vessels ... prior to the rendering of a final award on the merits in the above arbitration".[6]

3. LCIA

In the period 1 January 2004 to the date of writing 245 arbitrations were commenced at the LCIA. In sixteen of those cases applications were received, under Art. 9 of the Rules, for the expedited formation of the tribunal. Ten of the sixteen succeeded. Eight of the sixteen Art. 9 cases were accompanied by applications for interim measures.

Four applications were to restrain a party from dealing in shares. All were granted. One application was for the expedited submission of documents (not one of the Art. 9 cases). One application was for the preservation of goods the subject matter of the arbitration and this was granted. Another which was granted was for an expert to inspect the goods. Another application was for a provisional payment on account of the value of the claim or alternatively for security for the claim both of which were denied.

In a further eight cases (but not Art. 9 cases) six were applications for security for costs. Two were granted, three were rejected and one is pending. Two applications for security for the claim were made but rejected.[7]

4. ICC

ICC case officers see a wide range of interim measures applications. The most frequent is security for costs but these also emanate from non-UK parties and counsel. Other interim measures noted include attempts to stop calls on guarantees, attempts to restrict contractual non-performance and applications relating to confidentiality.[8]

IV. PERSONAL EXPERIENCE

The interim measure that frequently comes across my desk is an application for security for costs. I would guess that in 30 per cent of the cases with which I deal an application for security for costs is made. Some are not proceeded with. Some fail but a fair

---

6. I am grateful to Ulf Franke, Secretary General of SCC for providing this information.
7. I am grateful to Adrian Winstanley, Registrar of LCIA, for providing these statistics.
8. See fn. 3.

proportion succeed. The obvious reaction is to comment that this is a particularly English approach. Whereas few English parties appear in front of me it has to be said that English law firms and counsel are frequently involved. It is difficult nowadays, with the globalization of legal practice, to compartmentalize firms into common law/civil law, etc. Many large firms practising in, say, Paris will have American and English lawyers who will bring to the practice common law methods of acting. I understand from the ICC that security for costs applications are quite common in ICC arbitrations and that they do not only emanate from English lawyers nor are they granted solely by English or American arbitrators.

The application for security for costs has to be dealt with very carefully. The applicant thinks it may be a knock-out blow. The respondent to it sees it as a method of stifling a genuine claim. The arbitrator must first be satisfied that the respondent to the claim will be unable to pay the winning parties' costs if such an order is made. Frequently anecdotal evidence is supplied which is not helpful. Some applications fail at the proof stage. Then there is the quantum aspect. Not surprisingly the applicant attempts to estimate what the total costs will be. This sometimes throws up some surprising figures. In one recent case an estimate included counsel's fees at £900 per hour (apparently soon to be increased!). I think it can be said that most tribunals are capable of looking at an estimate of costs and bring to it an air of reality. Rather than ordering security for costs in one lump sum to cover the whole arbitration it may be fairer to order it in stages.

I have only had one application for security for the claim which was based on somewhat unusual facts. I think this is surprising especially since the power has existed in England and Hong Kong (firstly with the court and now with the tribunal) for some time. The power also exists under certain rules now in existence.

Anti-suit injunctions granted by courts have been the subject of much discussion of late. However as an arbitrator I have only received one such application. The tribunal declined to grant it but did order that if either party intended to make an application to a national court that party should first give notice to the other party and the tribunal. This form of order enables the tribunal to consider the actual order sought rather than grant a blanket injunction.

I have never received an application for an injunction apart from the anti-suit injunction to which I have just made reference.

I have made an order for testing of the subject matter of the dispute. This was complicated by the fact that the subject matter had to be taken some distance to the nearest place where examination could be carried out and this obviously required very stringent conditions and protections. Substantial issues of confidentiality also arose.

V.   ARBITRATORS' EXPERIENCE

Unlike Kaj Hobér I have not prepared a survey nor taken any formal soundings. I was however interested to discover whether my personal experience was typical so I contacted a number of leading arbitrators and interestingly their experience was similar to mine: several applications for security for costs but very few others. There was no stream of interim applications but occasionally an interesting one. I propose to set them out to show the nature of them.

Some of my colleagues have granted injunctions. In one case the tribunal was asked to order a party to continue performance under a long-term supply contract pending the tribunal's decision on the merits. In another an application was sought to restrain a government from appointing a new concessionaire until the validity of the determination of the first concession had been determined. These are surely all examples of tribunals granting orders the aim of which is to preserve the status quo pending the result of the arbitration. Presumably most arbitrators would be prepared to do this unless very unusual circumstances existed because to refuse might render the arbitral process nugatory.

One of my colleagues had to deal with an application to order one party to permit the other to enter on and inspect a facility. Clearly orders for inspection of goods the subject matter of the dispute are frequently made. Similarly, applications to inspect ships are not uncommon in maritime cases. Orders to inspect infrastructural projects are rare, at least, in my experience.

One commentator ventured the view that in London at least there is still a reaction in favour of going to court to get an injunction doubtless based on the perception that judges are more likely to grant them than are arbitrators.

However the same commentator noted an increase in applications for injunctions to restrain breaches of contract, restrain the holding of board meetings and security for costs. Anti-suit injunctions he thought were more frequently made to courts.

A leading maritime arbitrator confirmed that in his experience there was little call for interim measures in maritime cases, although it was sometimes necessary to order the inspection of a ship or cargo. In a few cases it was necessary to order the retention of documents.

Confidentiality was mentioned by several of those I contacted and I too have had to deal with that issue. My tribunal was faced with an admission in our London arbitration that various sums had been paid but a denial of receipt in another arbitration between one of the parties in our arbitration and its managing director. We permitted the pleading that contained the admission to be so used but subject to strict confidentiality.

In another LCIA case in London concerning a project in Singapore there was a parallel arbitration in Singapore not between identical parties but arising out of the same project the delays in which were crucial to our arbitration. Citing SIAC Rule 34.6 it was argued that we could not see any award, pleading or witness statement from the other arbitration. We would have had to construe the SIAC Rule very carefully but good sense broke out before we had to do so.

VI.   COMMENTS

As stated above, regrettably most of the above was written before I had sight of Kaj Hobér's excellent Report. However it seems that his conclusions are not materially different from those stated above.

However I do have some comments on his Report. I agree that in recent years arbitration has become more aggressive. This is regrettable. If this has led to more applications for interim measures – so be it. But it is important that the application for an interim measure should not take on a life of its own and detract from the primary aim of the arbitration which is to resolve the substantive issues as speedily as possible. Too often interim measures applications deflect the parties, and the tribunal, from the real work at hand. Accordingly, they should be handled as speedily as possible and should not be allowed to become a vehicle for delay whether intended or not.

In dealing with national arbitration legislations it is worth noting that in Hong Kong the wording of Art. 17 of the Model Law was not thought clear enough and accordingly Sect. 2 GB of the Arbitration Ordinance was introduced in 1996. Arbitrators in Hong Kong have very wide and specific powers to order interim measures,[9] unlike the position

---

9. Sect. 2GB provides as follows:

"(1) When conducting arbitration proceedings, an arbitral tribunal may make orders or give directions dealing with any of the following matters –
(a) requiring a claimant to give security for the costs of the arbitration;
(b) requiring money in dispute to be secured;
(c) directing the discovery of documents or the delivery of interrogatories;
(d) directing evidence to be given by affidavit;
(e) in relation to relevant property –
(i) directing the inspection, photographing, preservation, custody, detention or sale of the property by the tribunal, a party to the proceedings or an expert; or
(ii) directing samples to be taken from, observations to be made of, or experiments to be conducted on the property;
(f) granting interim injunctions or directing other interim measures to be taken.
(2) Property is relevant property for the purposes of subsection (1)(e) if –
(a) the property is owned by or is in the possession of a party to the proceedings; and
(b) the property is subject to the proceedings, or any question relating to the property arises in the proceedings.
(3) An arbitral tribunal must not make an order requiring a claimant to provide security for costs only on the ground that the claimant –
(a) is a natural person who is ordinarily resident outside Hong Kong; or
(b) is a body corporate that is incorporated, or an association that is formed, under a law of a place outside Hong Kong, or whose central management and control is exercised outside Hong Kong.
(4) An arbitral tribunal –
(a) must, when making an order to provide security for costs, specify a period within which the order is to be complied with; and
(b) may extend that period or an extended period.
(5) An arbitral tribunal may dismiss or stay a claim if it has made an order requiring the claimant to provide security for costs and the order has not been complied with within the period allowed under subsection (4).
(6) In conducting arbitration proceedings, an arbitral tribunal may decide whether and to what extent it should itself take the initiative in ascertaining the facts and the law relevant to those proceedings.
(7) An arbitral tribunal may –
(a) administer oaths to, or take the affirmations of, witnesses and parties; and
(b) examine witnesses and parties on oath or affirmation; and
(c) direct the attendance before the tribunal of witnesses in order to give evidence or to produce documents or other material evidence.
(8) A person cannot be required to produce in arbitration proceedings any document or other material evidence that the person could not be required to produce in civil proceedings before a court.

in the mainland of China. Sect. 2GG of the Hong Kong Arbitration Ordinance provides for enforcement of awards, orders or decisions made by a tribunal.[10]

I was interested that none of Kaj Hobér's responses dealt with the situation where an ICC tribunal orders a recalcitrant respondent to pay its share of the deposit on costs. One of my colleagues was a member of a tribunal that did just that in order to enable security provided by the claimant to be released.

My experience and enquiries did not indicate that there was any distinction to be drawn between the subject matter of the cases nor did it appear that there was any common law/civil law divide. However, having heard Marc Blessing speak and having read his Comments[11] it seems to me that the civil law approach may well be different. I agree with him and with Kaj Hobér that there are more interim measure applications now than they were ten to fifteen years ago. But of course there are also more arbitrations today than there were then. Tribunals may have become more robust and this will continue so long as they are supported by local courts. However the picture painted by Marc Blessing relating to interim measures is not the picture that I or my correspondents see in practice.

Finally, I am not convinced that the reason why most of us see relatively few interim measure applications is simply because parties go to court to obtain them. Many courts are reluctant to interfere when the tribunal has been constituted and has jurisdiction to make the order sought and indeed some modern statutes strive to create that result. The simple answer may well be that in the majority of commercial disputes all that is really needed from the tribunal is a speedy resolution of the substantive issues without too many unnecessary sideshows.

---

(9) Subsections (6) and (7) are subject to any agreement to the contrary of the parties to the relevant arbitration proceedings."

10. Sect. 2GG provides as follows:

"(1) An award, order or direction made or given in or in relation to arbitration proceedings by an arbitral tribunal is enforceable in the same way as a judgment, order or direction of the Court that has the same effect, but only with the leave of the Court or a judge of the Court. If that leave is given, the Court or judge may enter judgment in terms of the award, order or direction.
(2) Notwithstanding anything in this Ordinance, this section applies to an award, order and direction made or given whether in or outside Hong Kong."

11. Marc Blessing's Comments are not reproduced in this volume.

Working Group B

5. Round Table on Legal Experts

Commentary on Using Legal Experts in International Arbitration

Kap-You (Kevin) Kim* and John P. Bang**

I. DO WE NEED LEGAL EXPERTS?

Applying a governing law the tribunal is either not qualified in, or not familiar with, raises complex issues and therefore requires legal counsel to consider various strategies prior to and during the arbitration process. Indeed, tribunal members (particularly the chairman), who are not well versed in the applicable governing law of the arbitration, face the challenge of understanding and properly applying the applicable law to the case. Under these circumstances, either the parties may offer or the tribunal may seek assistance through legal experts in international arbitration.

1. Proving Governing Law as a Matter of Fact or a Matter of Law?

In civil law court proceedings, "foreign" law is treated as a matter of law rather than a matter of fact, and the court is in charge of investigating a foreign law. In the civil law tradition, the maxim *"la Cour sait le droit"* – the court knows the law – applies.[1] But in the common law tradition, "foreign" law is treated as a matter of fact that the parties must prove before the court. In international arbitrations, unless the tribunal is sufficiently familiar with the governing law, the parties must prove the substance of the law before the tribunal regardless of legal traditions, and legal experts perform that role.

---

* Partner and head of the International Arbitration & Litigation Practice Group, Bae, Kim & Lee, Seoul, Korea. Adjunct Professor of Law, College of Law, Seoul National University and College of Law, Sogang University.

** Senior Foreign Legal Consultant of the International Arbitration & Litigation Practice Group, Bae, Kim & Lee, Seoul, Korea.

1. Bernard HANOTIAU, "The Conduct of the Hearings", *The Leading Arbitrators' Guide to International Arbitration* (Juris 2004) p. 386.

2. When Counsel Are Familiar With, or Qualified in, the Governing Law Jurisdiction

When counsel for the parties are qualified lawyers of the governing law, which is frequently the case, the counsel themselves may provide the tribunal with legal opinions on the law. In such cases, the tribunal may require the counsel to submit an affidavit confirming the accuracy of the opinion. Alternatively, counsel may be asked to present their respective legal opinions through oral argument.

Many tribunals and parties in practice, however, regularly use legal experts even if counsel are qualified to provide legal opinions on the governing law. They do so because a third-party legal expert, whether appointed by the tribunal or the parties, is able to provide a neutral expert opinion, although parties frequently appoint experts whose "neutral" opinions are favorable to their case.

Notwithstanding the concern about neutrality, it may actually be more effective and efficient for the counsel to introduce and prove the relevant aspects of the governing law themselves. The introduction of law by counsel may be more appropriate in cases that do not involve many key issues of law, but more issues of fact, or also in complicated cases where the relevant legal points of the case would be best explained by a person who is intimately familiar with the case, such as the counsel. In a fact-intensive or complicated case, a legal expert may simply be unnecessary and actually be counter-productive because the expert could confuse the tribunal, or even worse, inadvertently mislead it unless the expert possesses sufficient familiarity with the facts and their nuances, twists and turns.

3. When the Arbitrators Are Familiar with the Governing Law

When all the members of the tribunal are qualified in the governing law or are from a jurisdiction with a similar legal system, it is quite natural that the tribunal may not want any legal expert.

What if, however, only one member of the tribunal is qualified in the governing law? For example, when the chair of the tribunal is qualified, would it be satisfactory to the parties for the chair to essentially act as the legal expert on the case? Or when one party-appointed member of the tribunal is qualified in the governing law, while the other members have little to no knowledge of the governing law, should the tribunal rely solely on the opinion of that member of the tribunal without the assistance of any legal expert? These are difficult questions to answer.

In practice, the party who did not appoint a tribunal member qualified in the governing law will usually want to use a third-party expert in order to minimize potential bias. The party may worry that the "qualified" tribunal member may be able to influence the other members unfavorably against the party that did not appoint such member. By using a legal expert in such a situation, the party may be able to level the legal-expertise balance that may otherwise have been weighted against it.

The appropriateness of a legal expert becomes more difficult to decide when the governing law is similar to the laws under which some members of the tribunal are qualified. For example, if the governing law is Singaporean law or Hong Kong law and two members of the tribunal are qualified barristers in the United Kingdom, would the case need legal experts?

To answer all of the questions in this Section, the parties and the tribunal must consider how much impact the governing law has on the case and, moreover, how many of the unique aspects of the governing law are relevant in the case. In some cases, it is obvious that the critical issues are fact-oriented or involve very general, universal legal principles, while in other cases, the critical issues require a more precise interpretation, or a finer understanding, of the governing law. The more critical the governing-law-specific issues a case contains, the more likely that the parties and the tribunal will, and should, want to use legal experts.

4.   *Should You Choose Co-arbitrators and/or a Chairman Licensed or Familiar with the Applicable Governing Law?*

In I.3 above we mentioned that in cases where only one of the parties appoints a tribunal member qualified in the governing law, the other party usually seeks the use of a legal expert to reduce any possible bias. Such reaction implies that appointing a tribunal member qualified in the pertinent jurisdiction is an advantage which the other party must counter. Alternatively, prior to deciding whether legal experts should be involved, a party may counter an appointment of a co-arbitrator qualified in the governing law by appointing its own co-arbitrator who is qualified in the governing law.

However, in I.3 we also mentioned that, as in all issues herein, every decision must be made on a case-by-case basis. The degree of familiarity with the governing law that an arbitrator should have will obviously depend on how heavily the critical issues of the arbitration case are legally oriented and, sometimes more precisely, governing-law-specific. In arbitration cases where legal issues will play a smaller role, there is less of a need to focus on legal qualifications when selecting an arbitrator, and therefore, other qualities of a potential arbitrator can be given further consideration.

5.   *General Attitude of Tribunals*

In my experience, many tribunals prefer not to use legal experts, particularly if: (i) a member or members of the tribunal are qualified in the governing law jurisdiction; and/or (ii) all of the parties are represented by counsel qualified in that jurisdiction.

It will almost always be the case that the parties' counsel will be qualified in the governing law. A counsel not qualified in the governing law representing a party in an arbitration case alone would carry an obvious risk. But whether to select an arbitrator who is qualified in the governing law is the more important issue that, of course, must be decided on a case-by-case basis.

II. WHO WILL APPOINT THE LEGAL EXPERTS?

1. Tribunal-appointed Expert

In the civil law tradition, the arbitral tribunal normally appoints a legal expert when necessary, whether upon a party's request or at its own discretion.[2] The tribunal as well as the parties may present a list of questions or issues to be responded to by the legal expert. After review, the legal expert will provide the tribunal with an opinion. An expert appointed by the tribunal will raise fewer concerns regarding neutrality and conflict of interest.

2. Party-appointed Expert

In the common law tradition, it is the parties that normally appoint their own legal experts and present such experts to the tribunal. Each party obtains the opinion of its appointed legal experts, and presents the opinions to the tribunal. Appointment of experts by the parties is, by far, more commonly seen in international arbitration than expert appointments by the tribunal.[3]

When a party appoints a legal expert, such expert too often "crosses the line" and acts more as an advocate rather than a neutral legal expert. In principle, however, even though a legal expert was appointed by a party, the expert is required to assist the tribunal rather than the parties by providing a neutral and objective opinion.

III. WHO SHOULD BE A LEGAL EXPERT?

1. Professor or Lawyer?

For various reasons including depth of knowledge and perceived neutrality, law professors are frequently appointed as legal experts. Professors generally project a more neutral and independent image and therefore, the opinions that they provide to the tribunal appear less biased. Lawyers, on the other hand, are almost reflexively regarded as "hired guns", despite being appointed to serve in a neutral capacity as an expert.

---

2. See Art. 26 of the UNICTRAL Model Law:

"(1) Unless otherwise agreed by the parties, the arbitral tribunal (a) may appoint one or more experts to report to it on specific issues to be determined by the arbitral tribunal...."

3. See Art. 20(3) and (4) of the ICC Rules of Arbitration:

"(3) The Arbitral Tribunal may decide to hear witnesses, experts appointed by the parties or any other person, in the presence of the parties, or in their absence provided that they have been duly summoned.
(4) The Arbitral Tribunal, after having consulted the parties, may appoint one or more experts, define their terms of reference and receive their reports. At the request of a party, the parties shall be given the opportunity to question at a hearing such expert appointed by the Tribunal."

Additionally, attempting to use practicing, or even recently retired lawyers, as legal experts may prove to be difficult because of conflict issues which could, in fact, bias their opinion. Even if lawyers could be more than qualified to serve as experts, because of the aforementioned inherent disadvantages, professors are generally favored over lawyers to be appointed as legal experts in international arbitration.

2.   Qualifications of the Expert?

The party or counsel should select a legal expert based on the candidate's actual expertise in the area where the expert opinion is required, together with the candidate's reputation in the area. In most cases, whether an individual is professionally licensed to practice law may be an appropriate or important condition, but it is not absolutely essential. Some law professors have experience as lawyers, prosecutors or judges, while other professors have no experience as a legal practitioner. In certain countries such as Korea and Japan, many law professors are not professionally qualified as lawyers in such jurisdictions but, nevertheless, are certainly well qualified to provide expert testimony on particular areas of the law.[4]

3.   Language?

Many international arbitration cases involving parties from different countries are conducted in English and therefore, it is ideal if the legal expert is fluent in English. Legalese and legal concepts are sometimes difficult to express and understand in any language. It is a huge asset if an expert is able to communicate his or her ideas directly in English.   No matter how good the translator, something is inevitably lost in translation. At best, just a slight shade in meaning may be lost, but at worst, key points can be entirely misinterpreted. Moreover, a legal expert who is able to communicate effectively not only minimizes any misunderstandings but also projects a more authoritative image that may add weight when legal experts offer differing opinions.

Unavoidably, the use of an interpreter for the legal expert will be necessary in many instances. In such situations, it is imperative on the part of counsel to attentively monitor the interpretation to ensure that it is being accurately conveyed to the tribunal.

IV.   WHAT IS THE ROLE OF THE LEGAL EXPERT?

1.   Neutral, or Is There a Conflict of Interest?

Whether a legal expert is appointed by a party or the tribunal, the legal expert is required to be neutral and independent from the parties. In that sense, the legal expert should be free from any conflict of interest. This situation raises the issue of what should be the appropriate criteria by which the conflict of interest of a legal expert is determined. While the legal experts must be independent, provide unbiased opinions

---

4. These professors are law college graduates who have also obtained masters (LLM) and doctorate (PhD) degrees in a particular area of the law.

to assist the tribunal, and not advocate the parties' position in theory, the legal experts appointed by the parties tend to and are generally expected to assist the parties' position to a certain extent in practice. Given the reality of the situation, in my opinion, the required standard for neutrality of legal experts should be less stringent than that of arbitrators.

2. General Opinions or Case-specific Comments?

Legal experts are supposed to provide the tribunal with opinions on the legal issues arising in the arbitration. In principle, the legal experts provide general opinions on the issues rather than specific conclusions regarding the specific circumstances of the case. Only certain limited information and documents are given to the legal expert and therefore, legal experts are generally not in a position to provide case-specific opinions. Nevertheless, in practice, legal experts often provide their opinions on specific issues while making the appropriate qualifications.

V. CROSS-EXAMINATION, EXPERT CONFERENCING OR QUESTIONING IN WRITING: WHICH OF THESE PROCEDURES IS MORE EFFECTIVE?

1. Cross-examination

Arbitration professionals have debated whether it is desirable to allow cross-examination of a legal expert in international arbitrations. In Korea for example, cultural sensitivity presents difficulties when counsel cross-examine legal experts, particularly law professors who are more senior and are alumni from the same law college. In practice, however, it is still common and expected for counsel to cross-examine legal experts in arbitration cases.

2. Expert Conferencing

In recent years, the developing and preferred trend is for arbitral tribunals to conduct expert conferencing rather than just cross-examination. Along with the expert conferencing, tribunals also require experts to prepare joint expert lists that summarize the positions of the experts, list the issues on which the experts agree and disagree and provide comments and reasons for their disagreement. In my experience, expert conferencing is quite useful and more efficient than cross-examination in many cases. It is especially helpful in those jurisdictions where the cross-examination of legal experts may be discouraged.

3. Questioning Through Writing

Rather than live testimony through cross–examination or expert conferencing, another alternative is to have the parties write out specific questions to the opposing legal experts. This method may be better than live testimony in the sense that, by providing the experts the opportunity to work out their thoughts, they will be able to provide more accurate opinions. On the other hand, given more time, the experts may be able to draft their "neutral" opinions with a slant that is favorable to the party that appointed them.

VI.   CONCLUSION

When one is appointed as legal counsel for an international arbitration, there are various issues and strategies that one must consider during the constitution of the tribunal and presentation of the case. Two important issues that must be remembered are whether it is important and appropriate to appoint a member(s) of the tribunal who is/are qualified in the governing law jurisdiction and whether it is necessary and effective to appoint legal experts.

Working Group B

6. Round Table on Damages and Technical Experts

Some Thoughts from Experiences in Construction Arbitrations

*Nael G. Bunni**

I. BACK TO BASICS

In construction arbitrations, as in others where technical and scientific matters often form an important part of the dispute between the parties, expert evidence is valuable and sometimes necessary. Whether simply valuable or in fact necessary, expert witnesses perform a vital role either in establishing the cause and effect or ultimately in the assessment of damages due from one party to the other.

Expert evidence is valuable when the tribunal is familiar with the technical matters in dispute, but not so when the tribunal in itself has the expert knowledge in that technical field. Furthermore, expert evidence is also valuable even if the tribunal has the expertise in the field but it is not appropriate for it to carry out the often lengthy and complex analysis for reasons of time or other constraints, such as, for example, the requirement for direct contact with the parties themselves or their employees.

However, expert evidence is necessary in technical disputes when the tribunal is not familiar with the technical issues involved and, therefore, requires genuine assistance in understanding the scientific basis behind the issues involved and how these issues operate in practice.

Even if the technical issues are resolved and the cause and effect are established, the assessment of damages and the calculation of quantum can be an awesome task that would require expertise to quantify the loss incurred – and that to be incurred if the dispute involves future consequences.

II. APPOINTMENT

It is accepted that the appointment of party-appointed experts should take place by both parties as soon as practicable after the commencement of the arbitration proceedings.

---

* Past President of the Chartered Institute of Arbitrators; Board Member, London Court of International Arbitration (LCIA); Visiting Professor in Construction Law & Contract Administration, Trinity College, Dublin; Chartered Engineer and Chartered Registered Arbitrator; Member of ICCA.

The tribunal generally deals with this matter at the preliminary meeting by establishing a date by which each party should identify its appointed expert along with the expert's qualification, experience, curriculum vitae, and publications. The tribunal would also normally set out the procedure for the form and content of the reports required to be submitted by the experts. This should obviously be done as early as possible and generally at the same preliminary meeting. However, the rules of the various arbitral institutions differ as to the precise procedure to be followed.

In this connection, Art. 5 of the IBA Rules on the Taking of Evidence in International Commercial Arbitration suggests that a report should be submitted first by the experts appointed by both parties following which the tribunal may order that they should meet and confer on the issues discussed in their report. The IBA Rules add that at such meeting(s), the experts should attempt to reach agreement on the issues upon which they differed in their reports. However, in recent trends and in an increasing pattern, tribunals require the experts to submit draft reports in the first instance, which would be followed by meeting(s) where they attempt to reach agreement on any different views they had expressed in their reports. This trend is logical, since once an expert submits an opinion, it is difficult to obtain a retraction of any views previously expressed unless such views are considered in advance as provisional and subject to such discussions between the experts.

The instructions given to an expert by the appointing party and the material provided to him are of the utmost importance. This information should be disclosed to the other party to avoid the possibility of the two appointed experts working on two different cases that have no relationship with each other. The instructions should identify clearly the issues upon which the expert's opinion is required. The expert, with the involvement of the appointing party and its technical personnel, should then devise the tests and the analyses to be carried out for the purposes of the expertise required.

It is important and necessary for at least one of the tribunal members to become familiar with the area of expertise and to understand the mechanism through which the experts are required to carry out the tests and analyses that were deemed necessary. Otherwise the decision-making process when making the award becomes a lottery.

III.   THE EXPERT'S ROLE

The first role that the party-appointed expert plays is to assist the party that appointed him/her, and in particular that party's legal advisers, in connection with the technical issues involved and to provide a truthful opinion regarding the strengths and weaknesses of the case being put forward. The opinion provided by the expert in this connection is obviously not subject to disclosure to the other party. Therefore, the first opinion that the expert would provide may include advice to the appointing party on the merits of the case and the manner in which it may be presented. As this opinion and its embedded advice, when finally formulated, and if adopted, becomes the expert's evidence upon which the appointing party relies in the case, it is important to ensure that the facts given to the expert are complete and fully reliable in that they can be proved if tested.

The second role undertaken by the party-appointed expert, once his/her opinion is submitted to the other party and to the tribunal, is to reduce the areas in conflict between the parties by establishing a "*proper*" basis for the dispute with reference to the expertise in question. This includes the task of: achieving agreement between the parties on as much as possible of the facts surrounding the case; reaching agreement on a chronology of the relevant events; and establishing how the consequences of these events affect the parties and how they could be calculated, if quantum is implicated.

In this connection, the expert's opinion or report submitted in the arbitration should be an objective one. Such objectivity means that whilst the report should advance the case being made so far as it could "*properly*" be advanced on the basis of the facts; and the tests and analyses made, it should, at the same time, assist the tribunal in regard to the relevant technical aspects by pointing the path to where the *whole* truth lies. Thus, the party-appointed expert, once presented as a witness in the arbitration, must ensure that he/she remains independent, impartial and objective and must offer his/her evidence in a dispassionate manner aimed at a fair and balanced view of the conflicting contentions of the parties. If that principle is not upheld by the expert and is not supported by the appointing party, the tribunal will not be served and the expert would become a "*hired gun*" whose testimony deserves nothing but a total discounting.

The third role that the party-appointed expert may have is to calculate precisely the effect of the consequences of the relevant events and the quantum of the damages due from one party to the other, if responsibility and liability are established. In this connection, one has to differentiate between the two terms: responsibility and liability. A party may be responsible for an event, but not liable for its consequences and for the damages that flow therefrom, and vice versa.

In the second role described above, i.e., that of narrowing down the issues between the parties, the experts appointed by both parties are expected to hold a series of meetings to:

— identify and list the technical matters between the parties on which they are to provide an opinion;
— identify and list the tests and/or analyses which need to be carried out;
— attempt to reach agreement on the technical matters and their relevant characteristics, and on the results of the tests and analyses which had been conducted; and
— prepare and exchange draft outline opinions for the purposes of these meetings. These opinions must be without prejudice to the parties' respective positions in the arbitration, but in the case of quantum experts, the figures calculated by them should be on the basis of "*figures as figures*", i.e., assuming that the submissions of either party are correct and, therefore, subject to subsequent decision on liability.

Once the discussions are completed, the experts should be required to prepare a statement setting out the results of their discussions in the form of a Scott Schedule showing the matters on which they agree and others upon which they differ. Where they differ, each of the experts should provide the reasons for the relevant difference in opinion. The matters referred to in the Scott Schedule could include the facts; the tests performed or to be performed; the analyses carried out or to be carried out; the methods used or to be used; and any other relevant factor in the expertise provided.

In this connection a Scott Schedule is drawn in such a way that it should show the following columns and the material to be provided in them in order to enable the experts to define their positions so that the tribunal may be able to analyse, conclude and decide on the various characteristics of the expertise carried out by the experts:

1. Item number;
2. The claimant's expert's views;
3. The respondent's expert's views;
4. Agreement if achieved;
5. Agreement with minor reservation, indicating in precise terms the nature of the reservation;
6. Disagreement with precise reasons against each disagreement in such detail so as to enable the tribunal to fully understand and appreciate the experts' respective views on the matter in disagreement; and
7. A space provided for use by the arbitral tribunal.

It should be noted that the success of such a Schedule will depend, in part, on each expert grappling and dealing positively with the principal characteristics of the expertise in question. Furthermore, the experts must adopt a constructive approach so that reasoning must be complete and if a different or additional analysis is claimed to be necessary, it must be run and its results indicated; or if a fault is alleged, the Schedule should include how this fault might be corrected. This Schedule should be submitted in hard and electronic copies for the tribunal's use.

The preparation of a Scott Schedule and the process of using it described above are rarely successful without the active involvement of the tribunal. Hence, the importance of the requirement that the tribunal be familiar with the technical matters in dispute becomes clear. Otherwise, the tribunal may reach conclusions that are essentially flawed through misunderstanding or lack of understanding of the expertise provided, as has happened on numerous occasions within this author's experience as an expert.

IV.   AN EXPERT'S DECLARATION:

It should always be required that a party-appointed expert provides at the beginning a signed and dated declaration stating the following:

> "A. I understand that my duty in providing written reports and offering evidence in this arbitration is to assist the Arbitral Tribunal decide the issues in respect of which expert evidence is being adduced. I confirm that I have complied and will continue to comply with this duty.
>
> B. I confirm insofar as the facts stated in my report are within my own knowledge, I have made clear which they are and I believe them to be true and that the opinions I have expressed represent my true and complete professional opinion.
>
> C. I have endeavoured to include in my report, those matters of which I have knowledge; or of which I have been made aware, that might adversely affect the validity of my opinion. I have clearly stated any qualification that may exist to my opinion.

D. I have shown, by footnotes, the sources of all the information I have used.

E. I have not without forming an independent view included or excluded anything which has been suggested to me by others, including my instructing solicitors.

F. I will notify those instructing me immediately, and confirm in writing, if for any reason my existing response requires correction or qualification.

G. I understand that:—

(1) My report, subject to any corrections before swearing as to its correctness, will form the evidence to be given under oath or affirmation.

(ii) I may be cross-examined on my report by a cross-examiner assisted by an expert.

(iii) I am likely to be the subject of public adverse criticism by the Arbitral Tribunal if it finds that I have not taken reasonable care in trying to meet the standards set out above.

H. I confirm that I have not entered into any arrangement where the amount or the payment of my fees is in any way dependent on the outcome of the case."

In some jurisdictions, such as in England, it is not unusual to find that the undertaking expressed in item A above, is supplemented by the following text:

"I also confirm that this duty to the Tribunal overrides any obligation to the party by whom I am engaged or the person who has paid or is liable to pay my fees."

The declaration, and certainly the above supplementary text, may be controversial to a number of arbitrators, particularly from the civil law jurisdictions, due to the presumption that the party-appointed expert must continue to maintain full loyalty to the appointing party, irrespective of any duty that might be held towards the tribunal. However, in the end analysis, to counter such a view, suffice to say that the value of such an opinion to the tribunal must diminish and could approach nil if the views advocated by the party-appointed expert were to be viewed as unsafe.

V.   IN CASE OF DEADLOCK

If the process of seeking expertise through party-appointed experts is unsuccessful and the assessment of damages ends in a deadlock between the parties, then there are three possibilities for the arbitral tribunal:

1. The arbitral tribunal should carry out the assessment and the necessary calculations by itself, which could only be done if the tribunal or one of its members has the necessary expertise in the particular field;

2. The arbitral tribunal should appoint a tribunal expert with all the advantages and disadvantages that go with such an appointment, but that involves further time input and additional cost; or

3. If the party-appointed experts have been observing a reasonable measure of independence and impartiality, but cannot reach an answer acceptable to both of them, the arbitral tribunal could take over the party-appointed experts to form a joint tribunal's experts who could then carry out the arbitral tribunal's instructions. This, of course, can only be done with the agreement of the parties and if the options under two and three are unavailable, too expensive or too time consuming. This process can be extremely useful in providing answers by the experts for resolving some of the intermittent issues that may arise between the parties very quickly. However, once again the importance of whether or not the tribunal has sufficient knowledge to understand the process that is being followed by the experts is self-evident. The experts would be helped, for example, in providing decisions where conflict arises between the experts as their work develops. In adopting this option the arbitral tribunal must of course continue to observe the rules of natural justice.

Each of the three routes described in the previous paragraph requires careful consideration, which should be viewed critically as soon as practicable in the arbitral process. With each route, the latest developments envisaged by experienced arbitrators should be examined and considered for adoption. In my experience the third route described above has been successfully used on a number of occasions and should be seriously considered whenever there is a deadlock between the parties or their experts.

Working Group B

7. Round Table on Techniques for Eliciting Expert Testimony

The Different Types of Experts with Special Emphasis on Legal Experts (*Jura Novit Curia*)

*Ahmed S. El-Kosheri**

I. INTRODUCTION

Within the context of contemporary international arbitrations, arbitral tribunals give particular attention to the issues pertaining to evidence in order to elaborate their awards on solid grounds of sufficiently proven data. The data in question extend to a variety of subjects, ranging from materially established facts to sound legal applicable rules, as well as appropriate economic, financial, auditing, engineering and technological information as the case may be.

If the elaboration of the relevant material facts can normally be accomplished through the examination and cross-examination of the witnesses provided by both parties, the tribunal's task becomes more complicated with regard to other aspects which require recourse to experts.

Basic differences in the legal traditions prevailing under various legal systems worldwide and in cultural juridical traditions necessarily influence the attitudes of both the arbitrators and counsel representing one party or the other.

Participants in the arbitral process educated in the common law system, whether arbitrators or counsel representing a given party, tend to rely basically on party-appointed experts well prepared in advance to appear before the arbitral tribunal in order to be examined and cross-examined with a view to sustaining that party's points of view and submissions.

In contrast, those belonging to the civil law and similar legal systems have a natural tendency to question the credibility of paid party-appointed experts acting in conformity with a scenario reminiscent of a Perry Mason TV episode, and prefer recourse to experts chosen by the arbitral tribunal itself from among recognized neutral and qualified persons to undertake an assignment reflected in specific terms of reference established by the arbitral tribunal after consultation with the parties.

It has to be noted, however, that in real life matters do not go in accordance with either model, and the prevailing pattern achieves a mixture of common law and civil law systems, since in an increasing number of cases there is a degree of co-existence between

---

* Partner, Kosheri, Rashed & Riad Law Firm; Member of ICCA.

party-appointed experts and experts chosen by the arbitral tribunal to undertake a given assignment and submit findings that the parties and their experts have the right to comment on and discuss in due time, before the tribunal starts its deliberation to elaborate its own conclusions in the light of all the data in its possession.

A survey of many cases – encountered during four decades of my involvement in arbitration practice – illustrates the success of this mixed pattern in a variety of arbitration subjects, whether large construction projects, exploitation of natural resources, industrial complexes, or with regard to important investment joint ventures in the fields of technology transfers, electronic services, telecommunication cooperation, or co-financing of transnational groups of companies. Each party, is normally assisted by one or more experts specialized in one or another branch of professional activity, and the final outcome of their expert opinions is analyzed and evaluated by the arbitral tribunal's own expert or group of experts, in order to provide the arbitrators with comprehensive objective information they can digest, scrutinize and utilize in formulating their ruling on each technical issue needed to render the final award, particularly as in most cases the three arbitrators, or at least two among them, are jurists without adequate background in sophisticated technical subject matters.

The picture is totally different with regard to issues related to the recourse to legal experts who are called upon to educate the arbitral tribunal about the rules that should be considered applicable to a certain aspect of the dispute.

In this respect, a basic difficulty stems from the existence of an established principle commonly referred to as *jura novit curia*, traditionally defined to mean that an international jurisdiction "is not solely dependent on the argument of the parties before it with respect to the applicable law".[1]

The above principle is considered applicable not only to international jurisdictions dealing with intergovernmental disputes, but is also equally applicable to all tribunals adjudicating transnational relationships whether between private business entities or between a governmental agency, on the one hand, and a private foreign entity, on the other hand.

In this respect, there should be a basic distinction between three situations:

(a) Circumstances under which the applicable rules are those of international law;
(b) Issues with regard to which the applicable rules are simply rules pertaining to a given domestic legal system; and
(c) Issues that are supposed to be governed by usages of trade, or other rules belonging to what is currently known as lex mercatoria, lex petrolia, professional codes of conduct governing a given branch of activity, as well as a certain commodity agreement.

---

1. The Permanent Court of International Justice, the *Lotus* case, 1927, Series A, no. 10 at p. 31, and the International Court of Justice, in the *Nicaragua* case, *ICJ Reports* (1986) at p. 24, para. 29.

II.   EXPERTISE IN INTERNATIONAL LAW

The Latin maxim *jura novit curia* has to be considered fully applicable within the first category; i.e., in the presence of a rule of public international law, whether the rule invoked relates to customary international law, general principles of law, or treaty provisions, such as the New York Convention of 1958 on the Recognition and Enforcement of Foreign Arbitral Awards and the ICSID Convention of 1965 governing the investment disputes falling within the jurisdiction of that Centre.

The arbitral tribunal concerned has to consider, on its own initiative, the interpretation and application of the said rules of international law in the given circumstances of the pending case, since "the law lies within the judicial knowledge of the Court", as stated by the International Court of Justice in the *Nicaragua* case.[2]

In essence, the arbitrators chosen to participate in a tribunal faced with such issues of international law are assumed to be sufficiently competent in this respect, and not in need of education from certain learned professors who produce paid legal opinions for one party or the other, as the case may be.

Therefore, I personally hope that counsel, in the best interests of the parties they represent, would refrain from using that counter-productive practice, and avoid the embarrassment of having an arbitral tribunal confronted with the task of questioning prestigious professors on what they wrote or failed to write. It seems more appropriate to leave it up to counsel and other members of the defense team to comprehensively prepare their case and plead it themselves, indicating what they think is the proper interpretation and application of the relevant international law rules.

III.   EXPERTISE IN SPECIFIC DOMESTIC LEGAL SYSTEMS

The position is basically different with regard to the other alternative when the applicable rules are those legislative provisions or established jurisprudence of a given domestic legal system. In such situation the principle *jura novit curia* loses a great deal of its significance, as the arbitral tribunal – as a whole or at least the majority thereof – is by definition not assumed to be knowledgeable about the foreign law in question. Therefore, it would be appropriate that each party calls upon a qualified jurist belonging to the legal system in question – whether a recognized professor or an eminent former judge – to provide a legal opinion explaining the rules deemed applicable to the issue under consideration. Occasionally, the arbitral tribunal may appoint its own legal expert requesting him to respond to the question put to him by the tribunal, with regard to which it has not received convincing answers from the party-appointed legal experts.

However, it has to be emphasized that the recourse to experts on legal issues is habitually limited to controversial issues that substantially differ from one country to the other, such as the periods of prescriptions or time-bars, the importing and exporting rules and regulations, construction permits and other necessary licenses, the

---

2. *ICJ Reports* (1986) at p. 25.

convertibility of local currency, the maximum rate of interest or whether compound interest is permitted under that applicable law.

For the majority of fundamental issues pertaining to the validity of the contracts, the canons of interpretation, the liability and remedies for non-performance of the contractual obligations, there are common principles similar, if not identical in all modern legal systems, and with regard to which *jura novit curia* regains its importance, in the sense that the arbitrators themselves can form their final opinion on these issues and evaluate the relevance or irrelevance of what was submitted to them by the respective counsels and their legal experts.

IV.   EXPERTISE IN TRANSNATIONAL LAW

As for the transnational rules which do not belong to either one of the two above-stated categories (international or national legal systems), they have to be treated differently due to their particular nature which can not be assimilated to either public international law rules basically subject to the *jura novit curia* principle, or to the domestic rules of national legal systems where that principle plays a more limited role.

In this respect, it has to be emphasized that most of the arbitrators in charge of international commercial cases are familiar with the frequently raised issues related to trade usages prevailing generally or in a particular type of business transaction, as well as regarding a given commodity agreement. Hence, the need for assistance from party-appointed experts within that context should be considered minimal, and a priori I am personally unaware of cases in which the arbitrators appointed experts entrusted with the task of educating them on such issues. In other words, the *jura novit curia* plays, as a general rule, an important role in this respect.

However, with regard to certain specific matters, such as determining whether the extraction of oil from wells located in a given strata was or was not conducted in conformity with the prevailing good oil practices, as part of the lex petrolia applicable in the industry, the recourse to professional highly qualified experts becomes a must, and such experts could be those appointed by the parties themselves, assisted by additional experts chosen by the arbitral tribunal to assist in arriving at a definitive solution that will bring an end to the controversies persisting among the party-appointed experts. The cost of the various experts engaged in such cases can be perfectly justifiable, since the claims could amount to billions of dollars.

Summing up, with regard to the third category of establishing evidence about trade usages, lex mercatoria requirements or specific technological patterns of conduct, normally the *jura novit curia* principle permits the arbitrators to establish the rules to be applicable, except in exceptional circumstances under which the sophistication of the technologies used in the industrial operations renders mandatory the reliance on the final outcome of the expert opinions provided and evaluated by the arbitral tribunal.

The Arbitral Tribunal-Appointed Expert

*Claus von Wobeser**

I.   INTRODUCTION

I cannot find a better way to start than rephrasing part of the presentation of this Session:

> "[t]he need for expert testimony in arbitral proceedings is generally unquestioned, but the proper way to bring it to bear is hotly contested. The use of tribunal-appointed experts may be on the upswing, but if so, so is the intensity of the debate over their proper role. Are they just another expert, whose views are subject to full disclosure and whose testimony is subject to full examination by the parties, or are they private advisors to the tribunal?"

And I could add the following questions: What are the bases to designate the tribunal-appointed experts? How should the terms of reference of such tribunal-appointed experts be established? And, how can tribunal-appointed experts be made most useful?

In the following paragraphs I will indicate generally the bases governing experts designated by the arbitral tribunal and I will try to makes some recommendations based on my theoretical knowledge, but above all on my practical experience (as arbitrator and as party counsel), for avoiding or, at least, attenuating problems arising from tribunal-appointed experts.[1]

Evidence or the evidentiary phase, one of the most important elements in every adversarial proceeding such as commercial arbitration, is one of the most complex in practice; perhaps even more so because the different arbitral laws or rules do not exhaustively regulate the handling of evidence[2] before the arbitrator or arbitral tribunal.

---

*   Managing partner, Von Wobeser y Sierra, S.C., Mexico City.

1. It is important to mention from the beginning that, given the scope of this document, I will not be able to go into detail about the regulation of expert evidence in general or recommendations in that respect.

2. When speaking of the *handling of evidence* we refer to the establishment and implementation of the rules with respect to the offering, admission, preparation, presentation and weighing of the different evidentiary materials during the arbitral proceeding.

This lack of exhaustive provisions in relation to evidence, as in many other aspects of the arbitral procedure, is not the result of negligence or omission on the part of the drafters. On the contrary, it reflects one of the most important principles of commercial arbitration: that of the flexibility of the proceedings. The flexibility with regard to procedure within arbitration reflects the aspiration for efficiency, which should be understood as getting the best result possible in terms of legal certainty with the least cost in terms of time and money. Evidence is treated differently in arbitration than in judicial proceedings, given that the judicial formalism of the latter does not and should not exist in arbitration.[3]

The evidence demonstrates to the arbitrator the truth of the version of the facts that each of the parties invokes as the foundation of its claim or answer. The lack of evidence negatively affects the parties,[4] which is why the offering and submission of the evidence constitutes what in general procedural theory is called a procedural burden: the burden of proof.[5] Notwithstanding the above, the great majority of the existing arbitral rules and laws grant the arbitrator or arbitral tribunal full investigative powers to make use of the means they consider appropriate to resolve the dispute.[6] This authority of the arbitral tribunal, based in part on the principle of procedural flexibility, is limited, on the other hand, by two other fundamental premises: (i) the duty of equal and impartial treatment of the parties; and (ii) providing the parties with a full opportunity to present their case. In addition, the duty of the arbitrator to observe due legal process[7] must not be forgotten, even in the case of an arbitration where powers to act as amiable compositeur or to decide ex aequo et bono have been conferred.

As a result of the above, the procedural forms and practices for the handling of the evidence vary a great deal in commercial arbitration, above all in international cases due,

---

3. See, among others, Francisco GONZÁLEZ DE COSSÍO, *Arbitraje* (Edit. Porrúa, Mexico 2004) p. 244.

4. This becomes still more obvious in countries with a civil law tradition, as is the case with the majority of Latin American countries, where, according to the principle governing commercial proceedings, if the parties do not offer or render evidence, the judge cannot ask for any evidence not requested by the parties (ultra petita).

5. According to this principle, it is left to the parties and their legal representatives to determine the necessity or relevance of offering evidence, given that it redounds to their own benefit by demonstrating to the judge, or in this case the arbitrator, the premises of their respective points of view in the dispute in question. The general doctrine in this respect is that evidence is a burden but not an obligation. It is an optional activity of the parties, but if they do not present it they will suffer the consequences of their procedural inactivity, which will redound in the invalidity of their claims or defenses. The party asserting a fact has the burden of proof and therefore it must be understood that it is not just the claimant or plaintiff who must prove, from a procedural point of view, but rather whoever asserts a claim, plea or defense.

6. That is to say, the parties to an arbitration must present their case and try to evidence or prove their assertions, this in addition to the powers of the arbitral tribunal to make determinations with respect to the admissibility, relevance or weight of the elements of evidence presented by the parties.

7. For more information on this topic the following is recommended: Matti S. KURKELA and Hannes SNELLMAN, *Due Process in International Commercial Arbitration* (Oceana Publications, Inc., New York 2005).

among other things, to the complexity of the matters in dispute, the involvement of parties of different nationalities and the existence of arbitrators trained under different legal systems.

This variety of procedural forms and practices (which should be mentioned, is not bad per se, and on the contrary benefits the versatility of commercial arbitration to adapt to the circumstances and complexity of a particular dispute) extends to the practice of expert evidence or expert witnesses testimony.

II.   THE IMPORTANCE OF EXPERT TESTIMONY

The unquestioned importance of expert evidence in commercial arbitration arises from, among many other elements, the fact that it is a useful tool that provides to the arbitral tribunal arguments or reasoning for the formation of its opinion with respect to certain facts, the perception or understanding of which, due to their technical nature, is beyond the knowledge of the members of the tribunal. On the one hand, it is an activity engaged in by persons with specialized knowledge of a certain science, art, technical matter or trade, and on the other hand, such knowledge has to do with particular facts that require such specialized knowledge in order to adequately interpret their causes, effects, meaning, relationships, weight, etc.[8]

As indicated by Yves Derains and Eric A. Schwartz, the use of expert testimony in international arbitration would seem surprising at first glance in the understanding that one of the repeatedly cited advantages of arbitration is the power or opportunity given to the parties to select arbitrators with specialized technical knowledge in the area of the matters in dispute. Furthermore, the designation of an expert considerably elevates the cost of the proceedings and, in the majority of cases, inevitably lengthens the evidentiary phase. Nevertheless, as these authors go on to mention, some international disputes are very complex, containing legal, technical, financial and other problems for which it is necessary to possess several specialized areas of knowledge in order to reach a satisfactory solution.[9]

In relation to the manner of appointing an expert, two types of experts can be identified: those designated by the parties (party-appointed experts) and those designated by the arbitral tribunal (tribunal-appointed experts). Further on, some

---

8. See Jorge L. KIELMANOVICH, *Teoría de la Prueba y Medios Probatorios* (Abeledo-Perrot, Buenos Aires, Argentina 1996). In this same line of thought, Matti S. Kurkela and Hannes Snellman stated:

"[t]he purpose of hearing expert witnesses is to elucidate issues of a technical, legal, medical, biological or other discipline of some sophistication to better understand the relevant facts and their significance. Expert testimony does not in general relate to direct reconstruction of past facts although it may offer explanations and establish causes and effects, but it may be used for pure fact finding or fact establishing purposes."

Matti S. KURKELA, and Hannes SNELLMAN, *op. cit.*, fn. 7.

9. *See* Yves DERAINS, and Eric A. SCHWARTZ, *A Guide to the New ICC Rules of Arbitration* (Kluwer Law International, The Hague/London/Boston 1998) p. 258.

comments will be made regarding the appointment of the expert by the arbitral tribunal, but for now it is sufficient to say that this authority of the tribunal is expressly recognized by the great majority of existing arbitral rules and laws.[10] Such rules also, with some variation, establish the bases for the presentation of this evidence.[11] In all cases, the only restriction on the appointment of experts is that such appointment be in accordance with the will of the parties.

The parties and/or the arbitral tribunal in a specific case, above all in order to fully respect due process and in an effort to ensure the normal development of the proceeding, must have a very clear understanding of the legal framework applicable to the handling of expert evidence. As a general rule, the first thing that must be observed is the will of the parties involved. Moreover, the following must be kept in mind: (i) the local laws applicable to arbitration, (ii) the applicable arbitration rules and (iii) the international regulations (applicable conventions and/or treaties).

For example: if an international commercial arbitration is carried out between a US company and a Mexican company, in which the place of arbitration designated by the parties is Mexico City and in which the ICC Rules of Arbitration have been chosen to govern the procedure, the arbitral tribunal, at the time of designating an expert should:

(i) take into account the will of the parties (in this example, the parties did not indicate anything in this respect, they simply chose the ICC Rules to govern the proceeding);
(ii) analyze the arbitration rules chosen by the parties (in this case, Art. 20(4) authorizes the arbitral tribunal to designate an expert, define his or her mission and receive his or her opinions);

---

10. As an example of this we can mention, among many others, the following: (i) Art. 20(4) of the ICC Rules of Arbitration ("The Arbitral Tribunal, after having consulted the parties, may appoint one or more experts, define their terms of reference and receive their reports...."); (ii) Art. 22(1) of the Rules of International Arbitration of the American Arbitration Association (AAA) ("The tribunal may appoint one or more independent experts to report to it, in writing, on specific issues designated by the tribunal and communicated to the parties."); (iii) Art. 21.1(a) of the Rules of Arbitration of the London Court of International Arbitration (LCIA) ("Unless otherwise agreed by the parties in writing, the Arbitral Tribunal: (a) may appoint one or more experts to report to the Arbitral Tribunal on specific issues, who shall be and remain impartial and independent of the parties throughout the arbitration proceedings..."); (iv) Art. 27(1) of the UNICTRAL Arbitration Rules ("The arbitral tribunal may appoint one or more experts to report to it, in writing, on specific issues to be determined by the tribunal...."); (v) Art. 26(1)(a) of the UNCITRAL Model Law on International Commercial Arbitration ("Unless otherwise agreed by the parties, the arbitral tribunal: (a) may appoint one or more experts to report to it on specific issues to be determined by the arbitral tribunal...") and (vi) Art. 1444 of the Commercial Code of Mexico ("Unless agreed otherwise by the parties, the arbitral tribunal may appoint one or more experts to inform it with regard to specific matters and request any of the parties to provide to the expert all the relevant information, or present it for inspection or provide the expert access to all the relevant documents, merchandise and other goods."), among many other examples.
11. Even in the case of silence in some rules or in a law on arbitration, it can be asserted that one or both parties can offer this or other evidence, based on the principle of the opportunity to present a defense.

(iii) analyze if the lex fori is open to the designation of an expert by the tribunal (in this case Art. 1442 of the Mexican Commerce Code, the law of arbitration of my country, inspired almost in its entirety by the UNCITRAL (United Nations Commission on International Trade Law) Model Law on International Commercial Arbitration, allows the arbitral tribunal to designate an expert without restriction other than it is not opposed by the parties); and

(iv) analyze the international rules that may be applicable (in this case, there are basically two international instruments applicable in Mexico in relation to commercial arbitration: the New York Convention[12] and the Panama Convention.[13] Although neither of these conventions contains express provisions on expert evidence, not even on evidence in general, they do include important guidelines that the parties and the arbitrators should take into account for achieving due compliance with the arbitral award or, in the absence thereof, to guarantee its forced execution).

III.   GUIDELINES FOR THE TRIBUNAL

As a preamble to the specific analysis and recommendations regarding the expert designated by the arbitral tribunal, it is very important that the reader have in mind the following premises that I consider fundamental:

– The arbitral tribunal should regulate the matter of expert evidence with flexibility seeking the best result possible in terms of legal certainty and the least cost in time and money;
– It is very important that the tribunal be sufficiently sensitive and take the necessary steps to establish rules with respect to the designation, preparation, presentation and weighing of the expert evidence, considering the circumstances of the case and the complexity of the matter under arbitration (always looking to reveal the truth in the disputed facts without undermining the procedural rights and obligations of the parties);
– The flexible treatment should have, as its only limit, the observance of the principles of procedural equality and a full opportunity to present a defense;
– The arbitral tribunal should, at all times, involve the parties in the process of designation of the expert, the determination of his or her purpose and the setting of the rules for the presentation and acceptance of the evidence. To the extent that the arbitral tribunal procures the consensus of the parties, more confidence in the handling of the evidence will be generated and a greater acceptance of the results therefrom, and even of the final award; and
– Given the lack of specific rules regarding evidence, several institutions and groups of experts in arbitration have taken on the task of preparing guidelines or more detailed rules for the administration of evidence. for example, the IBA (International Bar

---

12. Convention on the Recognition and Enforcement of Foreign Arbitral Awards and Judgments executed in New York on 10 June 1958.
13. Inter-American Convention on International Commercial Arbitration executed in Panama on 30 January 1975.

Association) Rules on the Taking of Evidence in International Commercial Arbitration[14] and the UNCITRAL Notes on Organizing Arbitral Proceedings. From my point of view, it is very advisable for arbitrators to use and/or look to these types of documents for guidance in the handling not only of expert evidence, but of all evidence in general.

IV. THE TRIBUNAL'S AUTHORITY TO APPOINT EXPERTS

The power of the arbitral tribunal to designate experts has been very polemical in theory and in practice. Numerous questions have been formulated in that regard, such as: are the experts designated by the tribunal really experts subject to the scrutiny of the parties or simply advisors of the arbitral tribunal? Doesn't the power of the tribunal to appoint an expert affect or invade the procedural rights, obligations and responsibilities of the parties?

With respect to the first question, in my opinion, the expert designated by the tribunal, on one hand is obviously an advisor of the tribunal in that he or she is responsible for using his or her technical, scientific and/or artistic knowledge to clarify certain facts or make them accessible to the members of the tribunal. On the other hand, the expert designated by the tribunal not only can but should be submitted to the scrutiny of the parties. The parties should have, among other things: (i) the power to intervene in the appointment of the expert, the setting of the criteria for his or her appointment and/or the power to object to or challenge his or her appointment; (ii) the possibility of participating in the establishment of the purpose of the expert; (iii) the opportunity to provide to the expert the necessary and opportune information to allow him or her to prepare the opinion; (iv) to have knowledge of all the documents and other information the expert uses to prepare his or her opinion; (v) an opportunity to review, comment on and object to the expert's opinion; and (vi) the opportunity to question the expert in a hearing.

The second question is clearly more difficult that the first. Obviously the tribunal must respect the parties' right to a full defense, and therefore in principle the invasion of the procedural rights, obligations and responsibilities of the parties should be avoided. The arbitral tribunal should be very careful that the request for a technical opinion does not constitute a delegation of decision-making powers to the expert, but also that it does not serve to liberate either of the parties from the burden of proving its case.[15]

In order to avoid problems such as those just mentioned and above all in order to respect the principle of due process in the designation of an expert, the arbitral tribunal, from my point of view, should be very careful with regard to the following four specific

---

14. According to the preamble of the IBA Rules, they were drafted "as a resource to parties and to arbitrators in order to enable them to conduct the evidence phase of international arbitration proceedings in an efficient and economical manner". Such rules are detailed and seek to systematize the general principles recognized internationally in relation to the handling of evidence. Moreover, as also recognized in the Rules themselves, the IBA Rules of Evidence reflect procedures in use in many different legal systems, and they may be particularly useful when the parties come from different legal cultures.

15. See Yves DERAINS, and Eric A. SCHWARTZ, *op. cit.*, fn. 9, p. 260.

points of time: (i) in the designation of the expert; (ii) in establishing the terms of reference of the expert; (iii) at the time of the preparation and acceptance of the expert evidence; and (iv) at the time of weighing the value of the expert opinion.

I will refer below to each of these points, making some practical recommendations in respect thereto.

1.   Appointment of the Expert by the Arbitral Tribunal

Perhaps the appointment of the expert together with the establishment of his or her terms of reference are the two most crucial moments when the tribunal should take the greatest care in order to avoid future delays.

The first point the arbitral tribunal should cover when appointing an expert witness is that such appointment be made at an appropriate time. To appoint a neutral expert at an inappropriate time could create confusion and irritation among the parties, in addition to increasing costs and delaying the proceeding. It is very difficult to determine a specific time within the procedure for the designation of an expert; this depends on the circumstances of the case. The most important point is that as soon as the arbitral tribunal realizes the importance or necessity of appointing an expert, it should initiate the appropriate steps and inform the parties as soon as possible in order to receive their perspectives.

The second commentary and perhaps the most important one in relation to the designation of the expert, is that aside from being appropriate it should be necessary or relevant. The right to an expert, derived from the right of due process, does not exist outside of the necessity for such, or at least the utility thereof, for establishing the facts of the case. The arbitral tribunal should not only consult the parties with respect to the relevance of the appointment of the expert, but it should also provide them with the arguments justifying it.[16]

Once the topics of appropriateness and relevance of the appointment of the expert have been addressed, the arbitral tribunal, assuming it is possible or advisable with the agreement of the parties (taking into account the circumstances of the case and the prior behavior of the parties), should appoint the expert witness. Regarding the appointment as such, we find two obstacles to overcome: (i) defining and establishing the qualities of the expert, and (ii) establishing the procedure for the appointment.

In relation to the qualities of the expert, the tribunal and the parties must keep the following in mind at the time of the appointment or identification of candidates: (i) the expert must be independent from the parties and the arbitral tribunal; (ii) it should be ensured that the expert acts with professionalism and neutrality; (iii) the specialty, experience and technical competence of the expert should be taken into account; (iv) the advantage of the expert mastering the languages necessary to analyze the documents and other information in order to prepare and render his or her opinion should be kept in mind; (v) another practical characteristic or quality is the proximity of the expert to the objects to be analyzed and his or her availability to travel from one place to another;

---

16. Arbitral tribunals should think twice before designating an expert, given that it frequently becomes costly and prolongs the duration of the arbitral process. See *ibid*.

and (vi) finally, but not least important, the costs that may be entailed from the fees and expenses of the expert and the form in which they will be paid by the parties must be considered.

In principle, the power to appoint the expert belongs to the arbitral tribunal, without any requirement or condition other than that the parties be consulted in advance. However, as we mentioned previously, it is advisable to involve the parties in the designation process. In this regard it will be the task of the arbitral tribunal, according to the circumstances of the specific case, to make use of the means it considers appropriate for the appointment. There are various appointment procedures such as the so-called "lists". According to these procedures, a list of candidates is submitted to the consideration of the parties and they may: (i) agree on a candidate; (ii) rank the candidates according to their preferences and return the lists to the arbitrators so that, after a comparison thereof, the most qualified candidate can be chosen, etc. Another possibility within these methods is that each of the parties submits a list of candidates numbered in order of preference and the best-positioned candidate is chosen.

There are many other problems related to the appointment of experts depending on the circumstances of the case; for example, when the matter is so technical that there are few experts available and, to complicate it even more, the only experts there are, are direct competitors or have a conflict of interest with one or both of the parties in the arbitration.

In such cases, when looking for adequate specialists the arbitral tribunal may want to request the assistance of appointing institutions such as the ICC International Centre for Expertise, which was established in 1976 and has acquired considerable experience in this regard, in order to propose independent experts for international disputes.[17]

Whatever the designation process chosen, the arbitral tribunal should request the expert candidate(s) to present, prior to accepting their designation, a declaration of availability to perform the task and of independence from the parties and the arbitral tribunal. Such declaration should be provided to the parties and they should be granted a period of time to state any objections.

2.   The Terms of Reference of the Tribunal-Appointed Expert

The great majority of the authors that address this topic, if not all, agree that it is necessary to precisely define the scope of the functions entrusted to the expert appointed by the tribunal. The terms of reference of an expert can contain, among other elements, the questions that the expert should answer, the documentation and information the expert will review in order to prepare his or her opinion and, in general, all the organizational aspects corresponding to expert evidence.[18]

The UNCITRAL Notes on Organizing Arbitral Proceedings, with respect to the task of the expert, indicate the following:

---

17. *Ibid.,* p. 261.
18. Among many others, see Graham TAPIA and Luis ENRIQUE, *El arbitraje comercial* (Edit. Themis, Mexico 2004) p. 39.

"71. The purpose of the expert's terms of reference is to indicate the questions on which the expert is to provide clarification, to avoid opinions on points that are not for the expert to assess and to commit the expert to a time schedule. While the discretion to appoint an expert normally includes the determination of the expert's terms of reference, the arbitral tribunal may decide to consult the parties before finalizing the terms. It might also be useful to determine details about how the expert will receive from the parties any relevant information or have access to any relevant documents, goods or other property, so as to enable the expert to prepare the report. In order to facilitate the evaluation of the expert's report, it is advisable to require the expert to include in the report information on the method used in arriving at the conclusions and the evidence and information used in preparing the report."

The importance of the expert's terms of reference is clear and, as a recommendation, the following should be taken into account for their preparation:

— Taking the necessary precautions given the particular circumstances of the proceeding, the parties should be involved in the process of preparing the terms of reference, given that they can make very valuable contributions in identifying the points to be resolved by the expert and the possible obstacles that may have to be confronted.
— The purpose and role of the expert during the proceeding (whether as permanent assistant of the arbitral tribunal, in the case of very complex arbitrations, or simply to address a specific consultation) should be established as clearly as possible.
— If applicable, the points that the expert opinion should address should be identified (normally this is done in the form of a questionnaire).
— The documentation, information or other elements on which the expert should base his or her report, or if applicable, the manner in which the expert can collect such information should be indicated.
— Establish, if necessary, the rules under which the expert can contact the parties to collect information or hold interviews with them.
— Establish in detail all the aspects of organization, preparation and presentation of the evidence. For example: (i) the format in which the expert opinion should be presented; (ii) a detailed time table for the preparation and presentation of the opinion for the scrutiny of the parties; (iii) the tentative calendar for holding hearings for the questioning of the expert.
— Take all the measures necessary to ensure the expert keeps the information used to prepare the opinion confidential.[19]
— The determination of the amount of the expert's fees and expenses (as well as the way they will be calculated), and how they will be paid.

---

19. In relation to experts, the case may arise that one of the parties does not want certain aspects of its company to be revealed because they are commercial or industrial secrets. In this case, among other aspects to consider, the necessary care should be taken to guarantee that the designated expert keeps confidential the information he or she uses or has access to for the preparation of the opinion.

– Any other aspects considered necessary and appropriate for the best handling of the expert evidence.

– It is preferable for the final approved version of the expert's terms of reference to be signed by the expert, the member(s) of the arbitral tribunal and the parties (or their legal representatives). A copy of such terms of reference should be delivered to both the parties involved and the expert.

3. Preparation and Presentation of the Expert Evidence

The phase of the preparation and presentation of the expert evidence goes from the expert's acceptance of his or her appointment until the delivery of his or her opinion and, if applicable, until the expert has appeared at a hearing to be questioned by the parties.

The most important elements of this phase are: (i) the preparation of the expert opinion; (ii) the presentation and delivery of the opinion to the arbitral tribunal and the parties; and if applicable, (iii) the hearing to question the expert.

Certain comments and recommendations in this respect are made below.

a. Preparation of the expert opinion

Respecting the procedural rules established by the parties and/or by the arbitral tribunal itself, the expert should be guaranteed access to all the information, documentation and any other element necessary to prepare his or her opinion.

Information may be provided to the expert by the parties in the following ways, among others: (i) through a request and delivery of documentation, information, materials or any other element to be analyzed; (ii) the holding of meetings between the parties; and/or (iii) the holding of inspection visits at specific places.

The arbitral tribunal, depending on the circumstances of the proceeding, should decide if the request for information may be made by the expert directly to the parties or through the tribunal.

The arbitral tribunal must always ensure that all the parties have a copy of all the documents requested and analyzed by the expert.

In the case of the holding of meetings or inspections, the parties should be notified sufficiently in advance and the reasonable and necessary measures should be taken to guarantee the independence and impartiality of the expert.

The expert should indicate in his or her final report the cases in which the parties or even a third party did not provide the information requested and to the extent possible the causes for not doing so.

The arbitral tribunal should ensure that the expert opinion contains, at a minimum, the following information:

– The complete name and domicile of the expert, his or her relationship, present or past, with any of the parties and/or members of the arbitral tribunal, the description of his or her academic background, his or her accreditation as an expert in the matters involved. The expert can be asked to attach a copy of the corresponding corroborating documents.

– A detailed list of the facts or assumptions on which the expert based his or her opinions and conclusions.

– An explanation of the conclusions and/or opinions of the expert, including the methods used and the information and documentation analyzed to reach such conclusions and opinions.

– All the circumstances that affected, negatively or positively, the preparation of the opinion (e.g., failure of one of the parties to deliver information).

– If advisable, a statement of the expert that he or she has acted truthfully and honestly.

– The date and place of its issuance and the signature of the expert.

– All the material supporting the preparation of the opinion should be attached to it.

– The presentation of the graphic material supporting the conclusions of the expert, especially in the case of materials about which little is known or which are very complicated and require the expert to use graphs, photographs, videos, etc.

b.   *The presentation and delivery of the opinion to the arbitral tribunal and the parties*
In relation to due process, except in extraordinary circumstances that suggest the contrary, the arbitral tribunal should ensure that the parties receive the expert report sufficiently in advance and give them the opportunity to make their comments thereon.

c.   *The hearing for the questioning of the expert*
Notwithstanding the above, the right of the parties to request a hearing to listen to and question the expert should be recognized, as the great majority of arbitration rules do.

The arbitral tribunal, depending on the circumstances of the case, should conduct the hearing in a manner so as to best illuminate the expert evidence (e.g., it may permit the parties to bring their own experts to the hearing to ask questions of the tribunal-appointed expert, etc.).

d.   *Weighing of the expert evidence*
With regard to the weighing of the expert evidence, it is very important to emphasize what we mentioned above, that the request for a technical opinion by the tribunal from an expert cannot and should not constitute a delegation of decision-making powers.

It is important that the expert does not become involved in the deliberations of the arbitral tribunal, given that this can sometimes lead to confusion with regard to the role of the expert. The decision-making power belongs to the arbitral tribunal, while the expert only issues an opinion or report that is put to the consideration of the arbitral tribunal and the latter is who in the end will recognize the probatory weight it deems appropriate.

The principle of the free weighing of the evidence followed in international commercial arbitration applies equally to expert evidence. Based on this, the tribunal is not bound by the opinion and/or conclusions of the expert, even though the expert is independent and neutral with respect to the parties. In this regard the arbitral tribunal frequently disregards parts of an expert opinion in light of comments of the parties, revelations in the hearing from the counter-arguments of one of the experts of the parties or simply the failure to be persuaded by the arguments presented by the tribunal-appointed expert.[20]

V. CONCLUSION

In conclusion, we would like to emphasize the unquestionable importance expert evidence plays in international commercial arbitration, specifically when it has been requested directly by the arbitral tribunal. We would also like to caution that the handling of this evidence is quite complex and there are no magic formulas for doing so. Nevertheless, certain principles and general guidelines can (and I would say should) be followed in order to help the arbitral tribunal and the parties, among which are the following: (i) the enormous importance and advisability of involving the parties in the handling of the expert evidence; and (ii) the unquestionable benefit provided by the proper preparation and issuance of terms of reference establishing the purpose of the expert.

---

20. The opinion can be disregarded if from an analysis thereof (either from the comments of the parties or from questioning during the hearing) it is found that: (i) the conclusions are not consistent with the arguments set forth by the expert; (ii) the research methodology is not appropriate; and/or (iii) the sources consulted were inadequate or were insufficient.

Contemporary Practice in the Conduct of Proceedings: Techniques for Eliciting Expert Testimony — How Party-Appointed Experts Can Be Made Most Useful

*Dushyant Dave**

I. INTRODUCTION

Alexander Borodin, (1833-1887, the great Russian composer, Professor of Chemistry and Medicine, known for his role in the revitalization of Russian music and for such compositions as the Opera 'Prince Igor') was once called upon to testify as an expert witness in a case in which two young composers had accused one another of plagiarism. Upon their respective compositions having been played, Borodin was asked which he believed to be the injured party? His verdict? "My friend Mussorgsky!"

Are party appointed experts always like Borodin?

As long ago as the sixteenth century, Justice Saunders exclaimed that it is an honorable and commendable thing in our law to apply for the aid of science or faculty.[1]

Yet Lord Jessel, Master of the Roles, harshly expressed,

> "in matters of opinion, I very much distrust Expert Evidence. Although the evidence is given on oath, the person knows that he cannot be indicted for perjury. But this is not all. Expert evidence of this type is the evidence of persons who sometimes live by their business but in all cases are remunerated for their evidence. It is but natural that his mind should be biased in favor of the person employing him and accordingly we find such bias."[2]

In international commercial arbitration, like litigation, each party has the burden of proving the facts relied on to support his claim or defence. A party may therefore rely on a party-appointed expert as a means of evidence on specific issues. Undoubtedly many cases have been won or lost on the testimony of the expert witness contrary to the statement in *Last Man Standing* by David Baldacci[3] that, "Most people didn't realize that trials were often won before anyone stepped foot inside a courtroom."

---

* Senior Advocate, India; Member of ICCA.

1. *Buckley v. Rice Thomas* (1554) 1 Plowden 118.
2. *Abinger v. Asthoa*, L.R., 17 Equity.
3. David BALDACCI, *Last Man Standing* (Simon & Schuster, London 1997).

It has been said:

> "some issues of fact can only be determined by the arbitral tribunal becoming involved in the evaluation of elements that are essentially matters of *opinion*. Thus, in a construction dispute, the contemporary documents, comprising correspondence, progress reports and other memoranda, and the evidence of witnesses who were present on the site may enable the arbitral tribunal to determine what actually happened. There may then be a further question to be determined; namely whether or not what actually happened was the result of, for example, a design error or defective construction practices. The determination of such an issue can only be made by the arbitral tribunal with the assistance of experts, unless it possesses the relevant expertise itself."[4]

As a general proposition of law, opinion evidence is inadmissible. To this proposition there are some exceptions, including the opinion of experts. It has been universally held, including in India, that "An expert witness is one who has made the subject upon which he speaks a matter of particular study, practice or observation; and he must have a special knowledge of the subject."[5] As Mansfield LJ said, "in matters of science, no other witnesses may be called".[6]

The fundamental principle is, "the purpose of expert evidence is to provide the Court with information which is outside the experience and knowledge of a judge and jury".[7] It is however important to bear in mind, as was stated by the Supreme Court of the United States, "that an expert, whether basing testimony upon professional studies or personal experience, employs in the courtroom the same level of intellectual rigor that characterizes the practice of an expert in the relevant field".[8] An expert gives evidence on the "ultimate issue". But experts give evidence and do not decide the issue, the principle being, "the trier of fact rather than the expert has the power and duty of ultimate decision".

An authoritative Canadian statement on the role of the expert evidence is found in *Kelliher (village of) v. Smith*[9] in which the Supreme Court of Canada concluded that for testimony to be considered expert "the subject matter of the inquiry must be such that ordinary people are unlikely to form the correct judgment about it, if unassisted by persons with special knowledge". In *R v. Mohan*[10] the Supreme Court emphasized that the expert evidence must be both necessary in assisting the trier of fact and relevant.

---

4. Alan REDFERN, Martin HUNTER, Nigel BLACKABY and Constantine PARTASIDES, *Law and Practice of International Commercial Arbitration*, 3d edn. (Sweet & Maxwell 2004) p. 308.

5. *State of HP v. Jai Lal and others*, (1999) 7 SCC 280 at p. 284 para. 13).

6. *Folks v. Chadd* (1782) 3 Doug K.B. 157.

7. *R v. Turner* (1975) 1 QB 834.

8. *Kumho Tire Company, Ltd. v. Patrick Carmichael, etc.*, 526 U.S. 137 (1999).

9. [1931] SCR 672.

10. [1994]2 SCR 9 at 23.

II.   HOW CAN PARTY-APPOINTED EXPERTS BE MADE MOST USEFUL?

1.   *First and Foremost, Decide Whether Expert Evidence Is Actually Necessary*

It is important to bear in mind that if direct evidence is available and is acceptable, it is hardly necessary to consider expert opinion.

2.   *Choosing an Expert*

Choice of an expert witness is critical, a wrong choice being fatal to the case of the party on whose behalf the expert witness is called; whilst qualifications and affiliations together with personal knowledge or reliable references are a must, ability to communicate or articulate conclusions to the tribunal is equally important.
    It would be worthwhile to inquire into the following:

– How many times has the expert acted as a consultant?
– In how many cases has the expert actually testified?
– Were the issues in previous cases similar to the issues in the case before the tribunal?
– Has the expert expressed views to the contrary, at any time in publications or testimony, on the subject upon which he is now expected to opine?
– Has the expert ever been employed by the opposing party or counsel?
– Has the expert been repeatedly engaged by the law firm or the counsel representing the party?
– Is the expert going to be available for cross-examination on the future dates that may be fixed by the tribunal?
– Has the expert disclosed unused material or any contrary tests or opinions (even if carried out by someone else) of which he/she is aware?
– It would be greatly helpful to remember the principles set out by the US Supreme Court in *Daubert v. Merrell Dow Pharmaceuticals*[11] and *Kumho Tire* (supra) while choosing an expert because it must be clear that his testimony will constitute "scientific knowledge" or "technical and other specialized knowledge" required to assist the tribunal in reaching the ultimate conclusion.
– To know the exact nature of the dispute to be decided in Arbitration and whether the expert is indeed proficient in the particular subject. For example in a dispute involving chemical technology it would be unwise to choose an expert from the field of civil engineering.

3.   *The Expert must Be Made Aware of the Nature of the Role and Duties to Be Performed*

Lord Wilberforce once stated, "Expert evidence presented to the Court should be and be seen to be the independent product of the expert, uninfluenced as to form or content

---

11. 509 U.S. 579 (1993).

by the exigencies of litigations."[12] Equally important is to remind the expert not to give evidence, "as to the result of their opinions and as to the effect of them" which Lord Atkin in *Florence A. Deeks v. H.G. Wells & Ors* said was, "not to be within the domain of expert evidence at all".[13] This case is an authority for the proposition that an expert must not give his conclusions on the ultimate question. The expert must also be made aware that his opinion must be based on facts which are either on record or are within the expert's own knowledge so as to avoid those facts being required to be proved independently.

4. Pre-conferencing

Although there are differing approaches in common law jurisdictions and civil law jurisdictions on preparation of an expert witness by a party's lawyer, the former permitting while the later prohibiting it, in international arbitration the prevailing practice permits such preparations (subject to applicable professional rules of conduct). But it must be remembered that the primary purpose is to assist the expert in becoming familiar with the subject matter of the dispute before the tribunal without actually telling the expert what to say. It cannot be forgotten that witnesses, even if experts on their subject, can be counterproductive if "coached" since they would generally, if not invariably, lose credibility under cross-examination.

Experts must be provided with the entire material relating to the dispute and such other information as may assist them in making inquiry and forming an opinion.

But it may greatly help if the experts chosen by the two parties were to have a preliminary conference amongst themselves for deciding the outline of methodology to be adopted by them for constructing their opinions. Of course, unless the parties have agreed to the same, they should be allowed to challenge the same before the tribunal as a preliminary issue, failing which the methodology would be final and binding.

5. Production of Expert Evidence

Expert evidence, as per prevailing universal practice in international arbitration is produced in the form of written reports. But such evidence must be on specific issues. It is therefore necessary to consider at an early stage of arbitration, the stage and the manner of exchange of expert reports. The stage of exchange of expert reports is crucial in respect of cost as well as content. It would be therefore desirable for the tribunal to direct or for counsel to ensure through agreed procedure complete factual evidence for the parties before submitting expert reports. Such a procedure has been recognized by the courts in England and is also accepted in international commercial arbitration. Equally, the exchange of reports must be simultaneous so as to ensure objectivity and avoid subjectivity in the respective reports.

---

12. *Whitehouse v. Jordan* [1981] 1 WLR246 at p. 256. Subsequently followed in *National Justice Compania Naviera S.A. v. Prudential Assurance Co. Ltd.* (*"The Ikarian Reefer"*) (1993, 2 Lloyds Reports 68 at p. 81).

13. *Florence A. Deeks v. H.G. Wells & Ors.*, AIR 1933 PC 26 at p. 28.

The contents of the written reports must conform to well-established principles on evidence and also to the agreement between the parties and the legislative enactments and institutional rules under which the arbitration is conducted. Art. 5 of the IBA

Rules[14] and Rule 35.10 of the CPR, 1998 in England[15] are useful guides as to the contents of experts' reports.

Needless to emphasize, that the report must be disclosed to the opposite side well in advance.

6. *Post Written Reports*

Each party must be allowed to put written questions to the expert of the opposite party seeking clarifications, if any. Response by the experts to these should be treated as part of the report. Failure of the expert to respond to the question must disentitle the party submitting his report from relying on that issue, unless otherwise directed by the tribunal. This procedure, to be found in Rule 35.6 of the CPR,[16] will reduce disagreement amongst the parties as well as cost by avoiding cross-examination to that extent.

Once this is completed, preferably within a specified time, the tribunal can draw an agenda of disputed, "expert matters" and either allow the parties to cross examine the expert or invite the experts together to sit across the tribunal to discuss these matters and seek clarification. But the latter procedure must be in presence of parties to avoid the process being declared unfair (see *How Engineering Services Ltd v. Lindner Ceiling Floors, Partitions plc*).[17]

Of course, as Redfern and Hunter[18] have recognized, "there are many different ways in which an arbitral tribunal may seek to educate itself on 'expert' issues, and it should not shrink from pursuing innovative solutions". Every tribunal when confronted with a specific situation must devise a tailor-made procedure.

7. *Value of Expert Evidence*

"The duty of an expert witness is to furnish the Judge with the necessary scientific criteria for testing the accuracy of the conclusions so as to enable the judge to form his

---

14. IBA Rules on the Taking of Evidence in International Commercial Arbitration available at <www.ibanet.org/images/downloads/IBA%20rules%20on%20the%20taking20of%20Eviden ce.pdf > (last accessed 20 May 2006).

15. Statutory Instrument 1998 No. 3132 (L.17) The Civil Procedure Rules 1998, Part 35 *Experts And Assessors Rule 35.10 Contents of reports* available at <www.opsi.gov.uk/si/si1998/98313215. htm#35.10>, (last accessed 20 May 2006).

16. Statutory Instrument 1998 No. 3132 (L.17) The Civil Procedure Rules 1998, Part 35 *Experts And Assessors Rule 35.6 Written Questions to Experts* available at <www.opsi.gov.uk/si/si1998/ 98313215.htm#35.6> (last accessed 20 May 2006).

17. (1999) 64 CLR 67.

18. Alan REDFERN, Martin HUNTER, Nigel BLACKABY and Constantine PARTASIDES, *Law and Practice of International Commercial Arbitration*, op. cit., fn. 4, p. 313.

independent judgment by the application of this criteria to the facts proved by the evidence of the case. The scientific opinion evidence, if intelligible, convincing and tested becomes a factor and often an important factor for consideration along with the other evidence of the case. The credibility of such a witness depends on the reasons stated in support of his conclusions and the data and materials furnished which form the basis of his conclusions."[19]

Per contra, no reliance can be placed upon the evidence of an expert witness if the evidence was merely an opinion unsupported by any reasons. Rules of evidence clearly demand that expert testimony be not only relevant but must be reliable, although it is proverbial that expert witnesses are, perhaps unwittingly, biased in favor of the side which calls them, as well as over-ready to regard neutral facts as confirmation of preconceived theories. At the same time international tribunals have become much more dependent on expert testimony, and the accelerating process of scientific and technological advance enhances this tendency. As a result arbitrators and even lawyers have had to become proficient in weighing competing expert evidence. Modern arbitration process, having lost its early simplicity, has become complex and legalistic. Increasingly members of the tribunal chosen by the parties or appointed by the institutions are themselves experts in diverse fields. They have accordingly become masters in the conduct of the proceedings although deriving their authority or jurisdiction from the parties. With general acceptance that intellectual rigor be applied while evaluating the testimony of expert witnesses, the arbitrators have become "gatekeepers" who ensure the quality and reliability of expert's testimony.

III.   IN CONCLUSION

International commercial disputes in the present day – being highly complex, legal, and most times technical – involve determination of issues by tribunals where truth in absolute terms is not forthcoming. The relevance of party-appointed experts so as to enable the tribunal to examine various ways of determining issues, is ever increasing. Burden of proof placed on the parties by legal systems or by institutional rules cannot be displaced or substituted by tribunal-appointed experts.

So what are the new ways, in addition to the ways enumerated above, which can help in achieving the fundamental objective of making available to the tribunal reliable, intellectual and relevant expert opinion and to do so at reduced costs?

1. To avoid any possibility of bias in experts towards parties appointing them, it may be made obligatory that while the parties may retain the freedom to choose their experts, their fees may be paid out of the costs and fees deposited by the parties with institutions under which the arbitration is conducted.

2. Although the practice has been condemned as being inquisitorial, experts may be called to give evidence-in-chief in hearings before the tribunal, which has the power and the duty to disallow any irrelevant and unspecific evidence given while retaining the

---

19. *State of HP v. Jai Lal and others*, (1990) 7 SCC 280 at p. 286 para 18).

advantage of witnessing the demeanor of the expert witness. This process can reduce cost and time substantially.

3. Always insist on the recording of expert evidence after the entire factual evidence of the parties has been completed. This will automatically limit the expert evidence to specific issues if left untouched or open, thus minimizing cost.

4. Arbitration is a highly flexible process and can enable the parties to create a unique hearing procedure tailored to suit the technical, scientific, financial or other types of disputes which arise for determination. Customizing the arbitration process can be achieved even by tribunals with a pro-active approach at the pre-hearing stage, with possible consent of parties, by adopting different measures including but not limited to prescribing standards for expert testimony, their qualifications, pre-qualifying their reports, etc.

5. Last but not least, by devising and adopting a Code of Conduct for Expert Witnesses to ensure such independence and objectivity as is expected of them as experts. This will ensure that their evidence contains "The truth, the whole truth and nothing but the truth." The Code may also provide for identifying expert witnesses who have misconducted themselves and for barring them from future participation in other arbitrations.

With some endeavor, we can hope and trust that the party-appointed expert ceases to be a "hired gun".

Unlike Borodin, Henry Rowland (another distinguished professor), while testifying as an expert witness in a trial one day, was asked during cross-examination what qualified him to serve as such a witness. "I am," the professor replied, "the greatest living expert on the subject under discussion."

Sometime later a friend, well aware of Rowland's usual modesty and unassuming manner, expressed his surprise at this uncharacteristically grandiose remark. "Well, what did you expect me to do? Rowland asked. "I was under oath!"

Like Professor Rowland, party-appointed experts may do well to remember that they are also under oath to speak "truth and nothing but the truth!"

Expert Conferencing and New Methods

*Martin Hunter**

I.   INTRODUCTION

The role of "experts" in the context is to assist, educate and advise the arbitral tribunal, in a fair and impartial manner, in specialist fields (e.g., technical, forensic accountancy, legal, etc.) in which the arbitrators (or some of them) do not themselves have relevant expertise in specific issues in dispute between the parties.

Historically, the practices of arbitrators and advocates in relation to the use of experts, from both common law and civil law countries, have tended to mirror the procedures and techniques adopted by the national court systems into which they were originally educated as litigation practitioners. In most cases this is neither necessary nor appropriate.

II.   COMMON LAW AND CIVIL LAW PRACTICES

The main disadvantage of the common law system is that the expert "evidence"[1] presented to the arbitral tribunal is "bought" by the party presenting it. The party in question simply would not present the testimony to the tribunal if the expert's opinion was unfavourable to its case. Judges in national courts have rules and sanctions at their disposal that are designed to eliminate, or at least discourage, blatantly partisan experts.

In arbitrations no such rules exist (unless applied by express or implied agreement), and in any event an arbitral tribunal cannot impose effective sanctions. The result is that tribunals find themselves faced with deciding between the opinions of opposing experts

---

*   Barrister; Professor of International Dispute Resolution, Nottingham Law School; Visiting Professor, King's College London University; Chairman, Dubai International Arbitration Centre; Hon. Dean of Postgraduate Studies, T.M.C. Asser Instituut, The Hague; Member of ICCA.

1. In the arbitration context, as opposed to a criminal trial, it is far from certain that experts should be described as "witnesses", or give "evidence" or "testimony", as implied by the title of this Session (Techniques for Eliciting Expert Testimony). In a commercial dispute, experts provide "opinions" or "information" to a national court or arbitral tribunal.

who have provided diametrically opposite opinions to questions such as, for example, "Why did the bridge fall down?",[2] with little or no unbiased expert advice to guide them.

The civil law system suffers from the disadvantage that the parties (or their advocates) tend to think that their dispute will be decided by the tribunal-appointed expert, rather than by the arbitral tribunal that was appointed by the parties to resolve it. The parties' advocates tend to distrust tribunal-appointed experts because they feel that their ability to control the manner in which what may be the most critical element in their case will be presented has been taken away from them.[3]

Over the last thirty years or so various efforts have been made to develop a satisfactory hybrid system for the presentation of independent expert assistance to arbitral tribunals. The 1976 UNCITRAL Arbitration Rules[4] provide that, where the tribunal appoints an expert, the parties may require a hearing at which they may "interrogate" the tribunal's expert and produce their own experts to rebut the advice or conclusions of the tribunal's expert. This is an unwieldy and expensive exercise that rarely justifies, in terms of cost, the effort spent on it. The ICC Rules are less explicit, but ICC arbitrators rarely refuse consent to a party that wishes to present expert testimony to the tribunal even where the tribunal has already appointed its own expert.[5]

The 1999 edition of the IBA Rules on the Taking of Evidence in International Commercial Arbitration provides more sophisticated procedures.[6] However, these Rules are aimed at regulating and codifying compromise solutions between the existing alternative civil law and common law practices rather than at "advancing the science". What is needed is a search for new and reliable cost-effective ways of assisting the arbitral tribunal to perform its task; at the same time as satisfying the fondness of the parties (or, more frequently, their advocates) for the formalistic and often lengthy rigmarole of direct examination, cross-examination and re-examination of experts.

III.   TWENTIETH-CENTURY DEVELOPMENTS

Within the scope of the regimes established by the existing sets of arbitration rules, including the IBA Rules, a number of experienced international arbitrators have experimented with "expert conferencing" techniques, usually limited to circumstances in which the parties and their counsel are willing to participate in this format. In this kind of procedure the parties first present their written expert reports, as under the IBA

---

2. One side's expert says, with great conviction, "faulty design of the bridge". Equally convincingly, the other side's expert says "defective materials used in construction of the bridge". Cross-examination of experts by counsel is considered by many international arbitrators as an inadequate tool to assist them in making a determination between the opposing views of such experts.

3. For a description of the comparative practices adopted in various national systems, see *Comparative Arbitration Practice*, ICCA Congress Series no. 3 (1986) pp. 107-111.

4. UNCITRAL Arbitration Rules, Art. 27(4). Broadly similar provisions appear in the LCIA Arbitration Rules, Art. 12.2.

5. CRAIG, PARK and PAULSSON, *International Chamber of Commerce Arbitration*, 2nd edn. (Oceana 1990) p. 404.

6. IBA Rules on the Taking of Evidence in International Commercial Arbitration, Arts. 5 and 6.

Rules; then the experts are required to meet in advance of the hearing to draw up lists of (a) matters on which they agree, and (b) matters on which they do not agree.

Based on list (b), the tribunal prepares an agenda designed to encompass the matters on which the experts are not agreed, and presents it to the parties and their advocates in advance of the hearing.[7] Then, after all the fact witnesses from both sides have been heard, the independent experts retained by the opposing parties come before the arbitral tribunal and are seated alongside each other at the witness table.

The chairman of the arbitral tribunal[8] then takes the experts though the agenda, item by item. The experts are requested to explain in their own words the basis for reaching the opinions set out in their written reports, and to answer each other's main points. They may also be encouraged to debate these points directly with each other if the arbitral tribunal considers that this would be useful. Experience indicates that the transcript of such a debate is of infinitely more assistance to the arbitral tribunal than the transcript of a traditional "sparring match" between one side's expert and the other side's cross-examining advocate. It is rare for such a cross-examination to be more useful to the arbitral tribunal than a childish "Yah-Sucks-Boo" type of exchange of repetitive and unanswered propositions.

Arbitral tribunals do not usually adopt an expert conferencing procedure unless the parties (through their advocates) agree to it. Further, the parties' advocates are usually permitted, if they wish, to conduct a traditional cross-examination after the expert conferencing session has been completed. This is both reasonable and appropriate. There may be matters that the arbitral tribunal has not raised, such as apparent inconsistencies between an expert's prior published works and his or her opinion in the current case.

IV.   CURRENT DEVELOPMENTS

Experience indicates that an expert conferencing system such as the one described above works well, *provided that* the experts are genuinely independent and not taking instructions from the counsel representing the party that retained them. For the procedure to work efficiently the arbitral tribunal must take the task of drawing up the agenda for the conference seriously, and ensure that the session is chaired firmly but fairly by the arbitrator charged with organizing the process.

However, the system still suffers from the habitual tension that exists between the arbitrators and the advocates. The interest of the arbitrators is to understand the technical aspects involved in the disputed specialist area, and to receive honest opinions and advice from the experts, so that they may decide the specialist issues in dispute fairly

---

7. For the sake of efficiency, this may be done at an early stage of the hearing after the experts have arrived at the hearing location, and during the period in which the fact witnesses for each side are giving their oral testimony.

8. Or one of the other arbitrators designated by the others, on the basis of his or her understanding of the technical issues, or simply because that arbitrator designed the agenda on the basis of the experts'(a) and (b) lists.

as between the parties. It is not the function of the arbitral tribunal to decide the issues on which side has the best advocate, or team of advocates.[9]

The interest of the attorneys is to win the case for their client; and for this purpose they want to be able to control the territory that their experts are to be asked to cover. The process of the direct examination of their experts is often rehearsed against a script, sometimes in front of a video camera and/or a "mock tribunal".

Skilled cross-examiners are trained in the techniques for controlling the scope of an expert's answers by posing a series of "closed" questions that deny the expert the opportunity to expand on his or her answers, or to put them in a particular context. This scenario is frustrating for experienced arbitrators, who may feel that they are learning only to admire the forensic skills of the cross-examiner rather than the merits of the expert's opinion.

In the civil law system, where the practice of judges and arbitrators is to appoint their own experts to assist and advise them, these vices are largely absent. In international arbitrations in which the parties are represented by lawyers from civil law countries it is common for the parties to raise no objection to such a procedure. In such countries cross-examination is virtually unknown, so the arbitral tribunal will not often have the benefit of a skilled cross-examination of fact witnesses. In some (but by no means all) cases cross-examination of fact witnesses, probing the story told by a witness by testing it against the contemporaneous documents and other collateral evidence can be useful.

Nevertheless, by 2006 the science had not advanced sufficiently to permit "expert conferencing" to be described as an accepted or routine international practice. It was still in its relative infancy and regarded with suspicion at least by many common law advocates.

V. THE FUTURE: BACK TO BASICS?

A possible way forward might be to eliminate some long-established *habits*. It was not an accident that the word "habitual" was used, earlier in this paper, to describe the inherent tension between the interest of the arbitral tribunal, as the decision-making body, to gain as much knowledge about the issues to be decided as possible and the interest of the advocates to gain strategic and/or tactical advantages over the opposing party.

The interest of the advocates is to maximize the impact on the arbitral tribunal of the strongest aspects of their clients' contentions, and to minimize the impact of the weakest. One well-trodden path for achieving the latter is to submerge the debate on the weak points to the level of excruciating detail, complicating everything that can be made more complicated and obfuscating everything that can be obfuscated – often by repetition of the same points in slightly different clothing, accompanied by an avalanche of barely relevant documents.

Practitioners who have experience of serving both as members of arbitral tribunals and as advocates over the course of their careers are well aware of the "tricks of the

---

9. Still less on the basis of which side has the most expensive team of advocates.

trade", and – on both sides of the table – have developed techniques for dealing with most different scenarios. However, this paper is not concerned with making opening or closing speeches, seeking the production of documents or examining, cross-examining and re-examining fact witnesses; it is concerned with the role of experts.

It may be possible to reform outdated twentieth century habits for handling experts by focusing on their underlying role – that is, as described above, to assist, educate and advise the arbitral tribunal. Perhaps, when the experts are heard, the layout of the hearing room might be changed so that it would be more like a classroom,[10] with the experts seated on a platform, or stage.

The "audience" could be arranged around them in a semi-circle with the tribunal in the centre, flanked by the advocates and other players. In a scenario like this, surely the old cross-examination habits would evaporate? It would not prevent the experts from being challenged, either by each other or by the parties' advocates – or indeed by members of the arbitral tribunal. A transcript would be taken in the normal way (accompanied by a video, where appropriate); and visual aids could be used as in a conference or seminar. It would be necessary for the arbitral tribunal to devise a system for maintaining an orderly and fair proceeding as between the parties, but this should not create any insurmountable difficulties. In the twenty-first century it is frequently done this way when taking the testimony of absent fact witnesses by videoconference.

VI.   SUMMARY AND CONCLUSIONS

It is clear that the participation of experts in international commercial arbitration is here to stay for the foreseeable future. The complexity of process design and construction technologies are way beyond the comprehension of "ordinary" engineer/technical arbitrators, let alone law professors or other legal practitioner arbitrators. Taken together with the ever-increasing ability of human beings and their computers to produce huge quantities of data either in electronic and/or hard copy form, this has made the presentation of expert assistance and advice to arbitral tribunals an enormously expensive and time-consuming operation. Traditional habits for presenting and testing the contributions of experts to the process have contributed to lack of efficiency in providing arbitral tribunals with the assistance and advice they need to enhance their ability to decide technical issues in a manner that is fair between the parties.

In the interest of procedural efficiency and limiting the ever-increasing cost of dispute resolution in international commerce it is desirable that the arbitration community should work towards finding better ways of determining specialist technical issues that are not within the expertise of the members of the tribunal. The alternative practices currently adopted by arbitral tribunals and advocates are either unwieldy and/or unreliable (party-experts tested by cross-examination); or present an impression of delegation by the arbitral tribunal of its decision-making mandate (opinions of tribunal-experts untested by the parties); or are potentially unacceptably expensive (such as the UNCITRAL and IBA models).

---

10. Or, even better, for the session with the experts to be held in a different room.

It is not the purpose of this paper to suggest that a "classroom" option on the lines suggested above is the only feasible solution, or indeed that it would necessarily be the best way. The purpose is to encourage the community of international arbitration practitioners to search for imaginative solutions to replace outdated twentieth century litigious habits with more efficient and cost-effective methods of transferring specialist technical knowledge to arbitrators whose background and training is usually in the field of law. Possible solutions could be tested in experimental form by using "mock" and/or "moot" case studies, in a controlled environment under the auspices of academic institutions.[11]

---

11. For example, as at the annual Institute for Transnational Arbitration events in Dallas.

Working Group B

8. Round Table on Oral Argument

"Oral Argument": Report of the Session*

I.   INTRODUCTION

The Moderator opened the Session, explaining that the Panel intended to initiate a revolution at ICCA: the Speakers would all come from the floor; and all the questions would come from the Panellists. Each Panellist would be addressing in turn one of the five topics of the Moderator's Notes (distributed to the floor and reproduced below);[1] the floor-speakers would then have to speak for at least one hour, and the Panellists' questions could not last for more than the remaining half hour.

---

*   The Moderator for this Session is V.V. Veeder, Essex Court Chambers, London ; Member of ICCA.
    The Panellists for this Session are:

    Robert Briner, Honorary Chairman, International Court of Arbitration of the International Chamber of Commerce (ICC); Past President, Iran-United States Claims Tribunal, The Hague; Member of ICCA.
    Albert Jan van den Berg, Hannotiau & van den Berg, Brussels; General Editor of ICCA.
    L. Yves Fortier, Past President, London Court of International Arbitration; Chair, Hong Kong International Arbitration Court; Past Ambassador and Permanent Representative of Canada to the United Nations; Member, United Nations Compensation Commission; Member of ICCA.
    Teresa Cheng, Deputy President for 2007 and President for 2008, Chartered Institute of Arbitrators; Vice Chairperson, Hong Kong International Arbitration Centre; Member of ICCA.
    David A.R. Williams, QC, Chief Justice of the Cook Islands; President, Arbitrators and Mediators Institute of New Zealand; Member of ICCA.

    The Rapporteur for this Session is *Salim Moollan,* Essex Court Chambers.

1. See Annex, this volume, pp. 000-000.

II.   TOPIC A — PURPOSES OF ORAL ARGUMENT

The first Panellist, *Mr. Robert Briner*, addressed this topic. He commenced his intervention by noting that ICCA was supposed to be to a large degree all about war-stories. He had two such stories. First, in 1980-1982, he attended a meeting in Berne for the inauguration of the ASA. After that meeting, on the train back to Geneva, he sat opposite a member of the Swiss Federal Supreme Court. This gentleman had spent all his life as a judge; and Mr. Briner asked him: "In all your experiences as a judge, has oral argument ever changed your mind following your reading of the documents?". The judge thought long and hard and said: "Yes – once in thirty-five years." Secondly, Mr. Briner referred to his time at the Iran-US Claims Tribunal. One Monday morning, he met an American colleague and told him about how busy his own week-end had been, reading all the files in preparation for the hearings which he was to have that week. His American colleague simply answered that he never looked at a file before the hearing.

What was the purpose, Mr. Briner asked, of oral argument? Was it just a tradition in the line of Pericles, Demosthenes or Cicero? Rhetoric is what made the reputation of ancient lawyers. Although this is still true to a certain degree, it was so mainly in criminal matters. What is the situation today? In commercial arbitration, there is an expectation that arbitrators will have actually looked at the file before the hearing. What then is the role of oral presentation and of a hearing? Mr. Briner made it clear that he was not concerned with the hearing of witnesses, but was discussing oral presentation proper. He put it to the floor-speakers that the purpose of oral submissions was twofold. First, to provide the parties with the opportunity to highlight what in their opinion the case was all about. Secondly, and more importantly, it was the time for a dialogue where the arbitrators put to the parties questions which *they* felt were important. This second purpose was the only real purpose where there was an informed tribunal who had studied the file. The Moderator stated that the real question raised by Topic A was "Why bother?" Mr. Briner concluded that the Swiss judge in his first war-story had failed to indicate whether, in the one case where oral argument had changed his mind over 35 years, it had changed its mind in favour of, or against, the party addressing him!

From the floor, *Mr. Carl Walton* stated that oral argument was the opportunity to establish your credibility with the tribunal, in particular by not overstating your evidence and position and by conceding points where this was required. It was also the time to show that you were committed to, and convinced of, your case.

From the floor, *Professor Dr. Karl-Heinz Böckstiegel* stated that he wished to continue Mr. Briner's war-story. Mr. Briner and himself were both at the Iran-US Claims Tribunal at the same time. Mr. Briner was in Chamber Two, and he was chairman of Chamber One. He soon started to have deliberations the morning immediately following the hearing. Accordingly, he had to know the documents before the hearing. Young German judges are trained to look at a case on paper to identify what is relevant before hearing any witnesses etc. This is the tradition Dr. Böckstiegel came from, but he had to admit that a case very often developed during oral hearing.

From the floor, *Lord Slynn* described his experience at the European Court of Justice, with its panel of fifteen judges. The attitude of all fifteen judges in a particular case at the beginning of a hearing had been: "what a waste of time to have oral argument". Five minutes later, every judge except the English judge had a question. Two hours later, the judges stated that there seemed to be something in this. Six months later, the decision went the other way. Lord Slynn concluded: "Long live oral argument, for ever and ever."

From the floor, *Mr. Diwan* asked the panel what an advocate should do where it was clear that one member of the arbitral tribunal was not up to speed. Mr. Briner answered that this depended on whether the advocate in question had appointed that particular arbitrator or not! The advocate should then go more into the details of the case than he otherwise would.

From the floor, a distinguished speaker from Chicago[2] stated that oral presentation now included PowerPoint presentations and equivalent technologies. This was now required. Outlines, time lines and video-clips were all persuasive as a roadmap.

From the floor, *Lord Mustill* stated that the English Court process had been dependent on a dialogue between the advocate and the judge for the past 700 years or so, when the English records disappear in the mist of history. Nothing had changed, and the same methods were used, in particular that of using an analogy, and of changing the analogy to test a proposition. That Socratic method enabled the law to be very thoroughly explored. Five hundred and fifty years ago, two cases were argued by the same advocate in the same Court before the same judge in the same term. In the first case the issue was: "When do hides change character when turned into boots." The advocate was Lord Kay, and he appeared before Haleford. Kay unsuccessfully argued that the hides had not changed their substance. In the second case six weeks later, the issue was: "When does a tree change character when turned into planks." Kay was arguing the point the other way. He lost. He told the judge: "Have you forgotten the case of the boots?" The judge answered: "Nay, it was different. The only difference is that you spell boots with two o's and boats with one o." Lord Mustill concluded that now that England had a mixed system where there were both written skeleton arguments and oral argument he was reminded of counsel's usual question to a judge: "Has Your Lordship had a chance to read the affidavits?" "Yes", the judge would answer, "but I have not taken it". Lord Mustill was for his part not so sure about the importance of written submissions.

From the floor, a distinguished speaker from New York stated that the Court of Appeals in New York was a so-called "Hot Court". All seven judges had received their briefs, had studied them and had preliminary opinions. The argument was strictly Question and Answer. The conclusion was that the process of oral argument in a Hot Court was a very helpful one, which helped the advocate to sharpen his or her own opinion and to see what was wrong with his or her argument. He wished to state a good word for the help which oral argument could provide in the proper context. As an arbitrator, the situation was not quite the same and oral argument did not provide him with much help; but as an appellate judge, it did.

From the floor, *Mr. John Kay* stated that two weeks before, he had attended a Circuit Conference in the United States, where the judges had opened up. The figures were consistent. In about twenty per cent of the cases, a judge would tell you that he had

---

2. Regrettably, not all speakers from the floor introduced themselves by name; and it was not therefore possible for the rapporteur to identify them here.

changed his mind after hearing oral argument. In almost fifty per cent of the cases, judges asked questions. Judges liked oral argument; and so did arbitrators.

From the floor, *Mr. Dushyant Dave* stated that he had been acting as arbitrator for sixteen years, and that oral argument was an insurance against arbitrators who had not read their files, or who had not understood them.

Mr. Briner concluded that this was not an ideal world. From his notes, he could see that only one of the speakers from the floor was not from the common law world. The latter were the converted. That was interesting. He reminded the floor that the panel was clearly only concerned about oral argument; this should not be confused with cross-examination. The two should not be mixed.

III.   TOPIC B — FORMS OF ORAL ARGUMENT

The second Panellist, *Ms. Teresa Cheng*, addressed this topic. She stated that when one came to think of this area, three matters should be considered viz. (i) the state of the proceedings, (ii) the purpose of the argument and (iii) whose perspective.

As for (i), interlocutory or procedural matters could often be dealt with over the telephone, or through video-conferencing. These were matters where "seeing people" was not of the essence. Oral argument as discussed here could properly be confined to substantive hearings. These could in turn be divided in two stages, opening and closing. Oral openings had to be done physically and in person, and the questions were: in what form and with what content. She was reminded of the instance where counsel had been addressing the Court for one-and-a-half to two hours when the judge told him: "Mr. X, I have read this." He answered: "Yes my Lord, but I have not." This could be one reason for oral argument.

As for (ii), there were two purposes to oral argument, the first was highlighting the case and the second to create the opportunity for a dialogue between counsel and judge. If the latter was not a purpose, then counsel might as well prepare a videotape or CD-ROM and give it to the arbitrators. That was the most important part. It involved communication skills. Body language was important and could be read. The arbitrator is frowning; he is nodding off; he has no files with him: counsel must get very worried. People tended to come out with a preconceived view; and it was not unlikely that they would change their minds. Counsel should plough on.

As for (iii), it should be borne in mind that arbitrators want a speedy resolution to cases. On the other hand, advocates and parties want a fair run. Has the arbitrator really understood their points? At the end of the day, we were all servants of the parties.

As to form, was the current mix of written and oral argument the worst of both worlds? It could in fact be the best of both worlds. Ms. Cheng wished to turn the question back to the floor and ask participants: "What form of oral hearing have you had?"

The Moderator stated that there appeared to be a difference of approach between civilists and common lawyers present on the floor. Taking the example of a terms of reference procedural meeting under the ICC Rules, these almost always took place in person. Where they did not, problems almost always developed later in the proceedings. This showed that there was something about people making personal contact. Mr. Briner expressed his full agreement and stated that exchanges of this sort were also required after a tribunal had heard the witnesses.

From the floor, a distinguished speaker from London described the experience which she had in a civil court a few years previously. The case was about the application of paint to a ship. The judges did not have a clue. She spoke about nail polish; and used it as an analogy. It worked. Ms. Cheng concluded that this proved her earlier point: the fact that the advocate could see that the judge was troubled enabled her to address the issue and find a solution. From the floor, a distinguished speaker from India stated that a judge faced with the question: "Are you with me?" faced a difficult situation. What was the correct answer , "Yes" or "I can't say"?

IV. TOPIC C – STYLES OF ORAL ARGUMENT

The third Panellist, *Mr. David A.R. Williams, QC*, addressed this topic. He observed that the Moderator's Notes contained a whole range of questions on the topic which were all essentially asking the following question: "What actually works in the arbitral setting, and what does not?" His view was that effective advocacy in international arbitration was founded upon the same principles that applied to advocacy in ordinary civil litigation, especially appellate litigation. Those fundamental principles had never been better articulated than in the famous article by US Solicitor General, John W. Davis, entitled "The Argument of an Appeal". Mr. Williams said he proposed to refer to several of Davis' ten fundamental principles in the course of his remarks.

Starting with Question 12 of the Moderator's Notes (*"As to the style of oral argument, how should an advocate address a tribunal generally?"*), the answer was that the advocate's style should be concise and focused because of the time limits which generally apply in international commercial arbitration. Mr. Williams favoured the restrained conversational style which treated the tribunal as interested and intelligent human beings and concentrated on following John W. Davis' advice to concentrate on the three Cs: Chronology, Candour and Clarity. The advocate should welcome dialogue with the tribunal. With respect to candour, Mr. Williams agreed with the previous intervention from the floor: the advocate should seek to earn the trust of the tribunal.

Problems frequently arose where there was no order, no clarity and no end to the oral argument. To appeal to the tribunal there should be a fairly low-key presentation which helpfully analyzed the key issues. After all, the tribunal must eventually provide an answer in the award to the issues posed and would be hoping to receive material that would provide such answers. As John W. Davis said, the advocate must "furnish the materials for decision". This was the purpose of the pre-hearing written submissions on which the advocate should elaborate orally.

The advocate should always bear in mind the tenth principle in the Davis decalogue, namely "Sit Down!" As an arbitrator, it can sometimes be a challenge to close down a garrulous advocate. Mr. Williams referred to a three-stage approach to the problem starting with "Mr. X, your submissions were very helpful, and we fully understand your case," hoping that this will be a signal to the advocate to cease. If the advocate continues, one moves to stage two where the arbitrator says "Mr. X, you have said all that could be said in support of your client's case and much, much more." Finally, if that does not have the desired result, in desperation one can move to the third stage where the arbitrator says "Mr. X, I am going to sleep now, and I don't want to see you here when I wake up." This third option was inherently risky and dangerous, especially if one was sitting as a sole arbitrator!

As for Question 17 of the Moderator's Notes ("*is a legal representative more forceful on the merits when forensically angry or calm? In practice, is the advocate's audience the tribunal or the paying client, or both? Does it assist an advocate to attack an opposing counsel, as distinct from the opposing party? Whilst a client may appreciate its lawyer's libellous attacks on the opposing party, does a tribunal appreciate that style?*"), Mr. Williams stated that there was always a danger in attacking opposing counsel. As John W. Davies put it in another of his propositions: "an advocate should never irritate the mind which he or she seeks to persuade. Rhetorical denunciation of opposing counsel may create sympathy for the person so denounced and may irritate the tribunal; it can never persuade."

From the floor, a distinguished speaker from Toronto addressed Question 18 of the Moderator's Notes ("*Where arbitrations are private hearings, an advocate's style is traditionally more conversational than a ranting public speech. Now that certain arbitral hearings are held in public (such as NAFTA), has the arbitral style of advocacy significantly changed? Has this in turn provoked a different treatment of oral argument by an arbitral tribunal? Just as Judge Judy has emerged on US television, will there be an "Arbitrator Judy", particularly if NAFTA or other hearings are filmed and broadcast to the general public?*"). He stated that he currently appeared before two members of the panel. Looking at the first two sentences of the question, had there been a change? He had appeared as counsel for NAFTA claimants in both scenarios. The first such public hearing had been a jurisdictional hearing. On the first day, four members of the public attended. On the second day, three. So, is anybody really listening out there? As counsel, it made absolutely no difference to his style of advocacy; if anything his arguments were even more tampered and even-keeled, although this could have more to do with age setting in! There was no reason not to have hearings in the open; the form of the process had not changed.

From the floor, Lord Mustill stated that when he had read Question 12 drawn as it is, he had completely misunderstood it: could one use "Hi Guys" as a form of address? As for the question asked earlier by Mr. Diwan, Lord Mustill had produced for the benefit of Mr. Diwan the following formula: "If that damn idiot sitting on the left were to listen to me for more than three minutes...." That should resolve the problem. More seriously, the style of argument depended on the nature of the tribunal. It was not the same for an appellate tribunal on a patent issue as for a fraud case at first instance. The common elements were calm, lucidity and structure. The personality of the speaker must be completely submerged. The judge or arbitrator could not care less. All the great advocates after World War II shared this quality. As for attacks on opposite counsel, one is guaranteed to lose a case by attacking the opposite party, for instance with ferocious or vitriolic attacks on the other side. You see this fellow blasting away and you just think: "Oh, shut up." There should be use of the arbitrator's disciplinary powers – seriously. Modern arbitration practice was being bogged down by too many codes, rules and the like. Where was the discretion of the arbitral tribunal? One does not need Rule No. 17 paragraph No. 43 of the IBA Rules. All disputes are different. Finally, as for the question on Contingency Fees (Question 21), Lord Mustill thought this a wonderful question, and was looking forward to seeing a lawyer instructed on a contingency fee basis kneeling on a desk in front of a tribunal explaining with his hands clasped in prayer: "It's been a miserable year for me, Sir."

From the floor, *Mr. John Townsend* from Washington DC expressed "a new principle of advocacy": never try to speak after Lord Mustill. He stated that a good advocate depended much more on his eyes and ears than his voice. He should take the cue from the judge. In an appeal hearing in New York where his opponent was given a hard time, he had simply told the Court that he would be happy to answer any questions it may have, and had sat down. The cardinal principle was to shut up at the right time.

(The Moderator observed that while there were relatively few oral contributions from civil lawyers, he was getting numerous written notes from them, as they were more used to written submissions. He invited more civil lawyers from the floor to intervene orally in the debate).

V. TOPIC D — CONTENTS OF ORAL ARGUMENT

The fourth Panellist, *Mr. Yves Fortier*, addressed this topic. He stated that everything that he had wanted to say had already been said. One of the cardinal rules was: if the point has already been made, do not belabour it. He wished to say as one would say in Court: "I adopt." But he had five minutes which he would use. He would speak of his experience as counsel and as arbitrator. As counsel, he had been and had remained until the end of his career as an advocate an aficionado of oral argument for all the reasons given so far. He had started out as a fan with a strong bias in favour. At the end of his career, he was still convinced that the greatest satisfaction for an advocate was to engage with the judge and the arbitrators; there was no more rewarding moment than to note that you are convincing your judge or arbitrators. The advocate can usually see it when this is happening. Mr. Fortier had looked up in Black's law dictionary the definition of an advocate; this read: "a person who assists, defends, pleads or prosecutes *for another*". It was vital for an advocate never to forget that he was a mouthpiece or a spokesperson. Mr. Fortier stated that he did believe in the power of the spoken word. The point had been made that an advocate had to establish credibility; this was indeed crucial to the success of any argument.

Turning to more direct pointers, Mr. Fortier recommended that counsel involved in an opening argument (i) set markers, indicating to the tribunal what the issues and answers were and (ii) try to ensure that the members of the tribunal know from Day 1 where the main lines of argument will lie (the "drawing of lines in the sand"). As for closing submissions, that was the last chance. The advocate should seek to provoke questions from the tribunal and try to get the arbitrators to tell him what concerns and worries his case is causing them. It needs to be an interactive and dynamic process.

As arbitrator, Mr. Fortier had not changed his mind on the usefulness of oral advocacy, particularly with respect to closing submissions. When sitting with continental colleagues in Europe, he had often noted an initial resistance, if not actual objections to oral closing submissions. Usually however, these colleagues started being persuaded and then became in favour of the exercise. In every instance, they said: "Yves, you were right." Even half-an-hour or one hour can be very useful. Mr. Fortier concluded with a few final recommendations. These were (1) Don't overstate your welcome; (2) Don't speak only to the arbitrator you appointed; (3) Don't treat the tribunal as a jury; and (4) Be respectful. On this last point, Mr. Fortier recalled one instance of US counsel being very respectful indeed. This was a case where both of his wingmen had not been well. The advocate was speaking; he looked at Mr. Fortier; he looked to his right; he looked to his left; but he said nothing. Mr. Fortier got the message.

From the floor, Mr. Dushyant Dave stated that this reminded him of a particular Indian judge who had a habit of sleeping post-lunch. The Attorney-General gathered a couple of advocates saying "let's do something without being disrespectful". One afternoon, the judge in question started sleeping some five to ten minutes into the hearing. After he had been sleeping for half-an-hour, one of the advocates took a very heavy book and dropped it. When the judge jumped, he stated: "My apologies my Lord, the recorder was sleeping; she thinks she is the judge." Mr. Fortier answered that they had had a similar problem in the Quebec Court of Appeal. One ought to be careful however for, although the judge in question appeared at first glance to be sleeping, he was in fact very much awake and only pretending.

From the floor, *Professor Philip Capper* stated that twenty years previously he had been involved with Me Matthieu de Boisséson, Lord Grabiner and many others in the *Eurotunnel* case. He remembered that, in the course of Lord Grabiner's very careful oral submissions, Matthieu de Boisséson and others expressed their thoughts as to how boring he was. By contrast, the Bâtonnier on the other side said nothing: he simply slammed his documents on the table. The problem was that the slamming did not find its way into the transcript. Lord Grabiner's careful words on the other hand did. Victor Borge actually pronounced punctuation. Transcripts thus change the nature of oral argument. There is now also a final opportunity to get one's views across before the tribunal's deliberations; that is written closing submissions which are now universal practice. Professor Capper wondered whether prior oral argument was still so important in the light of this development. Mr. Fortier's answer to this question was a simple "Yes".

From the floor, a distinguished speaker from Warsaw stated that he was a continental lawyer practicing in Warsaw in the US format, and that he had vast experience of such practice. He thought that this whole subject was intellectual provocation. Oral argument was the essence of the advocate's profession. Without it, advocacy would be but a boring and mechanical exercise. What does the practitioner want to achieve? He wants to be effective, win a maximum number of cases and lose the minimum. Questions of style, body language and persuasiveness are essential. The lawyer who gives those up is careless. Oral argument is important in a close case; in clear cases the documents speak for themselves. His general advice was to be active, and to be a good oralist.

VI. TOPIC E – VISUAL AND OTHER AIDS TO ORAL ARGUMENT

The fifth and final Panellist, *Mr. Albert Jan van den Berg*, addressed this topic. The question is: "What makes international arbitrators listen today?" That was a question about arbitrator psychology, a subject that is still in the infancy of scientific research. This panellist professed to have no such knowledge other than his own experience. Of course, there are many scientific studies on the psychology of judges and jurors, especially in the Untied States, but international arbitrators may be a different population for study. Advocacy, also before international arbitrators, is in essence an exercise in communication and persuasion. You have to convince them of your case, and to disprove the other side's case.

If you believe trial consultants (and others): "Words alone are not enough", to which they also add: "We're here to make you look good." It seems that there is indeed a psychological connection between visual aids, one the one hand, and verbal communication and persuasion on the other. It is claimed that, inter alia, visual aids reinforce key messages, improve memory recall and assist in explaining and simplifying key concepts or complex matters. It may also ensure a greater impact and a longer-lasting impression long after counsel have been speaking. This Panellist was inclined to accept that proposition, but not in all cases under all circumstances. Thus, he believed that you should always ask yourself the question: "Do I need it for my case?" Here, there is a tremendous challenge for counsel because you have to inquire what the arbitrator is thinking and what he or she needs for deciding the case. However, in many cases it is difficult to know before the hearing what his or her state of mind and necessity is. In many international arbitrations today, four types of visual and other aides are frequently used:

— First, hard copy. One use is the written outline of the oral argument. Many arbitrators appreciate having such an outline in front of them so they can follow counsel better. Next, there are pleading notes: much in use in civil law settings but unknown in the common law environment where they are considered a "stealth pleading". Then, you may wish to have a bundle of core documents to which you can take the arbitrators during your presentation. It is powerful and saves time, but you must be mindful that arbitrators have already seen the core documents and have annotated them. The better practice, therefore, seems to be a core bundle in advance of the hearing. Hard copy is also useful for time-lines and/or chronologies, as well as lists of dramatis personae, but here again it is preferable to provide them in advance of the hearing.
— Second, the whiteboard (or flip chart). That is useful to make a simple drawing or simple calculation. The problem is that in many cases it is not saved one way or the other. The preferred approach is to hand out, simultaneously or shortly thereafter, a hard copy of the drawing or calculation.
— Third, demonstrative exhibits. They are used for graphs, bar-charts, time-lines, diagrams, blowing up key passages in documents, photographs, decision trees and many other things. If well done, they can be very powerful. A few rules: (1) They should be based on what is in the record; (2) They should speak for themselves (although, first tell, then show); (3) They should not be overloaded; (4) They should be numbered sequentially (for the transcript and case of reference); (5) Make sure that everyone can see them (and leave the really important ones in sight as long as you can); and (6) A hard copy should be given simultaneously to the arbitrators and the other side.
— Fourth, PowerPoint. This enjoys great popularity amongst counsel in international arbitrations these days. Yet, they should be aware of certain disadvantages. First, you have the visibility problem. The projection screen is usually too far away for certain distinguished international arbitrators to read what is on it. And even if your

distinguished arbitrator is able to read it, the light in the hearing room has to be dimmed to nightclub level with the attendant problem that the arbitrator is unable to take notes (and some also drift away in their thoughts). Second, it may become a dazzling show in which the succession of slides may obfuscate the message. This is not to say that PowerPoint may not be useful. This Panellist would, however, recommend: (1) always provide a hard copy of the PowerPoint presentation at the outset of your oral argument (so that the arbitrators can make notes on it); and (2) leave the lights on.

Those are the four most commonly used visual and other aids in current international arbitration. The overhead projector with transparencies is apparently no longer in favour. On the other hand, in some arbitrations (in particular, in licencing disputes) the use of the models can assist oral argument if it concerns the subject matter of a case, e.g., perfume, slot/skill machines, sportswear apparel etc.

Less common in current international arbitration is the use of the following visual and other aids, but it may well be that within five years from now that is different. First, projection of documents and transcripts. Software programs, such as TrialMax, are used to project almost instantly, with so-called "call outs", the document or passage in the transcript that counsel is referring to. In this Panellist's experience, it is a useful tool in that it shows you where to look on the relevant page. Second, Excel on screen. In a damages phase, for example, it is sometimes useful to project the expert's calculation of damages on screen and show how the change of one input dramatically affects the outcome. Here, you have to be really careful. For one, you should be fully proficient in the use of Excel. Also, there are not many international arbitrators who understand programs such as Excel. Frankly, this Panellist had seen cases in which arbitrators, who were believed to be financial experts, got hopelessly lost with Excel. Third, videos and films. Their use depends entirely on the type of case you are in. They can be powerful, but counsel should be mindful that the other side can produce a video or film that shows just the opposite. Fourth, computer animations. Here again, their use depends on the type of case. One last important word of caution: international arbitrators have a healthy suspicion for slick and fanciful computer animations and similar presentations.

That last observation led to this Panellist's conclusion. Visual and other aids are what they are: aids. They should not overtake counsel's *viva voce* presentation, but only support it. International arbitration is not a multimedia show for the promotion of some product. This Panellist, therefore, wished to reiterate what was said earlier: Always ask yourself the question: "Do I need it for my case?"

From the floor, *Mr. Hew Dundas* from Scotland stated that the use of the words "the learned arbitrator" by counsel could be a sign of respect, but also sometimes a sign of disdain. He asked Mr. Fortier whether this is something which should be taken into account by a tribunal. Mr. Fortier replied that it would be easy to simply answer "No"; but one had to try to ascertain whether counsel used the adjective only for the tribunal or also for opposite counsel. He would be more influenced if this was done to the other side.

From the floor, *Mr. John Kidd* from Florida stated that there had been an interesting survey in the United States over a period of twenty years as to what people remember forty-eight hours after hearing or seeing it. This had involved 20,000 "ordinary citizens" and 500 judges. The results were that they had a very sharp and good recollection of eighty per cent of the visuals presented, whereas they could only recollect about twenty per cent of what they had heard. Mr. van den Berg stated that most of the research conducted had been aimed at juries and US judges. Could these be applied to international arbitrators? That may be a different population.

From the floor, a distinguished speaker stated that visual aids were very helpful in each case. One very rustic study had also shown that the colour of the visual aid was important. The best colours were blue and gold. Mr. van den Berg replied that, as counsel, he used green for his position, and red for his opponent's position.

From the floor, *Professor Hans van Houtte* from Belgium stated that one important thing to remember when using slides was not to put too much information on each slide. Mr. van den Berg replied that there were some basic rules to be adhered to for slides: they should be based on what's in the record – that's the rule of the game; they should speak for themselves; they should not be overloaded; they should be sequentially numbered; they should be positioned so that everybody can see them; and a hard copy of the slides should be given simultaneously to the arbitrators and to the other side.

VII.   TOPIC F – THE THREE BEST AND THREE WORST THINGS IN ORAL ARGUMENT (AS SEEN BY AN ARBITRATOR

The Moderator then asked each of the Panellists to state what in their experience were the three best and three worst things in oral argument by an advocate.

David Williams' "best" list was: (A) An argument which starts with a clear statement of the undisputed facts; (B) An argument that contains a short and succinct summary of the key issues for determination; and (C) An argument which uses the power of understatement. As an example, an overstatement would be something along the following lines: "the claimant's argument is a ridiculous litany of orchestrated lies". The more effective understatement would be: "The tribunal may be surprised that, even at this late stage of the case, the claimant is pursuing this claim notwithstanding that its unsoundness has been readily accepted by its main witness...." His "worst" list was: (X) Instead of presenting an attractive argument, producing a sustained tirade against the opposing party; (W) Going at a speed which makes note-taking impossible and prevents the stenographers from keeping up – failing to slow down even after repeated requests from the tribunal to do so; and (Z) Exceeding all time limits set for oral argument and refusing to take hints from the tribunal that all that needs to be said has been said.

Ms. Cheng's "worst" list was: (X) Counsel does not answer the question raised; (Y) Counsel reads from the written submissions. Ms. Cheng could remember a case where the judge told her opposing counsel: "I have been taught to read at the age of six. Now tell me what your main points are"; and (Z) Counsel does not watch the arbitrator's pen; this misses the whole point of the exercise. Her "best" list would be the reverse of the above.

Mr. van den Berg's "best" list was: (A) Keep it simple; (B) Be concise; and (C) Tell a story. His "worst" list was: (Y) Overrun of time by more than fifty per cent; and (Z) Treating the arbitrators as if they are 'missing in action'.

Mr. Fortier's "worst" list was: (X) Refusing to answer the question or obfuscating; (Y) Reading from a script; and (Z) Taking the tribunal for a bunch of idiots. His "best" list was: (A) Addressing the tribunal's real concerns; and (B) Finishing on time.

Mr. Briner stated his negative points: (Y) Jumping from one slide to another: the advocate should hand out hard copies not just of the slides but also of the record referred to; and (Z) Advocates should realize that, in most cases, not all members of the tribunal will have the same degree of fluency, especially in English. Advocates should keep it slow, consistent and coherent. It is better for the arbitrator to fall asleep for a time than for him not to understand a single word.

ANNEX

Notes from the Moderator

*V.V. Veeder**

The Program Committee's Brief:

> *"Oral argument is one of the great challenges and, it must be said, greatest satisfactions of the arbitration practitioner. But setting aside the stories and the tradition, what actually works, and what doesn't? Do sophisticated tribunals need argument, or just answers? And how does oral argument intersect with written submissions?"*

Almost invariably (but not invariably), the procedures for transnational commercial arbitration have included oral argument at an oral hearing with the parties' legal representatives, as confirmed by many arbitration rules. The following list is illustrative (without being complete):

— Art. 15(2) of the UNCITRAL Arbitration Rules provides: "If either party so requests at any stage of the proceedings, the arbitral tribunal shall hold hearings for the presentation of evidence by witnesses, including expert witnesses, or for oral argument. In the absence of such a request, the arbitral tribunal shall decide whether to hold such hearings or whether the proceedings shall be conducted on the basis of documents and other materials."
— Art. 20(2) of the ICC Rules provides: "After studying the written submissions of the parties and all documents relied upon, the Arbitral Tribunal shall hear the parties together in person if any of them so requests or, failing such a request, it may of its own motion decide to hear them."
— Art. 19.1 of the LCIA Rules provides: "Any party which expresses a desire to that effect has the right to be heard orally before the Arbitral Tribunal on the merits of the dispute, unless the parties have agreed in writing on documents-only arbitration."
— Art. 25(1) of the Stockholm Rules provides: "An oral hearing shall be arranged if requested by either Party or if the arbitral tribunal considers it appropriate."

This Session is not intended to address arbitration rules providing for oral argument, but rather to examine why, what and how is (or should be) "oral argument".

The intensely practical nature of these questions suggests a substantial contribution from the floor, which will include, inevitably, many oral (and vocal) arbitration arbitrators and advocates with questions or comments. It has therefore been suggested that the five

---

*   Essex Court Chambers, London; Member of ICCA.

speakers should be limited at first to about five minutes each, introducing in turn each of five topics to be followed by substantial questions and comments from the floor. The five speakers' written record of this session, to be published in the ICCA Congress Series, will incorporate much of the ideas and conclusions reached during these exchanges between the floor and the speakers.

These five topics (listed below under A-E) are intended to be self-contained for the purpose of this Session. There is, of course, a degree of overlap. Nonetheless the speakers will try to keep their topics separate; and interventions from the floor are requested to do the same. Lastly, the whole subject-matter is potentially vast: it cannot extend in this Session to other potentially overlapping topics, eg cross-examination; codes of conduct generally; good faith in the conduct of the arbitration; letter-writing and pre- and post-hearing briefs etc.

TOPIC A – PURPOSE(S) OF ORAL ARGUMENT

(1) What is the purpose of oral argument by the parties' legal representatives to members of an arbitration tribunal? Is it in fact now necessary at all? In the early days of the English jury, oral argument was necessary because most jurors were illiterate. Is this true of arbitrators?

(2) Is oral argument suited to any purpose? It can duplicate, almost exactly, the parties' written submissions, which can be assimilated by a tribunal more quickly, cheaply and easily than oral argument at an oral hearing. If the oral argument takes place at an evidential hearing, it can delay or obscure evidence from factual and expert witnesses testifying to the tribunal.

(3) Given users' increasing complaints at the high cost of international arbitration, is oral argument now an expensive luxury which should be dispensed with, or at least severely curtailed?

(4) Does the purpose change if the arbitrators or advocates are civilian or common or other lawyers?

(5) Does the purpose change if the arbitrators are non-specialists, non-lawyers or not familiar with the applicable law(s)?

(6) Outside of an oral hearing, no one can now seriously suggest that a tribunal should require the parties to dispense completely with all legal advisers and all representation. Given, therefore, the inevitable involvement of the parties' lawyers in the arbitral process, should oral argument by those same lawyers ever be completely curtailed by a tribunal, if desired by one or more parties?

(7) Is it not also, possibly, a case of oral argument having not one but several different purposes? First, should the tribunal be sensitive to each parties' desire to have its case placed before and understood by the tribunal, as part of due process? Second, is there

a cathartic purpose in having a party's opponent listen and respond to that party's oral argument at an oral hearing? Third, does oral argument allow a tribunal a unique opportunity to understand and (if not) to pose questions to a party's legal representatives. And is there any better, or fairer, way for a tribunal to probe or clarify a party's case than during oral argument?

(8) If oral argument serves one or more essential purposes, is it now necessary to codify or otherwise regulate the procedure(s) for oral argument in arbitration rules, including new proposals to reform the UNCITRAL Arbitration Rules?

TOPIC B – FORMS OF ORAL ARGUMENT

(9) Historically, it has been necessary for oral argument to take place at oral hearings held in person between the parties' legal representatives and the members of the tribunal. (The possible exception being the use of telepathy in ancient arbitrations under the rules of the AAA, in pre-Colonial Australia).

(10) With busy arbitrators and lawyers and with arbitral venues far from their respective homes, such oral in-person hearings can be now very difficult to schedule and very expensive. Occasionally an oral hearing need last only a few hours (or less), a period of time wholly disproportionate to the time spent travelling to the venue by arbitrators, lawyers and clients. Is there another practical form to the historical oral in-person hearing?

(11) For example, increasingly oral argument for procedural meetings is taking place by telephone conference-call and multi-site video-link conference. Is this a Good Thing? Whilst a telephone conference-call may be better than a prolonged exchange of party-correspondence and whilst a video-link may be better than a telephone conference-call, there is no doubt that an oral hearing held in person is the best form of all hearings, particularly in a difficult case or a case where temperatures have risen between the parties and their legal representatives. But why is this? Do human beings respond more reasonably when meeting another human being in person? Is direct eye-contact necessary with an arbitrator? Does this depend upon the cultural background of the parties or their lawyers? Or is all this an old arbitral myth?

TOPIC C – STYLES OF ORAL ARGUMENT

(12) As to the style of oral argument, how should an advocate address a tribunal generally?

(13) Is it attractive to a tribunal to hear from a party a succession of different advocates on distinct points? Is it better for a party to have one or many voices? Can, and if so how, does a tribunal discipline an emerging Tower of Babel?

(14) Should an oral advocate encourage and prepare for questions and other interruptions from the tribunal? If so, how?

(15) Where there are language differences between the tribunal's members and the oral advocate, how does the latter prepare for them? Is there a different oral style pertaining to particular languages?

(16) Should the advocate be or only appear to be "pleasant" and "helpful" to the tribunal, treating them as interested and intelligent human beings? Is it ever wise for an oral advocate to "harangue" a tribunal on the verge of arbitral misconduct, including excess of jurisdiction? If so, when and how is this best done?

(17) Is a legal representative more forceful on the merits when forensically angry or calm? In practice, is the advocate's audience the tribunal or the paying client, or both? Does it assist an advocate to attack opposing counsel, as distinct from the opposing party? Whilst a client may appreciate its lawyer's libellous attacks on the opposing party, does a tribunal appreciate that style?

(18) Where arbitrations are private hearings, an advocate's style is traditionally more conversational than a ranting public speech. Now that certain arbitral hearings are held in public (such as NAFTA), has the arbitral style of advocacy significantly changed? Has this in turn provoked a different treatment of oral argument by an arbitral tribunal? Just as Judge Judy has emerged on US television, will there be an "Arbitrator Judy", particularly if NAFTA or other hearings are filmed and broadcast to the general public?

(19) Is there a recognisably different oral advocacy style between a party's legal representative as a qualified lawyer and as a non-lawyer, eg a claims consultant?

(20) Is there a recognisably different oral advocacy style between lawyers subject to different professional codes of conduct, or none? Is there any present attempt to impose a uniform code of conduct on oral advocates, (as suggested by Professor Catherine Rogers in the USA)?

(21) Is there a recognisably different style consequent upon the mode of payment received by a party's legal representative? Does a success fee or a conditional fee agreement affect an oral advocate's style or its reception by an arbitration tribunal?

TOPIC D – CONTENTS OF ORAL ARGUMENT

(22) As to content, what should an advocate be trying to achieve in oral argument generally? Is there a difference between particular stages of the arbitration? Oral opening argument before the evidence at the main hearing may have a different content than closing oral argument after that evidence. May there also be a difference as regards such arguments depending on the existence of pre-hearing written skeleton arguments or

post-hearing briefs? How should an advocate address procedural issues arising during an oral hearing, if different?

(23) More particularly, what are the specific aims of opening oral argument? In such oral argument before the oral evidence, is it helpful for an oral advocate to indicate what is agreed and not agreed between the disputing parties? Is it likewise helpful to list, objectively, each the legal and factual issues dividing the parties? Is it useful to provide a preview of the oral evidence, as to what will or will not established by that evidence for the client-party, at least from the witnesses called that party?

(24) More particularly. what are the specific aims of closing oral argument? In oral argument after the oral evidence, is it helpful for an oral advocate to return to a list of issues, indicating how the oral evidence has actually affected each issue? And what else?

(25) Is it easier to say what the oral advocate should not do? First, should the oral advocate merely read aloud a written script? Second, should the oral advocate be repeating what is already written (and read by the tribunal) in pre-hearing memorials and written submissions? What other examples can be given of what an oral advocate should not do in opening or closing argument?

(26) To what extent should the oral advocate refer to written evidential materials. How should such reference be made, so as to allow the arbitration tribunal to find the materials later? Should the oral advocate give the tribunal page references to the exhibits or other materials to which reference is made? Should the oral advocate take the tribunal to particular pages in the written materials? Should the oral advocate make use of a "core" bundle or bundle of key documents? Should it be assumed that the arbitrators have brought any of their files to the hearing?

(27) Is it helpful for an oral advocate specifically to address legal materials? If so, is it more helpful to cite cases without reading the judgment (US style) or more helpful to identify the particular passage(s) on which the advocate relies as the statement of relevant legal principle (British Commonwealth style). How does a tribunal control the over-citation of legal materials, especially the string citation of duplicative authorities merely illustrative of the general principle?

(28) Does it make a difference for the oral advocate if a verbatim transcript is being made of the oral argument? Where a tribunal is relying only on its own notes, how does this affect the content of oral argument? What is the purpose of a transcript of oral argument? For what is the advocate or tribunal to use it later in the proceedings?

(29) What can a tribunal do when there is marked imbalance in the content of the disputing parties' oral argument?

(30) What policy should a tribunal adopt in interrupting oral argument with questions? Never, until the end of the oral argument? Limited through the tribunal's president? At will, at any time, by any arbitrator?

TOPIC E – VISUAL AND OTHER AIDS TO ORAL ARGUMENT?

(31) Does the human voice need any props for oral argument? At a low level, how useful to oral argument are written documents handed-in to the Tribunal for oral argument, including written lists of issues, dramatis personae, chronologies, summaries etc? And at a high level, how useful are elaborate visual aids, including film and models etc?

(32) In particular, how attractive is the increasing use of presentations using PowerPoint and other more sophisticated software. eg "Trial Max"? While such technology can save time (particularly by replacing the time-consuming references to hard-copy exhibits filed a short odyssey from the arbitral chair), does it impose its own tyranny in removing an oral advocate's flexibility, particularly in response to questions from the arbitral tribunal?

(33) In presenting slides or film to a tribunal requiring the lights to be dimmed in the hearing room, is there a timing problem? After a healthy liquid lunch, as darkness looms in the afternoon, is there any danger of the arbitrators being lulled inadvertently to sleep?

(34) Where visual aids are used in oral argument, should the tribunal require the distribution of hard copies before the presentation begin? Should a tribunal provide for the marking of such visual aids as exhibits etc, particularly so as to make a written transcript subsequently intelligible; and if so how?

(35) Is there a procedural difficulty where such hard copies are distributed or exhibited if either conflicts with an earlier procedural order by the Tribunal regarding the exchange of written memorials or written submissions before the oral hearing? Where is the line drawn between old written argument, new oral argument and a fresh case?

TOPIC F – THE THREE BEST AND THREE WORST THINGS IN ORAL ARGUMENT (AS SEEN BY AN ARBITRATOR)

(36) For this session's sixth topic, each speaker will introduce list the three most attractive and the three most irritating things any advocate can do in argument before an arbitration tribunal, based upon that speaker's arbitration experience. The floor will be asked to add their own contributions.

(37) Lastly, in the long term, what is the role of arbitration tribunals in promoting best practice in oral argument, if any? Can a tribunal reprove a wayward advocate, without risk of unfairness or offence? Is it best done privately after the arbitration, directly or indirectly? Or not done at all?

Plenary Session

1. Commercial Arbitration and Transnational Public Policy

Law, International Public Policy (So-called) and Arbitral Choice in International Commercial Arbitration

W. Michael Reisman[*]

"Public policy — it is an unruly horse and when once you get astride it, you never know where it will carry you. It may lead you from the sound law. It is never argued at all but when other points fail."
Burroughs J. in Richardson v. Mellish[1]

I.   LIMITS TO ARBITRAL CHOICE

Policy is a central and inescapable part of the enterprise of law. Policies are authoritative political objectives; in some instances, they also include the authoritative legal means for their achievement. All legislation as well as all the rules and principles of a body politic which have not originated in legislation may be seen as instruments for achieving that body politic's policies.

Two recurring and quite distinct questions in legal theory are, first, the extent to which those charged with *applying* legislation may themselves make policy and, second, the extent, if any, to which they may depart, in their applications, from the explicit directions of legislation or rules in an effort to implement the policies which, the applier believes, actually animate the legislation and rules.

The second question — which presents itself frequently and seems to be the more complex — actually admits of a simple answer: do what the law which governs the matter prescribes. In some circumstances, legal prescriptions are designed to allow relatively little or even no contextual adjustment by the person designated to apply them in particular cases. To take an extreme example, the sergeant sitting in a silo housing ICBMs is given the strictest instructions about the circumstances under which he is to flip a switch and send the missiles in his charge hurtling toward their target. Those who have established the rules (and indeed all the rest of us) do not want that soldier to do any contextual appraisal, even less to do a Derrida-style deconstruction of his commands. The sergeant is expected to confine himself to a drastically limited normative universe in which one and only one relevant rule contains a single binary choice which is to be taken on the occurrence of one and only one specific contingency.

---

[*]   Myres S. McDougal Professor of International Law, Yale Law School.
1. *Richardson v. Mellish*, 2 Bing. 229 (1824) at 303.

In other circumstances, the legislature frames its prescriptions in a more open-textured fashion. Then the implication is clear: the persons assigned to apply them are authorized and required to make certain adjustments in their application so as to ensure that the policies animating the prescriptions are given effect in that particular situation. In these circumstances, which are the more common, the applier, whether judge or arbitrator, must view the prescriptions which he or she is called upon to apply not as black-letter rules but as authoritative communications conveying information about (i) the policy or policies to be achieved as well as (ii) an indication of the range of circumstances in which those policies are to be applied. Where a rule formulation is the vehicle chosen for the achievement of a policy and it proves ill-adapted to do so in a particular case, whether because of the anachronism of the rule in the face of subsequent social changes or the idiosyncratic character of the fact situation, the appliers, whoever they may be, must consult and apply the policy. They must, as our French colleagues put it, engage in *actualisation*.

A conception of application which tried to model itself only on the sergeant in the silo and to insist exclusively upon strict application of the rules is likely, in these circumstances, to produce anachronistic decisions at odds with the contemporary objectives of the legislature. Sensitivity to policy is also important in complex cases: Because real life controversies rarely engage a single law, rule or, indeed, a single policy, the judge or arbitrator may have to make extensive adjustments in the accommodation of a policy in order to shape the package of remedies to be awarded so that they approximate all the policy objectives of the legal system which are engaged in that case.

In these respects, the international commercial arbitrator, like all other appliers, is obliged to be sensitive to policy, but it must be emphasized that it is the policy of that legal system — its authorized political objectives and the means for their achievement — which the parties have selected or to which the arbitrators are directed by principles of conflict of laws. This use of policy is a highly disciplined teleological exercise. It bears repeating that it is the policy of the legal system which governs the dispute and not an artifacted policy created by the arbitrators for that particular case.

It is important to emphasize that none of these tasks involves making *new* policy, i.e., creating new political goals and new instruments for achieving those goals. Creating new political goals and new instruments for achieving those goals is a province assigned to others in the community whose law is being applied. To be sure, some civil codes explicitly authorize and require a judge confronted by a *lacuna* to act as if he or she were the legislator rather than return a judgment of *non liquet*. An arbitrator applying that choice of law of the parties would similarly have a derivative competence to "legislate" *pro hac vice* but without effects beyond that case. Some legal systems — one thinks of the United States in certain historical periods — are more generally comfortable with the vocation of judge-made law or judicial legislation. There, the legislature is the designated law-maker but judges are deemed to have a contingent law-making role. Whatever one's view of that particular conception, it seems to me *not* to be part of the province and vocation of the international commercial arbitrator, other than in those circumstances in which the applicable law explicitly authorizes an applier to act as the legislator where there is a real *lacuna*. The reason for this is hardly recondite. It lies in the essential role of the international commercial arbitrator.

Arbitrators execute the mandate of the parties, whose common consent is the source of their jurisdiction. If parties expressly authorize arbitrators to decide ex aequo et bono, they may depart from law otherwise applicable and the terms of otherwise applicable contracts and decide according to their individual sense of justice. National courts, which play an indispensable role in international commercial arbitration, should have no hesitation in lending the powers of the state to the enforcement of such an ex aequo et bono award. After all, the parties had effectively authorized the arbitrators to rewrite their contract so the action of doing so is within the boundaries of their contractual consent. And of course, the state has already decided that if the parties consent to waive their right to adjudication and elect instead to privatize the resolution of their dispute, the state apparatus will implement that agreement.

The situation is entirely different when there has been no such authorization by the parties. In that situation, the arbitrator purporting to decide ex aequo et bono or an arbitral system that purports to endorse such excursions may still expect the apparatus of the state to ignore both its own commercial and constitutional policies as well as the fact that its own citizen has not agreed to waive them (insofar as they are *jus dispositivum*) yet still to implement the idiosyncratic vision of the arbitrators. This is, I submit, an unreasonable expectation which is likely to remain unrequited. And properly so. After all, national jurisdictions exist to protect the legitimate interests of the community concerned, which is the *raison d'être* both of the state and of the international law of jurisdiction. It is entirely reasonable to ask governments to yield judicial jurisdiction (i) when the parties manifest national diversity; (ii) when they wish, for licit reasons, to privatize the mode of resolution of their dispute and clearly indicate their wish; and (iii) when those private proceedings, including the application by the arbitrators of the parties' choice of law, are fair. But it is unreasonable to ask governments to surrender the application of their law and policy to matters within their jurisdiction just because arbitrators, without being so authorized by the parties, assign themselves a general legislative power or, more modestly, a norm-making power on a case by case basis.

My point is not that international commercial arbitrators should behave like the sergeant in the silo. Far from it. Every lawyer quickly learns that, though the law is beautiful in its complexity, reality is often more complex, while particular legislative or general law arrangements are insufficiently so. By its very nature, every application of the policies expressed in an open-textured rule to new situations supplements existing law. Particularly in modern industries, like biotechnology or information technology, in which national legislation lags behind technical or scientific developments, the most scrupulous application of the parties' choice of a national law may still require the identification of the relevant policies of that state and their extrapolation to new situations. In this sort of situation, supplementing law *infra* and *praeter legem* is sometimes required and proper; fashioning prescriptions *contra legem* is not. Wholly aside from the jurisdictional limit, aggressive law-making by international commercial arbitrators is ill-advised, because of the lack of aptitude of the international commercial arbitral process for law-making. I turn to that.

Modern law-making incorporates the efforts of many participants or stake-holders, all of whom bring both information about preferred policy and their respective views of the consequences of different arrangements on the aggregate goals of a community. This openness of the process of law-making is a critical part of the legitimacy of the

851

process. Now obviously, the many stake-holders have their own preferred outcomes, which will influence the information they gather and they will present it in a way most favorable to themselves. But the openness of the process and the wide range of participation ensure that a rich trove of information and a wide diversity of proposals will be available to the law-maker. Thus, the modern legislature, thanks to the structured openness of the law-making process, benefits from a wide range of viewpoints and rich and detailed projections of the probable consequences of the different alternatives available to it. In addition, the modern legislature, thanks to this open process, develops an acute sense of the relative power positions of different stakeholders, a factor which will be critical in securing economic implementation. This also alerts the law-maker to the intensity of the resistance which certain possible prescriptions are likely to encounter and, hence, the quantum of political capital which will have to be diverted for enforcement. Contrast this polycentric and information-rich process with three arbitrators, deciding a bilateral international commercial dispute in a process which is closed to the participation of all outsiders and could well be unknown to them. This arbitral process benefits from none of the advantages enjoyed by the modern law-maker. Hence arbitral efforts to play the role of Solon are likely to produce bad law, unenforceable law or both.[2]

II.   A FEW CONCERNS

Contracts presuppose a legal system. Ordinarily, one would expect those engaged in the competitive collaborative process of designing international commercial agreements between parties of different jurisdictions to select a system of national law which can recommend itself for its statutory precision, rich and relevant judicial illumination and

---

2. International investment arbitration, which has become quite distinct from international commercial arbitration even as it uses many of the same techniques, may have slightly more of a law-making vocation, for a host of reasons. For one thing, national courts are the default appliers for international commercial matters; investment tribunals are the default appliers for international investment disputes. It would be rather odd for a domestic lawyer, trying to determine the law of his or her jurisdiction to expect to digest, not the work of local courts but the work of international commercial tribunals applying that national law. By the same token, it would be odd, for a digest of international investment law, to include national judgments rather than the awards of international tribunals. Certainly international investment law, if it looks to public policy, should look to international public policy, if it is admissible. The law applied in investment arbitration is authentically international and not national as in commercial arbitration. Insofar as this arbitration continues to be more public and to experiment with being more open to outside participation, through, for example, amicus participation, the information and policy preferences of stakeholders other than the immediate parties to the dispute are increasingly brought to the attention of an investment tribunal. Moreover, the increasing practice of publishing international investment arbitral awards necessarily produces a body of jurisprudence which is available to parties and subsequent tribunals and can be evaluated on its merits by the college of international lawyers and only then given some precedential persuasion. But none of that applies to international commercial arbitration.

comparative research accessibility. So it can occasion no surprise, for example, that the law of New York or Delaware will be selected by American lawyers for contracts about corporate transactions or the law of Texas or Oklahoma will be selected for "farming-in" options in oil exploration contracts. The point is that national legal systems will be chosen.

There have been some curious exceptions to this common-sense practice. In an interesting sub-chapter in the history of international commercial arbitration, petroleum concessions concluded through the middle of the twentieth century – a period in which the jurisdictional theory of territoriality still prevailed – were subject to the law of the host state. Petroleum companies and, indeed, even arbitrators called upon to decide disputes arising under them chafed under this regime. The governing law was sometimes evaded or sometimes simply ignored by the arbitrators, as in Lord Asquith's astonishing award in the *Abu Dhabi* case. Governing law for these types of agreements was eventually contractually wrested from the host states by applicable law formulae on the order of "the law of the host state and international law and in case of a conflict between them general principles of law". This assured the application of international law or of general principles of law, a part of international law. But these were investment agreements with a state party and not commercial agreements between two private parties. In an investment, context, the imprecision of this sort of formula was apparently deemed preferable to the application of Libyan or Saudi law. The trend was finally confirmed by Maître Dupuy in *CALTEX v. Libya*.

On rare occasions, one will still find choices of international law as applicable or governing law in international commercial contracts or, indeed, governing law provisions that are even more idiosyncratic, like the inimitable clause in the *Aminoil v. Kuwait* arbitration:

> "The law governing the substantive issues between the Parties shall be determined by the Tribunal, having regard to the quality of the Parties, the transnational character of their relations and the principles of law and practice prevailing in the modern world."

Clearly, in cases in which the parties have selected international law, the same type of policy analysis and application I have proposed earlier would be applied, but now with respect to the animating policies of the pertinent parts of the corpus of international law. In addition, where a system of national law which has been selected by the parties incorporates international law, either as a supplement or a corrective to its own law, the same sorts of policy analyses with respect to international law would apply.

But when international law has *not* been adopted as governing law by the parties to an international commercial transaction nor directly incorporated and self-executing in the system of national law which was selected, would it not be inappropriate to allow a norm of international law to override the applicable norm of the national law selected by the parties on the ground that the international norm is "different" and "higher"? The issue does not turn on grand theories of monism or dualism but on common sense. That the norms are different is obvious. The predicate of the selection of governing law – the whole idea of bothering to make a selection – is that different legal systems address particular legal and factual issues differently. And, as for the relative "spatial" positions of different systems of law, when parties have the power to select the law which will govern their transaction, whether the law which they select is "higher" or "lower" is irrelevant. Imagine an international commercial arbitration tribunal deciding to apply to the construction of the commercial contract in dispute Art. 31 of the Vienna Convention on the Law of Treaties rather than the interpretative regime of the national governing law which the parties had selected on the ground that international law is "higher". Would not that be bizarre, if not a ground for annulment?

But is there some "transnational (or truly international) public policy", to borrow the title of Maître Lalive's famous report to ICCA in 1986, which can trump the national law that would otherwise govern the transaction and which should be applied by an international commercial arbitration tribunal? I am considerably more cautious than Maître Lalive about the space for – and propriety of – application of so-called international or transnational public policy in international commercial arbitration, though I acknowledge that it has on occasion been done. My own reservation is not simply Lord Burrough's acerbic observation that "public policy is never argued at all but when other points fail." My opposition to the use of international public policy in international commercial arbitration arises from systemic features of international commercial arbitration and of international law itself. Let me set out a few of my concerns:

First, international public policy is a term of almost unlimited and protean potential. In a decision this year by the Swiss Federal Tribunal, albeit on the use of public policy in the context of Art. V of the New York Convention and Art. 190(2) of the Swiss Law on Private International Law, the Court observed:

> "The fleeting character of public policy may be inherent to the concept, due to its excessive generality; the wide scope of the almost countless opinions proffered in this regard would tend to prove it.... As a commentator pointed out, all attempts to answer the numerous recurring questions raised by the interpretation of this concept merely resulted in raising further thorny or polemical question...."[3]

If that is the situation in Swiss law, imagine *a fortiori* what it is in international law! International law is rife with precatory statements. Moreover, not all of them were made with the intention of being effective; indeed, some were made with the intention of not being effective. International law abets this by maintaining categories of legal statements that are intended *not* to be binding or are subject to derogation on conditions to be determined by the derogating state itself. So-called "soft law" has become an industry in its own right. International public policy is indeed fleeting and the authorization of its application by international commercial arbitrators would lead to great uncertainty.

---

3. *Tensaccia S.P.A. v. Freyssinet Terra Armata R.L.* (March 8, 2006). The English translation of the judgment will be published, with a doctrinal note by Dr. Charles Poncet of the Geneva Bar, in the July issue of World Arbitration & Mediation Report. I am indebted to Dr. Poncet for an advance copy of the translation.

Second, even where international law has established a firm and not soft policy, it will often carefully exclude national and even specific international agencies from enforcing it. Recall George W. Bush's not implausible presumption that when important Chapter VII Security Council Resolutions concerning the maintenance of international security have been repeatedly ignored by the state to which they were directed, they may then be coercively enforced by self-selected willing states or coalitions of such states without additional UN authorization. As we all know, his presumption was resoundingly rejected. And it was no surprise to students of international law. Or consider the issue of slavery, apparently a favorite of those who urge transnational public policy to trump national law in arbitrations. Slavery is a practice which still persists and on the prohibition of which the international legal system has not distinguished itself. One of the reasons why is clearly explained in the famous nineteenth century *Le Louis* judgment. There Lord Stowell (then Sir William Scott) affirmed that British ships could not enforce a slavery prohibition against flag vessels of other nations, on the principle that no matter how reprehensible the practice, it was more important to maintain the freedom of the oceans which depended on the principle that no state could purport to exercise jurisdiction on the vessels of any other state. So the slave ship and its human cargo was permitted to go its way. In 1982, the United Nations Law of the Sea Convention in Art. 99 prescribed, in relevant part, that

> "Every State shall take effective measures to prevent and punish the transport of slaves in ships authorized to fly its flag and to prevent the unlawful use of its flag for that purpose."

Plus ça change, plus c'est la même chose. Yet using transnational public policy to hoist his bootstraps, the arbitrator who is so inclined may take the softest international law and simply present it as transnational public policy and thereby make it directly effective without regard to the way it would be handled in international law itself or the reasons why it would be handled that way.

Third, and related to the previous observation, is the extraordinary caution of international law about disturbing agreements, because they constitute one of its most important and most fragile lines of defense, itself built on the doctrine of *pacta sunt servanda*. While the Vienna Convention on the Law of Treaties nonetheless created a category of so-called peremptory norms or *jus cogens*, which have the effect of annulling any treaties that are inconsistent with them, the only *jus cogens* upon which the drafters of the Vienna Convention could agree was the prohibition of the use of force in Art. 2(4) of the UN Charter. Though the human rights advocacy bar and its literature are constantly discovering new *jus cogens*, to date only one international tribunal has applied the Vienna Convention's provision and, at that, in a way which seems quite bizarre. If international law is so careful about using a potentially disruptive device lest it disturb the effectiveness of international agreements, it would seem curious that international commercial arbitrators would invoke the "public policy" of the same international law to disturb the stability of expectation and effectiveness of international commercial agreements.

Fourth, public policy in domestic law is a legal concept with a verifiable judicial history. Not so in international law. When an alleged international public policy is given the force of law by an international commercial arbitral tribunal, it is not subjected to the discipline of customary international law analysis which requires that the state practice justifying the inference that a customary rule has been produced must be shown to be wide and extensive and to be accompanied by *opinio juris*. Without this discipline, the invocation of "transnational public policy" becomes an easy way for those claiming to have an insight into the heart and the soul of international law to effect their own preferences without having to prove that they have become customary international law.

Fifth, does international commercial arbitration really need such a slippery and malleable concept in order to protect its virtue? After all, what practice before an international commercial arbitration tribunal that has been alleged to violate an international or transnational public policy was permitted by the national governing *law*? Is there a national legal system that does not prohibit bribery of public officials? A national legal system that does not prohibit slavery....

If international public policies are treaty-based and their application extends to parties before an international commercial arbitral tribunal, then they can be applied as part of the governing law. If the policies have been confirmed by customary international law, then their application may be appropriate insofar as the governing national law incorporates customary international law. But if they are simply invoked as international public policy and that is their only basis in authority, I doubt that they have a proper role in international commercial arbitration.

And, finally, a personal plea. As a public international lawyer who believes that international law is a real and important system of law, I object to a concept whose notorious imprecision and subjectivity gives international law a bad name. The parties to an international commercial arbitration and the system of international law itself deserve better.

Transnational Public Policy

Catherine Kessedjian[*]

I. INTRODUCTION

Public policy has always been and indeed continues to be a hot topic. When public policy collides with arbitration, it becomes a burning issue. Some may wish to close their eyes and deny such a thing to avoid the risk of being burned. They flee when they hear the expression "transnational public policy" as if they had heard the worst curse ever. Unfortunately, denying it or running away won't make something disappear. A number of scholars have tried to shed light on the phenomenon but nobody really agrees on what transnational public policy is and how it should play out in arbitration.[1]

When Pierre Lalive used that expression for the first time in an article published in the Revue de l'arbitrage,[2] he felt compelled to add that he equated transnational public policy with a "truly international" public policy. We are not certain that this subtitle clarifies the concept, but we will try to elucidate this in light of the experience we have gained from the developments of the past twenty years (II). We will then turn to the question why arbitrators have to apply or consider transnational public policy when they

---

[*] Professor, Université Panthéon-Assas Paris II.

1. In the French language only and only in the past ten years, a number of monographs or collective works have been published which deal more or less with transnational public policy : Philippe KAHN and Catherine KESSEDJIAN, L'illicite dans le commerce international, (Paris, Litec 1996); Jean-Baptiste RACINE, L'arbitrage commercial international et l'ordre public (LGDJ, Bibliothèque de droit privé, vol. 309, 1999) ; Christophe SERAGLINI, Lois de police et justice arbitrale internationale (Paris, Dalloz 2001); Lotfy CHEDLY, Arbitrage commercial international et ordre public transnational (Tunis, Centre de publication universitaire 2002); Ali MEZGHANI, Méthodes de droit international privé et contrat illicite, Recueil des cours de l'Académie de droit international de La Haye, vol. 303 (2003); Alexandre COURT DE FONTMICHEL, L'arbitre, le juge et les pratiques illicites du commerce international (Paris, Editions Panthéon-Assas 2004); Homayoon ARFAZADEH, Ordre public et arbitrage international à l'épreuve de la mondialisation, (Bruylant, LGDJ, Schultess 2005). The concept of transnational public policy is discussed also in FOUCHARD, GAILLARD, GOLDMAN, Traité de l'arbitrage commercial international (Paris, Litec 1996), essentially at no.1525 et seq.; and by Jean-Francois POUDRET and SebastianBESSON, Droit comparé de l'arbitrage international (2003) nos. 708, 824 and 826.

2. Pierre LALIVE, "Ordre public transnational (ou réellement international) et arbitrage international", Rev. Arb. (1986) p. 329.

are confronted with cases that call for such an action. Finally, the purpose of this commentary is also to try to give some substance to a notion that is not yet well established in some parts of the world.

II.   WHAT IS TRANSNATIONAL PUBLIC POLICY?

Whether we like it or not, we are living in a world of legal pluralism. This means that transnational human activities, whether commercial or not, are no longer regulated only by State-made law. We may take a positivist attitude and deny the existence of legal pluralism. However, taking such an attitude will make it very difficult to describe with accuracy the world as it has evolved at least in the past two or three decades.[3] Many sources of law other than State law are available, including – not to a minor extent – norms created by the actors themselves. And this is not new. Indeed the central idea of Kant's philosophical system, "autonomous", i.e., "I am my own law", clearly shows that for any person (and hence entity), there is a good part of his or her activities which is regulated by norms created by that person or entity. In modern times, whether one accepts calling these norms lex mercatoria or gives them another name, or does not call them anything, does not change the nature of the process.[4] States are no longer the only source of law.[5]

And even when States are, in fine, the source of law – for example when they agree to adopt an international convention – very often, at least in the commercial areas, companies, the economic actors, are the ones who came up with the idea and even led the negotiations. Two recent examples of such a trend may be cited: the Hague Convention on the Law Applicable to Certain Rights in Respect of Securities Held with an Intermediary[6] and the Unidroit Convention on International Interests in Mobile Equipment.[7]

---

3. We are no historian and, thus, have no real way to say when the phenomenon started. One may also plead that even in ancient Greece, non-state-made law already existed as shown by some of Aristotle's best known pages. See for example, *Ethique de Nicomaque*, (GF Flammarion, vol. 43; *Politique*, Tel Gallimard, vol. 221).

4. J.-H. MOITRY, "*Arbitrage international et droit de la concurrence vers un ordre public de la lex mercatoria?*", Rev. Arb. (1989) p. 3.

5. For a more detailed analysis of this phenomenon, see Catherine KESSEDJIAN, "*Codification du droit commercial international et droit international privé – De la gouvernance normative pour les relations économiques transnationales*", Recueil des Cours de l'Académie de La Haye, vol. 300 (2004) passim. A number of authors, in recent years, have attributed this phenomenon to the globalization of the economy. Because the economy is global, "transnational" in nature, it calls for norms which are also global and transnational. For such a position, see Ali MEZGHANI, *op. cit.*, fn. 1, at p. 363; Homayoon ARFAZADEH, *op. cit.*, fn. 1, passim.

6. Adopted on 13 December 2002, this Convention was recently signed by the United States and Switzerland. The text and the status of the Convention are available on <www.hcch.net>.

7. Adopted in 2001, it came into force on 1 April 2004. The text and the status of the Convention are available on <www.unidroit.org>.

There are limits to what an actor on the international scene may do. Those limits fall into three categories, national public policy or mandatory rules; international public policy and transnational public policy. The three concepts must be distinguished. Ideally, in a world where all fundamental values of human dignity and well-being were to be achieved universally, the three notions should not be different. But in our world, they are still different and will remain so for a long time.

National public policy is the most commonly used. It is comprised of those fundamental rules, developed by each State, which are of utmost importance for that State's society and from which citizens (and very often residents) of that State cannot derogate. It is territorial in nature. In order to apply those rules we must conduct a conflict-of-laws analysis. Obviously, if they are included in the law chosen by the parties, they must be applied by arbitrators as part of that law. However, this is not the only time when they must be applied. In international arbitration, they must be applied because the place of arbitration is located in that country. Indeed, if the lex arbitri contains some mandatory rules which call for their application even in international matters, they have to be applied by the arbitral tribunal in order for the award to be fully secure in the country where the arbitration takes place. The third possibility, much more difficult in practice, is to look at the law of the country (and perhaps countries) where the award will be enforced or is likely to be enforced. We are all familiar with the weaknesses of the conflict analysis.[8] One of the ways to fight against these weaknesses is to allow room for the concept of transnational public policy[9] because, as we will see below, transnational public policy norms impose their force on everyone. Indeed, if arbitrators have considered the norms of transnational public policy they greatly reduce the risks that their award will be contrary to the public policy of the country of enforcement.[10]

International public policy is of a different nature but is still State-made law. It consists of norms, included in international conventions that are in force, that are mandatory in nature, i.e., from which the parties cannot derogate. The obvious example is taken from Arts. 11, 29 and the whole second part of the Vienna Convention on International Sales of Goods, which the parties cannot exclude or derogate from, when the Convention applies, in accordance with Art. 12, although they may exclude or derogate from any other rule of the text. In order for such international public policy to apply, the Convention must be applicable to the case by its own rules or must be applicable because it has been incorporated into a national law deemed to be applicable

---

8. See for example, R. PRIOUX, "*Le droit international privé et les contrats illicites dans le commerce international*", Journal des Tribunaux (1990) pp. 733-739.

9. Ali MEZGHANI, *op. cit.*, fn. 1, at p. 363:

"*L'éclatement des ordres étatiques n'est pas de nature à permettre la saisie de l'illicite qui prend, lui, une dimension transnationale. La compétence d'un seul ordre juridique et la mise en œuvre de ses solutions ne sont pas de nature à saisir l'ensemble du processus illicite.*"

10. As already stated, ideally all countries should have the norms of transnational public policy embedded in their own legal system.

to the case at issue.[11] In the latter situation, that national law is either applicable as the law chosen by the parties, or as the one the arbitral tribunal deems applicable in the absence of choice by the parties; or it is the law of the place of the arbitration or that of the place of enforcement. Hence, we, again, fall into the same conflict analysis as for national public policy. In our view, international public policy may not apply apart from those cases. It has no standing on its own, unless the situation at issue clearly falls into its ambit, via the activity of the State "interested" in the case.[12] Consequently, if a State has not ratified a convention, and even if that convention has entered into force and contains some mandatory provisions, these provisions are not part of the international public policy for that State. Apart from Conventions, an international public policy may also stem from what is now called *jus cogens*. But we all know that the concept of *jus cogens* is still a controversial one and States resent applying those norms they have not fully accepted. If a State law that has incorporated neither mandatory norms of international conventions nor norms of *jus cogens* is deemed applicable to the case, it is not international public policy that will help in rendering a better award but, rather, transnational public policy.

Transnational public policy is of a different species. This is one of the reasons we said earlier that we thought it was unclear and not very useful when we try to explain that concept by saying it is a "truly international" public policy.[13] First, by using the word "international", we are doomed to confuse the phenomenon we want to describe with the classic international public policy as defined in the preceding paragraph. Second the adverb "truly" is unfortunate because it adds some qualification impossible to prove and does not lead the interpreter either to the sources or to a method which is useful in finding its content. Hence, we prefer to explain the concept for what it is and not to try to compare it with something else.[14] Thus, if transnational public policy has a meaning, it is outside the ambit of the State in two ways.

---

11. The expression "incorporate into national law" is closer to dualist systems whereby international conventions must be transposed into national law by a domestic legislation. But in our view it also covers the monist systems whereby an international convention is directly applicable in a country once it has been ratified and has generally entered into force.

12. The concept of "State interested in a case" is a vague one and has no legal characteristic. It simply means that the dispute deals with circumstances which, partly or wholly, are located in the territory of that State: be it the localization of one or more parties; the performance of the activities at issue or some of them; the use of the banking system of that country, etc.

13. Of course, it is quite understandable that Professor Lalive did so at a time when he had invented the concept and he wanted to make sure his idea would be well understood.

14. For a confusion between international and transnational public policy, see the ILA New Dehli Resolution 2/2002 adopted upon the proposal of the Committee on International Commercial Arbitration which explains in Sect. 2 (b):

"... the existence ... of a consensus within the international community as regards the principle under consideration (international conventions may evidence the existence of such a consensus) ... [may allow the use of] the term 'transnational public policy' ... to describe such norms".

(in Report of the Seventieth Conference (2002) p. 18).

First, part of transnational public policy is created by non-State actors. This is not to say that States are necessarily excluded. Indeed, they may want to participate in the process and very often do. But they are not at the origin of the norm. Sometimes they arrive very late in the creation process. The issue of corruption is a good example of this. There is much literature to show that bribery is unanimously condemned not only by societies around the world, but also by the major religious and moral schools of thought.[15] State-made law long condemned corruption of local government officials, but States could not agree on an international norm to fight corruption in foreign countries. However, some corporations had already incorporated into their own codes of conduct unilateral norms explaining that it was the company's policy not to obtain business via corruption. Nowadays, the example is less interesting since there is the OECD Convention.[16] But it is not entirely obsolete because the OECD Convention is limited in its scope and there are some aspects of corruption that are still not regulated by international law. For this reason some aspects of the fight against corruption still fall under transnational public policy.[17]

Second, the other part of transnational public policy is comprised of norms created by governmental international organizations which are not conventional in nature (guidelines, recommendations, best practices etc. …); or, if they are conventional, they are not ratified by States; or if ratified, even by a large majority of States, not by all of them. Let's take an example outside commercial law, but on a topic that has great impact on economic activities: the rights of children. Who can deny that the values incorporated into the UN Convention on the Rights of Children are transnational public policy and can be imposed on market actors around the world? Who can deny that this is true even if those actors come from a country that has not ratified the Convention? Who can deny that, far from the legal niceties imposed by some States (for example, the fact that those rights are not directly enforceable), these values must be applied each time there is an occasion to do so.

In conclusion of this first section, we would say that transnational public policy is composed of mandatory norms which may be imposed on actors in the market either because they have been created by those actors themselves or by civil society at large, or because they have been widely accepted by different societies[18] around the world.[19]

---

15. See, for example, Philip M. NICHOLS, "Outlawing Transnational Bribery Through the World Trade Organisation", 28 Law and Pol'y Int'l Bus. (1997) p. 305 at pp. 318-321.

16. The Convention on Combating Bribery of Foreign Public Officials in International Business Transactions of 21 November 1997 entered into force on 15 February 1999. It was in force in thirty-six countries as of 25 November 2005.

17. In a collection of papers published by the American University International Law Review, (vol. 20, no. 5) Andrew DE LOBTINIÈRE MCDOUGALL explains the problem of arbitrations intended to disguise the criminal origin of assets. These cases are telling for the necessity of transnational public policy that applies regardless of the national law applicable to the dispute.

18. We avoid using the expression "international community" as it is a somewhat difficult concept and also a fairly controversial one.

19. Compare our definition with that given by the report of the ILA Committee on International Commercial Arbitration at the London meeting in 2000.

These norms aim at being universal.[20] They are the sign of the maturity of the international communities (that of the merchants and that of the civil societies) who know very well that there are limits to their activities.[21]

III.   WHY SHOULD ARBITRATORS APPLY TRANSNATIONAL PUBLIC POLICY?

The first factor in why arbitrators should apply transnational public policy is one for which very little controversy will exist. Even though arbitration, nowadays, is being criticized, its scope of application is continuously increasing. Many activities that were not amenable to dispute resolution via arbitration some years ago are no longer excluded from it, be it labour relations, consumer activities, family matters, intellectual property, investment disputes, and even public policy issues such as competition or some matters where an embargo has been imposed by the United Nations.[22] Consequently, arbitrators have more and more powers. The development of the law is now left in their hands. The regulation of society is left in their hands. The regulation of transnational activities is

---

"The concept of 'transnational public policy' ... comprises fundamental rules of natural law, principles of universal justice, *jus cogens* of public international law, and the general principles of morality accepted by what are referred to as 'civilised nations'."

(in Report of the Sixty-Ninth Conference, London, 2000, pp. 345 and 346. The meeting in London was reported by Loukas MISTELLIS, "Keeping the Unruly Horse in Control or Public Policy as a Bar to Enforcement of (Foreign) Arbitral Awards", 2 International Law Forum (2000) p. 248.

20. Kant's *radikal bose,* may be summarized in this one sentence: "Always act under such a maxim that you would also want it to become a universal law" (our interpretation and translation). It is not without interest to read again Richard Hare, the main representative of the twentieth century ethical theory called "universal prescriptivism". For Hare, a moral judgment is both prescriptive and universal or capable of becoming universal. In *Freedom and Reason* (Oxford University Press 1963) p. 123, Hare explains that in order for a moral judgment to be justified, it must be equally legitimate for all parties concerned with the situation. Hare remains a utilitarian because he prescribes that when confronted with contradictory interests, the moral judgment must aim at the maximization of all interests at stake (HARE and his critics, *Essays on Moral Thinking* (Oxford University Press 1988) with comments by Hare himself on each essay, pp. 199-293).

21. The late Philippe Fouchard had it right when he started his speech at the Académie des Sciences Morales et Politiques with a few thoughts about virtue. He explained that: *"... le bien commun international [exige] que l'on s'abstienne de faire commerce avec n'importe quoi"* and that *"[la vertu] consisterait à renoncer aux profits attendus de tels échanges".*

See Philippe FOUCHARD, *"Droit et morale dans les relations économiques internationales"*, Revue des Sciences morales et politiques (1998) p. 1 at p. 5.

22. We know that in many countries, labour law matters were arbitrable for a long time before this became true in a large majority of countries. We also know that it is now widely accepted that a matter is arbitrable even though it may involve public policy issues, but this has not always been the case. See the embargo case decided by the Quebec Court of Appeals on 31 March 2003, Rev. Arb. (2003) p. 1365.

also left in their hands. When States started to use arbitration clauses in their bilateral agreements on investment, they probably did not foresee the important development this would lead to and they did not foresee that many of the disputes would be resolved by persons who were more used to solving pure commercial disputes rather than public affairs. Power does not accrue without responsibility. And we probably would all agree that it is a huge responsibility for arbitrators to decide on a number of disputes that may have an impact on a large number of people in addition to the parties to the dispute themselves. This is why not everybody can be entrusted to be an arbitrator in all cases. This is why we have to think twice before accepting cases when we are already overloaded with current work. This is why we have to be very careful when money becomes the only driving force and arbitrating becomes nothing other than a business.

This is not to say that our topic does not entail an analysis of the balance of interests. On one side there is the development we just highlighted; on the other side, arbitrators are entrusted by parties who ask them to resolve a dispute which, at first glance, is privy to them. Reasonable expectations of the parties[23] should not be subject to surprises and very often, there will be no public interest at stake in that dispute and no room for transnational public policy to apply. It would be far from us to say that transnational public policy has to apply in each and every case. However, if we find ourselves in the presence of a clear norm of transnational public policy, how can it be said to be contrary to the parties' expectations? They must know the content of that public policy and have the means to respect it. In addition, arbitrators, as major actors in society, must be aware and alert and must recognize the cases in which fundamental norms are at stake. They must do their job in calling the parties' attention to the problem and asking them to discuss it fully. It would be a disservice to the parties, to the arbitration process and to society at large to say that arbitrators can only look at issues which have been posed by the parties. By doing so, they would become accomplice to the grossest violations of transnational public policy and fuel the debate against arbitration that has already started. In the arbitration process as in all dispute resolution mechanisms, the tribunal is faced with facts, circumstances, documents, testimonies and it is for the parties and the arbitrators together to formulate the issues at stake. We all know that the art of drafting the terms of reference is a difficult one because it must do justice to the matters in dispute, only the matters in dispute, but all the matters in dispute.

A few years ago, we might have argued that, after all, the award would be subsequently examined by a national judge, either at the review or enforcement level, and that the most important violations would be condemned under the exception of public policy which is the one exception always invoked by the parties and present in all the lex arbitrii around the world and in international conventions. This may have been true before but is no longer the case. Indeed, studies have shown that judges are very reluctant to use the public policy exception and that among all the cases where a party

---

23. We are avoiding the usual and often-heard claim for legal certainty. Indeed, in the world in which we live, nothing is certain, far from it. The law, in most countries, has become so detailed, so specific, so numerous, that legal certainty has become an expression devoid of real meaning. International/transnational law is not immune from this disease.

has tried to use it, very few have succeeded.[24] And this is the second reason why arbitrators must apply transnational public policy. Indeed, even before the most recent developments regarding the public policy exception in the enforcement of awards in some national case law, it was doubtful that a national court would apply something other than its own concept of public policy. For example, a judge would probably never have applied a *jus cogens* norm stemming from a convention its country would not have ratified, even less so some transnational public policy. But now that the public policy exception is left for exceptional cases, there is very little chance that a judge would do what the arbitrators have not done. It is also true that domestic public policy regarding international activities shrinks every day and that, at least in countries such as France or Switzerland, there are very few cases in which a judge has nullified an award on public policy grounds.

The latest development in this respect is worrisome for society. It is, in fact, a decision by the Swiss Federal Court rendered on 8 March 2006 which has already triggered many comments[25] and which seems to lead the way for an ever-decreasing control, at the enforcement level, of awards. By saying that competition law is not part of a universal concept of public policy, the highest Swiss court is certainly going too far given that since the 1960s as many as ninety-seven countries have now started to have sophisticated competition rules. And even countries in which such rules still do not exist, who today could argue that if these countries aim at establishing a market economy (which is what all of them – even China – want, apart from North Korea and perhaps Cuba) they have to establish some kind of competition safeguard. A market economy without competition is an oxymoron. However, even if we disagree with what the Federal Court has done, it remains the law in Switzerland and it increases the role and responsibility of arbitrators.

Some may argue that arbitrators lack legitimacy. This argument is very close to the one that says that outside the parties' mandate the arbitrators have no legitimacy. We have already answered that argument and we wish to tackle the legitimacy issue in a broader context. It is true that, at first glance, arbitrators have no legitimacy – no more, no less for that matter, than national judges. They are not elected through a democratic process and even in countries where judges are elected, the process is very often criticized. Having said that, however, we would argue that arbitrators' legitimacy[26] is one "by default", one which exists de facto for lack of a better system. Currently, the parliamentarian democratic system is widely criticized for a number of reasons, one of which is the lack of trust citizens have in politicians. In addition, the contractualization of activities essentially via self-regulation and the lack of true societal regulation via

---

24. In France, this is demonstrated every year by the cases rendered by the Paris Court of Appeals and the *Cour de cassation* as published by the Revue de l'arbitrage.
25. 1ère *Cour civile*, 4P.278/2005, extracts Bulletin ASA (2006) p. 363.
26. The same is true for judges' legitimacy.

preventive norms have rendered the role of the judge or the arbitrator an essential one for the regulation of society.[27]

If we turn now to the process itself, it is not the first time that arbitrators would apply norms that are different from those chosen by the parties or those, absent such a choice, they deem applicable to the case. We have not conducted a thorough analysis of arbitration practice for that purpose, but there is no doubt that the practice exists.[28] Let's take only one example. In a special activity like sports, it is not uncommon that the *Tribunal Arbitral du Sport* (TAS) would apply different norms (for example, those of the European Union) even though Swiss law applied to the cases.[29] The duty to apply a transnational public policy probably will be upheld in the right cases by some national judges. Indeed, the existence and working of the very concept was already accepted by Lord Steyn in his speech for the House of Lords decision in *Kuwait Airways Corp. v. Iraqi Airways Co.*[30] It was used to deny any effect to a foreign law applicable to the matter. It is clear to us that any norm of transnational public policy, if clearly identifiable and identified, will have to be used against the outcome under the applicable law if that law violates the transnational public policy norm. The criticism often heard against such a proposal is that the parties are mainly interested in the enforcement of the award. Applying public policy norms against the applicable law is often said to put the award at risk of not being enforced in the State whose law was displaced.[31] This is only partially true. Arbitration is a consensual process and by choosing such a process, parties commit themselves to respect the result.[32] Most of the time, the award is willingly enforced by the losing party. If not, very often the choice is between rendering an award refusing the remedy requested and hence there will be nothing to enforce, or accepting the remedy contrary to the applicable law and hence being able to enforce the award in a number of countries, even if not in the country whose law was displaced. This was the very option in the *Kuwait Airways* case. In many countries an award may be enforced over a

---

27. This is far from being the only example where private means of regulation and enforcement have replaced public means. See also, the private policing of corruption with compliance officers now at work in a number of large corporations and private independent firms whose job is to police the activities of other firms. Michael LEVI, "Private policing of corruption" in Cyrille FIJNAUT and Leo HUBERTS, *Corruption, Integrity and Law Enforcement* (Kluwer Law International 2002) pp. 443-452.

28. We can cite at least two awards: GAFTA, 11 January 1982, ICCA *Yearbook Commercial Arbitration* VIII (1983) p.158; ICC no. 6320 (1992), JDI (1995) p. 986 note D.H.

29. TAS 98/200 award of 20 August 1999, *AEK Athènes and SK Slavia Prague v. UEFA*; TAS 98/201, award of 7 January 2000, *Celtic Pic v. UEFA*. For an award applying Art. 1 of the Dutch Constitution when Swiss law was applicable to the case, see TAS award of 3 June 2003 *PSV Eindhoven v. UEFA*, JDI (2004) p. 294, note E. LOQUIN.

30. [2002] UKHL 19, para. 115.

31. This argument is found inter alia in William PARK, *Arbitration of International Business Disputes* (New York, Oxford University Press 2006) at p. 494.

32. William PARK, "The nature of arbitral authority: A comment on *Lesotho Highlands*", 21 Arbitration International (2005) p. 483.

long period of time,[33] so that it is quite possible to find assets belonging to the losing party somewhere in a country that will accept to enforce the award.

IV.   WHERE TO FIND THE CONTENT OF TRANSNATIONAL PUBLIC POLICY?

This is the most difficult part of our inquiry. For many, transnational public policy is no more than the result of the arbitrator's sense of morality or ethics. Hence, it becomes too uncertain, fuzzy and, therefore, dangerous, to be applied in practice. In the following paragraphs we will demonstrate that sources of transnational public policy are more concrete than just the arbitrator's ethics even though these certainly do play a role in the analysis, at least in the identification of the problem.[34]

Let's start by saying where transnational public policy should not be found. First, it should not be found in international conventions already in force. Indeed, any policy codified in positive international law is part of international public policy as defined earlier in this paper. For example, for any proceeding taking place in Europe, Art. 6 of the European Human Rights Convention is part of international public policy. The only time when an international convention may be part of transnational public policy is when a few States have begun to use it but it has not yet gained wide adherence, or even if it has, for cases in which the applicable law would not lead to the application of that particular convention. In such a case, a norm included in a convention may be considered as sufficiently established to be taken into consideration or even applied by an arbitral tribunal.

Second, transnational public policy is not to be found in national law. Whether some States have developed the same norms as those found in transnational public policy adds some credibility to them but is not consubstantial to them. Hence, the number of States that have gone in the same direction does not matter.

The content of transnational public policy, in the arbitration context, deals both with procedure and substance. For the procedural side of it, we will take two examples, one from arbitration practice and one from a document issued by a think tank.

When dealing with procedural aspects of the arbitration process, it is now amply demonstrated that arbitration practice has created uniform rules of procedure specifically crafted for arbitration purposes.[35] Some of these rules have lent themselves to an exercise in private codification, for example, the rules of evidence of the IBA or the more controversial IBA rules on conflicts of interest. However, not all of these

---

33. In most civil law countries, an award may be enforced for a period of thirty years from the date it was rendered. In many common law jurisdictions, even if the first period is shorter, the award may always be "revived" for enforcement purposes.

34. In the context of this commentary, we will not discuss whether transnational public policy has now formed a separate ethical order. For such a proposal, see Ali MEZGHANI, *op. cit.*, fn. 1, at p. 406: "*L'ordre spontané autorégulé: l'éthique*". See also our paper for the conference organized in Alexandria (Egypt) in honour of Philippe Fouchard, entitled: "*L'éthique dans les relations économiques internationales*" (Paris, Pedone 2006) pp. 229-264.

35. See, for example, D. HASCHER, "*Principes et pratique de procédure dans l'arbitrage commercial international*", 29 RCADI (1999) (The Hague, Martinus Nijhoff Publishers 2000) pp. 55-193.

uniform practice rules can be characterized as public policy norms. Only those considered the most fundamental for arbitration practice (equality of the parties, due process, and the like) may be said to be part of a transnational procedural public policy. Again, let's take an example. Perhaps we will all agree that, in appropriate cases, the principle according public access to arbitration proceedings, either through full participation in the hearings or by a more modest *amicus curiae* written submission only, has become part of transnational procedural public policy. The analysis conducted by the arbitral tribunal in the ICSID case *Aguas Argentinas S.A. et al, v. Argentine Republic*[36] is probably the best analysis so far of the type of considerations to be scrutinized by arbitrators before allowing such participation. A quote from the tribunal's order best illustrates this idea:

> "[i]n examining the issues at stake in the present case, the Tribunal finds that the present case potentially involves matters of public interest ... [t]he factor that gives this case particular public interest is that the investment dispute centers around the water distribution and sewage systems of a large metropolitan area, the city of Buenos Aires and surrounding municipalities".

The tribunal then concluded: "Any decision rendered in this case ... has the potential to affect the operation of those systems and thereby the public they serve."[37]

A second example may be found in what today is called "grey literature", such as the work of legal scholars and practitioners within the framework of think tanks such as the International Law Association. This is the case of the ILA resolution adopted in 1996 saying that the principle "*le criminel tient le civil en l'état*" is not a principle of public policy for arbitration purposes.[38] Hence, according to the arbitration specialists who worked under the auspices of the ILA, an arbitral tribunal may consider that a pending criminal case will have an impact on its decision and decide to suspend arbitral proceedings to await the criminal decision, but it is not obliged to do so. Some may regret that criminal proceedings are not given a prominent, influential role, including in international arbitration, as it is sometimes considered that criminal law crystallizes the "ethics" of globalization.[39] However, criminal proceedings are very often too parochial in nature

---

36. ARB/03/19. Order on Petition for Transparency and Participation as Amicus Curiae, 19 May 2005.
37. Para. 19 of the Order of 19 May 2005.
38. Resolution adopted at the Helsinki meeting of the ILA:

    "The fact that a pending or forthcoming court case, whether civil or criminal, is related to an arbitral proceeding should not, in itself, cause the discontinuation or suspension of the arbitral proceedings."

39. The expression is that of Mireille DELMAS-MARTY, "*Le droit pénal comme éthique de la mondialisation*", Rev. Sc. Crim. (2004) p. 1. See also Jean-Baptiste RACINE, "*La contribution de l'ordre public européen à l'élaboration d'un ordre public transnational en droit de l'arbitrage*", Law and European Affairs (2005 no. 2) p. 227 at p. 229.

and are but one of the many other ways to enforce public policy norms considered as paramount to arbitral proceedings.[40]

On the substantive side of the concept, inspiration may be derived from the principles of Corporate Social Responsibility[41] which have been developed both in the United States and via informal transnational groups such as the *Table ronde de Caux*.[42] These principles are currently discussed extensively at least within the United Nations[43] and the European Union.[44] They are elaborated through a process different from the traditional processes of norm creation. It is done either unilaterally by corporations themselves,[45] or within the framework of NGOs, or under the auspices of an international governmental organization but essentially by non-state actors, corporations not being the last ones to participate. The latest example comes from the investment community. On 27 April 2006, the Secretary General of the United Nations came to the Stock Exchange in New York City where he launched the Principles for Responsible Investment.[46] Those Principles were prepared by a group of leaders from the investment community with no participation from States. The institutions involved manage two trillion dollars in assets. The Principles are "a set of global best practice which offer a path for integrating environmental, social and governance criteria into investment analysis and ownership practices".

The case of competition law is an interesting one. We will dare posing as a given that, in our globalized, market-oriented society, competition is a must and should be safeguarded each time it is put in jeopardy. This is one of the prices to pay for more freedom in economic activities. We would also say that competition has now become a universal policy. Having said that, we do not necessarily disagree with the Swiss Federal Court when it says that competition rules are not universal. If the policy is universal, it is true that rules remain different from one country to another, from one continent to another. However, as comparative law often teaches, commonalities are

---

40. This principle was recently upheld by the French *Cour de cassation* in *Société Omenex v. Hugon*, Civ. 1, 25 October 2005, Rev. Arb. (2006) p.103, note J.-B. RACINE; D. 2005 pp. 3052 and 3060, obs. Th. CLAY, D. 2006, p. 199, *avis* J. SAINTE ROSE, JDI (2006) note F.-X. TRAIN. Several decisions of the Paris Court of Appeal had been previously decided in the same way. See Paris 23 May 2002 and 20 June 2002, Rev. Arb. (2002) p. 971. The Swiss Federal Court (ATF 119, 1993, II, 386) also decided similarly. However, we also know that it is still not accepted in Tunisia and the Emirates. See Rev. Arb. (1993) p. 229. It is to be noted that the rule as defined by the French *Cour de cassation* in 2005 does not apply at the review or enforcement level, where the principle "*le criminal* etc. ..." is still applicable as long as the criminal proceedings take place in France.

41. The concept is now used outside the United States. See, for France, Michèle DESCOLONGES and Bernard SAINCY, *Les entreprises seront-elles un jour responsables?* (Paris, La Dispute 2004).

42. In 1986, business leaders from Europe, the Americas and Japan, meet in Caux for the first time to develop the principles leading to a "moral capitalism". See <www.cauxroundtable.org>.

43. See mainly the UN Global Compact. See also Resolution no. 2003/16 of the Human Rights Sub-commission; the decision no. 2004/116 of the Human Rights Commission and its resolution no. 2005/69.

44. See the European Forum for Corporate Social Responsibility and the Green Paper of July 2001.

45. For a very good set of working principles as they apply in the day-to-day activity of a bank, see the yearly reports published by Rabobank at <www.rabobank.com>.

46. <http://www.unpri.org/principles/>.

more numerous than divergences even if it is more fun and fashionable to stress the differences than the convergences. Hence if arbitrators are asked to render a decision on an activity they consider a violation of competition principles, and even if neither party has raised the matter, they should call the parties' attention to and ask them to discuss the issue. The next question is: What precise rules should they apply? They should conduct, with the help of the parties, a comparative law analysis and see how the matter is treated in different countries and try to find a common ground. If no common ground can be found, it may mean that the transnational public policy is not certain enough yet and, therefore, if no national rule is applicable, use the rule of the place of arbitration. This is not entirely satisfactory but it may be the best-possible solution for the time being.

Last but not least, transnational public policy is about human dignity and fundamental principles without which our society would be tantamount to a nightmare. Let's imagine that an arbitral tribunal is confronted with a dispute between a buyer and a seller, the buyer refusing to pay the price of the "goods". Let's further imagine that the "goods" are in fact human organs which have been taken from human beings, at best under uncertain conditions, at worst against their will. Let's finally assume the law chosen by the parties in their contract has no provision prohibiting such a sale. Would the tribunal stand by and decide the matter as if the contract were dealing with any goods? For us, the answer is clearly "no". The contract should be nullified. And if some "goods" have already been delivered, the buyer should have to pay the price into some kind of escrow account to be used for the people who have been deprived of their integrity.

For a less dramatic case, let's assume that a company has issued a code of conduct with principles of fair dealing towards its clients, partners, agents and distributors. Let's further imagine that a dispute arises between that company and one of its distributors regarding the implementation of the distributorship agreement that contains an arbitration clause. It would be the duty of the arbitral tribunal to take into consideration unilateral declarations of the corporation in its code of conduct, if pertinent to the dispute, as a measure of the corporation's liability, if any, even if the corporation's acts were not illegal per se under the applicable law. Such a view seems to be a consequence of the bone fide principle which is clearly part of transnational public policy.

A similar analysis could be done for arms traffic and other kinds of traffic still not covered by international law.

To conclude this section of our inquiry, we would propose that transnational public policy contains both prohibitions and positive obligations. On the prohibition side, we would list corruption; fictitious schemes; tax evasion; abuse of dominant position and other unfair practices; and dealing in dangerous goods. On the positive obligations side, we find the sustainable protection of the environment, human dignity, health, cultural objects and social justice.[47] International commercial economic activities cannot be isolated from the needs and interests of society at large.

---

47. The Japanese precept of *kyosei* is very helpful: live and work together for the common good by reconciling cooperation and mutual prosperity with fair competition.

V.   CONCLUSION

At the end of the analysis, we wish to stress that any application of transnational public policy goes along with at least two major, strong principles. First, arbitrators who wish to apply a transnational policy must always give ample room for discussion by the parties, who should not be taken by surprise. Second, arbitrators should operate with self-restraint. Not all cases, far from it, may lend themselves to such an analysis. In addition, the norms of transnational public policy are very often not in the form of hard, black-letter rules. Most of the time, they would take the form of principles or just policies. Hence, the role of the arbitrator is often a delicate one in drawing the fine line beyond which it will allow interference of a transnational policy to influence the decision to be rendered. It is not suitable for arbitrators who wish to apply a legal norm mechanically. But it is in tune with the great powers arbitrators enjoy nowadays.

Fred Vargas, speaking through her main character Adamsberg in her latest published thriller,[48] explains that human beings tend to complicate things. But when they complicate them, they understand them better and when they understand them better, they finally simplify them. Transnational public policy follows exactly the same mental path: it may seem complicated at first glance. But if we truly try to understand it, it is, in the end, fairly simple.

---

48. Fred VARGAS, *Dans les bois éternels,* (Paris, Viviane Hamy 2006).

Comments on Commercial Arbitration and Transnational Public Policy

*Alan Redfern**

I.   LEX ARBITRI AND APPLICABLE LAW

The *Aminoil* arbitration, to which Professor Reisman refers in his paper,[1] was based on an ad hoc submission to arbitration. The parties agreed that the *law* governing the oil concession between the Government of Kuwait and the American Independent Oil Company was to be determined by the Tribunal,

> "having regard to the quality of the parties, the transnational character of their relations and the principles of law and practice prevailing in the modern world".

The team of lawyers representing Aminoil included Pierre Lalive; and it is not fanciful to see his influence in the reference to the "transnational character" of the parties' relationship and the "principles of law prevailing in the modern world". Indeed, two years after the *Aminoil* Award, and precisely twenty years ago at a similar event to this, Pierre Lalive gave his seminal talk on "Transnational (or Truly International) Public Policy".

Even twenty years ago, the term "transnational law" was not a new one. In his lectures at Yale, thirty years earlier, Judge Jessup had referred to "transnational law" as a term that included:

> "all law which regulates actions or events that transcend national frontiers. Both public and private international law are included, as are other rules which fit into such standard categories."

This is a very wide remit. Any scholar, charged with the task of codifying such law, would be entitled to shed a bitter tear. Now, for the purpose of this discussion, the elusive concept of "transnational law" is refined to the equally elusive concept of "transnational public policy". The vagrant nature of national (or domestic) public policy is well recognized: "uncertainly and ambiguity as to its actual content is one of its

---

* One Essex Court, London.
1. See this volume, pp. 849-856 at p. 853.

essential characteristics", as Julian Lew has said. Public policy changes as public convictions or beliefs change. At any one time and in any one country, it may or may not be against public policy to allow the consumption of alcohol, or on-line gambling, or the payment of interest on loans. Transnational public policy, which Pierre Lalive called "truly international" public policy, is perhaps built on less shifting sands.

Professor Hunter[2] has suggested that transnational public policy is better called "supra-national": it is meant to reflect "*internationally* and *commonly* recognized shared values of morality". This strikes me as a useful definition; but whilst the word "morality" may, for example, encompass the principle of compensation for breach of an international obligation, or for the unlawful seizure of property, it may well need to be extended to cover, for instance, environmental harm.

Considerations of transnational public policy may very well have an important role to play in arbitrations involving states (as in the *Aminoil* arbitration); and this is even more likely in the new, growth-industry of international investment arbitrations, where references to public international law, to governmental policies and decrees, to the general principles of law and so forth are likely to be commonplace. But there is a distinct, parallel universe – that of international *commercial* arbitration. Whilst international investment arbitrations may catch the headlines, considerably more purely commercial international disputes are being settled by arbitral tribunals throughout the world. The amounts at stake may run into millions of dollars; the survival of one or other of the parties may depend upon it; and yet there will be no reference to transnational law or to its offspring, transnational public policy.

This is not due to some legal lacuna. On the contrary, many different systems of law may bear on an international commercial arbitration. These include the law of the place of performance of the contract; the law governing the substantive issues in dispute ("the applicable law"); the law of the place of arbitration (the lex arbitri); and the law, or laws, of the place of enforcement of the arbitral award. Most commercial arbitrators, however, will be concerned with only two systems of law: the lex arbitri and the applicable law. The *lex arbitri* will depend upon the place of arbitration. The applicable law will generally be chosen by the parties, but in default will be chosen by the arbitral tribunal itself.

Taking the applicable law first, this may itself be international law[3] or it may, as Professor Reisman has noted, be a formulae devised by the parties ("ex aequo et bono", "general principles of law recognized by civilized nations" and so forth). Usually, however, the applicable law will be a recognized legal system organized on a national or state level (which I refer to as a "national law" or a "national legal system").

Where international law or transnational public policy finds expression through the *applicable law*, whether because this is international law or a certain devised formulae or because, as Professor Reisman recognised, the applicable law may give effect to international law or to international or transnational public policy, the application of such rules of international or transnational public policy as may clearly be found to exist

---

2. HUNTER and E. SILVA, "Transnational Public Policy and Its Application in Investment Arbitrations," The Journal of World Investment, June 2003, Volume 4, No.3 at 378

3. See, for example, *Republic of Ecuador v. Occidental Exploration and Production Co* [2006] 2 WLR 70,93

would seem unexceptional. The arbitrator in such a case is not applying international or transnational public policy as a separate body of rules. He or she is simply applying it as part of the applicable law, which is after all the law governing the parties' agreement. (Application of mandatory rules in this way is as inevitable as it is unobjectionable. The reality is that the range of legal issues which can and should properly be considered amenable to party autonomy is limited. No legal system will or should allow the criminality of an agreement, or of the agreed conduct, to depend upon the law chosen to govern the agreement. Nor will (or should) any legal system allow the same result to be obtained through an arbitration agreement.) It is when the applicable law is inconsistent with, and in Professor Reisman's words "may be trumped by", rules of international or transnational public policy, that one can see the first question begin to arise. Even then, however, it may well be that the lex arbitri requires the arbitrator to give effect to such public policies. The *applicable law* may be inconsistent with the lex arbitri's fundamental public policies or overriding mandatory laws, or the lex arbitri's choice of law rules may require effect be given to the mandatory or overriding substantive rules of a third legal system, which is not the lex arbitri or the applicable law but which has some relevant connection to the dispute.

The displacement by an arbitrator of rules of the applicable law in accordance with the public policy or overriding rules of the lex arbitri, or in accordance with mandatory rules of a third system of law which the lex arbitri's choice of law rules declare to be applicable, should equally be unobjectionable. In this way, the lex arbitri, either of its own accord or through a third system of law, may give effect to international or transnational public policy. Again, this should be unobjectionable.

II.   THE DEVIL IN THE DETAIL

So, the first question really is, is it appropriate for an arbitral tribunal to apply rules of international or transnational public policy other than at the direction of the applicable law or the lex arbitri? Professor Reisman has suggested that this is not appropriate so far as international or transnational public policy is said to be part of international law. I would agree with him. I would further suggest that it is not appropriate where international or transnational public policy is not part of international law, but instead comprises some discrete body of rules forming part of the international commercial arbitration landscape, which is the product of comparative analysis but does not represent the position under either the *applicable law*, the lex arbitri or an applicable national law to which the lex arbitri requires reference be given. In my view, mandatory rules and public policies, so far as they interfere with contractual bargains, should be clear and identifiable and should represent the policy and position of a particular legal system. The devil of public policy and mandatory law lies in its detail, just as the devil of all law lies in its detail. Generalized reference by arbitrators to "transnational public policy", without reference to particular national rules and an acceptable choice of law framework for their application, risks appearing an easy way out and a substitute for rigorous analysis.

The ILA's Final Report on Public Policy as a Bar to Enforcement of International Arbitral Awards falls, in my view, into this trap. At paragraphs 27-30 it suggests that the rules of international public policy should include such rules as *pacta sunt servanda*, good faith, abuse of rights, prohibitions against uncompensated expropriation, prohibitions against discrimination, antitrust or competition law rules (including price fixing), currency controls, environmental protection laws, embargoes and trade sanctions, tax laws and consumer protection laws.

Consider antitrust law. While it is true that many countries have now adopted antitrust laws (more than eighty, according to reports dated 2000), most antitrust laws do not purport to apply universally. Instead they contain internal choice-of-law rules limiting their application to conduct within the relevant jurisdiction or having a substantial effect upon its economy. This is entirely inconsistent with status as "transnational" public policy. Moreover, the antitrust laws of different nations may well differ fundamentally on key details of antitrust law, policy and remedy.

Or consider tax law. All countries have tax laws, but no two tax laws are alike; in general they are limited, in accordance with the international law of jurisdiction, to persons or matters having a relevant connection with the taxing jurisdiction. Even in respect of matters such as bribery and corruption, which purport to apply universally, the devil lies in the detail. In the context of international commercial arbitration, issues of bribery normally arise in respect of an allegation that a contract has been procured by a bribe and should not be enforced. Obvious questions arise. Was the payment made with the intention of inducing the contract, and was the contract in fact procured by the payment? These questions are notoriously difficult to prove, and in many jurisdictions – English law is one of them – the law requires irrefutable presumptions of intent and causation. (Even in English law, however, the reach of those presumptions is unclear. If a $50,000 secret payment is made ten months before a $10 million contract is awarded, is the contract impeachable? What if the payment was $5,000, and was made two years before the contract?) No amount of reference to the OECD Convention on Combating Bribery of Foreign Public Officials in International Business Transactions will supply an arbitral tribunal with the precise rules required to determine the effect of a bribe on the case before it. The arbitrator must turn to the lex arbitri and the applicable law.

III. COMMON PROCEDURAL PATTERNS

If there is a role for transnational public policy in international commercial arbitration, it is not one of providing a basis for an arbitrator's ruling on a particular issue, still less one of compelling a particular ruling in a particular case. It is, instead, a role of influence or persuasion, so that commonly accepted notions of morality underpin arbitral rulings and procedures.

It is in fact in the area of procedure that one sees a truly "transnational" approach. One of the most striking features of international commercial arbitrations is the way in which a common procedural pattern has emerged. Arbitrators are required to act fairly and impartially. The parties must be given a proper opportunity of presenting their respective cases. Submissions are usually presented in writing, accompanied by the documents on which reliance is placed. Under such rules as those of the IBA on the Taking of Evidence, requests for disclosure of documents are limited: there is no time or taste for "warehouse discovery". The tribunal will be expected to give effect to rules such as those governing legal professional privilege, which are themselves inspired by public policy considerations. The direct testimony of witnesses will be given in writing; and there may be limited time for cross-examination. The tribunal's award will be a reasoned award capable of being enforced – and also capable of being challenged (on grounds of procedural irregularity or national public policy) – under the New York Convention of 1958.

But this common procedural pattern has not come about as part of some doctrinal campaign. It has come about on the basis of hard-won practical experience, which has been translated both into rules of arbitration and into modern laws of arbitration.

Plenary Session

2. Treaty Arbitration and International Law

International Arbitration and the Generation of Legal Norms:
Treaty Arbitration and International Law

*Jan Paulsson**

I.   THE PRESENT

What is the status of awards rendered by ephemeral arbitral tribunals deciding claims of investors under treaties? Although they are not binding on subsequent tribunals, they are assuredly read by them. That they may have an influence is evidently believed by advocates whose pleadings treat them with great attention, as precedents to be invoked, distinguished, or rejected. That scholars of international law deem awards worthy of sustained attention is equally evident, and testifies to a perception that they matter. But what – if any – is the dignity, or shall we say legitimacy, of such awards as instruments susceptible of generating international law?

It takes no great insight to realize that the generation of norms of international law is unlikely to be a straightforward business. Although treaties are the pre-eminent source of international law, they may be invoked against a state only if they establish rules "expressly recognized" by that state. This formulation, which all international lawyers recognize as that of Art. 38 of the Statute of the International Court of Justice (ICJ), on reflection seems somewhat odd, but there can be little difficulty in understanding the impulse: the reluctance of states, jealous of their sovereignty, to consider themselves bound by arrangements made by other states. This is why the very notion of "law-making treaties" is controversial; like resolutions of the UN General Assembly or those of other gatherings of states, treaties are more likely to assume the status of law if they can be said to reflect or conform to "international custom", or "general principles of law". These are indeed two other sources of applicable norms recognized by Art. 38. But these two woolly categories – enshrined in sub-paras. (b) and (c) of Art. 38(1) – are in many cases unlikely to produce specific answers to precise questions. Lawyers naturally search for *precedents*.

But the role of precedents in international law is a matter of considerable delicacy. Just as jealous sovereign states may be averse to any suggestion that compacts other than those to which they have consented may be invoked against them, so too they are often

---

* Freshfields Bruckhaus Deringer, Paris; Member of ICCA.

disinclined to submit to the elaboration of international law by anything resembling the accretion of binding precedents known as common law.

This explains why even the judgments of the ICJ are expressly subject to the caveat of Art. 59 of that Court's Statute, which reads:

> "The decision of the Court has no binding force except as between the parties and in respect of that particular case."

With this in mind, we immediately see how cautiously the drafters of the Statute approached the fourth and final category of sources of international law in Art. 38(1), that is to say the category of concern to this essay.

The wording of sub-para. (d) of Art. 38(1) is this:

> "subject to the provisions of Article 59, judicial decisions and the teachings of the most highly qualified publicists of the various nations, as subsidiary means for the determination of rules of law".

Is this fourth category of sources of law the poor cousin in the list of Art. 38(1)? Such a possibility springs quite naturally to mind when one considers that sub-para. (d) both begins and ends with a qualification, the first being (by the reference to Art. 59) that decisions have no binding effect on third parties, the second that this fourth category is but a "subsidiary means for the determination of rules of law". Indeed, one might say that the very wording of the second qualification includes a third limiting factor, as it refers to the *determination* of norms rather than their *establishment*.

Instead of viewing sub-para. (d) as a poor cousin, however, it is perhaps more accurate to recognize its in-built limitations are a tribute to its potential potency. Treaties do not affect non-signatories, and "customs" and "general principles" evolve with glacial speed and, in most cases, at a level of considerable generality. The first three sub-paragraphs of Art. 38(1) are therefore relatively unthreatening. Precedents, on the other hand, may provide immediate and bold answers to highly specific questions. That is why, no doubt, they are regarded with circumspection.

And so we find that even judgments of the ICJ do not, as such, create binding jurisprudence, but only a "subsidiary means" to determining the norms of international law.

International arbitral awards, it would seem, are of an equal – and equally limited – dignity, as the functional if not terminological equivalent of "judicial decisions". And in many cases, depending on the composition of the tribunal, they are also exceptionally well-considered pronouncements of "the most highly qualified publicists" (assisted, one might add, by detailed and skilled legal argument).

So much for the theory. The reality, of course, is that effective advocates before the ICJ, and indeed before the ever-expanding variety of other international courts and tribunals, must be steeped in the precedents of the World Court; it is fundamental to their art, because international adjudicators themselves rely on other international judgments. Advocates must also be familiar with important arbitral awards. One of the most often quoted international awards was rendered by a sole arbitrator, Max Huber, whose decision in the *Islands of Palmas* case was in fact referred to by the Permanent

Court of International Justice itself in the *Eastern Greenland* case. And it raised no eyebrows when the ICJ, in the *Gulf of Maine* case, quite naturally referred to the prior analysis of the tribunal in the *UK-France Continental Shelf* arbitration which had faced similar quandaries of maritime geography.

So it is pointless to resist the observation that precedents generate norms of international law. It is a fact of life before international courts and tribunals. What is more pertinent is to understand that the influence of international awards and judgments – even those emanating from the *same* court – is highly variable. This is quite unlike the traditional concept of common law systems, where the precedent of the highest court is binding, no matter how unpersuasive it may seem to lower-court judges, until it is reversed at the same level. International courts and tribunals, on the other hand, are not part of a hierarchical system. This may result in some untidiness; there is no catalogue where one might locate a reference to the judgment of the PCIJ in the *Lotus* case and see at a glance the word "reversed" beside it; one must simply *know* that it has long been discredited.[1] And much in the same way, while hierarchically undistinguishable, there are awards and awards, some destined to become ever brighter beacons, others to flicker and die near-instant deaths. Perhaps the most salient example of an investment award to meet the latter fate will be *Loewen v. United States*, decided by three eminent national judges whose grasp of the international law of continuous nationality – the point on which they decided the case – proved unfortunately tenuous.

In his introductory chapter on "Sources of the Law", Professor Brownlie puts it about as concisely as one could:

> "The literature of the law contains frequent reference to decisions of arbitral tribunals. The quality of arbitral tribunals has varied considerably, but there have been a number of awards which contain notable contributions to the development of the law by eminent jurists sitting as arbitrators, umpires, or commissioners."[2]

The corpus of decided cases in the field of international investment arbitration is of recent vintage, but it has come into existence with remarkable speed. Its legal status as a source of law is in theory equal to that of other types of international courts or tribunals. In practice, it will also doubtless turn out to be subject to the same Darwinian imperative: the unfit will perish.

Against this background, one can hardly fail to remark that among the most frequently appointed members to international investment tribunal panels may be found former Presidents of the International Court of Justice (Guillaume, Schwebel, Bedjaoui), a former President of the WTO Appellate body and member of his country's Supreme Court (Feliciano), a former President of the UN Security Council (Fortier), the rapporteur of the International Law Commission's draft Articles on State Responsibility (Crawford), and the present and immediate past Presidents of the leading

---

1. As should be clear from the discussion above, international arbitral tribunals are just as free to resist the influence of judgments of the World Court. Thus, investment arbitration awards have been unenthusiastic about extending *Barcelona Traction* to deny the standing of foreign shareholders seeking to recover derivatively on account of prejudice suffered by local corporations; see *CMS v. Argentina* and *GAMI v. Mexico*.

2. Ian BROWNLIE, *Principles of Public International Law*, 6th edn. (2003) p. 19.

international arbitral institution: the International Court of Arbitration of the International Chamber of Commerce (Briner, Tercier). Indeed, the current President of the International Court of Justice (Higgins) chaired the oft-cited ICSID tribunal which decided the second *Amco v. Indonesia* case. The list could be extended to include numerous scholars and practitioners of international renown, but no more is needed, it seems, to conclude that among the authors of these awards are those who must surely qualify for consideration as "the most highly qualified publicists of the various nations".

This may do as a summary of where we are today. But before we turn to imagine the future, the past deserves a look. Perhaps we shall see, as one often does, that the past is not what it used to be – it is perhaps different, more ambiguous, than what we had perceived.

II.   THE PAST

The first proposition that emerges from a retrospective overview is that at the time the wording of Art. 38 was conceived, there was no particular attempt to posit *judgments* of the permanent international court then in gestation as being of an inherently superior genus than *awards* rendered by ad hoc tribunals or commissions which had been a familiar feature of the landscape of international relations for many generations.[3]

For our purposes, Art. 38 is substantively identical to its predecessor in the Statute of the Permanent Court of International Justice – which also happened to be numbered Art. 38 there. It is of interest to note the close connection between the notion of an International Court and the familiar mechanism of international arbitration in the Covenant of the League of Nations, which provided as follows (in Art. 14):

> "The Executive Council shall formulate plans for the establishment of a Permanent Court of International Justice and this Court shall, when established, be competent to hear and determine any matter which the parties recognise as suitable for submission to it for arbitration... ".

---

3. Given the prodigious expansion of international commercial arbitration over the past half-century (the increase of trade being its fundamental cause, and the 1958 New York Convention on the Recognition and Enforcement of Foreign Arbitral Awards its primary instrument) modern practitioners may be excused for believing that we are living in an unprecedented golden age of international arbitration. They would be surprised to learn how vast international arbitral jurisprudence was in the Nineteenth Century. In the period between 1814 and 1898, for example, one study enumerated no less than 158 different international tribunals, including the celebrated commissions created in 1853 between Britain and the United States; in 1868 between Mexico and the United States; and in 1880 between France and the United States. (W. Evans DARBY, *International Tribunals: A Collection of Various Schemes Which Have Been Propounded, and of Instances Since 1815* (Peace Society, London 1899) pp. 285-304 (Darby titled its little annex: "The Proved Practicability of International Arbitration"). The list did not include the commissions created under the famous Jay Treaty, United Kingdom/United States, 8 *Stat.* 116, which was concluded in 1794 for the purpose, inter alia, of adjudicating claims of British creditors who were unsatisfied by their treatment at the hands of US courts, and vice versa.) All of these bodies were created by treaty, some to resolve only one dispute, but others to deal with many cases over a period of years.

The drafters and negotiators may well have felt that the body they were contemplating would be selected in a manner that would give it higher political legitimacy internationally than arbitral tribunals constituted by the agreement of two disputants alone. But there is no evidence that they believed that they were creating an inherently superior body as a matter of legal hierarchy; such a distinction would be hard to square with the fact that either type of decision-making body has an identical constitutional foundation: the consent of the states being subjected to its authority. There is nothing startling about differences in terms of political legitimacy; such differences, susceptible of much subjective debate, have forever been perceived when comparing arbitral bodies *inter se* (for example, by reference to the relative bargaining power of those who agreed to their establishment).

A second observation is that Art. 38 has never been immutable. As noted, the ICJ itself is not bound by precedent when it comes to interpreting Art. 38. One generation ago, for example, it adopted a conservative approach in the *North Sea Continental Shelf* case, insisting that customary international law could be established only on the basis of evidence of actual state practice; subsequently, Professor Jonathan Charney has ventured,

> "the ICJ moved away from the traditional analysis of state practice in the real world towards greater reliance on activities at intergovernmental forums ... the meaning of article 38 is not fixed".[4]

And if Art. 38 is not "fixed" in its effects on the Court itself, a fortiori it should be recalled that Art. 38 binds only the ICJ; the international community can devise other approaches outside the domain of cases before the ICJ. (Although ICSID arbitrators, who are authorized to apply international law under the 1965 Washington Convention, find in para. 40 of the Report of the Executive Directors of the World Bank the explicit statement that the term "international law" as used in Art. 42(1) of that Convention should be "understood in the sense given to it by Article 38(1) of the ICJ Statute".)

However imperfect it remains, the international legal order has a far greater structure, and a far greater complexity, than it did at the creation of the PCIJ. This institutional transformation of the arena of international law would not admit of a frozen conception of the source of international law conceived back then. It seems useful to note in this connection that the ICJ has accepted – in the *Namibia Advisory Opinion* (1971) – that the interpretation of a treaty is to be effected in the context of the legal environment *at the time an interpretation is called for.*

Finally, it is permissible to doubt that the drafters of Art. 38 themselves were innocently unaware of the potential power of the fourth category, or that they would

---

4. "International Lawmaking – Article 38 of the ICJ Statute Reconsidered" in Jost DELBRÜCK, ed., *New Trends in International Lawmaking – International "Legislation" in the Public Interest* (1997) pp. 175-176. While his sense of the ICJ's jurisprudence as a whole is that it adopted a "more dynamic vision of the evolution of the law" between 1969 to 1986, Professor Pierre-Marie DUPUY considers that the Court at present prefers "*une conception plus classique*"; "*La pratique de l'article 38 du Statut de la Cour internationale de justice dans le cadre des plaidoiries écrites et orales*" in *Collection of Essays by Legal Advisers of States, Legal Advisers of International Organizations and Practitioners in the Field of International Law* (UN publication 1999) p. 378.

have been alarmed if they had perceived it clearly. In an explanatory statement entitled simply "The Permanent Court of International Justice", prepared in 1921 by Åke Hammarskjöld, then a member of the PCIJ Secretariat, as a presentation to a visiting delegation from the United Kingdom, these sentences appear, one following the other:

> "It is for the Court itself to make out what is international law, and it is in this domain that the jurisprudence of the Court will have its greatest importance as a means of codifying the law of nations. It is expressly stipulated that judicial decisions and the teachings of the most highly qualified publicists of the various nations may be taken into account, but as ... in the case of precedents, only as indicative and not as decisive factors."[5]

This passage is irremediably schizophrenic. The first sentence could have been drafted by a utopian One-Worlder; it speaks of a *jurisprudence* which will serve to *codify* international law. The second sentence, on the other hand, might have been designed for ultra-nationalists wanting no truck with multilateral organizations or any law but municipal law; as though its author rather hoped that they would not have heard or understood the first sentence, this audience is told that judgments and scholars may be "taken into account", but as is the case with respect to "precedents" – and here comes the anaesthetic mumbo-jumbo – "only as indicative and not as decisive factors". And this from the very pen which moments earlier had referred to the greatest importance of the jurisprudence of the Court as that of codifying international law!

The truth is that anyone who had thought about it would know that *non liquet* was proscribed; that the only way to ensure that the international court could indeed decide every dispute, even in the absence of dispositive rules articulated by treaty, was to allow reference to inherently malleable "general principles"; and that the infinite variety of principles to be found in the universe of comparative law would make it absolutely inevitable that "general principles" for the purposes of Art. 38 would find its exposition *par excellence* in the decisions of international courts and tribunals.

Who can resist in this connection recalling the splendidly pragmatic observation of Jules Basdevant, the French delegate in the Washington Committee of Jurists which met to prepare the Statute of the new Court to be born in 1946:

> "while Article 38 was not well drafted, it would be difficult to make a better draft in the time at the disposal of the Committee. He also called attention to the fact that the [PCIJ] had operated very well under Article 38. He felt, therefore, that time should not be spent in redrafting it."[6]

As Rapporteur, the same Professor Basdevant expressed himself somewhat differently in recommending that Art. 38 be maintained – recording the view that the Article had

---

5. At p. 17. The HAMMARSKJÖLD paper exists in a folio printed by Atar, Geneva; the present author was able to consult it in the Library of the Peace Palace in The Hague. (Hammarskjöld was elected Judge of the PCIJ in 1936.)

6. Quoted in Alain PELLET, "Article 38" in ZIMMERMANN, TOMUSCHAT and OELLERS-FRAHM, eds., *The Statute of the International Court of Justice: A Commentary* (Oxford University Press 2006) p. 689.

engendered greater controversy in "doctrine than in practice" and that "its implementation should be a matter of trust in the new Court".[7]

And as a long-serving member of the ICJ (1946-1964), the same Judge Basdevant was undoubtedly pleased to find himself to exercise a broad and intelligent discretion.

No criticism is intended – quite the contrary. But on the other hand, we need to discern what happened. Like many fledgling organizations, the PCIJ needed time to shore up its foundations. Asking for too much at the outset may have resulted in tighter restrictions; an open-textured Statute left room for authority by development and accredition. The drafters of the ICJ Statute saw no reason to tinker with a successful formation.

As Professor Pellet puts it in his authoritative 115-page contribution on Art. 38 in the OUP Commentary on the Statute,

> "in practice, Art. 38, while a useful directive, has not prevented the Court from deciding on the basis of other sources of international law, the theory of which it has greatly advanced".[8]

It would be fatuous to quarrel with the words "useful directive", and to insist that Art. 38 lays down a mandatory restriction. For there is no appeal from the decisions of the ICJ; nor is there from most international tribunals. This observation underscores the importance of *self-restraint* on the part of international adjudicators. The judicious application of evolving sources of law is at the heart of the process of building an international *system* where perceptions of legitimacy are often more important than the elusive "proof" of abstract legal propositions. It seems appropriate to conclude this backward glance with words written by Judge Manley more than sixty years ago:

> "The role of an international tribunal in finding the applicable law is not one of unbridled freedom, as is sometimes popularly assumed. The categories of materials to be considered have been more or less determined by a long development of international jurisprudence, and standards are available for appraising their value."[9]

III.   THE FUTURE

One of the reasons for the inescapable fuzziness of the formal sources of law identified in Art. 38(1) is that it was intentionally worded in such a way as to give the World Court sufficient flexibility to avoid *non liquet*.[10] This proposition should apply to ICSID tribunals as well; and there is every reason to presume that a BIT which gives an option to select either ICSID or another mechanism (such as the UNCITRAL Rules) is intended

---

7. *Idem.* An example may be of interest. One of the often-identified omissions among the categories in Art. 38(1) is that of unilateral acts. In the *Nuclear Tests* case in 1974 the ICJ expressly recognized that unilateral acts may create legal obligations.

8. *Op. cit.*, fn. 6, p. 700.

9. Manley O. HUDSON, *International Tribunals: Past and Future* (1944) p. 107.

10. Hersch LAUTERPACHT, *The Function of Law in the International Community* (1933) pp. 134-135.

to create a uniform regime in this regard.[11] The ICJ Statute does not allow the Judges to conclude that they cannot reach a decision because they have not found an applicable norm. Such a *duty to decide*, in the field of public international law, is inconceivable unless international adjudicators are free to devise new solutions within the interstices of established norms which are too general or too abstract to yield a definite answer. When the PCIJ was created, it should be noted, a respectable minority were not opposed to *non liquet*.[12] Had they won the day, judicial creativeness would have been curtailed, and international law deprived of room for development.

It should however be recognized that the topic remains controversial. The counter-argument is precisely that judicial creativeness *should be curtailed*, and that the development of international law on an enduring foundation may require diffidence by international adjudicators. For if one is charged with applying law, and at the heart of the issue lies a void, untouched by those who have the authority to make the law, would it not be a dangerous usurpation by decision-makers to make up the law as they go along? The notion of *finding* a solution in the "interstices" of positive law may indeed be a subtle but questionable justification for *inventing* a rule to fit one's predisposition.[13]

These observations are obviously relevant to investment arbitrations, because it is a domain where new issues are constantly confronted. Professor Dolzer has noted the absence of a *jurisprudence constante*, and the multiplicity of interpretative approaches to treaty texts, in respect of several issues relating to the concept of "investment" in investment-treaty law.[14]

Still, when conflicts arise the jurisprudence will evolve, and all the more so in a realm where historical precedents tend to be both rarefied and outdated. As Professor Orrego Vicuña observed in his Lauterpacht Lectures in 2001, "questions relating to major areas of international law, such as those dealing with trade, finance and investments, are never brought" before the International Court of Justice.[15] *Never* was perhaps too strong a word, since international lawyers working in the economic field will immediately think of *Barcelona Traction* and *ELSI*, but in fact those two unique exceptions serve to make the

---

11. The Model Rules on Arbitral Procedure adopted by the ILC in 1958 (reprinted in [1956-II] YBILC 83) expressly precluded the possibility of *non liquet*: Art. 11. It was thought that this rule itself reflected a mandatory general principle of law; see ILC SECRETARIAT, *Commentary on the Draft Convention on Arbitral Procedure* (1955) pp. 49-52 and the references.

12. A leading member of this group, the former US Secretary of State Elihu ROOT, explained his position by stating that the "Court must not have the power to legislate", *Procès-Verbaux of the Proceedings of the Advisory Committee of Jurists* (1920) Annexe No. 3, p. 309.

13. Hersch LAUTERPACHT wrote of "the animated, but highly unreal, controversy as to whether judges create the law or whether they merely reveal the rule already contained *in gremio legis*" and "the paradoxical assertion that judges are at the same time docile servants of the past and tyrants of the future". His point was that "the distinction between the evidence and the source of many a rule of law is more speculative and less rigid than is commonly supposed". *The Development of International Law by the International Court* (rev. edn. 1958; first published as *The Development of International Law by the Permanent Court of International Justice* in 1934) p. 21.

14. Rudolf DOLZER, "The Notion of Investment in Recent Practice" in CHARNOVITZ, et al., eds., *Law in the Service of Human Dignity: Essays in Honour of Florentino Feliciano* (2005) p. 261, in particular pp. 272 et seq.

15. *International Dispute Settlement in an Evolving Global Society* (Cambridge University Press 2004) p. 19.

point even stronger: two cases in half a century is a starvation diet.[16] Based on the experience of the last decade, it is hardly an understatement that major disputes between investors and states are being resolved by adjudication every month. This pace requires resources beyond those of a single world court, and expertise of quite a different kind.

The notion of leading cases in specialized areas of international law seems likely to become an ever more familiar element of our mindset, regardless of the fact that tribunals which render such decisions are not bodies formally constituted by treaties. (In that sense investment awards may be said to occupy a higher, perhaps *intermediate*, level, for they are frequently rendered *pursuant* to a treaty.) Indeed the expression "leading case" was used – and properly so – by Professor Orrego Vicuña in relation to the *de Merode* judgment of the World Bank Administrative Tribunal in defining the scope of review of the administrative policies of an international organization.[17] The same, to give just one additional example, may be said of the award rendered under the rules of the Court of Arbitration for Sport in *Aanes*,[18] often cited for its approach to the fundamental distinction between disqualification and suspension in relation to the policing of doping offences by international sports federations.

That a special jurisprudence is developing from the leading awards in the domain of investment arbitration can only be denied by those determined to close their eyes.

First of all, the contribution of the sizeable body of awards rendered in the course of more than a quarter of a century by the Iran-US Claims Tribunal is well recognized:

"As a pragmatic matter, it seems inevitable that the Tribunal's jurisprudence will be highly influential. The Tribunal has issued several hundred decisions in contested cases that are relevant to the Law of State Responsibility: it covers most aspects of the Law of State Responsibility for injuries to aliens and nearly every type of commercial activity. Some of that commercial activity is of relatively recent origin. Joint ventures, for example, are a relatively new and very important form of doing business. The Tribunal is the only international body to have considered the legal treatment of joint ventures in a systematic fashion; thus the Tribunal's holdings about joint ventures comprise virtually the entire field of international jurisprudence in this field. The Tribunal thus almost certainly will have a profound influence in this area, if only because there is not much else at which to look."[19]

---

16. Most cases that predate the foundation of the ICJ – from *Oscar Chinn* to *Chorzów Factory* – are a mixed bag, of little use today except with respect to the most general of propositions.

17. *Op. cit.*, fn. 15, p. 78. *De Merode*, WBAT Decision No. 1 (1981) was decided by the Tribunal in a noteworthy composition, presided by Jiménez de Aréchaga and also including Elias, Weil, Lauterpacht, Abul-Magd, Gorman and Kumarayya.

18. *Aanes v. FILA*, CAS 2000/A/317.

19. Daniel B. MAGRAW, "The Tribunal in Jurisprudential Perspective", in R.B. LILLICH and D.B. MAGRAW, eds., *The Iran-United States Claims Tribunal: Its Contribution to the Law of State Responsibility* (1998) p. 19. See also Veijo HEISKANEN, "The Contribution of the Iran-United States Claims Tribunal to the Development of the Doctrine of Indirect Expropriation", 5 International Law Forum (August 2003) p. 176.

In the half-decade since the last sentence was written, there have of course been many more important awards "to look at" in the field of investment arbitration. That they are given close attention as indicators of international normative developments is beyond cavil, as evident in a series of studies by OECD's Investment Committee, UNCTAD, and a host of Internet websites.[20]

A couple of incidental but important points merit mention.

First, there is a danger associated with the fact that all decisions of all courts or tribunals have in principle equal status as concerns their *potential* for normative influence.[21] One must be aware of the perils of conflating the learning to be derived from the great variety of courts and tribunals which coexist in the modern world. This is not the place to consider the complex issue of cross-fertilization between areas of international law where great issues overlap, such as the notion of "discrimination" in WTO parlance and in bilateral investment treaties. To take another particularly salient example, property rights are protected under human rights conventions as well as under BITs. Yet there one must surely recognize that there must be a potential difference between treaties intended to promote investments and to cause investors to rely on undertakings made with the direct and explicit intent of creating incentives, on the one hand, and the minimum treatment as understood in terms of human rights, applying even to investments which the state may not have desired.

Secondly, there is an important issue which appears not yet to have been considered in the depth it obviously deserves: whenever they are created by treaties which refer to the applicability of international law, are international tribunals in investment disputes organs of the international legal system and therefore bound to apply international law *whether or not it is pleaded by the parties?* The parallel with the ICJ and Art. 38 of its Statute is obvious, and the implications are equally clear, as the ICJ put it in the *Fisheries Jurisdiction* cases:

> "The Court ... as an international judicial organ, is deemed to take judicial notice of international law, and is therefore required ... to consider on its own initiative all rules of international law which may be relevant to the settlement of the dispute. It being the duty of the Court itself to ascertain and apply the relevant law in the given circumstance of the case, the burden of establishing or proving rules of international law cannot be imposed upon any of the parties for the law lies within the judicial knowledge of the Court."[22]

In other words, a tribunal in an investment dispute cannot content itself with inept pleadings, and simply uphold the least implausible of the two. Furthermore, as the PCIJ put it in *Brazilian Loans*, an international tribunal "is deemed itself to know what

---

20. For a compendium in a more traditional form, see Todd WEILER, ed., *International Investment Law and Arbitration: Leading Cases* (2005).

21. Much has been written on the related issue of the perceived threat to the unity of international law posed by the multitude of regional or specialized international tribunals. For an early but important contribution see R.Y. JENNINGS, "The Judiciary, International and National, and the Development of International Law", 45 ICLQ (1996) p. 1.

22. *ICJ Reports* (1974) pp. 3, 9 (para. 17) and pp. 175, 181 (para. 18).

[international] law is",[23] and this thought should be a sobering one to parties making appointments of arbitrators, and to arbitrators accepting appointment. There have indeed been some questionable decisions in investment arbitrations, which suggest that the arbitrators had an insufficient grounding in international law, but this comment must be seen in perspective; the PCIJ and the ICJ themselves have authored discredited judgments, and the normative influence of those judgments simply dissipates over time. We are in an early phase of dramatic extension of investment arbitration, and the fact that so many investment arbitrators are of a premier rank as international lawyers – as indicated by the very partial enumeration above – suggests that there is no cause for alarm. The intense attention of the international community of scholars and practitioners will undoubtedly have a salutary effect: good awards will chase the bad, and set standards which will contribute to a higher level of consistent quality.

These and other inquiries will continue to challenge us. Nevertheless, we should hear and heed the echo of the concluding words of the chapter on "Law Applicable by International Tribunals" in Manley Hudson's *International Tribunals: Past and Future*, written in 1944, which are certainly truer today, and perhaps less likely to be dismissed as an instance of hope triumphing over experience than they were in the bitter wake of global war:

> "... international tribunals applying the law which regulates the conduct of States can play an important role in world affairs. More than this, the judgments of such tribunals tend to become important sources for the development of international law."[24]

---

23. PCIJ Series A, No. 21, p. 124.
24. P. 110. Hudson was a Judge of the Permanent Court of International Justice (elected in 1936).

The Role of Treaty Arbitration in Rebalancing the Development of International Law

*Francisco Orrego Vicuña**

I.   INTRODUCTION

The Report introduced by Jan Paulsson[1] is a most timely contribution to the discussion of the role of awards and decisions as a source of international law, with particular reference to its meaning in the context of Art. 38(1) of the Statute of the International Court of Justice.

The discussion was necessary to assess the ongoing process of use and abuse of the various sources of international law taking place in today's world, a process in which awards frequently play a prominent part.

II.   ADVANCING THE LAW AND ITS LIMITS

There is of course much need to ensure a measure of progress in the legal framework that governs the international community, but it is one thing to advance the law, which must be favoured, and quite another thing to distort the meaning of the law, which must be stopped. There is thus a legitimate function of awards in the development of international law, occasionally clouded by an illegitimate use of judicial authority.

III.   ENSURING THE PRIMACY OF CONSENT IN TREATY INTERPRETATION

The process of use and abuse affects today every source of international law, beginning with treaties. It is well known that consent is the essence of treaties, yet a number of

---

*   Professor, University of Chile, Santiago, Chile; Member of ICCA.
1. See this volume, pp. 879-889.

developments appear to suggest that in a given view the traditional requirement of consent is no longer necessary.

Much has been done and can still be done in terms of adapting the operation of consent to the needs of contemporary international transactions, including experience. Yet, there is still a line clearly distinguishing what has been consented to from what has not been so consented to, a line which in turn separates a legal obligation from what it is not.

Under the theory of relative normativity, so well developed by Professor Prosper Weil, many efforts are currently being undertaken to blur this line so as to make non-legal obligations into a binding rule for States, or for that matter in many respects for individuals. Everything that is convenient for a given point of view or interest appears to be justified as a binding rule, just as everything that is not equally convenient appears to be dismissed as non-binding.

The so-called "soft law" developed by means of the action of international organizations and conferences, which is not law but yet purports to be binding, is perhaps the paramount example of this phenomenon.

IV.   TREATY ARBITRATION AND THE REBALANCING OF INTERPRETATION

It is interesting to note in this context that treaty arbitration has led on occasions to a rebalancing of the role of treaties as a source of international law. This is first done by means of the interpretation of treaties. Many times awards will result in a legitimate advancement of the law by the interpretation of the applicable treaties, but this will be done within the limits set by the rules on interpretation laid down in the Vienna Convention on the Law of Treaties, that is, within the limits that States themselves have established.

There will be quite naturally difficult problems to solve, particularly in connection with whether an award should assign greater weight to the original intention that the parties to a treaty had at the time of consenting to it rather than to the intention they might be sharing at a later point in time.

There can be no doubt that States are free to create new law by means of their treaty-making power if they consider that a new rule is necessary or more convenient to their interests, but they cannot do this in disregard of rights legitimately acquired under an existing treaty that denotes a different interpretation by those same States.

Since the very treaties concerned have recognized the interest of individuals, it will be for the awards issued under those treaties to give recognition to such interests to the extent that it is so justified under the terms of the treaty and its interpretation.

The *Plama* decision has done so in holding that the modification of rights cannot be made retroactive because individuals have been recognized under the pertinent treaty as subjects of the law and not mere objects of the law. So too an English court in *OPEC*, in deciding on an issue of non-justiciability, has established that individuals have rights of their own under treaties made between States that can be brought to the courts, a matter which otherwise would be excluded from their jurisdiction.

It then becomes apparent how these developments in treaty arbitration help the advancement of the law, but do so within the limits of a legal framework set by the very States concerned as interpreted by courts and tribunals.

V.   THE DANGERS OF A TAILOR-MADE CUSTOMARY LAW AND ITS OFFSETTING BY AWARDS

An identical process of use and abuse takes place today in connection with the role of customary international law. The issue here is whether a rule identified as customary law will be the result of a genuine practice and *opinio juris* of States, or it will be so considered just because it is convenient to a given interest as if it were a rule tailor-made to that particular view.

Quite unexpectedly, treaty arbitration has also come to rebalance the role of customary law in the cases submitted to the consideration of international tribunals. This rebirth of customary law has been prompted by the fact that often investment treaties remit to custom, as is the case, for example, of the operation of necessity as a rule excluding the wrongfulness of a government act, or they rely on concepts that are inextricably linked to customary law, as is the case of the standard of fair and equitable treatment.

By means of this rebalancing function, awards will ensure that practice is what it is genuinely proved to be and not simply what States will say it is in support of a given interest, as it is happening only too often in international law.

To the extent that awards and decisions keep within the strict requirements laid down by international law for the identification of a customary rule, the role of awards will be helping to avoid the distortions noted in the general use of this source of law. In so doing, such awards will also be ensuring that the rule of law is kept intact and it is not replaced by a dangerous new form of authorization in international law which privileges interests in disrespect of a legal outcome or right.

VI.   THE ABUSE OF FLEXIBILITY AND THE ROLE OF THE JUDICIARY

General principles of law are also subject to this process of use and abuse in international law. Flexibility with the law is necessary and welcome, yet stepping beyond the law is not. After a process of abstraction, generalization and implantation of general principles in international law, objective findings can be made and subjective deductions must be avoided.

The distorted application of equity by the International Court of Justice in the early cases of maritime delimitation before it, is perhaps the paramount example of this phenomenon. The role of equity was in fact conceived as extending far beyond the realm of law, so much so that such abuse prompted a strong reaction by learned authors, in awards and ultimately in the very decisions of the Court that came to correct the distortion.

This rebalancing is what explains the importance that awards have attained today as a subsidiary means for the determination of international law. As Jan Paulsson has well stated, the balanced decisions often displace the unbalanced. To this end, it must be ensured that the role of the judge will be to ascertain the existence of a rule of law and to avoid an interested interpretation that would only add to the distortion. This is done by means of the proper interpretation of the law before the judge, the adequate use of precedents to the extent appropriate and, above all, a reasoning that will allow no selectivity or politicization.

VII. THE MANDATES OF PRUDENCE

A successful result in this rebalancing of the sources of international law will be attained only by means of introducing an indispensable prudence in the judicial function, which is of the essence in the judge's role in adjudicating a dispute.

In referring to the role of equity, this is what Selden had to say in his famous allusion to the Chancellor's foot:

> "What an uncertain measure this would be! One chancellor has a long foot, another a short foot, a third an indifferent foot. 'Tis the same thing in the Chancellor's Conscience."

This is the same prudence with which all sources of international law should be used in today's world and on which all awards should be based.

Comments on Treaty Arbitration and International Law

*Rudlolf Dolzer**

I,   INTRODUCTION

In his paper, Jan Paulsson, with his usual brilliance, lays out and dissects the parameters of the topic of Treaty Arbitration and International Law.[1]

I agree with him that the framework of the sources laid down in Art. 38 of the International Court of Justice (ICJ) Statute leaves ample space for creative reasoning of arbitrators and that this is indeed necessary to allow for the decision of individual cases and for a healthy evolution of the law in accordance with the contemporary context. In practice, arbitral tribunals do generate legal norms within the framework of the applicable rules, and the role of individual decisions in guiding subsequent tribunals properly depends on the quality of their reasoning. Paulsson is also correct to underline the fact of specialization of investment tribunals (and lawyers, for that matter), and that assertions of "cross-fertilization" from the realms of the WTO or the field of human rights usually lead to more dead-end roads than to helpful navigational signs.

It is also right to point out, as Paulsson does, the parallels between arbitral tribunals and the ICJ specifically in regard to the common constitutional foundations. The role of consent of the state to investment arbitration is often overlooked in this context, and I shall return to the role of the states generally in a moment.

My own observations build upon and reflect on Paulsson's study mainly in regard to the broader question of the legitimacy of the arbitral process and the various fronts of criticism with which this process has been confronted more recently.

II.   POWER OF NORM CREATION

The topic of Treaty Arbitration and International Law with the emphasis on "norm generation", may suggest to critics that arbitral tribunals have usurped the power of

---

* University of Bonn.

1. See this volume, pp. 879-889.

norm creation which should rest in principle with the states. For those critics, what are the real issues raised by the current international arbitral process?

One of the difficulties concerning those real issues lies in the fact that no consensus exists on whether there are any real issues and if so, how one should approach and address them. It is true that occasionally the impression is created of an amorphous general uneasiness about the process. This may be the result of several factors. First, we occasionally hear more or less general attacks on the very concept of international arbitration. Second, the idea of instituting arbitration specifically between states and foreign enterprises seems to be suspect in some corners. Third, the debate on the homogeneity and consistency of the broader process has been going on, has not found any conclusion and may have contributed to an impression that the results are not firmly anchored in laws and principles but are idiosyncrasies of arbitrators chosen at random. Some observers question the integrity of the process in view of what they consider the bias which may arise from the fact that arbitrators exercise other professional activities which may be in conflict with the duties of neutral arbitration. Finally, still others suggest that the process seems to work only in favor of the investor and tends to shut out other goods such as environmental values or labor rights.

What makes the broader debate especially confusing is that critical voices come from rather different corners. Legal nationalists who mistrust international legal processes in general are as opposed to investment arbitration as are some environmentalists or some proponents of labor rights whose political philosophy otherwise have nothing in common with legal nationalism. The image of strange bedfellows comes to mind which may cooperate to undermine the public image of investment arbitration from the outside of the process, while more thoughtful and differentiated voices of reform come from within the arbitration community.

To what extent is it correct that the process of investment arbitration is driven by private claimants and by arbitrators acting as private actors without governmental legitimation? In other words: Is it true that the process of norm-interpretation or norm-generation has been privatized in the field of investment arbitration?

When we speak about ICSID arbitration, the influence of the states on the process is by no means absent. States have created ICSID, the defendant states have agreed to ICSID jurisdiction, and states have laid down the applicable law. These are the constitutional foundations to which Jan Paulsson rightly refers. The applicable law may be found in investment treaties, in the laws of the host state or in the general sources of international law. When it comes to investment agreements, the host state has consented to these rules and the value of the decision as a precedent with persuasive power will be limited to the understanding of corresponding clauses of investment agreements and not to the sphere of general international law.

From a broader perspective, the process of investment arbitration reflects the values held and the choices made by the international community. If we consider the agreements on investment and trade together as the central body of rules governing international economic relations, it is clear that states agreed on three basic principles. First, the current order as reflected in investment treaties and the rules of the WTO is based on the conviction that a rule-oriented rather than a power-oriented approach of dispute settlement shall govern. Second, the ICJ has not been chosen, but panels with a significant degree of specialization in their field. The need for specialization as emphasized by Jan Paulsson notwithstanding, it will not be doubted that this framework laid down by the states is common to the investment and the trade fields and that this framework largely determines the operation of the arbitral process. Any argument that the process is out of tune with international economic relations in general or has been created without the will of the international community does not reflect reality.

Of course, it is appropriate to continuously review the process and to consider new aspects and new solutions which the states might adopt for the future. But let us briefly consider the basic alternatives to the current system. And, of course, anyone with a fundamental criticism of this current system will have to consider and to propose more viable and constructive realistic options.

III.   ALTERNATIVES TO THE CURRENT SYSTEM

A first alternative would be to abandon the decision in favor of a rule-oriented approach based on third-party dispute settlement. Essentially, this would mean a return to the process of diplomatic protection, to the political process of negotiation with all of its vagaries, to the role of power as is inherent in bilateral negotiations, sometimes of raw power, to the open-endedness of such a process, to sanctions on the bilateral level and to schemes of the unilateral determination of a dispute as was true in the area of trade before 1994. This might be a return to economic power policies and welcomed by proponents of legal nationalism, but on the international level I fail to see the attractiveness of this scheme of the past and I see no majority in favor of such a turnaround: Ibrahim Shihata, the late Secretary General of ICSID, was right in his steady emphasis that at its heart, ICSID can be seen as an attempt to depoliticize investment disputes, and anyone who would contribute to an abandoning of international investment arbitration without proposing a viable alternative must be reminded that then the rules on diplomatic protection will come back into play.

Moreover, all those who would argue directly or indirectly for abandoning an international system of dispute settlement would also do away with an effect which economists call the externally anchored discipline of the domestic legal system of the host state. International treaties embedded in a system of international dispute settlement create a powerful incentive for the host state to live by the rules of an investment-friendly climate, and such an international system provides advantages for those authorities in the host state which are competent to defend these disciplines. China is by far the largest recipient of foreign direct investment in the Third World. It may not have a strong national machinery to enforce rules protecting the private investor, but it has concluded about 110 BITs, most with ICSID jurisdiction, more than any other developing country. The disciplinary effect of such treaties not just in regard to the foreign investor, but also in regard to the general legal climate of the host state should not be underrated, and a return to the system of diplomatic protection and legal nationalism would do away with this effect. It is true that the role of BITs has been contrasted with the demand of policy space for the host state, and there may be a need for a fine-tuning of rules along these lines. But in principle it is also true that investment rules in essence are meant to reduce only the space for such policies which are undesirable both from the international and the national point of view, including policies based on arbitrariness, instability and unpredictability. In the terminology of international financial institutions, these are core elements of any code of good governance.

Of course, an international surrogate of the present ICSID system might be seen in a permanent court of some sort. As is well known, the debate over such a court in the past years has led to no consensus. The pros and cons have been weighed and laid on the table. For the time being, it appears that a formal proposal for the establishment of a new tribunal would not be greeted by a majority. We all know as well that a permanent institution replacing ad hoc tribunals would itself raise new questions regarding efficiency, timing and costs, and it would show that no single model exists which combines all ideal features of an arbitration system.

IV. DEGREE OF HOMOGENEITY AND CONSISTENCY OF INVESTMENT JURISPRUDENCE

In my view, however, the debate on the future contours of the international arbitral architecture has not really been closed inasmuch as it left open a question that is central when we ask whether the current process works. What I refer to is the question of the degree of homogeneity and consistency of investment jurisprudence which is essential for the functioning, the acceptance, and the survival of the process. Perhaps the most remarkable aspect of the debate has been the failure to come even close to a consensus on whether or not the current state of investment jurisprudence is characterized more by homogeneity and consistence or by heterogeneity and divergence. In my view, some of the contributions on this point have been glossing over the realities of the jurisprudence. It is true that a degree of divergence is inherent in every decentralized or even centralized legal system and that out of this divergence may arise, in a flexible process, the optimal solution which is most persuasive from the point of view of the international community. It is also true that the jurisprudence of the past decade has led to results in key areas of investment law which lack consistency and are not conducive to legal security and predictability.

The parallels between investment arbitration and the ICJ to which Jan Paulsson rightly refers have their limit when it comes to what be might called an institutional sense for memory and self-preservation of a standing court. In the decentralized ICSID system, such a sense may not be entirely absent, but this sense does not enjoy the same degree of priority when every tribunal has new members with their own background, their own talents, and their own jurisprudential philosophy.

In my view, there is no rush at this moment to continue or reopen the debate on new mechanisms conducive to more uniformity. Possibly, we should pay attention to the argument that modern investment jurisprudence is still in its infancy, being just about a decade old, and that it simply needs to develop in an organic manner over the coming years. In a few years, the air may have cleared, presumably when dozens of decisions have been rendered in the Argentinean cases before ICSID which share basic features and which in an ideal world would not diverge in a dramatic manner. A longer period of investment jurisprudence characterized by sustained divergence and inconsistency would certainly lead to sense of crisis and urgent reform. I am aware that some voices also disagree on this point and apparently assume that the sheer settlement of a dispute is more important than the principles underlying the decision as explained by the tribunal. In my view, such a version of decisionism should not and would not be accepted by the international investment community.

V.   PRINCIPLES OF INTERPRETATION

In this context, some observations concerning principles of interpretation may be in order. There is general agreement that investment treaties will have to be interpreted in accordance with Art. 31 of the Vienna Convention on the Law of Treaties. As is the case with Art. 38 of the ICJ Statute we also know that Art. 31 will in the more difficult cases only provide for a starting point and leave room for adaption in the light of the circumstances of the case; in principle, neither an approach based on a broad interpretation in favor of the investor nor a narrow interpretation in favor of the host state can be reconciled with Art. 31. However, the object and purpose of an investment treaty will necessarily come into play, as is recognized in Art. 31. And it is also generally recognized in treaty law that the preamble to a treaty may give expression to the object and purpose as envisaged by the parties. Whether this function of the preamble has been as widely recognized as appropriate in the past by those who have drafted investment treaties may be a matter of speculation. In any event, tribunals have no choice but to rely, here as well, on the wording upon which the parties have agreed.

One specific issue of interpretation may merit attention here which has been at the basis of some appearance of jurisprudential divergence. I refer to the question whether broad standards and concepts such as fair and equitable treatment, national treatment, the most-favored-nation clause or also indirect expropriation should be addressed by individual tribunals by way of developing and designing broad and abstract formulae covering the full range of conceivable factual scenarios or whether tribunals ought to refrain from such an attempt at what may be called norm generation at the level below the text and the wording of the rule in question, and to decide the case on a much narrower grounded application of the rule to the specific circumstances of the case before the tribunal. Virtues and disadvantages for both approaches may be cited. In favor of broad abstract formulae it may be argued that a rule will become more transparent and predictable in its application, but this would, of course, not be so if every tribunal were to engage in a kind of competition for such efforts of eye-catching passages readily available for citation by academics or other tribunals.

The process of interpretation must also be seen in the context of the debate whether or not investment arbitration amounts to a kind of privatization of dispute settlement. In a rather simplified picture consisting of broad strokes, the legitimacy of the arbitral process has occasionally been placed in doubt with the rhetorical question of why three arbitrators as individuals without any specific mandate should be responsible for deciding major investment issues. From such a vantage point, the entire process of international arbitration can be put in question, including all the historical decisions rendered by arbitral tribunals a long time ago. Jan Paulsson's paper correctly points to the long and successful history of arbitration, and I think he would share the view that in principle arbitral awards reflect the collective experience of the international community, to rephrase Max Huber's position on international law in general. The crux of the matter is, of course, whether it is true or not that the process is steered by three individuals. The reality is much more complex and multifaceted, and, as has been pointed out above, ultimately it is much more correct to state that the three arbitrators decide the case on behalf of the states concerned, appointed in accordance with rules accepted by states and applying rules created and accepted by states. Indeed, states not only set the rules in advance. They also monitor the results, and they have the freedom and right to change and to revamp the rules if deemed necessary. Within NAFTA, for example, the right of the member states to issue an Authoritative Interpretation has existed and has been exercised when the states determined that NAFTA tribunals had interpreted the principle of fair and equitable treatment in a manner inconsistent with the will of the governments. More broadly, there is sufficient evidence showing that governments monitor the jurisprudence of arbitration tribunals. As is well known, the revision of the US Model BIT in 2004 reflects in significant part the US reaction to lines of arbitral jurisprudence. In capitals around the world executive and legislative authorities review the state of jurisprudence and consider whether new approaches are desirable. From a systematic viewpoint this is a healthy development because it ensures that treaties and arbitral awards based on these treaties will not depart in a broad way from the will of the states and therefore retain their legitimacy derived from the mandate of the states in the same way as other international tribunals.

VI. LEGITIMACY OF THE ARBITRAL PROCESS

Concerning the legitimacy of the arbitral process one issue that is raised directly and indirectly concerns the question whether the current process is in its procedural and substantive setting loaded in favor of private interests to the detriment of the public good. The right of the investor to bring a claim without the consent of his home state, the fact that the investor will design and present the case to protect its private interests and the limited professional or personal background and horizon of the selected arbitrators have been mentioned in this context. In my view, none of these elements necessarily translate into decisions ignoring the public good as reflected in the applicable rules.

When it comes to the right of an individual to bring a claim, the general tendency is to welcome this elevation of individuals in relation to the sovereign state when it comes to human rights. I think that in principle the same perspective should apply when it comes to economic rights and freedoms.

When it comes to the content of the rules applicable to the dispute, these are determined by the agreements among the parties to the dispute, by the laws of the host state and by the applicable rules of international law. Presumably, the public good is reflected in the laws of the host state and in public international law. Concerning investment agreements between the host state and the investor, Resolution 1803 (XVII), passed nearly unanimously by the UN General Assembly in 1962, states in its eighth declaration that such investments freely entered into must be observed in good faith, and there is no reason to change that rule today. In other words, neither the substantive nor the procedural rules are subject to the will of the arbitrators, and there is no ground to speak of privatization of the process in this respect.

This setting is also relevant when it comes to the manner in which the case is presented to the tribunal by the lawyers of both parties. The arguments are conceived in view of the pre-existing rules, with the usual legitimate effort on the side of each party to characterize and present the law in a favorable light.

At the next stage of the arbitral process, the arbitrators will weigh the factual evidence and determine the law applicable. Here it depends as always on the experience and the qualities of the arbitrators. As Jan Paulsson has shown, there is no basis to argue that the profile of international investment arbitrators in practice is somehow inferior to judges of other tribunals. Given the role of international law for the decision of investment cases, it is, of course, desirable that sufficient expertise is present among the tribunals in this field with its growing complexity. There may be cases in which such expertise may have been lacking in part and where the decision reflected this deficit. However, this would certainly have been the odd exception, and today most parties are fully aware that it is in their own interest to select an arbitrator familiar with the rules of public international law.

In summary, when we look at the arbitral process in some detail in its entirety, it is difficult to see in what respect a privatization should have occurred. Inasmuch as it is assumed that the rules of the host state or the rules of public international law are inadequate and do not reflect the public good, this cannot be attributed to the arbitral process and necessary reforms must come through the appropriate channels of the law-making process on the respective levels. It would be incorrect to assume that the arbitral process and the law-making process under the auspices of the states are in practice bifurcated and that the states have no influence or control over the law applicable.

VII. CONCLUSION

When the ICSID Convention was negotiated and created in the early 1960's, this was a rather extraordinary effort to forge a mechanism for dispute settlement in spite of the absence of a consensus on the substantive law to be applied. Art. 42 was no more than a compromise at the lowest level, investment treaties were just beginning to be negotiated, and customary law on foreign investment consisted of a disorderly patchwork with more holes than patterns. The wisdom of those who created ICSID became only apparent and bore fruits with the advent of bilateral and multilateral treaties containing substantive rules decades later. Combined, ICSID and these treaties in the past decade formed the legal framework for an unprecedented number of cases. In the wake of a quadrupling of foreign investment within a decade, and being at the highest recorded level in 2005, international investor-state arbitration had clearly become the preferred form of international dispute settlement. In my view, the most direct testimony in favor of the mechanisms and principles underlying this system comes from the more recent practice of countries from the Southern hemisphere in their own mutual relations. Essentially, this practice has been built and is being built in reliance on the same principles and patterns which had emerged in the North/South context. The quasi-universality of the acceptance of these principles clearly stands as a mark for their functionality in practice.

The system without doubt will have to mature and evolve in accordance with new changing values and issues. But the central message is that the main principles have turned out to contribute to an orderly constructive process of international economic cooperation. At a time when the arbitral system is questioned from so many different sides, this message may be the most important one for the continuing debates on the creation of norms specifically and the role of arbitration tribunals in general.

Plenary Session

3. Closing Ceremony
In Honour of Pieter Sanders

Closing Ceremony
In Honour of Pieter Sanders

*Gerold Herrmann**

Ladies and Gentlemen:

We have reached what in our program is called "Closing Ceremony". Some of you might be sad about having reached the closing. But, in fact, you should all rejoice: the only people who may justifiably be sad are the local taxi drivers. But nobody here in the room. We will first have a wonderful ceremony and only then a short, automatic, painless closing. The reason for the heartbreaking ceremony is that we have amongst us a great man of honour, a laureate who will receive the newly created ICCA Lifetime Merit Award ... and that will in fact be a truly unique event, at least for the foreseeable future.

When I attended my very first ICCA Congress 1982 in Hamburg I was deeply impressed by the fact that the world's leading group of arbitrators took the time during a busy congress to celebrate the seventieth birthday of one of its members. What a decent group of people, I thought.

You can imagine how happy I was when twenty years later my first honourable task as President of ICCA was to congratulate that same person on his ninetieth birthday, again at a special dinner.

And today my happiness is truly unbounded when I am given the opportunity of handing to that very same person the newly created ICCA Lifetime Merit Award. May I now ask our Secretary General to escort Mr. Arbitration, our Pieter Sanders, to the podium.

Dear Pieter, I congratulate you wholeheartedly and give you this very special award on behalf of ICCA, and that means on behalf of all its members. Since you are always present at our meetings, I had, of course, to prepare the matter by written communications. And since signatures may only be used with the consent of the signer, I invited anyone not willing to sign to let me know within a fixed period of time. Instead, I got rousing replies, such as

Ahmed El Kosheri: "I certainly full-heartedly welcome Gerold's initiative toward our mentor and extraordinary figure as honorary President."

Tinuade Oyekunle: "Splendid idea! Professor Pieter Sanders, a father of all, has done a lot to enhance the image of ICCA internationally It is an award well deserved."

Yves Derains: "As always, Gerold has had a splendid idea. I fully support it."

---

* President of ICCA.

Ivan Szasz: "It is a wonderful idea. I wholeheartedly support it."

Giorgio Bernini: "Simply to express my enthusiastic consent to the initiative honouring Pieter Sanders with the newly established ICCA Lifetime Achievement Award. The idea of handing him a silver tray as a token is excellent and I shall be honoured to have my signature engraved on the tray."

Neil Kaplan: "I am delighted to support the gift to Pieter. It's a wonderful and appropriate gesture."

Marc Lalonde: "My first arbitration ever was with Pieter as chairman. What a wonderful experience it was! I think the idea of a special and exclusive gift is more than appropriate in this case."

Martin Hunter: "Of course, I wholeheartedly approve and will not be able to prevent tears coming to my eyes on the occasion."

This is also a good moment to mention that it was Werner Melis who proposed the silver tray and arranged for its perfection, with all the signatures and a Viennese-style rim. Thank you, Werner.

Now to the most important part of our ceremony: the description of the merits of our laureate. He personifies as no one else the development and progress of arbitration.

Already the beginning of his career is of special importance in this respect. When he joined his first law firm, it was then the general practice that new members could freely use the logistical infrastructure of the firm, on the assumption that they had only a few clients, if any at all, of their own. However, in Pieter's case, soon half the law firm was working for him, because he rapidly became known as an expert in this absolutely new field called arbitration.

To describe the following decades of his achievements in arbitration, allow me to quote from my keynote address delivered at the ICCA Congress 1998 in Paris:

> "Pieter the Great (also known as Professor Sanders) ... has done (and still does) more than anyone else in the vineyard of international commercial arbitration, as an active arbitrator, as a prolific author of seminal articles and encyclopaedic treatises, and as an expert rule-maker or law-giver.
>
> Here I am thinking in particular of his contribution as main consultant in the preparation of the UNCITRAL Arbitration Rules. It is a tribute to his unmatched expertise and vision that these worldwide used rules, even after twenty-two years, are not in need of revision."

(I should like to add from today's perspective that UNCITRAL currently undertakes a revision and it shows Pieter's largesse to his own product that he has made proposals therefor.)

> "At least equally important was his much earlier legislative contribution to the 1958 New York Conference, as one of the veterans we are happy to have with us

today, together with Dr. Glossner. When reading the Summary Records of that Conference, one is struck by his insightful and influential interventions that helped shape provisions which turned out to be of fundamental importance in the years to come: Art. II with its referral instruction to courts so as to enforce arbitration agreements; Art. V with its now classic list of exhaustive grounds for refusing enforcement, to be proven by the opposing party; and the abolition of 'double-exequatur'.

(I am happy to learn from Pieter, however, that it survived as the name of a cocktail, with added pleasure because of my preference for doubles.)

Professor Sanders' foresight is also evidenced by the fact that, anticipating the almost chronic financial crisis of the United Nations, he decided to collect and analyse, in the context of the ICCA Yearbooks, the court decisions applying and interpreting the New York Convention. This invaluable work has later been taken over by his former disciple, Professor van den Berg, while Pieter himself became General Editor of the ICCA Handbook."

By the way, Pieter's influence on the 1958 New York Convention is still very conspicuous today, although subtle. As you know, the title speaks only of arbitral awards, but not of arbitration agreements. The reason is that the important Art. II dealing with agreements was introduced together with other articles during the last part of the conference, based on a draft version invented and typed on a Sunday by the Dutch delegate Pieter Sanders. At that late time, one did not want to change the title of the Convention.

Pieter contributed, also greatly, to the progress at the 1961 Geneva Conference, elaborating the European Convention. In connection with this Conference, a historically significant meeting took place in Chambésy where, although under a different name, ICCA was founded.

Clearly a highlight in the history of ICCA were the eight years (from 1978 to 1986), really the formative years, when Pieter was our President. As former Secretary of UNCITRAL, I remember particularly fondly the good and close cooperation with Pieter in the elaboration of UNCITRAL texts on dispute settlement. As already mentioned, Pieter was our main consultant for the UNCITRAL Arbitration Rules and, I can say, he was the principal draftsman. These Rules are not only the ones most frequently used in ad hoc proceedings, but they are also very widely used in administered or institutional arbitrations. Traditional arbitration institutions offer services under these Rules in addition to their own rules, and the great majority of institutions established or internationalized after 1976 use the UNCITRAL Arbitration Rules as they are institutional rules.

I mention this only because there are still some people on this globe who view the UNCITRAL Rules as ad hoc rules. Only a few weeks ago I was invited by a lawyer to contribute to a new book an article on these Rules to form the first part of a chapter entitled "Ad Hoc Arbitration". And I thought that by now everyone knows the truth: the Rules themselves do not say that they are only for ad hoc proceedings. In fact, there existed for some time two separate drafts, until it was realized that the proceedings themselves are the same; the only differences lie in the appointment of arbitrators and certain administrative formalities which could be dealt with by appropriate additions.

When we noted in 1981 that many institutions used our Rules and invented various administrative additions, we drafted and circulated the well-known Recommendations to assist arbitral institutions in using the UNCITRAL Arbitration Rules. The whole ad hoc saga was really a PR ploy of the ICC and its supporting countries. They also managed to include the reference to "ad hoc" in the relevant General Assembly resolution.

Please excuse me that I elaborate on this issue of ad hoc v. institutional arbitration. It is not only relevant to the background and use of the UNCITRAL Arbitration Rules, but also for ICCA. As you know, for many years we had members in ICCA who were really there as representatives of certain arbitral institutions and remained members even after having left their post in the institution. Since the establishment of IFCAI, the International Federation of Commercial Arbitration Institutions, this is no longer necessary. ICCA can perform a useful role for institutional as well as ad hoc arbitration and act as a kind of world conscience or forum for international commercial arbitration.

Pieter also told me another anecdote concerning the ICC. In 1982 I was asked to give a report at an ICCA Congress, although I was not yet a member of ICCA. The topic was conciliation (since UNCITRAL had just concluded its Conciliation Rules, again with the expert assistance of Pieter Sanders). In my report I spoke of the benign neglect of conciliation at the time and mentioned as one typical example that the ICC did not envisage any fee for the conciliator. The reason given for that gap was that no remuneration was justified for that short ritual before any real proceeding, i.e., arbitration. When Pieter suggested as a member of the ICC Arbitration Commission that the ICC should take the UNCITRAL Conciliation Rules and offer real conciliation services, the answer by its then Secretary-General, Frédéric Eisemann, was: the day we accept a text of the UN, we can close our boutique.

I am happy to report that the relationship between the ICC and UNCITRAL has considerably improved. Obviously, Paris has realized that UNCITRAL is not really a competitor and has made great improvements in the world of arbitration, especially by its Model Law.

Speaking of the Model Law reminds me of another interesting situation showing Pieter's practical no-nonsense approach to problems. One of the most controversial issues was whether a party which was unhappy about an arbitral tribunal's decision that it had jurisdiction should immediately go to court (so as to avoid unnecessary waste of money and time) or only once the award was made (in order to prevent dilatory tactics). Faced with this question Pieter gave the (Dutch law) answer: Of course only at the end, because that party might win in the arbitration and would then, of course, not object to the jurisdiction.

Ladies and gentlemen, you would not get a complete picture of Pieter if I would not tell you that he is by far the most active and industrious member of ICCA, always with useful proposals concerning our publications and congresses. He is indeed a living encyclopaedia of ICCA products. He is also a living encyclopedia of modern art. In fact, he probably has the largest collection thereof, with two museums exhibiting exclusively his objects of art. And he is a great patron of the arts, having discovered many young talents, e.g., Karel Appel, who today ranks as No. 2 on the Dutch hit list after de Kooning.

Moreover, Pieter follows a very strict timetable during the day and still has many plans to realize. When I called him some time ago and asked whether he would come to Montreal (what a question!), he replied that on Thursday 1 June, his son was to be given a farewell party as director of the Concertgebouw (Concert Hall) in Amsterdam and that he had to be there, but that he could fly on Friday to Montreal ... as he did, so as to be with us today.

My final remark concerns what I regard as the most touching aspect, which best illustrates what a wonderful human being Pieter is: despite his high age, he continues to care for and to lift himself his charming wife Ida, who is confined to a wheelchair.

Ladies and gentlemen, please honour Pieter Sanders by the longest standing ovation in the history of ICCA, and thereby we close.

ICCA MONTRÉAL CONGRESS LIST OF PARTICIPANTS

Argentina

Capparelli, Santiago
Baker & McKenzie
Av. Leandro N.Alem 1110, 13th Floor
Ciudad de Buenos-Aires
santiago.capparelli@bakernet.com.ar

de San Martín, Inés
de San Martín & Asociados
Montevideo 666, 7th Floor
C1019ABN Buenos Aires
idesanmartin@desanmartinabogados.com.ar

Tawil, Guido Santiago
Member of ICCA
M. & M. Bomchil
Suipacha 268, 12th floor
C1008AAF Buenos Aires
guido.tawil@bomchil.com

Australia

Bonnell, Max
Mallesons Stephen Jaques
Level 53, Governor Phillip Tower
Sydney, NSW 2000
max.bonnell@mallesons.com

Brown, Neil, QC
PO Box 2140
St Kilda West, Victoria 3182
nabrownqc@yahoo.com

Easton, Graham
73 Carlotta Street
Greenwich, NSW, 2065
geaston@bigpond.net.au

Farmer-Maloney, Ellen
Baulderstone Hornibrook Pty Ltd
40 Miller Street
North Sydney, 2060
EFarmer-Maloney@bh.com.au

Griffith, Gavan, Q.C.
Barrister Essex Court Chambers
205 William Street
Melbourne, Victoria 3000
Griffithqc@aol.com

Hoyle, Jonathan
Clayton Utz
Levels 19-35, No.1 O'Connell Street
Sydney NSW, 2000
jhoyle@claytonutz.com

Jones, Doug
Clayton Utz
C/- Clayton Utz, PO Box H3
Sydney NSW, 2000
djones@claytonutz.com

Megens, Peter
Mallesons Stephen Jaques
Level 50, Bourke Place
600 Bourke Street
Melbourne ,Victoria 3000
peter.megens@mallesons.com

Pryles, Michael
Member of ICCA
Clayton Utz
333 Collins Street,
Melbourne, Victoria 3000
mpryles@claytonutz.com

Stephenson, Andrew
Clayton Utz
Level 18, 333 Collins Street,
Melbourne, Victoria 3000
astephenson@claytonutz.com

Austria

Haugeneder, Florian, Mag.
Wolf Theiss Rechtsanwalte GMBH
Schubertring 6
1010 Vienna
florian.haugeneder@wolftheiss.com

Herrmann, Gerold
President of ICCA
Reimersgasse 16 B2
1190 Vienna
Gerold.Herrmann@aon.at

Melis, Werner
Honorary Vice President of ICCA
International Arbitral Center in Vienna
Wiedner Hauptstraße 63

1045 Vienna
arb@wko.at

Reiner, Andreas
Arp Andreas Reiner & Partner
Freyung 6/12
1010 Vienna
office@reiner-arp.at

Riegler, Stefan
Baker & McKenzie
Schubertring 2
1010 Vienna
stefan.riegler@bakernet.com

Sekolec, Jernej
United Nations Commission on International
Trade Law
Vienna International Centre
PO Box 500
1400 Vienna
jernej.sekolec@uncitral.org

Zeiler, Gerold
Schonerr Rechtsanwalte
Tuchlauben 17, A-10 14
1014 Vienna
g.zeiler@schoenherr.at

Belgium

Keutgan, Guy
Cepani
Rue des Sols 8
1000 Brussels
gk@cepina-cepani.be

Hanotiau, Bernard
Member of ICCA
Hanotiau & Van Den Berg
Avenue Louise 480
1050 Brussels
bernard.hanotiau@hvdb.com

Matray, Didier
Matray Matray & Hallet SC
Rue Des Fories 2
4020 Liege
matray.hallet@matray.be

Olofsson, Rolf
White & Case

62 rue de la Loi
1040 Brussels
rolf.olofsson@whitecase.com

Van den Berg, Albert Jan
Hanotiau & van den Berg
IT Tower, 9th Floor, Avenue Louise 480
1050 Brussels
ajvandenberg@hvdb.com

Van Houtte, Hans
Law School
Tiense Straat
3000 Leuven
hans.vanhoutte@law.kuleuven.be

Bermuda

Elkinson, Jeffrey
Conyers Dill and Pearman
2 Church Street
Hamilton HMCX
jpelkinson@cdp.bm

Brazil

Baptista, Luiz Olavo
L. O. Baptista, Avocats
Avenida Paulista 1294,8th Floor
01310-100 Sao Paulo
lob@baptista.com.br

Batista Martins, Pedro Antonio
Barbosa, Müssnich & Aragão Advogados
Ave Almirante Barroso, 52 - 32nd Floor
20031-000 Rio de Janeiro
pbm@bmalaw.com.br

Cavalcanti, Fabiano Robalinho
Escritório de Advocacia Sergio Bermudes
Praça XV de Novembro No. 20, 8th Floor
20010-010 Rio de Janeiro
fabianorobalinho@sbadv.com.br

Cezar Aragao, Paulo
Barbosa, Mussnich & Aragao
50, Avenida Presidente Juscelino Kubitschek
4th floor
04543-000 São Paulo, SP
pca@bmalaw.com.br

Costa, Marcio Vieira Souto
Escritório de Advocacia Sergio Bermudes
Praça XV de Novembro No. 20, 8th Floor
20010-010 Rio de Janeiro
marciocosta@sbadv.com.br

Ferro, Marcelo
Marcelo Ferro Advogados
Avenida Rio Branco, No. 85, 13th Floor
20040-004 Rio de Janeiro
marcelo.ferro@ferroadv.com.br

Giusti, Gilberto
Pinheiro Neto Advogado
Rua Boa Vista, 254, 9th floor
01014-907 São Paulo
gilberto@pinheironeto.com.br

Gonçalves, Eduardo Damião
Barretto Ferreira, Kujowski, Brancher &
Goncalvez-Sociedade de Advogados
Rua Dr. Eduardo de Souza Aranha 387
15th Floor
04543-121 São Paulo
goncalves@bkbg.com.br

Moreira Franco, Alice
Marcelo Ferro Advogados
Avenida Rio Branco, No. 85, 13th Floor
20040-004 Rio de Janeiro
alice.franco@ferroadv.com.br

Nehring Netto, Carlos
Member of ICCA
Nehring & Associados
Avenida Paulista, 1294, 12th Floor
1310915 Sao Paulo
nehring@nehring.com.br

Pitombo, Eleonora Bagueira Leal Coelho
Castro, Barros, Sobral, Gomes
Rua do Rocio 291, 11th Floor
Sao Paulo, SP, 04552 000
eleonora.pitombo@cbsg.com.br

Pucci, Adriana
Veirano Advogados
Avenida das Nações Unidas, 12.995
18th Floor Brooklin Novo
04578-000 São Paulo
adriana.pucci@veirano.com.br

Brunei

Ong, Colin Y. C.
Dr. Colin Ong Legal Services
Suites 2-2 to 2-4
Gadong Properties Centre
KM 3-5, Jalan Gadong
BE4119 Bandar Seri Begawan
onglegal@brunet.bn

Canada

Alary, Christiane, The Hon.
1, rue Notre Dame Est, Suite 15.39
Montreal QC H2Y1B6

Alvarez, Henri
Fasken Martineau DuMoulin
2100-1075 West Georgia Street
Vancouver BC V6E 3G2
halvarez@van.fasken.com

Antaki, Nabil
Université de Montréal
Centre de Droit des Affaires et du Commerce
Pavillon Maximilien-Caron
3101 chemin de la Tour
Montreal QC H3T 1J7
nabil.antaki@umontreal.ca

Appleton, Barry
Appleton & Associates International Lawyers
77 Bloor Street west, Suite 1800
Toronto ON, M5S 1M2
bappleton@appletonlaw.com

Bachand, Frédéric
McGill University
3674 Peel Street
Montreal QC H3A 1W9
frederic.bachand@mcgill.ca

Barin, Babak
Woods
2000 McGill College, Suite 1700
Montreal QC H3A 2A5
bbarin@woods.qc.ca

Bertrand, Carolyn
International Trade Canada
125 Sussex Drive, Tower C, 7th Floor

Ottawa ON K1A0G2
carolyn.bertrand@international.gc.ca

Bjorkquist, Sonia
Osler, Hoskin & Harcourt
PO Box 50, 1 First Canadian Place
Toronto ON M5X 1B8
sbjorkquist@osler.com

Branson, Cecil, QC
Cecil Branson Barrister & Solicitor
886 Walkers Hook Road
Saltspring Island BC V8K 1B6
codbqc@saltspring.com

Cadieux, René
Fasken Martineau DuMoulin
800 Place Victoria, Bureau 3400
Montreal QC H4Z 1E9
rcadieux@mtl.fasken.com

Cameron, Cara
Davies Ward Phillips & Vineberg
1501 McGill College Avenue, Suite 2600
26th Floor
Montreal QC H3A 8N9
ccameron@dwpv.com

Casey, Brian
Baker & McKenzie
181 Bay Street, Suite 2100
PO Box 874
Toronto ON M5J 2T3
j.brian.casey@bakernet.com

Cherniak, Earl
Lerners
2400 -130 Adelaide Street West
Toronto ON M5H 3P5
echerniak@lerners.ca

Chiasson, Edward
Borden Ladner Gervais
1200-200 Burrard Street
Vancouver BC V7X 1T2
echiasson@blgcanada.com

Cicchetti, Tina
Fasken Martineau DuMoulin
2100-1075 West Georgia Street
Vancouver BC V6E 3G2
tcicchetti@van.fasken.com

Cochlin, Christopher
International Trade Canada
125 Sussex Drive, Tower C, 7th Floor
Ottawa ON K1A 0G2
christopher.cochlin@international.gc.ca

Colas, Bernard
Gottlieb & Pearson
2020 University Street, Suite 1920
Montreal QC H3A 2A5
bcolas@colas.ca

Cooper, George
Clark Drummie
777 Main Street, Suite 400
Moncton NB E1C 1E9
glcooper@clark-drummie.com

Craig, John
Bennett Jones
4500 Bankers Hall East
Calgary AL, T2P 4K7
craigj@bennettjones.ca

Cuddihy , Margaret
1321 Sherbrooke St. W., Apt. C-41
Montreal QC H3G 1J4
margaretcuddihy@hotmail.com

Cullen, Peter
Stikeman Elliott
155 René-Lévesque Blvd West
Montreal QC H3B 3V2
pcullen@stikeman.com

Dagenais, Catherine
Ogilvy Renault
1981 McGill College, Suite 1100
Montreal QC H3A 3C1
cdagenais@ogilvyrenault.com

D'Allaire, Dominique
Ministère de la Justice Canada
284 rue Wellington, Pièce 5303
Ottawa ON K1A 0H8
ddallair@justice.gc.ca

Debrun, Laurent
Davies Ward Phillips & Vineberg
1501, McGill College Avenue
26th floor
Montreal QC H3A 3N9
ldebrun@dwpv.com

914

Der Mestral, Armand
McGill University
3674 Peel Street
Montreal QC H3A 1W9

Desgagnés, Richard L.
Ogilvy Renault
1981 McGill College Avenue, Suite 1100
Montreal QC H3A 3C1
rdesgagnes@ogilvyrenault.com

Després, Olivier
6, rue du Périgord
La Prairie QC J5R 5Y6
o.despres@videotron.ca

Dolea, Oana Irina
McGill Faculty of Law
2015 De La Montagne, No. 306
Montreal QC H3G 1Z9
oana.dolea@mail.mcgill.ca

Drymer, Stephen L.
Ogilvy Renault
1981 McGill College Avenue, Suite 1100
Montreal QC HG3A 3C1
sdrymer@ogilvyrenault.com

Dumberry, Patrick
Ogilvy Renault
1981 McGill College Avenue
Suite 1100
Montreal QC H3A 3C1
pdumberry@ogilvyrenault.com

Dupoy, Dominic
Osler, Hoskin & Harcourt
1000, rue de la Gauchetière Ouest
Bureau 2100
Montreal QC H3B 4W5
ddupoy@osler.com

Eltis, Karen
Université d'Ottawa
3450, rue Drummond, app. 1610
Montreal QC H3G 1Y2

Fortier, L. Yves
Member of ICCA
Ogilvy Renault
1981 McGill College Avenue, Bureau 1100
Montreal QC H3A 3C1
yfortier@ogilvyrenault.com

Franklin, David
Franklin & Franklin
4141 Sherbrooke Street West No. 545
Montreal QC H3Z 1B8
d.franklin@franklinlegal.com

Gelinas, Fabien
McGill University
3644 Peel Street
Montreal QC H3A 1W9
fabien.gelinas@mcgill.ca

Greenberg, Benjamin J., Q.C.
Stikeman Elliott
1155 Blvd René Levesque West, 40th Floor
Montreal QC H3B 3V2
bgreenberg@stikeman.com

Guérard-Langlois, Annie
McGill University
1530, Doctor Penfield
Montreal QC H3G 1C1
annie.guerard-langlois@mail.mcgill.ca

Haigh, David
Burnet Duckworth & Palmer
1400, 350-7th Avenue S.W.
Calgary AL T2P3N9
drh@bdplaw.com

Halpin, Matthew
Ogilvy Renault
45 O'Connor Street, 15th Floor
Ottawa ON K1P 1A4
mhalpin@ogilvyrenault.com

Heafey, Eve
Université d'Ottawa
192 Beaulac
Gatineau QC J9H 6Z5
eve_heafey@hotmail.com

Horton, William G.
Blake, Cassels & Graydon
199 Bay Street
Toronto ON M5L1A9
william.horton@blakes.com

Hussain, Azim
Ogilvy Renault
1981 McGill College Avenue, Suite 1100
Montreal QC H3A 3C1
ahussain@ogilvyrenault.com

915

Judge, John
Stikeman Elliott
5300 Commerce Court West
Toronto ON M5L 1B9
jjudge@stikeman.com

Juricevic, Diana
Stikeman Elliot
5300 Commerce Court West
Toronto ON H5L 1B9
djuricevic@stikemanelliott.com

Khadjavi, Hodjat
Penn State University
Montreal QC
hadjat@hotmail.com

Kinnear, Meg
Trade Law Bureau/Department of Justice and
International Trade
Lester B. Pearson Building, C7-167
Ottawa ON Canada K1A 0G2
meg.kinnear@international.gc.ca

Knobel, Carolyn
International Trade Canada
125 Sussex Drive, Tower C, 7th Floor
Ottawa ON K1A 0G2
carolyn.knobel@international.gc.ca

Laird, Ian
Davis & Company
159, Fulton Ave
Toronto ON M4K 1Y2
mail@ianlaird.com

Lalonde, Marc, The Hon.
Advisory Member of ICCA
Stikeman Elliott S.E.N.C.R.L., S.R.L
1155, Boulevard René-Lévesque West
Bureau 4000
Montreal QC H3B 3V2
mlalonde@stikeman.com

Lalonde, Paul
Heenan Blaikie
200 Bay Street, Suite 2600
Toronto ON M5J 2J4
plalonde@heenan.ca

Langlois, Raynold
Langlois Krontrom Desjardins

1002 rue Sherbrooke Ouest, 28e étage,
Montreal QC H3A 3L6
raynold.langlois@lkd.ca

Leon, Barry
Torys
79 Wellington Street W., Suite 300
Box 270, TD Centre
Toronto ON M2S 1N2
bleon@torys.com

Leroux, Eric
International Trade Canada
125 Sussex Drive, Tower C, 7th Floor
Ottawa ON K1A0G2
eric.leroux@international.gc.ca

Loong, Anne-Marie
McGill University
150 Windmill
Pointe-Claire QC H9R4Y7
aloong1@po-box.mcgill.ca

Ludwig, Marcos
Veirno Advogados
1535 Summerhill Avenue, apt. 506
Montreal QC H3H 1C2
marcos.ludwig@veirano.com.br

Martin, Tim
Nexen Inc.
801 7th Avenue SW
CalgaryAL T2T 2L4
tim_martin@nexeninc.com

McDonald, Daniel J.
Burnet, Duckworth & Palmer
1400, 350 - 7th Avenue SW
Calgary AL T2P 3N9
djm@bdplaw.com

Michaud, Kristofer
McGill University
Montreal QC
kristofer.michaud@mail.mcgill.ca

Michaud, Pierre A. The Hon., O.C., Q.C.
Ogilvy Renault
1981 McGill College Avenue, Suite 1100
Montreal QC H3A 3C1
pmichaud@ogilvyrenault.com

Mills, Janet
Baker & McKenzie
181 Bay Street, Suite 2100
Toronto ON M5J 2T3
janet.e.mills@bakernet.com

Moore, Greg
McCarthy Tétrault s.e.n.c.r.l., s.r.l.
1000 rue de la Gauchetière ouest
Bureau 2500
Montreal QC H3B 0A2
gmoore@mccarthy.ca

Newcombe, Andrew
Faculty of Law, University of Victoria
PO Box 2400 STN CSC,
Victoria BC V8W3H7
newcombe@uvic.ca

Novinger Grant, Louise
Burnet, Duck&Palmer
1400, 350-7th avenue S.W
Calgary AL T2P 3N9
lng@bdplaw.com

Nyer, Damien
McGill University
3620 Lorne Crescent
Montreal QC H2X 2B1
damien.nyer@mail.mcgill.ca

Ouimet, Eric J.
BCF
1100 Boulevard René-Lévesque Ouest
25th Floor
Montreal QC H3B 5C9
ejo@bcf.ca

Paquette, Marie-Anne
Woods & associés
2000 McGill College Avenue
Montreal QC H3A 3H3
mapaquette@woods.qc.ca

Pepper, Randy
Osler, Hoskin & Harcourt
100 King Street West, Box 50
Toronto ON M5X 1B8
rpepper@osler.com

Potter, Simon
McCarthy Tétrault

1000, de la Gauchetière Ouest, Bureau 2500
Montreal QC H3B 0A2
spotter@mccarthy.ca

Rabkin, Eric
NCA
33 Millcroft Way
Thornhill ON L4J 6P2
ericrabkin@yahoo.ca

Redmond, James, Q.C.
J.E. Redmond Prof. Corp
1000 Manulife Place, 10180-101
Edmonton AL T5J 3S4
james.redmond@shaw.ca

Richter, Christopher
Woods
2000, ave McGill College, Bureau 1700
Montreal QC H3H 3H3
crichter@woods.qc.ca

Rigaud, Marie-Claude
Université de Montréal
611 Walpole Avenue
Montreal QC H3R 2A5
mcrigaud@videotron.ca

Robb, James
Stikeman Elliott
1155 René-Lévesque West, 40th Floor
Montreal QC H3B 3V2
jrobb@stikeman.com

Rowley, J. William, QC
McMillan Binch Mendelsohn
181 Bay Street, Bay Wellington Tower
Suite 440
Toronto ON M5J 2T3
wrowley@mcmbm.com

Schenke, Steve
McCarthy Tétrault
1000 de la Gauchetière St. West, Suite 2500
Montreal QC H3B 0A2
sschenke@mccarthy.ca

Sébastien, Pierre
Sébastien Downs Astell
408, rue McGill
Montreal QC H2Y 2G1
psebastien@sdal.ca

Sharma, Rajeev
Heenan Blaikie
200 Bay Street, Suite 2600
Royal Bank Plaza
Toronto ON M5J 2J4
rsharma@heenan.ca

Smith, Murray
Smith Barristers
1300- 355 Burrard Street
Vancouver BC V6C 2G8
msmith@smithbarristers.com

Steele, Gregory, Q.C.
Steele Urquhart Payne
1090 West Georgia Street, Suite 1340
Vancouver BC V7V 2Z7
gsteele@steelelawyers.com

Steger, Peter
Navigant Consulting
One Adelaide Street East,
Toronto ON M4E 1N9
psteger@navigantconsulting.com

Tabet, Sylvie
International Trade Canada
125 Sussex Drive, Tower C, 7th Floor
Ottawa ON K1A0G2
sylvie.tabet@international.gc.ca

Talbot, Lisa
Torys
TD Centre, Suite 3000
Toronto ON L6W 2W7
ltalbot@torys.com

Terry, John
Torys
79 Wellington Street West, Suite 3000
Toronto ON M5K 1N2
jterry@torys.com

Thériault, Renée
Ogilvy Renault
45 O'Connor, Suite 1500
Ottawa ON K1P 1A4
sljette@ogilvyrenault.com

Thompson, Kevin
International Trade Canada
125 Sussex Drive, Tower C, 7th Floor

Ottawa ON K1A 0G2
kevin.thompson@international.gc.ca

Torrie, Jake
University of Toronto
125 Perry Street
Cobourg ON K9A 1N8
jake.torrie@utoronto.ca

Tremblay, Bernard
BCF s.e.n.c.r.l.
800, Place d'Youville, 19e étage
Quebec QC G1R 3P4
bt@bcf.ca

Ullrich, Dierk
Fasken Martineau DuMoulin
2100-1075 West Georgia Street
Vancouver BC V6E 3G2
dullrich@van.fasken.com

Valasek, Martin
Ogilvy Renault
1981 McGill College Avenue, Suite 1100
Montreal QC H3A 3C1
mvalasek@ogilvyrenault.com

Van Duzer, Tony
Common Law, University of Ottawa
57 Louis Pasteur
Ottawa ON K1N 6N5

Vlavianos, George
Bennett Jones
4500 Bankers Hall East
855 2nd Street SW
Calgary AL T2P 4K7
vlavianosg@bennettjones.ca

Woods, James A.
Woods s.e.n.c.l.
2000, McGill Collège, Suite 1700
Montreal QC H3A 3H3
jwoods@woods.qc.ca

Woods, Michael
Gottlieb & Pearson
2020 University St., Suite 1920
Montreal QC H3A 2A5
woods@gottliebpearson.com

Yates, George, The Hon.
222 Sulphur Springs Road

918

Ancaster ON l9G 4T7
gyates@primus.ca

Chile

Armer, Angie
Alvarez Hinzpeter Jana & Valle
Av. Andres Bello 2711, piso 8
Las Condes, Santiago
aarmer@ahjv.cl

Biggs, Gonzalo
Figueroa & Valenzuela
Moneda 970 piso 5
Santiago

Jana, Andres
Alvarez Hinzpeter Jana & Valle
Av. Andres Bello 2711, piso 8
Las Condes, Santiago
ajana@ahjv.cl

Orrego-Vicuña, Francisco
Member of ICCA
20 Essex Street Chambers
Avenida El Golf No. 40, 6th Floor
755-0107 Santiago
forrego@uchile.cl

China

Chen, Cong
Beijing Arbitration Commission
7/F, China Merchants Tower, No.118
Jian Guo Road, Chaoyang District
100022 Beijing
chencong@bjac.org.cn

Hongsong, Wang
Beijing Arbitration Commission
7/F, China Merchants Tower, No. 118
Jian Guo Road, Chaoyang District
100022 Beijing
wanghs@bjac.org.cn

Hongsong, Wang
Beijing Arbitration Commission
7/F, China Merchants Tower,
No. 118, Jian Guo Road
100022 Beijing
wanghs@bjac.org.cn

Houzhi, Tang
Advisory Member of ICCA
China International Economic and Trade
Arbitration Commission
6/F Golden Land Building
32 Liangmaqiao Road
100016 Beijing
tanghouzhi@cietac.org

Jianlong, Yu
China International Economic and Trade
Arbitration Commission
6/F, Golden Land Building
32 Liangmaqiao Road
100016 Beijing
yujianlong@cietac.org

Jing, Zhao
International Economic and Trade Arbitration
Commission, 7/F
28-2 Jin Ling Rd.W.,
200021 Shanghai
zhaojing@cietac.org

Munro, Susan
O'melveny & Myers
37th floor, Plaza 66
1266 Nanjing Road West
200040 Shanghai
smunro@omm.com

Yan, Gu
China International Economic and Trade
Arbitration Commission
6/F, Golden Land Building
32 Liangmaqiao Rd
100016 Beijing
guyan@cietac.org

Ye, Zhang
China International Economic and Trade
Arbitration Commission
6/F, Golden Land Building
32 Liangmaqiao Road
100016 Beijing
zhangye@cietac.org

Czech Republic

Klein, Bohuslav
Arbitration Court

C2-11000 Prague
marovcova@arbcourt.cr

Pohunek, Milos
Arbitration Court
C2-11000 Prague
praha@arbcourt.cr

Denmark

Spiermann, Ole
University of Copenhagen
Faculty of Law, Studiestraede 6,
K 1455 Copenhagen
ole.spiermann@jur.ku.dk

Egypt

Aboul-Enein, Mohamed
Cairo Centre for International Commercial
Arbitration
1 Al-Saleh Ayoub St.
Zamalek
11211 Cairo
info@crcica.org.eg

El-Kosheri, Ahmed
Member of ICCA
Kosheri, Rashed and Riad
16A Manuel El-Sokkar Street
Garden City
11451 Cairo
samiafr@link.net

Hafez, Karim
Hafez & Associates
5 Ibrahim Naguib Street
Garden City Cairo
11451
k.hafez@hafeznet.com

El Salvador

Brett, Zygmunt
Arias & Muñoz
85 avenida norte,
825 San Salvador
zbrett@ariaslaw.com

Finland

Möller, Gustaf
Arbitration Institute of the Central Chamber
of Commerce of Finland
Ritarikatu 7 A 7
FI-00170 H Helsinki
gmoller@welho.com

France

Ahdab, Jalal
Orrick
78, Av. de Sufrene
75007 Paris
jahdab@orrick.com

Baum, Axel
Hughes Hubbard & Reed
47, Av. Georges Mandel
75116 Paris
baum@hugheshubbard.com

Bensaude, Denis
Bensaude
12, rue Déodat de Séverac
75017 Paris
bensaude@orange.fr

Bernard, Patrick
Bernard Hertz Befot
8, rue Murillo
Paris
pbernard@bhbfrance.com

Bertrand, Edouard
Slaughter and May
112, Av. Kleber
75116 Paris
e.bertrand@slaughterandmay.com

Bond, Stephen R.
White & Case
11, Bd de la Madeleine
75001 Paris
sbond@whitecase.com

Bondy, Christophe
Hughes Hubbard & Reed
47, Av. Georges Mandel
75116 Paris
bondy@hugheshubbard.com

Branson, David
Wallace King Domike & Branson
26, rue Saint André des Arts
75006 Paris
dbranson@wallaceking.com

Brown, David
Sahdbolt & Co
52, Av. De La Grande Armée
75017 Paris
David_Brown@shadboltlaw.com

Camboulive, Christian
Cabinet Gide Loyrette Nouel
26, cours Albert 1er
Paris 75008
camboulive@gide.com

Colaiuta, Virginie
Hughes Hubbard & Reed
47, Av. Georges Mandel
75116 Paris

Craig, W. Laurence
Orrick Herrington & Sutcliffe
25, Bd de l'Amiral Bruix
16 75782 Paris Cedex
wlc@craigarbitration.com

Crestohl, Leigh
Clifford Chance
112, Av. Kléber, BP 163
Trocadéro
16 75770 Paris Cedex
leigh.crestohl@cliffordchance.com

Davis, Frederick T.
Debevoise & Plimpton
21, Av. George V
75008 Paris
ftdavis@debevoise.com

de Boisséson, Mathieu
Darrois Villey Maillot Brochier
69, Av. Victor Hugo
75783 Paris CEDEX 16
mdeboisseson@darroisvilley.com

Degos, Louis
Eversheds Frere Cholmeley
8, Place D'Iéna
Paris 75116
louisdegos@eversheds.com

Delanoy, Louis Christophe
Cabinet Brediw Prat
130, rue du Faubourg Saint Honoré
Paris 75008
lcd@bredinprat.com

Derains, Bertrand
Derains & Associés
167 bis, Av. Vistor Hugo
75116 Paris
bderains@derains.com

Delvolvé, Jean-Louis
Devolvé Rouche
5, rue Marguerite
75017 Paris
delvolve.et.rouche@gofornet.com

Dugué, Christophe
Shearman & Sterling
114, Av. des Champs-Elysées
75008 Paris
cdugue@shearman.com

Duprey, Pierre
Darrois Villey Maillot Brochier
69, Av. Victor Hugo
75783 Paris Cedex 16
cparpet@darroisvilley.com

Kleiman, Elie
Freshfields Bruckhaus Deringer
2, rue Paul Cezanne
75008 Paris
elie.kleiman@freshfields.com

Gaillard, Emmanuel
Member of ICCA
Shearman & Sterling
114, Av. des Champs Elysées
75008 Paris
egaillard@shearman.com

Gélinas, Paul-A.
69, Av. Victor Hugo
75783 Paris Cedex 16, Seine
pgelinas@pgelinas.com

Genot-Delbeque, Françoise
CMS Bureau Francis Lefebvre
1/3 villa Emile Bergerat
92200 Neuilly Sur Seine, Hauts de Seine
francoise.genot-delbecque@cms-bfl.com

Gharavi, Hamid
Salans
9, rue Boissy d'Anglas
75008 Paris
hgharavi@salans.com

Grierson, Jacob
Jones Day
120, rue du Faubourg Saint Honoré
75008 Paris
jgrierson@cgsh.com

Harb, Jean-Pierre
Baker & McKenzie
32, Av. Kléber
16 75771 Paris Cedex
jean-pierre.harb@bakernet.com

Hautot, Isabelle
6, Place D'Alleray
75505 Paris
isabelle.hautot@francetelecom.com

Henry, Marc
Lovells
6, Av. Kléber
Paris 75116
marc.henry@lovells.com

Honlet, Jean Christophe
Salans
9, rue Boissy d'Anglas
Paris 75008
jhonlet@salans.com

Horrigan, Brenda
Salans
9, rue Boissy D'Anglas
EC4V4AJ Paris
bhorrigan@salans.com

Jaeger, Laurent
Latham & Watkins
53 Quay D'Orsay
75007 Paris
laurent.jaeger@lw.com

Jarvin, Sigvard
Jones Day
120 Faubourg Saint Honoré
75008 Paris
sjarvin@jonesday.com

Kaplan, Charles
Herbert Smith
20, rue Quentin Bauchart
75008 Paris
charles.kaplan@herbertsmith.com

Kessedjian, Catherine
Université Panthéon - ASSAS Paris II
19, Villa Seurat, Boite B
75014 Paris
ckessedjian@u-paris2.fr

Leboulanger, Phillippe
Leboulanger & Associés
5, rue de Chaillot
75116 Paris
phl@leboulanger-avocats.com

Lécuyer-Thieffry, Christine
Thieffry & Associés
23, Av. Hoche
75008 Paris
christine.thieffry@thieffry.com

Legum, Barton
Debevoise & Plimpton
21, Av. George V
75008 Paris
blegum@debevoise.com

Lesguillons, Henry
Université de Paris X
26, Villa de la Réunion
75016 Paris Seine
henrylesguillons@iblj.com

Leurent, Bruno
Winston & Strawn
21, Av. Victor Hugo
75116 Paris
bleurent@winston.com

Mariani, Nicola
Freshfields Bruckhaus Deringer
2, rue Paul Cézanne
75008 Paris
nicola.mariani@freshfields.com

Mc Dougall, Andrew de Lotbinière
White & Case
11, Bd. de la Madeleine
75001 Paris
amcdougall@whitecase.com

Meese, Richard
Cabinet Meese
24, Place du Général Catroux
75017 Paris
cabinetrmeese@aol.com

Michou, Isabelle
Herbert Smith
20, rue Quentin Beauchart
75008 Paris
isabelle.michou@herbertsmith.com

Mohtashami, Reza
Freshfields Bruckhaus Deringer
2/4, rue Paul Cézanne
75008 Paris
reza.mohtashami@freshfields.com

Mondoloni, Dominique
Willkie Farr & Gallagher
21-23, rue de la Ville L'Evêque
75008 Paris
dmondoloni@willkie.com

Mourre, Alexis
Castaldi Mourre Sprague
3, rue du Boccador
75008 Paris
amourre@cmdslaw.com

Nelson, Karen
Salans
9, rue Boissy d'Anglas
75008 Paris
knelson@salans.com

Ostrove, Michael
Debevoise & Plimpton
21, Av. George V
75008 Paris Ile de France
mmostrove@debevoise.com

Paulsson, Jan
Member of ICCA
Freshfields Bruckhaus Deringer
2, rue Paul Cézanne
75008 Paris
jan.paulsson@freshfields.com

Pedone, Priscille
Castaldi Mourre
3, rue du boccador

75008 Paris
ppedone@cmdslaw.com

Perrot, Amance
Perrot law firm
5, Av. Gambetta
06600 Antibes Paca
agc.perrot@laposte.net

Peterson, Patricia
Linklaters
25, rue de Marignan
75008 Paris
patricia.peterson@linklaters.com

Petrochilos, Georgios
Freshfields Bruckhaus Deringer
2, rue Paul Cézanne
75008 Paris
georgies.petrochilos@freshfields.com

Philippe, Mirèze
International Chamber of Commerce
38, cours Albert 1er
75008 Paris
mireze.philippe@iccwbo.org

Pinsolle, Philippe
Shearman & Sterling
114, Av. des Champs-Elysées
75008 Paris
ppinsolle@shearman.com

Rosell, José
Hughes Hubbard & Reed
47, Av. Geiorges Mandel
75116 Paris
rosell@hugheshubbard.com

Rouche, Jean
Delvolve Rouche
5, rue Marguerite
75017 Paris
delvolve.et.rouche@gofornet.com

Schwartz, Eric
Freshfields Bruckhaus Deringer
2, rue Paul Cézanne
75008 Paris Ile de France
eric.schwartz@freshfields.com

Seppala, Christopher
White & Case

11, Bd de la Madeleine
75001 Paris

Stern, Brigitte
Université Paris 1, Panthéon Sorbonne
7, rue Pierre Nicole
75005 Paris
stern@univ-paris1.fr

Tercier, Pierre
Member of ICCA
ICC International Court of Arbitration
38, Cours Albert 1er
75008 Paris
pte@iccwbo.org

Turner, Peter
Freshfields Bruckhaus Deringer
2, rue Paul Cézanne, Paris
75006 France
peter.turner@freshfields.com

Van Leeuwen, Melanie
Loyens & Loeff
1, Av. F.D. Roosevelt
75008 Paris
melanie.van.leeuwen@loyensloeff.com

Verhoosel, Gaetan
Debevoise & Plimpton
21, Av. George V
75008 Paris
gverhoosel@debevoise.com

Wetmore, Todd
Shearman & Sterling
114, Av. des Champs-Élysées
75008 Paris
twetmore@shearman.com

Willems, Jane
Avocat à la Cour
24, Place du Général Catroux
Paris
janewillems@wanadoo.fr

Yannaca-Small, Katia
OECD
2, rue Andre Pascal
75116 Paris
catherine.yannaca-small@oecd.org

Germany

Behrens, Peter
University of Hamburg
Parkallee 2
20144 Hamburg
peter.behrens@uni-hamburg.de

Berger, Klaus Peter
University of Cologne
Albertus Magnus Platz
50968 Cologne NRW
kp.berger@uni-koeln.de

Böckstiegel, Karl-Heinz
Member of ICCA
Parkstraße 38
51427 Bergisch-Gladbach NRW
khboeckstiegel@aol.com

Bredow, Jens
German Institution of Arbitration
Beethovenstraße 5-13
50674 Cologne NRW
Bredow.Jens@dis-arb.de

Dolzer, Rudolf
University of Bonn
Institut für Völkerrecht
Adenauerallee 24-42
53113 Bonn
rdolzer@jura.uni-bonn.de

Friedrich, Bettina
Friedrich & Korch
Feldbergstrasse 23
60323 Frankfurt am Main, Hessen
friedrich@friedrichkorch.de

Hanefeld, Inka
Renzenbrink Raschke von Knobelsdorff
Heiser
Wexstrasse 16
20355 Hamburg
hanefeld@rrkh.de

Kreindler, Richard H.
Shearman & Sterling
Gervinusstr. 17
60322 Frankfurt am Main, Hessen
bwiechmann@shearman.com

Kuhn, Wolfgang
Heuking Kuhn Luer Wojtek
Cecilienallee 5
40474 Duesseldorf
w.kuehn@heuking.de

Nacimiento, Patricia
Nörr Stiefenhofer Lutz
Friedrichstraße 2-6
60323 Frankfurt am Main, Hesse
patricia.nacimiento@noerr.com

Pfitzner, Tanja V.
Freshfields Bruckhaus Deringer
Taunusanlage 11
60329 Frankfurt am Main, Hesse
tanja.pfitzner@freshfields.com

Schäfer, Erik
Cohausx & Florack
Annabergstrasse 15
Ratingen Hösel 40883
eschaefer@cohausz-florack.de

Greece

Antonias Dimolitsa
A. Dimolitsa and Associates
12 Milioni Street
10673 Athens
adoffice@hellasnet.gr

Hong Kong

Aglionby, Andrew
Baker & McKenzie
14/F Hutchison House
10 Harcourt Road
852 Central
andrew.aglionby@bakernet.com

Barrington, Louise
City University Law School
83 Tat Chee Avenue, 5/Floor
louiseb@netvigator.com

Cheng, Teresa, SC, JP
Member of ICCA
Des Voeux Chambers
10/F. Bank of East India Building

10 Des Voeux Road
tywcheng@netvigator.com

Harpole, Sally
Sally Harpole & Co.
G.P.O. Box 12153
sallyharpole@sallyharpole.com

Lin, Mark
Lovells
23/F, Cheung Kong Center
2 Queen's Road
Central
mark.lin@lovells.com

Moser, Michael J.
Freshfields Bruckhaus Deringer
11/F Two Exchange Square
mmoser@omm.com

Hungary

Horvath, Dr. Eva
Arbitration Court attached to the HCCI
Kossurh Lajos rér 6-8
H-1055 Budapest
vb@mail.mkik.hu

Szász, Iván
Vice President of ICCA
Squire Sanders & Demprey
Andrassy – Út 64
1062 Budapest
iszasz@ssd.com

India

Chandrasekaran, P.
Chandrasekar Associtates
48 Second Main Road
Rajaanamalaipuram, Chennai
600028 Tamilnadu
p_c_barrister@yahoo.com.in

Dave, Dushyant
Member of ICCA
43, Prithviraj Road
110011 New Delhi
dushyantdave@gmail.com

925

Dholakia, Shishir
Allied Law Practice
D-97, Panchseel Enclave
110017 New Delhi
shishir.dholakia@dholakias.com

Ganguli, Amal Kumar
Supreme Court of India
10 Lawyers' Chambers
110001 New Delhi
akg@ganguli.org

Parekh, Pravin H.
M/S P.H. Parekh & Co.
Parekh Chambers
30 School Lane
110001 New Delhi
phparekh@phparekh.com

Parikh, Devan
Behind Abhijeet-III, Near Law Garden
380006 Ellisbridge, Ahmedabad
sheelparikh@hotmail.com

Popat, Dharmasinh
M/S Mulla & Mulla & Craigie Blunt & Caroe
Mulla House
51 Mahatma Gandhi Road
400001 Mumbay, Maharashtra
dmp@mullas.net

Reddy, Vijaynandan
Tricons
2-2-12/A, D.D.Colony
500 007 Hyderabad, A.P.
iprtricons@yahoo.com

Sabharwal, Yogesh. K, The Hon.
Supreme Court of India
5 Krishna Menon Marg
110011 New Delhi
yksabharwal@hotmail.com

Indonesia

Budidjaja, Tony
Baker & McKenzie
Hadiputranto, Hadinoto & Partners
The Jakarta Stock Exchange Building Tower
II, 21st Floor
Jakarta Selatan
tony.budidjaja@bakernet.com

Ireland

Carrigan, Michael
Eugene F. Collins Temple Chambers
3 Burlington Road
Dublin 4
mwcarrigan@efc.ie

Lehane, Sheila
Law Library, Four Courts
Dublin 7
barrister@sheilalehane.com

Moran, Michael
The Law Society of Ireland
Blackhall Place
Dublin 7
michaelmoran@deloitte.ie

Reichert, Klaus
Law Library
145-151 Church Street
Dublin 7
klaus@indigo.ie

Israel

Kapeliuk, Daphna
Radzyner School of Law
Interdisciplinary Center
46150 Herzliya
daphnak@post.tau.ac.il

Italy

Azzali, Stefano
Chamber of National and International
Arbitration
Via Meracigli 91B
20123 Milan
azzali@mi.camcom.it

Caputo, Calogero Massimiliano
Law Firm Vassallo
Via Musumeci 107
95129 Catania
maxcaputo62@hotmail.com

Cicogna, Michelangelo
De Berti Jacchia Franchini Forlani

Via San Paolo 7
20121 Milan

Corapi, Diego
Studio Legale Corapi
Via Flaminia 318
196 Rome
diego.corapi@studiolegalecorapi.it

De Berti, Giovanni
De Berti Jacchia Franchini Forlani
Via San Paolo 7
20121 Milan
g.deberti@dejalex.com

Fumagalli, Luigi
Studio Legale Pavia E Ansaldo
Via des Lauro 7
20129 Milan
luigi.fumagalli@pavia-ansaldo.it

Radicati Di Brozolo, Luca G.
Bonelli Erede Pappalardo
Via Borozzi 1
20122 Milan
luca.radicati@beplex.com

Japan

Eastman, Richard
Holland & Knight
Akasaka Tokyu Building Ste 7C
2-14-3 Nagatacho, Chiyoda-ku
100-0014 Tokyo
richard.eastman@hklaw.com

Hayakawa, Yoshihisa
Rikkyo University
3-34-1 Nishi-Ikebukuro, Toshima-ku
171-8501 Tokyo
haya@rikkyo.ac.jp

Nakamura, Tatsuya
The Japan Commercial Arbitration
Association
1-9-1, Yurakucho, Chiyoda-ku
100-0006 Tokyo
nakamura@jcaa.or.jp

Oghigian, Haig
Paul Hastings - Gaikokho Kyodo Jigyo
347 Ark Mori Bldg

PO BOX 577
1-12-32, Akasaka
107-6034 Tokyo
haigoghigian@paulhastings.com

Onuki, Masaharu
The Japan Commercial Arbitration
Association
2-8, Hommachibashi, Chuo-ku
540-0029 Osaka
onuki@jcaa.or.jp

Sawai, Akira
Osaka Prefecture University
1-1 Gakuencho, Naka-ku, Sakai
599-8531 Osaka
sawai@eco.osakafu-u.ac.jp

Taniguchi, Yasuhei
Member of ICCA
Matsuo & Kosugi/WTO
Fukoku-Seimei Bldg. 18th Floor
2-2 Uchisaiwai-cho
100-0011 Tokyo
tanigy@mknet.jp

Tezuka, Hiroyuki
Nishimura & Partners
ARK Mori Bldg. 1-12-32
Akasaka, Minato-ku
1076029 Tokyo
h_tezuka@jurists.co.jp

Yanase, Shuji
Nagashima Ohno & Tsunematsu
Kioicho Building, 3-12
Kioicho, Chiyoda-ku
102-0094 Tokyo
shuji_yanase@noandt.com

Jordan

Obeidat, Sufian
Obeidat & Freihat
PO Box 926544
11190 Amman
sufian@obeidatfreihat.com

Kenya

The Hon. S. Amos Wako

927

Member of ICCA
PO Box 15053
Nairobi, Lagata

Korea

Bang, John
Bae, Kim & Lee
Hankook Tire Bldg
647-15 Yoksam-dong, Gangnam-gu
135-723 Seoul
jpb@bkl.co.kr

Choi, John Hyouk
Shin & Kim
Ace Tower, 4th Floor
1-170, Soonhwa-Dong, Chung-Ku
100-712 Seoul
jhchoi@shinkim.com

Kim, Beom Su
Shin & Kim
Ace Tower, 4th Floor
1-170 Soonhwa-Dong Chung-Ku
100-712 Seoul
bskim@shinkim.com

Kim, Kap-You (Kevin)
Bae, Kim & Lee
Hankook Tire Building
647-15 Yoksam-dong, Gangnam-gu
135-723 Seoul
kyk@baekimlee.com

Lee, Jae-Woo
The Korean Commercial Arbitration Board
World Trade Tower, Room 4303
159, Samsung-Dong
135-729 Seoul
mohikan@kcab.or.kr

Park, Sam Kyu
The Korean Commercial Arbitration Board
World Trade Tower, Room 4303
159, Samsung-Dong
138-759 Seoul
dipre@kcab.or.kr

Park, Eun-Young
Kim & Chang
Seyang Building, 8th Floor

Naeja-dong 223
110-720 Seoul
zjykim9@kimchang.com

Lebanon

Comair-Obeid, Nayla
Obeid Law Firm
116-2234, Palais de Justice
1109-2020 Beirut
info@obeidlawfirm.com

Malaysia

Abraham, Cecil
Member of ICCA
Shearn & Co.
Wisma Hamzah, 7th Floor
Kwong Hing
1Leboh Ampang
50100 Kuala Lumpur
cecil@shearndelamore.com

Idid, Syed
Kuala Lumpur Regional Centre for Arbitration
12 Jalan Oonlay
45500 Kuala Lumpur
director@rcakl.org.my

Loo, Yvan Y. F.
Skrine
Unit No. 50-8-1, 8th Floor
Wisma UOA Damansara
50 Jalan Dungun
50490 Kuala Lumpur
il@skrine.com

Mexico

Abascal, José Maria
11 Cda Flor de Agua
1030 Mexico City, D.F.
jma@abascal-asociados.com

Gonzalez de Cossio, Francisco
Barrera, Siqueiros y Torres Landa, S.C.
Montes Urales No. 470-1
Lomas de Chapultepec

11000 Mexico City
fgc@bst1.com.mx

Magallanes, Adrian
ELD
Guillermo Gonzalez Camarena 1100
7th floor, Santa Fe, Alvaro Obregon
1210 Mexico City D.F.
adrianmagallanesp@hotmail.com

Navardo-Velasco, Javier
Baker & McKenzie
Oficinas en el Parque Piso10
Boulevard Antonio L. Rodriguez 1884
64650 Monterrey, Nuevo Leon
javier.navarro-velasco@bakernet.com

Reyes-Retana, Ygnacio
Baker & McKenzie
Boulevard Agua Caliente 10611-1
22420 Tijuana, Baja California
ygnacio.reyes-retana@bakernet.com

Von Wobeser, Claus
Von Wobeser y Sierra, S.C.
Guillermo González Camarena
No. 1100, 7th Floor
Delegación Alvaro Obregón 1210
CVonWobeser@vwys.com.mx

Netherlands

Borelli, Silvia
Permanent Court of Arbitration
Peace Palace, Carnegieplein 2
2517 KJ The Hague
silvia.borelli@pca-cpa.org

De Groot, Diederik
DLA Piper Rudnick Gray Cary
PO Box 75258
1071 ZX Amsterdam
diederik.degroot@dlapiper.com

De Ly, Filip
Erasmus University
Johan Buziaulaan 33
3584 ZT Utrecht
dely@frg.eur.nl

Freedberg, Judith
Permanent Court of Arbitration

Peace Palace, Carnegieplein 2
2517 KJ The Hague
icca@pca-cpa.org

Meijer, Gerard
de Brauw Blackstone Westbroek
PO Box 90851
2509 LW The Hague
gerard.meijer@debrauw.com

Sanders, Pieter
Honorary President of ICCA
Burg. Knappertlaan 134
3117 BD Schiedam
psansders@tref.nl

Siegel, Alice
Permanent Court of Arbitration
Peace Palace, Carnegieplein 2
2517 KJ The Hague
asiegel@pca-cpa.org

Van Haersolte-Van Hof, Jackie
Freshfields Bruckhaus Deringer
PO Box 75299
1070 AG Amsterdam,
jacomyn.vanhaersolte@freshfiels.com

Van den Hout, Tjaco
Permanent Court of Arbitration
Peace Palace, Carnegieplein 2
2517 KJ The Hague
bureau@pca-cpa.org

van der Bend, Bommel
De Brauw Blackstone Westbroek
PO Box 90851
2509 LW The Hague
bommel.vanderbend@debrauw.com

Van Leyenhorst, Max
Nauta Dutilh
PO Box 1110
3000 BC Rotterdam
max.vanleyenhorst@nautadutilh.com

New Zealand

Williams, David A. R.
Member of ICCA
Essex Court Chambers & Bankside Chambers
4 Bankside Chambers, Level 22

The Lumley Center
88 Shorthand Street
PO Box 405
1001 Auckland
david.williams@darwilliams.co.nz

Nigeria

Ufot, Dorothy
Dorothy Ufot & Co
5 Idowu Taylor Street, 4th Floor
Victoria Island, Lagos
dufot@infoweb.com.ng

Pakistan

Khan, Muhammad Naeem
Muhammad Akram & Sons Trading &
Investment
PO BOX 1029 G.P.O.
46000 Rawalpindi, Punjab
makramsonsti@yahoo.com

Sarwana, Ahmed
Abraham & Sarwana
Mezzanine Floor, PIDC House
75530 Karachi, Sindh
abrahams@cyber.net.pk

Poland

Nowaczyk, Piotr
Court of Arbitration at the Polish Chamber of
Commerce
Trabacka 4 Str
00-074 Warsaw
info@sakig.pl

Okolski, Józef
Court of Arbitration at the Polish Chamber of
Commerce
Trabacka 4 Str
00-074 Warsaw
info@sadarbitrazowy.pl

Pieckowski, Sylwester
Court of Arbitration
UL. Flory 9 Lok. 3
00-586 Warsaw
sadarbitrazoxy@prywetni.pl

Poczobut, Jerzy
Court of Arbitration
UL. Flory 9 Lok. 3
00-586 Warsaw
sadarbitrazowy@prywatni.pl

Szumanski, Andrzej
Court of Arbitration
Ul. Flory 9 Lok. 3
00-586 Warsaw
sadarbitrazowy@prywatni.pl

Szurski, Tadeusz
Advisory Member of ICCA
Court of Arbitration
Ul. Flory 9 Lok. 3
00-586 Warsaw
sadarbitrazowy@prywatni.pl

Zbiegien, Tomasz
Court of Arbitration
Ul. Flory 9 Lok. 3
00-586 Warsaw
sadarbitrazowy@prywatni.pl

Russia

Aitkulov, Timur
Clifford Chance
Sadovaya-Sarnotechnaya Street 24/27
127051 Moscow
timur.aitkulov@cliffordchance.com

Komarov, Alexander
Member of ICCA
International Commercial Arbitration Court
at the
Russian Chamber of Commerce and Industry
6, Ilyinka St.
109012 Moscow
komarov@tpprf.ru

Lebedev, Sergei
Honorary Vice President of ICCA
Maritime Arbitration Commission
at the Russian Chamber of Commerce and
Industry
6, Ilyinka Street
109012 Moscow
privitlaw@mgimo.ru

Saudi Arabia

Altuwaigri, Waleed
The High Judicial Institute
in Riyadh in Saudi Arabia
PO Box 33294
11448 Riyadh
wstuwaigri@yahoo.com

Singapore

Boo, Lawrence
Singapore International Arbitration Centre
City Hall
3 St Andrew's Road
178958 Singapore
lawrenceboo@siac.org.sg

Hwang, Michael S.C.
Vice President of ICCA
One Marina Boulevard, No. 25-01
18989 Singapore
michael@mhwang.com

Koh, Swee Yen
Blk 26 Marsiling Drive, No. 04-233
730026 Singapore
sweeyen@singnet.com.sg

Lau, Christopher
Alban Tay Mahtani & de Silva
39 Robinson Road
07-01Robinson Point
068911 Singapore
christopherlau@atmdlaw.com.sg

Spooner, Guy David Anthony
Norton Rose
5 Shenton Way, No. 33-08 UIC Building
68808 Singapore
guy.spooner@nortonrose.com

Tan, Chuan Thye
Baker & McKenzie
27-01 Millenia 1 Temack Avenue
Singapore 39192

Spain

Arias, David
Perez - Llorca

Alcala 61
28014 Madrid
darias@perezllorca.com

Claros, Pedor
Cuatrecasas
C/ Velázquez, No. 63
28001 Madrid
pedro.claros@cuatrecasas.com

Cremades, Bernardo
Member of ICCA
Goya 18
B. Cremades y Asociados
28001Madrid
constanza@bcremades.com

Fernández-Armesto, Juan
Armesto & Asociados
General Pardiñas 102
28006 Madrid
loc@jfarmesto.com

Fernandez-Ballesteros, Miguel Angel
Gomez-Acebo & Pombo
Paseo de la Castellana 216
28046 Madrid
mfeernadezh@gomezacebo.com

Fröhlingsdorf, Josef
Froehlingsdorf Abogados Asociados
Paseo de la Castellana 120 −5
28046 Madrid
jfroehlingsdorf@froehlingsdorfabogados.es

Hamilton, Calvin
Monereo Meyer Marinel-lo Abogados
Barbara de Braganza 11, 2 Dcha
28004 Madrid
chamilton@mmmm.es

Mondragón-López, Omar
Uría Menéndez
c/ Príncipe de Vergara 187
28002 Madrid
omarmondragon@gmail.com

Rueda Garcia, José-Ángel
University of Salamanca
c/ El Greco. No 10-12, 5 F
37004 Salamanca
joseangelruedagarcia@hotmail.com

Venegas Grau, Carmen
Linklaters
Jerónimo de la Quintana, 10, 4th Floor
28010 Madrid
venegas@gmx.net

Sweden

Adolfsson, Sara
Arbitration Institute of the Stockholm
Chamber of Commerce
PO Box 16050
10321 Stockholm
sara.adolfsson@chamber.se

Bagner, Hans G.
Vinge
PO Box 1703
11187 Stockholm
hans.bagner@vinge.se

Bendrik, Mats
Advokatfirman Cederquist
Box 1670
11196 Stockholm
mats.bendrik@cederquist.se

Eklund, Jonas
Gernandt & Danielsson Advokatbyra KB
PO BOX 5747
Stockholm 11487
jonas.eklund@gda.se

Fohlin, Paulo
Advokatfirman Vinge KB
POBox 11025
40421 Gothenburg
paulo.fohlin@vinge.se

Franke, Ulf
Honorary Secretary General of ICCA
Arbitration Institute of the Stockolm
Chamber of Commerce
PO Box 16050
10321 Stockholm
ulf.franke@chamber.se

Gernandt, Johan
Gerdandt & Danielsson Advokatbyra KB
PO Box 5747
11487 Stockholm
johan.gernandt@gda.se

Hobér, Kaj
Mannheimer Swartling Advokatbyrå
Box 1711
11187 Stockholm
mh4@msa.se

Heuman, Lars
Stockholm University
10691 Stockholm
lars.heuman@juridicum.su.se

Johansson, Tom
Cederquist
PO Box 1670
11196 Stockholm
tj@ceq.se

Jonson, Lars
Advokatfirman Vinge KB
PO Box 11025
404 21 Gothenburg
lars.jonson@vinge.se

Magnusson, Annette
Baker & McKenzie Advokatbyrå KB
PO Box 5719
114 87 Stockholm
annette.magnusson@bakernet.com

Shaughnessy, Patricia
University of Stockholm
Rotella AB, Parksätravägen 3
18161 Lidingö
Patricia.Shaughnessy@juridicum.su.se

Söderlund, Christer
Vinge
PO Box 1703
11187 Stockholm
christer.soderlund@vinge.se

Wiwen-Nilsson, Tore
Mannheimer Swartling
Sodergatan 22
PO Box 4291
20314 Malmo
twn@msa.se

Switzerland

Appert, Nicole V.
Tavernier Tschanz

11 bis, rue Toepffer
1206 Geneva
appert@taverniertschanz.com

Baizeau, Domitille
Lalive
35, rue de la Mairie
1207 Geneva
dbaizeau@lalive.ch

Blessing, Marc
Baer & Karrer
Brandschenkestrasse 90
8027 Zurich
m.blessing@baerkarrer.ch

Briner, Robert
Member of ICCA
Lenz & Staehelin
Route de Chêne 30
1211 Geneva
robert.briner@lenzstaehelin.com

Casserly, David
Court of Arbitration for Sport
Château de Bethusy, Ave de Beaumont 2
1012 Lausanne, Vaud
david.casserly@tas-cas.org

Dasser, Felix
Homburger
PO Box 338
8035 Zurich
felix.dasser@homburger.ch

Favre-Bulle, Xavier
Lenz & Staehelin
30, route de Chêne
1211 Geneva 17
xavier.favre-bulle@lenzstaehelin.com

Genton, Pierre Michel
PMG Ing.-Econ. Conseils
72, rue du Centre
1025 Saint-Sulpice/Lausanne
pgenton@pmg-ing.ch

Giovannini, Teresa
Lalive
35, rue de la Mairie
1207 Geneva
tgiovannini@lalive.ch

Grégoire, Nicolas
SGS Société Générale de Surveillance S.A
1 Place des Alpes
1201 Geneva
nicolas.gregoire@sgs.com

Habegger, Philipp
Walder Wyss & Partners
Münstergasse 2
PO Box 2990
8022 Zurich
phabegger@wwp.ch

Hirsch, Laurent
Hirsch Kobel
8, rue Eynard
1205 Geneva
laurent.hirsch@hirsch-law.ch

Ibig, Eugène
Lenz & Staehelin
Route de Chêne 30
1211 Geneva
eugene.ibig@lenzstaehelin.com

Jolles, Alexander
Schellenberg Wittmer
Loewenstrasse 19
PO Box 6333
8023 Zurich
alexander.jolles@swlegal.ch

Kaelin-Nauer, Claudia
Froriep Renggli Attorneys at Law
Bellerivestrasse 201
8034 Zurich
ckaelin@froriep.ch

Karrer, Pierre A.
Lavaterstrasse 98
8002 Zurich
karrer@pierrekarrer.com

Kaufmann-Kohler, Gabrielle
Member of ICCA
Schellenberg Wittmer
15 bis, rue des Alpes
1211 Geneva
gabrielle.kaufmann@swlegal.ch

Koch, Christopher
Georgana & Koch
42, rue du Rhône

1204 Geneva
christopher@gklaw.gr

Knoepfler, François
KGG & Associés
Serre 4
2000 Neuchâtel
knoepfler@kgg.ch

Koenig, B. Gino
Gloor & Sieger
PO Box 581
8024 Zurich
bgkoenig@gloor-sieger.ch

Landolt, Phillip
Tavernier Tschanz
11 bis, rue Toepffer
1206 Geneva
landolt@taverniertscanz.com

Lévy, Laurent
Schellenberg Wittmer
15 bis, rue des Alpes
1211 Geneva
laurent.levy@swlegal.ch

Loungnarath, Vilaysoun
Organisation Mondiale du Commerce
154, rue de Lausanne
1211 Geneva
vilaysoun.loungnarath@wto.org

Nardin, Michel
PMG Consulting Engineers
Rue du Centre 72
1025 St-Sulpice, Vaud
mnardin@pmg-ing.ch

Oetiker, Christian
Vischer
Aeschenvorstadt 4
PO Box 526
4010 Basel
coetiker@vischer.com

Peter, Wolfgang
Python Schifferli Peter
9, rue Massot
1206 Geneva
wpeter@psplaw.ch

Preti, Philippe
Baker&McKenzie
4, Chemin des Vergers
1208 Geneva
philippe.preti@bakernet.com

Raboin, Michael
37 Route de Tannay, Coppet
1296 Geneva
mraboin@gmail.com

Reichert, Douglas
Etude Reichert
1, rue Etienne Dumont
CP 5327
1211 Geneva
dreichert@swissonline.ch

Roney, David
Schellenberg Wittmer
15 bis, rue des Alpes
PO Box 2088
1211 Geneva
David.roney@swlegal.ch

Schneider, Michael E.
Lalive
35, rue de la Mairie
1207 Geneva
meschneider@lalive.ch

Stutzer, Hansjorg
Thouvenin Rechtsanwalte
Klausstrasse 33
PO BOX
8034 Zurich
h.stutzer@thouvenin.com

Von Segesser, Georg
Schellenberg Wittmer
Löwenstrasse 19
PO Box 6333
8023 Zurich
georg.vonsegesser@swlegal.ch

Vermeille, François
PMG Ingénieurs-Economistes Conseils
72, rue du Centre
Lausanne-St Sulpice
1025 Vaud
fvermeille@pmg-ing.ch

Wiebecke, Martin
Anwaltsburo Wiebecke
Kohlrainstrasse 10
8700 Kusnacht, Zurich
info@wiebecke.com

Wilbers, Erik
WIPO Arbitration and Mediation Center
34, chemin des Colombettes
1211 Geneva
erik.wilbers@wipo.int

Wuehler, Norbert
IOM
Morillons
Geneva
nwuehler@iom.int

Yasseen , Rabab
Mentha & Partners
4, rue de l'Athénée
1205 Geneva

Thailand

Henderson, Alastair
Herbert Smith (Thailand)
1403 Abdulrahim Place
990 Rama 4 Road
10500 Bangkok
alastair.henderson@herbertsmith.com

Norton, James
Norton Arbitration
88 Pimarn Chaopraya Building, 5th floor
Bangkok 10600
james@fernandeshearn.com

Turkey

Yeşilirmak, Ali
Cihangir Caddesi, No. 15/16
34433 Istanbul
ayesilirmak@hotmail.com

Ukraine

Alyoshin, Oleg
Vasil Kisil & Partner

5/60 Zhylyanska Street, Suite 1
1033 Kiev

Slipachuk, Tatyana
Vasil Kisil & Partners
5/60 Zhylyanska Street, Suite 1
1033 Kiev

United Kingdom

Adaralegbe, Adebayo
CEPMLP, University of Dundee
Dundee Tayside, Scotland DD2 1DU
aogadaralegbe@dundee.ac.uk

Altuwaigri, Waleed
The High Judicial Institute, in Riyadh in Saudi
Arabia
Flat 3/2, 56 Hughenden Lane
Glasgow UK G12 9XJ
wstuwaigri@yahoo.com

Beechey, John
Clifford Chance
10 Upper Bank Street
London E14 5JJ
john.beechey@cliffordchance.com

Bogan, Sean
LeBoeuf Lamb Greene & MacRae
No. 1 Minster Court, Mincing Lane
London EC3R 7YL
sean.bogan@llgm.com

Brekoulakis, Stavros
School of Inteternational Arbitration-London
13-14 Charterhouse Square
London, Barbican EC1M 6AX
stbreko@gmail.com

Canham, Anthony
The Old School
School Lane
Norwich, Norfolk NR7 0EP
arbitrator@tonycanham.com

Capper, Phillip
Lovells
Atlantic House, Holborn Viaduct
London UK EC1A 2FG
phillip.capper@lovells.com

Commission, Jeffery
University College London – LLM
1 Gardner Court, 1 Brewery Square
London C1V 4JH
jeffery.commission@gmail.com

Connerty, Anthony
Lamb Chambers
Lamb Building, Temple
London EC4Y 7AS
anthonyconnerty@lambchambers.co.uk

Dang, Hop
University of Oxford
Brasenose College
Oxford OX1 4AJ
hop.dang@law.ox.ac.uk

Dervaird, Lord John, Hon.
Faculty of Advocates
4 Moray Place
Edinburgh, Scotland EH3 6DS
murraydervaird@talk21.com

Diwan, Ricky
Essex Court Chambers
24 Lincoln's Inn Fields
London WC2A 3ED
rdiwan@essexcourt.net

Dobry, George, QC, Hon.
Serle Chambers
Whitelandhouse 105
Cheltonham SW34RA
george@georgedobry.com

Dundas, Hew
International Arbitrator & Mediator
One St Colme Street
Edinburgh, Scotland EH3 6AA
dundas.energy@btinternet.com

Entwistle, Mark
CIArb
80, Glanrhyd, Cwmbran
Torfaen NP44 6TZ
markentwistle@consultant.com

Foyle, Andrew
One Essex Court Temple
London EC4Y 9AR
afoyle@eoclaw.co.uk

Frey, Harold
Wilmer Cutler Pickering Hale and Dorr
4 Carlton Gardens
London SW1Y 5AA
harold.frey@wilmerhale.com

Gal, Daniel
LeBoeuf Lamb Greene & MacRae
No. 1 Minster Court, Mincing Lane
London EC3R 7YL
dgal@llgm.com

Gearing, Matthew
Allen & Overy
One New Change
London EC4M 9QQ
matthew.gearing@allenovery.com

Goldberg, David
S.J. Berwin
10 Queen Street Place
London EC4R 1BE
david.goldberg@sjberwin.com

Griffin, Peter
Baker Botts
41 Lothbury
London EC2R 7HF
peter.griffin@bakerbotts.com

Hannon, Paul
47/E Lennox Garden
London SWI ODF
info@paulbhannon.com

Horrigan, Brenda
SCP Salans & Partners
Millenium Bridge House
2 Lambeth Hill
London EC4V4AJ
opidard@salans.com

Hunter, Ian QC
Essex Court Chambers
24 Lincoln's Inn Fields
London WC2A 3EG
hunter@essexcourt.net

Hunter, Martin
Member of ICCA
Essex Court Chambers
24 Lincoln's Inn Fields

936

London WC2A 3EG
mhunter@essexcourt.net

Inglis, William
Deloitte & Touche
Stonecutter Court
London EC4A 4TR
winglis@deloitte.co.uk

Jagusch, Stephen
Allen & Overy
One New Change
London EC4M92Q
stephen.jagusch@allenovery.com

Kaplan, Neil
Member of ICCA
Pine House
The Square, Stow on Wold
Gloucestershire GL541AF
neilkaplan@btconnect.com

Key, Paul
Essex Court Chambers
24 Lincolns Inn Fields
London WC2A 3EG
pkey@essexcourt.net

Knutson, Robert
Corbett & Co.
78 Dulwich Village
London UK SE228UL
robert@robertknutson.com

Krishan, Devishish
Baker Botts
41 Lothbury
London EC2R 7HF
dev.krishan@bakerbotts.com

Landau, Toby
Essex Court Chambers
24 Lincolns Inn Fields
London WC2A 3EG
ttlandau@aol.com

Lee, Michael
20 Essex Street
London WC2R3AL
michaeljalee@aol.com

Leaver, Peter, Q.C.
One Essex Court

London EC4Y9AR
pleaver@oeclaw.co.uk

Lew, Julian
20 Essex Street
London WC2R3AL
jlew@20essexst.com

Mistelis, Loukas
School of International Arbitration
Queen Mary University of London
Centre for Commercial Law Studies
13-14 Charterhouse Sq.
London EC1M 6AX
L.Mistelis@qmul.ac.uk

Moollan, Salim
Essex Court Chambers
24 Lincoln's Inn Fields
London WC2A 3ED
smoollan@essexcourt.net

Mustill, Lord Michael
Essex Court Chambers
24 Lincoln's Inn Fields
London WC2A 3EG
lpaterson@essexcourt.net

Nairn, Karyl
Skadden Arps Slate Meagher & Flom (UK)
40 Bank Street, Canary Wharf
London E14 5DS
knairn@skadden.com

Nappert, Sophie
Denton Wilde Sapte
1 Fleet Place
London EC4M 7WS
sophie.nappert@dentonwildesapte.com

Nesbitt, Simon
Lovells
Atlantic House, Holborn Viaduct
London EC1A 2FG
simon.nesbitt@lovells.com

O'Connor, Mary
Kilpatrick Stockton
One Canada Square, Canary Wharf
London E14 5NZ
moconnor@kilpatrickstockton.com

Redfern, Alan
Essex Court
3 Essex Court, Temple
London EC4Y 9AR
alanredfern@hotmail.com

Redmond, Catherine
Oxford University Press
70 Baker Street
London WIU 7DN
catherine.redmond@oup.com

Reed, David
Shearman & Sterrling
Broadgate West, 9 Appold Street
London EC2A 2AP
david.reed@shearman.com

Rees, Peter
Debevoise & Plimpton
Tower 42, Old Broad Street
London EC2N 1HQ
pjrees@debevoise.com

Reid, Greg
Linklaters
One Silk Street
London EC2Y 8HQ
greg.reid@linklaters.com

Roberts, Anthea
Debevoise & Plimpton
Tower 42, Old Broad Street
London EC2N 1HQ
aeroberts@debevoise.com

Ruff, Deborah
Lebouef Lamb Greene & MacRae
1 Minister Court, Mincing Lane
London EC3R7YL
druff@llgm.com

Schorr, Edward
Lovells
Atlantic House, Holborn Viaduct
London EC1A 2FG
michael.davison@lovells.com

Shackleton, Stewart
Eversheds
Senator House, 85 Queen Victoria Street
London EC4V 4JL
Stewartshackleton@eversheds.com

Sheppard, Audley
Clifford Chance
10 Upper Bank Street
Canary Wharf, London E14 5JJ
audley.sheppard@cliffordchance.com

Slynn, The Right Hon. Lord Gordon
One Essex Court
Temple
London EC4Y 9AR
clerks@oeclaw.co.uk

Smith, Michael Forbes
The Chartered Institute of Arbitrators
12 Bloomsbury Square
London WC1A 2LP
directorgeneral@arbitrators.org

Strizhova, Tatiana
Gaz Export
Dock lands Business Center
10-16 Tiller road
London E148PX
t.strizhova@gazexport.gazprom.ru

Taylor, Timothy
S J Berwin
10 Queen Street Place
London WC4R1BE
tim.taylor@sjberwin.com

Tirado, Joseph
Baker Botts
41 Lothbury
London EC2R7HF
joe.tirado@bakerbotts.com

Veeder, VV
Member of ICCA
Essex Court Chambers
24 Lincolns Inn Fields
London WC2A3EG
vvveeder@compuserve.com

Wall, Colin J.
The Chartered Institute of Arbitrators
12 Bloomsbury Square
London WC1A 2LP
president@arbitrators.org

Winter, Jeremy
Baker & McKenzie
100 New Bridge Street

London EC4V 6JA
jeremy.winter@bakernet.com

Woolhouse, Sarita
Watson, Farley & Williams
15 Appold Street
London EC2A 2HB
spwoolhouse@wfw.com

Wyld, David
David Wyld & Co
8-12 New Bridge Street
London EC4V 6AL
info@davidwyld.co.uk

York, Stephen
Kilpatrick Stockton
One Canada Square, Canary Wharf
London E145NZ
syork@kilpatrickstockton.com

United States

Abudu, Ollie
Skadden, Arps, Slate, Meagher & Flom and
Affiliates
4 Times Square, Room 48-426
New York, NY 10038
oabudu@skadden.com

Andersen, Steve
ICDR
American Arbitration Association
600 B. Street Suite 1450
San Diego, CA 92101
AndersenS@adr.org

Andreeva, Yulia
Debevoise & Plimpton
919 Third Avenue
New York, NY 10022
yandreeva@debevoise.com

Aksen, Gerald
875 Third Avenue, 10th Floor
New York, NY 10022
gaksen@thelenreid.com

Altieri, Peter
Epstein Becker & Green
250 Park Avenue

New York, NY 10177
paltieri@ebglaw.com

Arkin, Harry L.
Arkin and Associates, P.C.
Suite 2830, Lincoln Center
1660 Lincoln Street
Denver, CO 80264
hla@arkinandassociates.com

Astigarraga, José
Astigarraga Davis
701 Brickell Avenue, 16th Floor
Miami, FL 33131
jia@astidavis.com

Alexander, Jay
Baker Botts
1299 Pennsylvania Avenue, NW
Washington, DC 20004
jay.alexander@bakerbotts.com

Alexandrov, Stanimir
Sidley Austin
1501 K Street NW
Washington, DC 20005
salexandrov@sidley.com

Baker, Mark
Fulbright & Jaworski
1301 McKiney, No. 5100
Houston , TX 77010-3095

Baker, William H.
Ropes & Gray
1251 Avenue of the Americas
New York, NY 10020
william.baker@ropesgray.com

Barnes, Stacey
Barnes & Associates, PLLC
4309 Yoakum
Houston, TX 77006
staceylbarnes@eathlink.net

Battle, Thomas
The Battle Law Firm
38 Redbud Ridge Pl.
The Woodlands, TX 77380-3411
battlelaw@houston.rr.com

Bedard, Julie
Skadden, Arps, Slate, Meagher & Flom

939

4 Times Square, Room 47-108
New York, NY 10036
jbedard@skadden.com

Berghoff, Ethan
Baker & McKenzie
One Prudential Plaza, 130 East Randolph
Chicago, IL 60601
ethan.a.berghoff@bakernet.com

Bowker, David
WilmerHale
399 Park Avenue
New York, NY 10022
david.bowker@wilmerhale.com

Brennan, Lorraine
ICC International Court of Arbitration
1212 Avenue of the Americas
New York, NY 10036
lbrennan@uscib.org

Brown, William J.T.
LeBoeuf, Lamb, Greene & MacRae
125 West 55th St.
New York, NY 10019
wbrown@llgm.com

Buckley, John
Williams & Connolly
725 12th St NW
Washington, DC 20005
jbuckley@wc.com

Burton, Steven
University of Iowa
College of Law
Iowa City, IA 52242
steven-burton@uiowa.edu

Cann, Frederic
Cann Lawyers USA
Suite 2750 Wells Fargo Tower
1300 SW Fifth Avenue
Portland, OR 97201-5617
fec@cannlawyersusa.com

Carska, Andrea
Harvard Law School
1525 Massachusetts Ave
Cambridge, MA 02138
acarska@law.harvard.edu

Carter, James
Sullivan & Cromwell
125 Broad St., 32nd Floor
New York, NY 10004-2498
carterj@sullcrom.com

Clay, Steve
Kilpatrick Stockton
1100 Peachtree Street
Atlanta, GA 30309-4530
sclay@kilpatrickstockton.com

Coe, Jack
Pepperdine University
24255 PCH, Law Faculty
Malibu, CA 90263
jack.coe@pepperdine.edu

Cohen, Stephanie
White & Case
1155 Avenue of the Americas
New York, NY 10036
stephcohen@whitecase.com

Crook, John
George Washington University Law School
10610 Belfast Place
Potomac, MD 20854
jrc1648@yahoo.com

Cymrot, Mark
Baker & Hostetler
1050 Connecticut Avenue, NW, Suite 1100
Washington, DC 20036
mcymrot@bakerlaw.com

Dasteel, Jeffrey
Skadden Arps Slate Meagher & Flom
300 S. Grand Avenue, Suite 3400
Los Angeles, CA 90071
jdasteel@skadden.com

Davidson, George
Hughes Hubbard & Reed
One Battery Park Plaza, 12th Floor
New York, NY 10004
davidson@hugheshubbard.com

Day, Peter R.
Law Offices of Peter R. Day
6915 SE 33rd St
Mercer Island, WA 98040-3323
peterrday@comcast.net

de By, Robert A.
Dewey Ballantine
1301 Avenue of the Americas
New York, NY 10019-6092
rdeby@deweyballantine.com

De Gramont, Alexandre
Crowell & Moring
1001 Pennsylvania Avenue, NW
Washington, DC 20004-2595
adegramont@crowell.com

Delman, David
Pepe & Hazard
225 Asylum Street, Goodwin Square
Hartford, CT 06103-4302
ddelman@pepehazard.com

Dombrow, Russell
Nova Southeastern University
2831 NE 11th Avenue
Pompano Beach, FL 33064

Donahey, M. Scott
M. Scott Donahey
3790 El Camino Real, Suite 171
Palo Alto, CA 94022
adr@scottdonahey.com

Drahozal, Christopher R.
University of Kansas School of Law
Green Hall, 1535 W. 15th Street
Lawrence, KS 66045-7577
drahozal@ku.edu

Elbaz, Jessica M.
United Nations
Office of Legal Affairs
General Legal Division
New York, NY 10017
elbazj@un.org

Elul, Hagit
Hughes Hubbard & Reed
One Battery Park Plaza
New York, NY 10004
elul@hugheshubbard.com

Fantechi, Massimo
Law Offices Fantechi
730 Fifth Avenue, 9th Floor
New York, NY 10019
fantechi@fantechilaw.com

Fellas, John
Hugues Hubbard & Reed
One Battery Park Plaza
New York, NY 10004-1482
fellas@hugheshubbard.com

Friedland, Paul D.
White & Case
1155 Avenue of the Americas
New York, NY 100036
pfriedland@whitecase.com

Gans, Gary E.
Richards, Watson & Gershon
355 South Grand Avenue, 40th Floor
Los Angeles, CA 91354
ggans@rwglaw.com

Garfinkel, Barry H.
Skaden Arps Slate Marther & Flom
4 Times Square, Room 47100
New York, NY 10036
bgarfink@skaden.com

Gluck, George
Gluck
One City Place, Suite 3201
White Plains, NY 10601
george.gluck@gmail.com

Goldstein, Marc
Hodgson Russ
230 Park Avenue
New York, NY 10169
mgoldstein@hodgsonruss.com

Goldsmith, Aren
Cleary Gottlieb Steen & Hamilton
1 Liberty Plaza, 42 Floor
New York, NY 10006
agoldsmith@cgsh.com

Greenblatt, Jonathan
Shearman & Sterling
801 Pennsylvania Avenue, NW, Suite 900
Washington, DC 20004
jgreenblatt@shearman.com

Hancock, Stewart, Jr.
Hancock & Estabrook
1500 Tower 1
PO Box 4976
100 Madison Street,

Syracuse, NY 13221-4976
shancock@hancocklaw.com

Hanessian, Grant
Baker & MacKenzie
1114 Avenue of the Americas, 42nd Floor
New York, NY 10036
grant.hanessian@bakernet.com

Hayden, Don
Baker & McKenzie
1111 Brickell Avenue, Suite 1700
Miami, FL 33131
donald.hayden@bakernet.com

Hosking, James
Clifford Chance, US
31 West 52nd Street
New York, NY 10019
james.hosking@cliffordchance.com

Huckstep, Lee
The Halliburton Company
1401 McKinney, Suite 2400
Houston, TX 77010
lee.huckstep@halliburton.com

Hulbert, Richard
Cleary Gottlieb Steen & Hamilton
One Liberty Plaza
New York, NY 10006
rhulbert@cgsh.com

Johnson, Ian
Orrick Herrington & Sutcliffe
405 Howard Street
San Francisco, CA 94105
ijohnson@orrick.com

Kehoe, Edward
King & Spalding
1185 Avenue of the Americas, 35th Floor
New York, NY 10036
ekehoe@kslaw.com

Kerr, John J., Jr.
Simpson Thacher & Bartlett
425 Lexington Avenue
New York, NY 10017-3954
jkerr@stblaw.com

Kessler, Judd
Porter Wright Morris & Arthur

1919 Pennsylvania Ave NW, 5th Floor
Washington, DC 20006
jkessler@porterwright.com

Kidd, John
The Savoy ADR Group
401 So Palm Avenue
Sarasota, FL 34236
johnkiddadr@aol.com

Kim, Grant
Morrison & Foerster
425 Market Street,
San Francisco, CA 94105-2482
gkim@mofo.com

Kimball, Astri
O'Melveny & Myers
1625 Eye Street, NW
Washington, DC 20006
akimball@omm.com

Kimmelman, Louis B.
O'Melveny & Tower
Time Square Tower, 7 Times Square
New York, NY 10036
bkimmelman@omm.com

Kitzen, Michael
Juris Publishing
71 New Street,
Huntington, NY 11743
mkitzen@jurispub.com

Knox, Susan
Baker & MacKenzie
114 Avenue of the Americas
New York, NY 10036
susan.r.knox@bakernet.com

Knull, William H., III
Mayer Brown Rowe & Maw
700 Louisiana, Suite 3600
Houston, TX 77002
wknull@mayerbrownrowe.com

Kostadinova, Milanka
ICSID
The World Bank
1818 H Street, NW
Washington, DC 20433
mkostadinova@worldbank.org

Lamm, Carolyn
White & Case
701 13th Street
Washington, DC 20005
clamm@washdc.whitecase.com

Landsman, Kim
Patterson Belknap Webb & Tyler
1133 Avenue of the Americas
New York, NY 10036-6710
kjlandsman@pbwt.com

Levine, Judith
White & Case
1155 Avenue of the Americas
New York, NY 10036
jlevine@whitecase.com

Lichtenstein, Cynthia Crawford
Boston College Law School
22 Water Street
Stonington, CT 06378
lichtens@aya.yale.edu

Lindsey, David
Clifford Chance, US
31 West 52nd Street
New York, NY 10019
david.lindsey@cliffordchance.com

Lurie, Paul
Schiff Hardin
233 S. Wacker Drive
Chicago, IL 60606
plurie@schiffhardin.com

Luz, Mark A.
White & Case
1155 Avenue of the Americas
New York, NY 10036
mluz@whitecase.com

McLaren, Earl
Bechtel SAIC Company LLC
955 L'Enfant Plaza SW, Suite 8000
Washington, DC 20024
demclaren@aol.com

Medeiros, Suzana
NYU
4515 Willard Av., Apt. 1512 S
Chevy Chase, MD 20815
sdm306@nyu.edu

Micarelli, Carl
Debevoise & Plimpton
919 Third Avenue
New York, NY 10022
cmicarelli@debevoise.com

Michaels, Steven
Debevoise & Plimpton
919 Third Avenue
New York, NY 10022
ssmichaels@debevoise.com

Michaelson, Peter
Michaelson & Associates
PO Box 8489
328 Newman Springs Road
Red Bank, NJ 07701-8489
pete@mandw.com

Molineaux, Charles
Construction Arbitration Worldwide
1660 International Drive, Suite 400
McLean, VA 22102
CMlnx@aol.com

Morkin, Michael
Baker & McKenzie
130 E Randolph Drive, Suite
Chicago, IL 60601
michael.l.Morkin@bakernet.com

Naimark, Richard
ICDR
American Arbitration Association
335 Madison Avenue
New York, NY 10017
Naimarkr@adr.org

Nairac, Charles
White & Case
1155 Av of the Americas
New York, NY 10036
cnairac@whitecase.com

Nelson, Nancy
International Institute for Conflict Prevention
& Resolution
418 Central Park West,
New York, NY 10025
nnelson111@aol.com

Nelson, Timothy G.
Skadden, Arps, Slate, Meagher & Flom

4 Times Square
New York, NY 10036
tinelson@skadden.com

Neuhaus, Joseph
Sullivan & Cromwell
125 Broad Street
New York, NY 10011
neuhausj@sullcrom.com

Newman, Lawrence
Baker & McKenzie
1114 Avenue of the America
New York, NY 10036
lwn@bakernet.com

Nolan, Michael
Milbank, Tweed, Hadley & McCloy
1850, K Street NW, Suite 1100
Washington, DC 20006
mnolan@milbank.com

Oustalniol, Xavier
Aon Consulting Inc.
199 Fremont Street, 17th Floor
San Francisco, CA 94105
xavier_oustalniol@aon.com

Parada, Luis
LeBoeuf, Lamb, Greene & MacRae
1875 Connecticut Ave, NW, Suite 2100
Washington, DC 20009
Lparada@llgm.com

Park, William W.
Member of ICCA
Boston University Law Faculty
765 Commonwealth Avenue
Boston, MA 2215
wwpark@bu.edu

Parra, Antonio R.
Secretary General of ICCA
ICSID
1818 H Street, NW
Washington, DC 20433
arparra@earthlink.net

Pearsall, Patrick
Cleary Gottlieb Steen & Hamilton
One Liberty Plaza
New York, NY 10006
ppearsall@cgsh.com

Pierce, John
Wilmer Hale
399 Park Avenue
New York, NY 10022
john.pierce@wilmerhale.com

Port, Nicola
Debevoise & Plimpton
919 Third Avenue
New York, NY 10022
ncport@debevoise.com

Prager, Dietmar W.
Debevoise & Plimpton
919 Third Avenue
New York, NY 10022
dwprager@debevoise.com

Primps, William G.
LeBoeuf, Lamb, Greene & MacRae
125 West 55th Street
New York, NY 10019
wprimps@llgm.com

Rawding, Nigel
Freshfields Bruckhaus Deringer
520 Madison Avenue
New York, NY 10022
nigel.rawding@freshfields.com

Reed, Lucy
Freshfields Bruckhaus Deringer
520 Madison Ave, 34th Floor
New York, NY 10022
lucy.reed@freshfields.com

Reeves, Barbara
JAMS
707 Wilshire Blvd, 46th Floor
Los Angeles, CA 90017
breeves@jamsadr.com

Reisenfeld, Kenneth
Haynes and Boone
1615 L Street, NW, Suite 800
Washington, DC 20036-5610
Ken.Reisenfeld@haynesboone.com

Reisman, W. Michael
Yale Law School
127 Wall Street
New Haven, CT 6511
michael.reisman@yale.edu

Rivkin, David W.
Debevoise & Plimpton
919 Third Avenue
New York, NY 10022
dwrivkin@debevoise.com

Robinson, Anthony
F.L.I.C.
245 East 58th Street
New York, NY 10022
robinsoninparis@aol.com

Robinson, The Hon. Davis R.
3729 Fordham Road, NW
Washington, DC 20016-1933
drrobins@llgm.com

Rovine, Arthur
Baker & McKenzie
215 East 68th St.
New York, NY 10021
Arthur.W.Rovine@bakernet.com

Rubinstein, Javier
Mayer, Brown, Rowe & Maw
71 South Wacker Drive
Chicago, IL 60606
jrubinstein@mayerbrownrowe.com

Ryan, Christopher M.
Shearman & Stearling
801 Pennsylvania Avenue NW
Washington, DC 20004-2634
christopher.ryan@shearman.com

Sampliner, Gary
U.S. Treasury Department
1500 Pennsylvania Avenue, NW
Washington, DC 20220
gary.sampliner@do.treas.gov

Schaner, Lawrence
Jenner & Block
One IBM Plaza
Chicago, IL 60611
lschaner@jenner.com

Schnabl, Marco
Skadden, Arps, Slate, Meagher & Flom
4 Times Square, Room 47-416
New York, NY 10036-6522
mschnabl@skadden.com

Schwebel, Stephen M.
1501 K Street, NW, Suite 410
Washington, DC 20005
judgeschwebel@aol.com

Sherman, Fredrick
Jones Day
222 East 41st Street
New York, NY 10017
fsherman@jonesday.com

Siefert, Roger
Aon Consulting Inc.
55 Park Avenue Plaza, 31st Floor
New York, NY, USA 10055
roger_siefert@aon.com

Smit, Robert
Simpson Thacher & Bartlett
425 Lexington Avenue
New York, NY 10017
rsmit@stblaw.com

Smith, Stephen
Northwestern University School of Law
357 E. Chicago Avenue
Chicago, IL 60611
s-smith8@law.northwestern.edu

Stevens, Margrete
ICSID
1818 H Street, N.W.
Washington, DC 20433
mstevens1@worldbank.org

Syme, Carrie
Patterson, Belknap, Webb & Tyler
1133 Ave of the Americas
New York, NY 10036
casyme@pbwt.com

Townsend, John
Hughes Hubbard & Reed
1775 I Street, NW
Washington, DC 20016
townsend@hugheshubbard.com

Wagoner, David E.
International Arbitration Chambers
1420 5th Avenue, Suite 2200
Seattle, WA 98101
email@davidwagoner.com

Walsh, Mark A.
LeBoeuf, Lamb, Greene & MacRae
1875 Connecticut Ave, NW, Suite 1200
Washington, DC 20009-5728
mwalsh@llgm.com

Yanos, Alexander
Freshfields Bruckhaus Deringer
520 Madison Avenue, 34th Floor
New York, NY 10022
alex.yanos@freshfields.com

Venezuela

De Jesus O., Alfredo
Venezuelan Arbitration Committee
Centro Lido, Torre C, Piso 7
Oficina 73-C, Avenue Francisco de Miranda
El Rosal
1060 Caracas, Estado Miranda
adejesuso@cvarbitraje.com

Droulers, Diana
Caracas Chamber Arbitration Center
PO Box 2835
1010 Caracas, Libertador
dianadroulers@arbitrajeccc.org

INTERNATIONAL COUNCIL FOR COMMERCIAL ARBITRATION (ICCA)

Correspondence address:
Mr. Antonio R. Parra
Secretary General ICCA
c/o International Centre for Settlement of Investment Disputes
1818 H Street, NW
Washington, DC 20433
USA
Phone:+1-202 458 8511
Fax:+1-202 522 2615
E-mail: aparra@worldbank.org; aparra@earthlink.net

LIST OF OFFICERS AND MEMBERS

July 2007

OFFICERS

Honorary Presidents

THE HON. GIORGIO BERNINI (Bologna, Italy)
Former Minister of Foreign Trade and Member of Parliament; Former Member, Italian Antitrust Authority; Professor, University of Bologna, Chair of Arbitration and International Commercial Law; President, Association for the Teaching and Study of Arbitration (AISA); Member, Executive Committee, Italian Arbitration Association; Advocate, Studio Bernini Associato a Baker & McKenzie

MR. FALI S. NARIMAN (New Delhi, India)
Past President, Bar Association of India; Honorary Member, International Commission of Jurists; Past President, Law Association for Asia and the Pacific (LAWASIA); Member, Court of the LCIA; Past Vice Chairman, International Court

of Arbitration of the International Chamber of Commerce (ICC); Past Co-Chair, Human Rights Institute of the International Bar Association (IBA); Senior Advocate, Supreme Court of India

PROF. PIETER SANDERS (Schiedam, The Netherlands)
Honorary President, Netherlands Arbitration Institute; Professor Emeritus, Faculty of Law, Erasmus University, Rotterdam

President

DR. GEROLD HERRMANN (Vienna, Austria)
Former Secretary, United Nations Commission on International Trade Law (UNCITRAL); Honorary Professor, University of Vienna; International Dispute Resolver

Honorary Vice Presidents

JUDGE HOWARD M. HOLTZMANN (New York, USA)
Honorary Chairman of the Board, American Arbitration Association (AAA); Substitute Judge, Iran-United States Claims Tribunal, The Hague

PROF. SERGEI LEBEDEV (Moscow, Russian Federation)
President, Maritime Arbitration Commission; Member of the Presidium, International Commercial Arbitration Court of the Russian Federation Chamber of Commerce and Industry; Professor, Moscow Institute of International Relations

DDR. WERNER MELIS (Vienna, Austria)
President, International Arbitral Centre of the Austrian Federal Economic Chamber, Vienna; Past Vice President, LCIA

MS. TINUADE OYEKUNLE (Lagos, Nigeria)
Arbitrator and Notary Public; Member, Association of Arbitrators of Nigeria; Fellow, Chartered Institute of Arbitrators, London; Member, Arbitration Committee of the Lagos Chamber of Commerce; Chartered Arbitrator; Chairman, Education & Training Committee of the Chartered Institute of Arbitrators; Member, Board of

948

Management of the Chartered Institute of Arbitrators, London; Regional Representative for Promotion of Arbitration in the West African Region; Past Chairman, Chartered Institute of Arbitrators, Nigeria Branch; former Member, London Court of International Arbitration; Correspondent of UNIDROIT; Barrister and Solicitor of the Supreme Court of Nigeria, Arbitrator and Notary Public

Vice Presidents

MR. DONALD FRANCIS DONOVAN (New York, USA)
Adjunct Professor, New York University School of Law; Immediate Past Chair, Institute for Transnational Arbitration; Former Chair, U.S. National Committee International Chamber of Commerce (ICC), International Court of Arbitration; Board of Directors, Human Rights First

MR. MICHAEL HWANG, SC (Singapore)
Former Vice Chair, Committee D, International Bar Association; Member, Permanent Court of Arbitration; Vice-Chair, International Court of Arbitration of the International Chamber of Commerce (ICC); Exco Member, Institute of Transnational Arbitration; Member, LCIA; Former Acting High Court Judge, Singapore; Fellow, Chartered Institute of Arbitrators; Fellow, Singapore Institute of Arbitrators; Adjunct Professor, National University of Singapore; Deputy Chief Justice, Dubai International Financial Centre; Advocate and Solicitor, Singapore

PROF. DR. IVÁN SZÁSZ (Budapest, Hungary)
Professor of Law, University of Economic Sciences, Budapest; Member, Presidential Council of the Arbitration Court and Honorary President, Legal Commission at the Hungarian Chamber of Commerce; Past Ambassador of Hungary to the European Communities; Member, International Court of Arbitration of the International Chamber of Commerce (ICC); Attorney-at-law, Squire Sanders & Dempsey

Honorary Secretary General

MR. ULF FRANKE (Stockholm, Sweden)
Past Secretary General, ICCA; Secretary General, Arbitration Institute of the Stockholm Chamber of Commerce; President, International Federation of Commercial Arbitration Institutions (IFCAI)

Secretary General

MR. ANTONIO R. PARRA (Washington, DC, USA)

Past Deputy Secretary-General and Legal Adviser, International Centre for Settlement of Investment Disputes (ICSID); Past Senior Counsel, World Bank; Visiting Professor, University College London Faculty of Laws; Editor-in-Chief, ICSID Review—Foreign Investment Law Journal; Fellow, Chartered Institute of Arbitrators

MEMBERS

MR. CECIL ABRAHAM (Kuala Lumpur, Malaysia)

Fellow, Chartered Institute of Arbitrators; Fellow, Malaysian Institute of Arbitrators; Past Member, LCIA Court; Past President, Inter-Pacific Bar Association; Vice President, Asia Pacific Arbitration Group (APRAG); Partner, Shearn Delamore & Co.

MR. GUILLERMO AGUILAR-ALVAREZ (Mexico D.F., Mexico)

Past General Counsel, International Court of Arbitration of the International Chamber of Commerce (ICC); Principal Legal Counsel for the Government of Mexico for the Negotiation and Implementation of NAFTA; Partner, Weil Gotshal & Manges

DR. HUSSAIN M. AL BAHARNA (Manama, Bahrain)

Former Minister of Legal Affairs, Bahrain; Member, Arbitration Board of the Bahrain Centre for International Commercial Arbitration; Member, UN International Law Commission, Geneva; Practising Advocate, Court of Cassation, Bahrain; Barrister-at-law of Lincoln's Inn, London

PROF. DR. ALBERT JAN VAN DEN BERG (The Netherlands)

General Editor, ICCA (*Yearbook Commercial Arbitration*); President, Netherlands Arbitration Institute; Professor of Arbitration Law, Erasmus University, Rotterdam; Attorney

PROF. DR. PIERO BERNARDINI (Rome, Italy)
Professor of Arbitration Law, LUISS University, Rome; Vice-President, Italian Arbitration Association; Past Vice-President, International Court of Arbitration of the International Chamber of Commerce (ICC)

PROF. DR. KARL-HEINZ BÖCKSTIEGEL (Bergisch-Gladbach, Germany)
Professor Emeritus of International Business Law, University of Cologne; Chairman, German Institution of Arbitration (DIS); Past President, International Law Association; Past President, LCIA; Past President, Iran-United States Claims Tribunal, The Hague

PROF. DR. NAEL G. BUNNI (Dublin, Ireland)
Past President, The Chartered Institute of Arbitrators; Board Member, LCIA; Visiting Professor in Construction Law & Contract Administration, Trinity College, Dublin; Chartered Engineer and Chartered Registered Arbitrator

MS. TERESA CHENG, BBS, SC, JP (Hong Kong)
Deputy President for 2007 and President for 2008, Chartered Institute of Arbitrators; Vice Chairperson, Hong Kong International Arbitration Centre; Adjunct Professor, School of Law at the City University of Hong Kong; Barrister

PROF. BERNARDO M. CREMADES (Madrid, Spain)
Professor, Faculty of Law, Madrid University; Member of the Madrid Bar

MR. DUSHYANT DAVE (New Delhi, India)
Senior Advocate, Supreme Court of India; Member, National Legal Services Authority of India; President, Asia Pacific Users' Council, LCIA; Member, LCIA Court

Mᴱ YVES DERAINS (Paris, France)
Past Secretary General, International Court of Arbitration of the International Chamber of Commerce (ICC); Member of the Paris Bar

951

PROF. AHMED S. EL-KOSHERI (Cairo, Egypt)
Professor of International Economic Law and Former President, International University for African Development (Alexandria); Member, *l'Institut de Droit International*; Partner, Kosheri, Rashed & Riad Law Firm

MR. L. YVES FORTIER, CC, QC (Montreal, Canada)
Past President, London Court of International Arbitration; Chair, Hong Kong International Arbitration Court; Past Ambassador and Permanent Representative of Canada to the United Nations; Member, United Nations Compensation Commission

PROF. DR. EMMANUEL GAILLARD (Paris, France)
Professor of Law, University of Paris XII; Member, LCIA Court; Chairman, International Arbitration Institute; Past Chairman, International Arbitration Committee, International Law Association

PROF. DR. BERNARD HANOTIAU (Brussels, Belgium)
Professor of International Dispute Resolution, University of Louvain; Vice-President, London Court of International Arbitration; Vice Chairman, Institute of Transnational Arbitration; Vice Chairman, CEPANI (Belgium); Member, Brussels and Paris Bars

PROF. J. MARTIN H. HUNTER, SC (London, United Kingdom)
Professor of International Dispute Resolution, Nottingham Trent University; Visiting Professor, King's College London University; Chairman, Dubai International Arbitration Centre; Honorary Dean of Postgraduate Studies, T.M.C. Asser Instituut, The Hague; Barrister

MR. NEIL KAPLAN, CBE, QC (London, England)
Former Judge, High Court, Hong Kong; Chairman, Hong Kong International Arbitration Centre 1991-2004; Honorary Professor, City University of Hong Kong; Past President, The Chartered Institute of Arbitrators

PROF.DR. GABRIELLE KAUFMANN-KOHLER (Geneva, Switzerland)
Professor, Private International Law and International Dispute Resolution, Geneva University Law School; Honorary President, Swiss Arbitration Association (ASA); Attorney, Member of the Geneva Bar

DR. FATHI KEMICHA (Tunis, Tunisia)
Member, International Law Commission of the United Nations; Member, World Bank Group Sanctions Board; Member, Board of Trustees and Executive Committee, Dubai International Arbitration Centre; First appointed Secretary General, Constitutional Court of the Kingdom of Bahrain (January 2003 - December 2005); Former Vice President, London Court of International Arbitration; *Avocat a la Cour*, Member of the Paris and Tunisia Bars

PROF. ALEXANDER S. KOMAROV (Moscow, Russian Federation)
International Chamber of Commerce (ICC) Russian National Committee, Arbitration Commission, Chairman; Professor, Russian Academy of Foreign Trade; President, International Commercial Arbitration Court at the Russian Federation Chamber of Commerce and Industry

MR. ARTHUR MARRIOTT, QC (London, United Kingdom)
Board Member, LCIA; Board Member, Hong Kong International Arbitration Centre; Solicitor

M^E CARLOS NEHRING NETTO (São Paulo, Brazil)
Former Member, International Court of Arbitration of the International Chamber of Commerce (ICC); Member, LCIA

PROF. FRANCISCO ORREGO VICUÑA (Santiago, Chile)
Professor of Law, University of Chile and first Director of the LL.M. on Investments, Trade and Arbitration offered jointly with the University of Heidelberg and the Max Planck Institute; Judge and former President, Administrative Tribunal of the World Bank; Member, Chairman's List of ICSID Arbitrators; former Vice President, London Court of International Arbitration; Member, Latin American Committee of Arbitrators of the ICC

PROF. WILLIAM W. PARK (Boston, USA)
Professor of Law, Boston University; General Editor, Arbitration International; Vice President, London Court of International Arbitration; Past Chairman, American Bar Association Committee on International Commercial Dispute Resolution

PROF. JAN PAULSSON (Paris, France)

General Editor, ICCA (*International Handbook on Commercial Arbitration*); President, LCIA; President, World Bank Administrative Tribunal

PROF. DR. MICHAEL PRYLES (Melbourne, Australia)

President, Australian Centre for International Commercial Arbitration; Member, LCIA Court; Co-Chairman, ICC Asia Pacific Arbitration Commission; Former Commissioner, United Nations Compensation Commission; Former Commissioner, Australian Law Reform Commission; Former Henry Bournes Higgins Professor of Law, Monash University, Melbourne; Visiting Professor of Law, University of Queensland, Bond University, Murdoch University; Consultant, Clayton Utz

MR. WILLIAM K. SLATE II (New York, USA)

President and Chief Executive Officer, American Arbitration Association (AAA); Founder, Global Center for Dispute Resolution Research; Member, Arbitrator and Mediator, Panels of the International Court of Sport (Switzerland); Member, International Commercial Arbitration Court at the Ukraine Chamber of Commerce and Industry; Member, China International Economic and Trade Arbitration Commission (CIETAC)

PROF. YASUHEI TANIGUCHI (Tokyo, Japan)

Professor Emeritus, Kyoto University; President, Japan Association of Arbitrators; Special Advisor to the Japan Commercial Arbitration Association (JCAA); Member, Appellate Body of the World Trade Organization (WTO); Of Counsel, Matsuo & Kosugi

PROF. DR. GUIDO SANTIAGO TAWIL (Buenos Aires, Argentina)

Professor, University of Buenos Aires School of Law; Vice Chair, IBA Arbitration Committee; Attorney at Law, Partner, M.&M. Bomchil

PROF. PIERRE TERCIER (Fribourg, Switzerland)

Professor and Past Dean, Faculty of Law, University of Fribourg; Chairman, International Court of Arbitration of the International Chamber of Commerce (ICC)

MR. V.V. VEEDER, QC (London, United Kingdom)

Former Vice President, London Court of International Arbitration; Council Member, ICC Institute of World Business Law and of the Arbitration Institute of the

Stockholm Chamber of Commerce; Visiting Professor on Investment Arbitration, King's College, University of London

THE HON. S. AMOS WAKO, F.C.I.ARB, SC. (Nairobi, Kenya)
Attorney General, Republic of Kenya; Former Chairman, Arbitration Tribunal, Kenya Chamber of Commerce and Industry; Former Vice President, LCIA – Africa Region; Arbitrator, Vienna Convention on Law of Treaties, Centre for Settlement of International Disputes; Former Chairman, Law Society of Kenya; Former Member, International Advisory Committee of WIPO Centre for Settlement of Disputes; Former Member, International Commission of Jurists; Former Deputy Secretary General, International Bar Association (IBA); Former Secretary General, African Bar Association; Former President, Asian-African Legal Consultative Organisation; Senior Partner, Kaplan & Stratton

DR. WANG SHENG CHANG (Beijing, People's Republic of China)
Vice Chairman and Secretary General, China International Economic and Trade Arbitration Commission (CIETAC); Vice Chairman, China Maritime Arbitration Commission (CMAC); Vice Chairman, Asia Pacific Region Arbitration Group (ARPAG); Professor of Law, University of International Economics and Business, Beijing

MR. DAVID A. R. WILLIAMS, QC (Auckland, New Zealand)
Former Judge of the High Court of New Zealand; Former Judge of the High Court and Court of Appeal of the Cook Islands; Chief Justice of the Cook Islands; President, Arbitrators and Mediators Institute of New Zealand; Member, LCIA

Advisory Members

DR. ROBERT BRINER (Geneva, Switzerland)
Honorary Chairman, International Court of Arbitration of the International Chamber of Commerce (ICC); Past President, Iran-United States Claims Tribunal, The Hague

MR. ROBERT COULSON (Connecticut, USA)
Former President, American Arbitration Association (AAA)

PROF. DR. RADOMIR DJUROVIČ (Belgrade, Yugoslavia)
Former President, Arbitration Court of Yugoslavia; Professor of International Commercial Law, Belgrade University

DR. MAURO FERRANTE (Rome, Italy)
Secretary General, Italian Arbitration Association; Managing Director, ICC-Italy

DR.DR. OTTOARNDT GLOSSNER (Kronberg, Germany)
Past Chairman, International Chamber of Commerce (ICC) Commission on International Arbitration; Honorary President, German Institution of Arbitration (DIS) Cologne/Berlin; Attorney-at-law

PROF. DR. PIERRE LALIVE (Geneva, Switzerland)
Président d'honneur, Swiss Arbitration Association (ASA); Professor Emeritus, Geneva University; Honorary Chairman, Institute of International Business Law and Practice (ICC); Member (Former President), *l'Institut de Droit International*; Attorney-at-law, Lalive & Partners, Geneva

THE HON. MARC LALONDE (Montreal, Canada)
Ad-hoc Judge, International Court of Justice; Former Minister of Justice and Attorney General; Former Minister of Energy, Mines and Resources; Former Minister of Finance; President, LCIA North American Users Committee

MR. MARK LITTMAN, QC (London, United Kingdom)
Barrister

MR. ALAIN PLANTEY (Paris, France)
Former Member of the *Conseil d'État de France*; Member and Former President, *Institut de France*; Member and Former President, Academy of Moral and Political Sciences (*Institut de France*); Former Ambassador of France; Former Professor of Law, University of Paris I; *Président d'honneur*, International Court of Arbitration of the International Chamber of Commerce (ICC)

THE HON. ANDREW JOHN ROGERS, QC (Sydney, Australia)
Former Chief Judge, Commercial Division, Supreme Court of New South Wales; Chairman, National Dispute Centre, Sydney; Adjunct Professor, University of Technology, Sydney

DR. JOSÉ LUIS SIQUEIROS (Mexico City, Mexico)
Past President, Mexican Academy of International Commercial Arbitration; Past President, Inter-American Bar Association; Past Chairman, Inter-American Juridical Committee (OAS)

PROF. DR. HEINZ STROHBACH (Berlin, Germany)
Board Member, German Institution of Arbitration (DIS), Cologne/Berlin; Vice President, Federation on the Promotion of Arbitration, Berlin; President, Berlin Court of Arbitration

DR. HABIL. TADEUSZ SZURSKI (Warsaw, Poland)
Past President, Court of Arbitration at the Polish Chamber of Commerce; Vice President, Polish Arbitration Association; Member, Polish Bar; Member of the Scientific Council of the Institute of International Law, Warsaw University; Honorary President of the Court of Arbitration at the Polish Confederation of Private Employers Leviatan

PROF. TANG HOUZHI (Beijing, People's Republic of China)
Honorary Vice Chairman, China International Economic and Trade Arbitration Commission (CIETAC); Vice Chairman, CCPIT/CCOIC Beijing Conciliation Centre; Professor, Law School of the People's University of China; Visiting Professor, Amoy University School of Law; Arbitration Adviser, UN International Trade Centre; Fellow and Chartered Arbitrator, The Chartered Institute of Arbitrators; Former Court Member, LCIA; Honorary Professor, Hong Kong City University School of Law; Vice President, International Federation of Commercial Arbitration Institutions (IFCAI)